SOUTHERN LITERARY STUDIES
Fred Hobson, Editor

SOUTHERN WRITERS

A New Biographical Dictionary

EDITED BY

JOSEPH M. FLORA

AND

AMBER VOGEL

BRYAN GIEMZA, ASSISTANT EDITOR

LOUISIANA STATE UNIVERSITY PRESS

BATON ROUGE

Published by Louisiana State University Press
Copyright © 2006 by Louisiana State University Press
All rights reserved
Manufactured in the United States of America
First Printing

Designer: Melanie Samaha
Typeface: Aldus, Whitman
Typesetter: G&S Typesetters, Inc.
Printer: Data Reproductions, Inc.
Binder: Dekker Bookbinding

Library of Congress Cataloging-in-Publication Data

Southern writers : a new biographical dictionary / edited by Joseph M. Flora and
Amber Vogel ; assistant editor, Bryan Giemza.
    p.   cm.   —   (Southern literary studies)
  ISBN 0-8071-3123-7 (alk. paper)
1. Authors, American—Homes and haunts—Southern States—Dictionaries.
2. Authors, American—Southern States—Biography—Dictionaries.   3. Southern
States—Intellectual life—Dictionaries.   4. Southern States—In literature—
Dictionaries.   5. Authors, American—Biography—Dictionaries.   6. Southern
States—Biography—Dictionaries.   I. Flora, Joseph M.   II. Vogel, Amber.
III. Giemza, Bryan Albin.   IV. Series.
PS261.S595   2006
810.9′975′03—dc22

                                                             2005023668

For Les Phillabaum and John Easterly
Their extraordinary service to southern letters endures.

CONTENTS

PREFACE

Like its predecessor, *Southern Writers: A New Biographical Dictionary* provides in a single volume informative sketches of the lives of authors associated with the American South. This new edition continues as a repository of information about the major figures to whom readers must often refer, and also about the minor figures whose contributions and shaping influences provide necessary context that might otherwise be lost to readers if not gathered here.

The earlier edition of *Southern Writers* quickly proved its usefulness to scholars, students, and dedicated readers of southern literature. But much has happened in the field since 1979, and with each new year the need for a revised, updated resource has become more pressing. Numerous southern writers who have since risen to prominence (one thinks of Lee Smith, Robert Morgan, Rick Bragg, Richard Ford—to name but a few) assuredly deserve inclusion in this standard reference work. Furthermore, many of the writers in the earlier version have published new work, and important changes had occurred in many of those lives. An updated record is in order.

To be sure, the 1979 work served as a solid base for the planning of the new edition, even as we considered additional authors. Seeking the names of writers whose work clearly marked them as having made important or noteworthy contributions to the field, we consulted colleagues, prize and best-seller lists, and recent major overviews of southern literature such as *The Companion to Southern Literature*. The Internet, a research

tool unavailable to scholars in 1979, alerted us—through its online libraries and bookstores—to the interest of specialist and general readers in various authors' works and lives. Throughout the editorial process, we also remained open to suggestions from the scholars who worked on the new and revised sketches.

We sought to include all the new talent that had emerged since 1979, provided that the author either had at least five published books to his or her credit or had unquestionably made an impact on the national scene, as with Charles Frazier. We were also eager to acknowledge interesting older talents previously unknown or unacknowledged, as with Hannah Crafts and Zelda Fitzgerald. Doubtless, some author will shortly emerge who will make a similar impact. We welcome the ongoing contributions to our literature and understand that in another quarter century an update of this dictionary will again be necessary. Meanwhile, for what we may have overlooked, we beg pardon.

The sketches in this volume come in three categories. For most entries, the sketch is about 350 words long. Writers in a second group have sketches about 750 words long; this group is for writers who count among the chief shapers of southern literature, those writers most often discussed in overviews of the field, and those most regularly taught in courses in southern literature. Because of their eminence, a select few have entries of 1,000 or so words. The chronological sweep again covers writers from the colonial period to the contemporary. Following each sketch the reader will again typically find a chronological listing of the books by the author; in the case of colonial writers, the listed works are sometimes found in periodicals.

Of the 379 sketches in the 1979 edition, our review confirmed that for some there had been no new information about the writer and the original sketch continued to sparkle. We could identify no contemporary scholar who could give a more authoritative or graceful review. And so we retained some of the earlier sketches. For most of the writers, however, we favored a new sketch, a different way of looking.

Many persons have played important roles in the making of this book. John Easterly at Louisiana State University Press first encouraged us to undertake the challenge of an updated edition. During John's sojourn at the *Southern Literary Review*, his replacement at the Press, Sylvia Frank Rodrigue, patiently waited for us to gather all of the pieces. By the time our manuscript arrived in Baton Rouge, we detected no wavering of enthusiasm at the Press, despite some retirements and roster changes. There was poetry in the fact that John Easterly had returned and was now assigned to work with us as we began the review and editing process. MaryKatherine Callaway, director, and Lee Sioles, managing editor, added their supporting voices. When Lee assigned Marie Blanchard to serve as our copy editor and George Roupe as our production editor, she put us in skilled hands. Suddenly the inevitable frustrations that go with so large a project faded from memory.

Closer to home, we are greatly in the debt of James Thompson, chair of the UNC English Department. During times of great budgetary strain, he provided graduate student support for clerical and research duties. Amanda Page and Cindy Current proved efficient and prompt in fulfilling their assignments. Susan Marston and Christine Flora again gave us the benefit of their skilled editorial expertise whenever we turned to them. Bryan Giemza's broad understanding of the southern mind and southern literature was repeatedly an asset to the project. Young scholars of his ilk bode well for the vibrant scholarship in southern literature.

A special tip of the hat goes to Fred Hobson, William Andrews, and Trudier Harris for reviewing our proposed list of writers meriting inclusion. They were also helpful in identifying scholars who might be enlisted to write those sketches. As always, we are grateful to Louis D. Rubin, Jr., who even in retirement must be regarded the godfather, if not the father, of this new edition of *Southern Writers*.

It is fitting that this review of our many indebtednesses concludes by highlighting the splendid men and women who have taken time to write the informative and authoritative biographical entries that follow. Their knowledge of southern literature and their commitment to its dissemination have made them our partners. Without them, this book would not be exist.

Here then is a volume of 604 southern writers. We are grateful to the hundreds of scholars who have collaborated with us to explore these biographies. Taken together, the sketches in this edition trace the landscape of southern letters arrived at in the first years of the twenty-first century. Surveying that panorama, we are once again reminded how diverse and complex is that entity known as southern writing.

JOSEPH M. FLORA
AMBER VOGEL

SOUTHERN WRITERS
A New Biographical Dictionary

ALICE ADAMS (1926–1999). Alice Boyd Adams, the only child of Nicholson Barney Adams and Agatha Erskine Boyd Adams, was born in Fredericksburg, Va., on August 14, 1926. Shortly after her birth, the family moved to Chapel Hill, N.C., where her father taught Spanish at the University of North Carolina. At sixteen Adams enrolled at Radcliffe College. She graduated in 1946 and married Mark Linenthal, Jr., in 1947. Following a year in Paris, where Linenthal studied at the Sorbonne, the couple moved to California. In 1951 their only child, Peter Adams Linenthal, was born. Linenthal taught English at San Francisco State University and in 1957 received his Ph.D. from Stanford University. Meanwhile Adams was living in an unhappy marriage and struggling to launch her literary career.

Following her divorce in 1958, Adams supported herself and her son with various office jobs and continued to write. During these years she received encouragement from Robert K. McNie, an interior designer with whom she lived in San Francisco for about twenty years. In 1966 Adams published her first novel, *Careless Love*, to mixed reviews. She achieved a major literary breakthrough in November 1969, when "Gift of Grass" appeared in the *New Yorker* and was selected for inclusion in *Prize Stories: The O. Henry Awards* (1971). For the next twenty-five years, her stories were regularly published in this collection.

In *Families and Survivors*, her second novel, she firmly established the theme of her fiction, contemporary woman's search for self-identity and stable interpersonal relationships. The novel was nominated for a National Book Critics Circle Award, and other honors followed over the course of her career. She received a grant from the National Endowment for the Arts (1976), a Guggenheim Memorial Fellowship (1978), the O. Henry Special Award for Continuing Achievement (1982), and an Academy and Institute Award in Literature from the American Academy and Institute of Arts and Letters (1992). In addition to writing, Adams occasionally taught creative writing at Stanford University and the University of California at Davis and at Berkeley. She died at her home in San Francisco on May 27, 1999.

WORKS: *Careless Love* (1966; published in England as *The Fall of Daisy Duke*, 1967). *Families and Survivors* (1975). *Listening to Billie* (1978). *Beautiful Girl* (1979). *Rich Rewards* (1980). *To See You Again* (1982). *Molly's Dog* (1983). *Superior Women* (1984). *Return Trips* (1985). *Second Chances* (1988). *After You've Gone* (1989). *Mexico: Some Travels and Some Travelers There* (1990). *Caroline's Daughters* (1991). *Almost Perfect* (1993). *A Southern Exposure* (1995). *Medicine Men* (1997). *The Last Lovely City* (1999). *After the War* (2000). *The Stories of Alice Adams* (2002).

—BARBARA A. HERMAN

BETTY ADCOCK (1938–). Betty Adcock was born Elizabeth Sharp in Fort Worth, Tex., and raised in San Augustine, a small East Texas town. An only child in a large extended family, she has described her childhood as growing up "in the nineteenth century." She was educated at Hockaday Preparatory School in Dallas and, for one year, at Texas Tech; some time later she also attended North Carolina State University and Goddard College. In 1957 she married Don Adcock, a director of music at North Carolina State University, and moved to Raleigh. An advertising agency copywriter and producer for eleven years during the 1960s and 1970s, she worked on her poems whenever possible, encouraged by Guy Owen of N.C. State and *Southern Poetry Review*. Of that struggle to become a poet she wrote, in the essay "Permanent Enchantments": "What is it to be a southern woman poet of the generation now over fifty? The only certain answer I can give is that it has been lonely."

Her first book of poems, *Walking Out,* was published in 1975 by Louisiana State University Press, which has issued her four subsequent volumes. Adcock's intense poetry is distinguished by its vulnerable but tough voice, its quick wit, its subtle formal accomplishment, and its relentless pursuit of what the first poem in her first book called "Identity," the lost self that keeps leading her back to the landscape and relatives and stories of home, "knowing there's no place else. Not anywhere."

Betty Adcock has been Kenan Writer-in-Residence at Meredith College in Raleigh since 1983. She has received many prizes for her poetry, including the Great Lakes Colleges Association "New Writer" Award (1976), a National Endowment for the Arts Fellowship (1984), the North Carolina Award for Literature (1996), and a Guggenheim Fellowship (2002).

WORKS: *Walking Out* (1975). *Nettles* (1983). *Beholdings* (1988). *The Difficult Wheel* (1995). *Intervale: New and Selected Poems* (2001).

—MICHAEL MCFEE

JAMES AGEE (1909–1955). Born in Knoxville, Tenn., on November 27, 1909, James Rufus Agee was the first child of Hugh James Agee and Laura Whitman Tyler, an unlikely couple. His father was an ambitious mountain man with a fourth-grade education and a taste for alcohol, his mother a city girl with a degree from the University of Tennessee and a profound devotion to Anglo-Catholicism. The contrast between his parents established strains in Agee that shaped his personality and much of his writing.

The central event of his life was the death of his father in an automobile accident on May 18, 1916, a tragedy that in his view robbed him of his southern heritage. Agee attended St. Andrew's, an Episcopal boys school near Sewanee, Tenn., Knoxville High School, and Phillips Exeter Academy, from which he graduated in 1928. He continued his education at Harvard, where as editor of the literary magazine the *Advocate* he oversaw the publication of a parody of *Time*, which, in 1932, landed him a job at *Time's* sister publication *Fortune*.

He found business writing stultifying, but his marriage in 1933 (the first of three) and the publication of *Permit Me Voyage*, a volume of poetry, in 1934 brightened his early years at *Fortune*. In 1936 the magazine sent him and photographer Walker Evans to Alabama to do a story on cotton sharecropping. The material he developed and his plans for its presentation proved too ambitious for a mere article. In 1939 he left *Fortune* to devote more time to his Alabama book and other writing but soon found himself employed as a book reviewer for *Time* and a film critic for the *Nation*. The reviews he wrote for the *Nation* transcend their immediate subjects and can today be read for their sharp wit and masterful prose. In 1941 the Alabama material was published as *Let Us Now Praise Famous Men,* generally regarded as the finest literary documentary of the 1930s.

During the 1940s Agee abandoned journalism in favor of fiction and screenwriting. His most notable achievement in the latter field was his collaboration with director John Huston on *The African*

Queen. By 1949 he had begun major works of fiction, a novel about his father's death, and another about his experiences at St. Andrew's. Agee saw only the St. Andrew's project to completion with the publication of *The Morning Watch* in 1951.

On May 16, 1955, Agee died of heart attack in New York City. Editor David McDowell knitted the pieces of his nearly finished novel about his father's death into *A Death in the Family*, which won the Pulitzer Prize in 1957. Under the title *All the Way Home*, it was adapted into a play, a film, and a television special. Michael Lofaro is preparing a new edition of the novel, arranging it as Agee had planned. The reconstruction, scheduled for 2007 release, will be part of the ten-volume *Works of James Agee*, to be published by the University of Tennessee Press.

WORKS: *Permit Me Voyage* (1934). *Let Us Now Praise Famous Men* (with Walker Evans, 1941). *The Morning Watch* (1951). *A Death in the Family* (1957). *Agee on Film: Reviews and Comments*, vol. 1 (1958). *Agee on Film: Five Film Scripts by James Agee*, vol. 2 (1960). *The Collected Poems of James Agee* (1962). *The Collected Short Prose of James Agee* (1962). *The Letters of James Agee to Father Flye* (1962). *Four Early Stories of James Agee* (1964). *Selected Journalism* (1985). *Agee: Selected Literary Documents* (1996).

—RICHARD R. SCHRAMM

CONRAD AIKEN (1889–1973). Conrad Potter Aiken was born in Savannah, Ga., on August 5, 1889, to talented but stormy parents transplanted from New England. His father, William Ford Aiken, was a surgeon who dabbled in the arts. In 1900 William Aiken shot his wife, Anna Potter Aiken, and then himself, leaving eleven-year-old Conrad and his three siblings parentless.

Aiken was sent to New Bedford, Mass., to live with a great-great-aunt. He went to Harvard during an auspicious time. T. S. Eliot and E. E. Cummings were among his classmates. But Aiken marched to his own beat, and when he was placed on academic probation for poor class attendance, he responded by striking out to Europe for half a year. He was later to serve as a kind of ambassador for American poetry in England.

Aiken did graduate, and began his prolific career as a major-minor modernist, which led to more than forty separate volumes of poetry, plays, novels, short stories, and voluminous criticism. His best poetry fills *Collected Poems*; his five collections of short stories are brought together in the *Collected Short Stories of Conrad Aiken*; his sundry critical articles are collected in *A Reviewer's ABC*.

As he explored his childhood, Aiken became fascinated with psychoanalytical writing, and Freud himself praised Aiken's highly autobiographical second novel, *Great Circle*. *Ushant: An Essay* gives further insight into Aiken's life, albeit from a third-person perspective. Literary expatriates including Eliot, Ezra Pound, and Malcolm Lowery appear in thinly veiled analogs. *Selected Poems* (1929) was laureled with the Pulitzer Prize. Aiken served as poetry consultant to the Library of Congress (the precursor to the office of poet laureate) in 1950–52. He also received the National Book Award (1954) and the Bollingen Prize (1956).

Aiken completed his own circle by wintering in a house adjacent to his childhood home in Savannah. Although he was very much an international citizen, he once said, "In a way, I never stopped writing about Savannah." Some critics have noted the southern sensibility in his work, particularly in certain treatments of religion and place. He fathered three children by his first wife, and married two more times before he died of a heart attack on August 17, 1973. He is buried in Savannah's famous Bonaventure Cemetery, where his tombstone epitaph identifies him, "Cosmos Mariner, Destination Unknown." In 2004 the *Wall Street Journal* reported that Sotheby's was auctioning Aiken's childhood home, asking $1.5 million. No mention was made of what transpired there.

WORKS: *Earth Triumphant and Other Tales in Verse* (1914). *Turns and Movies and Other Tales in Verse* (1916). *The Jig of Forslin* (1916). *Nocturne of Remembered Spring and Other Poems* (1917). *The Charnel Rose* (1918). *Senlin: A Biography, and Other Poems* (1918). *Skepticisms: Notes on Contemporary Poetry* (1919). *The House of Dust* (1920). *Punch: The Immortal Liar* (1921). *Priapus and the Pool* (1922). *The Pilgrimage of Festus* (1923). *Changing Mind* (1925). *Priapus and the Pool and Other Poems* (1925). *Bring! Bring! and Other Stories* (1925). *Blue Voyage* (1927). *Costumes by Eros* (1928). *Prelude* (1929). *Selected Poems* (1929). Ed., *A Comprehensive Anthology of American Poetry* (1929, 1944). *John Deth: A Metaphysical Legend, and Other Poems* (1930). *Gehenna* (1930). *The Coming Forth by Day of Osiris Jones* (1931). *Preludes for Memnon* (1931). *And in the Hanging Gardens* (1933). *Great Circle* (1933). *Landscape West of Eden* (1934). *Among the Lost People* (1934). *King Coffin* (1935). *Time in the Rock: Preludes to Definition* (1936). *A Heart for the Gods of Mexico* (1939). *Conversation; or, Pilgrim's Progress* (1940). *And in the Human Heart* (1940). *Brownstone Eclogues and Other Poems* (1942). *The Soldier: A Poem by Conrad Aiken* (1944). Ed., *Twentieth Century American Poetry* (1944). *The Kid* (1947). *Skylight One: Fifteen Poems* (1949). *The Divine Pilgrim* (1949). *Short Stories* (1950). *Ushant: An Essay* (1952). *Wake II* (1952). *Collected Poems* (1953, 1970). *A Letter from Li Po and Other Poems* (1955). *The Fluteplayer* (1956). *Mr. Arcularis: A Play* (1957). *Sheepfold Hill: Fifteen Poems* (1958). *A Reviewer's ABC: Collected Criticism of Conrad Aiken from 1916 to the Present* (1958). *Collected Short Stories* (1960). *Selected Poems* (1961). *The Morning Song of Lord Zero* (1963). *The Collected Novels of Conrad Aiken* (1964). *A Seizure of Limericks* (1964). *Cats and Bats and Things with Wings: Poems* (1965). *Collected Short Stories of Conrad Aiken* (1966). *The Clerk's Journal* (1971). *A Little Who's Zoo of Mild Animals* (1977). *Selected Letters of Conrad Aiken* (1978).

—BRYAN GIEMZA

JAMES LANE ALLEN (1849–1925). A writer whose professional identity and literary reputation owed almost everything to association with his native state, James Lane Allen exiled himself from Kentucky for much of his life. When his body was returned to Lexington for burial, he had not even visited the Bluegrass State for almost three decades. A purveyor—in classically wrought, highly self-conscious style—of the romantic, the genteel, and the idealistic, he had such wide popularity in the age of realism and naturalism and the beginnings of modernism that several of his books created controversy when they seemed to reflect the tenets and outlooks of the new order.

The youngest of seven children, Allen was born on December 21, 1849, near Lexington, Ky., to Richard and Helen Jane Foster Allen. With a B.A. and an M.A. (1872, 1877) from Kentucky University (now Transylvania University), he entered upon a twelve-year teaching career that included appointments at public and private schools in Kentucky and Missouri and the Latin professorship at Bethany College in West Virginia. After achieving his first national publication with a critical article on Henry James in 1883, he soon placed other articles, poems, essays, and short stories in major periodicals. His first book, *Flute and Violin and Other Kentucky Tales and Romances,* was highly successful and marked the beginning of Allen's sustained ability to earn a living from his writing. In 1893 he moved from Kentucky to New York City, which remained his home until his death on February 18, 1925. Having assumed support of his sister Annie after their mother's death in 1889, he never married.

Although two short-story collections enclose Allen's extensive, nineteen-book career (*The Landmark* appeared posthumously in 1925), he mainly wrote longer fiction. He published a book a year from 1891 through 1897, then had three years between each of his next two before publishing nothing at all between 1903 and 1909. Eight new titles by Allen came out between 1909 and 1919, and after a hiatus of three years another was issued in 1923, before his final volume two years later.

Allen's most popular novel was *The Choir Invisible.* For two novelettes he wrote immediate sequels: *Aftermath* followed *A Kentucky Cardinal,* and *The Doctor's Christmas Eve* reintroduced characters of the mythic *The Bride of the Mistletoe.* To Allen, who waged critical war against the literary realists, it must have seemed strange when two of his books were similarly attacked, *Summer in Arcady* for its treatment of sex and *The Reign of Law* for its dealing with evolution.

In his own time either too realistic or too romantic for various readers' taste, neither Allen himself nor many subsequent critics would think of his work as anything approaching modern literary realism. The most evident constant in his genteel output, and the reason for his usual categorization with writers of local color fiction, is his focus on the place and people of Kentucky, which figure in some way in almost every one of his books, early and late.

WORKS: *Flute and Violin and Other Kentucky Tales and Romances* (1891). *The Blue-Grass Region of Kentucky and Other Kentucky Articles* (1892). *John Gray: A Kentucky Tale of the Olden Time* (1893). *A Kentucky Cardinal: A Story* (1894). *Aftermath* (1895). *Summer in Arcady: A Tale of Nature* (1896). *The Choir Invisible* (1897). *The Reign of Law: A Tale of the Kentucky Hemp Fields* (1900). *The Mettle of the Pasture* (1903). *The Bride of the Mistletoe* (1909). *The Doctor's Christmas Eve* (1910). *The Heroine in Bronze; or, A Portrait of a Girl* (1912). *The Last Christmas Tree: An Idyll of Immortality* (1914). *The Sword of Youth* (1915). *A Cathedral Singer* (1916). *The Kentucky Warbler* (1918). *The Emblems of Fidelity: A Comedy in Letters* (1919). *The Alabaster Box* (1923). *The Landmark* (1925).

—BERT HITCHCOCK

DOROTHY ALLISON (1949–). Born in Greenville, S.C., Dorothy Allison dealt with both poverty and abuse throughout her childhood. She was the first in her family to finish high school, and she went on to graduate from Florida Presbyterian College (now Eckerd College) in 1971. As a young adult, Allison became aware of the feminist movement, which she credits with giving her the inspiration and courage to write. Grounded in her experiences as a child and young woman, Allison's writing encompasses southern and working-class literature, as well as feminist and lesbian-feminist politics.

Allison has written six books, including poetry, short stories, novels, and nonfiction prose. The act of confronting the stories of life, and telling them as fully and honestly as possible, is a central theme of each of her works. Fittingly, her first book, *The Women Who Hate Me,* is primarily a collection of narrative poems portraying lives in poverty. Likewise, her 1988 collection of short stories, *Trash,* focuses on the necessity of storytelling to survival.

Allison is best known for her first novel, *Bastard out of Carolina,* which was a finalist for the National Book Award and has been translated into over a half dozen languages. The novel follows the life of Bone, a young girl who, after suffering abuse by her stepfather and betrayal by her mother, ultimately comes to terms with the harshness of her life. *Cavedweller,* Allison's second novel, was a *New York Times* best-seller; it also explores the ways families experience both betrayal and healing.

Allison's nonfiction includes *Skin: Talking about Sex, Class, and Literature,* which won the 1995 American Library Association Gay and Lesbian Book Award, and an autobiography, *Two or Three Things I Know for Sure.* In telling her own life story, Allison claims that "stories are the one sure way I know to touch the heart and change the world."

Allison now lives in Northern California with her partner and son.

WORKS: *The Women Who Hate Me* (1983). *Trash* (1988). *Bastard out of Carolina* (1992). *Skin: Talking about Sex, Class, and Literature* (1993). *Two or Three Things I Know for Sure* (1995). *Cavedweller* (1998).

—CAROLYN PERRY

WASHINGTON ALLSTON (1779–1843). Washington Allston was born on November 5, 1779, at Brookgreen, a rice plantation on Waccamaw Neck, Georgetown District, S.C. His father, William Allston, Jr., died while serving as an officer in the Revolutionary army. His mother, Rachel (Moore) Allston, then married Henry Collins Flagg, a physician. After boarding school in Charleston, S.C., Allston was educated at a Newport, R.I., preparatory school and then Harvard College (1796–1800).

Following graduation, Allston pursued a painting career and would become celebrated for his atmospheric color technique. He began studying art in London (1801–3) and later resided in Paris

(1803–4) and Rome (1804–8), where he befriended Samuel Taylor Coleridge. Back in Boston (1808–11), Allston married Ann Channing, then resumed his career in London (1811–18). Coleridge and William Wordsworth wrote favorably of his paintings and praised his book *The Sylphs of the Seasons with Other Poems*. After his wife's death, Allston intensified his commitment to large-scale religious paintings, especially *Belshazzar's Feast* (1817–43).

Returning to Boston in 1818, Allston received the patronage of the social elite. Nevertheless, he was troubled by indebtedness and his failure to finish *Belshazzar*. Marrying Martha R. Dana, he moved to Cambridgeport, Mass., in 1830. Written about 1819–22, Allston's *Monaldi: A Tale*, a gothic romance, complemented the religious tone of his paintings. Allston died on July 9, 1843. Afterward, the Boston Athenaeum exhibited the unfinished *Belshazzar's Feast* as a symbol of the artist's struggle for moral and aesthetic perfection. Allston's *Lectures on Art and Poems* posthumously solidified his reputation as a poet-philosopher in the tradition of Coleridge. Advocating a sisterhood of the arts, Allston equated poetry and music with color and drawing in revealing spiritual truths.

WORKS: *The Sylphs of the Seasons and Other Poems* (1813). *Monaldi: A Tale* (1841). *Lectures on Art and Poems* (1850).

—DAVID BJELAJAC

GEORGE ALSOP (1636?–1673?). Biographical information for George Alsop is sketchy, and most reliable data is provided by the author himself in his single published work. He was born, probably in 1636, in Westminster, London, the son of Rose and Peter Alsop. Because his father was a tailor, George served a two-year handicraft apprenticeship before his Anglican and Royalist sympathies led him to migrate to Maryland, in 1658, in order to escape Cromwell's regime. He served a comfortable four-year term of indenture to Thomas Stockett of Baltimore County. After his indenture expired in 1662, Alsop developed a serious illness, returning to England in late 1663 or early 1664.

Once home, Alsop began writing a book on his American experiences, published in 1666, his only known literary effort but one of such historical and literary importance that it served to rescue him from oblivion. Usually referred to as *A Character of the Province of Mary-Land*, the actual title of the work is over a hundred words long and clearly indicates the topics, organization, and style of the text. The four numbered sections describe the geography and "plenty" of the province; the laws, customs, and "natural demeanor" of the inhabitants; the benefits of indentured servitude in America; and the variety of commercial opportunities. Appended to the volume is a short treatise on "the wild and naked" Indians, together with a collection of letters written by Alsop, during his adventures abroad, to relatives in England. The book is based on the popular literary tradition of the character sketch, which treated character types or places in a satiric and sometimes bawdy manner.

Various factors contributed to the historical and literary value of *A Character*. Alsop, unlike the typical indentured servant, was not only literate but well read; he knew Latin and French, was familiar with contemporary literary forms, and could compose verse as well as prose. At the same time Stockett, his master, shared his religious and political views and seems to have utilized Alsop as a secretary-accountant, giving Alsop acquaintance with a broad range of Maryland life. Stockett was socially prominent and engaged in an impressive number of endeavors—as planter, fur trader, Baltimore County justice, legislator, and military officer. The neighboring Susquehanna Indians had to stop at his plantation to obtain traveling passes, providing Alsop with unique access to them. As colonial promotion literature, Alsop's book is both entertaining and positive, suggesting to both men and women the edenic possibilities of the new world.

After finishing *A Character,* Alsop became a minister; he is mentioned in his father's will in 1672 and thought to have died in 1673.

WORKS: *A Character of the Province of Mary-Land* (1666).

—K. HUNTRESS BALDWIN

LISA ALTHER (1944–). Lisa (Elisabeth Greene Reed) Alther was born on July 23, 1944, in Kingsport, Tenn., one of five children of a surgeon and a former English teacher. She attended public schools in Kingsport and in 1966 graduated from Wellesley College with a B.A. Later that year she married Richard Alther, a painter. Their daughter, Sara Halsey, was born November 15, 1968. Alther is now divorced and lives in rural Vermont and New York City.

Alther's early interest in science led to writing on ecology, gardening, and cooking—and her first publication, in the *Vermont Freeman* in the early 1970s. Her interest in the works of the older generation of southern women writers—Eudora Welty, Flannery O'Connor, Katherine Anne Porter, Carson McCullers—led her to choose writing as a career, with the novel as her preferred genre. She continued to write and publish journalistic pieces and worked on writing fiction. After 250 rejection slips, she says, in 1976 she published her first novel, *Kinflicks,* which was written in the vein of sexual frankness made popular by Erica Jong in *Fear of Flying* (1973); it soon became a best-seller.

That success enabled Alther to write slowly, as she preferred; she writes four or five drafts of each work before submitting it for publication. Her novels, all best-sellers, have appeared at long intervals: *Original Sins* in 1981 and *Other Women* in 1984, both Book-of-the-Month-Club selections; *Bedrock* in 1990; and *Five Minutes in Heaven* in 1995. Though she has written many short stories, she has been satisfied enough with only five to allow publication.

Alther has continued to write scientific articles, critical articles, and reviews; she has taught and lectured widely both in the United States and abroad. Though her first two novels were set in the South and the second two in New England, she writes for a universal audience; her ironic comic tone covers serious topics such as racism, religion, and gender issues. Her works have been translated into fifteen languages and have sold over six million copies. A novella, *Birdman and the Dancer,* was published in Amsterdam, Copenhagen, and Hamburg in the 1990s.

WORKS: *Kinflicks* (1976). *Original Sins* (1981). *Other Women* (1984). *Bedrock* (1990). *Birdman and the Dancer* (1993). *Five Minutes in Heaven* (1995).

—MARY ANNE FERGUSON

A. R. AMMONS (1926–2001). Archie Randolph Ammons, who always called himself "A. R. Ammons" in print, was born in Columbus County, N.C., on February 18, 1926, and died in Ithaca, N.Y., on February 25, 2001, a week after his seventy-fifth birthday. After a modest beginning on a farm in a rural section of southeastern North Carolina and a rather slow start—serving in the navy during World War II, receiving a B.S. in general science from Wake Forest College, and working a while in business—he emerged in his fortieth year as a poet of prodigious originality and scope, eventually publishing dozens of volumes, many of which won prestigious prizes.

When his first book appeared, in a subsidized edition, in 1955, few readers noticed; when his second appeared, some years later, more readers paid attention; but it was the enthusiastic attention of the brilliant critic Harold Bloom, as early as *Ringers in the Tower* (1971), that brought Ammons to prominence. Bloom located Ammons as an important member of the generation of his near contemporaries, such as John Ashbery (born 1927) and James Merrill (1926–1995), although many regard Ammons as less esoteric and more accessible. Bloom also argued for the placement of Ammons in a sturdy tradition of American romanticism going back to Emerson, Whitman, and Dickinson. Ammons can also be situated in a nativist-modernist tradition that includes Wallace Stevens (1879–1955), from Pennsylvania, and William Carlos Williams (1883–1963), from neighboring New Jersey, where Ammons also spent some important years of his life. Ammons combines the vernacular authenticity of Williams's lyrics with the philosophical elevation of Stevens's longer poems.

In 1964 Ammons was invited to take a temporary teaching job at Cornell University, in Ithaca, N.Y., but in time the temporary low-level appointee received one of the most distinguished titles that Cornell could bestow, the Goldwin Smith Professorship in Poetry. Ammons was a member of a community of writers, many of whom (such as Phyllis Janowitz and Robert Morgan) taught creative writing—although one, Roald Hoffmann, was best known as a Nobel laureate in chemistry. For about the last quarter of the twentieth century, Cornell boasted two poets of genius—Ammons and Morgan—who were both from rural North Carolina, Ammons toward the Atlantic coast, Morgan in the mountains.

He was married to Phyllis Plumbo for more than fifty years; they had one son, John Randolph Ammons.

WORKS: *Ommateum, with Doxology* (1955). *Expressions of Sea Level* (1964). *Corsons Inlet: A Book of Poems* (1965). *Tape for the Turn of the Year* (1965). *Northfield Poems* (1966). *Selected Poems* (1968). *Uplands* (1970). *Briefings* (1971). *Collected Poems, 1951–1971* (1972). *Sphere: The Form of a Motion* (1973). *Diversifications: Poems* (1975). *Recording* (1975). *For Doyle Fosso* (1977). *Highgate Road* (1977). *The Selected Poems, 1951–1977* (1977; expanded, 1987). *The Snow Poems* (1977). *Breaking Out* (1978). *Six-Piece Suite* (1978). *Selected Longer Poems* (1980). *Changing Things* (1981). *A Coast of Trees: Poems* (1981). *Hopes: Poems* (1982). *Lake Effect Country: Poems* (1982). *The Really Short Poems of A. R. Ammons* (1990). *Sumerian Vistas: Poems* (1990). *Garbage* (1993). *The North Carolina Poems*, ed. Alex Albright (1994). *Rarities* (1994). *Stand-in* (1994). *Brink Road: Poems* (1996). *Set in Motion: Essays, Interviews, and Dialogues* (1996). *Glare* (1997). *Collected Poems, 1951–1971* (2001). *A Coast of Trees: Poems* (2002). *Bosh and Flapoodle: Poems* (2005).

—WILLIAM HARMON

RAYMOND ANDREWS (1934–1991). Born and raised near Madison in Morgan County, Ga., Raymond Andrews was the fourth of ten children in an African American sharecropping family. At age fifteen, Andrews departed for Atlanta, where he attended evening courses at Booker T. Washington High School before joining the air force and serving a tour of duty in Korea. Following his military service, Andrews enrolled at Michigan State University and then moved to New York City in 1958. He eventually returned to his native Georgia, settling near Athens in 1984.

Andrews drew on his youthful experience in rural Georgia to create his best-known fiction, the Muskhogean trilogy: *Appalachee Red, Rosiebelle Lee Wildcat Tennessee,* and *Baby' Sweet's. Appalachee Red* was his first novel, and it earned the inaugural James Baldwin Prize for fiction in 1979. Set in the fictional Muskhogean County of north Georgia, the trilogy explores African American life in the Deep South between World War I and the 1960s. Andrews's novels draw widely on African American oral culture and emphasize the traditions of preaching, music, and storytelling. He prioritized good stories over political agendas in his writing, and he tended to concentrate on demonstrating a shared humanity across racial lines. Although his fiction does not avoid racial strife, the violent aspects of his writing are often tempered by the comic aspects.

In addition to the Muskhogean trilogy, Andrews published two novellas jointly under the title *Jessie and Jesus; and, Cousin Claire.* A memoir of his childhood years, *The Last Radio Baby,* appeared in 1991.

His brother, the renowned artist Benny Andrews, illustrated all of his books. Andrews's career was cut short when he took his own life in 1991.

WORKS: *Appalachee Red* (1978). *Rosiebelle Lee Wildcat Tennessee* (1980). *Baby' Sweet's* (1983). *The Last Radio Baby: A Memoir* (1991). *Jessie and Jesus; and, Cousin Claire* (1991). *Once Upon a Time in Atlanta* (1998).

—ANDREW B. LEITER

MAYA ANGELOU (1928–). Marguerite Johnson, who through a name change and marriage became Maya Angelou, was born in St. Louis, Mo., on April 4, 1928. Her parents' marriage failed when she was three, and Angelou and her brother, Bailey, moved to Stamps, Ark., where they lived with their paternal grandmother. In 1940 the grandmother, concerned about violence in the South, sent Maya and Bailey to San Francisco to live with their mother, who had recently remarried. At age sixteen, Angelou gave birth to a son, Guy Bailey Johnson. In 1945 she graduated from Mission High School in San Francisco.

Working at menial jobs, Angelou supported herself and her child, then married Tosh Angelos, a Greek American, in 1952. When the marriage ended two years later, Angelou worked in San Francisco nightclubs. She took the name Maya Angelou when she debuted as a dancer at the Purple Onion cabaret. After several years as a cabaret entertainer, she moved in 1952 to New York to work in theater. She also joined the Harlem Writers Guild, becoming an energetic political activist.

In 1960, after seeing the Reverend Martin Luther King, Jr., speak at a Harlem church rally, she co-wrote a musical review, *Cabaret for Freedom,* which helped to raise money in support of the Southern Christian Leadership Conference. In 1960–61, at Dr. King's request, she worked with the SCLC as its northern coordinator. She was the editor for an English-language magazine in Egypt, the features editor for the *African Review* in Ghana, and a television director and producer. She has written several autobiographies as well as children's books. *I Know Why the Caged Bird Sings* ranks with the most acclaimed American autobiographies of her time.

In 1981 Wake Forest University named Angelou its first Reynolds Professor of American Studies. Since then she has made Winston-Salem her home. On January 20, 1993, she read a new poem at President Clinton's first inauguration.

Divorced from her third husband, Paul du Feu, she enjoys being grandmother to Colin, Guy Johnson's son. She is a popular commencement speaker and seems ever ready for new ventures. *Down in the Delta* (1998) marked Angelou's directorial debut in the world of commercial films. The film is set in the rural South, suggesting again the influence of the region on the author's life and her creative imagination.

WORKS: *I Know Why the Caged Bird Sings* (1970). *Just Give Me a Cool Drink of Water — fore I Diiie* (1971). *Gather Together in My Name* (1974). *Oh Pray My Wings Are Gonna Fit Me Well* (1975). *Singin' and Swingin' and Gettin' Merry Like Christmas* (1976). *And Still I Rise* (1978). *The Heart of a Woman* (1981). *Shaker, Why Don't You Sing?* (1983). *All God's Children Need Traveling Shoes* (1986). *Now Sheba Sings the Song* (1987). *I Shall Not Be Moved* (1990). *Wouldn't Take Nothing for My Journey Now* (1993). *Phenomenal Woman* (1994). *The Complete Collected Poems of Maya Angelou* (1994). *Even the Stars Look Lonesome* (1997). *A Song Flung up to Heaven* (2002).

—NORLISHA F. CRAWFORD

TINA McELROY ANSA (1949–). Reviewers have praised this award-winning novelist, short-story writer, essayist, freelance journalist, college instructor, lecturer, and editor for creating four novels that, despite crafting issues, present a realistic, provocative, and vibrant southern African American community. Ansa situates her novels in fictional Mulberry, Ga., an insular African American town, to discuss the changing nature of the African American community as it makes the transition from segregation to integration, lower class to middle and upper middle class, and folk tradition to modern life.

Tina McElroy was born in Macon, Ga., in 1940 and educated there at Mount DeSales, a Catholic school. After graduating from Spelman College in Atlanta, she worked as a journalist. In addition to freelancing, she worked for the *Atlanta Constitution* and the *Charlotte Observer*. She is married to Jonée Ansa, a filmmaker.

Ansa's first novel, *Baby in the Family,* was published in 1989. The *New York Times Book Review* named it a "Notable Book." It won the 1989 Georgia Author Series Award and was cited as a best book by the American Library Association. Her success soon brought invitations to conduct writing workshops. The Ansas live on St. Thomas Island in Georgia. In 2005 Tina Ansa received the Stanley W. Lindberg Award in recognition of her contribution to the literary culture of Georgia.

works: *Baby of the Family* (1989). *Ugly Ways* (1993). *The Hand I Fan With* (1996). *You Know Better* (2002).

—Mildred R. Mickle

JAMES APPLEWHITE (1935–). The poetry of James Applewhite is centered in Stantonsburg, the small tobacco-farming town of eastern North Carolina where he was born. His grandfather was a tobacco farmer there, and his father owned the local Esso station, where James worked during the summers when he was growing up. He enrolled at Duke University, where his classmates included Reynolds Price, Anne Tyler, and Fred Chappell. He acknowledges the importance of his creative-writing teacher James Blackburn, who enabled him "to see myself as a writer, and he became to me an appropriate role model for a male in the South." At the age of twenty, Applewhite married Janis Forrest, also a native of Stantonsburg. They have two sons and a daughter. After graduating from Duke in 1958, he stayed on to earn his M.A. in English with a thesis on Faulkner's *The Sound and the Fury.*

For three years he was an instructor at Woman's College (today the University of North Carolina at Greensboro). Randall Jarrell, his colleague there, became for him what Applewhite calls a personal "paradigm," and he attended his lectures. With a Danforth Teaching Study Grant, he returned to Duke in 1963 to work for a Ph.D. His dissertation on Wordsworth was later published, with revisions, as *Seas and Inland Journeys: Landscape and Consciousness from Wordsworth to Roethke.* He returned to Woman's College, where he taught for four years before joining the faculty at Duke in 1971 to teach creative writing and Romantic and Modern poetry.

Applewhite had published poems in *Harper's Magazine, Shenandoah,* and *Southern Poetry Review* before publishing his first volume, *Statues of the Grass,* in 1975, when he was forty. The critic Harold Bloom has said of one of his later volumes, *River Writing: An Eno Journal,* that it is "one of the few authentic and strong American poetic sequences of his generation." Applewhite's work has been recognized with a National Endowment for the Arts grant, a Guggenheim Fellowship, the North Carolina Poetry Society Award, the Jean Stein Award in Poetry from the American Academy and Institute of Arts and Letters, and a North Carolina Award in Literature.

works: *Statues of the Grass* (1975). *Following Gravity* (1980). *Foreseeing the Journey* (1983). *Seas and Inland Journeys: Landscape and Consciousness from Wordsworth to Roethke* (1985). *Ode to the Chinaberry Tree and Other Poems* (1986). *River Writing: An Eno Journal* (1988). *Lessons in Soaring* (1989). *A History of the River* (1993). *Daytime and Starlight* (1997). *Quartet for Three Voices: Poems* (2002). *A Diary of Altered Light: Poems* (2006).

—George S. Lensing

HARRIETTE ARNOW (1908–1986). Harriette Arnow stands as the premier Appalachian feminist writer of the mid-twentieth century, and her meticulous realism has attracted an audience beyond the region.

Harriette Louisa Simpson was born in Wayne County, Ky., on July 7, 1908, the second of six children. As she reveals in her memoir, *Old Burnside,* her parents urged her to pursue a teaching career. To that end she graduated from Burnside High School in 1924 and received a teacher's certificate from Berea College in 1926. Her first job, teaching in a one-room school in Pulaski County, where she boarded with the family of one of her nineteen students, is memorialized in her first novel, *Mountain Path.* Although she earned a B.S. at the University of Louisville in 1932, she did not stay long in teaching.

In 1934 she moved to Cincinnati to try a "five-year-plan" to establish herself as a writer, working variously as a waiter, a clerk, and a writer for the Federal Writers' Project. There she met Harold Arnow, whom she married in 1939. In those years she published her first two short stories and her first novel, and completed a manuscript, *Between the Flowers,* a novel of a rural marriage that was published posthumously in 1999.

For six years the Arnows attempted subsistence farming at "Submarginal Manor" near Somerset, Ky. They had two children, Marcella and Thomas. When in 1945 Harold took a reporter's job in Detroit, the family went to live in a Wartime Housing Project. Like Thomas Wolfe, an author she admired, Arnow wrote about her early rural life after moving to a city. Her highly acclaimed novel *Hunter's Horn* is a mountain *Moby-Dick* in which the protagonist, Nunnely Ballew, searches obsessively for King Devil, a red fox.

In 1950 the family moved to a farm near Ann Arbor, where Arnow lived until her death on March 22, 1986. There she wrote her masterpiece, *The Dollmaker,* which describes the efforts of Gertie Nevels, uprooted from rural Kentucky, to hold her family together in wartime Detroit. Still in print, it was an instant best-seller and the runner-up to the National Book Award, won that year by Faulkner. Jane Fonda's production of a 1984 television film version of *The Dollmaker* further enlarged its audience.

Arnow's other works include two social histories, *Seedtime on the Cumberland* and *Flowering of the Cumberland;* a novel set in Michigan, *The Weedkiller's Daughter;* and a revolutionary novel, *The Kentucky Trace.* She was also a sought-after speaker and, from 1978 to 1985, she returned to teaching, conducting legendary creative writing classes at Hindman Settlement School in Kentucky. Her papers, including several unpublished works, are housed at the University of Kentucky.

WORKS: *Mountain Path* (1936). *Hunter's Horn* (1949). *The Dollmaker* (1954). *Seedtime in the Cumberland* (1960). *Flowering of the Cumberland* (1963). *The Weedkiller's Daughter* (1970). *The Kentucky Trace: A Novel of the Revolution* (1974). *Old Burnside* (1979). *Between the Flowers* (1999).

—NANCY CAROL JOYNER

DAPHNE ATHAS (1923–). Although she was born in New England, Daphne Athas is a southerner by choice: first her father's choice, then her own. When Athas was a teenager, her family moved to Chapel Hill, N.C., in order to escape the Great Depression. Educated at Chapel Hill High School and the University of North Carolina, Athas left the South to pursue graduate education at the Harvard University School of Education. She then taught near Boston and later served as the director of a service club for the U.S. Air Force in London for several years (1952–58). Athas returned to North Carolina in 1964, teaching at Durham Technical Institute before joining the creative writing program at the University of North Carolina.

Athas's publications include four novels, a play, a personal reminiscence, and a volume of poetry, as well as many essays, short fictions, and poems published in little magazines and anthologies. Her most interesting writing reflects her personal experiences. Exploring her Greek heritage, Athas has sometimes set her work in Greece and depicted her larger-than-life Greek father. Athas's best-known work is her semi-autobiographical novel *Entering Ephesus,* which is about the coming of age of a young girl in fictionalized pre–World War II Chapel Hill (Ephesus) and Carrboro (Haw), a setting that provides a creatively charged mix of intellectual arrogance and southern poverty.

Athas makes a substantial contribution to the literary life of Chapel Hill and the Research Triangle area through teaching and public lecturing, inspiring others to pursue language as a crucial window on the world.

WORKS: *The Weather of the Heart* (1947). *The Fourth World* (1956). "Sit on the Earth" in *The Observer Plays,* ed. Kenneth Tynan (1958). *Greece by Prejudice* (1963). *Entering Ephesus* (1971). *Cora* (1978). *Crumbs for the Bogeyman* (1991).

—HARRIETTE CUTTINO BUCHANAN

MARILOU AWIAKTA (1936–). Born Marilou Awiakta Bonham on January 24, 1936, in Knoxville, Tenn., to Bill and Wilma Bonham, Marilou Awiakta descended from Cherokee and white Appalachian ancestry. In 1945 the future author moved with her family to nearby Oak Ridge, Tenn., where she grew up fascinated by that community's atomic energy research. The worldview that infused her writings blended her Cherokee/Appalachian identity with her scientific knowledge.

In 1958 Awiakta received her B.A. in French and English from the University of Tennessee at Knoxville. Although she would reside for much of her adulthood in Memphis, she lived during the mid-1960s in France, where her husband Paul Thompson was fulfilling a three-year assignment with the U.S. Air Force. In France, Awiakta worked as an interpreter and translator. By the 1970s, her writings—poems and articles—had appeared in numerous smaller-circulation periodicals; by the 1980s major regional periodicals and anthologies were publishing her work.

Awiakta's first book, *Abiding Appalachia: Where Mountain and Atom Meet,* attempted to reconcile traditional values and modern, science-influenced values. *Rising Fawn and the Fire Mystery* was based on a historical incident from the nineteenth century; ostensibly for children, the narrative chronicled the plight of a Native American girl forced to reside in mainstream white society. *Selu: Seeking the Corn-Mother's Wisdom* combined essays, stories, and poems that celebrate the Corn-Mother, a mythic figure found in many Native American cultures. Awiakta's best-known work, *Selu* reinterpreted this myth in an effort to carry traditional Native American wisdom into contemporary life.

In 1985 the U.S. Information Agency included her first two books as part of a traveling exhibition entitled "Women in the Contemporary World." *Selu* has been incorporated into many schools' curricula, and it has inspired a Grammy Award-nominated audiotape production. Awiakta has received honorary awards from several literary organizations, including the Tennessee Mountain Writers Association and the Appalachian Writers Association.

WORKS: *Abiding Appalachia: Where Mountain and Atom Meet* (1978). *Rising Fawn and the Fire Mystery* (1983). *Selu: Seeking the Corn-Mother's Wisdom* (1993).

—TED OLSON

THOMAS BACON (1700?–1768). He was probably a native of Cumberland County, England, but little is known about Thomas Bacon before he appears as a customs collector in Dublin in the

1730s. He published a study of the Irish tax system in 1737 and edited two Dublin newspapers in 1742–43. Bacon entered the Anglican priesthood in 1745 and sailed for Maryland, where he was rector of St. Peter's Parish, Talbot County, for thirteen years. From 1758 until his death he served All Saints, Frederick County, the richest parish in the province.

Along with James Sterling and Thomas Cradock, Bacon represented the best that the Anglican ministry contributed to colonial Maryland culture. He became an honorary member of the Tuesday Club in 1745 and frequently attended the Annapolis organization's meetings, where his poetry, violin playing, and musical compositions enlivened the proceedings. He was the most widely published author in colonial Maryland, and his sermons on charity schools and the education of slaves were printed and reprinted in America and Britain, with the last edition appearing seventy-five years after his death. As a political writer, Bacon remained an articulate champion of the proprietary party and the interests of the established church. As a humanitarian, he advocated educational opportunities for poor whites, slaves, and German immigrants in the province.

Bacon is best known for his compilation of the *Laws of Maryland,* which Lawrence C. Wroth acclaimed as "the most important of the legal publications of the Province of Maryland . . . and a specimen of typography which was not exceeded in dignity and beauty by any production of an American colonial press." Surveying the totality of his contributions, J. A. Leo Lemay concluded: "In an age when clergymen dominated literature and society, Bacon led the Maryland clergy."

WORKS: *A Compleat System of the Revenue of Ireland . . .* (1737). Ed., *Dublin Mercury* (Jan. 23–Sept. 25, 1742). Ed., *Dublin Gazette* (Sept. 28, 1742–July 12, 1743). *Two Sermons, Preached to a Congregation of Black Slaves . . .* (1749). *Four Sermons, Upon the Great and Indispensible Duty of All Christian Masters and Mistresses to Bring Up Their Negro Slaves in the Knowledge and Fear of God . . .* (1750). *A Sermon Preached . . . Before a Society of Free and Accepted Masons . . .* (1753). *An Answer to the Queries on the Proprietary Government of Maryland . . . ,* with Cecilius Calvert (1764). *Laws of Maryland . . .* (1765). *Four Sermons . . . Viz. Two Sermons to Black Slaves and Two Sermons for the Benefit of a Charity Working School . . .* (1753, 1783 reprint only copy now extant). *Writings . . .* (1843). "Proceedings of the Parochial Clergy," *Maryland Historical Magazine* 3 (1908): 257–73, 364–84.

—DAVID CURTIS SKAGGS

GEORGE WILLIAM BAGBY (1828–1883). Journalist, essayist, and humorist, George William Bagby was born on August 13, 1828, in Buckingham County, Va. His mother suffered years of poor health and died when Bagby was eight. Thus he grew up mainly on the plantations of his aunt and of his grandfather and was educated in field schools in Buckingham and Prince Edward counties. The ambience of the "spring and gourd" Virginia of his youth would furnish in later years the material for his best writing.

When Bagby was ten, his father, a Lynchburg merchant, sent him north for his education, first at Edgehill School, in Princeton, N.J., and later to M. L. Hurlbut's school in Philadelphia. In 1849 he graduated from the University of Pennsylvania with a degree in medicine and returned to Lynchburg to practice. By 1853, however, he had turned to journalism, joining with George W. Latham to publish the *Lynchburg Express.*

After the failure of the *Express* in 1856, Bagby continued to contribute sketches and essays to local newspapers. From 1857 to 1859 he served as Washington correspondent for several newspapers. From February to December of 1858 he contributed eight "Mozis Addums" letters to the *Southern Literary Messenger.* These popular dialect letters of a semiliterate rural Virginian were no doubt partly responsible for Bagby's being named editor of the *Messenger* in May 1860. Poor health forced Bagby to leave the Confederate army after short service in 1861. He returned to Richmond, continued as editor of the *Messenger* until 1864, and became Richmond correspondent for newspapers throughout Virginia and the South.

After an unsuccessful postwar attempt to establish a newspaper in rural Virginia, Bagby accepted a post as custodian of the state library, which he held from 1870 to 1878. During this difficult financial period he supplemented his income by writing excursion guides and promotional pamphlets for Virginia railroads, which remain in the collection of the Library of Virginia in Richmond. He also wrote some of his most accomplished sketches of antebellum life in the Old Dominion. His gently irreverent and lightly satirical portraits, such as "The Old Virginia Gentleman" and "The Southern Fool," moved him beyond the idealized plantation romances of the period and made him popular on the lecture circuit. He died in Richmond on November 29, 1883.

WORKS: *Mozis Addum's New Letters: Lettur Wun* (1860). *The Letters of Mozis Addums to Billy Ivvins* (1862). *John M. Daniel's Latch Key: A Memoir of the Late Editor of the Richmond Examiner* (1868). *What I Did with My Fifty Millions* (1874). *Meekin's Twinses: A Perduckshun uv Mozis Addums* (1877). *Canal Reminiscences: Recollections of Travel in the Old Days on the James River and Kanawha Canal* (1879). *A Week in Hespidam: Being the First and Only True Account of the Mountains, Men, Manners and Morals Thereof* (1879). *John Brown and William Mahone: An Historical Parallel Foreshadowing Civil Trouble, 1860–1880* (1880). *Selections from the Writings of Dr. George W. Bagby* (1884). *The Old Virginia Gentleman and Other Sketches*, ed. Thomas Nelson Page (1910). *The Old Virginia Gentleman and Other Sketches*, ed. Ellen M. Bagby (1938).

—RITCHIE D. WATSON, JR.

JOSEPH GLOVER BALDWIN (1815–1864). Jo Baldwin, as he was called and usually signed his name, published only two books during his lifetime. Both classified by the Library of Congress as works of "American History," the first gained for him a durable literary reputation.

In broad outline Baldwin's life reflects nineteenth-century America in its ambitious, relentless westward movement. Born to parents of New England ancestry in Friendly Grove Factory, Va., on January 21, 1815, he was one of seven children of businessman Joseph Clarke Baldwin and Eliza Cook Baldwin. Growing up in Winchester and Staunton, Va., and educated at home and in schools at Staunton, he relinquished formal studies at age fourteen to become a chancery court deputy clerk in order to contribute to family finances. After a few years he began to study law and was licensed to practice at age twenty-one. In 1836, after short tenures as a newspaperman in Lexington and Buchanan, Va., he departed by horseback for the Southwest and established a flourishing legal business. He settled first in DeKalb, Miss., but then moved to Sumter County, Ala., where he lived in Gainesville from 1837 to 1850, and from 1850 to 1854 in Livingston. He was married to Sidney Gaylard White, in 1840, and they became the parents of six children. In 1843 Baldwin, a Whig, was elected to the state legislature, and he was narrowly defeated in a run for Congress in 1849. Twice, in 1837 and 1850, Baldwin made trips to Texas, and by 1854 he had decided to relocate to California.

In San Francisco he again gained high reputation as an attorney and ran for public office. Now a Democrat, he was elected to a three-year term (1859–62) as an associate justice of the California Supreme Court and was nominated but not chosen in 1860 for the U.S. Senate. Practicing law and managing mining investments in Nevada, Baldwin, a former slave owner, regarded the Civil War distantly only in terms of geographic separation. In 1863 he briefly traveled east in an unsuccessful attempt to see relatives in Virginia. Contracting tetanus after relatively minor surgery, he died in the early morning of September 30, 1864.

Baldwin is remarked for the short sketches he began writing in the 1850s. They capture the colorful, memorable individuals and incidents he observed in the judiciary of the Old Southwest. Seventeen were published in the respected *Southern Literary Messenger,* and, in late 1853, Appleton's of New York collected these pieces plus nine new ones in *The Flush Times of Alabama and Mississippi.* Having clear affinity with the work of other Old Southwest humorists, writings he obviously knew, Baldwin's sharp, astute sketches are distinctively different. His classical style is consciously literary and impressively allusive, his basic genre more the essay than the short story. Humor, history, literature, and moral education may all be among his purposes in this volume.

A second book, based on the success of the first, was published in 1855: sober and serious, *Party Leaders* contained essays on "distinguished American statesmen" such as Thomas Jefferson, Alexander Hamilton, Andrew Jackson, Henry Clay, and John Randolph. A final book publication for Baldwin was posthumous, over a century after his death. He had written and published a letter from a fictitious emigrant to California in 1850, but later he produced a manuscript for *The Flush Times of California* based on his actual experience.

WORKS: *The Flush Times of Alabama and Mississippi: A Series of Sketches* (1853). *Party Leaders: Sketches of Thomas Jefferson, Alex'r Hamilton, Andrew Jackson, Henry Clay, John Randolph, of Roanoke, Including Notices of Many Other Distinguished American Statesmen* (1855). *The Flush Times of California* (1966).

—BERT HITCHCOCK

BENJAMIN BANNEKER (1731–1806). Benjamin Banneker was a mostly self-taught mathematician, astronomer, naturalist, farmer, inventor, writer, musician, and almanac maker. He was born on November 9, 1731, in Baltimore County, Md., the first child of free African American parents, Mary Banneky and Robert, a former slave whose freedom she had purchased and who took her surname. They owned and lived on a large tobacco farm, which they cultivated and which Benjamin later inherited. He received little formal schooling, though he learned to read and write from his white grandmother. For short times he did attend a local Quaker interracial school, where his interest in math first developed. All of his life he continued to learn and to develop remarkable powers of observation and induction.

Banneker was of an independent nature and never married. In 1771 he became acquainted with George Ellicott and his wealthy and educated Quaker family, who had large flour mills on property adjoining the Banneker farm. They encouraged his interests and introduced him to others who were helpful to him, and when Andrew Ellicott was appointed to survey what was to become the District of Columbia, Banneker became his field assistant. From the Ellicotts he borrowed books, tools, and instruments, and trained himself to calculate what the positions of the sun, moon, and stars would be during the coming year.

This activity turned him toward almanac making, and he began publishing his own almanacs, which became very successful and widely known. The first was published in 1791 (for 1792), and for the next five years he continued this endeavor, in many editions, in varying versions with varying titles (sometimes even the same year), published in Baltimore, Philadelphia, Wilmington, Trenton, and/or Richmond—all together at least twenty-eight separate editions, each featuring his astronomical tables, with almost all other material apparently by others and chosen by the printers.

These endeavors seem to have encouraged Banneker to write, even some verse. It is known that he wrote about various aspects of nature, especially bees, but most of those writings have not survived. The letter that he wrote to Secretary of State Thomas Jefferson in August 1791, and sent to him along with a manuscript copy of calculations for his almanac, is now his chief claim to fame. The calculations were sent to demonstrate Banneker's abilities (and, by extension, those of his race), and the letter urged Jefferson to be more active against prejudice and, in accord with his widely expressed ideals, to promote freedom and rights for African Americans. Though the letter was not as successful with Jefferson as Banneker had hoped, it was published and often used in the antislavery cause. At age fifty-nine Banneker had retired from farming, and during the remaining years of his life he spent much time in recording in his journal items on math, astronomy, and his observations of nature. He died on October 9, 1806.

WORKS: *Benjamin Banneker's Pennsylvania, Delaware, Maryland and Virginia Almanack and Ephemeris, for the Year of Our Lord, 1792* (1791). *Copy of a Letter from Benjamin Banneker to the Secretary of State, with His Answer* (1792).

—JULIAN MASON

GERALD W. BARRAX (1933–). Born on June 21, 1933, in Attalla, Ala., to Aaron Barrax and Dorthera Hedrick Barrax, Gerald William Barrax moved with his family to Pittsburgh in 1944. His studies at Duquesne University were interrupted by service in the U.S. Air Force (1953–57), but he later earned his B.A. in English from Duquesne. After receiving the M.A. in English at the University of Pittsburgh in 1969, he began teaching at North Carolina Central University. The next year he began teaching at North Carolina State University. He married Geneva Catherine Lucy in 1954; they had three sons, but divorced in 1971. With his second wife, Joyce Dellimore, he had two daughters. His family roles have been important in the poetry that is central to his professional life. Since 1986, he has edited *Obsidian II: Black Literature in Review.*

Barrax's poems celebrate the obstacles and triumphs of his life, discussing how he defines himself through his art. In "To My Mother, in Heaven," he reveals how his family is a microcosm of the movement of African Americans from the South to the North, and he comments on the toll, represented by the loss of his mother's ability to play music on their piano, that that movement takes. He describes his relocation from Attalla to Pittsburgh at age ten, summarizes his family's experiences living in poverty in that city for several decades, and returns him literally and figuratively to the South, to North Carolina, a place where he and his children find another piano and attempt to make music. The return to playing the piano marks a way for him to praise his mother as an artist; to record for posterity and reclaim for her the act of making art; and to comment on the legacy of artistry his mother inspired in him and that he in turn has inspired in the next generation.

WORKS: *Another Kind of Rain* (1970). *An Audience of One* (1980). *The Deaths of Animals and Lesser Gods* (1984). *Leaning against the Sun* (1992). *From a Person Sitting in Darkness: New and Selected Poems* (1998).

—MILDRED R. MICKLE

JOHN BARTH (1930–). John Barth's birth on May 27, 1930, in Cambridge, Md., a small port on the Choptank River, placed him in the part of the state, the Eastern Shore, with the strongest ties to the rural Tidewater South. His parents were Georgia Simmons and John Jacob Barth, owner of a combination candy store and restaurant. Barth's twin sister was named Jill, his older brother, William. John attended public schools and graduated in 1947 from Cambridge High, where he played drums in the band and wrote a column for the school paper. In 1947 he entered the Juilliard School of Music, but soon returned to Maryland to study journalism at Johns Hopkins University, from which he received an B.A. (1951) and an M.A. in creative writing (1952).

At Hopkins, he fell in love with Scheherazade and the framed narratives of Burton's *Arabian Nights.* One of his teachers, Pedro Salinas, showed him the nobility of a life devoted to literature. Another, Louis D. Rubin, Jr., strengthened his awareness of the modernist tradition in southern writing. On January 11, 1950, Barth, only nineteen, married Harriette Anne Strickland. They would have a daughter and two sons.

Although he had begun study for a Ph.D. in the aesthetics of literature in the summer of 1952, a growing family forced him in the fall of 1953 to become an instructor of freshman English at Pennsylvania State University. His first published novel was the parodic existential comedy *The Floating Opera*, a work that conveyed a sense of place, the Eastern Shore, almost as rich as that of nineteenth-century southern local color fictions. Its successor, the sardonic, nihilistic *The End of the Road*, resembled local color less but still carried a realistic flavor of eastern Maryland. After 1958, Barth abandoned allegiance to realistic traditions by crafting an 806-page, eighteenth-century-style, existential epic burlesquing the adventures of Ebenezer Cooke, whose satirical poem *The Sot-Weed Factor* gave the novel its title. Setting the novel 250 years in the past provided the largely blank slate Barth needed to imagine more completely the contrasting possibilities of personality integrity and identity mutability investigated in his previous books.

The contrast between characters governed by fixed ideas and those who embrace Proteus-like shape-shifting resurfaced in *Giles Goat-Boy; or, The Revised New Syllabus*. Here Barth cut his ties to realism and history altogether by using two fantasy universities from the future as a doubled metaphor for contemporary uprisings in American universities and for the universe at large. He moved solidly out of the reality-copying tradition dominating American fiction into an aesthetics-focused approach associated with southern storytellers including Poe, Twain, and James Branch Cabell.

Experiments in Barth's next two book-length works made him the leader of the American wing of the movement eventually called postmodernism. Stories and sketches from *Lost in the Funhouse* combine parodic echoes of classical myths and his "southern" heritage with the most complicated framed stories ever created by an American. *Chimera* underscores an important function served by Barth's various experiments with parodies, frames, metafictions, and fantasies. All four modes of writing yield ontological effects: they enable a blocked author, a mythic hero, or a culture (whether Greek, southern, or Cold War) to transcend exhausted versions of reality and to replenish them with more imaginative, "as-if" perspectives. In *Chimera*, the blocked writer, a figure reexamined in later works including *LETTERS: A Novel* and *The Tidewater Tales*, emerged as Barth's metaphor for Western civilization in its recurring conflicts between East and West, women and men, whites and peoples of color, etcetera. *Chimera* earned Barth the 1973 National Book Award.

In 1965 Barth left Penn State to become professor of English at the State University of New York at Buffalo. In 1971 he moved back to Johns Hopkins, where he taught creative writing from 1973 to 1990. In 1969 Harriette Anne Strickland and John Barth divorced, and on December 27, 1970, he married Shelly I. Rosenberg, a teacher.

Barth has received, in addition to his National Book Award nominations and prize, the Brandeis University Creative Arts Award (1965), a Rockefeller Foundation grant (1965–66), a National Institute of Arts and Letters grant (1966), a Litt.D. from the University of Maryland (1969), the F. Scott Fitzgerald Award for outstanding achievement in American literature (1997), the PEN Malamud Award for Excellence in the Short Story (1998), the Lannan Foundation Lifetime Achievement Award (1998), and the Enoch Pratt Society Lifetime Achievement in Letters Award (1999).

WORKS: *The Floating Opera* (1956; rev. 1967). *The End of the Road* (1958; rev. 1967). *The Sot-Weed Factor* (1960; rev. 1967). *Giles Goat-Boy, or The Revised New Syllabus* (1966; rev. 1967). *Lost in the Funhouse: Fiction for Print, Tape, Live Voice* (1968). *Chimera* (1972). *A Conversation with John Barth* (1972). *LETTERS: A Novel* (1979). *Sabbatical: A Romance* (1982). *The Literature of Exhaustion: and, The Literature of Replenishment* (1982). *The Friday Book: Essays and Other Nonfiction* (1984). *The Tidewater Tales: A Novel* (1987). *The Last Voyage of Somebody the Sailor* (1991).

Once Upon a Time: A Floating Opera (1994). *Further Fridays: Essays, Lectures, and Other Nonfiction* (1995). *On with the Story: Stories* (1996). *Coming Soon!!! A Narrative* (2001). *The Book of Ten Nights and a Night: Eleven Stories* (2004).

—JULIUS ROWAN RAPER

FREDERICK BARTHELME (1943–). Born in Houston, Tex., on October 10, 1943, Frederick Barthelme comes from a literary family (one including brothers Donald and Steve) that has strongly influenced postmodern writing in the United States. Despite his Texas roots, Barthelme is now most associated with the Mississippi Gulf Coast, the fictional terrain of most of his fiction.

Barthelme began his artistic career not as a writer but as a painter. After attending Tulane University for a year, he studied for three years at the University of Houston. He received the B.A. from the Museum of Fine Art in Houston in 1965. His work was exhibited in galleries and museums around the country, including the Seattle Art Museum and New York's Museum of Modern Art. He was also, for a short time, the drummer for the psychedelic band Red Crayola, and can be heard on the band's classic album *The Parable of Arable Land*.

In the mid-1970s, Barthelme shifted his emphasis from paint to prose. After receiving his M.A. in 1977 from Johns Hopkins University, where he studied with John Barth, he joined the faculty in the department of English at the University of Southern Mississippi, where he still teaches creative writing and edits the *Mississippi Review.*

Barthelme's first collection of stories, *Moon Deluxe,* appeared in 1981, immediately catapulting him to the forefront of literary minimalism—a style of writing noted for its spare prose, quirky dialogue, and slice-of-life plots. Since *Moon Deluxe,* Barthelme has published eight novels, two short-story collections, and a memoir, co-authored with his brother Steven, on their adventures and problems with gambling. His writing style has progressively moved away from the spare minimalism of the early 1980s, to a richer, denser prose, with the plots and subjects still focused on the quiet nuttiness of postmodern suburban life.

Barthelme's fiction is set almost exclusively in the cities and suburbs of the Mississippi Gulf Coast, a world of high-rises, shopping malls, and casinos, and characteristically focuses on the everyday lives of everyday people. Amidst a world steeped in popular culture and the media, Barthelme's characters celebrate small victories and small defeats, struggling to endow their lives with wonder, hope, and beauty.

WORKS: *Moon Deluxe* (1983). *Second Marriage* (1984). *Tracer* (1985). *Chroma* (1987). *Two against One* (1988). *Natural Selection* (1989). *The Brothers* (1993). *Painted Desert* (1995). *Bob the Gambler* (1997). *Double Down: Reflections of Gambling and Loss,* with Steven Barthelme (1997). *The Law of Averages: New and Selected Stories* (2000). *Elroy Nights* (2003).

—ROBERT H. BRINKMEYER, JR.

WILLIAM BARTRAM (1739–1823). William Bartram, son of botanist John Bartram, was born outside Philadelphia on April 9, 1739. As a boy he studied at the academy that would become the University of Pennsylvania and showed evidence of the artistic skill he would later demonstrate in his detailed sketches of native American plants and animals.

Encouraged by his father to seek out a business career, Bartram grew frustrated with a Philadelphia apprenticeship and left in 1761 for North Carolina to work unsuccessfully at an uncle's trading post. In 1765 William joined his father—now botanist to King George III—on a year-long expedition into newly acquired British Florida. He would try becoming a planter near St. Augustine in 1766 only to return to Pennsylvania within the year, but by that time the work he had done with his father had made its mark. Bartram was now convinced that he wanted to work as a naturalist, and his Florida paintings won the attention of a wealthy British botanist, John Fothergill, who served as his patron from 1768 until 1780.

In 1773 Bartram set forth from Charleston, S.C., on a meandering 2,400-mile journey that took him as far west as Louisiana. Living alone or among native tribes for four years, Bartram compiled the diary that was eventually published as *Travels*. One of the most distinctive books to come out of the early Republic, it influenced a generation of European Romantics before coming full circle when Thomas Carlyle recommended it to Emerson as an American classic.

After his father's death in 1877, Bartram traveled occasionally—turning down Thomas Jefferson's request that he join the Lewis and Clark expedition—but primarily he assisted his brother in running the family botanical garden in Philadelphia. He died on July 22, 1823, in the house where he had been born.

WORKS: *Travels through North and South Carolina, Georgia, East and West Florida, the Cherokee Country, the Extensive Territories of the Muscogulges, or Creek Confederacy, and the Country of the Chactaws* (1791). *William Bartram: Botanical and Zoological Drawings, 1756–1788* (1968). *William Bartram on the Southeastern Indians* (1995). *William Bartram: Travels and Other Writings* (1996).

—FARRELL O'GORMAN

RICK BASS (1958–). Despite a career that began in the petroleum industry, Rick Bass has emerged as an important writer of fiction and nonfiction deeply concerned with humanity's ties with the natural world and with the preservation of the wilderness.

Bass was born on March 7, 1958, in Fort Worth, Tex. He received his B.S. from Utah State University in 1979, and not long after went to work as a petroleum geologist. He later wrote about this work in *Oil Notes*, a memoir that explores the tensions between his deeply felt connection with the earth and his enthusiasm for extracting oil from its depths.

Bass began his writing career with *The Deer Pasture*, a collection of essays focused on the Texas hill country. Like much of his later work, the essays emphasize the rejuvenating power of the wilderness and our primal ties with the land. After another collection of essays, *Wild to Heart*, Bass published his first book of fiction, *The Watch: Stories*.

Bass's life took a momentous turn when he and his wife moved to the largely isolated Yaak Valley in Montana. There they would raise their two sons, and Bass would write and work for environmental preservation. Numerous works have followed, both fiction and nonfiction, most focusing on life in the wilderness West.

Through such works as *The Ninemile Wolves: An Essay*, *The Lost Grizzlies: A Search for Survivors in the Wilderness of Colorado*, *The Book of Yaak*, and *The New Wolves: The Return of the Mexican Wolf to the American Southwest*, Bass is now recognized as an important nature writer and wilderness activist. His fiction' characteristically explores people struggling to untangle the confusions of their lives, frequently by immersion into the natural world.

WORKS: *The Deer Pasture* (1985). *Wild to Heart* (1987). *The Watch: Stories* (1989). *Oil Notes* (1989). *Winter: Notes from Montana* (1991). *The Ninemile Wolves: An Essay* (1993). *Platte River* (1994). *The Lost Grizzlies: A Search for Survivors in the Wilderness of Colorado* (1995). *In the Loyal Mountains: Stories* (1995). *The Book of Yaak* (1996). *The Sky, the Stars, the Wilderness: Novellas* (1997). *The New Wolves: The Return of the Mexican Wolf to the American Southwest* (1998). *Where the Sea Used to Be* (1998). *Fiber* (1998). *Brown Dog of the Yaak: Essays on Art and Activism* (1999). *Colter: The True Story of the Best Dog I Ever Had* (2000). *The Roadless Yaak: Reflections and Observations about One of Our Last Great Wilderness Areas* (2002). *The Hermit's Story* (2002).

—ROBERT H. BRINKMEYER, JR.

JOHN SPENCER BASSETT (1867–1928). Born on September 10, 1867, in Tarboro, N.C., to Mary Wilson and Richard Baxter Bassett, John Spencer Bassett was educated in public and private schools of eastern North Carolina, at Trinity College (later Duke University), from which he was graduated in 1888, and at Johns Hopkins University, where he received his doctorate in 1894. With his wife of two years, Jessie Lewellin, he then returned to Trinity as professor of history.

In addition to teaching, Bassett wrote articles and books, increased library holdings of southern materials, initiated publication of the *Historical Papers of the Trinity College Historical Society,* and founded and edited the *South Atlantic Quarterly* (1902–5). A liberal stand on the race question, highlighted in an editorial praising Booker T. Washington, nearly caused his dismissal from Trinity in 1903. Sustained by the college, he withstood attacks from without, winning a significant victory for academic freedom. Even so, the deep-seated intolerance in the South caused him to leave the region a few years later.

Bassett's interest in the history of North Carolina yielded monographs on its colonial government, the Regulator movement, and slavery. In 1906 *The Federalist System,* his contribution to the prestigious *American Nation* series, brought him wider recognition. That same year he accepted an appointment at Smith College in Massachusetts.

Although Bassett broadened his scholarly interests at Smith, he continued to work in regional history, publishing a two-volume *Life of Andrew Jackson,* his finest book. Bassett believed sectionalism to have been the formative force in the Jacksonian era. He viewed Jackson himself as a product of, and spokesman for, the frontier, portraying him sympathetically, yet fairly. Some years later, Bassett supplied a needed source by editing *The Southern Plantation Overseer as Revealed in His Letters,* long the standard work on the subject. On January 27, 1928, accidental death cut short his work as editor of the *Correspondence of Andrew Jackson.*

The author or editor of twenty-five books, Bassett was a pioneer in the critical study of southern history. His courage, competence, and commitment to seek the truth give him a high place among historians of the South.

WORKS: *The Constitutional Beginnings of North Carolina, 1663–1729* (1894). *Regulators of North Carolina* (1895). *Slavery and Servitude in the Colony of North Carolina* (1896). *Anti-Slavery Leaders of North Carolina* (1898). *Slavery in the State of North Carolina* (1899). Ed., *The Writings of "Colonel William Byrd of Westover in Virginia, Esqr."* (1901). *The Federalist System, 1789–1801* (1906). *Life of Andrew Jackson,* 2 vols. (1911). *A Short History of the United States* (1913). *The Plain Story of American History* (1916). Ed., *Correspondence of George Bancroft and Jared Sparks, 1823–1832* (1917). *The Middle Group of American Historians* (1917). *The Lost Fruits of Waterloo* (1918). *Our War with Germany: A History* (1919). Ed., *Selections from the Federalist* (1921). Ed., *The Westover Journal of John A. Selden, Esqr., 1858–1862* (1921). Ed., *Major Howell Tatum's Journal While Acting Topographical Engineer (1814) to General Jackson, Commanding the Seventh Military District* (1922). Ed., *Letters of Francis Parkman to Pierre Margry* (1923). Ed., *The Southern Plantation Overseer as Revealed in His Letters* (1925). Ed., *Correspondence of Andrew Jackson,* 7 vols. (1926–35; 3 vols. completed at Bassett's death). *Expansion and Reform, 1889–1926* (1926). Ed., with others, *The Writing of History* (1926). *The League of Nations: A Chapter in World Politics* (1928). *Makers of a New Nation* (1928). *Martin Van Buren, Secretary of State,* in Samuel Flagg Bemis, ed., *The American Secretaries of State and Their Diplomacy,* vol. 4 (1928).

—WAYNE MIXON

HAMILTON BASSO (1904–1964). When Hamilton Basso's ninth novel, *The View from Pompey's Head*, hit the *New York Times* best-seller list in 1954, he already had a prolific writing career behind him as a journalist for the *New Republic, Time, Life, Holiday,* and the *New Yorker.*

Born in New Orleans on September 5, 1904, Joseph Hamilton Basso was the son of an Italian-American shoe manufacturer and, after dropping out of Tulane University in 1926, got his start as a reporter on the city's newspapers, the *Tribune,* the *Item,* and the *Times-Picayune.* Stirred by H. L. Mencken's criticism of the South, he joined the writers of the innovative literary magazine the *Double Dealer,* in which he had his first two poems published.

After publishing his debut novel *Relics and Angels* in 1929, he married Etolia Simmons in 1930 and moved to a cabin in North Carolina's Pisgah Forest. His next book, a biography of Civil War general P. G. T. Beauregard, was followed by the local color novels *Cinnamon Seed, Courthouse Square,* and *Days before Lent,* which deal with a southern protagonist who is torn between his love for the land and his contempt for southern prejudice, hate crimes, and provincialism. *Days before Lent* earned Basso the Southern Authors Award in 1939.

After travels in Europe and various short-stint residences up and down the East Coast, the Bassos moved to Weston, Conn., in 1942. Not wanting to be labeled a southern novelist, Basso wrote *Wine of the Country* and *The Greenroom,* but looked to the South for *Sun in Capricorn,* his novel about Huey Long.

Though Basso criticized southern ancestor worship in his 1954 best-seller, he seemed nostalgic for the Old South in *The Light Infantry Ball.* His final novel, *A Touch of the Dragon,* was a departure from the southern scene altogether and was soon forgotten after Basso's death from lung cancer in New Haven, on May 13, 1964.

WORKS: *Relics and Angels* (1929). *Beauregard: The Great Creole* (1933). *Cinnamon Seed* (1934). *In Their Own Image* (1935). *Courthouse Square* (1936). *Days before Lent* (1939). *Wine of the Country* (1941). *Sun in Capricorn* (1942). *Mainstream* (1934). Ed., *The World from Jackson Square,* with Etolia S. Basso (1948). *The Greenroom* (1949). *The View from Pompey's Head* (1954). *The Light Infantry Ball* (1959). *A Quota of Seaweed* (1960). *A Touch of the Dragon* (1964).

—INEZ HOLLANDER

RICHARD BAUSCH (1945–). Richard Bausch was born on April 18, 1945, in Fort Benning, Ga., to Robert Carl, a natural storyteller, and Helen (Simmons) Bausch, an artist; they created for Bausch and his twin brother, Robert, an environment rich with artistry and imagination. Bausch served in the U.S. Air Force as a survival instructor in 1966–69. He received his B.A. in 1974 from George Mason University and his M.F.A. from the University of Iowa in 1975, and later taught at Northern Virginia Community College. After his marriage in 1969 to Karen Miller, a photographer, the couple had five children.

The author of nine novels and six short-story collections, Bausch is the recipient of many prestigious awards and has collaborated on several important anthologies, including the sixth edition of *The Norton Anthology of Short Fiction.* Bausch's stories have appeared in such literary journals and magazines as the *New Yorker, Atlantic Monthly, Esquire,* the *Southern Review,* and *Ploughshares,* where he published his first story, "The Wife's Tale," in 1978. In addition, his stories have been anthologized in the *O. Henry Prize Stories* and *Best American Short Stories.* In 1994 a feature film of Bausch's novel *The Last Good Time* starred Maureen Stapleton, Armin Mueller-Stahl, Lionel Stander, and Olivia D'Abo.

His novel *Take Me Back* was nominated for a PEN/Faulkner Award, as was his inaugural collection of stories, *Spirits and Other Stories.* Bausch received a National Endowment for the Arts grant in 1982 and a Guggenheim Fellowship in 1984, won one of the Lila Wallace–Reader's Digest Writers' Awards in 1992, and was recognized by the American Academy of Arts and Letters with their Award in

Literature in 1993. The Fellowship of Southern Writers granted Bausch membership in 1997. Currently, Bausch holds the Heritage Chair in Writing at George Mason University.

Bausch wrote introductions to *Bad Man Blues: A Portable George Garrett* (1998) and Eudora Welty's *On Writing* (2002). *Hello to the Cannibals: A Novel,* published by HarperCollins in 2002, testified to Bausch's continued commitment to the creation of original, evocative fiction. His seventh collection of shorter fiction, *Wives and Lovers,* appeared in 2004.

WORKS: *Real Presence* (1980). *Take Me Back* (1981). *The Last Good Time* (1984). *Spirits and Other Stories* (1987). *Mr. Field's Daughter* (1989). *The Fireman's Wife and Other Stories* (1990). *Violence* (1992). *Rebel Powers* (1993). *Aren't You Happy for Me? and Other Stories* (1995). *Rare and Endangered Species: A Novella and Stories* (1996). *The Selected Stories of Richard Bausch* (1996). *Good Evening Mr. and Mrs. America and All the Ships at Sea* (1996). *In the Night Season* (1998). *Someone to Watch over Me: Stories* (1999). Ed., *The Norton Anthology of Short Fiction,* with R. V. Cassill (6th ed., 2000). Ed., *The Cry of an Occasion: Fiction from the Fellowship of Southern Writers* (2001). *Hello to the Cannibals* (2002). *Wives and Lovers: Three Short Novels* (2004).

—PATRICK SAMWAY, S.J.

FRANCES COURTENAY BAYLOR (1848–1920). Frances Courtenay Dawson was born on January 20, 1848, in Fort Smith, Ark., the youngest of four sons and two daughters born to James Lowes Dawson and Sophie E. Baylor Dawson. Her father was in the military, and the family later moved to posts in San Antonio and New Orleans. Her parents separated around the time of the Civil War, and her mother resumed her maiden name and changed Dawson's name to Frances Courtenay Baylor. After the war Baylor and her mother returned to her mother's native Virginia, moving to Winchester to live with Baylor's sister, Sophie Baylor Walker, and her husband, Confederate general John George Walker. The families moved to England around 1865 and stayed about two years.

Beginning in the 1870s Baylor wrote short pieces that were published in newspapers. Her stories and poems were published in magazines such as the *Atlantic Monthly, Harper's, Ladies Home Journal, Lippincott's Magazine,* and the *New England Magazine.* Two of the stories originally published in *Lippincott's* were combined and published in 1886 as a novel entitled *On Both Sides,* humorous accounts of social misadventures of Americans visiting England and of an English family visiting America. In 1887 her next novel appeared, *Behind the Blue Ridge,* set in western Virginia, the only one of her novels to be set entirely in the United States. Her story for children, *Juan and Juanita,* became a juvenile classic. Some of her best short stories and sketches were collected in 1889 and published as *A Shocking Example and Other Sketches.* Her writing style—melodramatic, sentimental, and lacking a strong plot—was typical of fiction in the United States in the late nineteenth century, though *Behind the Blue Ridge* demonstrates some of the speech, customs, and manners of western Virginia.

In addition to her writing, Baylor was a supervisor in Virginia with the John F. Slater Fund, which aided the welfare and education of African American children. She also helped set up industrial schools in Virginia in the 1890s.

On August 24, 1896, Baylor married George Sherman Barnum, a railway official in Savannah, Ga. Barnum died not long after their marriage, and Baylor returned to Virginia. They had no children. She died in Winchester on October 15, 1920, and is buried in Mount Hebron Cemetery.

WORKS: *On Both Sides* (1886). *Behind the Blue Ridge* (1887). *Juan and Juanita* (1887). *A Shocking Example and Other Sketches.* (1889). *Claudia Hyde* (1894). *Miss Nina Barrow* (1897). *The Ladder of Fortune* (1899). *A Georgian Bungalow* (1900).

—ALICE R. COTTEN

JOHN BEECHER (1904–1980). John Henry Newman Beecher lived a remarkably varied life that fed his vigorous, plain-spoken poetry—poetry that often derides America's treatment of its working-class and African American citizens. Great-great nephew of abolitionists Harriet Beecher Stowe and Henry Ward Beecher, he was born on January 22, 1904, in New York City to Isabel Garghill and Leonard Thurlow Beecher, an executive of the Tennessee Coal, Iron, and Railroad Company (TCI). Within three years of Beecher's birth, the family moved to the new company headquarters in Birmingham, Ala.

Educated until age fifteen in the Birmingham public schools and in military summer camps, Beecher seemed headed for a military career, but in 1920 he withdrew in disillusionment from the Virginia Military Institute. He spent much of the ensuing year working the long day or night shifts in the open-hearth furnaces of a TCI mill in Birmingham. After an unsuccessful two years as an engineering student at Cornell, his father's alma mater, Beecher returned to work in the steel mills. He finally acceded to his mother's influence, and began taking college courses in creative writing and the liberal arts, though he continued working on and off in the mills until seriously injured in 1925.

In 1926 Beecher enrolled as a graduate student of language and literature at Harvard. He married just before returning to Harvard that fall, instructed at Dartmouth the spring semester of 1927, and then spent several years traveling and studying with his wife in Europe, working as a metallurgist for TCI, teaching college English, finishing his M.A., and studying sociology for a year in Chapel Hill at the University of North Carolina. This work in sociology produced his 1934 study *The Sharecropper's Union in Alabama* and may have gained him a number of jobs over the next several years under Roosevelt's New Deal—as researcher and administrator of labor and relief programs in several southern states.

Meanwhile, Beecher wrote poetry about his country's oppression of the people he was trying to help. His first long poem, *And I Will Be Heard,* was published by Twice a Year Press in 1940. After a stint working as editor for a Birmingham newspaper and staff writer for the *New York Post,* in 1943 Beecher became a sailor on the first racially integrated American ship in World War II, the account of which he published in 1945 as *All Brave Sailors.*

After the war he returned to teaching at San Francisco State College, but in 1950 he lost his position for refusing to sign the loyalty oath required by the McCarthy-inspired Levering Act. Blacklisted from college teaching, Beecher purchased a ranch north of San Francisco, where, in collaboration with his fourth wife, Barbara, he began Morning Star Press, later renamed Rampart Press. With this press he printed a number of his own poems in small, artful editions—typeset, sewn together by hand, and illustrated with his wife's block prints. *Report to the Stockholders and Other Poems, 1932–62,* first published by Rampart, was reprinted by a New York press and propelled him to national recognition as a poet.

From July 1964 to January 1965, Beecher left his position as poet-in-residence at the University of Santa Clara to cover the southern civil rights movement as a newspaper and magazine correspondent. The next decade of his life involved increasing recognition and success as a poet. A number of new books of his poetry appeared, perhaps the most important being *To Live and Die in Dixie and Other Poems* (1966). He was poet-in-residence at several colleges, gave endowed readings at colleges and universities throughout the nation, and became a visiting scholar at Duke University. He died on May 11, 1980, in San Francisco.

He lacks the aesthetic complexity and philosophical depth of Walt Whitman, with whom he is sometimes compared, but Beecher's poetry can searingly articulate the ironic distance in America and the American South between outward dominance and inward moral impoverishment, between societal hope and the laboring man's despair, between official report and vital colloquial account.

works: *The Share Croppers' Union in Alabama* (1934). *And I Will Be Heard: Two Talks to the American People* (1940). *Here I Stand* (1941). *All Brave Sailors* (1945). *Land of the Free: A Portfolio of Poems on the State of the Union* (1956). *Observe the Time: An Everyday Tragedy in Verse* (1956). *To Alexander Meiklejohn* (1956). *Just Peanuts* (1957). *Inquest: A Poem* (1957). *Moloch: A Poem* (1957). *Poems for the People: Broadsides* (1957). *Day of Strange Gods* (1959). *In Egypt Land* (1960). *Phantom City* (1961). *Undesirables* (1962). *Report to the Stockholders and Other Poems, 1932–1962* (1962). *Bestride the Narrow World* (1963). *Conformity Means Death* (1963). *On Acquiring a Cistercian Breviary* (1963). *Yours in the Bonds* (1963). *An Air That Kills* (1963). *A Humble Petition to the President of Harvard* (1963). *To Live and Die in Dixie and Other Poems* (1966). *Hear the Wind Blow!: Poems of Protest and Prophecy* (1968). *Collected Poems, 1924–1974* (1974). *Tomorrow Is a Day: A Story of the People in Politics* (1980). *One More River to Cross: The Selected Poetry of John Beecher* (2003).

—WHIT JONES

MADISON SMARTT BELL (1957–). Born on August 1, 1957, Madison Smartt Bell grew up on the family farm outside Nashville, Tenn. Both his parents had attended Vanderbilt and were friends with Allen Tate, Andrew Lytle, Donald Davidson, and Madison Jones. As a child, Bell was in contact with and in awe of these writers, and as a high school student he immersed himself in the fiction of Southern Renascence authors. When he left for college, his ambition was to follow in their footsteps.

In 1979 Bell graduated summa cum laude from Princeton University, where he participated in the creative writing program for undergraduates, was mentored by George Garrett, and won four awards for his fiction. In 1981 he completed an M.A. at Hollins College. Bell's first published novel, *The Washington Square Ensemble*, was written while he was at Hollins.

A prolific writer, Bell has published eleven novels and two collections of short stories, as well as a textbook. He has also published numerous stories, essays, book reviews, nonfiction pieces, and screenplays. His most acclaimed novel has been *All Souls' Rising*. A finalist for the National Book Award (1995) and the PEN/Faulkner Award (1996), it won the Maryland Library Association Award (1996) and the Annisfield-Wolf Award (1996). Other awards and recognition Bell has received include the Lillian Smith Award (1989), a Guggenheim Fellowship (1991), a National Endowment for the Arts Fellowship (1992), selection as one of *Granta*'s "Best American Novelists under Forty" (1996), the John Dos Passos Prize for Excellence in Literature (2001), and induction into the Fellowship of Southern Writers (2003).

Bell is writer-in-residence at Goucher College, where he has taught since 1984 and where his wife, poet Elizabeth Spires, also teaches. He has also taught in several other creative writing programs, including the Iowa Writers' Workshop, the 92nd Street Y in New York, and the Johns Hopkins University Writing Seminars.

works: *The Washington Square Ensemble* (1983). *Waiting for the End of the World* (1985). *Straight Cut* (1986). *Zero db* (1987). *The Year of Silence* (1987). *Soldier's Joy* (1989). *Barking Man* (1990). *Doctor Sleep* (1991). *Save Me, Joe Louis* (1993). *All Souls' Rising* (1995). *Ten Indians* (1997). *Narrative Design: A Writer's Guide to Structure* (1997). *Master of the Crossroads* (2000). *Narrative Design: Working with Imagination, Craft, and Form* (2000). *Anything Goes* (2002). *The Stone That the Builder Refused* (2004).

—VERBIE LOVORN PREVOST

KATHERINE BELLAMANN (1877–1956). In 1945, after the death of her husband, musician-novelist Henry Bellamann, Katherine McKee Jones Bellamann returned to her native Mississippi to resume a writing career that had lapsed since the publication of her first novel, *My Husband's Friends* (1931). At the time of her death in 1956 she had completed a novel that her husband had left unfinished, *Parris Mitchell of Kings Row*, composed a modest amount of poetry, and written a novel based on the life she had known as a child in rural Mississippi growing up near the small town of Carthage where she had been born on October 7, 1877.

She met Henry Bellamann at Methodist Girls' College in Tuscaloosa, Ala. They were married on September 3, 1907, at Carthage and moved to Columbia, S.C., where Henry was dean of the School of Fine Arts at Chicora College from 1907 to 1924. Having studied voice in Europe and New York, Katherine was preparing to make her debut at the Opéra Comique de Paris when she developed asthma and was forced to abandon her career as a professional singer. As a voice teacher in New York, where she and Henry moved in 1924, she achieved distinction. Desi Arnaz and Eddy Arnold were among her pupils.

Bellamann's writing career was strongly influenced by that of her husband. Although Henry Bellamann, who grew up in Fulton, Mo., was primarily interested in music, serving as chairman of the examining board of the Juilliard School, as a director of the Curtis School of Music, and briefly as head of the Department of Music at Vassar, he completed seven novels and one book of poems. *Kings Row* (1940) was his most successful novel.

Katherine Bellamann died in Jackson, Miss., on November 8, 1956. The Bellamann papers were given to Mississippi College at Clinton.

WORKS: *My Husband's Friends* (1931). *Parris Mitchell of Kings Row*, with Henry Bellamann (1948). *The Hayvens of Demaret* (1951). *Two Sides of a Poem* (1955). *A Poet Passed This Way* (1958).

—ROBERT L. PHILLIPS, JR.

LERONE BENNETT (1928–). Lerone Bennett was born in Clarksville, Miss., on October 17, 1928, the son of Lerone and Alma Reed Bennett. He went to public schools in Jackson before heading to Atlanta in 1945. There he edited the student newspaper at Morehouse College, the *Maroon Tiger*; he received his B.A. in 1949. Bennett flirted with going to graduate school but found himself pulled toward a journalism career. He first worked as a reporter with the *Atlanta Daily World* (1949–51), then was promoted to city editor (1952–53) before moving to Chicago to assume the associate editorship of *Ebony* magazine (1953–58). He married Gloria Sylvester and fathered four children.

Bennett was tapped as senior editor of *Ebony* in 1958, bringing his distinctive style—and longevity—to the post. As of this writing, he remains the editor, and his presence is to be detected in the magazine's continuing emphasis on black history. His first book, *Before the Mayflower*, was uncompromising in its center-stage analysis of black American history-making. Many of the historical actors that Bennett studied have been the subjects of continuing scholarly interest, including Nat Turner, John Menard, and the principals of the civil rights movement. He also published some of his more acerbic, and interesting, essays in a collection called *The Negro Mood and Other Essays*. His next book was a biography of Martin Luther King, Jr., *What Manner of Man*.

Bennett has not shied away from controversy. His latest, highly thesis-driven book, *Forced into Glory: Abraham Lincoln's White Dream*, contravenes—to put it mildly—the prevailing understanding of Lincoln's comparatively enlightened racial politics.

WORKS: *Before the Mayflower: A History of the Negro in America, 1619–1964* (1962; rev. 1966). *The Negro Mood and Other Essays* (1962). *What Manner of Man: A Biography of Martin Luther King, Jr.* (1964). *Black Power, U.S.A.: The Human Side of Reconstruction, 1867–1877* (1967). *Pioneers in Protest* (1968). *The Challenge of Blackness* (1972). *The Shaping of Black America* (1975). *Wade in the Water: Great Moments in Black History* (1979). *Succeeding against the Odds* (1987). *Forced into Glory: Abraham Lincoln's White Dream* (2000).

—BRYAN GIEMZA

WENDELL BERRY (1934–). Born in New Castle, Ky., on August 5, 1934, Wendell Berry left his childhood home for higher education and a teaching career. At the University of Kentucky he earned the B.A. and M.A. in English. He taught for a year at Georgetown College in Kentucky, then entered Stanford University on a Wallace Stegner Fellowship. With him were his wife Tanya (Amyx) and an infant daughter, Mary Dee. In 1961 the Berrys were back in Kentucky, but a Guggenheim took them to Florence, Italy. The next year the Berrys were briefly again in Kentucky; son Pryor Clifford was born in August. Berry was director of freshman English at the Bronx campus of New York University from 1962 to 1964. Ready to begin permanent residence in Kentucky, he accepted a position at the University of Kentucky. In 1965 the Berrys purchased Lane's Landing, a farm near the family retreat on the Kentucky River. In 1971 Berry was named Distinguished Professor of English at the university. He retired from teaching in 1993. With his wife, he continues farming and writing at the "native and chosen place."

Berry's work reveals a profound dedication to a responsible use of the world's resources by individuals, families, and communities; the interconnection of all the parts, the natural and the social together, is simply the basis of being. Perhaps Berry is more widely known as an essayist than as a writer of fiction or poetry, owing to his recognition by the back-to-the-earth community, his advocacy of local economies, and his philosophy of the unity of the natural and human worlds. His fiction is, however, of the highest order, replete with the drama and subtlety of human relationships and of lives grounded in the land and local community. We may well term it spiritual (if not directly religious) in its themes: life has sanctity; responsibility and conviviality are spiritual; grace and mystery inform living. Berry's skill at weaving that commitment into prose and poetry marks him as a major man of letters. Often honored as a writer, he has received Guggenheim and Rockefeller fellowships and, as well, a grant from the NEA, in addition to an award from the National Academy of Arts and Sciences and the T. S. Eliot Award.

Berry holds a unique place among American literary figures, as both artist and prophet. The mantle of the Vanderbilt Agrarians rests gracefully on his shoulders; indeed, he may be counted the perfecter of their vision.

WORKS: *Nathan Coulter* (1960). *The Broken Ground* (1964). *A Place on Earth* (1967). *The Hidden Wound* (1968). *Openings* (1968). *Findings* (1969). *The Long-Legged House* (1969). *Farming: A Hand Book* (1970). *The Unforeseen Wilderness: Kentucky's Red River Gorge* (1971). *A Continuous Harmony: Essays Cultural and Agricultural* (1972). *The Country of Marriage* (1973). *The Memory of Old Jack* (1974). *Sayings and Doings* (1975). *Clearing* (1977). *The Unsettling of America: Cultural and Agricultural* (1977). *A Part* (1980). *The Wheel* (1980). *Recollected Essays, 1965–1980* (1981). *The Gift of Good Land: Further Essays Cultural and Agricultural* (1981). *Standing by Words* (1983). *The Collected Poems, 1957–1983* (1985). *The Wild Birds* (1986). *Home Economics: Fourteen Essays* (1987). *Recollected Essays* (1987). *Sabbaths: Poems* (1987). *Remembering* (1988). *Traveling at Home* (1988). *Harland Hubbard: Life at Work* (1990). *What Are People For?* (1990). *The Discovery of Kentucky* (1991). *Fidelity* (1992). *Sex, Economy, Freedom and Community: Eight Essays* (1992). *Entries* (1994). *Watch with Me and Six Other Stories of the Yet-Remembered Ptolemy Proudfoot and His Wife, Miss Minnie, Née Quinch* (1994). *A World Lost* (1996). *Two More Stories* (1997). *A Timbered Choir: The Sabbath Poems, 1979–1997* (1998). *The Selected Poems of Wendell Berry* (1998). *Jayber Crow* (2000). *Life Is a Miracle: An Essay against Modern Superstition* (2000). *In the Presence of Fear: Three Essays for a Changed World* (2001). *The Art of the Commonplace: The Agrarian Essays of Wendell Berry*, ed. Norman Wirzba (2002). *Three Short Novels* (2002). *Citizens Dissent: Security, Morality, and Leadership in an Age of Terror* (2003). *Citizenship Papers* (2003). *That Distant Land: The Collected Stories* (2004). *Hannah Coulter: A Novel* (2004). *The Long-Legged House* (2004).

—SAMUEL S. HILL

DORIS BETTS (1932–). Doris June Waugh Betts, the only child of mill worker William Elmore and Mary Ellen Freeze Waugh, was born on June 4, 1932, in Iredell County, N.C. She received her early education in the Statesville public schools. In 1950 she entered the Woman's College of the University of North Carolina (now the University of North Carolina at Greensboro) and in 1952 married Lowry M. Betts. She left college following the first semester of her junior year, moving to Columbia, S.C., where daughter Doris LewEllyn was born, an event heralded by Betts's learning that she had won the Mademoiselle College Fiction Contest. In the fall the family moved to Chapel Hill, and Lowry entered the law school of the University of North Carolina. Two other children followed: David Lowry (b. 1954) and Erskine Moore (b. 1960).

The writing habit was entrenched. In 1954 Betts published her first collection of stories, *The Gentle Insurrection,* which earned the UNC Putnam Prize. Journalism was also a habit: she wrote for the *Statesville Daily Record* (1946–50), the *Chapel Hill Weekly* (1953–54), and the *Sanford Herald* (1957–58). She held a Guggenheim Fellowship in creative writing in 1958–59. In 1966 she began teaching creative writing at the University in Chapel Hill. Popular as teacher and colleague, Betts soon had a full-time appointment and was named Alumni Distinguished Professor in 1980. When she retired in 1998, the Doris Betts Professorship in Creative Writing was established.

A dedicated writer and teacher, Betts has always recognized an obligation to service. While living in Sanford (where her husband practiced law), Betts served on the Sanford school board and the Lee County library board of trustees. At UNC, she directed freshman-sophomore English from 1972 to 1977. She served on numerous departmental and university committees, and was elected to a three-year term as chair of the university faculty in 1982. She was the first woman to hold that position.

Acclaimed for her short stories, Betts came to see the novel as the greater challenge. Her third novel, *Heading West,* brought her national recognition and challenged earlier judgment that she was primarily a short-story writer; her novel was named a Book-of-the-Month selection. Her subsequent novels have been praised similarly for their skill and intellectual fiber. In 1981 her most famous short story, "The Ugliest Pilgrim," was filmed as *Violet* and won an academy award. "Violet" also achieved success as a musical. Betts's story "This Is the Only Time I'll Tell It" was filmed for television in 1999.

The Bettses now live in retirement on an eighty-acre horse farm, Araby, outside Pittsboro, N.C. Both Lowry (who became district judge of Orange and Chatham counties) and Doris have favored space between their public and private lives. For Doris, the commutes from Sanford and Pittsboro aided the writing under way.

WORKS: *The Gentle Insurrection* (1954). *Tall Houses in Winter* (1957). *The Scarlet Thread* (1964). *The Astronomer and Other Stories* (1965). Ed., *Young Writer at Chapel Hill* (1968). *The River to Pickle Beach* (1972). *Beasts of the Southern Wild and Other Stories* (1973). *Heading West* (1981). *Souls Raised from the Dead* (1994). *The Sharp Teeth of Love* (1997).

—JOSEPH M. FLORA

ROBERT BEVERLEY (ca. 1673–1722). Robert Beverley's *The History and Present State of Virginia, in Four Parts* (1705) remains the first known account of the colony's history and geography by an American. Like Thomas Jefferson's *Notes on the State of Virginia* (1785) and William Byrd II's *A History of the Dividing Line* (ca. 1730), Beverley's *History* represents early Americans' attempts to synthesize geographical, historical, social, and cultural epistemologies of the "New World."

Beverley was born about 1673 in Middlesex County, Va., to Major Robert Beverley, a wealthy planter and prominent politician who had immigrated to North America in 1663 from Yorkshire. He was educated in England, possibly at Yorkshire's Beverley Grammar School. In 1697 he wed Byrd's sister Ursula, but was widowed less than one year later, upon her death during the birth of their son, William. After serving in various bureaucratic offices, Beverley was elected to represent Jamestown in the House of Burgesses in 1700–1702 and 1705–6. While on business in England in 1703–5, he wrote letters disparaging the political actions of colonial governor Francis Nicholson and his administration. The letters led to his exit from politics. Before his death on April 21, 1722, he amassed one of Virginia's largest estates.

Beverley's *History* grew out of London bookseller Richard Parker's request that he proofread John Oldmixon's manuscript of *British Empire in America* (1708). He instead chose to write his own account. He wittily describes the colony's history, geography, and natural resources, Native Americans, and politics and culture. Most striking is his sustained, sympathetic interest in Native American life on its own terms. He revised *The History* in 1722, softening it (to later critics' chagrin). In addition to *The History,* he is credited with composing "Mr. Beverley's Acct of Lamhatty" and *An Abridgement of the Public Laws of Virginia.*

WORKS: *The History and Present State of Virginia, in Four Parts* (1705, 1722). "Mr. Beverley's Acct of Lamhatty" (w. 1707). *An Abridgement of the Public Laws of Virginia* (1722).

—SCOTT HICKS

JOHN PEALE BISHOP (1892–1944). John Peale Bishop was born on May 21, 1892, in Charles Town, W.Va. His father, of New England descent, died when he was ten, and after his Virginian mother remarried in 1906 the family moved to Maryland. In 1910 Bishop, never in good health, developed an eye ailment that prevented him from entering college. His mother and sister cared for him over the next three years, reading him poetry and fostering the love of verse that resulted in the publication of his first poem in *Harper's Weekly* in 1912.

A year later, his vision restored, Bishop entered Princeton. There he met Edmund Wilson and F. Scott Fitzgerald, who were to remain friends for life, and wrote poems for Princeton's *Nassau Literary Magazine.* Many of these were collected in the privately published *Green Fruit.* Upon graduation, Bishop took an army commission and served until 1919, mostly in France, where he did not see combat but first experienced the strong attraction to European culture that would mark him for life.

In 1920 Bishop moved to New York, where he became junior editor and then managing editor of *Vanity Fair.* In 1922 he married Margaret G. Hutchins. From 1924 to 1926 he would work again at *Vanity Fair* and write screenplays for Paramount in New York, but otherwise he and his bride spent their first decade as husband and wife abroad, primarily in France, where they met such figures as Ezra Pound, Ernest Hemingway, and Allen Tate. Bishop became much more productive, however, upon his return to the United States in 1933. In the 1930s he published substantial works of poetry, criticism, and fiction, achieving critical if not popular acclaim. He served as chief poetry reviewer for the *Nation* and contributed regularly to the *New Republic.* Appointed assistant to Archibald MacLeish at the Library of Congress in 1943, Bishop was soon forced to retire because of worsening heart trouble and emphysema. He died on April 4, 1944, on Cape Cod. His posthumous reputation was advanced by the collections that appeared in 1948 as well as by the essays Allen Tate collected from Bishop's friends and admirers in *A Southern Vanguard: The John Peale Bishop Memorial Volume* (1947).

WORKS: *Green Fruit* (1917). *The Undertaker's Garland* (1922). *Many Thousands Gone* (1931). *Now with His Love* (1933). *Minute Particulars* (1935). *Act of Darkness* (1935). *Selected Poems of John Peale Bishop* (1941). *Collected Essays of John Peale Bishop* (1948). *Collected Poems of John Peale Bishop* (1948).

—FARRELL O'GORMAN

ARTHUR BLACKAMORE (ca. 1679–post-1722). The novelist Arthur Blackamore has left few traces. He appears to have been born in England in 1679 and matriculated at Christ Church College, Oxford, on May 17, 1695. In September 1707, he journeyed to Virginia as a tutor, but once in Williamsburg took an appointment as master of the grammar school attached to the College of William and Mary and possibly as professor of humanities at the college. Contemporary documents indicate that Blackamore had a serious drinking problem; in two entries in 1709, the diary of William Byrd II refers to his drunkenness and concerns by the college governors over the master's fitness. Earning the dislike of the college president and Anglican commissary, James Blair, Blackamore was granted a final six months of service in June 1716, and departed in mid-1717 for England. After an attempt to enter orders and a brief literary career there, he disappears from the record after November 17, 1722.

Blackamore's first known literary work is a Latin poem, "Expeditio Ultramontana," composed in the autumn of 1716 in honor of the governor, Alexander Spotswood, and his exploratory trip to the Shenandoah River. Although the original is lost, a translation in English couplets celebrates the extension of empire and the naming of mountains for King George I and the governor. Back in England, Blackamore produced a series of three novellas, dedicated to Spotswood, the intent of which is to pillory dissenters and assert Anglican orthodoxy. After publishing an abridged version of Joseph Bingham's eight-volume *Origines Ecclesiastica* in 1722, the author produced his final known work, the novel *Luck at Last*. Sylvia is a virtuous young Englishwoman who, after fleeing home when her father contracts her marriage to an elderly man, survives several years incognito as a servant. Her story, modeled after Aphra Behn's *The Wandering Beauty*, not only anticipates Richardson's *Pamela* but has some original and realistic touches, including an episode in which Sylvia lives among a gang of beggars.

WORKS: *The Perfidious Brethren; or, The Religious Triumvirate, Display'd in Three Ecclesiastical Novels. I. Heathen Priestcraft; or, The Female Bigot. Being the History of Decius Mundus, and Paulina. II. Presbyterian Piety; or, The Way to Get a Fortune. III. The Cloven-Hoof; Or, The Anabaptist Teacher Detected* (1720). *Ecclesiae Primitivae Notitia; or, A Summary of Christian Antiquities*, 2 vols. (1722). *Luck at Last; or, The Happy Unfortunate* (1723); repr. as *The Distress'd Fair; or, Happy Unfortunate* (1737); also in William H. McBurney, ed., *Four before Richardson* (1963). "Expeditio Ultramontana," trans. George Seagood, *Maryland Gazette*, June 17 and 24, 1729; repr. *William and Mary Quarterly*, 1st series, 7 (1898): 33–37, also ed. Earl G. Swem (1960).

—JEFFREY H. RICHARDS

JAMES BLAIR (1655?/1656?–1743). James Blair, prominent for half a century in Virginia's political and religious life, was born in rural Scotland, in May 1655 or 1656. The son of a Church of Scotland clergyman, he attended Marischal College, a Calvinist institution in Aberdeen, and received the M.A. from the University of Edinburgh (1673), after six years of theological study there. He was ordained in 1679 and was minister of a parish near Edinburgh until 1682, when his refusal to take the Test Oath recognizing James II as head of the Church of Scotland forced him from his ministry. Backed by Henry Compton, Bishop of London, he was clerk of the Master of Rolls in London for three years, then traveled to Virginia in 1685, to become rector of the frontier parish of Henrico.

Blair's marriage to the seventeen-year-old Sarah Harrison (1687) allied him with one of Virginia's wealthiest families. A pugnacious man of indomitable will, idealism, and relentless political ambition, he exploited his family's influence and his high Anglican connections in England to secure appointment to numerous positions of power: as the bishop of London's commissary (1690), as rector of Bruton Parish in Williamsburg (1710), and twice as a member of the Governor's Council. A staunch supporter of the colonists' political rights, he effected the removal of three royal governors, all the while continuing to lead the Anglican clergy in Virginia.

Blair was widely known as a powerful pulpit orator and tireless writer. His five-volume edition of sermons, *Our Saviour's Divine Sermon on the Mount,* remained a standard homiletic work for a century. He achieved his enduring legacy as the founder of the College of William and Mary, for which he secured the royal charter in 1693. He served as its first president for nearly fifty years, until his death in 1743.

WORKS: *Our Saviour's Divine Sermon on the Mount, Contain'd in the Vth, VIth, and VIIth Chapters of St. Matthew's Gospel explained, And the Practice of it recommended in divers Sermons and Discourses,* 5 vols. (1722, 1740). *The Present State of Virginia, and the College,* with Henry Hartwell and Edward Chilton (1727). *A Paraphrase of Our Saviour's Sermon on the Mount, Contained in V, VI, VII Chap. of St. Matthew's Gospel* (1729).

—ELSA NETTELS

RICHARD BLAND (1710–1776). Richard Bland was born into a prominent and well-connected Tidewater family. His grandfather was a councilor and speaker of the House of Burgesses. Orphaned in 1720 and raised by Randolph uncles, Richard and William, Bland was educated at William and Mary and later learned enough law to qualify for the bar in 1746. From 1742 until he died, he continuously represented Prince George County in Virginia's legislatures. His poem to Landon Carter, which almost seems a prologue to his nephew Robert Munford's *The Candidates,* powerfully articulates Bland's sense of the gentry's political responsibility. Described by Thomas Jefferson as "the most learned and logical man of those who took prominent lead in public affairs," Bland provided significant legislative leadership in each of Virginia's political crises beginning with the Pistole Fee controversy, in which the lower house charged that Lt. Governor Robert Dinwiddie had imposed an unlawful tax on land patents, endangering colonial liberty.

Legislative experience, wide reading, and deep antiquarian interest enabled Bland, a formidable controversialist, to evolve a Whiggish defense of colonial Assemblies based on principles of *salus populi est suprema lex,* natural right theory, and English constitutional history. Opposing parliamentary interference into internal colonial affairs and virtual representation, Bland argued for a divided sovereignty that prefigured later commonwealth relationships. If he wrote an anti-bishopric essay, its thinking is probably similar to that expressed in a letter of August 1, 1771, to Thomas Adams (1730–1785), a prominent Virginia compatriot then in London.

Jefferson, a generation younger, remembered that Bland always drew back from the precipice; but Edmund Randolph praised his "boldness." While Bland frequently cautioned moderation during the 1770s, he also stood at the forefront of much Revolutionary activity. He was a signer of all three associations and a member of all three conventions, the Virginia House of Delegates, and the first two Continental Congresses. Declining election to the third Congress, Bland died serving as a member of the House of Delegates, but his intellectual legacy had already made its impact on Patrick Henry and Jefferson.

WORKS: *A Modest and True State of the Case* (1753); surviving only in part as *A Fragment on the Pistole Fee,* ed. W. C. Ford (1891). *"An Epistle to Landon Carter, Esq., upon hearing that he does not intend to stand a Candidate at the next Election of Burgesses"* (June 20, 1758, in Moncure Daniel Conway, *Barons of the Potomack and the Rappahannock,* 1892, 138–41). *A Letter to the Clergy of Virginia* (1760). *The Colonel Dismounted; or, The Rector Vindicated* (1764). *An Inquiry into the Rights of the British Colonies* (1766). Letter to Thomas Adams, August 1, 1771 (in *William and Mary College Quarterly Historical Magazine,* 1st ser., 5 [Jan. 1897]: 149–57).

—JON C. MILLER

ALBERT TAYLOR BLEDSOE (1809–1877). Albert Bledsoe was born on November 9, 1809, the eldest son of Moses Bledsoe, editor of the *Frankfort (Ky.) Commonwealth.* At West Point he was a classmate of Robert E. Lee and Jefferson Davis, but after his graduation in 1830 he left the army to study philosophy and theology at Kenyon College in Ohio. The mathematics he had learned at West Point was of practical value at Kenyon, where he taught it to support himself. Similarly, he was an instructor in mathematics at Miami University while studying law. In 1836 he married, and in 1838 moved to Springfield, Ill., where he practiced law for ten years. He knew Abraham Lincoln and Stephen Douglas, who practiced in the same courts, but his real interests were still in theology. He completed his brilliant and surprising study *Examination of President Edwards' Inquiry into the Freedom of the Will* while living in Springfield. A development of these ideas resulted in *Theodicy* in 1853, the most widely used southern theological work of the century, which with his reputation in religious circles as a polemicist led to his nickname, "The Arminian Sledge Hammer."

Bledsoe taught mathematics at the University of Mississippi from 1848 to 1854, and at the University of Virginia from 1854 to 1861. He became assistant secretary of war under Jefferson Davis, who sent him, as the region's best controversialist, to London to explain the southern side. He returned in February 1865, and the following year published his most impassioned work, *Is Davis a Traitor; or, Was Secession a Constitutional Right Previous to the War of 1861?* In 1867 he went to Baltimore to edit the *Southern Review,* with initial help from William Hand Brown and later assistance from his talented daughter, Sophia Bledsoe Herrick. Widely known as the most trenchant defender of the Lost Cause, Bledsoe consumed his great mental and physical energy in endless controversies in a journal the impoverished region could not support. Yet the magazine, brilliantly combative as it was, is his monument, for his daughter could continue it only a few months after his death on December 8, 1877.

WORKS: *An Examination of President Edwards' Inquiry into the Freedom of the Will* (1845). *A Theodicy; or, Vindication of the Divine Glory, as Manifested in the Constitution and Government of the Moral World* (1853). *Three Lectures on Rational Mechanics; or, The Theory of Motion* (1854). *An Essay on Liberty and Slavery* (1856). *Is Davis a Traitor; or, Was Secession a Constitutional Right Previous to the War of 1861?* (1886). *The Philosophy of Mathematics, with Special Reference to the Elements of Geometry and the Infinitesimal Method* (1867).

—C. CARROLL HOLLIS

JOSEPH BLOTNER (1923–). Born and raised in New Jersey, educated at Drew, Northwestern, and the University of Pennsylvania, Joseph Blotner was elected to the Fellowship of Southern Writers in 1999, thereby becoming a certified southerner. Of this he writes in his memoir, *An Unexpected Life:* "Walter Sullivan told me that I was the only Yankee among them. Marnie and I flew to Chattanooga where I was inducted into the Fellowship, deeply proud of the beribboned medallion for my neck and the rosette for my lapel." Blotner belongs because of his critical and scholarly contributions over many years, the fruits of a lifetime of labor, to the study of two great twentieth-century southern masters—William Faulkner and Robert Penn Warren. He was the authorized biographer for both. As biographer, Blotner came to know personally many of the writers of the Renascence as well as the leading scholars in the field of southern letters.

An only child, Joseph Leo Blotner was born on June 21, 1923, in Plainfield, N.J., where his father had a restaurant. After graduation from the local high school, he entered nearby Drew University, initially drawn to a career in radio. His college education was interrupted because of World War II. He enlisted in the air force, training in Nevada and at Kirtland Air Force Base in Albuquerque, N.M., before transfer to England and assignment to bombing raids. One flight did not return, and Blotner found himself a prisoner of Germany. He spent the last eight months of the war uncertain of his fate.

The war ended, Blotner returned to New Jersey. Like many veterans, he put his life on fast track. Returning to Drew, he claimed English as his major and graduated in 1947. Eight months later, he had an M.A. from Northwestern, and then proceeded to Penn for his Ph.D. (1951). His dissertation "Thorne Smith: A Study in Popular Fiction" gave little indication of his future interests and direction. In 1946 he married Yvonne Wright, with whom he would father three daughters.

After two years as an assistant professor at the University of Idaho, Blotner joined the faculty at the University of Virginia, where he would have the good fortune to meet William Faulkner, who had come to Charlottesville as writer-in-residence. Faulkner was sympathetically drawn to the young academic, and the Blotners and the Faulkners became good friends. When Blotner left Virginia in 1968 to accept a professorship at the University of North Carolina at Chapel Hill, he was deep into the research and writing of the Faulkner biography. In 1972 Blotner moved to the University of Michigan, where he would teach until his retirement in 1993. An outstanding teacher of American literature, Blotner enjoyed a number of distinguished visiting appointments at home and abroad; twice a Guggenheim Fellow and Fulbright Lecturer, he has received many national and international awards. In retirement, Blotner has remained active in Faulkner scholarship, co-editing with Noel Polk facsimiles of the manuscripts.

A widower when he retired, he married Marnie Courtelyou Allen, who also had important links to Charlottesville, where they soon relocated. Of the future he has written in the final paragraph of *An Unexpected Life:* "With luck there might be time for another book, and in some form the South would be intrinsic to it."

WORKS: *The Political Novel* (1955). *The Fiction of J. D. Salinger,* with Frederick L. Gwynn (1958). Ed., *Faulkner in the University,* with Gwynn (1959). *William Faulkner's Library: A Catalogue* (1964). *The Modern American Political Novel, 1900–1960* (1966). *Faulkner: A Biography,* 2 vols. (1974). Ed., *Selected Letters of William Faulkner* (1977). Ed., *Uncollected Stories of William Faulkner* (1979). *William Faulkner: A Biography* (1984). *Robert Penn Warren: A Biography* (1997). *An Unexpected Life* (2005).

—GEORGE GARRETT

ROY BLOUNT, JR. (1941–). Born in Indianapolis of southern parents, Roy Alton Blount grew up in Georgia, attended Vanderbilt University, worked for the *Atlanta Journal* and, though he has lived in the northeast since 1968, writes from a southern perspective.

Blount grew up in a middle-class home in Decatur, Ga.; his father was a savings and loan executive. In school he played sports and wrote about them, earning a scholarship to Vanderbilt, where he majored in English and graduated magna cum laude in 1963. He attended Harvard for an M.A. in English and after two years in the army began writing columns for the *Atlanta Journal.* In 1968 he joined *Sports Illustrated;* since 1975 he has been a freelance writer. He has two grown children and two grandchildren.

He has written a dizzying variety of things, including sports pieces, songs, one-act plays, one-man shows performed on Broadway, crossword puzzles, a screenplay; he has written a book on hair, a book of songs about food, three books about animals. In addition to his seventeen books he has contributed to 125 different periodicals, including the *New Yorker* and the *Atlantic Monthly* as well as *Organic Gardening;* he also has contributions in more than 152 books. His own "self-promotional" description identifies him as a "humorist-novelist-journalist-dramatist-lyricist-lecturer-reviewer-performer-versifier-cruciverbalist-sportswriter-screenwriter-anthologist-columnist-philologist of sorts."

About Three Bricks Shy of a Load, his first book, was about the Pittsburgh Steelers. About half of his books gather his own short humor pieces (parodies, personal essays, short stories, ruminations), some of them more topically united (*Crackers,* for instance, is mostly about the South and southerners), others more miscellaneous. He is the author of one novel, *First Hubby,* about the husband of the first female American president, and a memoir, *Be Sweet.* He edited *Roy Blount's Book of Southern Humor,* and he co-authored the nation's best-selling dog book. Blount may be the most versatile writer in America, and among the best, though he suffers from America's tendency to undervalue comic writers until they are dead.

He lives in Manhattan and western Massachusetts.

WORKS: *About Three Bricks Shy of a Load* (1974). *Crackers* (1980). *One Fell Soup* (1982). *What Men Don't Tell Women* (1984). *Not Exactly What I Had in Mind* (1985). *It Grows on You* (1986). *Soupsongs/ Webster's Ark* (1987). *Now, Where Were We?* (1988). *About Three Bricks Shy . . . and the Load Filled Up* (1989). *First Hubby* (1990). *Camels Are Easy, Comedy's Hard* (1991). *Roy Blount's Book of Southern Humor* (1994). *If Only You Knew How Much I Smell You,* with Valerie Shaff (1998). *Be Sweet* (1998). *I Am Puppy, Hear Me Yap,* with Shaff (2000). *Am I Pig Enough for You Yet?* with Shaff (2001). *Robert E. Lee: A Penguin Life* (2003).

—MERRITT W. MOSELEY, JR.

ROBERT BOLLING (1738–1775). Born on August 17, 1738, in Chellowe County, Va., Robert Bolling was the great-great-grandson of Pocahontas and John Rolfe. He was educated at the Wakefield School in England and later returned to Virginia to become a New World Renaissance man. He worked in a law office in Williamsburg before serving as the sheriff of Buckingham County and holding a seat in Virginia's House of Burgesses. Bolling also led his county militia and was a delegate to the July Convention of 1775. He accomplished all this in addition to a hearty literary career before dying at the age of thirty-seven in Richmond.

Like many other writers during the colonial period, Bolling was published in popular journals in both England and America. But he stood out from his contemporaries because of his classical education and ability to write well in a number of genres and languages. With many humorous essays to his credit, he is most famous for the narrative grotesque poem "Neanthe." Bearing the traits of the Restoration dramas Bolling saw during his years in England, "Neanthe" stands as one of the South's earliest exercises in grotesque humor and piercing satire. Most likely written in 1763, the poem combines historical events and personalities with Bolling's own imagined elements. Highlighting his deep knowledge not only of English literature but also of French and Italian Renaissance literature, "Neanthe" is prefaced by eight lines of Francisco Berni's "Al Cardinal Ippolito De' Medici."

Bolling was linked to the Virginia Wits, a loosely connected group of writers who were the colonial predecessors to the Transcendentalists. The Wits saw themselves as somewhat apart from their contemporaries, and their satires evidenced their scathing humor and intelligence. The group often used the *Virginia Gazette* and the *Richmond Argus* as the publishing vehicles for their work. Bolling is now considered to be *the* formidable mind of the Wits, and his work is only recently beginning to be collected from the three manuscript collections he left behind and the many contemporary publications that are now found only in small collections. Much credit goes to J. A. Leo Lemay for bringing Bolling's work to a contemporary readership.

WORKS: *Robert Bolling Woos Anne Miller: Love and Courtship in Colonial Virginia* (1760). *A Collection of Diverting Anecdotes, Bon Mots, and Other Trifling Pieces by Bolling* (1764). *Pieces Concerning Vineyards and Their Establishment in Virginia* (1772). *La Gazzetta de Parnaso or Poems, Imitations, Translations etc. by Bolling* (no date). *A Memoir of a Portion of the Bolling Family of Virginia,* no. 4, *Wynne's Historical Documents from the Old Dominion* (1868).

—MATTHEW SCIALDONE

JOHN HENRY BONER (1845–1903). John Henry Boner—poet, editor, and printer—was born in the Moravian community of Salem, N.C., on January 31, 1845. He was educated in local schools until the age of thirteen, when he began work as an apprentice in a newspaper office. Boner started his own newspaper in Salem in 1865, but it was short-lived due in part to his clear Republican bias. Boner's political connections helped him to gain a position as a clerk in the Republican-controlled state government, where he worked for a couple of years before moving to Washington, D.C., to begin a long career at the Government Printing Office. Boner spent sixteen years in Washington before, with the change to a Democratic administration in 1885, he was dismissed for "excessive partisanship."

Boner began publishing poetry in the late 1870s. The success of his first collection, *Whispering Pines,* enabled him to secure several editorial staff positions in New York. In the late 1890s he became the editor of the *Literary Digest,* a position he had held for only a short time when a dispute with the publishers led to his resignation. Boner left New York and was rehired by the Government Printing Office, but his health began to fail and he was often too weak to work. He died in Washington, from tuberculosis, on March 6, 1903.

Boner wrote romantic and allegorical poems, many showing the influence of Edgar Allan Poe. His descriptive nature poetry often focused on southern scenes, with his "Back to the Old North State" being especially popular in his home state. Boner's best-known work is "Poe's Cottage at Fordham," about Poe's home in Fordham, N.Y.

Boner's reputation remained strong in the years after his death. In newspaper and magazine articles he was referred to as "North Carolina's First Man of Letters." His burial in an unmarked grave in Washington, D.C., was a matter of concern to his friends and admirers, who formed the Boner Memorial Association to raise funds to return the poet's body to North Carolina. In December, 1904, Boner was reinterred in the Moravian Cemetery in Salem.

WORKS: *Whispering Pines* (1883). *Some New Poems* (1901). *Poems* (1903; cover title, *Boner's Lyrics*).

—NICHOLAS GRAHAM

SHERWOOD BONNER (1849–1883). Born in Holly Springs, Miss., on February 26, 1849, Katharine Sherwood Bonner McDowell enjoyed a brief but turbulent literary career as "Sherwood Bonner," a name she first used in 1875. Never large slaveholders or plantation owners (Bonner's father was a medical doctor), the Bonners nonetheless suffered personal and financial losses during the Civil War and the years immediately following; Bonner's mother and sister died of illness during the war and her father and brother were victims of the yellow fever epidemic of 1878. Bonner's marriage to fellow Holly Springs resident Edward McDowell began to fail shortly after it was sealed in 1871. They divorced in 1881.

In 1873 Bonner had left her husband and only child, a daughter called Lillian, and moved to Boston to pursue a literary career. There she served as secretary to Henry Wadsworth Longfellow and alienated much of the Boston literati by poking fun at them in an initially anonymous poem called "The Radical Club," written in imitation of Poe's "The Raven." Diagnosed with breast cancer, Bonner died on July 22, 1883, back in Holly Springs, nearly insolvent, and certain that she had failed to make any lasting literary contribution.

Bonner published a single novel, *Like unto Like,* and a serialized novelette, *The Valcours* (1881), in addition to numerous travel letters, essays, poems, and short stories in magazines including *Harper's Weekly* and *Lippincott's.* A number of those stories she included in her two collections, *Dialect Tales* and *Suwanee River Tales.* Notable for its consistent wit and its thinly veiled disregard for literary and social authority, Bonner's work frequently functions as cultural criticism. Her reconciliation romance, *Like unto Like,* for instance, subverts expectations for the genre by interrogating both northern and southern motivations for reunion and by leaving its heroine unmarried by choice, revealing Bonner's feminist sympathies. Recent critical attention to Bonner's work has suggested its diversity and complexity, thus expanding her reputation beyond that of a writer of dialect fiction.

WORKS: *Like unto Like* (1878). *Dialect Tales* (1883). *Suwanee River Tales* (1884).

—KATHRYN B. McKEE

ARNA WENDELL BONTEMPS (1902–1973). Although Arna Bontemps was physically removed from Louisiana at an early age, and in spite of his parents' desire to rid him of the implications of southern African American tradition, he maintained a lasting appreciation for his ethnic heritage. This admiration formed the basis for all that Bontemps wrote, and for his recurring themes: the return; race and protest; alienation and exile; religion and meditation; escape and revolt; the African American folk tradition; and the lonesome boy. His academic career placed him in the South, where he produced the bulk of his literary efforts; but his best artistic achievements were the result of his affiliation with the New Negro Renaissance.

Arnaud Wendell Bontemps was born on October 13, 1902, in Alexandria, La. His physical appearance would always accent his French Creole heritage. When he was three, his family fled the South, and young Arna grew up in Los Angeles. After graduation from Union Pacific College in 1923, he moved east and soon found himself involved in the Harlem Renaissance. He became a lifelong close friend of Langston Hughes.

Bontemps married and enjoyed a large family. During the 1920s he taught in New York City, and in the 1930s in Alabama and Chicago, earning an advanced degree at the University of Chicago. From 1943 until 1965 he served as university librarian at Fisk University; from 1965 until 1968 he was director of university relations. In 1968 he returned to teaching, first at Chicago Circle of the University of Illinois, then at Yale, returning finally to Fisk as writer-in-residence. He died in Nashville on June 4, 1973.

Throughout his varied career he continued to write—poetry, novels, short stories, essays. Although Bontemps has never received the attention accorded Langston Hughes, he must be counted a major figure of the Harlem Renaissance.

WORKS: *God Sends Sunday* (1931; dramatized as *St. Louis Woman,* 1966). *Popo and Fifina: Children of Haiti,* with Langston Hughes (1932). *You Can't Pet a Possum* (1934). *Black Thunder* (1936). *Sad-Faced Boy* (1937). *Drums at Dusk* (1939). Ed., *Golden Slippers: An Anthology of Negro Poetry for Young People* (1941). *Father of the Blues: The Autobiography of W. C. Handy,* with W. C. Handy (1941). *The Fast Sooner Hound,* with Jack Conroy (1942). *We Have Tomorrow* (1945). *They Seek a City,* with Jack Conroy (1945; rev. as *Anyplace but Here,* 1966). *Slappy Hooper: The Wonderful Sign Painter,* with Jack Conroy (1946). *The Story of the Negro* (1948). *The Poetry of the Negro: 1746–1949,* with Langston Hughes (1949). *George Washington Carver* (1950). *Chariot in the Sky* (1951). *Sam Patch, the High, Wide and Handsome Jumper,* with Jack Conroy (1951). *Lonesome Boy* (1955). *Frederick Douglass: Slave Fighter* (1958). *The Book of Negro Folklore,* with Langston Hughes (1958). *100 Years of Negro Freedom* (1961). Ed., *American Negro Poetry* (1963). *Personals* (1964). *Famous Negro Athletes* (1964). Ed., *Hold Fast to Dreams* (1969). Ed., *Great Slave Narratives* (1969). Ed., *The Harlem Renaissance Remembered* (1972). *The Old South: "A Summer Tragedy" and Other Stories of the Thirties* (1973).

—BETTY TAYLOR-THOMPSON

KATE LANGLEY BOSHER (1865–1932). Kate Lee Langley was born to Charles Henry Langley and Portia Deming on February 1, 1865, the cusp of the Civil War's end. Having grown up in Norfolk, Va., she graduated from the Norfolk College for Young Ladies in 1882. In 1887 she married Charles Gideon Bosher, who was part owner of a carriage manufacturing business in Richmond. Bosher devoted herself to a wide array of civic, social, and political organizations in addition to writing ten novels.

Bosher's community involvement focused on two causes: women's suffrage and orphans' welfare. Alongside Lila Meade Valentine, she was instrumental in the Equal Suffrage League of Virginia. For the league, she published a pamphlet that argued for women's right to vote on the basis of their citizenship, taxability, rationality, and responsibility to and for the family. She (and others) spoke before the Virginia House of Delegates in 1912 and before the Virginia Press Association in 1916. Once women's suffrage was achieved in 1920, Bosher became a leader in the League of Women Voters. Childless herself, Bosher was an advocate for the education and caretaking of abandoned children. She was appointed by the governor to the board of the Virginia Home and Industrial School for Girls in 1916 and 1922. Bosher was also a member of the Woman's Club of Richmond, the Country Club of Virginia, the Richmond Writer's Club, the Artists' Club, the Cosmopolitan Club of New York, the Daughters of the American Revolution, the United Daughters of the Confederacy, and the Daughters of the American Colonists.

Bosher wrote what she knew and what mattered to her: the post–Civil War South, the rescue of an orphan protagonist, and the differences between the public and private spheres. Her work is sentimental and romantic; her characters are lively and their adventures amusing. Of her novels, only the first, "Bobbie," appears under the pseudonym Kate Cairns. Bosher's third novel, *Mary Cary, "Frequently Martha,"* sold 100,000 copies in 1910 and continued to sell well. Its success and the popularity of *Miss Gibbie Gault, Kitty Canary,* and *His Friend Miss McFarlane,* as well as her own charisma, secured Bosher's much enjoyed position as a celebrated Richmond woman novelist.

Bosher died on July 27, 1932, a little more than six months after her husband's death. She was buried in Richmond's Hollywood Cemetery.

WORKS: *"Bobbie"* (1899). *When Love Is Love* (1904). *Mary Cary, "Frequently Martha"* (1910). *Miss Gibbie Gault* (1911). *The Man Is Lonely Land* (1912). *The House of Happiness* (1913). *How It Happened* (1914). *People Like That* (1916). *Kitty Canary* (1918). *His Friend Miss McFarlane* (1919).

—MELISSA GRAHAM MEEKS

DAVID BOTTOMS (1949–). Georgia Poet Laureate David Bottoms embodies the tradition of the southern realist poet-novelist as established by Robert Penn Warren and James Dickey. His writing has garnered critical praise and public acceptance since *Shooting Rats at the Bibb County Dump,* his first book of poems, was chosen by Warren for the 1979 Walt Whitman Award.

Born in Canton, Ga., on September 11, 1949, to David H. Bottoms, a funeral director, and Louise Ashe Bottoms, a registered nurse, Bottoms grew up in an area changing from rural to suburban in character, where he was deeply impressed by the southern rural tradition and by the Baptist faith. Both influences remain central to his writing.

Bottoms graduated from Mercer University in 1971, married Margaret Lynn Bensel in 1972, received the M.A. from West Georgia College in 1973, and began his teaching career in the Douglasville, Ga., high school in 1974. He completed a Florida State University Ph.D. in 1982, already recognized as a talented poet. Bottoms's marriage to Bensel ended in 1987, and he married Kelley Jean Beard in 1989. Combining writing success with a distinguished academic career, he began teaching at Georgia

State University in 1982, and currently holds the John B. and Elena Diaz-Verson Amos Distinguished Chair in English. Bottoms has contributed to many anthologies, co-edited *The Morrow Anthology of Younger American Poets*, and is founding editor of *Five Points Review*. His poems have been published in journals such as the *New Yorker* and the *Paris Review*, and he has conducted writing workshops at over 150 colleges.

Bottoms's poems in the 1970s and 1980s were most often narrative accounts of life in the South with a focus on the blue-collar world and on young men trying themselves against the culture's concept of manhood. These works are permeated with the yearning for spiritual meaning Bottoms found compelling in Warren, Dickey, Flannery O'Connor, and Charles Wright, and could never be mistaken for testosterone-charged red-neck romps. Twice in the 1980s he received the Book of the Year Award in Poetry from the Dixie Council of Authors and Journalists, and a selection of his poems also received the Levinson Prize from *Poetry* magazine.

In 1987 *Any Cold Jordan*, his first novel, was published to good reviews and modest sales. A second novel, *Easter Weekend*, followed in 1990. Both these books share with Bottoms's poetry the quality of discovering moral and spiritual significance in ordinary situations. Through direct narrative and exceptionally acute descriptions, Bottoms charges with metaphysical weight what might pass for mundane.

In recent years Bottoms has addressed the concerns of a more mature writer, such as his role as father and the progression of generations, but he has never left the themes or the geography that have always been the focus of his writing. He has said that a characteristic of all good poetry is "the simple but insistent longing to discover significance in the world, the need to understand not only how the world works, but why."

WORKS: *Jamming with the Band at the VFW* (chapbook, 1978). *Shooting Rats at the Bibb County Dump* (1979). *In a U-Haul North of Damascus* (1983). *Under the Vulture Tree* (1987). *Any Cold Jordan* (1987). *Easter Weekend* (1990). *Armored Hearts: Selected and New Poems* (1995). *Vagrant Grace* (1999). *Oglethorpe's Dream: A Picture of Georgia*, with Diane Kirkland (2001). *Waltzing through the Endtime* (2004).

—CY DILLON

JONATHAN BOUCHER (1738–1804). Known today as an articulate Loyalist, Jonathan Boucher was born in Blencogo, Cumberland Country, England, on March 12, 1738. Despite the family's penury, the boy received schooling at Bromfield and later at Wigton. Key to Boucher's progress was his association at St. Bees' School with the Reverend John James, who became a surrogate father and long-term mentor.

In 1759 Boucher became a tutor to a planter's children in Port Royal, Va. Not initially religious, Boucher in 1762 was ordained a priest in the Anglican Church. He first served at Hanover and later at St. Mary's Parish in Virginia. Besides being a parson, he ran a boys' school and became a planter. He developed a friendship with George Washington through tutoring his stepson, John Parke Custis.

Boucher believed in and supported traditional institutions of church and government even while he defended minority rights. Governor Robert Eden helped Boucher became rector of St. Anne's Church in Annapolis. There he was active in a literary society, the Homony Club, and was noted for his wit and poetry.

Boucher married three times, first to Eleanor Addison (who died in 1784), then to Mary Elizabeth Foreman (1787), and to Elizabeth Hodgson James, widow of John James, Jr., by whom he had eight children.

Initially, Boucher opposed British actions such as the Stamp Act and the Townshend Duties. However, he won Patriot enemies by defending accommodation with Great Britain, the supremacy of Parliament, an Anglican bishop in America, and maintenance of high clerical salaries. Preaching in May 1775 on a day of public fasting proclaimed by the extralegal Maryland Convention, he faced down two hundred armed men by challenging their leader.

In September 1775, Boucher returned to England, where he eventually became vicar of Epsom Parrish, Surrey. There he wrote thirteen reconstructed sermons arguing the case for monarchy, an autobiography, and an unfinished book of Americanisms and provincialisms.

WORKS: "A Letter from a Virginian to the Members of the Congress to Be Held at Philadelphia, on the First of September, 1774" (1774). *A View of the Causes and Consequences of the American Revolution* (1797). *Reminiscences of an American Loyalist, 1738–1789* (1797; repr. 1925). *Boucher's Glossary of Archaic and Provincial Words* (1832–33).

—RICHARD D. RUST

JAMES BOYD (1888–1944). James Boyd was born in Harrisburg, Pa., on July 2, 1888, the son of John Yeomans Boyd and Eleanor Gilmore Herr Boyd. He attended the Hill School in Pottstown, Pa., from 1901 to 1906, was graduated from Princeton University in 1910, and received a master's in English literature from Trinity College, Cambridge, in 1912. After several years' teaching English and French at Harrisburg Academy, he moved in 1914 to Weymouth, a family estate established by his grandfather near Southern Pines, N.C. He hoped rest and the milder climate there would aid his recovery from a mild case of polio.

In the fall of 1916, Boyd served on the editorial staff of *Country Life in America.* Rejected several times for military service because of his poor health, he secured a commission as second lieutenant in the U.S. Army Ambulance Service in 1917, serving in Italy and France. In 1919 he returned to Southern Pines, planning a career as a writer. Boyd soon began contributing short stories to prominent national magazines, including *Scribner's, Century,* and *American Mercury.* In 1925 he published *Drums,* his first novel, which sold more than 50,000 copies. Some critics have called it the best novel written about the American Revolution. In 1927 his second historical novel, *Marching On,* appeared, telling the story of a poor North Carolina farmer during the Civil War. Three years later, he produced *Long Hunt,* his first realistic rather than historical novel, although he again used North Carolina as his setting.

Still battling poor health, Boyd continued to write, publishing *Roll River* in 1935. This novel about four generations of a wealthy Pennsylvania family includes significant autobiographical elements. *Bitter Creek,* Boyd's fifth and final novel, is set in Wyoming cattle country. In 1940 Boyd organized and served as national chairman of the Free Company Players, a group of American writers, producers, and broadcasters who developed eleven original radio plays on democratic themes and freedom. In 1941 he edited a collection of these plays, *The Free Company Presents.* Boyd began to concentrate on poetry, with his work appearing in a number of national journals. In 1941 he purchased and assumed editorship of the *Pilot,* a small, unprofitable Southern Pines weekly, transforming it into a widely respected, award-winning newspaper.

Boyd married Katherine Lamont of Millbrook, N.Y., on December 15, 1917. The couple had three children, James Jr. (b. 1922), Daniel Lamont (b. 1924), and Nancy (b. 1927). James Boyd died on February 25, 1944.

Among honors Boyd received were election to the National Institute of Arts and Letters and the Society of American Historians. In 1996 he was one of the fifteen initial inductees into the North Carolina Literary Hall of Fame, which is located in his former study at Weymouth. Boyd's papers and manuscripts are at the Firestone Library, Princeton University, and the University of North Carolina at Chapel Hill's Southern Historical Collection.

WORKS: *Drums* (1925). *Marching On* (1927). *Long Hunt* (1930). *Roll Finger* (1935). *Bitter Creek* (1939). Ed., *The Free Company Presents* (1944). *Eighteen Poems* (1944). *Old Pines and Other Stories,* ed. Richard Walser (1952).

—ROBERT G. ANTHONY, JR.

ROARK BRADFORD (1898–1948). If Roark Bradford's name is still known today, it is because of Marc Connelly's Pulitzer Prize–winning play *Green Pastures,* based on Bradford's collection of stories *Ol' Man Adam an' His Chillun.* The story collection was published in 1928; the play opened in February 1930, ran on Broadway for seventy-three weeks, and was made into a motion picture (only the second ever to feature an all-black cast) in 1936. Bradford and Connelly received a Pulitzer for the "collaboration."

Roark Whitney Wickliffe Bradford, descended from a historic New England family, was born in rural western Tennessee on August 21, 1896. He was educated at home and in local schools before entering the University of California Law School, from which he graduated shortly before the outbreak of World War I. He served throughout the war as an artillery office in the Panama Canal Zone. In World War II, Bradford served in North Africa, where he contracted amebiasis, from which he died in New Orleans on November 13, 1948.

As a young man growing up in Tennessee, he had been fascinated by the African American culture surrounding him. He had a keen ear for dialect and frequently attended local black churches. These influences emerged when he began to write fiction. Among his first published works was the story "Child of God," which won an O. Henry Prize in 1927. *Ol' Man Adam* portrayed Heaven and God ("De Lawd") as Bradford understood them to be perceived by African Americans. Nearly all his subsequent fiction concentrated on similar themes, most notably his novel *John Henry,* a humorous rendering of the legend of the competition between the "steel-driving man" and a locomotive. *John Henry,* too, was adapted for the stage in 1939. Bradford's last collection, *Green Roller,* was published in 1949.

Much admired in his time, today Bradford is seen as exemplifying the patronizing and simplistic attitude of whites toward blacks that vanished in the Harlem Renaissance. His black characters are invariably childish, superstitious, and still very much beholden to their white "masters." Though none of Bradford's fiction possessed the quality of enduring art anyway, its portraits of African Americans doomed it to an early demise.

WORKS: *Ol' Man Adam an' His Chillun* (1928). *This Side of Jordan* (1929). *How Come Christmas* (1930). *John Henry* (1930). *Ol' King David and the Philistine Boys* (1930). *Kingdom Coming* (1933). *Let the Band Play Dixie* (1934). *The Three-Headed Angel* (1937). *Green Roller* (1949).

—TOM WILLIAMS

JOHN ED BRADLEY (1958–). John Edmund Bradley, Jr., was born on August 12, 1958, in Opelousas, La. He attended Louisiana State University, earning a B.A. in English in 1980. Bradley was an All-S.E.C. center and team captain in football; his senior year coincided with the final season for legendary coach Charlie McClendon. This experience informs Bradley's first two novels. *Tupelo Nights* features a former LSU All-American whose professional dreams are thwarted by an overbearing mother; *The Best There Ever Was* features a cantankerous college coach in his final season.

Bradley's novels are set in his native Louisiana, with the last two taking place in his adopted home of New Orleans, and he embraces the southern tradition of the grotesque and macabre. Cemeteries are prominent features in *Tupelo Nights* and *My Juliet,* and the protagonist of *Love and Obits* is a writer of obituaries. Although his incorporation of gothic settings, race, debauchery, and sex into his work is typical of many lesser New Orleans writers, Bradley's comic touch, poignant characterization, and realistic dialogue keep it fresh and original.

Inspired by his uncle Joe Bradley, Bradley enjoys painting and is a collector of southern art, and he mines his knowledge of the art world in his latest novel, *Restoration.*

Bradley's novels have been translated into several languages, including Spanish, French, Italian, Dutch, and Japanese. Bradley has made a name for himself as a journalist as well as a novelist. From 1983 to 1989 he was a writer for the *Washington Post.* He has written for *GQ,* and he has been a contributing editor of *Esquire* since 1991 and a contributing writer for *Sports Illustrated* since 1993.

WORKS: *Tupelo Nights* (1988). *The Best There Ever Was* (1990). *Love and Obits* (1992). *Smoke* (1994). *My Juliet* (2000). *Restoration* (2003).

—PETER J. FLORA

RICK BRAGG (1959–). Award-winning journalist and best-selling memoirist Rick Bragg was born in Calhoun County, Ala., on July 26, 1959, to Charles and Margaret Bundrum Bragg. After local public schools he attended Jacksonville State University.

Working in his home state for the *Jacksonville News, Talladega Daily Home, Anniston Star,* and *Birmingham News,* he reported stories on topics ranging from cockfights to speed traps, George Wallace to Bear Bryant. In 1989 he became Miami bureau chief for the *St. Petersburg Times,* covering stories in south Florida, the outbreak of the Gulf War, and violence in Haiti. A Harvard University Nieman Fellow in 1992–93, he worked for the *Los Angeles Times* before taking a position with the *New York Times* in 1994. While a national *Times* correspondent, Bragg was awarded the 1996 Pulitzer Prize for feature writing, being cited for his "elegantly written stories about contemporary America." Included in his more than fifty journalism awards are two prestigious American Society of Newspaper Editors Distinguished Writing Awards.

Bragg's two acclaimed memoirs chronicle growing up poor in the Appalachian foothills of northeast Alabama. *All Over but the Shoutin'* was written to honor his mother. When Bragg's father was unable to defeat the memories of the Korean War and the ravages of alcohol, Margaret Bragg sacrificed for her three sons by picking cotton, taking in laundry, and going eighteen years without a new dress. Bragg's second memoir, the best-seller *Ava's Man,* is a tribute to Margaret's parents, Charlie and Ava Bundrum. Charlie, a hero to his family and community, worked with his hands to keep his family together during the Great Depression, never allowing his fondness for liquor or his success as a moonshiner to destroy his core values. For Bragg, Charlie exemplifies the best of the people from the hill country, and a breed now essentially extinct.

Widely recognized as a spokesman for the underclass, and himself from the underclass, Bragg was selected to write the authorized biography of Pvt. Jessica Lynch, the soldier from Palestine, W.Va., whose capture and rescue during the Iraq War had garnered national attention. Also in the spring of 2003, Bragg resigned from the *New York Times* after being suspended for not crediting the reporter who had conducted interviews for him in connection with an article on oyster fishing in Apalachicola, Fla. Bragg insisted such practice was commonplace and acceptable journalism.

WORKS: *All Over but the Shoutin'* (1997; reprinted as *Redbirds: Memories from the South*, London, 1999). *Somebody Told Me: The Newspaper Stories of Rick Bragg* (2000). *Ava's Man* (2001). *I Am a Soldier Too: The Jessica Lynch Story* (2003).

—CYNTHIA B. DENHAM

TAYLOR BRANCH (1947–). Taylor Branch, journalist and novelist, is best known as the author of a trilogy on the life and times of Rev. Martin Luther King, Jr. The first volume in the trilogy, *Parting the Waters: America in the King Years, 1954–63*, won the Pulitzer Prize for history and the National Book Critics Circle Award for nonfiction, and was nominated for a National Book Award. Branch's interest in race relations in the United States began when he was growing up in the South; this interest focused on King while Branch was an undergraduate at the University of North Carolina at Chapel Hill (1964–68). He graduated the year King was assassinated. Branch refined his interest in race relations by doing graduate work at the Woodrow Wilson School of Public and International Affairs at Princeton University (1968–70), where his research project involved voter registration in rural Georgia.

After graduate work, Branch became an editor at the *Washington Monthly* (1970–73), where he continues to hold the position of contributing editor. He worked as a volunteer in the George McGovern campaign in Texas in 1972. Two fellow volunteers in that doomed campaign were Bill Clinton and Hillary Rodham. His friendship with the future president, whom he advised on civil rights policy, led to Branch's being awarded the National Humanities Medal in 1999.

After leaving the *Washington Monthly*, Branch wrote for *Harper's Magazine* (1973–75) and *Esquire* (1975–76). Both magazines are famous as incubators of liberal, politically savvy writers. Activist politics characterizes Branch's published work. Branch has co-authored two books: *Blowing the Whistle: Dissent in the Public Interest* and *Labyrinth*, an investigation of the tangled international politics surrounding the assassination of Chilean ambassador Orlando Letelier. Branch's other collaborative works include the ghostwriting of John W. Dean's *Blind Ambition: The White House Years* and an "as told to" book, *Second Wind: The Memoirs of an Opinionated Man*, for Boston Celtics star Bill Russell. His single novel, *Empire Blues*, was, in Branch's words, "an eminently predictable failure."

Branch's biographies of the civil rights movement and King—*Parting the Waters, Pillar of Fire*, and *At Canaan's Edge*—have consumed most of his writing life. The first volume took four years to finish; the second, nine. The third and final volume of the trilogy was *Time* magazine's cover story when it appeared in early 2006.

WORKS: *Blowing the Whistle: Dissent in the Public Interest*, with Charles Peters (1972). Ghost, John W. Dean, *Blind Ambition: The White House Years* (1976). *Empire Blues* (1981). *Labyrinth*, with Eugene M. Propper (1982). *Parting the Waters: America in the King Years, 1954–63* (1988). *Memoirs of an Opinionated Man*, with Bill Russell (1991). *Pillar of Fire: America in the King Years, 1963–65* (1998). *At Canaan's Edge: America in the King Years, 1965–68* (2006).

—MICHAEL KREYLING

BENJAMIN GRIFFITH BRAWLEY (1882–1939). Born in Columbia, S.C., on April 22, 1882, Benjamin Brawley was a precocious child nurtured on Greek and Roman classics. As a youth, he excelled in his studies, graduating with honors from Atlanta Baptist College (now Morehouse College) in 1901. After teaching one term in Georgetown, Fla., he began his career as an instructor of English and Latin at Morehouse, where he remained from 1902 to 1910. During this period, he continued advanced study, earning a second A.B. at the University of Chicago (1906) and an M.A. at Harvard University

(1908). From 1910 to 1912, Brawley taught at Howard University, but returned to Morehouse for a second eight-year period (1912–20). Then, embarking upon two new ventures, he conducted a six months' socio-educational survey of the Republic of Liberia and, after his return to America, became an ordained minister on June 2, 1921. He served as pastor of Messiah Baptist Church in Brockton, Mass., in 1921–22, before returning to teaching, an occupation which was for him as sacred a calling as the ministry. In his professorships at Shaw University (1923–31) and Howard University (1931–39), as at Morehouse earlier, he distinguished himself as a master teacher and scholar.

Brawley was also a minor poet, a frequent contributor to periodicals, and a prolific writer of social and literary history. Among his books, two emphases covering three stages of his career may be noted: race-centered books (1913–21), general interest books (1921–32), and race-inspired books (1933–38). Although Brawley explored racial themes, he did not use folk materials such as jazz and the blues reflected so popularly in race literature of the 1920s. On this point, he differed with many Harlem Renaissance writers. In literature, as in other areas, he observed standards of traditional morality, correctness, and classical good taste, which developed into the "Brawley Tradition" of excellence in personal and scholarly conduct.

Following a stroke, Brawley died at his home in Washington, D.C., on February 1, 1939. He was survived by his wife, Hilda Prowd Brawley.

WORKS: *A Toast to Love and Death* (1902). *The Problem and Other Poems* (1905). *The Dawn and Other Poems* (1911). *A Short History of the American Negro* (1913). *History of Morehouse College* (1917). *The Seven Sleepers of Ephesus: A Lyrical Legend* (1917). *Africa and the War* (1918). *The Negro in Literature and Art in the United States* (1918). Ed., *New Era Declamations* (1918). *Your Negro Neighbor* (1918). *Women of Achievement* (1919). *A Short History of the English Drama* (1921). *A Social History of the American Negro* (1921). *A New Survey of English Literature* (1925). *Freshman Year English* (1929). *Dr. Dillard of the Jeanes Fund* (1930). *A History of the English Hymn* (1932). Ed., *Early Negro American Writers* (1935). *Paul Laurence Dunbar, Poet of His People* (1936). *Negro Builders and Heroes* (1937). Ed., *The Negro Genius* (1937). *The Best Stories of Paul Laurence Dunbar* (1938). *Sojourner Truth,* with Arthur Huff Fauset (1938).

—PATSY B. PERRY

CLEANTH BROOKS (1906–1994). Born on October 16, 1906, in Murray, Ky., Cleanth Brooks, Jr., was the son of Cleanth Brooks, a Methodist minister, and Bessie Lee Witherspoon Brooks. After high school, where—despite his small size—he captained the football team, he entered Vanderbilt University in 1924. He studied with the Fugitive circle that included the poet-critics John Crowe Ransom, Allen Tate, and Robert Penn Warren. After graduating with Phi Beta Kappa honors, Brooks earned an M.A. at Tulane and then went to Oxford on a Rhodes Scholarship, obtaining a B.Litt. in 1932. The following year he joined the English faculty at Louisiana State University.

In 1934—the same year he married Edith Amy Blanchard (better known as Tinkum)—Brooks began a lifelong collaboration with Robert Penn Warren, newly arrived at Louisiana State University. During the next decade, they founded the *Southern Review* and created the textbooks *An Approach to Literature, Understanding Poetry,* and *Understanding Fiction,* which would bring New Criticism into thousands of classrooms and transform the teaching of literature across the nation. Brooks's *Modern Poetry and the Tradition* and *The Well Wrought Urn: Studies in the Structure of Poetry* became pivotal texts of the New Criticism.

In 1947 Brooks accepted a professorship at Yale, where Robert Penn Warren rejoined him in 1950 for more collaboration, most notably on the four-volume anthology *American Literature: The Makers and the Making* (with R. W. B. Lewis). Among Brooks's numerous works of this later period, the major books on William Faulkner seem most conspicuous, notably *William Faulkner: The Yoknapatawpha*

Country, Toward Yoknapatawpha and Beyond, William Faulkner: First Encounters, and *On the Prejudices, Predilections, and Firm Beliefs of William Faulkner: Essays.* After his retirement in 1975, Brooks continued a steady production of scholarship up to the time of his death on May 10, 1994, in New Haven.

WORKS: *The Relation of the Alabama-Georgia Dialect to the Provincial Dialects of Great Britain* (1935). Ed., *An Approach to Literature,* with Robert Penn Warren and John Thibaut Purser (1936). Ed., *Understanding Poetry,* with Robert Penn Warren (1938). *Modern Poetry and the Tradition* (1939). Ed., *Understanding Fiction,* with Robert Penn Warren (1943). Ed., *Understanding Drama: Twelve Plays,* with Robert B. Heilman (1945). *The Well Wrought Urn: Studies in the Structure of Poetry* (1947). Ed., *Modern Rhetoric,* with Robert Penn Warren (1949). Ed., *Fundamentals of Good Writing: A Handbook of Modern Rhetoric,* with Robert Penn Warren (1950). Ed., *An Anthology of Stories from the Southern Review,* with Robert Penn Warren (1953). Ed., with others, *Tragic Themes in Western Literature* (1955). *Literary Criticism: A Short History,* with William K. Wimsatt, Jr. (1957). Ed., *The Scope of Fiction,* with Robert Penn Warren (1960). *The Hidden God: Studies in Hemingway, Faulkner, Yeats, Eliot, and Warren* (1963). *William Faulkner: The Yoknapatawpha Country* (1963). *American Literature: A Mirror, Lens, or Prism?* (1967). *The Writer and His Community: The Twenty-First W. P. Ker Memorial Lecture Delivered in the University of Glasgow, 15th October 1965* (1968). *A Shaping Joy: Studies in the Writer's Craft* (1971). Ed., *American Literature: The Makers and the Making,* with Robert Penn Warren and R. W. B. Lewis (1973). *William Faulkner: Toward Yoknapatawpha and Beyond* (1978). *William Faulkner: First Encounters* (1983). *The Language of the American South* (1985). *On the Prejudices, Predilections, and Firm Beliefs of William Faulkner: Essays* (1987). *Historical Evidence and the Reading of Seventeenth-Century Poetry* (1991). *Community, Religion, and Literature* (1995).

—VICTOR STRANDBERG

LARRY BROWN (1951–2004). William Larry Brown was born in Oxford, Miss., on July 9, 1951, to Knox Brown, a farmer, and Leona Brown, a postmaster and store owner. Brown spent his childhood in Memphis, Tenn., and in Oxford, where he developed a profound love for the outdoors and a sense of connection to the area. After graduating from high school, he joined the U.S. Marines in 1970, an experience he credits with having inspired parts of his novel *Dirty Work,* although he never saw active duty. He returned to Oxford in 1973 and joined the fire department, where he was promoted to captain in 1986. He describes his life as a firefighter in his memoir *On Fire.* In 1990 he resigned to write full-time, having begun his initially self-taught apprenticeship as a writer in 1980. He married Mary Annie Coleman in 1974; they had three children.

Brown's work is characterized by his depiction of blue-collar southern life as alternately humorous and tragic. His gritty realism and understated style have been commended in numerous awards, including the Mississippi Institute of Arts and Letters Award for Literature, the Southern Critics Circle Award for Fiction in 1992 and 1997, the Lila Wallace–Reader's Digest Award, and the Thomas Wolfe Prize from the University of North Carolina at Chapel Hill in 2001. Brown's life and work have been the basis for two films: *Big Bad Love* (2001), directed by and starring Arliss Howard, and Gary Hawkins's documentary *The Rough South of Larry Brown,* which was released in 2000.

On November 24, 2004, a fatal heart attack claimed Brown at his Oxford home.

WORKS: *Facing the Music* (1988). *Dirty Work* (1989). *Big Bad Love* (1990). *Joe* (1991). *On Fire* (1994). *Father and Son* (1996). *Fay* (2000). *Billy Ray's Farm* (2001). *The Rabbit Factory* (2003).

—AMY E. WELDON

RITA MAE BROWN (1944–). Rita Mae Brown was born in Hanover, Pa., and lived there with her adoptive parents until she was eleven, when they moved to Fort Lauderdale. A Civil War enthusiast from a young age, Brown visited many battlefields as a girl and learned to love the South from her grandfather's stories of his experiences as a Confederate soldier. She matriculated at the University of Florida in Gainesville in 1962, but when her civil rights activism got her into trouble, Brown left for New York, where in 1968 she received a B.A. from New York University and a cinematography certificate from the New York School of Visual Arts. In 1973 she received her Ph.D. from the Institute for Policy Studies in Washington, D.C.

Nineteen seventy-three was also the year she published her first novel, *Rubyfruit Jungle,* about a working-class southern lesbian in New York who longs to return to a simpler life in the South. This novel established Brown's reputation and introduced the character types, conflicts, and desires that define her fiction. Her protagonists are often southern, lesbian, working-class survivors at odds with the conventional yet deeply engaged with history and tradition. Brown's work has been praised for its exuberance and its loving portrayal of strong women; it has been criticized for its embrace of extreme individualism and what is sometimes seen as the absence of social consciousness. Brown has published novels, essays, a writers' manual, poetry, a memoir, a cookbook, and screenplays and teleplays. She lives near Charlottesville, Va., with her cat, Sneaky Pie Brown, who is identified as co-author for many of the novels in the series of Mrs. Murphy mysteries that Brown began publishing in 1990 with *Wish You Were Here.*

WORKS: Trans., *Hrotsvitha: Six Medieval Latin Plays* (1971). *The Hand That Cradles the Rock* (1971). *Rubyfruit Jungle* (1973). *Songs to a Handsome Woman* (1973). *In Her Day* (1976). *A Plain Brown Rapper* (1976). *Six of One* (1978). *Southern Discomfort* (1982). *Sudden Death* (1983). *High Hearts* (1986). *Bingo* (1988). *Starting from Scratch: A Different Kind of Writer's Manual* (1988). *Wish You Were Here* (1990). *Rest in Pieces* (1992). *Venus Envy* (1993). *Dolley: A Novel of Dolley Madison in Love and War* (1994). *Murder at Monticello, or, Old Sins* (1994). *Pay Dirt, or, Adventures at Ash Lawn* (1995). *Riding Shotgun* (1996). *Murder She Meowed* (1996). *Rita Will: Memoir of a Literary Rabble Rouser* (1997). *Murder on the Prowl* (1998). *Loose Lips* (1999). *Cat on the Scent* (1999). *Sneaky Pie's Cookbook for Mystery Lovers* (1999). *Outfoxed* (2000). *Pawing through the Past* (2000). *Alma Mater* (2001). *Claws and Effect* (2001). *Catch as Cat Can* (2002). *Tale of the Tip-Off* (2003). *Cat's Eyewitness* (2005).

—BARBARA LADD

STERLING A. BROWN (1901–1989). Poet, critic, anthologist, and teacher, Sterling Allen Brown devoted his multifaceted career to the reclamation of African American expressive culture. He was born in Washington, D.C., on May 2, 1902, to Adelaide and the Reverend Sterling Brown. After graduating from D.C.'s Dunbar High, he entered Brown College, where he graduated Phi Beta Kappa. He then took an M.A. at Harvard. After brief stints at Virginia Seminary and College, Lincoln University, and Fisk University, in 1929 he joined the faculty at Howard University.

During his forty-year career as scholar at Howard, Brown wrote books of poetry and criticism and a corpus of essays and reviews; he researched and wrote for the Federal Writers' Project and the Gunnar Myrdal study *An American Dilemma* (1944); and he co-edited the most comprehensive anthology of African American expressive culture to date. All of his work directly addressed the issue of representation: how would African Americans be portrayed in American literature, theater, film, and popular culture?

With Zora Neale Hurston, Langston Hughes, and others, Brown worked with the radical wing of the New Negro arts movement (the Harlem Renaissance), focusing on African American vernacular and folk culture. His poetry written in the late 1920s and throughout the Depression addresses a historical and cultural context in which racist stereotypes in literature and popular culture contributed directly to the political agenda of white supremacy, particularly as it was practiced in the South. Freed from the reduction and simplicity of plantation tradition dialect, Brown's poetry reinvents black vernacular in pursuit of fully realized black personas. Brown creates mythic figures such as Calvin "Big

Boy" Davis, Revelations, Slim Greer, and Sister Lou, all in the process of using the rich folk culture around them to create meaning in a chaotically hostile racial milieu. His use of folk forms—work songs, spirituals, blues ballads, and the blues—delivers a range of emotions and psychological states heretofore unseen in American literature.

Brown worked for the Federal Writers' Project as national editor of *Negro Affairs*, supervising research and writing on African American culture for guide books to the southern states. He also oversaw the writing of two seminal FWP studies, *Washington: City and Capital* (1937) and *The Negro in Virginia* (1940). He served as lead editor for *The Negro Caravan*, an eclectic compilation of literary and folk expression, further evidence of a vibrant and evolving African American expressive culture. Brown's essays provide models for reading race and racist ideology in literature. They address the presence of African Americans in American literature and culture, critiquing racist stereotypes and examining the more accurate and enduring contributions African American writers have made in opposition to caricature.

Brown helped to nurture a generation of artists and activists (including Amiri Baraka, Kwame Ture, and Michael S. Harper), all deeply invested in the humanity inherent in African Americans and their art. He helped to lay the foundation for contemporary African American literature and criticism, providing both theory and example for the representation of African American culture. He died on January 13, 1989, in Takoma Park, Md.

WORKS: *Outline for the Study of the Poetry of American Negroes* (1931). *Southern Road* (1932). *Negro Poetry and Drama* (1937). *The Negro in American Fiction* (1937). Ed., *The Negro Caravan: Writings by American Negroes*, with Arthur P. Davis and Ulysses Lee (1941). *The Last Ride of Wild Bill and Eleven Narrative Poems* (1975). *The Collected Poems of Sterling A. Brown* (1980). *A Son's Return: Selected Essays of Sterling A. Brown*, ed. Mark A. Sanders (1996).

—MARK A. SANDERS

WILLIAM GARROTT BROWN (1868–1913). William Garrott Brown was born in Marion, Ala., on April 24, 1868, and remained there until 1889. After preparatory schooling in his native town, he graduated from Howard College in 1886. He devoted a year to independent study and writing for the *Montgomery Advertiser,* after which he taught English for two years at the Marion Military Institute. He then entered Harvard, where he spent thirteen years: three as a student, nine as an assistant in the university library, and one as a lecturer in American history. Increasing deafness prevented either an academic or a political career; he turned to writing, soon winning an enviable reputation as a literary historian and essayist. Albert B. Hart asserted that Brown was "one of the few men in the country who has got something to say and can say it."

A textbook *History of Alabama* appeared in 1900. Brown contributed volumes on Andrew Jackson and Stephen A. Douglas to Houghton Mifflin and Company's Riverside Biographical Series. His reputation as a southern historian rests largely upon *The Lower South in American History,* a collection of lectures and essays dealing in part with the civilization of the cotton states from 1820 to 1860. Brown's antebellum novel, *A Gentleman of the South: A Memory of the Black Belt,* revealed that fiction was not his forte. A life of Oliver Ellsworth was his last book except for a posthumous collection on political topics, *The New Politics and Other Papers.*

In 1906 Brown found that he had tuberculosis and abandoned projected historical studies; however, he kept up a lively interest in politics and was a regular contributor to newspapers and periodicals until his death on October 19, 1913.

WORKS: *A History of Alabama* (1900). *Andrew Jackson* (1900). *Stephen Arnold Douglas* (1902). *The Lower South in American History* (1902). *A Gentleman of the South: A Memory of the Black Belt, from the Manuscript Memoirs of the Late Colonel Stanton Elmore* (1903). *The Foe of Compromise and Other Essays* (1903). *The Life of Oliver Ellsworth* (1905). *The New Politics and Other Papers* (1914).

—NORMAN D. BROWN

WILLIAM WELLS BROWN (1814–1884). The first African American to achieve distinction in belletristic literature, William Wells Brown was born on a plantation near Lexington, Ky., the son of a white man and a slave woman. Brown spent his first twenty years mainly in St. Louis, Mo., and its vicinity, working in a variety of occupations, including as handyman for a Missouri slave trader, before escaping on New Year's Day, 1834.

After seizing his freedom, Brown worked for nine years as a steamboatman on Lake Erie and a conductor for the Underground Railroad in Buffalo, N.Y. In 1843 he became a lecturer for the Western New York Anti-Slavery Society. Moving to Boston in 1847, he wrote *Narrative of William W. Brown, A Fugitive Slave*, which went through four American and five British editions before 1850, earning its author international fame. During an extended stay in England and Europe, Brown wrote *Three Years in Europe*, the first travel book authored by an African American. A year later *Clotel, or the President's Daughter*, generally regarded as the first African American novel, was published in London, its major plot centering on the decades-old rumor of President Thomas Jefferson's sexual relationship with a slave mistress.

After returning to the United States in 1854, Brown continued his path-breaking literary work, publishing *The Escape*, the first drama by an African American, and two volumes of black history, one of which, *The Negro in the American Rebellion*, is the first military history of the African American in the United States. Active in reform circles after the final abolition of slavery in 1865, Brown practiced medicine in Boston, Mass. His final book, *My Southern Home*, is based on his experience as a slave and his travels in the post–Civil War South. Brown died in Chelsea, Mass., on November 6, 1884.

WORKS: *Narrative of William W. Brown, A Fugitive Slave* (1847). *Three Years in Europe* (1852). *Clotel, or the President's Daughter* (1853). *The Escape* (1858). *The Negro in the American Rebellion* (1867). *My Southern Home* (1880).

—WILLIAM L. ANDREWS

WILLIAM HAND BROWNE (1828–1912). Author, editor, educator, and historian, William Hand Browne was born in Baltimore City and lived in the immediate area for his entire life. His parents were members of established Maryland families. His father, William Browne, was a prominent commission merchant who traded mainly with the West Indies; his mother, Patience Hand Browne, was the daughter of the renowned landscape and portrait painter Moses Hand. Brown received a medical degree from the University of Maryland in 1850, but never practiced that profession; instead he involved himself in the commission business with a cousin for ten years before devoting himself fulltime to his literary and antiquarian interests. In 1863 he married Mary Catherine Owings and moved to Baltimore County. During the Civil War, he traveled throughout the South without taking an active role in military affairs.

By the end of the war, Browne had found his mission, the restoration of the cultural life of the South to its antebellum prominence. This work of cultural restoration, achieved most notably through his connections with various literary periodicals, had much to do with making Baltimore a focal point for southern writers. In 1867 he co-founded the *Southern Review* and served as editor for two years, after which he became co-editor of the *New Eclectic Magazine*, later renamed the *Southern Magazine*. By the time he left it in 1875, the *Southern Magazine* was the principal literary journal in the South.

During this time, he also tried editing a weekly, the *Statesman*, which covered literature, art, music, and politics, but dropped the project after a year and a half. Browne, who obviously enjoyed working with others, was joint editor of textbooks on English literature and the history of Maryland, and a concise English dictionary.

Browne's academic career began in 1879 with his appointment as Librarian of the Johns Hopkins University. He was affiliated with Hopkins for the rest of his life; at the time of his death he was professor emeritus of English literature. Although his bibliography contains other highlights—various translations, for example, or editions and explorations of early Scottish poetry—his achievement in colonial history is usually considered most noteworthy. In 1882 the Maryland General Assembly deposited the provincial records with the Maryland Historical Society with provision for publication. Browne was appointed editor, a position requiring both immense scholarly knowledge and editorial exactness; by the time of his death he had brought out thirty-two large quarto volumes of these *Archives of Maryland*. All the while he continued teaching at Hopkins and bringing other major projects to fruition: authoring two volumes on the Calverts, editing the Calvert papers, serving as founding editor of the quarterly *Maryland Historical Magazine*. Even the briefest biographical sketches of Browne mention his wit, refinement, and graciousness.

WORKS: *Speech in the House of Delegates of Virginia, on the Removal from the Commonwealth of the Free Colored Population* (1853). *Wheat, Its Worth and Waste*, with Thomas J. Hand (1862). Trans., Friedrich Spielhagen, *Hammer and Anvil* (1870). *An Historical Sketch of English Literature*, with Richard Malcolm Johnston (1872). Trans., Ivan Turgenev, *A Lear of the Steppe* (1874). *School History of Maryland*, with J. Thomas Scharf (1877). *Life of Alexander H. Stephens*, with Richard Malcolm Johnston (1878). *The Clarendon Dictionary*, with S. S. Haldeman (1882). Trans., Jakob von Falke, *Greece and Rome, Their Life and Art* (1882). *Archives of Maryland*, vols. 1–32 (1883–1912). *Maryland, the History of a Palatinate* (1884). *Maryland Historical Society Fund Publications*, vols. 27 and 34 [first two vols. of Calvert papers] (1889–94). *George Calvert and Cecelius Calvert, Barons Baltimore of Baltimore* (1890). *Selections from the early Scottish Poets* (1896). *Writings of Severn Teakle Wallis* (1896). *The Tail of Rauf Coilyear: A Scottish Metrical Romance of the Fifteenth Century* (1903).

—K. HUNTRESS BALDWIN

JAMES LEE BURKE (1936–). James Lee Burke was born on December 5, 1936, in Houston, Tex., but his home is New Iberia, La., where the Burke family has lived for generations. Burke attended the University of Southwestern Louisiana in nearby Lafayette for two years (1955–57) and later enrolled at the University of Missouri, where he earned a B.A. and an M.A. (1959–60). Before becoming one of America's premier writers of detective fiction in the late 1980s, Burke worked in a variety of positions: oil pipeline roughneck, reporter, social worker, and college English instructor. He and his wife, Pearl Pai, married since 1960, now have homes in Missoula, Mont., and New Iberia.

Burke began writing when he was an undergraduate in Lafayette, and by the 1970s had published both short stories and novels. But it was not until the publication of *The Lost Get-Back Boogie* and the subsequent detective novels starring Dave Robicheaux that Burke achieved the popular success and critical acclaim he now enjoys.

The Robicheaux novels are good examples of Burke's ability to create popular fiction that is both entertaining and thematically complex. The novels are exciting adventures in which New Iberia police detective Dave Robicheaux tracks down murderers, rapists, child molesters, and Mafia hit men in the lush, tropical landscapes of Cajun southwest Louisiana. But Burke also examines the troubled psyche of his hero. Tortured by his memories of the violence and depravity he has witnessed in Vietnam, in south Louisiana, in his family, and in himself, Dave is in search of a way to live with dignity in a world that seems to him hopelessly unredeemed. A middle-aged recovering alcoholic shamed and guilt-ridden by his past failures to defeat the immorality he has seen in himself and others, he tries daily to muster the moral strength he will need in order to construct a future less ignoble. Dave's desperate search for these moral resources is the dominant theme of the Robicheaux novels and a recurring theme in all of Burke's fiction.

WORKS: *Half of Paradise* (1965). *The Bright and Shining Sun* (1970). *Lay Down My Sword and Shield* (1971). *Two for Texas* (1982; published as *Sabine Spring*, 1989). *The Convict and Other Stories* (1985). *The Lost Get-Back Boogie* (1986). *The Neon Rain* (1987). *Heaven's Prisoners* (1988). *Black Cherry Blues* (1989). *A Morning for Flamingos* (1990). *A Stained White Radiance* (1992). *In the Electric Mist with Confederate Dead* (1993). *Dixie City Jam* (1994). *Burning Angel* (1995). *Cadillac Jukebox* (1996). *Cimarron Rose* (1997). *Sunset Limited* (1998). *Heartwood* (1999). *Purple Cane Road* (2000). *Bitterroot* (2001). *Jolie Blon's Bounce* (2002). *White Doves at Morning* (2002). *Last Car to Elysian Fields* (2003). *In the Moon of Red Ponies* (2004).

—ALLEN PRIDGEN

THOMAS BURKE (ca. 1747–1783). Thomas Burke—poet, congressman, and governor—was born in Ireland around 1747. He emigrated to North America in 1763, settling in Northampton County, Va., where he worked briefly as a doctor before beginning a more lucrative career in the law.

Burke moved to Hillsborough, N.C., in 1772 and continued his legal practice. In 1776 he was a delegate to the North Carolina Provisional Congress at Halifax that urged the Continental Congress to declare independence from Great Britain. Burke was elected to the Continental Congress in late 1776 and was an outspoken advocate for the rights of states in the new federal government, introducing the clause in the Articles of Confederation that those powers not explicitly granted to the federal government would belong to the states.

Although Burke was outspoken and often quarreled with other politicians, his popularity at home was evident in the ease with which he was returned to office, even after receiving a formal censure from Congress. He was elected governor of North Carolina in 1781 and held office for only a short time before he was captured by a band of Loyalists and held prisoner in a British fort. Burke escaped after a few months and returned to office, but refused to run for reelection. After his term ended, he went back to his home in Hillsborough, where he died on December 2, 1783.

As a contemporary of Thomas Jefferson and Benjamin Franklin, Burke lived in an age when it was not unusual for a statesman to show a strong interest in the arts. Burke wrote poetry throughout his life, and many of his early pastoral and love poems have survived in manuscript. His satiric works were influenced by the work of fellow Irishman Jonathan Swift and by the Latin verse of Juvenal, and he was an admirer of the English poet Edmund Waller. Burke began publishing poetry, often unsigned, in Virginia newspapers in the 1760s and was the center of a lively correspondence in the *Virginia Gazette*. His "Triumph America!" celebrating the repeal of the Stamp Act was reprinted throughout the colonies.

WORKS: *The Poems of Governor Thomas Burke of North Carolina*, ed. Richard Walser (1961).

—NICHOLAS GRAHAM

FRANCES HODGSON BURNETT (1849–1924). Frances Hodgson Burnett was born in Manchester, England, on November 24, 1849. She was four when her father's death left her mother to raise five children and run the family furniture store. Hard times forced her mother to sell the business and, when Frances was six, immigrate to America. They settled near Knoxville, Tenn.

Frances Hodgson's writing career began early. In her mid-teens, she wrote and sold stories to women's magazines to supplement the family income, publishing in nearly every popular American magazine. In 1873 she married Swan Burnett, an ophthalmologist, and bore a son, Lionel. They moved to Paris, and she continued to publish in American magazines. In France she had another son, Vivian, before the family returned to the United States to settle in Washington, D.C., where her husband established a medical practice.

Throughout the 1870s Burnett published several novels, but it was not until 1886, when she entered the genre of children's literature with the publication of *Little Lord Fauntleroy,* that she achieved major success. *Little Lord Fauntleroy* was so successful with both American and British readers that Burnett adapted it for the stage. The highly successful play redoubled the already substantial book sales, making it one of the best-selling works of the period.

Though Burnett's career soared, her marriage failed. When Lionel was fifteen he contracted tuberculosis, and Burnett traveled to Europe with him seeking, to no avail, a sanatorium and a cure. After his death, she traveled to Italy, where she wrote two melancholy collections of stories and a memoir about her enthusiasm for writing.

Returning to the United States, Burnett married Stephen Townesend, ten years her junior, creating a scandal. In the 1890s she began again to write adult fiction with a sensational murder novel, *A Lady of Quality,* which critics panned and her reading public loved. In 1905 Burnett reworked an earlier story, *Sara Crewe,* into *A Little Princess.* The revision received widespread acclaim; it remains one of her most successful works.

Though Burnett produced more than fifty book-length titles (many were collections of stories) and a dozen plays, it was with *The Secret Garden* that her fame skyrocketed and she became a major contributor to the canon of children's literature. *The Secret Garden* depicts three children who restore and tend a neglected garden in which they, too, begin to grow and flourish.

Burnett continued to write and publish until her death in 1924. Before she died at her Long Island estate, Plandome, she enjoyed entertaining and indulged her passion for gardening.

WORKS: *That Lass o' Lowrie's* (1877). *Surly Tim* (1877). *Theo* (1877). *Dolly* (1877). *Pretty Polly Pemberton* (1877). *Earlier Stories* (1878). *Kathleen* (1878). *Earlier Stories 2nd Series* (1878). *Miss Crespigny* (1878). *A Quiet Life and The Tide on the Moaning Bar* (1878). *Our Neighbor Opposite* (1878). *Jarl's Daughter* (1879). *Natalie* (1879). *Haworth's* (1879). *Louisiana* (1880). *A Fair Barbarian* (1881). *Esmeralda* (1881). *Young Folks' Ways* (1883). *Through One Administration* (1883). *Little Lord Fauntleroy* (1886). *A Woman's Will, or Miss Defarge* (1887). *Sara Crewe* (1887). *Editha's Burglar* (1888). *The Fortunes of Philippa Fairfax* (1888). *The Real Lord Fauntleroy* (1888). *The Pretty Sister of José* (1889). *Phyllis* (1889). *Little Saint Elizabeth* (1890). *Nixie* (1890). *Giovanni and the Other [Children I have Known]* (1892). *The Drury Lane Boys' Club* (1892). *The Showman's Daughter* (1892). *The One I knew Best of All* (1893). *Piccino and Other Child Stories [The Captain's Youngest]* (1894). *The Two Little Pilgrims Progress* (1895). *A Lady of Quality* (1896). *His Grace Osmonde* (1897). *The First Gentlemen of Europe* (1897). *In Connection with the De Willoughby Claim* (1899). *The Making of a Marchioness* (1901). *The Methods of Lady Walderhust* (1901). *A Little Princess* (1902). *In the Closed Room* (1904). *That Man and I* (1904). *The Dawn of a Tomorrow* (1906). *The Troubles of Queen Silver-Bell* (1906). *Racketty-Packetty House* (1906). *The Cozy Lion* (1907). *The Shuttle* (1907). *The Spring Cleaning* (1908). *The Good Wolf* (1908). *Barty Crusoe and His Man Saturday* (1909). *The Land of the Blue Flower* (1909). *The Secret Garden* (1911). *My Robin* (1912). *T. Tembaron* (1913). *The Lost Prince* (1915). *Little Hunchback Zia* (1916). *The White People* (1917). *The Head of the House of Coombe* (1922). *Robin* (1922). *In the Garden* (1925).

—Ruth Moose

OLIVE ANN BURNS (1924–1990). Although she completed only one novel, Olive Ann Burns is a nationally and internationally known southern writer. Published in 1984, *Cold Sassy Tree* caught the popular imagination and quickly became a best-seller, appealing to readers as diverse as Barbara Bush and B. F. Skinner. The novel tells the story of fourteen-year-old Will Tweedy's coming of age in a small southern town, Cold Sassy, during the early years of the twentieth century. Will's growing understanding of the complexity and change that characterize adult lives is paralleled by Cold Sassy's reluctant entry into the modern world.

Cold Sassy Tree is set in the pre-Depression world of Burns's father, Arnold Burns, and Cold Sassy is modeled on the town of Commerce, Ga., where he spent his childhood. Olive Ann Burns's own childhood was colored by the hardships the South endured during the Depression. The youngest of Ruby and Arnold Burns's four children, she was born on July 17, 1924, on a farm owned first by her great-great grandfather. In 1931 the Depression forced her father to give up farming and to move into the town of Commerce. Her nostalgic yearning for the farm gives the setting of Cold Sassy.

Although Burns did not publish *Cold Sassy Tree* until she was sixty, writing held a central place throughout her professional and personal life. Her interest in writing began in high school in Macon, Ga., where she wrote for her school newspaper. At Mercer University, where she began her college education, she edited the literary magazine. After transferring to the University of North Carolina, she majored in journalism, graduating in 1946. Within a year after graduation, Burns became a staff writer at the *Atlanta Journal Sunday Magazine.* There her training in writing continued under the magazine's founding editor, Angus Perkerson.

While working at the *Sunday Magazine,* Burns met and married another staff writer, Andy Sparks, in 1956. Their daughter was born in 1957, and their son in 1960. Between 1957 and 1972, Burns wrote very little. Not until her mother was diagnosed with stomach cancer in 1971 did she begin writing down the family stories that would become the basis of her novel. After her mother's death in 1972, Burns drew upon her father's stories about his childhood, including the tale of Grandpa Power, who remarried several weeks after his first wife's death. When her father died the following year, Burns continued her family history project to preserve her parents' voices and stories for her own children.

In 1974 Burns herself was diagnosed with cancer, and she then began the process of transforming her family histories into a novel as a means of coping with her illness. Her father provided the model for Will Tweedy, *Cold Sassy Tree*'s first-person narrator, and Grandpa Power became Enoch Rucker Blakeslee, whose marriage to Miss Love a mere three weeks after the death of his wife of thirty-five years provides the opening complication in the novel.

Following the success of *Cold Sassy Tree,* Burns began a sequel, continuing the story of Will Tweedy into adulthood and narrating his courtship and marriage to Sanna Klein. Work on her second novel, "Time, Dirt, and Money," was interrupted by a recurrence of her cancer. During her last three years, Burns was bedridden with congestive heart failure. She died on July 4, 1990. Her unfinished novel, along with her notes, was published posthumously in 1992 as *Leaving Cold Sassy.*

WORKS: *Cold Sassy Tree* (1984). *Leaving Cold Sassy* (1992).

—SUZAN HARRISON

JACK BUTLER (1944–). Jack Butler's impressive range as a writer is rooted in a very diverse biography. He was born in Alligator, Miss., and raised in the Delta, the son of a Southern Baptist preacher. In 1966 he received undergraduate degrees in English and mathematics at Central Missouri State College. In subsequent years, he was an ordained Southern Baptist minister, graduate student, bread company route man, fried pie salesman, poet in the schools, and maintenance man. In 1979 he earned an M.F.A. in creative writing from the University of Arkansas, after which he worked as a science writer, an actuarial analyst, a depreciation specialist for the Arkansas Public Service Commission, an assistant dean at Hendrix College, and—finally—a professor of creative writing at the College of Santa Fe in New Mexico, where he has been since 1993.

All this time, Butler was writing steadily, and these wide-ranging experiences (and many others as well—he is an avid cook and painter) are evident in his books: four novels, two collections of poetry, one collection of short stories, and a sort of cookbook. As a poet, Butler is a formalist: he has organized several conferences featuring "expansive poets," who favor restoring the narrative traditions of verse as a way of expanding and recovering poetry's audience. His novels, however, are more experimental, employing various conventions—of tragicomic realism, thrillers, science fiction, murder mysteries, and the southern gothic, among others—in unconventional ways. Whatever the genre, Butler's work is entertaining yet deadly serious, and always characterized by a lively imagination, a poet's ear for language, vivid characters and voices, and a powerful narrative drive.

His audacious novel *Living in Little Rock with Miss Little Rock* was nominated for a Pulitzer Prize by its New York publisher, Alfred Knopf.

WORKS: *West of Hollywood: Poems from a Hermitage* (1980). *Hawk Gumbo and Other Stories* (1982). *The Kid Who Wanted to Be a Spaceman and Other Poems* (1984). *Jujitsu for Christ* (1986). *Nightshade* (1989). *Living in Little Rock with Miss Little Rock* (1993). *Jack's Skillet: Plain Talk and Some Recipes from a Guy in the Kitchen* (1997). *Dreamer* (1998).

—MICHAEL MCFEE

ROBERT OLEN BUTLER (1945–). The son of Robert Olen Butler, Sr., a college professor, and Lucille Hall Butler, an executive secretary, Robert Olen Butler, Jr., was born on January 20, 1945, in the St. Louis suburb of Granite City, Ill. He took a B.S. in theater from Northwestern University in 1967, and an M.A. in playwriting from the University of Iowa in 1969.

Butler served in the army from 1969 to 1972. He became fluent in Vietnamese and worked in intelligence, as a translator, in Vietnam from 1971 to 1972, eventually rising to the rank of sergeant. In 1972 Butler married the poet Marylin Geller, with whom he has a son, Joshua. After his discharge from the army he settled in New York. He became an editor of trade journals and began writing novels using his experiences in Vietnam, striving especially to depict the humanity of the Vietnamese people.

In 1985 Butler joined the faculty at McNeese State University in Lake Charles, La., as an assistant professor of English. The Louisiana setting is central to his collection of stories *A Good Scent from a Strange Mountain*, as well as to stories in *Tabloid Dreams* and the novel *Mr. Spaceman*. Butler is currently the Francis Eppes Professor of English holding the Michael Shaara Chair in Creative Writing at Florida State University, where he teaches with his second wife, the playwright and novelist Elizabeth Dewberry.

Since becoming a surprise Pulitzer Prize winner in 1983 for *A Good Scent from a Strange Mountain*, Butler has received a Guggenheim Fellowship in fiction, a National Endowment for the Arts grant, and the Richard and Hinda Rosenthal Foundation Award from the American Academy of Arts and Letters. His works have been translated into Vietnamese and several other languages. A Catholic, Butler cites biblical influences on his writing, and *Mr. Spaceman*, for example, is rife with Christian imagery. Butler is distinguished by his ability to inhabit different characters—an alien, a nine-year-old hit man, a Catholic Vietnamese stripper in New Orleans, an auctioneer—and to imbue them with longing and sympathy.

WORKS: *The Alleys of Eden* (1981). *Sun Dogs* (1982). *Countrymen of Bones* (1983). *On Distant Ground* (1985). *Wabash* (1989). *The Deuce* (1989). *A Good Scent from a Strange Mountain* (1992). *They Whisper* (1994). *Tabloid Dreams* (1996). *Deep Green Sea* (1997). *Mr. Spaceman* (2000). *Fair Warning* (2002). *Had a Good Time: Stories from American Postcards* (2004). *From Where You Dream: The Process of Writing Fiction*, ed. Janet Burroway (2005).

—PETER J. FLORA

KATHRYN STRIPLING BYER (1944–). Poet Kathryn Stripling Byer was born and raised in south Georgia. Her parents are farmers, a background especially evident in the poems collected in *The Girl in the Midst of the Harvest.* After graduating from Wesleyan College with a B.A. in 1966, she studied creative writing at the University of North Carolina at Greensboro, where she received her M.F.A. in 1968. That year she began teaching English at Western Carolina University in Cullowhee, N.C. She worked at the university off and on for three decades, and from 1990 to 1998 served as its poet-in-residence. In 1970 she married James Byer, with whom she lives in Cullowhee; they have a daughter.

Byer has always shown an interest in speaking through poetic personae. In a sequence in *The Girl in the Midst of the Harvest,* she writes in the voice of her pioneer great-grandmother. Her second collection, *Wildwood Flower,* develops the persona of Alma, a woman living in the Blue Ridge wilderness at the turn of the twentieth century. Byer's third book, *Black Shawl,* includes several poems voiced by Delphia, an Appalachian quilter, and other poems in the book are spoken by various unnamed mountain women. Her fourth collection, *Catching Light,* includes a sequence in the voice of Evelyn, a former artist's model now in late life.

Another distinctive aspect of Byer's work is her prosody: whereas most of her contemporaries adopt either iambic or free verse, she tends to prefer the quick but regular pace of the anapest, the amphibrach, and the dactyl. She frequently uses short lines that break mid-foot, so that the poems cascade down the page.

Among her awards are the Academy of American Poets' Lamont Prize for a best second book (for *Wildwood Flower*), a National Endowment for the Arts Fellowship, and the North Carolina Award for Literature. In 2005 the governor selected Byer to be North Carolina's poet Laureate, the first woman in that role.

WORKS: *Search Party: Poem,* with drawings by Joyce Stills (1979). *Alma: Poems,* with drawings by Sharyn Jayne Hyatt (1983). *The Girl in the Midst of the Harvest* (1986). *Wildwood Flower: Poems* (1992). *Black Shawl: Poems* (1998). *Catching Light: Poems* (2002). *Coming to Rest: Poems* (2006).

—ROBERT M. WEST

WILLIAM BYRD II OF WESTOVER (1674–1744). Born to William Byrd I, a Virginia planter and trader in frontier furs who was the son of an English goldsmith, and Mary Horsmanden, William Byrd II reflected in his literary works the values and eclectic interests of an eighteenth-century English gentleman. Modern students of American literature know him best for writings unpublished in his lifetime: his personal diaries and his diary of a surveying expedition that he led along the Virginia and North Carolina border. He also amassed the largest private library in the South and wrote witty verses as well as scientific treatises.

Educated at the Felsted School in England in 1681, Byrd later apprenticed to merchants in the Netherlands and eventually studied law at the Middle Temple in London, where his literary apprenticeship occurred in the rich cultural life of the city. A protégé of Sir Robert Southwell, Byrd was inducted into the Royal Society for the Improving of Natural Knowledge and was appointed an English agent for the Virginia Colonial House of Burgesses.

Eventually returning to Virginia, Byrd became a leader in the political and economic life of the colony. A voracious reader and bibliophile, he collected a library of some three thousand volumes, at the time second only in size to that of Cotton Mather, the Boston Puritan divine. This library might have become the nucleus of a great southern university, had Byrd's son not sold off the volumes in order to pay his debts.

Byrd is best known as a diarist who, while not rivaling Samuel Pepys in style or incidents (the Virginian's social circle was more provincial), nonetheless documented the routines he employed in gentlemanly self-fashioning. His coded personal diaries show a man struggling to balance his appetites and passions, particularly his sexual appetites, while daily managing an extensive estate and improving his mind. In two versions of his surveying journal, one intended for print publication and the other for limited circulation among friends, Byrd offered a sympathetic ethnography of Native Americans and a satirical view of the differences between Carolinians and Virginians. In this picaresque narrative Byrd casts himself as the redoubtable "Colonel Steddy."

Byrd owned extensive properties to the west of the James River and laid out the future cities of Petersburg and Richmond on its banks. His account of that territory, *A Journey to the Land of Eden*, was apparently intended as a promotional text in the hopes of bringing German Swiss immigrants. Traveling to Fredericksburg in 1732, he visited an old political nemesis, Alexander Spotswood, who had pioneered in iron mining and milling. The resulting *A Progress to the Mines* is a more personal and "autumnal" piece, written by a man who has come to accept the limitations of his career and who even comes to terms with past animosities.

During the eight years between his first and second marriages, Byrd kept a gentleman's commonplace book, a record of his reading and conversations. His reading ranged widely, from the classics to Christian patristic writing to treatises on medical lore and nature.

Byrd's letters and "characters" (a popular Augustan literary form in which the foibles of character types or actual persons were satirized) circulated among friends, offering this small audience an unsentimental view of love, feminine beauty, and lust. His self-portrait in the character "Inamorato l'oiseaux" reveals a man who struggled with sexual passion even in childhood.

Several anonymous or pseudonymous works are attributed to Byrd. It is generally believed that he collaborated with William Burnaby, a colleague in the Middle Temple, on a translation of Petronius's *Satyricon* (London, 1694), from which Byrd's notebooks translate the anecdote of "The Ephesian Matron." Visiting the English spa of Tunbridge Wells in 1719, Byrd published several poems under the name of "Mr. Burrard" in *Tunbrigalia; or, Tunbridge Miscellanies* (London, 1719). Byrd and other dilettante "Water Poets" (as Richard Steele named them) wrote verses describing the habitués of Tunbridge Wells and other spa resorts. An early proponent of inoculation against smallpox (which had taken Byrd's first wife, Lucy), Byrd anonymously published *A Discourse Concerning the Plague* in 1721 in London. In this work he offered an account of historical plagues in classical literature and the Bible and suggested remedies derived from medical writers whom he had read, providing a naturalist's history of epidemic disease.

Satirist, naturalist, and diarist, Byrd provided a fascinating image of a Colonial gentleman in Virginia.

WORKS: *An Essay upon the Government of the English Plantations on the Continent of America: An Anonymous Virginian's Proposals for Liberty under the British Crown, with Two Memoranda by William Byrd* (1701). *A Discourse Concerning the Plague* (1721). *The Westover Manuscripts: Containing the History of the Dividing Line Betwixt Virginia and North Carolina; A Journey to the Land of Eden, A.D. 1733; and A Progress to the Mines; Written from 1728 to 1736, and Now First Published* (1841). *The Secret Diary of William Byrd of Westover, 1709–1712* (1941). *Another Secret Diary of William Byrd of Westover, 1739–1741, with Letters and Literary Exercises, 1696* (1942). *The London Diary, 1717–1728 and other Writings* (1958). *The Commonplace Book of William Byrd II of Westover* (2001).

—THOMAS L. LONG

JAMES BRANCH CABELL (1879–1958). James Branch Cabell, America's greatest purveyor and creator of myth for comic purposes through the mid-twentieth century, was born on April 14, 1879, in Richmond, Va. On both sides Cabell descended from aristocratic Virginia families; many of his fictions probe the vanities of the Virginia aristocracy. By nature intellectual and meditative, Cabell pondered the inconsistencies in the stories he heard his elders relate about the fallen Confederacy. To the contemporary myths connected with the Confederacy, he supplemented a keen appreciation of classical myth. He became a lifelong student of the mythic and the occult.

Cabell was a brilliant student at the College of William and Mary, and he later published poems written for the college literary magazine, as well as a college paper on William Congreve. As an upperclassman Cabell taught French and Greek; both literatures were to color his major fictions. In 1898 Cabell graduated with highest honors, an event briefly threatened when Cabell withdrew his name, angry at being a victim of campus gossip because he was a good friend of a college librarian accused of being homosexual. Ultimately Cabell's name was cleared and his graduation proceeded. In this time of uncertainty he met Ellen Glasgow, who was visiting the campus. Later the association would become major for both writers.

After graduation Cabell worked briefly as a copyreader for the *Richmond Times,* but the next year (1899) he was working for the *New York Herald.* By 1901 he was back with the *Times;* strangely he was soon the subject of Richmond gossip again—this time as the probable murderer of one of his mother's cousins. Angered and hurt by the accusations, Cabell fancied himself something of the devil's own dear son as he labored during the next ten years as a genealogist, a profession that would be reflected in his future books, especially in his magnum opus, *The Biography of the Life of Manuel.* During these years, he began publishing stories in national magazines, and in 1904 he published his first novel, *The Eagle's Shadow.* Surprisingly, Cabell worked in coal mine operations in West Virginia during 1911–13. By his own testimony he was gathering material for his writing by living the life of a Restoration rake, but this pattern ended decisively when he met Priscilla Bradley Shepherd at the Rockbridge Alum, a popular summer resort in Virginia. Mrs. Shepherd, some four and a half years Cabell's senior, was a widow with five children. He and Mrs. Shepherd were married on November 8, 1913. Their only child, a son—Ballard Hartwell—was born on August 25, 1915.

In 1919 Cabell became editor of the Virginia War History Commission, a post he held through 1926. In 1919 he also became genealogist for the Virginia chapter of the Sons of the America Revolution. The real event of 1919, however, was the publication of *Jurgen,* the book that made the quiet, shy Cabell one of the most controversial writers in America. He became an international figure when on January 14, 1920, his publisher was summoned to appear in court for violating New York's pornography law. The Cabell boom was on, and it would last through the 1920s. *Jurgen* was exonerated on October 19, 1922. The event was an important milestone in the struggle for a freer treatment of human sexuality. *Jurgen* and its author were taken as symbols of the ultrasophistication of the 1920s. Cabell was aligned closely with the "smart set," and H. L. Mencken was one of his staunchest defenders.

Following publication of *Jurgen,* Cabell revised his earlier work to make it conform to his scheme for Manuel's biography. The definitive edition of the biography appeared in eighteen volumes from 1927 to 1930 as the Storisende Edition of *The Works of James Branch Cabell.* Cabell marked the completion of this labor by publishing for a time thereafter under the shortened name Branch Cabell. Much of his later writing was autobiographical and philosophical, with Cabell meditating on the ironies, pleasures, and pains of the creative life. He did write three fictional trilogies in succeeding years, but never regained the public he had enjoyed in the 1920s, sometimes known as the James Branch Cabell era.

From 1932 to 1935 Cabell served—with George Jean Nathan, Ernest Boyd, Theodore Dreiser, Eugene O'Neill, and Sherwood Anderson—as an editor of the *American Spectator.* After 1935 he was plagued by attacks of pneumonia and began making frequent removals to St. Augustine, Fla. Florida's legendary past and history came to absorb him much as Virginia's had, and this interest found expression in his last fictional works. In St. Augustine, Priscilla Bradley Cabell died on March 25, 1949. On June 15, 1949, Cabell married Margaret Waller Freeman, a younger woman with whom he had been associated in 1921, when he had edited three issues of the *Reviewer,* Richmond's literary magazine. Cabell died on May 5, 1958, in Richmond.

WORKS: *The Eagle's Shadow* (1904). *The Line of Love* (1905). *Branchiana* (1907). *Gallantry* (1907). *Chivalry* (1909). *The Cords of Vanity* (1909). *Branch of Abingdon* (1911). *The Soul of Melicent* (1913). *The Majors and Their Marriages* (1915). *The Rivet in Grandfather's Neck* (1915). *The Certain Hour* (1916). *From the Hidden Way* (1916). *The Cream of the Jest* (1917). *Beyond Life* (1919). *Jurgen* (1919). *Domnei* (1920). *The Judging of Jurgen* (1920). *Figures of Earth* (1921). *The Jewel Merchants* (1921). *Joseph Hergesheimer* (1921). *The Lineage of Lichfield* (1922). *The High Place* (1923). *Straws and Prayer-Books* (1924). *Retractions* (1926). *The Silver Stallion* (1926). *The Music from behind the Moon* (1926). *Something about Eve* (1927). *The Works of James Branch Cabell* (Storisende Edition, 1927–30). *Ballades from the Hidden Way* (1928). *The White Robe* (1928). *Sonnets from Antan* (1929). *The Way of Ecben* (1929). *Some of Us* (1930). *Townsend of Lichfield* (1930). *Between Dawn and Sunrise* (1930). *These Restless Heads* (1932). *Special Delivery* (1933). *Ladies and Gentlemen* (1934). *Smirt* (1934). *Smith* (1935). *Preface to the Past* (1936). *The Nightmare Has Triplets* (1937). *Smire* (1937). *The King Was in His Counting House* (1938). *Of Ellen Glasgow* (1938). *Hamlet Had an Uncle* (1940). *The First Gentleman of America* (1942). *The St. Johns* (1942). *There Were Two Pirates* (1946). *Let Me Lie* (1947). *The Witch-Woman* (1948). *The Devil's Own Dear Son* (1949). *Quiet, Please* (1952). *As I Remember It* (1955). *Between Friends: Letters of James Branch Cabell and Others,* ed. Padraic Colum and Margaret Freeman Cabell (1962). *The Letters of James Branch Cabell,* ed. Edward Wagenknecht (1975).

—JOSEPH M. FLORA

GEORGE WASHINGTON CABLE (1844–1925). One of the first progressive writers of the New South, George Washington Cable was born in New Orleans on October 12, 1844, the son of Rebecca Boardman and G. W. Cable. His father's German background and his mother's New England Protestantism contributed to his own sense of isolation in a community whose leaders were primarily French and Catholic. Cable's position as an outsider may have stimulated his interest in sociological problems and made him more sensitive to the needs of minorities, especially southern blacks.

At his father's death, Cable, only fifteen, terminated his formal education and took a job at the local customhouse until his enlistment as a Confederate soldier at nineteen. After the Civil War he continued his old job. He married Louise Bartlett on December 7, 1869; they had four daughters and a son. In February 1870, Cable accepted a position on the *New Orleans Picayune,* where his "Drop Shot" column, though occasionally controversial, was well received. At this time Cable began writing a series of short stories and was discovered by Edward King of Scribner's, who was touring Louisiana in search of materials for his "Great South" series. Although Scribner's rejected "Bibi," Cable's story of a tormented slave prince, on the grounds of its unpleasant subject matter, they published his character sketch of an old Creole, "Sieur George," in 1873. Richard Watson Gilder, editor of *Scribner's Monthly* and the *Century,* considered Cable one of the leading local colorists who would contribute to Gilder's plan for reconciling the North and South through literature. H. H. Boyesen also took an interest in Cable's writing and initiated a correspondence helpful to the latter's career.

In 1879 Cable's *Old Creole Days,* a collection of short stories, was published, and the first installments of *The Grandissimes,* which incorporated the "Bibi" materials, appeared in *Scribner's Monthly.* In 1880 *The Grandissimes* was published in book form, as was *Madame Delphine,* a novella. These two books represent Cable's highest achievement, anticipating the complex drama of Faulkner's works.

Each deals with racial injustice, the continuing problems caused by exploitation of the black community, and the Creoles' resistance to social change.

By 1882 Cable began a full-time career as a writer, completing *Dr. Sevier,* a serious novel dealing with prison reform, which was followed by a *Century Magazine* exposé, "The Convict Lease System in the Southern States," and a history, *The Creoles of Louisiana.* These three works, openly polemical, offended Gilder and caused tremendous resentment throughout the South. A reading tour with Mark Twain brought Cable some additional income and popularity, but his increasingly fervent publications on the Negro's dilemma, especially "A Freedman's Case in Equity" and the first edition of *The Silent South,* made him notorious in New Orleans. He felt pressured to move his family to Northampton, Mass., in 1885.

There, in 1886, Cable organized the Home Culture clubs, racially integrated reading groups designed to raise the educational level of average citizens. The success of the movement was due in part to the national atmosphere of self-improvement and upward mobility in the last quarter of the nineteenth century. The clubs published a journal in 1892, called first the *Letter* and later, in 1896, the *Symposium.*

When Cable was fifty he published *John March, Southerner,* an ambiguous portrait of a southern aristocrat during the Reconstruction era; this was his last attempt at social satire. He continued to be an outspoken essayist, but his fiction became unashamedly romantic. The public taste of the period and his editors reinforced his tendency toward sentimentalism. *The Cavalier* was Cable's greatest popular success, with Julia Marlowe starring in a dramatic version of the novel a year later.

Cable's first wife died in 1904. Afterwards he was married to Eva Stevenson, who died in 1923, and to Hannah Cowing, who survived him. Energetic till the end, he published three novels while in his seventies; he died on January 31, 1925, at age eighty-one. Cable shaped an optimistic vision of technological progress in the New South and the eventual integration of the races. Perhaps because he remained too dependent on the family magazine audience and the taste of his editors, Cable did not live up to his early potential as a major southern writer. Nevertheless, in his best fiction he transcended the limitations of the local color genre and revealed a daring and prophetic intelligence.

WORKS: *Old Creole Days* (1979). *The Grandissimes* (1880). *Madame Delphine* (1881). *The Creoles of Louisiana* (1884). *Dr. Sevier* (1884). *The Silent South* (1885). *Bonaventure* (1888). *Strange True Stories of Louisiana* (1889). *The Negro Question* (1890). *The Busy Man's Bible* (1891). *A Memory of Roswell Smith* (1892). *John March, Southerner* (1894). *Strong Hearts* (1899). *The Cavalier* (1901). *Bylow Hill* (1902). *Kincaid's Battery* (1908). *"Posson Jone" and Père Raphaël* (1909). *Gideon's Band* (1914). *The Amateur Garden* (1914). *The Flower of the Chapdelaines* (1918). *Lovers of Louisiana* (1918).

—KIMBALL KING

ERSKINE CALDWELL (1903–1987). America's best-selling author from the 1930s to the 1970s, Erskine Caldwell virtually defined modern popular culture's conceptions of the rural, "backwoods" South.

Caldwell was born on December 17, 1903, in White Oak, near Moreland, Ga., southwest of Atlanta. His father, Ira Sylvester Caldwell, was an itinerant minister in the Associate Reformed Presbyterian Church. Caldwell's mother, Caroline Preston Bell Caldwell, was a teacher. She home-schooled her only son, shaping both his intellect and his values, while modeling moral responsibility through active support of her husband's ministry.

In 1918 the Caldwells settled in Wrens, Ga., near Augusta. What he discovered in the red-clay countryside impressed Caldwell deeply: hungry sharecroppers, black and white, living in physical conditions so far substandard as to be criminal. In 1920 Caldwell enrolled in his father's alma mater, Erskine College, but he soon dropped out. He obtained a scholarship to the University of Virginia and matriculated there in 1923, taking summer courses in 1924 at the University of Pennsylvania. He returned to Charlottesville in 1925. Rather than graduating, he married Helen Lannigan, daughter of the university's famous track coach, and moved with her to Atlanta, where he worked as a reporter for the *Atlanta Journal*. In 1927 the couple moved to Mount Vernon, Maine, where Caldwell declared he would concentrate on writing fiction.

After countless rejections, in 1929 Caldwell saw his first short story published in the French avant-garde magazine *Transition*. He published two apprentice novels, *The Bastard* and *Poor Fool*, while placing stories in the most important American "little magazines" of the day. When Maxwell Perkins accepted two of his stories for *Scribner's Magazine* in 1930, Caldwell's ascent began. Under Perkins's mentorship, Caldwell developed his first book, a collection of stories titled *American Earth*, and his first great novel, *Tobacco Road*, both published by Scribner's. In 1933 a play based on *Tobacco Road* began a record-setting run on Broadway.

With Viking's publication of *God's Little Acre* in 1933—the same year he won the *Yale Review*'s prize for fiction for "Country Full of Swedes"—Caldwell found himself at the center of controversy when charges of obscenity brought against the novel by the New York Society for the Suppression of Vice were dismissed in a landmark court case. In 1937 Caldwell collaborated with photographer Margaret Bourke-White to publish *You Have Seen Their Faces*, a photo-text documentary that would illustrate the reality behind his fiction. After his first divorce, he and Bourke-White married in 1939 and produced three other books together.

In the late 1930s and 1940s, Caldwell wrote for Hollywood and worked as a foreign correspondent, publishing three books on his experiences in Russia. In 1942 he and Bourke-White divorced, and the next year he married June Johnson. That marriage ended in 1956, and he married Virginia Moffett Fletcher, a talented artist and champion of his work. He died of lung cancer in 1987.

Into the 1970s, Caldwell published both fiction and nonfiction at a rate approaching a book per year. Despite the fact that Faulkner once named Caldwell with himself, Wolfe, Dos Passos, and Hemingway as the five best writers of his generation, and that in 1984 Caldwell was elected to the American Academy of Arts and Letters, his critical reputation suffered with his immense popularity. Serious efforts to appraise his achievement have appeared with increasing frequency since the 1990s, however, and scholars are recognizing the genius of Caldwell's untamed blending of humor, pathos, and social conscience in writing about the South's dispossessed.

WORKS: *The Bastard* (1929). *Poor Fool* (1930). *American Earth* (1931). *Tobacco Road* (1932). *God's Little Acre* (1933). *We Are the Living: Brief Stories* (1933). *Journeyman* (1935; rev. ed., 1938). *Kneel to the Rising Sun* (1935). *Some American People* (1935). *Tenant Farmer* (1935). *The Sacrilege of Alan Kent* (1936). *You Have Seen Their Faces*, with Margaret Bourke-White (1937). *Southways* (1938). *North of the Danube*, with Margaret Bourke-White (1939). *Jackpot: The Stories of Erskine Caldwell* (1940). *Trouble in July* (1940). *Say, Is This the U.S.A.?* with Bourke-White (1941). *All Night Long: A Novel of Guerrilla Warfare in Russia* (1942). *All-Out on the Road to Smolensk* (1942). *Russia at War*, with Bourke-White (1942). *Georgia Boy* (1943). *A Day's Wooing and Other Stories* (1944). *Stories by Erskine Caldwell: Twenty-four Representative Stories* (1944). *Tragic Ground* (1944). *A House in the Uplands* (1946). *The Caldwell Caravan* (1946). *The Sure Hand of God* (1947). *This Very Earth* (1948). *Place Called Estherville* (1949). *A Woman in the House* (1949). *Episode in Palmetto* (1950). *Call It Experience: The Years of Learning How to Write* (1951). *The Humorous Side of Erskine Caldwell* (1951). *The Courting of Susie Brown* (1952). *A Lamp for Nightfall* (1952). *The Complete Stories of Erskine Caldwell* (1953). *Love and Money* (1954). *Gretta* (1955). *Gulf Coast Stories* (1956). *Certain Women* (1957). *Claudelle Inglish* (1958). *Molly Cottontail* (1958). *When You Think of Me* (1959). *Men and Women: Twenty-two Stories* (1961). *Jenny by Nature* (1961). *Close to Home* (1962). *The Last Night of Summer* (1963). *Around*

About America (1964). *In Search of Bisco* (1965). *The Deer at Our House* (1966). *Miss Mamma Aimee* (1967). *Writing in America* (1967). *Deep South: Memory and Observation* (1968). *Summertime Island* (1969). *The Weather Shelter* (1969). *The Earnshaw Neighborhood* (1971). *Annette* (1973). *Afternoons in Mid-America: Observations and Impressions,* with Virginia Caldwell (1976). *The Black and White Stories of Erskine Caldwell* (1984). *With All My Might* (1987). *Erskine Caldwell: Selected Letters, 1929–1955* (1999).

—ROBERT L. McDONALD

FRANCES BOYD CALHOUN (1867–1909). *Miss Minerva and William Green Hill,* Frances Boyd Calhoun's only book-length title, is much better known than its creator. She was born on Christmas Day 1867, in Mecklenburg County, Va. Before moving to Tennessee in 1880, she lived in Warrenton, N.C., for some two years. She attended the Tipton Female Seminary in Covington, Tenn., from which she graduated in 1885. Thereafter she helped her father edit a local newspaper. Some of her early poetic efforts were published here and in one of the Memphis dailies.

After teaching for seven years in the Covington city school, she married George Barret Calhoun, in 1903. He died a year later, and it was not until the spring of 1908 that she mailed to a Chicago publisher the manuscript of her novel, on which she had worked for two years. She broke the publisher's silence with a prodding letter in late summer, and the manuscript was quickly accepted and published (it appeared on February 6, 1909). Four months later, on June 8, 1909, Frances Calhoun died, without ever knowing the success her book was to achieve.

Miss Minerva and William Green Hill became a minor classic of popular southern fiction. It ultimately went through more than fifty printings, and in 1918 a sequel appeared, titled *Billy and the Major.* This continuation, written by Emma Speed Sampson, was but the first of eleven continuations, the last being *Miss Minerva's Vacation* (1939), all by Sampson.

The germs of Calhoun's fictional treatment were found among individuals and incidents she witnessed in Covington, but research has shown that she exercised considerable authorial license. Attention in the novel is focused upon three groups of characters: the spindly old maid, Miss Minerva, and the rotund Major, her long-time suitor and a Confederate veteran; Minerva's nephew "Billy" Hill and his three playmates; and various black characters. Calhoun was sharply attuned to the local ambience, but her story concerns the universal problem of the distance that separates the child and adult worlds. Though the stiff Aunt Minerva at first listens to Billy "in frozen amazement and paralyzed silence," she ultimately comes to love him, in spite of his pranks and frequent scrapes with authority.

WORKS: *Miss Minerva and William Green Hill* (1909).

—WELFORD DUNAWAY TAYLOR

WILL D. CAMPBELL (1924–). Born in Amite County, Miss., in 1924, Will (Davis) Campbell showed signs of being an unusual boy when he became convinced at age nine of his "calling" to be a preacher. Preparing to study for the Baptist ministry, he enrolled at the denomination's Louisiana College. After his freshman year he enlisted in the U.S. Army, serving two years in the Pacific theater. During that time, he read Howard Fast's *Freedom Road,* which "converted" him to the belief that black people and white people are equals, opening the door to his conviction that segregation and racial prejudice are totally incompatible with Christian love.

Campbell's studies continued at Wake Forest College and the Yale Divinity School. Following a brief pastorate in Louisiana, he became Director of Religious Life at the University of Mississippi in 1954. His progressive views on race occasioned his ouster from that position in 1956. For seven years he was Race Relations Specialist for the National Council of Churches. Always critical of institutional life, he found his niche in 1963, becoming independent and self-supporting for the rest of his career. From 1956, he and his family lived in the village of Mt. Julian, a few miles east of Nashville, where he owned "forty acres and a goat."

Campbell has written extensively ever since, both fiction and personal recounting, with the South as a setting. The recurrent theme has been that "we're all bastards but God loves us anyway," since the Gospel calls for reconciliation with God and all people. As greatly concerned with the oppressor as the oppressed, he has been minister to "rednecks," including the Ku Klux Klan and other staunch segregationists.

Identifying himself always as a Baptist preacher, one who has no "steeple," Campbell has lived simply and radically. Known far and wide for his unique style in living, his courage, and his advocacy of justice in human relationships and opposition to capital punishment, his reputation derives from both action and writing.

WORKS: *Race and the Renewal of the Church* (1962). *Up to our Steeples in Politics* (1970). *Brother to a Dragonfly* (1977). *The Glad River* (1982). *God on Earth: The Lord's Prayer for Our Time*, with Bonnie Campbell (1983). *Cecilia's Sin* (1984). *Forty Acres and a Goat: A Memoir* (1986). *The Convention: A Parable* (1988). *Chester and Chun Ling* (1989). *Providence* (1992). *The Stem of Jesse: The Costs of Community at a 1960s School* (1995). *The Pear Tree that Bloomed in the Fall* (1996). *Bluebirds Always Come on Sunday* (1997). *Shugah and Doops* (1997). *And Also with You* (1997). *Soul among Lions: Musings of a Bootleg Preacher* (1999). *Robert G. Clark's Journey to the House: A Black Politician's Story* (2003). Ed., *The Failure and the Hope: Essays of Southern Churchmen* (2005).

—SAMUEL S. HILL

TRUMAN CAPOTE (1924–1984). Truman Streckfus Persons was born on September 30, 1924, in New Orleans, La., the son of Archulus Persons, a man who drifted between jobs, and Lillie Mae Faulk Persons, a sixteen-year-old beauty queen. The couple divorced when Truman was four years old, and he was sent to live with relatives in Monroeville, Ala. There he met Harper Lee, whose *To Kill a Mockingbird* reflects this period, as does Capote's own *A Christmas Memory*. When Truman was eight, his mother married Joseph G. Capote, a wealthy textile manufacturer, and Truman moved to New York. He was adopted by Joseph Capote and took his stepfather's surname.

Truman Capote attended the Trinity School and St. John's Academy in New York and Greenwich High School in Millbrook, Conn., but dropped out of school at the age of seventeen. He went to work at the *New Yorker* as a clerk and began writing stories for several magazines. In 1945 "Miriam," which appeared in *Mademoiselle* magazine, won an O. Henry Award. Random House offered him a contract, and in 1948 Capote released his first book, *Other Voices, Other Rooms*, a coming-of-age story set in the Deep South in which a young man becomes involved with a transvestite. The book's discussion of homosexuality made it controversial, but the novel also brought Capote celebrity. He was lionized by the social elite and began to lead a high-profile life.

The 1950s and 1960s were Capote's most productive decades. His novel *Breakfast at Tiffany's*, later made into a successful movie, drew on themes of childhood isolation and loneliness that characterize much of his fiction. In 1959 Capote undertook the writing of his pioneering "nonfiction novel," *In Cold Blood*, which delved into the murder of the Clutter family in Holcomb, Kans.

Following the publication of this best-selling book, considered by many critics to be his best work, Capote began work on a project exploring the lives of his socially prominent friends. In 1975 the appearance of the first few chapters of *Answered Prayers* in *Esquire* magazine outraged those depicted in the book, and Capote became a social pariah. The shock of this alienation and the resulting depression sapped Capote of his creativity. He died at the age of fifty-nine in Los Angeles, Calif., of liver disease complicated by multiple drug intoxication, on August 25, 1984.

Among Capote's literary honors are the O. Henry Award (1946, 1948, and 1951); membership in the National Institute of Arts and Letters and the institute's creative writing award (1959); the Edgar Award (1966) and National Book Award nomination (1967) for *In Cold Blood*.

WORKS: *Other Voices, Other Rooms* (1948). *A Tree of Night, and Other Stories* (1949). *Local Color* (1950). *The Grass Harp* (1951; drama, 1952). *Beat the Devil* (screenplay, 1954). *The House of Flowers* (drama, 1954; 1968). *The Grass Harp, and A Tree of Night, and Other Stories* (1956). *The Muses Are Heard* (1956). *Breakfast at Tiffany's* (1958). *Observations: Photographs by Richard Avedon*, with Richard Avedon (1959). *The Innocents* (screenplay, 1961). *Selected Writings* (1963). *In Cold Blood* (1965). *A Christmas Memory* (1966). *The Thanksgiving Visitor* (1968). *Trilogy: An Experiment in Multimedia* (1969). *The Dogs Bark: Public People and Private Places* (1973). *Then It All Came Down* (1976). *Music for Chameleons* (1980). *Miriam* (1982). *One Christmas* (1983). *Three by Truman Capote* (1985). *Jug of Silver* (1986). *Answered Prayers: The Unfinished Novel* (1987). *I Remember Grandpa* (1987). *Truman Capote: Conversations* (1987). *Capote Reader* (1987). *Marilyn Monroe: Photographs, 1945–1962* (1994). *Marlon Brando: Portraits and Film Stills, 1946–1995* (1996). *A House on the Heights* (2002).

—REGINA AMMON

FORREST CARTER (1925–1979). Asa Earl Carter was born on September 4, 1925, in Anniston, Ala., one of five children of Ralph and Hermione Weatherly Carter. Under his pen name Forrest Carter (short for Bedford Forrest Carter) he published four books: *Gone to Texas, The Vengeance Trail of Josey Wales, The Education of Little Tree*, and *Watch for Me on the Mountain* (originally published as *Cry Geronimo*). Carter died under mysterious circumstances on June 7, 1979.

All of Carter's published books were novels, though *The Education of Little Tree*—the only one that was not a western—proclaimed on its original cover that it was "a true story." *Little Tree*, written in the first person, conveyed the experiences of a Cherokee boy who lived in rural east Tennessee during the Great Depression. The book cover's suggestion that the book chronicled its author's own life story was eventually exposed as a fraud. Several people—especially journalist Wayne Greenhaw and scholar Dan T. Carter—revealed that Forrest Carter was in fact Asa Carter, a white supremacist who in the 1960s had organized a Birmingham-based hate group, written for racist publications, and scripted speeches for segregationist Alabama governors George and Lurleen Wallace.

Widespread doubt about the moral legitimacy of *Little Tree* was challenged in 1991 when scholar Henry Louis Gates, Jr., in an influential *New York Times* article, asserted that a work of fiction—which *Little Tree* was by then known to be—and the reputation of its author should be judged separately. That year, the book not only entered the *New York Times* best-seller list but was also awarded the American Booksellers Book of the Year (ABBY) Award. A critically acclaimed movie version of *Little Tree* was released in 1997. Actor/director Clint Eastwood's popular movie *The Outlaw Josey Wales* adapted Carter's novel *Gone to Texas*.

Unpublished manuscripts of Carter's writings include an unfinished sequel to *Little Tree* and a collection of his poetry.

WORKS: *Gone to Texas* (1973). *The Vengeance Trail of Josey Wales* (1976). *The Education of Little Tree* (1976). *Watch for Me on the Mountain* (1978).

—TED OLSON

HODDING CARTER (1907–1972). One of the most prominent southern newspaper editors of his era, Hodding Carter, Jr., crusaded against Louisiana politician Huey Long and racial discrimination. A recipient of a 1946 Pulitzer Prize for his journalism, Carter also distinguished himself as a writer, earning a Guggenheim Fellowship in 1945 and publishing numerous books of history, biography, fiction, and poetry.

Born on February 3, 1907, to William Hodding Carter and Irma Dutart Carter, he grew up in Hammond, La., and attended Maine's Bowdoin College, from which he graduated in 1927. After studying at Columbia University, he launched his journalism career in 1929 when he became a reporter for the *New Orleans Item-Tribune*. After brief stints with United Press International and the Associated Press, he collaborated with his wife, Betty Werlein Carter, to found the *Daily Courier* in Hammond in 1932. Still in his twenties, Carter drew national attention with his attacks on Long, whom he accused of corruption and demagoguery.

After Long's assassination and his own failed run for a seat in the Louisiana House of Representatives, Carter sold the *Daily Courier* and moved to Greenville, Miss., where in 1936 he founded the *Delta Star*. As editor of this paper and the *Delta Democrat-Times*, Carter developed a national reputation, particularly for his coverage of the civil rights movement. As a white southern moderate who argued against racial discrimination, he faced enormous opposition in segregated and turbulent Mississippi, where the state house of representatives formally accused him of slander and betrayal. In 1962 he handed over the *Delta Democrat-Times* to his son, William Hodding Carter III, who, in addition to taking a highly visible role as a spokesman in the Carter presidential administration, would also distinguish himself in journalism. After leaving the newspaper, Hodding Carter, Jr., published eight more books before his death of a heart attack in 1972.

WORKS: *Civilian Defense of the United States,* with R. Ernest Dupuy (1942). *Lower Mississippi* (1942). *The Winds of Fear* (1944). *Flood Crest* (1947). *Southern Legacy* (1950). *Gulf Coast Country,* with Anthony Ragusin (1951). *John Law Wasn't So Wrong: The Story of Louisiana's Horn of Plenty* (1952). *Where Main Street Meets the River* (1953). *Robert E. Lee and the Road of Honor* (1955). *So Great a Good: A History of the Episcopal Church in Louisiana and of Christ Church Cathedral, 1805–1955,* with Betty Carter (1955). *Marquis de Lafayette: Bright Sword for Freedom* (1958). *The Angry Scar: The Story of Reconstruction* (1959). *The South Strikes Back* (1959). *Doomed Road of Empire: The Spanish Trail of Conquest,* with Betty Carter (1963). *First Person Rural* (1963). *The Ballad of Catfood Grimes and Other Verses* (1964). *So the Heffners Left McComb* (1965). *The Commandos of World War II* (1966). *The Past as Prelude: New Orleans, 1718–1968* (1968). *Their Words Were Bullets: The Southern Press in War, Reconstruction, and Peace* (1969). *Man and River: The Mississippi* (1970).

—MARK CANADA

JIMMY CARTER (1924–). James Earl Carter, Jr., was born on October 1, 1924, in Plains, Ga. His father, James Earl, was a successful farmer and businessman, prominent in the county. His mother, Lillian (Gordy), was a spirited woman who instilled habits of reading and moral integrity in Jimmy and his younger siblings—William ("Billy"), Gloria, and Ruth. Like Ferrol Sams, who had similar roots, Jimmy Carter was one born "to run with the horsemen."

Always good in school, Carter aimed for a career in the navy. After graduating from Plains High School, he studied for one year at Georgia Southwestern College and another at Georgia Institute of Technology, then was admitted to the U.S. Naval Academy in 1941. Following graduation in 1946, he married Rosalynn Smith, also from Plains. There would be four children—John William (b. 1947), James Earl III (b. 1950), Donald Jeffrey (b. 1952), and Amy Lynn (b. 1967). Carter excelled in the navy, progressing to the rank of lieutenant. In 1953, following the death of his father, Carter felt obligated to resign his commission and return to Plains to take over the family business.

His intelligence and energy revived the lagging family enterprises, but Carter grew restless. He decided to enter politics, running for the Georgia Senate in 1962. After losing the election, against all odds he challenged the outcome and was declared winner. After winning a second senate term, Carter took aim at the governorship. Victorious, he used his inaugural address in January 1971 to mark a new era in southern politics by proclaiming an end to racial discrimination in government.

Few gave the one-term governor of Georgia much chance when he decided to run for president. No southerner had been elected directly into the office since 1848. (Lyndon Johnson won reelection in his own right but first entered the presidency through the vice presidency after the assassination of John F. Kennedy.) First out of the gate, Carter ran hard and fast, securing the nomination in 1976. In a close election, he defeated incumbent Gerald Ford.

Elected as an outsider, Carter found governing as an outsider difficult. His administration inherited a weak economy and high unemployment; both worsened. His chances for reelection were jeopardized further after Iranian militants took over the U.S. embassy in Teheran in 1979 and efforts to secure the hostages' release were stymied. His greatest achievement was the Camp David Accords, in which Egypt and Israel compromised unyielding positions that threatened the peace. His record as environmentalist surpassed that of all presidents who followed Theodore Roosevelt.

Though he was only fifty-six when denied a second term, Carter's commitment to service did not diminish. An avowed born-again Christian, Carter believed that faith had to be lived. Again facing overwhelming odds, he secured the funding to establish in Atlanta the Carter Center, a nonpartisan, nonpolitical organization aimed at alleviating human suffering, securing human rights, and advancing peace and freedom in the world. In addition, he and Rosalynn have been untiring in their work for Habitat for Humanity. In 2002 he received the Nobel Peace Prize.

Highly articulate, Carter has also been a prolific writer and has published memoirs, meditations, and poetry. With the advent of his novel depicting the Revolutionary War in North Carolina, *The Hornet's Nest*, he became the first president to publish in that genre. Withal, he has continued to be rooted in the red soil of Plains.

WORKS: *Why Not the Best? The First Fifty Years* (1975). *A Government as Good as Its People* (1977). *Keeping Faith: Memoirs of a President* (1982). *Negotiation: The Alternative to Hostility* (1984). *Blood of Abraham: Insights into the Middle East* (1985). *Everything to Gain: Making the Most of the Rest of Your Life*, with Rosalynn Carter (1987). *An Outdoor Journal: Adventures and Reflections* (1988; rev. ed. 1994). Ed., *Conference for Global Development and Cooperation* (1992), with Boutras Boutras-Ghali. *Turning Point: A Candidate, a State, and a Nation Come of Age* (1992). *Science, Technology, and Government for a Changing World: The Concluding Reports of the Carnegie Commission on Science, Technology, and Government* (1993). *Talking Peace: A Vision for the Next Generation* (1993). *An Outdoor Journal: Adventures and Reflections* (1994). *Always a Reckoning and Other Poems* (1995). *Little Baby Snoogle-Fleejer*, illustrated by Amy Carter (1995). *Living Faith* (1996). *Sources of Strength: Meditations on Scripture for a Living Faith* (1997). *Sunday in America: 75 Photographers Celebrate Faith and Family* (1997). *The Virtues of Aging* (1998). *Atlanta: The Right Kind of Courage* (1999). *An Hour before Daylight: Memories of a Rural Boyhood* (1999). Ed., *Century's Journey: How the Great Powers Shape the World* (1999), with Robert A. Pastor,. *Christmas in Plains: Memories* (2001). *The Hornet's Nest* (2003). *Sharing Good Times* (2004). *Our Endangered Values: America's Moral Crisis* (2005).

—JOSEPH M. FLORA

WILLIAM ALEXANDER CARUTHERS (1802–1846). Born in Lexington, Va., William Alexander Caruthers was one of eleven children born to William and Phoebe Caruthers. He attended, but did not graduate from, Washington College (now Washington and Lee University). He completed medical school at the University of Pennsylvania in 1823, the year that he also married Louisa Gibson of Savannah, Ga. They eventually had five children. In 1829–35 he practiced medicine in New York City, and began his writing career amongst the members of the New York literati. After time spent back in Lexington, Caruthers relocated to Savannah in 1837. There he wrote, served as a member of the town legislature, and practiced medicine. He died from tuberculosis on August 26, 1846, in Marietta, Ga. He is buried there in an unmarked grave in the cemetery of St. James Episcopal Church.

Caruthers was one of the earliest progenitors of the southern cavalier myth that helped shape the view of Virginia as the "Old Dominion," a sophisticated area replete with classically influenced architecture and ruling-class gentility. His plantation romances drew influence from the novels of Walter Scott and the romantic revival of his day. His 1834–35 two-volume *The Cavaliers of Virginia, or the Recluse of Jamestown,* which uses Bacon's Rebellion as its setting, is one of the earliest examples of cavalier fiction.

While historical record provided a fertile land for creation, Caruthers's portraits, especially that of Nathaniel Bacon as a romantic hero, were often historically inaccurate. Caruthers further propagated the vision of the genteel plantation aristocrat with his 1845 work, *The Knights of the Golden Horse-Shoe.* His work often portrayed the plantation system in an overly sentimental and idealized manner. As the horrors of the Civil War made the romanticized portraits of the plantation system seem more and more like relics, Caruthers and other cavalier fictionists such as John Esten Cooke, George Tucker, John Pendleton Kennedy, and Nathaniel Beverley Tucker faded in popularity.

WORKS: *The Kentuckian in New York; or, The Adventures of Three Southerns [sic], by a Virginian,* 2 vols. (1834–35). *The Cavaliers of Virginia; or, The Recluse of Jamestown; An Historical Romance of the Old Dominion,* 2 vols. (1834–35). "Daniel Boone," *National Portrait Gallery of Distinguished Americans,* 4 vols. (1834–39). "A Musical Soiree," *Knickerbocker Magazine* (1835). "Climbing the Natural Bridge. "By the Only Surviving Witness of That Extraordinary Feat," *Knickerbocker Magazine* (1838). "The Ruins of Jamestown," in *Magnolia; or, Southern Monthly* (1841). "Excerpts from the Portfolio of a Physician. Blushing," in *Magnolia; or, Southern Quarterly* (1841). "Mesmerism," in *Magnolia; or, Southern Monthly* (1842). "Excerpts from the Portfolio of an Old Novelist," in *Family Companion and Ladies' Mirror* (1842). "The Bardolphian Nose," in *Orion: A Monthly Magazine of Literature, Science, and Art* (1842). *The Knights of the Horse-Shoe: A Traditionary Tale of the Cocked Hat Gentry in Old Dominion* (1845). "Dr. Caruthers Aids a Lady," *Georgia Historical Quarterly* (Winter 1972).

—MATTHEW SCIALDONE

W. J. CASH (1900–1941). Wilbur Joseph Cash was born on May 2, 1900, in Gaffney, S.C., a Piedmont cotton-mill town. His father, John William Cash, was manager of the company store of Limestone Mills; the Cashes, of Scotch-Irish and German descent, were devout Baptists. After an early education in Gaffney and across the state line in Boiling Springs, N.C., and after brief stays at two colleges, W. J. Cash in 1920 entered Wake Forest College, a Baptist institution in North Carolina. Wake Forest was in many ways a liberal and progressive institution, and it was here that Cash began to read in earnest such iconoclasts as H. L. Mencken and James Branch Cabell. He also reaffirmed his earlier vow to become a writer, especially an interpreter of the southern mind.

After graduating from Wake Forest and briefly holding jobs as a teacher and reporter, Cash joined the staff of the *Charlotte News* in 1926. In 1929 he began to contribute essays on the South, largely satirical pieces, often overwritten, to Mencken's *American Mercury,* and it is obvious that Mencken was the greatest early influence on Cash. In the late 1920s Cash also began to work on the book he was to entitle *The Mind of the South.* He continued to work on the book during the 1930s, and in 1937 returned to the *Charlotte News* as associate editor and editorial writer. In February 1941, *The Mind of the South* was published to great acclaim. That spring Cash left for Mexico, where he was to spend a year working on a novel under a Guggenheim Fellowship. On July 1, 1941, depressed, confused, and under the delusion that he was being pursued by Nazi agents, he committed suicide in Mexico City.

Cash's single book, *The Mind of the South,* is regarded as perhaps the best attempt to define and explain the nature of the white male southerner. Writing basically from the viewpoint of a liberal southerner—but one with a distaste for undiscriminating "progress" and boosterism—Cash helped to demolish the myth of the aristocratic Old South. He contended that "the old ruling class had never been a fully realized aristocracy," that in fact virtually no aristocrats had existed in southern states other than Virginia, and that "the intellectual and aesthetic culture of the Old South was a superficial and jejune thing . . . not a true culture at all." In his book Cash treated most thoroughly the Carolina Piedmont he knew so well—the rise of the upland cotton planter in the early nineteenth century, the growth of the textile mill and mill village in the late nineteenth century. But he also concerned himself with the antebellum southern frontier of Alabama and Mississippi and with the more general topics of southern race relations, politics, and religion.

Cash was one of many southerners who have attempted to interpret and "explain" the South to out-siders and to themselves. He spent virtually his entire adult life in the writing of his single book, and it is in this book, despite its flaws and shortcomings, that the white southern mind received perhaps its fullest treatment.

WORKS: *Eight Essays on the South in the American Mercury* (1929–35). *The Mind of the South* (1941).

—FRED HOBSON

CLARENCE CASON (1896–1935). Clarence Cason had two great passions: writing and teaching. He excelled at both. Cason was born in Ragland, Ala., and raised in Talladega. He graduated from the University of Alabama in 1917. After service in World War I, he took up journalism and learned his craft at several newspapers, including the *Louisville Courier.* Later he enrolled at the University of Wisconsin, where he earned an M.A. in English and observed a pioneering program to educate journalists. While teaching at the University of Minnesota, he began to develop his own ideas for making journalism a respected discipline within the traditional liberal arts. In 1928 the University of Alabama hired Cason to organize its first journalism department. The thirty-year-old professor enjoyed freedom to design courses that would incorporate principles of writing and editing, but also education in contemporary events and thought.

Cason saw universities not as ivy-walled bastions for privilege, but rather as great schools for twentieth-century democracy. He had faith in common people's ability to govern themselves. A free and vigorous press would guide the public's deliberations, he wrote. Over the next seven years Cason published his ideas in elegant essays for scholarly journals. He also continued to write fever-ishly for newspapers and popular magazines. Along with his colleague Hudson Strode in the English department, Cason became one of the best-known faculty members at Alabama.

In 1935 Cason prepared to publish *Ninety Degrees in the Shade*, a book about his native region. His editor, W. T. Couch at the University of North Carolina Press, saw the volume as a major contribu-tion to southern letters. Cason would join a small but influential group of southern intellectuals who argued for progressive change in their region—a movement Cason labeled "a quiet revolution."

Apparently worried that public reaction to *Ninety Degrees in the Shade* would be angry, Cason went to his office on campus and killed himself just days before the book's publication. His death shocked the university community, as well as Cason's many friends outside Tuscaloosa. The book received favorable reviews from major publications, many critics complimenting Cason's insights into the southern mind.

The University of Alabama Press has twice republished Cason's book. In 1998 the university's journalism department showed gratitude to its founder by establishing the Clarence Cason Writing Award. Winners have included Gay Talese, E. O. Wilson, and Howell Raines.

WORKS: *Ninety Degrees in the Shade* (1935).

—BAILEY THOMSON

MADISON JULIUS CAWEIN (1865–1914). Madison Julius Cawein was born and died in Louisville, Ky., and lived there all his life except for three years in his early teens spent across the river in New Albany, Ind. He was born on March 23, 1865. His father, "Dr." William Cawein, an herbalist and compounder of "vegetable" family medicines, may have had some influence on the poet's dedication to nature. His mother was a spiritualist who thought she had the capacities of a medium, possibly a generative factor in the supernatural fantasies of much of Cawein's poetry. For six years after graduation from Louisville Male High in 1886, he was cashier in the local Newmarket Pool Hall, a center for the off-track betting industry legal then. Thereafter Cawein depended on the uncertain income from his books and contributions to periodicals in one of the least lucrative of literary genres. His dependence on literary production for a livelihood could account for his virtual enslavement to Romantic and Victorian lyric traditions, which held a firm appeal for traditional readers of poetry through Cawein's lifetime. He had a wide circle of literary acquaintances in Kentucky and in the nation, and often visited, for example, Edward Arlington Robinson in New York, Henry van Dyke in Princeton, and James Whitcomb Riley in Indianapolis. He died on December 8, 1914.

Cawein wrote some 2,700 lyrics, of which about 1,500 are originals, the remainder revisions. Although his genuine passion for nature, in the best Romantic tradition, inspired many admirers, the consensus today is that most of his work is the product of a fatigued genius with a few purple patches that have found their way into anthologies. In his own day he was generally respected, with the solid endorsements of such figures as William Dean Howells and Edmund Gosse. Richard H. Stoddard condemned his work as "execrable," but later he mistook Cawein's "Noera," published anonymously in a newspaper, for a hitherto unknown Elizabethan lyric. From a regional standpoint, Cawein is the first Kentucky poet with national recognition before the 1930s.

WORKS: *Blossoms of the Berry* (1887). *The Triumph of Music and Other Lyrics* (1888). *Ascolon of Gaul, with Other Poems* (1889). *Lyrics and Idyls* (1890). *Days and Dreams* (1891). *Moods and Memories: Poems* (1892). *Poems of Nature and Love* (1893). *Red Leaves and Roses* (1893). *Intimations of the Beautiful, and Poems* (1894). *The White Snake and Other Poems; Translated from the German into the Original Meters* (1895). *The Garden of Dreams* (1896). *Vndertones [sic]* (1896). *Idyllic Monologues* (1898). *Shapes and Shadows* (1898). *Myth and Romance, Being a Book of Verse* (1899). *One Day and Another, a Lyrical Eclogue* (1901). *Kentucky Poems* (1902). *A Voice on the Wind and Other Poems* (1902). *Weeds by the Wall* (1904). *The Vale of Tempe* (1905). *Nature-Notes and Impressions, in Prose and Verse* (1906). *An Ode August 15, 1907, at the Dedication of the Monument Erected at Gloucester, Massachusetts, in Commemoration of the Founding of Massachusetts Bay Colony in the Year Sixteen Hundred and Twenty-Three* (1908). *The Poems of Madison Cawein*, 5 vols. (1908). *The Giant and the Star: Little Annals in Rhyme* (1909). *New Poems* (1909). *The Shadow Garden (a Phantasy) and Other Plays* (1910). *Poems* (1911). *So Many Ways* (1911). *The Poet, the Fool and the Faeries* (1912). *The Message of the Lilies* (1913). *Minions of the Moon: a Little Book of Song and Story* (1913). *The Republic: A Little Book of Homespun Verse* (1913). *The Poet and Nature and the Morning Road* (1914). *The Cup of Comus, Fact and Fancy* (1915).

—LAWRENCE S. THOMPSON

FRED CHAPPELL (1936–). Fred Chappell was born on May 28, 1936, and grew up on the one-hundred-acre farm of his maternal grandparents near Canton, in Appalachian North Carolina. His grandfather built the house in which Fred grew up with his parents, James Taylor (J.T.) and Anne Davis Chappell. Fred's parents worked the farm but found it necessary to augment family income by serving as schoolteachers and eventually operating a retail furniture business. Canton is also home to the Champion paper mill, which frequently appears in Chappell's writing, demonstrating his concern about the threat of industrialism to agrarian culture.

In addition to wide reading in the classics of the Western tradition, his boyhood tastes ran to science fiction and horror stories, and his earliest publications, during high school, were in these genres. Eager to leave the farm and discover the modern world, Chappell matriculated in 1954 at Duke University, where he studied with the legendary William Blackburn and formed important literary friendships with fellow students James Applewhite and Reynolds Price. After a three-year interval back in Canton, Chappell completed his B.A. at Duke in 1961, followed by an M.A. in 1964, for which he wrote an eleven-hundred-page concordance to the poetry of Samuel Johnson. His growing interest in the classical and neoclassical poets served to balance his earlier fascination with darkly romantic writers such as Poe and the French Symbolists. The influence of Mark Twain and of Appalachian folk tales has also figured largely in his writing.

Widely recognized as one of the South's preeminent men of letters, Chappell has published more than twenty books, including novels, poetry, short fiction, and criticism. His early four novels explore the psychic fragmentation of the alienated self. With the volumes of poetry he began publishing during the 1970s, Chappell found a more hopeful vision, one he would continue to develop in his later quartet of novels that serve as an extended *kunstlerroman* depicting the maturation of a mountain-born poet named Jess Kirkman. The Kirkman tetralogy and the four poetry volumes published as *Midquest* form an octave of thematically and structurally related works that many consider Chappell's greatest achievement.

His many awards include the Bollingen Prize in Poetry (for *Midquest*), France's Prix de Meilleur des Livres Étrangers for the best foreign novel (for *Dagon*), the Award in Literature from the National Institute of Arts and Letters, a Rockefeller grant, the T. S. Eliot Award, the Aiken/Taylor Award, and the poet laureateship of North Carolina (1997–2002). In 2005 he received the Thomas Wolfe prize. From 1964 to his retirement in 2004, Chappell taught creative writing and literature at the University of North Carolina at Greensboro. He and his wife, Susan, have one son, Heath.

WORKS: *It Is Time, Lord* (1963). *The Inkling* (1965). *Dagon* (1968). *The World between the Eyes* (1971). *The Gaudy Place* (1973). *River* (1975). *Bloodfire* (1978). *Wind Mountain* (1979). *Earthsleep* (1980). *Moments of Light* (1980). *Midquest* (1981). *Castle Tzingal* (1984). *Source* (1985). *I Am One of You Forever* (1985). *The Fred Chappell Reader* (1987). *Brighten the Corner Where You Are* (1989). *First and Last Words* (1989). *More Shapes Than One* (1991). *C: 100 Poems* (1993). *Plow Naked* (1993). *Spring Garden: New and Selected Poems* (1995). *Farewell, I'm Bound to Leave You* (1996). *A Way of Happening* (1998). *Look Back All the Green Valley* (1999). *Family Gathering* (2001). *Backsass* (2004).

—GEORGE HOVIS

BRAINARD CHENEY (1900–1990). Born on June 3, 1900, in Fitzgerald, Ga., Brainard Bartwell Cheney grew up in Lumber City, Ga., on the banks of the Ocmulgee River, and spent most of his adult life in and around Nashville, Tenn. He was educated at the Citadel (1917–19) and Vanderbilt University (1920, 19243–25). In 1928 he married Frances Neel, a reference librarian and member of the faculty of the former George Peabody Library School.

Cheney worked at various jobs before joining the staff of the *Nashville Banner* (1925–42). Noted as a political reporter, he also served as executive secretary to U.S. Senator Tom Stewart (1943–44) and on the public relations staff of Governor Frank Clement (1952–58). He published four novels and an occasional short story; two plays, *Strangers in This World* and *I Choose to Die*, were produced. After publishing *Lightwood,* Cheney was a Fellow at the Bread Loaf Writers Conference (1940) and a Guggenheim Fellow (1941), enabling him to complete *River Rogue*. He later received an award from the Georgia Writers' Association. By sponsorship of Allen Tate and Caroline Gordon, Cheney and his wife became Roman Catholic converts in 1953.

Cheney's novels preserve the history and culture of the Georgia pine barren country of his youth, beginning in the 1870s. *This Is Adam* and *Devil's Elbow* carry the Hightower family into the twentieth century; Cheney planned a trilogy concluding with *In Pursuit of Happiness,* announced by Crown but never published. As interesting as his fiction and his criticism (primarily on fellow Catholic writers Flannery O'Connor and Caroline Gordon) are the Cheneys' papers, purchased by Vanderbilt in 1972. The letters therein—to correspondents such as O'Connor, Gordon, Tate, Robert Penn Warren, and Andrew Lytle—constitute a significant body of literary criticism and biographical information. Brainard Cheney died in Nashville on January 15, 1990.

WORKS: *Lightwood* (1939). *River Rogue* (1942). *This Is Adam* (1958). *Devil's Elbow* (1969). *The Correspondence of Flannery O'Connor and the Brainard Cheneys,* ed. Ralph Stephens (1986).

—MARTHA E. COOK

KELLY CHERRY (1940–). The daughter of musician parents, Kelly Cherry was born in Baton Rouge, La., on December 21, 1940. Cherry spent her childhood in Virginia and graduated from Mary Washington College in 1961 with a B.A. in philosophy and mathematics. She pursued graduate study at the University of Virginia and received an M.F.A. from the University of North Carolina at Greensboro in 1967.

Early in her career, Cherry worked as an editor for several different publishers, including Charles Scribner's Sons. Although she has taught at a number of colleges and universities, including Southwest Minnesota State College, Rhodes College, and Vermont College, the largest part of her career was spent at the University of Wisconsin–Madison, where she was Eudora Welty Professor of English and Evjue-Bascom Professor in the Humanities. In recent years, Cherry served as Visiting Eminent Scholar at the Humanities Center of the University of Alabama–Huntsville and Wyndham Robertson Writer-in-Residence at Hollins University.

Cherry has published over twenty books, including novels, collections of short fiction, nonfiction works, poetry collections, and translations. Her work has been translated into Russian, Lithuanian, Chinese, Dutch, Swedish, and Arabic. The recipient of numerous awards, Cherry received the first James G. Hanes Poetry Prize of the Fellowship of Southern Writers and has been awarded an NEA Fellowship and a Romnes Fellowship. Her stories have won O. Henry and Pushcart awards and have been published in *Best American Short Stories.* Her memoir, *The Exiled Heart,* has received wide critical acclaim; the reissue of her 1979 novel *Augusta Played* further attests to the significance of her work. Cherry's writing reflects her broad interest in fields as diverse as music, paleontology, and cosmology.

Cherry retired from teaching at the University of Wisconsin to move to a Virginia farmhouse, where she lives with her husband, Burke Davis III, a fiction writer.

WORKS: *Sick and Full of Burning* (1974). *Lovers and Agnostics: Poems* (1975). *Relativity: A Point of View: Poems* (1977). *Conversion* (1979). *Augusta Played: A Novel* (1979). *Songs for a Soviet Composer* (1980). *In the Wink of an Eye:*

A Novel (1983). *The Lost Traveller's Dream: A Novel* (1984). *Natural Theology: Poems* (1988). *My Life and Dr. Joyce Brothers: A Novel in Stories* (1990). *The Exiled Heart: A Meditative Autobiography* (1991). *God's Loud Hand: Poems* (1993). *Benjamin John* (1993). *Writing the World* (1995). *Time out of Mind* (1995). *Death and Transfiguration: Poems* (1997). *The Society of Friends: Stories* (1999). *Rising Venus: Poems* (2002). *We Can Still Be Friends: A Novel* (2003). *History, Passion, Freedom, Death, and Hope: Prose about Poetry* (2005).

—MARY LOUISE WEAKS

MARY BOYKIN CHESNUT (1823–1886). Born on March 31, 1823, into a socially and politically important family and married, at age seventeen, to James Chesnut, Jr., later a prominent South Carolina leader, Mary Boykin Miller was the eldest child of Mary Boykin and Stephen Decatur Miller. Privately educated in Camden and Charleston, she had more than a finishing school sheen, since she became genuinely interested in German, French, history, and literature. Her schooling in Charleston was interrupted by a six-month stay at her father's cotton plantation in Mississippi.

Following their marriage on April 23, 1840, she and her husband settled in Camden, where he practiced law, but split time during the next twenty years between Camden and Mulberry, the Chesnut family plantation. Her husband's election to the U.S. Senate in 1858 took her to Washington, where she met many of the men who later were instrumental in forming the Confederacy. Because Jefferson Davis chose her husband as an aide, she traveled to Montgomery, Ala., and Richmond, Va., before going to Columbia to accompany her husband in his new role as commander of the South Carolina reserve forces.

Beginning in February 1861, and continuing, with gaps, until July 1865, Chesnut recorded her experiences in diaries, coming back later to fill in a few of the gaps. She never rounded her diaries and memoirs into a publishable work. Her papers, however, yielded riches when edited, providing firsthand information about Confederate leaders and offering insightful social commentary on southern life. She attempted to write two novels, leaving both in a fragmentary state at her death on November 22, 1886. Until re-edited to conform to modern editorial standards, her diary was called *A Diary from Dixie* and won a secure place for her in southern and American letters.

WORKS: *Mary Chesnut's Civil War*, ed. C. Vann Woodward (1981). *The Private Mary Chesnut: The Unpublished Civil War Diaries*, ed. C. Vann Woodward and Elisabeth Muhlenfeld (1985). *Two Novels by Mary Chesnut*, ed. Elisabeth Muhlenfeld (2002).

—JOHN L. IDOL, JR.

CHARLES W. CHESNUTT (1858–1932). Charles W. Chesnutt was known for his writings about problems not only of very light-skinned African Americans but of African Americans in general; and he also was an important regional writer, particularly about the area around Fayetteville, N.C., where his ancestral roots were deep and where he lived during his formative years.

Charles Waddell Chesnutt was born on June 20, 1858, in Cleveland, Ohio, because in 1856 his parents had left North Carolina to escape the oppressions of slavery. In 1866 the family returned to Fayetteville, where Chesnutt was to grow up and then marry and begin a family. Because of his light color, he could easily pass as white, but he chose to live as an African American, a situation that in the South severely limited his possibilities for learning.

After teaching and serving as a principal in Fayetteville, Charlotte, and surrounding areas, and then in Fayetteville again, Chesnutt decided to seek better social and cultural circumstances. In 1883 he moved to New York, planning to put to use his self-taught ability to take shorthand at two hundred words per minute. Before long he moved to Cleveland, where his family joined him. He lived in Cleveland the rest of his life, enjoying a reputation as: court reporter; lawyer; interested citizen; member of many local civic and cultural organizations; member of Booker T. Washington's Committee of Twelve, the Open-Letter Club, and the General Committee of the NAACP; member of the bibliophile Rowfant Club; and, of course, author. In 1928 he was awarded the Spingarn Medal by the NAACP. He died on November 15, 1932.

Chesnutt published his first story when he was fourteen, in a small African American weekly newspaper. In 1885 one of his stories was published by the new McClure newspaper syndicate. He was to publish a great many articles and pieces of short fiction in such magazines as the *Atlantic Monthly*, the *Overland Monthly*, the *Outlook*, *Family Fiction*, *Puck*, *Crisis*, the *Southern Workman*, the *Century*, and *Youth's Companion*, as well as in newspapers of various larger cities. He believed that he understood and knew more about the South and especially African Americans than did most people writing about them. Both his fiction and nonfiction usually dealt with problems of African Americans, particularly in the South. One of his interests was folklore, which is reflected in his skillful dialect and especially in the plots of the stories of his first book, *The Conjure Woman*, in 1899. These are told by Uncle Julius, a well-drawn former slave who cleverly uses tales of conjuring to his own ends. A second volume of stories, *The Wife of His Youth and Other Stories of the Color Line*, was published in 1899. These stories are of a different type from those of *The Conjure Woman* and are of a sociological bent. Chesnutt's life of Frederick Douglass was also published in 1899.

Chesnutt published three novels: *The House behind the Cedars*, dealing with the pathos of miscegenation and "passing"; *The Marrow of Tradition*, based on the 1898 race riot in Wilmington, N.C.; and *The Colonel's Dream*, with a plan for economic and social help for the Reconstruction South. Although Chesnutt published no more books, his social concerns continued to be invested in public involvement both locally and nationally and in further articles and short fiction. Altogether he published between 1885 and 1931 sixty-one pieces of short fiction (including those in his first two books); one biography; thirty-one speeches, articles, and essays; seven poems; and three novels. He left much unpublished writing, the majority of which has now also been published, including three more novels about African Americans (one each focusing on North Carolina, Harlem, and New Orleans).

Chesnutt was the first important African American writer whose primary genre was fiction, and the first African American writer to be published primarily by major publishers and major periodicals. He wrote fiction both to provide entertainment and to call attention to racism and social injustice. He believed that the sources of, as well as the solutions to, these problems were in the South, so he wrote mostly about the South, with the hope of assisting better understanding and awareness of the positive and often complex humanity and variety of African Americans.

WORKS: *The Conjure Woman* (1899). *Frederick Douglass* (1899). *The Wife of His Youth and Other Stories of the Color Line* (1899). *The House behind the Cedars* (1900). *The Marrow of Tradition* (1901). *The Colonel's Dream* (1905). *The Short Fiction of Charles W. Chesnutt* (1974). *The Journals of Charles W. Chesnutt*, ed. Richard H. Brodhead (1993). *Mandy Oxendine* (1997). *"To Be an Author": Letters of Charles W. Chesnutt, 1899–1905*, ed. Joseph R. McElrath and Robert C. Leitz III (1997). *Paul Marchand, F.M.C.* (1999). *The Quarry* (1999). *Charles W. Chesnutt Essays and Speeches*, ed. McElrath, Leitz, and Jesse S. Crisler (1999). *An Exemplary Citizen: Letters of Charles W. Chesnutt, 1906–1932*, ed. Crisler, McElrath, and Leitz (2002). *A Business Career*, ed. Matthew Wilson and Marjan van Schaik (2005). *Evelyn's Husband*, ed. Wilson and van Schaik (2005).

—JULIAN MASON

ALICE CHILDRESS (1916–1994). Alice Childress was born in Charleston, S.C., on October 12, 1916. When she was five years old, her parents separated and sent her to Harlem, N.Y., to live with Eliza Campbell White, her maternal grandmother. By the end of her sophomore year at Wadleigh High School, the deaths of her grandmother and mother, Florence, forced her to discontinue her education and support herself. As a working-class Harlemite, Childress encountered the "genteel poor"—common people in simple settings—who later shaped her entire literary career.

In the 1940s Childress started an acting career with the American Negro Theatre. A 1944 Broadway debut in *Anna Lucasta* earned her a Tony Award nomination, but growing frustration with male-centered dramas and racial stereotyping compelled her to craft her own plays. This led to the first of three writing phases, the treatment of female interracial conflict. The results were *Florence, Trouble in Mind,* the nondramatic *A Hero Ain't Nothin' but a Sandwich,* and *Wedding Band.*

Plays conceived during a Radcliffe Institute internship in the late 1960s defined the locus of her second writing phase, intraracial conflict, which produced a trio of short plays. The first of three books for junior readers, *A Hero Ain't Nothin' but a Sandwich,* the story of a teenage drug addict, inaugurated her third phase devoted to the concerns of adolescents. *A Hero* became popular among readers of all ages when New World Pictures released a film version in 1978. During this phase, Childress published her only adult novel, *A Short Walk.*

Childress died of cancer on August 14, 1994. Nathan Woodard, her jazz musician husband of thirty-seven years, and granddaughter, Marilyn Alice Lee, survived her. A daughter, Jean R. Childress, died in 1990. An account of her grandmothers, a prelude to writing about her own life, was unfinished.

WORKS: *Florence: A One Act Drama* (1950). *Trouble in Mind: A Comedy Drama in Two Acts* (1955). *Like One of the Family . . . Conversations from a Domestic's Life* (1956). *Wedding Band: A Love/Hate Story in Black and White* (1966). *String* (1969). *Wine in the Wilderness: A Comedy Drama* (1969). *Mojo: A Black Love Story* (1970). *The World on a Hill,* in *Plays to Remember,* ed. Henry B. Maloney (1970). *The African Garden,* in *Black Scenes,* ed. Alice Childress (1971). *A Hero Ain't Nothin' but a Sandwich* (1973). *When the Rattlesnake Sounds* (1975). *Let's Hear It for the Queen* (1976). *A Short Walk* (1979). *Rainbow Jordan* (1981). *Those Other People* (1989). *Moms: A Praise Play for a Black Comedienne* (1993).

—LA VINIA DELOIS JENNINGS

MARK CHILDRESS (1957–). Mark Childress was born in Monroeville, Ala., on September 21, 1957, to Roy and Mary Helen (Gillion) Childress. He attended Louisiana State University in Shreveport, La. (1974–75), and completed a bachelor's degree at the University of Alabama in 1978. He began his writing career as a journalist for the *Birmingham News* and *Atlanta Journal and Constitution* and as a feature editor for *Southern Living,* before becoming a full-time fiction writer. Childress is the author of five novels and three children's books; his articles and reviews have appeared in the *New York Times,* the *Los Angeles Times,* the *Times of London,* and other publications.

Although Childress's novels all have been well received, *Tender,* a coming-of-age story about a young man who resembles Elvis Presley, was the first to appear on best-seller lists. Success followed success with the publication of Childress's most ambitious and best-known work, *Crazy in Alabama,* another coming-of-age story about two boys and their newly liberated aunt.

Childress's novels are set in remote locations, small towns in the rural South or, as in *Gone for Good,* an island in the Pacific Ocean. The characters are southerners, often orphans or people alienated from their families, who transcend their dysfunctional backgrounds to emerge mature and self-aware. The stories approach magic realism in style: extraordinary events and unusual turns of plot occur against realistic, detailed settings. In *A World Made of Fire*, a man acquires mysterious powers as the result of surviving a terrible fire; a German submarine surfaces in the Gulf of Mexico during World War II in *V for Victor*; in *Tender* and *Crazy in Alabama*, voices of deceased relatives chastise and confer with the living; a rock star crash lands on an island inhabited by Amelia Earhart and other missing celebrities in *Gone for Good*.

Though elements of his plots turn fantastic, Childress has been praised for his intimate knowledge and rendering of southern landscapes and mores. His prose evokes the milieu of Alabama just before World War I, during the World War II, in the 1960s during the civil rights movement, and in the recent past.

WORKS: *A World Made of Fire* (1984). *V for Victor* (1988). *Tender* (1990). *Joshua and Bigtooth* (1992). *Crazy in Alabama* (1993). *Henry Bobbity Is Missing and It Is All Billy Bobbity's Fault!* (1996). *Joshua and the Big Bad Blue Crabs* (1996). *Gone for Good* (1998).

—REGINA AMMON

THOMAS HOLLEY CHIVERS (1809–1858). Known today primarily for his association with Edgar Allan Poe, Thomas Holley Chivers published ten books of poetry, drama, and expository prose, all at his own expense.

The son of Colonel Robert Chivers, a cotton planter, Chivers was born near Washington, Ga., on October 18, 1809. In 1827 he married a first cousin, Elizabeth Chivers, who left him within a year. After earning a medical degree from Transylvania University in 1830, he briefly practiced medicine near Oaky Grove, the family plantation. In 1832 he published a collection of eighteen poems called *The Path of Sorrow*. Two years later, he published *Conrad and Eudora*, a play based on the Kentucky Tragedy, a well-known murder that also inspired Poe's *Politian*. In 1837 another poetry collection, *Nacoochee*, followed.

After his marriage to a Massachusetts woman, Harriett Hunt, in 1837, Chivers lived in Connecticut and New York between 1838 and 1842. Between 1842 and 1844, he lost four children. The loss of his three-year-old daughter Allegra Florence was particularly devastating and inspired poems in his 1845 collection *The Lost Pleiad*. After a return to Georgia in 1845, he published the prose exposition *Search After Truth* in 1848. Between 1850 and 1852, Chivers again lived in New York and Connecticut, writing "Letters from the North" for the *Georgia Citizen* and publishing the poetry collection *Eonchs of Ruby* in 1851. In 1853, while living in Boston, he published a narrative poem called *Atlanta; or, The True Blessed Isle of Poesy* and the poetry collection *Virginalia*. He returned to Georgia in 1855 and, in 1856, delivered and published *Birth-Day Song of Liberty*. His play *The Sons of Usna* appeared in 1858. He died that year, on December 18, in Decatur, Ga.

A minor poet, Chivers nevertheless drew positive attention from William Gilmore Simms and Poe, who both praised *The Lost Pleiad*. A Romantic poet with a taste for love, death, and the beautiful, Chivers also explored current events, Native American folklore, and Swedenborgian theology. The author of some decidedly florid and sentimental verse, he has also been recognized as a serious versifier who experimented with poetic forms and even African American dialect.

More enduring than any of his work has been Chivers's connection with Poe. The two corresponded from 1840 until Poe's death in 1849 and seem to have relied on each other for both support and inspiration. Poe solicited Chivers's help with his proposed "Penn" magazine and his failing *Broadway Journal*. In 1847 Chivers even offered to take in his ailing friend and care for him. As poets, they were of one mind and, at times, seem even to have written with the same pen. Chivers's poems about Isadore and the "child-like" and "beautiful, dutiful" Lily Adair, for instance, are remarkably similar to Poe's treatments of Lenore and Annabel Lee. Simms suggested to Chivers that he depended too much on Poe, but Chivers argued, in letters and articles after Poe's death, that the influence sometimes flowed in the other direction. In any case, it is unlikely that Chivers will soon come out from under the shadow of his idol, whom he called "one of the greatest men that ever lived"—and who called him "one of the best and one of the worst poets in America."

WORKS: *The Path of Sorrow; or, The Lament of Youth: A Poem* (1832). *Conrad and Eudora* (1834). *Nacoochee; or, The Beautiful Star, with Other Poems* (1837). *The Lost Pleiad, and Other Poems* (1845). *Search after Truth; or, A New Revelation of the Psycho-Physiological Nature of Man* (1848). *Eonchs of Ruby: A Gift of Love* (1851). *Atlanta; or, The True Blessed Isle of Poesy. A Paul Epic in Three Lustra* (1853). *Virginalia; or, Songs of My Summer Nights. A Gift of Love for the Beautiful* (1853). *Memoralia; or, Phials of Amber Full of the Tears of Love. A Gift for the Beautiful* (1853). *Birth-Day Song of Liberty: A Paean of Glory for the Heroes of Freedom* (1856). *The Sons of Usna: A Tragi-Apotheosis, in Five Acts* (1858). *Chivers' Life of Poe*, ed. Richard Beale Davis (1952). *The Correspondence of Thomas Holley Chivers*, ed. Emma Chase and Lois Parks (1957). *The Unpublished Plays of Thomas Holley Chivers*, ed. Charles M. Lombard (1980).

—MARK CANADA

KATE CHOPIN (1850–1904). Kate Chopin's early years gave little indication of the literary success she would come to enjoy in post–Civil War St. Louis. Kate O'Flaherty was born on February 8, 1850, in St. Louis, Mo., to Irish-born Thomas O'Flaherty, a businessman with railroad interests, and his sixteen-year-old second wife, Eliza Faris, the daughter of Creole aristocrats who could give her husband the social standing that his money alone could not. Shortly after Kate's fifth birthday, her father was killed when a suspension bridge over the Gasconade River collapsed, plunging railcars into the river several hundred feet below.

Despite the early loss of her father, Chopin continued her education at the elite Sacred Heart Academy, until she was forced to withdraw following the onset of the Civil War. She became fluent in French, which she learned from her grandmother Madame Charleville. Following a successful debut into St. Louis society, the young Kate captured the attention of Oscar Chopin, a Creole from Louisiana, and soon married him. By the time the Chopins returned to New Orleans following a European honeymoon, Kate was expecting her first child. The couple spent several happy years in New Orleans, despite financial constraints imposed by Oscar's failing cotton business, as well as the political unrest that culminated in the Battle of Liberty Place in 1874. By 1879, Oscar lost his brokerage and relocated his family to the Chopin estate in rural Cloutierville, La. While living in Cloutierville, Oscar ran a store, and Kate conducted herself in ways that the locals found shocking: she flirted with married men, rode her horse down the main street of town during the heat of the afternoon, and dressed extravagantly. Oscar contracted malaria and died in 1882, leaving Kate with substantial debts and six young children.

Chopin remained in Cloutierville for several years, maintaining the store and working diligently to repay all of Oscar's debts. Her methods met with disapproval from the townspeople, who considered her unforgiving and inflexible in her money collection efforts. During this time, Chopin reputedly engaged in a notorious affair with the married plantation owner Albert Sampite. The reasons for the demise of this relationship are murky, ranging from suggestions by Cloutierville locals that the affair never took place to allegations that Sampite physically abused Chopin in much the same way he abused his own wife. Chopin ultimately returned to St. Louis, where she lived the remainder of her life.

In St. Louis, Chopin needed to supplement her income in order to support her children adequately. She capitalized on her aptitude for writing, publishing her first poem, "If It Might Be," in 1889. Chopin enjoyed widespread success, publishing her short fiction in well-regarded periodicals ranging from *Youth's Companion* and the avant-garde *Vogue* to literary mainstays such as the *Atlantic* and *Century*. Her first novel, *At Fault*, was privately published in 1890 to positive reviews.

Readers relished Chopin's local color fiction, which provided glimpses of life on the exotic bayous of Louisiana, and she had soon written enough stories to publish her first collection, *Bayou Folk*, in 1894; a second collection, *A Night in Acadie*, appeared in 1897. In each of her collections, Chopin's themes gradually became more unconventional, showing women questioning the roles expected of them by nineteenth-century society, and chafing under the restrictions of these roles. Her master-piece, *The Awakening*, was published in 1899 to a firestorm of criticism. Despite the fact that the novel was praised by some critics for its deft and poetic use of language, many readers found its topic—a woman's seeking satisfaction outside the confines of her marriage—unsavory and resorted to con-demning the book and its author equally. Some critics were so virulent that Chopin herself quipped rather caustically that if she had known that Mrs. Pontellier would accomplish "her own damnation as she did," she would have "excluded her from the company" of characters populating the novel.

Although *The Awakening* received more negative criticism than its predecessors, legends of its being banned in St. Louis are overstated. Multiple copies of the novel were owned by both of the St. Louis lending libraries, and the copies were not removed from circulation until the books had be-come too worn for continued use. When *The Awakening* appeared, Chopin held a contract to publish a third collection of stories, *A Vocation and a Voice*, but because of the limited commercial success of *The Awakening*, the publisher opted not to publish the collection. *A Vocation and a Voice* appeared for the first time, arranged as Chopin seems to have intended, in 1991.

Rumors abound that Chopin was crushed by the negative reception of *The Awakening*, and that she never wrote again after this experience. Biographer Emily Toth suggests that Chopin continued to write on a limited basis, despite her failing health. In the summer of 1904, after attending the World's Fair in St. Louis, Chopin succumbed to a stroke. Her work fell into obscurity for over sixty years, but in recent decades it has enjoyed a resurgence of popularity, both for the artistry of the writing style and the sophistication of the themes for the time in which Chopin was writing. *The Awakening* is now counted among the most significant American novels.

WORKS: *At Fault* (1890). *Bayou Folk* (1894). *A Night in Acadie* (1897). *The Awakening* (1899). *The Complete Works of Kate Chopin*, ed. Per Seyersted (1969). *A Vocation and a Voice*, ed. Emily Toth (1991).

—SUZANNE DISHEROON-GREEN

EMILY TAPSCOTT CLARK (1893–1953). Clever and witty from childhood, Emily Clark was red-headed and homely. She was the daughter of the rector of St. James Episcopal Church in Richmond, Va., and she attended Miss Jennie Ellett's School. Although she prepared for Bryn Mawr, she chose instead to remain in Richmond and write for newspapers.

In 1921 Clark was founder of the *Reviewer*, a literary magazine. In her role as chief editor and regular contributor to the journal, Clark met many of the well-known literary figures of the day and published works by such writers as H. L. Mencken, Gertrude Stein, and Sinclair Lewis. She gave up the *Reviewer* in 1924 to marry Joseph Swift Balch, sixty-eight, an explorer, sportsman, and writer, who was a wealthy and socially prominent Philadelphian.

After her husband's death in 1927, Clark remained in Philadelphia, where she contributed articles and book reviews to various newspapers and where she was a patron of the arts. She left two-thirds of her estate to the University of Virginia upon her death on July 2, 1953, the income from the fund to be used for the purpose of "stimulating appreciation and creation of American literature."

Seven of her satirical portraits of thinly disguised Richmonders were collected in her first book, *Stuffed Peacocks.* In a second volume her gift at characterization was again demonstrated: *Innocence Abroad,* which relates her experiences with the *Reviewer,* includes twelve chapters that present portraits of prominent writers who contributed to the journal.

Clark also published pieces in *Saturday Review, Smart Set, American Mercury,* and *Virginia Quarterly Review.* Her lively letters to novelist Joseph Hergesheimer during the *Reviewer* days were published in *Ingénue among the Lions.*

WORKS: *Stuffed Peacocks* (1927). *Innocence Abroad* (1931). *Ingénue among the Lions: The Letters of Emily Clark to Joseph Hergesheimer,* ed. Gerald Langford (1965).

—DOROTHY McINNIS SCURA

JOHN HENRIK CLARKE (1915–1998). John Henrik Clarke was born on January 1, 1915, in Union Springs, Ala., to a family of sharecroppers. In 1919 the family moved to Columbus, Ga., where Clarke learned to read and began to develop an interest in literature. In 1933 he boarded a freight train and left the South to involve himself in the literary and activist communities of New York City. He studied creative writing at the League of American Writers School, Columbia University, and New York University, and became involved in the Harlem History Club and the Harlem Writers' Guild.

During his lifetime, Clarke rose to prominence as one of the world's leading black Africanists and African historians. He traveled and lectured across America and in almost every African country, collecting and archiving African and African American cultural materials. He published short stories, including the widely anthologized "The Boy Who Painted Christ Black," and a volume of poetry. In 1949 he co-founded the *Harlem Quarterly,* and also served as associate editor of the journal *Freedomways.* He worked extensively in journalism, most notably as feature writer on African subjects for the *Pittsburgh Courier.* He also wrote a book-review column, "African World Bookshelf," that was distributed internationally.

Throughout the 1960s, Clarke served as the director of the Heritage Teaching Program at Haryou-Act, an antipoverty agency in Harlem. He was a founding member of the Black Academy of Arts and Letters and the African American Scholars' Council, and became the first president of the African Heritage Studies Association in 1968. In 1969 he was the founding chairman of the Black and Puerto Rican Studies Department at New York City's Hunter College. He lectured at Columbia University, New York University, the New School for Social Research, and Cornell University (where the Africana library is named for him). In 1983 he received the Thomas Hunter Professorship at Hunter College. Although he lost his sight toward the end of his life, Clarke continued to write and work. He died in New York City on July 16, 1998.

WORKS: *Rebellion in Rhyme* (1948). Ed., *The Lives of Great African Chiefs* (1958). Ed., *Harlem, a Community in Transition* (1964). Ed., *American Negro Short Stories* (1966). Ed., *Black American Short Stories: Century of the Best Black American Short Stories* (1967). Ed., *Harlem, U.S.A.: The Story of a City within a City, Told by James Baldwin* (1967). Ed., *William Styron's Nat Turner: Ten Black Writers Respond* (1968). Ed., *History and Culture of Africa* (1969). Ed., *Malcolm X: The Man and His Times* (1969). Ed., *What's It All About?* (1969). Ed., *Harlem: Voices from the Soul of America* (1970). Ed., *Slave Trade and Slavery* (1970). Ed., *Black Titans: W. E. B. Du Bois* (1970). Ed., *Marcus Garvey and the Vision of Africa* (1974). Ed., *Paul Robeson: The Great Forerunner* (1978). Ed., *The End of the Age of Grandeur and the Beginning of the Slave Trade* (1981). *New Dimensions of African World History* (1991). *Christopher Columbus and the African Holocaust: Notes for an African World Revolution* (1991). *Notes for an African World Revolution: Africans at the Crossroads* (1991). *African People in World History* (1993). *Who Betrayed the African Revolution and Six Major Speeches* (1994).

—TESSA JOSEPH

JOHN BELL CLAYTON (1906–1955). Born on October 28, 1906, into a Craigville, Va., farm family that traced its American ancestry to before the Revolution, John Bell Clayton was the son of John Bell and Mary McCausland Clayton. Educated at local public schools, he left the University of Virginia without a degree to pursue a career in journalism on the *Charlottesville Daily Progress* and the *Washington News*. During World War II, he served in the Office of War Information, at one point working with Ernie Pyle in San Francisco, and later settled there to become an associate editor of the *San Francisco Chronicle*. Clayton was married twice: first to Millicent Pearsall in 1930, a union that ended in divorce after the birth of an only child, John Bell Clayton, Jr.; and then to Martha Carmichael, in 1945.

Clayton began writing fiction after the war, and met with enough success to leave newspaper work in 1950. His second published story, "The White Circle," won the O. Henry Prize in 1947, and his first novel, *Six Angels at My Back,* earned critical and commercial success in 1952. *Wait, Son, October Is Near,* probably his best and best-known novel, followed in 1953, with *Walk toward the Rainbow* also winning attention in 1954. Clayton had started a fourth novel when he died suddenly on February 10, 1955. A posthumous volume, *Strangers Were There,* collected published and unpublished short fiction in 1957, and the best of these pieces became perhaps his major contribution to southern letters, appearing often in anthologies until the end of the twentieth century.

WORKS: *Six Angels at My Back* (1952). *Wait, Son, October Is Near* (1953). *Walk toward the Rainbow* (1954). *Strangers Were There* (1957).

—JOSEPH R. MILLICHAP

PEARL CLEAGE (1948–). Born in Springfield, Mass., on December 7, 1948, Pearl Michelle Cleage grew up in Detroit, Mich., where her mother, Doris, taught elementary school and her father, Albert, a prominent minister, ran for governor in 1962 on the Freedom Ticket. He also became an active civil rights leader and African American nationalist, racial influences that pervade Cleage's work.

Besides being an accomplished playwright, Cleage is also a journalist, essayist, poet, novelist, and composer of performance pieces that have been performed internationally. Following an impressive high school career, Cleage in 1966 enrolled in Howard University, where she studied playwriting and dramatic literature and saw two of her one-act plays produced. In 1969 she left the university to marry Atlanta politician Michael Lomax, with whom she had one daughter; the marriage ended in 1979.

Cleage graduated from Spelman College with a degree in drama. She subsequently hosted an African American radio program, contributed articles to several newspapers and magazines, and served as director of communications for the city of Atlanta as well as press secretary for Maynard Jackson, the first southern African American mayor elected since the Civil War.

In the 1980s Cleage expanded her stage writing, producing *puppetplay, Hospice, Good News,* and *Essentials.* But it was her 1992 play *Flyin' West*—a daring look at the westward move of African Americans to attain land and freedom—that earned her national attention as a dramatist. It premiered at Atlanta's Alliance Theatre, which subsequently supported much of Cleage's work. Her reputation was further enhanced with *Blues for an Alabama Sky*—performed as part of the 1996 Atlanta Cultural Olympiad in conjunction with the Olympic Games—and *Bourbon at the Border*. Cleage has noted that her writing attempts to examine the juncture of racism and sexism, with her prevailing characters being strong African American women. Her debut novel, *What Looks Like Crazy on an Ordinary Day*, was an Oprah Book Club selection, vaulting her to national prominence as well as the *New York Times* best-seller list and earning a BCALA Literary Award. Cleage's other honors include five AUDELCO Awards for Outstanding Achievement Off Broadway for *Hospice*, the 1983 Bronze Jubilee Award for Literature, and the Atlanta Association of Black Journalists Award for Outstanding Columnist (1991), as well as grants from the NEA, the City of Atlanta Bureau of Cultural Affairs, and the Georgia Council for the Arts.

Cleage teaches playwriting at Spelman College in Atlanta, where she lives with her husband Zaron W. Burnett, Jr., writer and director of the Just Us Theater Company. She also co-founded and edits a literary journal *Catalyst* and serves as artistic director for Just Us Theater.

WORKS: *We Don't Need No Music* (1972). *puppetplay* (1981). *Hospice* (1983). *Mad at Miles: A Blackwoman's Guide to Truth* (1990). *The Brass Bed and Other Stories* (1991). *Chain and Late Bus to Mecca* (1992). *Deals with the Devil: and Other Reasons to Riot* (1993). *Flyin' West* (1995). *What Looks Like Crazy on an Ordinary Day* (1997). *Blues for an Alabama Sky* (1999). *Flyin' West and Other Plays* (1999). *I Wish I Had a Red Dress* (2001). *Some Things I Never Thought I'd Do* (2003). *Babylon Sisters* (2005).

—KAREN C. BLANSFIELD

IRVIN SHREWSBURY COBB (1876–1944). During the first half of the twentieth century Irvin Cobb was—along with a fellow Paducahan, U.S. vice president Alben Barkley—the most famous living Kentuckian. Best known as a humor writer in the local color tradition, Cobb was a journalist, fiction writer, film writer, radio personality, lecturer, and Hollywood actor and consultant. The son of Joshua (a Confederate veteran) and Marie Saunders Cobb, he published more than sixty books, which are little read today.

Cobb became a writer at age sixteen when he began reporting for the *Paducah Evening News*. For the next twenty years, he wrote humor columns and news for the *Louisville Post*, the *New York Sun*, and Joseph Pulitzer's *New York World*. In 1909 he became a staff contributor for the *Saturday Evening Post*, which published his short fiction and humorous essays, and twice sent him to Europe (in 1915 and 1917) to report on the war. From 1922 to 1932, he worked for William Randolph Hearst's *Cosmopolitan*. He published more than seventy stories about Judge Priest, his most famous character, an amalgam of several figures from his Kentucky childhood. His stories, often promulgating southern stereotypes, won several O. Henry Prizes.

In 1934 Cobb went to Hollywood to consult with his friend Will Rogers, who was playing Judge Priest in a movie. He stayed on and appeared in several films, wrote screenplays, and broadcast a radio show, *Paducah Plantation*.

His most successful books were *"Speaking of Operations—,"* about his appendectomy, and *Exit Laughing*, his autobiography. Much of his writing portrayed country characters lost in an industrialized world. An outdated sentimentality largely accounts for the obsolescence of his work. After World War I he took a strong stand against racism, particularly against Ku Klux Klan activities in the 1920s. He was married in 1900 to Laura Spencer Baker of Savannah. They had one child, Elisabeth. Cobb is buried in Paducah under a boulder inscribed "Back Home."

WORKS: *Home: Being the Narrative of Judge Priest and His People* (1912). *Cobb's Anatomy* (1912). *Cobb's Bill-of-Fare* (1913). *The Escape of Mrs. Trimm: His Plight and Other Plights* (1913). *Europe Revised* (1914). *Roughing It De Luxe* (1914). *Paths of Glory: Impressions of War Written at and near the Front* (1915). *"Speaking of Operations—"* (1915). *Fibble, D.D.* (1916). *Local Color* (1916). *Old Judge Priest* (1916). *Those Times and These* (1917). *"Speaking of Prussians—"* (1917). *The Glory of the Coming: What Mine Eyes Have Seen of the Americans in Action in This Year of Grace and Allied Endeavor* (1918). *The Thunders of Silence* (1918). *Eating in Two or Three Languages* (1919). *The Life of the Party* (1919). *From Place to Place* (1920). *One Third Off* (1921). *J. Poindexter, Colored* (1922). *Sundry Accounts* (1922). *A Laugh a Day Keeps the Doctor Away: His Favorite Stories as Told by Irvin S. Cobb* (1923). *Snake Doctor and Other Stories* (1923). *Stickfuls: Compositions of a Newspaper Minion* (1923). *Goin' on Fourteen, Being Cross-Sections out of a Year in the Life of an Average Boy* (1924). *Indiana* (1924). *Kansas* (1924). *Kentucky* (1924). *Maine* (1924). *New York* (1924). *North Carolina* (1924). *Alias Ben Alibi* (1925). *"Here Comes the Bride—" and So Forth* (1925). *"Oh, Well, You Know How Women Are!"* (1926). *On an Island That Cost $24,000* (1926). *Prose and Cons* (1926). *Some United States: A Series of Stops in Various Parts of the Nation with One Excursion across the Line* (1926). *Chivalry Peak* (1927). *Ladies and Gentlemen* (1927). *All Aboard: Saga of the Romantic River* (1928). *The Abandoned Farmers: Humorous Account of a Retreat from the City to the Farm* (1929). *Irvin Cobb at His Best* (1929). *The Man's World* (1929). *Red Likker* (1929). *Both Sides of the Street* (1930). *To Be Taken before Sailing* (1930). *Incredible Truth* (1931). *Down Yonder with Judge Priest* (1932). *Many Laughs for Many Days: Another Year's Supply (365) of His Favorite Stories as Told by Irvin S. Cobb* (1933). *Murder Day by Day* (1933). *One Way to Stop a Panic* (1933). *Faith, Hope and Charity* (1934). *Irvin S. Cobb's Own Recipe Book, Written by Mr. Cobb for Frankfort Distilleries, Incorporated* (1934). *Azam: The Story of an Arabian Colt and His Friends* (1937). *Judge Priest Turns Detective* (1937). *Favorite Humorous Stories of Irvin Cobb* (1940). *Four Useful Pups* (1940). *Glory, Glory, Hallelujah!* (1941). *Exit Laughing* (1941).

—JANE GENTRY VANCE

PAT CONROY (1945–). Pat Conroy primarily writes autobiographical fiction; reading it, one can almost follow the chronology of his life. Critics and reviewers have been quick to notice that Conroy's novels focus on his love/hate relationship with his family and the South. Although he actively resists such comparisons, Conroy has been likened to William Faulkner, Thomas Wolfe, and even Margaret Mitchell, who have written about similar themes. He is, however, quick to acknowledge Wolfe as his first literary inspiration; in 2003 Conroy received the Thomas Wolfe Prize.

Donald Patrick Conroy was born to Donald Conroy, a pilot in the Marines, who retired from the military and provided the inspiration for *The Great Santini*, Conroy's first novel. His mother, Peggy Egan Peek, a beauty queen from the South, was determined to raise her children to become true southerners. Conroy's relationship with her is the focus of both *The Prince of Tides* and his most recent novel, *Beach Music*. Conroy attended the Citadel, where he focused on literary pursuits and basketball. His experiences at the Citadel led to *The Boo*, a portrait of Lt. Colonel Thomas Courvoise, the instructor he most admired; *The Lords of Discipline*; and *My Losing Season*, which depicts the dynamics of his basketball career at the Citadel and provides a nonfiction assessment of his father. Following graduation, Conroy taught English and coached basketball at his alma mater, Beaufort High School in South Carolina. Following this position and prior to writing full-time, he taught for a year on Daufuskie Island, and the experiences there provided the basis of *The Water Is Wide*. The book was quickly translated to film as *Conrack*. From *The Boo* onward, Conroy has been sympathetic to the underdogs and the misunderstood.

It is a testament to his skill as storyteller, widely acknowledged, that several of Conroy's books, both fiction and nonfiction, have been made into successful movies. Conroy's family, on the other hand, is more critical, and his sister, Carol, who is the model for the suicidal Savannah in *The Prince of Tides,* no longer speaks to him. Conroy currently lives in South Carolina, where he is working on nonfiction and screenplays.

WORKS: *The Boo* (1970). *The Water Is Wide* (1972). *The Great Santini* (1976). *The Lords of Discipline* (1980). *The Prince of Tides* (1986). *Beach Music* (1995). *My Losing Season* (2002). *The Pat Conroy Cookbook: Recipes from My Life,* with Suzanne Williamson Pollak (2004).

—SUSIE SCIFRES KUILAN

MONCURE DANIEL CONWAY (1832–1907). Born in Stafford County, Va., on March 17, 1832, Moncure Daniel Conway, son of Margaret Eleanor Daniel and Walker Peyton Conway, grew up in comfortable, slaveholding circumstances. In 1847, he enrolled in Dickinson College in Carlisle, Pa., as the youngest student in his class and graduated two years later. Following a brief career as a circuit-riding Methodist preacher, during which his orthodoxy and support for slavery eroded, Conway followed his Emerson-inspired star to the Harvard Divinity School, where he completed a degree in 1854. Friends with Emerson, Thoreau, and Theodore Parker, the new Unitarian minister adopted radical abolition as his creed, for which beliefs he was removed after two years as pastor of a Washington, D.C., church.

In late 1856, he was called to Cincinnati, where his politics and increasing skepticism over the divinity of Christ were better received, despite causing a church schism. Unhappy with the course of the Civil War and Lincoln's slowness to adopt emancipation, Conway moved to London in 1863. As minister to South Park Chapel in that city for twenty years, Conway became a convinced rationalist, incorporating selected aspects of the world's creeds into his preaching. Following a trip to India in 1883–84, he returned with his family, including wife Ellen Dana, to New York. After a second stint at South Park Chapel in the mid-1890s, he came back to New York, only to leave again during the Spanish-American War. He spent most of his last years in Paris and died there on November 15, 1907.

Conway's considerable output includes newspaper columns; anti-slavery books and sermons; biographies of Emerson, Carlyle, and Hawthorne; and two novels. His most important works are his biography of Thomas Paine and his autobiography, the latter of which charts the transformation of the son of a Virginia Methodist slaveholder to free-thinking abolitionist and religious rationalist.

WORKS: *Free-schools in Virginia: A Plea of Education, Virtue and Thrift, vs. Ignorance, Vice and Poverty* (1850). *A Discourse on the Life and Character of the Hon. William Cranch, LL.D., Late Chief Justice of the District of Columbia* (1855). *The Old and the New: A Sermon Containing the History of the First Unitarian Church in Washington City* (1855). *Pharisaism and Fasting* (1855). *The True and the False in Prevalent Theories of Divine Dispensations* (1855). *The One Path; or, The Duties of North and South* (1856). *Spiritual Liberty* (1856). *Virtue vs. Defeat* (1856). *The Theater* (1857). *Tracts for Today* (1858). *East and West* (1859). *The Natural History of the Devil* (1859). *Thomas Paine: A Celebration* (1860). "Excalibur," *Dial* 1 (Jan. 1860): 38–48. *The Rejected Stone; or, Insurrection vs. Resurrection in America* (1861). *The Golden Hour* (1862). "Then and Now in the Old Dominion," *Atlantic Monthly* 9 (Apr. 1862): 493–502. "Benjamin Banneker, the Negro Astronomer," *Atlantic Monthly* 11 (Jan. 1863): 79–84. *Testimonies Concerning Slavery* (1864). *The Earthward Pilgrimage* (1870). *The Voysey Case from an Heretical Stand-point* (1871). *Mazzini* (1872). *The Parting of the Ways: A Study on the Lives of Sterling and Maurice* (1872). *Republican Superstitions as Illustrated in the Political History of America* (1872). *In Memoriam: A Memorial Discourse in Honor of John Stuart Mill* (1873). Ed., *The Sacred Anthology: A Book of Ethical Scriptures* (1874). *David Friedrich Strauss* (1874). *Consequences* (1875). *The First Love Again* (1875). *Intellectual Suicide* (1875). *Revivalism* (1875). *Human Sacrifices in England* (1876). *Christianity* (1876). *Our Cause and Its Claims upon Us* (1876). *The Religion of Children* (1877). *Alcestis in England* (1877). *Idols and Ideals, with an Essay on Christianity* (1877). *Unbelief: Its Nature, Cause, and Cure* (1877). *Entering Society* (1877). *Atheism: A Spectre* (1878). *Liberty and Morality* (1878). *The Peril of War* (1878). *Demonology and Devil-Lore,* 2 vols. (1879).

The Criminal's Ascension (1879). *A Last Word* (1880). *A Necklace of Stories* (1880). *What Is the Religion of Humanity?* (1880). *The Rising Generation* (1880). *Laureate Despair* (1881). *Thomas Carlyle* (1881). *The Wandering Jew* (1881). *The Oath and Its Ethics* (1881). *The Life and Death of Garfield* (1881). *Chronicles of Christopher Columbus: A Poem in Three Cantos* (1882). *Travels in South Kensington: With Notes on Decorative Art and Architecture in England* (1882). *Emerson at Home and Abroad* (1882). *Lessons for the Day* (1882–83; 1907). *Emerson and His Views of Nature* (1883). *Farewell Discourses* (1884). *Three Lyrical Dramas: Sintram, The Friends of Syracuse, The Lady of Kynast* (1886). *Passages from Some Journals and Other Poems* (1886). *Pine and Palm*, 2 vols. (1887). *Unitarianism and Its Grandchildren* (1887). *Omitted Chapters of History Disclosed in the Life and Papers of Edmund Randolph* (1888). *George Washington's Rules of Civility* (1890). *Life of Nathaniel Hawthorne* (1890). *Prisons of Air* (1891). *Barons of the Potomack and Rappahannock* (1892). *The American Utopia* (1892). *The Life of Thomas Paine*, 2 vols. (1892). Ed., *The Writings of Thomas Paine*, 4 vols. (1894–96). *Centenary History of the South Place Society* (1894). *Solomon and Solomonic Literature* (1899). *L'Alliance internationale pour l'arbitrage / The International Arbitration Alliance* (1899). *Thomas Paine et la Revolution dans les Deux Mondes* (1900). *Emerson's Centenary: His Thought and Teaching* (1903). *Autobiography, Memories and Experiences of Moncure Daniel Conway*, 2 vols. (1904). *My Pilgrimage to the Wise Men of the East* (1906). *On the Eve of Seventy-Four* (1906). *Addresses and Reprints, 1850–1907* (1909). Ed., *The Age of Reason*, by Thomas Paine (1909). *Fate* (1930). *Exploring the Lake District One Hundred Years Ago*, ed. Stuart D. Ludlum (1985).

—JEFFREY H. RICHARDS

J. GORDON COOGLER (1865–1901). Sounding his barbaric yawp over southern rooftops, James Gordon Coogler once sniffed: "Oh you critics!—if an author errs in a single line / That line you'll surely quote, / And will give it as a sample fair / Of all he ever wrote."

The South Carolina-born poetaster achieved a strange sort of celebrity within his lifetime, scribbling his deathless verses while his patrons snickered in their sleeves. An unadoring public was just one of the unhappy circumstances that Coogler faced. When his father died in 1880, young J. Gordon was left to provide for his mother and two sisters, a duty he discharged with filial devotion. He ceremoniously hung up his shingle and thus became the first (and probably last) poet-for-hire in South Carolina. The placard in his shop window announced simply: "Poems Written While You Wait." As one who recognized the importance of flaunting one's gifts, Coogler circulated booklets of his own verse and—rather disastrously—sent out his self-published work for review.

His best-known collection, *Purely Original Verses*, offered anything but, and the hapless poet soon became a running joke among the ink-stained wretches of his day, ridiculed in journals such as *Munsey's*, *Puck*, and the *Literary Digest*. The poet had a sense of what might now be termed niche marketing. His tailor-made collections numbered five thousand by the time of his death in 1901, according to the *Columbia State*.

But Coogler has been consecrated to fame primarily for his memorable plaint, which Mencken resounded in his searing "Sahara of the Bozart": "Alas! for the South, her books have grown fewer— / She never was much given to literature." How much Coogler hastened that decline is another matter. Mencken added insult to injury by calling Coogler "the last bard of Dixie," and indeed, the Baltimore curmudgeon can fairly be credited with rescuing him from a richly deserved oblivion. So the spirit (and quality) of Coogler's work endures. Today a number of mock-serious Coogler societies flourish and even dispense awards for their namesake, ensuring that wherever prosodic dullness reigns, there too goeth Coogler.

WORKS: *Purely Original Verse* (ca. 1891, ca. 1893, 1894, 1895, 1897). *Purely Original Verse: Complete Works, and a Number of New Productions, in One Volume* (1897, 1901).

—BRYAN GIEMZA

EBENEZER COOKE [COOK] (1667?–post-1732). Ebenezer Cooke, poet laureate of early Maryland, remains one of the most shadowy colonial authors; though his life was given a certain zany plausibility in John Barth's *The Sot-Weed Factor* (1960), we are not even sure whether the poet's title was self-assumed or playfully or seriously bestowed by others. He first signed himself poet laureate in October 1726, but there is evidence—notably a versified letter from the Virginia lawyer John Fox to Thomas Bordley, attorney general of Maryland—that the title had been familiarly applied to him before 1724.

The son of a Maryland merchant and his wife, Andrew and Anne Bowyer Cooke, Ebenezer was born in St. Michael's Parish, Bassingshawe, London, sometime in the late 1660s; his name first appears in Maryland records in 1694, when he signed a petition protesting the removal of the colonial capital from St. Mary's City to Annapolis. Apparently he returned to London shortly thereafter, possibly to oversee publication of his satire *The Sot-weed Factor*, which came out in 1708. He remained long enough to probate his father's will on January 2, 1712, by the terms of which he and his sister Anna each received half of the family estate, Malden, at Cooke's Point, Md. By 1717 he was back in the colony and, hard pressed for cash, had sold his share of Malden. From then on through the 1720s, he attempted to support himself by becoming a lawyer, by acting as a land agent for the proprietors' receivers-general Henry and Bennett Lowe, and by turning once again to the poet's trade he seems to have relinquished between 1708 and 1726, the year of his *ELOGY* on the death of Thomas Bordley.

The first belletristic writing published in the colonial South, Cooke's *ELOGY* initiated his association with the printer William Parks, who was also to publish *Sotweed Redivivus* and "The History of Bacon's Rebellion" in the next several years. But if Cooke's frequent complaints of his empty purse can be trusted, the venture with Parks seems to have brought in little money . The impoverished poet lived just long enough after the second of these pieces to mourn the passing of two friends, Justice William Lock and Benedict Leonard Calvert, in 1732. The rest, so far as history is concerned, is silence.

Although Cooke favored Samuel Butler's hudibrastic verses and lifted more than one line from *Hudibras*, he possessed a significant comic talent of his own and was more than merely an imitator. His treatment of Maryland's drunken rabble, his creation of a snobbish foreign persona who is himself the object of the poet's satire, and his attempt to maintain the point of view of a gentleman even while appreciating the vitality of backwoods language make him an important innovator in, if not indeed the founder of, the southern comic tradition.

WORKS: *The Sot-weed Factor; or, A Voyage to Maryland* (1708). *An ELOGY on the Death of Thomas Bordley* (1726). "An Elegy on the Death of the Honourable Nicholas Lowe" (1728). *Sotweed Redivivus* (1730). "The Sot-Weed Factor" (3rd ed.?) and "The History of Colonel Nathaniel Bacon's Rebellion in Virginia," in *The Maryland Muse* (1731). "An Elegy on the Death of the Honourable William Lock" (1732). "A Poem in Memory of the Hon[ble] Benedict Leonard Calvert" (1732).

—ROBERT D. ABNER

JOHN ESTEN COOKE (1830–1886). Often identified as a historian and novelist, John Esten Cooke was a prolific writer comfortable in any genre, though he most characteristically wrote prose works that romanticized history and historicized romance and dealt with questions of southern identity.

One of thirteen children, he was the son of John Rodgers Cooke, an attorney, and Maria Pendleton Cooke. Born in Winchester, Va., he spent his early years at Glengary, his father's country estate in the Upper Valley of the Shenandoah, a landscape that became a permanent part of his artistic imagination. When the plantation burned in 1839, the family moved to Richmond and to diminished financial circumstances. Since he could not afford to attend the University of Virginia, the young Cooke obtained a law license and became his father's partner in 1851. At the same time, he wrote essays, stories, and poems for various newspapers and periodicals, including *Harper's* and the *Southern Literary Messenger*. Instead of his father, he quickly and clearly chose an older brother, Philip Pendleton Cooke, a successful poet, as a vocational model.

In 1854 Cooke published his first novel, *Leather Stocking and Silk*, a frontier romance that stylistically and thematically imitated James Fenimore Cooper, John Pendleton Kennedy, Washington Irving, and other respected writers. A two-volume plantation novel, *The Virginia Comedians*, often considered his best single work, appeared in the same year. By the time of the Civil War, Cooke was probably the South's most financially successful writer, and he had managed to become quite popular with northern audiences.

Cooke was an ardent secessionist, and joined the Confederate army as a sergeant; he fought in almost every major battle on Virginia soil and was with Lee at Appomattox for the surrender. The war itself did little damage to Cooke's writing career, since between battles he managed to compose poems as well as war dispatches for Richmond newspapers. His accounts of the battlefield and camp life (published posthumously as *Outlines from the Outpost*) formed the core of his Confederate classic, *Wearing of the Grey*. Additionally, the war provided new subject matter: material for biographies of Stonewall Jackson and Robert E. Lee, as well as fictionalized versions of each (*Surrey of Eagle's-Nest* and *Mohun*).

In 1867 Cooke married Mary Francis Page, and they moved permanently to The Briars, an estate she had inherited. Life with their three children was idyllic, and Cooke became a gentleman farmer of the Old Dominion. Realism replaced romanticism as the accepted norm for faithfully reflecting life, and while Cooke approved, he said that he was too old to change. Nevertheless, he published a score of major works in his later phase, ranging from local color (*The Virginia Bohemians*) to regional history (*Virginia: A History of the People*) as well as countless short stories and newspaper articles that have yet to be collected.

WORKS: *Leatherstocking and Silk* (1854); repr. as *Leather Stocking and Silk: A Novel* (1892). *The Virginia Comedians*, 2 vols. (1854); vol. 1 repr. as *Beatrice Hallam* (1892); vol. 2 as *Captain Ralph* (1892). *The Youth of Jefferson* (1854). *Ellie* (1855). *The Last of the Foresters* (1856). *Henry St. John, Gentleman* (1859); repr. as *Bonnybel Vane* (1883); as *Miss Bonnybel: A Novel* (1892). *The Life of Stonewall Jackson* (1863); revised as *Stonewall Jackson: A Military Biography* (1866). *Surry of Eagle's-Nest* (1866). *Wearing of the Gray* (1867); repr. as *Personal Portraits, Scenes, and Adventures of the War* (1871). *Fairfax* (1868); repr. as *Lord Fairfax* (1888). *Hilt to Hilt* (1869). *Mohun* (1869). *Hammer and Rapier* (1870). *The Heir of Gaymount* (1870). *Out of the Foam: A Novel* (1871); repr. as *Westbrooke Hall: A Novel* (1891). *A Life of Gen. Robert E. Lee* (1871); repr. as *Our Leader and Defender: Gen. Robert E. Lee* (1889). *Dr. Vandyke: A Novel* (1872). *Her Majesty the Queen: A Novel* (1873). *Pretty Mrs. Gaston and Other Stories* (1874). *Justin Harley* (1875). *Cannolles* (1877). *Professor Pressensee* (1878). *Mr. Grantley's Idea* (1879). *Stories of the Old Dominion* (1879). *The Virginia Bohemians: A Novel* (1880). *Fanchette* (1883). *Virginia: A History of the People* (1883). *My Lady Pokahontas* (1885). *The Maurice Mystery* (1885); repr. as *Colonel Ross of Piedmont* (1893). *Poe as a Literary Critic* (1946). *Stonewall Jackson and the Old Stonewall Brigade* (1954). *Outlines from the Outpost* (1961). *John Esten Cooke's Autobiographical Memo* (1969).

—K. Huntress Baldwin

PHILIP PENDLETON COOKE (1816–1850). Philip Pendleton Cooke was the eldest son of John Rogers and Maria Pendleton Cooke and the brother of John Esten Cooke, the novelist and Civil War writer. Born in Martinsburg, Va. (now West Virginia), on October 26, 1816, he moved with his family to Winchester, Va., in 1828. After graduating from Princeton in 1834, Cooke returned to Glengary, the family estate near Winchester. For the next three years he studied law; wrote poetry and critical essays that were published in the *Southern Literary Messenger*; and unsuccessfully courted his cousin,

Mary Evalina Dandridge, an endeavor that seemingly provided the basis for his most famous poem, "Florence Vane." By age twenty-one he had been admitted to the bar, had acquired local fame for both his writing and his hunting skills, and married Anne Burwell. They were to have five children before his death at age thirty-three. The financial panic of 1837 and the burning of Glengary in 1839 severely disrupted the landed-gentry lifestyle, but in 1845 his wife inherited an estate called Vineyard—a thousand acres and a new house twelve miles from Winchester. She lived there until her death in 1899. Cooke had a resurgence of literary effort after the move to Vineyard, but he died on January 20, 1850, after contracting pneumonia while on a hunting trip.

While at Princeton, Cooke had three poems published in the *Knickerbocker Magazine*. The *Southern Literary Messenger* printed many of his poems and, in 1835, published his essay on English poetry and his first widely popular poem, "Young Rosalie Lee." In 1839 Edgar Allan Poe asked Cooke to contribute to *Burton's Gentleman's Magazine*. Cooke's response, the sentimental "Florence Vane," which was published in the spring of 1840, brought him fame. Poe highly praised "Florence Vane" in a New York lecture and reprinted it in the *Broadway Journal*. Inclusion in Rufus Griswold's *Poets and Poetry of America* (1842) and encouragement by his cousin, the novelist John Pendleton Kennedy, prompted Cooke to bring out his only book, *Froissart Ballads and Other Poems*, in 1847.

Cooke's developing interest in prose appeared in his critical writings, with the *Southern Literary Messenger* publishing "Living Novelists" in 1847. It also published the most important of his longer tales, including "John Carper, the Hunter of Lost River" (1848) and "The Two Country Houses" (1848). At the time of his death, Cooke was working on a historical romance, "The Chevalier Merlin."

WORKS: *Froissart Ballads and Other Poems* (1847).

—VICTOR L. THACKER

ANNA J. COOPER (1858?–1964). Anna Julia Haywood Cooper was born a slave in Raleigh, N.C. The exact date, even the year, is uncertain, but she celebrated August 10, 1858. Her father was her white master, George Washington Haywood. Inspired by her much-admired mother, shortly after the conclusion of the Civil War Anna entered St. Augustine's Normal School and Collegiate Institute, which had been established by the Episcopal Church to educate newly freed slaves. In 1877 she married George A. C. Cooper, who was training for the ministry. He died two years later; Anna never remarried. Childless, in 1915 she adopted the five young children of her half-brother.

Education as the essential tool for a new order for her race remained central to Cooper's vision and mission. Following graduation from St. Augustine's in 1881, she entered Oberlin College in northern Ohio. The first college to admit women, Oberlin had been a major stop along the Underground Railroad. Its liberal heritage was conducive to the extraordinary career that Cooper would shape. As early as 1886, much in advance of her time, she addressed black clergymen in Washington, D.C., on feminist concerns. At Oberlin, she chose mathematics—a "male" discipline—for her major. Her M.A. from Oberlin in hand, in 1887 she moved to Washington to teach in the high school that would eventually be named for Paul Laurence Dunbar. In 1892 she published *A Voice from the South; by a Black Woman from the South*. This book would secure her place as the major black feminist of the nineteenth century.

A co-founder of the Colored Women's League, Cooper wrote essays and spoke to numerous organizations in diverse locales (including Chicago and London) about race, women's issues, and the South. In Washington, she worked with the poor, but was never for long away from the classroom, where she taught a variety of subjects.

Nor did she cease to keep the bar high for her own educational growth. At the Sorbonne in 1925 she defended her doctoral dissertation on France and slavery. Howard University awarded her the doctorate in December of that year.

Ever receptive to the new challenge, following her retirement from high school teaching in 1930, she served for the next decade as the president of Frelinghuysen University, a night school for working people. Sometimes she taught classes in her home.

Cooper celebrated her hundredth birthday in 1958. She died in her Washington home on February 27, 1964, and was buried in Raleigh, N.C.

WORKS: *Christmas Bells: A One-Act Play for Children* (n.d.). *A Voice from the South; by a Black Woman from the South* (1892). *L'attitude de la France a l'égard de l'esclavage pendant le Revolution* (1925). Ed., *Voyage à Jerusalem et à Constantinople: Le Pèleringe de Charlemagne, publié avec un glossarie, par Anna J. Cooper* (1929). Ed., *Life and Writings of the Grimké Family* (1951).

—JOSEPH M. FLORA

PATRICIA CORNWELL (1956–). Born on June 9, 1956, in Miami, Fla., to Sam and Marilyn Zenner Daniels, Patricia Cornwell moved at the age of seven with her mother and two brothers to Montreat, N.C., after her parents' separation. There her mother began to suffer from severe depression and appealed to her neighbors Billy and Ruth Graham to keep Patricia and her brothers while she received hospital treatment. The Grahams placed the children with missionaries for the duration of their mother's commitment.

It was Ruth Graham who encouraged the young Patricia's early writing efforts. When Patricia showed herself a very bright college student, Ruth advised her to get her degree in English, which she did in 1979 at Davidson College. She soon thereafter married one of her former professors, Charles Cornwell, seventeen years her senior, and took her first job with the *Charlotte Observer*. She rapidly rose from a lowly copy assistant's position to reporting stories no one else wanted. When her investigative flair became evident, she was made a reporter, and within her first year she was covering crime stories. She won an award for a series on prostitution from the North Carolina Press Association in 1980. At this time her husband chose to go into the seminary, and the two moved to Richmond.

Not entirely satisfied with crime reporting, Cornwell decided to write a biography of Ruth Graham. The warm reception for *A Time for Remembering* made Cornwell want to write more. Crime interested her, but she found herself wanting to solve the crimes, not report them. She was directed to Marcella Fierro, a Virginia medical examiner whose work soon fascinated her. She became a volunteer police officer, interviewed staff at the morgue, and was hired in 1984 as a technical writer and computer analyst. At this time she began writing novels, modeling them on Agatha Christie and P. D. James, among others, until an editor told her to write what she saw at work. Thus Cornwell's distinctively southern settings and the forensic emphasis emerged.

Based on an actual serial-killer case in Richmond, her first novel, *Postmortem*, achieved the exceptional distinction of winning the John Creasy Award from the British Crime Writers Association, the Edgar from the Mystery Writers of America, the Anthony and Boucheron from the World Mystery Convention, and the Macavity from Mystery Readers International, all for the best first crime novel for 1990, and the French Prix du Roman d'Aventure (1991).

Meanwhile, her marriage to Charles Cornwell ended in 1990. Reportedly keeping to a fourteen-hour-per-day schedule, she has regularly produced one crime novel a year. In keeping with her commitment to forensics, she contributed $1.5 million to found the Virginia Institute for Forensic Science and Medicine. Recently she has carried the forensic search into the nonfiction arena, spending several million dollars of her own to reexamine the infamous Jack the Ripper case, the London Whitechapel Murders from 1888. Cornwell suggests that paper, ink, and phrasing in the murderer's letters to police, as well as mitochondrial DNA, match those of artist Walter Sickert.

Cornwell divides her time between Virginia and New York.

WORKS: *A Time for Remembering: The Story of Ruth Bell Graham* (1983). *Postmortem* (1990). *Body of Evidence* (1991). *All That Remains* (1992). *Cruel and Unusual* (1993). *The Body Farm* (1994). *From Potter's Field* (1995). *Cause of Death* (1996). *Hornet's Nest* (1997). *Ruth: A Portrait* (1997). *Unnatural Exposure* (1997). *Point of Origin* (1998). *Scarpetta's Winter Table* (1998). *Southern Cross* (1998). *Black Notice* (1999). *Life's Little Fable* (1999). *The Last Precinct* (2000). *Isle of Dogs* (2001). *Food to Die For: Secrets from Kay Scarpetta's Kitchen* (2001). *Portrait of a Killer: Jack the Ripper—Case Closed* (2002). *Blow Fly* (2003). *Trace* (2004). *Predator* (2005).

—REBECCA ROXBURGH BUTLER

JOHN WILLIAM CORRINGTON (1932–1988). John William Corrington was born on October 28, 1932, in Memphis, Tenn., to John Wesley and Viva Shelley Corrington. He was raised in a Catholic household and attended Catholic as well as public schools, which may explain in part his lifelong debate with Catholic doctrine. He earned a B.A. at Centenary College, in Shreveport, La., where he came to love literature and the Shreveport area, which he would revisit time and again in his fiction.

He earned an M.A. and pursued a Ph.D. at Rice University, and while there, married Joyce Elaine Hooper (a chemistry professor and writer). Frustrated by a dispute with a professor, Corrington eventually left Rice and moved to England, where he studied with David Daiches at the University of Sussex, earning his D.Phil. in 1964. During and after his work in England, Corrington taught on the faculty at Louisiana State University and began to write poetry, eventually publishing four collections of poems between 1962 and 1965.

While at LSU, Corrington was asked by the University Press to read a manuscript by historian Eric Voegelin. He was fascinated by Voegelin's theories on biblical history and began to use them in his fiction, seeking to apply a historical overview to localized events. Corrington's career at LSU was intense, if short-lived; he continued to publish fiction while simultaneously editing several collections of southern literature. Ultimately disillusioned by academic politics, in 1973 he left academia for law school.

This change in career reflected a similar change in Corrington's fiction; from the early 1970s on, his novels and stories explored themes of justice, from the local and personal to the universal and even metaphysical. He practiced law for only four years (1975–79), however, and while still in private practice he began to write screenplays and television scripts with his wife. This writing partnership culminated in the co-authorship of four "New Orleans Mysteries" (*So Small a Carnival, A Civil Death, A Project Named Desire,* and *The White Zone*) published for mass-market consumption during the 1980s (the last would appear posthumously in 1990). In addition to the extensive oeuvre he produced with his wife, Corrington continued to write what he termed "serious" fiction during this period.

Corrington's death on November 24, 1988, from a sudden heart attack cut off a writing career marked by a constant quest for new modes of expression—from poetry to historical fiction to screen writing to contemporary metaphysics. He constantly sought to understand through the written word man's place in the physical and metaphysical worlds, seeking transcendence over the violence and suffering he saw around him.

WORKS: *Where We Are* (1962). *The Anatomy of Love and Other Poems* (1964). *And Wait for the Night* (1964). *Mr. Clean and Other Poems* (1964). *Lines to the South and Other Poems* (1965). Ed., *Southern Writing in the Sixties: Fiction,* with

Miller Williams (1966). Ed., *Southern Writing in the Sixties: Poetry,* with Williams (1967). *The Upper Hand* (1967). *The Lonesome Traveler and Other Stories* (1968). *The Bombardier* (1970). *The Actes and Monuments* (1978). *The Southern Reporter* (1981). *Shad Sentell* (1984). *So Small a Carnival,* with Joyce H. Corrington (1986). *All My Trials: Two Novellas* (1987). *A Civil Death,* with Corrington (1987). *A Project Named Desire,* with Corrington (1987). *The White Zone,* with Corrington (1990). *The Collected Stories of John William Corrington* (1991).

—TERRY ROBERTS

JOHN COTTON OF QUEEN'S CREEK, VA. (1643?–post-1680). Author of what Louis Rubin has called "the best poem written in America in the seventeenth century—and quite possibly the best during the colonial era," planter John Cotton of Queen's Creek turned to poetry to reflect on an important political event of his time: the uprising of Nathaniel Bacon against the authority of Governor William Berkeley. Berkeley was slow to respond to the increasingly diverse population of his jurisdiction and its demand for some part in Berkeley's government. Because Berkeley had been indecisive in offering a clear policy against the increasingly hostile Indians, in May 1676 the disgruntled planter Bacon led an unauthorized expedition against the Indians. When Berkeley countered, Bacon's troops forced the governor from Jamestown to the eastern shore, then re-engaged the Indians and burned Jamestown when Berkeley's forces attempted to return. The struggle ended abruptly in October when Bacon died from dysentery and exhaustion. Berkeley promptly executed many of Bacon's followers, causing King Charles II to recall Berkeley.

Cotton immediately responded to the events by writing "A History of Bacon's and Ingram's Rebellions." The account includes two contrapuntal poems that present the two sides of the conflict. The stronger of the two poems, "Bacon's Epitaph, Made by His Man," in forty-four iambic lines portrays Bacon from the standpoint of the rebels. "Upon the Death of G. B. [General Bacon]" in forty-eight lines portrays Bacon from the perspective of the Loyalists. Seemingly, Cotton does not take sides.

Cotton was not a politically active member of the merchant-planter class, and the record of his life is sparse. The second son of William Cotton, minister of Hungar's Parish, Va., Cotton was born around 1643. He married Ann (or Hannah) Harrison (or Bernard) and continued to reside in Hungar's Parish until he moved to a tract lying between Queen's Creek and Townsend (later Yorktown) Creek that he had purchased on December 31, 1666. The new plantation adjoined Ringfield, the estate of the elder Colonel Nathaniel Bacon. The colonel's nephew and namesake headquartered at Ringfield a decade later—an immediacy that gave Cotton a vantage point that led to his account of what has been seen as the first resistance to the crown in the colonies.

Cotton had two children. A daughter Mary was born on October 21, 1660, and a son John on December 8, 1666. The date of Cotton's death is uncertain.

WORKS: "A History of Bacon's and Ingram's Rebellions" (1676). "To his Wife A. C. at Q. Creek" (1676).

—JOSEPH M. FLORA

VICKI COVINGTON (1952–). Vicki Marsh Covington was born on October 22, 1952, in Birmingham, Ala. The daughter of Jack H. Marsh, a metallurgical engineer, and Katherine Jennings Marsh, a teacher, Covington attended public schools in Birmingham. She received a bachelor's degree in sociology from the University of Alabama in 1974 and a master's in social work in 1976. In 1977 she married Dennis Covington, a writer and journalist, and they have two daughters.

While living temporarily in Ohio, Covington became homesick and began writing short stories set in her native Alabama. After returning to Birmingham, she continued writing while working as a social worker in substance abuse programs. Following a series of rejections, three of Covington's stories appeared in small literary magazines. In 1986 two stories, "Magnolia" and "Duty," were published by the *New Yorker*. At the request of an editor at Simon and Schuster, Covington developed an unpublished short story into her first novel, *Gathering Home*, which examines the impact of a congressional campaign on the lives of a Birmingham minister and his family.

Grants from the Alabama State Council on the Arts and the National Endowment for the Arts allowed Covington to leave her job as a social worker in 1988 and write full-time. Covington's second novel, *Bird of Paradise*, tells the story of a widow whose well-ordered life is disrupted by a family member's death and an unexpected romance. *Bird of Paradise* received the 1991 Fiction Award from the Alabama Library Association. *Night Ride Home* explores the relationships between people living in a fictional Alabama coal-mining town, and the community's reaction to a mine accident. *The Last Hotel for Women* is set in Birmingham during the civil rights movement and examines the impact of social change on the residents of a boarding house that once served as a brothel.

In 1999 Covington co-authored *Cleaving: The Story of a Marriage* with her husband Dennis. A frank examination of the Covingtons' marriage, including drug use and numerous infidelities, *Cleaving* was well received by some critics but not by the media and general public in the authors' hometown of Birmingham. In 2001 and 2002 Vicki Covington wrote a column entitled "Meditations for Bad Girls" for the *Oxford American*. Her 2002 book *Women in a Man's World, Crying: Essays* is a collection of short autobiographical essays, most previously published in the *Birmingham News*.

Covington's novels and stories are set in Alabama and often involve characters facing social upheaval or personal loss. Critics have complimented Covington for her strong character development but less so for her plot development. Her nonfiction is usually autobiographical and often addresses issues relating to women and their life choices, including choices about career, family, and sexual relationships.

WORKS: *Gathering Home* (1988). *Bird of Paradise* (1990). *Night Ride Home* (1992). *The Last Hotel for Women* (1996). *Cleaving: The Story of a Marriage* (1999). *Women in a Man's World, Crying: Essays* (2002).

—JAMES L. BAGGETT

ALFRED LELAND CRABB (1884–1979). Alfred Leland Crabb was an educator, novelist, and historian. Born in Warren County, Ky., in January 1884, he taught in rural schools and earned an undergraduate degree at George Peabody College for Teachers, an M.A. from Columbia University, and a Ph.D. from Peabody. He was a school principal in Louisiana and Kentucky, taught at Western Kentucky State Normal School beginning in 1916, and in 1927 joined the faculty at Peabody, where he stayed until he retired in 1950.

An avid student of the Civil War, Crabb began his career as a fiction writer with *Dinner at Belmont: A Novel of Captured Nashville*, which is set in his home city and treats the area from 1858 to 1865. The next novel, *Supper at the Maxwell House: A Novel of Recaptured Nashville*, treats Reconstruction in the Nashville area. The third, *Breakfast at the Hermitage*, deals with the rebuilding of Crabb's adopted city. The fourth, *Lodging at the Saint Cloud: A Tale of Occupied Nashville*, treats events during the Civil War.

Crabb wrote about the devastating conflicts of the Civil War in *A Mockingbird Sang at Chickamauga*, followed by treatment of Reconstruction in *Reunion at Chattanooga*. He recounts the war's aftermath in *Home to Tennessee: A Tale of Soldiers Returning*. His *Peace at Bowling Green* is a more extended treatment of the lives of Kentuckians in Bowling Green before, during, and after the war. He treats Andrew Jackson and his wife in *Home to the Hermitage*, Henry Clay in *Home to Kentucky*, and James Robertson and the founding of Nashville in *Journey to Nashville*. Besides fiction, Crabb wrote poetry and radio scripts, as well as articles and books pertaining to education. He died on October 1, 1979.

WORKS: *Standard Speller*, with A. C. Ferguson and August Dvorak (1931–34). *The Genealogy of George Peabody College for Teachers*, with Altstetter and Newton (1935). *America Yesterday and Today*, with L. E. Broaddus and J. P. Cornette (1937). *Modern English Handbook with Exercises* (1941). *Dinner at Belmont* (1942). *Supper at the Maxwell House* (1943). *Breakfast at the Hermitage* (1945). *Lodging at the Saint Cloud* (1946). *Home to the Hermitage* (1948). *A Mockingbird Sang at Chickamauga* (1949). *Reunion at Chattanooga* (1950). *Home to Tennessee* (1952). *Home to Kentucky* (1953). *Peace at Bowling Green* (1955). *Nashville: Personality of a City* (1955). *Journey to Nashville* (1957). *Andrew Jackson's Nashville* (1966). *Acorns to Oaks: The Story of Nashville Baptist Association and It's [sic] Affilliated [sic] Churches*, with J. Tresch, H. D. Gregory, J. F. Freeman, and Guard Green (1972). *A Cannon for General Marion* (1975).

—RICHARD D. RUST

THOMAS CRADOCK (1718–1770). Thomas Cradock was born in Staffordshire, England, baptized on November 8, 1718, attended Oxford, and in 1743 became eligible for the Anglican priesthood. Emigrating to Maryland in 1744, Cradock was appointed rector of a new parish, St. Thomas, in 1745, and remained there the rest of his life. In 1746 he married Catherine Risteau of Maryland, by whom he had four children: Arthur, John, Thomas, and Anne. In 1747 he began a school at the farm he received as part of the marriage settlement. A poet, Cradock circulated among Maryland's literary clubs, becoming an honorary member of the Tuesday Club of Annapolis. As a preacher of note, he sometimes spoke outside his normal duties, including delivering a sermon on October 7, 1753, that was highly critical of the kind of men then in the Anglican priesthood in Maryland. He became infirm in 1765, but continued preaching until death overtook him on May 7, 1770.

Cradock's literary career runs through most of his adult life. A number of sermons, in the neoclassical homiletic tradition, survive in manuscript. His poems, most of which were not published until 1983, include religious verses and satiric pieces. His translation of the Psalms, one of Cradock's major achievements, puts into couplets the Latin psalter of George Buchanan. His best satires are the "Maryland Eclogues," a set of nine poems on local themes built on equivalent eclogues by Virgil. In the second, "Daphne," the poet adopts the voice of Pompey, a slave who laments the loss of his lover to his white master. One of Cradock's most impressive works is his blank-verse drama (some lines are missing) on the death of Socrates. The parson's Athenian is a man of pure virtue, supported not only by the historically known pupils but also by a fictional woman, Apame, whose commitment to Socrates inspires the others. Until his illness in his last years, Cradock proved an active participant in a dynamic Chesapeake literary culture.

WORKS: *Two Sermons, with a Preface* (1747). "A Poem Sacred to the Memory," *Maryland Gazette*, Mar. 15, 1753. *A Poetical Translation of the Psalms of David* (1754). *A New Version of the Psalms of David* (1756). "To Thyrsis," *American Magazine* 1 (1757–58): 605–7. "Hymn for Whitsunday," "Sacramental Hymn," *American Church Review* 7 (July 1854): 308–11. "Thomas Cradock's Sermon on the Governance of Maryland's Established Church," *William and Mary Quarterly* 27 (1970): 630–53. *The Poetic Writings of Thomas Cradock, 1718–1770*, ed. David Curtis Skaggs (1983).

—JEFFREY H. RICHARDS

HANNAH CRAFTS (18?–?). Hannah Crafts (possibly a pseudonym) arrived on the literary scene nearly 150 years after she penned her only known novel, *The Bondwoman's Narrative*. The novel details the enslavement and ultimate escape of a woman named Hannah and blends autobiographical detail with gothic and sentimental conventions. The protagonist was born in Virginia (likely in Charles City County) and grew up on a plantation near the James River. After escaping from her first master, she eventually finds herself in the employ of Mr. Wheeler, a character who was likely based on the real-life John Hill Wheeler, a historian and bureaucrat from North Carolina who spent most of the 1850s in Washington, D.C. Within the novel, Hannah makes her escape from the Wheeler plantation in coastal North Carolina and ultimately finds her way to New Jersey, where she marries and becomes a teacher.

The handwritten manuscript by Crafts was virtually unknown until it was purchased at an auction in 2001 by Henry Louis Gates, Jr., chair of the department of African American studies at Harvard University. Forensic evidence obtained from the manuscript, along with links between novelistic characters and geography and historical people and places, led Gates and other researchers to agree that the novel was written between 1853 and 1861 by an African American woman who had once been a slave. No researchers have located a woman named Hannah Crafts residing in the United States during the period most likely to encompass her life. Nonetheless, her novel is an important document for students and teachers of African American and southern literature because it appears to represent the unmediated voice of a former slave who has the freedom to examine the sexual depravity of white masters, illuminate relationships between mistress and slave, and reveal the class hierarchies within the slave community.

WORKS: *The Bondwoman's Narrative* (2002).

—BRYAN C. SINCHE

WILLIAM CRAFTS (1787–1826). The son of a Boston merchant who settled in Charleston, S.C., and married a native of Beaufort, S.C., William Crafts, a handsome, popular man with a reputation for wit, was a minor poet and essayist. He was born in Charleston, on January 24, 1787. As a boy he studied under tutors, and entered Harvard as a sophomore, being graduated in 1805. For three years he read law in Charleston but seemingly learned little. He returned to Harvard in 1807 to work for a master's degree, and established a name for himself, particularly for a famous lecture he delivered in "execrable Latin." Admitted to the South Carolina bar in 1809, his ignorance of the law forced him into criminal practice, where his ability to dazzle juries proved useful. He entered politics as a Federalist in 1810, being elected to the state lower house. He was defeated for re-election, but was elected again two years later. The last six years of his life he was a member of the South Carolina senate.

A popular occasional speaker, Crafts was the author of numerous essays that faintly echoed Addison in the *Charleston Courier*. He wrote occasional verse, imitative of Pope and later of Moore. In 1810 he published *The Raciad and Other Occasional Poems*; the title poem, along with his Anacreontics, is his best work, an amusing account of Charlestonians at Race Day. *The Sea Serpent* was published in 1819, and *Sullivan's Island, The Raciad, and Other Poems* in 1820. Always torn between New England, which he treasured, and the South, which he loved, he bound the two together by marriage to a Boston cousin in 1823. He died in Lebanon Springs, N.Y., on September 23, 1826, and was buried in Boston. A posthumous collection of his work appeared in 1828. Crafts is well summed up by Vernon L. Parrington as "a graceful imitator of doubtful models."

WORKS: *The Raciad and Other Occasional Poems* (1810). *The Sea Serpent; or, Gloucester Hoax: A Dramatic Jeu d'Esprit in Three Sets* (1819). *Sullivan's Island, The Raciad, and Other Poems* (1820). *A Selection, in Prose and Poetry, from the Miscellaneous Writings of the Late William Crafts*, ed., with a memoir by, Samuel Gilman (1828).

—C. HUGH HOLMAN

HUBERT CREEKMORE (1907–1966). Hubert Creekmore was born on January 16, 1907, in Water Valley, Miss., into a family with deep southern roots. Interested in writing from an early age, he graduated from the University of Mississippi in 1927, studied drama at the University of Colorado and play writing at Yale, and earned an M.A. in American literature from Columbia University in 1940. Creekmore worked with the Federal Writers' Project, and he saw active duty in the Pacific during World War II, serving in the navy in 1942–45. Stationed on the Pacific island New Caledonia, he wrote many of the poems published in *The Long Reprieve*.

Creekmore published three other volumes of poetry: *Personal Sun*, "*The Stone Ants*," and *Formula*. In his novels, Creekmore explored the lives of marginalized southerners. *The Fingers of Night* portrays a young girl struggling against patriarchal religious zeal. *The Welcome* examines the difficulty that southern gay men, inculcated with repressive social mores, had in accepting their own sexual orientation; it also looks at the stultifying effects of traditional southern women's roles. *The Chain in the Heart* is a multigenerational saga of a southern African American family.

Creekmore's literary activities also included translating and editing classical and Europe authors. Creekmore died on May 23, 1966, in New York, where he had made his home and had a wide circle of friends.

WORKS: *Personal Sun, the Early Poems of Hubert Creekmore* (1940). "*The Stone Ants*" (1943). *The Fingers of Night* (1946). *The Long Reprieve, and Other Poems of New Caledonia* (1946). *Formula* (1947). *The Welcome* (1948). Trans., *Erotic Elegies of Albius Tibulus, with Poems of Sulpicia Arranged as a Sequence Called No Harm to Lovers* (1950). Ed., *A Little Treasury of World Poetry: Translations from the Great Poets of Other Languages* (1952). *The Chain in the Heart* (1953). Ed. and trans., *Lyrics of the Middle Ages* (1959). Ed. and trans., *Satires of Decimus Junius Juvenalis* (1963). *Daffodils Are Dangerous* (1966).

—Theresa Lloyd

HARRY CREWS (1935–). Harry Eugene Crews was born on June 7, 1935, to Ray and Myrtice Crews, sharecroppers in rural Alma, Ga. In 1937, at age thirty-five, Ray died of a heart attack, leaving Myrtice to care for Harry and his older brother, Hoyett. Later that year, Pascal Crews, Ray's hard-drinking older brother, divorced his wife and married Myrtice. In 1941 Myrtice—overcome by Pascal's incessant abuse—gathered her boys and moved south to Jacksonville, Fla., where she rolled tobacco leaves in a cigar factory and lived among other displaced Georgians.

Discharged from the U.S. Marines in 1956, Crews enrolled at the University of Florida in Gainesville, where he studied creative writing with Andrew Lytle. In January 1960, Crews married fellow student Sally Ellis, and that September, Patrick Scott was born. After graduating, Crews taught junior-high English in Jacksonville, and a year later returned to Gainesville to enter the master's program for English education. Because Crews was absorbed by his graduate studies and increasingly devoted to writing, the family suffered. He and Sally divorced in 1962, and Crews moved to Fort Lauderdale to teach English at Broward Community College. Feeling settled, he persuaded Sally to join him there and to remarry, and in August 1963, Byron Jason was born. Earlier that spring, Crews also celebrated his first story publication, "The Unattached Smile," in the *Sewanee Review*. In July 1964, tragedy struck when Patrick drowned in a neighbor's swimming pool. Shortly after, Harry and Sally were divorced again.

Spurred by the publication of his first novel, *The Gospel Singer,* in 1968, Crews left Broward to become assistant professor of English at the University of Florida. Avidly pursuing tenure, Crews lectured in class and at writers' conferences, published essays on the writer's craft in academic journals, and, after receiving an Atherton Scholarship to the Bread Loaf Writers' Conference, continued on another four years as summer faculty. By 1974 Crews had written seven novels. After a leave of absence to visit his uncle's farm in Georgia, Crews wrote an essay developing the incipient themes of *A Childhood*. "One Morning in February," published in *Shenandoah*, won the Best Nonfiction Award from the Coordinating Council of Literary Magazines. In 1974 the university granted Crews full professorship. On this success, *Playboy* magazine paid Crews to travel and write about the construction of the oil pipeline in Alaska. "Going Down in Valdeez," selected by *Playboy* as its best nonfiction piece of 1975, also marked Crews's transition into journalism. By December, Crews had written twice more for *Playboy* and once for *Esquire*, leading, in 1976, to the *Esquire* column "Grits," which lasted fourteen months. During this time, Crews wrote *A Feast of Snakes* and *A Childhood*, the two books that bear the greatest weight of his reputation as a writer. After writing *A Childhood*, which documents his upbringing, the traumas of his early adolescence, and the attempts of an older Crews to reconcile, as an adult, to his past, Crews did not publish another novel for nearly ten years, as though the intensity and demands of *A Childhood* had burned him out. But in 1987 he published *All We Need of Hell*, and since then five other novels.

The 1990s brought a resurgence of critical and popular interest in the United States and Europe for Crews as writer, teacher, and celebrity. The anthology *Classic Crews: A Harry Crews Reader* collected two out-of-print novels, *Car* and *The Gypsy's Curse*, as well as *A Childhood* and a selection of essays. *Where Does One Go When There's No Place Left to Go?* is a companion novel to *The Gospel Singer*. In 1997, after nearly thirty years at the University of Florida, Crews retired from teaching. He has since published chapters from *Assault on Memory*, a follow-up to his autobiography, and worked on a novel titled *Pit Bull*.

WORKS: *The Gospel Singer* (1968). *Naked in Garden Hills* (1969). *This Thing Don't Lead to Heaven* (1970). *Karate Is a Thing of the Spirit* (1971). *Car* (1972). *The Hawk Is Dying* (1973). *The Gypsy's Curse* (1974). *A Feast of Snakes* (1976). *A Childhood: The Biography of a Place* (1978). *Blood and Grits* (1979). *The Enthusiast* (1981). *Florida Frenzy* (1982). *Two by Crews* (1984). *All We Need of Hell* (1987). *The Knockout Artist* (1988). *Body* (1990). *Madonna at Ringside* (1991). *Scar Lover* (1992). *Classic Crews: A Harry Crews Reader* (1993). *The Mulching of America* (1995). *Celebration* (1998). *Where Does One Go When There's No Place Left to Go?* (1998).

—DAMON SAUVE

DAVY CROCKETT (1786–1836). David (Davy) Crockett was born on August 17, 1786, in Green County, Tenn., the son of John and Rebecca Hawkins Crockett. In part the inventor of his own myth, Crockett was a relatively unknown backwoods hunter with a talent for storytelling until his election to the Tennessee legislature in 1821 and then to the U.S. House of Representatives in 1827. He promoted himself as a simple, honest country boy, an unassuming yet expert hunter who was literally a "straight-shooter." Re-elected in 1829, he split with President Jackson on land reform issues and the Indian removal bill. Crockett was defeated in his bid for a third term in 1831 when he vehemently opposed Jackson's policies, was re-elected in 1833, and defeated again in 1835, a loss that encouraged him to explore opportunities in Texas, where he died at the Battle of the Alamo on March 6, 1836.

Already a legend before his death, by 1831 Crockett had become the model for Nimrod Wildfire, the hero of James Kirke Paulding's popular play *The Lion of the West*. In 1834 Crockett published his autobiography, *A Narrative of the Life of David Crockett of the State of Tennessee*, to counteract the outlandish stories printed in 1833 under his name as the *Sketches and Eccentricities of Colonel David Crockett of West Tennessee*, a work that helped to initiate the humor of the Old Southwest. The more outrageous stories were soon expanded by anonymous eastern hack writers who spun out tall tales for the *Crockett Almanacs* (1835–56). In their hands Davy became a backwoods screamer who could save the world by wringing the tail off Halley's Comet and flinging it back into outer space as easily as he could ride his pet alligator up Niagara Falls.

The image of Crockett in American culture was continued by the Davys played by Fess Parker in the Disney-inspired Crockett craze of the mid-1950s and by John Wayne in *The Alamo* (1960), and in the 1990s fiction of Cameron Judd and David Thompson. These did much to reinforce Crockett's stature as a preeminent hero of the American frontier.

WORKS: *Sketches and Eccentricities of Colonel David Crockett of West Tennessee* (1833; first issued earlier that year as *The Life and Adventures of Colonel David Crockett of West Tennessee*). *A Narrative of the Life of David Crockett of the State of Tennessee* (1834). *Col. Crockett's Tour to the North and Down East* (1835). *Life of Martin Van Buren* (1835). *Col. Crockett's Exploits and Adventures in Texas* (1836).

—MICHAEL A. LOFARO

HAL CROWTHER (1945–). The son of a naval officer, Harold Baker Crowther, Jr., was born on March 26, 1945, in Halifax, Nova Scotia. Before he was two, his family returned to Charleston, S.C. As a child he lived in the navy towns of Charleston and Norfolk, Va. He was educated in the North, at Williams College (B.A., English) and the Columbia University Graduate School of Journalism.

In New York he was a staff writer, editor, and critic for *Time* and *Newsweek,* and a columnist and film and drama critic for the *Buffalo News.* His essays and book reviews have been published in *The Humanist,* the *New York Times,* and the *Washington Post,* among many other places, and regularly in the *Atlanta Journal-Constitution.*

Returning to the South in 1980, Crowther served as executive editor of *Spectator,* for which he wrote a syndicated column addressing a variety of political and cultural issues. His column later appeared in the *Independent Weekly* of Durham, N.C.; in 1995 many of these essays were collected in *Unarmed but Dangerous.* Crowther's *Independent* essays won the *Baltimore Sun's* H. L. Mencken Writing Award (1992) and the first prize for commentary from the American Association of Newsweeklies (1998). He has received the Russell J. Jandoli Award for Excellence in Journalism (2000), and in 2002 he delivered the annual H. L. Mencken lecture in Baltimore. Crowther has been described as a "cultural pathologist," and like Mencken he has consistently sought to describe the varieties of illness afflicting American culture: the hypocrisy of its politicians, the shortcomings of its social and environmental policies, and the lack of substance in its various media, including what passes for serious journalism.

Since 1994, "Dealer's Choice," Crowther's column on southern letters and culture, has been featured in the *Oxford American.* Many of these essays were collected in *Cathedrals of Kudzu* (2000). Nominated for the Pulitzer Prize (his seventh Pulitzer nomination) and the National Book Award, *Cathedrals* won the Lillian Smith Book Award and the Fellowship Prize for Non-Fiction from the Fellowship of Southern Writers. *Foreword* magazine gave it the Book of the Year prize for essays.

Crowther has one daughter, Amity, and one stepson, Page Seay, and lives in Hillsborough, N.C., with his wife, novelist Lee Smith. Another stepson, Josh Seay, died in 2003.

WORKS: *Unarmed but Dangerous: Withering Attacks on All Things Phony, Foolish, and Fundamentally Wrong with America Today* (1995). *Cathedrals of Kudzu: A Personal Landscape of the South* (2000). *Gather at the River: Notes from the Post-Millennial South* (2005).

—GEORGE HOVIS

GEORGE WASHINGTON PARKE CUSTIS (1781–1857). The son of John Parke Custis, who was the stepson of George Washington, and Eleanor Calvert Custis, a descendant of Cecil Calvert, the second Lord Baltimore, George Washington Parke Custis was born at Mt. Airy, Md., on April 30, 1781. When his father, wealthy southern landowner and aide-de-camp to General Washington, died six months later, Custis was adopted by George and Martha Washington and raised at Mt. Vernon. He received a classical education at St. John's College, Annapolis, and Princeton, but his education was permanently interrupted when he was commissioned into the U.S. Army in 1799, as a cornet of horse with the rank of colonel. Following the death of his grandmother in 1802, he erected "Arlington House" on the heights near Washington, on a thousand acres he had inherited from his father (now the site of Arlington National Cemetery). Custis lived there with his wife, Mary Lee Fitzhugh, until his death. Their daughter Mary Custis married Robert E. Lee.

Although he was an accomplished orator and amateur painter, Custis merits a place in southern literary history as a playwright. Indeed, he was the dramatist laureate of his day, writing patriotic plays to celebrate national spirit or achievements. His first play, *The Indian Prophecy,* billed as a "national drama," was written as a birthday tribute to George Washington and first performed on July 4, 1827. The prophecy referred to involves the recognition, by an Indian leader who is fighting with the French against Washington, that the Great Spirit protects Chief Washington and that "he cannot die in battle." His next play, *The Eighth of January,* celebrated Andrew Jackson's bid for the presidency as well as his victory at the Battle of New Orleans.

Antebellum drama valued scenic spectacle as well as patriotic appeal, and Custis obliged with elaborate painted panoramas as well as the use of such props as a real locomotive. Although he is known to have written and produced at least eight plays, only two were published, *The Indian Prophecy* and his most successful effort, *Pocahontas, or the Settlers of Virginia.* The popularity of *Pocahontas* encouraged him to pursue the Native American theme in *The Pawnee Chief* (performed in 1832) and *Monongahela* (performed in 1836). Although Custis spent only a small part of his life penning and producing plays, he considered himself a writer above anything else. Besides plays, he published "Conversations with Lafayette" in the *Alexandria Gazette* and, starting in 1826, he published his recollections of Washington's private life in the *United States Gazette*; his daughter published the essay along with her memoir of her father.

WORKS: *The Indian Prophecy: A National Drama in Two Acts* (1828). *Pocahontas, or the Settlers of Virginia* (1830). *Recollections and Private Memoirs of Washington by his Adopted Son* (1860).

—K. HUNTRESS BALDWIN

JAMES McBRIDE DABBS (1896–1970). The offspring of parents from two distinct types of South Carolina families—his mother (Maude McBride) from plantation society, his father (Eugene Whitefield Dabbs) from the yeoman class—James McBride Dabbs, born May 8, 1896, in Mayes-Ville, S.C., grew up to study the competing and cooperative forces represented in these social classes in relation to churches, education, politics, history, industry, law, and race.

Dabbs attended public schools near the family plantation, Rip Raps, before enrolling at the University of South Carolina for undergraduate studies and pursuing graduate studies at Clark University and Columbia University. Before beginning a career in teaching, he served in the U.S. Army (1917–19). He returned to the University of South Carolina as an instructor in English in 1921, but left to join the English faculty at Coker College in Hartsville, S.C., in 1925 and remained there until 1942. He left teaching to become a freelance writer and a farmer, but his sense of civic responsibility led him to assume posts that enabled him to promote human relations. Among the groups he helped to guide were the Southern Regional Council, which he served as president from 1957 to 1963, and the Fellowship of Southern Churchmen.

His writings, in both essay and book form, serve to help define the character of southerners, offering explanations of the forces shaping that character. Numbering more than one hundred, his essays appeared in many American journals and in such collections as *The Lasting South, This Is the South*, and *We Dissent*.

WORKS: *Pee Dee Panorama*, with Carl Julien (1951). *The Southern Heritage* (1958). *The Road Home* (1960). *Who Speaks for the South?* (1964). *Civil Rights in Recent Southern Fiction* (1969). *Haunted by God* (1972).

—JOHN L. IDOL, JR.

RICHARD DABNEY (1787–1825). Born in 1787 in Louisa County, in central Virginia, Richard Dabney was one of twelve children born to Samuel and Jane Dabney. Through his mother, a Meriwether, he was first cousin to the explorer Meriwether Lewis.

Because of financial circumstances, Dabney was unable to attend college. Instead, at sixteen he entered a classical academy, where he showed a great talent for Greek and Latin, languages he was himself soon teaching at a boys' school in Richmond.

Seriously burned in the Richmond Theatre fire in 1811, Dabney sought treatment for his pain in the use of opium, a drug to which he became addicted. In 1812 he moved to Philadelphia, where he was employed by the publisher Matthew Carey. In that same year Dabney brought out his first volume of verse, *Poems, Original and Translated*, an expanded version of which appeared in 1815. As its title suggests, the book contains both Dabney's original compositions and translations from the Greek, Latin, Italian, and French. Neither volume received much critical notice. Dabney is also thought to have contributed to the writing of Carey's *The Olive Branch; or, Faults on Both Sides, Federal and Democratic* (1814), a call to resolving American factional conflict during the War of 1812. For a brief time also, and presumably because of his training in the classics, Dabney was incorrectly identified as the author of "Rhododaphne," a poem written by Thomas Love Peacock.

In 1815 Carey dismissed Dabney, and he returned to his family estate in Louisa County. There he spent the remaining years of his life, teaching some, reading, and suffering from considerable emotional and physical pain. Addicted to opium and drink, Dabney died unmarried at age thirty-eight in 1825.

WORKS: *Poems, Original and Translated* (1812, 1815).

—JOHN N. SOMERVILLE, JR.

THOMAS DALE (1700–1750). Thomas Dale was born in Hoxton, England, the son of an apothecary and nephew of the author of *Pharmacologia* (1693). Dale went to Oxford University (1717–20) and studied medicine at the University of Leyden (1721–23). He set up as a physician in London, and also translated medical texts out of a number of modern and classical languages. In 1732 personal and financial difficulties caused him to immigrate to Charleston, S.C., where his first wife, Maria, died soon after their arrival. He married Mary Brewton, the daughter of a merchant prominent in Charleston, on March 28, 1733. Dale was to be married twice more—to Anne Smith on November 26, 1738, and to Hannah Simons on June 30, 1743. Only one of his children survived to adulthood; Thomas Simons Dale became a physician in Scotland.

Dale was appointed assistant justice in 1733, justice of the peace in 1737, judge of the court of general sessions in 1739, and judge of the court of common pleas in 1746. He also served as an elected representative in the Royal Assembly, administrator of the slave detention workhouse, and overseer of the public slave markets. Dale's medical background is evident in his other activities. He collected "Dryed Plants as well as other Natural Rarities," which were eventually willed to a medical friend in Leyden. He fought against the practice of medicine by those without credentials. And when smallpox broke out in the area, the *South Carolina Gazette* published his views on inoculation, a controversial practice he opposed in "The Case of Miss Mary Roche" (November 2, 1738) and "The Puff; or, A Proper Reply to Skimmington's Last Crudities" (January 25, 1739).

Dale's literary interests ranged beyond the medical to the theatrical. In the 1730s he was instrumental in the founding of Charleston's first theater; and he is thought to have written a number of companion pieces for performances given there, including a prologue and epilogue to Otway's *The Orphan*, published in the *South Carolina Gazette* (February 8 and 22, 1735), and an epilogue to Farquhar's *The Recruiting Officer*, published in the *Gentleman's Magazine* (May 6, 1736). Such efforts appear to have established him as a significant regional poet. Dale died in Charleston on September 16, 1750.

WORKS: *Dissertatio medico-botanica inauguralis de pareira brava et serapia off., etc.* (1723). Trans., John Freind, *Emmenologia* (1729). Trans., John Freind, *Nine Commentaries upon Fevers: and Two Epistles Concerning the Small-pox, Addressed to Dr. Mead* (1730). Trans., Henry Frances Le Dran, *A Parallel of the Different Methods of Extracting the Stone out of the Bladder* (1731). Trans., N. Regnault, *Philosophical Conversations; or, A New System of Physics, by Way of Dialogue*, 3 vols. (1731). Trans., Jodocus Lommius, *A Treatise of Continual Fevers: in Four Parts* (1732). *An Epistle to Alexander Pope, Esq., from Southern Carolina* (1737). *The Case of Miss Mary Roche, more fairly related, &C* (1738). *The Puff* (1739).

—AMBER VOGEL

DANSKE DANDRIDGE (1854–1914). Caroline Lawrence Bedinger Dandridge, nicknamed "Danske" (Little Dane), was born in Copenhagen, Denmark, in November 1854, to Henry and Caroline Bedinger. Her father was America's first ambassador to Denmark, and after his death the family purchased Rose Brake, an estate near Shepherdstown, Va. (now West Virginia), that Dandridge called home almost all her adult life. She married Adam Stephen Dandridge, Jr., in 1877, and in 1880 they took possession of Rose Brake. There, for almost thirty years, Dandridge raised her family, tended her remarkable gardens, and wrote poetry, gardening articles, and history.

Dandridge's first poem appeared in *Godey's* in 1885. *Joy and Other Poems*, her first volume, contained primarily lyrics exploring the connection between nature and the spirit. *Rose Brake* continues these traditional forms. From 1892 through 1904 Dandridge wrote more than two hundred gardening articles, published in *Forest and Stream, Garden and Forest, Gardening*, and other magazines. She also examined with gentle wit the vicissitudes of family life.

In 1904 Dandridge moved from the personal to the historical, focusing on early America. The last shift to history has been attributed to emotional withdrawal and grief over the deaths of two of her children. An ongoing fragility of health and the tragedy of her personal life led on June 13, 1914, to her death, sometimes reported as suicide, a claim disputed by the family.

WORKS: *Joy and Other Poems* (1888; 2nd enl. ed. 1900). *Rose Brake* (1890). *George Michael Bedinger: A Kentucky Pioneer* (1909). *Historic Shepherdstown* (1910). *American Prisoners of the Revolution* (1911).

—GAIL GALLOWAY ADAMS

OLIVE TILFORD DARGAN (1869–1968). Olive Tilford Dargan—long-lived, peripatetic, and highly productive—was born in Tilford Springs, Ky., on January 11, 1869. When she was about ten, the family moved to Missouri, then to Arkansas, where she became a schoolteacher at fourteen. She graduated from Peabody College in Nashville, Tenn.; taught in Missouri and Texas; studied at Radcliffe College in Cambridge, Mass.; taught in Nova Scotia; worked for a rubber company in Boston; and then went to Blue Ridge in the north Georgia hills for her health in 1897.

Pegram Dargan, a South Carolina poet she had known in Cambridge, trailed her to Georgia, where they were married in 1898. They moved to New York City, where Olive Tilford Dargan produced acclaimed blank verse drama (*Semiramis and Other Plays* and *Lords and Lovers*). In England for her health for some years, she published plays (*The Mortal Gods*), nonfiction (*The Welsh Pony*), and poetry (*Path Flower*).

Dargan returned to New York, but moved back to the South soon after her husband was lost while sailing off the coast of Cuba in 1915. *The Cycle's Rim* (1916), her sonnets dedicated "to one drowned at sea," won the $500 poetry award of the Southern Society of New York. Until 1923 she made her home at a Swain County, N.C., farm. During this time she published over half a dozen books, including more poetry (*Lute and Furrow*) and plays (*Flutter of the Gold Leaf*, with Frederick Peterson). Her Nantahala River farmstead burned in 1923.

In 1924 the University of North Carolina saluted Dargan's achievements with an honorary doctorate, and in 1925 she brought out what is probably her best-known book, *Highland Annals,* stories about people she knew in Swain County. Another edition of this book—*From My Highest Hill: Carolina Mountain Folks*—appeared in 1941, illustrated with the work of the pioneering woman photographer Bayard Wooten.

Dargan turned to the novel late in life. Writing as Fielding Burke, she produced three "proletarian novels"—*Call Home the Heart* (about the Gastonia textile-mill strike); its sequel, *A Stone Came Rolling;* and *Sons of the Stranger*—all after she was sixty. Her poetry collection *The Spotted Hawk* won the 1959 Roanoke-Chowan Award, and she published the short-story volume *Innocent Bigamy* when she was ninety-three. She died on January 22, 1968, at Bluebonnet Lodge, Asheville, her home since 1925. In October 2000 she was inducted into the North Carolina Literary Hall of Fame at Weymouth in Southern Pines, N.C.

WORKS: *Semiramis and Other Plays* (1904). *Lords and Lovers and Other Dramas* (1906). *The Mortal Gods and Other Plays* (1912). *The Welsh Pony* (1913). *Pathflower* (1914). *The Cycle's Rim* (1916). *The Flutter of the Gold Lead and Other Plays*, with Frederick Peterson (1922). *Lute and Furrow* (1922). *Highland Annals* (1925). *Call Home the Heart* (1932). *A Stone Came Rolling* (1935). *From My Highest Hill* (1941). *Sons of the Stranger* (1947). *The Spotted Hawk* (1958). *Innocent Bigamy and Other Stories* (1962).

—BLAND SIMPSON

GUY DAVENPORT (1927–2005). Guy Mattison Davenport, Jr., erudite writer of unconventional short stories and novellas as well as wide-ranging essays, was born into a large extended family in Anderson, in western South Carolina. His mother was Marie Fant Davenport; his father worked as an express clerk. He graduated from Duke University in 1948, and then, as a Rhodes Scholar, earned a B.Litt. at Merton College, Oxford, in 1950. He served in the U.S. Army Airborne Corps from 1950 to 1952.

Davenport was a classicist, poet, critic, translator (notably of Herakleitos and Sappho), and book illustrator before he started publishing fiction, for which he became best known, with *Tatlin!* in 1974. He began teaching, which held a central place in his life, at Washington University in St. Louis (1952–55), after which he went to Harvard University, where he earned a Ph.D. in 1961. While serving as a tutor at Harvard, he was section man under Archibald MacLeish and Douglas Bush. He taught at

Haverford College in Pennsylvania (1961–63) before he joined the English faculty at the University of Kentucky (1963). He remained there until 1990, when he was awarded a MacArthur Fellowship.

Davenport's stories are *tours de force*, allusive, full of intellectual play and imaginative connections. Collages of fact and fantasy most often set in historical time, partially peopled with historical characters, they demand of readers close attention, wide learning, a willing suspension of disbelief, and a sense of fun. His fictions often provide a stage on which his favorite ideas can be enacted, as in *Eclogues* and *Apples and Pears*, where Charles Fourier's utopian vision of "harmonie" is explored. Davenport has said that fiction's essential activity is to imagine how others feel, which his stories do, usually without conventional beginning, middle, and end. This essentially modernist aesthetic places him in a line with Pound and Joyce.

Davenport served as a Pulitzer Prize juror and won many awards, including the Blumenthal-Leviton Prize for Poetry in 1970 and the American Academy of Arts and Letters Fiction Award in 1981. In 1998 he was elected to the American Academy of Arts and Sciences.

On January 4, 2005, he died of lung cancer in Lexington, Ky., which had remained his home. He was survived by Bonnie Jean Cox, his companion for forty years.

WORKS: *Carmina Archilochi: The Fragments of Archilochos* (1964). *Sappho: Poems and Fragments* (1965). *Tatlin!: Six Stories* (1974). *Da Vinci's Bicycle: Ten Stories* (1979). *Herakleitos and Diogenes* (1979). *Archilochos, Sappho, Alkman: Three Lyric Poets* (1980). *Eclogues: Eight Stories* (1981). *The Geography of the Imagination: Forty Essays* (1981). *The Mimes of Herondas* (1981). *Cities on Hills: A Study of I–XXX of Ezra Pound's "Cantos"* (1983). *Apples and Pears* (1984). *The Bicycle Rider* (1985). *Thasos and Ohio: Poems and Translations, 1950–1980* (1986). *Every Force Evolves a Form: Twenty Essays* (1987). *The Jules Verne Steam Balloon: Nine Stories* (1987). *A Balthus Notebook* (1989). *The Drummer of the Eleventh North Devonshire Fusiliers* (1990). *A Table of Green Fields: Ten Stories* (1993). *7 Greeks* (1995). *The Cardiff Team: Ten Stories* (1996). *The Hunter Gracchus* (1996). *Twelve Stories* (1997). *Objects on a Table* (1998). *The Death of Picasso: New and Selected Writing* (2003).

—JANE GENTRY VANCE

DONALD DAVIDSON (1893–1968). The descendant of Scottish pioneers and the son of a rural schoolmaster and a music teacher, Donald Grady Davidson was born in Campbellsville, Tenn., on August 18, 1893. After attending Lynnville Academy and the Branham and Hughes School, he enrolled in Vanderbilt University in Nashville at age sixteen. Because of a lack of funds, he left after one year to teach in several small Tennessee towns. In 1914 he returned to Vanderbilt, and finished his undergraduate degree just as he entered the U.S. Army in 1917 to fight as an infantryman in some of the last but toughest battles in France. Before leaving for Europe, he had married Theresa Sherrer, an artist and later lawyer and classical scholar.

Following his discharge, he taught at Kentucky Wesleyan College. In 1920 he began graduate studies for an M.A. at Vanderbilt and at the same time served as an instructor in the English department. Except for his adjunct position as book-page editor for the *Nashville Tennessean* (1924–30) and his summers teaching as a faculty member at the Bread Loaf School of English at Middlebury College in Vermont (beginning in 1931), Davidson was to spend his entire professional career at Vanderbilt until his retirement in 1964. After purchasing a home near that of Robert Frost, Davidson spent his summers in Vermont and the academic year in Nashville, where he died on April 25, 1968.

Davidson fell in with a group of young scholars and students who met regularly to discuss philosophy, art, and literature in Nashville in 1920. This group, which evolved into the Fugitives, included John Crowe Ransom, Allen Tate, and Robert Penn Warren, among others. In 1922 the first issue of the *Fugitive* appeared under their editorship. In the three and one-half years of its existence, the

Fugitive became an influential outlet for the regional voice in American poetry and helped inaugurate the Southern Literary Renascence that dominated the national scene in writing for several decades.

The same four young poets, with Davidson serving as the cohesive force, became interested in the encroachments of the technological society on the southern culture in the 1920s and led a second group of thinkers to make an appeal for an agrarian-based economy in America through a symposium published as *I'll Take My Stand* (1930). While the other central figures modified their philosophies with the passage of time, Davidson stood behind his carefully formulated beliefs and steadily developed them through a series of essays that remain admirable for their rhetorical facility. Many of these essays were collected in *The Attack on Leviathan* and *Still Rebels, Still Yankees.*

From his early contributions to the *Fugitive* through his retirement, Davidson continued to write and to develop as a poet, moving from a romantic, experimental stance toward the use of regional experience and history in poetic forms based on the ballad and narrative verse. His best works are considered to be *The Tall Men,* a probing analysis of modern man torn between his traditional past and the coming technological apocalypse, and "Lee in the Mountains" (1934), a partisan but historically accurate analysis of Robert E. Lee's reflections on the Civil War, a stream-of-consciousness poem that brings Lee's fate to the level of Christian tragedy. Davidson also taught and influenced several generations of younger southern writers and scholars, wrote literary criticism and historical studies, and produced several successful textbooks on teaching composition. He even tried his hand at fiction in a novel set in the country music world of Nashville and published posthumously as *The Big Ballad Jamboree.*

WORKS: *An Outland Piper* (1924). *The Tall Men* (1927). "A Mirror for Artists," in *I'll Take My Stand: The South and the Agrarian Tradition,* by Twelve Southerners (1930). *British Poetry of the Eighteen-Nineties* (1937). *The Attack on Leviathan* (1938). *American Composition and Rhetoric* (1939). *Readings for Composition from Prose Models* (1942). *The Tennessee,* 2 vols. (1946, 1948). *Twenty Lessons in Reading and Writing Prose* (1955). *Still Rebels, Still Yankees* (1957). *Southern Writers in the Modern World* (1958). *The Long Street* (1961). *The Spyglass: Views and Reviews* (1963). *Poems 1922–1961* (1966). Ed., *Selected Essays and Other Writings of John Donald Wade* (1966). *The Big Ballad Jamboree* (1996).

—M. THOMAS INGE

SAMUEL DAVIES (1723–1761). Samuel Davies was born on November 3, 1723, in New Castle County, Del., to David and Martha Davies. Educated early in his life by his mother, then at schools attached to local churches, he in time felt a call to the ministry and at age fifteen was sent to study at Samuel Blair's "log college" classical academy at Fagg's Manor, Chester County, Pa. There Davies received his theological training, one particularly influenced by the New Light Presbyterianism of William Tennent.

After completing his studies in 1746, Davies wed Sarah Kirkpatrick, who died unexpectedly less than one year later. In that same year he was ordained in the Presbyterian Church, spending his time first as an evangelist in the middle colonies, then in 1748 settling into a position at Hanover, Va., the only permanent pastorate of his career. He married again, this time to June Holt, with whom in the following years he had six children.

Celebrated for his eloquence as a preacher, Davies published a number of sermons during his lifetime. Several volumes of these, published posthumously, enjoyed numerous printings well into the nineteenth century. Throughout his time at Hanover, Davies also published a number of essays and poems, many in the *Virginia Gazette.* One volume of verse, *Miscellaneous Poems: Chiefly on Divine Subjects,* appeared in 1752. These poems, some written as meditative exercises in preparation for sermons he was composing, show the influence of such figures as Milton and Pope. Davies was best known for his poems written as hymns; indeed, he was one of the earliest American colonists to make a regular practice of writing hymns and one of the first to have them published.

While at Hanover Davies was active in a variety of ways—undertaking missionary journeys to outlying counties, committing himself to the teaching of slaves in his region, working to encourage religious toleration in Virginia, and in the mid-1750s traveling to Britain to raise funds for the recently established College of New Jersey.

In 1759 Davies accepted a call to become president of the school, following the death of Jonathan Edwards. Davies's tenure was brief, as he took sick and died within two years, on February 4, 1761, at age thirty-seven.

WORKS: *Miscellaneous Poems: Chiefly on Divine Subjects* (1752). *The Reverend Samuel Davies Abroad; The Diary of a Journey to England and Scotland, 1753–55* (1967). For a bibliography of Davies's numerous published sermons and essays, see George W. Pilcher, *Samuel Davies: Apostle of Dissent in Colonial Virginia* (1971), 196–202.

—JOHN N. SOMERVILLE, JR.

JAMES PAXTON DAVIS, JR. (1925–1994). James Paxton Davis, Jr.—fiction writer, journalist, and educator—was born on May 7, 1925, in Winston-Salem, N.C., son of James Paxton Davis and Emily McDowell Davis. He grew up in Winston-Salem, then attended Virginia Military Institute in 1942–43 before joining the army and serving in India and Burma.

Following military service, Davis resumed his education at Johns Hopkins University, intent on becoming a novelist. After receiving a B.A. from Johns Hopkins in 1949, Davis found it financially necessary to return to Winston-Salem and work as a reporter. He worked first with the *Winston-Salem Journal*, moving in 1951 to the *Richmond Times-Dispatch* (where he received an award for interpretive reporting), returning to Winston-Salem in 1952 to work with the *Twin City Sentinel*.

In 1953 Davis began teaching journalism at Washington and Lee University; he taught there until 1976, when he retired for health reasons. As book editor (1961–81) and editorial and op-ed columnist (1976–94) for the *Roanoke Times and World-News,* he blasted conservative politicians and penned elegant essays on the literary arts.

Davis had ten books published, ranging from novels set in World War II and the Civil War to "biographical fiction" about explorers and Robert E. Lee. His last three books were autobiographical novels about growing up in Winston-Salem during the Depression, serving in World War II, and returning to a changed world. This trilogy was so successful that Books on Tape released all three, unabridged. At his death, Davis left behind an unfinished manuscript for a book about the unsolved death of Zachary Smith Reynolds, heir to a tobacco fortune, who was shot and killed in his home in Winston-Salem in 1932. Davis was named a fellow in the Virginia Center for the Creative Arts in 1983.

Davis married Wylma Elizabeth Pooser in 1951. They had three children: Elizabeth Keith, Anne Beckley, and James Paxton III. That marriage ended in divorce in 1971. In 1973 he married Peggy Painter Camper. Troubled by heart problems since 1976, Davis died in Fincastle, Va., on May 28, 1994, after open-heart surgery.

WORKS: *Two Soldiers* (1956). *The Battle of New Market: A Story of V.M.I.* (1963). *One of the Dark Places* (1965). *The Seasons of Heroes* (1967). *A Flag at the Pole: Three Soliloquies* (1976). *Ned* (1978). *Three Days: With Robert E. Lee at Gettysburg* (1980). *Being a Boy* (1988). *A Boy's War* (1990). *A Boy No More* (1992).

—ALICE R. COTTEN

OSSIE DAVIS (1917–2005). Raiford Chatman Davis was born on December 18, 1917, in Cogdell, Ga., the oldest of Kince Charles and Laura Cooper Davis's five children. He was also named by the clerk filing his birth certificate, who misunderstood the pronunciation of his initials, "R.C.," as "Ossie." He attended high school in Waycross, Ga., a town on the fringe of the Okefenokee Swamp. Alain Locke mentored him at Howard University, and Davis dropped out to pursue stage ambitions in New York. His dramatic career began somewhat inauspiciously; in the early years, the main part he played was that of a starving artist. World War II called him into service with the army, where he staged several plays for GIs. Upon his return, he accepted the title role (and plaudits) in Robert Audrey's *Jeb*. He married Ann Wallace (better known as Ruby Dee), a member of the cast, in 1949. The couple had a son and two daughters.

A long and illustrious acting career led Davis also to produce and direct, on stage and screen, and to write his own material. *Purlie Victorious* follows a fast-talking black minister who wants a church of his own but must first outmaneuver an antagonistic white landholder. *Purlie* was adapted to film in *Gone Are the Days* and was later made into a Broadway musical.

Davis advocated strongly in the civil rights movement. He served as master of ceremonies at the March on Washington, where Martin Luther King, Jr., delivered his "I Have a Dream" speech. Davis would see the dream deferred; he eulogized both King and Malcolm X. His concern with race relations inspires much of his work. The action of his novel for young adults, *Just Like Martin*, takes place in 1963. A father straddles a generation gap, as he struggles with his conflicted feelings about a promising son's attraction to the civil rights struggle.

Davis's energy seemed boundless. Over the years he acted in dozens of plays and films, and had a hand in scripting or directing many more. His influence extends into latter-day ruminations on the color line, including many appearances in Spike Lee's films. Davis died on February 4, 2005, in Miami Beach, Fla.

WORKS: *Purlie Victorious* (1961). *Escape to Freedom: A Play about Young Frederick Douglass* (1976). *Langston: A Play* (1982). *Just like Martin* (1992). *With Ossie and Ruby: In This Life Together*, with Ruby Dee (1998).

—BRYAN GIEMZA

REBECCA HARDING DAVIS (1831–1910). Rebecca Blaine Harding Davis, daughter of Richard and Rachel Harding, was born on June 24, 1831, in Washington, Pa. The Harding family lived in Big Spring, Ala., until 1837, when they moved to Wheeling, W.Va. Rebecca attended Washington Female Seminary, graduating in 1848 with highest honors. A life of uneventful spinsterhood seemed her destiny when, at age thirty, she published anonymously "Life in the Iron Mills" in the *Atlantic Monthly*. This short story became a landmark of American realism. The narrative recounts the sordid details of a frustrated iron mill worker who aspires to become an artist but ends his life by suicide. Davis's next work, a novel, is just as grim. Published serially in the *Atlantic Monthly* as "A Story of Today," *Margret Howth* depicts the degrading conditions of mill workers and the evils of social inequality. Davis considered it an attempt "to dig into this commonplace, this vulgar American life, and see what it is."

In 1863 Rebecca Harding married Clarke Davis and moved to Philadelphia, where Clarke became a prominent journalist. Rebecca served as an associate editor for the *New York Tribune* from 1869 to 1875. The couple had three children, one of whom, Richard Harding Davis, became one of the most popular journalists of his generation. Rebecca Harding Davis continued to crusade for the poor and the dispossessed in her nonfiction social criticism, but her voluminous fictional output never fulfilled the promise of her early work. Her stories, many published in the *Atlantic Monthly*, *Lippincott's*, and *Scribner's*, became repetitious, sentimental, and didactic. Nevertheless, two more of her novels did show potential: *Waiting for the Verdict*, a Reconstruction story about miscegenation, and *John Andross*, an indictment of corrupt politics and the Whiskey Ring scandal.

Rebecca Harding Davis died at her son Richard's home at Mount Kisco, N.Y., on September 29, 1910.

WORKS: "Life in the Iron Mills" (April 1861). *Margret Howth: A Story of To-Day* (1862); repr. as *Margaret* (1970). *The Second Life* (ser. in *Peterson's*, Jan.–June, 1863). *Atlantic Tales* (1866). *Waiting for the Verdict* (1868). *Dallas Galbraith* (1868). *Kitty's Choice* (1873). *Pro Aris et Focis* (1869, England; 1870, U.S.). *Earthen Pitchers* (ser. in *Scribner's Maga- zine*, Nov. 1873–Apr. 1874). *John Andross* (1874). *A Law unto Herself* (1878). *Gleanings from Merrimac Valley* (1881). *Natasqua* (1886). *Silhouettes of American Life* (1892). *Kent Hampden* (1892). *Stories of the South* (1894). *Doctor Warrick's Daughters* (1896). *Frances Waldeaux* (1897). *Bits of Gossip* (1904). *Rebecca Harding Davis Reader: "Life in the Iron-Mills": Selected Fiction and Essays*, ed. Jean Pfaelzer (1995).

—HAROLD WOODELL

WILLIAM DAWSON (1704–1752). William Dawson is a rare kind of writer; he achieved a place in American literary history with a book of English poems. That thin thirty-page book, the only known volume and once the personal property of George Washington, is now lodged in the Boston Athenaeum library. The Facsimile Text Society reprinted it in 1930.

Poems on Several Occasions by a Gentleman of Virginia is a beautifully printed little book, contain- ing "the casual Productions" of Dawson's youth. He probably wrote these poems while a student at Queen's College in Oxford, which he entered at the age of fifteen and where he remained (until 1728 or 1729) before coming to America. Dawson imitated Anacreon and Horace and also Shakespeare, Milton, and James Thomson. Yet his poetry has some originality and spontaneity. He avoids the man- nered style of some of the contemporary English neoclassical verse. Brooks and rills, for example, don't "babble" in Dawson's poetry—they "gurgle." He also had a touch of the Cavalier, at times reminding one of Herrick or Waller—particularly in his addresses to Sylvia, that paragon of her sex and object of his desire. He wrote in a variety of forms—epistles, epigrams, fables with morals, hymns, songs, light satires—but all of it is pure English poetry, far removed from our native American tradition.

Little is known of Dawson's life in England. He was born in Cumberland County, spent nine years at Oxford, taking his M.A. there in 1728, and leaving to become Professor of Moral Philosophy at William and Mary in 1729. In a letter to the bishop of London (June 2, 1740) he mentions being elected a Fellow at Oxford in 1733—after he had left.

In Virginia the Reverend Dawson married Mary Randolph Stith, a niece of Sir John Randolph. In succession to James Blair, he became second president of William and Mary, receiving a D.D. there in February 1747. His papers are in the Library of Congress.

WORKS: *Poems on Several Occasions by a Gentleman of Virginia* (1736).

—RICHARD E. AMACHER

JAMES DUNWOODY BROWNSON DE BOW (1820–1867). Born on July 10, 1820, in Charles- ton, S.C., De Bow attended Cokesbury Institute and was graduated from the College of Charleston (1843). He practiced law briefly and then launched his career as a magazinist with the *Southern Quarterly Review*, publishing essays on history and law and performing minor editorial work. As a delegate to the Southern Commercial Convention of 1845, he took an interest in regional economic problems and subsequently moved to New Orleans to found a monthly devoted to "trade, com- merce, commercial polity, and manufacturers." First appearing in January 1846, *De Bow's Review* regularly featured articles on agricultural commodities, transportation and communication, com- mercial conventions, industrialization, and trade laws. The editor envisioned a southern prosperity based upon education, economic diversification, and slavery. In 1848 De Bow became head of the

Louisiana Bureau of Statistics and lectured on commerce at the University of Louisiana. He published a collection of essays from the *Review* in 1852–53 and then moved to Washington, where he became superintendent of the Census Bureau. He oversaw the tabulation of the important 1850 census and published the results in three major works.

Meanwhile his *Review* had become the main repository of arguments for slavery and sectional rights. As president of the Southern Commercial Convention of 1857, De Bow preached regional loyalty, spoke of a possible "separate confederation," and urged the reopening of the African slave trade. During the war he acted as general agent for the Confederate Produce Loan Agency. The fall of New Orleans in 1862 curtailed publication of the *Review*, which De Bow could not resume regularly until 1866. In the face of Reconstruction, he continued to champion southern causes and encourage economic development; he became president of the Tennessee and Pacific Railroad in 1866. After De Bow's death on February 27, 1867, the influential *Review* survived only a few years, but its place in the cultural history of the South was already secure.

WORKS: *Political Annals of South Carolina* (1845). *De Bow's Review* (1846–62; 1866–67). *The Industrial Resources, etc., of the Southern and Western States* (1852–53). *Seventh Census of the United States: 1850* (1853). *Statistical View of the United States* (1854). *Mortality Statistics of the Seventh Census of the United States, 1850* (1855). *The Interest in Slavery of the Southern Non-slaveholder* (1860).

—J. GERALD KENNEDY

EDWIN DE LEON (1818–1891). Edwin De Leon was born in Columbia, S.C., on May 4, 1818. He was the second son of Dr. Mardici Heinrich and Rebecca Lopez-y-Nuñez De Leon, and the elder brother and guardian of the journalist and author Thomas Cooper De Leon. De Leon graduated from South Carolina College in 1837 and was admitted to the South Carolina bar in 1840. From 1842 to 1848 he worked as coeditor of the *Republican* of Savannah, Ga. In 1850, by request of the southern wing of Congress, he moved to Washington, D.C., where he and Ellwood Fisher founded the *Southern Press*, a mouthpiece for the southern cause.

In 1854 De Leon embarked on a diplomatic career as consul general and diplomatic agent to Egypt and its dependencies, where he distinguished himself in a dramatic confrontation with Abbas Pasha, the Egyptian ruler who threatened to murder the Greeks in Alexandria. In 1861, at the outbreak of the Civil War, De Leon's southern allegiances forced him to resign his position. In the following year Jefferson Davis appointed him the Confederate diplomatic agent to Europe, a post he held until 1867, when he returned to the South. After the war De Leon went back to Egypt and Europe, returning briefly in 1879 to negotiate arrangements for introducing a telephone system to Egypt. This he accomplished in 1881.

Throughout his life De Leon demonstrated a talent and interest in writing. He edited his college journal, and after graduation made frequent contributions to magazines and periodicals. Later in life he cultivated the friendship of such literary figures as Hawthorne, Longfellow, Dickens, Tennyson, and Thackeray. Most of De Leon's writings draw on his experiences abroad, especially those of Egypt. He died in New York City on December 1, 1891, shortly after returning to the United States, where he planned to give a series of lectures on his experiences in foreign lands.

WORKS: *Three Letters from a South Carolinian, Relating to Secession, Slavery, and the Trent Case* (1862). *La Vérité sur les États Confédérés d'Amérique* (1862). *Askaros Kassis, the Copt* (1870). *The Khedive's Egypt* (1877, 1882). *Under the Stars and under the Crescent, a Romance of East and West* (1879). *Thirty Years of Life in Three Continents* (1890).

—JAMES A. LEVERNIER

THOMAS COOPER DE LEON (1839–1914). Although his name is associated with Alabama, Thomas Cooper was born in Columbia, S.C., on May 21, 1839, to Dr. Mardici Heinrich and the beautifully named Rebecca Lopez-y-Nuñez De Leon. Thomas graduated from Georgetown College in Washington, D.C., and served as an audit clerk in the Bureau of Topographical Engineering until 1862, when sectional loyalties obliged him to accept his commission as captain in the Confederate army. Thereafter he served as a secretary to President Davis. The De Leon family had literary leanings: Thomas's older brother, Edwin De Leon, also made his mark as a journalist and political appointee.

With the end of the war, Thomas De Leon channeled his energies into his literary aspirations, working as a journalist in New York and then Baltimore, where he edited the magazine *Cosmopolite* (1866). Like many of his southern literary contemporaries, he published a collection of Confederate ballads, called *South Songs*. In 1867 he moved to Mobile and made it his home for the rest of his life. His lively humor shone in a number of projects, including his direction of the Mobile Theatre (1873–85), his work as principal organizer and long-time coordinator of the Mobile Mardi Gras, and his own press, which printed the cheeky periodical *Gossip*.

De Leon was prolific and ranged across subjects. His war romances typify the popular conciliatory postbellum novels of the day; his war trilogy includes *The Puritan's Daughter*, *John Holden, Unionist*, and *Crag-Nest*. His best-known works are told from the standpoint of a wartime insider, and include the biographical *Four Years in Rebel Capitals* and *Belles, Beaux and Brains of the 60's*. Like fellow Confederate writer John Banister Tabb, he suffered from blindness in late life. De Leon wrote until his death on March 19, 1914.

WORKS: *South Songs* (1866). *Cross Purposes* (1871). *Coqsureus* (1887). *The Soldiers' Souvenir* (1887). *The Rock or the Rye* (1888). *Creole and Puritan* (1889). *Four Years in Rebel Capitals* (1890). *Juny* (1890). *Our Creole Carnivals* (1890). *Society as I Have Foundered It* (1890). *A Fair Blockade-Breaker* (1891). *The Puritan's Daughter* (1891). *Sybilla* (1891). *John Holden, Unionist* (1893). *Schooners That Bump on the Bar* (1894). *Out of the Sulphur* (1895). *The Rending of the Solid South* (1895). *East, West, and South* (1896). *Crag-Nest* (1897). *A Novelette Trilogy* (1897). *Creole Carnivals* (1898). *An Innocent Cheat* (1898). *The Pride of the Mercers* (1898). *War Rhymes, Grave and Gay* (1898). *Confederate Memories* (1899). *Joseph Wheeler* (1899). *Inauguration of President Watterson* (1902). *Tales from the Coves* (1903). *The Passing of Arle Haine* (1905). *Belles, Beaux and Brains of the 60's* (1909).

—BRYAN GIEMZA

BABS H. DEAL (1929–2004). Babs Hodges Deal was born in Scottsboro, Ala., on June 23, 1929, to Hilburn Tyson and Evelyn Coffey Hodges. She worked as a substitute teacher in the Jackson County school system in 1950, clerk-typist for the U.S. Army, judge advocate general in Washington, D.C., in 1951, and typist for the Birmingham Brass Company in 1951–52. In 1952 she married Borden Deal. That year they graduated from the University of Alabama, where they had both studied in Hudson Strode's creative writing program. They had three children together, and Babs was also a stepmother to Borden's child from a previous marriage. Babs and Borden Deal divorced in 1975. She lived in Sarasota, Fla., for many years before moving to Gulf Shores, Ala. She died in Montgomery on February 20, 2004.

Deal produced thirteen novels over a twenty-year period. Her work was received with popular as well as critical acclaim: she was nominated for an Edgar Award in 1966 for *Fancy's Knell*, received the Mystery Writers of America Award in 1967, and won the Alabama Library Association's Author Award in 1969 for *The Walls Came Tumbling Down*. Deal was a frequent contributor to *Redbook*, *Ladies' Home Journal*, and *Good Housekeeping* magazines. She also wrote for television, including an episode of *Alfred Hitchcock Presents* titled "Make My Death Bed" (1961) and *Friendships, Secrets, and Lies* (1979), the adaptation of *The Walls Came Tumbling Down*. In 1990 the University of Alabama Press reprinted her novel *It's Always Three O'Clock*.

Although the majority of her work is set in small-town Alabama, part of Deal's popularity can perhaps be attributed to her diverse subjects. *The Grail*, for example, captures the traditions and rituals of college football in the South, and *High Lonesome World* depicts the life of a country and western musician as told by his friends and colleagues. This range of interests, along with her work in other mediums, places Deal as a notable figure in the contemporary literary landscape of the South.

WORKS: *Acres of Afternoon* (1959). *It's Always Three O'Clock* (1961). *Night Story* (1962). *The Grail* (1963). *Fancy's Knell* (1966). *The Walls Came Tumbling Down* (1968). *High Lonesome World: The Death and Life of a Country Music Singer* (1969). *Summer Games* (1972). *The Crystal Mouse* (1973). *The Reason for Roses* (1974). *Waiting to Hear from William* (1975). *Goodnight Ladies* (1978).

—JOHN KWIST, JR.

BORDEN DEAL (1922–1985). Born Loysé Youth Deal on October 12, 1922, in Pontotoc, Miss., and raised in Union County near New Albany, Borden Deal was the author of more than twenty novels, approximately one hundred short stories, and numerous essays sometimes using the pseudonyms Lee Borden and Leigh Borden. During the Depression, Roosevelt's rehabilitation program moved Deal's family to the communal, government-sponsored farming project in Enterprise, Miss.—a location that Deal fictionalized as Bugscuffle Bottoms in *The Least One*. The family later moved to Darden community, another farming venture that Deal incorporated into his fiction as Hell Creek Bottom in *The Other Room*. After his father's death, Deal left his family in 1938 and worked as a migrant wheat farmer and as a firefighter for the Civilian Conservation Corps, as well as on a showboat, before joining the navy in Ft. Lauderdale, Fla., in 1942.

Following World War II, Deal studied English and creative writing under Hudson Strode at the University of Alabama (1946–49). During this time, Deal's first published story, "Exodus," appeared in *Tomorrow*. He attended graduate school in Mexico City before meeting his second wife, writer Babs Hodges; they divorced in 1975.

Much of Deal's fiction is set in the South. His most popular works include *Dunbar's Cove* and *The Insolent Breed*. *Dunbar's Cove*, which dramatizes the impact of the Tennessee Valley Authority, was combined with William Bradford Huie's *Mud on the Stars* (1942) to make Elia Kazan's film *Wild River* (1960). *The Insolent Breed*, the story of a small-town musical family, was the basis for Oscar Brand and Paul Nassau's Broadway musical *A Joyful Noise* (1966). Also notable are Deal's New South Saga, a series of novels that follow protagonist John Bookman through southern political intrigues, and *The Tobacco Men*, a novel about the Kentucky tobacco wars that Deal wrote using notes from Theodore Dreiser and Hy Kraft. Deal won a Guggenheim Fellowship (1957), an American Library Association Liberty and Justice Award (1956), and an Alabama Library Association Literary Award (1963). After a prolific lifetime of writing, he died of a heart attack in Sarasota, Fla., on January 22, 1985.

WORKS: *Walk through the Valley* (1956). *Dunbar's Cove* (1957). *Search for Surrender* (1957). *Killer in the House* (1957). *The Secret of Sylvia*, as Lee Borden (1958). *The Insolent Breed* (1959). *Dragon's Wine* (1960). *Devil's Whispers*, as Lee Borden (1961). *The Spangled Road* (1962). *The Loser* (1964). *The Tobacco Men* (1965). *A Long Way to Go* (1965). *The Least One* (1967). *The Advocate* (1968). *Interstate* (1970). *A Neo-Socratic Dialogue on the Reluctant Empire* (1971). *The Winner* (1973). *The Other Room* (1974). *Bluegrass* (1976). *Legend of the Bluegrass*, as Leigh Borden (1977). *Adventure* (1978). *There Were also Strangers: A Novel* (1985). *The Platinum Man* (1986).

—SEAN H. WELLS

JAMES DICKEY (1923–1997). Poet, novelist, essayist, critic, James Dickey enjoyed the reputation as one of the most eminent southern men of letters in the 1960s and 1970s. Born in a suburb of Atlanta in 1923, and son of a successful lawyer there, he went on to enroll at Clemson College, where he was a freshman starter on the varsity football team before withdrawing from college to join the army air corps during World War II. He flew more than a hundred missions in the Pacific theater. After the war he enrolled at Vanderbilt University and, as an English major, came under the influence of Professor of English Monroe K. Spears. He published poems in the local literary magazine. He also won the Tennessee state championship for running the 120-yard high hurdles. In November 1948, he married Maxine Syerson and graduated magna cum laude. He won a graduate fellowship at Vanderbilt, where he earned his M.A. in English in 1950.

Dickey began his teaching career as an instructor of English at Rice Institute, but was called back into the military during the Korean War. He returned to his teaching position at Rice in 1954 and went on to teach at the University of Florida. After a controversy arose following his public reading of his poem "The Father's Body," about discovering sexual identity, he resigned from Florida and joined the New York advertising firm McCann-Erickson, where he worked on the Coca-Cola account as a copywriter. He later worked for other advertising agencies in Atlanta. Continuing to write poetry during these years, he published *Into the Stone* in 1960 and *Drowning with Others* two years later. Awarded a Guggenheim Fellowship, he resigned from the business world. His fourth book, *Buckdancer's Choice*, was awarded the National Book Award in 1966, and his *Poems 1957–1967* won him national acclaim. He served two years as poetry consultant to the Library of Congress (an office that later became poet laureate). In 1969 he became poet-in-residence and First Carolina Professor of English at the University of South Carolina in Columbia. A year later, he published his best-selling novel *Deliverance*, later made into a major motion picture. Following the death of his first wife, he married Deborah Dodson in 1976. Newly elected president Jimmy Carter solicited a poem from Dickey, who recited his "The Strength of Fields" at the inaugural celebration in 1977.

Dickey eventually published more than twenty books of poetry, fiction, criticism, and other essays. He was inducted into the National Institute of Arts and Letters in 1972 and the American Academy and Institute of Arts and Letters in 1988. He won the Harriet Monroe Prize for lifetime achievement in poetry in 1996. Dickey died in 1997 following a long illness.

WORKS: *Into the Stone and Other Poems* (1960). *Drowning with Others* (1962). *Helmets* (1964). *The Suspect in Poetry* (1964). *Two Poems of the Air* (1964). *Buckdancer's Choice* (1965). *Poems 1957–1967* (1967). *Spinning the Crystal Ball: Some Guesses at the Future of American Poetry* (1967). *The Achievement of James Dickey: A Comprehensive Selection of His Poems* (1968). *Babel to Byzantium* (1968). *The Eye-Beaters, Blood, Victory, Madness, Buckhead and Mercy* (1970). *Deliverance* (1970). *The Self as Agent* (1970). *Self-Interviews* (1970). *Sorties: Journals and New Essays* (1971). *Exchanges, by James Dickey, Being in the Form of a Dialogue with Joseph Trumbull Stickney* (1971). *Jericho: The South Beheld* (1974). *The Zodiac* (1976). *God's Images: The Bible: A New Vision* (1977). *Veteran Birth: The Gadfly Poems, 1947–1949* (1978). *Tucky the Hunter* (1978). *The Enemy from Eden* (1978). *The Strength of Fields* (1979). *In Pursuit of the Grey Soul* (1979). *Head-Deep in Strange Sounds: Free-Flight Improvisations from the unEnglish* (1979). *Falling, May Day Sermon, and Other Poems* (1981). *The Early Motion* (1981). *The Starry Place between the Antlers: Why I Live in South Carolina* (1981). *Puella* (1982). *Värmland* (1982). *The Poet Turns on Himself* (1982). *The Central Motion: Poems 1968–1979* (1983). *False Youth: Four Seasons* (1983). *Intervisions: Poems and Photographs* (1983). *Night Hurdling: Poems, Essays, Conversations, Commencements, and Afterwords* (1983). *For a Time and Place* (1983). *Bronwen, The Traw, and the Shape-Shifter: A Poem in Four Parts* (1986). *Alnilam* (1987). *Wayfarer: A Voice from the Southern Mountains* (1988). *The Eagle's Mile* (1990). *The Whole Motion: Collected Poems 1949–1992* (1992). *To the White Sea* (1993). *Striking In The Early Notebooks of James Dickey* (1996). *Crux: The Letters of James Dickey* (1999). *The James Dickey Reader* (1999).

—GEORGE S. LENSING

SAMUEL HENRY DICKSON (1798–1872). Born in Charleston, S.C., on September 20, 1798, Samuel Henry Dickson enrolled at Yale at the age of thirteen. He completed his M.D. degree at the University of Pennsylvania in 1819, then returned to his native state to take charge of the Marine and Yellow Fever Hospitals in Charleston. He was a leading figure in medical circles throughout his long career in Charleston; having helped to found the Medical College of South Carolina in 1833, he served on that institution's faculty until 1847. He then taught at the University of the City of New York (1847–50), returned to teach and practice in Charleston (1850–58), and finished his career at Jefferson Medical College in Philadelphia, where he taught until his death on March 31, 1872.

A friend of William Gilmore Simms, Dickson moved freely in the nineteenth-century Charleston literary world, frequenting Russell's bookstore and helping to found *Russell's Magazine,* the most successful and influential of the many short-lived antebellum Charleston literary journals. Dickson himself was an occasional poet, his reputation secured by his popular 1830 topographical poem "I Sigh for the Land of the Cypress and the Pine." That same year Dickson published a lecture on temperance, and over the next three decades he produced a variety of works, including a collection of poems, medical texts, and articles on literary topics for the *Southern Literary Messenger* and the *Southern Quarterly Review.*

WORKS: *Address before the South Carolina Society for the Promotion of Temperance* (1830). *On Dengue: Its History, Pathology, and Treatment* (1839). *Poems* (1844). *Essays on Pathology and Therapeutics* (1845). *Essays on Life, Sleep, Pain, Etc.* (1852). *Elements of Medicine: A Compendious View of Pathology and Therapeutics* (1855).

—DANIEL J. ENNIS

R. H. W. DILLARD (1937–). Richard Henry Wilde Dillard—poet, fiction writer, literary critic, film critic, film writer, editor, and distinguished teacher—was born in Roanoke, Va., and is a Phi Beta Kappa graduate of Roanoke College. He earned an M.A. (1959) and a Ph.D. (1965) at the University of Virginia, where he held Woodrow Wilson and DuPont fellowships.

Best known as a poet and as an enthusiast of popular culture generally and of fantasy/horror films particularly, he has published six volumes of poetry, in the course of which his work has moved away from its original modernist influences, becoming more personal and emotional and less allusive, while retaining its distinctive wit and erudition.

Dillard received the Academy of American Poets Prize in 1961; the O. B. Hardison, Jr., Poetry Award in 1994; and, in 2003, the Hanes Award for Poetry from the Fellowship of Southern Writers.

His two novels, *The Book of Changes* and *The First Man on the Sun,* and his collection of short stories, *Omniphobia,* are also charged with his wondering, funny take on the world. He has published essays, articles, and reviews in an array of journals. He was vice president of *Film Journal* from 1973 to 1980, and from 1966 to 1977 was contributing editor of *Hollins Critic,* of which he has been editor since 1996.

His academic life has been spent at Hollins University, where his work and personality have infused the English department and shaped its creative writing program, since he began there as instructor in 1964. As chair of creative writing, a position he assumed in 1971 and continues to hold, he has taught and influenced many accomplished writers, including Annie Doak Dillard (to whom he was married in 1965 and from whom he was divorced in 1975), Cathryn Hankla (whom he married in 1979 and from whom he was divorced in 1992), Henry Taylor, Lee Smith, Lucinda MacKethan, Anne Jones, Rosanne Coggeshall, Wyn Cooper, Jill McCorkle, Madison Smartt Bell, and Julia Johnson.

WORKS: *The Day I Stopped Dreaming about Barbara Steele and Other Poems* (1966). *Frankenstein Meets the Space Monster* (screenplay), with George Garrett and John Rodenbeck (1966). *News of the Nile: A Book of Poems* (1971). Ed., *The Sounder Few: Essays from the Hollins Critic,* with Garrett and John Rees Moore (1971). *After Borges: A*

Sequence of New Poems (1972). *The Book of Changes* (1974). *Horror Films* (1976). *The Greeting: New and Selected Poems* (1981). *The First Man on the Sun: A Novel* (1983). *Understanding George Garrett* (1988). *Just Here, Just Now: Poems* (1994). *Omniphobia: Stories* (1995). *Sallies: Poems* (2001). Ed., *Twayne Companion to Contemporary Literature in English, from the Editors of the Hollins Critic*, with Amanda Cockrell (2002).

—JANE GENTRY VANCE

THOMAS DIXON (1864–1946). Minister, legislator, lawyer, novelist, actor, film producer, real estate investor, and lecturer—a versatile man of multiple talents—Thomas Dixon was born on a farm near Shelby, N.C., on January 11, 1864. Shaped by the Reconstruction era, young Dixon experienced poverty and observed firsthand social conflicts that precipitated the violence and lawlessness of the Ku Klux Klan, materials that would provide the subjects for some of his novels.

Despite his impoverished upbringing and lack of opportunity for much formal schooling, Dixon entered Wake Forest College in 1879, distinguishing himself as an outstanding scholar and graduating with a master's degree in four years. Awarded a scholarship to Johns Hopkins in political science in 1883, Dixon studied politics and history and developed an interest in dramatic arts, an interest that was shared by Woodrow Wilson, with whom Dixon became friends. Dixon left Johns Hopkins without finishing his degree and, hoping to pursue a career in acting, he entered the Frobisher School in New York City as a drama student. Because Dixon's physical appearance worked against his attaining acting roles, he returned home to North Carolina, where, in 1884, he was elected to the state legislature, serving only one term.

Desiring a more practical livelihood than the theater promised, Dixon entered the Greensboro (N.C.) Law School and completed his law degree in 1885. A year later he married Harriet Bussey, the daughter of a minister. Becoming disenchanted with the law profession, Dixon next decided on the Baptist ministry.

After his ordination in 1886, he served pastorates in Goldsboro and Raleigh, N.C., Boston, Mass., and New York City, where in 1895 he founded a nondenominational church. During his ministry in New York, Dixon also used the pulpit to express his views on political matters, including Cuba's independence from Spain and the corruption of the Tammany Hall political machine, and on current social issues such as miscegenation and the promotion of justice for immigrants who lived in the New York slums. As his popularity as a speaker increased, Dixon in 1895 turned to the lecture platform and eventually lectured in many parts of the United States, carrying his social views to larger and more diverse audiences, a practice he followed until 1903.

During a midwestern lecture tour, Dixon attended a dramatization of Harriet Beecher Stowe's *Uncle Tom's Cabin* and was angered by what he perceived as the falsification of southern life. Beginning with *The Leopard Spots* in 1903 and continuing in other novels, Dixon used fiction as a propagandistic tool to correct misconceptions and false impressions about the South and its history, addressing controversial national social issues such as the evils of capitalism, socialism, communism, and the liberation of women. *The Clansman,* which glorifies the activities of the Ku Klux Klan and portrays African Americans in a dehumanizing manner, inspired D. W. Griffith's widely popular and controversial epic film *The Birth of a Nation* (1915).

Unsuccessful in his first venture into the theater world in the 1880s, Dixon turned to drama again in 1915, when he adapted *The Clansman* into a play. Other dramatic adaptations of his novels followed, as did several one-act plays. Dixon acted in several of his plays. After the success of *The Birth of a Nation,* he became a film producer himself, moving to California and opening his own studio in Los Angeles, where he adapted several of his works into films.

In the remaining years of his life, Dixon again became involved in politics. In 1932 he engaged in a national speaking tour supporting Franklin Delano Roosevelt and his New Deal policies, but four years later he abruptly repudiated the Roosevelt administration, fearing that it was being influenced by communism. In 1937 Dixon's first wife, Harriet, died. Two years later, after being stricken by a cerebral hemorrhage, he married Madelyn Donovan, who had played the lead in his film *The Mark of the Beast*. From 1939 until his death on April 3, 1946, Dixon lived as an invalid in Raleigh, N.C.

WORKS: *What Is Religion? An Outline of Vital Ritualism* (1891). *Dixon on Ingersoll: Ten Discourse Delivered in Association Hall, New York* (1892). *The Failure of Protestantism in New York and Its Causes* (1896). *Dixon's Sermons, Delivered in the Grand Opera House, 1898–1899* (1899). *Living Problems in Religion and Social Science* (1899). *The Leopard Spots: A Romance of the White Man's Burden 1865–1900* (1903). *The One Woman: A Story of Modern Utopia* (1903). *The Clansman: An Historical Romance of the Ku Klux Klan* (1905). *The One Woman: A Drama* (1906). *The Traitor: A Story of the Fall of the Invisible Empire* (1907). *Comrades: A Story of Social Adventures in California* (1909). *The Root of Evil: A Novel* (1911). *The Sins of the Father: A Romance of the South* (1912). *The Southerner: A Romance of the Real Lincoln* (1913). *The Victim: A Romance of the Real Jefferson Davis* (1914). *The Life Worth Living: A Personal Experience* (1914). *The Foolish Virgin: A Romance of Today* (1915). *The Fall of a Nation: A Sequel to the Birth of a Nation* (1916). *The Way of a Man: A Story of the New Woman* (1919). *A Man of the People: A Drama of Abraham Lincoln* (1920). *The Man in Gray: A Romance of North and South* (1921). *The Black Hood* (1924). *The Love Complex* (1925). *The Hope of the World: A Story of the Coming War* (1925). *Wildacres: In the Land of the Sky* (1926). *The Sun Virgin* (1929). *Companions* (1931). *The Inside Story of the Harding Tragedy*, with Harry M. Daugherty (1932). *A Dreamer in Portugal: A Story of Bernarr Macfadden's Mission to Continental Europe* (1934). *The Flaming Sword* (1939).

—ED PIACENTINO

J. FRANK DOBIE (1888–1964). Although J. Frank Dobie is more identified with the literature of the West than the South, he shared central beliefs with the Vanderbilt Agrarians (and was contemporary with them). Scornful of the industrial, the urban, the mechanical, and the consumeristic, he championed the land and the natural world. More than the Vanderbilt group, he remained rooted in his place and close to the earth.

James Frank Dobie was born on a ranch in Live Oak County, Tex., on September 26, 1888. He earned an A.B. from Southwestern University in 1910 and an M.A. from Columbia University in 1914. In 1916 he married his college sweetheart, Bertha McKee. He was principal of a high school in Alpine, Tex. (1910–11), and taught at Southwestern (1911–13) and the University of Texas (1914–17, 1919–20, 1921–23) before leaving for military service. After the war, he returned to teaching at Texas, Oklahoma A&M, and again Texas. Reflecting his commitment to place and appreciation of the past, he served as editor of the *Texas Folklore Society* for twenty years. His popular course "Life and Literature of the Southwest" led to his *Guide to Life and Literature of the Southwest*.

Feisty defender of unpopular causes and critic of Texas politics, he resigned from the University of Texas in 1947 after the regents refused to extend a leave of absence. Governor Coker Stevenson had called for his dismissal.

Dobie recounted his experience as a visiting professor of English at Cambridge during World War II in *A Texan in England*. He also taught in Germany and Austria. And he continued to write and publish about the land and the people who struggled for a living on it. His most important books are *A Vaquero of the Brush Country* and *The Longhorns*, his most popular book.

On September 14, 1964, President Lyndon Johnson awarded Dobie the Medal of Freedom. Four days later Dobie died. He remains a vivid presence in Texas and Southwest studies.

WORKS: *The Mexican Vaquero of the Texas Border* (1927). *A Vaquero of the Brush Country* (1929). *Coronado's Children* (1930). *On the Open Range* (1931). *Tongues of the Monte* (1935). *Tales of the Mustang* (1936). *The Flavor of Texas*

(1936). *Apache Gold and Yaqui Silver* (1939). *John C. Duval: First Texas Man of Letters* (1939). *The Longhorns* (1941). *The Mexico I Like* (1942). *Guide to Life and Literature of the Southwest* (1942, 1952). *A Texan in England* (1945). *The Voice of the Coyote* (1949). *The Ben Lilly Legend* (1950). *The Mustangs* (1952). *Tales of Old-Time Texas* (1955). *Up the Trail from Texas* (1955). *I'll Tell You a Tale* (1960). *Cow People* (1964). *Rattlesnakes*, ed. Bertha McKee Dobie (1965). *Rainbow in the Morning* (1965). *Carl Sandburg and St. Peter at the Gate* (1966). *Some Part of Myself*, ed. McKee Dobie (1967). *Out of the Old Rock*, ed. McKee Dobie (1972). *Prefaces*, ed. McKee Dobie (1975).

—WAYNE J. POND

ELLEN DOUGLAS (1921–). Ellen Douglas is the pseudonym of Josephine Ayres Haxton, who was born on July 12, 1921, in Natchez, Miss., the home of both sets of her grandparents. Richardson and Laura Davis Ayres raised their four children in Hope, Ark., and Alexandria, La., where Richardson worked as a civil engineer. Douglas has said that family, tale-telling, and church (Presbyterian) were important influences on her childhood.

Josephine Ayres graduated from the University of Mississippi in 1942. During World War I she worked at a radio station in Alexandria, at a nearby army induction center, and at a book store in New York City. In 1945 she married Kenneth Haxton, Jr., and they moved to his hometown of Greenville, Miss., where he entered the family's clothing business and composed music. Josephine stayed home to raise the couple's three sons, Richard, Ayres, and Brooks.

After her youngest son entered nursery school, she began to pursue her long-time passion, writing. She became Ellen Douglas with her first book, the novel *A Family's Affairs*, published in 1962 and winner of the Houghton Mifflin–Esquire Fellowship Award. Both *A Family's Affairs* and the story collection *Black Cloud, White Cloud* were selected for the *New York Times*'s annual lists of outstanding fiction. In 1976 she received a grant from the National Endowment for the Arts. Her novels *A Lifetime Burning* and *Can't Quit You, Baby* have received much acclaim.

Douglas has published six novels, a collection of stories, a collection of retold fairy tales, a book of four nonfiction narratives, and another of essays. She has taught at colleges in Louisiana, Virginia, and Mississippi. In 1983 she moved to Jackson, Miss., and she and Haxton divorced in the mid-1990s.

WORKS: *A Family's Affairs* (1962). *Black Cloud, White Cloud* (1963). *Where the Dreams Cross* (1968). *Apostles of Light* (1973). *A Rock Cried Out* (1979). *A Lifetime Burning* (1982). *The Magic Carpet and Other Tales* (1987). *Can't Quit You, Baby* (1988). *Truth: Four Stories I Am Finally Old Enough to Tell* (1998). *Witnessing* (2004).

—CAROL S. MANNING

FREDERICK DOUGLASS (1818–1895). The most influential African American writer of the nineteenth century, Frederick Douglass was born on Maryland's Eastern Shore in February 1818, the son of Harriet Bailey, a slave, and an unknown white man. Sent to Baltimore in 1826 by his master's son-in-law, Thomas Auld, Frederick spent five years as a servant in the home of Hugh and Sophia Auld. Sophia treated the slave boy with unusual kindness, giving him reading lessons until her husband forbade them. Rather than accept his master's dictates, Frederick taught himself clandestinely to read and write.

In 1833 a quarrel between the Auld brothers brought Frederick back to his home in St. Michaels, Md., where Thomas Auld hired him out as a farm worker under the supervision of Edward Covey, a local slave-breaker. After six months of unstinting labor and repeated beatings, the desperate sixteen-year-old slave fought back. Douglass's dramatic account of his struggle with Covey became the heroic turning point of his future autobiographies and one of the most celebrated scenes in all of African American literature.

In the spring of 1836, after a failed attempt to escape from slavery, Frederick was sent back to Baltimore to learn the caulking trade. With the aid of his future spouse, Anna Murray, and masquerading as a free black merchant sailor, he boarded a northbound train out of Baltimore on September 3, 1838, and arrived in New York City the next day. Before a month had passed Frederick and Anna were reunited, married, and living in New Bedford, Mass., as Mr. and Mrs. Frederick Douglass, the new last name recommended by a friend in New Bedford's thriving African American community. Less than three years later Douglass joined the American Anti-Slavery Society as a full-time lecturer.

After years of honing his rhetorical skills on the antislavery platform, Douglass wrote *Narrative of the Life of Frederick Douglass, an American Slave* in 1845. The book sold more than thirty thousand copies in the first five years of its existence. After a triumphal twenty-one-month lecture tour in Great Britain, Douglass returned to the United States in the spring of 1847 to launch his own newspaper, the *North Star*. While journalism occupied his pen for the most part, he found time to author a novella, *The Heroic Slave*, generally regarded as the first work of long fiction by an African American writer. A rupture between Douglass and his abolitionist mentor William Lloyd Garrison occasioned a period of reflection and reassessment that culminated in Douglass's second autobiography, *My Bondage and My Freedom*, in which he revised his heroic individualist self-image in the *Narrative* to emphasize his identity formation in Maryland slave communities. Welcoming the Civil War as a final means of ending slavery, Douglass lobbied President Lincoln in favor of African American recruitment for the Union army. When the war ended, Douglass pleaded with President Andrew Johnson for a national voting rights act that would enfranchise African American men. Douglass's loyalty to the Republican Party won him appointment to several national offices: federal marshal and recorder of deeds for the District of Columbia, president of the Freedman's Bureau Bank, consul to Haiti, and chargé d'affaires for the Dominican Republic.

The income Douglass earned from these positions, coupled with the fees he received for his popular lectures and his investments in real estate, allowed him and his family to live in comfort at Cedar Hill, a fifteen-acre estate he purchased in 1878 in Anacostia, D.C. Sixteen months after the death of Anna Murray Douglass in 1882, Douglass married Helen Pitts, his white former secretary, in 1884. His final memoir, *Life and Times of Frederick Douglass*, appeared in 1881 and in an expanded edition in 1892. *Life and Times* shows Douglass dedicated to the ideal of building a racially integrated America in which skin color would cease to determine an individual's social value and economic options. In the last months of his life Douglass decried the increasing incidence of lynching in the South and disputed the notion that by disenfranchising the African American a more peaceful social climate would prevail throughout the nation. After returning from a women's rights rally, Douglass died of a heart attack on February 20, 1895, at his home in Anacostia.

WORKS: *Narrative of the Life of Frederick Douglass, an American Slave* (1845). *The Heroic Slave* (1853). *My Bondage and My Freedom* (1855). *Life and Times of Frederick Douglass* (1882, 1893). *The Oxford Frederick Douglass Reader* (1996).

—WILLIAM L. ANDREWS

RITA DOVE (1952–). Rita Frances Dove was born in Akron, Ohio, on August 28, 1952, the second of four children. After first being barred from such a job because of his race, her father, Ray, became the Goodyear Tire and Rubber Company's first African American chemist. Her mother, Elvira (Hord), worked in the home. Rita graduated from Miami University of Ohio with a B.A. in English (summa cum laude, 1973) and from the University of Iowa Writers' Workshop with an M.F.A. (1977). In 1974–75 a Fulbright Fellowship took her to Germany, where she studied at the University of Tübingen.

Dove's poetry career has followed a somewhat typical pattern for success among contemporary po-ets—academic appointments (Arizona State University, 1981–89; University of Virginia, 1989–pres-ent), regular output of collections, and rounds of readings. But, like her father, she has also blazed trails. In 1987 she was the second African American woman awarded the Pulitzer in poetry. In 1993 she became the second woman, the first African American, and the youngest person ever appointed Poet Laureate of the United States and Consultant in Poetry to the Library of Congress. She served in that capacity for two years (1993–95), before returning to Charlottesville, where she has been Com-monwealth Professor of English since 1993.

Dove has been awarded many honorary degrees and received many prizes, including, in 1996, the lucrative Heinz Award in the Arts and Humanities and the National Humanities Medal. In 1999–2000 she was the Library of Congress's Special Consultant in Poetry. In 2004 she became poet laureate of the Commonwealth of Virginia.

In addition to her growing eminence in Virginia letters, Dove's ties to southern literature include her Pulitzer Prize–winning collection, *Thomas and Beulah*. These poems trace the lives of her mater-nal grandparents, who took part in the Great Migration of African Americans from their southern homes to the North, where economic and social opportunity seemed to await. Dove has delved into journalism (a weekly column, "Poet's Choice," appeared in the *Washington Post* in 2000–2002), fic-tion writing, and drama. *The Darker Face of the Earth*, a verse play set on a South Carolina plantation before the Civil War, was performed at the Kennedy Center, the Royal National Theatre, and other venues. Dove narrated *Tell about the South: Voices in Black and White* (2000), a public television series about southern literature.

Dove married Fred Viebahn, a German novelist, in 1979. Their daughter, Aviva Chantal Tamu Dove-Viebahn, was born in 1983. Dove's childhood involvement with music continues; it is a creative source for her work, including textual accompaniments to compositions by John Williams and other collaborators. Seeking distraction after fire burned their home and possessions in 1998, Dove and her husband took up ballroom dancing, an interest that informs the recent collection *American Smooth*.

WORKS: *Ten Poems* (1977). *The Yellow House on the Corner* (1980). *Mandolin* (1982). *Museum* (1983). *Fifth Sun-day* (1985). *Thomas and Beulah: Poems* (1986). *Grace Notes* (1989). *Through the Ivory Gate* (1992). *Selected Poems* (1993). *Lady Freedom among Us* (1993). *The Darker Face of the Earth: A Verse Play in Fourteen Scenes* (1994). *The Poet's World* (1995). *Mother Love* (1995). *Darker Face of the Earth* (1996). *On the Bus with Rosa Parks* (1999). Ed., *The Best American Poetry 2000* (2000). *American Smooth* (2004).

—AMBER VOGEL

CLIFFORD DOWDEY (1904–1979). Clifford Dowdey was born in Richmond, Va., on January 23, 1904. He graduated from John Marshall High School in Richmond and attended Columbia University in 1921–22 and 1923–25. In 1925 he returned to Richmond to work for a few months on the *Richmond News Leader,* but by 1926 he was back in New York. There for the next ten years he worked as an edi-tor of various pulp magazines and, as a freelance writer, contributed large numbers of westerns and confession romances to these magazines.

Through the worst of the Depression years Dowdey gave his days to freelance and editorial du-ties, but many of his nights were spent researching Civil War history. Out of this research came a short story which the *Atlantic Monthly* immediately accepted, with an option for a novel dealing with a similar background. The result was *Bugles Blow No More,* an account of Richmond under siege that won Dowdey a Guggenheim Fellowship. Over the next eight years he combined writing with travel, living in such diverse places as Vermont, Hollywood, and Texas. During this period he published four more historical novels.

In 1945 Dowdey returned to Richmond, where he eventually established permanent residence in his boyhood home. Here he researched his first nonfictional history, *Experiment in Rebellion*. This account of the Confederacy in Richmond, the initial choice of the History Book Club, was well received by both readers and critics and marked the beginning of Dowdey's career as a distinguished historian. He wrote four novels after *Experiment in Rebellion*, but by 1960 he was best known for a series of Civil War histories that made him an authority on the background and the events of the war, on the Army of Northern Virginia, and on the men who profoundly influenced the Virginia campaigns—Robert E. Lee and "Stonewall" Jackson. In later years Dowdey published two histories of colonial Virginia and of its planter aristocracy. He died at his home in Richmond on May 30, 1979.

WORKS: *Bugles Blow No More* (1937). *Gamble's Hundred* (1939). *Sing for a Penny* (1941). *Tidewater* (1943). *Where My Love Sleeps* (1945). *Experiment in Rebellion* (1946). *Weep for My Brother* (1950). *Jasmine Street* (1952). *The Proud Retreat: A Novel of the Lost Confederate Treasure* (1953). *The Land They Fought For: The Story of the South as the Confederacy, 1832–1865* (1955). *The Great Plantation: A Profile of Berkeley Hundred and Plantation Virginia from Jamestown to Appomattox* (1957). *Death of a Nation: The Story of Lee and His Men at Gettysburg* (1958). *Lee's Last Campaign: The Story of Lee and His Men against Grant—1864* (1960). Ed., *The Wartime Papers of R. E. Lee*, with Louis Manarin (1961). *Last Night the Nightingale* (1962). *The Seven Days: The Emergence of Lee* (1964). *Lee* (1965). *The Virginia Dynasties: The Emergence of "King" Carter and the Golden Age* (1969). *The Golden Age: A Climate of Greatness, Virginia 1732–1775* (1970). *The History of Henrico County*, with Louis H. Manarin (1984).

—RITCHIE D. WATSON, JR.

HARRIS DOWNEY (1907–1979). Born on May 12, 1907, in Baton Rouge, La., the son of Lawrence and Florence Chiek Downey, Harris Downey was educated at local schools and at Louisiana State University. After earning his B.A. (1929) and M.A. (1930), the latter with a thesis on George Washington Cable, Downey completed additional graduate study at New York University before returning to Baton Rouge as an assistant professor of English. During World War II, he served with the air force in the European theater, and then came back to Louisiana State after the war. His literary success allowed Downey to retire from the university, but he continued to live and write in Baton Rouge, his lifelong home.

Downey began to produce serious fiction after his experience in Europe, and his stories appeared in literary and popular periodicals; for example, the ironic combat story, "The Hunters," won the first prize in the 1951 O. Henry Awards. His first novel, *Thunder in the Room*, narrates one day in the life of a small southern city and is focused by the execution of a veteran detective caught up in political corruption. The book received mixed reviews, as did his two later novels, *The Key to My Prison*, the suicide diary of a listless belle, and *Carrie Dumain*, the harshly realistic story of a restless black girl and her dysfunctional family.

WORKS: *Thunder in the Room* (1956). *The Key to My Prison* (1964). *Carrie Dumain* (1966).

—JOSEPH R. MILLICHAP

ANDRE DUBUS (1936–1999). Although Andre Dubus lived the last three decades of his life in Massachusetts and set much of his fiction there, his roots are deeply southern. Brother to two older sisters, Dubus was born on August 11, 1936, in Lake Charles, La., and grew up in Baton Rouge and Lafayette. He and his cousin James Lee Burke played and watched baseball games together in Lafayette, and in later years Dubus would maintain his passion for the game through the Boston Red Sox. Graduating from the Christian Brothers Cathedral High School, Dubus knew that his Cajun-Irish culture was a major shaping force in the man that he would become. In numerous short stories Dubus explores the passage from childhood into maturity: Paul Clement is a recurring figure in many of these stories, serving Dubus much as the character Nick Adams served Ernest Hemingway, an important influence on Dubus.

In 1954 Dubus entered McNeese State College in Lake Charles, and in 1958 he received his B.A. in English and journalism, married Patricia Lowe, and was commissioned lieutenant in the U.S. Marine Corps. The intensity that became Dubus's hallmark is mirrored in his rapidly growing family—Suzanne born in 1958, Andre III in 1959, Jeb in 1960, and Nicole in 1963. Following his father's death in 1963, Captain Andre Dubus resigned his commission in the Marine Corps to enter the Iowa Writers' Program. That same year, the *Sewanee Review* published "The Intruder," his first publication.

M.F.A. in hand, in 1965 Dubus accepted a position as lecturer in English at Nicholls State College in Thibodaux, La. The following year he began teaching modern fiction and creative writing at Bradford College in Bradford, Mass. He retired from that post in 1984. Although he published two novels, he returned regularly to the short story and the novella, winning important critical praise for those efforts. In 1976 he received a Guggenheim Fellowship and two years later a grant from the National Endowment for the Arts, to be followed by another in 1985. Other honors include the PEN/Malamud Award, the Rea Award for excellence in short fiction, the Jean Stein Award from the American Academy of Arts and Letters, the Lawrence L. Winship Award, and in 1988 a fellowship from the MacArthur Foundation.

Dubus's first marriage ended in divorce in 1970. He married Tommie Gale Cotter in 1975; divorce followed three years later. In 1979 he married Peggy Rambach, with whom he had two daughters: Candace (1982) and Madeline Elise (1987). In 1986 Dubus lost a leg when he was struck by a car, having stopped to give aid to victims of an accident. Divorce followed soon after the accident, and Dubus would live in pain for the rest of his life, the avid runner now confined to a wheelchair.

One gift to emerge from the tragedy was Dubus's *Meditations from a Movable Chair.* The meditation, a genre associated more with earlier centuries, becomes an appropriate vehicle for Dubus to share the spiritual lessons he learned from his ordeal. The book is at once a profile in courage and an account of his abiding religious faith.

Shortly after Dubus's death, his short story "Killings" was filmed as *In the Bedroom,* one of the most acclaimed films of 2001. Film and story touch issues central in much of Dubus's work: father-son relationships, parental love and testing, and strained marriages. The 2004 film *We Don't Live Here Anymore,* based on two of Dubus's stories, explores the suffering and turmoil in two faltering marriages. Andre Dubus III continues his father's legacy in his novel *House of Sand and Fog* (1999), which in 2004 also became a searing motion picture. In 2001 *Andre Dubus: Tributes* was published; it gathers appreciations from a host of writers, many from the South.

WORKS: *The Lieutenant* (1967). *Separate Flights: A Novella and Seven Short Stories* (1975). *Adultery and Other Choices: Nine Short Stories and a Novella* (1977). *Finding a Girl in America: Ten Stories and a Novella* (1980). *The Times Are Never So Bad: A Novella and Eight Short Stories* (1983). *Land Where My Fathers Died* (1984). *Voices from the Moon* (1984). *We Don't Live Here Anymore* (1984). *The Last Worthless Evening: Four Novellas and Two Stories* (1986). *Blessings* (1987). *Selected Stories of Andre Dubus* (1988). *Broken Vessels* (1991). *Dancing After Hours* (1996). *Meditations from a Movable Chair* (1998). *Leap of the Heart,* ed. Ross Gresham (2003).

—JOSEPH M. FLORA

JAMES DUFF (1955–). Playwright and Hollywood screenwriter James Duff was born Daryl Wayne Rogers on September 3, 1955, in New Orleans, La. The adopted son of James Henry Duff and Blanche Ainsworth, Duff was raised in Texas. His father, who worked for Sears, Roebuck, and Co., often uprooted the family, moving from town to town, and Duff attended eleven different schools throughout Texas. Despite this transient lifestyle, the Duff family was active in the Southern Baptist Church and upheld conservative values, which Duff used as the antagonistic backdrop for his most celebrated play, *Home Front*. Set in Dallas on the eve and day of Thanksgiving 1973, *Home Front* depicts the return of Jeremy, a Vietnam veteran, to his suburban family.

Duff attended three years of college: a year and a half at Texas Tech University in Lubbock and a year and a half at Tarrant County Junior College. At Texas Tech, he acted in several plays, though his father opposed his majoring in theater because it was not likely he would make a living at it. After dropping out of college, Duff lived in Dallas from 1976 to 1981, working as a bartender, actor, and writer. He began his professional career as a playwright when Theater Three of Dallas and the Grimm Magician Players staged his *Breman Town Musicians, The Golden Goose,* and *The Firebird,* three as-yet-unpublished plays for children.

In 1981 Duff moved to New York, where he worked in bars and restaurants while pursuing a life in the theater. A year later, with the help of friends and a meager production budget, *The War at Home* was staged at the Carter Hotel. The play was subsequently performed in England at the Hampstead Theatre Club in June 1984. It returned to New York in January 1985 and ran at the Royale Theater, where it was retitled *Home Front*. Duff's second play, *A Quarrel of Sparrows,* was presented in Dallas in 1988, ran at the Cleveland Play House in 1992, and was off-Broadway a year later. But *Home Front* is to date his most successful work.

In 1989 Duff moved to Los Angeles and began writing for television. *Doing Time on Maple Drive* (1992), a television drama set in suburban middle America, revisits some of the themes of *Home Front,* as a family struggles to accept the homosexuality of its picture-perfect son. Unlike *Home Front, Doing Time on Maple Drive* ends happily, with the reconciliation of father and son after the son's unsuccessful suicide attempt. The screenplay of *Home Front,* written by Duff and under the original title *The War at Home,* was released by Avatar Entertainment in 1996. In the 1990s Duff wrote for several television programs, including *Felicity, Star Trek: Enterprise,* and *The Agency.* More recently, he has worked as creator, executive producer, and writer of *The D.A.* and *The Closer,* television series involving law enforcement.

WORKS: *Home Front* (1985). *A Quarrel of Sparrows* (1994).

—MATTHEW SPANGLER

JOHN DUFRESNE (1948–). Novelist and short-story writer John Dufresne was born in Worcester, Mass., on January 30, 1948. He attended public schools there and graduated from Worcester State College in 1970. He was a social worker and crisis intervention counselor from 1970 to 1982. He entered the University of Arkansas in 1982 and earned an M.F.A. in 1984. He held his first teaching job at Northeast Louisiana University (now the University of Louisiana–Monroe) from 1984 to 1987; he took graduate courses toward a Ph.D. at SUNY–Binghamton in 1987–88, but left to become an English instructor at Augusta College for 1988–89. Since 1989 he has worked at Florida International University, where he is now a full professor. He is married and has a son.

Dufresne won the *Transatlantic Review* Award in 1983, a PEN Syndicated Fiction Award in 1984, a *Yankee* magazine Fiction Award in 1988, and a Florida State Arts Council grant in 1992. With such other Florida writers as Dave Barry and Carl Hiaasen, he contributed a chapter to *Naked Came the Manatee,* a serial novel published over thirteen weeks in the *Miami Herald* in 1996.

Five of the thirteen stories in *The Way that Water Enters Stone* are postmodern versions of Faulkner/ Caldwell/Welty/O'Connor stories, in that Dufresne deconstructs the myths and stereotypes about the South and about "white trash" southerners the earlier authors helped to invent. His first novel, *Louisiana Power and Light,* expands the longest story in his collection, "The Fontana Gene," an account of a cursed family living in and around Monroe. His third novel, *Deep in the Shade of Paradise,* continues to chronicle the last of the Fontanas in a way reminiscent at once of *A Midsummer Night's Dream* in plot and *Tristram Shandy* in its digressions. All of Dufresne's works are marked by the rich textures of his language and the grace and compassion of his tragicomic vision.

WORKS: *The Way that Water Enters Stone* (1991). *Louisiana Power and Light* (1994). *Love Warps the Mind a Little* (1997). *Deep in the Shade of Paradise* (2002). *The Lie That Tells a Truth: A Guide to Writing Fiction* (2003). *Johnny Too Bad* (2005).

—DAVID K. JEFFREY

DANIEL DULANY, THE ELDER (1685–1753). Daniel Dulany the Elder, born in Queens County, Ireland, attended the University of Dublin before embarking for Maryland as an indentured servant in 1703. His services were bought by a prominent lawyer, who turned Dulany toward the law. After his term of service he rapidly established himself as a leading attorney.

Honors and wealth came his way in such plenitude that his life is an almost unparalleled example of the American success story. He first held elective offices but soon began accumulating the lucrative appointive posts possible in an age that tolerated plural office holding: the posts of attorney general, receiver general, chief judge in admiralty, chief probate judge, and councilor of state. In his private capacity he simultaneously practiced law, ran a mercantile business, engaged in iron manufacturing, and speculated in land. In all of these he prospered, but his land speculations proved a bonanza, raising a "handsome" fortune to a fabulous one before his death on September 6, 1753.

Dulany's literary work came early in his career. He wrote *The Right of the Inhabitants of Maryland to the Benefit of the English Laws* in the autumn of 1728 when the popularly elected house of the assembly battled the lord proprietor over the question of the extension of English statute law to the province. As a leader in the lower house Dulany supported the popular view in this pamphlet, notable for its early use of fundamental or natural law and its novel legal argument. Dulany premises the right of Englishmen to the rule of law, the common law compounded of the "Law of Nature, the Law of Reason, and the revealed Law of God." But, he argues, the depravity of men over the years necessitated the passage of statutes which declared, altered, and strengthened the common law. Accordingly, denial of this essential statute law rendered "Life, Liberties, and Properties Precarious."

WORKS: *The Right of the Inhabitants of Maryland to the Benefit of the English Laws* (1728).

—AUBREY C. LAND

DANIEL DULANY, THE YOUNGER (1722–1797). Eldest son of Daniel the Elder, Daniel Dulany the Younger was born in Annapolis, Md., on June 28, 1722. As heir of a well-to-do social and political leader, Dulany went to England for the most complete education available to a colonial: Eton, Cambridge, and the Inns of Court, where he was called to the bar of the Middle Temple. On his return to the province in 1747 he embarked in law practice that won him even greater acclaim than his father's, and his marriage in 1749 to Rebecca Tasker brought him into kinship with the squirearchy of Maryland and Virginia.

As a beneficiary of his father's wealth, young Dulany encountered few obstacles to his political advancement. Even his opponents admired his astute dealings with the tight but highly competitive elite that ruled Maryland. Within half a decade Dulany rose to the top in the political scramble. Curiously, he managed to command the respect of both leading political factions in Maryland.

During the Stamp Act troubles, Dulany presented the case for American rights in a brilliant pamphlet, *Considerations on the Propriety of Imposing Taxes in the British Colonies*, instantly reprinted throughout the colonies and in London. His reputation suffered no ill effects from a second pamphlet later in the same year, *The Right to the Tonnage*, which argued the lord proprietor's legal right to collect the unpopular ship taxes in the province. Dulany became such a power in the politics of equilibrium that the governor sarcastically dubbed him "the patriot councillor."

During the decade of his ascendancy Dulany added considerably to the family fortune and enhanced his reputation as "oracle of the law," quoted admiringly by Lord Chief Justice Camden. But the Revolution shattered his world forever. His two sons divided in loyalty, one to the crown and one to the patriot cause. Dulany himself became a neutral and went into permanent retirement until his death in Baltimore on March 17, 1797.

WORKS: *Considerations on the Propriety of Imposing Taxes in the British Colonies, For the Purpose of Raising a Revenue, By Act of Parliament* (1765). *The Right to the Tonnage* (1765).

—AUBREY C. LAND

HENRY DUMAS (1934–1968). Born on July 20, 1934, Henry Dumas lived in Sweet Home, Ark., until the age of ten, when he moved to Harlem in New York City. Upon graduation from Commerce High School in 1953, Dumas enrolled at City College, but dropped out to join the air force. First stationed at Lackland Air Force Base in San Antonio, Tex., Dumas later spent a year in the Middle East before his discharge in 1957.

Dumas married Loretta Ponton on September 24, 1955, and they had two children, David and Michael. In 1958 Dumas enrolled at Rutgers University, where he studied for two years, until he needed more time to work and care for his family and give further attention to the civil rights movement and his writing. From 1963 to 1964, Dumas worked as a printing machine operator at IBM, while continuing as a part-time student at Rutgers until 1965, when he left without graduating. Dumas later held a position as Hiram College's assistant director of Upward Bound. In 1967 he became the director of language workshops at Southern Illinois University's Experiment in Education, where he met the poet Eugene B. Redmond.

Despite the demands of his many other roles, Dumas edited and published numerous "little magazines," such as *Black Ikon, Anthologist, Untitled, Camel*, and *Hiram Poetry Review*, in which his own work appeared. In his writing, Dumas presents a powerfully mythic and often supernatural vision of the African American experience. Though he was quite prolific, his work was not published in book form until after his death, when Redmond began to collect and publish it. Dumas was shot and killed by an NYC Transit Authority policeman in a Harlem subway station on May 23, 1968, in a case of mistaken identity.

WORKS: *Poetry for My People* (1971); repr. as *Play Ebony, Play Ivory* (1974). *Ark of Bones and Other Stories* (1974). *Jonah and the Green Stone* (1976). *Rope of the Wind and Other Stories* (1979). *Goodbye, Sweetwater* (1988). *Knees of*

Natural Man: The Selected Poetry of Henry Dumas (1989). *Echo Tree: The Collected Short Fiction of Henry Dumas* (2003).

—AMANDA PAGE

JOSEPH DUMBLETON (fl. 1740–1750). Joseph Dumbleton was an author of newspaper verse in Virginia and, later, South Carolina during the first half of the eighteenth century. His identity remains an almost complete mystery, and the full name under which he published is known only because he attached the signature to his "Ode for St. Patric's Day" in lieu of his customary "J. Dumbleton." Indeed, most authors who, like Dumbleton, published in the *South Carolina Gazette* and the *Virginia Gazette*, left their work unsigned or used a pseudonym.

Dumbleton's limited poetic production is not original in its form or subject matter, but he clearly possessed a classical background and a lively sense of humor. One of his most famous pieces is the 1744 mock-heroic "The Paper Mill. Inscribed to Mr. Parks." In this poem, Dumbleton asks the citizens of Williamsburg, Va., to donate their rags to Mr. Parks for his paper mill; however, the poem is full of double entendres and suggestive metaphors that give it a burlesque quality. Dumbleton's other major production is "A Rhapsody on Rum," which was first published in the *South Carolina Gazette* in 1749 (suggesting that Dumbleton had taken up residence there by this time). Like "The Paper Mill," the "Rhapsody" is an energetic mock-heroic that showcases, through allusions and puns, the author's knowledge and sense of humor. Though Dumbleton's poetry is not particularly noteworthy for its literary quality, his work gives readers an illuminating glimpse into aspects of life and culture in the colonial South.

WORKS: "A Transient View of Solomon's Pursuit after Content," *Virginia Gazette*, ca. 1740, credited to the *Virginia Gazette* by *General Magazine and Historical Chronicle* 1 (Apr. 1741): 276–78. "The Paper Mill. Inscribed to Mr. Parks," *Virginia Gazette*, July 26, 1744; repr. in *Virginia Magazine of History and Biography* 7 (Apr. 1900): 442–44. "Ode for St. Patric's Day. Humbly Inscribed to the President and Members of the Irish Society," *South Carolina Gazette*, Mar. 20, 1749, p. 1. "A Rhapsody on Rum," *South Carolina Gazette*, Mar. 20, 1749, p. 1; also printed in *Gentleman's Magazine* 19 (Sept. 1749): 424. "The Northern Miracle. A Tale," *South Carolina Gazette*, Jan. 8, 1750, pp. 1–2.

—BRYAN C. SINCHE

ALICE DUNBAR-NELSON (1875–1935). Alice Ruth Moore Dunbar-Nelson's main claim to fame was her brief marriage to poet Paul Laurence Dunbar. Although she did not achieve the financial stability and social cachet she desired until the last few years of her life, Dunbar-Nelson worked her entire life as a writer, educator, newspaper columnist, public speaker, and social activist.

Alice Ruth Moore, the second child of Patricia Wright and Joseph Moore, was born in New Orleans on July 19, 1875. A spirited young woman, she attended Straight University (now Dillard University) in New Orleans, graduating in 1892. Although she spent most of her adult life in the Mid-Atlantic, the light-skinned, racially mixed Dunbar-Nelson always felt a deep connection to New Orleans, and much of her fiction centers on Creole life and culture in Louisiana. In 1895 she published her first book, *Violets and Other Tales*, a collection of poems and short stories that received generally positive reviews. Her work was also published in various newspapers and magazines, and Paul Dunbar sent the young woman a letter after seeing a poem and photo in the *Monthly Review* in 1897. The two corresponded by mail for a year. They married in 1898, and moved to Washington, D.C. The marriage was tempestuous, ending in divorce in 1902. (He died in 1906.)

Dunbar-Nelson was active in numerous social movements, including the struggles for women's suffrage and education. She studied education at Cornell University and co-founded schools for underprivileged and delinquent African American girls in New York and Delaware. She also advocated the introduction of African American history and literature into the curriculum.

After a brief, secret marriage to Arthur Hope Callas in 1910, Dunbar-Nelson married for the last time in 1916, to journalist and activist Robert J. Nelson. Dunbar-Nelson's journalism represents the bulk of her published writing; she continued to write poetry, short stories, and plays throughout her life, but they were largely rejected by publishers.

Dunbar-Nelson died of heart failure in 1935.

WORKS: *Violets and Other Tales* (1895). *The Goodness of St. Rocque and Other Stories* (1899). *Masterpieces of Negro Eloquence* (1914). *The Dunbar Speaker and Entertainer: The Poet and His Song* (1920).

—KRISTINA D. BOBO

WILMA DYKEMAN (1920–). Wilma Dykeman was born on May 20, 1920, in Asheville, N.C., to Willard Jerome and Bonnie Cushman Cole Dykeman. She grew up in the French Broad River valley in the mountains of western North Carolina, the only child of a mother whose family had lived in the southern Appalachians since the eighteenth century. After graduating from Biltmore Junior College in Asheville, Dykeman earned a B.A. in speech from Northwestern University in 1940.

After graduating from Northwestern, Dykeman married James R. Stokely, Jr., of Newport, Tenn., a poet and nonfiction writer, as well as a member of the influential Tennessee farming family that created the Stokely canning company. For many years, the couple maintained homes in Asheville and Newport, as well as traveling extensively in Asia and Europe. They had two sons: Dykeman Cole Stokely and James (Jim) R. Stokely III. They also collaborated on a number of writing projects, including *Neither Black Nor White* and *Seeds of Southern Change,* books directly concerned with social progress in the South, especially with regard to race. During her long and successful writing career, Dykeman also addressed these concerns as a lecturer and adjunct professor (1975–95) at the University of Tennessee at Knoxville.

One of Dykeman's best known books, however, was her first. *The French Broad,* in the well-known "Rivers of America" series, was a characteristic mix of history, sociology, and biography (of Thomas Wolfe, among others), reflecting Dykeman's wide-ranging interests. Even Dykeman's fiction—notably *The Tall Woman* and *The Far Family*—reflects her lifelong concern with the social evolution of the South, specifically the southern mountains. In addition to her biographies and fiction, Dykeman's fascination with the southern Appalachians manifested itself in two book-length historical studies, *The Border States* and *Tennessee: A Bicentennial History.* She was named the state historian of Tennessee in 1980.

In a wide variety of genres, Wilma Dykeman has examined the way in which significant global issues—race, gender, the environment—have manifested themselves in her own local arena, the mountains of western North Carolina and eastern Tennessee. In a career spanning decades, she has sought both to understand, through her fiction, and promote, through her nonfiction, the social evolution of her mountain home.

WORKS: *The French Broad* (1955). *Neither Black Nor White,* with James Stokely (1957). *Seeds of Southern Change: The Life of Will Alexander,* with James Stokely (1962). *The Tall Woman* (1962). *The Southern Appalachian Region: A Survey* (1962). *The Far Family* (1966). *Prophet of Plenty: The First Ninety Years of W. D. Weatherford* (1966). *Look to This Day* (1968). *The Border States: Kentucky, North Carolina, Tennessee, Virginia, West Virginia,* with James Stokely et al. (1968). *Return the Innocent Earth* (1973). *Too Many People, Too Little Love* (1974). *Tennessee: A Bicentennial History* (1975). *Highland Homeland: The People of the Great Smokies*, with Jim Stokely (1978); revised as *At Home in the Smokies* (1984). *Tennessee*, with Edward Schell. *Appalachian Mountains* with Dykeman Stokely and Clyde H. Smith (1980). *Explorations* (1984). *Haunting Memories: Echoes and Images of Tennessee's Past*, with Christine P. Patterson (1996). *Montgomery Morning*, with James Stokely.

—TERRY ROBERTS

TONY EARLEY (1961–). After two of Tony Earley's stories, "Charlotte" and "The Prophet of Jupiter," appeared in *Harper's* in 1992 and 1993, the *New Yorker* featured him in its best young fiction writers issue, and *Granta* selected him as one of the twenty best young novelists in America—all before his first novel, *Jim the Boy*, was completed. Though he was born in San Antonio, Tex., on June 15, 1961, Earley's family soon relocated to Rutherford County, N.C., which has provided the setting for most of his work. "I consider myself a southern writer," Earley says, "because that's where I'm from and that's what I write about. More specifically, I suppose, I'm a North Carolina writer. Even my stories set in other places are about North Carolinians."

Earley graduated with a degree in English from Warren Wilson College, and spent time as a newspaperman before obtaining his M.F.A. in creative writing at the University of Alabama. In 1993 he married Sarah Bell, and the couple moved to Pittsburgh, where she attended seminary. Earley's short-story collection *Here We Are in Paradise* was published in 1994. It was his wife's reading of *Charlotte's Web* aloud in bed that inspired *Jim the Boy*, also a work of innocence and profound sadness. *Jim the Boy* was published in 2000, and received much critical attention, including the cover of the *New York Times Book Review*. A nonfiction collection, *Somehow Form a Family*, appeared in 2001. Earley now lives in Nashville, Tenn., where he teaches at Vanderbilt University.

WORKS: *Here We Are in Paradise* (1994). *Jim the Boy* (2000). *Somehow Form a Family* (2001).

—ROB TRUCKS

CHARLES EDWARD EATON (1916–). Charles Edward Eaton was born on June 25, 1916, in Winston-Salem, N.C., to Mary and Oscar Benjamin Eaton, a ten-term mayor of the city. Early in his childhood Eaton displayed an interest in writing, an interest he continued to pursue in the years following and one that brought its first significant recognition when, during high school, he won a statewide essay competition.

Eaton began his college studies with a year at Duke University (1932–33). He transferred to the University of North Carolina, from which he graduated in 1936. Following a year of graduate work in philosophy at Princeton, Eaton spent the 1937–38 school year teaching at a high school in Puerto Rico, after which he returned to the United States and the M.A. program in English at Harvard. During his two years at Harvard, he studied under Robert Frost, with whom he developed a lifelong friendship.

Eaton taught at the University of Missouri in 1940–42. In 1942 he published *Bright Plain*, his first book of poems. Unable because of poor vision to serve in the military during World War II, he spent the years 1942–46 as United States vice-consul in Rio de Janeiro, Brazil. In 1946 he returned to Chapel Hill, where he began teaching creative writing at the university. In 1950 Eaton married Isobel Patterson, and in 1952 he and his wife moved to Connecticut.

Dividing his time between North Carolina and Connecticut for the next three decades, Eaton left teaching and pursued his writing full-time. In that time and in the years since, he has been unusually prolific, publishing an impressive array of poetry, fiction, and nonfiction. In 1980 he moved back to Chapel Hill, where he continues to live and write.

WORKS: *Bright Plain* (1942). *The Shadow of the Swimmer* (1951). *The Greenhouse in the Garden* (1956). *Write Me from Rio* (1959). *Countermoves* (1963). *On the Edge of the Knife* (1970). *The Girl from Ipanema* (1972). *The Man in the Green Chair* (1977). *The Case of the Missing Photographs* (1978). *Colophon of the Rover* (1980). *The Thing King* (1983). *The Work of the Wrench* (1985). *New and Selected Poems, 1942–1987* (1987). *New and Selected Stories, 1959–1989* (1989). *A Guest on Mild Evenings* (1991). *A Lady of Pleasure* (1993). *The Country of the Blue* (1994). *The Fox and I* (1996). *The Scout in Summer* (1999). *The Jogger by the Sea* (2000). *The Man from Buena Vista: Selected Nonfiction, 1944–2000* (2001). *Between the Devil and the Deep Blue Sea* (2002). *The Work of the Sun* (2004).

—JOHN N. SOMERVILLE, JR.

WILLIAM EDDIS (1738–1825). A native of England, William Eddis came to Maryland in 1769 under the patronage of Governor Robert Eden to be a surveyor and customs searcher. With Eden, he traveled throughout the Chesapeake area and rose in the bureaucracy to be a commissioner of finance. Having a love of literature and the theater from an early age, Eddis became active in the Homony Club in Annapolis—in which he became the poet laureate and eventually president. He was also active in the Jockey Club and the Annapolis races.

A consummate letter writer, Eddis wrote friends in England about Maryland geography, history, people, agriculture, politics, and events leading to and during the Revolutionary War. In 1792 he published his collection of correspondence as *Letters from America, Historical and Descriptive; Comprising Occurrences from 1769 to 1777.*

Eddis viewed the increasing conflict between the colonies and England with sympathy for the grievances of the colonists but with cautionary comments. In an anonymous poem published in the *Annapolis Gazette* in 1772, he expressed his desire that Heaven would bring about a cessation of jarring factionalism and diffuse peace over the land. Writing anonymously in February 1775, as "A Friend to Amity," he recommended that the colonists practice reason and moderation. In July 1775, Eddis lamented the "popular fury" of persons setting fire to a ship as "burnt offering to liberty." In a letter dated July 8, 1776, he described the Declaration of Independence and contemplated "with horror the complicated miseries which appear ready to overwhelm this devoted country." Holding to his Loyalist sympathies, Eddis left Maryland in June 1777. Subsequently, he received a modest allowance from the British government to compensate him for his losses when he was forced to leave his employment in Maryland and give up his salaries. He lived another forty-eight years in England.

WORKS: *Letters from America, Historical and Descriptive; Comprising Occurrences from 1769 to 1777, Inclusive* (1792).

—RICHARD D. RUST

CLYDE EDGERTON (1944–). Clyde Carlyle Edgerton was born on May 20, 1944, in Durham, N.C., and grew up nearby in the small community of Bethesda. Although he was an only child, he was raised among twenty-three aunts and uncles and many cousins. His reading of Hemingway as a sophomore at the University of North Carolina at Chapel Hill inspired him to become a high school English teacher, but another dream—advanced by his membership in the university's Air Force ROTC—beckoned. After gaining an English-education degree in 1966, he became a pilot for five years, serving as a forward air controller in Southeast Asia from 1970 to 1971.

Back in Chapel Hill in 1973, Edgerton completed an M.A. in teaching and accepted an English faculty position at his old high school in Durham County. He returned to UNC in 1974 for a doctoral program, and accepted a faculty position at Campbell University in 1977. When his first novel, *Raney,* was published in 1985, the Campbell administration suggested that the novel did not promote the goals and purposes of Campbell, a conservative Baptist institution, and withheld his contract. Edgerton resigned and moved on to St. Andrews Presbyterian College, where he taught until 1989. At St. Andrews he wrote two more novels, *Walking across Egypt* and *The Floatplane Notebooks,* the latter based on his military service.

In 1998, after nine years of full-time writing and four more novels, including *Killer Diller, In Memory of Junior, Redeye: A Western,* and *Where Trouble Sleeps,* Edgerton began teaching creative writing at the University of North Carolina at Wilmington. His eighth novel, *Lunch at the Piccadilly,* was published in 2003. Edgerton's humor and his talent as a singer and guitarist make him a popular figure at literary events.

He has received a Guggenheim Fellowship, a Lyndhurst Fellowship, and the North Carolina Award for Literature. Five of his novels have been selected as "Notable Books" by the *New York Times. Walking across Egypt* and *Killer Diller* have been made into motion pictures. His first marriage, to Susan Ketchin, ended in divorce; his daughter, Catherine, is the product of this marriage. He lives with his wife Kristina and two young sons, Nathaniel and Ridley, in Wilmington, N.C., where he continues to teach at UNCW.

WORKS: *Raney* (1986). *Walking across Egypt* (1988). *The Floatplane Notebooks* (1989). *Killer Diller* (1992). *In Memory of Junior* (1994). *Redeye: A Western* (1995). *Where Trouble Sleeps* (1997). *Lunch at the Piccadilly* (2003). *Solo: My Adventures in the Air* (2005).

—R. STERLING HENNIS

RANDOLPH EDMONDS (1900–1983). Widely known as the "dean of the black academic theater," Randolph Edmonds was born in Lawrenceville, Va. After graduating from the high school department of St. Paul's Normal and Industrial School, he received degrees from Oberlin College and Columbia University. He received a Rockefeller Fund Fellowship and studied at the Yale University School of Drama. Subsequently, he studied drama in England, Ireland, Scotland, and Wales on a Rosenwald Fund Fellowship. He took courses at Dublin University and at the London School of Speech Training and Dramatic Arts.

For more than forty years Edmonds was associated with predominantly black colleges as a teacher of English and drama and as a director of drama. These institutions included Morgan College, Dillard University, and Florida Agricultural and Mechanical College.

Edmonds founded the two most outstanding drama organizations among black colleges and universities: the Negro Intercollegiate Drama Association and the National Association of Dramatic and Speech Arts. He organized high school associations in Louisiana and served as chief consultant for associations throughout the South. He received a Doctor of Letters from Bethune-Cookman College.

Edmonds's works are chiefly of three types: folk plays, problem plays, and plays of fantasy. His many short plays appear in numerous anthologies.

WORKS: *Shades and Shadows* (1930). *Six Plays for a Negro Theatre* (1934). *The Land of Cotton and Other Plays* (1942).

—ELAINE MITCHELL NEWSOME

MURRELL EDMUNDS (1898–1981). A native of Halifax, Va., Thomas Murrell Edmonds was born on March 23, 1898, to John Richard and Willie Thurman Murrell Edmunds. Among his ancestors were several prominent Virginians, including two members of the United States Congress and a judge who sat on the first Virginia Supreme Court. Edmunds received his undergraduate degree in 1917 from the University of Virginia, where he was a member of the Raven Society. After a year's service in the U.S. Army during World War I, he returned to Charlottesville to study law. He excelled in law school, earning a spot on the editorial staff of the *Virginia Law Review.* After being admitted to the Virginia bar in 1921, he taught English for a year at Episcopal High School in Alexandria, Va., and then began his law practice, clerking in Virginia circuit courts and serving for a brief time as an assistant Commonwealth's attorney.

In 1926 Edmunds left the law to pursue a career as a writer, driven, as he put it, by his devotion to "writing books of fiction, drama, and verse, all carefully attuned to history's evolving mandate: the gradual relaxation of old patterns and tensions and a forthright new articulation of the eternal Brotherhood of Man." Especially in his short stories and novels, Edmunds sought to work out this thesis within a southern setting, treating familiar regional themes of race and politics in light of his historical theories and his belief in the possibility of social change. Edmunds's work is at once unsentimental and idealistic, fully aware of the South's benighted past but hopeful of genuine progress, especially in relationships between African Americans and whites. Edmunds realized modest success as a writer, publishing several short stories and poems in little magazines and frequently contributing to anthologies of regional literature and verse. In 1963 the *Arizona Quarterly* awarded him its annual award for poetry.

WORKS: *Music-makers* (1927). *Earthenware* (1930). *Sojourn among Shadows* (1936). *Between the Devil* (1939). *Time's Laughter in Their Ears* (1942). *Red, White and Black* (1945). *Behold, Thy Brother* (1950). *Moon of My Delight* (1961). *Passionate Journey to Winter* (1962). *Laurel for the Undefeated* (1964). *Beautiful upon the Mountains* (1966). *Shadow of a Great Rock* (1969). *Dim Footprints along a Hazardous Trail* (1971). *Reservoir* (1977).

—H. COLLIN MESSER

HARRY STILLWELL EDWARDS (1855–1938). Short-story writer, poet, novelist, newspaperman, and political activist, Harry Stillwell Edwards was born on April 23, 1855, in Macon, Ga. Tutored in private schools, at age fifteen he left Macon for Washington, D.C., where he served as a clerk in a branch of the Treasury Department. Three years later he returned to Macon, graduating with a Bachelor of Laws from Mercer University in 1876. On January 13, 1881, he married Mary Roxie Lane of Sparta, Ga.; they had four children.

From 1881 to 1888, Edwards held a number of editorial positions with Macon newspapers, including that of co-owner and editor of the *Macon Telegraph and Messenger* and *Macon Evening News,* before devoting full time to writing. In 1904 he was delegate-at-large to the Republican National Convention in Chicago, seconding the nomination of his friend Theodore Roosevelt. Other achievements included being appointed postmaster in Macon (1900–13) and federal district referee in Georgia by President McKinley, helping to establish the Georgia School of Technology, running for the U.S. Senate in 1920 as an independent candidate, and, in 1924, promoting the Stone Mountain Memorial half-dollar. In demand as a speaker, he lectured on the Lyceum Circuit.

Edwards's humorous sketches first appeared in Macon newspapers, but his first well-received short story, "Elmer Brown's Backslide," appeared in *Harper's Magazine* in 1885. Of his estimated hundred known short stories, sketches, dialect verses, and stories for children, at least sixty appeared in the nation's best-known periodicals, including the *Century, Scribner's, Life, Atlantic Monthly, Saturday Evening Post,* and *Youth's Companion.* In addition, Edwards composed music for several of his short poems in Negro dialect.

In 1889 Edwards published his first collection, *The Two Runaways and Other Stories.* In 1896 his first of two novels, *Sons and Fathers,* was selected by the *Chicago Record* to receive its first prize of $10,000. Edwards is best known for *Eneas Africanus,* a short story told in letters about a faithful, old Negro who was guardian of treasured family heirlooms; it first appeared in the *Macon News* in 1919. To date, it has sold more than three million copies.

Edwards was elected to the American Academy of Arts and Letters in 1913, the only southerner to be so honored at that time. Following the death of his wife in 1922, he lived at Holly Bluff, his country home, a few miles from Macon. His popular column, "Coming Down My Creek," appeared in the *Atlanta Journal* from 1922 until his death, at age 84, on October 22, 1938.

WORKS: *The Two Runaways and Other Stories* (1889). *Sons and Fathers* (1896). *The Marbeau Cousins* (1897). *His Defense and Other Stories* (1899). *The Fifth Dimension* (1900). *Bypaths in Dixie: Folk Tales of the South* (1912). *Eneas Africanus* (1919). *The Adventures of a Parrot* (1920). *Brother Sim's Mistake* (1920). *Isam's Spectacles* (1920). *Just Sweethearts* (1920). *Eneas Africanus, Defendant* (1921). *The Blue Hen's Chickens* (1924). *The Tenth Generation* (1928). *Little Legends of the Land* (1930).

—GARY KERLEY

GEORGE CARY EGGLESTON (1839–1911). George Cary Eggleston did not limit his literary talents to any one age group. He wrote juvenile instructional books, conscientious historical accounts, historical fiction, and novels; he also regularly published articles in several high-profile journals, edited collections of poetry and fiction, and acted as literary editor for such influential magazines as the *Evening Post* and the *New York World.*

The Egglestons had settled in Virginia in 1635 (and the Carys in 1750). George Cary Eggleston was born on November 26, 1839, in Vevay, Ind. In 1856 he moved to Amelia County, Va., where he lived for nine years, attending Richmond College in 1856–57, studying law, and eventually going to war for the Confederacy. At the war's end, disillusioned and in need of employment, Eggleston moved north to Cairo, Ill., and eventually settled in New York, where he became associated with several of the more prominent journals, including the *Brooklyn Daily Union* (1870–71) and *Hearth and Home* and *American Homes* magazines (1872–75). He served as literary editor of the *Evening Post* (1875–81), reader at Harper publishing house (1881–85), and editor of the *Commercial Advertiser* (1885–89) and the *New York World* (1889–1900). After his retirement from the *World,* Eggleston continued to publish articles and books. He died on April 14, 1911.

Eggleston was a prolific writer. His writing is generally of the popular sort, given to sentimentality and patriotism, conspicuously concerned with the South (most often using Virginia as its backdrop), and frequently centered on the Civil War. Eggleston's narratives look back nostalgically to the times before the war, exemplified in such works as his *Dorothy South: A Love Story of Virginia Just before the War* and *Love Is the Sum of It All: A Plantation Romance.* His Civil War fiction portrays the war's participants, both Confederate and Union, in ultimately admirable terms; his philosophical perspective remained positive and uplifting throughout his life. Despite his idealism, Eggleston is not afraid of recording and decrying greed, moral corruption, and inhumanity, his courage stemming from his belief that a writer must remain true to even the dark aspects of human nature, dealing "wholesomely with the unwholesome things of life." Deeply moral, patriotic, and proud of his heritage, Eggleston was a man who believed in the redemptive power of literature and its ability to reform.

WORKS: *How to Educate Yourself with or without Masters* (1872). *A Man of Honor* (1873). *The Big Brother* (1875). *How to Make a Living* (1875). *A Rebel's Recollections* (1875). *Captain Sam* (1876). *The Signal Boys* (1877). *Red Eagle and the Wars with the Creek Indians of Alabama* (1878). *The Wreck of the Red Bird* (1882). *Strange Stories from History for Young People* (1885). Ed., *American War Ballads and Lyrics* (1889). *Juggernaut, a Veiled Record*, with Dolores Marbourg (1891). Ed., *Liber Scriptorum I*, with Rossiter Johnson and John Champlin (1893). *Southern Soldier Stories* (1898). *The Last of the Flatboats: A Story of the Mississippi and Its Interesting Family of Rivers* (1900). *American Immortals* (1901). *Camp Venture: A Story of the Virginia Mountains* (1901). *A Carolina Cavalier: A Romance of the American Revolution* (1901). *The Bale Marked Circle X: A Blockade Running Adventure* (1902). *Dorothy South: A Love Story of Virginia Just before the War* (1902). *The First of the Hoosiers, Edward Eggleston* (1903). *The Master of Warlock: A Virginia War Story* (1903). *Captain in the Ranks* (1904). *Evelyn Byrd* (1904). *Running the River: A Story of Adventure and Success* (1904). *A Daughter of the South: A War's End Romance* (1905). *Life in the Eighteenth Century* (1905). *Our First Century* (1905). *Blind Alleys: A Novel of Nowadays* (1906). *Jack Shelby: A Story of the Indiana Backwoods* (1906). *Long Knives: The Story of How They Won the West* (1907). *Love Is the Sum of It All: A Plantation Romance* (1907). *Two Gentlemen of Virginia: A Novel of the Old Regime in the Old Dominion* (1908). *The Warrens of Virginia* (1908). *Irene of the Mountains: A Romance of Old Virginia* (1909). *Westover of Wanalah: A Story of Love and Life in Old Virginia* (1910). *The History of the Confederate War, Its Causes and Its Conduct: A Narrative and Critical History*, 2 vols. (1910). *Recollections of a Varied Life* (1910). *What Happened at Quasi: The Story of a Carolina Cruise* (1911).

—JOHN T. BICKLEY

JOHN EHLE (1925–). John Marsden Ehle, Jr., was born in Asheville, N.C., on December 13, 1925. He served in the U.S. Army during World War II, then earned his B.A. in 1949 from the University of North Carolina at Chapel Hill, where he majored in the Department of Radio, Television, and Motion Pictures. In 1952 he received an M.A. in drama there. Ehle married Gail Oliver on August 30, 1951. They were divorced in 1967, and later that year Ehle married British actress Rosemary Harris. The couple has one child, Jennifer Anne (born in 1969), also an actress.

From 1949 to 1962 Ehle worked as writer-producer in the communications center at the University of North Carolina at Chapel Hill and taught (1952–62) in his home department. From 1962 to 1964, he served on Governor Terry Sanford's staff as a special assistant. In that capacity Ehle conceived and helped establish the North Carolina Governor's School, the nation's first such program; the North Carolina School for the Arts; and the North Carolina Fund, the first statewide antipoverty program in the United States. Under Governor James B. Hunt, Jr., he subsequently initiated the North Carolina School of Science and Mathematics. His public service during the 1960s, before he turned to writing full-time, also included membership on the White House Group on Domestic Affairs (1964–66) and on the first National Council on the Humanities (1966–70), along with a year at the Ford Foundation as a program officer.

Ehle's writing career began at the University of North Carolina with a set of twenty-six half-hour radio dramas, the American Adventure series, broadcast by the National Association of Educational Broadcasters and by NBC during 1952 and 1953. His first novel, *Move Over, Mountain,* grew out of a short story that Paul Green encouraged him to expand. With the publication of his third novel, *Lion on the Hearth,* Ehle began to explore what has remained his principal subject: the history, landscape, people, and culture of his native region, the mountains of western North Carolina. His eight novels depicting the Wright, King, and Plover families over three centuries have made him a major figure in Appalachian literature, but Ehle is also the author of several books of nonfiction, most notably *The Free Men,* an account of the civil rights struggle in Chapel Hill, and *Trail of Tears.* His writing has earned him many awards, including the Sir Walter Raleigh Prize (on five occasions), the Mayflower Cup for *The Free Men,* the Lillian Smith Award for *The Winter People,* and the Thomas Wolfe Award for *Last One Home.*

WORKS: *Move Over, Mountain* (1957). *The Survivor* (1958). *Kingstree Island* (1959). *Shepherd of the Streets* (1960). *Lion on the Hearth* (1961). *The Land Breakers* (1964). *The Free Men* (1965). *The Road* (1967). *Time of Drums* (1970). *The Journey of August King* (1971). *The Cheeses and Wines of England and France, with Notes on Irish Whiskey* (1972). *The Changing of the Guard* (1974). *The Winter People* (1982). *Last One Home* (1984). *Trail of Tears* (1988). *The Widow's Trial* (1989). *Dr. Frank: Living with Frank Porter Graham* (1993). *The Road* (1998).

—JOHN LANG

LONNE ELDER III (1931–1996). Lonne Elder was born in Americus, Ga., but was raised by an aunt in New Jersey following his parents' untimely deaths. He is best known as a playwright and a screenwriter.

Elder was drafted into the army before completing his freshman year at New Jersey State Teachers College. While in the military, he met poet Robert Hayden, who encouraged him to pursue writing. After being discharged, he moved to New York City and joined the Harlem Writer's Guild.

In New York, Elder roomed with playwright Douglas Turner Ward, whose friendship influenced his artistic turn toward drama. Elder's first play, *A Hysterical Turtle in a Rabbit's Race,* was written in 1961 and remains unpublished. In 1963 Elder married Mary Gross, and in 1964 they had a son. In his art, Elder moved to rendering more gripping portraits of the black family, as in his 1965 drama *Ceremonies in Dark Old Men.*

In 1965 Elder won a fellowship to study drama and filmmaking at Yale University, but his marriage was troubled, and he divorced in 1967. He remarried in 1970, wedding Judith Ann Johnson, who had played a minor character in a production of *Ceremonies.*

At the height of his career as a dramatist, Elder turned his attention to screenwriting. Among his many acclaimed screenplays was the 1972 ABC adaptation of the children's book *Sounder.* Elder also wrote for NBC, including the made-for-television movie *A Woman Called Moses* (1978), starring Cicely Tyson. In addition, he wrote the screenplay for *Bustin' Loose* for Universal Pictures in 1981. Elder died at the age of sixty-nine. He had three children. Several of Elder's plays remain unpublished.

WORKS: *Ceremonies in Dark Old Men* (produced 1965, published 1969). *Charades on East Fourth Street* (produced 1967, published 1971).

—TOMEIKO R. ASHFORD

SARAH BARNWELL ELLIOTT (1848–1928). Born in Savannah, Ga., Sarah Barnwell Elliott was the daughter of Stephen Elliott, the first Episcopal bishop of Georgia. In 1871 she moved with other family members to Sewanee, Tenn., home of the University of the South; her father was one of its founders. She lived in Sewanee much of the rest of her life, with the exception of 1895–1902, when she lived in New York.

Elliott's principal educational opportunity came in 1886 when she attended summer lectures at Johns Hopkins. In that year her first story ("Jack Watson—A Character Study") was published, and she began a visit to Europe and the Holy Land, which she described in a series of sixteen travel letters printed in the *Louisville Courier-Journal* (January 9–August 27, 1887).

Elliott's first novels dealt with issues of faith, but with *Jerry,* serialized in *Scribner's* in 1890–91 and published in book form the following year, she turned more to the mountains as a subject. The title character, a boy from the Cumberland mountains, escapes a brutal father and stepmother, goes to the West, is adopted by a gold prospector, and is eventually corrupted by mercenary interests. The novel, sometimes described as an early example of naturalism in American literature, proved to be Elliott's most popular. *The Durket Sperret,* a later novel, is set in the mountains near Sewanee and depicts some interaction between the mountaineers and the university students. Some reviewers thought its depiction of mountain life superior to that of the more celebrated Mary Noailles Murfree.

Besides her novels, Elliott wrote some forty short stories, many of which were published in such magazines as *Harper's*, *Harper's Bazaar*, *McClure's*, *Scribner's*, *Youth's Companion*, and *Independent*. In 1899 eight of these were collected as *An Incident and Other Happenings*. Elliott's one venture into nonfiction was her biography of native Tennessean Sam Houston.

In time Elliott became active in the movement to obtain voting rights for women. In 1912 she was elected president of the Tennessee Equal Suffrage Association, serving until 1914. She died at Sewanee on August 30, 1928.

WORKS: *The Felmeres* (1879). *A Simple Heart* (1887). *Jerry* (1891). *John Paget* (1893). *The Durket Sperret* (1898). *An Incident and Other Happenings* (1899). *Sam Houston* (1900). *The Making of Jane* (1901).

—ALLISON R. ENSOR

WILLIAM ELLIOTT (1788–1863). The eldest son of William and Phoebe Waight Elliott, born in Beaufort, S.C., on April 27, 1788, William Elliott received his education in the schools at Beaufort and at Beaufort College. He also attended Harvard University and received his A.B. and A.M. there. At an early age he acquired a sportsman's taste for hunting and fishing. The broad waters of Port Royal Sound became the scene for his extraordinary tales of harpooning the devil-fish. These colorful sketches were to provide him with a reputation as a writer on rural sports.

Elliott served for eighteen years as representative and senator in the state legislature. He aligned himself with the Unionists against nullification and secession. In 1832 he resigned from the state senate rather than bow to a mandate from his constituents who had instructed him to vote for nullification of the federal tariff laws.

Following his father and grandfather, Elliott became a planter in the Beaufort area, where his plantations produced large crops of rice and cotton. Elliott became widely known for his leadership and influence in agricultural circles and spoke frequently to agricultural societies. He wrote articles on agriculture, advocating better farming practices and crop diversification.

Elliott is best known as a writer of sporting sketches, which were collected and published in 1846 as *Carolina Sports by Land and Water Including Incidents of Devil-Fishing, Wild Cat, Deer and Bear Hunting, Etc.* The sketches, many of which had been published in Charleston newspapers, are lively accounts of his own hunting and fishing experiences. The book has been published in six separate editions and one reprint edition. Elliott also wrote a five-act drama based on the sixteenth-century conspiracy of John Lewis de Fiesco, a Genoese nobleman, against the Dorias, the ruling family of Genoa. The drama, entitled *Fiesco: A Tragedy*, was privately published in 1850.

Elliott died in Charleston, S.C., on February 3, 1863.

WORKS: *Address to the People of St. Helena Parish* (1832). *Examination of Mr. Edmund Rhett's Agricultural Address: On the Question "Who Is the Producer?"* (1841). *The Planter Vindicated: His Claims Examined to Be Considered a Direct Producer: The Chief Producer: And Chief Tax-Payer of South Carolina* (1842). *Carolina Sports by Land and Water Including Incidents of Devil-Fishing, Wild Cat, Deer and Bear Hunting, Etc.* (1846). *Anniversary Address of the State Agricultural Society of South Carolina, Delivered in the Hall of the House of Representatives, November 30, 1848* (1849). *Address Delivered by Special Request before the St. Paul's Agricultural Society* (1850). *Fiesco: A Tragedy* (1850). *Letters of Agricola* (1852). *Report of the Honorable William Elliott, Commissioner of the State of South Carolina to the Universal Exhibition of Paris* (1856). *Address to the Imperial and Central Agricultural Society of France, Read before Them at Paris, July 4, 1855* (1857). "A Trip to Cuba," *Russell's Magazine*, 2, 3 (Oct.–Dec. 1857; Jan.–Feb., Apr. 1858).

—B. N. SKARDON

RALPH ELLISON (1913?–1994). Ralph Waldo Ellison was born on March 1, 1913 (?), the son of Ida and Lewis, an ice and coal dealer. His brother, Herbert, was born in June 1916, just weeks before their father died of injuries resulting from a workplace accident.

Ellison studied music from an early age, and he enrolled in Tuskegee University's music school in 1933 to become a symphony conductor., training there with William L. Dawson. In Tuskegee's library he stumbled across T. S. Eliot's "The Waste Land." By 1936 he had met Langston Hughes in New York City; a year later he met Richard Wright. Under the influence of Hughes and Wright he began to explore modern literature and the radical Left movement for political and social justice.

In the 1940s Ellison published essays and reviews in *New Masses, Negro Quarterly, Direction, New Republic,* and *Antioch Review.* He also wrote short fiction using folklore and the techniques of social realism and surrealism. In 1947 he published a short story called "Battle Royal" that served as the first chapter to his epic novel *Invisible Man.* More than any single work of American fiction, *Invisible Man* has embodied the anguish and beauty of African American life, the historic and intellectual struggle to tame injustice, and the fundamental crisis of modern existence, articulated in a formal narrative structure of elegance and refinement. *Invisible Man* won the National Book Award for 1952.

Ellison continued his career by publishing two collections of highly regarded essays: *Shadow and Act* and *Going to the Territory.* In the face of a generation of criticisms, he held fast to his belief that "most American whites are culturally part Negro American without even realizing it."

Ellison's first marriage, to Rose Poindexter, an actress, ended in 1945. In 1946, he married Fanny McConnell Buford, who supported him financially and intellectually during the writing of *Invisible Man.* He and Fanny remained married until his death of cancer in New York City on April 16, 1994. Ellison's literary estate published portions of his unfinished fiction, posthumously called *Juneteenth.* In the tale of an orphaned boy named Bliss who is raised by Hickman, a jazz musician turned preacher, Ellison reveals the folds of American life with his inimitable style and considerable irony.

WORKS: *Invisible Man* (1952). *Shadow and Act* (1964). *Going to the Territory* (1986). *The Collected Essays of Ralph Ellison* (1995). *Flying Home and Other Stories* (1996). *Juneteenth* (1999). *Trading Twelves: The Selected Letters of Ralph Ellison and Albert Murray,* ed. Albert Murray and John F. Callahan (2000). *Ralph Ellison's Jazz Writings,* ed. Robert O'Meally (2002).

—LAWRENCE JACKSON

PERCIVAL EVERETT (1956–). Percival L. Everett was born on December 22, 1956, in Fort Gordon, Ga., son of Percival Leonard, a dentist, and Dorothy (Stinson) Everett. He grew up in Columbia, S.C., graduated from A. C. Flora High School, earned a B.A. in philosophy at the University of Miami in 1977, attended the University of Oregon from 1978 to 1980, and earned an A.M. in writing from Brown University in 1982. He is one of the emerging elite postmodern writers of fiction (though Everett dislikes such categorization). Critics regard *Suder* as his earliest important work, a novel of an African American third baseman for the Seattle Mariners who leaves the team and his family on a quixotic odyssey that finds him, at the novel's end, Icarus-like learning to fly. The settings and topoi of his novels, story collections, and one children's book erect often experimental narratives that appropriate elements of realism, Greek mythology, the western, science fiction, and the carnivalesque. Many have won prizes.

With specialties in creative writing, American studies, and critical theory, he has held academic positions at the University of Kentucky (1985–89), University of Notre Dame (1989–92), University of Wyoming, where he held the William Robertson Coe Chair in American Studies (1992), and

University of California–Riverside (1992–99). In 1999 Everett joined the faculty of the University of Southern California. He is also a jazz musician and painter.

Everett's awards and honors include the D. H. Lawrence Fellowship at the University of New Mexico (1984), New American Writing Award for *Zulus* (1990), Lila Wallace–Reader's Digest Fellowship of the Woodrow Wilson Foundation (1994), and PEN/Oakland–Josephine Miles Award for Excellence in Literature for *Big Picture* (1997). He has served as a judge for the PEN/Faulkner and National Book Awards, and as an editor of *Callaloo*. He received the 2002 Hurston/Wright Legacy Award for Fiction for *Erasure*, which was also nominated for the 2003 IMPAC Dublin Literary Award.

WORKS: *Suder* (1983). *Cutting Lisa* (1986). *Walk Me to the Distance* (1985). *The Weather and Women Treat Me Fair* (1987). *For Her Dark Skin* (1990). *Zulus* (1990). *The One that Got Away* (1992). *The Body of Martin Aguilera* (1994). *God's Country* (1994). *Watershed* (1996). *The Big Picture* (1996). *Frenzy* (1997). *Glyph* (1999). *Grand Canyon, Inc.* (2001). *Erasure* (2001). *American Desert* (2004). *Damned If I Do: Stories* (2004). *A History of the African-American People (Proposed) by Strom Thurmond: A Novel*, with James Kincaid (2004).

—JOHN R. PFEIFFER

WILLIAM CLARK FALKNER (1825–1889). William Clark Falkner was born on July 6, 1825, in Knox County, Tenn. His parents thereafter resumed their journey from North Carolina to Missouri, where they settled in Ste. Genevieve. About 1840, fleeing punishment or seeking means to support his widowed mother, the boy settled in Ripley, Miss., where he had relatives. An energetic worker, studying law and profitably serving as amanuensis for a condemned ax-murderer, Falkner made his way.

His equivocal service in the Mexican War provided the substance for an autobiographical poem, *The Siege of Monterey.* Later the same year he published an adventure novel called *The Spanish Heroine.* In the ten years before the outbreak of the Civil War he prospered at law and farming, killed two men in affrays, and was widowed and re-wed. (John Wesley Thompson Falkner, the only child of his first marriage, would become William Faulkner's grandfather.) Like other men of his class, he apparently fathered a child, Fannie Mae, on one of his slaves, Emmeline, to form a "shadow family," not unlike that in his great-grandson's novel *Go Down, Moses.*

After leading with distinction at the First Manassas, Colonel Falkner was defeated for re-election as commander of his regiment. Raising a regiment of Partisan Rangers, he waged guerrilla warfare until that command was destroyed and he was forced to go underground.

After the war he wrote an eight-scene play, *The Lost Diamond*, the proceeds helping to reopen a local school renamed Stonewall College. Although preoccupied with expanding the Ripley Railroad, Falkner found time to write a serial for the *Ripley Advertiser* called *The White Rose of Memphis*. With a Mississippi riverboat journey for a frame setting, Falkner's characters—costumed for a masquerade ball—took turns telling stories, but a central plot involved violence, betrayal, and true love rewarded. Published in 1881, it went through many editions. *The Little Brick Church* of the next year was set partly on the Hudson but showed a number of similarities to its predecessor, sharing many of the same faults without the compensating vitality and ingenuity. A trip to Europe produced *Rapid Ramblings in Europe*, a book of travel sketches distinguished by clear narration and exposition and good handling of dialect. This was Falkner's last work, as railroad building and politics occupied him until his death at the hands of a former business partner on November 6, 1889.

WORKS:. *The Siege of Monterey* (1851). *The Spanish Heroine* (1851). *The Lost Diamond* (1867). *The White Rose of Memphis* (1881). *The Little Brick Church* (1882). *Rapid Ramblings in Europe* (1884).

—JOSEPH BLOTNER

JOHN WESLEY THOMPSON FAULKNER III (1901–1963). John Wesley Thompson Faulkner III—burdened with the name and family aspirations of his great-grandfather, The Colonel—was steamrolled by brother William's Faulkner Express. Consigned to second-place status from the start, John Faulkner's writing has been largely passed over, despite its legitimate place among the latter descendants of southwestern humor traditions. Fortunately, John Faulkner inherited something of his great-grandfather's versatility. Like him, he worked at various times in transportation, as a highway engineer and railroad worker. He also dabbled in such suitably dashing pursuits as aviation.

John Faulkner (like William, he added a "u" to the family name) was born on September 24, 1901, in Ripley, Miss. He was the third of the four Faulkner boys, and he made his literary debut after his famous brother was well established. Brother William had asked John (affectionately known as "Johncy") to manage his mule farm outside of Oxford, despite waning demand for the beasts. It was, he discovered, a world apart. John received a sympathetic education in the hard-scrabble ways of the modern Mississippi yeoman.

His first novel, *Men Working*, took satiric aim at government "improvement" schemes, particularly the "W P and A." Next came *Dollar Cotton*, an account of monocrop disaster. *Chooky* followed, a sort of book for boys based on John's son. *Cabin Road* sketched, with broad humor, the innocent ways of the boisterous folk in John's own slackwater, dubbed "Beat Two." The four novels that followed are of a piece, in their recurring themes and characters. His plain style and his eye for character owe much to George W. Harris's *Sut Lovingood* (one of William's favorites, too).

John's last book memorialized his brother. Serious William Faulkner biographers downplay the relevance of *My Brother Bill*, but it remains a touchingly human and humane account of Faulkner family life, invested with John's good humor. The anecdotes illuminate a number of William Faulkner's sources. John Faulkner died on March 28, 1963, not long after the book's publication.

WORKS: *Men Working* (1941). *Dollar Cotton* (1942). *Chooky* (1950). *Cabin Road* (1951). *Uncle Good's Girls* (1952). *The Sin Shouter of Cabin Road* (1955). *Ain't Gonna Rain No More* (1959). *Uncle Good's Weekend Party* (1960). *My Brother Bill* (1963).

—BRYAN GIEMZA

WILLIAM FAULKNER (1897–1962). William Cuthbert Faulkner was born in the north Mississippi town of New Albany on September 25, 1897. Fifteen months later his parents moved to nearby Ripley where his great-grandfather had settled about 1840. A lawyer planter, and slave owner, William Clark Falkner had led a regiment north in 1861 to fight valiantly at First Manassas, and later he had served near home as colonel of his regiment of partisan cavalry. A successful novelist and railroad builder in the postwar years, he was fatally shot by a onetime business rival the day he was elected to the legislature. Precocious as Billy Falkner was, he may well have absorbed some of this family lore before his parents moved southwest to Oxford just before his fifth birthday.

There with his three younger brothers he enjoyed a comfortable small-town boyhood. He was a bright student but eventually lost interest and dropped out during high school. He quit a job in his grandfather's bank to pursue his real interest: writing verse. Encouraged by Phil Stone, an older and better-educated friend, he remained in Oxford until the spring of 1918 when, his sweetheart about to be married to a successful lawyer, he traveled north to share Stone's student lodgings at Yale. That July, spelling his name Faulkner, he began pilot training in Toronto with the RAF–Canada. Although this experience ended with the war, it profoundly affected his imagination and supplied material for future writing.

At home again, he led an existence deceptive in appearance. Roaming the countryside, taking odd jobs when he chose, he was still reading widely and experimenting in verse and prose. A brief taste of New York in 1921 and nearly three onerous years as postmaster at the University of Mississippi whetted his appetite for Europe. He planned to travel there via New Orleans, where he visited late in 1924 just before the appearance of *The Marble Faun,* a sequence of pastoral verses financed by himself and Stone.

He had met Sherwood Anderson in New Orleans, and in the genial company of the older writer and his circle he settled in for half a year, writing prose and verse, much of it published in the *Times-Picayune.* After sending a novel manuscript to Anderson's publisher, Faulkner sailed for Europe in July with his friend, architect William Spratling. From Genoa they journeyed through Switzerland to Paris, where Faulkner spent the rest of the year but for brief trips into the French countryside and to England. He worked on stories and novels, elements of which he would salvage later.

On February 25, 1925, Boni & Liveright published *Soldiers' Pay,* Faulkner's Lost Generation novel of postwar disillusionment. Returning to New Orleans, he worked on a novel set there called *Mosquitoes,* which suggested Huxleyan bohemians and dilettantes. Faulkner found his unique métier and voice in *Flags in the Dust,* a novel of the north Mississippi Sartoris clan (based on the Falkners). Several times rejected, it was published as *Sartoris* by Harcourt, Brace in 1929, when Faulkner was completing a highly experimental book called *The Sound and the Fury,* which Cape & Smith issued that October. Fusing poetic imagery with stream-of-consciousness narration, Faulkner used the disintegrating Compson family in both a realistic and a symbolic manner. Some reviewers recognized the novel as a masterpiece.

These two works of 1929 signaled the beginning of more than a decade of productivity and brilliance unmatched by any other American novelist. Pushing into other regions of his mythic Yoknapatawpha County, Faulkner extended his use of the stream-of-consciousness technique in a story of country people called *As I Lay Dying,* which operated on a realistic level yet also suggested symbolic Christian and pagan analogues as *The Sound and the Fury* had done. *Sanctuary* was a shocking novel of violence that brought Faulkner notoriety, sales, and a Hollywood offer. Married to his divorced childhood sweetheart, and now owner of an antebellum house much in need of repair, he went to Hollywood as a screenwriter the next spring, beginning a remunerative but burdensome second career that would continue intermittently for more than two decades.

He was at the height of his powers, as he showed in *Light in August,* a massive contrapuntal novel portraying self-isolated characters against the complex Yoknapatawpha society. But he was far from financially secure, and he now spent much energy on short stories in the hope of quick returns from major magazines. He was publishing a book a year now, culminating in 1936 in *Absalom, Absalom!* issued by Random House, his publisher thenceforward. Here Quentin Compson, of *The Sound and the Fury,* tried to understand, through the life of Colonel Thomas Sutpen, larger meanings extending into the realms of southern history and human values. Exploring the quintessentially southern matters of the Civil War and race relations, Faulkner fashioned short stories into novels with *The Unvanquished* and *Go Down, Moses. The Hamlet* emerged from similar reworkings to inaugurate in novel form the Snopes saga, which engaged Faulkner during two decades in a fictional view of sweeping historical and socioeconomic change.

Gaining increasing recognition but modest sales, Faulkner had worked for three other studios before going to Warner Brothers in 1942. Much of the next three years was spent there on ephemeral scenarios, but *Intruder in the Dust,* a popular novel of detection and race relations, brought him financial security and renewed popularity in 1948.

Faulkner's international stature was confirmed by the Nobel Prize in 1950. During this decade he traveled extensively on State Department cultural missions, but he worked intensively to complete *A Fable*, his recasting of the Christ story set in 1918, and his Snopes trilogy. In *The Town* he followed the incursion of the Snopeses into Jefferson, the seat of Yoknapatawpha County, and in *The Mansion* he brought the triumph and fall of Flem Snopes into the contemporary period.

Residing half the year in Charlottesville, where he was associated with the University of Virginia, he lived the life of a venerated artist and fox-hunting country gentleman. *The Reivers* was a grandfather's mellow reminiscence of a boy's coming of age in the early years of the century. The most honored of living writers, secure as one of America's greatest artists, he died in Mississippi on July 6, 1962, just short of his sixty-fifth birthday.

WORKS: *The Marble Faun* (1924). *Soldiers' Pay* (1926). *Mosquitoes* (1927). *Sartoris* (1929); longer version published as *Flags in the Dust* (1973). *The Sound and the Fury* (1929). *As I Lay Dying* (1930). *Sanctuary* (1931). *These 13* (1931). *Light in August* (1932). *A Green Bough* (1933). *Doctor Martino and Other Stories* (1934). *Pylon* (1935). *Absalom, Absalom!* (1936). *The Unvanquished* (1938). *The Wild Palms* (1939); repr. as *If I Forget Thee Jerusalem* (1995). *The Hamlet* (1940). *Go Down, Moses* (1942). *The Portable Faulkner*, ed. Malcolm Cowley (1946). *Intruder in the Dust* (1948). *Knight's Gambit* (1949). *Collected Stories of William Faulkner* (1950). *Requiem for a Nun* (1951). *A Fable* (1954). *Big Woods* (1955). *The Town* (1957). *The Mansion* (1959). *Faulkner in the University*, ed. Frederick L. Gwynn and Joseph L. Blotner (1959). *The Reivers* (1961). *Early Prose and Poetry*, ed. Carvel Collins (1962). *Faulkner at West Point*, ed. Joseph L. Fant III, and Robert Ashley (1964). *The Wishing Tree* (1964). *Essays, Speeches and Public Letters*, ed. James B. Meriwether (1965). *Lion in the Garden: Interviews with William Faulkner*, ed. Meriwether and Michael Millgate (1968). *New Orleans Sketches*, ed. Collins (1968). *Mayday* (1976). *Selected Letters of William Faulkner*, ed. Blotner (1977). *The Marionettes: A Play in One Act*, ed. Noel Polk (1978). *Uncollected Stories of William Faulkner*, ed. Blotner (1979). *Helen: A Courtship and Mississippi Poems*, ed. Collins and Blotner (1981). *Father Abraham*, ed. Meriwether (1984). *Vision in Spring*, ed. Judith Sensibar (1985). *Thinking of Home: William Faulkner, Letters to His Mother and Father, 1918–1925*, ed. James G. Watson (1992).

—JOSEPH BLOTNER

JESSIE REDMOND FAUSET (1886–1961). Daughter of a minister, Jessie Fauset was a member of the African American aristocracy of Philadelphia—"O P's," as these Old Philadelphians were called. She attended Cornell University (B.A., 1905) and the University of Pennsylvania (M.A., 1906). She taught Latin and French at Douglass High School in Baltimore, later moving to Dunbar High School in Washington, D.C. She left the public school system in 1919 to serve as literary editor of *Crisis*, the official publication of the NAACP. In this capacity, according to Langston Hughes, she helped to midwife the "Negro" or Harlem Renaissance of the 1920s. Fauset herself wrote stories, poetry, essays, and book reviews for the magazine before she began her major career as a novelist. She married Herbert E. Harris in the late 1920s.

In 1920 Fauset and W. E. B. Du Bois put together the *Brownies' Book*, a children's periodical; and in 1921 Du Bois sent her to Europe to cover the second Pan-African Congress for *Crisis*. Infatuated with Paris, she spent the entire year of 1924 studying French at the Sorbonne.

Resigning her position as literary editor in 1926, Fauset returned to teaching, next at DeWitt Clinton High School in New York City, where she taught until 1944. She became a visiting professor of English at Hampton Institute in 1949, and late in life she taught Latin and French at Tuskegee Institute. She died in Philadelphia on April 30, 1961.

Fauset wrote four novels, all dealing with upper-middle-class black life, but it is a mistake to think that this was the only social milieu that she was capable of writing about. William Stanley Braithewait called her "the potential Jane Austen of Negro literature," yet the gothic subtext beneath her novels of manners links her with Hawthorne, Poe, Melville, and even Faulkner. Indeed, the genealogy of the white and black sides of the Bye family at the beginning of *There Is Confusion* anticipates the complicated bloodlines of *Go Down, Moses* (1942). Her black characters are often haunted by ghosts from their racial past, and all four of her heroines try, with various degrees of success, to escape the burdens of history. Perhaps her most successful work is *Plum Bun*, a city novel that brilliantly interweaves the southern theme of transplantation and return with the expatriate theme of Old World versus New.

WORKS: *There Is Confusion* (1924). *Plum Bun* (1929). *The Chinaberry Tree* (1931). *Comedy: American Style* (1933).

—CHARLES SCRUGGS

PETER STEINAM FEIBLEMAN (1930–). Peter Steinam Feibleman, the only child of James Kern and Dorothy (Steinam) Feibleman, was born in 1930 in New York City but was raised and educated in New Orleans, where his father was a professor of philosophy at Tulane University. This childhood was not without trauma, being disrupted by both sexual molestation and his parents' divorce. Although both parents remarried, Feibleman was and has remained particularly estranged from his father's second wife, the New Orleans novelist Shirley Ann Grau, and her four children.

Transplanted to New York in his teens, Feibleman later studied drama at Carnegie Tech and Columbia University and lived in Spain for much of the 1950s, acting, working as a theatrical manager, and completing his first novel, *A Place without Twilight*. (It later became the basis of his play *Tiger, Tiger, Burning Bright*, which opened on Broadway at the Booth Theatre in 1962.) He returned to the United States to live in various places as a freelance writer and as a recipient of a Guggenheim Fellowship in 1959.

In the early 1960s, after a phase he characterizes as sexually "experimental," Feibleman became the longtime companion of the much older New Orleans-born playwright Lillian Hellman, traveling with her and often sharing a residence on Martha's Vineyard. During this period Feibleman published three additional novels—*The Daughters of Necessity, The Columbus Tree*, and *Charlie Boy*—and *Strangers and Graves*, a collection of four novellas, as well as two cookbooks. His relationship with Hellman, which lasted until her death in 1984, is documented in *Eating Together: Recipes and Recollections*, which he was writing with Hellman when she died; it also led to his memoir *Lilly: Reminiscences of Lillian Hellman* and his play *Cakewalk*. Later married, Feibleman continues to write from his homes in New York and Martha's Vineyard.

WORKS: *A Place without Twilight* (1958). *The Daughters of Necessity* (1959). *Tiger, Tiger, Burning Bright* (1963). *Strangers and Graves* (1966). *The Cooking of Spain and Portugal* (1969). *American Cooking: Creole and Acadian* (1971). *The Columbus Tree* (1973). *The Bayous* (1973). *Charlie Boy* (1980). *Eating Together: Recipes and Recollections*, with Lillian Hellman (1984). *Lilly: Reminiscences of Lillian Hellman* (1988). *Cakewalk* (1998).

—GARY RICHARDS

ROBERTO G. FERNÁNDEZ (1952–). Cuban-born novelist Roberto Fernández was raised and educated in South Florida. He earned his B.A. and M.A. at Florida Atlantic University and teaches at Florida State University, where he earned his doctorate and is professor of Hispanic American literature. He has two daughters, Tatiana and Larisa.

Living in Tallahassee, Fernández calls himself an exile from a sultry and technicolor Miami. His exile analogy aptly reflects the major themes in his fiction: dislocation and the complex, and often wildly comic, effects of diaspora, geographically, culturally, and psychologically. His novels treat characters who find themselves caught up in the rhythms, so often unnerving and disconcerting, of living in America while longing for, and mythologizing, their past life in Cuba. The humor and the pathos can cut three ways. First, his characters romantically idealize their lost way of life that was never really as fulfilling as the characters fantasize; second, they can easily misread their chances for success in the present world; third, they try to re-create, or imagine that they have re-created, their past lives in the middle of their disconcerting present existence. The overlapping of all three modes of attempted life produces an often surreal, even insane, existence in a supercharged present.

Fernández's most popular works, *Raining Backwards* and *Holy Radishes!* treat immigrants searching for community in America, the importance of memory, and the inevitability of cultural disconnections. In *Raining Backwards,* a Cuban American girly Santeria priest becomes Pope; his brother launches a guerrilla war to cut the Florida peninsula off from the rest of the United States; and their sister fantasizes about becoming a cheerleader for the Miami Dolphins. In his satiric *Holy Radishes!* Fernández uses grotesque zoological and botanical metaphors in showing how members of the Cuban exile community and southerners reinvent themselves, or imagine that they have reinvented themselves, in their parodic quests for earthly paradise in America. Throughout his works, however, Fernández reminds his multicultural readership that none of us should forget we all have our own success fantasies, and that we should not take our American dreaming too seriously, either.

WORKS: *Cuentos sin Rumbo* (1975). *La Vida es un Special* (1981). *Biographical Index of Cuban Authors (Diaspora 1959–1979): Literature,* with José B. Fernández (1983). *La Montaña Rusa* (1985). *Raining Backwards* (1988). *Holy Radishes!* (1995). *En la Ocho y la Doce* (2001).

—R. BRUCE BICKLEY, JR.

JULIA FIELDS (1938–). Julia Fields, an African American poet and fiction writer, was born in Perry County, Ala., on January 21, 1938. Her father was a preacher, farmer, carpenter, and storekeeper. Growing up in country solitude, fascinated by the botanical world, the rhythms of poetry (early on memorizing scripture, Wordsworth, Shakespeare, and Burns), and African American church music, she also experienced the practical world of cotton picking, selling vegetables, waitressing, and working in a factory. This mingling of the practical and lyrical worlds has been maintained in her poetry, which expresses a distrust of effete intellectualism, as it reaches out to the religious, political, and workaday practical.

Fields graduated from the Presbyterian Knoxville College in Tennessee in 1961 and completed an M.A. in English from the Bread Loaf School at Middlebury College in Vermont in 1972. She also attended the University of Edinburgh in 1963. In London she met Langston Hughes, who became a mentor. She taught high school in Alabama and English classes at Hampton Institute, East Carolina University, Howard University, St. Augustine's College, and North Carolina State University. In 1968 her first book, *Poems,* was published in New York. While living there, she was identified by Kenneth Rexroth as a promising poet. Leaving the literary limelight to settle in Scotland Neck, N.C., she was hailed by Clarence Major in *The Dark and Feeling* (1974) as an enduring African American poet because of her intellectual crispness.

Her poems range in theme, hallowing the natural world, with farmers as poets, and criticizing a stultifying suburbia, hollow imitations of jazz, or obsessive materialism; they encompass love spent, outrage at lynching and other racial injustices, touching portraits of those in occupations limited by race, and a joyous cry of freedom from a lifestyle racially constricted, in "High on the Hog."

WORKS: *Poems* (1968). *East of Moonlight* (1973). *A Summoning, a Shining* (1976). *Slow Coins* (1981). *The Green Lion of Zion Street* (1988).

—SARA ANDREWS JOHNSTON

JOHN FINLAY (1941–1991). John Finlay was born in Ozark, Ala., on January 24, 1941, and grew up working on his parents' dairy and peanut farm in Enterprise, Ala. He graduated from the University of Alabama with a B.A. in English in 1964, earning his M.A. two years later. He taught at the University of Montevallo in Alabama for three years before leaving to pursue his Ph.D. in English at Louisiana State University, where he studied under Donald E. Stanford, who wrote that Finlay's poems possess "fundamental importance." Once he completed his dissertation in 1980, he made two important decisions: he left academia to work in peace at his family farm and converted from Episcopalianism to Roman Catholicism. By 1982 he was diagnosed with the AIDS virus, which was just then beginning to make serious inroads in America.

Critic Jeffrey Goodman has speculated that it was his looming mortality that inspired Finlay to his more important poetic accomplishments. In the years after his diagnosis, Finlay wrote the majority of poems published in his posthumous collection *Mind and Blood,* as well as most of the literary essays that appeared in *Hermetic Light: Essays on the Gnostic Spirit in Modern Literature and Thought.* He also compiled fourteen precepts under the title *Notes for the Perfect Poem.* Based on an aesthetic both classical and realistic, these precepts demand that a poem be literal yet also symbolic, truthful and moral but also beautiful; most of all, a poem aiming for perfection must come from a mature author who has mastered language and history. David Middleton edited *In Light Apart: The Achievement of John Finlay* (1999), a commemorative volume of Finlay's prose and poetry, as well as a critical examination of his work and lasting impact.

WORKS: *The Wide Porch and Other Poems* (1984). *Between the Gulfs* (1986). *The Self of Exposure* (1988). *A Prayer to the Father* (1992). *Mind and Blood* (1992). *Notes for the Perfect Poem* (1993). *Hermetic Light: Essays on the Gnostic Spirit in Modern Literature and Thought* (1994).

—PATRICK SAMWAY, S.J.

ZELDA FITZGERALD (1900–1948). Zelda Sayre was born on July 24, 1900, in Montgomery, Ala., the youngest of six children. Her mother, Minnie Machen Sayre, daughter of a Kentucky politician, was noted "a brilliant woman" and "clever writer" in the local paper; her father, Anthony Dickinson Sayre, was a longtime Alabama supreme court justice. When she graduated from Sidney Lanier High School in May 1918, Zelda was already known for her talent, vivacity, and beauty. That summer at the Montgomery Country Club, she met Francis Scott Fitzgerald, a first lieutenant stationed at Camp Sheridan. As World War I ended, Scott pursued his literary ambitions and the fitful relationship with Zelda. They married in New York on April 3, 1920, a week after his first novel, *This Side of Paradise,* was published. Their only child, a daughter named Frances Scott but known as Scottie, was born on October 26, 1921.

Under the banner "Children of the Alabama Judiciary," an interview in the *Montgomery Advertiser* on March 26, 1911, records Zelda Sayre's declaration, "I dearly love the theatre." Her early enthusiasm for the arts extended to reading stories ("because there are such beautiful tales in the books"), drawing, painting, and dancing. In adulthood Zelda pursued all these interests, but it was as a high-living avatar of the Jazz Age that she was celebrated. Scott, who successfully chronicled the period at its apogee, also traced the downward trajectories of the Jazz Age, his marriage, and Zelda's mental health.

In 1940 a fatal heart attack claimed Scott in Hollywood, where he was involved with a show-biz columnist, managing Zelda's care from afar, and attempting to earn their living as a scriptwriter. Zelda died on March 10, 1948, one among nine victims of a fire at the Highland Hospital in Asheville, N.C. Her last years had been divided between the sanitarium and her mother's house in Montgomery. She was buried with Scott in Rockville, Md.

Public interest in Zelda as a creative force in her own right was focused by Nancy Milford's best-selling biography *Zelda* (1970), and furthered when her literary output was identified (some of her stories and literary journalism had been published under Scott's more marketable name) and collected by Scottie and the scholar Matthew J. Bruccoli. Scott's venerable editor at Scribner's, Maxwell Perkins, had seen to the publication of Zelda's autobiographical novel *Save Me the Waltz*. A second novel, *Caesar's Things*, was left unfinished. *Scandalabra: A Farce Fantasy in a Prologue and Three Acts* ran in Baltimore from June 26 to July 1, 1933; and the aphoristic snap of Zelda's dialogue suggests that her talent, rather than Scott's, might have been for the movies.

WORKS: *Save Me the Waltz* (1932). *Bits of Paradise: Twenty-one Uncollected Stories by F. Scott Fitzgerald and Zelda Fitzgerald*, ed. Scottie Fitzgerald Smith and Matthew J. Bruccoli (1974). *Scandalabra: A Farce Fantasy in a Prologue and Three Acts* (1980). *The Collected Writings*, ed. Bruccoli (1991). *Dear Scott, Dearest Zelda: The Love Letters of F. Scott and Zelda Fitzgerald*, ed. Jackson R. Bryer and Cathy W. Barks (2002).

—AMBER VOGEL

GEORGE FITZHUGH (1806–1881). Lawyer, pro-slavery advocate, and editor, George Fitzhugh was born on November 4, 1806, in an isolated rural community along the Potomac River in Prince William County, Va. When he was six, his parents moved to a plantation in a neighborhood of Alexandria, where he lived until he was twenty-seven. Educated in a field school, Fitzhugh never attended college but was a voracious reader and largely self-educated, reading law. In 1829 he met Mary Metcalf Brockenbrough of Port Royal, Caroline County, Va., and the couple began living there in 1830; they had nine children, three of whom died in infancy. In Port Royal, whose population was half free Negroes and slaves, Fitzhugh had a law practice specializing in criminal cases.

Fitzhugh became convinced in 1844 that slavery was right and necessary, and he began contributing editorials and articles on that and other socioeconomic issues to the *Federalsburg Democratic Review* (1849–51) and, as an editorial writer, to the *Richmond Examiner* (1854–56), which had the largest newspaper circulation in the South. Other outlets for Fitzhugh's writings were the *Richmond Enquirer*, the *Southern Literary Messenger, Lippincott's Magazine*, the *Fredericksburg (Va.) News*, and especially *De Bow's Review*, where an estimated one hundred of his writings were published from 1846 to 1880.

While writing for these publications, Fitzhugh also published two pamphlets, *Slavery Justified* and *What Shall Be Done with the Free Negroes?* both appended to his first book, *Sociology for the South; or, The Failure of Free Society*. In the latter work and in *Cannibals All! or, Slaves without Masters*, Fitzhugh attacked the free-capitalist system and liberalism as being largely responsible for the problems that freed slaves were creating in Virginia and elsewhere. As a pro-slavery advocate, Fitzhugh won popularity in the South and angered abolitionists and prominent northerners, especially Abraham Lincoln, by advocating that only by enslaving blacks could they be free.

In 1856 Fitzhugh made his only trip to the North, lecturing in Boston and New Haven; he also met Harriet Beecher Stowe and became friends with a number of abolitionists. In 1857 he was appointed by President Buchanan as a law clerk in the attorney general's office.

For a year following the war, Fitzhugh served at Camp Lee as part of the Freedman's Bureau in the Johnson administration. He was a local court agent and an associate judge of the Freedman's Court, deciding Negro cases. His wife died in October 1877. In 1878, at seventy-two, Fitzhugh left Virginia to live with his son in Frankfort, Ky. Three years later, he moved to Huntsville, Tex., to live with his daughter and her veteran husband. There, in 1881, nearly blind and suffering from insomnia, Fitzhugh died on July 30, 1881.

WORKS: *Slavery Justified* (1850). *What Shall Be Done with the Free Negroes?* (1851). *Sociology for the South; or, The Failure of Free Society* (1854). *Cannibals ALL! or, Slaves without Masters* (1857).

—GARY KERLEY

WILLIAM FITZHUGH (1651–1701). The son of a wealthy woolen draper, William Fitzhugh was born in Bedford, England, and baptized on January 10, 1651. Little is known of his early life, but when he arrived in Virginia about 1670 he was an educated lawyer. He had fortune enough to purchase land, or he received certain tracts on August 26, 1674, as part of the dowry of Sarah Tucker, the eleven-to thirteen-year-old daughter of influential Virginians. Family tradition insists that she was sent to Europe for two years before the marriage was consummated. By 1676 Fitzhugh had settled on a large Stafford County estate where he prospered as a lawyer, member of the House of Burgesses, and gentleman-farmer who grew and exported tobacco. A recognized authority on colonial law, he earned fame for his defense of Major Robert Beverley, who had refused to supply the royal governor copies of the house's journals without that body's permission (1682–84/85). Fitzhugh also became a lieutenant-colonel of the Stafford County militia and a justice of the peace (1684), and one of two resident agents for the Culpeper heirs and Lord Fairfax in the Northern Neck Proprietary (1693). Fitzhugh's agency established a pattern of land grant and patenting that significantly influenced future American land speculation and development.

Fitzhugh's literary importance derives from a collection of 212 letters, which together with William Byrd I's give the clearest picture of seventeenth-century Virginia life. Through these letters (May 15, 1679–April 26, 1699) Fitzhugh chronicles colonial economic and governmental development. He reveals his self-made success, personal piety, emphasis upon moderation in all things, introduction of large-scale slave labor, fear of Indian attack, and a fairly sophisticated social life, and he gives the best description of a seventeenth-century plantation. Fitzhugh completed a short history of Virginia as a preface to his edition of its laws (1693; never published, not extant), and projected a longer history to encourage settlement (1697). The final two years of Fitzhugh's life escaped record except for a trip to England (1699–1700) and his death on October 21, 1701.

WORKS: *William Fitzhugh and His Chesapeake World, 1676–1701: The Fitzhugh Letters and Other Documents*, ed. Richard Beale Davis (1963).

—MICHAEL A. LOFARO

FANNIE FLAGG (1941–). Patricia Neal, known to audiences and readers as Fannie Flagg, has enjoyed prominence as an actress, screenwriter, and novelist. Born on September 21, 1941, in Birmingham, Ala., she became a successful actress, appearing in lead roles on stage and in film, as well as making more than five hundred television appearances. Already an established performer, Flagg turned her attention to writing in her thirties, receiving encouragement from Eudora Welty after winning a short-story contest.

Flagg has discussed publicly how her battles with dyslexia and attention deficit disorder discouraged her at first from becoming a writer. Nonetheless, her first novel spent ten weeks on the *New York Times* best-seller list. Her second novel, for which she is known best, *Fried Green Tomatoes at the*

Whistle Stop Cafe, remained first on the list for thirty-six weeks, and was praised by Welty, Harper Lee, and other well-known literary colleagues. These and Flagg's subsequent novels are characterized by strong southern female characters, small-town settings, and humor. Flagg has continued her acting and screenwriting careers, though she considers herself primarily a novelist. She received the Scripters Award, as well as an Academy Award nomination, for her 1991 screenplay *Fried Green Tomatoes.* The hit movie adaptation of her novel featured Kathy Bates and Jessica Tandy. Flagg divides her time between her home in Montecito, Calif., and her native Alabama.

WORKS: *Coming Attractions: A Wonderful Novel* (1981); repr. as *Daisy Fay and the Miracle Man* (1992). *Fried Green Tomatoes at the Whistle Stop Cafe* (1987). *Fannie Flagg's Original Whistle Stop Cafe Cookbook* (1993). *Welcome to the World, Baby Girl!* (1998). *Standing in the Rainbow* (2002). *A Redbird Christmas* (2004).

—TARA POWELL

INGLIS FLETCHER (1879–1969). Minna Towner Englis Clark Fletcher, called "Peggy" by her friends and known as Inglis Fletcher in the literary world, is best known for her historical novels about eastern North Carolina, though she also wrote some poetry, an autobiography, and movie scripts. Born on October 20, 1879, in Alton, Ill., she studied sculpture before marrying an engineer with whom she moved between mining camps in the American Northwest and Alaska before settling in Spokane, Wa. Interest in witchcraft took her for a seven-month trip to British Central Africa.

Fletcher's first two novels were based on research gathered during her travels in Africa. Though she remained interested in Africa and even did some later work transcribing African music, she became fascinated by eastern North Carolina after researching some of her ancestors from Tyrell County. The twelve novels beginning with *Raleigh's Eden* and concluding with *Rogue's Harbour* became known as her "Carolina" series, and were immensely popular, selling millions of copies. Fletcher was known for her meticulous research, and these books taken together cover more than two hundred years of the region's history, tracing the fortunes of different fictional families against a backdrop of historical figures and events between 1585 to 1789. Characterized by their complex plots and loving evocation of the region in which they are set, these novels continue to be interesting resources—not only for students of North Carolina history, but also for fans of the historical novel.

After her 1944 move to Bandon Plantation in Edenton, N.C., Fletcher remained a familiar public figure until her death, taking active part in the preservation of the state's history and development of its literary community. She and her husband were buried in Wilmington, N.C.

WORKS: *The White Leopard* (1931). *The Red Jasmine* (1932). *Raleigh's Eden* (1940). *Men of Albemarle* (1942). *Lusty Wind for Carolina* (1944). *Toil of the Brave* (1946). *Roanoke Hundred* (1948). *Bennett's Welcome* (1950). *The Young Commissioner* (1951). *Queen's Gift* (1952). *The Scotswoman* (1954). *The Wind in the Forest* (1957). *Pay, Pack, and Follow: The Story of My Life* (1959). *Cormorant's Brood* (1959). *Wicked Lady* (1962). *Rogue's Harbour* (1964).

—TARA POWELL

JOHN GOULD FLETCHER (1886–1950). John Gould Fletcher was born in Little Rock, Ark., to the wealthy banker and politician John G. Fletcher. The prominence and wealth of his family provided Fletcher with the best education available in Arkansas, culminating with his enrollment at Harvard University in 1903. At Harvard, in spite of his affinity for languages, he was an apathetic student at best. When his father died in 1906, Fletcher left Harvard without receiving a degree, his inheritance allowing him to pursue his poetic interests.

After a brief trip to the American West to study Mesa Verde civilization, Fletcher left the United States for Europe. After sojourns in Italy and Paris, he settled in London, where he published five books of poetry at his own expense in 1913. Shortly thereafter, he met Ezra Pound. Fletcher became active in the Imagist movement of Pound and his compatriots, but his mistrust of Pound's true intentions made it impossible for him to remain loyal. He allied himself with Amy Lowell and was published in each of her annual *Some Imagists* anthologies. In 1915 Fletcher's *Irradiations: Sand and Spray* established him at the forefront of American poetry. He began publishing in the major poetry magazines of the time and befriended the by-then-famous T. S. Eliot.

On a lecture tour in the United States, Fletcher met the Agrarians in Nashville. He contributed an essay on education to the group's manifesto *I'll Take My Stand* (1930). In an effort to make his agrarian ideas manifest, Fletcher returned in 1933 to his southern home in Arkansas, where he continued to write poetry. In 1936 he married the popular novelist Charlie May Simmons. Two years later, his *Selected Poems* took the Pulitzer Prize. Though Fletcher continued to write poetry, depression ultimately drove him to suicide by drowning in 1950.

WORKS: *The Book of Nature* (1913). *The Dominant City* (1913). *Fire and Wine* (1913). *Fool's Gold* (1913). *Visions of the Evening* (1913). *Irradiations: Sand and Spray* (1915). *Goblins and Pagodas* (1916). *Japanese Prints* (1918). *The Tree of Life* (1918). *La Poésie d'Andre Fontainas* (1919). *Some Contemporary American Poets* (1921). *Breakers and Granite* (1921). *Paul Gauguin: His Life and Art* (1921). *Preludes and Symphonies* (1922). *Parables* (1925). *Branches of Adam* (1926). *The Black Rock* (1928). *John Smith—Or Pocahontas* (1928). *The Crisis of Film* (1929). *The Two Frontiers: A Study in Historical Psychology (On Russia and America)* (1930). "Education, Past and Present," in *I'll Take My Stand: The South and the Agrarian Tradition*, by Twelve Southerners (1930). *XXIV Elegies* (1935). *The Epic of Arkansas* (1936). *Life Is My Song* (1937). *Selected Poems* (1938). *South Star* (1941). *The Burning Mountain* (1946). *Arkansas* (1947).

—HARRIS W. HENDERSON

HORTON FOOTE (1916–). One of the most distinguished and prolific American playwrights, Horton Foote was born on March 14, 1916, in Wharton, Tex., the descendant of a prominent family that includes the state's first lieutenant governor. That family provides a central theme for much of Foote's realistic drama. Most of his plays incorporate southern history, culture, and music, and are usually set in the fictional town of Harrison, Tex., based on his hometown.

Though playwriting is his primary interest, Foote has made rich contributions to both early television and contemporary film. After graduating from Wharton High School in 1932, he studied acting at the Pasadena Playhouse (1933–35) and Tamara Daykarhanova's Theatre School in New York (1937–39); in 1938 he joined the American Actors Company, for which he began writing plays. In 1945 Foote married Lillian Vallish (who died in 1992); they had four children: Hallie, Horton, Jr. (both of whom are actors), Walter, and Daisy. After helping establish a theater school and a theater in Washington, D.C., Foote and his wife returned to New York, where he took teaching jobs to support his writing endeavors.

Foote's first play, *Wharton Dance* (1940), centers on the small-town life he would become known for, and his Broadway debut came with *Only the Heart* (1942). A central dramatic accomplishment is his epic nine-play cycle *The Orphan's Home*, about four generations of a Texas family named Robedaux, based on Foote's own ancestors. His writing for television's "Golden Age" included *The Trip to Bountiful* (1954), which he later also produced for the big screen (1985). His wide variety of film work includes screenplays adapting texts by Faulkner, O'Connor, Steinbeck, and Flaubert; the screenplay *Baby, the Rain Must Fall* (1965) was based on his own drama *The Traveling Lady* (1954).

Foote won Academy Awards for two of his screenplays—*To Kill a Mockingbird* (1962), based on the novel by Harper Lee, and *Tender Mercies* (1980)—as well as the 1995 Pulitzer Prize for his drama *Young Man from Atlanta*. His many honors include the Lucille Lortel Award (1995), Gold Medal for Drama from the Academy of Arts and Letters (1998), William Inge Award for Lifetime Achievement in American Theatre (1989), Lifetime Achievement Award from Writers Guild of America (1999), Master American Dramatist Award of the PEN American Center (2000), and National Medal of Arts (2000). He was elected to the Theater Hall of Fame in 1996 and the American Academy of Arts and Letters in 1998. He also served as playwright-in-residence at New York's Signature Theatre Company (1994–95) and received an Outer Critics Circle Special Achievement Award for the four of his plays presented there.

WORKS: *Only the Heart* (1944). *The Trip to Bountiful* (1954). *The Traveling Lady* (1955). *The Chase* (1956). *Harrison, Texas: Eight Television Plays* (1956). *The Midnight Caller* (1959). *Roots in a Parched Ground* (1962). *Three Plays* (1962). *The Roads to Home* (1982). *A Young Lady of Property* (1983). *Courtship* (1984). *Tomorrow and Tomorrow and Tomorrow*, ed. David G. Yellin and Marie Connors (1985). *Blind Date* (1986). *Valentine's Day* (1987). *The Widow Claire* (1987). *Lily Dale* (1987). *1918* (1987). *Three Plays from the Orphans' Home Cycle* (1987). *The Road to the Graveyard* (1988). *The First Four Plays of the Orphans' Home Cycle* (1988). *Cousins* (1989). *The Death of Papa* (1989). *The Final Two Plays of The Orphans' Home Cycle* (1989). *The Man Who Climbed the Pecan Trees* (1989). *Three Screenplays* (1989). *Selected One-Act Plays of Horton Foote*, ed. Gerald C. Wood (1989). *Horton Foote's Three Trips to Bountiful*, ed. David G. Yellin and Barbara Moore (1993). *The Habitation of Dragons* (1993). *Four New Plays* (1993). *The Young Man from Atlanta* (1995). *Night Seasons* (1996). *Laura Dennis* (1996). *Talking Pictures* (1996). *Collected Plays* (1996). *Getting Frankie Married—and Afterwards; and Other Plays* (1998). *Farewell: A Memoir of a Texas Childhood* (1999). *Vernon Early* (1999). *The Orphans' Home Cycle* (1999). *The Last of the Thorntons* (2000). *Beginnings: A Memoir* (2001). *The Carpetbagger's Children* (2002). *Horton Foote's "The Shape of the River" : The Lost Teleplay about Mark Twain*, with Mark Dawidziak (2003). *Carpetbagger's Children and The Actor : Two Plays* (2003). *Genesis of an American Playwright*, ed. Marion Castleberry (2004).

—KAREN C. BLANSFIELD

SHELBY FOOTE (1916–2005). A good name is rather to be chosen than riches—so says the good book. Shelby Foote's patrimony included both. The only scion of two prominent Mississippi families, Foote was born in Greenville, Miss., on November 17, 1916, to Shelby Dade Foote and Lillian Rosenstock Foote. His maternal grandfather was once a wealthy businessman, his other grandfather was a planter, and a great-grandfather was a cavalry officer at Shiloh. Yet the family fortunes dwindled precipitously, leaving young Shelby with more in the way of name than riches. Shelby Sr. died when Foote was just five years old.

A Greenville upbringing made him a classmate of Walker Percy, whose father also died when he was young. Walker was Shelby's brother-of-the-heart, and the two became lifelong friends. Percy's uncle, William Alexander Percy, was well connected in literary circles. He spurred young Foote's literary interests, taking him under his wing as he had Walker, and granting him access to his library, where Foote was a self-described "colt in clover."

Foote attended the University of North Carolina for a while starting in 1935, but found it pretentious. The library was the part of Carolina that he liked, and he spent most of his time there. An academic dabbler, he attended only classes that interested him, and those infrequently. In 1937 he drifted back to Greenville, where he took a string of odd jobs and started the manuscript of a first novel based loosely on his grandfather's life; *Tournament* was shelved at an editor's suggestion. In the meantime, true to Percy's observation that a southerner "never met a war he didn't like," Foote joined the Mississippi National Guard, found his way into the army, and became a captain before his "sharp elbows" led to his discharge.

In the postwar years, Foote returned to Greenville with his first wife and worked as a reporter for a time with Hodding Carter's *Delta Democrat-Times*. He revised *Tournament* and saw it published in 1949. The book established his fictional landscape: Jordan County and Bristol, Miss. In the extraordinarily productive five years that followed, pen famously in hand and working from a garage behind his mother's house, Foote cranked out a series of novels: *Follow Me Down, Love in a Dry Season, Shiloh,* and *Jordan County: A Landscape in Narrative*. With the exception of *Shiloh,* they are largely of a piece in their themes and locus. They concern recurring characters in Jordan County, and focus on the South's transition into modernity, loneliness, and the crises produced by an honor-inflected sense of manhood. The failure of love and the immanence of violence attach to Foote's fascination with war. No less an authority than William Faulkner reckoned Foote one of America's most promising writers.

In 1954 Foote moved to Memphis to begin work on his magnum opus, *The Civil War*. This authoritative history, certainly one of the best yet written in America, would require twenty years to complete and span three volumes. After completing the series in 1974, he published *September, September,* a novel about a racially motivated kidnapping.

He was three times a Guggenheim Fellow and once a Ford Fellow, a lecturer at the University of Virginia and at Memphis State University, and writer-in-residence at Hollins College. Foote was drawn into the cultural limelight again when he was a featured narrator in Ken Burns's television documentary *The Civil War*. The nation delighted in his homespun accounts of a war he had, in a very real sense, lived through. An irascible and hugely talented presence in American literature, among fiction writers he deserves special acclaim for accomplishment in writing history, and among historians he deserves special recognition for bringing poetry to historical writing.

Shelby Foote died in Memphis on June 27, 2005, leaving his wife, Gwyn; a daughter, Margaret Selby; and a son, Huger Lee.

WORKS: *Tournament* (1949). *Follow Me Down* (1950). *Love in a Dry Season* (1951). *Shiloh* (1952). *Jordan County: A Landscape in Narrative* (1954). Ed., *The Night before Chancellorsville and Other Civil War Stories* (1957). *The Civil War: A Narrative,* 3 vols. (1958, 1963, 1974). *Jordan County: A Landscape in the Round (A Play)* (1964). *September, September* (1977). *Conversations with Shelby Foote* (1989). *Chickamauga and Other Civil War Stories* (1993). *Stars in Their Courses: The Gettysburg Campaign, June–July 1863* (1994). *The Beleaguered City: The Vicksburg Campaign, December 1862–July 1863* (1995). *The Correspondence of Shelby Foote and Walker Percy,* ed. Jay Tolson (1997).

—BRYAN GIEMZA

JESSE HILL FORD (1928–1996). Jesse Hill Ford, born in Troy, Ala., on December 28, 1928, received his B.A. from Vanderbilt University (1951) and his M.A. from the University of Florida (1955). He married Sarah Anne Davis of Humboldt, Tenn., in 1951. They had two sons and two daughters, but divorced in 1973; Ford later remarried.

After serving in the U.S. Navy, Ford worked in journalism, in public relations, and as writer-in-residence at Memphis State University (1969–71) and Vanderbilt (1987). He is best known for his works of fiction. Mostly set in west Tennessee, they are filled with conflict, often involving characters who are struggling with change, from the settlement of the frontier to the Civil War to the racial and political upheaval of the 1960s. Ford also wrote two screenplays, an adaptation of his play *The Conversion of Buster Drumwright* for CBS-TV and, with Stirling Silliphant, the 1970 movie version of *The Liberation of Lord Byron Jones,* directed by William Wyler.

Ford was recognized with a Fulbright Scholarship (1961), a Guggenheim Fellowship (1966), an honorary D.Litt., Lambuth College, Jackson, Tenn. (1966), and awards for his short fiction (mostly collected in *Fishes, Birds and Sons of Men*). The novel *The Liberation of Lord Byron Jones* was a Book-of-the-Month Club selection. However, the movie seemed to exacerbate racial tension in Ford's home in Humboldt, where the schools had recently been integrated. In November 1970, Ford was charged in the death of an African American soldier on his property. In July 1971 he was acquitted by a jury of eleven whites and one African American. Ford's only subsequent major work of fiction was *The Raider*. Later he wrote for *USA Today*. On June 4, 1996, Ford committed suicide. He had authorized Anne Cheney to publish *The Life and Letters of Jesse Hill Ford, Southern Writer*.

WORKS: *Mountains of Gilead* (1961). *The Conversion of Buster Drumwright: The Television and Stage Scripts* (1964). *The Liberation of Lord Byron Jones* (1965). *The Feast of St. Barnabas* (1969). *Fishes, Birds and Sons of Men* (1967). *The Raider* (1975).

—MARTHA E. COOK

RICHARD FORD (1944–). Richard Ford was born on February 16, 1944, in Jackson, Miss., an only child. His father, a traveling salesman for the Faultless Starch Company, was home only on weekends. During summers, Ford and his mother would travel with him, and Ford also spent time during summers and school vacations with his grandfather, who managed a hotel in Little Rock, Ark. His father died of a heart attack when Ford was sixteen. So in his early years Ford was exposed to an itinerant life and itinerant people.

At age eighteen, he enrolled at Michigan State University, intending to major in hotel management and follow his grandfather, but changed his major to literature. In 1968 he married Kristina Hensley, who has a Ph.D. in urban and regional planning and to whom all his books are dedicated. He received an M.F.A. in creative writing in 1970 from the University of California at Irvine.

As an adult Ford has himself been itinerant, living in at least fourteen different places. Since 1989 his home has been New Orleans, where Kristina is executive director of the New Orleans City Planning Commission, but Ford has houses in Maine and Montana where he also spends substantial time. The Fords have no children.

Ford is accomplished in both the short story and the novel. His first novel, *A Piece of My Heart*, was published in 1976, but it was not until the 1986 publication of his third novel, *The Sportswriter*, as a paperback original in the influential Vintage Contemporaries series that he received wide acclaim. *Independence Day*, a later novel featuring the protagonist of *The Sportswriter*, was published in 1995 and won both the Pulitzer Prize and the PEN/Faulkner award. Only his first novel is set in the South, but Ford is frequently linked with Walker Percy in their shared concern with personal alienation and the issue of place and placelessness. He is widely regarded as one of the finest postmodern writers from the South.

WORKS: *A Piece of My Heart* (1976). *The Ultimate Good Luck* (1981). *The Sportswriter* (1986). *Rock Springs* (1987). *Wildlife* (1990). *Independence Day* (1995). *Women with Men* (1997). *A Multitude of Sins* (2002).

—FRANK W. SHELTON

ALCÉE FORTIER (1856–1914). Born in 1856, in St. James Parish, La., Alcée Fortier dedicated his life to studying Louisiana history and culture. Following two years at the University of Virginia, from which he did not graduate, and two years studying law, he worked various jobs in the New Orleans area before becoming a professor of romance languages and dean of the Graduate College at the University of Louisiana (currently Tulane University).

While employed in these various pursuits, Fortier turned his talent for research into a means of preserving the ways and customs of the Louisiana people. His publications on Louisiana include *Bits of Louisiana Folk-Lore*, *Louisiana Studies*, *Louisiana Folk-Tales*, the four-volume *History of Louisiana*, and *Louisiana, Comprising Sketches of Parishes, Towns, Events, Institutions, and Persons, Arranged in Cyclopedic Form*. Additionally, Fortier wrote articles for literary and historical journals. With his work on his home state, Fortier joined the ranks of Charles Gayarré in capturing Louisiana in the words of history and folklore.

Readily recognized as a prominent Louisiana historian and folklorist during his life, Fortier held various positions: president of the board of curators for the Louisiana State Museum, 1906–11; president of the Louisiana Historical Society, 1894–1912; president of l'Athénée Louisianais, 1894–1914; president of the Modern Language Association, 1908; president of the American Folklore Society, 1894–95; president of the Fédération de l'Alliance Française des Etats-Unis et Canada, 1906–7. He also received honorary degrees as doctor of letters from the University of Virginia, Washington and Lee University, and Laval University of Canada. Completing his collection of honors was the cross of Chevalier de la Légion d'Honneur from the French government. Fortier died in 1914, and is buried in St. Louis Cemetery in New Orleans.

WORKS: *Gabriel d'Ennerich* (1886). *Bits of Louisiana Folk-Lore* (1888). *Histoire de la Littérature Française* (1893). *Louisiana Studies* (1894). *Louisiana Folk-Tales* (1894). *Voyage en Europe* (1895). *Précis de l'Histoire de France* (1899). *History of Louisiana*, 4 vols. (1904). *History of Mexico* (1907). *Louisiana, Comprising Sketches of Parishes, Towns, Events, Institutions, and Persons, Arranged in Cyclopedic Form* (1914).

—MARIA P. HEBERT

JOHN FOX, JR. (1862 or 1863–1919). Son of a schoolmaster, John William Fox, Jr., was born on December 16, 1862 or 1863, in the middle years of the Civil War, in bluegrass country near the town of Paris, Ky. The war's ferocity altered almost everything in America. This background of radical transformation provided a deep well of conflict for the stories Fox wrote just before and after the beginning of the twentieth century. Fox's narratives often centered on the wrenching nature of change in human experience. Before the start of a writing career focused on the ways and circumstances of mountain folk in western Virginia, Fox traveled widely enough (a Harvard degree in 1883 and some time in New York City as a journalist) to become concerned about the survival of backcountry life, a situation later addressed by the Agrarian Manifesto group of the 1920s and 1930s.

The extraordinary charm of country customs is knowingly represented in all of Fox's fiction, but so are the brutish implications of extreme backwardness—the killing intoxications and bloodlusts beyond the reach of enlightenment. Sometimes, a kind of chivalric honor or a form of Christian justice prevails, as in the outcome of the "On Hell-Fer-Sartain Creek" story in Fox's *Hell Fer Sartain* collection. Complications multiply whenever some form of sophistication from outside—for example, an enchanting northern city woman called "The Blight" in *A Knight of the Cumberland*—joins the mountain landscape. Fox himself experienced the stress of city/country conflict in the failure of his five-year (1908–13) marriage to Fritzi Scheff, first known to Fox through her leading roles at the Metropolitan Opera.

Forgotten elsewhere, Fox's work continues to be celebrated in Big Stone Gap, Va., Fox's home for twenty years preceding his death (from pneumonia) on July 8, 1919. Each summer since 1964, a group of local dramatists, Lonesome Pine Arts and Crafts, stages an outdoor production of Fox's 1908 best-seller, *The Trail of the Lonesome Pine*, which features southern mountain life enthusiastically.

WORKS: *A Cumberland Vendetta and Other Stories* (1895). *Hell-Fer-Sartain and Other Stories* (1897). *The Kentuckians* (1897). *A Mountain Europa* (1899). *Crittenden* (1900). *Blue-grass and Rhododendron* (1901). *The Little Shepherd of Kingdom Come* (1903). *Christmas Even on Lonesome and Other Stories* (1904). *Following the Sun Flag: A Vain Pursuit through Manchuria* (1905). *A Knight of the Cumberland* (1906). *The Trail of the Lonesome Pine* (1908). *The Heart of the Hills* (1913). *In Happy Valley* (1917). *Erskine Dale, Pioneer* (1920).

—OWEN W. GILMAN, JR.

WILLIAM PRICE FOX (1926–). William Price Fox, Jr., was born in Waukegan, Ill., on April 9, 1926, one of four sons of William Price and Annette Fanta Fox. When he was two, his family moved to Columbia, S.C., where Fox attended public schools. After leaving school in the tenth grade, he joined the army air corps at the age of sixteen, qualified as a navigator/bombardier, and became a second lieutenant before leaving the service in 1946. Fox then returned to Columbia, completing his high school work in five months, and entered the University of South Carolina, graduating with a degree in history in 1950. He taught at the Miami Military Academy in 1951, but soon left, and subsequently hitchhiked to New York City.

While working in sales positions in the late 1950s, Fox began his literary career in earnest by attending the New School for Social Research, where he studied under Caroline Gordon, and by publishing his first short stories. In 1962 he began to receive national recognition with the publication of a forty-cent paperback titled *Southern Fried*. This collection of sixteen short stories, only three of which had been published previously, established Fox as a perceptive observer of character types in the southern scene, particularly in and around Columbia. In both his fiction and his personal essays, he displays an appreciation for the humorous, the idiosyncratic, and the courageous in the human condition.

During the 1960s Fox continued his writing career with two novels, through television (including episodes of *The Beverly Hillbillies*) and movie scriptwriting in Hollywood (1964–65), and by publishing several short stories and personal essays, many of which appeared in the *Saturday Evening Post, Holiday*, and *Sports Illustrated*. In 1968, at the request of Kurt Vonnegut, Jr., Fox became a teacher at the Writer's Workshop at the University of Iowa. In 1975 he returned to his hometown of Columbia as a writer-in-residence at the University of South Carolina and eventually became a producer for the *Writer's Workshop*, a program on South Carolina educational television.

WORKS: *Southern Fried* (1962). *Dr. Golf* (1963). *Moonshine Light, Moonshine Bright* (1967). *Southern Fried Plus Six* (1968). *Cold Turkey* (movie, 1968). *Ruby Red* (1971). *Dixiana Moon* (1981). *Chitlin Strut and Other Madrigals* (1983). *How 'bout Them Gamecocks!* (1985). *Golfing in the Carolinas* (1990). Ed., with others, *Tales of the Diamond: Selected Gems of Baseball Fiction* (1991). *Lunatic Wind: Surviving the Storm of the Century* (1992). *South Carolina: Off the Beaten Path* (1996). *Wild Blue Yonder* (2002). *Satchel Paige's America* (2005).

—HAROLD WOODELL

JOHN HOPE FRANKLIN (1915–). Historian, professor, and lifelong civil rights activist, John Hope Franklin is one of the country's leading scholars on the African American experience. The youngest of four children, he was born on January 2, 1915, in Rentiesville, Okla. His father was a lawyer, and his mother, who taught school, was his first and best teacher. A high school valedictorian at age sixteen, Franklin earned his B.A. in history from Fisk University in 1935 and his M.A. and Ph.D. in history from Harvard in 1936 and 1941 respectively. He married Aurelia E. Whittington, a Fisk University graduate, in 1940. The couple had one son, John Whittington Franklin, in 1952.

A prolific scholar, Franklin has written more than 125 scholarly articles and more than a dozen books, and edited ten others. Franklin taught at Fisk University, North Carolina Central University, Howard University, Brooklyn College, and the University of Chicago. In 1982 he retired from the University of Chicago and ended his academic career as the James B. Duke Professor of History Emeritus at Duke University.

Franklin's involvement with the civil rights movement is a long one. He helped write the 1954 Supreme Court decision ending legal segregation in public schools and marched with Martin Luther King, Jr., in Montgomery, Ala., in 1965. He was awarded the Presidential Medal of Freedom in 1995 and appointed chair of the President's Initiative on Race in 1997. When the John Hope Franklin Center for Interdisciplinary and International Studies opened at Duke University in 2000, hundreds of adults, many with their children, lined up for his picture and autograph. Franklin remarked, "They know I'm old. They want their children to get a chance to see me." Recent days have been spent writing his autobiography and tending to orchids in his North Carolina greenhouse.

WORKS: *The Free Negro in North Carolina* (1943). *From Slavery to Freedom: A History of African Americans* (1947). *The Militant South, 1800–1860* (1956). *Reconstruction after the Civil War* (1961). *The Emancipation Proclamation* (1963). *Land of the Free* (1965). *Color and Race* (1968). *An Illustrated History of Black Americans* (1970). *A Southern Odyssey: Travelers in the Antebellum North* (1976). Ed., *Black Leaders of the Twentieth Century*, with August Meier (1982). *Racial Equality in America* (1976). *George Washington Williams: A Biography* (1985). *Race and History: Selected Essays, 1938–1988* (1990). *The Color Line: Legacy for the Twenty-first Century* (1993). *Runaway Slaves: Rebels on the Plantation*, with Loren Schweninger (1999). *Mirror to America: The Autobiography of John Hope Franklin* (2005).

—KAREN JEAN HUNT

CHARLES FRAZIER (1950–). Charles Robinson Frazier was born on November 4, 1950, in Asheville, N.C. He grew up in Andrews and Franklin, small towns in the western part of the state; but it was Cold Mountain, a majestic Blue Ridge rising 6,030 feet in southern Haywood County, that Frazier made famous with the publication of his celebrated novel of the same name. Although his paternal grandparents owned a farm in Bethel near the bottom of Cold Mountain, it was his maternal grandparents from neighboring Canton, a paper mill town, who are credited with getting him to climb the mountain's peak to camp and pick huckleberries as a young boy. His parents, C. O. (Charles Oldridge) and Betty Robinson Frazier, instilled in him and his two younger siblings a love of reading and storytelling.

Frazier earned his B.A. (1973) at the University of North Carolina at Chapel Hill. He then attended Appalachian State University, where in 1974 he met Katherine Beal, an accounting major. After receiving his M.A. in English (1975), he and Katherine continued graduate studies at the University of South Carolina. They were married on June 5, 1976. Before completing his Ph.D. in American literature in 1986, Frazier traveled extensively throughout South America and wrote a travel guide to the Andes with Donald Secreast (1985). He and Katherine also became parents during this period. Their only child, Annie Elizabeth Frazier, was born August 17, 1985.

For a short time, Frazier and his wife taught at the University of Colorado in Boulder before moving to Raleigh to take teaching positions at North Carolina State University. While Frazier published a few short stories in academic journals, his real interest was in writing a book on the Appalachian region. When his father told him about W. P. Inman—Frazier's great-great-uncle, a Confederate soldier who was wounded badly, hospitalized in Raleigh, deserted, and walked home to the mountains where he was shot in a fight with the Home Guard, the local militia—Frazier had a story. When researching additional facts on Inman's life proved futile, Frazier decided to create a life for him by writing a novel. His wife, who with the help of Kaye Gibbons was responsible for submitting the novel, persuaded Frazier to give up his teaching job, become the at-home parent to their daughter, and work seriously on the book. Determined to make the landscape and language in *Cold Mountain* as authentic as possible, Frazier researched everything that he could pertaining to life in western North Carolina during the Civil War. His efforts and talent resulted in an intense bidding war, which Atlantic Monthly Press won by purchasing *Cold Mountain* in December 1995. Frazier still had to finish the ending of the book, which he did with great skill.

Hailed as a modern classic and epic love story, *Cold Mountain* became a best-seller, and won the National Book Award in 1997. In the same year, Frazier sold film rights to United Artists for $1.25 million. The movie, directed by Anthony Minghella, was released on December 25, 2003. Frazier relishes his privacy and is working on a second novel, which Random House reportedly purchased with an $8 million advance. He currently lives on a horse farm outside Raleigh with his family.

WORKS: *Adventuring in the Andes: The Sierra Club Travel Guide to Ecuador, Peru, Bolivia, the Amazon Basin, and the Galapagos,* with Donald Secreast (1985). *Cold Mountain* (1997).

—TONY PEACOCK

EDWIN WILEY FULLER (1847–1876). Poet and novelist Edwin Wiley Fuller was born on November 30, 1847, and lived his entire life in Louisburg, seat of Franklin County, N.C. He was the only son of Jones Fuller, a cotton broker and merchant, and of Anna Long Thomas, great-granddaughter of Colonel Nicholas Long of Halifax, N.C., Continental line quartermaster general for the southern colonies during the American Revolution.

A short, trim man, Fuller was a skillful hunter and horseman known for quick wit, droll humor, and conversational ability. Letters from schoolmates note his strong character. After college he taught Methodist Sunday school and was active in the Friends of Temperance. Entering the war-depleted University of North Carolina in 1864, he was Delta Psi fraternity anniversary orator as a freshman and a sophomore declaimer at commencement his second year. The next year he worked in his father's store, pondered entering the ministry, and decided to study law. In the fall of 1867, Fuller attended the University of Virginia. There, seemingly influenced by the ghost of Poe, he wrote poetry and short fiction for the university magazine. In 1868 his father's ill health forced a return home to manage the family business until his own death, of pneumonia, on April 22, 1876. In 1871 he married Mary Elisabeth Malone. They had two daughters, Ethel Stuart Fuller, who died at sixteen months, and another, born March 19, 1876, only a month prior to her father's death and given the masculine name Edwin Sumner Fuller. The mother seems to have been determined to name the couple's only surviving child after her husband, regardless of its gender.

Fuller's two books had made him the best-known writer in the state when he died at age twenty-eight. *The Angel in the Cloud,* a long philosophical poem, received favorable reviews in northern newspapers. *Sea-Gift,* his autobiographical novel of student life, was published while he was mayor of Louisburg. It became known as the "Freshman's Bible" at the University of North Carolina and contains folktales, Dickensian humor, and an adaptation of the state's "Dromgoole Legend" about a campus duel. Published during the five years when the university was closed following the Civil War, *Sea-Gift* evoked sharp criticism from Fuller's cousin, Professor Kemp Plummer Battle, eventual president of the reopened institution, who charged that its depiction of campus events was sensationalized and caused the university to lose the support of many conservative citizens of the state.

WORKS: "The Corpse and the Cat," *University (Va.) Magazine*, Feb. 1868. *The Angel in the Cloud* (1871). *Sea-Gift: A Novel* (1873).

—E. T. MALONE, JR.

CHRISTOPHER GADSDEN (1724–1805). Son of an English customs official and an Anglo-Irish mother, Christopher Gadsden was born on February 16, 1724, in Charleston, S.C., and lived most of his life there. Following the death of his first stepmother, "Kittie" was sent to England to live with relatives and receive schooling. He returned in 1740 and was apprenticed to Thomas Lawrence of Philadelphia to learn business. After reaching his majority, Gadsden served as purser aboard a British naval ship, married Jane Godfrey, and fathered daughter Elizabeth before setting up as a merchant in Charleston in 1748. Gadsden used his sizable inheritance to become a successful factor and wharf builder, not to mention absentee plantation owner and major slaveholder. He had another child, Christopher, Jr., with his first wife, and with his second, Mary Hasell, he had four others: Thomas, Philip, Mary, and Ann. Gadsden outlived all but two or three of his children and at his death on August 28, 1805, was survived by his third wife, Ann Wragg.

As a writer, Gadsden played a prominent role in Revolutionary-era politics. His Philopatrios letters attacked British military incompetence against the Cherokee in 1760–61, while praising provincial prowess. A vocal opponent of the Stamp Act, he championed Charleston's mechanics in the Home-spun Free-man letters, while in other articles he argued against parliamentary authority to regulate trade, putting himself in the vanguard of independence sentiment. His principled but radical and often hyperbolic writing alienated moderate Whigs, yet he supported reconciliation with Tories even before the war ended. Following his imprisonment in British-held St. Augustine in 1780–81, Gadsden supported strong central government, the 1787 constitution, and Federalist candidates. Despite his seeming switch from radical to conservative, he consistently maintained Lockean rights for white male property owners, including those outside the low-country elite, but never seriously challenged the slavery that helped make him rich.

WORKS: "Philopatrios to Peter Timothy," *South Carolina Gazette*, Dec. 18, 1761. Philopatrios, *Some Observations on the Two Campaigns against the Cherokee Indians, in 1760 and 1761* (1762). Letters, *South Carolina Gazette*, Dec. 3 and 24, 1764. Homespun Free-man letters, *South-Carolina Gazette and Country Journal*, Feb. 11, 25, Mar. 18, and Apr. 1, 1766. "To be published as speedily as possible" [mock advertisement], *South-Carolina Gazette and Country Journal*, Feb. 18; repr. Mar. 4, 1766. William Henry Drayton, et al., *The Letters of Freeman, Etc*, numbers 5, 15, 17 (1771); repr. ed. Robert M. Weir (1977). *A Few Observations on Some Late Public Transactions in and out of Congress* (1797). "Letter of Messrs. R. Smith and Christopher Gadsden, of Charleston, S.C. 1768," *New England Historical and Genealogical Register* 29 (July 1875): 246. "Gen. Chris Gadsden: A Great Revolutionary Letter" [to John Rutledge, June 7, 1777], *American Autograph Journal* 4.3 (1940): 330–32. *The Writings of Christopher Gadsden, 1746–1805*, ed. Richard Walsh (1966). "Two Letters by Christopher Gadsden, February 1766," ed. Robert M. Weir, *South Carolina Historical Magazine* 75.3 (1974): 169–76.

—JEFFREY H. RICHARDS

ERNEST J. GAINES (1933–). Ernest Gaines knows Louisiana. The son of Manuel and Adrienne Colar Gaines, he was born in Oscar, La., on February 15, 1933. He was of the fifth generation to be born on the River Lake plantation in Pointe Coupée Parish. The rhythm of life there had not changed much: his parents were laborers, and as a boy Gaines chopped cane with the rest. The storied area offered him a wellspring for his fictional settings, in particular "the quarter" of *A Gathering of Old Men* and *A Lesson before Dying*. He was educated—in the sense of learning manners and absorbing oral history—by his handicapped aunt, Miss Augusteen Jefferson, who would serve as the inspiration for many of Gaines's lively fictional female characters. It was she who served as Gaines's primary guardian during his childhood.

Gaines's literary interests began gelling after he followed his stepfather and mother to Vallejo, Calif., in 1948, where he could pursue educational opportunities without the impediments of segregation. The homesick youth spent much of his time in the public library and resolved to create some of the voices that he found missing in literature. He was moved to try to write a first novel at age sixteen. After high school, Gaines matriculated at a junior college in Vallejo, but his time there was cut short when he was drafted into the army in 1953. After service, he attended San Francisco State College on the G.I. bill in 1955 and graduated with a B.A. in 1957. While an undergraduate, Gaines tried his hand at short-story writing. Two of his tales helped gain him a Wallace Stegner Creative Writing Fellowship in 1958 for graduate study at Stanford.

At Stanford, Gaines revived the novel he had tried to write as a teenager. In 1964 he published it under the title *Catherine Carmier*. In 1966 he received a grant from the National Endowment for the Arts. The following year he published *Bloodline*, a collection of stories related from the perspective of multiple narrators from rural Louisiana. He received a Guggenheim Fellowship in 1971, the same year that he released another work of short fiction for juveniles, *A Long Day in November*, adapted from one of the *Bloodline* stories.

Gaines owns to many influences, and has expressed admiration for works by Turgenev, Hurston, Ellison, Chekhov, Faulkner, and Baldwin, among others. Unlike other "regional expatriates," Gaines retained a fondness for the South, despite the acknowledged difficulties of life in the region. Indeed, Gaines enjoys taking pictures and has presented his native terrain in portraits both photographic and literary. The substance of his fiction derives from the rural Louisiana South, and it is out of this background that he produced his most critically successful work, *The Autobiography of Miss Jane Pittman*, a novel he described as "folk autobiography." So authentic was the voice of the title character that many took literally Gaines's conceit of "interviewing" her. But Jane Pittman's voice was a pastiche from Gaines's research in narrative and biography, his recollections, and, most important, his imagination. In 1974 the work was adapted for a popular television film. *In My Father's House* garnered weak reviews, but the multiple narrative perspectives of Gaines's next effort, *A Gathering of Old Men*, revealed a writer at the height of his powers. The novel concerns a murder that galvanizes a group of rural Louisiana African Americans. It is especially notable for its probing treatment of the subtleties of racial hierarchies and community empowerment. Gaines's novels are peopled with characters who are keenly aware of the difficulties in conforming oneself to contorted social codes.

Gaines's most recent novel, *A Lesson before Dying*, chronicles a wrongly convicted man's quest to regain basic human dignity before his execution. It won the 1993 National Book Critics Circle Award for fiction. In 1998 Gaines was inducted into the American Academy of Arts and Letters. He has worked as a writer-in-residence and professor of English at the University of Louisiana at Lafayette (formerly the University of Southwestern Louisiana) since 1983; he has lectured widely in the United States and abroad. Gaines met Dianne Saulney, an attorney, at a book fair, and married her on May 15, 1993.

The soft-spoken writer is more wont to affirm human similarities than differences in his explorations of the color line. When some of his students complained of having to read the views of a decidedly "white" Ernest (Hemingway), Gaines replied that Hemingway wrote about "grace under pressure"—a theme that applied equally to black and white students, and perhaps especially to the unheralded struggle of African Americans for familial dignity. Numerous honorary degrees and the worldwide translation of Gaines's work attest to the power and resonance of his voice.

WORKS: *Catherine Carmier* (1964). *Of Love and Dust* (1967). *Bloodline* (1968). *The Autobiography of Miss Jane Pittman* (1971). *A Long Day in November* (1971). *In My Father's House* (1978). *A Gathering of Old Men* (1983). *A Lesson before Dying* (1993). *Mozart and Leadbelly: Stories and Essays* (2005).

—BRYAN GIEMZA

FRANCES GAITHER (1889–1955). Frances Ormond Jones Gaither was born on May 21, 1889, in Somerville, Tenn., to Annie Smith and Paul Tudor Jones. Her father, a doctor and son of a substantial antebellum planter, moved his family to Corinth, Miss., soon after "Frankie" was born. In 1909 Frances was graduated with highest honors from Mississippi State College for Women (now Mississippi University for Women), where she had been student body president. After teaching senior high school English for a brief period in Corinth, she married journalist Rice Gaither, who had been her childhood sweetheart, on April 25, 1912. The couple lived first in Fairhope, Ala., and then in 1929 moved to New York City, where Rice Gaither was a reporter and feature writer for the *New York Times* until his death in 1953. Frances Gaither died in Cocoa, Fla., on October 28, 1955.

She began her career by writing ceremonial pageants and masques. Among these are *The Commencement Play of the Class of 1915* (including "The Pageant of Columbus"), "The Book of Words," and "The Clock and the Fountain," which she wrote for her alma mater, and "The Shadow of the Builder" and "Shores of Happiness" for the University of Virginia, the former celebrating that university's centennial. During the 1930s she wrote four children's books (stories entitled *The Painted Arrow, The Scarlet Coat,* and *Little Miss Cappo,* and one biography, *The Fatal River,* about La Salle). Turning to adult fiction in 1940 with *Follow the Drinking Gourd,* she found the antebellum plantation setting and theme upon which her reputation as a serious novelist rests. It was a world she knew through the tales told in Corinth and Sommerville. Her last novel, *Double Muscadine,* was a Book-of-the-Month Club selection for March 1949.

WORKS: *The Painted Arrow* (1931). *The Fatal River: The Life and Death of La Salle* (1931). *The Scarlet Coat* (1934). *Little Miss Cappo* (1937). *Follow the Drinking Gourd* (1940). *The Red Cock Crows* (1944). *Double Muscadine* (1949).

—ROBERT L. PHILLIPS, JR.

ALEXANDER GARDEN (1730–1791). Alexander Garden was born during January 1730 in Birse, Scotland, the son of a clergyman in the Church of Scotland. As an apprentice to a professor of medicine at Marischal College, Aberdeen, he developed an interest in natural history. Following brief service as a surgeon's first mate in the navy, he studied medicine at the University of Edinburgh. He received the A.M. in 1753 and the M.D. in 1754, both from Marischal.

Seeking a milder climate for health reasons, Garden joined a medical practice near Charles Town, S.C., in 1752. There he began extensive research and writing on the natural history of the American Southeast. On travels as far south as Florida and as far west as the Blue Ridge Mountains, he collected numerous specimens for shipment to natural scientists and physicians in Britain and Europe. His extensive correspondence with them and with fellow naturalists in the American colonies helped expand the scientific community's knowledge of the flora and fauna of North America. In 1755 he moved into Charles Town, becoming one of the city's most prominent physicians and developing an important garden at his plantation home, Otranto, at Goose Creek.

Garden received numerous honors for his research and writings on natural science, including election to the Royal Society of Arts of London, Philosophical Society of Edinburgh, Royal Society of London, Royal Society of Uppsala, American Society for Promoting and Propagating Useful Knowledge, Philadelphia Medical Society, and American Philosophical Society. He remained loyal to Great Britain during the American Revolution, and was banished, his property confiscated and turned over to his estranged son, Alexander (1757–1829), who had joined the American rebels. The elder Garden returned to England, continuing his natural history studies from his home in London, where he lived with wife Elizabeth Peronneau and their two daughters. He died in London on April 15, 1791.

WORKS: "The Description of a New Plant," in *Essays and Observations, Physical and Literary,* II (1756). *An Account of the Medical Properties of the Virginia Pink-Root* (1764). Description of the "Siren Lacertina" in Abraham Oester, *Amoenitates Academiae,* VII (1766). "An Account of the Indian Pink," *Essays and Observations, Physical and Literary,* III (1771). Description of a soft-shelled turtle in Thomas Pennant, "An Account of two new Tortoises; in a letter to Matthew Maty," *Transactions of the Royal Society of London,* LXI (1771). "An Account of the *Gymnotus Electricus,* or Electrical Eel, in a Letter from Alexander Garden, M.D., F.R.S., to John Ellis, Esq., F.R.S.," *Transactions of the Royal Society of London,* LXV (1775). Description of a tornado in Thomas Pennant, *Arctic Zoology: Supplement* (1788).

—ROBERT G. ANTHONY, JR.

GEORGE GARRETT (1929–). The range of George Garrett's work is unmatched in contemporary southern literature. Like Robert Penn Warren, he has written significant poetry, short fiction, novels, plays, and scholarly and critical essays and monographs, and he has also written screenplays and an opera libretto.

George Palmer Garrett, Jr., was born in Orlando, Fla., on June 11, 1929, into a family that included southern novelist Harry Stillwell Edwards, children's writer Helen Garrett, and prolific screenwriter Oliver H. P. Garrett. He attended Princeton University (B.A., 1952; M.A., 1956; Ph.D., 1985) and served in the U.S. Army (field artillery), stationed in the Free Territory of Trieste and Linz, Austria, for two years. He taught at numerous colleges and universities (among them Hollins College, the University of South Carolina, Bennington College, and the University of Michigan), until his retirement in 2000 from his position as Henry Hoyns Professor of Creative Writing at the University of Virginia.

Garrett's first book, the first of eight collections of poetry, was published in 1957, and he was named poet laureate of Virginia in 2002. He is also the author of seven highly regarded collections of short fiction. His nine novels have received the most notice, especially his formally innovative Elizabethan trilogy of historical novels, *Death of the Fox, The Succession,* and *Entered from the Sun.* Garrett's first collection of short fiction, *King of the Mountain,* prefigured the shape of the larger body of his fiction, moving from traditional forms through increasingly experimental fiction to a radical fusion of fiction and memoir. His work as a whole encompasses writing that is, at one extreme, wildly satirical and irreverent and, at the other, quietly and profoundly meditative.

Garrett married Susan Parrish Jackson in 1952; they have three children and two grandchildren and live in Charlottesville, Va.

WORKS: *The Reverend Ghost* (1957). *King of the Mountain* (1958). *The Sleeping Gypsy and Other Poems* (1958). *The Finished Man* (1959). *Abraham's Knife and Other Poems* (1961). *In the Briar Patch* (1961). *Which Ones Are the Enemy?* (1961). *Sir Slob and the Princess: A Play for Children* (1962). *Cold Ground Was My Bed Last Night* (1964). *Do, Lord, Remember Me* (1965). *For a Bitter Season: New and Selected Poems* (1967). *A Wreath for Garibaldi and Other Stories*

(1969). *Death of the Fox* (1971). *The Magic Striptease* (1973). *Welcome to the Medicine Show: Flashcards / Postcards / Snapshots* (1978). *To Recollect a Cloud of Ghosts: Christmas in England, 1602–1603* (1979). *Luck's Shining Child: A Miscellany of Poems and Verses* (1981). *Enchanted Ground: A Play for Readers' Theater* (1981). *The Succession: A Novel of Elizabeth and James* (1983). *The Collected Poems of George Garrett* (1984). *James Jones* (1984). *An Evening Performance: New and Selected Short Stories* (1985). *Poison Pen, or, Live Now and Pay Later* (1986). *Understanding Mary Lee Settle* (1988). *Entered from the Sun* (1990). *The Sorrows of Fat City: A Selection of Literary Essays and Reviews* (1992). *Whistling in the Dark: True Stories and Other Fables* (1992). *My Silk Purse and Yours: The Publishing Scene and American Literary Art* (1992). *The Old Army Game: A Novel and Stories* (1994). *The King of Babylon Shall Not Come against You* (1996). *Days of Our Lives Lie in Fragments: New and Old Poems, 1957–1997* (1998). *Bad Man Blues: A Portable George Garrett* (1998). *Going to See the Elephant: Pieces of a Writing Life* (2002). *Southern Excursions: Selected Essays and Critical Pieces on Southern Literature* (2003). *Double Vision* (2004).

—R. H. W. Dillard

HENRY LOUIS GATES, JR. (1950–). Henry Louis "Skip" Gates, Jr., was born in Piedmont, W.Va. His father worked in a paper mill and also as a janitor; his mother, Pauline, cleaned houses. Gates attended Potomac State College in Keyser, W.Va., in preparation for a medical career, before transferring to Yale University, where he earned a B.A. in history (1973). In 1970–71 he took time away from Yale to work in an Anglican mission hospital in Tanzania and hitchhike in Africa. At Clare College, Cambridge, where Gates received an M.A. and Ph.D. in English language and literature (1979), the Nigerian writer Wole Soyinka introduced him to Yoruba mythology and led him into African cultural studies. While in England, Gates also worked as a correspondent for *Time* magazine. In 1976–79, Gates was a lecturer and director of undergraduate education at Yale. In 1979 he was appointed assistant professor, and that year he married Sharon Adams, a potter he had met when they both worked in Jay Rockefeller's 1972 gubernatorial campaign in West Virginia. They have two daughters, Maggie and Liza.

Having begun work on the massive Black Periodical Fiction Project intended to recover all black fiction from nineteenth-century American periodicals, Gates came to national prominence with his rediscovery and republication of Harriet Wilson's *Our Nig; or, Sketches from the Life of a Free Black*, the first novel by an African American published in the United States (1859). In his introduction to *Our Nig* and in a series of critical essays, Gates argued that African Americans had a richer, longer literary history than conventional wisdom supposed, and he set out to dig up and validate their "lost texts." His most controversial find was the manuscript of Hannah Crafts's semi-autobiographical *The Bondwoman's Narrative*, which Gates claimed to be "the first novel written by a female fugitive slave." Gates collected slave narratives, prepared critical works on African American writers, and co-edited the *Norton Anthology of African American Literature*.

At the same time, Gates was engaged in remapping the full sweep of African American literature by approaching it through African culture. Gates argued that African American literature played on and against previous forms, an idea he explored in *Black Literature and Literary Theory* and *Figures in Black*. His *The Signifying Monkey: Towards a Theory of Afro-American Literary Criticism*, winner of the American Book Award, most fully laid out the hermeneutic basis of "signifyin(g)," Gates's metaphor for literary history.

By the early 1990s, Gates had become a national figure, at once literary critic, social commentator, and cultural arbiter. *Loose Canons: Notes on the Culture Wars* staked out his position that diverse approaches to multiculturalism promise constant discussion and negotiation and, thus, the most understanding, whether reading literature or "rappin'." As a regular contributor to the *New Yorker*, frequent reviewer and subject of comment in the *New York Times*, and guest on radio and television talk shows,

Gates became the fulcrum in debates among African American intellectuals about what "black" meant and ought to mean in America. He became involved in controversy in 1990 after testifying in the trial of the hip-hop group 2 Live Crew on obscenity charges. Drawing on his interviews with prominent African Americans to suggest how race shaped identity in America, *Thirteen Ways of Looking at a Black Man* further linked Gates with the famous in the public mind.

Fellowships and accolades, including a MacArthur "genius" grant (1981), came to Gates. He left Yale for Cornell in 1985; he went to Duke University in 1990; and in 1991 he went to Harvard University to rebuild the W. E. B. Du Bois Institute for Afro-American Studies. Seeking to realize Du Bois's dream of a world-renowned center of African and African American genius, Gates brought to Harvard many leading African American scholars.

With friend and co-editor K. Anthony Appiah, Gates completed another of Du Bois's projects, a pan-African encyclopedia, which was released as a CD-ROM called *Encarta Africana* (1999) and in book form under the title *Africana*. In 1999 PBS aired *Wonders of the African World*, a documentary featuring Gates's travels and his investigations into African history. The encyclopedia and documentary gave full compass to Gates's life-long passion to discover and recover African and African American culture and place it at the center of Americans' perception of the world and themselves.

WORKS: Ed., *Black Is the Color of the Cosmos: Charles T. Davis's Essay on Afro-American Literature and Culture, 1942–1981* (1982). Ed., Harriet E. Wilson, *Our Nig; or, Sketches from the Life of a Free Slave, in a Two Story White House* (1983). Ed., *Black Literature and Theory* (1984). Ed., *The Slave's Narrative: Texts and Contexts*, with Charles T. Davis (1985). Ed., *Wole Soyinka: A Bibliography of Primary and Secondary Sources*, with J. Gibbs and K. Katrak (1986). Ed., *"Race," Writing, and Difference* (1986). Ed., *In the House of Oshugbo: Critical Essays on Wole Soyinka* (1987). *Figures in Black: Words, Signs, and the "Racial" Self* (1987). *The Signifying Monkey: Towards a Theory of Afro-American Literary Criticism* (1987). Ed., *The Classic Slave Narratives* (1987). Ed., *The Oxford-Schomburg Library of Nineteenth-Century Black Women Writers* (1988–91). Ed., *Bearing Witness: Selections from African American Autobiography* (1991). *Loose Canons: Notes on the Culture Wars* (1992). *Colored People: A Memoir* (1994). Ed., *Frederick Douglass: Autobiographies* (1994). *Speaking of Race: Hate Speech, Civil Rights, and Civil Liberties* (1995). Ed., *The Dictionary of Global Culture*, with K. Anthony Appiah (1995). *The Future of the Race*, with Cornel West (1996). Ed., *Identities*, with Appiah (1996). Ed., *The Norton Anthology of African American Literature*, with Nellie Y. McKay (1996). *Thirteen Ways of Looking at a Black Man* (1997). Ed., *Africana: The Encyclopedia of the African and African American Experience*, with Appiah (1999). *Wonders of the African World* (1999). *The African American Century: How Black American Have Shaped Our Century*, with West (2000). Ed., Helen Crafts, *The Bondwoman's Narrative* (2002). Ed., *In Search of Hannah Crafts: Critical Essays on "The Bondwoman's Narrative,"* with Hollis Robbins (2003). *The Trials of Phillis Wheatley: America's First Black Poet and Encounters with the Founding Fathers* (2003). Ed., *African American Lives*, with Evelyn Brooks Higginbotham (2004). *America behind the Color Line: Dialogues with African Americans* (2004). Ed., *White Pages: Black Writers on Whites and Whiteness*, with Appiah and Michael Colin Vazquez (2005). Ed., *The African American Biography*, with Higginbotham (2006).

—RANDALL M. MILLER

TIM GAUTREAUX (1947–). Timothy M. Gautreaux was born in Morgan City, La., on October 19, 1947, and raised in southern Louisiana, where his father, Minos, was a tugboat captain. Gautreaux stayed in his native region to take a B.A. from Nicholls State University in Thibodaux in 1969. He earned a Ph.D. in English literature and creative writing from the University of South Carolina in 1972 and returned to Louisiana that year to teach at Southeastern Louisiana University in Hammond. At Southeastern he was a professor of English and the university's writer-in-residence until his retirement in 2002. In the fall of 1996 he was the John and Renee Grisham Southern Writer-in-Residence at the University of Mississippi. In 1999 he was the recipient of a fellowship from the National Endowment for the Arts. He and his wife, Winborne, have two sons and continue to live in Hammond.

Gautreaux's first novel, *The Next Step in the Dance*, was named novel of the year by the Southeastern Booksellers Association, and his second collection of short stories, *Welding with Children*, was acclaimed as a notable book of 1999 by the *New York Times Book Review*. In 1998 Gautreaux received the National Magazine Award for Fiction. His stories have appeared in the *Atlantic*, *Gentleman's Quarterly*, *Harper's*, *Story*, the *Virginia Quarterly Review*, and *Zoetrope*. He has also had stories selected for the anthologies *Best American Short Stories* and *New Stories from the South*.

Gautreaux considers himself a Catholic writer in the tradition of Walker Percy (who advised him to abandon poetry for fiction) and Flannery O'Connor, and he cites James Dickey as an early influence. In stories such as "Died and Gone to Vegas," he also places himself in the frontier tradition of the tall tale and Mark Twain. Southern Louisiana is the clearly and (particularly when juxtaposed with Texas) lovingly drawn setting for virtually all of his fiction, and many stories concern the struggle to maintain and cherish the distinct cultural heritage of the region. His characters tend to be poor, undereducated, and employed (if at all) at dirty, mechanical work. Though they are seemingly incapable of escaping their woeful circumstances, Gautreaux depicts his characters with sympathy, humor, and hope for redemption.

WORKS: *Same Place, Same Things* (1996). *The Next Step in the Dance* (1998). *Welding with Children* (1999). *The Clearing* (2003).

—PETER J. FLORA

CHARLES GAYARRÉ (1805–1895). On January 9, 1805, Charles Étienne Arthure Gayarré was born into one of Louisiana's most prominent families. In 1830, his legal education completed, the young lawyer published *Essai historique sur la Louisiane*, essentially a translation of François-Xavier Martin's *History of Louisiana* (1827). Gayarré rose from state senator (1830) to assistant attorney general (1831) to attorney general (1832) to presiding judge of the City Court of New Orleans (1832–35). Although he was elected to the U.S. Senate in 1835, poor health forced him to resign, and he spent most of the next eight years in France. After returning to New Orleans, he served as state senator and as Louisiana's secretary of state. Defeat in the 1853 election prompted him to attack political corruption in pamphlets and a "dramatic novel," *The School of Politics*.

The time spent in Europe and his political positions enabled Gayarré to collect documents from European archives, which he cited at great length in *Histoire de la Louisiane*. Desiring a larger readership, he abandoned French for English in *Romance of the History of Louisiana*, a series of lectures that grew into the four-volume *History of Louisiana*, his major work. Influenced by Scott, he at first tended to sacrifice fact to romance, but beginning with his coverage of the Spanish administration, the history became accurate as well as vivid.

His fortune lost during the Civil War, Gayarré lived in near-poverty until his death on February 11, 1895. He was a dominant figure in Louisiana's literary circles and the author of a psychological study, *Philip II of Spain*, an autobiographical novel, *Fernando de Lemos*, other fiction, a comedy, and many essays and pamphlets.

WORKS: *Essai historique sur la Louisiane* (1830). *Histoire de la Louisiane* (1846–47). *Romance of the History of Louisiana* (1848). *Louisiana: Its Colonial History and Romance* (1851). *Louisiana: Its History as a French Colony* (1852). *History of Louisiana: The French Domination* (1854). *History of Louisiana: The Spanish Domination* (1854). *The School for Politics: A Dramatic Novel* (1854). *Dr. Bluff in Russian, or The Emperor Nicholas and the American Doctor: A Comedy in Two Acts* (1865). *History of Louisiana: The American Domination* (1866). *History of Louisiana* (1866, 1879, 1885, 1903). *Philip II of Spain* (1866). *Fernando de Lemos: Truth and Fiction* (1872). *Aubert Dubayet; or, The Two Sister Republics* (1882).

—ALFRED BENDIXEN

DENISE GIARDINA (1951–). Denise Giardina lived her first twelve years in Black Wolf Coal Camp, near Bluefield, W.Va. Her grandfather and two uncles worked underground, while her father was a bookkeeper for Page Coal and Coke, her mother a nurse. With the closing of the mine in 1963, her family moved to Charleston, W.Va.

Giardina attended West Virginia Wesleyan College on a scholarship, graduating with honors in history and political science in 1973. Her Appalachian upbringing had roused her social consciousness, and study in London in her junior year awakened an interest in Anglican theology. Giardina considered law school but enrolled in the Virginia Theological Seminary (Episcopal). She graduated in 1979 with an M.A., was ordained a deacon, and returned to a church in southern West Virginia. When her public criticism of the coal companies led to differences with her superiors, she relocated to Washington, D.C., and worked in the peace movement. During this period she began her first novel, about Henry V, examining the moral dilemma faced by good people who wield power.

Giardina returned to Charleston and did secretarial work to support her writing, leading to the publication of *Good King Harry* in 1984. Though critically acclaimed, the novel did not sell well. Undeterred, Giardina began writing where her passion lay, on the history of the coal fields in southern Appalachia from the 1920s to the 1990s. *Storming Heaven,* a novel focusing on the miners' struggle to unionize, won the W. D. Weatherford Award for best published work about the Appalachian South (1988). *The Unquiet Earth* picked up the narrative with the newly unionized miners now fighting corporate corruption. This novel won Giardina her second Weatherford Award (1992), an American Book Award (1993), and the Lillian Smith Award for fiction (1992). Accepting a position as writer-in-residence at West Virginia State College, Giardina next wrote *Saints and Villains,* a fictional biography of Dietrich Bonhoeffer that was awarded the Fisk Fiction Prize in 1999.

Giardina has received fellowships from the National Endowment for the Arts (1988 and 1996); authored an award-winning screenplay for West Virginia Public Television, "The Gift Horse" (1996); and received the 2002 Appalachian Heritage Writers Award. A force in the coal-field struggles, she published articles on the 1989 Pittston Coal strike in the *Nation, Southern Exposure,* and the *Village Voice;* and her activism continues in her op-ed writing for major newspapers. Her outrage over the strip-mining practice of "mountaintop removal" led to her unsuccessful run for governor as the candidate of the West Virginia Mountain Party in 2000.

WORKS: *Good King Harry* (1984). *Storming Heaven* (1987). *The Unquiet Earth* (1992). *Saints and Villains* (1999). *Fallam's Secret* (2003).

—PETER L. STAFFEL

KAYE GIBBONS (1960–). Kaye Batts was born on May 5, 1960, in Wilson, N.C., and grew up on a tobacco farm in nearby Nash County, experiencing the agricultural seasons and relative poverty. Her mother, who had provided order and stability, killed herself in 1970. In 1971 Kaye moved to her aunt's home, and after her alcoholic father died in 1972 she moved to a foster home. In June 1973 her brother married, and she moved to his home in Rocky Mount, where she graduated from high school in 1978.

She then entered North Carolina State University in Raleigh. During her schooling she had become more and more fascinated with language and literature and had begun writing poetry, so she decided to major in English.

In the fall of 1980 she transferred to Chapel Hill; but in August 1981, because of manic depression, she entered a hospital in Raleigh, staying there until March 1982 while again attending State. In 1983 she had another attack and left school and worked at various jobs. In 1984 she married Michael Gibbons, a landscape architect; they had three daughters (in 1984, 1987, 1989). In 1985 she returned to Chapel Hill, and in classes there she became more aware of uses of everyday speech in literature and of relationships between language and place. She was encouraged in her writing by her teacher, Louis Rubin, and her first novel, *Ellen Foster,* was published in 1987. Since then she has published six other novels. Gibbons and her family moved to California in 1992, but the marriage deteriorated and eventually she returned to Raleigh and divorced. In 1993 she married Frank Ward, a Raleigh attorney with two children of his own. The marriage ended in an acrimonious divorce.

Gibbons's first two novels depend a great deal on her memories of her own life and her family. For subsequent novels, she has had to do more research in order to make her characters and their lives authentic to times and places of the past. The geographic and cultural emphases of her writings are southern, and her strongest characters are females of strength and courage. She has won numerous awards for her works, especially for *Ellen Foster.* In 2006 Gibbons began a new life in New York City.

WORKS: *Ellen Foster* (1987). *A Virtuous Woman* (1989). *A Cure for Dreams* (1991). *Charms for the Easy Life* (1993). *Sights Unseen* (1995). *On the Occasion of My Last Afternoon* (1998). *Divining Women* (2004). *The Life All around Me by Ellen Foster* (2006).

—JULIAN MASON

MARGARET GIBSON (1944–). Margaret Gibson was born in Philadelphia, but considers herself a native of Richmond, Va., where she grew up. The daughter of an engineer and a teacher, Gibson found need for a refuge in words and books within the conservative society of Richmond. She continued to read avidly and later flourished in the liberal arts environment of Hollins College. She graduated from Hollins in 1966 and went on to receive an M.A. from the University of Virginia in 1967. A summer stay in the artists' community of Yaddo in 1975 helped to refine her sense of herself and her art.

Gibson's poetry from the first has been profoundly relational. It is the voice of a speaker finding herself by working toward an adequate expression of her relation to the world about her. She is perhaps most identified with the nature-elegies and domestic lyrics collected in *Signs, Long Walks in the Afternoon,* and *Out in the Open.* But the personal and religious, for Gibson, cannot be separated from the political. Although present elsewhere, her socialist and feminist convictions most deeply inform *Memories of the Future,* in which she assumes the voice of the photographer Tina Modotti in postrevolutionary Mexico and the Spanish Civil War. Her consideration of the relationship between love and power can assume quieter forms as well, as it does in *The Vigil,* in which three generations of women come to terms with a death in the family. She synthesizes and expands upon many of the strands in her previous volumes in *Early Elegy.* Her recent volume *Icon and Evidence* reflects the power of Gibson's mature contemplative vision.

Gibson has taught and served as writer-in-residence at a number of universities, primarily in Virginia and Connecticut. She lives in Connecticut with her husband, the poet and nonfiction writer David McKain.

WORKS: *The Duel and Other Poems* (1966). *Lunes: Poems* (1973). *On the Cutting Edge* (1976). *Signs: Poems* (1979). *Long Walks in the Afternoon: Poems* (1982). *Memories of the Future: The Daybooks of Tina Modotti: Poems* (1986). *Out in the Open: Poems* (1989). *The Vigil: A Poem in Four Voices* (1993). *Earth Elegy: New and Selected Poems* (1997). *Icon and Evidence: Poems* (2001). *Autumn Grasses: Poems* (2003).

—DOUGLAS L. MITCHELL

ELLEN GILCHRIST (1935–). Mississippi native Ellen Gilchrist lived for much of her childhood in the Midwest, but she returned regularly to the Delta to visit her mother's family, and her family moved back to the South when she was in high school. She began her writing career at fifteen as a columnist for the Franklin, Ky., newspaper but had to give up her column when her father again moved their family. It was a foreshadowing event, for Gilchrist would eventually put aside her writing for her own family obligations: she wrote in college, but not professionally until her three sons were grown.

Gilchrist attended Vanderbilt University as a freshman, then the University of Alabama as a sopho- more, then dropped out to marry Marshall Walker, who would be the father of her children. These two divorced and remarried; in between, Gilchrist married and divorced James Bloodworth. After her second divorce from Walker, Gilchrist finished her B.A. at Millsaps College in Mississippi. She then married Frederick Kullman of New Orleans, where Gilchrist worked as a contributing editor of the *Vieux Carré Courier*. In 1976 she enrolled in the creative writing program at the University of Arkansas, first commuting, but taking up permanent residence in Fayetteville after her divorce from Kullman.

Although Gilchrist did not complete the M.F.A. program, during her matriculation Fayetteville's Lost Roads Press published a collection of her poems, and the university press published her first book of fiction. This short-story collection attracted the attention of Little, Brown, which has since published all of her books except for a second collection of poetry and *Anabasis,* a historical novel set in ancient Greece. Her second collection of short fiction, *Victory over Japan,* won the American Book Award for fiction.

In the Land of Dreamy Dreams introduces Rhoda Manning, the protagonist of numerous stories throughout Gilchrist's canon and of the novel *Net of Jewels*. Precocious, spoiled, strong-willed, and rebellious, Rhoda is the prototype for most Gilchrist protagonists, including Amanda McCamey in the novel *The Annunciation* and a few short stories in later collections, and Nora Jane Whittington and Crystal Manning Mallison Weiss, two other recurrent characters of Gilchrist's short fiction. In the novel *The Anna Papers,* Anna Hand fulfills the promise of the original prototype. Unable to overcome her conflict with her dominating father and brother or her belief that her value as a woman depends on the opinions of the men in her life, Rhoda focuses most of her energy toward finding a mate rather than on her ambition to write. In contrast, Anna has put behind her the experience of several miscar- riages and disappointing marriages and has focused her attention on her writing.

By continuing to create characters with Rhoda's weaknesses, Gilchrist reminds her readers that overcoming gender strictures is not easy, even for women growing up post-"women's lib." Whereas most of her other early protagonists are members of the author's own generation, many of the pro- tagonists of her post–*Anna Papers* works are girls and young women of the next generation—reaching maturity in the 1980s. Having a career may be more accessible to these women and more socially ac- ceptable in the world at large, but Gilchrist's plots suggest that not much is changing for these young women from old southern families, which still prize compliant daughters who find fine husbands and provide heirs.

In recent collections of fiction, Gilchrist has begun to write about a sixty-year-old Rhoda. These stories lack the poignancy and humor of the early Rhoda stories, which, though also based on Gil- christ's life, were set far enough in the past that the author had achieved some distance from her auto- biographical character. In the most recent collection, Rhoda has made her peace with her father—to such an extent that she seems to have decided that his conservative views may have been right all along. The fan of Gilchrist's younger rebel may be disappointed by this change of heart.

WORKS: *The Land Surveyor's Daughter* (1979). *In the Land of Dreamy Dreams* (1981). *The Annunciation* (1983). *Victory over Japan* (1984). *Drunk with Love* (1986). *Riding Out the Tropical Depression* (1986). *Falling through Space* (1987; expanded ed. 2000). *The Anna Papers* (1988). *Light Can Be Both Wave and Particle* (1989). *I Cannot Get You Close Enough* (1990). *Net of Jewels* (1992). *Anabasis* (1994). *Starcarbon* (1994). *The Age of Miracles* (1995). *Rhoda: A Life in Stories* (1995). *The Courts of Love* (1996). *Sarah Conley* (1997). *Flights of Angels* (1999). *The Cabal and Other Stories* (2000). *Ellen Gilchrist: Collected Stories* (2000). *I, Rhoda Manning, Go Hunting with My Daddy* (2002). *Nora Jane: A Life in Stories* (2005). *The Writing Life* (2005).

—MARGARET D. BAUER

JANICE GILES (1909–1979). Giles was born Janice Holt in Altus, Ark., on March 28, 1901, and then taken home by her parents to the Indian Territory. The Holts were teachers in the old Choctaw Nation (eastern Oklahoma) from 1901 to 1917, when they returned with their three children to Arkansas, settling in Fort Smith. Janice married Otto Moore in 1927, a marriage that produced one daughter but ended in divorce in 1939. Janice Moore then moved to Little Rock, serving as director of religious education at a local church. That led to her work as director of children's work for the Disciples of Christ—an activity she dovetailed with study at Little Rock Junior College and the University of Arkansas. For her religious work she began writing plays, articles, and poems.

The next move was to Louisville, Ky., to serve as assistant to the dean of the Louisville Presbyterian Seminary. On a trip in 1943 to visit her daughter, she met a soldier, Henry Earl Gates, who came from a family long established in Kentucky. The couple married on October 11, 1945. They moved from Louisville in 1949 to forty acres on Giles Ridge near Kiffney. When Henry took a position with the *News-Journal*, they moved to Campbellsville, Ky.

Janice Giles was the author of six contemporary novels set in the Kentucky hills, most notably her trilogy, *The Enduring Hills*, *Tara's Healing*, and *Miss Willie*. These books endeared her to readers because they offered a sympathetic view of rural Kentuckians, who often humanized outsiders coming into their communities to "do good." She also wrote eleven historical novels, seven set in the West and four in Kentucky. *The Believers* takes place in a Shaker community in Kentucky and illuminates religious fanaticism. *Hannah Fowler* probes the character of a strong eastern Kentucky pioneer woman who is captured by Indians.

Giles was the author of seven nonfiction memoirs. *Forty Acres and No Mule* is a popular account of her move to the country, and *A Little Better Than Plumb* describes the rebuilding of the same house on higher ground. *The Damned Engineers* is a critical commentary on the impact of the Army Corps of Engineers dam that required the move. Giles's work presents an unusual combination of precise historical research along with detailed grassroots wisdom about how nature, animals, and people really work.

Giles was one of Kentucky's most popular and respected literary figures from the 1950s through the 1970s. Although her work has been called sentimental, her literary legacy endures because she captured as completely and accurately as any twentieth-century writer the impact of America's westward expansion—from the Appalachians to the Pacific—upon women.

WORKS: *The Enduring Hills* (1950). *Miss Willie* (1951). *Tara's Healing* (1951). *Harbin's Ridge* (1951). *Forty Acres and No Mule* (1952). *The Kentuckians* (1953). *Hill Man* (1954). *The Plum Thicket* (1954). *Hannah Fowler* (1956). *The Believers* (1957). *The Land beyond the Mountains* (1958). *Johnny Osage* (1960). *Savanna* (1961). *Voyage to Santa Fe* (1962). *A Little Better Than Plumb* (1963). *Run Me a River* (1964). *The G.I. Journal of Sgt. Giles* (1965). *The Great*

Adventure (1966). *Shady Grove* (1967). *Six Horse Hitch* (1968). *The Damned Engineers* (1970). *Around Our House* (1971). *The Kinda Years* (1973). *Wellspring* (1975). *Act of Contrition* (2001).

—GEORGE BROSI

CAROLINE HOWARD GILMAN (1794–1888). The youngest daughter of Samuel Howard, an "Indian" of the Boston Tea Party, Caroline Gilman was born on October 8, 1794, in Boston. Reared by an older sister, Ann Marie White, whose own daughter married James Russell Lowell, Caroline wrote poetry, visited her brothers who were merchants in Savannah, and in 1819 married the Reverend Samuel Gilman. The Reverend Gilman and his bride moved immediately to Charleston, S.C., where he served as a famous Unitarian minister for almost forty years. After his death in 1858, Gilman continued to live in Charleston and the South until 1873, when she moved to her married daughter's home in the North. She died on September 15, 1888.

Her Boston upbringing was conducive to her conservatism, modesty, and piety, traits furthered by her marriage to a minister. Her love of Charleston and southern ways was a natural response to her years of active social and cultural involvement in her new home. Perhaps the only characteristic not predicated by her cultural environment was her delightful sense of humor, revealed throughout her life in her best writing and especially in her family letters.

An early interest in providing suitable reading for her own and other children led her in 1832 to found and edit the *Rose Bud,* later the *Southern Rose Bud,* and for the final four years, as a magazine for adults, the *Southern Rose.* It published some leading contemporaries, including Hawthorne and Simms, and was also the source for her own later books. Notable were her editing of the *Letters of Eliza Wilkinson* (eyewitness accounts of the Revolutionary War in Charleston) and her own lively *Recollections of a Housekeeper, Recollections of a Southern Matron,* and *Poetry of Travelling in the United States.* If her writing, especially her poetry, seems overly didactic now, her contemporary popularity was not thereby weakened. Indeed, she was clearly the best-known southern woman writer for a quarter of a century (1833–58). An overlooked resource for social histories is her lifelong effort to educate the North to the ways of life in the South, for she felt that as a daughter of New England she was in the best position to explain her adopted region.

WORKS: *The Rose Bud, or Youth's Gazette* (1832–33). *Southern Rose Bud,* 2–3 (1833–35). *The Southern Rose,* 4–7 (1835–39). *The Lady's Register and Housewife's Memorandum-Book* (1839–41). *Recollections of a Housekeeper* (1834, 1836, 1838, 1842). *Tales and Ballads* (1834, 1838, 1839, 1844). *Recollections of a Southern Matron* (1837, 1838, 1839, 1852, 1854). *The Poetry of Travelling in the United States* (1838). Ed., *Letters of Eliza Wilkinson, during the Invasion and Possession of Charleston, S.C. by the British in the Revolutionary War* (1839, 1969). *Love's Progress* (1840). *The Rose-Bud-Wreath* (1841). *Oracles from the Poets: A Fanciful Diversion for the Drawing-Room* (1844, 1845, 1847,1848, 1849, 1852, 1853, 1854). *Stories and Poems for Children* (1844, 1845). *The Little Wreath of Stories and Poems for Children* (1846). *The Sibyl, or, New Oracles from the Poets* (1848, 1849, 1852). *Verses of a Life Time* (1849). *A Gift Book of Stories and Poems for Children* (1850, 1854). *Oracles for Youth: A Home Pastime* (1852, 1853). "My Autobiography," in *The Female Prose Writers of America,* ed. John S. Hart (1852), 49–57. *Recollections of a New England Bride and of a Southern Matron* (1852, 1854). *Recollections of a Southern Matron, and a New England Bride* (1859, 1867, 1889). *Record of Inscriptions in the Cemetery and Building of the Unitarian, Formerly Denominated the Independent Church, Archdale Street, Charleston, S.C., from 1777 to 1860* (1860). *Stories and Poems by Mother and Daughter,* with Caroline Howard Jervey (1872). *The Young Fortune Teller; Oracles for Youth* (1874). *The Poetic Fate Book: New Oracles from the Poets* (1874). *Recollections of the Private Centennial Celebration of the Overthrow of the Tea, at Griffin's Wharf, in Boston Harbor, December 16, 1773, in Honor of Samuel Howard, One of the Actors, at Cambridge, Mass., December 1873* (1874). "Letters of a Confederate Mother: Charleston in the Sixties," *Atlantic Monthly* 137 (Apr. 1926): 503–15.

—JANICE J. THOMPSON

REBECCA GILMAN (1964–). The youngest of four children, playwright Rebecca Claire Gilman grew up in Trussville, Ala., the daughter of a Jewish father and a Southern Baptist mother. Gilman began her undergraduate career at Middlebury College but graduated from Birmingham Southern College. She went on to get her M.A. in English from the University of Virginia before receiving her M.F.A. in playwriting from the University of Iowa in 1991.

Gilman's work was performed in many small regional theaters before her play *The Glory of Living* was produced in Chicago, first by the Circle Theatre and then by the Goodman Theatre. After the play's run at the Royal Court Theatre in London, Gilman became the first American recipient of the *Evening Standard* Award for Most Promising Playwright, in 1999. Gilman's work is notable for its bold handling of controversial themes. *Spinning into Butter,* a play in which subtle forms of racism are exposed at a small liberal college in New England, had its New York premiere at the Lincoln Center Theater in 2000. That same year her play *Boy Gets Girl,* a story of one woman's struggle with a stalker, was named best play of the year by *Time* magazine. In 2001 *Blue Surge* premiered at the Goodman Theatre in Chicago, where Gilman currently lives with her husband, Charles. *The Sweetest Swing in Baseball,* about an artist who, after a nervous breakdown, pretends to be baseball player Darryl Strawberry in order to remain in a psychiatric hospital, premiered at the Royal Court Theatre in March 2004.

WORKS: *My Sin and Nothing More* (1997). *The Land of the Little Horses* (1998). *The Glory of Living* (1998). *Spinning into Butter* (2000). *Boy Gets Girl* (2000). *Blue Surge* (2001).

—AMANDA PAGE

FRANCIS WALKER GILMER (1790–1826). The tenth child of Dr. George Gilmer, Francis Walker Gilmer was born on October 9, 1790, at Pen Park, an estate across the river from Monticello. Christened Francis Thornton Gilmer, he assumed the name of his uncle Francis Walker after the latter's death in 1806. After his father's death in 1795, Gilmer remained in Albemarle County, Va., until he was eighteen as a guest/ward of his neighbors. He entered William and Mary College in 1809, and by January 1811 he was practicing law in Richmond under the tutelage of William Wirt. After moving to Winchester in July 1814, he returned to Richmond in 1818 to take over Wirt's substantial practice. Here Gilmer also served as the court reporter for the Virginia Court of Appeals (1820–21) and laid the foundation for an eminent legal career.

The extraordinary achievements predicted for Gilmer, whom his friend Jefferson called "the best educated subject we have raised since the Revolution," were never fully realized. Yet, despite his weak constitution, he became an accomplished lawyer, as well as an author, geologist, economist, botanist, and social scientist. He was elected the first professor of law at the University of Virginia and was enlisted by Jefferson to travel to Europe in 1824 to select and hire the institution's future faculty.

The range of Gilmer's erudition is evident in his varied writings. His claim to literary fame is founded upon his *Sketches of American Orators,* one of the first evaluations of America's then most widespread literary endeavor. His "On the Geological Formation of the Natural Bridge of Virginia" was the first treatise to suggest the still accepted theory of formation by erosion due to an underground stream. Gilmer's interest in Virginiana also led to his publishing the first scholarly American editions of Captain John Smith's *General Historie of Virginia* and Smith's *True Travels.* Although somewhat Romantic in taste, Gilmer, in his "Reflections on the Institutions of the Cherokee Indians," a result of his excursion to Georgia (1815), describes the Cherokees not as noble savages but as a "mixture of insensibility, vulgarity, and vice." In economics, his *Vindication* was a highly esteemed rebuttal of Jeremy Bentham's classic *Defense of Usury.* Gilmer's busy legal career and subsequent illnesses precluded any further publication. He died a bachelor on February 25, 1826, a victim of tuberculosis.

158

WORKS: *Sketches of American Orators* (1816). "On the Geological Formations of the Natural Bridge of Virginia," *Publications of the American Philosophical Society*, n.s., 1 (Feb. 1816). "Reflections on the Institutions of the Cherokee Indians, from Observations Made during a Recent Visit to That Tribe: In a Letter from a Gentleman of Virginia to Robert Walsh, Jan.–June 1st. 1817," *Analectic Magazine* 12 (July 1818). Editions of *The General Historie of Virginia, New England, and the Summer Iles . . . and The True Travels, Adventures and Observations of Captaine John Smith . . .* (1819). *A Vindication of the Laws, Limiting the Rate of Interest on Loans; from the Objections of Jeremy Bentham, and the Edinburgh Reviewers* (1820). *Reports of Cases Decided in the Court of Appeals of Virginia* (from April 10, 1820, to June 28, 1821) (1821). *Sketches, Essays and Translations* (1828).

—MICHAEL A. LOFARO

MARIANNE GINGHER (1947–). Because their daughter was born on one of the Marianna Islands on February 19, 1947, Roderick Buie, a navy physician, and his wife, Betty Jane Cannon, named her Marianne. By 1950 the family had moved permanently to North Carolina, where Marianne attended school. She received her B.A. in 1969 from Salem College in Winston-Salem and her M.F.A. from the University of North Carolina at Greensboro in 1974.

Gingher has two children, Roderick and Samuel, with Robert Gingher, whom she married in 1967 and divorced in 1991. She taught art in the public schools in 1969–75, was Visiting Writer at Elon College in Burlington, N.C., in the fall of 1987, and worked as an assistant professor of English at Hollins College in Roanoke, Va., in 1989–91. In 1976 Gingher began teaching in the creative writing program at the University of North Carolina at Chapel Hill, where she is currently an associate professor of English, serving as the director of creative writing in 1997–2002.

Gingher's early works, *Bobby Rex's Greatest Hits* and *Teen Angel and Other Stories of Wayward Love*, explore in fiction the adolescent struggles with identity and finding love in the world. Later nonfiction, *How to Have a Happy Childhood* and *A Girl's Life: Horses, Boys, Weddings, and Luck*, focuses on the impact of childhood and family.

Gingher has published short stories and nonfiction in numerous journals, magazines, and anthologies, including *Redbook, McCall's, Ladies' Home Journal, Southern Review, O: The Oprah Magazine,* and the *Oxford American,* and she has reviewed books for such well-known publications as the *New York Times, Los Angeles Times,* and *Washington Times.* She has received numerous fellowships, grants, and awards, including the PEN Syndicated Fiction Award in 1986 for her short story "Putting the Babies to Bed."

WORKS: *Bobby Rex's Greatest Hits* (1986). *Teen Angel and Other Stories of Wayward Love* (1988). *How to Have a Happy Childhood* (2000). *A Girl's Life: Horses, Boys, Weddings, and Luck* (2001).

—BARBARA BENNETT

NIKKI GIOVANNI (1943–). Yolande Cornelia (Nikki) Giovanni, Jr., was born on June 7, 1943, in Knoxville, Tenn. The younger daughter of Jones and Yolande Giovanni, she had a secure, middle-class upbringing. When she was very young, the family moved to Lincoln Heights, a predominantly African American suburb of Cincinnati, Ohio, where Giovanni attended public and parochial schools. In 1960 she enrolled at Fisk University, her maternal grandfather's alma mater, but was "released" in February 1961 because her attitudes were not those of a "Fisk woman."

In 1964 Giovanni returned to Fisk, proving herself a serious and productive student. She sharpened her literary skills by participating in the Fisk Writers Workshop, directed by celebrated author John Oliver Killens, and by editing *Elan,* Fisk's literary magazine. Politically, she shifted her position from Barry Goldwater conservative to Black Power revolutionary and led the reorganization of Fisk's chapter of the Student Nonviolent Coordinating Committee. Academically, she excelled, graduating magna cum laude with a B.A. in history in February 1967.

Concurrently, Giovanni's poetic talent burst forth, capturing the volatile 1960s—the black revolution, its leaders, and her role as a revolutionist. For many, she became chief among the new revolutionary black poets.

During 1969–71, Giovanni made important personal and artistic decisions. She gave birth to Thomas Watson Giovanni in August 1969, though she chose to remain single and to keep secret the father's name. Motherhood deepened her sense of family pride and expanded her priorities. She began exploring reforms needed for a personal, moral revolution. Although this shift from political to personal themes disappointed some readers, her new focus solidified a growing popularity. She received six honorary doctorates between 1972 and 1983; she continues to draw large audiences at poetry readings, and she is still attracting new readers who appreciate her artistic, ethical, and intellectual growth.

Since 1988, Giovanni has taught at Virginia Polytechnic and State University, where she is University Distinguished Professor of English.

WORKS: *Black Feeling, Black Talk* (1968). *Black Judgment* (1969). *Black Feeling, Black Talk/Black Judgment* (1970). *Re: Creation* (1970). *Gemini: An Extended Autobiographical Statement on My First Twenty-Five Years of Being a Black Poet* (1971). *Spin a Soft Black Song: Poems for Children* (1971). *My House* (1972). *A Dialogue: James Baldwin and Nikki Giovanni* (1973). *Ego-Tripping and Other Poems for Young People* (1973). *A Poetic Equation: Conversations between Nikki Giovanni and Margaret Walker* (1974). *The Women and the Men* (1975). *Cotton Candy on a Rainy Day* (1978). *Vacation Time: Poems for Children* (1980). *Those Who Ride the Night Winds* (1983). *Sacred Cows . . . and Other Edibles* (1988). Ed., *Appalachian Elders: A Warm Hearth Sampler*, with C. Dennison (1991). *Racism 101* (1994). Ed., *Grand Mothers: Poems, Reminiscences, and Short Stories about the Keepers of Our Traditions* (1994). *Shimmy Shimmy Shimmy like My Sister Kate: Looking at the Harlem Renaissance through Poems* (1995). *The Genie in the Jar* (1996). *The Selected Poems of Nikki Giovanni, 1968–1995* (1996). *The Sun Is So Quiet* (1996). *Love Poems* (1997). *Blues: For All the Changes: New Poems* (1999). Ed., *Grand Fathers: Reminiscences, Poems, Recipes, and Photos of the Keepers of Our Traditions* (1999). *Quilting the Black-Eyed Pea: Poems and Not Quite Poems* (2002). *The Prosaic Soul of Nikki Giovanni* (2003). *Just for You: Girls in the Circle* (2004). *Rosa* (2005). *The Collected Poetry of Nikki Giovanni, 1968–1998* (2006).

—Patsy B. Perry

ELLEN GLASGOW (1873–1945). Although modern southern literature grew out of ground cleared, and for the most part tended, by Ellen Glasgow, traditional attitudes about women have left important episodes of her life distorted by rumor and speculation. No official record exists to show whether she was born on April 21, 1874, or April 22, 1873. In either case, she was the eighth of ten children (eight lived to maturity) of Francis Thomas Glasgow, who managed Tredegar Iron Works in Richmond and whose roots ran back to the Scotch Presbyterians of the Shenandoah Valley. Her mother was the orphaned daughter of an orphaned mother, although her ties were to many of the oldest families of Tidewater Virginia. Ellen Glasgow received almost no formal education, but relatives and tutors taught her to read and write.

In her late teens she started a novel, and shortly thereafter fell under the guidance of Walter McCormack of Charleston, her sister Cary's husband-to-be, who directed her attention to Charles Darwin and to other thinkers who shaped her views of humankind and society. Her interest in critical realism hardened to pessimism when, within the period of a few years, she experienced difficulty hearing, rebelled against her father's inflexible religion, watched her mother die in 1893, failed to conclude either of two novels satisfactorily, and, finally in 1894, learned that McCormack, for whom she had developed a deep respect, had committed suicide under sordid circumstances.

To work out her bitterness she finished the second of the novels she had begun, a Darwinian study of New York's bohemia called *The Descendant,* which she followed with a second bohemian study before choosing her native state as the scene of *The Voice of the People,* the first of the novels eventually to compose her social history of Virginia. By 1905 this series included a Civil War novel and a powerful exploration of tensions that beset agrarian classes after the war.

During this fruitful period (1899–1905), she found herself involved in the most devastating of three important affairs, a sometimes ecstatic romance with a married man she later called "Gerald B." "Gerald B." has been variously identified as a figment of her imagination, as another woman, as a middle-aged New York hearing specialist, H. Holbrook Curtis (1856–1920), as an important New York neurologist, Pearce Bailey (1865–1922), as the fiction editor of Bobbs-Merrill, Hewitt Hanson Howland (1863–1944), and as a wealthy New York financier, William Riggin Travers. Some of these possibilities need not exclude one another, but certain evidence points toward Howland, whose wife of fifteen years sued for divorce in 1903 on grounds that he had failed to provide. Other circumstantial evidence leads to Travers, whose wife, Lily Harriman Travers, closely related to the Harriman and Vanderbilt families of New York and Newport society, was suing him for divorce in September 1905 when he committed suicide. Glasgow later became engaged twice: between 1906 and 1909 to Frank Ilsley Paradise, a roving Episcopal minister and author, and from 1917, off and on, to Henry Watkins Anderson, a prominent Richmond lawyer, adventurer, and experimental politician, who remained her frequent visitor long after their engagement wore itself out.

Glasgow reached her full power with *Virginia,* the best of her books before 1925. After her closest brother committed suicide in 1909 and her sister Cary died in 1911, Glasgow, now a feminist, took an apartment in New York, where she spent most of her time until 1915, the year before her father, from whom she still felt estranged, died. Thereafter she lived in the family home in Richmond, with a nurse-secretary. Her poorest work fell around 1918, when Howland remarried, her early publisher Walter Hines Page died, and rumors of Anderson's wartime flirtation with Queen Marie of Romania caused the author to attempt suicide. After these troubles forced her to confront deeper levels of herself, she exceeded her former powers in the lacerating *Barren Ground* and the two scintillant comedies of manners that preceded her finest book, *The Sheltered Life.* During this period many writers formed friendships with her, but her special confidant was James Branch Cabell. As woman of letters she reached her full height in 1931, when she presided in spirit and flesh at the first modern Southern Writers Conference, held at the University of Virginia.

With *Vein of Iron* the intensity of her characterization began to fail, and *In This Our Life,* written despite two heart attacks, revealed a weakening of stylistic control, although it brought her the Pulitzer Prize (1942). Her exceptional contribution to regional and national letters had previously earned special recognition from four universities, the National Institute of Arts and Letters (1932), the American Academy of Arts and Letters (1938 and 1940), and the *Saturday Review of Literature* (1941). Her collected prefaces (1943) presented Ellen Glasgow as master of the novel, the mask she wore for her public. When she died on November 21, 1945, she left in manuscript a sequel to *In This Our Life,* plus her autobiography, in which she exposed the victim's mask she wore for her intimates and, it seems, for herself.

WORKS: *The Descendant* (1897). *Phases of an Inferior Planet* (1898). *The Voice of the People* (1900). *The Battle-Ground* (1902). *The Freeman and Other Poems* (1902). *The Deliverance* (1904). *The Wheel of Life* (1906). *The Ancient Law* (1908). *The Romance of a Plain Man* (1909). *The Miller of Old Church* (1911). *Virginia* (1913). *Life and Gabriella* (1916). *The Builders* (1919). *One Man in His Time* (1922). *The Shadowy Third and Other Stories* (1923). *Barren Ground* (1925). *The Romantic Comedians* (1926). *They Stooped to Folly* (1929). *The Sheltered Life* (1932). *Vein of Iron* (1935). *In This Our Life* (1941). *A Certain Measure* (1943). *The Woman Within* (1954). *Letters of Ellen Glasgow,* ed. Blair

Rouse (1958). *The Collected Stories of Ellen Glasgow,* ed. Richard K. Meeker (1963). *Beyond Defeat,* ed. Luther Y. Gore (1966). *Ellen Glasgow's Reasonable Doubts: A Collection of Her Writings,* ed. Julius Rowan Raper (1988).

—JULIUS ROWAN RAPER

GAIL GODWIN (1937–). Novelist Gail Godwin was born in Alabama, spent much of her early life in Asheville, N.C., was graduated with a B.A. in journalism from the University of North Carolina at Chapel Hill, and received a Ph.D. in English from the University of Iowa. After two brief marriages, she began her productive, successful writing career. She has taught at Columbia University and Vassar College and has been honored by a Guggenheim Fellowship as well as by an award from the National Academy of Arts and Letters. She has lived for many years in the artists' colony at Woodstock, N.Y.

Godwin has published short fiction and libretti, but her substantial reputation rests on her novels, which to some extent reflect concerns she has faced in her life and career. Godwin's early novels, for example—*The Perfectionists* and *Glass People*—depict young women trapped in unhappy marriages. *The Odd Woman,* a transitional work, centers on an unmarried woman, Jane Clifford, who is self-supporting but who subordinates her scholarly work to that of her lover, Gabriel Weeks. By contrast, the major women characters in *A Mother and Two Daughters* and *A Southern Family* either abandon marriage altogether or subordinate domestic life to professional concerns.

Although male characters are important throughout her work, Godwin's writing in the 1970s and 1980s centers on the difficulties confronted by women figures. In her later fiction—*Father Melancholy's Daughter, The Good Husband,* and *Evensong*—Godwin explores her interest in Episcopalianism, granting male and female figures equal prominence. This is evidenced by the important role of the Reverend Walter Gower in *Father Melancholy's Daughter,* by the two male protagonists of *The Good Husband,* and by the priest Adrian Bonner in *Evensong. Evenings at Five* is a lightly fictionalized memorial tribute to her partner, the composer Robert Starer, that depicts the life they shared for many years.

The South is not Godwin's principal subject, but it is an important setting for most of her novels. This fact enables her to address issues characteristic of the region during the several decades of her writing career, such as racial tensions, interracial friendships, the disparities between Appalachia and other southern regions, and the increasing intrusion of technology, especially television, into the daily lives of ordinary people. The South of Godwin's fiction remains a recognizable historical section comprised of rural areas and mid-sized cities and marked by a mountain as well as an agrarian heritage. It is also, however, a part of modern America whose inhabitants wrestle with problems characteristic of contemporary life.

WORKS: *The Perfectionists* (1970). *Glass People* (1972). *The Odd Woman* (1974). *Dream Children* (1976). *Violet Clay* (1978). *A Mother and Two Daughters* (1982). *Mr. Bedford and the Muses* (1983). *The Finishing School* (1984). *A Southern Family* (1987). *Father Melancholy's Daughter* (1991). *The Good Husband* (1994). *Evensong* (1999). *Heart: A Natural History of the Heart-Filled Life* (2002). *Evenings at Five* (2003). *The Making of a Writer: Journals, 1961–1963* (2006). *Queen of the Underworld: A Novel* (2006).

—MARY ANN WIMSATT

CAROLINE GORDON (1895–1981). Time, place, the creation of art, and the preservation of human relationships meant much to the ever-migrating fiction writer Caroline Gordon. Born on October 6, 1895, at her maternal grandmother's home in Todd County, Ky., Gordon was tutored by her classically educated father, James Morris Gordon. Graduating from Bethany College in West Virginia in 1916, Gordon taught high school and worked as a journalist for the *Chattanooga News,* where she published, in 1923, an article on *The Fugitive.* Shortly thereafter, Gordon moved to New York and married Fugitive poet Allen Tate in 1924. The couple had one child, a daughter, Nancy, born in 1925. The couple divorced in January 1946 and remarried that April, finally divorcing in August 1959.

Mentored by Ford Madox Ford and having traveled to Europe with Tate, Gordon flourished as a writer. She and Tate settled in their Tennessee home, Benfolly, where they lived on and off for much of the 1930s, surrounded by family and friends, until 1938. At Benfolly, Gordon immersed herself in the southern past, producing many of her finest short stories and her Civil War novels, *Penhally* and *None Shall Look Back.* She also wrote *The Garden of Adonis,* a modernist novel of the fallen South, and *Aleck Maury, Sportsman,* which Gordon referred to as her father's autobiography. Intrigued by questions regarding the relationship between men and women, inspired by her fear of instability and of the chaos that she felt enveloped the modern world, Gordon wrote stories of pioneers, *Green Centuries* and "The Captive," and three autobiographical fictions, *The Women on the Porch, The Strange Children,* and *The Malefactors.*

Turning increasingly toward art and religion to discover an orderliness and authority she could not locate in her world, Gordon was baptized a Roman Catholic in 1947. Teaching appointments at numerous universities also gave meaning to her life. They began in 1938, when she was writer-in-residence at the University of North Carolina in Greensboro. Her final appointment, at age seventy-eight, took her to the University of Dallas, a Catholic institution. Gordon died in San Cristóbal, Mexico, on April 11, 1981.

WORKS: *Penhally* (1931). *Aleck Maury, Sportsman* (1934). *None Shall Look Back* (1937). *The Garden of Adonis* (1937). *Green Centuries* (1941). *The Women on the Porch* (1944). *The Forest of the South* (1945). Ed., *The House of Fiction: An Anthology of the Short Story,* with Allen Tate (1950). *The Strange Children* (1951). *The Malefactors* (1956). *How to Read a Novel* (1957). *Old Red and Other Stories* (1963). *The Glory of Hera* (1972). *The Collected Stories of Caroline Gordon* (1981).

—ANNE M. BOYLE

F. R. GOULDING (1810–1881). F. R. Goulding—teacher, minister, and inventor—wrote adventure books for the young that are largely forgotten today. His father, Thomas Goulding, was a Presbyterian minister who married Ann Holbrook of Wolcott, Conn. The two settled in Midway Community, Ga., where Francis Robert Goulding was born on September 28, 1810. The young Goulding graduated from the University of Georgia and took religious instruction at the school his father founded, the Columbia (S.C.) Theological Seminary. He then married Mary Wallace Howard in 1833, a union that produced six children.

Goulding's first work was *Little Josephine,* a religious tract for children. Next came *Robert and Harold; or, The Young Marooners on the Florida Coast.* The plot owes much to Defoe's *Robinson Crusoe,* but the terra incognita of Goulding's novel is Florida. It is a treasure trove of a book, with accounts of Indian encounters, the Florida devil-fish (a massive variety of ray), the lore of bygone storytellers, and the practical wisdom of Dr. Gordon. The book was so popular that Goulding wrote a sequel titled *Marooner's Island; or, Dr. Gordon in Search of His Children.* Both books read as a kind of nineteenth-century scout handbook, and are salted with religious lessons, useful skills, and lore. Their topics range from fishing and basic safety techniques to recovering an object from a well, identifying mysterious plants and obscure animals, and forecasting weather.

During the Civil War Goulding served as an unofficial Confederate chaplain and collected the *Soldiers Hymn Book.* The three novels of his Woodruff series fell into obscurity, yet they reveal Goulding's obsession with Indian folkways. *Sal-o-quah* relates tales of Sequoyah (Goulding greatly admired the

Cherokee scribe), native American medicine, and Indian "conversion" ("Injin want more Bible," are the words he puts in one convert's mouth). The principal characteristics of Indian character, wrote Goulding, are "taciturnity, and a proud self-reliance." Goulding was as fascinated by the developing frontier as by the South Carolina low country.

Goulding's books are the outpouring of a wide-ranging curiosity, and they provide a fascinating catalog of people, things, and phenomena largely vanished from this earth. He died on August 22, 1881.

WORKS: *Little Josephine* (1844). *Robert and Harold; or, The Young Marooners on the Florida Coast* (1852). *Soldiers Hymn Book* (1864). *Marooners Island* (1868). *Frank Gordon* (1869). *Life Scenes from the Gospel History* (1870). *Sal-o-quah* (1870). *Tah-le-quah* (1870). *Nacoochee* (1871). *Sapelo; or, Child Life in the Tide Waters* (1888).

—BRYAN GIEMZA

WILLIAM GOYEN (1915–1983). Charles William Goyen was born on April 24, 1915, in Trinity, Tex., to Charles Provine and Mary Inez Trow Goyen, natives of Mississippi and Texas. In 1923, after a short relocation to Shreveport, the family moved to Houston, where Goyen spent his adolescence. After graduating from Sam Houston High School in 1932, he attended Rice Institute (later Rice University), where he acted, garnered prizes in playwriting and short-story writing, and earned a B.A. in literature (1937) and an M.A. in comparative literature (1939). He briefly pursued a Ph.D. at the University of Iowa, but returned to Houston in 1939 to teach at the University of Houston. He enlisted in the navy that same year and served as an officer during World War II on the aircraft carrier *Casablanca* in the South Pacific.

Following his discharge, Goyen and companion Walter Berns moved to Taos, N.M., residing near benefactor Frieda Lawrence and devoting themselves to their writing begun during the war. By the late 1940s Goyen's short fiction was appearing in magazines such as *Mademoiselle* and the *Southwest Review*, which awarded him its literary fellowship in 1948. His first novel, *The House of Breath*, appeared in 1950 to significant acclaim. Guggenheim Fellowships in 1952 and 1954 and a teaching position at the New School of Social Research (1955–60) allowed for further European travel and literary productivity that included by the early 1960s short fiction, another novel, and plays for both stage and television. On November 10, 1963, Goyen married actress Doris Roberts. While continuing to write drama and fiction, he served as senior trade editor for McGraw-Hill (1966–71) and taught at various universities, including Columbia, Brown, Princeton, and the University of Houston.

The last decade of Goyen's life saw the reissue of *The House of Breath* and the publication of *Selected Writing* and *Collected Stories* as well as minor works in limited editions. He died on August 29, 1983, in Los Angeles, leaving significant fiction and letters to appear posthumously.

WORKS: *The House of Breath* (1950). *Ghost and Flesh: Stories and Tales* (1952). *In a Farther Country* (1955). *The Diamond Rattler* (1955). *The Faces of Blood Kindred* (1960). *A Possibility of Oil* (1961). *The Mind* (1961). *Christy* (1963). *The Fair Sister* (1963). *The House of Breath, Black/White* (1969). *A Book of Jesus* (1973). *Come, the Restorer* (1974). *Aimée* (1974). *Selected Writings of William Goyen* (1974). *The Collected Stories of William Goyen* (1975). *Nine Poems* (1976). *Arthur Bond* (1979). *Wonderful Plant* (1980). *Precious Door* (1981). *New Work and Work in Progress* (1983). *Arcadio* (1983). *Had I a Hundred Mouths: New and Selected Stories, 1947–1983* (1985). *Half a Look of Cain: A Fantastical Narrative*, ed. Reginald Gibbons (1994). *William Goyen: Selected Letters from a Writer's Life*, ed. Robert Phillips (1995).

—GARY RICHARDS

HENRY W. GRADY (1850–1889). Henry Woodfin Grady was born on May 24, 1850, in Athens, Ga., to Ann Gartrell and William Sammons Grady, a substantial merchant. Graduated from the University of Georgia in 1868, the following year Grady attended the University of Virginia, where he excelled in oratory and showed journalistic talent.

Returning to Georgia, Grady married Julia King in 1871 and began a career in journalism, working for various newspapers, including the *Atlanta Constitution,* during the 1870s. In 1880 he bought a quarter interest in the *Constitution.* Under his lead as managing editor, the paper soon became the pre-eminent organ of the New South movement, an attempt to effect regional prosperity mainly through industrialization.

Not only in the press but also at the podium, Grady, the foremost spokesman of the movement, hailed what he perceived to be the matchless material progress of the postbellum South. To sustain this progress he entreated the North and the South to surmount sectional animosity so that northern capital might more readily move south. To insure the social stability prized by northern investors, he proposed that the race problem be solved to the satisfaction of all. Granted northern restraint and trust, white southerners would respect the civil and political rights of black southerners but would maintain white supremacy and segregation, an arrangement merely reflecting the instinct of both races. These matters settled, nothing could hinder the South, with its abundant resources, from achieving the prosperity ordained by Providence. Late in his life, though, Grady began to view concentrated capital selfishly used as a threat to regional progress.

Throughout his writings and speeches, Grady prefaced his tribute to the new order with encomiums to the legendary Old South and the "hero in gray" of the Lost Cause. The emotional appeal of his addresses made him a figure of national stature.

After a speaking engagement in Boston late in 1889, Grady developed pneumonia and died in Atlanta on December 23. The dream of a prosperous New South, his own claims notwithstanding, remained far from fulfillment.

WORKS: *Life and Labors of Henry W. Grady: His Speeches, Writings, etc.* (1890). *The New South,* six articles first published in the *New York Ledger,* Nov. 16–Dec. 21, 1889 (1890). "Writings and Speeches," in *Life of Henry W. Grady,* by Joel Chandler Harris (1890). *The Speeches of Henry W. Grady* (1895). *The New South and Other Addresses* (1904). *The Complete Orations and Speeches of Henry W. Grady,* ed. Edwin DuBois Shurter (1910). *The New South: Writings and Speeches of Henry W. Grady* (1971).

—WAYNE MIXON

EDWIN PHILLIPS GRANBERRY (1897–1988). Born on April 18, 1897, in Meridian, Miss., Edwin Granberry lived in the Oklahoma Territory before moving at age ten to Florida, the setting for his most important work. An accomplished stylist, Granberry is considered not merely a "local colorist" but a distinguished regional novelist, along with Floridian Marjorie Kinnan Rawlings and Florida mystery writer John D. MacDonald.

Granberry's major period is the 1920s and 1930s. His 1920 A.B. in Romance languages from Columbia led to an assistant professorship at Miami University (Ohio) in 1920–22. He attended George Pierce Baker's 47 Workshop at Harvard in 1922–24, and his play *Hitch Your Wagon to a Star* was produced in 1924. From 1925 to 1930, while a private-school language teacher, Granberry published three novels. By 1933 he had translated three French novels and published the short story that ensured his reputation.

The Ancient Hunger, a novel of romantic attraction and tragedy set in Oklahoma, poetically evoked a bleak natural scene. Granberry's remaining fiction explores characters and customs in Florida scrub pine country. *Strangers and Lovers,* a richly lyrical rendering of innocence and doomed love realistically anchored in the backwoods, introduced to literature the Florida "Cracker." *The Erl King,* a tragic tale of adolescent love set at St. Augustine, is less realistic yet effective for its mythical atmosphere and primal images.

Granberry's most renowned story, "A Trip to Czardis," appeared in *Forum*, winning the O. Henry Memorial Prize for 1932. Presenting a mother taking two unwitting sons on a final visit with their father, this spare tale painstakingly crafts dialect and elemental imagery. The story sensitively under-scores the humanity of average persons facing an extraordinarily harsh reality—particularly the older son's unfolding realization of his father's imminent execution. "A Trip to Czardis," anthologized con-tinuously and adapted for radio and television, was incorporated in 1967 into Granberry's generally acclaimed final novel of the same title. The story constitutes the novel's last chapter.

After reading "A Trip to Czardis" in 1933, Rollins College president Hamilton Holt appointed Granberry to the faculty in 1933. Granberry served as Irving Bacheller Professor of Creative Writing from 1941 until retirement in 1971. The college produced his play *The Falcon* in 1951. For more than thirty years, Granberry co-authored, with creator Roy Crane, the nationally syndicated *Buz Sawyer* comic strip.

He died on December 5, 1988, in Winter Park, Fla.

WORKS: *The Ancient Hunger* (1927). *Strangers and Lovers* (1928). *The Erl King* (1930). Trans., Dominique Dunois, *A Lover Returns* (1931). Trans., Jacques de Lacretalle, *A Man's Life* (1931). "A Trip to Czardis," *Forum* 87 (Apr. 1932): 248–51. Trans., André Chamson, *The Mountain Tavern* (1933). *A Trip to Czardis* (1967).

—JOHN J. FENSTERMAKER

SHIRLEY ANN GRAU (1929–). Shirley Ann Grau was born on July 8, 1929, in New Orleans, La., and was raised both there and in Montgomery, Ala., where she attended Booth School. Grau earned a B.A. in English in 1950, graduating Phi Beta Kappa and with honors from Newcomb College, Tulane University, in New Orleans. She began graduate work in Renaissance and metaphysical poetry at Tu-lane, but did not receive a degree. As a college student, Grau decided she wanted to become a writer, and she began publishing her fiction soon after she graduated.

Grau is the author of six novels and three collections of short stories. Her first book, a collection of stories entitled *The Black Prince*, met high acclaim, and the first printing sold out within two weeks. Set in the bayous, the collection is still regarded by many as her best work. Grau's third book, *The Keepers of the House*, won the Pulitzer Prize. The novel was chosen as a selection of both the Literary Guild and the Book-of-the-Month Club, and it was published in a condensed form in *Ladies' Home Journal*.

Grau has commented that with *The Keepers of the House* she searched for a setting not connected to a specific place, but much of her work is set in the Gulf states. Grau is intensely interested in the relationships between African Americans and whites, and her portraits of African American life have been praised as some of the most accurate in American literature. *Nine Women* and *Roadwalkers* show her interest in women's narratives. Grau's stories and articles have appeared in various publications, including the *Atlantic*, *New Yorker*, *Southern Review*, *Saturday Evening Post*, and *Redbook*.

Married in 1955 to James Kern Feibleman, a Tulane philosophy professor, Grau is the mother of two sons and two daughters. She currently divides her time between New Orleans and Martha's Vineyard.

WORKS: *The Black Prince and Other Stories* (1955). *The Hard Blue Sky* (1958). *The House on Coliseum Street* (1961). *The Keepers of the House* (1964). *The Condor Passes* (1971). *The Wind Shifting West* (1973). *Evidence of Love* (1977). *Nine Women* (1985). *Roadwalkers* (1994). *Selected Stories* (2003).

—MARY LOUISE WEAKS

WILLIAM J. GRAYSON (1788–1863). William J. (John) Grayson was the son of William John Grayson, sheriff of the Beaufort District, S.C., and a Revolutionary artillery officer taken prisoner by the British upon the fall of Charleston in May 1780, and Susannah Greene Grayson, daughter of a local merchant. Grayson was born in the Beaufort District on November 12, 1788, was educated in schools in New York and New Jersey and at Beaufort Grammar School, and was graduated from South Carolina College in December 1809. His father having died in 1797 and his mother having married William Joyner, a wealthy Beaufort planter, Grayson lived a life of leisure until November 1813, when he was elected to the South Carolina legislature to fill an unexpired term. He was re-elected in 1815. In 1814 he married Sarah Matilda Somarsall, the child of a wealthy Charleston merchant and planter, and taught school in Beaufort and Savannah, Ga., until 1817, when a malaria epidemic in the latter city forced him to return to Beaufort and a subsequent outbreak of yellow fever in the same year led him to leave education and turn to the study of law. By 1822 he was in the state legislature again and served there until 1826, when he was elected to the state senate (1827–31). During this period he acquired property in Charleston and two plantations on the Wando River, and in 1832 he was elected to Congress for two terms (1833–37). Returning to Charleston in 1837, he became active in the Whig Party. He was appointed collector of customs in Charleston in July 1841 and served in that office until March 1853.

Concurrently, he took up the cause of opposing secession and published an open letter to Governor Whitemarsh Seabrook against "dissolution," a pamphlet entitled *The Union, Past and Future: How It Works and How to Save It,* and a collection of letters he had contributed to the *Charleston Courier* (*The Letters of Curtius*)—all seeking to make his readers aware of the folly of secession and of the rationality of maintaining the union. At the same time he was contributing essays to the *Southern Quarterly Review,* edited by William Gilmore Simms. In 1854 he published *The Hireling and the Slave,* a long poem in heroic couplets that contrasts the northern worker's desperate economic situation with the southern slave's secure and safe pastoral station and is also, according to Jay B. Hubbell, "the most notable of many replies to *Uncle Tom's Cabin.*" Despite this attack on abolition and the northern economy and its defense of slavery, Grayson, in keeping with his unionist views, nowhere advocates secession. The verse form, satire, and invective incorporated in the poem clearly demonstrate his preference for classical or neoclassical standards and methods. These attributes are clearly expressed, along with criticism of Wordsworth and Romanticism, in his essay "What Is Poetry?" published in *Russell's Magazine* for April 1857 (a piece Henry Timrod responded to on behalf of Wordsworth and Romanticism in another essay of the same title in the issue for October 1857).

Grayson's most important prose works—*James Louis Petigru: A Biographical Sketch* and *Witness to Sorrow: The Antebellum Autobiography of William J. Grayson*—were published posthumously (Grayson died in Newberry, S.C., on October 4, 1863), and provide substantial evidence of his accomplishment with two forms of life accounts, one dealing with the story of his lifelong friend and fellow unionist Petigru and the other with his own intellectual and cultural development.

WORKS: *Letter to His Excellency Whitemarsh B. Seabrook, Governor of the State of South Carolina, on the Dissolution of the Union* (1850). *The Union, Past and Future: How It Works and How to Save It* (1850). *The Letters of Curtius* (1851). *The Hireling and the Slave* (1854). *The Hireling and the Slave, Chicora, and Other Poems* (1856). *The Country* (1858). *Marion* (1860). *James Louis Petigru: A Biographical Sketch* (1866). *Selected Poems of William J. Grayson,* ed. Mrs. William H. Armstrong (1907). *Witness to Sorrow: The Antebellum Autobiography of William J. Grayson,* ed. Richard J. Calhoun (1990).

—RAYBURN S. MOORE

PAUL GREEN (1894–1981). Paul Green was born on March 17, 1894, in Lillington, N.C., the son of William Archibald and his second wife, Betty Byrd Green. He attended Buies Creek Academy, then served as principal of the country school in Olive Branch. After one year at the University of North Carolina, he served two years in the army engineers and returned to the university, where he studied with the influential professor Frederick Koch and his Carolina Playmakers theater group. Upon graduation in 1921, he received a fellowship to study philosophy at Cornell. He began teaching philosophy at the University of North Carolina at Chapel Hill in 1922. In the same year, he married Elizabeth Lay; they had four children. Except for occasional years in Hollywood and extended trips abroad, he lived in Chapel Hill, where he died on May 4, 1981.

Green's one-act folk plays served as apprenticeship for his overnight success in New York with three full dramas: *In Abraham's Bosom,* winner of a Pulitzer Prize, *The Field God,* and *The House of Connelly.* Critical acclaim ranked him then second only to O'Neill among American playwrights. In 1928–29, a Guggenheim Fellowship took him to Europe, where he met Alexis Gronowsky and Bertolt Brecht. He wrote four plays in their experimental form—a blend of dialogue, music, film, dance, chorus, and commentary; except for *Johnny Johnson's* modest success, all were failures. But they readied him for his outdoor "symphonic dramas." This form fuses music, stylized movement, and dialogue to stimulate ritual participation. Green's subjects are from American history. His outdoor drama *The Lost Colony* was first performed on Roanoke Island, N.C., in 1937 and, except for the World War II years, has continued since then.

Green's work attests to his belief in the heroic possibility of all men: humanity's value lies in the continuous reaffirmation of its own greatness. The heroes are Negro and white, for Green sees no distinction between them in potential and achievement. His writing is a profile of democracy, from his early short stories and novels about the land and those who love and hate it, to the "heritage dramas" that recount the pain and glory in the making of America.

WORKS: *Salvation on a String* (1924). *Contemporary American Literature,* with Elizabeth Lay Green (1925). *The Lord's Will and Other Carolina Plays* (1925). *Lonesome Road: Six Plays for the Negro Theater* (1926). *The Field God and In Abraham's Bosom* (1927). *In the Valley and Other Carolina Plays* (1928). *Wide Fields* (1928). *The House of Connelly and Other Plays* (1931). *The Laughing Pioneer* (1932). *Fixin's,* with Erma Green (1934). *This Body the Earth* (1935). *Shroud My Body Down* (1935). *Johnny Johnson* (1937). *The Lost Colony* (1937). *The Southern Cross* (1938). *The Lost Colony Song-Book* (1938). *The Critical Year* (1939). *Franklin and the King* (1939). *Out of the South* (fifteen plays revised, 1939). *The Enchanted Maze* (1939). Adapt., Richard Wright, *Native Son,* with Wright (1941). *The Highland Call* (1941). *The Hawthorne Tree* (1943). *Forever Growing* (1945). *Song of the Wilderness,* with music by Charles Vardell (1947). *The Common Glory* (1948). *Dog on the Sun* (1949). Adapt., Henrik Ibsen, *Peer Gynt* (1951). *The Common Glory Song-Book* (1951). *Dramatic Heritage* (1953). *Wilderness Road* (1956). *The Founders* (1957). *Drama and the Weather* (1958). *The Confederacy* (1959). *Wings for to Fly: Three Plays of Negro Life* (1959). *The Stephen Foster Story* (1960). *Five Plays of the South* (five plays revised, 1963). *Plough and Furrow* (1963). *Cross and Sword* (1966). *Texas* (1967). *Texas Song-Book* (1967). *Words and Ways* (1968). *Home to My Valley* (1971). *Honeycomb* (1972). *Trumpet in the Land* (1972). *The Land of Nod* (1976). *Paul Green's War Songs: A Southern Poet's History of the Great War, 1917–1920,* ed. John H. Roper (1993). *A Southern Life: Letters of Paul Green, 1916–1881,* ed. Laurence G. Avery (1994).

—VINCENT S. KENNY

BEN GREER (1948–). A man of many interests and talents, Ben Greer was born on December 4, 1948, to Bernard Eugene and Margaret Phillips Greer of Spartanburg, S.C. Greer is a musician, painter, impersonator, weight lifter, and cook. He is also a devout Roman Catholic who considered becoming a priest. During periodic retreats, he has spent time meditating with Trappist monks.

Greer graduated from Wade Hampton High School in Greenville, S.C., before entering the University of South Carolina, where he studied creative writing under James Dickey and George Garrett, graduating in 1971. To help pay his college expenses, he served as a prison guard, an experience transmuted into his best-known novel, *Slammer*. He continued his education in creative writing at Hollins College, receiving an M.A. in 1973. At Hollins, he worked with R. H. W. Dillard and William Jay Smith.

Wanting a fuller taste of life, he moved to York Harbor, Maine, finding jobs on a fishing boat and in construction. His New England sojourn found fictional expression in *Time Loves a Hero*. His circle of friends included May Sarton and John Yount, like Greer a southerner practicing the craft of a novelist while living in New England. After writing a draft of *Slammer*, Greer returned to South Carolina to revise and polish it.

Reviews were favorable: a snippet from the *New Republic* is representative: "In the slammer every character is matched with his antagonist, every gesture of generosity countered by perversity or greed. Like Flannery O'Connor, Greer illuminates his grotesques with the redemptive glare of Catholicism, and like her, he knows evil is contagious for travelers in infernal regions." The novel has been reprinted often and was chosen for canonization by the prestigious Voices of the South series.

South Carolina life figures prominently in a later novel, *The Loss of Heaven*, and in a nonfiction account of the politician Tim Wilkes's efforts to clear his name when charged with taking bribes, *Presumed Guilty: The Tim Wilkes Story*.

Aside from *Slammer*, Greer's most celebrated novel is *Halloween*, a work revealing him as an adept handler of southern gothic motifs and techniques.

Greer is on the faculty at the University of South Carolina.

WORKS: *Slammer* (1975). *Halloween* (1978). *Times Loves a Hero* (1986). *The Loss of Heaven* (1988). *Presumed Guilty: The Tim Wilkes Story* (1995). *Ivory Bed* (2000).

—JOHN L. IDOL, JR.

JOHN HOWARD GRIFFIN (1920–1980). A novelist and nonfiction writer, John Howard Griffin was born in Dallas, Tex., on June 16, 1920, to Jack Walter and Lena Mae Young Griffin. His education was French: a certificate of studies from the Institut de Tours in 1937 and studies at the University of Poitiers from 1938 to 1939. During World War II he served with the French resistance and then the army air corps—losing his sight from an injury but regaining it ten years later. After the war he entered the Conservatory of Fontainebleau, Abbey of Solesmes, from which he received certificates in piano and composition in 1947.

This wide range of interests is reflected in Griffin's first novel, *The Devil Rides Outside*, in which a young, American, sexually obsessed miscreant lives in a French monastery pursuing the study of Gregorian music. The novel suggests a debate between the body and the soul. His second novel, *Nuni*, indicates Griffin's increased consciousness of form: it is narrated in the first person and completely in the present tense. A stock situation involving a professor who survives a plane crash on a South Pacific island inhabited by savages transcends itself as it moves allegorically toward a "spiritual evolution." The emphasis on anthropological detail is a prelude to the author's social interests reflected in his nonfiction and journalism after 1936.

Most noted for his odyssey through the South in the disguise of a black man, Griffin first wrote about the venture in *Sepia* before publishing the account as the now famous *Black Like Me* in 1961. After 1956, his writing favored autobiography, biography, and sociology. The winner of several humanitarian awards, including the Pacem in Terris in 1963, Griffin wrote his final work on the subject of racism in 1977, *A Time to be Human*. He died in Fort Worth, Tex., on September 9, 1980.

WORKS: *The Devil Rides Outside* (1952). *Nuni* (1956). *Mansfield, Texas* (1957). *Land of the High Sky* (1959). *Black Like Me* (1961). *Scattered Shadows* (1963). *John Howard Griffin Reader* (1968). *The Church and the Black Man* (1969).

A Hidden Wholeness: The Visual World of Thomas Merton (1972). *Twelve Photographic Portraits* (1973). *Jacques Maritain: Homage in Words and Pictures* (1975). *The Biography of Thomas Merton* (1976). *The Problems of Racism* (1976). *A Time to Be Human* (1977).

—THOMAS BONNER, JR.

ANGELINA GRIMKÉ (1805–1879) AND SARAH GRIMKÉ (1792–1873). The sisters Sarah Moore and Angelina Emily Grimké were born into a large slave-owning family in Charleston, S.C. Although they were raised in a society in which slavery flourished and was rarely challenged, both sisters were affected at an early age when on separate occasions they witnessed the brutal punishment of a slave.

Sarah's glimpse of life outside the South came on a trip with her father to Pennsylvania and New Jersey. She met with Quakers in Pennsylvania and became interested in their religion. Growing increasingly despondent living in the midst of slavery, she moved to Philadelphia in 1821, joining the Society of Friends there. Younger sister Angelina, who had developed strong antislavery feelings on her own, joined Sarah in 1829.

The Grimkés were thrust into the heat of the debate over slavery when a letter Angelina wrote to abolitionist William Lloyd Garrison in 1835 was published in his newspaper *The Liberator*. The sisters were welcomed into the American Anti-Slavery Society, in which they became extremely active, producing in this connection the majority of the works for which they would be remembered.

Angelina published "An Appeal to the Christian Woman of the South" in 1836, and Sarah's "Epistle to the Clergy of the Southern States" was published the same year. Both works discussed the hypocrisy of holding slaves in a society that claimed adherence to Christian tenets and ideals. No other southern women had spoken out against slavery as forcefully and effectively as the Grimkés. They became popular lecturers throughout the North. Sometimes they met with opposition from clergy and editorialists who objected to their speaking before audiences composed of women and men. Angered by these rebukes, and by similar reprisals in the Quaker meeting, Sarah wrote a series of letters published in 1838 as "Letters on the Equality of Sexes, and the Condition of Women," a work widely recognized as one of the founding documents of the women's movement in the United States.

In 1838 Angelina Grimké married the abolitionist Theodore Weld. Weld and the Grimkés worked together to edit *American Slavery As It Is: Testimony of a Thousand Witnesses*, a compilation of newspaper articles and other firsthand accounts of slavery, later a source for Stowe's *Uncle Tom's Cabin*.

After the explosive years of the 1830s, the Grimkés stayed largely out of the public eye. Sarah continued to live with Angelina and Theodore Weld in New Jersey, where they ran a couple of schools, and later in Massachusetts, where Sarah died in 1873, followed by Angelina in 1879.

As southern women speaking out against slavery, and as women arguing for gender equality, they helped to lay the foundation for two of the most significant public debates of the nineteenth century.

WORKS: BY Angelina Grimké. *Appeal to the Christian Women of the South* (1836). *Letters to Catherine E. Beecher, in Reply to an Essay on Slavery and Abolitionism, Addressed to A. E. Grimke* (1838).

BY Sarah Grimké. *An Epistle to the Clergy of the Southern States* (1836). *Letters on the Equality of the Sexes, and the Condition of Woman: Addressed to Mary S. Parker, President of the Boston Female Anti-Slavery Society* (1838). Trans., Alphonse de Lamartine, *Joan of Arc: A Biography* (1867). *Letters on the Equality of the Sexes and Other Essays,* ed. Elizabeth Ann Bartlett (1988).

BY Angelina and Sarah Grimké. *American Slavery As It Is: Testimony of a Thousand Witnesses,* with Theodore Weld (1839). *Letters of Theodore Dwight Weld, Angelina Grimké and Sarah Grimké, 1822–1844,* ed. Gilbert Hobbes Barnes and Dwight Lowell Dumond (1934). *The Public Years of Sarah and Angelina Grimké: Selected Writings, 1835–1839,* ed. Larry Ceplair (1989).

—NICHOLAS GRAHAM

JIM GRIMSLEY (1955–). Jim Grimsley was born on September 21, 1955, in Rocky Mount, N.C., to Jasper Melton "Jack" Grimsley and Mary Elizabeth Brantham. Remaining in North Carolina until 1978, he attended the University of North Carolina at Chapel Hill and studied writing with Doris Betts and Max Steele. After three years in New Orleans, Grimsley moved to Atlanta in 1981 and began work in the healthcare industry. He continues to reside there as playwright-in-residence at 7 Stages and a member of the creative writing faculty at Emory University.

Adept in several genres, Grimsley is a prolific playwright. His first play, *The Existentialists*, was produced in the summer of 1983 at ACME Theatre. Subsequent works, many of which premiered at 7 Stages, include *The Earthlings* (1984), the award-winning *Mr. Universe* (1987), *Math and Aftermath* (1988), *Man with a Gun* (1989), *White People* (1989), *The Lizard of Tarsus* (1990), *Belle Ives* (1991), the adaptation *The Fall of the House of Usher* (1991), *The Decline and Fall of the Rest* (1997), *The Borderland* (1997), *In Berlin* (2000), and *Fascination* (2003). Several of the earlier plays are collected in *Mr. Universe and Other Plays*.

Over the last decade Grimsley has become even better known as a fiction writer. His short stories have appeared in numerous quarterlies since the early 1980s, but it has been his recent novels, those often drawing upon his childhood in rural eastern North Carolina and his gay adult life, that have garnered the most extensive praise. Initially published in Germany in translation in 1992, his first novel, *Winter Birds*, appeared in English in the United States in 1994. An exploration of rural poverty and familial abuse, it won the Sue Kaufman Prize for best first novel. Subsequent novels include: the award-winning *Dream Boy*, a lyrical account of two boys' adolescent relationship; *My Drowning* and *Comfort and Joy*, both of which develop characters from his first novel; and *Boulevard*, a coming-out narrative set in the French Quarter of New Orleans in the late 1970s. Grimsley has also recently published the fantasy novels *Kirith Kirin* and *The Ordinary* and several works of short science fiction.

WORKS: *Winter Birds* (1994). *Dream Boy* (1995). *My Drowning* (1997). *Mr. Universe and Other Plays* (1998). *Comfort and Joy* (1999). *Kirith Kirin* (2000). *Boulevard* (2002). *The Ordinary* (2004).

—GARY RICHARDS

JOHN GRISHAM (1955–). The son of a construction worker and a homemaker, John Grisham was born in Jonesboro, Ark., on February 8, 1955. Grisham stands in a long tradition of southern lawyers who have sought renown as fiction writers. What most often proved a dilettante pursuit for his predecessors, however, has brought Grisham tremendous popular acclaim.

After attending college at Mississippi State University, Grisham studied law at the University of Mississippi, and began practicing criminal law in 1982. In 1983 he was elected as a Democrat to the Mississippi legislature, where he served for six years. After witnessing a young rape victim's courtroom testimony against her assailant, he was inspired to write his first novel, *A Time to Kill*. That novel, which tells the story of an African American man who kills his young daughter's white rapist, was published in 1989. At first the book met with only middling success, but it demonstrated Grisham's knack for powerfully dramatizing age-old southern themes of race, sexuality, and class. It arguably remains his best book. His second novel, *The Firm*, was an instant success, and Grisham quickly gained renown as the master of the legal thriller, producing best-selling formula novels almost yearly throughout the 1990s. Nearly all of his novels have been commercially successful, and a majority of them have been turned into blockbuster films. Grisham's reception by literary critics, however, has been mixed, as has his attitude toward them. In a 1994 *Entertainment Weekly* interview, Grisham remarked, "I've sold too many books to get good reviews anymore. . . . There's a lot of jealousy, because [reviewers] think they can write a good novel or a best-seller and get frustrated when they can't. As a group, I've learned to despise them."

In recent years, Grisham has ventured into new fictional territory. *A Painted House* is a coming-of-age story set in Arkansas, and Grisham asserts in the foreword that the book contains not a single lawyer. His latest novel, *Bleachers*, is about a former high school football star.

Grisham and his wife Renee currently maintain homes in Charlottesville, Va., and Oxford, Miss.

WORKS: *A Time to Kill* (1989). *The Firm* (1991). *The Pelican Brief* (1992). *The Client* (1993). *The Chamber* (1994). *The Rainmaker* (1995). *The Runaway Jury* (1996). *The Partner* (1997). *The Street Lawyer* (1998). *The Testament* (1999). *The Brethren* (2000). *A Painted House* (2001). *Skipping Christmas* (2001). *The Summons* (2001). *The King of Torts* (2003). *Bleachers* (2003).

—H. COLLIN MESSER

LEWIS GRIZZARD (1946–1994). Lewis McDonald Grizzard, Jr., began life as a military brat. He was born on October 20, 1946, at Fort Benning, Ga., the only child of Lewis McDonald and Christine Word, a schoolteacher. He was raised, as he often said, "poor, proud, and patriotic," mostly in the hamlet of Moreland, Ga., which endowed him with an ample fund of material for his later stories.

Grizzard attended the University of Georgia, where he became a rabid football fan. (Years later, after Georgia lost to arch-rival Tech, his entire syndicated column consisted of just one terse line: "Frankly, I don't want to talk about it.") He left before graduating to begin a journalistic career. By age twenty-three, he was the executive sports editor of the *Atlanta Journal*. He joined the *Chicago Sun-Times*, but, homesick and unnerved by two divorces, he returned to Atlanta. Eventually, he began interjecting his trademark anecdotes and branched out from sports writing.

Grizzard once commented of southerners, "God talks like we do," and his columns clearly speak with a southern accent. The touchstones are all present: a dash of mother worship, beloved dogs and boyhood puppy love, stern patriarchs, manners and courtship. He was unabashedly a good old boy whose humor spoke to plain folks; as a self-described "quintessential southern male," he was no more politically correct than one might expect. Yet he was personable enough to win over many of those whose pretensions he plucked. At the height of his popularity, he faced the weekly grind of syndication in over 450 newspapers. He was given to tippling, as he freely admitted. He married four times (the last marriage was conducted while he was in hospital) and underwent four major heart surgeries to repair a congenital heart defect. He died of complications from the last operation on March 20, 1994.

Caught between the pull of forward-looking baby boomers and conservative-leaning southern roots, Grizzard always felt like a man out of time. And indeed, the vein of character-based humor that he tapped belonged to an older time, harkening back to southwestern humor tradition modeled in the work of fellow Georgian Augustus Baldwin Longstreet and Mark Twain. Some of his stories were too old to be attributed. But Grizzard gave them new life and made his mark in his own age, as a self-deprecating humorist and "personality" who ranked among the best homespun storytellers of the South in the twentieth century. Today, visitors to the Lewis Grizzard Museum in Moreland can take the Lewis Grizzard Highway to get there.

WORKS: *Kathy Sue Loudermilk, I Love You* (1979). *Glory! Glory! Georgia's 1980 Championship Season* (1981). *They Tore out My Heart and Stomped That Sucker Flat* (1982). *If Love Were Oil, I'd Be about a Quart Low* (1983). *Don't Sit under the Grits Tree with Anyone Else but Me* (1984). *Elvis Is Dead and I Don't Feel So Good Myself* (1984). *Won't You Come Home Billy Bob Bailey?* (1985). *My Daddy Was a Pistol and I'm a Son of a Gun* (1986). *Shoot Low Boys—They're*

Riding Shetland Ponies (1986). *When My Love Returns from the Ladies Room, Will I Be Too Old to Care?* (1987). *Don't Bend over in the Garden, Granny, You Know Them Taters Got Eyes* (1988). *Lewis Grizzard's Advice to the Newly Wed* (1989). *Lewis Grizzard on Fear of Flying* (1989). *If I Ever Get Back to Georgia, I'm Gonna Nail My Feet to the Ground* (1990). *Does a Wild Bear Chip in the Woods?* (1990). *Chili Dawgs Always Bark at Night* (1990). *Don't Forget to Call Your Momma—I Wish I Could Call Mine* (1991). *You Can't Put No Boogie-Woogie on the King of Rock and Roll* (1991). *I Haven't Understood Anything since 1962 and Other Nekkid Truths* (1992). *I Took a Lickin' and Kept on Tickin' and Now I Believe in Miracles* (1993). *The Grizzard Sampler: A Collection of the Early Writings of Lewis Grizzard* (1994). *The Last Bus to Albuquerque*, ed. Gerrie Ferris (1994). *It Wasn't Always Easy but I Sure Had Fun* (1994). *Grizzardisms: The Wit and Wisdom of Lewis Grizzard* (1995). *Southern by the Grace of God: Lewis Grizzard on the South*, ed. Ferris (1996).

—BRYAN GIEMZA

WINSTON GROOM (1944–). Born in Mobile, Ala., and educated at University Military School in Mobile and the University of Alabama in Tuscaloosa, Winston Groom served in Vietnam as a lieutenant in the U.S. Army's Fourth Infantry Division and returned to work as a journalist with the *Washington Star*. He also began an independent writing career, publishing a first novel of combat in Vietnam, *Better Times Than These*, which elicited favorable comparison with the work of such contemporaries as Philip Caputo, James Webb, and Tim O'Brien. Modest success followed with a mystery novel set on the Gulf Coast, *As Summers Die*; a children's book, *Only*; and a nonfiction account, with Duncan Spencer, of the captivity of the controversial Vietnam POW Robert Garwood, *Conversations with the Enemy*.

Groom followed with another novel, a highly inventive tale told from the distinctly Deep South perspective of an inspired "idiot" named Forrest Gump, whose achievements included playing All-American football for Bear Bryant, winning the Congressional Medal of Honor in Vietnam, and—as a ping-pong-playing emissary to Nixon's China—lifeguarding Mao Tse-tung's celebrated geriatric swim in the Yangtze River. Some Hollywood people got interested; and the rest, as they say, is history. Follow-up texts by Groom included a sequel, *Gump & Co.*, and a collection of sayings, *Gumpisms*. Groom also continued his novelistic career, publishing *Gone the Sun* and *Such a Pretty, Pretty Girl*. Meanwhile, he turned to narrative history, with *Shrouds of Glory*, about the Nashville-Atlanta campaigns of the American Civil War. *A Storm in Flanders* is about the horrific sequence of World War I battles fought over the course of the war in the Ypres Salient; *1942* treats pivotal events in World War II. Groom now divides the year between residences in Point Clear, Ala., and Cashiers, N.C. Married to Mary Winston Smith, he is the father of a daughter, Carolina Montgomery.

WORKS: *Better Times Than These* (1978). *As Summers Die* (1980). *Conversations with the Enemy*, with Duncan Spencer (1983). *Only* (1984). *Forrest Gump* (1986). *Gone the Sun* (1988). *Gumpisms* (1994). *Gump & Co.* (1995). *Shrouds of Glory* (1995). *Such a Pretty, Pretty Girl* (1999). *Crimson Tide: An Illustrated History of Football at the University of Alabama* (2000). *Storm in Flanders* (2002). *1942: The Year That Tried Men's Souls* (2005).

—PHILIP D. BEIDLER

ALLAN GURGANUS (1947–). Allan Gurganus was born on June 11, 1947, in Rocky Mount, N.C., the eldest of four sons of M. F. Gurganus, a merchant and small town entrepreneur, and Ethel Morris Gurganus, a school teacher. He first trained as a painter, studying at the University of Pennsylvania and the Pennsylvania Academy of Fine Arts. His drawings and oil paintings are represented in private and public collections. Following a three-year stint in the navy during the Vietnam War, Gurganus attended Sarah Lawrence College, where he worked with Grace Paley. At the University of Iowa Writers' Workshop, his teachers included Stanley Elkin and John Cheever. Cheever later observed Gurganus to be "the most technically gifted and morally responsive writer of his generation." Gurganus won a Wallace Stegner Fellowship at Stanford and has subsequently taught writing and literature at Stanford, Duke, the Iowa Writers' Workshop, and Sarah Lawrence. In 1991 he returned from Manhattan to live in his native North Carolina.

In his first novel, *Oldest Living Confederate Widow Tells All*, ninety-nine-year-old Lucy Marsden tells a history of the South from the Civil War until the late twentieth century. *Widow* won the Sue Kaufman Prize, and a CBS TV adaptation won four Emmys. His collection of stories and novellas *White People* won the Los Angeles Times Book Prize and was a finalist for the PEN Faulkner Award. Other awards include induction into the American Academy of Arts and Sciences and into the Fellowship of Southern Writers, and the Lambda Literary Award and the National Magazine Prize for *The Practical Heart*, a collection of four novellas. His short fiction has appeared in the *New Yorker, Atlantic Monthly, Paris Review, O. Henry Prize Collection, Norton Anthology of Short Fiction*, and *Best American Short Stories*. The *New York Times* has named all of Gurganus's works to its annual lists of "Notable Books."

Gurganus's political activism has included editorials in the *New York Times* and the co-founding of Writers Against Jesse Helms, an organization that raised tens of thousands of dollars toward an unsuccessful effort to defeat the senator.

WORKS: *Oldest Living Confederate Widow Tells All* (1989). *White People* (1990). *Plays Well with Others* (1997). *The Practical Heart* (2001).

—GEORGE HOVIS

R. S. GWYNN (1948–). Poet R. S. (Sam) Gwynn was born in Leaksville (now Eden), N.C. His father ran a chain of drive-in movie theaters before becoming sales manager at Industries of the Blind in Greensboro; his mother worked as a kindergarten teacher and daycare worker. He attended Davidson College, where he played football, receiving his B.A. in 1969. After studying at Middlebury College's Bread Loaf School of English, he entered graduate school at the University of Arkansas; there he received his M.A. (1972) and M.F.A. (1973). In 1973 he began work as an instructor of English at Southwest Texas State University, then moved in 1976 to Lamar University in Beaumont, Tex. Since 1997 he has held the title of University Professor, Lamar's highest academic rank. He lives in Beaumont with his wife, Donna; they have three sons.

Gwynn's oeuvre is distinctive in several respects. Whereas most of his contemporaries either write free verse or began their careers doing so, he has always cast his lines in meter and rhyme; often he adopts such fixed forms as the sonnet and the villanelle. His peers tend to work in the mode of the self-referential lyric, but he rarely dwells on his own life and feelings; many of his poems are in such self-effacing modes as the ballad, the elegy, and the epigram. He likes to play the satirist, as in his mock epic *The Narcissiad*, which lampoons the narcissistic tendencies of contemporary culture. Some of his poems also exhibit a virtuosic wit: examples include his cento "Approaching a Significant Birthday, He Peruses *The Norton Anthology of Poetry*" and his backwards villanelle "Ellenalliv for Lew: On His Retirement."

From 1987 through 1991 Gwynn wrote "The Year in Poetry" for the *Dictionary of Literary Biography*; he has also edited two volumes of the *D.L.B.*, as well as volumes in Penguin's Pocket Anthology Series and several other anthologies.

WORKS: *Bearing and Distance* (1977). *The Narcissiad* (1981). *The Drive-In* (1986). Ed., *American Poets since World War II, Second Series: Dictionary of Literary Biography*, vol. 105 (1991). Ed., *American Poets since World War II, Third Series: Dictionary of Literary Biography*, vol. 120 (1992). *The Area Code of God* (1993). Ed., *The Advocates of Poetry:*

A Reader of American Poet-Critics of the Modern Era (1996). Ed., *New Expansive Poetry: Theory, Criticism, History* (1999). Ed., *The Longman Anthology of Short Fiction: Stories and Authors in Context,* with Dana Gioia (2001). *No Word of Farewell: Selected Poems, 1970–2000* (2001). Ed., *The Longman Masters of Short Fiction,* with Gioia (2002). Ed., *The Art of the Short Story: 52 Great Authors, Their Best Short Fiction, and Their Insights on Writing,* with Gioia (2005). Ed., *Contemporary American Poetry: A Pocket Anthology,* with April Linder (2005).

—ROBERT M. WEST

ALEX HALEY (1921–1992). Alex Murphy Palmer Haley, the oldest son of Simon Alexander and Bertha Palmer Haley, was born on August 11, 1921, in Ithaca, N.Y., and raised in Henning, Tenn. He graduated from high school at the age of fifteen, after which he attended college for two years (1937–38). In 1939 Haley enlisted as a messboy in the U.S. Coast Guard, where he began writing stories and gaining some recognition; in 1952 he was given the title of chief journalist. After retirement from the Coast Guard in 1959, Haley began a career as a freelance journalist. He wrote for *Reader's Digest* and *Playboy,* where he began the now-famous *"Playboy* Interviews." His interviews with Malcolm X led to Haley's first book, the widely successful *Autobiography of Malcolm X.*

Haley's most successful book, however, was *Roots,* a historical novel based on family stories that his maternal grandmother told him when he was young. Haley spent twelve arduous years tracing his maternal family's genealogy back to an African named Kunta Kinte. The success of *Roots* was phenomenal, especially after the twelve-hour television series based on the book debuted in January 1977. *Roots* garnered both the National Book Award and the Pulitzer Prize in 1976. That year, Haley accepted the NAACP's Springharn Medal for historical achievement.

Haley followed this success with the novella *A Different Kind of Christmas,* which dramatized a group of slaves' successful escape in the 1850s. Haley was also chief consultant on the television drama *Roots: The Gift* (1988), about Kunta Kinte's desperate attempt to help free dozens of slaves during Christmas.

Haley died of heart failure on February 10, 1992. Several manuscripts were published posthumously, including *Queen,* which explored Haley's paternal lineage, and *Mama Flora's Family,* a bildungsroman.

WORKS: *The Autobiography of Malcolm X* (1965). *Roots: The Saga of an American Family* (1976). *A Different Kind of Christmas* (1988). *Queen,* with David Stevens (1993). *Mama Flora's Family,* "co-written" by Stevens (1998).

—KEITH MITCHELL

MARTHA HALL (1923–). Martha Lacy Hall was born in Magnolia, Miss., on August 19, 1923. She has lived in Baton Rouge since 1954. From 1968 to her retirement in 1980, she was an editor at Louisiana State University Press. Hall was educated at the Whitworth College for Women in Brookhaven, Miss.; she married in 1941 and has three children. She is best known for three collections of short stories: *Call It Living, Music Lesson,* and *The Apple-Green Triumph.* The title story of her third book won an O. Henry Award in 1981.

Walker Percy was the first to discover Hall's talents, describing the tales in *Music Lesson* as "quiet, well crafted and deceptive." "Under [their] calm surface," Percy declared, "lurk the secret and sometimes terrible motions of the human heart." Subsequent critical commentary on Hall's stories evoked comparisons with Eudora Welty and Peter Taylor. Like them, she writes of an "earlier, perhaps gentler time" in the South. Her stories draw on the "impeccable manners, social rituals and class demarcations" of the South of her childhood to penetrate the psyches of seemingly settled and contented characters in order to reveal the sometimes awful struggle to come to terms with personal losses and challenges to their ideas of order. The protagonist of "The Apple Green Triumph" confronts the loss of her eyesight, the deaths of all but one of her siblings, and a brother grown obese and distant from her. In "The Birthday Party," three sisters and their husbands gather to celebrate the birthday of their father, a bitter and disaffected man whose relationships with his children, and theirs with him, are dutiful, rather than loving. "Saturday Job," a story of black/white relations, and "Elinor and Peggy," with its undertones of female eroticism, are also notable tales from Hall's most recent collection.

WORKS: *An Historical Sketch of Magnolia, Mississippi: Centennial Celebration, Magnolia, Mississippi, 1856–1956* (1956). *Call It Living* (1981). *Music Lesson* (1984). *The Apple-Green Triumph and Other Stories* (1990).

—TOM WILLIAMS

ALEXANDER HAMILTON (1712–1756). Alexander Hamilton was born on September 26, 1712, in Edinburgh to Mary Robertson Hamilton and the Reverend William Hamilton, a professor of divinity and principal of the University of Edinburgh. After completing a medical degree at Edinburgh in 1737, Hamilton came to America in 1739 and established a medical practice in Annapolis. Almost immediately he began experiencing the health problems, probably related to tuberculosis, that would lead to his early death on May 11, 1756.

His illness seemingly exacerbated by the Maryland climate, Hamilton contemplated returning to Great Britain, but in 1744 he chose instead to escape the summer humidity with a four-month horseback trip to Maine. His candid personal record of this lengthy trip from May 30 to September 27, 1744, Hamilton's *Itinerarium*, probably was not intended for publication. Yet its publication in 1907 made accessible one of the most authentic accounts of mid-eighteenth-century colonial American life.

By the time he married Margaret Dulany, daughter of a prominent Annapolis family, in 1747, Hamilton had established himself professionally and socially in Maryland society. In 1745 he founded the Tuesday Club of Annapolis, seeking to establish in his adopted homeland the tradition of eighteenth-century British clubs. The club attracted the cultural and financial elite of the Chesapeake Bay area. For eleven years Hamilton kept minutes of club meetings, expanded those into a "Record of the Tuesday Club," and, most significantly, used them to create a prose mock epic entitled *The History of the Ancient and Honorable Tuesday Club*. First published in 1990, this exaggerated fictional account of the club is now regarded as one of the best humorous works from colonial America and serves as a valuable literary and cultural document.

Although he also authored numerous essays, usually humorous or satirical, which were published in the *Maryland Gazette* or other newspapers, Hamilton's *Itinerarium* and *Tuesday Club* are the works that have established his reputation as a significant writer of neoclassical prose in America.

WORKS: *A Defence of Dr. Thomson's Discourse on the Preparation of the Body for the Small Pox* (1751). *Hamilton's Itinerarium, Being a Narrative of a Journey from Annapolis, Maryland, through Delaware, Pennsylvania, New York, New Jersey, Connecticut, Rhode Island, Massachusetts and New Hampshire, from May to September, 1744*, ed. Albert Bushnell Hart (1907); repr. as *Gentleman's Progress: The Itinerarium of Dr. Alexander Hamilton, 1744*, ed. Carl Bridenbaugh (1948). *The History of the Ancient and Honorable Tuesday Club*, ed. Robert Micklus (1990). *The Tuesday Club: A Shorter Edition of the History of the Ancient and Honorable Tuesday Club by Dr. Alexander Hamilton*, ed. Micklus (1995).

—VERBIE LOVORN PREVOST

JAMES HENRY HAMMOND (1807–1864). Born into modest circumstances in Newberry, S.C., James Henry Hammond became a prosperous planter, prominent politician, and well-known defender of slavery. After studying at South Carolina College, Hammond taught school for a brief period before training for the bar. He soon found his true passion as a radical pro-nullification newspaper editor in the early 1830s, when he also married Catherine Fitzsimons, gaining a large plantation and almost 150 slaves. Hammond became a member of the U.S. Congress in 1835, the governor of South Carolina in 1842, and a member of the U.S. Senate in 1857.

Though he never produced a full-length book, Hammond wrote speeches and newspaper and journal articles on a range of subjects, including opposition to banks and railroads, scientific agriculture, and political and social commentary. He achieved most fame as an advocate of slavery and southern rights. In a renowned 1858 speech to the Senate, he predicted that no nation would wage war against an independent South because "Cotton is king," and declared that every society must rest on a "mudsill" class. Hammond had described his hierarchical social ideal in earlier writings, most notably his 1845 letters to English abolitionist Thomas Clarkson, arguing that slavery, benefiting master and slave, allowed for a stable republicanism that could counteract the menaces of materialism, "the mob," and false notions of progress.

Hammond was painfully ambivalent about himself and his world. Ever conscious of being a social outsider, he was never satisfied and never seemed able to follow through with his successes. His family life was often strained, in part because of his sexual relations with slaves and with several young nieces. Having threatened disunion in the 1830s, Hammond was less certain about the feasibility of secession during the 1850s and became disillusioned with Confederate policies during the war. He died in 1864, his society collapsing around him.

WORKS: *Selections from the Letters and Speeches of the Hon. James Henry Hammond, of South Carolina* (1866).

—PAUL D. QUIGLEY

JOHN HENRY HAMMOND (d. 1663). Up until his settling in the New World, little biographical information exists concerning this Englishman who became an early definer of the American Dream. Some scholars have speculated that John Henry Hammond's father was Dr. John Hammond, physician to Henry, Prince of Wales; however, genealogical records of Dr. Hammond's family reveal no descendants named John.

Hammond came to Virginia in either 1633 or 1634, settling in Isle of Wight County. He and his wife Ann raised four children—Mordecai, Bernard, Ann, and Daniel. In 1652 Hammond was elected as a burgess, but the Assembly of Virginia soon dismissed him for being "a scandalous person, and a frequent disturber of the peace of the country." Shortly thereafter Hammond and his family moved to Newtown, St. Mary's County, Md., where he had purchased a plantation, established an inn, assumed responsibility for ferrying persons across the Newtown River, and served as an attorney before the Provincial Court of Maryland.

Although John Henry Hammond never considered himself to be a writer, his reputation rests upon his authoring of two tracts. The first of these, *Hammond vs. Heamans*, responds to a pamphlet by Richard Heamans, captain of the merchant ship *The Golden Lyon*, whose crew helped the Puritan faction win the Battle of the Severn during Maryland's civil war. To avoid capture after the Puritan victory, Hammond, an ardent supporter of Lord Baltimore, disguised himself and then fled aboard the ship *Crescent* to England. There in 1655 he wrote a political pamphlet to vigorously expose Heamans's foolishness and villainy. While in England, Hammond was appalled by the wretched poverty he witnessed. Wishing to promote the "wholesome, healthy, and fruitfull" Chesapeake area and the opportunities to achieve a decent standard of living there, he published *Leah and Rachel; or, The Two Fruitfull*

Sisters Virginia and Mary-Land in 1656. Through this pamphlet Hammond became one of the first to describe the New World as a place evoking a dream of a better life, promoting self-reliance, and offering freedom from poverty and oppression.

In 1661 Hammond, no longer fearing for his safety, returned to his beloved Maryland. The next year he agreed to act as under-sheriff of St. Mary's County and won a defamation suit against Jacob Lumbroso. Hammond died in 1663.

WORKS: *Hammond vs. Heamans* (1655). *Leah and Rachel; or, The Two Fruitfull Sisters Virginia and Mary-Land* (1656).

—LYNNE P. SHACKELFORD

EARL HAMNER (1923–). Earl Henry Hamner, Jr., was born on July 10, 1923, in Schuyler, Va., the eldest of eight red-haired children. His parents—Doris (Gianinni) and Earl Hamner, Sr., a worker in the local soapstone factory and, after losing that job, the proprietor of a sawmill—encouraged their son's literary leanings. He wove from their family's life in the foothills of the Blue Ridge Mountains a reverie set against the background of the Depression and World War II. *The Waltons*, a television series based on Hamner's reminiscences, found an audience in the latter days of the Vietnam War and through the inflationary 1970s (September 14, 1972–June 4, 1981).

Hamner graduated from Schuyler High School (1940) and attended the University of Richmond on scholarship, before being drafted into the army, where he was trained in demolitions (1943–46). He attended Northwestern University briefly (1946), eventually graduating with a B.F.A. from the University of Cincinnati's College of Music (1958).

Hamner's varied, prolific literary career began early. He was seven years old when the *Richmond Times Dispatch* published one of his poems. As an adult, he wrote for the radio in Richmond, Cincinnati, and New York; got the first of many television credits with a script for *The Twilight Zone* ("The Hunt," January 26, 1962); published novels, typically based on his own life story; and wrote for the movies.

In 1963 his novel *Spencer's Mountain*—which tells how Clay-Boy Spencer's killing of a legendary white deer in rural Virginia marks him—was translated to celluloid. The movie, set in Wyoming, starred Henry Fonda and, as the young protagonist, James MacArthur. Clay-Boy appeared again in *The Homecoming: A Novel about Spencer's Mountain*, which became a holiday special for television, *The Homecoming: A Christmas Story* (December 19, 1971). On TV the protagonist, played by Richard Thomas, is named John-Boy Walton and the action is set again in Virginia, though in fictional Walton's Mountain. Like his creator, John-Boy Walton becomes a writer who recalls the days of his youth and the fortunes and misfortunes of the small rural community of which his family was part. Stories of the Walton family continued in television specials into the late 1990s. Hamner supplied the voice-over that framed each episode; and he had a small, nonspeaking role in one episode of the series, "The Journey" (September 13, 1973).

Hamner continued to write for the big screen, including scripts for *Where the Lilies Bloom* (1974), and, at E. B. White's request, *Charlotte's Web* (1973). He produced and wrote for a number of other television movies and series, including *Falcon Crest* (December 4, 1981–May 18, 1990), a nighttime soap opera that starred Jane Wyman and reflected yuppie interests in the lives of the rich and famous during the presidency of Ronald Reagan, Wyman's ex-husband. *Falcon Crest*'s Napa Valley setting also reflected the fact of Hamner's move to the West Coast in the early 1960s. *The Avocado Drive Zoo* recollects his settling—along with his wife, Jane, and their children, Scott and Caroline—into a home in the Hollywood Hills that they increasingly shared with domestic and exotic animals. On the other side of the country, the Hamners' homeplace, the Walton's Mountain Museum, and other sites dedicated to the iconic television series still make Schuyler a tourist destination.

WORKS: *Fifty Roads to Town: A Novel* (1953). *Spencer's Mountain* (1961). *You Can't Get There from Here* (1965). *The Homecoming: A Novel about Spencer's Mountain* (1970). *The Hollywood Zoo* (1997). *Lassie: A Christmas Story*, with Don Sipes (1997). *The Homecoming: A Musical*, with Christopher Sergel and Evelyn Swensson (1998). *The Avocado Drive Zoo: At Home with My Family and the Creatures We've Loved* (1999). *Murder in Tinseltown*, with Sipes (2000). *Goodnight John-Boy: A Celebration of an American Family and the Values That Have Sustained Us through Good Times and Bad*, with Ralph Giffin (2002). *The Twilight Zone Scripts of Earl Hamner*, with Tony Albarella (2003).

—AMBER VOGEL

CATHRYN HANKLA (1958–). Cathryn Anne Hankla was born on March 20, 1958, in Richlands, Va., and has always lived in the Appalachian landscape portrayed in her fiction and poetry. She received her undergraduate and masters degrees from Hollins College, where she studied with Dara Wier and William Goyen, among others. She is also a photographer and painter, and her writing draws on her expertise in visual art. Hankla's first poetry collection, *Phenomena: Poems*, received the Breakthrough Award in poetry.

Hankla's seven books of poetry are characterized by their focus on the natural world, especially Appalachian Virginia, familial relationships, and use of visions and dreams to explore the passing of time and individuals' coming to terms with personal and cultural histories. Although her early poems are primarily free verse, Hankla's later collections echo the possibilities of broken and remembered forms. Her travels in the American West and Southwest, the Czech Republic, England, France, Iceland, and Spain also inform her later poems. *Last Exposures: A Sequence of Poems* spans most of these landscapes and is framed by the accidental death of the poet's father, a veteran whose struggles with mental illness exert a powerful influence on Hankla's imagination. Though Hankla's poetry often is semi-autobiographical, her fiction is less clearly drawn from her life. Her short-story cycle and her two novels do draw on the author's Appalachian heritage, however, and are characterized by lyrical prose, visual energy, and exploration of identity.

Hankla is professor of English at Hollins University, where she has taught since 1982. She also taught at Washington and Lee University, Randolph-Macon Woman's College, and the University of Virginia. Her writing appears in various anthologies, including *Buck and Wing: Southern Poetry at 2000* (2000) and *Best American Short Stories* (2001). In 1989 she received a PEN Syndicated Fiction Award. Her thirteen-year marriage to R. H. W. Dillard ended in 1992. She lives in Roanoke. She has served as poetry editor of the *Hollins Critic* since 1997.

WORKS: *Phenomena: Poems* (1983). *Learning the Mother Tongue: Stories* (1987). *A Blue Moon in Poorwater* (1988). *Afterimages: Poems* (1991). *Negative History: Poems* (1997). *Texas School Book Depository: Prose Poems* (2000). *Poems for the Pardoned* (2002). *Emerald City Blues: Poems* (2002). *The Land Between* (2003). *Last Exposures: A Sequence of Poems* (2004).

—TARA POWELL

BARRY HANNAH (1942–). Born on April 23, 1942, Barry Hannah was the son of William Hannah, an insurance agent, and Elizabeth King Hannah. He spent his boyhood years in Clinton, Miss., which is home to Mississippi College, from which he graduated in 1964 with a pre-med degree. Although many doctors of diverse kinds show up in Hannah's stories, he himself moved quickly away from medicine with an M.A. (1966) and M.F.A. (1967) from the University of Arkansas, programs that headed him into a long and productive career as a fictionalist.

With his first wife, Meridith Johnson, Hannah had three children, Barry, Jr., Ted, and Lee. His early years as a writer/teacher involved frequent moves—Clemson University (1967–73), Middlebury College (three years), University of Alabama (five years), University of Iowa (1981), University of Mississippi (1982), University of Montana (1982–83)—and calamity in love (divorce from Meridith followed by a painfully short marriage with Patricia Busch). Hannah was hard drinking and hard living.

Hannah's first novel, *Geronimo Rex*, reflected much of his own youth, but with every incident ratcheted up several notches in intensity and strangeness. Hannah's narratives have all the wild energy of a pinball machine, and they rack up high scores in terms of gothic plot twists, grotesque sex, and lightning-bolt strokes of insight about life that are somewhere between raw and surreal. Hannah's life quieted down in the 1990s following his marriage to Susan Varas, but his fiction remains consistently lively, rich in surprises with each turn of phrase. His more recent works, *High Lonesome* and *Yonder Stands Your Orphan*, hold up well against the brilliance of *Airships* and *Ray* from early in his career. He held the Mitte Endowed Chair in Creative Writing at Texas State University in 2004–5, then returned to the University of Mississippi, where as writer-in-residence he directs the M.F.A. program.

WORKS: *Geronimo Rex* (1972). *Nightwatchmen* (1973). *Airships* (1978). *Ray* (1980). *The Tennis Handsome* (1983). *Captain Maximus: Stories* (1985). *Hey Jack!* (1987). *Boomerang* (1989). *Never Die* (1991). *Bats out of Hell* (1993). *High Lonesome* (1996). *Yonder Stands the Orphan* (2001).

—OWEN W. GILMAN, JR.

CHARLES HANSFORD (1685?–1761). Knowledge of Charles Hansford's life largely comes from two paragraphs written by his friend and patron Benjamin Waller into his own manuscript copy of four Hansford poems and from facts established by his editors. Hansford's grandfather was in Virginia by 1644; his father was significant enough to have been a militia and county officer in York County. Reporting that the poet "was bred a blacksmith and worked at his trade as long as his strength would permit," Waller notes that Hansford once kept school, even though his learning came from "borrowed books." He borrowed well, demonstrating knowledge of history, the Bible, several classical writers ("Of Body and of Soul" seems to be a response to Lucretius), and English writers such as Camden and Sidney. Hansford tells us that he once "delighted to pore on maps and globes," perhaps gleaning information displayed in "Barzillai." His selection as vestryman (1752) suggests piety and more than yeoman social status. His later years seem to have been successful despite deafness and diminished eyesight. Leo Lemay suggests that Hansford published a poem in the *Virginia Gazette* (1745). He inherited and operated an ordinary near Williamsburg (1755–59). Because Hansford's work (1745?–52?) is richly and intimately detailed, unlike the frequently anonymous and conventional poetry of his time, it also is a biographical source, telling about his family, friends, griefs, and infirmities. With an eye for physical detail, he also has an eye for Heaven; biographers must carefully consider whether sea stories are not "sea of life" parables.

Aware of his place in a deferential society and reflecting southern fears of Indian attack and slave uprising, Hansford calls upon Virginia's gentry for virtuous example and leadership. Nonetheless, voices such as Hansford's, John Harrower's, and James Reid's remind readers that an informed, thoughtful underclass contributed much to Virginia culture.

WORKS: *The Poems of Charles Hansford*, ed. J. A. Servies and C. Dolmetsch (1961). J. A. Leo Lemay, "A Poem Probably by Charles Hansford," *Virginia Magazine of History and Biography* 74 (1966): 445–47.

—JON C. MILLER

WILL N. HARBEN (1858–1919). Born and raised in Dalton, Ga., William Nathaniel Harben worked in the family mercantile business until he was thirty. He moved to New York City in 1888 and began a career as a writer. Between 1888 and his death in 1919, he wrote prolifically, publishing thirty books in a broad range of genres, including local color, detective fiction, social gospel, romance, science fiction, and literary realism. He made regular visits to his hometown throughout his life, marrying Maybelle Chandler on one such visit in 1896.

Most of Harben's works are set in the South, several in Darley, his fictional version of Dalton. His first novel, *White Marie: A Story of Georgia Plantation Life,* is a melodrama about a white woman raised as a slave. Its intentionally ambiguous attitude toward slavery and racism caused a significant amount of controversy at the time of its publication. Following *White Marie,* Harben published several experimental works, including a science fiction novel in the style of Jules Verne and three detective novels in the style of Arthur Conan Doyle. In 1900 Harben published a collection of stories, *Northern Georgia Sketches,* that came to the attention of influential editor William Dean Howells, who promoted Harben's work.

Harben's most significant works concern the lives of mountain people of North Georgia. The two most successful, *Abner Daniel* and *Ann Boyd,* portray the homespun pragmatism and deeply rooted religious conviction endemic to the insular Appalachian community. But he is perhaps most famous for his use of North Georgia mountain dialect and colloquialism. In his last years, Harben wrote a pair of melodramatic potboilers under the pseudonym Virginia Demarest and several novels under his own name.

WORKS: *White Marie: A Story of Georgia Plantation Life* (1889). *Almost Persuaded* (1891). *A Mute Confessor: The Romance of a Southern Town* (1892). *The Land of the Changing Sun* (1894). *The Carruthers Affair* (1898). *The North Walk Mystery* (1899). *Northern Georgia Sketches* (1900). *Westerfelt* (1901). *The Woman Who Trusted: A Story of Literary Life in New York* (1901). *Abner Daniel* (1902). *The Substitute* (1903). *The Georgians: A Novel* (1904). *Pole Baker: A Novel* (1905). *Ann Boyd* (1906). *Mam' Linda: A Novel* (1907). *Gilbert Neal: A Novel* (1908). *The Redemption of Kenneth Galt* (1909). *Dixie Hart* (1910). *The Fruit of Desire* (1910). *Jane Dawson: A Novel* (1911). *Nobody's* (1911). *Paul Rundel: A Novel* (1912). *The Desired Woman* (1913). *The New Clarion: A Novel* (1914). *The Inner Law* (1915). *Second Choice: A Romance* (1916). *The Triumph: A Novel* (1917). *The Hills of Refuge* (1918). *The Cottage of Delight* (1919). *The Divine Event* (1920).

—DAVID A. DAVIS

ISAAC HARBY (1788–1828). Isaac Harby was born in Charleston, S.C., where he spent all but the last six months of his life. Although Harby made many attempts to support himself and his large family as journalist, drama critic, and playwright, his private academy remained the most reliable source of income throughout his career.

Harby's journalistic career began with the publication of a short-lived literary magazine, *The Quiver* (1807), which was probably the first literary journal published by a Jew in the United States. In 1814 Harby purchased a newspaper called the *Investigator.* After a few months, he renamed this paper the *Southern Patriot and Commercial Advertiser,* which he owned and edited until 1817. From 1821 to 1823 he edited the *Charleston City Gazette* and, subsequently he wrote articles for the *Charleston Mercury* as well as other journalistic enterprises.

Harby is known to have written at least three plays, two of which have survived. His dramatic criticism was highly regarded, and his many critical essays stressed a belief in the moral purpose of the theater. In 1824 he published a series of essays on "The Presidency" in two Charleston newspapers that advocated the candidacy of Andrew Jackson and the democratic policies of republicanism.

Harby played a central role in the establishment of the Reformed Society of Israelites in 1825—the first organized expression of Jewish religious reform in North America. His widely circulated *Discourse*, delivered before the Society on November 21, 1825, explicates the group's original goals and aspirations. With David N. Carvalho and Abraham Moïse, Harby compiled the Society's prayer book, the first formal attempt to reform traditional Jewish liturgy in the United States.

In mid-1828 Harby moved to New York, where he contributed to the *New York Evening Post* and the *New York Mirror*, a leading literary journal. He died of acute typhoid fever in New York on December 14, 1828.

WORKS: *The Gordian Knot* (1810). *Alberti* (1819). *A Selection from the Miscellaneous Writings of the Late Isaac Harby, Esq.*, ed. Abraham Moïse and Henry L. Pinckney (1829).

—GARY PHILLIP ZOLA

ELIZABETH HARDWICK (1916–). Writing on subjects ranging from Herman Melville to the O. J. Simpson case, Elizabeth Hardwick is probably best known for her pioneering collection of feminist essays, *Seduction and Betrayal,* her novel *Sleepless Nights,* and an impressive body of literary and cultural criticism that has made her a formidable presence on the literary scene since the mid-1940s. One of the founders of the *New York Review of Books,* Hardwick has, in the words of Cynthia Ozick, "redefined the possibilities of the literary essay."

Hardwick was born on July 7, 1916, in Lexington, Ky., where she grew up in a family of ten brothers and sisters. She was educated at the University of Kentucky, from which she received a B.A. and, in 1939, an M.A. in English. Turning down a graduate-school fellowship at Louisiana State University, she moved to New York City to study English literature at Columbia University. Hardwick began reviewing for the *Partisan Review* after her novel *The Ghostly Lover* attracted the attention of the journal's notoriously demanding editor, Philip Rahv. By the late 1940s she had won both a Guggenheim Fellowship for fiction and the growing attention of writers ranging from Peter Taylor to Elizabeth Bishop for her take-no-prisoners reviews.

In 1949 she married Robert Lowell, already proclaimed the most prominent poet of his generation and certainly one of the most important influences on Hardwick's life and writing during their twenty-three-year marriage. Despite Lowell's long struggle with manic-depression, the couple traveled extensively in Europe and the United States, had a daughter, Harriet Winslow Lowell, and wrote several books, among them Lowell's landmark volume *Life Studies*. Hardwick herself produced a novel entitled *The Simple Truth,* a collection of her essays called *A View of My Own,* an edition of William James's selected letters, and a number of short stories for the *Partisan Review,* the *Kenyon Review,* and the *New Yorker*. Hardwick and Lowell divorced in 1972.

In 1963, during a printers' strike in New York, Hardwick helped found the *New York Review of Books* with Robert Silvers and Barbara Epstein. In the years that followed she contributed book reviews, social critiques, and theater reviews and essays, many of which have been collected in *Bartleby in Manhattan, Sight-Readings,* and *American Fictions*. She followed a series of essays on Herman Melville's fiction with a short critical biography, *Herman Melville,* in the Penguin Life series.

Hardwick remains best known, though, for her novel *Sleepless Nights,* published in 1979 to general acclaim and in 1980 nominated for a National Book Critics Circle Award. As a teacher of creative writing at Barnard College and Columbia University from the 1960s to the mid-1980s, Hardwick has also left her mark on a generation of writers, including Mary Gordon, Nancy Lehmann, Susan Minot, and Sigrid Nunez.

WORKS: *The Ghostly Lover* (1945). *The Simple Truth* (1955). Ed., *Selected Essays of William James* (1961). *A View of My Own: Essays in Literature and Society* (1962). *Seduction and Betrayal: Women and Literature* (1974). *Sleepless Nights* (1979). *Bartleby in Manhattan and Other Essays* (1983). Ed., *The Best American Essays, 1986,* with Robert Atwan (1987). *Sight-Readings: American Fictions* (1998). *American Fictions* (1999). *Herman Melville* (2000).

—SUSAN V. DONALDSON

DONALD HARINGTON (1935–). Born on December 22, 1935, in Little Rock, Ark., Donald Harington became strongly attached to the life and language of the rural Ozark Mountains where he spent summer vacations. That language, conveying his grandmother's stories, remained in his mental ear after he lost his hearing to meningitis at the age of twelve. He calls himself an *Arkansawyer,* and most of his work celebrates the Ozarks and their culture.

Harington received a B.A. in 1956 and an M.F.A. in art in 1958 from the University of Arkansas. He received an M.A. in art history from Boston University in 1959 and did doctoral work at Harvard University. For the next twenty-five years he wrote novels rooted in the Ozarks and Arkansas while he taught at Bennett College in New York, Windham College in Vermont, the University of Missouri–Rolla, the University of Pittsburgh, and South Dakota State University. In 1986 he returned to the University of Arkansas, Fayetteville, where he is professor of art history and has received awards for excellence in teaching.

Harington married Nita Harrison on July 20, 1957. They had three children: Jennifer, Calico, and Katy. On October 8, 1983, Harington married Kim Gunn McClish.

Harington has been more appreciated by other writers than by the general public. His books have not sold spectacularly, but steadily enough that two publishers have issued reprint editions. He has received several local and regional literary prizes, the Porter Prize in 1987, and the Heasley Prize at Lyon College in 1998. In 2002 *Southern Quarterly* published a "Donald Harington Special Issue." In 2003 the Fellowship of Southern Writers awarded him its Robert Penn Warren Award for fiction.

Although resisting definition as an Arkansas writer or even as a southern writer, Harington concedes a resemblance between his efforts to create a fictional place, Stay More, and those of Faulkner to create Yoknapatawpha County. Confining the physical setting of his fiction, Harington has said, frees the reader's imagination to enter the story. Far from being "hillbilly stories," Harington's novels have considerable literary sophistication. *Ekaterina,* for example, is an explicit tribute to one of the author's idols, Vladimir Nabokov. He uses postmodernist devices—playing with literary conventions, blurring the boundaries between author and story, shifting time sequences, and the like. This style, with his humor and his acute depiction of place, characters, and language, distinguishes Harington's work.

WORKS: *The Cherry Pit* (1965). *Lightning Bug* (1970). *Some Other Place. The Right Place* (1972). *Architecture of the Arkansas Ozarks: A Novel* (1975). *Let Us Build Us a City: Eleven Lost Towns* (1986). *The Cockroaches of Stay More* (1989). *The Choiring of the Trees* (1991). *Ekaterina* (1993). *On a Clear Day: The Paintings of George Dombeck* (1995). *Butterfly Weed* (1996). *When Angels Rest* (1998). *Thirteen Albatrosses (or, Falling off the Mountain)* (2002). *With* (2004). *The Pitcher Shower* (2005).

—ETHEL C. SIMPSON

WILLIAM HARMON (1938–). Poet William Harmon was born and raised in Concord, N.C.; his father was a textile executive, and his mother also worked in the textile business. After earning an A.B. in English at the University of Chicago, he joined the navy and served in the Vietnam War. He later received an A.M. in humanities from the University of Chicago, an M.A. in English from the University of North Carolina at Chapel Hill, and a Ph.D. in English from the University of Cincinnati. An English professor at UNC–Chapel Hill for over thirty years, he lives in nearby Durham with his second wife, Anne; they have a daughter. He also has a daughter and a son from his first marriage.

His book-length poem *Treasury Holiday* won the Academy of American Poets' Lamont Prize for a best first book; the poem parodies Walt Whitman's oracular voice to satirize America's obsession with money. His next book, the sequence *Legion: Civic Choruses*, continues to combine Whitman's long line with reflections on the national character. Both books describe themselves as sections of a projected long poem titled *Looms*.

Later books make no reference to that project, but continue to demonstrate an interest in large poetic structures. *The Intussusception of Miss Mary America*, like *Treasury Holiday*, is a book-length poem that questions America's idealization of itself. *One Long Poem* appears at first to collect miscellaneous poems, but turns out to operate like a sequence; it includes some of Harmon's most transparent and affecting work, such as "Mothsong" and "The Chariot." The sequence *Mutatis Mutandis*, his one largely metrical book, won (ironically) the Poetry Society of America's William Carlos Williams Award.

The author of a book on Ezra Pound and many critical articles on other writers, he has also edited *A Handbook to Literature* and several poetry anthologies.

WORKS: *Treasury Holiday* (1970). *Legion: Civic Choruses* (1973). *The Intussusception of Miss Mary America* (1976). *Time in Ezra Pound's Work* (1977). Ed., *The Oxford Book of American Light Verse* (1979). *One Long Poem* (1982). *Uneeda Review*, with Louis D. Rubin (1984). *Mutatis Mutandis: 27 Invoices* (1985). Ed., *A Handbook to Literature*, with C. Hugh Holman, beginning with the 5th ed. (1986–). Ed., *The Concise Columbia Book of Poetry* (1990). Ed., *The Top Five Hundred Poems* (1992). Ed., *The Classic Hundred: All-Time Favorite Poems* (1993). Ed., *Classic Writings on Poetry* (2003).

—ROBERT M. WEST

FRANCES E. W. HARPER (1825–1911). Recovery and reconsideration of the works of Frances Ellen Watkins Harper in the last two decades have proven her to be one of the important American authors, orators, and activists of the nineteenth century. Born in Maryland, a slave state, the only child of free black parents, she was raised by an aunt and uncle after her parents' early deaths. Her uncle, the Reverend William Watkins, ran a free school for blacks with a classic academic orientation and strong moral and religious values. There she learned literary and oratorical skills that she would soon put to singular use. Her education was further enhanced when she was first employed, at the age of thirteen, to do general housework and care for the children of a family who owned a bookstore. In addition to generally encouraging her literary inclinations, they employed her at the bookstore, giving her unusual cultural advantages for a nineteenth-century African American woman. At twenty, she published her first book, a collection of poems entitled *Forest Leaves*.

The passage of the Fugitive Slave Act of 1850 greatly increased the number of slaves heading north to freedom, and Maryland passed legislation making any free black discovered within the state subject to immediate enslavement. Harper chose to go to the free state of Ohio, where she became the first female teacher at Union Seminary, a school founded by the African Methodist Episcopal Church. Her commitment to social and political reform led her to move to Philadelphia, where she became actively involved in the abolitionist movement. Then, for six years, she traveled extensively, lecturing on abolitionist causes. In her lectures, she frequently used her own poetry to dramatize an issue, and those poems began to appear in abolitionist outlets. *Poems on Miscellaneous Subjects*, published in 1854 and her first extant volume, was extremely popular and brought her to a wide audience; the collection features "Bury Me in a Free Land," her best-known antislavery poem. The influence of popular poets of the period such as Henry Wadsworth Longfellow and John Greenleaf Whittier are evident; she also makes effective use of familiar biblical themes and imagery and typically composes in the oral style of the folk ballad. In 1859 Harper added fiction to her repertoire with the landmark publication of "The Two Offers," the earliest extant short story by an African American writer, in the *Anglo-African Magazine*. This story is strongly feminist and deals with the issue of choosing marriage or social commitment.

Somewhat surprisingly, Harper herself chose marriage in 1860 and devoted herself, mainly but not exclusively, to family and farm for four years. When her husband, Fenton Harper, died in 1864, she moved to New England with her daughter Mary and renewed her dedication to speaking and writing on a wide range of political, social, moral, and religious issues. For the next forty years, Harper was a whirlwind of activism and authorship. Important organizations marked by her influence include the Universal Peace Union, the American Woman Suffrage Association, the American Equal Rights Association, the National Women's Christian Temperance Union, and the National Association of Colored Women. In 1892 she achieved another literary landmark with the publication of *Iola Leroy; or, Shadows Uplifted*, one of the earliest novels written by an African American woman and a distinct commercial success. Although the novel is clearly in the nineteenth-century sentimental tradition, it is comprehensive in its treatment of issues of race, class, gender, and identity.

There are gaps in Harper's biography and bibliography, a situation complicated by the fact that she provided no autobiographical material for posterity.

WORKS: *Forest Leaves* (ca. 1845). *Poems on Miscellaneous Subjects* (1854; enl., 1855; enl. again, 1871). *Moses: A Story of the Nile* (1869; enl., 1889; enl. again as *Idylls of the Bible*, 1901). *Poems* (1871). *Sketches of Southern Life* (1872; enl., 1887). *Enlightened Motherhood: An Address by Mrs. Frances E. W. Harper before the Brooklyn Literary Society, November 15, 1892* (n.d.). *Eventide* [under pseudonym Effie Afton] (1854). *Iola Leroy; or, Shadows Uplifted* (1892). *The Sparrow's Fall and Other Poems* (ca. 1894). *The Martyr of Alabama and Other Poems* (ca. 1895). *Atlanta Offering: Poems* (1895). *Poems* (1895; enl., 1898; enl. again, 1900). *Light beyond the Darkness* (n.d.). *The Complete Poems of Frances E. W. Harper* (1988). *A Brighter Day Coming: A Frances Ellen Watkins Harper Reader* (1990). *Minnie's Sacrifice, Sowing and Reaping, Trial and Triumph: Three Rediscovered Novels by Frances E. W. Harper* (1994).

—K. HUNTRESS BALDWIN

THOMAS HARRIOTT [HARRIOT] (1560–1621). Though Thomas Harriott was by profession a mathematician, his intellectual abilities and fateful connections would not allow his employments to be so limited. By age twenty-five Harriott traveled across the Atlantic to the New World, where he proved a capable and important scientific explorer, ethnographer, cartographer, and linguist, and the author of a highly influential account of the first English colony in Virginia—an account now considered the first major text of English colonialism.

Harriott was born in Oxfordshire in 1560. On December 20, 1577, at age seventeen, he enrolled in Saint Mary's Hall at Oxford University. Harriott made his three-year stay at Oxford a productive one, forging important relationships with, among others, George Peele, Richard Hakluyt, Thomas Allen, and George Chapman. He received his B.A. in 1580. In London he provided private instruction in mathematics for the next three years. Harriott came into the service of Sir Walter Raleigh, whose fate from this point on would be closely tied to his own. By the spring of 1584, Harriott was aiding Raleigh in his preparations for an exploration of the New World, training Raleigh's seamen in navigation, and writing a manual, now lost, for the calculation of courses and distances.

In 1585 Raleigh sent Harriott on Sir Richard Grenville's expedition to the English colony of Virginia. Having studied the Algonquian language beforehand (possibly by means of a Native American, Wanchese, who had returned to England with Arthur Barlowe in 1584), Harriott acted as interpreter as well as cartographer, geographer, and scientific reporter. He created his own phonetic alphabet in order to transcribe the speech of Native Americans and recorded an extensive glossary of Algonquian terms for locations and goods.

Upon his return to England in July 1586, Harriott began his official record of the expedition. The result was his soon-to-be-famous account of the natural commodities, building resources, methods of cultivation, and "nature and manners of the people of the countrey," entitled *A Briefe and True Report of the New Found Land of Virginia*. Published in 1588, the account proved an essential description of the earliest English colony in America. Deftly positioning his political aims among lists of natural and marketable commodities and favorable and sympathetic descriptions of the manners and disposition of the Native Americans, Harriott successfully shapes a useful and rhetorically affective account of England's "new found land." The report records Harriott's indignation at the treatment of many of the Native Americans at the hands of the colonizers. *A Brief and True Report* was reprinted in 1589 in Hakluyt's *The Principal Navigations* (along with illustrations by John White, who was likewise present on the Grenville expedition) and was quickly translated into several languages.

After the Gunpowder Plot of 1605, Harriott's life became ever more private, as allegations of atheism and heresy became increasingly threatening. With a substantial pension at Henry Percy's Syon House (received in 1598), Harriott devoted the rest of his days to the passionate study of the sciences. He is identified as the discoverer of the fundamental elements of the binary notation and credited as the shaper of modern algebra, including the creation of the modern algebraic value signs. He also studied and wrote extensive notes on spherical geometry, astronomy, and light refraction. The extant folio pages of Harriott's theories and discoveries in these subjects number in the thousands. On July 2, 1621, Harriott died of nasal cancer.

WORKS: *A Briefe and True Report of the New Found Land of Virginia* (1588). *Artis Analyticae Praxis, as Aequations Algebraicas Nova, Expedita, & Generali Methodo, Resolvendas* (1631).

—JOHN T. BICKLEY

BERNICE KELLY HARRIS (1891–1973). Bernice Kelly was born on October 8, 1891, the third of seven children of William and Rosa Poole Kelly. The family farmed near Raleigh in Wake County, N.C., and Bernice was raised a Democrat and devout Baptist among turn-of-the-century Piedmont families. After graduating from Meredith College in 1913, she taught school. In 1919 and 1920, she studied playwriting under Frederick H. Koch in summer school at the University of North Carolina. She returned to her teaching job in Seaboard inspired by Koch's enthusiasm for writing about the experience, beliefs, and customs of common people in their own vernacular. Kelly organized a local theater group to write and produce plays.

In 1926 she married Herbert Kavanaugh Harris, a prosperous Seaboard farmer and businessman. Life as a childless matron left time to write. She began sending feature articles to newspapers in the region, sold a story to the *Saturday Evening Post* in 1934, and continued to write plays. Her first novel, *Purslane,* was about the world of her childhood. It was given the Mayflower Society Cup as the best North Carolina book of the year.

While collecting life stories for the Federal Writers' Project, Harris saw desperate poverty among North Carolinians and stored up characters and incidents for her subsequent novels. Her sequel to *Purslane,* the 1941 *Portulaca,* was highly critical of the comfortable white elite.

Harris's fourth novel, *Janey Jeems,* outraged many readers by not revealing until the end that the protagonists were black. Although sensitive to African Americans as individuals, in the 1960s she feared the changes brought by the civil rights movement would destroy much that had been worthy in southern culture.

Widowed in 1950, Harris wrote to support herself and in 1963 began teaching creative writing at Chowan College. She collected and edited her students' stories, which were published in two volumes, *Southern Home Remedies* and *Strange Things Happen*. She died on September 13, 1973.

WORKS: *Purslane* (1939). *Folk Plays of Eastern Carolina* (1940). *Portulaca* (1941). *Sweet Beulah Land* (1943). *Sage Quarter* (1945). *Janey Jeems* (1946). *Hearthstones* (1948). *Wild Cherry Tree Road* (1951). *The Very Real Truth about Christmas* (1961). *The Santa on the Mantle* (1964). *Southern Savory* (1964). Ed., *Southern Home Remedies* (1968). Ed., *Strange Things Happen* (1971).

—NANCY GRAY SCHOONMAKER

CORRA HARRIS (1869–1935). Corra Mae White was the daughter of Civil War veteran Tinsley Rucker White and his wife Mary Elizabeth Mathews. Born on March 17, 1869, in Elbert County, Ga., she spent most of her life in the mountains of Georgia. She married Lundy Harris, a Methodist clergyman, in 1887. Their honeymoon year on his rural Georgia circuit was the basis for her best-known book, *A Circuit Rider's Wife*. Lundy Harris was a professor of Greek at Emory College from 1889 until he suffered a nervous collapse in 1899. He was never entirely stable again, and Corra turned to writing to earn money. A rebuttal to an anti-lynching editorial in the *Independent* drew attention. Although not avowedly "pro-lynching," she resented northern meddling in southern affairs. The editors of that New York paper invited regular submissions. A decade of sprightly articles and book reviews followed. Harris deplored realism, the state of modern fiction, and post–Civil War southern literature mired in a romanticized past.

Her first book, *The Jessica Letters,* was co-written with a former editor from the *Independent*. Her next book was *A Circuit Rider's Wife,* her first great success, which initially appeared as a serial in the *Saturday Evening Post*. Readers assumed it was autobiographical, and ever after conflated Corra Harris with the wife of the novel. Harris denounced the Methodist Church for the hardships of the minister's life on the circuit, and was disappointed that the clergy did not seem disturbed by her book. Lundy Harris took his own life that same year.

Harris published nineteen books. Before the end of her life her popularity with the reading public waned. After a heart attack in 1927, she wrote only a newspaper column for the *Atlanta Journal* until her death on February 4, 1935.

WORKS: *The Jessica Letters,* with Paul Elmer More (1904). *A Circuit Rider's Wife* (1910). *Eve's Second Husband* (1911). *The Recording Angel* (1912). *In Search of a Husband* (1913). *Justice* (1915). *The Co-Citizens* (1915). *A Circuit Rider's Widow* (1916). *Making Her His Wife* (1918). *From Sun-up to Sun-down,* with Faith Harris Leech (1919). *Happily Married* (1920). *My Son* (1921). *The Eyes of Love* (1922). *A Daughter of Adam* (1923). *The House of Helen* (1923). *My Book and Heart* (1924). *As a Woman Thinks* (1925). *Flapper Anne* (1926). *The Happy Pilgrimage* (1927).

—NANCY GRAY SCHOONMAKER

GEORGE WASHINGTON HARRIS (1814–1869). George Washington Harris was born on March 20, 1814, in Allegheny City, Pa. In 1819 he moved to Knoxville, Tenn., with Samuel Bell, his half-brother. Bell became a successful metalworker in Knoxville, and Harris learned the trade from him. Harris was an apt pupil: by the age of twelve he was skilled enough to fashion and exhibit a working miniature steamboat. His early training in metalworking and jewelry-making seems to have given him a sense of craftsmanship that would later be evident in his writings.

Harris had almost no formal schooling, but he was mature and responsible beyond his years. At fifteen he was traveling as Bell's representative on business trips, and by the age of twenty-one, he was captain of a Mississippi steamboat. In 1835 he married Mary Emeline Nance. Four years later Harris left steamboating and attempted to establish himself as a gentleman landowner, but he was unsuccessful and was forced by debt to give up his farm. By 1843 he was back in Knoxville and had opened his own metalworking shop there.

In that same year, Harris began contributing epistles and reportage to the New York *Spirit of the Times*, a sporting, racing, and literary journal whose editor, William Trotter Porter, fostered much antebellum southern humorous writing. With Porter's encouragement, Harris wrote a number of realistic and humorous items for the *Spirit* under the pseudonyms "Mr. Free" and "Sugar-tail." Harris's most famous creation, Sut Lovingood, made his first appearance on November 4, 1854, in the *Spirit*.

In the 1850s Harris became deeply involved in politics as a Democrat and a secessionist. During this period he held a number of jobs, most of them connected with metalworking, glassworking, mining, or railroading. He also served as an alderman and later as postmaster in Knoxville. (Harris was not a good businessman; during his adult life he moved from one venture to another, always ready to make a new start but never able to establish himself in any profession.) In a literary sense, though, these years were productive: he published numerous sketches in the *Nashville Union and American* and in other newspapers and periodicals. In 1858 he made plans to collect some of his writings in a volume, but he was unable to find a publisher.

During the Civil War, Harris was forced to move from city to city with his wife and children. These troubled years of wandering, during which he saw the South crumble, disillusioned and embittered him. After the war, he worked for the Wills Valley Railroad and turned his pen increasingly to vicious and even scurrilous anti-northern satire. His wife died in 1867; two years later (just two months before his own death) Harris remarried. There was one bright spot after the war: in April 1867 the New York publisher Dick & Fitzgerald brought out Harris's now-famous collection *Sut Lovingood: Yarns Spun by a "Nat'ral Born Durn'd Fool."* Harris continued to write and publish sketches during the next two years, and by December 1869 he had assembled the manuscript of a second collection, this one entitled *High Times and Hard Times*. He took the manuscript to Lynchburg, Va., to negotiate with a printer, but on the train trip home he fell ill. He died the night of December 11, 1869. Harris is reputed to have uttered the word "poisoned" on his deathbed; perhaps he was the victim of foul play, but it is more likely that he died of apoplexy. The manuscript that he carried has never been recovered.

WORKS: *Sut Lovingood: Yarns Spun by a "Nat'ral Born Durn'd Fool"* (1867). *Sut Lovingood*, ed. Brom Weber (1954). *High Times and Hard Times*, ed. M. Thomas Inge (1967).

—JAMES L. W. WEST III

JOEL CHANDLER HARRIS (1845–1908). Joel Chandler Harris, the illegitimate son of Mary Harris and an unidentified father, was born on December 9, 1845, in Eatonton, Ga. Schoolmates remembered him for his carrot-red hair, stammer, and practical jokes. In 1862–66 Harris worked at nearby Turnwold as a printer's devil on America's only plantation newspaper, Joseph Addison Turner's weekly *The Countryman*. Turner encouraged Harris to explore his plantation library of a thousand volumes, meanwhile coaching his young apprentice about his own writing. Harris also spent long sessions in the slave quarters and in the Turner kitchen, absorbing the fascinating African American Brer Rabbit trickster tales told by Old Harbert, Aunt Crissy, and Uncle George Terrell—the prototypes for Uncle Remus, Aunt Tempy, Mingo, and other African American narrators whom Harris would re-create a decade later. Today, Eatonton's Uncle Remus Museum, a restored slave cabin, contains Harris memorabilia. Harris would later fictionalize his boyhood in *On the Plantation,* and illegitimacy is a major theme in his novel *Sister Jane.*

Harris's typesetting and writing experiences at Turnwold led him to newspaper positions in Macon and Forsyth. In 1870–76 Harris served as associate editor for William Tappan Thompson's *Savannah Morning News,* writing a popular local color and humor column, "Affairs in Georgia." Harris met and married French-Canadian Esther La Rose. They had the first two of their nine children in Savannah. In 1876 a vicious yellow fever outbreak sent the Harrises to the higher ground of Atlanta, where Harris was soon hired as associate editor, with Henry Grady, of the *Atlanta Constitution*—the most influential daily chronicle of what Grady himself, a decade later, would memorably term "the New South."

Harris's editorial writings became a demonstrable force for racial and sectional tolerance and mutual understanding during Reconstruction and post-Reconstruction, but his humorous sketches and his folk tales soon made him America's most recognized southeastern local color newspaper writer. To help him tell his folk stories, Harris invented Uncle Remus, who synthesized the rich cultural and linguistic legacy of the African American storytellers he had heard at Turnwold. The first collection of these widely reprinted stories, *Uncle Remus: His Songs and His Sayings,* appeared in 1880. *Nights with Uncle Remus* followed in 1883, and four more volumes of Uncle Remus tales were printed during his lifetime; two small collections appeared posthumously. In all, Harris wrote 185 Brer Rabbit stories— two-thirds of which are African in origin. Harris's collections comprise the world's largest and most important gathering of reconstructed African American trickster stories prior to more systematic field collecting in the later twentieth century.

The slave-master sociology of these engaging but often violent and amoral trickster stories is complex. But Harris found other important literary voices, too, during his quarter-century as associate editor of the *Constitution,* and afterwards, writing from his porch at The Wren's Nest in West End, Atlanta. This Queen Anne Victorian house-museum, now fully restored and a National Historic Landmark, draws thousands of visitors each year and is also the Joel Chandler Harris Association's headquarters.

Harris published six volumes of children's stories, as well as four Civil War and Reconstruction-era novels and seven books of local color short fiction. His best-known short story is "Free Joe and the Rest of the World," a poignant study of the plight of an African American freedman before Emancipation.

Two weeks before his death, Harris consummated his lifelong interest in spiritual practice by converting to Roman Catholicism. When he died on July 3, 1908, followed by his friend Mark Twain in 1910, America lost her two most beloved and internationally celebrated authors of the later nineteenth century. Both Harris and Twain had taught themselves to write by hand-setting type on regional newspapers. By the time they met in the early 1880s, they had both became famous for capturing, in print, important oral storytelling traditions—the word choices, dialects, natural rhythms, humor, ironies, and essential humanity of nineteenth-century African Americans and lower-class or poor whites who lived along Uncle Remus's and Jim's big road or in Brer Rabbit's and Huckleberry Finn's briar patches of life. Harris generously gave Twain permission to tell the Brer Rabbit and tar baby tale during his platform readings, and this was more frequently requested than any other piece in his repertoire. Uncle Remus's tar baby tale remains the best-known trickster story in America.

WORKS: *Uncle Remus: His Songs and His Sayings* (1880). *Nights with Uncle Remus* (1883). *Mingo and Other Sketches in Black and White* (1884). *Free Joe and Other Georgian Sketches* (1887). *Daddy Jake the Runaway and Short Stories Told after Dark* (1889). *Joel Chandler Harris' Life of Henry W. Grady* (1890). *Balaam and His Master and Other Sketches and Stories* (1891). *On the Plantation: A Story of a Georgia Boy's Adventures during the War* (1892). *Uncle*

Remus and His Friends (1892). *Little Mr. Thimblefinger and His Queer Country* (1894). *Uncle Remus: His Songs and His Sayings . . . New and Revised Edition* (1895). *Mr. Rabbit at Home* (1895). *The Story of Aaron (So Named) The Son of Ben Ali* (1896). *Stories of Georgia* (1896). *Sister Jane: Her Friends and Acquaintances* (1896). *Aaron in the Wildwoods* (1897). *Tales of the Home Folks in Peace and War* (1898). *Plantation Pageants* (1899). *The Chronicles of Aunt Minervy Ann* (1899). *On the Wing of Occasions* (1900). *The Making of a Statesman and Other Stories* (1902). *Gabriel Tolliver: A Story of Reconstruction* (1902). *Wally Wanderoon and His Story-Telling Machine* (1903). *A Little Union Scout* (1904). *The Tar-Baby and Other Rhymes of Uncle Remus* (1904). *Told by Uncle Remus: New Stories of the Old Plantation* (1905). *Uncle Remus and Brer Rabbit* (1907). *The Bishop and the Boogerman* (1909). *The Shadow between His Shoulder-Blades* (1909). *Uncle Remus and the Little Boy* (1910). *Uncle Remus Returns* (1918). *The Witch Wolf: An Uncle Remus Story* (1921). *Qua: A Romance of the Revolution* (1946). *Seven Tales of Uncle Remus* (1948). *The Complete Tales of Uncle Remus* (1955).

—R. Bruce Bickley, Jr.

CONSTANCE CARY HARRISON [MRS. BURTON HARRISON] (1843–1920). Born in Lexington, Ky., on April 25, 1843, Constance Cary was the daughter of Monimia Fairfax and Archibald Cary. She was connected to many of the most distinguished families of Virginia. After her father's death in Cumberland, Md., in 1854, his widow and three children returned to Vaucluse, the family home in Virginia.

Educated by a French governess at home and then at Mr. LeFebvre's boarding school in Richmond, she later spent the Civil War years as a refugee in Richmond with her family. Clever and beautiful, the auburn-haired Constance experienced firsthand the horrors of the war. She knew many of the Confederate leaders during the war. After studying in Europe for a year, she returned home to marry Burton Harrison, Jefferson Davis's secretary during the war years. The Harrisons lived in New York City, where he was a successful lawyer and she a prolific writer. They had three sons. After his death in 1904, she moved to Washington, D.C., where she remained until her death on November 21, 1920.

Her literary career began during the war when she wrote for Richmond newspapers under the pseudonym Refugitta. Later she began publishing pieces in magazines, drawing on her own background for material on William Byrd, George Washington, and Lord Fairfax. She then published short stories, novels, fairy tales, and plays. She drew on both her knowledge of New York City (*The Anglomaniacs*) and her Virginia past (*Flower de Hundred*) in her fiction, but her most valuable work is undoubtedly the autobiographical *Recollections Grave and Gay*, which includes a full account of life in Richmond during the Civil War.

WORKS: *Golden-Rod: An Idyl of Mount Desert* (1879). *The Story of Helen of Troy* (1881). *Woman's Handiwork in Modern Homes* (1881). *The Old Fashioned Fairy Book* (1884). *Bric-a-brac Stories* (1885). *Folk and Fairy Tales* (1885). *Bar Harbor Days* (1887). *Short Comedies for Amateur Players* (1889). *Alice in Wonderland: A Play for Children in Three Acts Dramatized by Mrs. Burton Harrison* (1890). *The Anglomaniacs* (1890). *Flower de Hundred* (1890). Adapt., A. E. Scribe, *A Russian Honeymoon* (1890). *Belhaven Tales* (1892). *A Daughter of the South, and Shorter Stories* (1892). *An Edelweiss of the Sierras: Goldenrod, and Other Tales* (1882). *The Mouse Trap: A Comedietta in One Act* (1892). *Tea at Four O'Clock: A Drawing Room Comedy in One Act* (1892). *Two Strings to Her Bow: A Comedy in Two Acts* (1892). Trans. and adapt., P. Siraudin, *Weeping Wives* (1892). Ed., *Short Stories* (1893, 1969). *Sweet Bells Out of Tune* (1893). *A Bachelor Maid* (1894). *An Errant Wooing* (1895). *A Virginia Cousin, and Bar Harbor Tales* (1895). *The Merry Maid of Arcady, His Lordship, and Other Stories* (1897). *A Son of the Old Dominion* (1897). *Good Americans* (1898). *The Well-Bred Girl in Society* (1898). *The Carcellini Emerald* (1899). *The Circle of a Century* (1899). *A Triple Entanglement* (1899). *A Princess of the Hills* (1901). *The Unwelcome Mrs. Hatch* (1901). *Sylvia's Husband* (1904). *The Carlyles* (1905). *Latter-Day Sweet-Hearts* (1906). *The Count and the Congressman* (1908). *Recollections Grave and Gay* (1911).

—Dorothy McInnis Scura

HENRY SYDNOR HARRISON (1880–1930). Born on February 12, 1880, in Sewanee, Tenn., Henry Sydnor Harrison was raised in Brooklyn, N.Y., where his father founded a Latin school. Harrison received his B.A. (1900) and M.A. (1913) from Columbia University. Journalism took Harrison back to the South, and he became the leading editorialist at the *Times-Dispatch* in Richmond, Va. Harrison never married, but seemed bound to a life of travel, experience, and observation that would help him craft a more three-dimensional universe in his fiction than some of his contemporaries.

In the years preceding World War I, Richmond was identified as a burgeoning hot spot for literature. Harrison and fellow Richmond writers Amelie Rivers, Mary Johnston, Ellen Glasgow, and James Branch Cabell emerged as important new southern voices. In 1910 Harrison published his first novel, *Captivating Mary Carstairs,* under the pen name Henry Second, and soon thereafter, he left the newspaper world to become a full-time novelist and relocated to Charleston, W.Va. Harrison's work as a newspaperman opened his eyes to a number of social problems such as the tobacco industry's exploitation of its poor workers that would inform his later fiction. His works *Queed* and *V. V.'s Eyes* were best-sellers. Although H. L. Mencken described Harrison as a "merchant of mush," contemporary scholars are investigating the nascent feminism and sociopolitical advocacy to be found in his work.

After publishing *Angela's Business* in 1915, Harrison became a member of the American Ambulance service in France, and he later served in the U.S. Navy (1917–19). At the conclusion of his military service, Harrison permanently settled in New York City, where he published *When I Come Back,* a nonfiction tribute to his brother who lost his life in World War I. He published two more works of fiction before his death in 1930, and *The Good Hope* was published posthumously in 1931. He died on July 14, 1930. He was buried in Richmond.

WORKS: *Captivating Mary Carstairs* (1910). *Queed* (1911). *V. V.'s Eyes* (1913). *Angela's Business* (1915). *When I Come Back* (1919). *Saint Teresa* (1922). *Andrew Bride of Paris* (1925). *The Good Hope* (1931).

—MATTHEW SCIALDONE

MILDRED EUNICE HAUN (1911–1966). Born in Hamblen County, Tenn., on January 6, 1911, Mildred Haun grew up in Haun Hollow, Hoot Owl District, Cocke County, in a typical Appalachian community rich in folklore, proverbs, music, and tall tales. At the age of sixteen, she moved to Franklin, near Nashville, to attend high school. Her intention was to study medicine and return to her community as an educated "granny-woman," one who traditionally tended the sick and acted as a midwife. She entered Vanderbilt University in 1931, and with the encouragement of John Crowe Ransom, and later Donald Davidson, Haun wrote her first fiction. For her master's thesis in 1937, she compiled a collection of "Cocke County Ballads and Songs," which has been of inestimable value to southern ballad specialists.

After studying with Wilbur Schramm at the University of Iowa, she gathered her stories together as a fictionalized chronicle of Cocke County. Bobbs-Merrill published it as *The Hawk's Done Gone* in 1941. Although she continued to write after 1941, she published only one story. During the last twenty-five years of her life, she did other professional writing as the book review editor of the *Nashville Tennessean,* an editorial assistant to Allen Tate on the *Sewanee Review,* an information specialist at the Arnold Engineering Development Center in Tullahoma, and for thirteen years a public relations editor and author of technical manuals for the Department of Agriculture in Memphis and Washington, D.C. Haun died in Washington on December 20, 1966. After her death Herschel Gower collected ten additional pieces and published them along with the text of her only book as *The Hawk's Done Gone and Other Stories.*

WORKS: *The Hawk's Done Gone* (1941). *The Hawk's Done Gone and Other Stories* (1968).

—M. THOMAS INGE

PAUL HAMILTON HAYNE (1830–1886). Paul Hayne was born in Charleston, S.C., on January 1, 1830, the only child of Paul Hamilton (1803–31) and Emily McElhenny Hayne (1806–79). Hayne's father, a naval officer and a member of a prominent South Carolina family, died shortly thereafter, and his uncle, Senator Robert Y. Hayne, became his guardian and a lifelong influence. Hayne was educated at Christopher Cotes's school (Henry Timrod was a schoolmate) and at the College of Charleston (1847–50). A publishing poet from 1845, he nevertheless studied law with James Louis Petigru. In 1852 he married Mary Middleton Michel, daughter of a well-known physician; in the same year he was admitted to the bar and served as assistant editor and then as editor of the *Southern Literary Gazette*. He sold his interest in this weekly in 1854, gave up the law, and thereafter devoted himself to literature, editing *Russell's Magazine* (1857–60) and publishing three volumes of poems by 1860. An early espouser of secession, Hayne embraced his state's cause, and though frail in health since youth (lung and gastrointestinal problems), served actively for four months in 1861–62 as aide-de-camp to Governor Francis Pickens. When his health failed, he continued to support the Confederacy with his pen.

The end of the Civil War brought not only defeat but near economic ruin, and Hayne moved his family (wife, son, and mother) to eighteen acres (later called Copse Hill) in Columbia County, Ga., near Augusta, and committed himself anew to literature. Struggling for bread, he served in various editorial capacities on numerous southern periodicals and contributed verse, essays, criticism, and occasional fiction to southern magazines and any northern journals—*The Old Guard, Round Table, Appleton's Journal, Lippincott's,* and the *Galaxy*—that would print his work. By the early 1870s his poems were appearing in the *Atlantic Monthly, Scribner's Monthly, Harper's New Monthly, Harper's Weekly,* and in most major northern literary magazines, and he was able to make a modest living. He collected new poems in 1872 and 1875, and in 1882 a misnamed "complete edition" came out.

During this period, particularly after the death of Simms in 1870, Hayne was widely known as the "representative poet of the South" or the "poet laureate of the South." In response to official requests he composed poems for such occasions as the centennials of the Battle of King's Mountain, the British surrender at Yorktown, and the sesquicentennial of the founding of the Colony of Georgia, along with many others, and he took seriously the duties associated with such a reputation. He corresponded with a number of prominent American and British writers, including Bryant, Longfellow, Whittier, Holmes, Whipple, Howells, Stedman, Taylor, Simms, Gayarré, Cooke, Lanier, Margaret Preston, and Constance Woolson among the Americans, and Tennyson, Swinburne, Charles Reade, R. D. Blackmore, Jean Ingelow, William Black, and Wilkie Collins among the British. His letters, indeed, may be his most important contribution to literature. As a poet, Hayne generally accepted the Anglo-American tradition and condemned Whitman and all attempts to modify it, and despite his role as southern laureate, his verse suggests his background only in its stress on verbal melody and in its occasional treatment of nature, politics, and theme. His prose is a different matter, and his essays and letters at times forcefully demonstrate his Carolina temperament and unreconstructed political views. His postwar experience illustrates more fully than that of his contemporaries the economic and cultural plight of a dedicated man of letters in the South. Hayne died of a stroke on July 6, 1886.

WORKS: *Poems* (1855). *Sonnets, and Other Poems* (1857). *Avolio: A Legend of the Island of Cos, with Poems, Lyrical, Miscellaneous, and Dramatic* (1859). *Legends and Lyrics* (1872). Ed., *The Poems of Henry Timrod* (1873). *The*

Mountain of Lovers; with Poems of Nature and Tradition (1875). *Poems* (complete ed., 1882). *A Collection of Hayne Letters,* ed. Daniel M. McKeithan (1944). *A Man of Letters in the Nineteenth-Century South: Selected Letters of Paul Hamilton Hayne,* ed. Rayburn S. Moore (1982).

—RAYBURN S. MOORE

LAFCADIO HEARN (1850–1904). Named after the Greek island of Leucadia (present-day Levkas) on which he was born in 1850, Patrick Lafcadio Hearn was the son of a British military doctor and a Greek woman. He was educated in Ireland, England, and France. By his sixteenth year, Hearn had reached his full height of five feet three inches; and an accident had blinded and scarred one eye, which he consciously tried to hide in pictures. At nineteen, he immigrated to the United States, where he eventually worked as a newspaperman for the *Cincinnati Commercial.*

Traveling to New Orleans in 1877 to write local color sketches for the *Commercial,* Hearn discovered a romantic and decaying city. He wrote for the *New Orleans City Item* and eventually moved on to the *Times-Democrat.* By this time he dropped his first name in print and became Lafcadio Hearn, the name by which he is still recognized. Hearn also wrote two texts that further preserve the Creole New Orleans culture: *La Cuisine Créole* and *"Gombo Zhèbes,"* both published in 1885. In 1883 George Washington Cable related to Hearn the story of Isle Dernière and the 1856 hurricane that destroyed the resort island, which Hearn captured in his novel *Chita: A Memory of Last Island.* Guy Davenport dubbed the novel a "lost classic."

After ten years in New Orleans, Hearn left the city and journeyed to Martinique before continuing on to Japan, where he spent the last decade of his life absorbing the culture while translating it for the English-speaking world. Hearn not only translated the culture but also adopted it as his own by becoming a Japanese citizen in 1896, and changing his name to Koizumi Yakumo. He died in Japan in 1904, and is buried in the northern part of Tokyo.

WORKS: *Stray Leaves from Strange Literature* (1884). *La Cuisine Créole* (1885). *"Gombo Zhèbes": Little Dictionary of Creole Proverbs* (1885). *Some Chinese Ghosts* (1887). *Chita: A Memory of Last Island* (1889). *Two Years in the French West Indies* (1890). *Youma: The Story of a West-Indian Slave* (1890). *Glimpses of Unfamiliar Japan* (1894). *Out of the East* (1895). *Kokoro* (1896). *Gleanings in Buddha-Fields* (1897). *Exotics and Retrospectives* (1898). *In Ghostly Japan* (1899). *Shadowings* (1900). *A Japanese Miscellany* (1901). *Kotto* (1902). *Kwaidan* (1904). *Japan: An Attempt at Interpretation* (1904). *The Romance of the Milky Way* (1905). *The Writings of Lafcadio Hearn* (1922). *Creole Sketches* (1924). *Complete Lectures on Art, Literature, and Philosophy,* ed. Ryuiji Tanabé, Teisaburo Ochiai, and Ichiro Nishizaki (1925–34). *Lafcadio Hearn, Japan's Great Interpreter: A New Anthology of His Writings, 1894–1904* (1992). *Inventing New Orleans: Writings of Lafcadio Hearn,* ed. S. Frederick Starr (2001).

—MARIA P. HEBERT

LILLIAN HELLMAN (1905–1984). Lillian Hellman, one of the most distinguished American and female playwrights, was born in New Orleans on June 20, 1905, the only child of Max Hellman and Julia Newhouse. Until age six, she lived in a boardinghouse run by two aunts; her father then moved the family to New York, although Hellman regularly returned to New Orleans each year until age sixteen, and her family background often figures in her plays.

After attending New York University and Columbia, Hellman worked in publishing and theatrical jobs. Her marriage to theatrical press agent Arthur Krober ended in divorce in 1932, not least because of Hellman's affairs, the most important and influential being her lifelong association with writer Dashiell Hammett, an emotional anchor and mentor until his death in 1959.

Hellman's first theatrical success came in 1934 with *The Children's Hour,* based on a British court case and dealing with the taboo issue of lesbianism. This was followed by a string of plays, including the unsuccessful *Days to Come; The Little Foxes*—probably her best-known work, one of her most highly acclaimed, and part of a planned trilogy about an enterprising Alabama family, the Hubbards; the politically charged *Watch on the Rhine; Another Part of the Forest,* depicting the Hubbard family twenty years earlier; the wistful but commercially unsuccessful *The Autumn Garden; Toys in the Attic;* and another political play, *The Searching Wind.* Though often criticized for her use of the well-made play formula, Hellman's works are marked by rich characterization, realistic dialogue, bold themes, and tightly structured plots. Hellman also wrote screenplays, adaptations, and three acclaimed memoirs, one of which spawned the film *Julia* (1980), starring Jason Robards and Jane Fonda.

For all her literary achievements, Hellman became equally well known for her passionate political activities and a tumultuous personal life filled with controversy, feuds, and self-fabrications. Like Hammett, she was ardently concerned with the labor movement of the 1930s, the progressive era in the 1940s, and the cold war politics of the 1950s, during which both she and Hammett were victimized by the House Un-American Activities Committee and blacklisted.

Zoë Caldwell's 1996 portrayal of this volatile woman in *Lillian,* a one-woman show written by William Luce, provides a testament to Hellman's enduring place in American theater.

WORKS: *The Children's Hour* (1934). *Days to Come* (1936). *The Little Foxes* (1939). *Watch on the Rhine* (1941). *Four Plays* (1942). *The North Star* (1943). *The Searching Wind* (1944). *Another Part of the Forest* (1946). *Montserrat,* adapted from the play by Emmanuel Roblès (1950). *The Autumn Garden* (1951). Ed., *The Selected Letters of Anton Chekhov* (1955). *The Lark,* adapted from the play by Jean Anouilh (1956). *Candide* (1957). *Toys in the Attic* (1960). *My Mother, My Father and Me,* based on the novel *How Much?* by Burt Blechman (1963). Ed., *The Big Knockover,* by Dashiell Hammett (1966). *An Unfinished Woman* (1969). *Pentimento* (1973). *Scoundrel Time* (1976). *Six Plays by Lillian Hellman* (1979). *Maybe: A Story* (1980). *Eating Together: Recipes and Recollections* (1984). *Conversations with Lillian Hellman* (1986).

—KAREN C. BLANSFIELD

HINTON HELPER (1829–1909). "The Notorious Helper," as Hinton Rowan Helper became known after the publication in 1857 of *The Impending Crisis of the South,* was born in the North Carolina Piedmont on December 27, 1829, the descendant of plain farmers of German origins. After early education in a private academy and a brief stay in New York, he traveled to the Far West at age twenty-one seeking wealth and adventure. What he found instead was material for his first book, *The Land of Gold,* in which he sought to puncture myths about California and expose the "rottenness, corruption, squalor, and misery" of the West.

Nothing in that book would have prepared readers for his *The Impending Crisis,* published two years later. Written from the point of view of an abolitionist who was also a racist (not an altogether rare combination among non-slaveholding whites), *The Impending Crisis* blasted the "slave-driving oligarchy" Helper held responsible for the inferiority of the American South in relation to the North. Helper contended that slaveholders were "more criminal than common murderers," that slavery was "the monstrous enemy that stalks abroad in our land," but he did not oppose it, principally for moral reasons. Rather he had in mind the interests of plain white southerners, who he contended had been held back by slavery, and he produced tables and statistics to show just how deficient, economically and socially, the South truly was. He was denounced for his book as few southerners had ever been denounced: possession of his abolitionist tract became a crime in most southern states, and three men in Arkansas were reported hanged for owning copies.

Helper's racism in *The Impending Crisis*, in fact, is very mild compared to that demonstrated in his three other books, all written during Reconstruction. Having helped to abolish slavery, he now sought to abolish the freed slave. In *Nojoque, The Negroes in Negroland,* and *Noonday Exigencies in America* he attempted to "write the negro out of America" and "to write him . . . out of existence." Those books, however, received little attention. Helper lived for nearly forty years after the publication of his last book, but he largely disappeared from public notice. He committed suicide in Washington in 1909.

WORKS: *The Land of Gold* (1855). *The Impending Crisis of the South* (1857; and *Compendium,* 1859, 1860). *Nojoque: A Question for a Continent* (1867). *The Negroes in Negroland; The Negroes in America; and Negroes Generally* (1868). *Noonday Exigencies in America* (1871).

—FRED HOBSON

GEORGE WYLIE HENDERSON (1904–1965). Little is known about George Wylie Henderson's life. The thin biographical record mainly touches on his two books without much revealing the man, but from what is known, the contours of his life typify those who participated in the Harlem Renaissance. His grandfather had been a farmer; his father, a minister; and he came from tiny Warrior's Stand, Ala., where he was born on June 14, 1904. After taking a printer's apprenticeship at the Tuskegee Institute, he set out for the hub of black culture in New York, joining the likes of Ralph Ellison, Langston Hughes, and Ellen Tarry.

Arriving inauspiciously during the Depression years, he eventually found employment in the printing shop of the *New York Daily News*. There he published his first short story, "Sinner Man's Wedding," in the January 14, 1932, edition, following it with eight others. From 1933 to 1947 he published occasional fiction in the pages of *Redbook*.

Henderson's novelistic debut garnered respectable acclaim. Part agrarian idyll, *Ollie Miss* relates the hardscrabble life of a farmhand who falls for a worker named Jule, and chooses to bear his illegitimate child on her own. A contemporaneous *New York Times* review trumpeted it as "an excellent novel of Negro life," and marked its "real achievement," particularly in Henderson's treatment of "Negroes as responsible individuals." Reviewers unanimously appreciated the authenticity of Henderson's characters, and its independent heroine has been compared to Janie Mae Crawford of Zora Neale Hurston's *Their Eyes Were Watching God* (1937).

But the sequel, *Jule*, did not fare so well, though it clearly contained autobiographical elements and borrows Ollie's illegitimate son for its protagonist. Readers will recognize shopworn elements from the southern black migration novel (and, for that matter, slave narratives), as this bildungsroman recounts Jule's trek to the North and his ensuing disillusionment. Henderson's few biographers repeat the assertion that *Jule*'s poor critical reception consigned him to oblivion, and many have faulted the novel for its poorly shaded characters and lack of psychological subtlety. But less has been written about Henderson's minimalist prose and its debt to modernist writers.

Ultimately, Henderson's two novels can be seen as a kind of diptych of black literary history, as they clearly show the transition from the Harlem Renaissance (*Ollie Miss*) to later social protest literature (*Jule*). According to his *Times* obituary, Henderson died suddenly on April 28, 1965, leaving behind his wife, Blanche, and a stepdaughter, Walda.

WORKS: *Ollie Miss* (1935). *Jule* (1946).

—BRYAN GIEMZA

BETH HENLEY (1952–). Beth Henley, the second of four daughters, was born Elizabeth Becker Henley on May 8, 1952, in Jackson, Miss. She attended local public schools. Because her mother was active in Jackson's New State Theater, Henley developed an early interest in theater. At Southern Methodist University (B.F.A., 1974) she pursued acting and began writing plays. Before beginning graduate work at the University of Illinois, she performed for the Dallas Minority Theatre. After a year and summer at Illinois, she moved to California to join her SMU boyfriend Stephen Tobolowsky and to try to find a place in the movie industry. Her break came when Frederick Bailey entered *Crimes of the Heart* in the Great American Play contest sponsored by the Actors Theatre of Louisville, Ky.

Crimes of the Heart, Henley's first full-length, professionally produced play, opened on Broadway in 1981 and received numerous awards, including a Pulitzer Prize. It describes the reunion of three quirky sisters in a small Mississippi town, and the entire action takes place in a kitchen. As a small cast of characters enters and exits this domestic space, the sisters' lives unfold, inviting the audience to examine the internal and external factors that shape—and often limit—them.

The darkly comic perspective on southern women's lives and the domestic focus that characterize this play also inform other early plays by Henley. *Am I Blue, The Wake of Jamey Foster, The Miss Firecracker Contest, The Lucky Spot,* and *The Debutante Ball* are all set in either Mississippi or Louisiana. Some of Henley's later plays have been set in the American West. *Abundance* focuses on the lives of two western women in the late 1860s. *Control Freaks,* which was produced in 1992 and marked Henley's directorial debut, focuses on contemporary California, and *Signature,* originally produced in 1990, takes place in Hollywood in the year 2052. Henley has become increasingly experimental in playwriting technique as well as in subject matter.

Her most recent plays include *Impossible Marriage* and *Revelers.* Critical recognition of her oeuvre has resulted in two collected works: *Four Plays* and *Collected Plays.* Henley has also written and co-written several screenplays, including one for the popular movie version of *Crimes of the Heart,* for which she received an Academy Award nomination in 1986. She lives in California with her son, Patrick.

WORKS: *Crimes of the Heart* (1982). *Am I Blue* (1982). *The Wake of Jamey Foster* (1983). *The Miss Firecracker Contest* (1985). *The Lucky Spot* (1987). *Abundance* (1990). *Four Plays* (1992). *The Debutante Ball* (1991). *Impossible Marriage* (1999). *Control Freaks* (2000). *Signature* (2000). *Collected Plays* (2000). *Revelers* (2003).

—EMILY WRIGHT

JOHN BELL HENNEMANN (1864–1908). John Bell Hennemann was born in Spartanburg,S. C., on January 2, 1864. Hennemann was educated at the University of Virginia and the University of Berlin. He was professor of English at the University of Tennessee (1893–1900), where, on September 7, 1897, he married Marion Hubard. In 1900 he moved to Sewanee, Tenn., where he became dean of the School of Arts and Sciences and professor of English at the University of the South (1900–1908). There he assumed the editorship of the *Sewanee Review* (1907–8), which had been founded in 1892 by his friend and colleague W. P. Trent.

Hennemann's career as educator, editor, literary historian, and critic is closely aligned with Trent's. In "The National Element in Southern Literature" (*Sewanee Review,* July 1903), he praises Trent's *Life of William Gilmore Simms* (1892) as an example of a seminal school of criticism then forming in the South—a school that included such scholars as William M. Baskervill of Vanderbilt and himself and which, he felt, was germinated by Sidney Lanier's literary lectures at Johns Hopkins (1880). Hennemann believed that romantic southern local color was more indicative of a national literary heritage and point of view than the realism of Howells and James, but in "The Modern Spirit in Literature" (*Sewanee Review,* August 1894) he had maintained that all regional and national literatures would shortly lose identities in world literature. His entry on Trent in *The Library of Southern*

Literature (1907) is a defense of this critical movement and of academic freedom. Here he again defends Trent's *Simms* and congratulates the University of the South for supporting Trent against irate Charlestonians.

While at Sewanee, Hennemann became a prominent editor whose interests ranged from Shakespeare to American short fiction. He died at Richmond, Va., on November 26, 1908.

WORKS: Ed., *Johnson Series of English Classics* (1900–1903). Ed., *The Complete Works of Thackeray,* with W. P. Trent (1904). Ed., *Shakespeare's "Twelfth Night"* (1906). Ed., Kemper Bocock, *Antiphon to the Stars* (1907). Ed., *Best American Tales,* with Trent (1907).

—JOHN T. HIERS

O. HENRY (1862–1910). Known to his readers as O. Henry, William Sydney Porter was born on September 11, 1862, in Greensboro, N.C., where he spent nearly half his life. Early on, he gained renown as a humorist, artist, and storyteller, absorbing local tales and character types while working in his uncle's drugstore. In 1882 Porter moved to Texas for health reasons and remained there until early 1898, working variously as a ranch hand, drugstore clerk, bookkeeper, draftsman, and—in a job that would change his life—a bank teller.

In 1887 he married Athol Estes; two years later their daughter, Margaret, was born. In 1894 Porter channeled his artistic interests into a weekly humorous newspaper, the *Rolling Stone,* which lasted only a year because of financial difficulties. After Porter quit his bank job, discrepancies in his accounts were discovered and he was suspected of embezzlement; a grand jury found insufficient evidence to indict him, and the case has never been clearly resolved. A few months later, while Porter was working for the *Houston Post,* the bank case was reopened, and this time Porter was indicted. On the eve of his trial he fled, seeking refuge in New Orleans, Honduras, Mexico, and other places that would eventually provide material for many of his stories. In 1897, learning that his wife was dying of tuberculosis, he returned home; after she died, Porter was tried, convicted, and remanded to the Ohio State Penitentiary, earning early release from his five-year sentence in 1901.

Using the literary pseudonym he had adopted in prison, Porter moved to New York, where he could live anonymously as O. Henry and hide from his past. He rapidly became one of the country's most popular writers, churning out nearly three hundred stories in a few short years. In 1907 he married Sarah Coleman, a childhood friend from Greensboro. Despite his income, Porter was perpetually broke, squandering money on friends and alcohol. On June 5, 1910, Porter died, deeply in debt. His style, stories, and famous "O. Henry twist" endings remain legendary.

WORKS: *His Courier* (1902). *Cabbages and Kings* (1904). *The Four Million* (1906). *The Gift of the Magi* (1906). *The Trimmed Lamp* (1907). *Heart of the West* (1907). *The Voice of the City* (1908). *The Gentle Grafter* (1908). *Roads of Destiny* (1909). *Options* (1909). *Strictly Business* (1910). *Whirligigs* (1910). *Let Me Feel Your Pulse: Adventures in Neurasthenia* (1910). *Sixes and Sevens* (1911). *The Complete Edition of O. Henry* (1911). *Rolling Stones* (1912). *Waifs and Strays* (1917). *The Ransom of Red Chief and Other O. Henry Stories for Boys* (1918). *O. Henryana* (1920). *Selected Stories from O. Henry* (1922). *Letters to Lithopolis* (1922). *The Best of O. Henry: One Hundred of His Stories* (1929). *Postscripts* (1923). *More O. Henry: One Hundred More of the Master's Stories* (1933). *Ten Plays from O. Henry,* adapt. Addison Geery Smith (1934). *O. Henry Encore,* ed. Mary S. Harrell (1939).

—KAREN C. BLANSFIELD

CAROLINE LEE HENTZ (1800–1856). Novelist Caroline Lee Hentz was born in Lancaster, Mass., on June 1, 1800, the eighth and youngest child of John and Orpah Whiting. The Whitings had lived in

Massachusetts for six generations, and Caroline's father and three of her brothers were career army officers. At twenty-four she married Nicholas Marcellus Hentz, a native of Metz, France, who had come to America for political reasons. Hentz was teaching at George Bancroft's Round Hill School in Northampton when he married Caroline; but in 1826 he moved south to teach modern languages at the University of North Carolina. In Chapel Hill she fostered the talent of slave poet George Moses Horton. Hentz's remaining years were lived in southern and border states, in which she and her husband established and conducted girls' schools. The Hentzes taught successively in Covington, Ky. (1830–32); in Cincinnati (1832–34); in Florence, Ala. (1834–43); in Tuscaloosa, Ala. (1843–45); in Tuskegee, Ala. (1845–48); and in Columbus, Ga. (1848–49).

During the years in which she raised four children and helped her husband teach, Hentz also found the time to write. She composed poetry, three plays, a novel, and a popular collection of short stories, *Aunt Patty's Scrap-Bag*. The breakdown of her husband's health in 1849 and the closing of their school in Columbus forced Hentz to write full time to support her family. Over the next seven years she completed an astonishing total of seventeen novels and short-story collections. A number of these works were popular and were reprinted well into the 1880s.

Hentz's novels and stories are sentimental and melodramatic renderings of the antebellum South. They project an idealized vision of plantation life—of refined ladies and gentlemen, contented slaves, and rustic and properly subservient backwoods farmers. Two of her novels, *Marcus Warland* and *The Planter's Northern Bride*, were spirited and popular refutations of the condemnatory view of slavery and the plantation system presented in *Uncle Tom's Cabin*. Hentz died on February 11, 1856, in Marianna, Fla., where she had moved to live with her grown children.

WORKS: *Lovell's Folly, a Novel* (1833). *De Lara; or, The Moorish Bride* (1843). *Aunt Patty's Scrap-Bag* (1845). *Linda; or, The Young Pilot of the Belle Creole* (1850). *The Mob Cap and other Tales* (1850). *Ugly Effie; or, The Neglected One and the Pet Beauty, and Other Tales* (1850). *Rena; or, The Snowbird* (1851). *The Banished Son and Other Stories of the Heart* (1852). *Eoline; or, Magnolia Vale* (1852). *Marcus Warland; or, The Long Moss Spring: A Tale of the South* (1852). *Helen and Arthur; or, Miss Thusa's Spinning Wheel* (1853). *The Victim of Excitement, The Bosom Serpent, etc., etc., etc.* (1853). *Wild Jack; or, The Stolen Child, and Other Stories* (1853). *The Planter's Northern Bride* (1854). *The Flowers of Elocution: A Class Book* (1855). *Robert Graham, a Novel* (1855). *Courtship and Marriage; or, The Joys and Sorrows of American Life* (1856). *Ernest Linwood, a Novel* (1856). *The Lost Daughter and Other Stories of the Heart* (1857). *Love after Marriage and Other Stories of the Heart* (1857). *The Planter's Daughter: A Tale of Louisiana* (1858).

—RITCHIE D. WATSON, JR.

SOPHIA BLEDSOE HERRICK (1837–1919). Editor and writer Sophia McIlvaine Bledsoe was born in Gambier, Ohio, on March 26, 1837, oldest child of Albert Taylor Bledsoe and Harriet Coxe Bledsoe. Her early education was at boarding schools, but she later studied math, drawing, and natural sciences in colleges where her father taught. In 1860 she married James Burton Herrick, an Episcopal clergyman, and moved to New York with him. They had three children—Albert, Virginia, and Louise.

In 1868 her husband joined the Oneida Community. Herrick did not go with him but instead took the children and moved to Baltimore, where her father was editor of the *Southern Review*. For a few years Herrick headed a school for girls in Baltimore. She began to write scientific articles for the journal her father edited. She also took a course in biology at Johns Hopkins and wrote and illustrated several scientific articles that *Scribner's Monthly* published. Herrick's three science books for children, published in the 1870s, are notable for their clarity and may be her most enduring achievement.

When her father died in 1877, Herrick assumed editorship of the *Southern Review*, though that journal folded soon afterward. She moved back to New York and continued contributing articles and editing at *Scribner's Monthly* and its successor, the *Century,* until 1906, when she retired. Herrick and her husband remained separated, but she resisted a formal divorce on moral grounds. In the 1870s Herrick had a relationship with Allen C. Redwood, a Civil War illustrator with a studio in Baltimore. She died in Greenwich, Conn. Her papers, not including letters to Redwood, which are privately owned, are in the Schlesinger Library at Radcliffe College.

WORKS: *The Wonders of Plant Life under the Microscope* (1883). *Chapters on Plant Life* (1885). *Essays and Reviews of George Eliot Not Hitherto Reprinted, Together with an Introductory Essay on the Genius of George Eliot* (1887). *The Earth in Past Ages* (1888). *A Century of Sonnets* (1902). *Public School Physiology: Perversion of Truth and Science in the Name of Temperance* (1908).

—ALICE R. COTTEN

DUBOSE HEYWARD (1885–1940). Edwin DuBose Heyward, whose enduring fame came from his creation of a black character immortalized in George Gershwin's opera *Porgy and Bess* (1935), was born in Charleston, S.C., on August 31, 1885, to Edward Watkins and Janie Screven DuBose Heyward. Although birth to a descendant of a signer of the Declaration of Independence placed him in the Charleston aristocracy, economic losses from the Civil War plagued the family. Heyward's father died when Heyward was two, compounding family woes. He abandoned formal education at age fourteen to work in a hardware store. At eighteen he was stricken with polio. At twenty he suffered from typhoid, then worked for a time as a wharf checker. A pleurisy attack in 1906 resulted in an eighteen-month recuperation in Arizona. In 1906 he entered an insurance and real estate partnership. Exhausted by overwork and a second pleurisy attack, in 1917 he took refuge in Hendersonville, N.C., where he took up painting, wrote stories, and bought a summer cottage.

In Charleston, Heyward became friends with northern writers Hervey Allen and John Bennett. Under their influence, he began to write poetry. In the fall of 1920 the trio founded the Poetry Society of South Carolina—in part a response to H. L. Mencken's "Sahara of the Bozart." Secretary of the Society, Heyward edited its yearbooks until 1924. *Carolina Chansons*, his first volume of poems, with Allen, appeared in 1922.

Invited to MacDowell Colony for the summers of 1922 and 1923, Heyward met playwright Dorothy Hartzell Kuhns. They married on September 22, 1923. (A daughter, Jennifer, was born in 1930.) In 1924 Heyward gave up his business and committed himself full-time to writing and to lecturing on southern literature. *Porgy,* his first novel, was based on Heyward's appreciation for black life and speech on the wharves of Charleston. He and his wife adapted the novel for the stage, where it had a highly successful run. Heyward later wrote the libretto for the opera. The couple also dramatized Heyward's *Mamba's Daughters,* another depiction of black life in Charleston.

Continuing to work in fiction, poetry, and drama, Heyward also wrote the movie scenarios for *The Emperor Jones* and *The Good Earth.* His realistic and compassionate portrayal of blacks won him praise and censure. He died on June 16, 1940, in Tryon, N.C.

WORKS: *Carolina Chansons: Legends of the Low Country,* with Hervey Allen (1922). *Skylines and Horizons* (1924). *Porgy* (1925). *Angel* (1926). *Porgy: A Play in Four Acts,* with Dorothy Heyward (1927). *The Half-Pint Flask* (1929). *Mamba's Daughters* (1929). *Jasbo Brown and Selected Poems* (1931). *Brass Ankle* (1931). *Peter Ashley* (1932). *Porgy and Bess,* with music by George Gershwin, libretto by Heyward, lyrics by Heyward and Ira Gershwin (1935). *Lost Morning* (1936). *Mamba's Daughters,* with Dorothy Heyward (1939). *Star Spangled Virgin* (1939). *The Country Bunny and the Little Gold Shoes* (1939).

—JOSEPH M. FLORA

CARL HIAASEN (1952–). Carl Hiaasen was born in Plantation, Fla., in 1953 and grew up on the edge of the Everglades, where his grandfather had moved in the 1920s from North Dakota. He developed an interest in writing at an early age, receiving a typewriter at the age of six. Hiaasen attended Emory University. He graduated from the University of Florida with a degree in journalism in 1974.

After writing what have been termed offbeat public interest stories for *Cocoa Today* (now *Florida Today*), Hiaasen went to work for the *Miami Herald,* where the focus of his numerous investigations has included drug smuggling and political crimes in south Florida. For the last sixteen years he has written a twice-weekly column for the *Herald.*

Hiaasen's work as an investigative reporter with the *Herald* inspired him to write fiction. With his editor, Bill Montalbano, he has written three novels as well as stories on the drug trade and cocaine wars in Miami in the late 1970s. After Montalbano moved to China, Hiaasen went on to write detective novels combining black humor, strange characters, and serious issues of vandalism to the environment and political corruption. He credits the south Florida region with providing plenty of inspiration in the form of real-life occurrences and characters for his fiction. His novel *Strip Tease* was made into a movie starring Demi Moore and Burt Reynolds.

Hiaasen has also turned his hand to songwriting. Among his works are two co-authored songs, "Seminole Bingo" and "Rottweiler Blues." Hiaasen lives in the Florida Keys.

WORKS: *Powder Burn,* with Bill Montalbano (1981). *Trap Line* (1982). *A Death in China* (1984). *Tourist Season* (1986). *Double Whammy* (1987). *Skin Tight* (1989). *Native Tongue* (1991). *Strip Tease* (1993). *Lucky You* (1997). *Team Rodent: How Disney Devours the World* (1998). *Kick Ass: Selected Columns of Carl Hiaasen* (1999). *Sick Puppy* (2000). *Paradise Screwed* (2001). *Basket Case* (2002). *Hoot* (2002). *Skinny Dip* (2004).

—ANNE E. ROWE

HOMER H. HICKAM, JR. (1943–). Homer Hickam was born and raised in Coalwood, W.Va., a small town in the heart of Appalachian coal country. He was the second son of a stern and demanding mine superintendent. The youthful Hickam's night-time observation of a satellite led to his fascination with space exploration and experimentation in rocket propulsion. This unlikely pursuit was rewarded by a National Science Fair prize and scholarship to Virginia Polytechnic Institute, from which he received a B.S. in industrial engineering in 1964.

Following college, Hickam served six years in the army. A tour in Vietnam (1967–68) brought him the Army Commendation and the Bronze Star. Leaving active duty, he worked as a civilian engineer in the U.S. Army Missile Command in Huntsville, Ala. (1971–81). Hickam began a twenty-year aerospace engineering career with NASA in 1981, working in propulsion, spacecraft design, and flight crew training. He was involved with most of the major space projects, including Spacelab, the Space Shuttle, the Hubble Space Telescope, and the International Space Station Program.

Hickam's writing career began during his NASA days with the military history *Torpedo Junction.* His memoir *Rocket Boys,* which relates his struggle to overcome the Appalachian coal-mining culture's insularity and his father's prejudice against a seemingly impossible career in science, brought national recognition. It was selected as a *New York Times* "Great Book of 1998" and nominated for Best Biography of 1998 by the National Book Critics Circle. A year after publication, the story was turned into the popular film *October Sky* (an anagram of *Rocket Boys*). The film's enormous success led to the reissue of his memoir as *October Sky,* which rose to number one on the *New York Times* best-seller list.

Hickam has since published the novels *Back to the Moon, The Keeper's Son,* and *The Ambassador's Son* (the latter following the career of Josh Thurlow, a coast guard officer during World War II); two further installments of memoirs, *The Coalwood Way* and *Sky of Stone*; and a self-help/inspirational title, *We Are Not Afraid*. Now a full-time writer and lecturer in great demand, Hickam lives with his wife, Linda, in Huntsville, Ala., and the Virgin Islands.

WORKS: *Torpedo Junction* (1989). *Rocket Boys: A Memoir* (1998; reissued as *October Sky*, 1999). *Back to the Moon* (1999). *The Coalwood Way* (2000). *Sky of Stone* (2001). *We Are Not Afraid: Strength and Courage from the Town That Inspired the #1 Bestseller and Award-Winning Movie "October Sky"* (2002). *The Keeper's Son* (2003). *The Ambassador's Son* (2005).

—PETER L. STAFFEL

LESLIE PINCKNEY HILL (1880–1960). Leslie Pinckney Hill was born in Lynchburg, Va., on May 14, 1880. He was educated in a Lynchburg elementary school, in an East Orange, N.J., high school, and at Harvard University, where he earned an A.B. (Phi Beta Kappa, 1903) and an A.M. (1904). He then taught at Tuskegee Institute (1904–7); served as principal of the Manassas, Va., Industrial Institute (1907–13); and headed the Cheyney, Pa., Institute for Colored Youth, a school that he guided to full recognition and state support by 1920. During his administration (1913–51), the Institute became Cheyney Training School for Teachers (1914), State Normal School (1920), and Cheyney State Teachers College (1951).

Besides being an educator and administrator, Hill was a poet, dramatist, lecturer, and essayist. The role that appears to have informed most of his literary efforts, however, is that of educator, a role highlighted in the foreword of two published works. In his 1921 volume *The Wings of Oppression* he announced his hope that some poems would exhibit the "indestructible spiritual quality of my race." Similarly, he stated that his blank-verse drama *Toussaint L'Ouverture*, together with other creative African American literature, "must correct and counter-balance this falsehood" that African Americans have made no substantial contributions. Not all of Hill's works, however, are "correctives" on behalf of his race; some poems are pure lyric expressions.

Both creative and civic-minded, Hill was founder and president of the West Chester Community Center, Pennsylvania State Negro Council, and Pennsylvania Association for Teachers of Colored Children (now Pennsylvania Teachers Association), and a member of many boards and committees. For his contributions, Hill won the Seltzer Award for distinguished service and received honorary doctorates from Lincoln University, Morgan State College, Haverford College, and the Rhode Island College of Education. Cheyney University of Pennsylvania established the Leslie Pinckney Hill Library.

Hill died on February 15, 1960, in Philadelphia.

WORKS: *The Wings of Oppression and Other Poems* (1921). *Toussaint L'Ouverture: A Dramatic History* (1928). *Jethro: A Biblical Drama* (1931).

—PATSY B. PERRY

CHESTER HIMES (1909–1984). Chester Bomar Himes was born in Jefferson City, Mo., on July 29, 1909, to middle-class, schoolteacher parents. Himes attended school in several southern and midwestern cities before graduating from a Cleveland, Ohio, high school in 1926. He then enrolled at Ohio State University, but his failure to adjust academically and socially resulted in his dismissal in the spring of 1927. Following his brief college experience, he became involved with small-time racketeers in Cleveland and, by December 1928, had drawn a twenty-to-twenty-five-year sentence in the Ohio State Penitentiary for armed robbery. Himes began writing while in prison and published his first story, "Crazy in the Stir," in *Esquire* (August 1934). By the time he was paroled in 1936, he had published stories in *Abbott's Monthly*, *Bronzeman*, and *Crisis*. Following his release, he worked on numerous nonliterary jobs and for the Ohio Writers' Project. In 1944 Himes received a Rosenwald Fellowship and, in 1948, his writing was further validated during his residence at the Yaddo artists' colony in Saratoga Springs, N.Y. Beginning in 1953, Himes lived in France and Spain; he died in Spain on November 12, 1984.

Between 1945 and 1955, Himes published five social protest novels. Often classified in the Richard Wright school of naturalism, these novels explore the emasculating effect of American racism on African American men. Himes also wrote detective novels that have been especially popular in France, where he was presented with the Grand Prix de Littérature Policière in 1958. One detective thriller, *Cotton Comes to Harlem,* was made into a successful American movie, but generally these novels were not valued in America until shortly before his death. Posthumous examinations of Himes's short stories, protest works, autobiographical fiction, detective novels, satires, and autobiographies credit him with the creation of diverse and complex characters who mirror the absurdity in various aspects of African American life.

WORKS: *If He Hollers Let Him Go* (1945). *Lonely Crusade* (1947). *Cast the First Stone* (1952). *The Third Generation* (1954). *The Primitive* (1955). *For Love of Imabelle* (1957); expanded as *La Reine des Pommes,* trans. Minnie Danzas (1958); revised as *A Rage in Harlem* (1965). *The Crazy Kill* (1959). *The Real Cool Killers* (1959). *All Shot Up* (1960). *The Big Gold Dream* (1960). *Cotton Comes to Harlem* (1965). *Pinktoes* (1965); original title *Mamie Mason,* published in Paris and London (1961). *The Heat's On* (1966); also published as *Come Back, Charleston Blue* (1974). *Run Man Run* (1966). *Blind Man with A Pistol* (1969); also published as *Hot Day, Hot Night* (1970). *The Quality of Hurt: Autobiography,* vol. 1 (1972). *Black on Black: Baby Sister and Selected Writings* (1973). *My Life of Absurdity: Autobiography,* vol. 2 (1976). *Plan B* (1983). *The Collected Stories of Chester Himes* (1990). *The End of a Primitive* (1990). *Conversations with Chester Himes,* ed. Michel Fabre and Robert Skinner (1995).

—PATSY B. PERRY

WILLIAM HOFFMAN (1925–). Henry William Hoffman was born in Charleston, W.Va., on May 16, 1925, but he has lived most of his adult life in Virginia. That his fictional locale and characterizations involve both Virginias, then, is not surprising. Reared by his grandmother in Charleston, he was drafted into the army immediately after finishing high school at Kentucky Military Institute in 1943. His World War II experience includes service with the medical corps at the Normandy invasion and at the "Battle of the Bulge," and it infuses the themes of many of his novels. Following service he attended Hampden-Sydney College, receiving the B.A. in 1949. He then attended law school at Washington and Lee University for one year (1949–50), but took a creative-writing course "just as a lark" and found his love of writing. His first story appeared in *Shenandoah* in 1950. Hoffman next attended the Writers' Workshop at the University of Iowa (1950–51). He worked briefly for the *Evening Star* in Washington, D.C., and for the Chase National Bank in New York, finally becoming an instructor in English at Hampden-Sydney College (1952–59). While there he published his first two novels, and also met Alice Sue Richardson, whom he married on April 17, 1957. They have two daughters—Ruth Beckley Hoffman and Margaret Kay (Hoffman) Huffman—and three grandchildren.

After leaving Hampden-Sydney in 1959, Hoffman returned as writer-in-residence in 1966, having written three novels in the interim. He published two more books before retiring from Hampden-Sydney in 1973. During the summer of 1967 he was playwright-in-residence at the Barter Theatre in Abingdon, Va., producing and publishing his only play, *The Love Touch,* that year. He and his wife reside on their farm, Wynyard, in Charlotte Court House, Va.

His numerous awards and honors include: National Endowment for the Arts Creative Writing Fellowship (1976); induction as Virginia Cultural Laureate (1986); Emily Clark Balch Prize (1988); Andrew Lytle Prize, *Sewanee Review* (1989); Jeanne Charplot Goodheart Prize, *Shenandoah* (1989);

John Dos Passos Prize for Literature (1992); O. Henry Prize (1996); election to the Fellowship of Southern Writers (1998); Hillsdale Prize (1998); D.Litt., Hampden-Sydney College (1980) and Washington and Lee University (1995). He is frequently invited to speak at colleges and universities, libraries, and book festivals. A prolific and disciplined writer, Hoffman continues to publish in scholarly magazines and periodicals.

Hoffman's fictional themes search out the complexities of the basic human condition; his war experiences changed his viewpoint on life, he says. Those themes involve war and peace, mysteries and murders, loves and jealousies, sacred and secular institutions, aspirations and failures of the American Dream. His scenes and characters examine the southern community and its inherent values depicted in family, community, religion, and language. Rooted in this sense of place, his fiction translates into the larger scene, his Virginias into the world.

WORKS: *The Trumpet Unblown* (1955). *Days in the Yellow Leaf* (1958). *A Place for My Head* (1960). *The Dark Mountains* (1963). *Yancey's War* (1966). *A Walk to the River* (1970). *A Death of Dreams* (1973). *Virginia Reels* ((1978). *The Land That Drank the Rain* (1982). *Godfires* (1985). *By Land, By Sea* (1988). *Furors Die* (1990). *Follow Me Home* (1994). *Tidewater Blood* (1998). *Doors* (1999). *Blood and Guile* (2000). *Wild Thorn* (2002).

—JEANNE R. NOSTRANDT

GEORGE FREDERICK HOLMES (1820–1897). Born on August 21, 1820, in British Guiana and briefly educated in England at the University of Durham, George Frederick Holmes, at the age of sixteen, sailed for Canada. Coming then to the United States, he moved about in Virginia, Georgia, and South Carolina for four years, finally being admitted to the practice of law, which he found unsatisfactory. Although as early as 1839 he had published a short story in the *Southern Literary Messenger,* his first creative efforts ultimately were supplanted by the periodical review, which was to become his literary forte. He accepted a professorship in classical languages at Richmond College in 1846; the following year he taught at the College of William and Mary. His election to the presidency of the newly created University of Mississippi did not provide the academic security he urgently needed: his short tenure was a virtual fiasco.

From 1849 to 1857 Holmes resided in self-imposed exile at his wife's western Virginia plantation. Although he was perpetually plagued by ineptitude in practical matters—principally financial—during these years he produced his most significant intellectual accomplishments, represented by a ponderous bibliography of reviews and articles for contemporary periodicals. Following the years of rustication, Holmes secured a position in the School of History and Literature at the University of Virginia, where he remained until his death on November 4, 1897.

WORKS: *Address Delivered before the Beaufort District Society* (1845). *Inaugural Address Delivered on Occasion of the Opening of the University of the State of Mississippi, November 6, 1848* (1849). *The Southern Elementary Spelling-Book for Schools and Families* (1866). *Holmes' Pictorial Primer, for Home or School* (1867). *An Elementary Grammar of the English Language* (1868). *Holmes' First (-Sixth) Reader* (1870–72). *A Grammar of the English Language* (1871). *A School History of the United States of America, from the Earliest Discoveries to the Year 1870* (1871). *The Science of Society* (1883). *New School History of the United States* (1883, 1886).

—LEONIDAS S. BETTS

MARY HOOD (1946–). The daughter of a native New Yorker and a Georgian, Mary Hood was born on September 16, 1946, in Brunswick. She received an A.B. in Spanish from Georgia State University in 1967, completing her degree in only three years. Hood has lived in Georgia all of her life, and many of her stories are set in the foothills of rural north Georgia.

How Far She Went, Hood's first collection of short stories, won the Flannery O'Connor Award for Short Fiction and the *Southern Review* Louisiana State University Short Fiction Award. A story from that collection, "Inexorable Progress," is included in *Best American Short Stories 1984.* In 1986 Hood's story "Something Good for Ginny" won the National Magazine Award in Fiction and a Pushcart Prize. Other stories by Hood have been anthologized in *New Stories from the South, The Pushcart Prize Anthology,* and *Georgia Voices: Fiction.* Hood's *And Venus Is Blue,* a novella and short stories, won the Townsend Prize for Fiction, the Lillian Smith Award, and the Dixie Council of Authors and Journalists Author-of-the-Year Award. In 1994 Hood received the Whiting Writers Award.

The author of one novel, *Familiar Heat,* Hood published stories in *Georgia Review, Kenyon Review,* and *Ohio Review.* Her prose has also appeared in *Harper's Magazine, North American Review,* and *Art & Antiques.* Hood's work has been translated into Dutch, French, Japanese, and Swedish.

Hood has worked at jobs ranging from substitute teacher to department store clerk, and at one time she made her living by painting rural scenes and portraits of people and animals. She has taught creative writing at the University of Georgia, the University of Mississippi (where she was the John and Renee Grisham Southern-Writer-in-Residence), and Berry College in Georgia.

WORKS: *How Far She Went* (1984). *And Venus Is Blue* (1986). *Familiar Heat* (1995).

—MARY LOUISE WEAKS

JOHNSON JONES HOOPER (1815–1862). The creator of Simon Suggs, one of the most vividly drawn characters in the antebellum humor of the Old Southwest, was born on June 9, 1815, in Wilmington, N.C. Johnson Jones Hooper was the youngest of six children. His father, Archibald Maclaine Hooper, was related to several prominent North Carolina families, and his mother, Charlotte DeBerniere, was descended from the English divine Jeremy Taylor and from an eminent Huguenot who had fled France after the revocation of the Edict of Nantes. The father, a competent journalist but a poor business manager, could ill support the large family, and Johnson went to work, as a printer's devil, instead of to college. At twenty he began reading law in the frontier town of La Fayette, Ala., though his studies were interrupted by trips to Louisiana and South Carolina as well as by a stint as census taker in 1840—experiences of which he later made humorous capital. In 1841 he started a law practice in Dadeville, Ala., and the next year married Mary Mildred Brantley, daughter of an Alabama merchant. They had three children: William (1844–1875), Annie (1845–1847), and Adolphus (1849–1895).

In 1842 Hooper founded the La Fayette *East Alabamian,* for which newspaper he wrote humorous and realistic sketches and tales of frontier life, later published as *Some Adventures of Captain Simon Suggs.* Actively promoted by William T. Porter, editor of the *Spirit of the Times,* the sporting weekly that introduced many of Hooper's pieces to a nationwide readership, Suggs—with the motto, "It is good to be shifty in a new country"—made the author immediately famous. Yet, because of his law practice, his editorship of the *Alabama Journal* in Montgomery (1846–49), and his political ambitions, Hooper's creative output declined in quantity. By 1849, after resuming the practice of law in La Fayette and despite new duties as editor of the *Chambers County Tribune,* he had written the pieces collected in *A Ride with Old Kit Kuncker.*

In the same year Hooper, a Whig, was elected solicitor of Alabama's Ninth District, but was defeated for reelection in 1853. The next year he co-founded the *Montgomery Mail,* a paper nominally independent but with cautious Know-Nothing inclinations despite Hooper's disapproval of that party's religious intolerance. He remained associated with the *Mail* until 1861, when he became secretary to the Provisional Congress of the new Confederacy and removed with that body to Richmond. When the unicameral congress reorganized as senate and house, Hooper was defeated for election as secretary of the Senate but soon gained a position as editor of the Provisional Congress records. His new labors were cut short by his death, probably from tuberculosis, on June 7, 1862.

Hooper left a number of pungent, realistic sketches and tales that rank with the best work of the humorists of the Old Southwest. Especially significant are the Simon Suggs pieces, which constitute the only effective picaresque novel by any of the southwest writers. In creating Suggs and his victims, Hooper broke out of regional humor and made a permanent contribution to the international literature of roguery.

WORKS: *Some Adventures of Captain Simon Suggs, Late of the Tallapoosa Volunteers; Together with "Taking the Census" and Other Alabama Sketches* (1845). *A Ride with Old Kit Kuncker and Other Sketches and Scenes of Alabama* (1849). *The Widow Rugby's Husband, A Night at the Ugly Man's, and Other Tales of Alabama* (1851). *Read and Circulate: Proceedings of the Democratic and Anti-Know-Nothing Party in Caucus; or, the Guillotine at Work, at the Capital, during the Session of 1855–'56* (1855). *Dog and Gun: A Few Loose Chapters on Shooting, among Which Will Be Found Some Anecdotes and Incidents* (1856).

—NORRIS YATES

GEORGE MOSES HORTON (ca. 1797–ca. 1883). George Moses Horton was born into slavery on the William Horton tobacco farm in Northampton County, N.C. Around 1800, the white Horton family relocated to Chatham County, N.C. In a series of property transfers, George Moses Horton eventually became the property of Hall Horton, from whom he fled when Union troops entered North Carolina during the Civil War. Horton, who hated the "cow-boy" work he was forced to do under slavery, taught himself to spell by using discarded spelling books and exploiting any opportunity to be around school children. Later, he memorized verses from the Bible and a hymnal. He accomplished several important firsts by publishing two volumes of poetry while he was enslaved, and a third in the final year of the Civil War.

Horton interacted with students and faculty at the nearby Chapel Hill campus, initially when he came to town as a young man to sell farm produce, and later when he performed a variety of odd jobs and janitorial services there. He eventually earned money making up poems for members of the all-male student body. Faculty wife and author Caroline Lee Hentz assisted Horton in first becoming a published poet, and several influential persons, including the editors of *Freedom's Journal,* interceded in a futile effort to purchase his freedom.

After the war, Horton moved to Philadelphia, leaving his wife and children behind. He purportedly emigrated to Liberia in December 1866. The last available note on his life locates him in Philadelphia in 1883 when he would have been around eighty-six years old. The University of North Carolina at Chapel Hill, now home of the George Moses Horton Society, maintains materials about Horton's life and work in its special collections. In 1996 the poet was inducted into the newly formed North Carolina Literary Hall of Fame. In 1997 the Chatham County Historical Society named Horton poet laureate of Chatham County and erected a marker in his memory. A Chatham County middle school bears Horton's name.

WORKS: *The Hope of Liberty* (1829). *Poetical Works of George Moses Horton, the Colored Bard of North Carolina, to Which Is Prefaced the Life of the Author, Written by Himself* (1845). *Naked Genius* (1865).

—LOVALERIE KING

JAY BROADUS HUBBELL (1885–1979). Jay Hubbell, the son of the Reverend David Shelton and Ruth Eller Hubbell, was born on May 8, 1885, in Smyth County, Va., and educated at Richmond

College (B.A. 1905), Harvard (M.A., 1908), and Columbia (Ph.D., 1922). He taught at Wake Forest, North Carolina, and Southern Methodist. He also served as an officer in the field artillery in World War I. He married Lucinda Smith of Dallas, Tex., in 1918 and became the father of two boys—Jay, Jr., and David. Subsequently he became chairman of the English department and E. A. Lilly Professor at Southern Methodist and edited the *Southwest Review*. In 1927 he went to Duke University and remained—with occasional breaks for exchange professorships in Vienna and Athens, and at Hebrew University—until he retired in 1954.

At Duke, Hubbell became a pioneer in the study of American literature. He was an early member and chairman (1924–27) of the American literature group of the Modern Language Association. In 1928 he became the founding editor of *American Literature*, the first scholarly journal in the field, and served as chairman of the board of editors until his retirement in 1954. His anthology *American Life in Literature* was chosen to be reprinted on three occasions in Armed Services editions in World War II, and his friendships and correspondence with such worthies as Robert Frost, Carl Sandburg, and John Hall Wheelock suggest his connections with American writing of his own day. His position in the vanguard of American literary scholarship was affirmed by his election to the executive council of MLA (1946–49) and to the vice presidency in 1951. His articles, his direction of theses and dissertations, and his magisterial *The South in American Literature* established him as dean among scholars in southern literature. Later books, *South and Southwest* and *Who Are the Major American Writers?* testified anew to his stature in both fields, a stature exemplified by the Hubbell Medallion awarded by the American Literature Group of MLA for lifetime contributions to the field (he was the first recipient) and by the Jay B. Hubbell Center for American Literary Historiography at Duke, a depository of papers and manuscripts of important scholars and teachers in American literature. Hubbell died in Durham, N.C., on February 13, 1979.

WORKS: *Virginia Life in Fiction* (1922). *An Introduction to Poetry*, with John O. Beaty (1922). *An Introduction to Drama*, with Beaty (1927). Ed., Robert Louis Stevenson, *Treasure Island* (1927). *The Enjoyment of Literature* (1929). Ed., John Pendleton Kennedy, *Swallow Barn* (1929). Ed., *American Life in Literature*, 2 vols. (1936, 1949). *The Last Years of Henry Timrod, 1864–1867* (1941). Ed., Robert Munford, *The Candidates*, with Douglass Adair (1948). *The South in American Literature, 1607–1900* (1954). "Edgar Allan Poe," in *Eight American Authors: A Review of Research and Criticism*, ed. James Woodress (1956, 1971). *Southern Life in Fiction* (1960). *South and Southwest: Literary Essays and Reminiscences* (1965). *Who Are the Major American Writers? A Study of the Changing Literary Canon* (1972).

—RAYBURN S. MOORE

DAVID HUDDLE (1942–). A versatile poet and fiction writer, David Huddle has incorporated some portion of his southern origins into most of his fifteen books. David Ross Huddle was born in Ivanhoe, a small town between Wytheville and Galax in southwest Virginia. In the guise of poet, Huddle embraces Sir Walter Scott's Ivanhoe impulse, repeatedly bringing his Virginia origins up close for loving reconsideration, even from the distance of Vermont, where he has lived since 1971 following graduate study at Hollins College (M.A., English, 1969) and Columbia University (M.F.A., 1971).

In the poems, Huddle deals with his father, Charles Richard Huddle, Jr. (1911–1986), a manager in a factory who mastered crossword puzzles and painted precisely by the numbers; with his mother, Mary Francis Akers Huddle (1919–1999), who talked with just about everybody in town, went with her son for a swim in muddy water, and kept a good house in traditional southern style, biscuits included; with his brothers, Charles Richard Huddle III and William Royal Huddle; with leaving Ivanhoe for the university (and Mr. Jefferson's serpentine wall) in Charlottesville, for Germany and

Vietnam in the army, and eventually for Burlington, Vt., and a long career of teaching at the University of Vermont, Bread Loaf, and several other institutions as visiting writer. His poems carry forward with his marriage to Lindsey Massie Huddle, a lawyer, and chronicle some key turning points in the lives of their two daughters, Bess and Molly.

Huddle has also worked his craft as a writer of essays, short fiction, and occasionally novel-length work. In fiction, Ivanhoe becomes Rosemary, and the autobiographical streak turns rather aggressively inventive, pushing fantasies into a reality where many boys/men are tantalized by many girls/women. Sex is the ache of the ages. Huddle's most imaginative story, a novel called *La Tour Dreams of the Wolf Girl*, presents a middle-aged woman from the Blue Ridge part of Virginia in an unsatisfying marriage who becomes enthralled with the creative life of a painter from the seventeenth century. Sometimes, though, even the fiction has the immediate feel of a life just lived, as in the splendid contrast of a mid-March day in Vermont (picture an ugly mud season compounded by a wet snow that further chills a dad watching a daughter go off to the movies with her first date) set off against some remembered and longed-for early spring day in Virginia (think lilacs greening and forsythias fully in bloom). Huddle does the north woods knowingly, but the South is never that far away down I-87, I-84, and I-81—all well-traveled roads for him.

WORKS: *A Dream with No Stump Roots in It* (1975). *Paper Boy* (1979). *Only the Little Bone* (1988). *Stopping by Home* (1988). *The High Spirits: Stories of Men and Women* (1989). *The Writing Habit* (1992). *The Nature of Yearning* (1992). *Intimates* (1993). *A David Huddle Reader* (1994). *Tenorman* (1995). *Summer Lake: New and Selected Poems* (1999). *The Story of a Million Years* (1999). *Not: A Trio—A Novella and Two Stories* (2000). *La Tour Dreams of the Wolf Girl* (2002). *Grayscale* (2004).

—OWEN W. GILMAN, JR.

ANDREW HUDGINS (1951–). The son of an air force officer, Andrew Leon Hudgins, Jr., was born in Killeen, Tex., and lived in several states before settling in Montgomery, Ala. There he attended Sidney Lanier High School, named for the post–Civil War poet whose life later inspired Hudgins's *After the Lost War*. High-strung, nervous, and extremely sensitive to sounds, Hudgins has not had a "normal" life—as he recounts in the essay "Sensitive" in the *American Scholar* (2002). He attended Huntingdon College, the University of Alabama, and the University of Iowa, from which he received an M.F.A. in 1983. In 1983–84 he was a Wallace Stegner Fellow at Stanford University.

His first book of poems, *Saints and Strangers*, was published in 1985, and was a finalist for the Pulitzer Prize. Also in 1985, Hudgins joined the faculty of the University of Cincinnati. There a sequence of poems in the voice of Sidney Lanier, which Hudgins had begun years earlier in Montgomery, took shape as a longer narrative and eventually became the 1988 book *After the Lost War*. This book received the Poet's Prize in 1989, and solidified Hudgins's reputation as a master of both narrative poetry and the blank verse form.

In 1991 Hudgins published *The Never-Ending*, a darker and more lyrical collection of poems, many of them taking their subject matter from autobiography or questions of faith. *The Never-Ending* was a finalist for the 1991 National Book Award in poetry. In 1992 Hudgins married the fiction writer Erin McGraw. *The Glass Hammer*, a book of almost exclusively autobiographical poems, was published in 1994, followed by *The Glass Anvil*, a collection of literary essays. In 1998 Hudgins published *Babylon in a Jar*, a book of loosely metered narrative and lyric poems that return to subjects from history and myth. Since 2001 Hudgins and McGraw have taught at Ohio State University. His most recent book of poems, *Ecstatic in the Poison*, appeared in 2003.

WORKS: *Saints and Strangers* (1985). *After the Lost War: A Narrative* (1988). *The Never-Ending: New Poems* (1991). *The Glass Hammer: A Southern Childhood* (1994). *The Glass Anvil* (1997). *Babylon in a Jar* (1998). *Ecstatic in the Poison* (2003).

—JULIANA GRAY

LANGSTON HUGHES (1902–1967). Langston Hughes is perhaps best remembered for the way his poetry reflected and celebrated the speech and musical rhythms of the black community of the Harlem Renaissance of the 1920s. However, Hughes wrote and published prolifically in a number of forms, including fiction, autobiography, children's fiction, stage works, screenplays, song lyrics, articles, and translations.

Hughes was born James Mercer Langston Hughes on February 1, 1902, in Joplin, Mo., to Carrie Langston, an aspiring stage actress, and James Hughes. Shortly after Langston was born, James Hughes left the family to settle in Mexico. After joining him briefly in 1907, Carrie and Langston returned to Lawrence, Kan., where Carrie left Langston in the care of his maternal grandmother, Mary Langston, who had been a fervent abolitionist. Langston was strongly shaped by the abolitionist heritage handed down to him from his grandmother, but he felt his mother's rejection keenly throughout his life. During this time, he developed an interest in literature, reading W. E. B. Du Bois, Paul Laurence Dunbar, and others.

In 1916 Hughes went to live with his mother in Cleveland, Ohio. Hughes enjoyed living in Cleveland, where he was for the first time part of a large black community, but in 1920 he moved to Mexico to live with his father. He lived there unhappily until 1921, when he left for New York and a brief enrollment at Columbia University. In that year, his well-known poem "The Negro Speaks of Rivers" was published in the NAACP's journal *Crisis,* and more publications followed. He left Columbia in 1922 to travel the world, working on board ships.

When he returned to the United States, his reputation as a promising young black poet had been established. In 1926 Alfred A. Knopf published his first book of poetry, *The Weary Blues,* to positive reviews, and Hughes entered Lincoln University, where he graduated in 1929. His influential essay "The Negro Artist and the Racial Mountain," written during this time, articulated the importance of the black writer's identification as a black writer, writing for a black audience. In 1931 he embarked on a speaking tour of black colleges across the country, traveling extensively in the segregated South at the time of the Scottsboro case and sparking controversy with such poems as "Christ in Alabama."

Later in life, Hughes worked as a playwright and established the black theaters the Suitcase Theater and the New Negro Theater. He continued to write poetry and political and humorous prose. He died in New York City at the age of sixty-five.

WORKS: *The Weary Blues* (1926). *Fine Clothes to the Jew* (1927). *Not without Laughter* (1930). *Dear Lovely Death* (1931). *The Negro Mother* (1931). *The Dream Keeper and Other Poems* (1932). *Scottsboro Limited* (1932). *Pop and Fifina,* with Arna Bontemps (1932). *The Ways of White Folks* (1934). *A New Song* (1938). *The Big Sea* (1940). *Shakespeare in Harlem* (1942). *Freedom's Plow* (1943). *Jim Crow's Last Stand* (1943). *Lament for Dark People and Other Poems* (1944). *Fields of Wonder* (1947). *Street Scene: An American Opera Based on Elmer Rice's Play* (1948). *Troubled Island* (1949). *One-Way Ticket* (1949). Ed., *The Poetry of the Negro, 1746–1949* (1949). *Simple Speaks His Mind* (1950). *Montage of a Dream Deferred* (1951). *Laughing to Keep from Crying* (1952). *The First Book of Negroes* (1952). *Simple Takes a Wife* (1953). *Famous American Negroes* (1954). *The First Book of Rhythms* (1954). *The First Book of Jazz* (1955). *Famous Negro Music Makers* (1955). *The Sweet Flypaper of Life* (1955). *I Wonder as I Wander* (1956). *A Pictorial History of the Negro in America* (1956). *The First Book of the West Indies* (1956). *Simple Stakes a Claim* (1957). *Famous Negro Heroes of America* (1958). *Tambourines to Glory* (1958). *The Langston Hughes Reader* (1958).

Ed., *The Book of Negro Folklore*, with Bontemps (1958). *Selected Poems of Langston Hughes* (1959). *Simply Heavenly* (1959). *The First Book of Africa* (1960). *Ask Your Mama: Twelve Moods for Jazz* (1961). *The Best of Simple* (1961). *Fight for Freedom: The Story of the NAACP* (1962). *Five Plays of Langston Hughes* (1963). *Something in Common and Other Stories* (1963). *Simple's Uncle Sam* (1965). *Black Magic: A Pictorial History of the Negro in American Entertainment* (1967). *The Panther and the Lash: Poems of Our Times* (1967). Ed., *The Best Short Stories by Negro Writers: An Anthology from 1899 to the Present* (1967). *Black Misery* (1969). *Don't You Turn Back* (1969). Ed., *The Poetry of the Negro, 1746–1970*, with Bontemps (1970). Ed., *The Poetry of the Negro, 1746–1970* (1970). *Good Morning Revolution*, ed. Faith Berry (1973). *The Arna Bontemps-Langston Hughes Letters*, ed. Charles Nichols (1980). *Collected Poems*, ed. Arnold Rampersad and David Roessel (1994). *The Return of Simple*, ed. Akiba Sullivan Harper (1994). *Langston Hughes and the Chicago Defender*, ed. Christopher C. De Santis (1995). *Short Stories [of] Langston Hughes*, ed. Donna Sullivan Harper (1996). *Remember Me to Harlem: The Letters of Langston Hughes and Carl Van Vechten, 1925–1964*, ed. Emily Bernard (2001).

—TESSA JOSEPH

T. R. HUMMER (1950–). A native of Noxobee County in eastern Mississippi, Terry Randolph Hummer is a metaphysical poet of the South. After earning bachelor's and master's degrees in English at the University of Southern Mississippi, he completed his Ph.D. (1980) in American literature and creative writing at the University of Utah under the tutelage of southern poet Dave Smith.

At the heart of Hummer's poetry is a persistent critique of Romantic idealism, which is made convincing by his authentic and often confessional record of the self's struggle actually to live in a world bereft of certainty. Suspicious as he is of their idealism, Hummer shares with the Romantics their desire for a passionate realization and expression of lived experience. As they pursue these problems, Hummer's poems consistently turn to universal questions of individualism, personal guilt, and the burden of fateful knowledge. In his often dialogical rhetoric, his self-consciousness as a southern male, and his awareness of human weakness, Hummer's southernness—particularly his debt to James Dickey and William Faulkner—is apparent. (Hummer co-edited a 1984 collection of essays on Dickey's poems.) True to tendencies that have marked southern poetry and prose over the last several decades, the settings for Hummer's poems are far from romantic or idealized. Rather he seems to go out of his way to remind us of the commonplace. His narrators often find themselves in truck stops or honky-tonks. His depictions of nature are seldom idyllic and often menacing, or at the very least ironic—hence the title of his long poem "Bluegrass Wasteland."

In addition to editing several major poetry magazines, Hummer has held teaching or writer-in-residence posts at several schools, including Kenyon College, Middlebury College, and Virginia Commonwealth University. He became editor of the *Georgia Review* in 2001.

WORKS: *Translation of Light* (1976). *The Angelic Orders: Poems* (1982). *The Passion of the Right-Angled Man: Poems* (1984). Ed., *The Imagination as Glory: The Poetry of James Dickey*, with Bruce Weigl (1984). *Lower-Class Heresy: Poems* (1987). *The 18,000-Ton Olympic Dream: Poems* (1990). Ed., *The Unfeigned Word: Fifteen Years of New England Review*, with Devon Jersild (1993). *Walt Whitman in Hell: Poems* (1996). *Useless Virtues: Poems* (2001). *The Infinity Sessions: Poems* (2005).

—H. COLLIN MESSER

WILLIAM HUMPHREY (1924–1997). Novelist and short-story writer William Humphrey was born on June 18, 1924, in Clarksville, Tex., the setting for many of his stories and novels. When Humphrey was thirteen, his father, a hard-drinking and self-destructive man, died in a car accident, an event central to Humphrey's critically acclaimed memoir, *Farther Off from Heaven*. After his father's death, he moved to Dallas with his mother and later attended the University of Texas and Southern Methodist University. In 1944 Humphrey left SMU without finishing his degree and moved north, settling in Greenwich Village in New York, where he met his wife, the painter Dorothy Feinman, whom he married in 1949.

Directed to the work of Katherine Anne Porter by Randall Jarrell, Humphrey became friends with his fellow Texan. Porter helped launch Humphrey's career and remained a friend and mentor for many years. While teaching at Bard College, Humphrey published his first book, *The Last Husband and Other Stories*. In 1958 his first novel, *Home from the Hill*, was published and became a best-seller. The success of this novel, which was later made into a movie, allowed Humphrey to quit teaching (except for short-term guest appointments later at Washington and Lee, Smith, and Princeton) and to travel and live in Europe for many years. He bought a farm in Hudson, N.Y., in 1965 and lived there until his death in 1997.

Humphrey remains best known for his first novel and for his fiction set in Texas, including the novel *The Ordways* and the story collection *A Time and a Place*. Later in his career, he wrote numerous pieces on fishing and the outdoors, a novel set in upstate New York (*Hostages to Fortune*), and a historical novel about the Trail of Tears, *No Resting Place*.

WORKS: *The Last Husband and Other Stories* (1953). *Home from the Hill* (1958). *The Ordways* (1965). *A Time and a Place* (1968). *Proud Flesh* (1973). *Ah, Wilderness! The Frontier in American Literature* (1977). *Farther Off from Heaven* (1977). *Hostages to Fortune* (1984). *The Collected Stories of William Humphrey* (1985). *Open Season: Sporting Adventures* (1986). *No Resting Place* (1989). *September Song* (1992).

—STEPHEN COOPER

JOSEPHINE HUMPHREYS (1945–). Born on February 2, 1945, in Charleston, S.C., the eldest child of a prominent family with long-time connections in the Carolinas, Josephine Humphreys was educated at suburban schools, Duke (B.A., 1967), Yale (M.A., 1968), and the University of Texas (doctoral work, 1968–70). Returning to Charleston in 1970, she married Thomas Hutcheson, a local attorney, taught English at Baptist College of Charleston, and raised two sons, Allen and William. In 1977 Humphreys left full-time teaching to complete her first novel with the encouragement of Duke writing mentor Reynolds Price, and since its publication in 1984 she has published three more, all to critical and popular acclaim.

Dreams of Sleep, set in contemporary Charleston and seen through an alienated male protagonist, reminded reviewers and critics of other works by southern women writers such as Gail Godwin, Lee Smith, and Bobbie Ann Mason. In 1985 the book won the PEN/Hemingway Prize for the best American first novel. Her second novel viewed the seaside suburbs of Charleston from the first-person viewpoint of a teen-aged female protagonist; the best-seller status of *Rich in Love* led to a filmed version directed by Bruce Beresford in 1993. *The Fireman's Fair* was focused by the destruction wrought on Charleston by Hurricane Hugo in 1989 as experienced by another ineffectual male protagonist.

For almost a decade, Humphreys worked on her fourth and most ambitious novel, *Nowhere Else on Earth*. This rich historical romance concerns the so-called Lowerie Wars, the fierce guerrilla resistance movement of the Lumbee Indians, during and after the Civil War, led by the heroic figure Henry Berry Lowerie. In an act of fictive daring, Humphreys chooses Rhoda Strong Lowerie, Henry's wife, as her protagonist and narrator, thus combining all of her earlier heroines, both the feisty teenagers and the disillusioned young wives and mothers. Humphreys remains important in her extension of

the romantic and feminine traditions of southern fiction into the feminist and realistic modes of contemporary letters in the South.

WORKS: *Dreams of Sleep* (1984). *Rich in Love* (1987). *The Fireman's Fair* (1991). *Nowhere Else on Earth* (2000).

—JOSEPH R. MILLICHAP

DANIEL ROBINSON HUNDLEY (1832–1899). Daniel Hundley was born in Madison County,
Ala., on December 11, 1832, to John Henderson and Melinda Robinson Hundley, both of Virginia. He
graduated from Bacon College, Harrodsburg, Ky., in 1850 and entered law school at the University of
Virginia. Continuing his study at Harvard, he received the LL.B. in 1853. He married his first cousin,
Mary Ann Hundley, of Charlotte County, Va., and moved, in 1856, to Chicago, where his father-in-law
had real-estate interests. There he practiced law, contributed to periodicals, and wrote *Social Relations
in Our Southern States*. An ardent Unionist, Hundley opposed both abolition and secession and urged
southern support of Douglas in 1860. After the fall of Fort Sumter and Lincoln's call for volunteers,
however, leaving considerable property in Illinois, he returned to Alabama and was elected colonel of
the 31st Alabama Infantry Regiment.

After seeing action in Tennessee, Hundley was wounded and captured at Port Gibson, Miss., in
the defense of Vicksburg. Exchanged after Vicksburg's surrender, he commanded his regiment in
the Army of Tennessee until his capture at Big Shanty, Ga., in June 1864. Imprisoned at Johnson's
Island, Ohio, he escaped but was recaptured in January 1865. After the war he settled in Lawrence
and Limestone counties, Ala., as a planter and attorney and, for a time, he edited a newspaper. In 1874
he published his journal of prison experiences. Hundley died in Mooresville, Ala., on December 27,
1899, without completing a planned work on the results of the war and Reconstruction.

Social Relations in Our Southern States is notable for its candid delineation of classes in southern society. Hundley insisted that southerners descended from the cavaliers were far outnumbered by those
of middle- and lower-class origins. Although he stoutly defended slavery, he admitted abuse of slaves
by some, such as the "Cotton Snobs," whom he satirized severely.

WORKS: *Work and Bread; or, The Coming Winter and the Poor* (1858). *Social Relations in Our Southern States* (1860).
Prison Echoes of the Great Rebellion (1874).

—WILLIAM MOSS

KERMIT HUNTER (1910–2001). The nation's most prolific writer of outdoor historical dramas,
Kermit Hunter was born in Hallsville, W.Va., on October 3, 1910. The son of Otis John Hunter and
Lillian Farley Hunter, he began writing at an early age; in high school he was a reporter and feature
writer for his hometown newspaper. He played piano and organ for silent movies. After graduation
from Ohio State University, he attended the Juilliard School of Music in New York City, followed by a
tour of Europe playing piano concerts. In the mid-1930s, after receiving advice from a distinguished
professor of music to go home and practice piano for seven more years, he returned to West Virginia
to assist in trading minor league baseball players for the Mountain State League.

At the outbreak of World War II, Hunter enlisted in the National Guard, and within three years was
on the general staff of the Pentagon. From Panama, he planned the American defense of the Caribbean, for which he won the Legion of Merit. Leaving the service as a lieutenant colonel, he became
business manager for the North Carolina Symphony in Raleigh.

In 1949 Hunter entered graduate school at the University of North Carolina at Chapel Hill. For
his M.A. thesis in dramatic art, he wrote the outdoor drama *Unto These Hills* depicting the removal
of Cherokee Indians from North Carolina to Oklahoma. Performed first in 1950, the drama played to

more than fourteen million people by the time of Hunter's death. Caught up in the university atmosphere at Chapel Hill, Hunter went on to earn a Ph.D. in English literature. After a year as a Guggenheim fellow, he accepted a position in drama at Hollins College in Roanoke, Va., becoming chairman
of the fine arts department in 1964. He ended his academic career as dean of the Meadows School of
the Arts at Southern Methodist University in Dallas, Tex.

Hunter wrote forty-three outdoor historical dramas for many communities across the United
States. (The most important are listed below.) All of them were fashioned with historical themes and
uplifting values. His *Horn in the West,* a story of the American Revolution and Appalachian frontiers-
man Daniel Boone, has been performed in Boone, N.C., since 1952. His *Honey in the Rock* has been
performed in Beckley, W.Va., since 1959. This legacy earned him the title of "Dean of Outdoor Drama
Playwrights."

WORKS: *Unto These Hills* (1950). *Forever This Land* (1951). *Horn in the West* (1952). *The Bell and the Plough* (1954).
Eleventh Hour (1956). *Voice in the Wind* (1956). *Chucky Jack* (1956). *Thy Kingdom Come* (1957). *Honey in the Rock*
(1959). *The Golden Crucible* (1959). *The Third Frontier* (1960). *The Golden Prairie* (1960). *Thunder on the River* (1961).
Bound for Kentucky (1961). *Next Day in the Morning* (1962). *Stars in My Crown* (1963). *The Liberty Tree* (1968). *Trail
of Tears* (1969). *Walk toward the Sunset* (1969). *Wings of the Morning* (1974). *Beyond the Sundown* (1975). *McIntosh
Trail* (1976). *Dust on Her Petticoats* (1976). *Daniel Shay's Rebellion* (1976). *Hernando de Soto* (1976).

—SCOTT J. PARKER

ZORA NEALE HURSTON (1891–1960). During the 1930s, Zora Neale Hurston became the most
popular, published, and respected African American woman writer of fiction and simultaneously was
acclaimed for her work in anthropology and folklore. After black protest writing became preferred
around 1940, she disappeared from view till 1974, when Robert Hemenway's biography and Alice
Walker's championing of her work restored her to prominence.

Hurston's origins did not suggest such a spectacular rise, but her family was relatively well off and
valued education. Her parents, the Reverend John and Lucy Hurston, met in Alabama, where Hurston
was born in 1891 in Notasulga, near Tuskegee Institute. Hurston always claimed to have been born in
1901 in the all-black town of Eatonville, Fla., where the family relocated during her childhood. John
became a popular preacher and served as mayor, and Lucy took care of their eight children. Hurston
grew up learning all the biblical stories, but also the wonderful tales she heard listening in on the "lyin'
sessions" townsmen had on the porch of Joe Clarke's store. She invented tales herself, imagining a
glorious world where she could mimic the deeds of Thor.

Hurston's childhood came to an abrupt end when Lucy died in 1904. Lucy had had a hard time
raising her children, as John often traveled for the state Baptist organizations; unfortunately, his journeys included philandering, which created domestic turmoil. After her death, John soon remarried,
much to young Zora's dismay. John responded by shipping Zora off to boarding school in Jacksonville,
a racially segregated city that taught her what it meant to be "colored." Sent to live with older siblings,
Hurston became bored with tending children and doing housework and ran off to work as a lady's
maid with a Gilbert and Sullivan troupe, where she acquired a lasting love of theater and perfected
her ability to use humor to deal with bossy white folks.

After the tour ended in Baltimore, Hurston enrolled at Morgan Academy (now Morgan State University) and completed her high school work. Moving in 1918 to Washington, D.C., she studied part-
time for five years at Howard University, where she took courses from Lorenzo Dow Turner and Alain
Locke. Although she left without finishing her degree, she had been active in the vibrant life at Howard.

Financial concerns and the desire to give more time to writing led Hurston to move to New York
City in 1925. Adept at attracting the attention of white philanthropists, she wangled scholarship money

to become the first black student at Barnard. There she discovered the exciting world of American anthropology with scholars Franz Boas and Ruth Benedict. "Papa Franz," setting Hurston on target for a Ph.D., sent her to Florida to collect folklore.

Hurston's arrival in New York had coincided with the eruption of the fabled Harlem Renaissance. Her student magazine writing at Howard proved excellent preparation for literary competitions offered by journals such as *Crisis* and *Opportunity*. Awarded second place for a story and first place for a short play, she was soon the published author of a story, "Spunk," which in 1925 appeared in *The New Negro*. A favorite at "rent parties" and Harlem nightspots for her raucous stories and "killing" humor, Hurston was compiling a legendary status in the literary movement, even though she would publish most of her major works years later. Her starry placement in Harlem's firmament had much to do with her close connections with other writers such as Countee Cullen, Wallace Thurman, and especially Langston Hughes. The latter joined Hurston and Thurman to publish the one-issue wonder *FIRE!!* (1926), a magazine they were determined would astonish and outrage more "polite" and "bougie" writers who, despite their zeal for social uplift, seemed to these "youngsters" to hew too closely to white standards of decorum.

Hurston helped make ends meet by becoming the secretary of white writer Fannie Hurst and became a favorite of Harlem's most famous Caucasian, Carl Van Vechten. Hurston's most significant white patron was Mrs. Charlotte Mason, who insisted that her protégés call her "Godmother of the Primitives." Hurston paid dearly for Mason's money, suffering hectoring and control of her publications. But without Mason's help, Hurston could not have made the trips to Florida, Louisiana, and the Caribbean that led to her two anthropological volumes, *Mules and Men* and *Tell My Horse*.

For her anthropological research, Hurston pioneered the "participant/observer" method. She bought a jazzy dress, loaded her things into a Chevy coupe, and sped off to the sawmill camps and turpentine woods with a tale about her bootlegging man, trouble with the law, and a need for a safe refuge. Once installed, she'd tell a "tale" herself and then sit back and soak up the "lie-swappin'" that ensued.

Hurston kept at her fiction, too, and when one of her best stories, a bittersweet tale about a tested marriage, "The Gilded Six-Bits," was published in *Story* in 1933, Lippincott wrote her asking if she had a novel they could see. She replied that she did and then had to write one. Needing a ready-made subject, she turned to the story of her parents' marriage. Melding Eatonville settings with doses of folk culture, the narrative became *Jonah's Gourd Vine*, an alternately comic and poignant novel that ends tragically. The Reverend John Pearson's talent in the pulpit derives from the same qualities that undo him—his powerful physical presence and appetite for life, which lead to multiple infidelities. Following the novel's successful reception, in 1935 Hurston was able to bring out her classic of American folklore, *Mules and Men*. It often reads like a novel, especially her initiation as a hoodoo priestess in New Orleans.

Hurston embarked for the Bahamas, Jamaica, and Haiti to collect material for *Tell My Horse*. While in Haiti, she wrote *Their Eyes Were Watching God*, in an attempt, she said, to embalm the love she had for an ex-lover. Set in Eatonville and the Everglades, the novel traces the marriages of Janie Mae Crawford Killens Stark Woods. Each union contributes, in complex ways, to Janie's inner growth and, eventually, to her solitary but transcendent personhood, even though she has had to kill and then bury her beloved third husband, Teacake, who contracts rabies and threatens her life. A celebration of folk culture, oral tradition, and rural hardships, *Their Eyes* has also been taught as a book about women's liberation; it speaks, however, at many registers for readers everywhere.

Throughout her career, Hurston sought success as a playwright; with Langston Hughes, she hoped to found a new Negro theater. She wrote some short plays during her New York days and constructed the three-act *Mule Bone* with Hughes. The project foundered when Hughes insisted that their typist be included in royalties. Hurston, enraged, called the play off, along with their friendship. *Mule Bone* finally came to life in 1990, when it opened on Broadway. The plot focuses on a rather slight romantic triangle, which is eclipsed by the surrounding and boisterous presentation of folk culture, children's games, and lying sessions on Joe Clarke's porch. Hurston wrote numbers of other plays, but most went unproduced. Most are set in Florida and are meant to amuse.

During the 1930s, Hurston worked for the Federal Writers' Project in Florida. Simultaneously, she wrote *Moses, Man of the Mountain*, a retelling of the events of Exodus, but from a black perspective and in dialect. Moses appears here as an African hoodoo man who comments cogently and powerfully on racial leadership, religion, and exceptionalist definitions of group identity.

Hurston's autobiography, *Dust Tracks on a Road*, often omits facts (such as date of birth, her three brief marriages, her involvement in the Harlem Renaissance), but the writing dazzles. Chapters originally expunged by her publisher during World War II have been restored and are highly critical of American imperialism and racism. The book presents an intriguing portrait of Hurston's aesthetics, while plumbing key conundrums of human existence.

Hurston, out of favor after the war, resorted to teaching and clerical jobs, then domestic work, but kept writing. Her final novel, *Seraph on the Suwanee*, was in some ways her most ambitious. Focusing on white figures and "cracker" culture, the book draws on Hurston's Federal Writers' Project work and her absorbed reading of Marjorie Kinnan Rawlings's Florida frontier narratives. Jim and Arvay Meserve's troubled marriage receives a Freudian presentation, *but* against the backdrop of an accurately observed cultural milieu. The novel shows Hurston's beloved Florida undergoing tremendous changes, as industrialization, tourism, and real estate developments pick up steam. Arvay's slow grappling with her psychological problems and her difficult marriage echoes *Their Eyes*, but with a different treatment and conclusion. The novel reveals Hurston experimenting with tone, voice, and modernist concepts of the self.

When Hurston was falsely accused of sexual corruption of a minor in 1948, the black press convicted her of charges that were ultimately dismissed by the courts. Hurston felt betrayed and briefly considered suicide. She subsequently turned away from her former material, concentrating on narratives set in the ancient past, most significantly a novel about Herod the Great. Publishers weren't interested in these projects, so she supported herself with more odd jobs, including working with William Bradford Huie to report the sensational trial of Ruby McCollum, a black woman accused of murdering a white lover. Hurston also found time to rail against the *Brown v. Board of Education* decision in 1954, which she felt insulted the achievements of black teachers and schools.

Hurston, ill and too proud to appeal to her family, found refuge in the county welfare home in Fort Pierce, Fla. She died there in 1960, penniless, but certainly not alone. Three ministers presided at her funeral service and hundreds attended. After her death, her papers were thrown on a fire, but someone rescued many of the manuscripts. As her books came back in print in the 1970s, Hurston was claimed by a new generation of African American women writers, who appreciated her experimentalism, her ear for dialect, her humor, and her metaphor-drenched prose. Her attentiveness to social issues, historical events, and national politics is often eclipsed by the power and beauty of her characters and language, but all these elements function integrally to form one of the most compelling and memorable portraits of African American and southern culture in American letters.

WORKS: *Jonah's Gourd Vine* (1934). *Mules and Men* (1935). *Their Eyes Were Watching God* (1937). *Tell My Horse* (1938). *Moses, Man of the Mountain* (1939). *Dust Tracks on a Road* (1942). *Seraph on the Suwanee* (1948). *The Sanctified Church: The Folklore Writings of Zora Neale Hurston* (1981). *Mule Bone: A Comedy of Negro Life in Three Acts*, with Langston Hughes, ed. George Houston Bass and Henry Louis Gates, Jr. (1991). *The Complete Stories of*

Zora Neale Hurston (1995). *Every Tongue Got to Confess: Negro Tales from the Gulf States*, ed. Carla Kaplan (2001). *Barracoon* (2005).

—JOHN LOWE

MAC HYMAN (1923–1963). Mac Hyman was born in Cordele, Ga., on August 25, 1923. He graduated from Cordele High School, spent a short time at North Georgia College and State University, and in 1947 earned a degree from Duke University. Two stints in the U.S. Air Force (1943–46, 1949–52) provided source material for *No Time for Sergeants*, a first novel that defined Hyman's literary career. A second novel, *Take Now Thy Son*, was published posthumously.

No Time for Sergeants follows a young man, Will Stockdale, from his father's rustic southern home and through the bureaucratic and subcultural byways of the air force into which he has been drafted during World War II. Naive but not stupid, eager to please but no pushover, Stockdale thwarts those who underestimate him in broadly comic scenes that he recounts in a southern patois.

After his own military service, Ira Levin (later better known for writing *Rosemary's Baby* and *The Stepford Wives*) adapted *No Time for Sergeants* for television (1955), Broadway (1955–57), and the movies (1958). All these successful versions starred Andy Griffith, a young actor from North Carolina. A television series (1964–65) starring Sammy Jackson did not fare as well.

In his own, eponymous television series, Griffith was to achieve iconic status playing a southern sheriff who exhibits Stockdale's unsuspected strength and knowingness, while Stockdale's down-home naiveté is transferred to a number of supporting characters, most notably a gas station attendant played by Alabamian Jim Nabors. When Nabors's character moved to his own series, *Gomer Pyle, USMC*, the tie to Hyman's creation was reinforced in many details, including the young marine's interactions with a gruff, long-suffering, and often-bested sergeant.

Hyman married Gwendolyn Holt in 1947, and they had three children. Daughter Gwyn Hyman Rubio, who grew up in Cordele, wrote the novel *Icy Sparks* (2001), which concerns a girl with Tourette syndrome. In 2001 television star Oprah Winfrey selected *Icy Sparks* for her well-known book club.

WORKS: *No Time for Sergeants* (1954). *Take Now Thy Son* (1965). *Love, Boy: The Letters of Mac Hyman*, ed. William Blackburn (1969).

—AMBER VOGEL

JOSEPH HOLT INGRAHAM (1809–1860). Although Ingraham was a popular and prolific novelist, many details of his life remain obscure. He was born to a wealthy mercantile family in Portland, Maine, probably on January 26, 1809. He claimed to have been graduated from Bowdoin College, but the school's records do not show that he ever attended it. In 1830 he left Portland on the sea voyage to New Orleans that he describes in his first book, *The South-West*, and on May 24, 1832, he married Mary Brooks, daughter of a Natchez planter.

Ingraham moved frequently between the North and South until 1847. He was in New York when his second book, the first two-volume romantic novel *Lafitte: The Pirate of the Gulf*, appeared in 1836. It was followed by three more historical novels modeled on Sir Walter Scott's work. Between 1842 and 1847, Ingraham concocted at least eighty more short (100 or fewer pages), lurid romances, mostly about pirates and the evils of big cities. They were published in paperback pamphlets by various Boston firms.

Suddenly in 1847 Ingraham's flood of cheap romances ended. He joined the Protestant Episcopal Church and became headmaster of a church school for girls near Nashville, Tenn. In April 1851 he took charge of St. John's Mission, Aberdeen, Miss.; and on February 8, 1852, he was received into the Episcopal priesthood at Jackson, Miss. In December 1853 he moved to St. John's Church, Mobile, Ala. During three years there he composed his most famous novel, *The Prince of the House of David*, the first best-selling fictionalization of the life of Christ. *The Sunny South*, a series of letters defending the plantation system, appeared in 1860.

Meanwhile, in 1857, Ingraham had become headmaster of a church school in Riverside, Tenn. Then in September 1858 he became rector of Christ Church in Holly Springs, Miss. Here he died mysteriously of a self-inflicted gunshot wound on December 18, 1860. Some have speculated that financial troubles drove him to suicide, but most contemporary accounts affirm that the gun fired accidentally.

WORKS: *The South-West, by a Yankee* (1835). *Lafitte: The Pirate of the Gulf* (1836). *Burton; or, The Sieges* (1838). *Captain Kyd; or, The Wizard of the Sea* (1839). *The American Lounger* (1839). *The Quadroone; or, St. Michael's Day* (1840). *Nobody's Son; or, The Life and Adventures of Percival Mayberry* (1851). *Man: A Sermon Preached at St. John's Church, Aberdeen, Mississippi* (1852). *Pamphlets for the People, in Illustration of the Claims of the Church and Methodism* (1854). *The Prince of the House of David* (1855). *The Pillar of Fire* (1859). *The Throne of David, from the Consecration of the Shepherd in Bethlehem to the Rebellion of Prince Absalom* (1860). *The Sunny South; or, The Southerner at Home* (1860); reissued as *Not "A Fool's Errand"* (1880) and *Kate's Experiences* (1891).

—WARREN FRENCH

WILLIAM IOOR (1780–1850). Of French Huguenot ancestry, born near Dorchester, S.C., in St. George's Parish on January 4, 1780, and educated in medicine at the University of Pennsylvania, William Ioor was South Carolina's first native playwright. His *Independence; or, Which Do You Like the Best, the Peer, or the Farmer?* was produced at the Charleston Theatre in 1805 and published later that year. The play celebrates the virtues of the "independent farmer" in Jeffersonian fashion, and Ioor's subject matter may well have been suggested by the playwright's own life near Dorchester, S.C., where he was both a farmer and served as the local physician. A second play, *The Battle of Eutaw Springs*, was acted in Charleston three times in 1807, once in 1808, and then produced in Richmond (1811) and Philadelphia (1813) by touring companies based in Charleston. Like John Daly Burk's *Bunker Hill* (1797) and William Dunlap's *The Glory of Columbia* (1803), Ioor's play glorifies the actions of the American rebels and urges defiance against Great Britain. The play features the engaging Jonathan Slyboots, the humorous, colorful, and chivalric prototype of the southern gentleman character. The latter part of Ioor's life was more and more taken up with his medical practice, and after fifteen years as a physician in Savannah he moved to upstate South Carolina where he died, near Pelzer, S.C., on July 30, 1850.

WORKS: *Independence; or, Which Do You Like the Best, the Peer, or the Farmer?* (1805). *The Battle of Eutaw Springs and Evacuation of Charleston* (1807).

—DANIEL J. ENNIS

MOLLY IVINS (1944–). Molly Ivins was born Mary Tyler Ivins on August 30, 1944, in Monterey, Calif., to Jim and Margo Ivins. She received a B.A. from Smith College and an M.A. from Columbia University, and studied at the Institute of Political Science in Paris.

Ivins, who had grown up in Houston, got her start in the complaints department of the *Houston Chronicle*, but soon moved to reporting. She wrote the police report at the *Star Tribune* in Minneapolis, but was lured away in 1970 to become co-editor of the *Texas Observer* in Austin. In 1976 she joined the staff of the *New York Times*, first reporting on New York politics and then heading the Rocky Mountain bureau. In 1982 she returned to Texas to work on the *Dallas Times Herald*. She currently writes a syndicated column for the Fort Worth *Star-Telegraph*. Her work is often reprinted in periodicals such as the *Nation, Mother Jones, Progressive,* and the *New York Times Book Review,* and her commentary has been heard on National Public Radio and the McNeil/Lehrer Report. She has published several collections of her essays.

Ivins is best known for her irreverent wit and aggressive attacks on public political figures. Texas politics has often been the target of her satire. As Texas politicians have moved to Washington, D.C., her scope has enlarged to encompass both the national and international scenes. Along with politics, Ivins lampoons such diverse topics as southern football, debutantes, barbecue, and religion. She is known for her uncanny ability to capture the absurdity of America's political and social scene accurately and savagely, but with disarming humor.

Ivins is a board member of the National News Council and is active in Amnesty International's Network and the Reporters Committee for Freedom of the Press. In 1992 she received the Headliner's Award for the best column in Texas, and she has been a finalist for the Pulitzer Prize three times.

WORKS: *Molly Ivins Can't Say That, Can She?* (1991). *Nothin' but Good Times Ahead* (1993). *You Got to Dance with Them What Brung You: Politics in the Clinton Years* (1998). *Shrub: The Short but Happy Life of George W. Bush*, with Lou Dubose (2000). *Bushwhacked: Life in George W. Bush's America*, with Dubose (2003). *Who Let the Dogs In? Incredible Political Animals I Have Known* (2004).

—BARBARA BENNETT

HARRIET A. JACOBS (ca. 1813–1897). Harriet Ann Jacobs was born into slavery in Edenton, N.C., to a woman whose first name was Delilah. Scholars speculate that her father was Elijah, the son of a white farmer named Henry Jacobs. Jacobs had one sibling, John, and two children, Joseph and Louisa Matilda.

In *Incidents in the Life of a Slave Girl,* Jacobs uses pseudonymous narrator Linda Brent to tell her own story. She describes an idyllic life before she learned that she was property, her subsequent persecution by a lecherous slaveholder, the birth of her two children by a white neighbor, and her escape from slavery after hiding in a crawlspace for almost seven years. Her narrative has been the subject of much scholarly study, including Jean Fagan Yellen's groundbreaking research into the author's life that lends validity to the novelized story.

Jacobs officially escaped from slavery in 1842. Though she had been temporarily separated from her children, they were reunited in New York. A harsh new Fugitive Slave Act in 1850 compelled Jacobs's employer, Cornelia Grinnell Willis, to purchase Jacobs's freedom from her former owners in 1853, though Jacobs was herself against the idea. Afterward, Jacobs worked on her narrative, eventually enlisting the aid of abolitionist author L. Maria Child as editor and agent.

During the Civil War, Jacobs and her daughter returned south to assist efforts to supply emergency relief to the thousands of homeless and destitute newly freed blacks. The two women assisted in reform efforts and established a free school in Alexandria, Va. Jacobs was also involved with the Women's Loyal National League, and her daughter lectured for the American Equal Rights Association. Though by 1877 they had settled in Washington, D.C., where Harriet Jacobs died on March 7, 1897, mother and daughter are both buried in Mt. Auburn Cemetery in Cambridge, Mass. Jacobs is now a member of the North Carolina Literary Hall of Fame.

WORKS: *Incidents in the Life of a Slave Girl* (1861).

—LOVALERIE KING

RANDALL JARRELL (1914–1965). Randall Jarrell was born in Nashville, Tenn., on May 6, 1914. At age nineteen, he entered Vanderbilt University (B.A. in psychology; M.A. in literature), where he met literary giants Robert Penn Warren, Allen Tate, and John Crowe Ransom, all of whom helped Jarrell in his early career as a literary critic and poet. In 1937 Ransom, who had left Vanderbilt for Kenyon College, asked Jarrell to teach writing at Kenyon. There Jarrell met other long-time friends and supporters: the confessional poet Robert Lowell and novelist Peter Taylor.

In 1940 Jarrell married Mackie Langham, whom he had met in 1939 while teaching in Austin at the University of Texas. At the outbreak of World War II, Jarrell joined the army air corps, where he instructed B-29 pilots in celestial navigation. Although he was distanced from fighting, military life influenced Jarrell's poetic imagination. *Little Friend, Little Friend,* his second poetry collection, dealt directly with death and war, as evidenced by his most anthologized poem, "The Death of the Ball Turret Gunner."

After the war, Jarrell's career as critic, poet, and teacher surged. He received a Guggenheim, spent a year in New York City teaching at Sarah Lawrence, served as poetry editor for the *Nation,* and published poems and criticism in the major literary journals of the time. He secured a professorship in 1947 at the Woman's College of the University of North Carolina (now the University of North Carolina at Greensboro), with his third book of poetry, *Losses,* nearly in hand. After teaching American poetry to Europeans at the Harvard Seminars in Salzburg in 1948, Jarrell must have found it hard to return to Greensboro. On returning, he separated from his first wife, and he devoted his time to writing about the lack of American cultural taste. Additionally, Jarrell wrote important literary criticism on E. E. Cummings, William Carlos Williams, and Robert Frost and reviewed contemporary poets; he was known as a piercing literary reviewer. By the time *Poetry and the Age,* his collection of criticism, appeared, he was a revered (and feared) critic.

In 1952 he married Mary von Schrader. They lived together in Greensboro, with her two daughters, but they traveled extensively for lectureships and seminars. At Greensboro, Jarrell was known as the tennis-playing intellectual who babied his beloved convertible Mercedes, wrote and revised poetry and criticism, translated Goethe and Grimm, and taught literature. In 1960 his fifth book of poems, *The Woman at the Washington Zoo,* for which he received the National Book Award, was published.

Though Jarrell's life was successful on many counts, he harbored darker regions in his psyche. In 1964 he was hospitalized for a "breakdown" in Chapel Hill, N.C. In the fall of 1965, at age fifty-one, Randall Jarrell was struck and killed by car on a highway outside of Chapel Hill. Much speculation exists concerning the poet's death. Some suspect that his death was a suicide; others see it as a tragic accident. *The Lost World,* Jarrell's last poetry collection, reconstructs the memories of childhood; it was published posthumously.

WORKS: *Blood for a Stranger* (1942). *Little Friend, Little Friend* (1945). *Losses* (1948). *The Seven-League Crutches* (1951). *Poetry and the Age* (1953). *Pictures from an Institution: A Comedy* (1954). *Selected Poems* (1955). *The Woman at the Washington Zoo* (1960). *A Sad Heart at the Supermarket* (1962). *The Gingerbread Rabbit* (1964). *The Bat-Poet* (1964). *The Lost World* (1965). *The Animal Family* (1965). *Complete Poems* (1969). *The Third Book of Criticism* (1969). *Kipling, Auden, and Co.* (1980).

—MARK ALLEN ROBERTS

THOMAS JEFFERSON (1743–1826). Thomas Jefferson was born on April 13, 1743, in the shadow of the Blue Ridge Mountains in what would soon become Albemarle County, Va. His father, Peter Jefferson, was a civil engineer and aspiring planter, and his mother, Jane Randolph, came from one of Virginia's first families. Growing up on the western frontier, however, distanced him from the entrenched Tidewater and provided him with his lifelong ideals of independence, equality, and the value of the modest freehold to a strong republic.

After graduating from the College of William and Mary in 1762 and completing his legal studies, the young lawyer and planter began his political career proper with his election to the Virginia House of Burgesses in 1768. Once launched in his career, he married the young widow Martha Wayles Skelton in 1772. Jefferson quickly established a reputation as a radical, opposing the more conservative views of the Tidewater elite. Jefferson as politician had one major flaw: he was considered a poor speaker in an age that prized oratory as the defining mark of a legislator. Fortunately, he more than made up for this deficiency with his skill as a writer, and it was this gift that led to his first widespread recognition as a revolutionary voice through *A Summary View of the Rights of British America*. He was chosen to serve as an alternate delegate to the Second Continental Congress in Philadelphia in 1775 and to return as a regular delegate in 1776.

In the summer of 1776, with hostilities well under way, the Congress approved a Virginia resolution for separation from Great Britain. Jefferson was part of a committee of five, including John Adams and Benjamin Franklin, charged with drafting the formal Declaration of Independence, and Jefferson, because of his reputation as a writer, was chosen to write the document. The committee and Congress made changes to Jefferson's draft, most notably the elimination of a long section charging the King with foisting the evil of slavery onto the colonies, but what remained is essentially Jefferson's own. His words marked the birth of the nation and have since become a rallying cry for human rights and democratic revolution throughout the world.

Jefferson returned to his home state in September 1776 to what he saw as more important duties in the convention then drafting the Virginia Constitution. Seeking to establish a solid foundation for republican governance against entrenched aristocratic interests, Jefferson successfully sought the abolition of entail and primogeniture, a reform of the penal code, and, his greatest achievement, a statute guaranteeing religious freedom. His most ambitious efforts, however, a proposal for the gradual abolition of slavery by 1800 and a plan for a system of public primary schools, failed to win the necessary support. In 1779–81, Jefferson served as a wartime governor of Virginia.

Closer to Jefferson's heart was his time at Monticello. The house itself, begun in 1767, would prove to be the greatest American architectural achievement of the century. Monticello provided Jefferson leisure to pursue his vast range of interests, including gardening and agricultural improvements, inventions such as the swivel chair and dumbwaiter, music, and astronomy, to name but a few.

During the interim between his governorship and his appointment to the diplomatic mission to France in 1784, Jefferson composed his only full-length book, a collection of essays entitled *Notes on the State of Virginia*. These essays are written to provide an understanding of the physical, cultural, economic, and political conditions of Virginia for a foreign observer. The book attempts to answer foreign critics who claimed that all things (from beasts to political life) degenerate in the New World. Jefferson answered such critics by describing geographical advantages, natural wonders, and an agrarian society adapted to a stable republic, but there are other parts of the book that reveal Jefferson's own misgivings, particularly the question of how a stable order could arise in a society divided between whites and blacks, whom he regarded as inherently inferior.

This contradiction between the champion of individual rights and the Virginia slaveholder has long troubled Jefferson's legacy. Much of the attention, from Jefferson's time forward, has focused on a possible sexual relationship with one of his house-servants, Sally Hemings, the half-sister of Jefferson's wife, in the years after the latter's death in 1782. Recent DNA testing has provided support for the long-standing claim of the Hemings descendants that Jefferson indeed fathered at least one of her children.

After his service in France, Jefferson became secretary of state to President Washington and soon found himself embroiled in a struggle with Alexander Hamilton over the constitutional limits of the federal government, particularly the executive branch. Hamilton favored a strong, centralized federal government and a loose reading of the constitution; Jefferson, out of his concern for the preservation of individual liberties, held to a strict reading, reserving to the states and the people all powers not specifically given to the federal government. These competing visions gave rise to the first two organized parties in American politics: the Hamiltonian Federalists and the Jeffersonian Republicans.

Jefferson ran for the presidency three times as the Republican candidate, finishing second to John Adams and thereby becoming vice president in 1796, then winning the office in 1800 and 1804. Jefferson strove to be a truly republican president, reducing the pomp and pageantry associated with the office and exercising fiscal restraint; his great legacy, however, was defined by acts of imagination and executive audacity. In 1803 Jefferson sent out the Lewis and Clark Expedition to explore the West to the Pacific, then succeeded in purchasing vast tracts of western lands from France in the Louisiana Purchase later that year.

After a second term marred by the ill-conceived Embargo Act, Jefferson refused nomination to a third term and left Washington to return to Monticello and "the tranquil pursuits of science." Along with entertaining the many young admirers who sought him out in his hilltop retreat, Jefferson renewed a remarkable correspondence with his old rival John Adams. His greatest energies were reserved for work on the University of Virginia, the "academical village" he intended to train a new generation of leaders in the liberal arts and the most advanced science. The buildings on the quadrangle, all designed by Jefferson, are an architectural triumph.

Thomas Jefferson died on July 4, 1826, fifty years after the signing of the Declaration and on the same day his friend John Adams passed away in Massachusetts. He was buried at Monticello.

WORKS: *A Summary View of the Rights of British America* (1774). "A Declaration by the Representatives of the United States of America, in General Congress Assembled" (1776). *Notes on the State of Virginia* (1785). *A Manual of Parliamentary Practice* (1801). *Autobiography* (1814). *The Writings of Thomas Jefferson*, 10 vols., ed. Paul L. Ford (1892–99). *Essay on Anglo-Saxon* (1851). *The Life and Morals of Jesus of Nazareth* (1902). *The Writings of Thomas Jefferson*, 20 vols., ed. A. A. Lipscomb and A. E. Bergh (1903). *The Papers of Thomas Jefferson*, 31 vols. to date, ed. Julian P. Boyd et al. (1950–2004).

—DOUGLAS L. MITCHELL

GEORGIA DOUGLAS JOHNSON (1877–1966). Georgia Blanche Douglas Camp was born in Atlanta, Ga., to George and Laura Jackson Camp, probably on September 10, 1877. Following secondary schooling in Rome, Ga., and Atlanta, Johnson graduated from the Atlanta University Normal School. A self-taught violinist, she studied piano, voice, and violin at the Oberlin Conservatory and at the Cleveland College of Music. In 1903 Johnson married successful local lawyer Henry Lincoln ("Link") Johnson, whose parents had been slaves. In 1910 the Johnsons and their two young sons moved to Washington, D.C. Link practiced law and served in William Howard Taft's administration, while Georgia attended Howard University and began to write lyric poetry.

Link and Georgia became well-recognized figures in Washington's upper-class African American society, and Georgia was active in several women and minority advocacy groups and in poetry clubs. Important writers began to endorse her creative work, including William Stanley Braithwaite, W. E. B. Du Bois, Alain Locke, and Zona Gale.

An early feminist, Johnson sought to establish herself primarily as a woman poet who also happened to be an African American. In the four-to-twelve-line rhymed poems that comprise her first book, *The Heart of a Woman and Other Poems*, Johnson explored a woman's youthful yearnings, quest for identity, joy, loss of innocence, and, occasionally, despair. Johnson organized her second volume,

Bronze, into seven major thematic clusters of poems; motherhood, the long shadow of slavery, and hope are dominant motifs. She also included fourteen "Appreciations" dedicated to people who had uplifted African Americans. *An Autumn Love Cycle*, her third book, is a five-part collection treating love and passion, separation, introspection, death, grief, recollection, and encouragement—a volume informed in part by the manifold consequences of Link's death in 1925 of a cerebral hemorrhage. Johnson also wrote a widely syndicated weekly newspaper column, "Homely Philosophy" (1926–32).

After Link's death, Johnson held a series of teaching and civil service jobs, raised her children resourcefully, and turned her attention to writing short plays. In her drama, she openly addresses troublesome racial issues. *A Sunday Morning in the South* examines prejudice, brutality, and lynching. *Paupaulekejo* treats the abuse of Africans by hypocritical white missionaries. *Blue Blood* confronts miscegenation, and *Plumes* stresses the centrality of African American folk beliefs in the face of death. *Safe* echoes the saga of Margaret Garner and anticipates Toni Morrison's *Beloved* (1987): an African American woman kills her healthy newborn baby to keep the child safe from lynchers.

Johnson's writing was stimulated by the authors and artists who frequented her "Saturday Soirées," also called the "Saturday Nighters Club"—a reading, discussion, and socializing salon and African American nexus that she maintained in Washington for some forty years. Her guests at these heady gatherings included Countee Cullen, May Miller, Jean Toomer, Langston Hughes, Angelina Grimké, Carter Woodson, Sterling Brown, Arna Bontemps, James Weldon Johnson, Zora Neale Hurston, as well as Locke, Du Bois, and Braithwaite. Intellectually active throughout her later years, Johnson kept a note pad and pencil around her neck. She assembled one final volume of new and reprinted poems, *Share My World*, in 1962. Following a stroke, she died at the Freedman's Hospital, Howard University, on May 14, 1966.

WORKS: *The Heart of a Woman and Other Poems* (1918). *Bronze: A Book of Verse* (1922). *A Sunday Morning in the South* (1925). *Blue Blood: A Play* (1926). *Paupaulekejo* (1926). *Plumes: A Play in One Act* (1927). *An Autumn Love Cycle* (1928). *Safe* (1929). *Share My World: A Book of Poems* (1962). *The Selected Works of Georgia Douglas Johnson* (1997).

—R. BRUCE BICKLEY, JR.

GERALD WHITE JOHNSON (1890–1980). Born on August 6, 1890, in the rural community of Riverton in eastern North Carolina, Gerald Johnson gained renown in the 1920s and 1930s as a journalist and biographer. His father, Archibald Johnson, was a newspaperman, and Gerald Johnson was educated in a Baptist institution, Wake Forest College. Upon graduation in 1911, he worked briefly for two small North Carolina newspapers before joining the *Greensboro Daily News* in 1913. He served as a reporter and editorial writer for the *Daily News* until 1924, and in 1922 his writing caught the eye of the Baltimore newspaperman H. L. Mencken, who proclaimed Johnson "the best editorial writer in the South." After spending two years (1924–26) as a professor of journalism at the University of North Carolina, Johnson joined Mencken on the *Baltimore Sunpapers* as an editorial writer, and he wrote for the *Sun* until 1943. After 1943 he wrote essays for numerous journals and magazines, particularly the *New Republic*, and also wrote novels and works of history.

Although Johnson became widely respected after 1930 as a national political analyst and a spokesman for the liberal viewpoint, his greatest contribution to southern life was his work as an iconoclastic essayist in the 1920s. He was second only to Mencken in his indictment of southern literary and cultural poverty and in his call for a new southern spirit. He was the boldest of writers for the new southern journals—especially the *Reviewer* of Richmond—and in national magazines such as Mencken's *American Mercury* he reigned as the leading native interpreter of the South. His subjects were religious frenzy, racial prejudice, the poor white, and the subculture of the southern mill town; his free-wheeling prose style equaled and sometimes surpassed Mencken's own. Johnson's criticism of the South, however, was tempered by a sympathy and an understanding foreign to many southern critics of the 1920s.

WORKS: Essays in the *Reviewer,* the *Journal of Social Forces,* and *American Mercury* (1922–30). *The Undefeated* (1926). *Andrew Johnson: An Epic in Homespun* (1927). *Randolph of Roanoke: A Political Fantastic* (1929). *By Reason of Strength* (1930). *The Secession of the Southern States* (1933). *A Little Night Music* (1937). *The Wasted Land* (1937). *America's Silver Age: The Statecraft of Clay, Webster, and Calhoun* (1939). *Roosevelt: Dictator or Democrat?* (1941). *American Heroes and Hero-Worship* (1943). *Woodrow Wilson* (1944). *An Honorable Titan: A Biographical Study of Adolph S. Ochs* (1946). *The First Captain* (1949). *Liberal's Progress* (1948). *Our English Heritage* (1949). *Incredible Tale: The Odyssey of the Average American in the Last Half Century* (1950). *The American People* (1951). *The Making of a Southern Industrialist: A Biographical Study of Simpson Bobo Tanner* (1952). *Pattern for Liberty: The Story of Old Philadelphia* (1952). *Mount Vernon* (1953). *Lunatic Fringe* (1957). *Peril and Promise: An Inquiry into Freedom of the Press* (1958). *The Lines Are Drawn* (1958). *The Man Who Feels Left Behind* (1960). *The Supreme Court* (1962). *The Congress* (1963). *Hod-Carrier* (1964). *Communism: An American's View* (1967). *Franklin D. Roosevelt* (1967). *The Imperial Republic* (1972). *South-Watching: Selected Essays of Gerald W. Johnson,* ed. Fred Hobson (1982).

—FRED HOBSON

JAMES WELDON JOHNSON (1871–1938). Though his career took him not only to the North but also to international destinations, James Weldon Johnson remained devoted to his southern roots and to the black folk culture so richly presented there. Born in Jacksonville, Fla., to a middle-class family (his mother was a teacher and his father a headwaiter at a luxury hotel), Johnson was provided with an unusually comprehensive education in the post-Reconstruction South. English literature and classical music were staples in the Johnson household. While a freshman at Atlanta University in the summer of 1891, Johnson found his educational focus. Teaching the children of former slaves in rural Georgia, he was drawn to the culture of the common people. In exploring black culture he probed the depths of his own identity. The folk would be central to his future art.

After college graduation in 1894, Johnson returned to Jacksonville to become principal of Stanton School, his alma mater. In 1895 he founded the *Daily American,* a newspaper devoted to exposing racial injustice while also touting the virtues of self-help espoused by Booker T. Washington. Though short-lived, the paper drew the attention of Washington and W. E. B. Du Bois, an achievement that served Johnson in his later career. Soon after the paper's demise, Johnson took up the study of law, ultimately establishing a successful practice conducted simultaneously with his duties as principal.

By the end of the decade, Johnson was collaborating on musical compositions with his brother, John Rosamond Johnson, an 1897 graduate of the New England Conservatory of Music. The two brothers divided their time between Jacksonville and New York. Working with the talented black performer Bob Cole, the brothers provided scores of compositions to Broadway musicals. In 1900, for a commemoration of Abraham Lincoln's birthday, Johnson wrote the now famous "Lift Ev'ry Voice and Sing," which his brother set to music. Over twenty years later it was adopted by the NAACP as the "Negro National Anthem." After 1901 Johnson was living solely in New York and moving easily in black society, where he met his future wife, Grace Nail.

In 1904 Johnson undertook a serious study of literature at Columbia University, working with famed critic and novelist Brander Matthews. Two years later he agreed to serve as consul to Venezuela, a post he earned as a result of his connections with Booker T. Washington, then an advisor to the Roosevelt administration. During the next three years, while in Venezuela, Johnson wrote his only novel, *The Autobiography of an Ex-Colored Man,* which he published anonymously in 1912. Addressing the plight of the "tragic mulatto," Johnson's novel is also the first to give fictional voice to Du Bois's notion of black double-consciousness.

After leaving Venezuela in 1909, Johnson became head of the U.S. consulate in Nicaragua, where he remained until 1913. The following year he was named editorial page editor of the *New York Age*, a weekly paper sympathetic to the Booker T. Washington agenda. Two years later, in 1916, he was made field secretary for the NAACP, and in 1920 he was elected to head the civil rights organization, where he remained until 1930. Within that decade, Johnson, one of the darlings of the Harlem Renaissance, produced some of his more ambitious literary works, most notably the seven poems featured in *God's Trombones*. Combining free verse with the black oral tradition, Johnson celebrated the dignity and force of black folklore. During this period, Johnson meticulously edited books on black poetry and spirituals.

From 1930 until his untimely death in an automobile accident in 1938, Johnson enjoyed the life of a scholar. Awarded the Adam K. Spence Chair of Creative Literature at Fisk University, he found the leisure to complete his autobiography, published in 1933, and in later years he lectured widely on civil rights and racial advancement.

WORKS: *The Autobiography of an Ex-Colored Man* (1912, 1927). *The Book of American Negro Poetry* (1927). *God's Trombones* (1927). *The Book of American Negro Spirituals* (1925). *The Second Book of American Negro Spirituals* (1926). *Black Manhattan* (1930). *Along This Way* (1933). *Negro Americans, What Now?* (1934). *Saint Peter Relates an Incident* (1934).

—CHARLES E. WILSON, JR.

MARY JOHNSTON (1870–1936). A popular and prolific writer, Mary Johnston is now remembered primarily for one of her early novels, the colonial Virginia romance *To Have and To Hold*. This book sold over 500,000 copies and was twice made into a movie. Her principal writings include twenty-three novels and thirty-eight short stories.

Born in Buchanan, Va., on November 21, 1870, Johnston was the eldest of six children. Her health was frail and her education took place largely at home. Her life was not sheltered because her father, John William, a former Confederate artillery officer, held significant public and business posts, requiring travels to Europe as well as moves to New York City, Birmingham, Ala., and Richmond, Va.

When her mother died in 1889, Mary took charge of the Johnston household. Some of her most successful early books appeared over the next several years as she strove to assist the family financially. In 1902 the family moved from Birmingham to Richmond, and this return to the Old Dominion furthered Johnston's interest in writing about her native state. Notable books of this period include *The Long Roll* and *Cease Firing*, both epic stories of the Civil War.

In the years following her father's death in 1905 Johnston rekindled interests in the Allegheny Mountains of Virginia, and in 1911–12 she and two of her sisters built a large house, Three Hills, in Warm Springs. Ties to Richmond remained, not only with longstanding friendships with writers such as Ellen Glasgow, but in various causes, such as the suffragist movement. She founded the Equal Suffrage League of Virginia in 1909, with Glasgow and Lila Meade Valentine. Johnston's novel *Hagar* reflected many of her strong feminist ideals. As an honorary officer of the league she addressed legislatures in West Virginia and Tennessee and also a governors' conference.

Never strong physically, Johnston contracted Bright's disease late in life and died at her Warm Springs home on May 9, 1936, following an extended hospitalization.

WORKS: *Prisoners of Hope* (1898). *To Have and To Hold* (1900). *Audrey* (1902). *Sir Mortimer* (1904). *The Goddess of Reason* (1907). *Lewis Rand* (1908). *The Long Roll* (1911). *Cease Firing* (1912). *Hagar* (1913). *Witch* (1914). *Fortunes of Garin* (1915). *Wanderers* (1917). *Foes* (1918). *Michael Forth* (1919). *Sweet Rocket* (1920). *Pioneers of the Old South* (1920). *1492* (1922). *Silver Cross* (1922). *Croatan* (1923). *Slave Ship* (1924). *The Great Valley* (1926). *Exile* (1927). *Hunting Shirt* (1931). *Miss Delicia Allen* (1933). *Drury Randall* (1934).

—WILLIAM W. KELLY

RICHARD MALCOLM JOHNSTON (1822–1898). A Georgia-born lawyer and teacher, Richard Malcolm Johnston spent the latter third of his life in Baltimore, where he achieved literary prominence for his novels and humorous sketches of small town and rural life in middle Georgia during the antebellum era.

Born in Powelton to a Baptist minister and his wife, Johnston was educated at Mercer College in nearby Macon. After his graduation in 1841, he practiced law in Hancock County and intermittently taught school until 1857, when he moved to Athens to take a position as professor of rhetoric and belles lettres at the University of Georgia. With the Civil War's outbreak, Johnston resigned his position and returned to Hancock County, where he opened his own school for boys. Dissatisfied with the course of Reconstruction and postwar recovery in Georgia, he moved to Baltimore in 1867, where he established another school that lasted until the early 1880s.

Johnston's literary career began in earnest with the publication of *Georgia Sketches*, a compilation of humorous stories published under the pseudonym "Philemon Perch" and inspired by Augustus Baldwin Longstreet's *Georgia Scenes* (1835). Encouraged by a fellow Georgia writer then in Baltimore, Sidney Lanier, Johnston produced a much-expanded version of *Georgia Sketches* in 1871 under the title *Dukesborough Tales*, which was expanded yet again in both 1874 and 1883 under the same title. Based on antebellum characters and incidents in Dukesborough, a fictionalized version of Powelton, the latter edition established Johnston's reputation as a southern humorist and local color writer. He published four novels between 1884 and 1898, all nostalgic treatments of life in middle Georgia before the war. He also produced several other volumes of short stories, literary criticism, and nonfiction, including a biography of fellow Georgian Alexander Stephens (the half-brother of his onetime law partner Linton Stephens) and an autobiography that appeared in 1900, two years after his death in Baltimore.

WORKS: *The English Classics* (1860). *Georgia Sketches* (1864). *Dukesborough Tales* (1871); rev. eds. (1874, 1883). *English Literature*, with William Hand Browne (1872). *Life of Alexander H. Stephens* (1878). *Old Mark Langston* (1884). *Two Gray Tourists* (1885). *Mr. Absalom Billinslea, and Other Georgia Folk* (1888). *Ogeechee Cross-Firings* (1889). *Widow Guthrie* (1890). *The Primes and Their Neighbors: Ten Tales of Middle Georgia* (1891). *Studies, Literary and Social* (1891, 1892). *Mr. Fortner's Marital Claims and Other Stories* (1894). *Mr. Billy Downs and His Likes* (1892). *Little Ike Templin and Other Stories* (1894). *Early Educational Life in Middle Georgia* (1896). *Lectures on Literature: English, French, and Spanish* (1897). *Old Times in Middle Georgia* (1897). *Pearce Amerson's Will* (1898). *Autobiography of Colonel Richard Malcolm Johnston* (1900).

—JOHN C. INSCOE

CHARLES COLCOCK JONES, JR. (1831–1893). Lawyer, historian, soldier, archaeologist, and politician, Charles Colcock Jones, Jr., was born on October 28, 1831, in Savannah, the son of a planter, Presbyterian minister, and seminary professor. He was privately tutored and spent his boyhood on three plantations in Liberty County. He attended South Carolina College in Columbia (1848–50), received his A.B. from the College of New Jersey (Princeton) in 1852, then went to Philadelphia to study and read law. In 1855 he graduated from the Dane Law School at Harvard University, where he also attended lectures by Longfellow, Holmes, and Lowell.

Jones was admitted to the bar in Savannah and was partner in a law firm. On November 9, 1858, he married Ruth Berrien Whitehead of Burke County, Ga.; they had two children. In 1859 he was a city alderman of Savannah, and in 1860–61 he was its mayor. In 1862 Jones joined the Confederate army and served with the Georgia Artillery, as a first lieutenant and then lieutenant colonel. He was chief of artillery during the Siege of Savannah. Soon after he joined the war, his wife and children died. On October 20, 1863, he married Eva Berrien Eve of Augusta; they had one child.

Following the war, Jones moved to New York, where he practiced law. In 1877 he returned to Georgia and settled at Montrose in Summerville, a suburb of Augusta, where he lived until his death. In 1879 he spent several months in England, and that year he organized, directed, and was elected president of the Confederate Survivors' Association of Augusta. He was awarded law degrees from City College of New York (1880) and Emory College (1882) and held membership in a number of national and international societies. At his death on July 19, 1893, Jones was given a soldier's burial.

Jones's literary career began in 1859 when an address he delivered to the Georgia Historical Society on Indian remains was published as a pamphlet. He collected historical relics, including some twenty thousand aboriginal remains of southern Indians. A popular lecturer and writer on southern history, he had a vast library of 4,500 volumes. So accomplished was Jones as a defender and historian of the Old South that he was given the nickname "Macaulay of the South."

WORKS: *The Religious Instruction of the Negroes in the United States* (1842). *Indian Remains in Southern Georgia* (1859). *The Monumental Remains of Georgia* (1861). *Historical Sketches of the Chatham Artillery* (1867). *Historical Sketches of Tomo-chi-chi, Mico of the Yamacraws* (1868). *Reminiscences of the Last Days of General Henry Lee* (1870). *Antiquities of the Southern Indians, Particularly of the Georgia Tribes* (1873). *The Siege of Savannah in 1779* (1874). *History of the Dead Towns of Georgia* (1878). *The Life and Services of Commodore Josiah Tattnall* (1878). *Hernando de Soto* (1880). *History of Georgia*, 2 vols. (1883). *Life, Labors, and Neglected Grave of Richard Henry Wilde* (1885). *Negro Myths from the Georgia Coast Told in the Vernacular* (1888). *History of Savannah, Ga.* (1890). *Memorial History of Augusta, Ga.* (1890).

—GARY KERLEY

GAYL JONES (1949–). Born on November 23, 1949, in Lexington, Ky., Gayle Jones attended Lexington public schools but went north for college. After earning her B.A. at Connecticut College (1971), she earned an M.A. and a D.A. in creative writing at Brown. She then became an assistant professor of English and Afro-American and African Studies at the University of Michigan. Her work was rewarded with a Howard Foundation Award (1975), a fellowship from the National Endowment for the Arts (1976), and a two-year fellowship from the Michigan Society of Fellows (1977–79). In the early 1980s, she resigned from Michigan, returning to Lexington and a life of seclusion.

Jones has attained fame and notoriety as a prolific and provocative writer, one frequently faulted for negative depictions of black men. She has suffered also the loss of her carefully guarded privacy as periodicals reported the circumstances under which her mentally troubled husband, Robert Higgins Jones, committed suicide and the toll it took on her.

As a scholar, professor of creative writing, novelist, short-story writer, poet, and playwright, Jones has portrayed and investigated the significance of the inflections and rhythms of African American oral and folk tradition. Using blues, jazz, African American vernacular English, and non-linearity as narrative strategies, Jones explores the complex layers of humanity. She presents and re-envisions the history of slavery in African American culture and in other cultures influenced by the transatlantic slave trade. Her settings range from maroon communities and slave plantations in Brazil to the American Southwest.

WORKS: *Chile Woman* (1974). *B.O.P. (Blacks on Paper)* (1975). *Corregidora* (1975). *Eva's Man* (1976). *White Rat: Short Stories* (1977). *Song for Anninho* (1981). *The Hermit-Woman* (1983). *Xarque and Other Poems* (1985). *Liberating Voices: Oral Tradition in African American Literature* (1991). *The Healing* (1998). *Mosquito* (1999).

—MILDRED R. MICKLE

HUGH JONES (1692–1760). The Reverend Hugh Jones arrived in Williamsburg, Va., in the spring of 1717 to become professor of mathematics at the College of William and Mary. His recently acquired Oxford B.A. and M.A. prepared him for clerical positions, which he soon assumed as chaplain to the Virginia House of Burgesses and as minister of a Jamestown church. Jones's participation in the political, religious, and intellectual affairs of the colony qualified him well for his most famous work, *The Present State of Virginia*, published in 1724 in London while Jones was living there. Returning to America in the same year with a wife and two adopted children, Jones was reassigned to a distant parish in King and Queen County, Va. In 1726 he removed to Charles County, Md., where his pastoral and educational labors, particularly among slaves, were rewarded in 1731 by a more substantial living in Sassafras Parish, Cecil County, in Maryland's upper Eastern Shore. Here with his family he spent the remainder of his years, defending the Church of England, working as Lord Baltimore's chief mathematician in a boundary line dispute between Maryland and Pennsylvania, and promoting scientific investigation and the regulation of arithmetic measurements and methodology.

Intended as an updated supplement to Robert Beverly's *History and Present State of Virginia* (1705, 1722), Jones's 150-page *Present State of Virginia* both defended the colony against its detractors and promoted its nascent myth as a haven for gracious Cavaliers. In an appendix, however, Jones went further to recommend improvements for the colony. Among these were the modernization of the curriculum and government of the College of William and Mary, the ordination of a "Dean of Virginia" to ensure clerical uniformity, and the relaxation of Britain's mercantile policy toward the colonies.

WORKS: *The Present State of Virginia* (1724). *An Accidence to the English Tongue* (1724). *The Pancronometer; or, Universal Georgia Calendar. . . and the Reasons, Rules, and Uses of Octave Computation, or Natural Arithmetic* (1753).

—WILLIAM L. ANDREWS

MADISON JONES (1925–). Madison Percy Jones was born in Nashville, Tenn., on March 21, 1925, and graduated from a private high school there. He dropped out of Vanderbilt after three semesters to work on the family farm for eighteen months, returned to Vanderbilt for another three semesters, and was then drafted. After serving in Korea as a military policeman in 1945 and 1946, Jones returned to Vanderbilt, studying with Donald Davidson and earning his B.A. in 1949. To continue his study of writing (under Andrew Lytle), Jones went to the University of Florida, earning his M.A. in 1951. That year he married Shailah McEvilley, with whom he has five children.

After two more years of graduate work at Florida, Jones began work on his first novel, *The Innocent*, and took a job as an English instructor at Miami University in Ohio. He held a *Sewanee Review* Fellowship in 1954–55 and taught at the University of Tennessee in 1955–56. He began teaching at Auburn University in 1956, became writer-in-residence there in 1967, full professor in 1968, and a chaired professor in 1982. He retired in 1987.

Jones was awarded a Rockefeller Foundation Fellowship in 1968 and a Guggenheim Fellowship in 1974. He is the recipient of the Harper Lee Award, the T. S. Eliot Award, and the Michael Shaara Award for Civil War Fiction. He was inducted into the Alabama Academy of Distinguished Authors in 1982 and into the Fellowship of Southern Writers in 1989. Jones has published short stories and criticism in *Sewanee Review, Perspective, South Atlantic Quarterly,* the *Washington Post,* and the *New York Times Book Review.*

The moral values and social views that inform all of Jones's work are clearly stated from the first. *The Innocent* details the protagonist's loss of innocence, tragic error, self-recognition, and expiation; the novel reveals Jones's grounding in Puritan theology and classical tragedy, as well as his admiration for both Hawthorne and Dostoevski. His short novel *An Exile* was filmed as *I Walk the Line* (1970), starring Gregory Peck and Tuesday Weld. His next novel, *A Cry of Absence,* is an impressive study of the effects of integration and racial conflict in the South. His novel *Nashville 1864: The Dying of the Light* has been favorably compared to *Huckleberry Finn* and *The Red Badge of Courage;* the novel was a Book-of-the-Month Club selection and Jones's most popular to that date.

WORKS: *The Innocent* (1957). *Forest of the Night* (1960). *A Buried Land* (1963). *An Exile* (1967); repr. as *I Walk the Line* (1967). *A Cry of Absence* (1971). *Passage through Gehenna* (1978). *Season of the Strangler* (1982). *Last Things* (1989). *To the Winds* (1996). *Nashville 1864: The Dying of the Light* (1997).

—DAVID K. JEFFREY

PRESTON JONES (1936–1979). Preston Jones was born in Albuquerque, N.M., on April 7, 1936. He became a playwright so that he could re-create, on the stage, everyday life in the rural Southwest. By design a regional writer, Jones at his best transcended his Texas and New Mexico settings to reveal a larger vision of a racist, sexist, materialistic society clinging to self-serving myths as it disregards religious values and a viable work ethic.

A graduate of the University of New Mexico, Jones began graduate study at Baylor University, then switched to Trinity College in San Antonio, Tex., where he received an M.A. in 1966. Jones began as an actor with the Dallas Theater Center and later directed plays as well. When his marriage to Gaye Jones failed, he married Mary Sue Fridge, who was also an actor, director, and general factotum for the company.

Jones decided in the early 1970s to try his own hand at writing plays, since he had a professional's knowledge of the theater and a personal gift of storytelling. He began a draft of *Lu Ann Hampton La-verty Oberlander,* the first of the three plays on which his reputation largely depends; but the second play of the trilogy, *The Last Meeting of the Knights of the White Magnolia,* was performed first, in the Down Center Stage at the Theater Center on December 4, 1973. In February 1974, *Lu Ann* was also performed in the same theater. Finally, in November 1974, *The Oldest Living Graduate* opened in the upstairs Kalita Humphreys Theater. The first two plays of the trilogy were revised and alternated in the repertory, referred to collectively as the Bradleyville Trilogy (later renamed *A Texas Trilogy*). In the final week of the *Trilogy*'s production, it was possible for audiences to see all these plays during a six-and-a-half-hour period each night.

The project was so successful that it established Jones as the most popular playwright at the theater center and spawned regional productions of his works in Chicago, Washington, and Seattle. New York, however, was not so receptive. Although the scheduling of the *Trilogy* was generously heralded by the popular press, some critics of the actual production were skeptical. The drama reviewers in the *New Yorker* and the *New Republic* found Jones's work derivative, sentimental, and insignificant. Stunned by the negative publicity, Jones retreated to the Theater Center with which he had been associated for nineteen years and where he remained a celebrity. Ultimately his heavy drinking and the late-night schedule of constant theater productions caught up with him, and he began to experience continuing difficulties with a stomach ulcer. Following an attack of bleeding ulcers, he underwent surgery and died in the intensive care unit on September 19, 1979, in Dallas, Tex.

A *Texas Trilogy* and *Santa Fe Sunshine* were published in 1976 and 1977, respectively. Produced but unpublished late plays by the writer include *A Place on the Magdalena Flats* (1976), *Juneteenth* (1979), and *Remember* (1979).

Perhaps Jones is most plausible as a twentieth-century "local colorist," propitiously writing in an era when promoting regional theater was an American obsession. His is a lonely but insistent voice, decrying the spiritual emptiness of the late twentieth century and recording futile attempts to recapture a more vital past or to create a more meaningful future.

WORKS: *A Texas Trilogy* (1976). *Santa Fe Sunshine* (1977).

—KIMBALL KING

RODNEY JONES (1950–). In his poetic sequence "Elegy for the Southern Drawl," Rodney Jones writes, "The old people in the valley where I was born / Still held to the brogue, elisions, and coloratura / Of the Scotch-Irish, and brandished / Like guns the iffens, you'uns, and narys / That linked by the labyrinthine hollers / Of the foothills of the Appalachian Mountains / The remnants of a people." Rodney Glenn Jones was raised outside Falkville, in rural northern Alabama, which he once said "resembled much of the present third world, essentially feudal, agrarian, and unelectrified until my sixth year." He received his B.A. at the University of Alabama (1971) and his M.F.A. at the University of North Carolina at Greensboro (1973). He taught poetry in the public schools of Tennessee, Alabama, and Virginia from 1974 to 1978, moving on to Virginia Intermont College in Bristol (writer-in-residence, 1978–84) and—since then—Southern Illinois University in Carbondale, where he is now professor of English.

In extended discursive lines, Jones writes candidly about traditional southern subjects (race, history, God, landscape, language, family, eccentrics, violence, humor, home) in a multilayered manner at once joking and serious. Though some of his best poetry addresses mules and glossolalia and other regional staples, his seven books also deal with the dark changes and raw edgy weirdness of life as many people really live it, here in late-twentieth- and early-twenty-first-century America: most of his poems (like the matter-of-factly bizarre "Serious Partying") are spoken by a troubled, bemused, thoughtful, thoroughly contemporary man who is himself "the remnants of a people."

Jones has won the Associated Writing Programs Award Series (1980), a Guggenheim Fellowship (1985), the National Book Critics Circle Award for Poetry for *Transparent Gestures* (1989), and many other prizes for his work.

WORKS: *The Story They Told Us of Light* (1980). *The Unborn* (1985). *Transparent Gestures* (1989). *Apocalyptic Narrative* (1993). *Things That Happen Once* (1996). *Elegy for the Southern Drawl* (1999). *Kingdom of the Instant* (2002).

—MICHAEL MCFEE

DONALD JUSTICE (1925–2004). This Florida-born son/husband/father/musician/teacher/editor/writer attended the University of Miami (B.A., 1945), the University of North Carolina at Chapel Hill (M.A., 1947), Stanford University (1948–49), and the University of Iowa (Ph.D., 1954). His education was enhanced by such teachers as the composer Carl Ruggles and writers Yvor Winters, Paul Engle, Karl Shapiro, Robert Lowell, and John Berryman, among others. His writing brought him numerous recognitions, including the Lamont Poetry Selection (1959), the Pulitzer Prize (1980), and the Bollingen Prize in Poetry (1991). Justice taught writing at several universities, ending at the University of Iowa, where he retired in 1992.

Justice's oeuvre includes short stories, essays, plays, librettos, and his first love, poetry. Critics have praised his poetic precision, the naturalness of his language, his vibrant meter, his memorable images and motifs, and his subtle themes—best described as "poetic elegance." Justice's poetry provides readers with a sensitivity to the rhythm of language, a marriage of music and vocabulary integrating sound, sense, and structure. *New and Selected Poems* provides in one volume a historical perspective on his poetic development in formal and free verse forms. In the section "New Poems," for example, traditional forms and variations on them include the distich ("On a Picture by Burchfield"), the sonnet ("The Artist Orpheus"), the pantoum ("Pantoum of the Great Depression"), and the virelay ("Sadness"), along with freer, more experimental verse ("Lorca in California" and "The Miami of Other Days").

An understanding of Justice's own poetry is illuminated by his essays about the poetry of Charles Baudelaire, T. S. Eliot, Wallace Stevens, Yvor Winters, and others in his collection *Oblivion: On Writers and Writing*. In that volume, the essay "Oblivion: Variations on a Theme" addresses the essential qualities of an artist's dimension of self and spiritual dedication to art. Those qualities are found in obscure poets and poem fragments, too, before oblivion sets in. They are qualities that serve Justice well in his poetry. Described as a "poet's poet," Justice strove to write in new and different ways and always for poetic perfection. He died on August 6, 2004, in Iowa City. He is survived by his wife, Jean Ross, and their son, Nathaniel.

WORKS: *The Summer Anniversaries* (1960). Ed., *The Collected Poems of Weldon Kees* (1960). *A Local Storm* (1963). Ed., *Contemporary French Poetry*, with Alexander Aspel (1965). *Night Light* (1967). *Sixteen Poems* (1970). *From a Notebook* (1972). *Departures* (1973). *Selected Poems* (1979). Ed., *Platonic Scripts* (1984). *The Sunset Maker: Poems/Stories/A Memoir* (1987). Ed., *The Collected Poems of Henri Coulette*, with Robert Mezey (1990). *A Donald Justice Reader: Selected Poetry and Prose*, ed. Robert Pack and Jay Parini (1991). *New and Selected Poems* (1995). Ed., *Comma after Love: Selected Poems of Raeburn Miller*, with Cooper R. Mackin and Richard D. Olson (1996). *Oblivion: On Writers and Writing* (1998). Ed., Joe Bolton, *The Last Nostalgia: Poems 1981–1990* (1999). *Donald Justice in Conversation with Philip Hoy* (2002).

—JAMES A. GRIMSHAW, JR.

JAN KARON (1937–). Jan Karon was born Janice Meredith Wilson in Lenoir, N.C. Karon came by her literary roots early in life: she was named after the title of Paul L. Ford's *Janice Meredith: A Story of the American Revolution,* and she crafted her first novel when she was ten years old. At eighteen, Karon took a job as a receptionist at an advertising agency. She worked her way up in the advertising field with assignments that took her from North Carolina to New York City and San Francisco.

At the age of forty-eight, Karon, then a creative vice president, left her award-winning, thirty-year career in advertising to become a full-time writer. She relocated to Blowing Rock, N.C., a small town much like the fictional one in her popular "Mitford Years" novels. *At Home in Mitford,* Karon's first novel in the series, was published in 1994, followed a year later by *A Light in the Window.* Karon's books have earned her a loyal following of readers, as well as numerous prizes, including the Evangelical Christian Publishers Association Gold Medallion Book Award and a Christy Award in 2000 for *A New Song.* Karon was also awarded a Parents' Choice Gold Award for *Jeremy: The Tale of an Honest Bunny,* a children's book. Karon's novels have appeared on best-seller lists across the country. *Out to Canaan* and *A Common Life* reached the top of the *New York Times* best-seller list.

Karon, the founder of the Mitford Children's Foundation, has one daughter and currently resides on a farm in Virginia.

WORKS: *At Home in Mitford* (1994). *A Light in the Window* (1995). *These High, Green Hills* (1996). *The Mitford Years Reading Guide* (1997). *Out to Canaan* (1997). *Miss Fannie's Hat,* illustrated by Toni Goffe (1998). *A New Song* (1999).

Jeremy: The Tale of an Honest Bunny, illustrated by Terry Weidner (2000). *A Common Life: The Wedding Story* (2001). *Father Timothy A. Kavanagh* (2001). *The Mitford Snowmen: A Christmas Story* (2001). *Patches of Godlight: Father Tim's Favorie Quotes* (2001). *Esther's Gift: A Mitford Christmas Story* (2002). *In This Mountain* (2002). *Shepherds Abiding: A Mitford Christmas Story* (2003). *The Trellis and the Seed: A Book of Encouragement for All Ages*, illustrated by Robert Gantt Steel (2003). *Jan Karon's Mitford Cookbook and Kitchen Reader*, ed. Martha McIntosh (2004). *A Continual Feast: Words of Comfort and Celebration, Collected by Father Tim* (2005). *Light from Heaven* (2005).

—SHANNON MCKENNA

ELIZABETH KECKLEY (ca. 1820–1907). Elizabeth Hobbs Keckley was born a slave in Dinwiddie Court House, Va., around 1820. Regularly loaned to her owner's family members and friends, Keckley was often abused as she moved around Virginia and North Carolina. Eventually she arrived in the household of Hugh and Anne Garland in the frontier town of St. Louis, Mo. There Keckley's talents as a seamstress were discovered. She earned enough to support the entire family and, in 1860, was able to purchase her freedom and move to Washington, D.C.

Keckley quickly established herself as a dressmaker and gained many prominent clients, including the wives of Charles Sumner and Jefferson Davis. Mrs. Davis was so taken with Keckley that she invited her to come south with the family after Mississippi seceded. Keckley declined, and soon after received her first commission to make a dress for Mary Todd Lincoln, wife of the president-elect.

Mary Lincoln and Keckley developed a close friendship that would last for the next seven years. Keckley served as her "modiste," advising her on fashion, designing her dresses, and helping her prepare for public events. In this role, Keckley earned the first lady's trust and was a witness to the domestic life of the family throughout Abraham Lincoln's presidency. After he was assassinated, Keckley traveled with his widow and their sons to Chicago and helped them settle there.

In 1868 Keckley published *Behind the Scenes; Or, Thirty Years a Slave and Four Years in the White House*. After an opening section describing her life as a slave, Keckley describes her years in the Lincoln White House. Her portrayals of the Lincoln children and her candid accounts of the character of Mary Lincoln have proven essential to historians and biographers of the Lincolns. Although Keckley claimed to have written the book in order to raise money to help the Lincoln family, Mary Lincoln was angered by the personal details revealed in the book and ended her friendship with Keckley.

Some critics have questioned Keckley's authorship of *Behind the Scenes*. It is known that during the period she would have been writing the book, she met regularly with Washington writer James Redpath. Despite these misgivings, the facts of Keckley's story are believed to be true.

After the publication of *Behind the Scenes*, Keckley lost many of her prominent white clients but remained in Washington, D.C., for most of the rest of her life, making her living by teaching dressmaking.

WORKS: *Behind the Scenes; Or, Thirty Years and Slave and Four Years in the White House* (1868).

—NICHOLAS GRAHAM

HELEN KELLER (1880–1968). A writer and distinguished human being who overcame blindness and deafness to become an international symbol of the indomitable human spirit, Helen Adams Keller was born on June 27, 1880, near Tuscumbia, Ala. Her father, Arthur Keller, a self-styled "gentleman farmer," served successively as a captain in the Confederate army, a weekly newspaper publisher, and a U.S. marshal. Her mother, Kate (Adams), was a Memphis belle with prominent New England connections. Having read of Dr. Samuel Gridley Howe's successful training of the blind Laura Bridgman at the Perkins Institution in Boston, Kate Keller arranged through Perkins for Anne Sullivan (later Macy) to come to Alabama to teach her daughter.

On March 3, 1887—which Helen Keller was to call her "soul's birthday"—began the legendary collaboration between innovative teacher and extraordinary pupil. After an initial tumultuous contest of wills, Keller learned—when Annie spelled W-A-T-E-R into her hand—that "everything had a name, and each name gave birth to a new thought. That living word awakened my soul, gave it light, hope, joy, set it free." Tutored privately, continuously, and intensively by Sullivan and others, Keller entered Radcliffe in 1900 with a reading knowledge of Latin, Greek, French, and German, continuing to work at the most difficult language of all—spoken speech. Before graduating cum laude in 1904, Keller had published her autobiography, *The Story of My Life*, which laid out the prototype for successful education of the deaf and blind and did much to dispel their socially imposed isolation in and out of demeaning asylums.

Keller's intelligence, principled stand on social justice (reinforced by her Swedenborgian faith), and gracious warmth made her an international spokesperson for humanitarian issues—particularly as addressed by the Socialist Party until 1921. Between 1920 and 1924, Keller and Macy toured the vaudeville circuit. Thereafter, from homes in Wrentham, Mass., and Forest Hills, N.Y., she devoted the bulk of her efforts to fund raising and social action efforts for the American Foundation for the Blind. Keller's optimistic activism, expressed in person and through her numerous writings, enhanced her work and brought her international acclaim, including the Presidential Medal of Freedom in 1964. She died on June 1, 1968.

WORKS: *The Story of My Life* (1902). *Optimism: An Essay* (1903). *The World I Live In* (1908). *Out of the Dark* (1913). *The Song of the Stone Wall* (1910). *Out of the Dark: Essays, Letters, and Addresses on Physical and Social Vision* (1913). *My Religion* (1927). *Midstream: My Later Life* (1929). *We Bereaved* (1929). *Double Blossoms* (1931). *Peace at Eventide* (1932). *Helen Keller in Scotland*, ed. J. K. Love (1933). *Helen Keller's Journal, 1936–1937* (1938). *American Foundation for the Blind, 1923–1938: A Report from Helen Keller to the Blind People of America* (1938). *Let Us Have Faith* (1941). *Teacher: Anne Sullivan Macy, A Tribute by the Foster-child [sic] of Her Mind* (1955). *Open Door* (1957). *Helen Keller, Her Socialist Years: Writings and Speeches*, ed. Philip S. Foner (1967).

—LYNN Z. BLOOM

RANDALL KENAN (1963–). Born in Brooklyn in 1963 to young parents, at the age of six weeks Randall Garrett Kenan was taken to live with his paternal grandparents in the coastal plains town of Wallace, N.C. Eventually, he would come to live in the nearby farming village of Chinquapin with his great-uncle Redden (who died when Kenan was six) and his great-aunt Mary, whom Kenan grew up calling "Mama." There he lived in the family's ancestral homeplace, on land that had been in the family for five generations.

From 1981 to 1985 he studied at the University of North Carolina at Chapel Hill, where he abandoned his boyhood dream of becoming a scientist and instead majored in English, studying fiction writing with Doris Betts and Max Steele. Afterward, he left North Carolina for the city of his birth to work in New York's publishing industry. With the publication of his own first novel, *A Visitation of Spirits*, Kenan began teaching writing—at Duke University, Sarah Lawrence, and the University of Memphis. In 2003 he became associate professor of English at his alma mater.

In *Visitation* and in the 1992 collection of stories *Let the Dead Bury Their Dead* (finalist for the National Book Critics Circle Award and a nominee for the Los Angeles Times Book Prize), Kenan fictionalizes his home town of Chinquapin as Tims Creek, an autonomous, unincorporated community of black farmers, with the Baptist church at its center. While he celebrates the African American folklore of eastern North Carolina, as a gay writer Kenan often finds problematic the rigid sexual mores of this traditional society. One of the predominant themes in his fiction and in his travelogue *Walking on Water: Black American Lives at the Turn of the Twenty-First Century* is the deracination of rural black communities in America that has resulted from urbanization and desegregation. Kenan has also published a young adults' biography of James Baldwin. His awards include a Guggenheim Fellowship, a Whiting Writers' Award, and the Sherwood Anderson Award.

WORKS: *A Visitation of Spirits* (1989). *Let the Dead Bury Their Dead* (1992). *James Baldwin* (1994). *Walking on Water: Black American Lives at the Turn of the Twenty-First Century* (1999).

—GEORGE HOVIS

JOHN PENDLETON KENNEDY (1795–1870). John Pendleton Kennedy was born in Baltimore on October 25, 1795, to John Kennedy, a Baltimore merchant, and Nancy Pendleton Kennedy. His mother's ancestral Shenandoah Valley estate in Martinsburg, Va., known as The Bower, became Kennedy's model for Swallow Barn, the plantation setting of his first novel, which for fictional purposes he moved from the western Virginia countryside to the Tidewater, James River area. Kennedy was loyal to the roots of both of his parents yet lived most of his life in Baltimore, where he married twice into prominent families (first wife Mary Tenant died in 1824; he married Elizabeth Gray in 1829), fashioned a distinguished law career, and served in the Maryland House of Delegates. He was also elected to the U.S. House of Representatives and served as Millard Fillmore's secretary of the navy, supporting Commodore Perry's expedition to Japan. Through his friendship with the philanthropist George Peabody, he directed the building of the Peabody Institute in Baltimore·and served as president of its board of directors. All of his papers and the contents of his extensive library are housed in the Peabody Library.

Kennedy was a man of letters as well as of politics, and a friend of William Thackeray and Washington Irving, whose "sketchbook" style was an important model. His most important literary friendship was with fellow Baltimorean Edgar Allan Poe. In 1833 Kennedy served as a judge on a panel that awarded Poe's "MS. Found in a Bottle" a literary prize. He became Poe's mentor, recommending him for the editorship of the *Southern Literary Messenger* and ranking him as "one of the best prose critics in this country." Kennedy's own literary reputation rests on the three southern-plotted novels that he wrote in the 1830s.

Horseshoe Robinson dealt with loyalist versus patriot conflict in South Carolina during the American Revolution, and *Rob of the Bowl* was set in seventeenth-century Baltimore. Both were historical romances built upon the Sir Walter Scott formula of conflicts between classes during times of social and political upheaval. It is Kennedy's first novel, *Swallow Barn,* that has endured as a classic antebellum example of the plantation novel genre, providing a sentimental rendering of the staples that would dominate southern local color fiction after the Civil War: happy slaves serving gentlemen and belles in an idyllic rural sanctuary. The book is actually gently satiric of the romantic notions and foppish manners of the planters, yet it is unquestionably slanted, particularly in its 1851 revision, to promote a paternalistic view of slavery and the nonmaterialistic gentility of the master class.

WORKS: *Swallow Barn; or, A Sojourn in the Old Dominion* (1832; rev. ed. 1851). *Horse-Shoe Robinson* (1835). *Rob of the Bowl: A Legend of St. Inigoe's* (1838). *Quodilebet* (1840). *Memoirs of the Life of William Wirt* (1849; rev. ed. 1856 [2 vols.]). *Autograph Leaves of Our Country's Authors* (1864). *At Home and Abroad: A Series of Essays, With a Journal in Europe in 1867–8* (1872).

—LUCINDA H. MACKETHAN

CHARLES WILLIAM KENT (1860–1917). Noted educator, editor, and lecturer Charles William Kent was born on September 27, 1860, in Kalona, Louisa County, Va. His parents were Robert Meredith and Sallie Garland Hunter Kent. Educated at schools in Louisa County, Kent entered the University of Virginia in 1878 and graduated in 1882 with an M.A. After graduation, he and his college friend Lewis Minor Coleman founded the University School in Charleston, S.C., where Kent taught from 1882 until 1884. Then he went to Germany to study English and modern languages at Göttingen, Berlin, and finally Leipzig, where he took a Ph.D. in 1887.

After a year spent teaching French and German at the University of Virginia, Kent became professor of English and modern languages at the University of Tennessee, where he remained until 1893. That year he accepted the newly established chair at the University of Virginia in the Linden Kent Memorial School of English Literature, named for his older brother. On June 4, 1895, he married Eleanor Miles. Professor Kent remained on the faculty at the University of Virginia until his death on October 15, 1917.

Kent was a member of Phi Kappa Psi fraternity, Phi Beta Kappa, the Virginia state board of education, and the executive committee of the Virginia Historical Society. He was president of both the Young Men's Christian Association and the Poe Memorial Association. He was a Progressive Democrat and a member of the Disciples of Christ Church. Gifted at oratory and a serious student of the Bible, he taught a Sunday school Bible class with a regular enrollment of 150.

Perhaps the best known of the many volumes edited by Kent is the *Library of Southern Literature*. In addition to serving as literary editor of that project, he contributed pieces on John James Audubon, Lafcadio Hearn, Thomas Nelson Page, and others.

WORKS EDITED: *Cynewulf's Elene* (1889). *Shakespeare Note-book* (1897). *Idyls of the Lawn* (1899). *The Cotter's Saturday Night* (1901). *The Princess: A Medley by Alfred Tennyson* (1901). *Selected Poems of Robert Burns* (1901). *The Unveiling of the Bust of Edgar Allan Poe in the Library of the University of Virginia* (1901). *Poems of Edgar Allan Poe* (1903). *The Book of the Poe Centenary*, with John S. Patton (1909). *Library of Southern Literature*, with Edwin Anderson Alderman and Joel Chandler Harris, 17 vols. (1909–23). *The Land Where We Were Dreaming and Other Poems of Daniel Bedinger Lucas*, with Virginia Lucas (1913). *Dramatic Works of Daniel Bedinger Lucas*, with Virginia Lucas (1913). *Southern Poems* (1913).

—DOROTHY MCINNIS SCURA

FRANCIS SCOTT KEY (1779–1843). Second of four children of John Ross Key, an army officer in the Revolutionary War, and the former Anne Phoebe Charlton, Francis Scott Key was born on August 1, 1779, at the family estate, Terra Rubra, south of Taneytown, Md. After graduating as salutatorian from St. John's College, Annapolis, in 1796, he studied law privately and commenced practice at Frederick in 1801. In 1802 he married Mary Tayloe Lloyd; they settled at Georgetown, where he practiced law with great success for some thirty years. He moved to Washington when he was appointed U.S. attorney for the District of Columbia in 1833, a position he held until 1841.

A combination of courage and circumstance led to his authorship of "The Star-Spangled Banner," originally written as a poem during the War of 1812, then sung to the tune of a popular English drinking song, "To Anacreon in Heaven," and finally declared the national anthem of the United States in 1931. Having invaded and captured Washington in August 1814, the British prepared for an attack on Baltimore by land and sea. A much-admired physician, Dr. William Beanes, had been captured by the British and was being held on the British flagship, where it was feared he would be hanged. Key was asked to negotiate with the British. With the help of a negotiator, Col. John Skinner, and flying a flag of truce provided by President Madison, Key sailed to the British flagship and arranged for the release of Beanes. However, the Americans had observed so much of the British preparations for the siege of Baltimore that they were placed under guard and forced to wait out the battle behind the British fleet.

From his unique vantage point, Key watched the bombardment of Fort McHenry on the night of September 13–14, 1814. An amateur versifier, he saw the fort's huge flag as a symbol of the American cause, and when the British decided to retreat in the morning, Key was moved to write the poem on the way to shore.

Although Key had been known to pen Episcopalian hymns and occasional poems, he did not regard himself as a literary person or seek publication. Ironically, his printed legacy consists almost exclusively of orations, discourses, and speeches. And at the time of his death, Key could not have conceived of the countless commemorations of his name as the author of "The Star-Spangled Banner."

WORKS: *An oration . . . Before the Washington Society of Alexandria* ([1814]). *A discourse on education, delivered in St. Anne's Church, Annapolis . . . February 22nd, 1827 . . . .* (1827). *Oration . . . in the rotunda of the Capitol of the U. States, on the 4th of July, 1831* (1831). *Speech . . . counsel for Gen. Samuel Houston . . . before the House of Representatives . . . .* (1832). *The Power of Literature and Its Connexion with Religion: An Oration . . . July 23, 1834 . . . .* (1834). *A Part of a Speech . . . on the Trial of Reuben Crandall, M.D. . . .* (1836). *Speech . . . Before the Colonization Convention, May 9, 1842* ([1842]). *Poems of the Late Francis S. Key, Esq.* (1857).

—K. HUNTRESS BALDWIN

FRANCES PARKINSON KEYES (1885–1970). Though born in Virginia and famous for fiction about Louisiana, Frances Parkinson Wheeler Keyes was of New England stock. Her father, John Henry Wheeler, a Bostonian, was head of the Greek department at the University of Virginia when his daughter was born on July 21, 1885. Her mother, Louise Fuller Johnson, was from Vermont, and after her husband died, when Frances was two, she returned to New England and remarried. Frances's formal education was erratic. Privately tutored and briefly a student at Miss Winsor's in Boston, she lived in Geneva when she was ten and later studied in Berlin, becoming fluent in several languages. She later received honorary degrees from George Washington University, Bates College, and the University of New Hampshire.

At eighteen, she married Henry Wilder Keyes, twenty-seven years her senior. The couple had three sons. Harry Keyes was elected governor of New Hampshire in 1916 and was a U.S. senator from 1918 until shortly before his death in 1938. Frances Keyes, who had wanted to be a writer since childhood, published her first novel in 1919. Her first success was a collection of *Good Housekeeping* articles about Washington life, *Letters from a Senator's Wife*. She wrote nonfiction throughout her career, often based on her extensive travels abroad. She became a Roman Catholic in 1939 and wrote a number of popular lives of saints. She received several honors for her religious activism, including the Siena Medal in 1946 as an outstanding Catholic woman.

Though Keyes preferred writing fiction, she had a journalist's eye for detail and commitment to facts. Her carefully researched settings, combined with inventive storytelling, romantic plots, and patrician characters, resulted in several best-sellers. A visit to New Orleans in 1940 launched a series of novels about Louisiana, including *Crescent Carnival* and *Dinner at Antoine's*. With over fifty volumes of fiction, biography, and travel writing—seven of which achieved best-seller status—Keyes was a popular writer, often translated, with a well-deserved reputation for the skillful evocation of place and period. For many years, she lived in the New Orleans residence of Confederate general P. G. T. Beauregard, which she restored in the 1950s, and where she died on July 3, 1970.

WORKS: *The Old Gray Homestead* (1919). *The Career of David Noble* (1921). *Letters from a Senator's Wife* (1924). *Queen Anne's Lace* (1930). *Silver Seas and Golden Cities* (1931). *Lady Blanche Farm* (1931). *Senator Marlowe's Daughter* (1933). *The Safe Bridge* (1934). *The Happy Wanderer* (1935). *Honor Bright* (1936). *Capital Kaleidoscope* (1937). *Pioneering People in Northern New England* (1937). *Written in Heaven* (1937); rev. as *Therese: Saint of a Little Way* (1950). *Parts Unknown* (1938). *The Great Tradition* (1939). *Along a Little Way* (1940). *The Sublime Shepherdess* (1940); rev. as *Bernadette of Lourdes* (1953). *Fielding's Folly* (1940). *The Grace of Guadalupe* (1941). *All That Glitters* (1941). *Crescent Carnival* (1942). *Also the Hills* (1943). *The River Road* (1945). *Came a Cavalier* (1947). *Once on Esplanade* (1947). *Dinner at Antoine's* (1948). *Joy Street* (1950). *All This Is Louisiana* (1950). *The Cost of a Best Seller* (1950). *Steamboat Gothic* (1952). *The Royal Box* (1954). *Frances Parkinson Keyes Cookbook* (1955). *Saint Anne: Grandmother of Our Savior* (1955). *Blue Camellia* (1957). *The Land of Stones and Saints* (1957). *Victorine* (1958). *Station Wagon in Spain* (1959). *Mother Cabrini: Missionary to the World* (1959). *Christmas Gift* (1959). *The Third Mystic of Avila* (1960). *Roses in December* (1960). *The Chess Players* (1960). *The Rose and the Lily* (1961). *The Restless Lady and Other Stories* (1961). *Madame Castel's Lodger* (1962). Ed., *A Treasury of Favorite Poems* (1963). *Three Ways of Love* (1963). *The Explorer* (1964). *I, the King* (1966). *Tongues of Fire* (1966). *The Heritage* (1968). *All Flags Flying* (1972).

—BARBARA C. EWELL

JOHN OLIVER KILLENS (1916–1987). John Oliver Killens was born in Macon, Ga., on January 14, 1916. He attended Edward Waters College, Brown College, and Howard University, and went on to study law at Terrell Law School, New York University, and Columbia University, though he later abandoned law to devote himself to writing.

Killens was deeply aware of racial and social injustice, and these themes shaped his life and work. From 1936 to 1942 he served on the National Labor Relations Board, where he became increasingly politicized. As a writer and activist, he was concerned with the development of black community and black heroism. His second novel, *And Then We Heard the Thunder,* draws on his own experience as a black soldier in World War II; novels such as *Youngblood,* *'Sippi,* and *The Cotillion* explore the consequences of racial prejudice and inequality. All of his novels are notable for their treatment of African American folklore and vernacular. Killens was a prolific essayist as well, publishing the collection *Black Man's Burden,* which articulated many of his controversial social and political positions. He also wrote and co-wrote screenplays and stage plays, including *Lower than the Angels,* which was produced in New York City.

Killens held a number of academic posts, including that of writer-in-residence at Fisk University (1965–68), at Columbia University (1970–73), and at Bronx Community College (1979–81). He founded the Harlem Writers Guild and served as vice president of the Black Academy of American Arts and Letters. He was writer-in-residence at Medgar Evers College of the City University of New York when he died of cancer on October 27, 1987.

WORKS: *Youngblood* (1954). *And Then We Heard the Thunder* (1963). *Black Man's Burden* (1965). *'Sippi* (1967). *Slaves* (1969). *The Cotillion; or, One Good Bull Is Half the Herd* (1971). *Great Gittin' Up Morning: A Biography of Denmark Vesey* (1972). *A Man Ain't Nothing but a Man: The Adventures of John Henry* (1975). *Great Black Russian: A Novel on the Life and Times of Alexander Pushkin* (1989). Ed., *Black Southern Voices: An Anthology of Fiction, Poetry, Drama, Nonfiction, and Critical Essays,* with Jerry W. Ward (1992).

—TESSA JOSEPH

NANCI KINCAID (1950–). Nanci Pierce Kincaid was born in Tallahassee, Fla., in 1950, the daughter of two educators. Her family lived in a neighborhood at the edge of Frenchtown, a predominantly

African American part of the city, and her childhood experiences there inspired her first novel, *Crossing Blood*. Kincaid recalls always wanting to be a writer, but had to defer her ambitions when she got married, at nineteen, to Al Kincaid, who became a football coach. They had two daughters. Nanci Kincaid went back to college and earned a B.A. at Athens State in 1987, then an M.F.A. at the University of Alabama in 1991. In Tuscaloosa, she finished *Crossing Blood*, which tells of the intense and risky friendship between Lucy, a white girl, and Skippy, the son of her family's housekeeper, in segregated Tallahassee. By the mid-1990s, Kincaid was divorced and living outside the South, but always revisiting it in her fiction. In 1997 she married Dick Tomey, who was at that time head football coach at the University of Arizona. After a number of relocations, Tomey became the head coach at San Jose State University in 2005.

Kincaid's characters are often women torn between old ideals of white southern ladyhood and the siren pull of self-actualization. In 1998 she published *Balls*, a novel about the tribal, testosterone-fired world of college football recounted through the voices of players' and coaches' wives, girlfriends, and mothers. A later novel, *Verbena*, is set in rural Alabama and tells the story of a widowed teacher with five children and a complicated relationship with the mailman. Kincaid's work shows the influence of Eudora Welty in its humor and attention to the domestic sphere, as well as of Zora Neale Hurston. She wittily borrows the multiple-narrator structure of *As I Lay Dying* for *Balls*, reinventing Addie Bundren as Dixie Carraway, a former homecoming queen turned football widow. Kincaid's South is a far cry from Faulkner's haunted landscape, but her fiction reveals that under the shiny veneer of *Southern Living*–style suburban affluence, the old race, class, and gender conflicts still rage.

WORKS: *Crossing Blood* (1992). *Pretending the Bed Is a Raft: Stories* (1997). *Balls: A Novel* (1998). *Verbena: A Novel* (2002). *As Hot as It Was You Ought to Thank Me: A Novel* (2005).

—DIANE ROBERTS

FLORENCE KING (1936–). Born on January 5, 1936, in Washington, D.C., humorist Florence King was the only child of Herbert King, a bookish English dance band musician, and Louise Ruding King, a chain-smoking baseball fan. King's acclaimed humorous *Confessions of a Failed Southern Lady* recounts her unconventional upbringing and her grandmother's vain attempt to turn Florence into a southern lady.

King attended American University on scholarship, receiving a B.A. in history in 1957. While in college, she joined a sorority and completed most of the training in the Marines' Woman Officer Candidate School at Quantico. She attended graduate school in history at the University of Mississippi on scholarship, and there fell in love with a female graduate student who died in an auto accident. King left without the M.A., encouraged to write by payments for stories written for true confessions magazines. She worked briefly for American Can, taught tenth grade, and was an assistant editor. She has lived in New Jersey, Massachusetts, Arizona, and Washington state, spending ten years in Seattle before returning to Virginia, where she has lived in Fredericksburg since 1982. She has never married, considering writing to be her first love.

King began by writing true confessions from 1958 to 1964, but she soon turned to journalism, which she has written throughout her career. From 1964 to 1967 she was the woman's page feature writer for the *Raleigh News and Observer*, winning two North Carolina Press Women awards for reporting and interviewing. Since 1968 she has supported herself as a free-lance writer. Under pseudonyms including Cynthia Veronica King, Emmett X. Reed, Niko Stavros, and Mike Winston, she penned thirty-seven "erotic adventures" between 1968 and 1973. King's iconoclastic essays have appeared in *Cosmopolitan, Harper's, Ms., Redbook*, and other magazines, and she has written reviews for many newspapers, including the *Philadelphia Inquirer, Baltimore Sun,* and *New York Times Book Review.* She began her continuing monthly column, "The Misanthrope's Corner," for the *National Review* in 1990. In 1993 she initiated her literary column, "The Open Book," for the *Raleigh News and Observer.* She has served on panels for the *American Heritage Dictionary* and the National Book Critics Circle.

Southern Ladies and Gentlemen earned King a reputation as a regional humorist in the late 1970s. Since then she has often employed a taxonomy of "types" (WASPs, American men, southerners, etc.) in her conservative satires of feminists, liberals, and politically correct sacred cows. *Confessions of a Failed Southern Lady* attracted a national readership in 1985. King considers it to be her first mature work. While some reviewers find her work ephemeral, most find it refreshing and hilarious.

WORKS: *Southern Ladies and Gentlemen* (1975). *WASP, Where Is Thy Sting?* (1977). *The Barbarian Princess,* as Laura Buchanan (1978). *He: An Irreverent Look at the American Male* (1978). *When Sisterhood Was in Flower* (1982). *Confessions of a Failed Southern Lady* (1985). *Reflections in a Jaundiced Eye* (1989). *Lump It or Leave It* (1990). *With Charity toward None: A Fond Look at Misanthropy* (1992). *Satan's Child: A Survivor Tells Her Story to Help Others,* as Laura Buchanan (1994). *The Florence King Reader* (1995).

—KATHRYN VANSPANCKEREN

GRACE KING (1852–1932). Native New Orleanian Grace Elizabeth King was known during her lifetime as a gracious southern lady of letters, but criticized by twentieth-century critics as an apologist for the southern ideology of racial oppression. Her short fiction, novels, histories, and memoir provide a contemporary view of life in the Reconstruction-era South. King is remembered for her use of local color to illustrate life in the thriving and racially complicated New Orleans society.

Grace King was born on November 29, 1852, into a family that enjoyed the privileges afforded by land ownership. Her mother, Sarah Ann Miller, was her father's second wife, and her father, William Woodson King, was a well-regarded attorney who believed that education would benefit his daughters. At the onset of the Civil War, the King family fled from New Orleans to their plantation in rural St. Martin Parish. Returning to New Orleans after the war, the Kings endured the financial hardships common to the former land-owning class during Reconstruction.

Grace King studied at the Institute St. Louis, graduating at sixteen, and continued her intellectual endeavors with private tutors. It was not until later in her life, however, that she embarked on a career as a writer. Although she published minor works prior to 1885, a conversation with the editor of *Century* magazine, Richard Watson Gilder, led her to begin writing in earnest. In her discussion with Gilder, she criticized the work of George Washington Cable, arguing that he portrayed Creole society inaccurately and taking exception to his depictions of African Americans as the equals of their white counterparts. Gilder challenged King to write stories that would counteract Cable's and articulate what, in her view, would be a more accurate representation of the racial and gender conflicts inherent in the South. As her writing career flourished, King maintained a lifelong relationship with Samuel and Olivia Clemens; her writing was also influenced by the feminism of Isabelle Hooker and Julia Ward Howe.

Examining race and gender, many of her stories are set in the antebellum South. Capitalizing on the growing national appetite for local color stories that showed the picturesque qualities of Louisiana life, King's fiction reinforced the racial caste system implicit in the region, often focusing specifically on the plight of the mixed-race woman in southern society. Other stories illustrated the effects of Reconstruction on the Old South and its supporters. King died of nephritis in 1932, leaving a body of work that examined women's lives, familial relationships, and the influence of race on a southern culture in the process of being redefined.

works: *Monsieur Mott* (1888). *Tales of a Time and a Place* (1892). *Jean Baptiste le Moyne, Sieur de Bienville* (1892). *Balcony Stories* (1893). *A History of Louisiana*, with John R. Ficklen (1893). *New Orleans, the Place and the People* (1895). *De Soto and His Men in the Land of Florida* (1898). *Stories from Louisiana History*, with Ficklen (1905). *The Pleasant Ways of St. Médard* (1916). *Creole Families of New Orleans* (1921). *Madame Girard, an Old French Teacher of New Orleans* (1922). *La Dame de Sainte Hermine* (1924). *The History of Mt. Vernon on the Potomac* (1929). *Memories of a Southern Woman of Letters* (1932). *Grace King of New Orleans: A Selection of Her Writings*, ed. Robert Bush (1973).

—Suzanne Disheroon-Green

LARRY L. KING (1929–). Freelance writer, novelist, and playwright, Larry King was born in Putnam, Tex., on January 1, 1929. He developed an interest in writing in elementary school and later in high school, where he wrote for the student newspaper and found inspiration for his writing in English teacher/football coach Aubra Nooncaster.

After working in the Texas oil fields, King joined the army in 1946, and served for two years as a reporter for the base newspaper. In 1949 he briefly attended Texas Technological College, where he majored in journalism. A year later he married Wilma Jeanne Casey, and subsequently worked as a sports and crime reporter for newspapers in Texas and New Mexico and as news director at a radio station in Midland, Tex. In the mid-1950s, King moved to Washington, D.C., where, for the next ten years, he worked for two Texas congressmen—first for J. T. Rutherford, and in 1962 for James C. Wright.

In 1964 King became a full-time freelancer, writing some of his most important articles, the best examining Texas life and culture and published in the *Texas Observer, Harper's, Sports Illustrated, Playboy*, and other magazines. King has collected some of his magazine essays, his best and most representative ones found in *And Other Dirty Stories, The Old Man and Lesser Mortals*, and *Of Outlaws, Con Men, Whores, Politicians, and Other Artists*. He published his first novel, *The One-Eyed Man*, in 1966. Yet the work that catapulted King to national prominence was *The Best Little Whorehouse in Texas*, a long-running Broadway musical. Since that time, King has written six additional plays. His other writings—television documentaries, screenplays, and short stories—attest to his versatility as a writer.

King has held fellowships at Harvard and Duke and an endowed chair at Princeton. He currently resides in Washington, D.C., with his wife, Barbara S. Blaine, who is also his lawyer and literary agent.

works: *The One-Eyed Man* (1966). *And Other Dirty Stories* (1968). *Confessions of a White Racist* (1971). *The Old Man and Lesser Mortals* (1974). *Wheeling and Dealing: The Best Little Whorehouse in Texas* (1978), with Peter Masterson and Carol Hall. *Confessions of a Capital Hill Operator*, with Bobby Baker (1978). *The Kingfish: A One-Man Play Loosely Depicting the Life and Times of the Late Huey P. Long of Louisiana*, with Ben Z. Grant (1979). *Of Outlaws, Con Men, Whores, Politicians, and Other Artists* (1980). *That Terrible Night Santa Got Lost in the Woods*, with Pat Oliphant (1981). *The Whorehouse Papers* (1982). *Warning: Writer at Work: The Best Collectibles of Larry L. King*, with Edwin Shrake (1985). *None but a Blockhead: On Being a Writer* (1986). *Christmas 1933* (1987). *The History of Calham and Vicinity, 1888–1988* (1987). *The Night Hank Williams Died* (1988). *The Golden Shadows Old West Museum* (1988). *The Best Little Whorehouse Goes Public*, with Peter Masterson and Carol Hall (1994). *The Dead Presidents' Club* (1996). *True Facts, Tall Tales and Pure Fiction* (1997). *Texas Short Stories 2* (1999). *Larry L. King: A Writer's Life in Letters; or, Reflections in a Bloodshot Eye* (1999), ed. Richard Holland. *The One-Eyed Man* (2001).

—Ed Piacentino

MARTIN LUTHER KING, JR. (1929–1968). Michael King, Jr., was born at home in Atlanta, Ga., on January 15, 1929. He was one of three children in an African American family steeped in a tradition of Baptist ministry and political action. While he was still a child, his father changed both their names to Martin Luther, after the sixteenth-century priest who sparked the Reformation. Mercurial but talented, King was able to enter Morehouse College at the age of fifteen, without graduating from Booker T. Washington High School. In 1948 he received a B.A. in sociology from Morehouse and became an ordained minister. He received a B.D. from Crozer Theological Seminary, in Chester, Pa. (1951), and a Ph.D. in theology from Boston University (1955). His dissertation was "A Comparison of the Conceptions of God in the Thinking of Paul Tillich and Henry Nelson Wieman."

In 1953 King married Coretta Scott, a voice student at the New England Conservatory of Music. The couple moved to Alabama, Coretta's home state, where Martin took leadership of the congregation of Montgomery's Dexter Avenue Baptist Church. In 1955 the activist E. D. Nixon called upon him to join the cause of Rosa Parks, a local black woman who had refused to give her bus seat to a white man, and King's course was set. His work during the Montgomery Bus Boycott brought him to national attention, which he parlayed into leadership of a new civil rights organization, the Southern Christian Leadership Conference. In 1959 he moved back to Atlanta, where the SCLC was based, and he and his father shared the pulpit at Ebenezer Baptist Church. In these years, Martin and Coretta began their own family, which eventually included four children: Yolanda, Martin Luther III, Dexter, and Bernice.

Taking inspiration from Thoreau and Gandhi, King was steadfastly nonviolent, even when physically attacked. Rather, he relied on the force of his example and on the strength of his words. King wrote much for publication: books such as *Stride toward Freedom*, which gives his account of the boycott and sets out his program for nonviolent direct action; and shorter pieces, most famously "Letter from Birmingham Jail," dated April 16, 1963, issued during one of his many arrests. But he excelled at oratory. His "I Have a Dream" speech, delivered before a quarter of a million civil rights marchers in Washington, D.C., on August 28, 1963, has become a rhetorical model for American students. The speech is notable for the clarity and beauty of its language, and for the parallel phrases that take their rhythm and structure from the high-flying sermon.

In January 1964 *Time* magazine named King "Man of the Year." In December of that year he received the Nobel Peace Prize and donated the cash award to civil rights groups. But despite such triumphs, King often despaired in the face of entrenched social and psychological opposition to racial equality. At an evening meeting in support of striking garbage workers in Memphis, Tenn., an exhausted but inspired King gave an address—often called "I've Been to the Mountaintop"—in which he surveyed his own life to that point and evoked the image of Moses gazing out on a promised land he would never reach. This was a kind of prophecy, for the next afternoon—April 4, 1968—King was shot as he stood chatting with colleagues on the balcony of the Lorraine Motel and died in St. Joseph's Hospital. James Earl Ray, a white drifter, pled guilty to the murder.

Even as the nuances of 1960s politics and prejudices were lost over time, events continued to stir memories, and resonances of King's life, death, and influence endured. In 1974 King's mother, Alberta, was shot to death during a service at Ebenezer Baptist Church. In the 1990s Ray, who had recanted his guilty plea and now sought a trial, found support in King's own family, who were open to conspiracy theories. Posthumous revelations of affairs with numerous women showed that King was no plaster saint; they also showed the extent to which J. Edgar Hoover's FBI spied on this private citizen. In counterpoise, Coretta Scott King, who never remarried, was a resolute, almost regal figure still championing her husband's memory and cause. Acolytes Andrew Jackson and Jesse Jackson, who witnessed King's shooting, carried his work forward into mainstream politics.

King's family, who hoped to benefit financially as they had not during his lifetime, laid legal claim to his literary output, including his speeches, which are frequently quoted. But their successful campaign to establish a national holiday in his honor signified the extent to which King has become part of the mass cultural consciousness. Martin Luther King, Jr., Day was first celebrated in the United States on January 20, 1986. This southern preacher, just thirty-nine when he died, now officially represents communally held ideas and ideals even more complex than celebrity and copyright.

WORKS: *Stride toward Freedom: The Montgomery Story* (1958). *The Measure of a Man* (1959). *Strength to Love* (1963). *Why We Can't Wait.* (1964). *Where Do We Go from Here: Chaos or Community?* (1967). *The Trumpet of Conscience* (1968). *A Testament of Hope* (1986). *The Papers of Martin Luther King, Jr.*, vols. 1–4, ed. Clayborne Carson, Ralph E. Luker, and Penny A. Russell (1992–2000).

—AMBER VOGEL

BARBARA KINGSOLVER (1955–). A writer known for her outspoken commitment to social justice and environmental preservation, Barbara Kingsolver has written powerful, engaging fiction, poetry, and nonfiction about the American West, southern Appalachia, and Africa.

Born on April 8, 1955, in Annapolis, Md., daughter of a county physician, Kingsolver spent most of her childhood in Carlisle, a town in eastern Kentucky. The family lived for almost a year in the Congo, when Kingsolver was in the second grade, while her father practiced medicine there. In Africa she began the lifelong habit of keeping a journal.

Although she entered DePauw University on a music scholarship, she switched her major to biology. She was in Greece and France as an archaeologist's assistant during her junior year. She received her degree in 1977. Degree in hand, Kingsolver lived for a time in France, then returned to the States to study ecology and evolutionary biology at the University of Arizona. She earned her M.A. in 1981. In 1985 she married Joseph Hoffman, a chemist. They had one daughter, Camille, but divorced in 1992. Abandoning plans for the Ph.D. in biology, Kingsolver accepted a position as a science writer for the Office of Land Studies at Arizona. Meanwhile, she began publishing poetry and short stories.

Kingsolver's immensely successful first novel, *The Bean Trees*, written in spare time while she was freelancing as a journalist, was published in 1988. About a young woman's flight west, *The Bean Trees* focuses on many of the issues that would become central to Kingsolver's work, including social and economic justice and racial tolerance. Kingsolver's fiction is anything but downbeat; her work, finally, is most concerned with the nurturing possibilities of community and family, of lives bound together in love and commitment.

Kingsolver's subsequent publications underscore her range of interests and talents: an oral history of a mine strike, *Holding the Line;* a short-story collection, *Homeland and Other Stories;* two more novels set in the West, *Animal Dreams* and *Pigs in Heaven;* a collection of poetry, *Another America: Otra América;* two collections of essays, *High Tide in Tucson* and *Small Wonder;* a work on Annie Griffiths Belt's nature photography, *Last Stand;* a novel set in Africa, *The Poisonwood Bible;* and a novel set in rural Appalachia, *Prodigal Summer.* All of her work exhibits her social and environmental activism.

Kingsolver lives with her second husband, Steven Hopp, and their two daughters, spending part of the year in Tucson and part on their farm in southern Appalachia. In recognition of her distinguished career, Kingsolver received the National Humanities Medal in 2000.

WORKS: *The Bean Trees* (1988). *Holding the Line: Women in the Great Arizona Mine Strike of 1983* (1989). *Homeland and Other Stories* (1989). *Animal Dreams* (1990). *Another America: Otra América* (1992). *Pigs in Heaven* (1993). *High Tide in Tucson: Essays from Now and Never* (1995). *The Poisonwood Bible* (1999). *Prodigal Summer* (2000). *Last Stand: America's Virgin Lands*, with Annie Griffiths Belt (2002). *Small Wonder* (2002).

—ROBERT H. BRINKMEYER, JR.

DAVID KIRBY (1944–). Born in Baton Rouge, La., David Kirby is the son of an elementary school teacher and Thomas Kirby, former chairperson of the Department of English at Louisiana State University. Kirby earned his Ph.D. at Johns Hopkins in 1969, under an experimental three-year doctoral program, and joined Florida State University's Department of English the same year. He is married to poet Barbara Hamby, with whom he has two sons, Will (winner, in 2001, of the U.S. version of the reality television show *Big Brother*) and Ian. Kirby has had a distinguished career teaching nineteenth- and twentieth-century American literature and poetry writing and has authored over twenty books and hundreds of poems, essays, and reviews. Now Guy McKenzie Professor and Robert O. Lawton Distinguished Professor of English at Florida State, Kirby has gathered many honors: grants from the National Endowment for the Arts, the Guy Owen and James Dickey prizes, four Pushcart Prizes, the Brittingham Prize, inclusion in *Best American Poetry* annuals twice, and a Guggenheim Fellowship.

Kirby's best works are his story-poems. He creates mostly unrhymed interpretations of actual events, in the natural cadences of spoken English. His agile and inviting poetry explores the sublime, the tragic, and the wryly or sometimes hilariously comic collocations and dislocations occurring daily in lives lived in this increasingly plural world—a world in which, Kirby discovers, the music of Sam Cooke can evoke Herman Melville and Little Richard's can evoke John Keats. His poetry chapbooks themselves include *The Opera Lover, Sarah Bernhardt's Leg, Saving the Young Men of Vienna, Big-Leg Music, The House of Blue Light,* and *The Ha-Ha.*

Kirby is also an energetic and prolific scholar. His resource guides to literary and intellectual traditions include a collection of essays on the individual and the community in American fiction; two annotated secondary bibliographies on American literature; and a useful and lively dictionary of terms that bridge fields in the arts, sciences, social sciences, and humanities in our "plural world." Among his critical books and discussions of literature are a bio-critical study of Grace King; an exploration of monism and quietism in Western culture; an analysis of Mark Strand's importance in the later twentieth century; examinations of melodrama in Henry James and of the picaro as recurring character and theme in Herman Melville; and an extended essay on what makes a book substantial and memorable, historically, intellectually, and aesthetically.

WORKS: *American Fiction to 1900: A Guide to Information Sources* (1975). Ed., *Individual and Community: Variations on a Theme in American Fiction,* with Kenneth H. Baldwin (1975). *The Opera Lover: Poems* (1977). *America's Hive of Honey; or, Foreign Influences on American Fiction through Henry James; Essays and Bibliographies* (1980). *Grace King* (1980). *The Sun Rises in the Evening: Monism and Quietism in Western Culture* (1982). *Sarah Bernhardt's Leg: Poems* (1983). *The Plural World: An Interdisciplinary Glossary of Contemporary Thought* (1984). *Diving for Poems* (1985). *Saving the Young Men of Vienna* (1987). *Writing Poetry: Where Poems Come From and How to Write Them* (1989). *Mark Strand and the Poet's Place in Contemporary Culture* (1990). *Boyishness in American Culture: The Charms and Dangers of Social Immaturity* (1991). *The Cows Are Going to Paris,* with Allen Woodman (1991). *"The Portrait of a Lady" and "The Turn of the Screw": Henry James and Melodrama* (1991). *Herman Melville* (1993). *Big-Leg Music* (1995). *My Twentieth Century: Poems* (1999). *The House of Blue Light: Poems* (2000). *The Travelling Library: Three Poems* (2001). *What Is a Book?* (2002). *The Ha-Ha: Poems* (2003). *I Think I Am Going to Call My Wife Paraguay: Selected Early Poems* (2004).

—R. BRUCE BICKLEY, JR.

ETHERIDGE KNIGHT (1931–1991). Born in Corinth, Miss., Etheridge Knight spent his young adulthood in the army, including a tour of combat duty in Korea, where he received a shrapnel wound. While in the army, he became addicted to heroin, and after his discharge in 1957 drifted from place to place until he was arrested for robbery in 1960 in Indiana. Encouraged by Gwendolyn Brooks and

Sonia Sanchez, who became his first wife, Knight wrote his first volume of poetry, *Poems from Prison*, while in jail. During the 1970s and 1980s, Knight continued to write poetry while teaching at a number of universities and winning prestigious awards, including a National Endowment for the Arts grant and a Guggenheim Fellowship, and he continued to struggle with his drug addiction. He remarried twice after his divorce from Sanchez. His second marriage produced two children, and his third, one before he died of cancer at age fifty-nine.

Although he has been linked with the Black Arts Movement, Knight's work does not demonstrate the overt militancy normally associated with the Black Aesthetic. His poems, instead, tend to be personal works dealing with the three most significant aspects of his experience: addiction, incarceration, and family. In his most southern and most famous work, "The Idea of Ancestry," a black inmate persona describes the pictures of his family taped to the wall of his cell and discovers that those faces are an inextricable part of his identity. Among his most moving poems is "Belly Song," which blends filial love and anguish as it compares the stretch marks on a pregnant woman's belly and the scars on a man's body. Although many of Knight's poems concern imprisonment—both literal and metaphorical—the dominant theme in his work is freedom, which he celebrates with the zeal of someone who has lived without it.

WORKS: *Poems from Prison* (1968). Ed., *Black Voices from Prison* (1970). *A Poem for Brotherman* (1972). *Belly Song and Other Poems* (1973). *Born of a Woman* (1980). *The Essential Etheridge Knight* (1986).

—DAVID A. DAVIS

YUSEF KOMUNYAKAA (1947–). Born James Brown in Bogalusa, La., in 1947, Yusef Komunyakaa changed his name to honor his grandfather, a stowaway from Trinidad. After high school, Komunyakaa joined the army and, as an information specialist, fulfilled a tour of duty in Vietnam (1969–70), where he saw combat and received a Bronze Star. Between 1975 and 1980, Komunyakaa earned a B.A. in English and sociology at the University of Colorado, an M.A. in creative writing at Colorado State University, and an M.F.A. in creative writing at the University of California at Irvine. After teaching at the University of New Orleans and Indiana University he became a professor at Princeton University in 1997.

Komunyakaa has published a dozen volumes of poetry, recorded three CDs of lyrical compilations with jazz musicians, and co-edited two editions of *The Jazz Poetry Anthology*. He won the 1994 Pulitzer Prize for poetry as well as the Kingsley-Tufts Poetry Award, was a finalist for the 1999 National Book Critics Circle Award, and was named a chancellor in the Academy of American Poets. He is most famous for his poetic recollections of Vietnam published in *Dien Cai Dau* and *Thieves of Paradise*.

Though he has built an impressive national reputation, Komunyakaa remains a poet of the South, writing from the vantage of an African American survivor of Jim Crow. His traumatic images of a racially vexed, poverty-stricken Louisiana explore intersections between the South and Vietnam, especially in bearing witness to racism at home and abroad. His style reflects a poetics of trauma: his terse, three- or four-beat lines are imbued with a frenetic energy through breakneck tonal shifts and a shockingly beautiful commingling of vernacular phrasings with surrealist imagery. Komunyakaa's verse reflects a strong and abiding claim for an African American presence in contemporary southern poetry.

WORKS: *Dedications and Other Darkhorses* (1977). *Lost in the Bonewheel Factory* (1979). *Copacetic* (1984). *I Apologize for the Eyes in My Head* (1986). *Toys in a Field* (1986). *Dien Cai Dau* (1988). *February in Sydney* (1989). *Magic City* (1992). Ed., *The Jazz Poetry Anthology*, 2 vols., with Sascha Feinstein (1991–96). *Neon Vernacular: New and*

Selected Poems (1993). *Thieves of Paradise* (1998). *Love Notes from the Madhouse,* poems read by Komunyakaa set to jazz by John Tchicai (1998). *Blue Notes: Essays, Interviews, and Commentaries* (2000). *Talking Dirty to the Gods: Poems* (2000). *Thirteen Kinds of Desire,* Komunyakaa's lyrics set to jazz and vocals by Pamela Knowles (2000). *Herido: Live at St. James Cathedral, Chicago,* Komunyakaa's lyrics set to jazz by Dennis Gonzalez (2001). *Pleasure Dome: New and Collected Poems* (2001). Ed., *The Best American Poetry* (2003). *Taboo* (2004).

—DANIEL C. TURNER

HARRY HARRISON KROLL (1888–1967). A realistic chronicler of southern rural and mountain life and a writer with a proletarian sensibility, Harry Harrison Kroll was born near Hartford City, Ind., on February 18, 1888. The son of a sharecropper, Kroll spent his formative years among farmers and share-croppers of Indiana, Tennessee, and Alabama. In 1905, with little formal schooling, he migrated to the Alabama coast, where he worked in the sawmills and as a photographer. Six years later he married Annette Heard, an Alabama schoolteacher, and the two of them taught in Alabama schools until 1921.

That same year Kroll entered Peabody College for Teachers in Nashville, where he received his B.A. in 1923 and his M.A. in 1925. He taught at Lincoln Memorial University in Harrogate, Tenn., from 1926 to 1928. This was followed by a short stint teaching journalis m at Iowa Wesleyan College, a posi-tion he relinquished in 1930 to become a full-time writer. In 1935 he returned to teaching as an Eng-lish instructor at the Tennessee Junior College in Martin, where he remained until he retired in 1958.

Kroll's first novel, *The Mountainy Singer,* celebrates the social customs and traditions of Tennessee mountaineers. *The Cabin in the Cotton,* his most heralded work, is reflective of his social consciousness and chronicles the conflict between a Mississippi plantation owner and his exploited tenants, the latter victims of a corrupt and inhumane system. *Their Ancient Grudge,* a best-seller, recounts the no-torious Hatfield-McCoy feud. Although Kroll also wrote an autobiography, *I Was a Sharecropper,* many additional novels, and numerous short stories, his most representative and memorable fiction treats southern small farmers, sharecroppers, and mountaineers and their impoverished and troubled lives. A few of his late and lesser known books explore a similar subject matter in a more romantic vein, but he never again reached the level of achievement of *The Cabin in the Cotton.* Kroll died on June 11, 1967.

WORKS: *The Mountainy Singer* (1928). *The Cabin in the Cotton* (1931). *Three Brothers and Seven Daddies* (1932). *I Was a Sharecropper* (1937). *The Ghosts of Slave Driver's Bend* (1937). *The Keeper's of the House* (1940). *The Usurper* (1941). *Dark Cabins,* selected and edited with Lealon N. Jones (1942). *The Rider on the Bronze Horse* (1942). *Perilous Journey: A Tale of the Mississippi River and the Natchez Trace,* with C. M. Sublette (1943). *Rogues Company: A Novel of John Murrell* (1943). *Waters over the Dam* (1944). *Fury in the Earth* (1945). *Their Ancient Grudge* (1946). *Darker Grows the Valley* (1947). *Lost Homecoming* (1950). *The Long Quest: The Story of John Wesley* (1954). *The Smoldering Fire* (1955). *The Savage Within: Destruction Was His Aim, Possession Hers* (1955). *Summer Gold* (1955). *My Heart's in the Hills* (1956). *For Chloe with Love* (1959). *The Brazen Dream* (1961). *Riders in the Night* (1965). *Bluegrass, Belles, Bourbon: A Pictorial History of Whisky in Kentucky* (1967). *Mounts in the Mist,* with Mildred Y. Payne (1969).

—ED PIACENTINO

CHARLES KURALT (1934–1997). Charles Bishop Kuralt, a Tar Heel who charmed television audi-ences with his down-home manner, was born on September 10, 1934, in Wilmington, N.C., a home-town he shares with newsman David Brinkley. He was the son of social worker Wallace Hamilton and teacher Ina Bishop. Kuralt's passion for journalism manifested itself early. He worked for local papers and a radio station while in high school. He edited the *Daily Tar Heel* at the University of North Caro-lina, and in 1955 left to work for the *Charlotte News,* where he wrote a column titled "People" (later collected in *Charles Kuralt's People*). Like Shelby Foote, he left Carolina without his degree, hampered by the absence of some physical education requirements. Ten years later, after the requirements were waived, he received his B.A. in history—not journalism!—reports to the contrary notwithstanding.

At age twenty-three he started working for the Columbia Broadcasting System (CBS), soon became a news writer, and by 1959, a correspondent. Kuralt's passion inclined toward the lives of ordinary Americans, and away from so-called hard news. In 1967 he landed on the idea for the format of a "just folks" segment that would become his celebrated "On the Road." His wanderings led him to a 104-year-old jogger and a man who lived in a house made of beer bottles, among others.

Kuralt was a master of the human interest story, and had a knack for drawing his subjects without saccharine flourishes. Perhaps that is why his work lends itself to printed collections. Most of his books are companions to his television journalism; mainly, they are tributes to those that they observe. But Kuralt's prose, always direct, could be memorably poetic. Of a Wisconsin marsh, he said, "This is a place where you can hear fall coming for miles." His wry touch shines through in his comment on modern road corridors: "Thanks to the interstate highway system, it is now possible to travel across the country from coast to coast without seeing anything."

Kuralt died of heart failure at New York Hospital on Independence Day, 1997. His reputation was sullied by a surprise will that precipitated the widespread revelation of a decades-long extramarital affair. Nevertheless, the Kuralt faithful may peruse his papers in the Southern Historical Collection at the University of North Carolina. They may also visit the Charles Kuralt Learning Center in UNC's Carroll Hall, where his former New York penthouse office has been relocated entire, enshrining his library, mementos, and honorary degrees.

WORKS: *To the Top of the World: The Adventures and Misadventures of the Plaisted Polar Expedition, March 28–May 4, 1967* (1968). *Dateline America* (1979). *On the Road with Charles Kuralt* (1985). *Southerners: Portrait of a People* (1986). *North Carolina: An Intimate View* (1986). *North Carolina Is My Home*, with Loonis McGlohan, ed. Patty Davis (1986). *A Life on the Road* (1990). *Charles Kuralt's America* (1995). *Charles Kuralt's American Moments*, ed. Peter Freundlich (1998). *Charles Kuralt's People*, ed. Ralph Grizzle (2002).

—BRYAN GIEMZA

TONY KUSHNER (1956–). Born in Manhattan, Tony Kushner was raised by his classically trained musician parents, William and Sylvia (Deutscher) Kushner, in Lake Charles, La., after they inherited a lumber business there. Kushner's mother performed in local plays, and as a Jewish and gay high school student in the Deep South, Kushner found he could best express himself in the theater. He matriculated to Columbia University in 1974, and took a B.A. in English (medieval studies) in 1978. While working as a hotel switchboard operator, he undertook graduate studies in direction at New York University, earning an M.F.A. in 1984.

Kushner worked as an assistant director of the Repertory Theatre of St. Louis in 1985–86, and was the artistic director of the New York Theatre Workshop in 1987–88, when he won a fellowship from the National Endowment for the Arts. He was the Juilliard School of Drama's playwright-in-residence in 1990–92.

A prolific playwright, he wrote and produced plays in New York, St. Louis, and Martha's Vineyard before bursting onto the drama scene in the early 1990s with his epic seven-hour, two-part Broadway production *Angels in America: A Gay Fantasia on National Themes.* Kushner won numerous awards for the play, including two Tony Awards and a Pulitzer Prize, and London's National Theatre named it one of the ten best plays of the twentieth century. *Angels in America* has been performed all over the world and was adapted into a film by HBO in 2003. Kushner's blending of fantasy with realism in this and other plays distinguishes him from his contemporary American dramatists.

In addition to his original plays, Kushner has adapted works by Goethe, Brecht, Ansky, and Corneille. He also composes one-act plays and opera. An outspoken socialist, Kushner cites Bertolt Brecht and Tennessee Williams as major influences and sees his plays as part of a political movement. His prescient play *Homebody/Kabul,* written pre-9/11, links modern New York and London to the politics of the Taliban.

Kushner currently teaches in New York University's dramatic writing program and is in demand as a public speaker. He is a regular columnist for the *Advocate,* and has contributed articles and essays to *Newsweek,* the *Nation, Mother Jones,* and other journals and newspapers. With Eric Ross, he wrote the screenplay for Steven Spielberg's film *Munich* (2006).

In 1994 Kushner's hometown university, McNeese State, awarded him with an honorary doctorate, and his recent musical *Caroline or Change* is set in the civil-rights-era Louisiana of his youth.

WORKS: *Angels in America, Part I: Millennium Approaches* (1992). *Plays by Tony Kushner* (1992). *Angels in American, Part II: Perestroika* (1994). *Thinking about the Longstanding Problems of Virtue and Happiness: Essays, a Play, Two Poems, and a Prayer* (1995). *A Dybbuk; and, The Dybbuk Melody and Other Themes and Variations* (1998). *Plays by Tony Kushner* (1999). *Death and Taxes: Hydriotaphia and Other Plays* (2000). Ed., *Disraeli's Jewishness,* with Todd M. Endelman (2002). *Homebody/Kabul* (2002). *Brundibar* (2003). *The Art of Maurice Sendak: 1980 to the Present* (2003). *Save Your Democratic Soul! Rants, Screeds, and Other Public Utterances* (2003). *Wrestling with Zion: Progressive Jewish-American Responses to the Israeli-Palestinian Conflict,* with Alisa Soloman (2003).

—PETER J. FLORA

MIRABEAU BUONAPARTE LAMAR (1798–1859). Poet, politician, educator, and statesman, Mirabeau Buonaparte Lamar was born on August 16, 1798, near Louisville, Ga., in Warren County. He grew up at Fairfield, his father's plantation, and attended academies in Milledgeville and Eatonton. In 1819 he had a brief partnership in Catawba, Ala., then the state capital. In 1821, for a few months, he was the joint publisher of *Catawba Press.* He returned to Georgia in 1823 and for three years was Governor George M. Troup's secretary and member of his household.

On January 1, 1826, Lamar married Tabitha B. Jordan of Twiggs County, Ga., and in 1828 he moved his wife and daughter to Columbus, Ga., where he established the *Columbus Enquirer,* a states' rights weekly. In 1829 he was elected state senator. On August 30, 1830, his wife died. Having run unsuccessfully for Congress as an Independent candidate, he founded the Georgia States Rights Party in 1833. He sold his interest in the newspaper in 1835 and moved to Texas, where he soon joined Sam Houston's army.

On April 10, 1836, Lamar won fame at the Battle of San Jacinto. Commissioned a colonel and assigned to command a cavalry, Lamar was promoted to major general and commander in chief of the Texan army. In 1836 Lamar was attorney general and then vice president of the Republic of Texas, and from 1838 to 1841 he was its second president. In 1839 Lamar was instrumental in moving the state's capital to Austin. Because of his leadership in establishing public land for education, which eventually led to the founding of the University of Texas and Texas A&M, he is often referred to as the "Father of Texas Education."

Lamar was a lieutenant colonel in Zachary Taylor's army at the battle of Monterrey in the Mexican-American War, and after the war, in 1847, he served one term in the Texas legislature. In 1851 he married Henrietta Maffitt of Galveston, and a daughter was born in 1852. That year Lamar was appointed, but did not serve, as U.S. minister to the Argentine Republic, but he did serve for twenty months, beginning in 1857, as U.S. minister to Nicaragua and Costa Rica. Resigning his position in Nicaragua, Lamar returned to Galveston on October 8, 1859, and died of a heart attack on his plantation in Richmond on December 19 of that year.

Although only one publication of Lamar's verses appeared in his lifetime—*Verse Memorials* in September 1857—he left behind an album of manuscript poetry and a seventy-page manuscript, *Journals of My Travels.* Many of his poems were printed in ladies' albums, newspapers, and magazines, and his most frequently anthologized poem, "The Daughter of Mendoza," on the death of his daughter, appeared in the *Southern Literary Messenger.*

WORKS: *Verse Memorials* (1857). *Papers of Mirabeau Buonaparte Lamar* (1920–27; repr. 1968).

—GARY KERLEY

PINKIE GORDON LANE (1923–). Pinkie Gordon was born to working-class parents in Philadelphia, and graduated from the Philadelphia School for Girls in 1940. After her father's death she worked in a sewing factory, then moved to Atlanta and Spelman College, where she received her B.A. in English and art (1949) and met and married Ulysses Lane (1948). After teaching for five years in public high schools in Georgia and Florida, she earned an M.A. from Atlanta University. When the couple moved to Baton Rouge, Lane began to write poetry, much of it inspired by her rapt appreciation of the tropical environment, but also by the emotions stirred by the birth of her son, Gordon. Her first collection, *Wind Thoughts,* came out shortly after her husband's death and was influenced by that tragic event. Electrified by the technical advances of the black aesthetic movement, she included inscriptions from LeRoi Jones, Gwendolyn Brooks, and Sonia Sanchez in her work.

Lane became the first African American woman to receive a Ph.D. at Louisiana State University (1967). She had a distinguished career at Southern University, where she enjoyed a long tenure as chair of English. She retired from Southern in 1986, but subsequently held visiting appointments at the University of Northern Iowa and Bridgewater College.

Her duties did not hinder her poetic production; she published *The Mystic Female* in 1978, *I Never Scream* in 1985, and after her retirement, *Girl at the Window* and *Elegy for Etheridge.* Lane's poetry has often been praised for its lyricism, and yet is punctuated by sharp, arresting images. Inspired by revolutionaries, she also owes debts to classical writers such as Milton, Keats, and Lao Tzu. Her poems have a wide range of reference, from simple observation of grasshoppers or opossums to shocking snapshots of addiction or abortion. Her complex investigations of social injustice are epitomized in poems such as "Sexual Privacy of Women on Welfare." She has also crafted poignant, often sensual love poems, which can alternately sear and soar, as in "St. Valentine's Eve Poem." Her most powerful works are her elegies for kin and friends, who take on full-bodied life in Lane's unflinching portraits. "Poems to My Father" bravely challenges, condemns, and ultimately accepts her parent in a re-creation of his moods and menace. Alternately, her tender and sorrowful treatment of her husband's fatal illness, "Songs to the Dialysis Machine," touches other frequencies, as does her moving tribute to her mother, "Prose Poem: Portrait." Her more recent poems have centered on musical themes, a tribute to her musician son, Gordon. Lane, who has traveled and lectured globally, is the recipient of many awards and honors, and was poet laureate of Louisiana (1989–92).

WORKS: *Wind Thoughts* (1972). *The Mystic Female* (1978). *I Never Scream* (1985). *Girl at the Window* (1991). *Elegy for Etheridge* (2000).

—JOHN LOWE

SIDNEY LANIER (1842–1881). Lanier is an unusual figure in American literature—a canonical poet who was also a professional musician. Throughout his short but intense career, Lanier was fascinated by the connections between poetry and music, and his energies were often torn between the two. His verse style developed as an attempt to convey musical impressions through words.

Born into a middle-class family in Macon, Ga., Lanier graduated from Oglethorpe College, then in Milledgeville, in 1860. He seemed destined to follow his father into the practice of law, but when the Civil War began he joined the Macon Volunteers, served on a blockade-runner, and was subsequently captured and held on a prison ship; this is where he most likely contracted the tuberculosis that was to kill him less than two decades later. After his release in a prisoner exchange, he made his way back to Georgia. He married Mary Day in 1867 and spent the next few years working in his father's law office, as a hotel clerk, and teaching. He published a Civil War novel, *Tiger-Lilies*, and composed a number of poems and songs. He also began to bristle under the restraints of his traditional society, which did not regard music as an appropriate profession for a southern gentleman. After a period of emotional and intellectual struggle, during which he continued to produce verse but also had to write potboilers in order to support his growing family, he finally determined to pursue an artistic career. By this time he had only seven years remaining, yet amazingly crammed a prodigious amount of work into this span.

To accomplish his goals, Lanier had to leave Georgia. He moved to Baltimore, where he auditioned for Asger Hamerik, the Danish musical director of the new Peabody conservatory. Hamerik introduced radical new "programme music," including compositions by Berlioz and Wagner. As Lanier became exposed to more varied styles of music, his poetry began to evolve from a simpler balladic style to a freer, more intricately textured verse. A comparison of his 1868 lyric "Little Ella" with his 1880 "Sunrise" reveals a drastic and bold development. Lanier's most renowned works are his later poems, including "The Marshes of Glynn," which reflect the influence of larger musical forms and the weaving of different themes, lines, and voices that is characteristic of the symphony. Lanier's experiences in the orchestra, studying sophisticated contemporary music, led him to create poetry that often anticipated modern verse.

Lanier believed that music and poetry were intimately related forms that ideally could combine and meld to express one thought. He expresses this ideal at the end of his poem "The Symphony," and it is probably his most famous phrase: "Music is Love in search of a word." Lanier was highly acclaimed for his proficiency as a flute player, but his poetry, because it became increasingly original, was not always appreciated. Still, he was a major enough figure to be commissioned to write the words for a cantata celebrating the centennial of the United States in 1876. In addition to playing in the Peabody orchestra and other ensembles, Lanier gave popular lectures on many literary subjects.

The center of a circle of devoted friends and family, Lanier was mourned widely when he succumbed at the age of thirty-nine to the illness he had fought for so long. How his poetry might have developed even further can only be speculated, but literary critics acknowledge that he can be considered a significant figure in early modern American literature. Lanier's life and works were the subject of great attention and adulation in the first half of the twentieth century, especially in the South.

WORKS: *Tiger-Lilies* (1867). *Florida: Its Scenery, Climate, and History* (1875). *The Centennial Meditation of Columbia* (1876). *Poems* (1877). *The Boy's Froissart* (1879). *The Boy's King Arthur* (1880). *The Science of English Verse* (1880). *The Boy's Mabinogion* (1881). *The Boy's Percy* (1882). *The English Novel and the Principle of Its Development*, ed. William Hand Browne (1883). *Poems*, ed. Mary Day Lanier (1884). *Music and Poetry*, ed. Henry Wysham Lanier (1898). *Retrospects and Prospects*, ed. Henry Wysham Lanier (1899). *Letters of Lanier: Selections from His Correspondence*, ed. Henry Wysham Lanier (1899). *Bob: The Story of Our Mocking-Bird*, ed. Henry Wysham Lanier (1899). *Shakespeare and His Forerunners*, ed. Henry Wysham Lanier (1902). *The Complete Works of Sidney Lanier*, ed. Charles R. Anderson and others (1945).

—JANE S. GABIN

HENRY LAURENS (1724–1792). Henry Laurens was born in Charleston, S.C., on February 24, 1724, the son of French Huguenots from New York. Laurens followed his father into the import/export business and in 1749 established a lucrative slave-trading network. He was an astute and industrious merchant who traded in many goods, but the great wealth he accumulated in the next two decades was founded on the approximately 7,600 Africans he sold in South Carolina. His view of slavery slowly reversed itself in the 1760s, and when the colony banned slave imports for three years in 1764, Laurens essentially retired from trafficking in humans.

Laurens, a lover of law and order, came late to the patriots' cause. During the Stamp Act crisis a mob suspected him of hiding the hated licenses in his home. But by 1774 he was a confirmed patriot, perhaps being influenced by the radical views of his own son, John Laurens (1754–1782), whom he had sent to Geneva to be educated. Henry tepidly supported John's hopes for the emancipation of slaves during the Revolution.

Beginning in 1757, Henry Laurens served as a member of the South Carolina Commons House for nearly fifteen years. He was a lieutenant colonel in the Cherokee War of 1761. He presided over South Carolina's Council of Safety in 1775–76. He was vice president of South Carolina in 1776–77 and achieved the nation's highest office as president of the Continental Congress in 1778. Congress sent him to Holland in 1780, but he was captured at sea, precipitating war between the English and the Dutch. In 1780–81 Laurens was imprisoned in the Tower of London, where his refusal to accept parole testified to the nobility of the American cause.

His son's death in 1782, in a useless skirmish with British troops, so disheartened him that he withdrew from public life and retired to his luxurious plantation, Mepkin, twenty-five miles up the river from Charleston. He died on December 9, 1792.

WORKS: *The Papers of Henry Laurens*, 16 vols., ed. George C. Rogers, Jr., David R. Chesnutt, and C. James Taylor (1972–).

—JOSEPH KELLY

JOHN LAWSON (d. 1711). Historians have disagreed as to the origins of John Lawson, some arguing that he was the son of Dr. John Lawson (1632–ca. 1690) of London, others that he was from Yorkshire, still others that he was a Scotsman. Later scholarship suggests that he was the son of Andrew Lawson, a salter of London, with identity of his mother still unknown. In 1675 Lawson apparently began service as an apprentice to a London apothecary and may have developed his interest in the natural sciences during this time.

Little else is known about Lawson until 1700, when he set sail from England for the Carolina colony in search of adventure and fame. Appointed by the colony's lords proprietor to survey the interior of Carolina, he left Charles Town on December 28 on a journey that would last fifty-nine days and cover approximately 550 miles. Accompanied by five other Englishmen and four Indians, Lawson recorded in a journal his observations about the region's topography, flora and fauna, and native peoples. The party followed a horseshoe-shaped route that carried it from Charleston into the Carolina piedmont, then eastward, ending near the Bath settlement on the Pamlico River in North Carolina.

Soon afterwards, Lawson built a home at present-day New Bern and from there periodically made shorter exploratory travels in the region. He became county clerk of court and public register, acquired considerable land, and was surveyor-planner and co-founder of the towns of Bath and New Bern. He also served as deputy surveyor of the colony, and then as surveyor-general.

In 1709 Lawson returned to England to seek publication of the journal from his exploration of the Carolina interior, to which he had added sections titled "Description of North-Carolina" and "An Account of the Indians of North-Carolina." His work was initially published in the April 1709 issue of John Stevens's serial anthology *A New Collection of Voyages and Travels. With Historical Accounts of Dis-*

coveries and Conquest in All Parts of the World. Later that year it was separately bound and issued under the title *A New Voyage to Carolina; Containing the Exact Description and Natural History of that Country: Together with the Present State thereof. And a Journal of A Thousand Miles, Travel'd thro' several Nations of Indians. Giving a particular Account of Their Customs, Manners, &c.* Considered the first significant effort to describe the natural history and the natives of North America, the book is a classic of early American literature.

After returning to North Carolina, Lawson continued his explorations. In September 1711, he and Baron Christopher von Graffenried, the other co-founder of New Bern, began a trip up the Neuse River to discover its source. As European settlement in the region increased, relations with the Indians in the region had deteriorated. Lawson and Graffenried were seized by a party of Tuscaroras and, according to Graffenried, Lawson was executed after an argument with a native king. Although Graffenried was released unharmed, a few days later the Tuscarora began widespread attacks on whites in the region, the beginning of two years of warfare.

Lawson fathered at least one child—a daughter, Isabella—by Hannah Smith, apparently his common-law wife.

WORKS: *A New Voyage to Carolina* (1709).

—ROBERT G. ANTHONY, JR.

LEROY LEATHERMAN (1922–1984). On February 10, 1922, LeRoy Leatherman was born of middle-class parents, LeRoy Sessums Leatherman and Mary Aline Dugger, in Alexandria, La. From 1939 to 1941 he attended Vanderbilt University, and he received a John Crowe Ransom Creative Writing Scholarship at Kenyon College for 1942. During World War II Leatherman worked in the intelligence division of the United States Army Air Corps from 1942 to 1946, attending the University of Illinois during the 1943–44 academic year. In 1948 he completed a B.A. at Southern Methodist University in Dallas, Tex., and received an M.A. the next year.

In 1950, while directing the film and recordings department of the Dallas Public Library, Leatherman published his first novel, *The Caged Birds,* a rendering of a young boy's struggle in the 1930s to choose among adults who pose conflicting demands of him. After managing the Martha Graham Dance Company's first appearances in Europe, Leatherman left Dallas in 1953 to become the director and personnel manager for the Martha Graham School and Dance Company in New York City until 1960. During these years he published his second novel, *The Other Side of the Tree,* and received a *Sewanee Review* Fellowship for 1957–58. After living in southern France for two years, Leatherman completed, with Dr. Heinz Westman, his third book, *The Springs of Creativity,* a nonfiction exploration of depth psychology and myth criticism's explanations of the psychic genesis of creativity.

By 1962 Leatherman had returned to New York City as a producer and writer of films for the International Film Foundation and in 1966 became the executive director of the Martha Graham Center of Contemporary Dance. His final book, *Martha Graham: Portrait of the Lady as an Artist,* explains how Graham's creative process exemplifies the ideas explored in *The Springs of Creativity.*

In 1972 Leatherman became the assistant dean of the School for the Arts at Boston University and the executive director of the Tanglewood Institute. Continuing to apply his administrative skills in the theater, Leatherman became the special assistant to the dean of the University of Southern California's School of Performing Arts in 1979 and then the public-information officer in 1982 in the university's School of Music. On April 9, 1984, Leatherman died in Daniel Freeman Hospital in Inglewood, Calif.

works: *The Caged Birds* (1950). *The Other Side of the Tree* (1954). *The Springs of Creativity* (1961). *Martha Graham: Portrait of the Lady as an Artist* (1966).

—ALAN T. BELSCHES

ARTHUR LEE (1740–1792). Arthur Lee, the tenth and last child of Thomas and Hannah Ludwell Lee, was born on December 21, 1740, in Westmoreland County, Va. When he was only nine, both parents died, leaving him under the guardianship of his eldest brother, Philip Ludwell Lee. At age ten Lee was sent to Eton College, his education in England financed by his brother Richard Henry Lee, also his mentor and closest friend. Subsequently, Lee received his M.D. from the University of Edinburgh (1764), but after a brief stint practicing medicine in Williamsburg, he abandoned that career and went to London to study law (1768).

Although he had written some earlier essays, his literary career blossomed in 1768 with a series of polemical political letters for the *Virginia Gazette* known as "The Monitor's Letters." Inspired by John Dickinson's *Letters from a Farmer in Pennsylvania,* Lee called for American resistance to all forms of taxation by Parliament and for British redress of American grievances. During the next decade Lee wrote numerous essays, petitions, letters, and pamphlets under a wide variety of pen names, including Junius Americanus, Bostonian, and Raleigh. In two widely read pamphlets, *An Appeal to the Justice and Interests of the People of Great Britain* and *A Second Appeal,* he attempted to persuade the British to resolve the dispute with America.

In America, Lee's reputation as a scribe for the colonial cause led to several political appointments. Eventually, he was sent with Benjamin Franklin and Silas Deane to negotiate a treaty with France and solicit aid for the revolutionary cause. Although the negotiators experienced some success, their relationship was fractious. The discord ultimately led to Lee's dismissal as a diplomat by Congress in 1779. On his return to America, he served in the Virginia House of Delegates and as a delegate to Congress, but his influence significantly diminished during his latter years. He settled into the role of gentleman farmer until his death on December 12, 1792.

works: *An Essay in Vindication of the Continental Colonies of America, From a Censure of Mr. Adam Smith, in His Theory of Moral Sentiments* (1764). "The Monitor's Letters," Rind's *Virginia Gazette* (Feb. 25–Apr. 28, 1968). *An Appeal to the Justice and Interests of the People of Great Britain in the Present Disputes with America by An Old Member of Parliament* (1774). *A True State of the Proceedings in the Parliament of Great Britain, and in the Province of Massachusetts Bay, Relative to the Giving and Granting the Money of the People of that Province, and of all America, in the House of Commons, in Which They Are Not Represented* (1774). *A Second Appeal to the Justice and Interest of the People on the Measures Respecting America by the Author of the First* (1775). *A Speech, Intended to Have Been Delivered in the House of Commons, in Support of the Petition from the General Congress at Philadelphia, by the Author of an Appeal to the Justice and Interest of Great Britain* (1775).

—VERBIE LOVORN PREVOST

HARPER LEE (1926–). In 1960 Harper Lee published her only novel. *To Kill a Mockingbird* arrived at the right moment to help the South and the nation grapple with the racial tensions that the accelerating civil rights movement had brought to the fore. Quickly selected by the Literary Guild and the Book-of-the-Month Club and soon condensed for *Reader's Digest,* in 1961 the novel won the Pulitzer Prize in fiction and the Brotherhood Award of the National Conference of Christians and Jews. In 1962 a superb film rendition was released, winning an Oscar for Gregory Peck. The novel, remaining in print and regularly taught in schools, ranks as one of the defining works of the twentieth century. The film has also taken its place among the classics.

Nelle Harper Lee was born in Monroeville, Ala., on April 28, 1926, daughter of lawyer Amasa Coleman and Frances Finch Lee. She joined a brother, Edwin, and a sister, Alice. Atticus Finch of the novel is her moving tribute to her father. The Finch family reflects her own; the narrative voice, herself. The eccentric little cousin who is companion to the Finch children is modeled on Truman Capote, who for six years lived in Monroeville with elderly unmarried cousins during the time of Lee's childhood. Lee and Capote remained close friends throughout his life. She aided him with the research for *In Cold Blood*, making several trips to Kansas for this effort.

After attending Huntingdon College in Montgomery for one year (1944–45), Lee transferred to the University of Alabama, writing there for student publications. Her liberated views on race were evident in that writing. In 1947 she enrolled in the University of Alabama Law School, spending one year at Oxford University in England as an exchange student. She left Tuscaloosa in 1950 without taking her degree, moving to New York to become a writer. She supported herself as a reservations clerk with Eastern Airlines and British Overseas Airways until friends made a gift, which Lee accepted as loan, so that she could write full-time. In 1958 the first draft of *Mockingbird* was finished. Having returned to Monroeville, Lee was positioned for continuing work with Capote and for the wave of publicity that followed the success of the novel and film. During the filming, Lee became a life-long friend of Peck, acknowledged by her gift to him of her father's watch. Peck named a daughter for her.

Although Lee started a second novel, the project faded. She has written nonfiction pieces for magazines, but she has made it clear that with *Mockingbird* she made her statement. She continues to live in Monroeville, guarding her privacy.

WORKS: *To Kill a Mockingbird* (1960).

—JOSEPH M. FLORA

RICHARD HENRY LEE (1732–1794). Born in Westmoreland County, Va., on January 20, 1732, to Thomas and Hannah Ludwell Lee, Richard Henry Lee was privately tutored as a child. He then attended Wakefield Academy in England. Returning to Virginia, Lee apparently read widely in history, law, and politics before embarking on a career of public service.

In 1757 Lee became a justice of the peace in his county, married Anne Aylette, and established residence near his boyhood home. Following Anne's death, he married Anne Pinckard in 1769. In the House of Burgesses (1758–75), he became an early spokesman against slavery and an outspoken opponent of the Stamp Act and the Townshend Acts. A member of the Continental Congress (1774–79), he was a major orator for independence, made the motion that led to the Declaration of Independence, and became one of its signers.

Health problems caused Lee to resign from Congress and return to Virginia in 1779, but in 1784 he returned to Congress. Following the drafting of the United States Constitution, Lee aligned himself with the anti-Federalists and produced his most significant literary achievement, *Letters from the Federal Farmer*. This pamphlet was composed of a series of articles first published in the *Poughkeepsie (N.Y.) Country Journal*. Lee expanded his views in a second collection the following year. Despite his efforts, the Constitution was adopted. His main concern then became the adoption of the Bill of Rights, of which he authored the tenth amendment. In poor health, he resigned from the Senate in 1792 and retired to Chantilly, where he died on June 19, 1794.

Although Richard Henry Lee is widely credited as the author of both series of *Letters from a Federal Farmer*, some scholars think the articles were actually written by or in collaboration with someone else, possibly Melancton Smith of New York.

WORKS: *Observations Leading to a Fair Examination of the System of Government Proposed by the Late Convention; and to Several Essential and Necessary Alterations to it, In a Number of Letters from the Federal Farmer to the Republican* (1787). *An Additional Number of Letters From the Federal Farmer to the Republican Leading to a Fair Examination of the System of Government Proposed by the Late Convention; To Several Essential and Necessary Alterations in It; And Calculated to Illustrate and Support the Principles And Positions Laid Down in the Preceding Letters* (1788).

—VERBIE LOVORN PREVOST

HUGH SWINTON LEGARÉ (1797–1843). Hugh Swinton Legaré (pronounced Le-gree) was born on January 22, 1797, in Charleston, S.C. His father died while Legaré was an infant, and he was raised by his mother. Her task was made particularly difficult after a negative reaction to a smallpox inoculation caused her son to develop a case of infantile paralysis. Though in time Legaré recovered his ability to walk, the disease stunted the growth of his legs, a deformity magnified as his upper body grew to a properly proportioned size.

Rendered timid and sensitive by his condition, Legaré devoted himself to intellectual pursuits, and he thrived under the instruction provided by his mother and a series of private schools. In 1811, and with the rank of sophomore, Legaré entered South Carolina College, from which he graduated first in his class three years later.

After three years of legal instruction in Charleston, Legaré traveled to Europe, where he pursued further studies before returning to South Carolina in 1820. In that year he was elected to the lower house of the South Carolina legislature, the first of a series of political positions he held over the remaining years of his life. Most notable among these were his terms as a United States congressman, American chargé d'affaires in Brussels, U.S. attorney general, and, at the time of his death, acting secretary of state.

Legaré's foremost literary contributions were as a member of the circle of writers associated with Russell's Bookstore in Charleston and as a founder of the *Southern Review,* the quarterly journal which Legaré served as editor and to which he contributed a number of pieces, many on classical subjects.

Legaré died in Boston in June 1843, after falling ill while attending the dedication of a monument at the site of the Battle of Bunker Hill.

WORKS: *Writings of Hugh Swinton Legaré,* 2 vols., ed. Mary S. Legaré Bullen (1845–46).

—JOHN N. SOMERVILLE, JR.

JAMES MATHEWES LEGARÉ (1823–1859). Writer, artist, and inventor James Mathewes Legaré was born in Charleston, S.C., on November 26, 1823, to agricultural editor John D. and Mary Doughty Mathewes Legaré. James rounded off his undergraduate years at the College of Charleston and Saint Mary's College, Baltimore, by staging an elaborate practical joke reminiscent of Edgar Allan Poe's "Balloon Hoax." In a Charleston lot, James buried an iron casket, stamped 1682, that contained a genealogical history validating the Legarés' royal lineage, originating in 912 A.D. with "Hubert, Earl de L'Egaré," first duke of Normandy. When a servant found the casket, even the Boston papers initially reported the story as factual. Harriet Beecher Stowe may have derived her brutal plantation overseer's name, Simon Legree, from the last Continental ancestor James listed—"Solomon Legaré."

Legaré was to put his creative talents to more productive uses. After briefly pursuing law, he wrote one of America's finest elegies, later titled "On the Death of a Kinsman," when his cousin Hugh Swinton Legaré died in 1843. He also composed sketches and paintings for Charleston expositions; both William Gilmore Simms and John James Audubon sponsored his artwork. Financial crises forced his family to relocate to Aiken, S.C. There Legaré wrote magazine fiction and poetry and ran a girls' school. He married Anne C. Andrews of Augusta, Ga., in March 1850, and moved into a cottage on the family property. Legaré's cottage in Aiken is now listed on the National Register of Historic Places.

Legaré wrote sentimental tales and romantic trans-Mississippi-west adventure stories for national periodicals. His neoclassical and romantic poetry, his best writing, typically celebrated the natural landscape and the rarefied emotions of love. He collected several of his poems in *Orta-Undis and Other Poems.*

Legaré experienced one last burst of creativity during his final seven years, while tuberculosis was progressively eroding his health. While serving as postmaster for the Millard Fillmore administration in 1852–53, he set up a laboratory and made valiant, but ultimately Sisyphean, attempts to design an air-powered machine that would compete with the cumbersome and dangerous steam engine. Yet Legaré succeeded in other experiments, earning local prizes and two national patents for a "plastic cotton" compound (which he called lignine, and molded into a variety of sturdy, still-usable furniture items and decorative pieces) and for an ivory-frame composite material. Legaré had almost brought lignine into commercial production when he succumbed to tuberculosis on May 30, 1859; he was only thirty-five. He gave many of his poems Latin and Greek titles and habitually included classical words and phrases in his poetry. The motto for James Mathewes Legaré's remarkable career is indeed "Ars longa—vita brevis."

WORKS: "Du Saye" (*The Charleston Book,* ed. William Gilmore Simms, 1845). *Orta-Undis, and Other Poems* (1848). "Thanatokallos" (*Knickerbocker,* Sept. 1849). "Pedro de Padilh" (*Graham's Magazine,* 1850). *Cap-and-Bells* (*Harper's,* 1863–64). *That Ambitious Mr. Legaré: The Life of James M. Legaré of South Carolina, Including a Collected Edition of His Verse,* ed. Curtis Carroll Davis (1971).

—R. BRUCE BICKLEY, JR.

NANCY LEMANN (1956–). Nancy Elise Lemann was born in New Orleans, La., on February 4, 1956, to Thomas, a lawyer, and Barbara Lemann, and she grew up in the Crescent City. Education was a priority in the family. (Lemann's brother Nicholas would become a professor and dean of the School of Journalism at Columbia University, with particular expertise in race relations.) Lemann graduated from Metairie Park Country Day School. In 1978 she received her B.A. from Brown University; in 1958 she received the M.F.A. from Columbia. She married Mark Paul Clein on October 5, 1991. With their two daughters, they currently reside in Chevy Chase, Md. Though Lemann lived in New York for fifteen years and San Diego for six, her writing has remained joyously southern.

Of her four novels, only one, *Lives of the Saints,* is set in her hometown. Yet of all the New Orleans writers, none captures its essence as well as Lemann. She alone depicts the New Orleanian's New Orleans—not Mardi Gras, not jazz funerals, not hurricanes, not the French Quarter. Her New Orleans is located "uptown," where the families that have inhabited (and run) the city for generations live. Whether the novels take place in Long Island (*Sportsman's Paradise*); Virginia, Istanbul, and North Africa (*The Fiery Pantheon*); or California (*Malaise*), their characters are uniquely and irreversibly New Orleanian. Lemann celebrates their decadence, their boozy charm, their tribalism, their antiquated manners, even their special vocabulary ("heart," as a term of address). In this world, nearly everyone is in "deep, deep trouble," failure is ubiquitous and counts more than success, and age is superior to youth.

In addition to her novels, Lemann has also written a nonfiction account of Louisiana governor Edwin Edwards's 1985–86 racketeering trials called *The Ritz on the Bayou.*

WORKS: *Lives of the Saints* (1985). *The Ritz on the Bayou* (1987). *Sportsman's Paradise* (1992). *The Fiery Pantheon* (1998). *Malaise* (2002).

—TOM WILLIAMS

HENRY CLAY LEWIS [MADISON TENSAS] (1825–1850). Henry Clay Lewis's father, David, came to the United States as an adult from Auvergne, France, to fight in the Revolution. His mother, Mary Salomon, was the daughter of a surgeon. Henry was born on June 26, 1825, in Charleston, S.C., where his father kept a furniture store. Before 1829 the family moved to Cincinnati, Ohio. Mary died there in 1831, and Henry went to live with a brother.

Missing the kindness and studious atmosphere of his cultured Jewish parents' home, the child ran away at ten to become a cook's helper and cabin boy on riverboats. At eleven he was taken off a Yazoo River packet by another brother, Joseph, a merchant in Yazoo City, Miss. Joseph promised Henry an education, but, failing in business, he put the boy to hard work in the cotton fields for the next five years. At sixteen Henry was apprenticed to a medical doctor, and in 1844 was sent to Kentucky to the Louisville Medical Institute. He graduated in 1846 and moved to Louisiana to practice in a backwoods community on the Tensas River, treating slaves and their masters on the great plantations and hunters and squatters in the swamps. In 1848 he moved to Richmond, La., where he prospered: he became active in Whig politics; he bought land, new instruments, law books, and a medical library in French, remembering perhaps the European culture of his childhood. Returning home exhausted during the 1850 cholera epidemic, he accidentally drowned in a flooded bayou on August 5, 1850.

In 1845 he had begun contributing sketches to the New York *Spirit of the Times*. These are partly picaresque autobiography, and partly accounts of backwoods life, often violent and brutal. Through the use of dialect, comic folk imagery, folklore, and the form of the mock oral tale, he presents a vigorous, grotesque, demonic vision of the southern backwoods.

WORKS: *Odd Leaves from the Life of a Louisiana Swamp Doctor* (1850), repr. as *Louisiana Swamp Doctor* (1962). *The Swamp Doctor's Adventures in the South-West* (1858).

—MILTON AND PATRICIA RICKELS

RICHARD LEWIS (ca. 1700–1734). Though he was a frequently reprinted poet during his lifetime, details of Richard Lewis's life are vague. He may have been the son of Richard Lewis of Llanfair, Montgomeryshire, Wales, who attended Balliol College, Oxford, in April 1718. He also may have attended Eton. Apparently he arrived in Maryland in 1718. In January 1719, a Richard Lewis married Elizabeth Batee at All Hallows Parish, Anne Arundel County, Md.

Lewis places himself in Maryland on October 22, 1725, in a 1732 letter to Peter Collinson of the Royal Society of London in which he describes an explosion in the air near Patapsco (present-day Baltimore). A letter by Maryland Governor Benedict Leonard Calvert to Thomas Hearne dated March 18, 1728–29, reveals that Lewis was serving as a schoolmaster in Annapolis at the time. In the early 1730s Lewis acted as a clerk in the Maryland general assembly. He died in 1734 around the age of thirty and was survived by his son, Richard, who became apprenticed to a saddler named Richard Tootel in March 1735.

The first extant work by Lewis is his translation of Edward Holdsworth's Latin poem *Muscipula*. Lewis celebrates it as the "FIRST ESSAY of *Latin Poetry*, in *English Dress*, which MARYLAND hath publish'd from the Press" and points to the great potential of the colony, a theme revisited in "Carmen Seculare" and "To Mr. Samuel Hastings." "A Journey from Patapsko" finds the American landscape more fit for poetry than those written about by Old World poets. The "Patapsko" narrator uses a one-day journey through the natural beauty and terror of rural Maryland to explore the role of the individual within the universe and the individual's relationship to God. Vivid descriptions of nature and the journey through nature as allegory appear as well in "A Rhapsody" and "Food for Criticks," a poem that mourns the loss of American wilderness. Lewis is a good candidate for authorship of "Upon Prince *Madoc*'s Expedition to the Country now called *America*, in the 12th Century," which appeared in 1743 under the pseudonym Philo Cambrensis.

WORKS: Trans., Edward Holdsworth's *Muscipula—The Mouse-Trap, or The Battle of the Cambrians and Mice* (1728). "To Mr. *Samuel Hastings* (Shipwright of Philadelphia) on his Launching the *Maryland-Merchant*, a Large Ship Built by Him at *Annapolis*," *Maryland Gazette* (Dec. 30, 1729); repr. *Pennsylvania Gazette* (Jan. 6–13, 1730). "A Journey from Patapsko to Annapolis, April 4, 1730," *Pennsylvania Gazette* (May 21, 1731). "Food for Criticks," *Maryland Gazette* (1731); repr. in altered form *New England Weekly Journal* (June 28, 1731) and *Pennsylvania Gazette* (July 10–17, 1732). "A Rhapsody," Annapolis, Mar. 1, 1731–32 [folio]; repr. *Maryland Gazette* (Feb. 9, 1732–33). "Verses, to Mr. Ross, on Mr. Calvert's Departure from Maryland, May 10th, 1732," *Maryland Historical Magazine* 32 (June 1937): 118–20. "Verses: To the Memory of His Excellency Benedict Leonard Calvert; Late Governor of the Province of Maryland who Died at Sea, June—1732," *Maryland Historical Magazine* 32 (June 1937): 121–27. "Congratulatory Verses, wrote at the Arrival of our Honourable PROPRIETARY [Thomas Penn]," *Pennsylvania Gazette* (Aug. 21, 1732). "Carmen Seculare" Annapolis, Nov. 25, 1732; portions repr. *Gentlemen's Magazine* (Apr. 1733 and May 1733). "An ELEGY on the much lamented Death of the Honourable CHARLES CALVERT, Esq. . . . ," *Maryland Gazette* (Mar. 8–15, 1734).

—DERRICK SPRADLIN

C. ERIC LINCOLN (1924–2000). Born on June 23, 1924, C. Eric Lincoln grew up in Athens, Ala., experiencing firsthand a brutal racism that would lead him to serious study of the African American experience in works of sociology, history, and fiction. In his memoir *Coming through the Fire: Surviving Race and Place in America,* Lincoln recalls a series of lessons he learned about his place as an African American in the segregated South. In particular, he recounts a brutal beating at the hands of a white manager of a cotton gin for daring to question what he should be paid for a bag of cotton. In his late teens, Lincoln moved to Chicago, only to find racism there as well. Shortly after arriving in Chicago, he was drafted and served in the U.S. Navy during World War II.

After the war, Lincoln received his undergraduate degree from Le Moyne College in 1947. He continued his education with degrees from Fisk University (M.A., 1954), University of Chicago Divinity School (B.D., 1956), and Boston University (Ph.D., 1960). His doctoral dissertation was published in 1961 as *The Black Muslims in America* and was immediately hailed as a seminal work on its subject. Lincoln's subsequent career consisted of a series of academic posts, including stints at Clark College, Union Theological Seminary, Fisk University, and Duke University, where he was William R. Kenan Distinguished Professor of Religion and Culture.

With his academic training in both sociology and theology, Lincoln's major works focused on the conjunction of race and religion in America. In addition to his scholarly works, he also published a novel, *The Avenue, Clayton City,* which won the Lillian Smith Award for Best Southern Fiction, and a collection of poems. He died in Durham, N.C., on May 14, 2000.

WORKS: *The Black Muslims in America* (1961). *My Face Is Black* (1964). *Sounds of the Struggle* (1967). *The Negro Pilgrimage in America: The Coming of Age of the Blackamericans* (1967). *Is Anybody Listening?* (1968). *A Pictorial History of the Negro in America*, with Langston Hughes and Milton Melzer (1968). *A Profile of Martin Luther King, Jr.* (1969). *The Blackamericans* (1969). *The Black Church since Frazier* (1974). *Race, Religion, and the Continuing Ameri-*

can Dilemma (1984). *The Avenue, Clayton City* (1988). *The Black Church in the African-American Experience*, with Lawrence H. Mamiya (1990). *This Road since Freedom: Collected Poems* (1990). *Coming through the Fire: Surviving Race and Place in America* (1996).

—Stephen Cooper

ROMULUS LINNEY (1930–). Author of novels, plays, and stories, Romulus Linney was born on September 21, 1930, in Philadelphia, Pa., descendant of a long lineage of western North Carolina ancestors. He spent much of his early childhood in Charlotte and Boone, N.C., as well as in Madison, Tenn., mountain settings that would figure largely in his work. His father died when he was thirteen, a loss that he has felt keenly throughout his life. Married twice, to Ann Legett Sims and Margaret Andrews, Linney has two daughters, one of whom is actress Laura Linney.

Linney graduated from Oberlin College in 1953 and went on to Yale University School of Drama as an actor, but was drafted into the army for two years. After returning to Yale, he shifted his focus to directing, earning an M.F.A. in 1958. Moving to New York, Linney worked in television and served as stage manager for the Actors Studio. His early fiction gradually evolved into drama, the genre for which he is most well known. In the early 1960s, Linney taught at the University of North Carolina at Chapel Hill and North Carolina State University; he later served on the faculty of the Manhattan School of Music and the University of Pennsylvania, and taught at Brooklyn College and Columbia University.

Linney writes three kinds of plays: Appalachian, historical, and personal. He adapted his first novel, *Heathen Valley*, a tale of strange occurrences in the Appalachian Mountains of the 1840s, into a play that won the National Critics Award. Historical works include *Sorrows of Frederick*, based on Frederick the Great, and *2*, about Hermann Goering and the Nuremberg Trials.

Recipient of fellowships from the National Endowment for the Arts as well as Yaddo and the MacDowell Colony, Linney has received Guggenheim and Rockefeller Foundation grants, the 1984 Award in Literature, the Lucille Lortel Award, the 1999 Award of Merit Medal for Drama from the American Academy and Institute of Arts and Letters, of which he is a member, the Hollywood Drama League Award, and the 2003 Annual William Inge Theatre Festival Award, as well as two Obie Awards—one in 1980 for *Tennessee*, the other in 1992 for "sustained excellence in playwriting." Signature Theatre, for which Linney was the first playwright-in-residence, devoted its 1991–92 season to five of his plays, four of which he directed.

works: *Heathen Valley* (1962). *Slowly, by Thy Hand Unfurled* (1965). *The Sorrows of Frederick* (1968). *The Love Suicide at Schofield Barracks* (1972). *Democracy and Esther* (1973). *Holy Ghosts* (prod. 1974). *Appalachia Sounding* (prod. 1976). *Just Folks* (commissioned 1976 by Kennedy Center, prod. 1978). *The Death of King Philip* (opera libretto, prod. 1976). *Old Man Joseph and His Family: A Play in Two Acts* (1978). *Tennessee* (1980). *The Captivity of Pixie Shedman: A Play in Two Acts* (1980). *Jesus Tales: A Novel* (1980). *El Hermano: A Play in One Act* (1981). *Childe Byron: A Play in Two Acts* (1981). *The Death of King Philip: A Play* (1984). *Laughing Stock* (1984). *Why the Lord Come to Sand Mountain* (1984). *Sand Mountain* (1985). *A Woman without a Name: A Play in Two Acts* (1986). *Pops* (1987). *April Snow* (prod. 1987). *Holy Ghosts* (1989). *Three Poets: Three Plays* (1990). *Unchanging Love*, adapt. of Anton Chekhov's story "In the Ravine" (1991). *Romulus Linney: Seventeen Short Plays* (1992). *2* (1993). *Ambrosio* (1993). *Spain* (1994). *True Crimes* (1996). *A Christmas Carol*, based on the story by Charles Dickens (1996). *Mountain Memory: A Play about Appalachian Life* (1997). *Gint*, based on Ibsen's *Peer Gynt* (1999). *Nine Adaptations for the American Stage* (2000). *A Lesson before Dying*, based on the novel by Ernest J. Gaines (2001). *Fugue, Fugue: A Play for Four Voices* (perf. 2001). *Heathen Valley: A Novel* (2004). *Slowly, by Thy Hand Unfurled: A Novel* (2004).

—Karen C. Blansfield

AUGUSTUS BALDWIN LONGSTREET (1790–1870). Born in Augusta, Ga., on September 22, 1790, Longstreet enrolled as a junior at Yale University in 1811 after having attended Dr. Moses Wadell's famous academy in Willington, S.C. He graduated from law school in Connecticut in 1815 and returned to Georgia to begin his practice. Shortly thereafter, Longstreet married Francis Eliza Parke, and the couple moved to her hometown of Greensboro, Ga., where he was elected to the state legislature in 1822. Following the death of his oldest son in 1824, Longstreet withdrew from a promising campaign for Congress. In the same year, he moved his family to Augusta, buying an unsuccessful plantation and opening his own law practice.

In 1830 Longstreet began writing the sketches that would make him famous. Three years later, these humorous pictures of daily life in Georgia began to appear in the Milledgeville *Southern Recorder,* and Longstreet continued to publish them in the *State's Rights Sentinel,* a paper he purchased in 1834. The next year the *Sentinel* published the entire collection as *Georgia Scenes: Characters, Incidents, &tc. in the First Half Century of the Republic.* With its publication, Longstreet contributed what is generally agreed to be the first major work of Southwest humor. Edgar Allan Poe called the work "a sure omen of better days for the literature of the South."

Longstreet did not, however, become a full-time author. He joined the Methodist clergy in 1838 and went on to serve as the president of Emory College in Oxford, Ga. Consequently, he served as president for several universities across the South, including Centenary College in Louisiana, the University of South Carolina, and the University of Mississippi. When most of the South Carolina students joined the Confederate army, Longstreet retired to Oxford, Miss., where he died on July 9, 1870, after living in Augusta with family during the Civil War.

WORKS: *Georgia Scenes: Characters, Incidents, &tc., in the First Half Century of the Republic* (1835). *A Voice from the South* (1847). *Master William Mitten; or, a Youth of Brilliant Talents Who Was Ruined by Bad Luck* (1864). *Stories with a Moral Humourous and Descriptive of a Southern Life a Century Ago* (1912).

—HARRIS W. HENDERSON

BEVERLY LOWRY (1938–). Beverly Lowry was born in Memphis, grew up in Mississippi, and moved to Texas, as the dust jackets of her first four novels repeat. She also attended the University of Mississippi and then transferred to Memphis State University, where she graduated. She married in the June following her college graduation.

Had her life continued on its orderly trajectory, Lowry would soon have been recognized as one of the finest southern women comic writers. Her early fictions were distinguished by an audacious style and a jaunty humor. In 1984, however, her world broke in two. First her diabetic father's legs required amputating and then her eighteen-year-old son Peter was killed in a terrible hit-and-run "accident" which has never been solved.

Catapulted into chaos by these events, Lowry landed in a new place. Her work, needless to say, became very different. It is now more varied, more melancholy, more profound. Yet out of the confusion came the volume on which Lowry's reputation may eventually rest: *Crossed Over: A Murder, A Memoir.* This meditation is secondarily the story of Beverly Lowry. Primarily, it is the story of Karla Faye Tucker, a confessed ax-murderess who converted in prison. Despite the efforts of the pope and capital punishment opponents, Tucker was executed in Texas on February 3, 1998. In her sensitive biographical study of Tucker, Lowry suggests that nothing human is alien to her.

WORKS: *Come Back, Lolly Ray* (1977). *Emma Blue* (1978). *Daddy's Girl* (1981). *The Perfect Sonya* (1987). *Breaking Gentle* (1991). *Crossed Over: A Murder, A Memoir* (1992). *The Track of Real Desires* (1994). *Her Dream of Dreams: The Rise and Triumph of Madam C. J. Walker* (2002).

—MERRILL MAGUIRE SKAGGS

SUSAN LUDVIGSON (1942–). Although a prominent poet of the South, Susan Ludvigson writes just as passionately about people and places far from her home in South Carolina. Born in Rice Lake, Wisc., on February 13, 1942, to Howard C. and Mabel Helgeland Ludvigson, Ludvigson was educated at the University of Wisconsin at River Falls. She married David Bartels, an audiologist, in 1961. The marriage produced a son, Joel David, before it ended in 1974. After moving to Charlotte, N.C., in 1971, she began writing poetry, and in 1973, she received an M.A. in English from the University of North Carolina. Her first collection, *Step Carefully in Night Grass,* was published in 1974. The next year she accepted a position as instructor in the English department at Winthrop University in Rock Hill, S.C., and she continues to teach there as professor and poet-in-residence. In 1988 she married the novelist Scott Ely.

Ludvigson's early collections, *Northern Lights* and *The Swimmer,* were recognized for her psychological portraits and her dark humor. Her experiences in Yugoslavia are reflected in *Defining the Holy;* subsequent collections contain numerous poems about experiences in France and Italy. *Trinity* includes daring portrayals of women's lives, such as the Gospel according to Mary Magdalene and the secret life of Emily Dickinson as portrayed through letters to her from God.

Ludvigson's early writing was supported by fellowships to the Virginia Center for the Creative Arts and to the MacDowell Colony (1979–81). Numerous awards followed, including a Guggenheim grant in 1983 and both a Fulbright award and a National Endowment for the Arts Fellowship in 1984. Her work has appeared in over eighty journals, including the *Atlantic Monthly, Poetry, Paris Review, Southern Review, Shenandoah,* and the *Nation.* As its title poem suggests, Ludvigson noticeably departs from her early work in the experimental *Escaping the House of Certainty.*

WORKS: *Step Carefully in Night Grass* (1974). *The Wisconsin Women* (1980). *Northern Lights* (1981). *The Swimmer* (1984). *Defining the Holy* (1985). *The Beautiful Noon of No Shadow* (1986). *To Find the Gold* (1990). *Everything Winged Must Be Dreaming* (1993). *Helle's Story* (1995). *Trinity* (1996). *Sweet Confluence: New and Selected Poems* (2000). *Escaping the House of Certainty* (2006).

—CAROLYN PERRY

GRACE LUMPKIN (1891–1980). Grace Lumpkin was born in Milledgeville, Ga., on March 3, 1891, daughter of William Wallace and Annette Morris Lumpkin. She graduated from high school in Columbia, S.C., attended the College for Women in Columbia and , and earned a B.D. in 1911 from Brenau College in Gainesville, Ga. After teaching school in Brunswick, Tenn., and Columbia, S.C., Lumpkin became an industrial secretary with the YWCA. She spent eighteen months in France as World War I was ending, and in 1924 moved to New York City to be a writer. She worked for the pacifist magazine *The World Tomorrow* and studied writing at Columbia University. She became involved in both the New Negro literary movement and the proletarian literature movement, publishing her first article on the convergence of these topics in *The World Tomorrow* in April 1926. Her first short stories were published in *New Masses* a year later.

Her first novel, *To Make My Bread,* depicted Appalachian subsistence farmers forced out of the mountains to work in the cotton mills and concluded with the Gastonia textile strike of 1929. The novel won the Maxim Gorky Prize, and a stage version by Albert Bein titled *Let Freedom Ring* was produced in 1935. Lumpkin's next novel, *A Sign for Cain,* was about sharecroppers, Communists, and racial violence in Alabama. Unlike her strongly class-conscious first two novels, *The Wedding* depicted the decline of a southern planter family. In 1933 she also published two potboiler romance novels under the pseudonym Ann Du Pre (*Some Take a Lover* and *Timid Woman*).

Influenced by her friend Whittaker Chambers, Lumpkin broke from the Communist Party. Her embrace of conservative political values and religion is reflected in her autobiographical novel *Full*

Circle and articles she wrote for *National Review*. She lived in rural Virginia in the 1960s and 1970s, moving back to Columbia a few years before her death on March 23, 1980. Her papers are in the University of South Carolina's South Caroliniana Library.

WORKS: *To Make My Bread* (1932). *Some Take a Lover* (1933). *Timid Woman* (1933). *A Sign for Cain* (1935). *The Wedding* (1939). *Full Circle* (1962).

—BRUCE E. BAKER

KATHARINE DU PRE LUMPKIN (1897–1988). Katharine Du Pre Lumpkin, the youngest child of William Wallace and Annette Morris Lumpkin, was born in Macon, Ga., on December 22, 1897. After the family moved to Columbia, S.C., in 1898, she attended the public schools there before entering Brenau College in 1912. Finishing her B.A. in 1915, Lumpkin stayed on at the school as student secretary of the YWCA. In 1918 and 1919 she earned an M.A. in sociology at Columbia University. For the next five years, she was the national student secretary for the YWCA. In 1928 she completed a Ph.D. in sociology at the University of Wisconsin, writing a dissertation on delinquent girls. After one year at Mt. Holyoke, Lumpkin began teaching at Smith College and directing research at the Council of Industrial Studies, where she collaborated with economist Dorothy Wolff Douglas on several studies. The pair became active in the Communist Party in the mid-1930s. In 1939 Lumpkin left Smith and turned her attention to the South.

The South in Progress examined the forces of progress in a region generally considered a political and economic backwater. Its historical perspective would be elaborated in Lumpkin's most important work, *The Making of a Southerner*. Cast as autobiography, this book also used history in a project of social critique. Using her own life story as an example, Lumpkin demonstrated how southerners learned race and class prejudice as children, and how the contradictions they sometimes saw in the South could lead them to question those beliefs and eventually transcend them. On the heels of this successful book, Lumpkin worked for several years on a novel about Reconstruction, but it never satisfied her or her editor and remained unpublished. From 1957 to her retirement in 1967, Lumpkin taught sociology at Wells College. She spent her retirement in Charlottesville, Va., and Chapel Hill, N.C., completing *The Emancipation of Angelina Grimké* at the age of seventy-seven. Katharine Du Pre Lumpkin died in Chapel Hill on May 5, 1988. Her papers are in the Southern Historical Collection at the University of North Carolina.

WORKS: *The Family: A Study in Member Roles* (1933). *Shutdowns in the Connecticut Valley: A Study of Worker Displacement in the Small Industrial Community* (1934). *Child Workers in America* (1937). *The South in Progress* (1940). *The Making of a Southerner* (1946). *The Emancipation of Angelina Grimké* (1974).

—BRUCE E. BAKER

ANDREW LYTLE (1902–1995). Over a long and distinguished career as novelist, critic, and editor, Andrew Nelson Lytle probably did more than any other writer to make the Agrarian vision of life a permanent part of the southern imagination. Born on December 26, 1902, in Murfreesboro, Tenn., Lytle received his B.A. from Vanderbilt University in 1925. After failing in his attempt to become an actor and playwright in New York, he returned to the South in 1929. In his contribution to the Agrarian symposium *I'll Take My Stand* (1930), he paints an idyllic picture of the life of the yeoman farmer. Throughout much of his subsequent life, Lytle tried unsuccessfully to experience such an existence at a succession of farms in Alabama, Tennessee, and Kentucky. He enjoyed much greater success as a teacher of creative writing at Southwestern University in Memphis, the University of the South, the University of Iowa (where Flannery O'Connor was one of his students), and the University of Florida.

As managing editor of the *Sewanee Review* in 1942–43, he helped transform that magazine into one of the major literary quarterlies. He returned as principal editor of the review in 1961–73.

Lytle's densely textured novels have enjoyed more critical than popular success. With the exception of two major works about the Spanish conquest of North America, *At the Moon's Inn* and *Alchemy,* Lytle's fiction deals with southern whites falling short of the divine plan in their stewardship of the earth. His final novel, *The Velvet Horn,* is considered his most technically accomplished work. Some of Lytle's most accessible and engaging writing can be found in his biography of Nathan Bedford Forrest, *Bedford Forrest and His Critter Company,* and his family memoir *A Wake for the Living.*

WORKS: "The Hind Tit," in *I'll Take My Stand: The South and the Agrarian Tradition,* by Twelve Southerners (1930). *Bedford Forrest and His Critter Company* (1931). *The Long Night* (1936). "The Small Farm Secures the State," in *Who Owns America?: A New Declaration of Independence* (1936). *At the Moon's Inn* (1941). *Alchemy* (1942). *A Name for Evil* (1947). *The Velvet Horn* (1957). *A Novel, a Novella, and Four Stories* (1958). *The Hero with the Private Parts: Essays by Andrew Lytle* (1966). Ed., *Craft and Vision: The Best Fiction from the Sewanee Review* (1971). *A Wake for the Living: A Family Chronicle* (1975). *Southerners and Europeans: Essays in a Time of Disorder* (1988). *From Eden to Babylon: The Social and Political Essays of Andrew Nelson Lytle* (1990). *Kristen: A Reading* (1992).

—MARK ROYDEN WINCHELL

DAVID MADDEN (1933–). Gerald David Madden was born in Knoxville, Tenn., on July 25, 1933, to James Helvy Madden and Emile Merritt Madden. In 1951 Madden entered the University of Tennessee, but left soon after to try Greenwich Village, a place he found disappointing. He served in the merchant marine, then the army, during the Korean War but did not see combat. In 1956 he enrolled at Iowa State Teachers College, now the University of Northern Iowa, and married Roberta Margaret Young. After completing his undergraduate degree at the University of Tennessee, he earned his M.A. in creative writing classes at San Francisco State College in 1958.

In 1958–59 Madden taught at Appalachian State Teachers College, then spent 1959–60 at the Yale School of Drama on a playwriting fellowship. Thereafter, he taught for two-year stints at Centre College, the University of Louisville, Kenyon College, and Ohio University. In 1968 he became the Donald and Velvia Crumbley Professor of Creative Writing at Louisiana State University and directed the program from 1992 to 1994. He created the United States Civil War Center at the University in 1993 and served as its director until May 1999.

Madden has worked in a number of genres, including essay, memoir, drama, and poetry, but he is primarily known as a fiction writer. His first novel, *The Beautiful Greed,* is a tale of the sea that borrows from his merchant marine experience; six other novels and two collections of short stories, *The Shadow Knows* and *The New Orleans of Possibilities,* followed relatively quickly, many based on his southern and Appalachian background. Since 1980 he has published only one novel, *Sharpshooter,* and no books of original short stories since 1982. Most of Madden's book publications after 1980 have emerged from his capacity as an editor of textbooks and essay collections on such writers as James Agee, Robert Penn Warren, and Thomas Wolfe.

WORKS: *The Beautiful Greed* (1961). *Wright Morris* (1964). Ed., *Proletarian Writers of the Thirties* (1968). Ed., *Tough Guy Writers of the Thirties* (1968). *Cassandra Singing* (1969). *The Poetic Image in Six Genres* (1969). *James M. Cain* (1970). *The Shadow Knows* (1970). Ed., *American Dreams, American Nightmares* (1970). Ed., *Rediscoveries: Informal Essays in Which Well-Known Novelists Rediscover Neglected Works of Fiction by One of Their Favorite Authors* (1971). *Brothers in Confidence* (1972). Ed., *The Popular Culture Explosion,* with Ray B. Browne (1972). Ed., *Nathanael West: The Cheaters and the Cheated* (1973). *Bijou* (1974). Ed., *Remembering James Agee* (1974). *The Day the Flowers Came: A Drama in One Act* (1975). *Creative Choices: A Spectrum of Quality and Technique in Fiction* (1975). *Harlequin's Stick, Charlie's Cane: A Comparative Study of Commedia dell'Arte and Silent Comedy* (1975). Ed., *Studies in the Short Story,* with Virgil Scott (1975; 6th ed. 1984). *The Suicide's Wife* (1978). *Pleasure-Dome* (1979). *On the Big Wind* (1980). *A Primer of the Novel: For Readers and Writers* (1980). Ed., *Writer's Revisions: An Annotated Bibliography of Articles and Books about Writers' Revisions and Their Comments on the Creative Process*, with Richard Powers (1981). *The New Orleans of Possibilities* (1982). *Cain's Craft* (1985). *Revising Fiction: A Handbook for Writers* (1988). Ed., *Rediscoveries II: Important Writers Select Their Favorite Works of Neglected Fiction*, with Peggy Bach (1988). *The Fiction Tutor* (1990). Ed., *Eight Classic American Novels* (1990). Ed., *The World of Fiction* (1990). Ed., *A Pocketful of Prose: Contemporary Short Fiction* (1992). *Sharpshooter: A Novel of the Civil War* (1996). Ed., *A Pocketful of Poems: Vintage Verse* (1996). Ed., *A Pocketful of Plays: Vintage Drama* (1996). Ed., *Remembering James Agee*, 2nd ed., with Jeffrey J. Folks (1997). Ed., *The Legacy of Robert Penn Warren* (2000). Ed., *Beyond the Battlefield: The Ordinary Life and Extraordinary Times of the Civil War Soldier* (2000). Ed., *A Pocketful of Essays* (2001). Ed., *Thomas Wolfe's Civil War* (2004).

—JEFFREY H. RICHARDS

JAMES MADISON (1751–1836). The fourth president of the United States, James Madison was born March 16, 1751, the eldest of ten children of James and Nelly Conway Madison, a substantial planter and slaveholding family in Orange County, Va. Following tutoring by local clergymen, Madison entered Donald Robertson's school at age twelve and continued there for five years. Robertson, a Scot, influenced Madison's decision to enroll at the College of New Jersey in 1769. For the first time he traveled beyond the Old Dominion, discovered at Princeton a lively collegiate community, and completed the baccalaureate program in two years. Awarded a B.A. in the fall of 1771, Madison remained for six months, studying under President John Witherspoon. There followed a difficult three-year period that found the young graduate at home, uncertain about the choice of a career, abandoning thoughts of the ministry and inclining toward the law, experiencing melancholy and recurring ill health, and concluding that he had but a short time to live. From indecision, introspection, and unhappiness he was suddenly catapulted by the revolutionary crisis into a lifetime of political leadership.

In the forty years following his election to the Orange County Committee on Safety in December 1774, Madison moved rapidly from local to state to national levels of influence. Election to the Virginia provisional convention in 1776 was followed by membership on the governor's council in 1778 and selection by the assembly in 1780 as a delegate to the Continental Congress. For the last three years of the Revolutionary War, Madison participated in the critical military, political, and diplomatic decisions made at the continental level. Upon his return to Virginia in December 1783, he professed a desire for the quiet life of a gentleman-scholar-planter, but he quickly put this aside when opportunities for an active political role presented themselves: election to the Virginia House of Delegates in 1784, attendance at the Annapolis Convention, representation of Virginia in the Confederation Congress in 1787, and selection as a delegate to the Constitutional Convention of 1787.

At Philadelphia in the summer of 1787, Madison led the fight for a strong national government. He left his countrymen greatly in his debt by keeping the only detailed notes of the convention debates and proceedings, and through his contributions to *The Federalist*, originally newspaper essays written with John Jay and Alexander Hamilton, in 1787–88, he played a major role in defining republican political theory and interpreting the intent and character of the Constitution. His reputation for political sagacity secured, Madison discovered that the practical tasks of fashioning a new national government afforded opportunities for demonstrating his leadership. As a member of the House of Representatives (1789–97), he quickly emerged as the spokesman for those opposing Hamilton's economic program and, in the wake of these legislative battles, set about organizing an opposition party, the first in the nation's political history. Next, as secretary of state (1801–9) during Jefferson's two presidential terms, he played an important role in charting a course designed both to preserve peace and defend

American trading rights as Europe was convulsed by war. Finally, as president (1809–17), the search for peace with honor having failed, he led an ill-prepared nation into a war with Great Britain that brought neither gain nor glory. But it also brought no substantial losses, and while this unhappy event continues to provoke questions about the quality of Madison's statesmanship, the conclusion of the war ushered in an era of dynamic national growth.

In 1794, at age forty-three, the shy, sober, dispassionate "Jemmy" Madison had married Dolley Payne Todd, a lively young widow who in her own right did much to make the nation's new capital a more tolerable place. Madison died on June 28, 1836, at Montpelier, their Virginia home. He had spent the last two decades of his life at Montpelier, entertaining friends and travelers, lending support to public causes, most notably the American Colonization Society, and attempting to discharge the substantial debts accumulated in a lifetime devoted to public service.

The preeminent political theorist in the Revolutionary generation, Madison was no ivory-tower scholar. His delineation of republicanism came in essays, tracts, and articles addressing immediate problems. His writings are marked by a tough-minded appraisal of human nature, a realistic grasp of the social and economic conditions underlying political issues and ideals, a calm elevated tone, and tightly reasoned arguments that evince an abiding faith in reason itself as the source of truth and equity. It is a mark of his genius that these products of the moment have proved timeless in their capacity to instruct and inspire.

WORKS: *Letters and Other Writings of James Madison*, 4 vols., ed. William C. Rives and Philip R. Fendall (1865). *The Writings of James Madison*, 9 vols., ed. Gaillard Hunt (1900–1910). *The Federalist* [1787–88], ed. Jacob E. Cooke (1961). *The Papers of James Madison, Congressional Series*, 17 vols., ed. various (1962–91). *Notes of Debates in the Federal Convention of 1787. Reported by James Madison [1840]*, ed. Adrienne Koch (1966). *The Mind of the Founder: Sources of the Political Thought of James Madison*, ed. Marvin Meyers (1973). *The Papers of James Madison, Presidential Series*, 5 vols., ed. Robert A. Rutland et al. (1984–). *The Papers of James Madison, Secretary of State Series*, 6 vols., ed. Robert J. Brugger et al. (1986–). *The Essential Federalist*, with Alexander Hamilton and John Jay, ed. Quentin P. Taylor (1998). *Writings*, ed. Jack N. Rakove (1999).

—JOHN K. NELSON

CLARENCE MAJOR (1936–). Poet, novelist, essayist, editor, educator, and visual artist, Clarence Major has sought throughout his career to break the boundaries of traditional concepts of literature and art. Major's fiction is often linked with that of Ishmael Reed and William Melvin Kelley because of its highly experimental style. Although much of his adult life has been spent outside the American South, the region figures importantly in his work. He once described his novel *No* as "very definitely a Southern novel." Many of his protagonists find themselves attempting to come to terms with the reality of their lives as black southerners.

Major was born in Atlanta, Ga., on December 31, 1936. He was the eldest child of Clarence Major and Inez Huff Major. After his parents divorced in the late 1940s, his mother moved the children to Chicago. As a youngster, Major originally desired to become a visual artist and was awarded lessons at the Art Institute of Chicago, but eventually abandoned that idea. After high school he spent two years in the U.S. Air Force, as a record specialist. Major married and divorced twice in the 1960s; those marriages resulted in six children. He married Pamela Jane Ritter in 1980.

Major entered the literary world in 1954 with a collection of poetry, *The Fires That Burn in Heaven*. His first novel, *All Night Visitors*, was released in 1969 to some controversy, as his publisher insisted the book be heavily edited before publication. (The book was reissued in unadulterated form in 1998.) Major earned a Ph.D. in literature and art from the Union for Experimenting Colleges and Universities in 1978 and has held faculty positions at numerous universities across the United States. Editor of several prominent literary journals and anthologies of African American writing, he has also compiled a dictionary of African American speech. Reclaiming his roots as a visual artist, he became a serious painter.

Major openly took issue with the existence of a "Black Aesthetic," a type of writing specific to African American authors, and criticized the openly propagandistic black fiction that arose in the late 1960s and early 1970s. For Major, artistic quality comes before political concerns, and he countered that all good writing was individual and self-referential, yet universal and understandable by anyone. He did not discount the influence of being African American on literary production, or the importance of exploring black experience, but did not agree that African American literature had to restrict itself to polemicizing about social concerns or to particular forms. While claiming several European and white American writers as influences, Major calls for a new concept of art that goes beyond the traditional and the expected, moving within itself and without to search for meaning and fulfill its purpose of enlightenment.

WORKS: *The Fires That Burn in Heaven* (1954). *Love Poems of a Black Man* (1965). *Human Juices* (1966). *Writers Workshop Anthology* (1967). *Man Is Like a Child: An Anthology of Creative Writing by Students* (1968). *All Night Visitors* (1969). *The New Black Poetry* (1969). *Dictionary of Afro-American Slang* (1970). *Swallow the Lake* (1970). *Black Slang: A Dictionary of Afro-American Talk* (1971). *Private Line* (1971). *Symptoms and Madness: Poems* (1971). *The Cotton Club: New Poems* (1972). *No* (1973). *The Dark and Feeling: Black American Writers and Their Work* (1974). *The Syncopated Cakewalk* (1974). *Reflex and Bone Structure* (1975). *Emergency Exit* (1979). *Parking Lots* (1982). *Inside Diameter: The France Poems* (1985). *My Amputations: A Novel* (1986). *Such Was the Season: A Novel* (1987). *Painted Turtle, Woman with Guitar: A Novel* (1988). *Some Observations of a Stranger at Zuni in the Latter Part of the Century* (1988). *Surfaces and Masks: A Poem* (1988). *Fun and Games: Short Fictions* (1990). *Calling the Wind: Twentieth Century African American Short Stories* (1993). *Juba to Jive: A Dictionary of African American Slang* (1994). *Dirty Bird Blues: A Novel* (1996). *The Garden Thrives: Twentieth Century African American Poetry* (1996). *Configurations: New and Selected Poems, 1958–1998* (1998). *Afterthought: Essays and Criticism* (2000). *Necessary Distance: Essays and Criticism* (2001). *Trips: A Memoir* (2001). *Come by Here: My Mother's Life* (2002). *Conversations with Clarence Major* (2002). *Waiting for Sweet Betty* (2002). *One Flesh* (2003).

—KRISTINA D. BOBO

WILLIAM MARCH (1893–1954). William March, once among the most widely read American novelists and short-story writers of the early twentieth century, is known today for *The Bad Seed*, a potboiler that became a cult movie, or a famous first novel, *Company K*, about combat in World War I France.

During March's career, he was regarded as a master of the magazine short story, with his fiction reprinted in popular collections, including *The Little Wife and Other Stories*, *Some Like Them Short*, and *Trial Balance*. He was also regarded as a prominent southern novelist, with a series of works such as *Come in at the Door*, *The Tallons*, and *The Looking Glass*, all centering, as do many of his stories, on a mythical Pearl County, Ala., with its central town of Reedyville.

In life, he was William Edward Campbell, known to most people not as a writer but as an executive of the Waterman Steamship Line, headquartered in Mobile but dispatching March for extended periods of residence in New York. March himself was a bona fide World War I hero, a member of the Fifth Marines, and a winner of the Croix de Guerre, the Distinguished Service Cross, and the Navy Cross.

March's great achievement will always be *Company K*, a collocation of first-person narratives, by a company of U.S. Marines. We realize eventually that many of the voices are those of the dead. Along with Thomas Boyd's *Through the Wheat, Company K* is one of the few works of World War I fiction about combat by a skilled writer who was an actual combatant. Comparisons of the Pearl County short stories and novels to Faulkner's Yoknapatawpha saga are unfair to March. He was a traditional realist-naturalist, quietly courageous about social issues of race, poverty, discrimination, cruelty, and the social pressures of conformity, and possessed of a gift for understanding buried lives. In *A William March Omnibus* (1956), Alistair Cooke called him "the unrecognized genius of our time."

WORKS: *Company K* (1931). *Come in at the Door* (1934). *The Little Wife and Other Stories* (1935). *The Tallons* (1936). *Some Like Them Short* (1939). *The Looking Glass* (1943). *Trial Balance* (1945). *October Island* (1952). *The Bad Seed* (1952).

—PHILIP D. BEIDLER

JEFF DANIEL MARION (1940–). Cherishing his heritage, Jeff Daniel Marion writes of the scenes and people of what he terms his "heart's true county," the area around Rogersville, Tenn., where he was born on July 7, 1940. His poetic sensibility was nurtured by an unusually close-knit family who gave him a legacy of reverence for nature, involvement in the Baptist Church, and a passion for story-telling. His parents, Eloise Gladson and J. D. Marion, grew up on nearby farms and knew each other from childhood. His mother's two sisters married his father's brothers.

Marion earned a B.S. from the University of Tennessee, then taught high school, first in Knoxville and then in Rogersville. In 1966 he earned a master's degree in English from the University of Tennessee, then did further graduate study at the University of Tennessee, the University of Southern Mississippi, and the University of Alabama. While pursuing his graduate studies, Marion became friends with a graduate of Carson-Newman College, a small Baptist school in Jefferson City, Tenn. His friend's fond memories of his college days inspired Marion to seek employment at Carson-Newman. He taught creative writing there from 1969 until his retirement in the spring of 2002. In addition, he served as the college's poet-in-residence, director of the Appalachian Center, and editor of *Mossy Creek Reader,* a literary review. Marion also participated in the Poet-in-the Schools program in North Carolina, Virginia, and Tennessee; taught at the Tennessee Governor's School of the Humanities; and founded the *Small Farm,* a journal focusing upon Appalachian poetry, which he edited from 1975 to 1980. Presently Marion resides with his wife, Linda Parsons, a fellow poet, in Knoxville, delights in the company of his two granddaughters, and operates Mill Springs Press, which produces chapbooks and broadsides from handset type. He continues to lecture and to conduct poetry workshops through-out the Appalachian region.

Throughout his career as poet, essayist, fiction writer, editor, and printer, Marion has celebrated the cultural richness of southern Appalachia and proudly proclaimed his revelation that the past launches us upon a pilgrimage of self-discovery and renewal.

WORKS: *Out in the Country, Back Home* (1976). *Tight Lines* (1981). *Vigils: Selected Poems* (1990). *Hello, Crow* (1992). *Lost and Found* (1994). *The Chinese Poet Awakens* (1999). *Letters Home* (2001). *Ebbing and Flowing Spring: New and Selected Poems and Prose, 1976–2001* (2002).

—LYNNE P. SHACKELFORD

DOUG MARLETTE (1949–). Doug Marlette, novelist and cartoonist, was born in Greensboro, N.C., in 1949 and raised in Durham, N.C., Laurel, Miss., and Sanford, Fla. Soon after graduating from Florida State University in 1972, he began work as an editorial cartoonist with the *Charlotte Observer.*

Marlette's cartoons have been both controversial and highly acclaimed. In 1981 he was the first car‑
toonist to be awarded a Nieman Fellowship to Harvard. In 1988, a year after he moved to the *Atlanta Constitution*, he won a Pulitzer Prize. He drew cartoons for *New York Newsday* from 1989 to 2001, and the *Tallahassee Democrat* beginning in 2002. Marlette has been criticized from both sides of the po‑
litical spectrum, and some of his editorial cartoons about religion have been especially controversial, though even-handed, drawing sharp attacks from Catholic, Muslim, Jewish, and Evangelical Christian groups.

In 1981 Marlette began drawing *Kudzu*, a daily comic strip set in the fictional small town of Bypass, N.C., and featuring a cast of quirky southern characters. Among these is the Reverend Will B. Dunn, an irreverent preacher whose prototype is the itinerant Mississippi Baptist minister and author Will D. Campbell. The strip is syndicated in more than three hundred papers and has appeared in sev‑
eral volumes of collected *Kudzu* cartoons. In 1996 Marlette and the Red Clay Ramblers collaborated on *Kudzu, the Southern Musical*, a stage adaptation of the comic strip.

Marlette's first novel, the semi-autobiographical *The Bridge*, tells of a successful but contentious editorial cartoonist who has returned home to the South from New York. The book is set alternately in the 1990s, as the protagonist adapts to his new surroundings and investigates his family's history, and in the 1930s, as his grandmother and other cotton-mill workers are challenged by mill owners and police during the 1934 General Textile Strike.

In the 1990s Marlette and his family moved to Hillsborough, N.C., and he taught some classes in the School of Journalism and Mass Communication at the University of North Carolina at Chapel Hill. Even as Marlette explored different art forms, his creative output did not wane. While researching and writing a novel, he continued to produce five editorial cartoons a week and a daily comic strip. In any format, his work is distinguished by humor, southern themes, and a willingness to challenge authority.

WORKS: *The Emperor Has No Clothes: Editorial Cartoons* (1976). *Drawing Book: Political Cartoons* (1980). *Kudzu* (1982). *It's a Dirty Job—But Somebody Has to Do It!* (1984). *Preacher: The Wit and Wisdom of Reverend Will B. Dunn* (1984). *Just a Simple Country Preacher: More Wit and Wisdom of Reverend Will B. Dunn* (1985). *Chocolate Is My Life: Featuring Doris the Parakeet* (1987). *There's No Business Like Soul Business* (1987). *"I Am Not a Televangelist!": The Continuing Saga of Reverend Will B. Dunn* (1988). *Shred This Book: The Scandalous Cartoons of Doug Marlette* (1988). *A Doublewide with a View: The Kudzu Chronicles* (1989). *'Til Stress Do Us Part: A Guide to Modern Love by Reverend Will B. Dunn* (1989). *In Your Face: A Cartoonist at Work* (1991). *Even White Boys Get the Blues: Kudzu's First Ten Years* (1992). *The Before and After Book* (1992). *Faux Bubba: Bill and Hillary Go to Washington* (1993). *Gone with the Kudzu* (1995). *I Feel Your Pain!* (1996). *The Bridge* (2001). *What Would Marlette Drive?* (2003).

—NICHOLAS GRAHAM

DON MARQUIS (1878–1937). Don Marquis was a celebrated New York newspaper columnist and humorist who is remembered today chiefly for his stories of Archy and Mehitabel, a lowercase-typing cockroach and *toujours gai* alley cat. In his lifetime, however, Marquis was known equally well for the Old Soak, a rummy foe of Prohibition whose tales were recounted in two books, a hit Broadway play, and two movies.

Donald Robert Perry Marquis was born on July 29, 1878, in Walnut, Ill. After brief stints as a reporter in Washington, D.C., and Philadelphia, he took a job at the *Atlanta News* in 1902, and then the *Atlanta Journal*, before Joel Chandler Harris hired him in 1907 as associate editor of *Uncle Remus's Magazine*. Marquis honed his storytelling talents there and also met his first wife, Reina Melcher, a freelance writer.

In 1909 Marquis moved to New York, and in 1912 the *Evening Sun* gave him a signed daily column, "The Sun Dial." It won fame for its mix of quips, commentary, and verse, and for its farcical characters who chronicled events and fashions of the time. The cast included the Old Soak, Archy and Mehitabel, and Hermione, a Greenwich Village dilettante.

Marquis jumped to the *New York Tribune* in 1922—his column renamed "The Lantern"—and then quit newspapers for good in 1925. He was exhausted by the work and heartsick from recent tragedies: the death of his only son in 1921 and Reina's unexpected death in 1923. He remarried in 1926, to the actress Marjorie Vonnegut, but the tragedies continued. His only daughter died in 1931, and Marjorie in 1936.

For ten years Marquis wrote regularly for *Collier's* and other magazines. He also worked as a playwright and screenwriter, but with limited success. He suffered debilitating strokes in 1935 and 1936 and died December 29, 1937.

WORKS: *The History of the Fighting Fourteenth* (1911). *Danny's Own Story* (1912). *Dreams and Dust* (1915). *The Cruise of the Jasper B.* (1916). *Hermione and Her Little Group of Serious Thinkers* (1916). *Prefaces* (1919). *The Old Soak; and, Hail and Farewell* (1921). *Carter, and Other People* (1921). *Noah an' Jonah an' Cap'n John Smith: A Book of Humorous Verse* (1921). *Poems and Portraits* (1922). *Sonnets to a Red-Haired Lady (by a Gentleman with a Blue Beard) and Famous Love Affairs* (1922). *The Revolt of the Oyster* (1922). *Mr. Hawley Breaks into Song* (1923). *The Old Soak's History of the World, with Occasional Glances at Baycliff, L.I., and Paris, France* (1924). *Pandora Lifts the Lid* (1924). *The Awakening and Other Poems* (1924). *Words and Thoughts: A Play in One Act* (1924). *The Dark Hours: Five Scenes from a History* (1924). *The Old Soak: A Comedy in Three Acts* (1926). *Out of the Sea: A Play in Four Acts* (1927). *The Almost Perfect State* (1927). *Archy and Mehitabel* (1927). *Love Sonnets of a Cave Man and Other Verses* (1928). *When the Turtles Sing and Other Unusual Tales* (1928). *A Variety of People* (1929). *An Ode to Hollywood* (1929). *The Nightcap: A Mystery in Three Acts* (1929). *Off the Arm* (1930). *Archys Life of Mehitabel* (1933). *Master of the Revels: A Comedy in Four Acts* (1934). *Chapters for the Orthodox* (1934). *Her Foot Is on the Brass Rail* (1935). *Archy Does His Part* (1935). *Sun Dial Time* (1936). *The Old Soak; The Old Soak's History of the World* (1937). *Sons of the Puritans* (1939). *The Lives and Times of Archy and Mehitabel* (1940). *The Best of Don Marquis* (1946). *Everything's Jake* (1978). *Selected Letters of Don Marquis* (1982). *Archyology: The Long Lost Tales of Archy and Mehitabel*, ed. Jeff Adams (1996). *Archyology II: The Final Dig: The Long Lost Tales of Archy and Mehitabel*, ed. Adams (1998).

—JOHN BATTEIGER

VALERIE MARTIN (1948–). Valerie Martin, novelist and short-story writer, has won increasing acclaim since the success of *Mary Reilly,* her rewriting of Robert Louis Stevenson's *The Strange Case of Dr. Jekyll and Mr. Hyde* from the point of view of a female servant. In 2003 she won Britain's prestigious Orange Prize for *Property,* a novel set in antebellum Louisiana.

She was born Valerie Metcalf on March 14, 1948, in Sedalia, Mo., and returned with her parents—John Roger, a sea captain, and Valerie Fleisher Metcalf—to her mother's native New Orleans in 1951. There she attended Mount Carmel Academy, a Catholic girls' school. She earned a B.A. in education at the University of New Orleans in 1970, and in the same year married Robert Martin, an artist. She worked for the Louisiana Department of Welfare before completing an M.F.A. at the University of Massachusetts in 1974. Returning to New Orleans, Martin in 1976 published the story collection *Love* and worked on *Set in Motion*—which drew on her brief experience in social work—in Walker Percy's writing seminar at Loyola University.

She soon published that novel with Farrar, Straus and Giroux, but lost their interest after *Alexandra.* She began teaching at her undergraduate alma mater in 1980. She and Robert Martin were divorced in 1984; they had one daughter, Adrienne. Having taken a position as a lecturer at Mount

Holyoke College (1986–89), Martin went on to teach at the University of Massachusetts (1989–97). *Mary Reilly,* made into a film in 1996, established both her critical and her popular reputation.

Now married to James Watson, Martin wrote *Italian Fever* while living in Rome in the late 1990s. That novel, about a young American woman's experiences abroad, reflects her consistent gothic themes as well as the intermittent engagement with Catholicism that strongly marked her subsequent foray into nonfiction in *Salvation.* Her ongoing interest in perverse and violent psychological states, especially in women, has perhaps reached its culmination in *Property,* which is narrated by the miserable and sadistic slaveholding mistress of an early-nineteenth-century sugar plantation. All of Martin's novels have been set in either Louisiana or Europe.

WORKS: *Love: Short Stories* (1976). *Set in Motion* (1978). *Alexandra* (1979). *A Recent Martyr* (1987). *The Consolation of Nature and Other Stories* (1988). *Mary Reilly* (1990). *The Great Divorce* (1994). *Italian Fever* (1999). *Salvation: Scenes from the Life of St. Francis* (2001). *Property* (2003).

—FARRELL O'GORMAN

BOBBIE ANN MASON (1940–). Chronicler of a changing South, Bobbie Ann Mason has struck chords that have resonated with a national audience. Mason's life mirrors the change that is a central theme of her work. Born on May 1, 1940, in Mayfield, Ky., daughter of Wilburn A., a dairy farmer, and Christie Lee Mason, she was the oldest of four children. Beginning her formal schooling in a small rural school, in Mayfield's high school she later experienced class divisions between town and country. Shy by nature, she had always been taken with books, but the passion that she shared with her parents for popular music would color her dream world and then lead her into an ever-widening orbit. As a young teen, she was an avid fan of the Hilltoppers, the popular music group born at Western Kentucky State College; her support of the group would lead her to the presidency of their national fan club, to interviews on radio and television, and to travel to towns and cities as far away as Detroit.

After graduating with a B.A. in English from the University of Kentucky in 1962, she moved to New York to work as a writer for various movie and television magazines, but she soon returned to academia, earning an M.A. in 1966 at the State University of New York at Binghamton and a Ph.D. in English from the University of Connecticut in 1972. Her dissertation on Nabokov's novel *Ada* was published as a book in 1974. In the same year, looking back to books that had helped mold her, Mason published *The Girl Sleuth: A Feminist Guide to the Bobbsey Twins, Nancy Drew, and Their Sisters.* From 1972 through 1979 she was an assistant professor at Mansfield State College in Mansfield, Pa., where she lived with her husband, Roger B. Rawlings, a magazine editor and writer. The couple had married in 1969; they have no children.

The other Roger who played a key role in her life is Roger Angell, one of the fiction editors at the *New Yorker.* Although he kept rejecting her stories, he continued to send her encouraging comments, eventually accepting "Offerings" in 1980. The career of the fiction writer was at last launched, and the *New Yorker* became an outlet for many of her stories. With the publication of *Shiloh and Other Stories,* winner of the PEN/Hemingway Award, Mason had earned a prominent place in the minimalist tradition of Raymond Carver.

Another flurry of attention followed in 1984 when she published her first novel. *In Country* portrays a young woman about to enter adulthood and her struggle to understand the Vietnam War (which had claimed the life of the father she never saw) and its legacy. The novel was dramatized as a Hollywood film in 1989.

The shy Mason had herself become the celebrity. She traveled frequently for readings and lectures. Meanwhile, she continued to write and publish accomplished stories, usually set in the corner of

Kentucky where she had lived her youth. A novella, *Spence + Lila*, is based on the solid marriage of her parents. *Feather Crowns*, a long novel set in rural Kentucky at the start of the twentieth century, is an important contribution to Mason's investigation of a changing South—an investigation that continues in her dedication to the short story.

Often portraying characters who wander from the home place and then return, Mason herself decided to return to the state that is omnipresent in her work. In 1990 she and her husband left Pennsylvania for a farm near Lexington, Ky. In *Clear Springs* Mason describes the place and the people who had shaped her. Befitting her interest in popular culture and celebrity, she wrote *Elvis Presley* for the Penguin Biography series.

WORKS: *The Girl Sleuth: A Feminist Guide to the Bobbsey Twins, Nancy Drew, and Their Sisters* (1974); repr. as *The Girl Sleuth: On the Trial of Nancy Drew, Judy Bolton, and Cherry Ames* (1995). *Nabokov's Garden: A Guide to "Ada"* (1974). *Shiloh and Other Stories* (1982). *In Country: A Novel* (1985). *Spence + Lila* (1988). *Love Life: Stories* (1989). *Feather Crowns: A Novel* (1993). *Midnight Magic: Selected Stories of Bobbie Ann Mason* (1998). *Clear Springs: A Memoir* (1999). *Zigzagging Down a Wild Trail: Stories* (2001). *Elvis Presley* (2003). *Atomic Romance: A Novel* (2005).

—JOSEPH M. FLORA

ARMISTEAD MAUPIN (1944–). Armistead Maupin was born on May 13, 1944, in Washington, D.C. He grew up in Raleigh, N.C., in a well-connected and (in his words) "very conservative and militaristic family." In 1966 he received his B.A. from the University of North Carolina at Chapel Hill, where he had been writing a right-wing column for the campus paper and had become a protégé of Jesse Helms, a family friend. He began law school at Chapel Hill, but a year later walked away in the middle of an equity exam. After working briefly for Helms at WRAL-TV in Raleigh, he trained as a navy ensign in Newport, R.I. His service (1968–70) included a posting on the Bassac River near the Vietnamese-Cambodian border.

In 1971 a job with the Associated Press brought Maupin to San Francisco. There he came to terms with his homosexuality, met his long-time partner Terry Anderson, and wrote *Tales of the City*, serialized in the *San Francisco Chronicle* (1976–89) after the first installments appeared in the *Pacific Sun*. *Tales* grew into eight volumes of immensely popular fiction, at once soap opera and soap-opera parody, with a gothic dénouement for the first volume. Though Maupin has the disillusioned narrator of a later novel, *The Night Listener*, disparage the *Tales* series in caustic terms, it remains an unrivaled evocation of San Francisco in the years of its cultural apotheosis, with plot twists and metamorphoses of character sometimes recalling Balzac, Dickens, and Proust.

In 1994 Richard Kramer's screen adaptation of *Tales of the City*, starring Olympia Dukakis and Chloe Webb, was broadcast by PBS, winning the Peabody Award. Its frank homoerotic content, however, led to a confrontation between PBS and the southern conservatives who had once considered Maupin one of their own. Maupin still lives and writes in San Francisco.

WORKS: *Tales of the City* (1978). *More Tales of the City* (1980). *Further Tales of the City* (1982). *Babycakes* (1984). *Significant Others* (1987). *Sure of You* (1989). *Maybe the Moon* (1992). *The Night Listener* (2000).

—DAVID A. CASE

DONALD McCAIG (1940–). Donald McCaig was born in Butte, Mont., in 1940 and earned his B.A. at nearby Montana State University. After graduation, he attended a number of graduate schools and taught philosophy at Wayne State University and at the University of Waterloo in Ontario. He moved to New York City in the 1960s to work as a copywriter for a Madison Avenue advertising agency.

McCaig soon began dating Anne Ashley, a Brooklyn social worker. In 1971, perhaps influenced by the "back-to-the-land" movement popular at the time, he and Anne and another couple moved to an abandoned 280-acre farm in the Virginia mountains in order to pursue a simpler life. The farm had no electricity, no running water, no heat. The nearest town was Williamsville, population twelve. Their two friends returned to New York after a few months on the farm, but Donald and Anne stayed and, eventually, began to produce hay and raise sheep.

McCaig also began his writing career at the farm. Since the early 1970s he has written eight novels, a book of poetry, a collection of essays about rural life, and a nonfiction book about border collies. In addition to contributing book reviews and essays to *Harper's*, *Atlantic*, and the *New York Times*, McCaig appears regularly on National Public Radio's *All Things Considered*.

The publication of *Nop's Trials* brought McCaig widespread recognition and financial success. Inspired by McCaig's border collie Pip, the novel chronicles the adventures of Lewis Burkholder as he searches the country for Nop, the sheep dog that has been stolen from his Virginia farm. McCaig's latest novel, *Jacob's Ladder*, is considered by most critics his best work. Set in the Virginia mountains during the Civil War period, the novel explores the social, psychological, and moral lives of plantation owners, slaves, and other settlers in the region. Noting the historical accuracy and compelling narrative of *Jacob's Ladder*, critics have compared it favorably with the Civil War novels by Shelby Foote, Michael Shaara, and Charles Frazier.

McCaig—writer, sheep farmer, dog trainer, community activist—continues to live happily with Anne and their five border collies on their sheep farm near Williamsville. Both he and Anne are active members of the local Presbyterian church and volunteer fire department.

WORKS: *Caleb, Who Is Hotter Than a Two-Dollar Pistol*, as Steven Ashley (1975). *Last Poems*, as Snee McCaig (1975). *Stalking Blind*, as Steven Ashley (1976). *The Butte Polka* (1980). *Nop's Trials* (1984). *The Man Who Made the Devil Glad* (1986). *Bamboo Cannon* (1989). *Eminent Dogs, Dangerous Men* (1991). *An American Homeplace* (1992). *Nop's Hope* (1994). *Jacob's Ladder: A Story of Virginia during the War* (1998).

—ALLEN PRIDGEN

CORMAC McCARTHY (1933–). Cormac McCarthy's position in American letters as a widely celebrated and sometimes best-selling author dates back only to 1992, when he published *All the Pretty Horses*, first of the novels in his Border Trilogy. Earlier, he had enjoyed critical appreciation but little popular acceptance for five difficult and uncompromising novels, each of them a stylistic triumph but concerned with subject matter that had been described variously as too arcane, too violent, too grotesque, or too shocking to appeal to a broad-based readership. Throughout his career, McCarthy has guarded his private life, refusing interviews, public appearances, and the like. He has no public persona—except his reputation for remaining elusive—and his biographical facts remain generally unelaborated.

At his birth in Providence, R.I., on July 20, 1933, he was named Charles Joseph McCarthy, Jr., and was the third of six children in the family of Charles, Sr., and Gladys McCarthy. Sources differ as to whether the Gaelic name Cormac—evidently from the Irish king associated with Blarney Castle—was used within the family or taken later by the author. In 1937 the family moved to Knoxville, Tenn., where the father held a position as attorney for the Tennessee Valley Authority. Cormac attended parochial schools while growing up in a comfortable rural environment south of the city. He graduated from Catholic High School in Knoxville in 1951 and enrolled as a freshman at the University of Tennessee, dropping out, perhaps to travel, the next year. From 1953 to 1957 he served in the United

States Air Force and spent part of his enlistment as a radio operator in Alaska. Upon his discharge he returned to the university, majoring successively in engineering and business administration and publishing in the *Phoenix,* a campus literary magazine, the first of his fiction (two short stories) to see print. McCarthy left college in 1961 without graduating, married Lee Holleman, and had a son, Cullen. Living in Chicago and working at various jobs to support his new family, McCarthy completed his first novel, *The Orchard Keeper,* published in 1965, a year after he and Holleman divorced. In 1966 he married Annie DeLisle, a singer, at a ceremony in her native England, after which they lived and traveled in Europe before returning to settle in the Rockford, Tenn., area in 1967. By the time they were divorced in 1968, McCarthy had moved to El Paso, Tex., where he lived an austere and private life, writing fiction and conducting some of the voluminous research on southwest history that was to go into *Blood Meridian* and the later Texas novels.

Throughout McCarthy's writing career a number of prestigious grants and awards provided subsistence and encouragement not yet available to him through the sale of his books. Among these were an Ingram-Merrill Foundation grant (1960); a William Faulkner Foundation Award and an American Academy of Arts and Letters Award (1965); a Rockefeller Foundation grant (1966); a Guggenheim Fellowship (1969); and the munificent MacArthur Fellowship (1981). Important early recognition of his talent came from his editor at Random House, Albert Erskine (who had also worked with William Faulkner in the same capacity), and from influential critics and fellow writers such as Shelby Foote and the psychologist Robert Coles.

With *All the Pretty Horses* McCarthy moved to a style and narrative method of much greater accessibility than in his earlier works, and was rewarded with a National Book Award, a National Book Critics Circle Award, and sales and public interest that extended to subsequent novels in the trilogy, *The Crossing* and *Cities of the Plain.* The Cormac McCarthy Society serves this interest with current postings on the Internet, although McCarthy himself remains far removed from public contact.

WORKS: *The Orchard Keeper* (1965). *Outer Dark* (1968). *Child of God* (1973). *The Gardener's Son* [screenplay for Public Broadcasting System] (1977). *Suttree* (1979). *Blood Meridian; or, The Evening Redness in the West* (1985). *All the Pretty Horses* (1992). *The Stonemason* [a play] (1994). *The Crossing* (1994). *Cities of the Plain* (1998). *No Country for Old Men* (2005).

—JERRY LEATH MILLS

ED McCLANAHAN (1932–). One of the most distinctive voices in southern writing sounds in Ed McClanahan's fiction and nonfiction. It is a voice at once satirical of heroic rhetoric, true to country diction, and infused with clear-eyed perception of himself, his characters, and their place in a larger scheme. His fictions are remarkable for their hilarity and their long gestation (twenty-two years for *The Natural Man* and thirty years for "Finch's Song: A Schoolbus Tragedy" in *A Congress of Wonders*).

A native of Brooksville in northeastern Kentucky, Edward Poage McClanahan knew early on that he wanted to be a writer, though as a young man he put in time driving a school bus and working construction. He began undergraduate school at Washington and Lee, where vain attempts to make a southern gentleman of him sent him hustling to Miami of Ohio, from which he graduated in 1955. Precociously, he sought instruction at writers' conferences (from May Sarton at one and Saul Bellow at another) and in graduate school, first at Stanford in 1955–56 (Richard Scowcroft and Malcolm Cowley), then at the University of Kentucky (Hollis Summers and Robert Hazel), where he got an M.A. in 1958. Subsequently, he taught writing at Oregon State College until 1962, when he won a Stegner Fellowship (as had Kentuckians Wendell Berry, James Baker Hall, and Gurney Norman before him).

This time, he remained at Stanford for ten years teaching creative writing with his mentor Wallace Stegner. He took up residence in Perry Lane, and, wearing biker boots, flowing red cape, shades, and big moustache, became "Captain Kentucky" in Ken Kesey's circle. His exuberant essays, which he first published in *Esquire, Playboy,* and *Rolling Stone,* often take their subjects from the 1960s. His 1973 *Esquire* piece on Little Enis, an early Elvis imitator who sang at the Zebra Bar in Lexington, is a classic of its genre.

He also has taught at the University of Montana (1973–75) and the University of Kentucky (several stints, the first in 1972–73). He has five children and lives in Lexington with his wife, Hilda.

WORKS: *The Natural Man* (1983). *Famous People I Have Known* (1985). *A Congress of Wonders* (1996). *My Vita, If You Will* (1998). *Fondelle; or, The Whore with a Heart of Gold* (2002). Ed., *Spit in the Ocean 7: All About Ken Kesey* (2003).

—JANE GENTRY VANCE

JILL McCORKLE (1958–). Novelist and short-story writer Jill McCorkle was born in Lumberton, N.C., on July 7 (the title of her second novel, published on the same day as *The Cheer Leader*), 1958. Her father, John Wesley McCorkle, Jr., was a postal worker; her mother, née Melba Collins, a medical secretary. As a child she spent much time with her grandmother, listening to family stories. The events, people, accents, and culture of the Lumberton area in which she grew up form the matrix of most of her geographically identifiable work. A graduate of Lumberton High School in 1976, where she was indeed a cheer leader, she entered the University of North Carolina at Chapel Hill as a recreation major. In her junior year, she studied creative writing with Louis Rubin, and later Lee Smith, switched her major to English—and changed her life. After graduating with highest honors in 1980, she earned an M.F.A. in creative writing from Hollins College in 1981.

McCorkle's first marriage, to Steven Alexander in 1981, ended in 1984. During this time she began publishing short stories, and held short-term jobs as a receptionist, teacher, librarian, and secretary. Favorable reviews of her debut novels brought invitations to teach creative writing part time, at Duke University and her alma mater; and in 1987–89 at Tufts University during the residency of her second husband, Daniel Shapiro, M.D., whom she married in 1987. Following the birth of their daughter, Claudia, in 1989, the couple returned to Chapel Hill, where McCorkle again taught at the University of North Carolina and published two more novels and a short-story collection: *Tending to Virginia, Ferris Beach* and *Crash Diet: Stories.* A son, Robert, was born in 1991. In 1992 the family returned to Boston, where they remain. McCorkle has taught creative writing at Harvard and at Bennington. Amidst ties of family and friends who both inspire and sustain her work, she continues to write reviews and fiction, including another novel, *Carolina Moon.*

WORKS: *The Cheer Leader* (1984). *July 7th* (1984). *Tending to Virginia* (1987). *Ferris Beach* (1990). *Crash Diet: Stories* (1992). *Carolina Moon* (1996). *Final Vinyl Days* (1998). *Creatures of Habit: Stories* (2001).

—LYNN Z. BLOOM

SHARYN McCRUMB (1948–). Award-winning novelist Sharyn McCrumb defies categorization. Combining her interest in Appalachian culture with her proven talents as a mystery writer, McCrumb has earned the respect of genre readers, mainstream critics, and literary scholars as well. Born Sharyn Elaine Arwood in Wilmington, N.C., in 1948, McCrumb traces her Scots Irish ancestry through late-eighteenth-century Smoky Mountain settlers and further to the old country. Her family legacy informs her fiction. With her husband, David, and children, Laura and Spencer, McCrumb lives in Shawsville, Va., in the heart of Appalachia.

Although McCrumb established her reputation as a mystery writer, her work transcends genre. Her satire can be devastating, as demonstrated in her murder mystery set at a science fiction convention, *Bimbos of the Death Sun,* and her withering analysis of American society's obsession with beauty, *The PMS Outlaws.* The latter novel features forensic anthropologist/amateur sleuth Elizabeth MacPherson, whose adventures fill nine novels to date. McCrumb has also developed a series of evocative "ballad novels," which she compares to quilts, in that they weave custom, legend, song, history, belief, and inquiry into a revelatory whole. Notable among the consistently well-respected ballad novels are *She Walks These Hills,* winner of the 1994 Agatha Award and the 1995 Macavity, Anthony, and Nero Wolfe Awards, and *The Ballad of Frankie Silver,* a historical novel based upon a North Carolinian mountain woman hanged for murder in 1833. Among her most acclaimed works, *The Songcatcher* offers a capsule history of Appalachian culture as it traces a folksong through seven generations. Like ballads, the novels explore a cultural resonance that transcends time and place, eliciting universal themes through rich regional detail. *St. Dale* is a novel inspired by the death of NASCAR legend Dale Earnhardt.

WORKS: *Sick of Shadows* (1984). *Lovely in Her Bones* (1985). *Highland Laddie Gone* (1986). *Paying the Piper* (1988). *Bimbos of the Death Sun* (1988). *The Windsor Knot* (1990). *If I Ever Return, Pretty Peggy-O* (1990). *Missing Susan* (1991). *Zombies of the Gene Pool* (1992). *McPherson's Lament* (1992). *The Hangman's Beautiful Daughter* (1992). *She Walks These Hills* (1994). *If I'd Killed Him When I Met Him* (1995). *The Rosewood Casket* (1996). *Foggy Mountain Breakdown and Other Stories* (1997). *The Ballad of Frankie Silver* (1998). *The PMS Outlaws* (2000). *The Songcatcher* (2001). *Ghost Riders* (2003). *St. Dale* (2005).

—THOMAS ALAN HOLMES

CARSON McCULLERS (1917–1967). Born Lula Carson Smith on February 19, 1917, in Columbus, Ga., McCullers was the first child of Marguerite Waters and Lamar Smith, a watchmaker and jeweler. In 1919 her brother, Lamar, Jr., was born, and in 1922 their sister, Margarita (Rita) Gachet. At nine McCullers was baptized in the First Baptist Church and attended Sunday school regularly for five years, then withdrew from every activity associated with the church. As a child, she read voraciously, took piano lessons for six years, first with Alice Kierce, then with Mary Tucker, to whom she became deeply attached. When Mrs. Tucker declared that the lessons must stop because of her husband's military transfer to another state, McCullers handled her teacher's dark pronouncement by insisting that she already had decided to be a writer, not a concert pianist. Given McCullers's frail health as a child and throughout her adult years, she lacked the stamina required of a performing artist, and perhaps the talent as well. At seventeen, she moved to New York City to study fiction writing with Dorothy Scarborough and Helen Rose Hull at Columbia University, and later, with Sylvia Chatfield Bates at New York University and Whit Burnett at Columbia. Burnett edited *Story* magazine and published McCullers's first story, "Wunderkind," a subtle mirror image of her emotional and physical break from Mary Tucker.

At twenty, she married James Reeves McCullers and moved with him to Charlotte, N.C., where she began her first novel, *The Heart Is a Lonely Hunter,* published by Houghton Mifflin in 1940, and dedicated to her husband and parents. Having aspired to be a writer himself, Reeves was jealous of his wife's success and resented having to nurse her through a variety of illnesses and perform the household chores she had no interest in or was too sick to do herself. Upon learning that her husband had forged checks on her account and had an affair with their best friend, McCullers divorced him in 1942, but remarried him in 1945 upon his return from the European front during World War II. As a company commander of a U.S. Army Ranger battalion, Reeves was injured in the D-Day invasion of Normandy and returned home a decorated war hero.

Meanwhile, McCullers had continued to write and to publish both fiction and nonfiction, including a number of short stories and three novels, *Reflections in a Golden Eye, The Ballad of the Sad Café*, and *The Member of the Wedding*. After her father's suicide in 1944 (it was reported that he died of a heart attack), her mother bought a house at 131 South Broadway in Nyack, N.Y., and moved there with Rita, then a fiction editor at *Mademoiselle*.

An estrangement of fifteen years had followed McCullers's break with Mary Tucker, relieved only when her former teacher wrote to congratulate her upon the successful Broadway production of *The Member of the Wedding*, a script McCullers also wrote. Mrs. Tucker had been McCullers's "we of me," just as in *The Member of the Wedding* her protagonist, Frankie, falls in love with her brother and his bride and insists that they are her "we of me." A number of McCullers's short stories are derived from such abject feelings of abandonment as a young woman; they also reflect her concept of the immense complexity of love and the disintegration of both of her marriages to Reeves, who committed suicide in Paris in 1953. McCullers died fourteen years later, at the age of fifty, after suffering a massive brain hemorrhage. She is buried beside her mother on a hill overlooking the Hudson River in Nyack, which she called home for the last twenty-five years of her life.

WORKS: *The Heart Is a Lonely Hunter* (1940). *Reflections in a Golden Eye* (1941). *The Ballad of the Sad Café* (1943). *The Member of the Wedding* (1946). *The Member of the Wedding* (play, 1949). *The Ballad of the Sad Café: The Novels and Stories of Carson McCullers* (omnibus ed., 1951). *The Square Root of Wonderful* (play, 1957; book version, 1958). *Sweet as a Pickle, Clean as a Pig* (children's verse, 1959). *Clock without Hands* (1961). *The Mortgaged Heart* (1971). *Collected Stories of Carson McCullers* (1987). *Illumination and Night Glare: The Unfinished Autobiography of Carson McCullers* (1999). *Carson McCullers: Complete Novels* (2001).

—VIRGINIA SPENCER CARR

MICHAEL McFEE (1954–). Born in Asheville, N.C., poet Michael McFee grew up in nearby Arden. His father was a postal clerk, and his mother worked for the Air Weather Service in Asheville before becoming a full-time mother; he has an older sister. After attending Buncombe County schools, McFee began studying design at North Carolina State University, but transferred to the University of North Carolina at Chapel Hill; there he earned a B.A. in English with highest honors in creative writing, then an M.A. in English. He taught creative writing at UNC-Greensboro, Cornell University, and Lawrence University before joining the English Department back at UNC–Chapel Hill. He served two years as poetry editor of the *Carolina Quarterly*, twelve as book commentator for the Chapel Hill public radio station WUNC-FM, thirteen as book editor of the Research Triangle magazine the *Spectator*, and three as assistant poetry editor of *DoubleTake*. A resident of Durham since 1979, he is married to Belinda Pickett, with whom he has a son.

One of the pleasures of McFee's oeuvre is its great variety, but certain topics and approaches do recur. Many poems recall his late parents: his collection *Sad Girl Sitting on a Running Board* tells the story of his mother's life, and his book *Earthly* focuses similarly on his father. Some of the poems in *Sad Girl* are based on family photographs, and McFee has written many other poems that draw their inspiration from other kinds of photos; the poems of *To See*, for instance, comment on landscapes and cityscapes taken by Elizabeth Matheson. His poems combine wit, technical virtuosity, and accessibility—a word he often uses in describing the poetry he admires.

Among his honors are an Ingram Merrill Foundation Fellowship, a Discovery/*The Nation* Award, and an NEA Fellowship.

WORKS: *Plain Air* (1983). Ed., *The Spectator Reader* (1985). *Vanishing Acts* (1989). *Sad Girl Sitting on a Running Board* (1991). *To See,* with photographer Elizabeth Matheson (1991). Ed., *The Language They Speak Is Things to Eat: Poems by Fifteen Contemporary North Carolina Poets* (1994). *Colander* (1996). Ed., *This Is Where We Live: Short Stories by Twenty-five Contemporary North Carolina Writers* (2000). *Earthly* (2001).

—ROBERT M. WEST

MARTHA McFERREN (1947–). Although Martha McFerren has family roots in Louisiana and currently lives in New Orleans with husband Dennis Wall, she was born in Henderson, Tex. She received a B.S. in education and an M.L.S. at North Texas State University in Denton. After earning an M.F.A. at Warren Wilson College, McFerren received a Yaddo Writer's Residency Fellowship in 1985.

Author of four books of poems, McFerren is also a contributing editor for *New Laurel Review* and has been associate director of the New Orleans Poetry Forum since 1978. McFerren's poems began appearing in journals and anthologies, including *Apple Street Anthology* and *Maple Leaf Rag: An Anthology of New Orleans Poetry,* in the late 1970s. Poems were also chosen for *Keener Sounds: Selected Poems from the Georgia Review* and *The Yellow Shoe Poets: Selected Poems, 1964–1999.* Her first book of poems, *Delusions of a Popular Mind,* was published in 1983.

McFerren was awarded a creative-writing fellowship by the National Endowment for the Arts (1991), and she received the Marianne Moore Poetry Prize for *Women in Cars.* In the introduction to this collection, Colette Inez notes McFerren's "sassy, off-beat, nose-thumbing and altogether original voice" as well as a "sense of place that transcends mere landscaping."

Fond of incorporating history (family as well as regional) into contemporary settings and situation, McFerren continues to write the "extraordinarily educated poems" that Dabney Stuart praised in the *Southern Review*'s notice of McFerren's first collection.

WORKS: *Delusions of a Popular Mind* (1983). *Get Out of Here!* (1984). *Contours for Ritual* (1988). *Women in Cars* (1992).

—BES STARK SPANGLER

RALPH McGILL (1898–1969). Ralph Emerson McGill was among the South's most influential journalists during the civil rights movement. As editor-in-chief and publisher of the *Atlanta Constitution* before and during that crucial era, he appealed for moderation in terms of race relations in Georgia and its capital city, and earned a national reputation as "the conscience of the South."

McGill was born on a mountain farm in Igou's Ferry, Tenn., in 1898. His family moved to the coal-mining town of Soddy a year later and then, five years after that, thirty miles south to Chattanooga, where McGill spent his childhood and adolescence. In 1917 he entered Vanderbilt University, though he soon left to serve in the Marine Corps during the last months of World War I. He returned to Vanderbilt after the war, but just months before his graduation was expelled because of a column in the student newspaper suggesting mismanagement of funds by the administration.

McGill quickly became a reporter for the *Nashville Banner,* spending much of the 1920s as its sports editor and columnist. In 1929 he was hired by the *Atlanta Constitution* as a sportswriter, but soon began to cover political, economic, and international topics as well. He served as a correspondent in Europe during the dark days of Hitler's rise to power, and when he returned to Atlanta in 1938, he was made the *Constitution*'s executive editor. He became its editor-in-chief in 1941, and continued in that role until he became its publisher in 1960.

During the postwar era, McGill turned his attention increasingly to the racial injustices of the South, and while not advocating integration, he wrote frequently about the economic plight of African Americans and the inequities of black educational facilities. After the Supreme Court's *Brown v. Board of Education* decision in 1954, he was among the few southern journalists to urge full and prompt compliance and to predict that blacks would soon come into their own politically and bring about considerable change in southern and national politics. His views won him widespread acclaim outside the South, as his writings began appearing regularly in national periodicals such as *Atlantic Monthly, Harper's*, the *New York Times Magazine*, and the *Saturday Evening Post*. His editorial column in the *Constitution* became nationally syndicated in the late 1950s, appearing in newspapers across the country. In 1959 he won a Pulitzer Prize for distinguished editorial writing, for his columns condemning the racist bombing of the Temple in Atlanta, the city's largest Jewish congregation, the year before.

McGill published four books over the course of his career. The first three consisted primarily of compilations of his newspaper columns: *Israel Revisited* focused on reports he made from his visit to the newly established nation in 1950, and reflected his long-term interest in the Middle East; *The Fleas Come with the Dog* gathered sixteen years worth of commentary on both southern and national issues, including McCarthyism, which he vehemently condemned, even as he was often charged with Communist leanings for his moderate racial views; and *A Church, a School* consisted largely of his editorials on the Temple bombing and other hate crimes by the Ku Klux Klan. McGill's most notable book is *The South and the Southerner*. A selective memoir of his East Tennessee upbringing and various facets of his early journalistic career, it is also a much broader social commentary on and sharp critique of the South, past and present, but one that also reflected his optimism for the region's capacity for progressive change. McGill died suddenly of a heart attack in Atlanta in 1969, just two days before his seventy-first birthday.

WORKS: *Israel Revisited* (1950). *The Fleas Come with the Dog* (1954). *A Church, A School* (1959). *The South and the Southerner* (1963). *The Best of Ralph McGill* (1980). *Southern Encounters: Southerners of Note in Ralph McGill's South* (1983). *No Place to Hide: The South and Human Rights,* ed. Calvin Logue (1984).

—JOHN C. INSCOE

TIM McLAURIN (1953–2002). Tim McLaurin's death on July 11, 2002, ended a thirteen-year battle with cancer, during which he wrote and published five books. A final novel was completed in typescript by mid-spring of his last year. Personal documentation of his short but eventful life occupies two autobiographical works, *Keeper of the Moon* and *The River Less Run*. Both memoirs develop themes prominent in his fiction as well—the struggle of individual will against social and physical pressures, and threats against traditional southern culture from both internal and external forces of change.

Timothy Reese McLaurin was born in Fayetteville, N.C., on December 14, 1953, and grew up as the second of Reese and Darlene McLaurin's six children in the nearly rural community of Beard. As a boy he worked in tobacco fields and delighted in the study of snakes—a lifelong avocation—and astronomy. At Cape Fear Regional High School he was a forward on the varsity basketball team. Upon graduation in 1972 he enlisted in the Marine Corps for tours of duty in Cuba and the Canal Zone. Discharged in 1975, he returned home to marry Janell Clark and to hold a variety of jobs, including those of Pepsi-Cola route man and supervisor in a furniture factory.

After the dissolution of his brief first marriage to his high school sweetheart, McLaurin undertook a succession of jobs, including traveling as Wild Man Mack with the Last Great Snake Show, a carnival act; performing various functions in the building trades; and reporting for newspapers. In 1979 he entered North Carolina Central University in Durham, N.C., later transferring to the University of North Carolina at Chapel Hill, where he eventually earned a degree in journalism in 1985, five years after his marriage to Katie Early of Memphis, Tenn.

With Katie, who became the mother of his two children, Meghan and Christopher, McLaurin served a two-year enlistment with the Peace Corps in Tunisia. In June 1989, McLaurin was diagnosed with myeloma. Some seven months later he underwent treatment in Seattle, Wash., involving a bone marrow transplant and a year of recuperation.

From 1988 to 1990 McLaurin held positions as lecturer in fiction writing at Duke University and North Carolina State University. Upon his return from Seattle he resumed teaching at N.C. State, where he was appointed visiting assistant professor in 1999. His second marriage, which disintegrated under the pressures of alcoholic bouts and his defiant life style, ended in divorce.

In the decade following a *New York Times* citation for *Keeper of the Moon* as among the Best Books of the Year in 1992, he received a succession of writing awards, including the Mayflower Cup (1992), the Sir Walter Raleigh Award (1995), the Rubin-Ragan Award (1999), and the R. Hunt Parker Award for lifetime contribution to the literary heritage of North Carolina. In July 2002 he married Carol Smolinski. His death in a hospital in Morehead City, N.C., occurred on the second anniversary of their vows.

WORKS: *The Acorn Plan* (1988). *Woodrow's Trumpet* (1989). *Keeper of the Moon: A Southern Boyhood* (1991). *Cured by Fire* (1995). *The Last Great Snake Show* (1997). *Lola* [book-length narrative poem] (1997). *The River Less Run* (2000). *Another Son of Man* (2004).

—JERRY LEATH MILLS

JOHN CHARLES McNEILL (1874–1907). John Charles McNeill, youngest of five children of Duncan and Euphemia McNeill, was born near Wagram in Scotland County, N.C., on July 26, 1874. Many of his poems are nostalgic evocations of a happy boyhood spent roaming the fields and woods, swimming and hunting and fishing, working along the rows with white and black laborers, and attending the "old field" school. Before entering Wake Forest College in 1894, he studied at Whiteville Academy, clerked in a store, and taught in Georgia. At Wake Forest, he was an exemplary student, contributed poems to and edited the literary journal, and took special law courses. Briefly he was on the faculties at Wake Forest and Mercer University.

When twenty-six, he opened a law office in Lumberton, where he wrote poems and stories for the local newspaper, but after several years he moved to Laurinburg to practice, and was elected to the state legislature. He had little interest in deeds and writs, and only the personalities of those involved in courtroom battles intrigued him. Meanwhile, the *Youth's Companion* in 1901 accepted a poem by him, and the *Century Magazine* over a four-year span used eighteen selections, both lyrics and dialect verse. In September 1904 the *Charlotte Observer* invited him to the staff to write when and what he wished. In the *Observer* over the next three years appeared 467 of his poems, only 134 of them collected in his two published books. Besides the columns of poetry, he wrote anecdotes, fables, reports on fires and funerals, and book reviews, and he covered special events in North Carolina and South Carolina. His popularity soared, and his byline became regionally famous. "The little loves and sorrows are my song," he said. His dialect verse and his poems on nature and religion are chaste productions of a man who was himself warm-hearted and uncomplicated. He died on October 17, 1907.

WORKS: *Songs Merry and Sad* (1906). *Lyrics from Cotton Land* (1907). *Select Prose of John Charles McNeill* (1936).

—RICHARD WALSER

JAMES ALAN McPHERSON (1943–). The son of a master electrician and a domestic worker, short-story writer James Alan McPherson was born on September 16, 1943, in Savannah, Ga. Growing up in an African American working-class neighborhood, he attended segregated schools but also enjoyed the aid and patronage of white friends of his parents. McPherson attended Morgan State University in Maryland for two years and completed his degree at Morris Brown College in Atlanta. He then went on to Harvard Law School, where he received his law degree in 1968. During his college career, he worked as a waiter on the Great Northern Railway and as a janitor, work experiences that provided material and inspiration for his fiction.

McPherson launched his writing career while still at Harvard when his short story "Gold Coast" won first prize in a fiction contest sponsored by the *Atlantic*. That story was included in his first collection, *Hue and Cry*, a book praised by Ralph Ellison. McPherson's emphasis on craft, pluralism, and integration was in keeping with Ellison's views, but put him at odds with the Black Arts Movement of the time. Also in 1969, McPherson became a contributing editor of the *Atlantic*.

After law school, McPherson briefly taught legal writing at the University of Iowa before earning his M.F.A. at the Iowa Writers' Workshop. After teaching at the University of California–Santa Cruz, Morgan State University, and the University of Virginia, he returned to the Iowa Writers' Workshop as a faculty member in 1981. Meanwhile, his second collection of fiction, *Elbow Room*, was awarded the Pulitzer Prize in 1978, making him the first African American to win the prize for fiction. In 1981 he was given a MacArthur Fellowship. With *Crabcakes* and *A Region Not Home* he has concentrated on memoir.

WORKS: *Hue and Cry* (1969). *Elbow Room* (1977). *Crabcakes* (1998). *A Region Not Home: Reflections from Exile* (2000).

—STEPHEN COOPER

DIANE McWHORTER (1953–). One book, one Pulitzer Prize. That book, *Carry Me Home: Birmingham, Alabama: The Climactic Battle of the Civil Rights Revolution*, took Diane McWhorter nineteen years to complete. The author was born in Tupelo, Miss., but her father's roots were in Birmingham, and the family returned there when McWhorter was five years old. She attended the private school her father's parents founded and served as president of the elite high school sorority Theta Kappa Delta in 1969, somewhat removed, if not shielded, from the racial turmoil that involved the city of Birmingham throughout the decade. After high school McWhorter moved north and received a degree in comparative literature from Wellesley College in 1974 before starting her journalism career with the alternative weekly *Boston Phoenix*.

The inspiration for *Carry Me Home* came when McWhorter was leafing through a nearly discarded book on Alabama given to her by her editor at the *Phoenix*, and discovered a quote from a cousin who had been one of the city leaders negotiating with Martin Luther King, Jr., during the civil rights demonstrations in 1963. From there McWhorter began her exhaustive research into both her city's and family's history as it crossed paths with the civil rights movement. She has written for *Harper's*, the *Nation*, the *New Republic*, *Newsday*, *People*, *Talk*, the *Wall Street Journal* and the *Washington Post*. She currently lives in New York City with her husband and two children, and is a frequent speaker on matters of race and culture, as well as a contributor to the *New York Times* and *USA Today*.

A Dream of Freedom: The Civil Rights Movement from 1954 to 1968 provides younger readers a history of the civil rights movement by focusing on the persons involved in the most dramatic moments of the struggle.

WORKS: *Carry Me Home: Birmingham, Alabama: The Climactic Battle of the Civil Rights Revolution* (2001). *A Dream of Freedom: The Civil Rights Movement from 1954 to 1968* (2004).

—ROB TRUCKS

MARY MEBANE (1933–1992). Writer and educator Mary Elizabeth Mebane was born on June 26, 1933, in Durham County, N.C. She was the second of three children born to Carrie Brandon Mebane and Samuel Nathaniel Mebane.

Mebane excelled in academics as a child. She attended historically black North Carolina College (now North Carolina Central University) in Durham, graduating with a B.A. in 1955. She then taught in segregated schools in the city of Durham and in rural North Carolina before entering graduate school at the University of North Carolina at Chapel Hill. After receiving the M.A. in English in 1961, she returned to North Carolina College, first as an instructor and later as assistant professor. She earned her Ph.D. in English from UNC in 1973, while teaching at South Carolina State University. She then went on to a faculty position at the University of South Carolina at Columbia, which she left in 1977. In 1980 she accepted a lectureship at the University of Wisconsin at Milwaukee.

While a graduate student, Mebane began writing her autobiography. *Mary,* the story of her childhood, was published in 1981 to great acclaim. The sequel, *Mary, Wayfarer,* detailed the struggles and difficulties Mebane faced in academia, and her experiences as a firsthand observer of the civil rights movement in the Carolinas. Both autobiographies are especially notable for Mebane's exploration of the life of the female intellectual in the black folk community. The narratives are marked with a strong sense of alienation and profound loneliness, as she struggles in solitude toward aspirations of academic accomplishment that no one in her life understands. Yet despite the resistance she encountered, Mebane retained a profound interest in and genuine concern for black communities, especially poor, often-ignored ones like her own in Durham County. This is demonstrated both in her academic projects and the op-ed articles she often wrote for the *New York Times* and other periodicals.

Mebane was notoriously reclusive. She never married or had children, and throughout her life was unable to sustain close friendships. Little is known of her life after the publication of *Mary, Wayfarer* in 1983. Despite the strong desire for recognition and respect she expresses in her autobiographies, she died in poverty and obscurity in a nursing home in Milwaukee, Wisc., on March 5, 1992. She was buried in Milwaukee by the county.

WORKS: *Mary* (1981). *Mary, Wayfarer* (1983).

—KRISTINA D. BOBO

ALEXANDER BEAUFORT MEEK (1814–1865). The son of Anne McDowell and Samuel Mills Meek, a physician and Methodist minister, Alexander Beaufort Meek was born on July 17, 1814, in Columbia, S.C. When he was five, his parents moved to Tuscaloosa, Ala., where Meek grew up and attended the university (A.B., 1833; A.M., 1836). He was admitted to the bar in 1835, but he was interested enough in literature to write for and edit a local paper, *Flag of the Union,* and, briefly in 1839, to edit his own literary magazine, the *Southron.* In the meantime he served as a noncommissioned officer in the Indian war in Florida and accepted appointments as attorney general of Alabama in 1836 and as probate judge of Tuscaloosa County in 1842.

In 1841 Meek published *A Supplement to Aikin's Digest of the Laws of Alabama* and in 1845 went to Washington and became a member of the U.S. Treasury Department in the Polk administration. Subsequently he was appointed U.S. attorney for the Southern District of Alabama and moved to Mobile.

In 1849 he became associate editor of the *Mobile Daily Register* and served two terms in the Alabama legislature, first in 1853–55, when he was responsible for legislation establishing a public school system, and again in 1859–61, when he was Speaker of the House. Though initially opposed to secession, he eventually supported the Confederate cause. He was married twice—to Mrs. Emma Donaldson Slatter in 1856 and, following her death in 1863, to Mrs. Eliza Jane Cannon in 1864. He had no children. He died of a heart attack on November 1, 1865, in Columbus, Miss.

Meek's chief contributions to literature, aside from essays and addresses such as "Americanism in Literature" (1844), are *The Red Eagle,* a long narrative poem dedicated to William Gilmore Simms; *Songs and Poems of the South,* his only collection; and *Romantic Passages in Southwestern History,* a miscellany of historical pieces. His failure to contribute more to literature, as *Russell's Magazine* pointed out in 1858, was the result of too much "society" and "partisan politics," factors all too common among gifted southerners then.

WORKS: *A Supplement to Aikin's Digest of the Laws of the State of Alabama* (1841). *The Red Eagle: A Poem of the South* (1855). *Songs and Poems of the South* (1857). *Romantic Passages in Southwestern History; Including Orations, Sketches, and Essays* (1857).

—RAYBURN S. MOORE

H. L. MENCKEN (1880–1956). Henry Louis Mencken was born on September 12, 1880, in Baltimore, Md., the son of August and Anna Abhau Mencken. His grandfather Burkhardt Ludwig Mencken had emigrated from Germany in 1848, and in the late nineteenth century the Menckens were still keenly aware and proud of their German heritage.

H. L. Mencken was educated in private and public schools in Baltimore, worked briefly in his father's cigar factory, and at the age of eighteen became a reporter on the *Baltimore Morning Herald.* In 1906 he joined the *Baltimore Sunpapers,* the newspapers for which he was to work—as reporter, columnist, and editor—for most of the rest of his life.

During his twenties and while he was a working newspaperman, Mencken produced a volume of verse and books on George Bernard Shaw and Friedrich Nietzsche. In 1908 he became literary editor of the *Smart Set,* and his monthly book reviews first brought him to national attention. He became co-editor of the *Smart Set* in 1914 and remained in that capacity until 1924. During this period Mencken championed such controversial writers as Theodore Dreiser and James Branch Cabell; he also led the fight against censorship and the genteel tradition in American letters and against provincialism, rotarianism, and mediocrity in American life. By the mid-1920s he was the nation's most notorious iconoclast, a role he continued to play during his editorship of the *American Mercury* from 1924 to 1933. Reading Mencken's *Mercury* became the badge of sophistication to many young Americans, and Walter Lippmann wrote in 1926 that Mencken was "the most powerful personal influence on this whole generation of educated people."

Mencken's reputation declined after 1930 as he turned from preachers and pedagogues and instead directed his barbs at Franklin D. Roosevelt and the New Deal. He continued to write essays and volumes on many subjects, and continued to expand his philological work, *The American Language,* the first version of which he had published in 1918. He also produced in the late 1930s and early 1940s a delightful series of autobiographical works, the first of which, *Happy Days,* has been described by one scholar as "Tom Sawyer in Baltimore." Mencken suffered a debilitating stroke in 1948 and died in Baltimore on January 29, 1956.

Mencken was one of the greatest American essayists and stylists and one of the most original, irreverent, and fearless American social critics. His best and most representative work is included in the six volumes of *Prejudices* published between 1919 and 1927. One of these essays, "The Sahara of the Bozart," an indictment of southern intellectual and literary sterility, probably occasioned a more hostile response than any other work by Mencken. It also inspired young southerners such as W. J. Cash, Gerald W. Johnson, and Paul Green, who themselves began to echo Mencken. Richard Wright, too, was emboldened by Mencken's irreverence.

In social and political thought Mencken was basically a Social Darwinist; he prized individual freedom and was critical of government intervention and reform. He was suspicious of causes and crusaders; yet the irony in Mencken's life is that he himself became a leading crusader for the liberation of American letters and American thought.

WORKS: *Ventures into Verse* (1903). *George Bernard Shaw: His Plays* (1905). *The Philosophy of Friedrich Nietzsche* (1908). *The Artist* (1912). *A Book of Burlesques* (1916). *A Little Book in C-Major* (1916). *A Book of Prefaces* (1917). *In Defense of Women* (1917). *Damn: A Book of Calumny* (1917). *The American Language* (1918 and later revisions). *Prejudices: First Series* (1919), *Second Series* (1920), *Third Series* (1922), *Fourth Series* (1924), *Fifth Series* (1926), *Sixth Series* (1927). *Notes on Democracy* (1926). *James Branch Cabell* (1927). *Treatise on the Gods* (1930). *Making a President* (1932). *Treatise on Right and Wrong* (1934). *Happy Days* (1940). *Newspaper Days* (1941). *Heathen Days* (1943). *A Christmas Story* (1946). *A Mencken Chrestomathy* (1949). *Minority Report: H. L. Mencken's Notebooks* (1956). *The Diary of H. L. Mencken,* ed. Charles A. Fecher (1989). *My Life as Author and Editor,* ed. Jonathan Yardley (1993). *Thirty-Five Years of Newspaper Work: A Memoir by H. L. Mencken,* ed. Fred Hobson, Vincent Fitzpatrick, and Bradford Jacobs (1994).

—FRED HOBSON

CAROLINE MILLER (1903–1992). Caroline Miller's two novels both illuminate the austere pioneer life of antebellum south Georgia. Born to Elias Moore and Levy Zan Hall Pafford on August 26, 1903, in Waycross, Ga., Carrie Pafford was the youngest of seven children. It was the life of her great-grandfather, who came to frontier Georgia as a Free Light minister, from which she would draw her fictional depictions.

As a child she demonstrated a natural talent for oral interpretation, and as a student she excelled in school drama productions. After graduation, besides writing short stories, she worked with a drama group creating and performing plays. In 1924 her prize-winning story "The Greatest of These" was published in the *Waycross Journal Herald*. In 1928 one of her original one-acts won an honorable mention from the Town Theater of Savannah.

Having married her former high school English teacher William Dews Miller immediately after graduation, Caroline Miller found herself in 1928 in Baxley, Ga., where William had been appointed superintendent of schools. By this time she had three small boys. Feeling overwhelmed, she turned to the examples of her own mother, her grandmother, and pioneer women who she knew had faced much worse frustrations. She drove her Ford around Baxley and into the countryside, gathering stories, notes, and samples of dialect in a notebook.

Lamb in His Bosom enjoyed the distinction of winning both the Pulitzer Prize and the Prix Femina Americain. The book charmed critics and readers alike, going into thirty printings. Classified as historical realism as practiced by the American regionalists of the time, the novel is actually a sequence of vignettes, highly pictorial, weaving incidents from her grandparents' memoirs into mesmerizing descriptions of nature, sketches creating a rhythm of unending daily toil against the backdrop of a lyrical backcountry Georgia.

Miller divorced Will Miller in 1936 and married Clyde Ray in 1937. The second marriage produced one son and one daughter. Miller continued publishing short stories, and in 1944 her second novel, *Lebanon,* appeared. Heeding criticisms that her first novel, compelling as it was, lacked a plot, Miller gave *Lebanon* a traditional plot structure and retained the pioneer themes and settings. Even more emphasis on the development of a woman's individual identity emerges in this story of a girl who loves a man she cannot marry. Reviews of the book were mixed, possibly because the presence of a plot worked against the naiveté so attractive in the first novel, or possibly because of drastic editorial cuts that Miller did not see until the book was in print.

Throughout the decades that followed, Miller divided her time between family activities and writing. Many unpublished manuscripts were left behind at her death in 1992. She is buried in a family plot in North Carolina.

WORKS: *Lamb in His Bosom* (1933). *Lebanon* (1944).

—REBECCA ROXBURGH BUTLER

HEATHER ROSS MILLER (1939–). Heather Ross Miller was born on September 15, 1939, in Albemarle, N.C., the daughter of Fred E. Ross and Geneva Smith Ross. Famed as "the writing Rosses," Fred Ross (a journalist), Eleanor Ross Taylor (a poet and the wife of Peter Taylor), Jean Ross Justice (a fiction writer and the wife of poet Donald Justice), and James Ross (also a fiction writer), encouraged her youthful reading and writing efforts.

Miller was graduated from the Woman's College, University of North Carolina, Greensboro, magna cum laude in 1961. While teaching at Pfeiffer College, she returned to Greensboro, completing her M.F.A. in 1969. Granted creative writing fellowships by the National Endowment for the Arts, Miller published both poetry and fiction during these years and did postgraduate work at the University of London. Her teaching career eventually led her to direct the M.F.A. program at the University of Arkansas and, in 1992, to Washington and Lee University, Lexington, Va., where she is currently Thomas H. Broadus, Jr., Professor of English.

Miller's awards include a Woodrow Wilson Fellowship in 1961; the National Association of Independent Schools Award for her first novel, *The Edge of the Woods;* the Sir Walter Raleigh Prize for Fiction for *Tenants of the House;* the Arnold Young Cup for Poetry for *The Wind Southerly;* the University of North Carolina at Greensboro's Alumni Award for Outstanding Achievement in Literature (1976); the North Carolina Prize for Literature (1983); and *Kentucky Poetry Review*'s Blaine Hall Award for "I Dream I Drown Myself on Purpose, Not on Purpose" (1988). A Heather Ross Miller issue of *Kentucky Poetry Review* was published in 1990.

Currently, Miller divides her time between Lexington, Va., and her home in Baden, N.C., to be near her children, Melissa and Kirk, and their families. The poetry collections *Hard Evidence* and *Friends and Assassins,* the short-story collection *In the Funny Papers,* and the 1999 novel *Champeen* (which revisits the character and setting of her 1976 novel *Confessions of a Champeen Fire-Baton Twirler*), along with a memoir of her "wilderness" years as a park ranger's wife, *Crusoe's Island,* indicate her continued vitality in both poetry and fiction.

WORKS: *The Edge of the Woods* (1964). *Tenants of the House* (1966). *The Wind Southerly* (1967). *Gone a Hundred Miles* (1968). *Horse Horse Tyger Tyger* (1973). *A Spiritual Divorce and Other Stories* (1974). *Confessions of a Champeen Fire-Baton Twirler* (1976). *Adam's First Wife* (1983). *Hard Evidence* (1990). *Friends and Assassins* (1993). *In the Funny*

Papers (1995). *Champeen* (1999). *Crusoe's Island: The Story of a Writer and a Place* (2000). *Miss Jessie Dukes and Kid Heavy* (2003).

—BES STARK SPANGLER

JIM WAYNE MILLER (1936–1996). Jim Wayne Miller spent his life defining and promoting the Appalachian South. He grew up in Buncombe County, N.C., and attended Berea College in Kentucky, strongly regional experiences that shaped his art and validated his public role as spokesperson for an Appalachian aesthetic. Miller married Mary Ellen Yates in 1958, and they became the parents of three children. After studying German and American literature at Vanderbilt on a National Defense Fellowship, in 1963 Miller joined the faculty of Western Kentucky University in Bowling Green. He received his Ph.D. from Vanderbilt in 1965.

Miller is best known as a poet, especially for his creation of the figure of the Brier—a synecdoche for the Appalachian Everyman. In his seven volumes of poetry, he explores the meaning of his own Appalachian experience, but always places it within a broader regional and national consciousness. He struggles to find creative ways that people in the mountain South can live in the modern world while not losing their own cultural heritage.

He is also well known for his satirical essays, articles about Appalachian history and culture, translations, reviews, editions of work by Jesse Stuart, anthologies, and fiction. He sometimes converted his short fiction into other genres; "His First, Best Country" eventually became both a novel and a play. In his satire, Miller attacks everything from American consumerism to the literary notion that the South is essentially homogeneous—exclusively a lowland South, not a mountain South. He is one of the editors of *Appalachia Inside Out*, a two-volume anthology of Appalachian literature.

Miller received numerous awards during his lifetime. Western Kentucky University, Berea College, and Emory & Henry College all honored him. In 1991 he received the Laurel Leaves Award from the Appalachian Consortium. Lung cancer brought an untimely end to Miller's promising talent and his tireless commitment to serving his region.

WORKS: *Copperhead Cane* (1964). *The More Things Change, the More They Stay the Same* (1971). *Dialogue with a Dead Man* (1974). Trans., *Figure of Fulfillment: Translations from the Poetry of Emil Lerperger* (1975). *The Mountains Have Come Closer* (1980). Ed., *I Have a Place* (1981). *Vein of Words* (1984). *Reading, Writing, Region: A Checklist, Purchase Guide, and Directory for School and Community Libraries in Appalachia* (1984). *Nostalgia for Seventy* (1986). *Sideswipes* (1986). *His First, Best Country* [chapbook] (1987). *Brier: His Book* (1988). *The Wisdom of Folk Metaphor* (1988). *Newfound* (1989). *The Examined Life: Family, Community, and Work in American Literature* (1989). *Round and Round with Kahlil Gibran* (1990). Ed., Cratis D. Williams, *Southern Mountain Speech*, with Loyal Jones (1992). Ed., Jesse Stuart, *Penny's Worth of Character*, with Jerry A. Herndon and James M. Gifford (1993). *His First, Best Country* [novel] (1993). *Copperhead Cane* (1995). Ed., *Appalachia Inside Out*, 2 vols., with Robert J. Higgs and Ambrose N. Manning (1995). *The Brier Poems* (1997).

—JOYCE DYER

VASSAR MILLER (1924–1998). Vassar Morrison Miller was born severely afflicted with cerebral palsy on July 19, 1924; her mother died a year later. Miller's wealthy Houston real-estate-developer father assumed that the clumsy child with a speech impediment was mentally retarded, but his second wife recognized her stepdaughter's intelligence and began to home-school her. Using an Underwood typewriter, operated with one hand steadying the other, she unlocked pent-up poems and short stories. Eventually Miller pursued creative writing at the University of Houston, writing her 1952 master's thesis on mysticism in Edwin Arlington Robinson's poetry.

Adam's Footprint introduced Miller as a religious poet writing in traditional forms in the era of the Beats. Her ironic wit and erotic imagery, however, caught the attention of poets Donald Hall, who helped her get her second book published, and James Wright, who reviewed the volume favorably in *Poetry*. Novelist Larry McMurtry, then a Rice University graduate student, sought Miller out and became her lifelong champion, calling her Texas's greatest writer. Seven more books and chapbooks and an edited anthology on disability preceded the collected poems of 1991. From the mid-1960s onward Miller's poems became increasingly confessional; in the mid-1970s she experimented with free verse. Proudly independent, she lived alone, helped by a housekeeper, until confined to a nursing home in 1991. On Sundays she would ride a motorized three-wheeled bike to Episcopal services in the mornings and Baptist services in the afternoons.

Separateness and longing were Miller's overarching themes: longing for knowledge of God, for physical union with a lover, and for death as a release from suffering. While her formal style and religious content may seem to align her with Emily Dickinson and the English metaphysical poets rather than with her contemporaries, Miller's feminism, unflinching self-examination, and frankness about disability unmask her as a postmodern writer.

WORKS: *Adam's Footprint* (1956). *Wage War on Silence* (1960). *My Bones Being Wiser* (1963). *Onions and Roses* (1968). *If I Could Sleep Deeply Enough* (1974). *Small Change* (1976). *Approaching Nada* (1977). *Selected and New Poems, 1950–1980* (1981). *Struggling to Swim on Concrete* (1984). Ed., *Despite This Flesh: The Disabled in Stories and Poems* (1985). *If I Had Wheels or Love: Collected Poems* (1991).

—JULIE KANE

WILLIAM MILLS (1935–). The oldest of five sons, William Mills was born on June 17, 1935, in Hattiesburg, Miss. His devoutly Methodist parents, William W. Mills, Sr., and Frances Finney Mills, moved their family frequently during the late 1930s, eventually settling in Baton Rouge, La., where the younger Mills spent the rest of his youth. Mills's apprenticeship included service as an itinerant Methodist preacher, a cattleman in Louisiana and Missouri, and a refinery worker in Louisiana and Nicaragua.

After attending Centenary College in Shreveport, La., for a year, Mills joined the U.S. Army in 1955, serving in Kyoto, Japan, until 1957. Subsequently, he moved to Germany, and studied philosophy in Tübingen, Munich, and at the Goethe Institute in Blaubeuren. He returned to Louisiana, enrolling at Louisiana State University, where he received his B.A. in 1959 and M.A. in 1961. Also in 1961, he married Sylvia Richard; their marriage dissolved in 1973. Mills received his Ph.D. from Louisiana State in 1972, having written a dissertation on the poetry of Howard Nemerov, eventually published as *The Stillness in Moving Things*. Mills has taught at several universities including the University of Arkansas and Oklahoma State University.

Mills is best known for his poetry, which tends to be regional, colloquial, sensory, and set in the natural world. Aside from poetry, he has also published fiction and travel narratives. In *Bears and Men: A Gathering* and *The Arkansas: An American River,* Mills provides a firsthand account of an expedition to the Hudson Bay and a geological and historical account of a river and its surroundings. His novel *Those That Blink* concerns the changing economic and social terrain of the South in the 1950s; his most recent collection of short stories, *Properties of Blood,* focuses on professional, middle-aged southern white men ending personal ordeals and finding solace in nature and through introspection. Mills lives in Columbia, Mo.

WORKS: *Watch the Fox* (1974). *The Stillness in Moving Things* (1975). *I Know a Place* (1976). *Introduction to Louisiana Cajuns* (1977). *Stained Glass* (1979). *The Meaning of Coyotes* (1984). *Bears and Men: A Gathering* (1986). *Those Who*

Blink (1986). *The Arkansas: An American River* (1988). *Properties of Blood* (1992). Ed., *John William Corrington, Southern Man of Letters* (1994).

—DANIEL GARRIEN

EDWIN MIMS (1872–1959). Edwin Mims was born in Richmond, Ark., on May 27, 1872; his parents were Andrew Jackson and Cornelia Williamson Mims, devout Methodists. He attended the Webb School in Bell Buckle, Tenn., before entering Vanderbilt University, where he studied under William Malone Baskervill and received an A.B. (1892) and an A.M. (1893). In 1894 Mims took a position as professor of English at Trinity College (later Duke University), where he remained until 1909, except for his absence beginning in 1896 while he went to Cornell University to study for his Ph.D., which he received in 1900. Mims married Clara Puryear on June 29, 1898, and they became the parents of two sons and two daughters. While at Trinity, Mims met Walter Hines Page, who became for him the quintessential New Southerner. In 1905 Mims published his biography of Sidney Lanier, in which he was much more concerned with Lanier the prophet of the New South than Lanier the Confederate soldier. From 1906 to 1909 he was joint editor of the *South Atlantic Quarterly*. In 1909 he went to the University of North Carolina in Chapel Hill as professor of English, remaining for three years.

In 1912 Mims went to Vanderbilt University to be chairman of the department of English (1912–42), and later chairman of the division of humanities (1928–42). It was in that capacity that he was associated with the Nashville Fugitive-Agrarians, for whom he was often an adversary since his views about the South and its future were quite different from theirs. His ideas were enthusiastically propounded in *The Advancing South: Stories of Progress and Reaction*. Mims's espousal of industrialism was not without qualification, for he insisted that it should not come "at the expense of the grace and charm of life," and throughout his life he was a part-time lay preacher and Sunday school teacher.

During 1935–36 Mims was Carnegie visiting professor at five British universities. He was named emeritus professor at Vanderbilt in 1942. He remained very active during his later years and was visiting professor at Emory University from 1951 to 1954. He died in his eighty-eighth year on September 15, 1959.

WORKS: Ed., Thomas Carlyle, *Essay on Burns* (1903). *The University in the South* (1903). *Sidney Lanier* (1905). Ed., *Southern Prose and Poetry for Schools*, with Bruce R. Payne (1910). Ed., *History of Southern Fiction*, vol. 8 of *The South in the Building of the Nation* (1910). Ed., Robert Louis Stevenson, *Inland Voyage and Travels with a Donkey* (1911). Ed., *The Van Dyke Book, Selected from the Writings of Henry Van Dyke* (1914). *A Handbook for Interracial Committees* (1920). *The Advancing South: Stories of Progress and Reaction* (1926). *God and the New Knowledge*, with Oswald E. Brown and James H. Kirkland (1926). *Adventurous America: A Study of Contemporary Life and Thought* (1929). *Chancellor Kirkland of Vanderbilt* (1940). *Great Writers as Interpreters of Religion* (1945). *History of Vanderbilt University* (1946). *The Christ of Poets* (1948).

—RANDALL G. PATTERSON

BENJAMIN BLAKE MINOR (1818–1905). Benjamin Blake Minor, known today chiefly for his editorship of the *Southern Literary Messenger* from 1843 through 1847, was born on October 21, 1818, in Tappahannock, Va. His family was a distinguished one, with plantation gentry on both sides. Unusually well educated for his time, Minor attended the University of Virginia for two years, then the College of William and Mary, where he studied under the famous judge and novelist Nathaniel Beverley Tucker.

Minor's professional career began with the practice of law, but finding letters more to his taste, he purchased the *Southern Literary Messenger* in 1843. In December 1845 Minor purchased from William Gilmore Simms the *Southern and Western Monthly Magazine and Review* of Charleston, S.C., and merged it with his own journal, but he continued as editor and proprietor only until October 1847. The most notable feature of Minor's editorship was his encouragement of southern writing, particularly in history.

After selling his magazine to John R. Thompson, Minor became primarily an educator, first as principal of the Virginia Female Institute in Staunton, Va., and then as founder and director of a girls' school in Richmond. On July 4, 1860, he became the president of the University of Missouri, but the university was closed in 1862. After several years as teacher, public lecturer, and life insurance representative in Missouri, Minor returned to Richmond in 1889, where he remained until his death on August 1, 1905.

Although Minor edited George Wythe's *Decisions of Cases in Virginia, by the High Court of Chancery*, the only book he wrote was his history of the *Southern Literary Messenger*, a rambling account of the journal's editors, contributors, and contents.

WORKS: *An Appeal to the Whole Country, for an Union of Parties, on the Basis of the Principles of Washington, Jefferson, Madison, and Monroe in Favor of Gen. Taylor's Administration, by a Republican of the School of 1800* (1850). Ed., George Wythe, *Decisions of Cases in Virginia, by the High Court of Chancery* (1852). *The Southern Literary Messenger, 1834–1864* (1905).

—ROBERT D. JACOBS

JOSEPH MITCHELL (1908–1996). Joseph Mitchell, journalist and short-story writer, was born on a cotton and tobacco farm in Robeson County, N.C., on July 27, 1908. He spent four years at the University of North Carolina, but left in 1929 without graduating to take a job at a newspaper in Durham. Mitchell moved to New York after a story he wrote about a tobacco auction in his hometown was reprinted in the *New York Herald-Tribune*. He worked as a police reporter for the *Herald-Tribune*, and then as a feature writer for the *World-Telegram*, where he wrote well-received stories about petty criminals, fishmongers, and the colorful denizens of dim bars and flophouses. "I specialized for years in writing about outcasts and cranks and about unusual groups," he wrote later. Mitchell joined the staff of the *New Yorker* in 1938, where he continued to publish pieces about the city's down and out. At the *New Yorker*, he was able to take more time with his stories and to explore the characters and places he wrote about in greater depth. Mitchell's spare, precise style, and the sympathetic but unsentimental manner in which he wrote about New York and New Yorkers became a hallmark of the magazine.

Mitchell published collections of his newspaper and magazine pieces in 1938, 1943, and 1948. *McSorley's Wonderful Saloon* featured several short stories set in the fictional Black Ankle County, N.C. Although Mitchell was able to purchase his family's farm and returned often to North Carolina throughout his life, these are the only stories he published about his native state.

Two of Mitchell's books were about individual New Yorkers. *Old Mr. Flood* contains three stories about the ninety-three-year-old Hugh G. Flood, a composite of several old men Mitchell knew around the Fulton Fish Market. Mr. Flood and his friends entertain each other with long stories about old New York, revealing Mitchell's fondness for the city's past. *Joe Gould's Secret* is about a well-known Greenwich Village bohemian who claimed to be able to speak the language of seagulls and who entertained poets and painters with stories about a monumental book he was writing. Gould's secret, Mitchell revealed, was that he had written nothing at all.

Mitchell is often said to have suffered from a legendary case of writer's block, but anecdotal evidence suggests that he wrote steadily, albeit privately, from his office at the *New Yorker*. If he labored on a manuscript, the shape of what he intended has been lost; for now, readers must content themselves with *Up in the Old Hotel and Other Stories,* the only book published during the period, which merely collects many of his previously published *New Yorker* pieces. Despite the dry spell, Mitchell is still considered by many to have been a stylist of the first rank who set the benchmark for prose-craft at the *New Yorker.* His well-bred southern instincts for listening exposed a broad readership to the authentic, strange, and rarely glimpsed beauties of Gotham.

Mitchell lived for thirty-one years after the publication of *Joe Gould's Secret,* and continued to visit the *New Yorker* offices every day. Not unlike McSorley's Old Ale House, the saloon that he celebrated for its fierce resistance to change, Mitchell may have been reluctant to accept rapid changes in New York City. He told a reporter in 1992, "I can't seem to get anything finished anymore. The hideous state the world is in just defeats the kind of writing I used to do." Mitchell died in New York on May 24, 1996, and was buried near his family's home in Robeson County, N.C.

WORKS: *My Ears Are Bent* (1938). *McSorley's Wonderful Saloon* (1943). *Old Mr. Flood* (1948). *The Bottom of the Harbor* (1959). *Joe Gould's Secret* (1965). *Up in the Old Hotel and Other Stories* (1992).

—NICHOLAS GRAHAM

MARGARET MITCHELL (1889–1973). Margaret Munnerlyn Mitchell's family roots extend to the days when Atlanta was called Marthasville, and beyond. She was born there on November 8, 1900, the daughter of Eugene Mitchell, a lawyer, and Maybelle Stephens, a suffragette leader and "sainted" mother who loomed large in her daughter's memory. Maybelle Stephens did not spare the rod, or rather, "the hairbrush and #3 slipper," but she taught her daughter to live by her own terms. Despite their deep southern pedigrees and upper-middle-class status, Mitchell's ancestors had always stood apart in one important respect: the family came of Anglo-Catholic stock by way of Maryland, with Irish Catholics and Protestants marrying in along the way. As a child, Margaret Mitchell read voraciously and absorbed the firsthand family lore of Civil War veterans and Reconstruction. The girl showed an early proclivity for writing, became a practiced equestrienne, and enjoyed sports.

While still in finishing school she wrote a novel, now lost, and a short story about a woman who avenges her sister by murdering her rapist. Mitchell went on to Smith College, ever the redoubt for southern ladies' education. There she awakened to the exhilarating possibilities of womanhood, and experienced heady times. She rechristened herself "Peggy," not as a diminutive nickname but as a variety of her chosen icon, the winged mythological horse.

Her time at Smith was cut short by her mother's death in 1919, when she returned home to keep house and provide comfort. Her bifurcated personality, with its contrasting shyness and sauciness, drew many suitors, and she enjoyed playing the "baby-faced vamp." In her politics and her flapper's attitude, she shared much in common with Zelda Fitzgerald, who also styled herself a southern belle fatale. At her father's urging, Mitchell debuted in 1921, and a year later she married Berrien K. Upshaw. He was abusive, and they divorced in 1923.

She began working for the *Atlanta Journal* in a period when men still dominated the newsroom. Her witty columns showed the influence of Ring Lardner and H. L. Mencken, whom she admired greatly. Mitchell was deeply influenced by the nascent southern literary renascence, and she loved the witty salaciousness of James Branch Cabell. Around this time she penned a novelette, "Ropa Carmagin," later discarded by her heirs. Accounts of it, however, describe a Faulkneresque southern gothic, replete with a decrepit big house and an interracial love affair.

Mitchell married again in 1925, taking for her husband John Marsh, the best man from her first wedding. Mitchell might have known about birthing babies, but she found the whole business repellent, and the couple never had a child. But marriage afforded her time to work on her own writing. For three years she labored furiously—and very secretively—in her apartment, producing the manuscript that would become *Gone with the Wind*, and contending with mostly hypochondriacal ailments. She apparently considered her volume unpublishable, stacked the reams in bags and folders, and closeted them. Indeed, she initially fibbed to her would-be editor, Harold Latham, and denied that she had been working on a book. At last she submitted a draft; it was quickly accepted. She spent the next year revising and fact checking her history. A million copies flew off the shelves in the first six months of publication, and it probably stands as the most popular novel of the twentieth century. It was Mitchell's novel, and not Faulkner's *Absalom, Absalom!* that garnered the Pulitzer Prize in 1937.

Like many other writers, Mitchell was a great one for unfinished projects. Unfortunately, the success of *Gone with the Wind* dominated the rest of her life and betokened considerable personal unhappiness. She spent the twelve years before her death "cleaning up after *GWTW*," engaging in charity work, settling her foreign royalties, and salvaging what remained of her privacy. At one point she employed a small army of full-time writers in an attempt to graciously answer *all* of her fan mail. She died on August 16, 1949, five days after being struck by a taxi. Her remains are interred at Atlanta's Oakland Cemetery.

Mitchell was caught between her own rebellious tendencies and the severe demands of her southern society. She was always tough-minded and contradictory—not unlike her most famous character. Like all stereotypes, the "steel magnolia" type that Mitchell coined contained a kernel of reality.

Her work has suffered outrageous critical reverses over the years. Once deigned a writer that critics love to hate, her stock is rising again, despite her single novel's unselfconscious racism and its historically counterfactual missteps. Part of the book's power may be gauged by the continuing literary and cultural fascination with it. Alexandra Ripley's *Scarlett* (1991) offers a sequel, and Alice Randall's *The Wind Done Gone* (2001) gives an African American complement. Scholars now properly acknowledge *Gone with the Wind*'s iconic power and centrality in defining the way the whole world perceives the South.

WORKS: *Gone with the Wind* (1936). *Margaret Mitchell's "Gone with the Wind" Letters*, ed. Richard Harwell (1976). *A Dynamo Going to Waste: Letters to Allen Edee, 1919–1921*, ed. Jane Bonner Peacock (1985). *Lost Laysen*, ed. Debra Freer (1996). *Before Scarlett: Girlhood Writings of Margaret Mitchell*, ed. Jane Eskridge (2000). *Margaret Mitchell: Reporter*, ed. Patrick Allen (2000).

—BRYAN GIEMZA

PENINA MOÏSE (1797–1880). Woman of letters, poet, educator, and hymnist Penina Moïse was the first Jewish woman in the United States to gain popularity for her literary endeavors. Born in Charleston, S.C., Penina was the sixth child of Abraham (Sr.) and Sarah Moïse. When her father died in 1809, the twelve-year-old Penina was forced to abandon formal studies to care for her mother and ailing brother. Her teacher and mentor, Isaac Harby of Charleston, encouraged her to pursue her literary interests.

For more than six decades, Moïse published her poems, short stories, and essays in newspapers, magazines, and literary journals throughout the country. Like most southern women of her era, Moïse focused in her personal life primarily on family, education, and caring for the afflicted. Her writings frequently addressed salient political issues and themes of social importance. Some of her poetry dealt with slavery, southern patriotism, the Civil War, the Irish famine of the 1840s, and persecuted foreigners seeking refuge in the United States. Moïse's work celebrated values that have frequently been linked to the antebellum South: chivalry, valor, loyalty, hospitality, and self-sacrifice.

Moïse venerated her Jewish heritage, and the depth of her religious devotion is reflected in the numerous hymns she composed for her beloved synagogue, Kahal Kadosh Beth Elohim (KKBE) in Charleston. More than a dozen of Moïse's hymns were later published in the *Union Hymnal,* a hymn book used by hundreds of Reform Jewish congregations in North America during the first half of the twentieth century.

Moïse supplemented her income through educational work. She was the superintendent of KKBE's Sunday school for many years, and after the Civil War she operated her own private academy with the help of a widowed sister and niece. Although persistent poverty and poor health plagued her life, Moïse impressed contemporaries with her charm and perennial good nature. At the time of her death on September 13, 1880, one eulogist crowned Penina Moïse a queen of Charleston's literary society. Some of Moïse's poems were published under the title *Fancy's Sketch Book,* but the vast majority of her literary writings remain scattered in various journals, periodicals, and newspapers that were published in Charleston and elsewhere. Two of her compositions will be found in *The Charleston Book: A Miscellany in Prose and Verse,* edited by William Gilmore Simms (1845). She often wrote under the initials "M.P.," and other writings were signed "P.M." It is to be hoped that, one day soon, a researcher will assume the task of gathering together much more of this historically significant harvest.

WORKS: *Fancy's Sketch Book* (1833).

—GARY PHILLIP ZOLA

MARION MONTGOMERY (1925–). Marion (Hoyt) Montgomery, Jr., was born in Thomaston, Ga., on April 16, 1925, to Marion Hoyt and Lottie Mae (Jenkins) Montgomery. After serving in the field artillery in Europe (1943–46), he attended the University of Georgia, where he earned his B.A. in 1950 and M.A. in 1953. In 1951 he married Dorothy Dean Carlisle of Camilla, Ga., with whom he has five children.

After teaching one year at Darlington School for Boys, in Rome, Ga., he returned to the university to teach in the English department. Except for study at the University of Iowa's Writers' Workshop (1956–58), and a term as writer-in-residence at Converse College (1963), he taught writing and literature, primarily twentieth-century poetry and lyric poetry, at the University of Georgia from 1954 until his retirement in 1987. He lives in nearby Crawford.

After three volumes of poetry, two novels, and a novella in the 1960s, critical treatments of Ezra Pound and of T. S. Eliot in 1970 marked a turn in Montgomery's writing. Since then, except for the novel *Fugitive,* in 1974, and some poems, his major works have been critical and increasingly reflective. While much of his criticism has focused on Flannery O'Connor, the Fugitives, American modernist poets, and major British Romantics, his three-volume *The Prophetic Poet and the Spirit of the Age* embraced much of the Western literary tradition. Maintaining the Agrarian perspective of his early work, his later works have offered moral and ontological critiques of modern culture and education, grounded in a view of God and man that he traces to Thomas Aquinas. The continuity of Montgomery's central concerns is suggested by his repetition of the opening words of his 1965 poem "On Fishing Creek" as the title of his 1990 volume *The Men I Have Chosen for Fathers.*

WORKS: *Dry Lightning* (1960). *The Wandering of Desire: A Novel* (1962). *Darrell* (1964). *Stones from the Rubble* (1965). *Ye Olde Bluebird: A Novelette* (1967). *The Gull and Other Georgia Scenes* (1969). *Ezra Pound: A Critical Essay* (1970). *T. S. Eliot: An Essay on the American Magus* (1970). *The Reflective Journey toward Order: Essays on Dante, Wordsworth, Eliot, and Others* (1973). *Fugitive* (1974). *Eliot's Reflective Journey to the Garden* (1979). *The Prophetic Poet and the Spirit of the Age,* vol. 1: *Why Flannery O'Connor Stayed Home* (1981); vol. 2: *Why Poe Drank Liquor* (1983); vol. 3: *Why Hawthorne Was Melancholy* (1984). *Possum and Other Receipts for the Recovery of "Southern" Be-*

ing (1987). *The Trouble with You Innerleckchuls* (1988). *Liberal Arts and Community: The Feeding of the Larger Body* (1990). *Virtue and Modern Shadows of Turning: Preliminary Agitations* (1990). *The Men I Have Chosen for Fathers: Literary and Philosophical Passages* (1990). *Romantic Confusions of the Good* (1997). *Concerning Intellectual Philandering: Poets and Philosophers, Priests, and Politicians* (1998). *The Truth of Things: Liberal Arts and the Recovery of Reality* (1999). *Making: The Proper Habit of Our Being: Essays Speculative, Reflective, Argumentative* (2000). *Romancing Reality: Homo Viator and the Scandal Called Beauty* (2002). *John Crowe Ransom and Allen Tate: At Odds about the Ends of History and the Mystery of Nature* (2003).

—WILLIAM MOSS

ANNE MOODY (1940–). As the author of the autobiography *Coming of Age in Mississippi*, Anne Moody is one of the best-known writers of the civil rights movement.

The eldest daughter of African American sharecroppers Fred and Elmire Moody, she was born in Wilkinson County, Miss., on September 15, 1940, and later entered the segregated school system. In 1959 she attended Natchez Junior College on a basketball scholarship. After her transfer to Tougaloo College in Jackson, Miss., she became heavily involved in the civil rights movement, working with the NAACP, helping to set up the Congress of Racial Equality (CORE), doing voter registration with the Student Non-Violent Coordinating Committee (SNCC), and taking part in a sit-in at a Woolworth's lunch counter in Jackson. She graduated from Tougaloo in 1964 and spent a year as civil rights project coordinator at Cornell University in Ithaca, N.Y. She then moved to New York City, where she wrote *Coming of Age in Mississippi*.

In sections titled "Childhood," "High School," "College," and "The Movement," Moody's autobiography recounts her struggles as the daughter of a poor working mother, as well as her reaction to the killing of Emmett Till, her encounters with racism, and her involvement with the NAACP. Published in 1968, the book received the Best Book of the Year Award from the American Library Association in 1969 and eventually made its way into classrooms. Moody's collection of short stories, *Mr. Death*, was also published.

She continues to live in New York, where she works for the Poverty Program.

WORKS: *Coming of Age in Mississippi* (1968). *Mr. Death* (1975).

—MARK CANADA

JOHN TROTWOOD MOORE (1858–1929). John Trotwood Moore was Tennessee's state librarian from 1919 until 1929, the father of poet Merrill Moore, and a notable man of letters in his own right. He was born on August 26, 1858, in Marion, Ala., and named John Moore, Jr. (He later dropped the *Jr.* and added *Trotwood* in honor of Charles Dickens's character.) Moore attended Howard College and worked as a teacher and as a journalist in Alabama, before moving to a Middle Tennessee farm in 1885. He lived in Tennessee until his death in 1929.

Moore was a popular writer whose stories and poems blend nostalgia for the Old South, portrayals of contemporary life, and the rough and rowdy comedy of southwestern humor. His love of horses and horse racing provided subject matter for much of his writing, as did his interest in African American life. Moore's most popular character was the shrewd and comic African American "Uncle Wash," whose tales were later collected as *Uncle Wash: His Stories*. In 1897 Moore published his first collection of writing, *Songs and Stories from Tennessee*, and in 1905 he founded *Trotwood's Monthly*, which later became *The Taylor-Trotwood Magazine*. While Moore was the primary contributor to this publication, he also published and encouraged younger writers such as T. S. Stribling.

Although Moore gained popularity with his entertaining sketches of local life, he also wrote novels of social indignation. His most successful novel, *The Bishop of Cottontown,* indicts working conditions and child labor in southern cotton mills, and *Jack Ballington, Forester* argues for the conservation of forests. Moore was also an active Tennessee historian, and his deep interest in Andrew Jackson provided the basis for his historical novel *Hearts of Hickory: A Story of Andrew Jackson and the War of 1812.*

WORKS: *Songs and Stories from Tennessee* (1897). *A Summer Hymnal: A Romance of Tennessee* (1901). *The Bishop of Cottontown: A Story of the Southern Cotton Mills* (1906). *Ole Mistis and Other Songs and Stories from Tennessee* (1909). *The Old Cotton Gin* (1910). *Uncle Wash: His Stories* (1910). *The Gift of the Grass: Being the Autobiography of a Famous Racing Horse* (1911). *Jack Ballington, Forester* (1911). *Hearts of Hickory: A Story of Andrew Jackson and the War of 1812* (1926). *Tom's Last Forage* (1926).

—ANDREW B. LEITER

MERRILL MOORE (1903–1957). Austin Merrill Moore is an oddity in the annals of southern literature—poet, psychiatrist, researcher, hospital administrator, conchologist, long-distance swimmer, photographer. One of the Fugitives at Vanderbilt University in the early 1920s, Merrill Moore is among America's most prolific poets. His surviving poems number well over fifty thousand, and those who knew him place his output much higher. Legends of Moore's prodigious productivity abound, making him a virtual Hercules among scribblers. Throughout most of his life he wrote at least five poems a day, almost all of them sonnets, loosely speaking. He kept a separate small domicile crammed with filing cabinets to house his verse. He called it the Sonnetorium. Unlike the better-known Fugitives—Donald Davidson, John Crowe Ransom, Allen Tate, and Robert Penn Warren—Moore did not become a literary professional.

Born on September 11, 1903, in Columbia, Tenn., Merrill Moore was the son of poet John Trotwood Moore and Mary Brown Daniel Moore, a music teacher and writer who became state librarian after her husband's death in 1929. When Moore was four years old he moved with his family to Nashville. He attended preparatory school at Montgomery Bell Academy, and there began his writing. At Vanderbilt (1920–24) he first published his poetry in the *Fugitive* magazine.

Moore proceeded from college directly into Vanderbilt Medical School, and upon receiving his M.D. in 1928 he was hired as a neurologist at Boston City Hospital. Within a few years he became a clinical psychiatrist who also taught neurology, neuropathology, and psychiatry at the Harvard Medical School. Moore published some 150 medical and psychological papers on alcoholism, drug addiction, suicide, venereal disease, the organization and administration of hospitals, Adolf Hitler, the psychoneurosis of war, migraine headaches, and other subjects, including conchology, the study of shells.

Moore married Ann Leslie Nichol in 1930. During World War II, at the rank of major, he served first as an army psychiatrist in New Zealand and the South Pacific and then, promoted to lieutenant colonel, as the U.S. Army director of medical operations in Nanking. He received commendation for "untiring energy, zeal and enthusiasm" and for "superior and outstanding" conduct. After the war he returned to Boston and continued to teach at Harvard, to work in free clinics, and to see private patients. He and his wife had four children. Throughout it all, sonnets flowed from his pen in a torrent. He died of cancer on September 20, 1957.

Just as Moore's subjects are "disconcertingly various," in Ransom's words, so is the quality of his verse. Not surprisingly, given their sheer number, plenty of his poems are mediocre, some are outright bad, but a significant number are superb—striking in their originality of thought and expression, profound in their depth of insight, vivid and precise in their imagery, yet also lighthearted and exhilarating in their play of language, frequently lacking recognizable meter, having little or no rhyme scheme, and often employing more than fourteen lines.

WORKS: *The Noise That Time Makes* (1929). *It Is a Good Deal Later Than You Think* (1934). *Six Sides to a Man* (1935). *Poems from the Fugitive, 1922–1926* (1936). *Sonnets from the Fugitive, 1922–1926* (1937). *Fifteen Poems from the Fugitive, 1922–1926, and One Additional Poem: Ego* (1938). *Sonnets from the Sewanee Review, 1928–1935* (1938). *Sonnets from New Directions* (1938). *M: One Thousand Autobiographical Sonnets* (1938). *The Fugitive: Clippings and Comment about the Magazine and the Members of the Group That Published It* (1939). *Some Poems for New Zealand* (1944). *Clinical Sonnets* (1949). *Illegitimate Sonnets* (1950). *Case Record from a Sonnetorium* (1951). *More Clinical Sonnets* (1953). *Merrill Moore and the American Sonnet* (1954). *Verse-Diary of a Psychiatrist* (1954). *Homo Sonetticus Moorensis* (1955). *Poems of American Life* (1958). *The Dance of Death* (1959).

—ROBERT E. JONES

VIRGINIA MOORE (1903–1993). Born in Virginia on July 11, 1903, Virginia Moore was the precocious daughter of John Fitzallen and Ethel Daniel Moore. She graduated from Hollins College with her A.B. at nineteen, earning her M.A. in English at Columbia University in 1924. In 1926 Moore published her first volume of poetry, *Not Poppy,* a gathering of Petrarchan sonnets and lyrics on youth and age, nature and self, courage, and metaphysical paradoxes, along with seven poems, four in dialect, about African Americans. Moore also married poet and anthologist Louis Untermeyer in 1926. Their marriage lasted only until 1928; their son, John Moore Untermeyer, was born the same year. That year, too, Virginia published a Civil War novel, *Rising Wind,* and a second volume of poems, *Sweet Water and Bitter,* which gathers some especially poignant sonnets on marriage, love powerful and fretful, and dejection and loneliness. Moore's final volume of poems, *Homer's Chain,* appeared in 1936.

Yet poetry was only part of Moore's literary output. She had co-authored an inspirational book for girls in 1927, and in 1934 she wrote a book on memorable women writers, from Sappho and Dorothy Wordsworth to Elinor Wylie and Katherine Mansfield. *The Life and Eager Death of Emily Brontë* followed in 1936. Moore showed her increasing fascination with religion and metaphysics in her next two books, both substantial in their scholarship. *Ho for Heaven! Man's Changing Attitude toward Dying* explores funeral practices and belief systems in ancient Egypt and Persia, the classical world, India, medieval times, and the eighteenth century. In writing her Ph.D. dissertation on William Butler Yeats and religion at Columbia (1952), Moore worked directly with Yeats's papers and with Mrs. Yeats. This evolved into a substantial study, *The Unicorn: William Butler Yeats' Search for Reality,* examining the poet's complex spiritual response to Irish lore, Druidism, Hermeticism, Rosicrucianism, spiritism, and other influences.

In 1945, during her shift away from publishing poetry to pursuing scholarly projects, Moore married John Jefferson Hudgins. She later spent several months with her sister Nancy on a tour of India and Greece and the Far and Near East, their cumulative experiences resulting in a discursive travelogue, *The Whole World, Stranger,* the subtext for which is the essential unity of mankind. Moore's last major work was a well-researched and readable biography of James and Dolley Madison. Virginia Moore died at eighty-nine in her beloved Scottsville, Va., in June 1993.

WORKS: *Not Poppy* (1926). *Girls Who Did: Stories of Real Girls and Their Careers,* with Helen Josephine Ferris (1927; rev. ed. 1937). *Rising Wind* (1928). *Sweet Water and Bitter* (1928). *Distinguished Women Writers* (1934). *The Life and Eager Death of Emily Brontë: A Biography* (1936). *Homer's Golden Chain* (1936). *Virginia Is a State of Mind* (1942).

Ho for Heaven! Man's Changing Attitude toward Dying (1946). *The Unicorn: William Butler Yeats' Search for Reality* (1954). *The Whole World, Stranger* (1957). *Scottsville on the James: An Informal History* (1969). *The Madisons: A Biography* (1979). *The Liberty Bell Papers: An Inquiry into American Values* (1980).

—R. Bruce Bickley, Jr.

BERRY MORGAN (1919–2002). The short-story writer and novelist Berry Morgan was born on May 20, 1919, in Port Gibson, Miss., to John Marshall and Bess Berry Taylor Brumfield. Although she only began writing in her thirties, she recalled telling stories as a child to amuse herself and later feeling the impulse to write. A Roman Catholic, she studied at Loyola University in New Orleans (1947) and at Tulane University (1948–49). Married and divorced and the mother of four children, she divided her time among Albena Plantation (near Port Gibson), a New Orleans home, and a West Virginia farm. In her later years she resided at Aylmere Farm, Summit Point, W.Va. Morgan died at the nearby Shenandoah Nursing Home on June 19, 2002.

Her literary career began in the early 1950s when she completed a long mystery story, which was rejected and later abandoned. At forty-three, she began writing again in the midst of her work for the civil rights movement in Mississippi. In 1966 she won the Houghton-Mifflin Fellowship for *Pursuit*, her first novel, the initial publication of a sequence called *Certain Shadows*, about a cross-section of people in mythical King County, Miss. *Pursuit* depicts the tortured struggle of Ned Ingles to obtain a meaningful relationship with his illegitimate son Laurence. Many of her stories appeared in the *New Yorker*; "Andrew" was included in *The Best American Short Stories of 1967*. Morgan became writer-in-residence at Northeast Louisiana University (now University of Louisiana–Monroe) in 1972 and subsequently at several universities in the Washington, D.C., area. She won another Houghton-Mifflin Fellowship in 1974 for *The Mystic Adventures of Roxie Stoner*, a series of linked stories told from the point of view of the black woman who works intermittently on the Ingles Plantation of *Pursuit* and who thus moves in both the black and white cultures. The stronger stories explore Stoner's experiences at the state mental hospital. For many years Berry worked on the third volume of the planned *Certain Shadows* trilogy. She once said, "I think all writers are struggling writers," a statement ultimately reflecting the experiences of her own lifetime.

WORKS: *Pursuit* (1966). *The Mystic Adventures of Roxie Stoner* (1974).

—Thomas Bonner, Jr.

ROBERT MORGAN (1944–). Robert Ray Morgan, born on October 3, 1944, shares more than a birthday with Thomas Wolfe (born October 3, 1900): both are gifted and versatile writers from the North Carolina mountains, Morgan from Henderson County, Wolfe from Buncombe County nearby. And both are artists to whom the mountains matter much, as landscape, history, symbol, language. The title of Morgan's first book, *Zirconia Poems*, honors a rural community near Hendersonville; a later volume of new and selected poems, *Green River*, is also given a title that honors Morgan's rural upbringing.

At sixteen, Morgan entered Emory University, intending to study mathematics and science. He transferred to North Carolina State University to pursue those interests. He also took a course in creative writing with Guy Owen. Owen was impressed with his student's potential and recommended that Morgan transfer again—this time to the University of North Carolina at Chapel Hill. In 1965 Morgan received his B.A., with honors in writing. Supporting himself briefly as a house painter, he next entered the M.F.A. program at the University of North Carolina at Greensboro, where Fred Chappell was his most influential mentor. Degree in hand (1968), Morgan taught briefly at Salem College in Winston-Salem, N.C., but in 1971 went to Cornell University in Ithaca, N.Y., as a lecturer. Writing and rising through the ranks at Cornell, Morgan eventually became the Kappa Alpha Professor of English. He even served a term as department chair. Another title—*At the Edge of the Orchard Country*—reflects his main homelands in North Carolina and New York, since both Hendersonville and Ithaca are in apple-growing regions. Morgan is married and has three children.

From the beginning, he wrote both fiction and poetry, but his first recognition came for poetry. Like A. R. Ammons, another writer from rural North Carolina who spent decades at Cornell, Morgan has written poems in various voices and patterns, including experiments in rare lyric forms (pantoum, chant royal) and brilliant long studies somewhat in the manner of Christopher Smart's *Jubilate Agno*. He even based a serious poem, "Mountain Graveyard," on anagrams (*sacred cedars, slate tales, stone notes,* and so forth).

Having published eleven volumes of poetry, Morgan turned increasingly to fiction, with a big break coming in 2000 when *Gap Creek* was chosen by Oprah Winfrey for her immensely influential book club. The novel sold hundreds of thousands of copies and also had a ripple effect on all other titles by Morgan, especially the fiction. *This Rock* followed in 2001 and *Brave Enemies* in 2003.

Morgan is in frequent demand as lecturer and reader. He has held numerous visiting appointments, including one as William Blackburn Visiting Professor of Creative Writing at Duke University in Spring 2002.

WORKS: *Zirconia Poems* (1969). *The Voice in the Crosshairs* (1971). *Red Owl* (1972). *Land Diving* (1976). *Trunk and Thicket* (1978). *Groundwork* (1979). *Bronze Age* (1981). *At the Edge of the Orchard Country* (1987). *The Blue Valleys: Stories* (1989). *Sigodlin* (1990). *Green River: New and Selected Poems* (1991). *The Mountains Won't Remember Us* (1992). *Good Measure: Essays and Interviews on Poetry* (1993). *The Hinterlands: A Mountain Tale in Three Parts* (1994). *The Truest Pleasure* (1995). *Wild Peavines: New Poems* (1996). *The Hinterland* (1999). *Gap Creek* (1999). *The Balm of Gilead Tree and Other Stories* (1999). *Topsoil Road: Poems* (2000). *This Rock* (2001). *Brave Enemies: A Novel* (2003). *The Strange Attractor: New and Selected Poems* (2004).

—WILLIAM HARMON

WILLIE MORRIS (1934–1999). Relative of a Mississippi governor, son of a City Service gasoline deliveryman, Willie Morris was born in Jackson, Miss., on November 29, 1934. He would live to earn national recognition as a journalist, novelist, storyteller, autobiographer, editor, essayist, and interpreter of the liberal and moderate South to the nation at large.

When he was six months old, his parents, Henry Rae and Marion Weaks Morris, moved the family to Yazoo City, Miss., on the edge of the Delta. Willie grew up as an intelligent but conventional white Protestant boy from a middle-class small southern town. In 1952 he entered the University of Texas and began his transformation into the muckraking editor of the school paper, able to support desegregation at the University and willing to attack the powerful oil and gas interests that ran the state. His boldness brought him a Rhodes Scholarship (1956–60) to New College, Oxford, where he earned a B.A. and M.A. and learned to see through nonsense when he encountered it. In 1958 he married Celia Buchan, with whom he had a son, David Rae Morris, in 1961. That year he became editor of the liberal *Texas Observer* in Austin, a position that allowed him to oppose the secretive John Birch Society and the increasing Dixie-fication of the nation supported by Senator Barry Goldwater of Arizona.

His work as journalist in Austin enabled Morris in 1963 to move to *Harper's* magazine in New York. He became editor-in-chief in 1967, the youngest individual in history to hold the position. Before ascending to the leadership of *Harper's*, Morris put together a special supplement, *The South Today*, that exhibited his own southern spin by including essays from commentators as diverse as C. Vann Woodward, William Styron, Whitney Young, and James Kilpatrick. The year he became *Harper's* editor he published his lyrical memoir of boyhood, *North Toward Home*, a Houghton Mifflin Literary Fellowship Book, his most admired work. Morris brought to the magazine a team of productive contributing editors, including David Halberstam and Larry L. King, in addition to such well-known contributors as William Styron, who published 45,000 words from *The Confessions of Nat Turner* in *Harper's*, and Norman Mailer, whose controversial work "The Prisoner of Sex" led the publisher, William S. Blair, to force Morris's resignation in 1971.

On leaving *Harper's*, Morris, whose marriage to Celia Buchan had ended in 1969, wrote from his home in Bridgehampton, Long Island. Of his books from the 1970s, *Yazoo: Integration in a Deep-Southern Town* stands with *North Toward Home* as among his finest works. In the same decade he published his first novel, *The Last of the Southern Girls*, a roman à clef of Washington social life, followed by a memoir titled *James Jones: A Friendship*.

After a Mississippi football weekend in 1979, Morris decided to reverse the direction of his life and returned South. In 1980 he became writer-in-residence at the University of Mississippi in Oxford, to which he was able to bring high-profile figures such as Styron, author John Knowles, and James Jones's widow, Gloria. His changed psychological orientation appears in the titles of two of his books from the 1980s, *Terrains of the Heart and Other Essays on Home* and *Homecomings*. The book from this decade that attracted most attention was *The Courting of Marcus Dupree*, the story of a talented black football player from an integrated high school in Philadelphia, Miss. This was the place where civil rights workers James Earl Chaney, Andrew Goodman, and Michael Schwerner were murdered in 1964, the year Dupree was born.

On September 14, 1990, Morris married JoAnne Prichard of Jackson, Miss. During the 1990s, he continued to write from Oxford, Miss., where he became closely connected with the Yoknapatawpha Press and its publishers, Larry Wells and Dean Faulkner Wells, whose uncle was William Faulkner. His sequel to *North Toward Home*, entitled *New York Days*, appeared in 1993. When Morris died on August 2, 1999, of heart failure at a hospital in Jackson, President Bill Clinton described him as a friend and a national treasure. Morris was sixty-four.

WORKS: Ed., *The South Today, 100 Years after Appomattox* (1965). *North Toward Home* (1967). *Good Old Boy: A Delta Boyhood* (1971). *Yazoo: Integration in a Deep-Southern Town* (1971). *The Last of the Southern Girls* (1973). *A Southern Album: Recollections of Some People and Places and Times Gone By*, ed. Irwin Glusker (1975). *James Jones: A Friendship* (1978). *Terrains of the Heart and Other Essays on Home* (1981). *The Courting of Marcus Dupree* (1983; repr. 1992). *Always Stand in against the Curve and Other Sports Stories* (1983). *Good Old Boy and The Witch of Yazoo* (1898). *Homecomings* (1989). *Faulkner's Mississippi* (1990). *After All, It's Only a Game* (1992). *New York Days* (1993). *My Dog Skip* (1995). *The Ghosts of Medgar Evers: A Tale of Race, Murder, Mississippi, and Hollywood* (1998). *My Cat Spit McGee* (1999). *Conversations with Willie Morris*, ed. Jack Bales (2000). *Taps: A Novel* (2001). *My Mississippi*, with photographs by David Rae Morris (2002). *Shifting Interludes: Selected Essays*, ed. Jack Bales (2002).

—JULIUS ROWAN RAPER

JOHN S. MOSBY (1833–1916). The Confederacy's most renowned cavalry raider, John Singleton Mosby led guerrilla units that harassed and frightened Federal forces throughout northern Virginia, especially from 1863 until after Appomattox. A lively and colorful writer, he published two volumes of postwar memoirs that convey powerful images of the Civil War as a romantic adventure.

Born to a slave-owning farm family in Powhattan County, Va., Mosby grew up outside Charlottes-ville and entered the University of Virginia in 1850. Jailed in 1853 for shooting a fellow student, Mosby won a pardon, and after studying the law, married Pauline Clarke, daughter of a leading lawyer and former congressman. The couple settled in Bristol, Va., where Mosby practiced his profession

A prewar Unionist, Mosby joined the 1st Virginia Cavalry after his state's secession and served under General J. E. B. Stuart. Distinguishing himself as a scout, he won Stuart's permission in January 1863 to form an independent unit of guerrilla raiders. Mosby's Raiders soon emerged as the Confed-eracy's most celebrated cavalry unit, operating behind enemy lines to collect information, cut com-munications, destroy supplies, and take prisoners. Perhaps his most famous exploit was the capture of Union General Edwin H. Stoughton in his own headquarters in Fairfax, Va., while the general lay fast asleep in bed. Mosby's exploits became the stuff of legend among Union and Confederate troops in northern Virginia, provoking widespread hatred and adulation respectively. After Confederate de-feat, Mosby disbanded his unit rather than surrender and was specifically excluded from the terms of Federal pardon until 1866.

Mosby developed a sincere admiration for his adversary Ulysses S. Grant during the war and en-dorsed him for the presidency in 1868. This decision brought condemnation from southerners but led to an appointment as U.S. consul in Hong Kong, then to service as an attorney for the Southern Pacific Railroad, and finally to a position in the U.S. Land Office. A series of lectures in 1886 led to the publication of *Mosby's War Reminiscences and Stuart's Cavalry Campaigns* the following year. In 1908 he defended his former commander in *Stuart's Cavalry in the Gettysburg Campaign,* and spent his final years in Washington on a more complete autobiography. This work appeared posthumously in 1917 as *The Memoirs of Colonel John S. Mosby,* edited by his son-in-law Charles Wells Russell.

WORKS: *Mosby's War Reminiscences and Stuart's Cavalry Campaigns* (1887). *Stuart's Cavalry in the Gettysburg Cam-paign* (1908). *The Memoirs of Colonel John S. Mosby* (1917).

—HARRY L. WATSON

MONTROSE J. MOSES (1878–1934).

A drama critic and editor, Montrose Jonas Moses was born in New York City on September 2, 1878, to Montefiore and Rose Jonas Moses. Of Alabama lineage, Moses's parents moved to Montgomery during his childhood, and there Moses received his early education. Later he returned to New York and graduated from the College of the City of New York in 1899. After graduation, Moses first served on the editorial staff of the *Literary Digest* (1900–1902), and then as dramatic editor of the *Reader* (1903–7), the *Independent* (1908–18), the *Book News Monthly* (1908–18), and the *Bellman* (1910–19). From 1919 until his death on March 29, 1934, Moses worked as a freelance writer.

In addition to his frequent contributions to magazines, Moses wrote, edited, or translated numer-ous books on drama. He compiled collections of British and Continental plays, which illustrated his-torical developments in drama, and wrote studies of two European playwrights. Especially interested in the history of his own nation's stage, Moses compiled several collections of American plays, helped edit a historical anthology of theater criticism, and wrote biographies of American stage personalities. He also published a survey of American drama, which discussed prominent playwrights and the the-ater of their times. Seeking to interest youngsters in the stage, Moses edited three collections of plays for children. Many of Moses's books appeared in several editions and some have been reissued.

Early in his career, Moses put aside the study of drama long enough to write a historical survey of southern literature. Including oratory, poetry, and fiction, he focused on the influence that social and economic conditions during each period of the South's history had on its literature. Published in 1910, *The Literature of the South* remained the standard treatment of its subject until succeeded by Jay B. Hubbell's *The South in American Literature* forty-four years later.

WORKS: *Famous Actor-Families in America* (1906). *Children's Books and Reading* (1907). *Henrik Ibsen: The Man and His Plays* (1908). *The Literature of the South* (1910). *The American Dramatist* (1911). *Maurice Maeterlick: A Study* (1911). *The Life of Heinrich Conried* (1916). *The Fabulous Forest: The Record of an American Actor* (1929).

—GAINES M. FOSTER

ROBERT MUNFORD (1737?–1783). Family background prepared Robert Munford to assume a significant place in Virginia's deferential society. Well connected by marriage, the family enjoyed William Byrd II's friendship. After his father's financial losses and death, Robert lived with his uncle, William Beverley (1745), and was educated in England (1750–56). Returning in 1756, he studied law under a cousin, Peyton Randolph. After serving as an officer at Fort Duquesne, he completed his legal studies, married Anna Beverley (1760), and established himself as a gentleman planter in the wide open Southside. Regularly a Mecklenburg burgess after 1765, Munford initially aligned himself with those "hot and giddy members" surrounding Patrick Henry; but as the Revolution approached, Munford's positions increasingly seemed moderate.

Containing two comedies, a translation (*The Metamorphoses,* "Book 1"), a Hudibrastic, a series of satiric epistles, a pastoral, and a patriotic song, Munford's *Collection* richly reveals the conventions of mid-eighteenth-century English literature. Shrewdly aware of Virginia's social, political, and literary culture, Munford satirizes women's fashions, brutal overseers, and wartime profiteers. "An Answer" participates in the small furor surrounding Robert Bolling's "A Winter Piece." The plays, *The Candidates* (set in the early 1770s) and *The Patriots* (written ca. 1777), anatomize Munford's Southside community. Aristocratic protagonists, finding themselves out of place and threatened in a crudely democratic, often simple-minded, nondeferential society, yearn for that thoughtfully ordered world that seems to be disappearing. Indeed, in *The Patriots* the aristocratic Trueman is largely removed from political power, just as Munford lost the 1774 Convention election, because he was too aristocratic.

Rehabilitated by 1779, Munford served as a member of the House of Delegates and as a militia commander at the battle of Guilford Courthouse. Nonetheless, his last years appear to have been financially and personally unhappy. Little read when published, his works vividly portray their time, while their themes and their tone anticipate the nostalgia and embattled stance of much antebellum Virginia writing.

WORKS: "The D—l to M— M—, of Meck—g," in Dixon and Nicholson's *Virginia Gazette,* August 21, 1779. *A Collection of Plays and Poems by the late Col. Robert Munford of Mecklenburg County, in the State of Virginia* (1798).

—JON C. MILLER

MARY NOAILLES MURFREE (1850–1922). A local color writer who published her stories and novels under the pseudonym Charles Egbert Craddock, Mary Noailles Murfree put Tennessee's Cumberland and Great Smoky Mountains on the literary map in the late-nineteenth century.

Murfree was born on January 24, 1850, at Grantland, her family's plantation on Stone's River, near Murfreesboro, Tenn., a town named for her great-grandfather. Her lawyer father, William Law Murfree, moved the family to Nashville a few years later. There Murfree attended the Nashville Female Academy and, following the Civil War, Philadelphia's Chegary Institute, a finishing school for young women. More pertinent to her writing about life in the mountains was the fact that the Murfree family spent fifteen summers at their cottage at Beersheba Springs, a popular resort in the Cumberland Mountains south of McMinnville. Later Murfree stayed at another popular Tennessee resort, Montvale Springs, south of Maryville. She was to spend nine years (1881–90) in St. Louis before returning to Tennessee. She died in Murfreesboro on July 31, 1922.

At first Murfree wrote comedy-of-manners sketches that appeared under the name R. Emmet Dembry, but she soon turned to other material. Though she submitted earlier mountain stories, her first real success came with "The Dancin' Party at Harrison's Cove" (*Atlantic Monthly*, May 1878), a story that reflects the interaction between the mountaineers and the summer people at Beersheba Springs. Murfree's first book was *In the Tennessee Mountains*, eight stories previously published in the *Atlantic Monthly*. The last of these, "The 'Harnt' That Walks Chilhowee," is most frequently reprinted. In addition to her stories, Murfree wrote a number of novels, of which *The Prophet of the Great Smoky Mountains* is usually thought to be her best. Most of her stories and novels take place in the Tennessee mountains, but two are set in Mississippi, where Murfree's father owned plantations. Some of her later novels depict Tennessee's past, telling stories of the pioneers and of the Cherokee Indians. A few of her novels and stories were written for younger readers.

Though initially high, Murfree's reputation did not hold up as years passed. She was, after all, an outsider who had little firsthand knowledge of the mountains. The distance between her narrators and the mountaineers was all too great, her scenic descriptions were considerably overblown, her plots showed a great deal of similarity, and her characters were all too often stereotypes.

WORKS: *In the Tennessee Mountains* (1884). *Where the Battle Was Fought* (1884). *Down the Ravine* (1885). *The Prophet of the Great Smoky Mountains* (1885). *In the Clouds* (1887). *The Story of Keedon Bluffs.* (1888). *The Despot of Broomsedge Cove* (1889). *In the "Stranger People's" Country* (1891). *His Vanished Star* (1894). *The Mystery of Witch-Face Mountain and Other Stories* (1895). *The Phantoms of the Foot-Bridge and Other Stories* (1895). *The Young Mountaineers* (1897). *The Juggler* (1897). *The Story of Old Fort Loudon* (1899). *The Bushwhackers and Other Stories* (1899). *The Champion* (1902). *A Spectre of Power* (1903). *The Frontiersmen* (1904). *The Storm Centre* (1905). *The Amulet* (1906). *The Windfall* (1907). *The Fair Mississippian* (1908). *The Raid of the Guerrilla and Other Stories* (1912). *The Ordeal: A Mountain Romance of Tennessee* (1912). *The Story of Duciehurst: A Tale of the Mississippi* (1914). *The Erskine Honeymoon* (posthumously published in the Nashville *Banner*, Dec. 29–Mar. 3, 1931).

—ALLISON R. ENSOR

ALBERT MURRAY (1926–). Albert Murray was born on May 12, 1926, in Nokomis, Ala., the son of John Young and Sudie Graham. He was adopted by Hugh and Mattie Murray. Albert Murray's education began in Mobile County Training School, where in 1935 he won a scholarship to Tuskegee Institute.

After graduating from Tuskegee with a B.S. in 1940, Murray enrolled in graduate school at the University of Michigan. That year he returned to Tuskegee to teach literature and composition. In 1941 he married Mozelle Menefee, who graduated from Tuskegee in 1943. In 1942 Murray became acquainted with Ralph Ellison, a fellow Tuskegean. Because of their shared love of literature and jazz, Murray and Ellison developed one of the important literary friendships of the twentieth century.

The same year as his marriage to Mozelle, Murray enlisted in the U.S. Air Force; he served on active duty until 1947. Almost immediately afterwards, he enrolled in graduate school at New York University. At the time, graduate courses were taught in the evening, and Murray often did not leave school until ten o'clock at night. The late departure proved serendipitous because it afforded him the opportunity to spend time at many of New York's great jazz clubs. He would often stop by the Three

Deuces to see jazz innovators such as Charlie Parker, Miles Davis, and Max Roach. At the Three Deuces, Murray's friend Harry Carney introduced him to Duke Ellington, who, among others, had a profound influence on Murray's views on literature.

A voracious reader, Murray has been much influenced by European and American writers: William Faulkner, Leo Tolstoy, Thomas Mann, T. S. Eliot, Ernest Hemingway. The greatest influence on Murray's aesthetic sensibility, outside of literature, is music, especially blues and jazz. In his work, Murray confronts the best and worst aspects of humanity through what he calls "swinging"—that is, relating humanity at its best, when it is most elegant, as well as tackling the immediate problems that everyday life affords, taking the chaos of life and giving it form and beauty through a blues aesthetic. Music is Murray's suggestion for elegantly "stomping the blues."

Albert Murray remains an active promoter and patron of the arts. He is both a board member and secretary of Jazz at Lincoln Center in New York City, through which he endeavors to promote jazz as fine art to be examined and re-examined in the same manner as great literature.

WORKS: *The Omni-Americans: New Perspectives on Black Experience and American Culture* (1970). *South to a Very Old Place* (1971). *The Hero and the Blues* (1973). *Train Whistle Guitar* (1974). *Stomping the Blues* (1976). *Good Morning Blues: The Autobiography of Count Basie,* with Count Basie (1986). *The Spyglass Tree* (1991). *The Blue Devils of Nada* (1996). *The Seven League Boots* (1996). Ed., *Trading Twelves: The Selected Letters of Ralph Ellison and Albert Murray,* with John F. Callahan (2000). *From the Briarpatch File: On Context, Procedure and American Identity* (2001). *Conjugations and Reiterations* (2001). *The Magic Keys: A Novel* (2005).

—KEITH MITCHELL

LAWRENCE NAUMOFF (1946–). Lawrence Naumoff was born in Charlotte, N.C., on July 23, 1946, to Esther and Philip Naumoff. Growing up in Charlotte as the son of a physician during the postwar years gave Naumoff perspective on the rapidly changing South in that most New South of cities. Like many promising young sons of the Piedmont, he attended the University of North Carolina at Chapel Hill, graduating in 1969. Naumoff developed an identity as the gifted young writer early on, an identity only strengthened by the heady days of the late 1960s.

Launched on a promising start, with fiction awards and a National Endowment for the Arts grant under his belt by 1970, he had already completed drafts of three novels and published several short stories under the pseudonym Peter Nesovich. This early burst of energy was not to last, however; Naumoff quit writing and worked as a carpenter and builder in 1971–88. His novels (and Peter Nesovich along with them) burned in a farmhouse in 1977.

The writer in Naumoff was not to be denied, and he began writing again in 1985. After 1988, with his first publication of a novel, *The Night of the Weeping Women,* he gave himself to writing full-time, having found a surer voice and a subject that would dominate his fiction—the strange relationships between men and women. Working in a style somewhere between the fabulous and the grotesque, Naumoff explored the nexus of gender, sexuality, and personal identity. Also, like many southern writers of the postwar generation, he and his characters rediscovered the need for place and tradition, even (or especially) in the postmodern South.

Since 1971, Naumoff has lived in Silk Hope, N.C. He currently teaches creative writing at his alma mater.

WORKS: The Night of the Weeping Women (1988). Rootie Kazootie (1990). Taller Women (1992). Silk Hope, NC (1994). A Plan for Women (1997). A Southern Tragedy in Crimson and Yellow (2005).

—DOUGLAS L. MITCHELL

Jane Thornhill on July 19, 1952, in Buckhanon, W.Va., she was reared with her two brothers in a culture where storytelling was a frequent pastime. Phillips earned a B.A. in English from West Virginia University in 1974, graduating magna cum laude. After traveling and working at odd jobs for several years, she enrolled in the University of Iowa Writers' Workshop and completed an M.F.A. in 1978.

The author of several collections of short stories and novels, Phillips began winning awards with *Sweethearts,* a collection of short fiction that received the Pushcart Prize and the Fels Award for Fiction. Also to her credit are the short-story collections *Black Tickets* and *Fast Lanes.* Her first novel, the critically acclaimed *Machine Dreams,* was honored with a *New York Times* best-book citation and a National Book Critics Circle Award nomination, and was called a Notable Book by the American Library Association. *Shelter,* her second novel, was praised for its lush language and its adept shifting of narrative perspectives. *MotherKind,* examines the contemporary family and the ways in which blended and extended families bond, dissolve, and redefine traditional constructions of "home."

Phillips resists identifying her work with a particular tradition, suggesting instead that such classifications more appropriately come from critics; yet a strong sense of place is evident in her writing. Though citing the influence of authors ranging from southerners (William Faulkner, Flannery O'Connor, Eudora Welty, Katherine Anne Porter, James Agee) to Continental writers (Franz Kafka, Bruno Schulz), she is most frequently associated with the Appalachian region. Phillips acknowledges the influence of the South and its values on her work, noting that "in order to live in the South in my imagination, I have to be separate from it. I feel fortunate that I lived in one place during my entire childhood and adolescence and didn't leave the area for good until I was in my 20s. The place that I use as a source no longer exists." A sense of connection to a bygone place and time in many ways serves to reinforce her connection to the South's rural past and the cultural value placed on family.

Over the course of her career, Phillips has held teaching positions throughout the Northeast, including stints at Radcliffe College, Boston University, and Harvard University, as well as at the University of Iowa. In 1996 she was named fiction writer-in-residence at Brandeis University. Phillips has received numerous awards, including two National Endowment for the Arts fellowships, the Guggenheim Fellowship, and the Sue Kaufman Prize for First Fiction for *Black Tickets.* She resides in Boston and continues to write fiction.

WORKS: *Sweethearts* (1976). *Black Tickets* (1979). *Fast Lanes* (1984). *Machine Dreams* (1984). *Shelter* (1994). *MotherKind* (2000).

—SUZANNE DISHEROON-GREEN

THOMAS HAL PHILLIPS (1922–). Born on a farm near Corinth, Miss., on October 11, 1922, Thomas Hal Phillips used his native state for the settings of much of his fiction. One of six children of W. T. Phillips and schoolteacher Ollie Fare Phillips, he was an all-around student and athlete at Alcorn Agricultural High School. He earned a B.S. in social science from Mississippi State University in 1943 and entered the navy as a lieutenant (j.g.). He saw action in the Mediterranean.

After the war, his literary career began at the University of Alabama, where, under Hudson Strode, he wrote a novel, *The Bitterweed Path,* as his thesis for the M.A. In 1947 Phillips won a Rosenwald Fellowship in Fiction, and a year later the Eugene F. Saxon Award.

He joined the faculty of Southern Methodist University in 1948. In 1950 he received a Fulbright Fellowship for study in France, the same year *The Bitterweed Path* was published. A sensitively composed narrative, it sets the interest of his later fiction: relationships among males and the coming-of-

FRANCES NEWMAN (1883–1928). In an allusive, modernist vein, Frances Newman satirized southern culture for its sexist and racist assumptions. Her novels focus on the inner lives of her female characters, revealing rebellious emotions and taboo thoughts beneath a thin veneer of socially sanctioned behavior.

Born into a prominent Atlanta family, Newman was the youngest daughter of William T. and Fanny Percy Alexander Newman. She attended Agnes Scott College and the University of Tennessee's Summer School of the South. In 1912 she received a library science degree from the Atlanta Carnegie Library. After working briefly for the Florida State College for Women, she returned to the Carnegie Library in 1914 and launched her writing career with witty reviews for the *Atlanta Journal* and *Atlanta Constitution*. In 1921 Newman wrote *The Gold-Fish Bowl*, a lighthearted comedy of manners about a librarian, but found no publisher.

In 1923 she studied at the Sorbonne, translating stories from five languages for *The Short Story's Mutations*. After working as a librarian at the Georgia Institute of Technology (1924–26), Newman completed *The Hard-Boiled Virgin* at the McDowell Colony in New Hampshire in 1926. Experimental in form, this episodic novel about a naive southern belle created a sensation with its allusions to women's sexual arousal, menstruation, and birth control. Its best-seller status enabled Newman to write full-time, and in 1928 she completed *Dead Lovers Are Faithful Lovers*. Narrated from the perspectives of two women, this novel deconstructs the literary conventions of the selfless angel of the house and the mistress.

In Europe, while working on a translation of Jules Laforgue's short fiction, Newman developed a serious eye problem and returned to New York for treatment. Although in intense pain and nearly blind, she completed this work by dictation before dying of a cerebral hemorrhage complicated by pneumonia on October 22, 1928.

WORKS: *The Short Story's Mutations* (1924). *The Hard-Boiled Virgin* (1926). *Dead Lovers Are Faithful Lovers* (1928). *Six Moral Tales from Jules Laforgue* (1928). *Frances Newman's Letters*, ed. Hansell Baugh (1929). *The Gold-Fish Bowl*, ed. Margaret Manning Duggan (1985).

—BARBARA A. WADE

CHARLES FENTON MERCER NOLAND (1816–1858). Born in Loudon County, Va., in 1816, to William Noland and Catharine Callender, Charles Noland grew up in Aldie, Va. His father served in the Virginia legislature and held federal appointments in Arkansas and in Washington, D.C., under six presidents.

After education at home, Noland was appointed to the U.S. Military Academy at thirteen, but was dismissed in 1825 for deficiency in drawing and mathematics. His father, recently appointed to the land office in Batesville, Ark., desired a rigorous discipline for his son and had him come out to the Arkansas territory in 1826. There he read law under another stern Virginian, and by 1829 was practicing. In a duel in 1831 he killed Governor John Pope's nephew. In 1833–36 he served with the U.S. Mounted Rangers in Vincennes, Prairie du Chien, and St. Louis before returning to Arkansas. A Whig, he served four terms in the state legislature. In 1840 he married Lucretia Ringgold and, until his death after a lifetime of tuberculosis, held various elective offices and federal and state appointments. He died in Little Rock on June 23, 1858.

Throughout his life he was fond of horse racing, shooting, and the ritualistic bear hunts of the American frontier. His topics for his newspaper sketches were the sports, politics, dances, and brutal fights of the settlements. His legacy is a series of mock Pete Whetstone letters written for the New York

Spirit of the Times from 1837 until 1856. His largely fictional character, carelessly but vigorously conceived, presents, in Noland's version of frontier dialect and perspective, one of our earliest sustained comic re-creations of the Old Southwest frontier.

WORKS: *Pete Whetstone of Devil's Fork,* ed. Ted R. Worley and Eugene A. Nolte (1957).

—MILTON AND PATRICIA RICKELS

LEWIS NORDAN (1939–). Born in Jackson, Miss., on August 23, 1939, Lewis Nordan grew up in the tiny Delta town of Itta Bena. After spending two years in the U.S. Navy—primarily, he has said, as a way to experience life beyond the Delta—he earned a B.A. from Millsaps College in 1963, followed by an M.A. from Mississippi State University. When he went to Auburn University to pursue a Ph.D. in English, he left his home state for good, though he retained an affinity for the Delta blues that still informs his writing. He completed the doctorate in 1973 with a dissertation on "Shakespeare's Dramatic Poetry."

Before breaking into print as a fiction writer, Nordan held a variety of jobs, working as a high school teacher, orderly, soda jerk, night watchman, fireworks salesman, and book reviewer. In 1977 he won the John Gould Fletcher Award from the University of Arkansas for his short story "The Rat Song"; it was to be the first of many awards. A National Endowment for the Arts grant a year later allowed him to complete his first book, a collection of short fiction that appeared in 1983. In that year he also moved from the University of Arkansas, where he had been an assistant professor, to the University of Pittsburgh. His first novel, *Music of the Swamp,* appeared in 1991.

His second novel, *Wolf Whistle,* won a Southern Book Award and a Notable Book Award from the American Library Association; *The Sharpshooter Blues* won both a Notable Book Award and the Best Fiction Award of the Mississippi Institute of Arts and Letters. In an essay "Growing Up White in the South" Nordan recounts the factors that motivated him to write *Wolf Whistle.*

Nordan married in 1962; the marriage ended after an only son committed suicide. He has since remarried, and lives in Pittsburgh. He is a creative-writing professor at the University of Pittsburgh.

WORKS: *Welcome to the Arrow-Catcher Fair* (1983). *The All-Girl Football Team* (1986). *Music of the Swamp* (1991). *Wolf Whistle* (1993). *The Sharpshooter Blues* (1995). *Sugar among the Freaks* (1996). *Lightning Song* (1997). *Boy with Loaded Gun: A Memoir* (2000).

—MARYANNE M. GOBBLE

MARSHA NORMAN (1947–). Born in Louisville, Ky., on September 21, 1947, Marsha Norman spent a solitary childhood, deprived by her mother's fundamentalist views of television, movies, and even playing with other children. But theater, piano, and reading helped offset the loneliness that would propel her to become a writer. Norman's early theatrical exposure included plays at the Actors Theatre of Louisville (ATL), a venue that would nurture her own playwriting career. Norman became part of a wave of important women dramatists emerging in the 1970s and 1980s, as well as one of many regional writers to attain Broadway success.

Norman earned her B.A. in philosophy from Agnes Scott College in Georgia and her M.F.A. from the University of Louisville. She worked as a journalist and arts reviewer for the *Louisville Times* and, in 1972–76, served as Kentucky arts commissioner. Encouraged by ATL's artistic director, Jon Jory, Norman began writing plays and made her theatrical debut with *Getting Out* (1977). Like some of Norman's other works, *Getting Out* draws on personal experience—in this case, her work with dis-

WORKS: *Something More Than Earth* (1940). *For the Glory of God* (1958). *The Christmas Wife: Stories* (1985). *More Than Seven Watchmen* (1985). *Water into Wine* (1988). *Walk with the Sickle Moon* (1989). *The Burning Glass: Stories* (1992). *Whatever Is Round* (1994). *One Day in the Life of a Born Again Loser and Other Stories* (2000).

—JOSEPH M. FLORA

SOLOMON NORTHUP (1808–1863?). Solomon Northup's life was the subject of one of the most famous slave narratives in American history. He was born free in Minerva, N.Y., and grew up working on his father's farm. Marrying Anne Hampton in 1829, Northup became a raftsman and gradually developed a reputation as a popular fiddler. In March 1841, Northup, now the father of three children, agreed to accompany two white men on a musical tour bound for Washington, D.C., where they promised him lucrative fiddling engagements. In the nation's capital, Northup was drugged, robbed, and delivered over to a slave trader who had him shipped to New Orleans. There he was purchased and sold to a succession of masters who held him in slavery in the Red River region of Louisiana for the next twelve years. "Platt," as he was known during his enslavement, worked as a carpenter, a sugarcane cutter, and a driver.

In 1852 Northup met Samuel Bass, a Canadian carpenter who had come to work for Northup's harsh master, Edwin Epps. Finding Bass fair-minded and outspokenly antislavery, Northup asked him to mail a letter to two white businessmen whom Northup knew in Saratoga, N.Y. In January 1853 a special agent of the governor of New York was dispatched to Bayou Boeuf to find the kidnapped black man and free him. Shortly after his return to his family in Glens Falls, N.Y., Northup contracted with a local white lawyer, David Wilson, to write his autobiography. *Twelve Years a Slave: Narrative of Solomon Northup, a Citizen of New-York* was published in the summer of 1853. The book sold over thirty thousand copies in England and the United States, rivaling the popularity of such classic slave narratives as *Narrative of the Life of Frederick Douglass*. Proceeds from the sale of *Twelve Years a Slave* enabled Northup to live comfortably in his own home until his death around 1863. He was never compensated for the crimes committed against him. His kidnappers were arrested and tried but never convicted.

WORKS: *Twelve Years a Slave: Narrative of Solomon Northup, a Citizen of New-York* (1853).

—WILLIAM L. ANDREWS

FLANNERY O'CONNOR (1925–1964). For so complex a person, the life of Flannery O'Connor was surprisingly unproblematic. O'Connor was born on March 25, 1925, in Savannah, Ga., only child to devout Irish Catholic parents Regina Cline and Edward Francis O'Connor, Jr. Baptized Mary Flannery, O'Connor was educated by nuns through grammar school in Savannah and Atlanta, to which the family moved in 1938 because of economic difficulties caused by the Depression. Within a year, the O'Connors relocated to the family farm outside Milledgeville, the antebellum capital of Georgia, where the Clines, O'Connor's maternal side, had substantial property and social prominence.

Milledgeville in middle Georgia was home. Here, in 1941, her father died of lupus, the autoimmune disease that O'Connor inherited. O'Connor graduated from the local high school and in 1945 received her B.A. from Georgia State College for Women (now Georgia College and State University). Her stories and poems in the college literary magazine revealed a born storyteller. She accepted a scholarship to the University of Iowa's graduate writing program, where she was introduced to great Modernists (Joyce, Faulkner, and Eliot) who stressed well-crafted structures, questions of faith, and the ability of language to explore intricate realms of consciousness.

In Iowa, O'Connor's faith and southern ties strengthened. She attended daily mass and wrote her mother every day. In 1948 she received her M.F.A. With an award to finish a novel, O'Connor went to Yaddo, the upstate New York artists colony. In 1949 she ventured to New York City, but the beaten path for young writers was not for her. O'Connor could not abide New York or any city. By September 1949 she rented a room over an attached garage owned by Sally Fitzgerald and Robert Fitzgerald near Ridgefield, Conn. Her stay with the Fitzgeralds began a lifelong relationship based on deep spiritual and professional affinities. In 1965 Robert Fitzgerald wrote an influential introduction to O'Connor's posthumous collection of stories *Everything That Rises Must Converge,* and with Sally Fitzgerald later edited *Mystery and Manners,* O'Connor's nonfiction prose. Sally Fitzgerald edited *The Habit of Being,* the volume of O'Connor's letters, as well as the definitive texts in O'Connor's *Collected Works.* Sally Fitzgerald was O'Connor's soul mate who laid the ground for the critical recognition of O'Connor's multiangled genius.

In Connecticut during December 1950, O'Connor at twenty-five developed pain and stiffness in her body that were diagnosed as lupus. Though her career might have been thwarted just as it began, O'Connor's determination to write won out. Medication enabled her to work, but her illness required her to return permanently to the 1500-acre farm outside Milledgeville. Though independent and ambitious, O'Connor was forced to rely on her mother for care and survival. She felt exiled: a single, aspiring, Catholic woman stuck in a Protestant, racist, and sexist hinterland. Constraints, however, catalyzed O'Connor's development. Insular Milledgeville became the magnetic field of her writing.

Isolation made mail eventful. Writing to friends and readers, O'Connor gave her best. Her letters express extraordinary grace and wisdom, revealing a warmth behind her stern fiction and principled mind. She read widely in theology, reviewed books for diocesan papers, and lectured at colleges and universities. But O'Connor led a secluded life (a telephone was installed in July 1956) that allowed her to refine her writing, pray, receive visitors, and raise her cherished peafowl. While nations were fighting hot and cold wars, she, sharing in the displacement and affliction of the era, led a simple, sane life. Work and leisure, solitude and sociability, struggle and ease, fatigue and convalescence composed a humanizing daily practice. God and writing were the founding calls of O'Connor's life.

From this quiet hermitage sprang tumultuous narratives. With home, faith, and the rural South as coordinates, O'Connor dramatized the search for ultimates in a broken world. Her two novels portray murderous firebrands: *Wise Blood* recounts a nihilist preacher finding God; *The Violent Bear It Away* details the brutal formation of a teenage prophet. O'Connor's stories also erupt: *A Good Man Is Hard to Find* unleashes the terror of assailants and victims encountering divine mercy; *Everything That Rises Must Converge* depicts tormented people breaking out of dread. A chronicler of sin, conversion, and grace, O'Connor is a writer of hope and joy.

O'Connor the storyteller and the letter writer also made her mark as literary critic and public intellectual. In treating God's relations with the universe, O'Connor can rightly be called a theologian. She achieved much during a short span. In February 1964, O'Connor underwent surgery. Her lupus prevailed, and she died on August 3, 1964, at thirty-nine.

WORKS: *Wise Blood* (1952). *A Good Man Is Hard to Find* (1955). *The Violent Bear It Away* (1960). Ed., *A Memoir of Mary Ann* (1962). *Everything That Rises Must Converge* (1964). *The Habit of Being: Letters of Flannery O'Connor,* ed. Sally Fitzgerald (1969). *The Complete Stories* (1971). *Mystery and Manners: Occasional Prose,* ed. Sally Fitzgerald and Robert Fitzgerald (1979). *The Presence of Grace and Other Book Reviews,* ed. Carter Martin (1983). *Conversations with Flannery O'Connor,* ed. Rosemary Magee (1987). *Flannery O'Connor: Collected Works,* ed. Sally Fitzgerald (1988).

—RICHARD GIANNONE

E. P. O'DONNELL (1895–1943). E. P. (Edwin Philip "Pat") O'Donnell was born on March 25, 1895, in New Orleans, La., and grew up near the wharves along the Mississippi River. Although it is unclear exactly how much education he received, he had certainly left school by the seventh grade to begin a varied career; he claimed later to remember holding at least thirty-three jobs, beginning as a newsboy and shoe shiner on the New Orleans ferry route. During World War I, he served in the adjutant general's department and drove an ambulance.

Back in New Orleans after the war, O'Donnell landed at the Ford assembly plant, where he worked his way up from the assembly line to become chief of publicity. In that capacity, he guided Sherwood Anderson around the plant when the author visited the area in the late 1920s. Anderson must have enjoyed his tour; at the end, he suggested that his guide become a writer. O'Donnell's first story appeared in a small magazine in 1929, followed quickly by appearances in Collier's, Harper's, and Scribner's. "Jesus Knew," which appeared in Harper's in 1935, won third prize in the O. Henry contest and helped him to win a $1,000 literary fellowship from Houghton Mifflin.

With the prize money, O'Donnell purchased a shack in the Delta country, where he worked on shrimp and oyster boats, helped orange and lily growers to establish cooperatives, and wrote his first novel, Green Margins, which appeared as a 1936 Book-of-the-Month-Club selection. Eudora Welty praised it for showing the rich human relationships of the materially poor. His second novel, The Great Big Doorstep, took a comic view of the same Delta culture that had been the setting for the tragic Green Margins. A stage adaptation of The Great Big Doorstep ran on Broadway for three weeks in late 1942.

O'Donnell died in April 1943, after a long illness, only six weeks after marrying his second wife, Mary King.

WORKS: Green Margins (1936). The Great Big Doorstep: A Delta Comedy (1941).

—MARYANNE M. GOBBLE

HOWARD W. ODUM (1884–1954). Howard Washington Odum, the South's most notable sociologist in the first half of the twentieth century, was born in Walton County, Ga., on May 24, 1884, to William Pleasants and Mary Ann Thomas Odum. "A native of the ruralest of the rural south," as Odum later wrote, and reared among people "from which is recruited our fundamentalists and often our Ku Klux folk," Odum was educated at Emory College (A.B., 1904), the University of Mississippi (A.M., 1906), Clark University (Ph.D., 1909), and Columbia University (Ph.D., 1910). Between 1904 and 1920 he served as a school principal in Mississippi, an instructor at the University of Mississippi, professor of sociology at the University of Georgia, and dean of the School of Liberal Arts at Emory.

In 1920 Odum became director of the School of Public Welfare at the University of North Carolina, and in 1924 became director of the Institute for Research in Social Sciences. In 1922 he founded the Journal of Social Forces, one of the leading organs of southern self-examination in the 1920s. During this period Odum joined with Gerald W. Johnson and other southerners in an attempt to bring about what Odum called a "critical-creative" revival in the South. In the 1930s he was widely identified as the leader of the southern Regionalists, a group concerned largely with defining and attacking southern social and economic ills. He and his philosophy were frequently challenged by the southern Agrarians, who were more concerned with preserving than reforming the South. He died on November 8, 1954, in Chapel Hill, N.C.

Odum was also a folk artist, a chronicler of the trials of southern African Americans. His folk trilogy—Rainbow Round My Shoulder, Wings on My Feet, and Cold Blue Moon—depicted with sympathy and understanding the life of a black laborer he called Black Ulysses. Odum was by discipline a sociologist, but as he showed in his folk trilogy and other work, his sociology was an all-encompassing study of what he called "the folk-regional society."

WORKS: *Social and Mental Traits of the Negro* (1910). *The Negro and His Songs* (1925). *Negro Workaday Songs* (1926). *Rainbow Round My Shoulder* (1928). Ed., *Southern Pioneers in Social Interpretation* (1929). *Wings on My Feet* (1929). *An American Epoch: Southern Portraiture in the National Picture* (1930). *Cold Blue Moon* (1931). *Southern Regions of the United States* (1936). *American Regionalism*, with Harry E. Moore (1938). *American Democracy Anew*, with others (1940). *Alabama, Past and Future* (1941). *Race and Rumors of Race* (1943). *The Way of the South* (1947). *Folk, Region, and Society: Selected Papers of Howard W. Odum*, ed. Katherine Jocher et al. (1964).

—FRED HOBSON

CHRIS OFFUTT (1958–). Chris Offutt was born on August 24, 1958, in Haldeman, Ky., a Rowan County village that no longer exists. He quit high school before graduating, opting instead to wander the country as a hitchhiker while supporting himself with a series of odd jobs. (His years of drifting are successfully recounted from the position of impending fatherhood in Offutt's memoir *The Same River Twice.*) He moved back to Kentucky (the first of several returns) to attend Morehead State University, where he received his B.A. in theater in 1981. In the mid-1980s Offutt met his future wife, Rita Lily, and together they moved to Iowa when Offutt was accepted into the University of Iowa's Writers' Workshop. Offutt received his M.F.A. from Iowa in 1990, and he left Iowa City to begin what would be a series of short-term teaching assignments at locations as diverse as the University of Montana, the University of New Mexico, and his alma mater. His second memoir, *No Heroes*, covers Offutt's return to Kentucky to teach creative writing at Morehead State, as well as his in-laws' Holocaust experiences. Although it was lauded nationally, many eastern Kentucky critics charged that *No Heroes* was filled with stinging inaccuracies. Offutt's fiction, nearly always either set in Kentucky or populated by characters who feel the pull of their Kentucky home, has been more universally accepted, and the unadorned and straightforward prose of his story collections, *Kentucky Straight* and *Out of the Woods*, has led more than one reviewer to describe him as a kind of Appalachian Raymond Carver. Offutt is the father of two sons, Sam and James, and currently resides in Iowa City.

WORKS: *Kentucky Straight* (1992). *The Same River Twice* (1993). *The Good Brother* (1997). *Out of the Woods* (1999). *No Heroes: A Memoir of Coming Home* (2002).

—ROB TRUCKS

THEODORE O'HARA (1820–1867). The fame of this Kentucky poet rests on one poem, "The Bivouac of the Dead," or more particularly on its first stanza, which is inscribed on the gateway to the Arlington National Cemetery. The son of Kean and Helen Hardy O'Hara, he was probably born (on February 11, 1820) in Frankfort, although Danville, Ky., also lays claim to being the place of his birth. His father, a well-educated Irish immigrant, provided his early schooling and prepared him for studies at St. Joseph's College in Bardstown. So advanced was O'Hara's preparation in Greek that he taught that language while pursuing his college degree.

Although he read law after leaving college and passed the bar examination, he spent most of his life as a journalist and soldier. He wrote for the *Frankfort Yeoman* (1843–44), during which time he apparently wrote "The Old Pioneer," a poem honoring Daniel Boone. Soldiering won out over journalism, however, and he volunteered for service in the Mexican War, receiving a commission as a captain and being appointed assistant quartermaster. For gallant behavior in battles at Contreras and Churubusco, he was brevetted major. Alcoholism was a persistent problem in his life, and he faced a court-martial from young lieutenant colonel Robert E. Lee for drunkenness on duty. To honor Kentuckians who fell at the battle of Buena Vista in 1847, he composed "The Bivouac of the Dead."

In the years remaining to him, he enlisted in the army of Narcisco López to help in the fight for Cuban independence and accepted a commission in the Confederate army, serving under Generals Albert Johnston and John Breckinridge, and held journalistic positions with the *Louisville Times* and the *Mobile Register*.

Following the Civil War, he settled in Columbus, Ga., where he dealt in cotton. He died on June 6, 1867, and was interred in Columbus, but his remains were later (1874) reburied in Frankfort.

WORKS: "The Old Pioneer" (1845). "The Bivouac of the Dead" (possibly as early as 1848).

—JOHN L. IDOL, JR.

BRENDA MARIE OSBEY (1957–). A native of New Orleans, poet Brenda Marie Osbey has used that city as locus and focus in virtually all of her published work. The Crescent City's rich, often troubled history, its crowded, multiethnic neighborhoods, it music, its moods, its violent weather and events constitute a vivid backdrop for her profoundly evocative and often provocative narrative figures. Osbey has, however, spent time elsewhere. After earning a B.A. from Dillard, she attended Paul Valery University, Montpellier, France, and received an M.A. from the University of Kentucky. Since then she has mostly lived in New Orleans, where she is currently writer-in-residence at Dillard. But she has also taught at UCLA, and spent a year as a fellow of the Bunting Institute at Radcliffe. The recipient of many awards (in 2005 she was named poet laureate of Louisiana), she is the author of four volumes of poetry.

Ceremony for Minneconjoux offers voices and visions of the women of New Orleans's black wards, whose poignant, often traumatic lives find soaring expression in long confessional passages. Occluded events, mysterious personages, shadowy backgrounds lend an air of intrigue and mystery to many of these poems, especially when the woman in question seems possessed by the spirits, mad from grief, or simply mad. Osbey's deep knowledge of two particular faubourgs (neighborhoods), the Tremé and the Marigny, allows her to localize some unique aspects of the city that ornament the lineaments of her stories. The Bahalia women with their roots and tambourines introduce us to Afro-Caribbean forms of devotion that circulate through the city.

In These Houses provides more portraits of such women, who are here called "Madhouses"; they are sometimes "swift, 'easy' women" who, Circe-like, lure men into disaster. Careless Reva's indifference causes her lover Diamond to hang himself. Thelma Picou runs out naked to eat dirt, driven mad by her dominating "Darling Henry." Several characters end up in "infirmary" or in Jackson, the state mental hospital. Osbey appends a helpful glossary of Louisiana ethnic expressions and place names to avoid having to spell out meanings in the poems themselves.

Desperate Circumstance, Dangerous Woman presents one long romantic drama, dominated by the tortured love affair of Marie Calcasieu ("Screaming Eagle") with Percy, the really desperate figure in this story; both consult the hoodoo woman Ms. Regina. Rites, rituals, and the haunted presence of interior rooms in the Faubourg Marigny carry secrets brought to the city from the Manchac Swamp.

Osbey won the American Poetry Award for *All Saints: New and Selected Poems*. The collection brought forward several of her classic pieces but was mostly composed of stunning new historical poems that excavate the terrible legacy of slavery. Osbey relates these poems to the book's overarching concern with the dead, and New Orleans as a city with a "particular fascination" for the dead. Moving elegies for relatives and for relatives of friends complement the central structure, which moves effortlessly from legendary figures such as the cult priestess Mother Catherine to contemporary musicians such as Nina Simone, whose long-ago impasse with a black audience occasions a mournful lament for lost connections and the early interbraiding of music and femininity in Osbey's own life.

More recently Osbey has composed a series of complicated love poems, and the libretto for an opera, *La Sultane*. Written in French, *La Sultane* portrays antebellum diasporan events and legendary figures against a tropical, often threatening backdrop, and provides many operatic opportunities for its yet-to-be-named composer.

Osbey has written several essays about New Orleans, including sharp, often witty, but ultimately meditative and respectful observations about jazz funerals and other burial rituals and traditions. Always alert to both the past and the present, ever creative and speculative, alternately elegant and startling, Osbey continues to blaze a unique and compelling path for African American and southern letters.

WORKS: *Ceremony for Minneconjoux* (1983). *In These Houses* (1988). *Desperate Circumstance, Dangerous Woman* (1991). *All Saints: New and Selected Poems* (1997).

—JOHN LOWE

GUY OWEN (1925–1981). From Welsh and English ancestors, Guy Owen was born on February 24, 1925, in Clarkton, N.C., the Clayton of his fictional and mythical "Cape Fear County." Eldest of four boys, he grew up in Florida and South Carolina, before the family returned during the Depression to Clarkton, where he learned about farm life and tobacco fields on his grandfather's farm. Graduating from high school in 1942, he entered the University of North Carolina that fall, but was soon called to military service. Following deployment to France and Germany, he returned to Chapel Hill. After receiving a B.A. (1947) and an M.A. (1949), he taught for two years at Davidson. In 1952 he married Dorothy Jennings, with whom he had two sons. He taught at nearby Elon College while completing his Ph.D. (1955) at Chapel Hill. He became an associate professor at Stetson University in Deland, Fla., where he wrote short stories, poems, and his first novel, *Season of Fear*. Set in "Cape Fear County" during the Depression, this is a novel of a lonely and God-obsessed man.

In 1962 Owen began teaching modern literature and creative writing at North Carolina State University, where he received numerous teaching awards. Until 1978 he also edited the *Southern Poetry Review* (a magazine founded in 1958 at Stetson as *Impetus*) and for five years co-edited *North Carolina Folklore*. He also served as co-editor of anthologies of southern and North Carolina poetry. He is the author of *The White Stallion*, a volume of poems, and many critical articles.

Owen received many awards in his home state and beyond, including a Bread Loaf scholarship (1960) and a Yaddo Fellowship (1968). Although he was vigorous in promoting excellence in poetry, he is now best known for Mordecai Jones, the Flim-Flam Man, an engaging con artist who with his young partner follows a comically adventurous path through eastern North Carolina. Introduced in *The Ballad of the Flim-Flam Man*, Jones's exploits continue in another novel and a collection of short stories. *Journey for Joedel*, a serious novel about the Depression, was nominated for the Pulitzer Prize and recounts the journey of a part-Lumbee Indian boy from innocence to moral ambiguity.

In his lectures throughout the South and in his teaching and editorial work, Owen encouraged southern writers; in his novels he recorded the life of his region. He died from cancer on July 23, 1981. He is buried in Clarkton.

WORKS: *Season of Fear* (1960). Ed., *Essays in Modern American Literature*, with Richard Langford and William E. Taylor (1963). *The Guilty and Other Poems* (1964). *The Ballad of the Flim-Flam Man* (1965). *The White Stallion and*

Other Poems (1969). *Journey for Joedel* (1970). *The Flim-Flam Man and the Apprentice Grifter* (1972). Ed., *Modern American Poetry: Essays in Criticism* (1972). Ed., *New Southern Poets: Selected Poems from Southern Poetry Review*, with Mary C. Williams (1975). *The Flim-Flam Man and Other Stories* (1976). Ed., *Contemporary Poetry of North Carolina*, with Williams (1977).

—WAYNE J. POND

THOMAS NELSON PAGE (1853–1922). Although Thomas Nelson Page is widely considered to be an apologist for the so-called Old South and an opponent of social and economic changes in that region following the Civil War, Page himself believed his was an authentic vision of a lamentably anachronistic culture. Born at Oakland Plantation in Virginia on April 23, 1853, Page was descended from colonial governors and other leaders of early American life. He attended Washington College (1869–72), while General Robert E. Lee was its president, and later studied law both in Kentucky and at the University of Virginia (1873–74). With a quick mind and attractive personality, he soon became a successful attorney.

Adding to his popularity as a member of Virginia's young elite was his publication of a short story, "Marse Chan," in 1884. The story's slave narrator claims that "dem wuz good ole times . . . de bes' guine Sam ever see," earning Page a reputation as a propagandist of the old order.

In 1886 Page married Anne Bruce, who died two years later. His grief was Poesque, and he romanticized aristocratic female characters in all his fiction afterward. In despair he moved his business to Europe and lingered there until the economic panic of 1891 drove him back to America and lecture tours with another local colorist, F. Hopkinson Smith. A second marriage, to Florence Lathrop Field, the widowed sister-in-law of Marshall Field, restored his lagging spirits and his financial solvency. Both in Washington, D.C., in a fine house designed by McKim, Mead, and White, and in York Harbor, Maine, the Pages entertained socialites, politicians, and writers. All the while considering himself a man of letters, Page wrote elegiac accounts of a doomed civilization.

After he had rallied much of the southern constituency behind Woodrow Wilson's nomination for president in 1912, Page was rewarded by being named ambassador to Rome. In Rome the Pages were known as champions of the poor. Returning to America after his ambassadorial appointment, Page gave a series of lectures on Dante and began recording antebellum southern fictional material. His wife died in 1921, and he returned to Oakland Plantation, which they had restored to its former architectural glory. He himself died on October 31, 1922, as he was planting a rosebush near the house where he was born.

WORKS: *Marse Chan: A Tale of Old Virginia* (1885). *In Ole Virginia; or, Marse Chan and Other Stories* (1887). *Befo' de War: Echoes in Negro Dialect*, with A. C. Gordon (1888). *Two Little Confederates* (1888). *Unc' Edinburg: A Plantation Echo* (1889). *Among the Camps; or, Young People's Stories of the War* (1891). *Elsket and Other Stories* (1891). *On Newfound River* (1891). *The Old South: Essays Social and Political* (1892). *Meh Lady: A Story of the War* (1893). *The Burial of the Guns and Other Stories* (1894). *Pastime Stories* (1894). *Polly: A Christmas Recollection* (1894). *The Old Gentleman of the Black Stock* (1897). *Social Life in Old Virginia before the War* (1897). *Red Rock: A Chronicle of Reconstruction* (1898). *Two Prisoners* (1898). *The Peace Cross Book: Cathedral of SS Peter and Paul, Washington* (1899). *Santa Claus's Partner* (1899). *A Captured Santa Claus* (1902). *Gordon Keith* (1903). *Bred in the Bone* (1904). *The Negro: The Southerner's Problem* (1904). *The Coast of Bohemia* (1906). *The Page Story Book* (1906). *Under the Crust* (1907). *The Old Dominion: Her Making and Her Manners* (1908). *Robert E. Lee, the Southerner* (1908). *Tommy Trot's Visit to Santa Claus* (1908). *General Lee, Man and Soldier* (1909); rev. as *Robert E. Lee, Man and Soldier* (1911). *John Marvel, Assistant* (1909). *Mount Vernon and Its Preservation, 1858–1910: The Acquisition, Restoration and Care of the Home of Washington by the Mount Vernon Ladies' Association for over Half a Century* (1910). *The Land of the Spirit* (1913).

The Shepherd Who Watched by Night (1913). *The Stranger's Pew* (1914). *Tommaso Jefferson, Apostolo della Libertà (1743–1826)* (1918). *Italy and the World War* (1920.) *Dante and His Influence* (1922). *Washington and Its Romance* (1923). *The Red Riders*, completed by Rosewell Page (1924). *The Stable of the Inn* (1959). *John Fox and Tom Page as They Were: Letters, an Address, and an Essay* (1969). *North Africa Journal, 1912, with Letters along the Way* (1970). *On the Nile in 1901* (1970). *Mediterranean Winter, 1906: Journal and Letters* (1971).

—KIMBALL KING

WALTER HINES PAGE (1855–1918). Born in what is now Cary, N.C., on August 15, 1855, Walter Hines Page—editor, publisher, writer, and diplomat—traveled far from his hometown but remained concerned with the post–Civil War South and encouraged political and social reforms to restore the region. As a journalist, Page contributed observations on the South to both newspapers and journals. He returned to Raleigh, N.C., in 1883, and founded the *State Chronicle*, a paper in which he encouraged and critiqued his own state and the South. After leaving the *Chronicle*, Page edited two prominent journals, the *Forum* (1891–95) and the *Atlantic Monthly* (1898–99), where he encouraged the careers of other southern writers, including Charles W. Chesnutt, Ellen Glasgow, and Mary Johnston.

In partnership with Frank Doubleday, he formed the publishing house Doubleday, Page, and Company in 1899 and served as its vice president. Page also edited the *World's Work*, a new journal, and published three books, including *The Rebuilding of Old Commonwealths*, a collection of three of his essays about the South; *A Publisher's Confession*, a collection of letters about his profession; and *The Southerner*, his only novel.

In 1913 Page entered another career when his old friend President Woodrow Wilson appointed him ambassador to Great Britain. As a result of his distinguished service during World War I, he is one of only three Americans honored in Westminster Abbey. He died in 1918, shortly after his return to the United States. He was subsequently honored when the Walter Hines Page School of Public Relations at Johns Hopkins University was named for him in 1924.

WORKS: *The Rebuilding of Old Commonwealths: Being Essays towards the Training of the Forgotten Man in the Southern States* (1902). *A Publisher's Confession* (1905). *The Southerner: A Novel* (1909).

—SHARON L. GRAVETT

F. V. N. PAINTER (1852–1931). Franklin Verzelius Newton Painter was born in Hampshire County, Va. (now W.Va.), on April 12, 1852, to Israel and Juliana Wilson Painter. His father, a millwright, was of German descent; his mother came from Scottish stock. He attended the public schools of Aurora, W.Va., and in 1870 entered Roanoke College, Salem, Va., receiving a B.A. four years later and winning first honor in his graduating class.

In 1878, upon graduation from Lutheran Theological Seminary in Salem, Painter became a Lutheran clergyman. That year he accepted an appointment to the faculty of Roanoke College, where he was professor of modern languages and literature for many years. In 1906 he retired from the ministry and from his professorship to devote his time to writing, but retained a lectureship in pedagogy and the history of education. In addition to his work as teacher and minister, he was active and outstanding as educator, author, scholar, and poet.

Painter's most notable contribution may be the large number of textbooks he wrote in the fields of literature, education, and religion. *A History of Education*, for example, went through many editions between 1886 and 1927, as did his *Introduction to American Literature* between 1897 and 1932. He published one volume of Wordsworthian poems, *Lyrical Vignettes*. In addition, he preached sermons, contributed articles to periodicals, and gave literary addresses. He was an ardent spokesman for the teaching of modern foreign languages as opposed to ancient languages in the college curriculum, a position approved by the Modern Language Association in 1885.

Painter married Laura Trimble Shickel on August 9, 1857. Eight children were born to them. He died on January 18, 1931.

WORKS: *A History of Education* (1886; rev., enl., and largely rewritten, 1904). *Luther on Education* (1889). *History of Christian Worship,* with J. W. Richardson (1891). *Introduction to English Literature* (1894; rev. and enl., 1919). *Introduction to American Literature* (1897). *Introduction to English and American Literature* (1899). *A History of English Literature* (1899). *Lyrical Vignettes* (1900). *The Reformation Dawn* (1901). *Elementary Guide to Literary Criticism* (1903). *Poets of the South* (1903). *Great Pedagogical Essays* (1905). *Poets of Virginia* (1907). *Introduction to Bible Study: The Old Testament* (1911).

—DOROTHY MCINNIS SCURA

BREECE D'J PANCAKE (1952–1979). Breece Dexter Pancake was born on June 29, 1952, in Milton, W.Va., the son of a World War II veteran and Union Carbide shipping clerk, and a public librarian. His middle initial was changed to "D'J" because of a galley proof error in his first story sold to the *Atlantic Monthly,* "Trilobites." He attended Milton High School, West Virginia Wesleyan College, and then Marshall University in Huntington, W.Va., from which he graduated in 1974. The death of his father, in 1975, and Pancake's inability to make a living in his home state had a profound impact on his writing. While teaching at Fork Union and Staunton military academies, he began writing short stories and attending creative writing classes at the University of Virginia. His teachers there were Peter Taylor, John Casey, James Alan McPherson, and the English poet Richard Jones.

Pancake published three stories before committing suicide in Charlottesville on April 8, 1979. Interest in his work and the circumstances of his death (similar to the case of John Kennedy Toole) resulted in the posthumous *The Stories of Breece D'J Pancake,* published by Little, Brown in 1983. Nominated for the Pulitzer Prize and the Weatherford Award, the book signaled the emergence of many contemporary Appalachian writers onto the national literary scene.

Pancake's fiction compares to that of an earlier generation of southern writers: Faulkner, Wolfe, O'Connor, and Walker Percy, depicting characters longing for the values of the past and place yet conflicted by the moral perplexity of a changing world. Like Quentin Compson, Eugene Gant, and Will Barrett, Pancake's characters struggle between the impulses to return to and escape from all that has formed them. Pancake himself entered the Roman Catholic faith before his death. Noted for his use of first-person, present-tense narration and a realistic, poetic texture, Pancake dramatized the moral dilemmas of coming of age during the Vietnam era.

WORKS: *The Stories of Breece D'J Pancake* (1983).

—THOMAS E. DOUGLASS

FRANCES GRAY PATTON (1906–2000). Born on March 19, 1906, in Raleigh, N.C., Frances Gray, daughter of a journalist, turned to writing almost as a birthright. After one year at Trinity College (now Duke University), she transferred to the University of North Carolina at Chapel Hill but left during her final semester. At Chapel Hill, she performed with the Carolina Playmakers and wrote a play, "The Beaded Buckle." At twenty-one, she married Lewis Patton, a professor at Duke. They had three children, a son (Robert) and twin daughters (Mary and Susannah).

As her children grew up, Patton resumed writing, and the short story seemed made for her schedule as well as her instinct. Her first published story, "A Piece of Bread" (1944), appeared in the *Kenyon Review* and was included in the annual *O. Henry Memorial Award Stories*. Other stories followed in numerous magazines, but especially the *New Yorker*. Her stories were carefully plotted and marked by clever twists. She wrote about the subjects she knew best: parents and children, husbands and wives, and teachers and pupils. Her work captures the traditions of southern womanhood in an upper-middle-class culture during the first half of the twentieth century. Her stories appear in three collections—*The Finer Things of Life, A Piece of Luck,* and *Twenty-Eight Stories*. Her best-known story, "The Terrible Miss Dove," a portrait of a demanding teacher who inspires a soldier in wartime, was the basis for a novel, *Good Morning, Miss Dove*. A book club selection, the novel quickly became a successful film (1955) starring Jennifer Jones. The next year, an adaptation for television starred Phyllis Kirk.

Patton was a three-time winner of the Sir Walter Raleigh Award for excellence in fiction by a North Carolinian and taught classes in creative writing at Chapel Hill, Duke, and the University of North Carolina at Greensboro. She died in Durham, N.C., on March 28, 2000.

WORKS: *The Finer Things of Life* (1951). *Good Morning, Miss Dove* (1954). *A Piece of Luck* (1955). *Twenty-Eight Stories* (all but one story reprinted from previous collections, 1969).

—WAYNE J. POND

LEONIDAS WARREN PAYNE, JR. (1873–1945). Leonidas Warren Payne, Jr., was born on July 12, 1873, in Auburn, Ala., the son of Leonidas Warren and Mary Jane Foster Payne. He married Mary Susan Bledsoe on October 27, 1897, and they were the parents of four children. He received his college education at Alabama Polytechnic Institute, now Auburn University (B.Sc., 1892; M.Sc., 1893) and the University of Pennsylvania (Ph.D., 1904); at the latter he was Harrison Fellow in English (1902–4). Payne held teaching positions at Southwestern Alabama Agricultural School, Evergreen, Ala. (1894–1901); Jacksonville, Ala., State Normal School (1901–2), Louisiana State University (1906), and the University of Texas (1906; professor of English, 1919). He was co-founder and the first president of the Texas Folklore Society (1910). He died on June 16, 1945.

In the field of linguistics and language, Payne served as associate editor of Worcester's *Dictionary* (1904–6), compiled *Word List of Eastern Alabama* and *Learn to Spell,* and edited a five-volume series, *Using Our Language,* for use in grades three to seven. He also helped to edit three other anthologies for use in secondary schools: *Literature for the Junior High School; Enjoying Literature* for grades nine to twelve; and *Enjoying Literature* for grades six to eight. He was author of *History of American Literature* and editor of *American Literary Readings, Selections from American Literature, Selections from English Literature,* and *Selections from Later American Writers*.

Payne's work in southern literature was extensive. He produced *A Survey of Texas Literature* and edited *Southern Literary Readings, Fifty Famous Southern Poems,* and *Texas Poems*. For the biographical eleventh and twelfth volumes of *The South in the Building of the Nation* (1909), Payne contributed sketches of William Gilmore Simms, George W. Cable, Joel Chandler Harris, Paul Hamilton Hayne, Mary Noailles Murfree, and Mary Johnston, among others.

WORKS: Ed., W. Smith, *Hector of Germanic* (1906). Comp., *Word List of Eastern Alabama* (1910). Ed., *Southern Literary Readings* (1913). Comp., *Learn to Spell* (1916). Ed., *American Literary Readings* (1917). *History of American Literature* (1919). Ed., *Selections from American Literature* (1919). Ed., *Fifty Famous Southern Poems* (1920). Ed., *Selections from English Literature,* with N. Hill (1922). Ed., *Selections from Later American Writers* (1927). *A Survey of Texas Literature* (1928). Ed., *Literature for the Junior High Schools,* 3 vols., with T. H. Briggs and C. M. Curry (1929).

Ed., *Using Our Language*, 5 vols., with A. Blount and C. S. Northrup (1935). Ed., *Enjoying Literature*, 4 vols., with M. A. Neville and N. E. Chapman (1936). Ed., *Texas Poems* (1936), with J. O. Beaty, R. W. Smith, and W. H. Vann. Ed., *Enjoying Literature*, 3 vols., with M. A. Neville (1942).

—Randall G. Patterson

T. R. PEARSON (1956–). Thomas Reid Pearson was born on March 27, 1956, in Winston-Salem, N.C. He graduated from Winston-Salem's R. J. Reynolds High School in 1974 and left home to pursue a degree at North Carolina State University. After earning a B.A. (1977) and an M.A. (1980) in English at the university, Pearson remained in Raleigh for a further year, teaching English at Peace College. In 1981 he began study toward a Ph.D. in English at Pennsylvania State University, but left the program after only one quarter and returned to Raleigh.

There he spent several years working as a carpenter and painter for a building contractor. Part of his time he also devoted to writing, and in 1982 he finished his first novel, *The Short History of a Small Place*. It was not until he had completed a second volume, however, that Pearson was able to find a publisher; he then saw his two books into print—*A Short History* in 1985 and *Off for the Sweet Hereafter* in 1986. With the publication of a third novel, *The Last of How It Was,* Pearson completed his "trilogy" set in the fictional town of Neeley, a community modeled on Reidsville, N.C., where Pearson's grandparents had lived.

After three further novels, Pearson did not publish again until 2000, an interval of seven years. In the fall semester of 1993 he was writer-in-residence at the University of Mississippi. And in the following several years he turned his talents to the writing of screenplays, including two on which he collaborated with the novelist John Grisham.

Pearson divides his time between his homes in New York and Carroll County, in rural southwestern Virginia, a region that provides the setting for his most recent work.

WORKS: *A Short History of a Small Place* (1985). *Off for the Sweet Hereafter* (1986). *The Last of How It Was* (1987). *Call and Response* (1989). *Gospel Hour* (1991). *Cry Me a River* (1993). *Blue Ridge* (2000). *Polar* (2002).

—John N. Somerville, Jr.

SAMUEL MINTURN PECK (1854–1938). Samuel Minturn Peck, Alabama's first poet laureate, was born on November 4, 1854, in Tuscaloosa, Ala., to Judge Elijah Wolsey Peck and Lucy Lamb Randall Peck. In 1876 he received his master's degree from the University of Alabama. In 1879, under pressure from his father, Peck received his M.D. from Bellevue Hospital Medical College in New York, although he never practiced medicine. He studied languages and literature at Columbia, then at the Alliance Français in Paris, before settling down to a long and apparently comfortable life of travel, study, and writing made possible by a family inheritance. His 1931 laureateship was no doubt assisted by the turn-of-the-century popularity of his poem "The Grapevine Swing," published in 1892, which was widely anthologized and set to music. Peck never married, and he maintained the Peck family home as his residence in Tuscaloosa throughout his life, considering himself rooted in Alabama despite his extensive travels.

A gentleman of letters rather than a true literary professional, Peck produced four unpublished novels and many local color stories and journalistic "sketches" in addition to his volumes of verse. His poetry is marked by ornamentally expressed nostalgia for a southern boyhood and a preference for floridly Victorian and sentimental diction, even well into the twentieth century; Peck deplored and resisted the influence of such modern voices as Amy Lowell, Carl Sandburg, and Harriet Monroe. At his best, however, as in "The Grapevine Swing" and some moments in his stories, Peck achieves simplicity and energy that hint at a promise and a maturity his career never quite fulfilled.

WORKS: *Cap and Bells* (1886). *Rings and Love-Knots* (1892.) *Rhymes and Roses* (1895). *Fair Women of To-day* (1895). *The Golf Girl* (1899). *Alabama Sketches* (1902). *Maybloom and Myrtle* (1910). *The Autumn Trail* (1925).

—AMY E. WELDON

WALKER PERCY (1916–1990). Walker Percy diagnoses in his novels and essays the existential malaise afflicting anxious, affluent Americans as they desperately pursue their happiness in their smart suburban homes. In childhood, he saw the possible consequences of this malaise in his parents' privileged but troubled lives. Percy was born on May 28, 1916, in Birmingham, Ala., to LeRoy Percy, a prominent attorney, and Martha Susan Phinizy Percy, a daughter of the distinguished Phinizy family of Athens, Ga. In 1929, when Walker was thirteen, his father shot himself to death in the attic of the Percys' fashionable home fronting the country club golf course. Percy's mother died in an automobile accident in 1932, an accident Percy always believed was a suicide.

After their father's death, Walker Percy and his two brothers were adopted by their bachelor cousin, William Alexander Percy, and in 1930 moved with their mother to Greenville, Miss., to live in "Uncle Will's" spacious home. "Uncle Will" was a genteel, Sewanee- and Harvard-educated planter, attorney, and poet who provided a cultured, refined environment for his adopted sons. In this new home, the precocious Walker enjoyed the sizable library, the classical music collection, and the frequent visits by literary celebrities.

But the teenage Walker was more interested in science than literature and music, having become convinced through his limited reading that whatever truth was available was available through the study of science. After his high school education in Greenville, he enrolled in 1933 at the University of North Carolina, where he majored in chemistry. At Chapel Hill he was elected to Phi Beta Kappa and graduated in 1937. He continued his education at Columbia University's medical school (M.D., 1941), where he specialized in pathology.

Percy contracted tuberculosis in 1942—probably from the cadavers he dissected at Columbia. His hospitalization for the disease at Trudeau Sanatorium in upstate New York proved to be a life-changing experience. Awakened for the first time to the blunt fact of his mortality, Percy realized that he knew very little about the life he could in a few months lose. Alone in his bed at Trudeau, he wondered, like the protagonists of the novels he would later write, who he was, where he was, and what he should do in a life that had so far passed like a dream while he was studying it in the laboratories at Chapel Hill and Columbia. Science had told him a great deal about the biological and chemical workings of existence, but nothing about the actualities of his private ontological experience.

In response to this disturbing realization of his ignorance, Percy began to read Aquinas, Kierkegaard, Marcel, Heidegger, Sartre, and Camus, writers who examine the particular existential experience of the unique self. For them, "life" is not merely the biological or social functions of the organism, but the world of meaning constructed by the self as it negotiates with other selves in comprehending its world through language. Biological need-satisfaction, acquisition of material comfort, occupational achievement, and conventional role-playing are necessary human activities, but they do not, these writers insist, constitute full and authentic being.

After his self-education at Trudeau, Percy pledged himself to a search for a way to know the world more fully and a way to live free from the ennui and despair Kierkegaard and Sartre warned him about. Convinced that this search would require radical changes in his personal and professional life, Percy returned to the South in 1946, married Mary Bernice ("Bunt") Townsend, converted to Catholicism in 1947, and settled in Covington, La., in 1950. He also gave up his medical career. He knew he needed a profession that would allow him to continue the philosophical and religious search initiated by his discoveries at Trudeau and therefore decided to become a writer and philosopher.

For the next forty years Percy lived quietly in Covington with Bunt and his daughters, Mary Pratt and Ann, and wrote essays and novels in which he set forth his Catholic Christian, existentialist understanding of the self and the world. The essays, many of them first published in scholarly journals, present Percy's ideas on culture, language, philosophy, theology, and literature. In his novels these ideas are reified in the stories of existential questers who search the ruins of modern American society for a life they have not yet been able to discover.

When Walker Percy died on May 10, 1990, he was already recognized as one of the most important American novelists and thinkers of the twentieth century. The two full-length biographies and the hundreds of critical studies of his work published since his death are evidence that his extraordinary artistic and intellectual achievements continue to be acknowledged.

WORKS: *The Moviegoer* (1961). *The Last Gentleman* (1966). *Love in the Ruins: The Adventures of a Bad Catholic at a Time Near the End of the World* (1971). *Why Don't You Linguists Have an Explanatory Theory of Language?* (1972). *The Message in the Bottle: How Queer Man Is, How Queer Language Is, and What One Has to Do with the Other* (1975). *Lancelot* (1977). *The Second Coming* (1980). *Lost in the Cosmos: The Last Self-Help Book* (1983). *Conversations with Walker Percy*, ed. Lewis A. Lawler and Victor A. Kramer (1985). *The Thanatos Syndrome* (1987). *Signposts in a Strange Land*, ed. Patrick H. Samway (1991). *More Conversations with Walker Percy*, ed. Lawler and Cramer (1993). *A Thief of Peirce: The Letters of Kenneth Laine Ketner and Walker Percy*, ed. Samway (1995). *The Correspondence of Walker Percy and Shelby Foote*, ed. Jay Tolson (1998).

—ALLEN PRIDGEN

WILLIAM ALEXANDER PERCY (1885–1942). Born on May 14, 1885, in Greenville, Miss., William Alexander Percy became an accomplished poet, a decorated war hero, a successful attorney, a wealthy owner of Delta plantations, and a respected civic leader. He is remembered now primarily for his popular *Lanterns on the Levee: Recollections of a Planter's Son*, a poignant memoir in which he eulogizes the aristocratic, Old South ethical and social codes that were his legacy from his distinguished family and the region's plantation culture.

Percy was educated at the University of the South at Sewanee and at Harvard Law School. After he returned from World War I, he settled into his family's home in Greenville, established his law practice, and assumed the family and civic duties expected of a gentleman of his social position and heritage. In the spirit of noblesse oblige, he was always ready to assist those in need. Percy, for example, directed the Greenville Relief Committee during the catastrophic flood of 1927. In an effort to improve racial relations and promote religious tolerance in the region, he was a fearless political advocate for the African Americans, Jews, and Catholics who were routinely threatened by Mississippi's Ku Klux Klan. In service to his own family, he adopted his three young cousins after their father's suicide in 1929 and insisted that the boys and their mother move into his spacious Greenville home. One of these boys was thirteen-year-old Walker Percy, who would later become one of America's most important men of letters.

William Alexander Percy began writing poetry while he was a student at Sewanee, and by the 1920s he had become a notable southern poet. His literary reputation at the time is suggested by the fact that Yale University Press in 1925 appointed him editor for their Series of Younger Poets. But his reputation soon declined, his melancholy, late-Victorian verse woefully old-fashioned in an emerging new literary world in which the Modernist aesthetics determined standards of poetic excellence.

WORKS: *Sappho in Levkas* (1915). *In April Once* (1920). *Enzio's Kingdom* (1924). *Selected Poems* (1930). *Lanterns on the Levee: Recollections of a Planter's Son* (1941; 1974, with an introduction by Walker Percy). *Collected Poems* (1943).

—ALLEN PRIDGEN

GUSTAVO PÉREZ FIRMAT (1949–). Born in Havana, Cuba, and raised in Miami, Fla., Gustavo Pérez Firmat, a scholar, poet, novelist, and critic, writes about the intersections between Cuban and American culture. After earning a B.A. at the University of Miami, he earned a Ph.D. in comparative literature at the University of Michigan, and then taught for twenty years at Duke University. He is now David Feinson Professor in the Humanities at Columbia University, and makes his home in Chapel Hill, N.C., with his wife Mary Anne. He has two children by a previous marriage. His numerous awards include a Guggenheim Fellowship, an NEH Fellowship, and a National Humanities Center Fellowship; in 2004 he was elected to the American Academy of Arts and Sciences.

Pérez Firmat's scholarly work and his creative writing both address the theme of dislocation. As a Cuban living in America, a Miamian living in Chapel Hill, and a Carolinian teaching in New York, he understands keenly the relationship between place and identity. In *Life on the Hyphen: The Cuban-American Way* he examines the peculiar role of Cubans in American culture, from the unlikely rise of Desi Arnaz as an early sitcom star to the Latin music boom of the early 1990s. He finds that Cubans, many of whom were exiled from their homeland after the revolution, have found ingenious ways to adapt themselves to the dominant culture of the United States and to adapt the dominant culture of the United States to them.

While Pérez Firmat identifies himself as an ethnic Cuban, he claims Miami as his hometown. In the poetry collection *Carolina Cuban* he explores that triangulation with North Carolina. In the poem "Before I Was a Writer" he describes himself leafing through the novels of Reynolds Price and Louis Rubin and feeling an urge to write his own version of the South, but feeling himself too connected to Miami to identify with the South. Later, he would write his own southern novel, *Anything but Love*.

WORKS: *Idle Fictions: The Hispanic Vanguard Novel, 1926–1934* (1982). *Literature and Liminality: Festive Readings in the Hispanic Tradition* (1986). *Carolina Cuban* (1987). *The Cuban Condition: Translation and Identity in Modern Cuban Literature* (1989). *Equivacaciones* (1989). Ed., *Do the Americas Have a Common Literature?* (1990). *Life on the Hyphen: The Cuban-American Way* (1994). *Bilingual Blues* (1995). *Next Year in Cuba* (1995). *My Own Private Cuba: Essays on Cuban Literature and Culture* (1999). *Anything but Love* (2000). *Cincuenta lecciones de exilio y desexilio* (2000). *Tongue Ties: Logo-Eroticism in Anglo-Hispanic Culture* (2003).

—DAVID A. DAVIS

JULIA PETERKIN (1880–1961). Born Julia Mood on October 31, 1880, in Laurens County, S.C., Julia Peterkin was first exposed to Gullah (the dialect of descendants of rice plantation slaves) by family servants who cared for her. As a young schoolteacher in Fort Motte, S.C., Julia married into a family that owned Lang Syne, a huge cotton plantation where hundreds of Gullah speakers worked. She became a writer by chance. While studying piano in an effort to combat depression, she told her teacher stories about the people of Lang Syne. The teacher encouraged her to write. Her earliest works appeared in the Richmond-based *Reviewer*, and in 1924 Knopf published these as *Green*

Thursday. In the 1920s she published in outlets as varied as *Poetry, American Mercury, Good Housekeeping,* and *Country Gentleman.*

At a time when few outside the South had heard of Gullah, Peterkin's fiction seemed to many reviewers to break new ground. Her characters had distinctive speech patterns and local customs, and they exhibited a wide range of behavior, sometimes noble and sometimes sordid. In 1929 she won the Pulitzer Prize for *Scarlet Sister Mary.* Other novels included *Black April* and *Bright Skin,* the latter involving a Harlem locale as well as her usual rural South Carolina setting. Peterkin also wrote the text for *Roll, Jordan, Roll,* a photo essay about southern African Americans by Doris Ullmann. In 1934 *A Plantation Christmas* chronicled the holiday traditions at Lang Syne and lamented "that strange thing called progress which so often means change without betterment" and that would cause many African Americans to leave the plantation.

Peterkin was distressed by postwar industrialization and, later, desegregation of the rural South, and she wrote little after the mid-1930s. She died in 1961.

WORKS: *Green Thursday* (1924). *Black April* (1927). *Scarlet Sister Mary* (1928). *Bright Skin* (1932). *Roll, Jordan, Roll* (1933). *A Plantation Christmas* (1934). *The Collected Stories of Julia Peterkin,* ed. Frank Durham (1970).

—JULIA EICHELBERGER

ROBERT DEANE PHARR (1916–1992). Robert Pharr was born on July 5, 1916, in Richmond, Va., the son of the Reverend John Benjamin and Lucie Dean Pharr. He was educated in St. Paul's College, Lawrenceville, Va. (1933); Lincoln University, Pa. (1934); and Virginia Union, where he received a B.A. in 1939. He also engaged in graduate study at Fisk University.

Success as a writer came late to Pharr. For many years he was employed as a waiter in New York's resort hotels and private clubs while his literary ambitions remained in limbo. *The Book of Numbers* was published in 1969, receiving general critical acclaim. It became a motion picture starring Raymond St. Jacques. It was followed by *S.R.O.* in 1971, a more complex and ambitious work considered less successful than *The Book of Numbers.*

The Book of Numbers is a penetrating analysis of black America, emphasizing the nuances and gamesmanship of hustlers in the street world. Pharr's protagonists, two waiters do become wealthy after organizing a numbers game, strive for independence but wind up being almost completely dependent. *S.R.O.* expands the locale and impetus of *The Book of Numbers,* developing the nuances of inner-city living. *S.R.O.* stands for single-room occupancy, a hotel of Kafkaesque derivatives. Both novels demonstrate Pharr's eye for detail and nuance.

Pharr then published *The Welfare Bitch* and *The Soul Murder Case: A Confession of the Victim* to little fanfare and limited sales. His final published novel is *Giveadamn Brown,* a study of a young southerner who moves to Harlem and becomes the head of a drug empire.

Pharr died in a Syracuse hospital on April 1, 1992, during surgery for an aneurysm. He left a son, a daughter, and a grandson.

WORKS: *The Book of Numbers* (1969). *S.R.O.* (1971). *The Welfare Bitch* (1975). *The Soul Murder Case: A Confession of the Victim* (1975). *Giveadamn Brown* (1978).

—BRIAN J. BENSON

JAYNE ANNE PHILLIPS (1952–). Novelist and short-story writer Jayne Anne Phillips describes herself as a "family chronicler from a small town in West Virginia." Born to Russell Phillips and Martha age experience. *The Golden Lie,* appearing in 1951, explores father-son and black-white conflicts. "The Shadow of an Arm" was included in the *O. Henry Prize Stories of 1951.* The following year, *Search for a Hero* explored the romantic theme of a youth's search for self-knowledge. Phillips received a Guggenheim Fellowship in 1953, and the following year *Kangaroo Hollow,* a chronicle of family life and class conflict from World War I, was published in England. In 1955 *The Loved and the Unloved,* an experiment with fiction as autobiography, had some critical success.

Since the 1950s, Phillips has worked in the film industry as well as state government and the insurance business. Among the films to which he contributed are *The Autobiography of Miss Jane Pittman, Thieves Like Us,* and *Nashville.* After nearly forty years, Phillips returned to fiction in 2002 with the novel *Red Midnight,* about an older and a younger convict who unite emotionally to survive. The author lives in Corinth, Miss.

WORKS: *The Bitterweed Path* (1950). *The Golden Lie* (1951). *Search for a Hero* (1952). *Kangaroo Hollow* (1954). *The Loved and the Unloved* (1955). *Red Midnight* (2002).

—THOMAS BONNER, JR.

OVID WILLIAMS PIERCE (1910–1989). A native of Weldon, N.C., where he was born on October 1, 1910, Ovid Williams Pierce won a prize for his essay "Epic Poetry" at the 1927 Halifax County Fair and went on to author five novels set in eastern Carolina: *The Plantation, On a Lonesome Porch, The Devil's Half, The Wedding Guest,* and *Judge Buell's Legacy,* as well as the collection *Old Man's Gold and Other Stories.*

Pierce was educated at Duke University (B.A., English, 1932) and Harvard (M.A., English, 1936) and, after serving in army counterintelligence during World War II, he taught at Southern Methodist University in Texas (1946–49) and Tulane University in Louisiana (1949–53). In 1953 *The Plantation* won Pierce his first Sir Walter Raleigh Award for Fiction from the North Carolina Literary and Historical Association, and in 1956, after living in Europe, he became writer-in-residence at East Carolina College (now University).

Of his twenty years at East Carolina, W. Keats Sparrow has written: "Pierce became noted for his cavalier attitude towards teaching. . . . His students often were disappointed that an author of such renown offered them so little of substance. Many students were nevertheless inspired by Pierce's joviality, easy manner, courtliness, and image as the quintessential country gentleman."

Pierce won a second Sir Walter Raleigh Award for *On a Lonesome Porch;* won the North Carolina Literature Award in 1969; received the Oliver Max Gardner Award in 1973, which cited him for producing "with artistry and integrity, an authoritative portrait of the South"; and won the Brown-Hudson Award from the North Carolina Folklore Society in 1982. Critic Jerry Leath Mills has called Pierce's *The Plantation* "a magnificent introduction to just about everything anybody needs to understand in order to read southern literature with real comprehension."

Suffering from declining health for several years, Pierce died on December 9, 1989, from cardiac arrest. He was buried in Weldon.

WORKS: *The Plantation* (1953). *On a Lonesome Porch* (1960). *The Devil's Half* (1968). *The Wedding Guest* (1974). *Old Man's Gold and Other Stories* (1976).

—BLAND SIMPSON

ALBERT PIKE (1809–1891). Born on December 29, 1809, in Boston, Mass., Albert Pike lived his formative years in that state. There he taught school from 1824 to 1831, reading widely all the while and writing poetry. His family was too poor to afford Harvard, but in 1859 the institution awarded Pike an honorary M.A. in recognition of his extraordinary ability to teach himself.

In 1831 Pike left Massachusetts, joining a party of hunters and traders bound for Santa Fe, N.M. In New Mexico he found material for poetry and sketches that resulted in *Prose Sketches and Poems.* In 1833 he joined another expedition, ending this time in Arkansas, where he became an important political figure. Settling in Little Rock, he earned a place on the *Arkansas Advocate* and became assistant clerk in the territorial legislature. He married Mary Ann Hilton on November 18, 1834. Her dowry enabled Pike to purchase an interest in the *Advocate,* and in 1835 he became sole owner and editor. To support a growing family, he sold the newspaper in 1837 to practice law, having been licensed in 1834 after another impressive instance of self-education.

Successful as a lawyer, he set law aside to fight for the United States in the war against Mexico. After the war he continued to be active in Whig politics, later championing the Know-Nothing Party. He moved his law practice to New Orleans in 1853, returning to Little Rock in 1857. When the Civil War began, he threw his support to the Confederacy, transforming Daniel Emmett's "Dixie" into a war hymn of several stanzas. Appointed to negotiate with the Indian tribes of the Southwest, Pike overstepped his authority, earning Confederate president Jefferson Davis's ire. During the war, Pike lost his reputation and his property.

The struggling romantic moved to Memphis, Tenn., in 1867 to practice law, and the next year moved to Washington, D.C., devoting his energies to Freemasonry, winning an international reputation. His massive *Morals and Dogma of the Ancient and Accepted Scottish Rite of Freemasonry* blended Masonic ritual with Pike's mystical philosophy. He died in Washington on April 2, 1891.

Although Edgar Allan Poe found him a talented poet and Pike's poems appeared widely in magazines, Pike's poetry is not now much valued. His accounts of life and people in the Southwest provide a compelling record of life in the territory.

WORKS: *Prose Sketches and Poems, Written in the Western Country* (1834). *Lays of the Humbuggers, &c. by Sam. Barnacle, Poet Laureate* (1836). *Nugae* (1854). "Letter to the Northern States" (1860). "Letter to the President of the Confederate States" (1862). *The Duties of Freemasonry* (1871). *Morals and Dogma of the Ancient and Accepted Scottish Rite of Freemasonry* (1871). "Hymns to the Gods" and Other Poems (1872). *The Silver Wedding: A Masque* (1878). *What Does Freemasonry Teach* (1892). *Masonic Justice* (1893). *Lyrics and Love Poems,* ed. Mrs. L. P. Roome (1899). *Gen. Albert Pike's Poems* (1900). *Albert Pike on Prayer* (1901). *Albert Pike on Blue Lodge Masonry* (1904). *Irano-Aryan Faith and Doctrine as Contained in the Zend-Avesta* (1924). Lengthy extract from MS autobiography in *New Age Magazine* (Aug. 1929–Sept. 1930). *Indo-Aryan Deities and Worship as Contained in the Rig-Vedau* (1930). *Lectures of the Arya* (1930).

—JOSEPH M. FLORA

ELIZA LUCAS PINCKNEY (1722–1793). Born on December 28, 1723, in the West Indies to British parents, Elizabeth Lucas was educated in England, and in 1738 moved with her family to Charleston, S.C., where her father hoped the climate would improve his wife's health. At seventeen, Eliza took charge of her father's several plantations while he resumed military duties in Antigua, and she began copying her personal and business letters into a letterbook. By 1740 she had begun experimenting with the cultivation of indigo, a crop that became highly profitable to the region. Pinckney harbored no antislavery sentiments, writing in 1742 of her dismay when a white evangelist predicted to a group of slaves that they would revolt and gain freedom.

In 1744 she married Charles Pinckney, and in 1753 moved to England. After Charles's death in 1758, Eliza managed the family plantations in Charleston, leaving her sons in England to be educated and teaching her daughter at home. Other pupils included two slave girls, whom she hoped would teach other slaves to read. Pinckney delighted in gardening and was a conscientious housekeeper.

The recipe book she kept includes such entries as "To prevent the Jaw Fallen in Children," "Plumb Marmalade," and "Little Pudings." But the letters of this highly educated woman also reflect an occasional deviance from social conventions of the Lowcountry planter class. At eighteen, she politely refuses a suitor offered by her father, saying she plans to remain single. Another letter says some women warn that her habit of rising at five will make her look old, and others say she reads too much and should burn her books. Pinckney records her study of French, music, and law, her reading of Locke and Richardson, and her own verses. Her correspondence reveals a woman of uncommon gifts and uncommon opportunities to develop them in eighteenth-century South Carolina. She died of cancer on May 23, 1793.

WORKS: *Journal and Letters of Eliza Lucas*, ed. Harriott Pinckney Holbrook (1850). *Recipe Book of Eliza Lucas Pinckney, 1756* (1936). *The Letterbook of Eliza Lucas Pinckney, 1739–1762*, ed. Elise Pinckney (1972).

—JULIA EICHELBERGER

JOSEPHINE PINCKNEY (1895–1957). Born on January 25, 1895, in Charleston, S.C., to Thomas and Camilla Scott Pinckney, Josephine Lyons Scott Pinckney was an only child. It has been said that her career as a writer was as much a matter of fate as of choice, descended as she was from Charles Pinckney and Charles Cotesworthy Pinckney, both signers of the Constitution (one a Federalist, one a Republican), and from Eliza Lucas Pinckney, rice planter and author.

As a student at Ashley Hall she started the student literary magazine *Cerberus*. After studying English at the College of Charleston, Columbia University, and Radcliffe, she returned to Charleston, where she helped found the Poetry Society of South Carolina in 1920. This group was at the forefront of the Southern Literary Renascence and was singled out by Donald Davidson as the one on which similar organizations modeled themselves.

She had written poetry for *Cerebus*, was a regular contributor to the Poetry Society yearbook, and in 1921 began seeing her work published in *Poetry*. She published in numerous literary reviews until 1935. Her only collection of poems is *Sea-Drinking Cities*. The subject of her poetry was the Carolina low country, its folklore, songs, superstitions.

In the 1930s she turned to fiction, publishing *Hilton Head* in 1941. A thoroughly researched treatment of the life of Henry Woodward, first English settler of Carolina, the work is more than a historical novel. As she would do in all her five books, Pinckney explores with wit and irony the interaction of character and fate in an individual's maturation. Her second novel was *Three O'Clock Dinner*, a Literary Guild Selection and still probably her best known.

During this time of energetic composition, Pinckney maintained a family plantation on the Santee River. She served as a trustee of the Charleston Museum, as a member of both the Carolina Art Association and the Historic Charleston Foundation, and as a founder of the Society for the Preservation of Spirituals. She lived until her death at 36 Chalmers Street in a house she restored in 1940. She had traveled to New York to oversee final editorial changes to her fifth novel when she fell ill, entered the hospital, and died on October 4, 1957. She is buried in Charleston's Magnolia Cemetery.

WORKS: *Sea-Drinking Cities* (1927). *Hilton Head* (1941). *Three O'Clock Dinner* (1945). *Great Mischief* (1948). *My Son and Foe* (1952). *Splendid in Ashes* (1958).

—REBECCA ROXBURGH BUTLER

EDWARD COOTE PINKNEY (1802–1828). Naval officer, lawyer, poet, and editor, Edward Coote Pinkney is rarely mentioned today except as an influence upon Edgar Allan Poe. He was born on October 1, 1802, in London, where his father, William Pinkney, served first as a U.S. commissioner and then as a minister to the Court of St. James. Returning to America in 1811, young Pinkney attended St. Mary's College in Baltimore, but at the age of thirteen he was appointed as a midshipman in the U.S. Navy.

Pinkney's career as a poet appears to have begun in 1822, during a tour of shore duty in Baltimore, but his first publication came in January 1823, when his poem "Serenade" was set to music and published. He wrote other poems in 1823, and one of them, *Rodolph*, was published as a pamphlet. This same year Pinkney challenged the writer John Neal to a duel over an unflattering description of Pinkney's father that had appeared in Neal's novel *Randolph*. Neal refused the challenge, and Pinkney posted him as a coward.

In 1824 Pinkney resigned from the navy and became a law partner of Robert Wilson, Jr., in Baltimore. He continued to write poems, however, and published a collection in 1825. When law did not yield adequate financial returns, Pinkney attempted without success to secure a commission in the Mexican navy. After his return from Mexico, he was asked in 1827 by a political group to edit the *Marylander*, a paper founded to support John Quincy Adams against the Jacksonians. In this paper he published four of his poems as well as editorials. His editorial activities involved him in a near duel with the editor of the *Philadelphia Mercury*, a Jacksonian newspaper. Pinkney died on April 11, 1828, in Baltimore.

Pinkney's poems are usually described as "Cavalier" lyrics, influenced in expression and subject matter by Thomas Moore and Lord Byron. Although he wrote longer poems in the manner of Byron, he was at his best in lyrics, usually love songs or graceful compliments to women.

WORKS: *Look Out upon the Stars, My Love* ("Serenade," poem set to music, 1823). *Rodolph: A Fragment* (1823). *Poems* (1825).

—ROBERT D. JACOBS

EDGAR ALLAN POE (1809–1849). Born in Boston on January 19, 1809, Edgar Allan Poe became a southerner by an act of fate. Already abandoned by his father, actor David Poe, Edgar was left an orphan in 1811 when his mother, actress Eliza Poe, died in Richmond, Va. There he was taken in by a well-to-do tobacco merchant, John Allan, and his wife, Frances. Although the Allans never formally adopted him, Poe spent his childhood and adolescence in their home, living with them in Richmond from 1811 to 1815, joining them for stints in Scotland and England between 1815 and 1820, and returning with them to Richmond in 1820.

In Richmond, he attended school and fell in love—first with a schoolmate's mother, Jane Stanard, who would inspire his poem "To Helen," and then with a neighbor girl named Elmira Royster. Engaged to Royster, Poe left for the University of Virginia in 1826, but both his engagement and his education faltered. Perhaps because he had not received adequate funds from Allan, Poe ran up gambling debts in Charlottesville and returned home in December.

After quarreling with Allan, Poe moved to Boston in 1827 and, under the name of Edgar A. Perry, enlisted in the U.S. Army. His first book, *Tamerlane and Other Poems*, appeared anonymously a few months later, attracting little attention. Before the year was out, he returned to the South when his battery was transferred to Fort Moultrie on Sullivan's Island, a South Carolina locale he would later use in his story "The Gold-Bug." Obtaining an honorable discharge in 1829, Poe moved to Baltimore and came out with *Al Aaraaf, Tamerlane, and Minor Poems*. Still largely unknown as a poet, he entered turbed children at Kentucky Central State Hospital. The American Theatre Critics Association voted *Getting Out* best new play produced by a regional theater; it also won the John Gassner Medallion and *Newsday*'s Oppenheimer Award.

Norman's best-known play is her Pulitzer Prize–winning *'Night, Mother* (1982), which also earned the Susan Smith Blackburn Prize, Hull-Warriner, and Drama Desk awards and four Tony nominations. The play incorporates several themes central to Norman's work: mother/daughter relationships, the need to claim control of one's life, the struggle to justify survival, and individual isolation. Another well-known work is Norman's adaptation of Frances Hodgson Burnett's *The Secret Garden* (1991), a Broadway musical that won a Tony Award and Drama Desk Award.

In addition to other plays—*Third and Oak*, comprising two plays (1978), *Circus Valentine* (1979), *The Holdup* (1980), *Traveller in the Dark* (1984), *Sarah and Abraham* (1988), *Loving Daniel Boone* (1992), and *Trudy Blue* (1994)—Norman has also written a novel, *The Fortune Teller*, several television scripts, and *Cooler Climate*, a screenplay (2000). Her numerous honors include grants from the National Endowment for the Arts, Rockefeller Foundation, and American Academy and Institute of Arts and Letters, and she serves on the council of the Dramatists Guild. Since 1994, Norman has been a professor of drama at the Juilliard School and co-director of its Playwrights Program.

WORKS: *Getting Out: Play in Two Acts* (1979). *Third and Oak—The Laundromat: A Play in One Act* (1980). *'Night, Mother: A Play* (1983). *Third and Oak—The Pool Hall: A Play in One Act* (1985). *The Fortune Teller* (1987). *Holdup* (1987). *Four Plays* (1988). *Secret Garden*, with Lucy Simon (1991). *Collected Plays* (1998).

—KAREN C. BLANSFIELD

HELEN NORRIS (1916–). Helen Norris, Alabama poet laureate (1999–2003) and accomplished fiction writer, was born on June 22, 1916, in Miami, Fla., to Elmer W. and Louise W. Brown Norris. In her second year, the family returned to a five-hundred-acre cotton farm outside Montgomery, Ala., where she had a privileged and happy childhood.

Like her parents, she was early drawn to literature, and she had the "itch" to write. After graduation from Lanier High School, she entered the University of Alabama, where she studied with Hudson Strode, legendary for encouraging students interested in writing. Norris earned her B.A. in 1938, winning election into Phi Beta Kappa, and remained at Alabama to write her first novel, which was published in 1940, the same year that she received her M.A. and married Thomas Reuben Bell. Her novel, *Something More Than Earth*, won second prize in the *Atlantic Monthly* contest.

Following their graduation, the couple moved to Birmingham, where her husband practiced law. While Reuben Bell served in the army air corps in 1942–45, the couple lived in Louisiana, Massachusetts, and Washington, D.C. They had two children, a son and a daughter. After the children were enrolled in school, Norris's writing again accelerated, though her Christian themes did not find a wide audience. (Norris is a devout Episcopalian.) Sadly, the daughter died in an accident.

Norris's marriage had been disintegrating, and in 1965 she resumed graduate study at Duke University. Divorced, she returned to Montgomery in 1966 and began teaching English at Huntingdon College. Thirteen years later, she resigned from Huntingdon to give priority to writing, and her career took flight. Her stories began appearing in *Sewanee Review* and other prestigious journals. She collected literary honors: four O. Henry Awards, four Christian Book Association Awards, two Andrew Lytle Awards, among others. In 1985 she was in residence at Yaddo and followed that with an appointment to the McDowell writers' colony. Adaptation of "The Christmas Wife" for Home Box Office in 1988 brought Norris a wider American audience than she had ever known.

the U.S. Military Academy at West Point in 1830, but became dissatisfied and got himself expelled the following year. After a brief stay in New York City, where he published *Poems*, he moved in with his aunt Maria Clemm and her daughter, Virginia, in Baltimore.

Now that he was somewhat settled back in the South, Poe's career began to take shape. In Baltimore, he wrote six stories and submitted them to a contest in 1833. He won first place for "MS. Found in a Bottle" and, more important, drew the notice of one of the contest's judges, John Pendleton Kennedy. Encouraged by his new mentor, in 1835 Poe wrote stories and reviews for Richmond's *Southern Literary Messenger*. The following year, Poe moved to Richmond and went to work for the *Messenger*. Over the next two years, he supplied it with reviews and stories, and the publication's circulation climbed. In 1836 he married his cousin Virginia, then thirteen.

Despite their success, Poe broke with publisher Thomas White in 1837 and moved to New York, then to Philadelphia, where he worked for *Burton's Gentleman's Magazine* from 1839 to 1840 and *Graham's Magazine* from 1841 to 1842. Even as he performed his various editorial duties, which included writing reviews and reading proofs, Poe churned out fiction, producing some of his most memorable stories. During this time, Lea & Blanchard came out with *Tales of the Grotesque and Arabesque*, which contained "William Wilson," "The Fall of the House of Usher," and twenty-three other stories, many of which had already appeared in *Burton's*, *Godey's Lady's Book*, and other publications. Over his remaining years in Philadelphia, he published "The Murders in the Rue Morgue," "The Masque of the Red Death," "The Pit and the Pendulum," and "The Tell-Tale Heart" in his own and other publications.

Poe's fiction was by now attracting favorable attention from reviewers and readers alike. His 1843 story "The Gold-Bug" was especially successful, winning a $100 prize and wide popular acclaim. He also began a successful lecturing career. On a personal level, however, the rising author was struggling and suffering. In 1842 his wife showed signs of tuberculosis. Meanwhile, poverty dogged the family, even while Poe's testy personality and drinking problems—perhaps the result of an oversensitivity to alcohol—caused him to alienate potential supporters.

In 1844 Poe moved to New York City and joined the staff of the *Evening Mirror*. In 1845 the *Mirror* published "The Raven," which quickly became his most famous work. Later the same year, after he had moved to the *Broadway Journal*, Wiley and Putnam published *Tales*, which included "The Purloined Letter," "The Man of the Crowd," and ten other stories. On the heels of this successful collection, the same publisher came out with *The Raven and Other Poems*.

Meanwhile, Poe's personal problems continued, as he drank excessively, flopped at a public reading, and published a bizarre attack on Henry Wadsworth Longfellow, accusing the poet of plagiarism. In Fordham, N.Y., where Poe moved the family in 1846, he suffered from illness, depression, and poverty as he watched Virginia's condition worsen. She died in 1847.

Poe's career was in marked decline. Over the next two years, he produced only a handful of notable works, including *Eureka* and "Annabel Lee," while apparently trying to fill the void left by Virginia's death. He poured out his heart in letters to a married woman named Annie Richmond, confessing to a suicide attempt in 1848, and proposed to fellow poet Sarah Helen Whitman. In 1849, his engagement to Whitman over, he returned to Richmond, where he reunited with Elmira Royster (now Elmira Shelton). More than two decades after their first engagement failed, the two planned marriage again. On his way back north, perhaps to pick up Maria Clemm, Poe mysteriously turned up partly conscious near a polling booth in Baltimore on October 3. Although the cause of his death on October 7 was listed as "congestion of the brain," the full circumstances remain a mystery.

The downward slope of Poe's life and career continued even after his death, thanks largely to his literary executor, Rufus Griswold, who marked his erstwhile friend's passing with an obituary and

"Memoir" portraying him as an unscrupulous madman. Later writers and scholars have resurrected Poe's reputation, and today he stands as one of the South's preeminent writers.

WORKS: *Tamerlane and Other Poems* (1827). *Al Aaraaf, Tamerlane, and Minor Poems* (1829). *Poems* (1831). *The Narrative of Arthur Gordon Pym* (1838). *The Conchologist's First Book* (1839). *Tales of the Grotesque and Arabesque* (1840). *The Prose Romances of Edgar A. Poe* (1843). *Tales* (1845). *The Raven and Other Poems* (1845). *Eureka: A Prose Poem* (1848).

—MARK CANADA

KATHERINE ANNE PORTER (1890–1980). Katherine Anne Porter was born Callie Russell Porter on May 15, 1890, at Indian Creek, Tex., to a poor farming family with Kentucky roots. After her mother died in 1892, Porter's family moved to Kyle, Tex., to live with her paternal grandmother, Catherine Anne Porter, whose strength of character would influence Porter for decades to come. Following Catherine Anne's death in 1901, the family moved to San Antonio. Borrowed money enabled Porter briefly to attend a private girls' school there and dream of becoming an actress. But soon she found herself moving to Victoria, Tex., and—together with her sister—supporting the family by teaching the dramatic arts. Her own formal education was at an end.

Porter met John Henry Koontz in Victoria and was married to him a month after her sixteenth birthday. Born a Methodist, she converted to her husband's Roman Catholic faith and professed it sporadically throughout her life despite her general religious skepticism. Her dissatisfaction with domestic life, strongly expressed when she traveled to Chicago to pursue acting work in 1914, culminated in her divorce from Koontz a year later, at which time she legally took the name Katherine Anne Porter. Nineteen fifteen was a turning point in other respects as well. After working several months in musical productions on Louisiana's Lyceum circuit—and marrying a Fort Worth man only to have the marriage quickly annulled—an exhausted Porter contracted tuberculosis. She spent the next two years recovering in Texas hospitals. During this time she befriended a journalist who led her to work as a society writer and drama critic for the *Rocky Mountain News;* but in Denver she also fell prey to an influenza epidemic, a nearly fatal experience that was later reflected in her novella "Pale Horse, Pale Rider" (1939).

Porter spent the 1920s living in the urban Northeast and in Mexico, establishing herself as a serious writer and building the fund of experience she would draw upon in her fiction. Moving to Greenwich Village in 1919 and supporting herself by ghostwriting and other marginally profitable literary ventures, she met a number of exiled Mexican artists and intellectuals who encouraged her to visit their native country in the midst of its ongoing political upheaval. Her first extended visit, in 1920, provided her with the material for "María Concepción" (1922), which she published in *Century* magazine and consistently claimed as her first story. With this piece and later stories of Mexico such as "The Martyr," "Virgin Violeta," and especially "Flowering Judas"—all collected in *Flowering Judas and Other Stories*—Porter first established her literary reputation.

In the second half of the decade Porter married and divorced a third man, the English veteran Ernest Stock, and during her time in New York and Connecticut she became acquainted with Allen Tate, Caroline Gordon, and Robert Penn Warren. A leisurely 1928 visit to Bermuda allowed her to imagine the aristocratic Old South she had once longed to be a part of and thereby to conceive the stories that would eventually become "Old Mortality" and "The Old Order." After a final trip to Mexico—where she met Eugene Pressly, the lover who would become her fourth husband—Porter traveled to Europe in 1931, living in Berlin for a time. She married Pressly in 1933, and they settled in Paris. Increasingly unhappy and unproductive, Porter returned to the United States in 1936 and, lodging at an isolated

Pennsylvania inn, completed two stories that had long been in progress—"Noon Wine" and "Old Mortality"—and nearly completed "Pale Horse, Pale Rider." These novellas were published together in 1939 and secured Porter's critical reputation.

In 1938 she divorced Pressly and married Albert Erskine, the young business manager of the *Sewanee Review*, in New Orleans. When that marriage faltered two years later, she moved to Yaddo and then Saratoga Springs in upstate New York, attempting to write a long novel about her 1931 transatlantic voyage. Instead she completed *The Leaning Tower and Other Stories*. In need of money, she worked as a Hollywood scriptwriter in 1945 before embarking on lecture tours and temporary teaching assignments at Stanford, Michigan, and Washington and Lee, as well as in Europe. After she finally completed *Ship of Fools*—her only full-length novel—her major writings were at an end. In 1966 her collected stories won both the National Book Award and a Pulitzer Prize. She lived the last years of her life in Silver Spring, Md., where she died on September 18, 1980. She is buried at Indian Creek, Tex.

WORKS: *Flowering Judas and Other Stories* (1930). *Katherine Anne Porter's French Song Book* (1933). *Hacienda* (1934). *Noon Wine* (1937). *Pale Horse, Pale Rider: Three Short Novels* (1939). *The Leaning Tower and Other Stories* (1944). *The Days Before* (1952). *Ship of Fools* (1962). *The Collected Stories of Katherine Anne Porter* (1965). *The Collected Essays and Occasional Writings of Katherine Anne Porter* (1970). *The Never-Ending Wrong* (1977). *This Strange, Old World and Other Book Reviews*, ed. Darlene Harbour Unrue (1991). *Uncollected Early Prose of Katherine Anne Porter*, ed. Ruth M. Alvarez and Thomas F. Walsh (1993). *Katherine Anne Porter's Poetry*, ed. Unrue (1996).

—FARRELL O'GORMAN

CHARLES PORTIS (1933–). Charles (McColl) Portis was born on December 28, 1933, to Samuel and Alice Waddell Portis in El Dorado, Ark. He pulled a hitch in the U.S. Marine Corps (1952–55) before attending the University of Arkansas to study journalism. His career in journalism led to work for the *Arkansas Gazette*, the *Commercial Appeal* in Memphis, and the *New York Herald Tribune*. He associated with such notable journalists as Tom Wolfe, Jimmy Breslin, and Dick Schaap but resigned his post with the *Herald Tribune* to devote his time to writing fiction.

His limited output as a novelist began with *Norwood*, a hilarious tale of an ex-Marine whose travels lead through American subculture and enable Portis to cast a watchful eye on the foibles of American life. His next work, *True Grit*, elevated him to the status of a best-selling author. His story of resourceful Mattie Ross pleased readers and moviegoers alike, and the portrayal of the novel's antihero, Rooster Cogburn, brought John Wayne his only Oscar. Ten years passed before *The Dog of the South* followed. Richly and tellingly satiric, this quirky novel traces the adventures and misadventures of a young man whose sentimental feelings for his Buick take him from Little Rock to Belize. Continuing in his comic and satiric vein, Portis next published *Masters of Atlantis*, a work examining all sorts of New Age societies. Portis's fifth novel, *Gringos*, presents other sects of New Agers amongst artifact smugglers in Mexico. It helped him to reclaim his identity as an apt student of Ring Lardner and Mark Twain as commentators on American society. His recent output has been limited to journalistic pieces.

When he decided to become a novelist, Portis returned to Arkansas, where he has continued to live, except for temporary residence in Mexico following the publication of *True Grit*.

WORKS: *Norwood* (1966). *True Grit* (1968). *The Dog of the South* (1979). *Masters of Atlantis* (1985). *Gringos* (1991).

—JOHN L. IDOL, JR.

JOHN PORY (1572–1636). Born in Thompson, Norfolk, of a well-to-do farming family, Pory was graduated from Caius College, Cambridge, the university with which relatives had been associated for many years. After teaching Greek at Caius for two years he began private study with Richard Hakluyt, geographer-historian, and assisted in the preparation of Hakluyt's *Voyages* (1600). Pory's own book, *A Geographical Historie of Africa*, appeared later that same year and became the source of most of the impressions of Africa and Africans held by Englishmen, including Shakespeare, well into the eighteenth century. His *Epitome of Ortelius*, a condensation of a larger work, was intended for the growing body of literate Englishmen who could not read Latin.

Pory served in Parliament (1605–11), afterwards traveling on the Continent and serving on the embassy staff in Constantinople (1613–16). He was a lifelong friend of John Donne; both were incorporated M.A. at Oxford at the same convocation, and Pory delivered letters to Donne in France. He was also a friend of Ben Jonson, and both men participated in a disputation in Paris in 1612, afterwards collaborating in the publication of *The Summe and Substance of a Disputation*.

In 1618 Pory became secretary in the colony of Virginia under Governor Sir George Yeardley, his cousin's husband. In this capacity Pory served as speaker of the first American legislature, organizing it along the lines of the House of Commons.

Pory is perhaps best known as a writer of newsletters, precursor of the newspaper. His letters from 1606 to 1633 touch numerable subjects but are of especial interest for their information about Virginia, the Thirty Years' War, affairs of the court of England, and personal observations of scores of his contemporaries, including literary figures, artists, royalty, and the nobility. While in Virginia, Pory explored in the vicinity of the Potomac River and down into what later became North Carolina. In returning to England, he also visited Plymouth, Mass.

WORKS: *A Geographical Historie of Africa* (1600). *An Epitome of Ortelius* (1602). "The observations of Master John Pory Secretarie of Virginia, in his travels," in John Smith, *The General Historie of Virginia* (1624). *The Summe and Substance of a Disputation*, with Ben Jonson (1630). Pory's newsletters and other minor writings are in William S. Powell, *John Pory, 1572–1636: A Man of Many Parts* (1976).

—WILLIAM S. POWELL

ALEXANDER POSEY (1873–1908). Alexander Lawrence Posey was born on August 3, 1873, in the Tulladega Hills west of Eufaula, Creek Nation, Indian Territory (later Oklahoma), the first of the twelve children of Lewis Henderson and Nancy Harjo Phillips Posey. His father was a non-Indian who had been orphaned as a child and raised in a Creek family; Posey's mother was Creek. Posey began his English education at age twelve, when his father hired a tutor. Two years later Posey enrolled in the Creek Nation Boarding School at Eufaula, transferring from there in 1890 to the Bacone Indian University in Muskogee, Creek Nation. He graduated from Bacone in 1895, won a seat in the House of Warriors, the lower house of the Creek National Council, and served one term.

In 1896 the council appointed him superintendent of the Creek Orphanage at Okmulgee. There he met and married Minnie Harris, the girls' matron. Together they had three children. Posey was appointed superintendent of public instruction in 1897; between 1899 and 1901 he was superintendent at the nation's two boarding schools, first at Eufaula and then at Wetumpka. In 1902 he joined a partnership that purchased the Eufaula *Indian Journal*, which he edited for over a year. After a brief stint as editor of the *Muskogee Evening Times*, in 1904 he began a three-year appointment with the Dawes Commission, the federal agency headquartered in Muskogee to administer allotment, the policy of breaking up the communally owned tribal land base and allotting parcels of land to individual Creeks. During the winter of 1907–8, Posey worked as a real estate agent. In the spring of 1908 he resumed editorship of the *Indian Journal*. On May 2 of that year he drowned in the Canadian River while trying to cross during a flood.

While a student at Bacone, Posey began publishing poems in the school newspaper. When he became editor of the *Indian Journal*, he had written more than two hundred poems. Romantic, derivative, most of them are about nature and love, and generally are not well regarded. Posey's literary fame began in October 1902 when the first Fus Fixico letter appeared in the *Indian Journal*. Fus Fixico (Heartless Bird in English), Posey's persona, was a rural Creek with an imperfect command of English who ostensibly wrote weekly letters to editor Posey about events in the countryside.

The letters quickly became political, and Posey used them to editorialize about the events of the day. As the subjects of the letters changed, so did their structure. Fus Fixico continued to write them, but instead of describing local doings they became accounts of conversations he had overheard or participated in with a group of regulars—Wolf Warrior, Cheola, Kono Harjo, Tookpafka Micco, Hotgun, and others—who gathered daily around the sofky pot, the Creek equivalent of the cracker barrel. Hotgun became the central character and his diatribes addressed such hot issues as Creek electoral politics, the benefits and disadvantages of allotment, the corruption of the Dawes commissioners and other federal officials, statehood, and the problems facing the Creeks as they adjusted to the new regime. By the summer of 1903 the Fus Fixico letters had won Posey national attention. Newspapers all over the country copied them and printed articles about how remarkable it was that their author was an Indian, the only one in the United States to edit a daily newspaper.

The topics of the Fus Fixico letters were less interesting to the nationwide newspaper-reading public than their style. Posey was a wit, the letters were funny, and his mastery of dialect put him firmly into the small but widely popular genre of dialect humor.

Posey's politics were controversial. His biographer calls him a "progressive" who supported allotment and believed that the Creeks should have the chance to sink or swim in the American market economy. His own plan to swim is evident in his activities during the last months of his life as a speculator in Creek allotments. Many contemporaries found his association with notorious grafters and swindlers of vulnerable Indians disquieting and hard to understand. A recent Creek scholar suggests that when he sank beneath the swollen waters of the Canadian River, his beloved Oktahutche, he was in the grip of the Tie-Snake, the legendary avenger of the Creeks.

WORKS: *Poems of Alexander Lawrence Posey, Creek Indian Bard,* ed. Minnie H. Posey (1910, 1969). *The Fus Fixico Letters,* ed. Daniel F. Littlefield and Carol A. Petty Hunter (1993).

—MICHAEL D. GREEN

PADGETT POWELL (1952–). Born in Gainesville, Fla., on April 25, 1952, and raised in Florida and South Carolina, Padgett Powell graduated from the College of Charleston in 1975 with what he calls "a poet's degree in chemistry." He briefly studied chemistry in graduate school at the University of Tennessee, withdrawing to write and travel around the Southeast. Powell worked as a roofer in Houston, Tex., before entering the M.F.A. Program at the University of Houston, where he studied with Donald Barthelme. In 1984 Powell's first novel, *Edisto,* was nominated for the National Book Award, and Powell returned to Gainesville, where he teaches at the University of Florida. He and his wife, the poet Sidney Wade, have two daughters. In the summer, Powell frequently serves on the faculty at the Sewanee Writers' Conference.

Powell drew on his South Carolina childhood, his abrupt departure from graduate school, and his experience as a day laborer to create the precocious child in *Edisto,* the displaced chemistry student in *A Woman Named Drown,* and the disaffected blue-collar workers in the short-story collections *Typical* and *Aliens of Affection.* Powell writes with wry humor about the decline of southern tradition and the victims of "the latest reconstruction in the south." Although Powell's fiction has moved from realistic narratives to a postmodern examination of perception and language, his southern roots can be found in his settings, his idiosyncratic blend of dialect and baroque rhetoric, and his sympathetic parody of the old South, particularly in the novels *Edisto Revisited* and *Mrs. Hollingsworth's Men*.

Powell's fiction and essays have appeared in the *New Yorker, Esquire, Harper's, Grand Street,* the *Paris Review,* and the *New York Times,* and have been selected for *The Best American Short Stories* and *The Best American Essays.* His honors include the Whiting Writers' Award, the Prix de Rome in Literature, the *Paris Review* John Train Humor Prize, the O. Henry Award, and the Pushcart Prize.

WORKS: *Edisto* (1984). *A Woman Named Drown* (1987). *Typical* (1991). *Edisto Revisited* (1996). *Aliens of Affection* (1998). *Mrs. Hollingsworth's Men* (2000).

—THOMAS M. CARLSON

MINNIE BRUCE PRATT (1946–). Born on September 12, 1946, in Selma, Ala., Minnie Bruce Pratt grew up in nearby Centreville. In 1964 she entered the University of Alabama in Tuscaloosa, where she received her B.A. and earned induction into Phi Beta Kappa. In 1979 she received the Ph.D. in English at the University of North Carolina at Chapel Hill.

Growing up in the South as a lesbian during the civil rights era, Pratt learned to identify with blacks as well as with homosexuals. She began writing for various feminist publications, including *Feminary: A Feminist Journal for the South, Emphasizing Lesbian Visions.* Her famous feminist essay "Identity: Skin Blood Heart" is located in *Yours in Struggle: Three Feminist Perspectives on Anti-Semitism and Racism* (1984), which she co-authored with Elly Bulkin and Barbara Smith.

Pratt has published five poetry collections that speak to her feminist and sexual agendas. She also authored the collection of autobiographical and political essays entitled *Rebellion: Essays 1980–1991* and a collection of prose stories, *S/HE.* Pratt's work has been honored repeatedly for its honest portrayal of homosexuality. In 1989 her collection *Crime against Nature,* which relates her experience as a lesbian mother of two sons, was chosen as the Lamont Poetry Selection by the Academy of American Poets, and won the 1991 American Library Association Gay and Lesbian Book Award for Literature. In 1991 she was chosen, along with two other lesbian authors, to receive the Fund for Free Expression's Lillian Hellman–Dashiell Hammett Award after the three became "targets of right wing and fundamentalist forces" during public debate about the National Endowment for the Arts' awards to artists and writers.

Rebellion: Essays 1980–1991 was chosen as a 1992 finalist in nonfiction for the Lambda Literature Awards. In 1995 *S/HE* was one of five finalists in nonfiction for the American Library Association Gay, Lesbian, and Bisexual Book Award, and one of three finalists for the Firecracker Award in nonfiction. In 1999 selected poems from *Walking Back Up Depot Street* were nominated for the Pushcart Prize, and the collection was chosen by *ForeWord: The Magazine of Independent Bookstores and Booksellers* as the Best Lesbian/Gay Book of the Year.

Pratt has also had success as a college teacher, with much of her teaching in black universities. Besides giving readings in colleges and universities, she is a member of the graduate faculty of the Union Institute and University, a nontraditional, nonresidential, Ph.D.-granting institution. She lives with her partner, Leslie Feinberg, in Jersey City, N.J.

WORKS: *The Sound of One Fork* (1981). *Yours in Struggle: Three Feminist Perspectives on Anti-Semitism and Racism,* with Elly Bulkin and Barbara Smith (1984). *We Say We Love Each Other* (1985). *Crime against Nature* (1990). *Rebellion: Essays 1980–1991* (1991). *S/HE* (1995). *Walking Back Up Depot Street* (1999). *Dirt She Ate* (2003).

—MARIA P. HEBERT

MARGARET JUNKIN PRESTON (1820–1897). Margaret Junkin Preston was born in Milton, Pa., on May 19, 1820. She was the daughter of a distinguished minister and educator, Dr. George Junkin. Under his tutelage Margaret learned to read both Latin and Greek by the age of twelve. Indeed, the intense reading associated with her studies may have seriously impaired her eyesight by the age of twenty-five.

In 1848, after serving as founding president of Lafayette College, Dr. Junkin accepted the presidency of Washington College (now Washington and Lee University) in Lexington, Va. Here Margaret spent nine happy years in her father's house, devoting her free time to writing. In 1856 her first novel, *Silverwood,* was published anonymously. The following year she married Major J. T. L. Preston, a professor of Latin at Virginia Military Institute and a widower with seven children. In 1861 her father, a Unionist, resigned from the presidency of Washington College and left Virginia with Margaret's sister. Margaret, however, was firmly loyal to her adopted state and remained in Lexington.

From 1862 to 1865, while her husband fought in the Civil War and served on the staff of General Stonewall Jackson, Margaret kept a detailed journal that became the source for her long narrative poem, *Beechenbrook: A Rhyme of War.* This story of a family whose father is serving in the Confederate army was reprinted eight times and spread Mrs. Preston's name throughout the South as the poetic spokeswoman for "proud Virginia."

Through Reconstruction Preston continued to combine the roles of housewife, mother, and poet. She published four collections of poetry and a travel book between 1870 and the loss of her eyesight in the late 1880s. In these collections she demonstrated a wide range of technique and subject matter, from European folk legends and American ballads, to sonnets and poetic vignettes drawn from Vasari's lives of the great Italian artists. She died in Baltimore at the home of her son on March 28, 1897.

WORKS: *Silverwood: A Book of Memories* (1856). *Beechenbrook: A Rhyme of War* (1865). *Old Song and New* (1870). *Cartoons* (1875). *Centennial Poem for Washington and Lee University: Lexington, Virginia, 1775–1885* (1885). *A Handful of Monographs, Continental and English* (1886). *For Love's Sake: Poems of Faith and Comfort* (1886). *Colonial Ballads, Sonnets and Other Verse* (1887). *Chimes for Church Children* (1889). *Semi-Centennial Ode for the Virginia Military Institute: Lexington, Virginia, 1839–1889* (1889). *Aunt Dorothy: An Old Virginia Plantation Story* (1890).

—RITCHIE D. WATSON, JR.

REYNOLDS PRICE (1933–). Edward Reynolds Price is one of America's most versatile writers, having published numerous acclaimed novels, essays, stories, poems, plays, and translations. Born February 1, 1933, in Macon, N.C., Price grew up in a family of avid readers, but lost both parents to cancer in his early twenties. He studied at Duke University in Durham, N.C., where he received encouragement on his writing from, among others, visiting writer Eudora Welty, who was later to assist him in publishing his first novel. Price spent 1955–58 as a Rhodes Scholar at Merton College, Oxford University, before returning to North Carolina, where he has spent most of his career writing and teaching at his alma mater.

Price's diverse body of work examines the psychology of familial relationships and sexual identity, while delving into the lingering complexities of race and class in the South. These themes are present in the trilogy that came to be called The Great Circle, novels exploring generations of the Mayfield family, considered Price's most ambitious project. Introduced in the 1975 novel *The Surface of Earth,* the Mayfield saga continued in *The Source of Light* and *The Promise of Rest.* These novels and his other writing also explore the promises of faith and the problems of mercy and redemption. Though he does not attend church, Christianity has remained important in his life. He has become a well-known essayist on theology, even publishing some of his own translations of the Gospels.

In 1984 Price was stricken with spinal cancer, recounted in *A Whole New Life*. Though the illness confined him to a wheelchair, he became still more prolific. He is currently James B. Duke Professor of English at Duke, where he teaches literature and creative writing. His many honors include the William Faulkner Award for his first novel, *A Long and Happy Life*, a National Book Critics Circle Award for *Kate Vaiden*, and membership in the American Academy of Arts and Letters.

WORKS: *A Long and Happy Life* (1962). *The Names and Faces of Heroes* (1963). *A Generous Man* (1966). *The Thing Itself* (1966). *Late Warning: Four Poems* (1968). *Love and Work* (1968). *Torso of an Archaic Apollo—After Rilke* (1969). *Permanent Errors* (1970). *Things Themselves: Essays and Sciences* (1972). *The Surface of Earth* (1975). *Early Dark* (1977). *Lessons Learned: Seven Poems* (1977). *Oracles: Six Versions from the Bible* (1977). *Christ Child's Song at the End of the Night* (1978). *A Palpable God: Thirty Stories Translated from the Bible with an Essay on the Origins and Life of Narrative* (1978). *Nine Mysteries (Four Joyful, Four Sorrowful, One Glorious)* (1979). *The Annual Heron* (1980). *A Start* (1981). *The Source of Light* (1981). *Vital Provisions* (1982). *Mustian: Two Novels and a Story* (1983). *Private Contentment* (1984). *Kate Vaiden* (1986). *The Laws of Ice* (1986). *House Snake* (1986). *A Common Room: Essays 1954–1987* (1987). *Good Hearts* (1988). *Real Copies: Will Price, Crichton Davis, Phyllis Peacock, and More* (1988). *Clear Pictures: First Loves, First Guides* (1989). *Back before Day* (1989). *The Tongues of Angels* (1990). *The Use of Fire* (1990). *New Music: A Trilogy* (1990). *Home Made* (1990). *The Foreseeable Future: Three Long Stories* (1991). *Conversations with Reynolds Price* (1991). *An Early Christmas* (1992). *Blue Calhoun* (1992). *Immediate Family*, with Sally Mann (1992). *Out on the Porch: An Evocation in Words and Phrases* (1992). *Full Moon and Other Plays* (1993). *The Collected Stories* (1993). *A Whole New Life* (1994). *The Honest Account of a Memorable Life: An Apocryphal Gospel* (1994). *The Promise of Rest* (1995). *The Three Gospels: The Good News According to Mark, the Good News According to John, an Honest Account of a Memorable Life* (1996). *Borrowed Time*, with Caroline Vaughan (1996). *The Collected Poems* (1997). *Winds of Fury, Circle of Grace: Life after the Palm Sunday Tornadoes*, with Dale Clem (1997). *Roxanna Slade* (1998). *Learning a Trade: A Craftsman's Notebooks, 1955–1997* (1998). *Letter to a Man in the Fire: Does God Exist and Does He Care?* (1999). *A Singular Family: Rosacoke and Her Kin* (1999). *Faggots*, with Larry Kramer (2000). *Feasting the Heart: Fifty-Two Commentaries for the Air* (2000). *A Perfect Friend* (2000). *Noble Norfleet* (2002). *The Good Priest's Son* (2005).

—TARA POWELL

WYATT PRUNTY (1947–). Many poets who came of age in the 1960s had one eye on writing folk song lyrics and one eye on writing literary poetry. A small number of them embarked on their literary careers with someone as intense and austere as Allen Tate looking over their shoulders, as Wyatt Prunty did when he was an undergraduate at the University of the South in Sewanee, Tenn. Prunty was born in Humbolt, Tenn., on May 15, 1947, but grew up primarily in Athens, Ga., where his father was a professor of geography at the University of Georgia. After graduation from Sewanee in 1969, Prunty served three years as a gunnery officer in the U.S. Navy.

Prunty attended the writing seminars at Johns Hopkins University, then proceeded to earn his Ph.D. at Louisiana State University, where he studied with Donald Stafford and Lewis Simpson, who were then the editors of the *Southern Review*. Prunty has taught at Louisiana State, Washington and Lee, Johns Hopkins, Virginia Tech, the Bread Loaf School of English, and the Bread Loaf Writers' Conference. He is currently Carlton Professor of English at the University of the South, where he directs the Sewanee Writers' Conference and edits the Sewanee Writers' Series, published by Overlook Press. He married Barbara Heather Svell in 1974; they have a son and a daughter.

In his poetry, Prunty casts his eye across quiet landscapes. Sometimes that landscape is the South of his past, at other times the suburbs of his present, and yet his sensibility is anything but suburban. He often writes with a half-hidden smile. For instance, in the final two lines of "The Actuarial Wife," a woman proclaims to her husband, "Darling, if one of us dies, / I'm going to live in Paris." His work is characterized by a mild yet ironic watchfulness, and he delights in jokes, misspoken phrases, and the many ways in which we perceive and interact with nature. Some of Prunty's influences can be traced to writers such as Howard Nemerov, J. V. Cunningham, and Philip Larkin, to name a few. But one can also detect at times soft and nostalgic tones that counterbalance the edginess of these poets who have had a large impact on his work.

WORKS: *Domestic of the Outer Banks* (1980). *The Times Between* (1982). *What Women Know, What Men Believe* (1986). *Balance as Belief* (1989). *Fallen from the Symboled World: Precedents for the New Formalism* (1990). *The Run of the House* (1993). *Since the Noon Mail Stopped* (1997). *Unarmed and Dangerous: New and Selected Poems* (2000). Ed., *Sewanee Writers on Writing* (2000).

—DANIEL ANDERSON

THOMAS RABBITT (1943–). Although born in Boston, Thomas Rabbitt lived in Alabama for twenty-six years, and the landscape and character of rural Alabama are the subject of much of his poetry. He studied at the Boston Latin School (Diploma, 1961), Harvard (A.B., 1966) and Johns Hopkins (M.A., 1968), then moved to San Francisco and worked for two years in advertising as a copy writer and an account executive. In 1970 he renewed his studies, entering the Writers' Workshop at the University of Iowa (M.F.A., 1972), where he was a teaching-writing fellow. In 1972 he began teaching at the University of Alabama in Tuscaloosa. There he founded and directed the M.F.A. program, founded and edited the Alabama Poetry Series for the university press (1979–90), and received the Outstanding Scholar Award (1980). He lived on several ranches in the outlying rural areas and raised livestock. He also raised and showed Arabian horses. In 1998 he retired from the university and moved onto Cape Cod; then in 2000 he moved to the west of Ireland, where he raised Arabians, Suffolk sheep, Christmas Geese, and pug puppies. He has since moved to Tennessee.

Rabbitt's poems have been reprinted in numerous anthologies, including *The Ohio Review: New and Selected, Real Things: An Anthology of Popular Culture in American Poetry, The Carnegie-Mellon Anthology of Poetry, New American Poets of the Nineties, Alabama Poets,* and *The Made Thing: An Anthology of Contemporary Southern Poetry.* His essay "Impossible Horses" appears in *Horse People* (1998), and "A Flat Rock: Poetry Perception, and Landscape" appears in *Landscape in America* (1995). Among the grants and awards he has received are the United States Award of the International Poetry Forum, later known as the Pitt Prize (1974, for *Exile*); a Pushcart Prize (1994); an Artists Fellowship in Literature from the Alabama State Council on the Arts (1996–97); a National Endowment for the Arts Literary Fellowship (1997); and inclusion in *The Best American Poetry 2000.*

WORKS: *Exile* (1975). *The Booth Interstate* (1981). *The Abandoned Country* (1988). *The Rehabilitation of Galileo Galilei* (1994). *Road Kills* (1995). *The Transfiguration of Dread* (1998). *The Capon Islands' News* (1999). *Enemies of the State* (2000). *Prepositional Heaven* (2002).

—JEFF MOCK

HOWELL RAINES (1943–). Howell Hiram Raines was born on February 5, 1943, in Birmingham, Ala. His father, W. S. "Wattie" Raines, operated a prosperous store-fixtures business. His mother, Bertha Walker Raines, read Hemingway to him and encouraged his writing. He played baseball, fished with his father, and was elected vice president of his senior class. In 1961 he enrolled at Birmingham-Southern College, just blocks away from his house. Raines was well-situated to observe the turmoil of the civil rights movement in Birmingham.

He graduated in 1964 and fully intended to ship off to Florida State University, envisioning a life of book writing and professing. Instead, he found himself drawn into journalism after taking a job at the

Birmingham Post-Herald, where he covered Bear Bryant and George Wallace. He worked briefly for a TV station, served a short stint in the National Guard (a consequence of Vietnam draft avoidance), and then enrolled in a master's program at the University of Alabama. While covering Robert Kennedy for the *Tuscaloosa News* in 1968 he met his future wife, Susan Woodley. They married in 1969.

In 1970 Raines worked for the *Birmingham News,* but soon moved to the *Atlanta Constitution,* where he became political editor in 1974. He was moonlighting as a novelist all the while, and in 1977, after years of shopping around his novel, it was published. *Whiskey Man* cynically examined the two-faced standards of provincial southern life. He had also been working on an oral history of the civil rights movement. *My Soul Is Rested* was published the same year.

With two sons to support, Raines turned back to bread-and-butter journalism. He became the *New York Times* Atlanta bureau chief (1979), then White House correspondent. A string of promotions led to his installation as Washington bureau chief (1988). His marriage was foundering around the same time, an experience he recounts in *Fly Fishing through the Midlife Crisis.* In 1992 he won the Pulitzer Prize for "Grady's Gift," an article in the *New York Times Magazine.* Starting in 1993 he served as the editorial page editor for the *Times,* where his iconoclastic style served him well.

In 2001 he was appointed executive editor, joining Clifton Daniel (North Carolina) and Turner Catledge (Mississippi) in the ranks of southern *Times* leaders. Raines was institutionally famous for his "sharp elbows" and his seersucker suits, and his hard-pushing editorship shone in the paper's coverage of September 11, 2001, which garnered six Pulitzers. But his autocratic decision-making redounded when Jason Blair, his golden boy, was revealed to be more of a fabulist-plagiarist than a reporter. In the bitter shake-up that followed, Raines did not go quietly, but eventually resigned (along with Rick Bragg and others), leaving at "a low point in the 152-year history of the paper," as the *Times* itself reported.

WORKS: *Whiskey Man* (1977). *My Soul Is Rested: Movement Days in the Deep South Remembered* (1977). *Fly Fishing through the Midlife Crisis* (1993). *Out of the Blue: The Story of September 11, 2001, from Jihad to Ground Zero,* with Richard Bernstein (2003).

—BRYAN GIEMZA

JAMES RYDER RANDALL (1839–1908). Born on January 1, 1839, in Baltimore, Md., James Ryder Randall was the son of John K. Randall, a merchant, and his wife, Ruth.

As a child, Randall studied under Joseph H. Clarke, who had taught Edgar Allan Poe when he was a boy in Richmond. Randall later attended Georgetown College in Washington, D.C., but he developed pneumonia in his last year and did not graduate. Seeking a healthier climate, he traveled in the West Indies and South America before returning to the United States, where in 1859 he settled in New Orleans. In 1860 Randall accepted a position as professor of English and classics at Poydras College, a Creole institution in Pointe Coupée Parish, La.

While there in April 1861, Randall read an account of a battle in Baltimore between local citizens and a detachment of Massachusetts troops passing through the city, an encounter in which a former classmate was killed. With this event in his mind, Randall sat down and wrote "Maryland, My Maryland." First published in the *New Orleans Sunday Delta,* the poem was later set to music by Jennie Carey of Baltimore, who adapted the words to the tune of "Tannenbaum, O Tannenbaum." As a song, it became one of the great hymns of the Confederacy.

Though as an enthusiastic secessionist he wished to support the southern cause through military service, Randall was prevented from doing so by his poor health. Following the war, he was employed in a variety of newspaper positions. For a period of time he was the Washington correspondent for the

Augusta Chronicle. In Washington he also served as personal secretary to Georgia Congressman W. H. Fleming and Georgia Senator Joseph E. Brown.

Married in 1866, Randall was the father of eight. He died in 1908, aged sixty-nine.

WORKS: *Maryland, My Maryland and Other Poems* (1908). *The Poems of James Ryder Randall,* ed. Matthew Page Andrews (1910).

—JOHN N. SOMERVILLE, JR.

JAMES INNES RANDOLPH, JR. (1837–1887). Frequently referred to as "Innes Randolph," causing some confusion in biographical and bibliographical attribution, James, Jr., was the second of many children of James Innes Randolph and Marguerite S. P. Armistead Randolph. He was born on October 25, 1837, at Barleywood Homestead, Winchester, Va. Although gifted and skilled in many areas of the arts, he published little in book form and seems not to have sought a wide reputation. When he died of heart disease on April 28, 1887, he was buried in Green Mount Cemetery, Baltimore, in an unmarked grave belonging to the Randolph family.

Randolph attended Hobart College in Geneva, N.Y., and graduated from the State and National Law School in Poughkeepsie, N.Y. In 1859 he married Anna Clare King of Georgetown, D.C.; the couple had four children. During the Civil War, he served the Confederacy as a topographical engineer and achieved the rank of major. Following the war, he became a newsman for the *Richmond Examiner,* and began to turn out light verse and prose fiction, in addition to his journalism. But none of the locally renowned tales have been identified, and his collected poetry was compiled and published by his son, Professor Harold Randolph, a decade after his death. Randolph's most familiar poems include "Twilight at Hollywood," "The Good Old Rebel," and "Ode to John Marshall." Randolph is best known for the song most often referred to as "Good Ol' Rebel Soldier," a jeremiad against the Union that is a notable literary folk effort. Penned by Randolph during the war at a meeting of the Mosaic Club, Richmond, the published form appeared in the Augusta, Ga., *Constitutionalist* on July 4, 1867.

Moving his family permanently to Baltimore in 1868, Randolph commenced a dual career, a law practice combined with various journalistic assignments for the many Baltimore newspapers. He eventually gave up law for the dual position of chief editorial writer and music critic for the *Baltimore American;* in 1884 he went to Europe as the political and social correspondent for the paper. Enthusiastic and capable, he was locally renowned as athlete, painter, sculptor, and musician; several of his pieces, including a marble bust, *William Pinckney (1764–1822),* are in the collection of the Peabody Museum.

WORKS: *The Grasshopper: A Tragic Cantata* (1878). *Poems* (1898).

—K. HUNTRESS BALDWIN

JOHN CROWE RANSOM (1888–1974). As poet, critic, and editor, John Crowe Ransom was one of the most influential men of letters to write in English during the first half of the twentieth century. The son of a Methodist minister, Ransom was born in Pulaski, Tenn., on April 20, 1888. After attending the Boman prep school in Nashville, where he completed a curriculum in the classics, he entered Vanderbilt University at age fifteen. After earning his undergraduate degree in 1909, Ransom, a Rhodes scholar, enrolled at Oxford University, where he received a B.A. in humanities in 1913. A year later, he joined the English faculty at Vanderbilt. Shortly after his return to Vanderbilt, Ransom joined an informal discussion group that met on alternate Saturday nights. After disbanding when several of it members (Ransom included) went off to fight in World War I, the group reformed in 1920 and published *The Fugitive: A Magazine of Poetry* in 1923–25. Ransom established his own reputation as a poet in *Chills and Fever* and *Two Gentlemen in Bonds*. He was also a key figure in the Agrarian social movement, which published *I'll Take My Stand* in 1930. Nevertheless, by the time he left Vanderbilt for a position at Kenyon College in 1937, Ransom was devoting the lion's share of his time and effort to literary criticism. Finally, from 1939 to 1959, he edited the *Kenyon Review*.

Although he wrote relatively few poems (and virtually none after the late 1920s), Ransom remains a fixture in anthologies of American literature. His verse is notable for its metrical precision, emotional restraint, pervasive irony, and occasional whimsy. As a teacher at Vanderbilt and Kenyon, Ransom influenced several generations of younger poets, including Donald Davidson, Allen Tate, Robert Penn Warren, Randall Jarrell, Robert Lowell, and James Wright. He was also instrumental in steering the academic study of literature away from historical and philological scholarship toward critical analysis. In his most influential book of criticism, *The World's Body*, he stresses the human need for aesthetic form—in religion and manners as well as poetry. A confirmed skeptic in his view of religious dogma, Ransom believed in the spiritual and psychological value of ritual. Like T. S. Eliot, he thought that poetry is best when it is impersonal, and even anonymous (as in Milton's "Lycidas"). His essay "Forms and Citizens" argues that people are most human when developing elaborate forms to restrain and guide their visceral impulses. In making his case in his book *The New Criticism* for what he terms a more "ontological" approach to literature, Ransom inadvertently named the critical approach with which he himself has been most frequently identified. Just as he eventually moved beyond the Fugitive and Agrarian movements, however, Ransom finally discarded New Criticism in favor of the eclectic discussion of literature featured in the quarterly installments of his magazine. Ransom died in Gambier, Ohio, on July 30, 1974, and is buried in the cemetery behind Chalmer's Library at Kenyon. He lies next to his wife, Robb Reavill Ransom.

WORKS: *Poems about God* (1919). *Chills and Fever* (1924). *Grace after Meat* (1924). *Two Gentlemen in Bonds* (1927). *God without Thunder: An Unorthodox Defense of Orthodoxy* (1930). "Reconstructed but Unregenerate," in *I'll Take My Stand: The South and the Agrarian Tradition*, by Twelve Southerners (1930). *Topics for Freshman Writing* (1935). *The World's Body* (1938). *The New Criticism* (1941). *A College Primer of Writing* (1943). *Selected Poems* (1945, 1963, 1969). Ed., *The Kenyon Critics* (1951). *Poems and Essays* (1955). Ed., *Selected Poems of Thomas Hardy* (1961). *Beating the Bushes: Selected Essays, 1941–1970* (1971). *The Selected Essays of John Crowe Ransom*, ed. Thomas Daniel Young and John Hindle (1984). *The Selected Letters of John Crowe Ransom*, ed. Young and George Core (1985).

—MARK ROYDEN WINCHELL

BEATRICE RAVENEL (1870–1956). Of the group of poets most active in the Poetry Society of South Carolina in the 1920s, Beatrice Witte Ravenel is perhaps least known, in large part because, unlike DuBose Heyward, Hervey Allen, and Josephine Pinckney, she did not subsequently achieve a reputation as a writer of fiction. During her long lifetime she published only a single book, *Arrow of Lightning*. Yet she produced some few poems that avoid the immediately exotic and picturesque uses of local color writing and are striking in their imaginativeness, in their richness and specificity of imagery, and in their strong sense of place and history.

Born in Charleston on August 24, 1870, she was the third of six daughters of Charles Otto Witte, German-born and a prominent businessman and civic leader, and Charlotte Sophia Reeves Witte. She was educated privately, and in 1889 enrolled in the women's division of Harvard University. There she played a prominent role in a group of literary young men and women that included William Vaughn Moody, Trumbull Stickney, and Norman and Hutchins Hapgood, wrote for the *Harvard Monthly* and the *Advocate,* and published poems in *Scribner's Magazine,* the *Chap-Book Magazine,* and the *Literary Digest.*

In 1900 she married Francis Gualdo Ravenel, whose mother, Harriet Horry Ravenel, was a writer and biographer of some note. For some years the Ravenels and their daughter, Beatrice St. Julien, born in 1904, lived on a plantation south of Charleston, the setting for several of her best poems, which deal with the Yemassee Indian heritage of the Carolina low country. Frank Ravenel was no businessman; by the late 1910s the sizable fortune left Beatrice Ravenel by her father was gone, and she helped support the family by writing fiction for *Ainslie's, Harper's,* and the *Saturday Evening Post,* and after 1919 she wrote editorials for the *Columbia* (S.C.) *State.*

In the late 1910s she began writing poetry again, and in the early 1920s came an abrupt change in her verse. Almost overnight she put aside the sentimental abstractions of the waning genteel tradition and began producing free verse with a notable economy of diction, precision of language, and vivid imagery. The formation of the South Carolina Poetry Society brought her into contact with other poets, including visitors such as Amy Lowell, with whom she formed a strong friendship.

In 1926, six years after her first husband's death, she married Samuel Prioleau Ravenel. It was no longer necessary for her to support her daughter and herself through journalism and fiction. The Ravenels traveled extensively. Though she wrote little poetry during her later years, one sequence based on the West Indies, unpublished in her lifetime, is among her most accomplished work. She died on March 15, 1956, at the age of eighty-five. A selection of her work was published in 1969.

WORKS: *Arrow of Lightning* (1925). *The Yemassee Lands,* ed. Louis D. Rubin, Jr. (1969).

—LOUIS D. RUBIN, JR.

MARJORIE KINNAN RAWLINGS (1896–1953).

Marjorie Rawlings was born on August 8, 1896, in Washington, D.C., and spent her childhood there. She graduated in 1918 from the University of Wisconsin. The following year she married Charles Rawlings and, while living in Rochester, N.Y., wrote short fiction that was not published.

In 1928 the Rawlings purchased seventy-four acres at Cross Creek, Fla., south of Gainesville. In Florida she found a setting that inspired her, and she soon began to publish her fiction. She sold "Jacob's Ladder," her first short story, in 1930. With encouragement from Scribner's editor Maxwell Perkins, her novel *South Moon Under* appeared in 1933. The relationship with Perkins, which lasted many years, led to her associations with Thomas Wolfe, Ernest Hemingway, Robert Frost, and F. Scott Fitzgerald. Rawlings's novel *The Yearling* won the Pulitzer Prize in 1939. It was made into a popular movie in 1946.

After her husband Charles grew tired of Cross Creek and the marriage ended in divorce, Rawlings remained there. She became known in her lifetime as one of the most extensive chroniclers of life in Florida's early years. Her *Cross Creek* has been called a Florida *Walden.* By the end of 1942, *Cross Creek* and *The Yearling* had been translated into thirteen languages.

In addition to her devotion to chronicling life in Florida, Rawlings became a strong advocate of civil rights. In 1941 Rawlings married Norton S. Baskin. In her later years alcohol increasingly was a problem, but she worked on a biography of Ellen Glasgow, never finished. She was the subject of a libel suit that went on for a number of years, and she survived two automobile accidents. At the time of her death she was dividing her time between Cross Creek and a cottage she had purchased at Crescent Beach, Fla. Her death on December 14, 1953, was the result of a brain hemorrhage. She was buried in Island Grove, Fla. A collection of her letters and manuscripts is located in the Smathers

Library at the University of Florida. Several "readers" and compilations of her poetry and stories have appeared posthumously.

WORKS: *South Moon Under* (1933). *Golden Apples* (1935). *The Yearling* (1938). *When the Whippoorwill* (1940). *Cross Creek* (1942). *Cross Creek Cookery* (1942). *The Sojourner* (1953). *The Secret River* (1955). *Selected Letters of Marjorie Kinnan Rawlings*, ed. Gordon E. Bigelow and Laura V. Monti (1983). *Short Stories by Marjorie Kinnan Rawlings*, ed. Rodger L. Tarr (1994). *Poems by Marjorie Kinnan Rawlings*, ed. Tarr (1997). *Max and Marjorie: The Correspondence between Maxwell E. Perkins and Marjorie Kinnan Rawlings*, ed. Tarr (1999). *Blood of My Blood* (2002).

—ANNE E. ROWE

OPIE READ (1852–1939). Newspaperman, humorist, traveling lecturer, and prolific novelist, Nashville native Opie Percival Read was born in 1852. Inspired as a boy by Benjamin Franklin's *Autobiography*, Read early determined to become a printer. After learning to set type at the *Franklin Patriot* in Kentucky, he began work at the *Scottsville Argus*, the first of his many publishing ventures. In 1882 Read founded the *Arkansaw Traveller*, a weekly magazine that enjoyed remarkable popularity during the greater part of its thirty-four-year run. In its heyday, the magazine had upwards of 85,000 subscribers.

An oft-repeated story about Read describes his encounter with Mark Twain when Read was a student at Neophegen College in Gallatin, Tenn. In a lecture delivered at Neophegen, Twain remarked that for writers "real knowledge lies in the close attention we pay to little things." Read took this wisdom from the storyteller to heart. As an editor and writer, he looked to his local surroundings for his materials, and such stock characters as the old southern colonel, dialect-speaking African Americans, and poor whites are commonplace in his work. Westerner that he was, Read had more in common with the Old Southwest humorists than he did with the "moonlight and magnolia" school of southern writing. His values, while sentimental, were decidedly homespun and fiercely individualistic, and he was consistently ironic when portraying the gentility of the Old South or of the East.

Read's most productive period as a novelist came in a fifteen-year period spanning the turn of the century. Between 1891 and 1906 he published more than thirty books, many of which found an eager popular readership. His novel entitled *The Jucklins*, a romance set in rural North Carolina, sold over a million copies. Late in his career, Read lectured extensively, claiming at one point to have lectured in every state in the Union.

WORKS: *Len Gansett* (1888). *Up Terrapin River* (1889). *A Kentucky Colonel* (1890). *Mrs. Annie Green: A Romance* (1890). *A Kentucky Editor* (1891). *Emmett Bonlore* (1891). *Selected Stories* (1891). *Twenty Good Stories* (1891). *Opie Read in Arkansas and What He Saw There; Comprising Popular Stories by this Famous Author* (1891). *The Colossus: A Story* (1893). *A Tennessee Judge* (1893). *The Tear in the Cup and Other Stories* (1894). *The Wives of the Prophet* (1894). *On the Suwanee River: A Romance* (1895). *My Young Master* (1896). *An Arkansas Planter* (1896). *The Captain's Romance* (1896). *The Jucklins* (1896). *Bolanyo* (1897). *Old Ebenezer* (1897). *Odd Folks* (1897). *The Waters of Caney Fork: A Romance of Tennessee* (1898). *The Carpetbagger* (1899). *Judge Elbridge* (1899). *A Yankee from the West* (1899). *In the Alamo* (1900). *Our Josephine and Other Tales* (1902). *The Starbucks* (1902). *The Club Woman and the Hero: A Comedietta* (1903). *The Fiddle and the Fawn and Other Stories* (1903). *The Harkriders* (1903). *The American Cavalier* (1904). *Confessions of Marguerite: The Story of a Girl's Heart* (1904). *Adventures of a Vice-President: A Fable of Our Times* (1904). *"Turk"* (1904). *"Turkey-Egg" Griffin* (1905). *An American in New York: A Novel of Today* (1905). *Old Lim Jucklins: The Opinions of an Open-Air Philosopher* (1905). *Opie Read in the Ozarks, Including Many of the Rich, Rare, Quaint, Eccentric, Ignorant, and Superstitious Sayings of the Natives of Missouri and Arkansaw* (1905). *Plantation Yarns and Bayou Stories* (1905). *The Son of the Swordmaker: A Romance* (1905). *Tales of the South* (1905). *By the Eter-*

nal (1906). *My Friends in Arkansas* (1906). *The Mystery of Margaret* (1907). *The Bandit's Sweetheart and Other Stories* (1907). *The Queen's Robe: A Dramatic Story* (1908). *Kentucky Yarns* (1909). *Tom and the Squatter's Son: A Stirring Tale of Adventure in the Pioneer Days for Boys from Seven to Sixty* (1910). *The New Mr. Howerson* (1914). *Opie Read on Golf* (1925). *"Come on Buck"* (1926). *The Gold Gauze Veil* (1927). *I Remember* (1930). *Mark Twain and I* (1940).

—H. COLLIN MESSER

JAY SAUNDERS REDDING (1906–1988). Jay Saunders Redding—scholar, educator, man of letters—was born in Wilmington, Del., on October 13, 1906. He attended Lincoln University in Pennsylvania for one year before entering Brown University, where he earned the Ph.B. (1928) and M.A. (1932). Eventually he received six honorary doctorates and many awards, including Rockefeller and Guggenheim fellowships, the National Urban League Service Award, and the Mayflower Award.

Redding taught at Morehouse College (1928–31), Louisville Municipal College (1934–36), Southern University (1936–38), Elizabeth City State Teachers College (now Elizabeth City State University, 1938–43), Hampton Institute (now Hampton University, 1943–66), and many other colleges and universities, including his alma mater, Brown University. When he retired in 1975, he was the Ernest I. White Professor of American Studies and Humane Letters at Cornell University. In addition, Redding lectured in India for the State Department, in Africa for the American Society of African Culture, and throughout America at scholarly assemblies. Redding served on the editorial board of *American Scholar;* directed the Division of Research and Publication, National Endowment for the Humanities; contributed to anthologies; and wrote numerous articles and reviews published in *American Scholar, Atlantic Monthly, Harper's, Nation, Negro Digest, Phylon, Saturday Review, Transition,* and other periodicals.

Among Redding's book-length publications, critics have judged *No Day of Triumph* his best work. It won the 1942 Mayflower Cup Award for the year's best book by a North Carolina resident. Combining autobiography with a report of observations made while traveling through the South, Redding presents a dramatic account of southern African American life in the 1940s. Redding wrote or edited thirteen other books, including fiction, autobiography, history, and literary criticism. In each work, his writing is effective and convincing in its depictions of African American history, literature, and culture. Redding died in Ithaca, N.Y., on March 2, 1988.

WORKS: *To Make a Poet Black* (1939). *No Day of Triumph* (1942). *Stranger and Alone* (1950). *They Came in Chains* (1950). *On Being Negro in America* (1951). Ed., *Reading for Writing,* with Ivan E. Taylor (1952). *An American in India* (1954). *The Lonesome Road* (1958). *The Negro* (1967). *Of Men and the Writing of Books* (1969). *Negro Writing and the Political Climate* (1970). Ed., *Cavalcade: Negro American Writing from 1760 to the Present,* with Arthur P. Davis (1971). Ed., *The New Cavalcade: African American Writing from 1760 to the Present,* with Arthur P. Davis and Joyce Ann Joyce (1991–92). *A Scholar's Conscience: Selected Writings, 1942–1977,* ed. Faith Berry (1992).

—PATSY B. PERRY

BYRON HERBERT REECE (1917–1958). Byron Herbert Reece was born on September 14, 1917, at the foot of Blood Mountain in north Georgia to Juan and Emma Reece. As a young boy Reece lived in a secluded mountain area, not seeing an automobile until he was eight years old. Before entering the Choestoe Elementary School in 1923, Reece had read *Pilgrim's Progress* and much of the Bible, upon which many of his later ballads were based.

In June 1935, Reece was graduated from Blairsville High School and entered Young Harris College in September. There he published numerous poems in the small poetry journals and attracted the attention of Ralph McGill, editor of the *Atlanta Constitution*. Reece left Young Harris College without being graduated because he refused to take the required courses in French, which he considered an affectation.

He returned to his parents' farm, where he did heavy farm work during the day and at night composed literary mountain ballads. He attracted the attention of Jesse Stuart, who had read his work in *Prairie Schooner*. On Stuart's recommendation E. P. Dutton published *Ballad of the Bones* in October 1945, to wide and favorable critical acclaim. After Reece published a novel, *Better a Dinner of Herbs*, he was invited to the University of California at Los Angeles as poet-in-residence. In 1953 he was invited to Young Harris College as poet-in-residence but was forced early in 1954 to enter Battey Hospital at Rome, Ga., because of tuberculosis.

By early 1956 Reece had recovered sufficiently to become poet-in-residence at Emory University. He returned the following fall to Young Harris College. The following summer he received a Guggenheim award, but illness and depression forced him to return to his mountain home. After another academic year at Young Harris College, he committed suicide on June 3, 1958.

WORKS: "The Hills Not Home," in *Three Lyric Poets* (1942). *Ballad of the Bones* (1945). *Remembrance of Moab* (1949). *Better a Dinner of Herbs* (1950). *Bow Down in Jericho* (1950). *A Song of Joy* (1952). *The Season of Flesh* (1955). *The Hawk and the Sun* (1955). *Fable in the Blood: The Selected Poems of Byron Herbert Reece*, ed. Jim Clark (2002).

—RAYMOND A. COOK

ISHMAEL REED (1938–). Ishmael Reed was born in Chattanooga, Tenn., on February 22, 1938, and raised by his mother, Thelma Coleman, and stepfather, Bennie Stephen Reed. Reed grew up in Buffalo, N.Y., and attended the State University of New York there, before dropping out and living for a time in a city ghetto. In 1960 he joined the *Empire Star Weekly*, where he wrote about civil rights conflicts; he would call the 1960s "the decade that screamed." Later, he met Malcolm X, moved to New York, joined the Umbra Writers Workshop, and involved himself in the nascent Black Arts Movement. Political activism has been the hallmark of his life and work. He was a proponent of multiculturalism before the term had been coined.

Poet, novelist, essayist, and editor, Reed is perhaps most remarked as a satirist and free-ranging iconoclast. He plucked oppressive whites and exploitative blacks alike in the menagerie of *The Free-Lance Pallbearers*. His *Yellow Back Radio Broke Down* is a western that features an African American cowboy. *Flight to Canada* controversially spoofed the slave narrative. *Reckless Eyeballing*, which satirized the feminist view of the Emmett Till murder, raised the ire of many commentators. Reed has nurtured a long-standing fascination with the subversive voodoo religion. Playfulness and hybridity characterize his genre-spanning, highly postmodern writing. That creativity has brought accolades. In addition to his nomination for the Pulitzer Prize and National Book Award, Reed has received a Guggenheim Foundation Award, fellowships from the National Endowment for the Arts, and a MacArthur "genius" grant. His ventures into the academy have found him where he seems most at home: at the center of controversy.

Reed moved to California in 1967 and has spent much of his life there. He recently published an extended ode to Oakland. Despite a largely northern upbringing, the South has served as a creative wellspring for much of Reed's work, and a good portion of his work is set there. A daughter from his second marriage is named Tennessee.

WORKS: *The Free-Lance Pallbearers* (1967). *Yellow Back Radio Broke Down* (1969). *catechism of d neoamerican hoodoo church* (1970). Ed., *Nineteen Necromancers from Now* (1970). *Conjure: Selected Poems, 1963–1970* (1972). *Mumbo*

Jumbo (1972). *Chattanooga: Poems* (1973). *The Last Days of Louisiana Red* (1974). *Flight to Canada* (1976). *A Secretary to the Spirits* (1978). *Shrovetide in Old New Orleans* (1978). *The Ace Boons* (1980). *Mother Hubbard* (1982). *God Made Alaska for the Indians: Selected Essays* (1982). *The Terrible Twos* (1982). *Reckless Eyeballing* (1986). *New and Collected Poems* (1988). *Writin' Is Fightin': Thirty-Seven Years of Boxing on Paper* (1988). *The Terrible Threes* (1989). *Japanese by Spring* (1993). *Airing Dirty Laundry* (1993). *Conversations with Ishmael Reed* (1995). *MultiAmerica: Essays on Cultural Wars and Cultural Peace* (1997). *The Reed Reader* (2000). *Another Day at the Front: Dispatches from the Race War* (2003). *Blues City: A Walk in Oakland* (2003). Ed., *From Totems to Hip-Hop* (2003).

—Bryan Giemza

JOHN SHELTON REED (1942–). John Reed has been called "the most accomplished and influential living sociologist of the U.S. South." More important, he is a sociologist who can *write*. He was born (without being asked) in New York City on January 8, 1942, a birthday he shares with Elvis Presley. Reed's father, John Shelton Reed, Sr., hailed from the mountains of Tennessee; his mother, from Rochester, N.Y. He was raised in Kingsport, Tenn., and went to the Massachusetts Institute of Technology, where he had a close brush with becoming a statistician. There, in the words of writer Doris Betts, "[he] first found himself called upon to define how the South was distinctive, then to defend it."

A Ph.D. in sociology at Columbia followed in 1969. His dissertation, later his first book, *The Enduring South,* eloquently put forth the case that southern culture was more redoubtable than commonly believed, a theme that would become the touchstone of his work. Reed became the finest spokesman of the position that the South endures, an important counterpoint to the oft-opined position that regional identity must give way to the bulldozer.

In the many books that followed, Reed continued to explore the meaning of southern identity. As a champion of jargon-free, plain-style prose, Reed reached beyond an academic audience, taking up such varied subjects as social types, latter-day agrarianism, and Anglo-Catholicism. His articles have been published in magazines ranging from *Science* to *Southern Living,* and many of his essays have been collected in books. He has been a Guggenheim Fellow, a Fulbright lecturer, and an NEH Fellow, and was elected to the Fellowship of Southern Writers in 2001. For thirty-one years he taught at the University of North Carolina, where he held a chaired professorship.

His work has garnered praise from such writers as Lee Smith and Roy Blount, Jr. Some of Reed's homespun witticisms have been so widely circulated that they have become instant truisms of southern identity (e.g., "[Atlanta] represents what a quarter of a million Confederates died to prevent," and his observation that "Barbeque divides the South and grits hold it together.") If southern literary studies pay curiously little attention to what constitutes the South in the first place, then Reed's work provides the best clarification.

works: *The Enduring South: Subcultural Persistence in Mass Society* (1972). *One South: An Ethnic Approach to Regional Culture* (1982). Ed., *Regionalism and the South: Selected Papers of Rupert Vance,* with D. J. Singal (1982). *Southerners: The Social Psychology of Sectionalism* (1983). *Southern Folk, Plain and Fancy: Native White Social Types* (1986). *Whistling Dixie: Dispatches from the South* (1990). *"My Tears Spoiled My Aim" and Other Reflections on Southern Culture* (1993). *Surveying the South: Studies in Regional Sociology* (1993). *Kicking Back: Further Dispatches from the South* (1995). *Glorious Battle: The Cultural Politics of Victorian Anglo-Catholicism* (1996). *1001 Things Everyone Should Know about the South,* with Dale Volberg Reed (1996). *Minding the South* (2003).

—Bryan Giemza

LIZETTE WOODWORTH REESE (1856–1935). Lizette Woodworth Reese was born on January 9, 1856, in Waverly, Md., a rural village two miles outside Baltimore. Her parents were immigrants to the United States; Louisa Gabler Reese moved from Germany, and David Reese from Wales. Her father fought for the Confederacy during the Civil War. Lizette and her twin, Sophia, were the first two of five children that included four girls and a boy. In 1873 she began teaching at St. John's Parish School and embarked upon a teaching career in Baltimore-area public schools that would last for forty-eight years. In 1875 she relocated to the Number Three English-German School, where she taught half the day in German, the other half in English. She taught English literature and composition at Baltimore's Colored High School from 1897 until 1901, what she called "the happiest years of my life." When the school board decided that black students should have black teachers, Reese was transferred to Western High School, an all-girls school, where she taught until she retired in 1921.

Reese published her first poem, "The Deserted House," in Baltimore's *Southern Magazine* in 1874. She formed her poetic style in youth and did not vary from it significantly. Her poems use traditional rhythms and meter along with an effective simplicity of language to represent memory and celebrate the beauty of nature. Reese's memory poems view the past with a nostalgic, rose-colored glow tempered with painful realities. Her sonnet "Tears," one of the most popular and celebrated poems during her lifetime, begins with a note of despair, but ends on one of hope. Although Reese was never married and had no children, "Rachel" and her long narrative poem *Little Henrietta* deal poignantly with the death of children. With the exception of her last volume of poems, *The Old House in the Country*, the majority of her poetry is not autobiographical, though much of her prose is. *A Victorian Village, The York Road*, and her unfinished novel *Worleys* contain personal essays and short stories set in rural Maryland. Her verbal concision and intensity influenced a generation of women American poets, including Louise Bogan and Edna St. Vincent Millay.

A schoolteacher and prolific poet, publishing over four hundred poems in eleven volumes, Reese was also a public figure. She founded the Woman's Literary Club of Baltimore and served as its chairwoman until her death. In 1931 she was named poet laureate of the General Federation of Women's Clubs, and she received an honorary degree from Goucher College, where she was called one of "the greatest living women poets in America." Reese died of a kidney infection on December 17, 1935.

WORKS: *A Branch of May* (1887). *A Handful of Lavender* (1891). *A Quiet Road* (1896). *A Wayside Lute* (1909). *Spicewood* (1920). *Wild Cherry* (1923). *Selected Poems* (1926). *Little Henrietta* (1927). *A Victorian Village: Reminiscences of Other Days* (1929). *White April* (1930). *The York Road* (1931). *Pastures* (1933). *The Old House in the Country* (1936). *Worleys* (1936).

—MATTHEW SPANGLER

JAMES REID (fl. 1768). Like so many southern colonial writers, James Reid left few discernible tracks. He was evidently born and schooled in Edinburgh, Scotland, where he was a classmate and contemporary of the blind poet Thomas Blalock. Reid had migrated to Virginia by the late 1760s, perhaps as a tutor, even an indentured tutor, to a planter. Evidence indicates that Reid served as schoolmaster to the family of Colonel Robert Ruffin, who during the winter of 1768–69 moved from his Mayfield plantation in Dinwiddie County to Sweet Hall or to the adjoining plantation of Windsor Shades in King William County to be nearer a daughter married to a Claiborne. Reid, whose religious sympathies have been characterized as Old Light Presbyterian, found the move to King William County unsatisfactory. He satirized the King Williamites as arrogant, crude, and ignorant.

Under the pseudonym of "Caledoniensis," Reid published between September 15, 1768, and March 30, 1769, nine or ten poems and four essays in the *Virginia Gazette* of Purdie and Dixon. Three of the essays deal with religious and theological problems, and the fourth with abuses of language. The poems range from mock elegies to love poems to verse satires.

Reid's long prose satire, *The Religion of the Bible and Religion of K[ing] W[illiam] County Compared,* written in 1769 but not published until 1967, depicts the young Virginia gentry not as esquires, but as "Ass-queers." The Ass-queer "drinks, fights, bullies, curses, swears, whores, games." "This," says Reid, "comprehends his whole life, and renders him a Polite Gentleman, or to use the modern elegant phrase—a damn'd honest Fellow." Reid presents a view of the Virginia gentleman current among immigrants and back-country people of the day, and his attitude counterpoints that of many romantic versions of the nineteenth century. Scholars have not discovered further biographical details.

WORKS: *The Religion of the Bible and Religion of K[ing] W[illiam] County Compared,* repr. in *The Colonial Virginia Satirist* (1967), ed. Richard Beale Davis.

—ROBERT BAIN

ALICE CALDWELL HEGAN RICE (1870–1942). Alice Caldwell Hegan Rice said she was born with a pen in her hand. As a child she told stories and wrote plays to entertain her young aunts and eight cousins, while they played in the "big, friendly house" of her maternal grandfather, Judge James Caldwell. She is best known for her novel *Mrs. Wiggs of the Cabbage Patch,* which has been translated into many languages.

Born on January 11, 1870, in Shelbyville, Ky., Rice was a sickly child, often kept at home, where she was read to extensively. She did not start formal schooling until she was ten, when she was sent to Miss Hampton's private school for girls in Louisville. She hated mathematics, devoured English, and was soon writing compositions for others in her class. The only medal she ever received was for handwriting.

Rice's work first saw print in the local newspaper when she was fifteen. At sixteen she began work in a mission Sunday school in a nearby slum called the Cabbage Patch. She admired the fortitude and cheerfulness of the poor, and continued as an active social worker. The Louisville authors' club encouraged her to write a novel based on her experience.

Mrs. Wiggs of the Cabbage Patch portrays a poor woman with a brood of children and a do-nothing husband. This woman had such a gay and courageous spirit that she touched the springs of human nature in both rich and poor and brought them closer to an understanding. *Mrs. Wiggs* was first produced as a play in Louisville, then later in New York and abroad. In 1934 it was made into a popular movie starring W. C. Fields. *Lovely Mary,* set in the Cabbage Patch, was also popular. With Louise Marshall, Rice established the Cabbage Patch Settlement House in a Louisville slum.

In 1902 Hegan married Cale Young Rice, the dramatist and poet, and they traveled extensively. They had no children. She died at home in Louisville in 1942, maintaining that in heaven she would "still have a pen in hand trying to chronicle the antics of the angels."

WORKS: *Mrs. Wiggs of the Cabbage Patch* (1901). *Lovely Mary* (1903). *Captain June* (1907). *Sandy* (1905). *Mr. Opp* (1909). *A Romance of Billy-Goat Hill* (1912). *The Honorable Percival* (1914). *Calvary Alley* (1917). *Quin* (1921) *The Buffer* (1929). *Mr. Pete & Co.* (1933). *The Lark Legacy* (1935). *Our Ernie* (1939). *On Being Clinnicked: A Bit of Talk over the Alley Fence* (1931). *My Pillow Book* (1937). *The Inky Way* (1940). *Happiness Road* (1942).

—RUTH MOOSE

ANNE RICE (1941–). Howard Allen O'Brien was born on October 4, 1941, at Mercy Hospital in New Orleans, the second of four daughters of Katherine Allen and Howard O'Brien. Unhappy with her masculine name, as a schoolgirl she adopted the name Anne. Though her well-educated parents provided her with a stimulating childhood rich in art and literature, she also dealt with her mother's alcoholism and the stigma of being poor and Irish in a highly segregated city. As a teenager, she met much upheaval: when Anne was fifteen her mother died, prompting her father to enroll her in a Catholic boarding school. Soon after, he remarried and relocated the family to Richardson, Tex. In high school there, Anne met the poet Stan Rice, whom she married in 1961. The Rices moved to San Francisco in 1962, beginning what she has called a twenty-six-year period of exile from her native city.

In 1964 Rice took a B.A. in political science from San Francisco State University, followed by an M.A. in creative writing in 1972. The same year, her daughter Michele died of leukemia just before her sixth birthday. Rice dealt with her grief by writing her first novel, the gothic horror tale *Interview with the Vampire,* which was published by Knopf in 1976 and remains her best-known and most highly regarded novel. In 1978 the Rices had a son, Christopher, who is now a published novelist. Following two historical novels, *The Feast of All Saints* and *Cry to Heaven,* Rice penned three pornographic novels under the pseudonym A. N. Roquelaure. In 1985, the year her celebrity peaked, Rice managed the publication of three novels under three names; after the success of the film version of *Interview,* she had four novels on the best-seller list.

Rice's tenth novel, *The Queen of the Damned,* reached the top of the *New York Times* best-seller list in 1989, enabling her to return to her beloved New Orleans. She became something of a cottage industry in New Orleans, having purchased several historical buildings that feature in her vampire chronicles, and having inspired Anne Rice–themed tours, an Anne Rice retail store, and a doll collection. After her husband's death from cancer in December 2002, Rice sought to simplify her life, selling off her many properties and relocating from the Garden District of New Orleans to the suburbs and eventually moving to La Jolla, Calif., to be near her son. Ever daring, she has written a novel based on the life of Jesus.

WORKS: *Interview with the Vampire* (1976). *The Feast of All Saints* (1979). *Cry to Heaven* (1982). *The Claiming of Sleeping Beauty,* as A. N. Roquelaure (1983). *Beauty's Punishment,* as A. N. Roquelaure (1984). *Beauty's Release,* as A. N. Roquelaure (1985). *The Vampire Lestat* (1985). *Exit to Eden,* as Anne Rampling (1985). *Belinda,* as Anne Rampling (1986). *The Queen of the Damned* (1988). *The Mummy; or, Ramses the Damned* (1989). *The Witching Hour* (1990). *The Tale of the Body Thief* (1992). *Lasher* (1993). *Taltos: Lives of the Mayfair Witches* (1994). *Memnoch the Devil* (1995). *Servant of the Bones* (1996). *Violin* (1997). *Pandora: New Tales of the Vampires* (1998). *The Vampire Armand* (1998). *Vittorio, the Vampire: New Tales of the Vampires* (1999). *Merrick* (2000). *Blood and Gold; or, The Story of Marius* (2001). *Blackwood Farm* (2002). *Blood Canticle* (2003). *Christ the Lord: Out of Egypt* (2005).

—PETER J. FLORA

CALE YOUNG RICE (1872–1943). Born on December 7, 1872, in Dixon, the seat of Webster County in western Kentucky, Cale Rice Young was educated in the schools of Evansville, Ind., and at Cumberland University in Lebanon, Tenn. He later earned a B.A. (1895) and M.A. (1896) at Harvard, where he studied with William James and George Santayana. After teaching at Cumberland for several years, he came back to Kentucky in 1902 to marry Alice Caldwell Hagan (1870–1842), the Louisville writer who penned the popular novel *Mrs. Wiggs of the Cabbage Patch* in 1901. Their union proved childless but literarily productive, as both published prodigiously in their chosen genres throughout their lives. Despondent following his wife's death in 1942, he committed suicide on January 23, 1943.

Alice Hagan Rice remained more of a popular favorite, particularly for *Cabbage Patch* sequels, local color tales of a sentimentalized Irish ghetto in Louisville. Cale Rice Young was regarded as a more serious poet and dramatist, as his work was most often concerned with classical and romantic matter and theme. Although her fiction is being reconsidered at present, his poetry and drama remain largely neglected and forgotten. In his day, however, critics as serious as William Dean Howells, James Huneker, and Gilbert Murray praised him as one of America's significant writers, and some later scholars have connected him to the rise of expressionism in American drama. The very best of his voluminous lyric and narrative poetry, if ever bridled by traditional verse forms, sometimes reminds the reader of the later Hardy, the early Yeats, or the first books of Edwin Arlington Robinson.

WORKS: *From Dusk to Dusk* (1898). *Song Surf* (1901). *Charles di Tocca: A Tragedy* (1903). *Plays and Lyrics* (1906). *Nirvana Days* (1908). *Many Gods* (1910). *The Immortal Lure* (1911). *Far Quests* (1912). *At the World's Heart* (1914). *Collected Plays and Poems* (1915). *Earth and New Earth* (1916). *Songs to A.H.R.* (1918). *Wraiths and Realities* (1918). *Sea Poems* (1921). *Mihrima and Other Poems* (1922). *Bitter Brew* (1925). *Selected Plays and Poems* (1926). *Early Reaping* (1929). *The Swamp Bird* (1931). *High Perils* (1933). *Love and Lord Byron* (1936). *Bridging the Years* (1939).

—JOSEPH R. MILLICHAP

AMELIE RIVES [PRINCESS TROUBETZKOY] (1863–1945). Born in Richmond, Va., on August 23, 1863, Amelie Louise Rives descended from Virginia antecedents that included a U.S. senator, a minister to France, an explorer, a Confederate officer, and several authors. Both her family background and her formative years, which were spent at Castle Hill, the Rives estate in Albemarle County, Va., proved important in shaping her temperament, talent, and social conscience.

She was educated by governesses and was allowed to read at will from the library of her grandfather, William Cabell Rives. She began to write almost as soon as she learned to read, though until she was twenty-three, she entertained no thoughts of publication. But when a house guest discovered one of her manuscripts, he was given permission to publish it anonymously. This story, "A Brother to Dragons," appeared in the *Atlantic Monthly* in March 1886. This and several subsequent stories were romantic tales of adventure, often narrated in dialect, and they gained the author a following. The publication of *The Quick or the Dead?* which sold more than 300,000 copies, introduced a strain of psychological realism that would be developed throughout the remaining years of her career.

Rives's personal life was also much publicized. One of the great beauties of her generation, she married John Armstrong Chanler, a wealthy descendant of John Jacob Astor, in 1888. After she separated from Chanler in 1894, Oscar Wilde introduced her to Prince Pierre Troubetzkoy, a noted portrait artist, whom she married in 1896. She enjoyed social and intellectual life in both England and America until World War I. Thereafter, believing that the England she had known as a young woman was permanently changed, she spent most of her time in New York and at Castle Hill. Her final fifteen years were generally unhappy, and she wrote little after 1930. She died in Charlottesville on June 16, 1945.

WORKS: *A Brother to Dragons and Other Old-Time Tales* (1888). *Herod and Marianne* (1888). *The Quick or the Dead?* (1888). *Virginia of Virginia* (1888). *The Witness of the Sun* (1889). *According to St. John* (1891). *Athelwold* (1893). *Barbara Dering* (1893). *Tanis, the Sand-Digger* (1893). *A Damsel Errant* (1898). *Seléné* (1905). *Augustine the Man* (1906). *The Golden Rose* (1908). *Trix and Over-the-Moon* (1909). *Pan's Mountain* (1910). *Hidden House* (1912). *World's-End* (1914). *Shadows of Flames* (1915). *The Ghost Garden* (1918). *As the Wind Blew* (1920). *The Sea-Woman's Cloak and November Eve* (1923). *The Queerness of Celia* (1926). *Love-in-a-Mist* (1927). *Firedamp* (1930).

—WELFORD DUNAWAY TAYLOR

ELIZABETH MADOX ROBERTS (1881–1941). Elizabeth Madox Roberts was born on October 30, 1881, in Perryville, Ky. Her family moved three years later to nearby Springfield, which later became the model for many of the rural towns she depicted in her work. As a child Roberts aspired to be a poet. Although she is now known primarily for her fiction, she also published a small body of good poetry.

Roberts attended a private academy in Springfield and then enrolled in high school in Covington, Ky. She attended the University of Kentucky in 1900 but withdrew because of illness. In 1900–1914 she taught at a number of public and private schools. At age thirty-six she enrolled as a freshman at the University of Chicago, where she was elected to Phi Beta Kappa. In her senior year she was president of the poetry club, a group that included Glenway Wescott, Yvor Winters, Monroe Wheeler, and Janet Lewis. She also began to publish her work in journals, including *Poetry* magazine, edited by Harriet Monroe. In 1922 she won the Fiske Poetry Prize.

At forty, artistically liberated in Chicago, Roberts embarked on a determined writing career, which she pursued for the next twenty-one years until her death. Roberts is most widely known for two of her novels, *The Time of Man* and *The Great Meadow.* Both novels treat the development of a female protagonist set against the rural Kentucky world and the passage of time from one generation to the next.

Suffering through the 1930s from numerous skin and respiratory illnesses, Roberts was diagnosed with Hodgkin's disease in 1936. Thereafter she wintered in Florida and spent the warmer seasons in Kentucky, the place she felt was her true home. She died in Orlando on March 13, 1941, and was buried in Springfield, Ky. A conference celebrating the centenary of her birth was held there in 1981. Remembered as an increasingly innovative poet, Roberts is celebrated for her sensitive depiction in novels and stories of Kentucky mountain people, their dialect, and customs.

WORKS: *In the Great Steep's Garden* (1915). *Under the Tree* (1922). *The Time of Man* (1926). *My Heart and My Flesh* (1927). *Jingling in the Wind* (1928). *The Great Meadow* (1930). *A Buried Treasure* (1931). *The Haunted Mirror* (1932). *He Sent Forth a Raven* (1935). *Black Is My Truelove's Hair* (1938). *Song in the Meadow* (1940). *Not by Strange Gods* (1941).

—ANNE E. ROWE

BEN ROBERTSON (1903–1943). Ben Robertson earned fame as an internationally respected journalist. He is now remembered chiefly for his memoir *Red Hills and Cotton: An Upcountry Memory.*

Robertson was born on June 22, 1903, in Clemson, S.C., son of Benjamin Franklin and Mary Bowen Robertson. His father, a chemist, was on the Agricultural Extension staff at Clemson University. After Ben's mother died when he was seven, he continued to visit her parents, who, like the Robertsons, had deep upland roots and valued education. Democrat and Baptist on both sides, Ben maintained both convictions. Although he majored in botany as a Clemson undergraduate, he took many literature courses, wrote for the student newspaper, and during his senior year edited the college yearbook. Following his graduation in 1923, Robertson began study in the journalism school at the University of Missouri. He interrupted those studies for a year with the *Charleston News and Courier.* He completed the B.A. in journalism the next year.

A position at the *Honolulu Star-Bulletin* helped satisfy his yen for travel and the exotic. After two years in Honolulu, he explored more distant parts of the Pacific—Borneo, Java, Surabaya—then worked for a year in Australia for the *Adelaide News.* The material he gathered eventually became feature articles in *Scribner's, Current History, Asia,* and *Travel.* In 1929 Robertson became a reporter for the *New York Herald-Tribune,* a springboard to becoming a political reporter for the Associated Press's Washington bureau. From 1934 to 1936, he served alternately as White House and Supreme Court correspondent.

He returned to Clemson to write a novel (its theme was the innate restlessness of Americans), but failed to find an established publisher. Eventually *Travelers' Rest* was published through the efforts of friends. Ever restless himself, he embarked on an around-the-world voyage on a freighter to study the professional wanderers who manned those ships. By December 1937, he was back in Clemson to finish a draft of "The Pilgrim"—the book he hoped to create from his travels. It remains unpublished.

Neo-populist and pro–New Deal, Robertson was active in several campaigns in the 1938 Democratic primary, supporting himself all the while as a freelance journalist. In 1940, putting aside his first flirtation with running for political office, he returned to New York to work for *PM*, the newly founded daily that favored intervention in World War II. In June of that year, Robertson went to Great Britain to cover the war. On furlough in January 1941, he completed *I Saw England*. His account of the Battle of Britain was widely praised on both sides of the Atlantic.

Back in South Carolina that fall, Robertson seriously contemplated running for a seat in Congress, but when Senator James F. Byrnes gave no encouragement, he used his time in Clemson to complete the book that became *Red Hills and Cotton*, celebrating his upcountry heritage. He envisioned the book as commentary on American democracy.

Early in 1942, Robertson resumed his duties for *PM*, covering the war in the Soviet Union, India, and northern Africa. He celebrated Christmas with his family in Clemson and was about to begin work as chief of the *Herald-Tribune's* London bureau. On February 22, 1943, his plane crashed in Portugal.

WORKS: *Travelers' Rest* (1938). *I Saw England* (1941). *Red Hills and Cotton: An Upcountry Memory* (1942).

—JOSEPH M. FLORA

LEON ROOKE (1934–). Short-story writer, novelist, playwright, editor, newspaper reviewer, anthologist, and critic, Leon Rooke was born at Roanoke Rapids, N.C., on September 11, 1934. He was educated at the University of North Carolina in Chapel Hill (1955–58, 1961–62) and drafted into the U.S. Army infantry, which he served in Alaska (1958–60). After studying screenwriting at Chapel Hill, Rooke turned to journalism and creative writing. In 1969 he married and moved with his wife, Constance, to Victoria, British Columbia, where she had accepted a job teaching English at the University of Victoria. In 1989 Rooke became the founder and artistic director of the popular Eden Mills Writers' Festival in an Ontario town near Guelph, where the couple had moved in 1988 in order for Constance to take up a position initially as an English professor and then as president of the University of Guelph. Currently, the Rookes live in Toronto.

Rooke is a prolific and energetic storyteller. His writing is characterized by inventive language, experimental form, and an extreme range of offbeat characters with distinctive voices. In spite of his distinctly southern linguistic idiom, cultural sensibility, and affinity with southern gothic writers, Rooke has regularly received praise from Canadian critics and reviewers, most notably for his novels. His first, *Fat Woman*, was nominated for both the 1982 Governor-General's Award for Fiction and *Books in Canada* First Novel Award. *Shakespeare's Dog* won the Governor-General's Award for Fiction in 1984.

In 2000 a stage adaptation of *Shakespeare's Dog* toured the Atlantic Seaboard by tall ship. Rooke also completed the screenplay for *A Good Baby*, a feature film released in 2001. Rooke has served as writer-in-residence at over a dozen Canadian and U.S. universities, including the University of North Carolina and Southwest Minnesota State University. He has also received numerous awards, including the 1981 Canada-Australia Prize, the 1990 North Carolina Award for Literature (for a body of work), and the 2002 W. O. Mitchell Literary Award for teaching and mentoring. He has edited numerous anthologies with John Metcalfe.

WORKS: *Last One Home Sleeps in the Yellow Bed: Stories* (1968). *Vault: A Story in Three Parts* (1973). *Krokodile* (1975). *The Love Parlour: Stories* (1977). *The Broad Back of the Angel* (1977). *Cry Evil* (1980). *Fat Woman* (1980). *Death Suite* (1981). *The Happiness of Others* (1981). *How I Saved the Province* (1981). *The Magician in Love* (1981). *The Birth Control King of Upper Volta* (1982). *Shakespeare's Dog: A Novel* (1983). *A Bolt of White Cloth* (1984). *Sing Me No Love Songs, I'll Say You No Prayers: Selected Stories* (1984). *Muffins* (1985). *A Good Baby* (1991). *The Coming* (1991). *Who Do You Love?* (1992). *Oh, No, I Have Not Seen Molly* (1996). *Oh!: Twenty-Seven Stories* (1997). *The Fall of Gravity: A Novel* (2000). *Painting the Dog: The Best Stories of Leon Rooke* (2001).

—DONNA COATES

ADRIEN-EMMANUEL ROUQUETTE (1813–1887). Adrien-Emmanuel Rouquette was born on February 13, 1813, in New Orleans but spent most of his childhood years at his family's home in the woods outside of the city, where he developed his love for solitude, nature, and the Choctaw Indians who lived nearby. After attending schools in New Orleans, Kentucky, and Pennsylvania, he went to France in 1829 and received his baccalaureate from Rennes in 1833. Then he studied law in France and Louisiana, but he abandoned his legal studies in 1839.

His lyric poems *Les Savanes* met with critical success when published simultaneously in Paris and New Orleans in 1841. Soon afterwards, Rouquette decided to enter the priesthood and was ordained in 1845. During the next fourteen years he sought permission to live as a hermit and missionary among the Indians. In 1852 he published his defense of the contemplative, eremitic life, *La Thébaïde*, and became a missionary to the Choctaws in 1859. He won acceptance from the Indians, who called him Chata-Ima (Choctaw-like), a name Rouquette often used to sign his works. An anti-secessionist, he saw the Civil War and postbellum change ruin his efforts to help the Choctaws. Throughout his life he remained close to his brother, François-Dominique Rouquette (1810–1890), the only other important author of French poetry in Louisiana. Rouquette died on July 15, 1887.

His works include an unpublished dictionary of Choctaw; numerous poems, reviews, and essays in periodicals; *Wild Flowers*, his English poems; *L'Antoiniade*, religious and patriotic poems; *La Nouvelle Atala*, a romance; and *Aboo and Caboo*, a pamphlet viciously attacking G. W. Cable's portrayal of the Creoles in *The Grandissimes*. Rouquette's writings reveal a deep love for the Indians and for the simple, primitive life close to nature, a religious mysticism, and a patriotic faith in America.

WORKS: *Les Savanes, poésies americaines* (1841). *Wild Flowers, Sacred Poetry* (1848). *La Thébaïde en Amérique; ou, Apologie de la vie solitaire et contemplative* (1852). *L'Antoniade; ou, La Solitude avec Dieu (trois âges) poème érémitique* (1860). *La Nouvelle Atala; ou, La Fille de L'esprit: Légende indienne* (1879). E. Junius (pseud.), *Critical Dialogue between Aboo and Caboo on a New Book; or, A Grandissime Ascension* (1880).

—ALFRED BENDIXEN

GIBBONS RUARK (1941–). Poet Gibbons Ruark was born in Raleigh, N.C., and grew up in various towns in eastern North Carolina. His mother taught high school Latin before having children; his father was a Methodist (and thus itinerant) minister. Ruark received an A.B. in English from the University of North Carolina at Chapel Hill in 1963 and an M.A. in English from the University of Massachusetts in 1965. From 1965 to 1968 he taught at the University of North Carolina at Greensboro, and in 1968 he joined the English Department of University of Delaware. He lives in Landenberg, Pa., with his wife, Kay, to whom he has been married since 1963; they have two daughters.

Like many contemporary southern poets, Ruark often writes about his family. His father is especially present in his work, and Ruark suggests a deep affection for him (in poems such as "Polio" and "Night Fishing") without approaching the excesses of sentimentality. Among the best poems about other family members are a pair of sonnets to his daughters, "To Emily, Practicing the Clarinet" and "To Jennifer, Singing at the Piano."

One of Ruark's most distinctive characteristics as a poet is his open preoccupation with elegy: among his selected poems are titles such as "Transatlantic Summer Elegy," "Postscript to an Elegy," "Autumn Elegy," "American Elegy," and "Elegiac Anyway." Yet Ruark is hardly a gloomy poet; his poems do not so much mourn loss as seek to redeem it. Equally distinctive is the depth of his feeling for Ireland; he has held two residencies at Annaghmakerrig (the Tyrone Guthrie Centre) in County Monaghan, and many of his poems deal with Irish landscape and culture. His interests in elegy and Ireland dovetail in his poem "The Enniskillen Bombing," which commemorates a 1987 attack by the I.R.A.

Among his awards are a National Arts Council Prize, a Pushcart Prize, and three NEA fellowships.

WORKS: *A Program for Survival* (1971). *Reeds* (1978). *Keeping Company* (1983). *Rescue the Perishing* (1991). *Passing through Customs: New and Selected Poems* (1999).

—ROBERT M. WEST

ROBERT RUARK (1915–1965). Robert Chester Ruark, Jr., was born on December 29, 1915, in Wilmington, N.C., son of Robert Chester Ruark, Sr., and Charlotte Atkins Ruark. He attended school in Wilmington but spent considerable time in and around nearby Southport with his maternal grandfather, from whom he learned about hunting, fishing, and training dogs. At fifteen, he enrolled in the University of North Carolina at Chapel Hill, from which he received an A.B. in journalism in 1935.

After brief stints as a reporter for the *Hamlet (N.C.) News-Messenger* and *Sanford (N.C.) Herald,* Ruark worked for a short time as an accountant with the Works Progress Administration in Washington, D.C., quitting to join the merchant marine. He soon returned to newspaper work, as a copy boy for the *Washington Post* in 1936, then moving to the *Washington Star* before accepting a more satisfying position at the *Washington Daily News*. He produced well-crafted, often confrontational and provocative essays and articles until enlisting as a gunnery officer in the navy during World War II, eventually serving as a press censor in the Pacific. Upon returning to the *Daily News* in 1945, he began a syndicated column, which by 1950 was earning $50,000 annually.

Especially skilled as a lampooner and satirist, Ruark wrote columns, essays, and magazine articles about topics as diverse as southern cooking, psychiatrists, women's fashion, and the state of Texas. His first significant attempt at fiction, the novel *Grenadine Etching,* poked fun at historical romances; it sold over 40,000 copies. Ruark followed it with *Grenadine's Spawn* in 1952. *I Didn't Know It Was Loaded* and *One for the Road,* collections of his columns, also were popular.

Upon the advice of his physician, Ruark stopped writing for a year and traveled to Africa to hunt big game. He returned to Africa frequently. In 1953 he published *Horn of the Hunter: The Story of an African Hunt,* followed in 1955 by *Something of Value,* a novel based on the Mau-Mau uprisings against the British colonialists. The latter earned him over a million dollars in royalties and movie rights.

Now a wealthy man, Ruark purchased a house in Spain, where he wrote five more books, including the autobiographical *The Old Man and the Boy, Poor No More,* and *The Old Man's Boy Grows Older.* Many critics consider *The Old Man and the Boy,* a reminiscence of time spent with his grandfather along the North Carolina coast, Ruark's best book.

Ruark married Virginia Webb, an interior decorator in Washington, D.C., in 1938. By the 1960s, the couple had divorced, and he became engaged to Marilyn Kaytor, a food editor for *Look* magazine. He had no children. He died on July 1, 1965, in London. His remains were returned to Spain and buried near his home there. Ruark's papers and manuscripts are in the Southern Historical Collection at the University of North Carolina at Chapel Hill. In recent years, Southport has hosted a Robert Ruark Festival in the fall. On October 15, 2000, Ruark was inducted into the North Carolina Literary Hall of Fame in Southern Pines.

WORKS: *Grenadine Etching* (1947). *I Didn't Know It Was Loaded* (1948). *One for the Road* (1949). *Grenadine's Spawn* (1952). *Horn of the Hunter* (1953). *Something of Value* (1955). *The Old Man and the Boy* (1957). *Poor No More* (1959). *The Old Man's Boy Grows Older* (1961). *Uhuru* (1962). *The Honey Badger* (1965). *Women* (1967).

—ROBERT G. ANTHONY, JR.

LOUIS D. RUBIN, JR. (1923–). Louis Decimus Rubin, Jr., is the master builder of southern literature as a field of academic study. As editor or co-editor of *Southern Renascence, South: Modern Southern Literature in Its Cultural Setting,* and *The History of Southern Literature;* as the author of more than a score of books of essays, literary biography, literary history, fiction, and memoir; as the teacher of generations of undergraduate and graduate students; as the teacher of many aspiring writers at Hollins College in the 1950s and 1960s; and again as editor of beginning and established writers at the press he founded, Algonquin Books of Chapel Hill, Rubin single-handedly set the agenda and redefined it over a career spanning the second half of the twentieth century.

Rubin's career started in newspaper rooms, moved to American studies when that field had barely begun to generate Ph.D.s, and became synonymous with the English department at the University of North Carolina at Chapel Hill (where he worked with colleagues C. Hugh Holman, Blyden Jackson, and many younger scholars) and with Louisiana State University Press (where he edited the Southern Literary Studies series of critical works and published most of his own foundational books).

Themes that distinguish Rubin's critical work have run steady from the beginning: a trust in the authenticity of experience as lived over the invented or solely imagined, the distinctiveness of lived experience in the South, the superiority of the South's writers and critics over those of any other American region, and the natural necessity for order and continuity in critical and literary historical accounts of southern literary life.

Thomas Wolfe was Rubin's early critical passion. One can hardly name a writer who was so fiercely insistent on the authenticity of experience, the moment of perception, and the thing perceived. The Nashville Agrarians, as intellectual critics, early gave Rubin some difficulty, for he leaned toward the Cash position in *The Mind of the South* that the Agrarian thesis smelled too much of the lamp—that is, Ransom and the other contributors theorized southern experience rather than basing their defense on living it. Gradually, however, Rubin reconciled *I'll Take My Stand* to his own temperament, and wrote introductions to 1962 and 1977 reissues of the 1930 volume.

Rubin's work is marked by a quest for continuities. Themes such as small town and rural life, the hunt, race relations, and the deracination of man in modern, urban concentrations knit his works into a whole. His monumental *The History of Southern Literature* strives to periodize and thematize a vast array of southern writers from the obscure to the household name, and to do so by employing multiple individual contributors. Thus, southern literary study as a field is both announced and arranged by rank from general editors to section editors to authors of headnotes to individual writers.

In addition to his scholarly writing, Rubin has written novels and essays on such diverse topics as baseball and boat building. After his retirement from UNC, Rubin has delved into autobiography—first with an account of his career as a newspaperman, *An Honorable Estate: My Time in the Working Press*, and then with *My Father's People: A Family of Southern Jews*, a memoir of the generation of his father's family, Jews in Charleston, S.C., at the turn of the century.

WORKS: Ed., *Southern Renascence: The Literature of the Modern South*, with Robert Jacobs (1953). *Thomas Wolfe: The Weather of His Youth* (1955). Ed., *The Lasting South: Fourteen Southerners Look at Their Home*, with James J. Kilpatrick (1957). Ed., *Teach the Freeman: The Correspondence of Rutherford B. Hayes and the Slater Fund for Negro Education* (1959). *The Golden Weather* (1961). Ed., *South: Modern Southern Literature in Its Cultural Setting*, with Robert Jacobs (1961). *The Faraway Country: Writers of the Modern South* (1963). *The Curious Death of the Novel: Essays in American Literature* (1967). *The Teller in the Tale* (1967). Ed., *The Hollins Poets* (1967) .*A Bibliographic Guide to the Study of Southern Literature* (1969). *George Washington Cable: The Life and Times of a Southern Heretic* (1969). *The Writer in the South: Studies in Literary Community* (1972). *William Elliott Shoots a Bear: Essays on the Southern Literary Imagination* (1975). *Virginia: A Bicentennial History* (1977). *The Wary Fugitives: Four Poets and the South* (1978). Ed., *The Literary South* (1979). Ed., *Southern Writers: A Biographical Dictionary* , edited with Robert Bain and Joseph M. Flora (1979). *The American South: Portrait of a Culture* (1980). *Surfaces of a Diamond* (1981). *A Gallery of Southerners* (1982). Gen. ed., *The History of Southern Literature* (1985). *The Edge of the Swamp: A Study of the Literature and Society of the Old South* (1989). *Mockingbird in the Gum Tree: A Literary Gallimaufry* (1990). *The Heat of the Sun* (1995). Ed., *A Writer's Companion*, with Jerry Leath Mills (1995). *Babe Ruth's Ghost and Other Historical and Literary Speculations* (1996). *An Honorable Estate: My Time in the Working Press* (2001). *My Father's People: A Family of Southern Jews* (2002). *Where the Southern Cross the Yellow Dog: On Writers and Writing* (2005).

—MICHAEL KREYLING

ROWLAND RUGELEY (ca. 1735–1776). Little is known about Rowland Rugeley's life. His exact year of birth is uncertain but is believed to have been 1735. He emigrated from England to South Carolina sometime around 1766, prior to which he published a volume of *Miscellaneous Poems and Translations from La Fontaine and Others* in London and made frequent contributions to the British magazines.

Local records indicate that in 1766 Rugeley purchased a large tract of land on the banks of the Ashley River near Charleston. A contemporary diary describes him as a "merchant" and mentions that he had three brothers and three sisters, also of Charleston. Rugeley died of unknown causes in the autumn of 1776, possibly from the same epidemic that killed his wife and youngest child a few weeks later. A death notice in the *South Carolina and American General Gazette* states that he was an honest man and a jovial companion whose poetry was "very generally admired" and entitled him to "some Rank in the Literary World."

Rugeley is perhaps best remembered today as the author of *The Story of Aeneas and Dido Burlesqued: From the Fourth Book of the Aeneid of Virgil*. This lively parody of Virgil written in the tradition of Paul Scarron and Charles Cotton was printed in Charleston by Robert Wells. It is the first classical burlesque written in America, and it reveals that Rugeley was a man of uncommon learning and.

WORKS: *Miscellaneous Poems and Translations from La Fontaine and Others* (1763). *The Story of Aeneas and Dido Burlesqued: From the Fourth Book of the Aeneid of Virgil* (1774).

—JAMES A. LEVERNIER

IRWIN RUSSELL (1853–1879). The son of a physician and a women's college teacher, Irwin Russell was born on June 3, 1853, in Port Gibson, Miss. Following a temporary relocation to St. Louis, the Russells returned to Port Gibson as the Civil War was breaking out. Irwin attended school in town and earned his baccalaureate, with distinction, in 1869 at the University of St. Louis; studied law; and began to practice when he was only nineteen. He read Milton, Burns, and the English Romantics as a youth, but was also drawn to the personal stories and language patterns of former African American slaves. Russell bought a small hand press and began to write plays and poetry, increasingly the focus of his short life. Starting in 1871, Russell published poems, including African American dialect verse, in *Scribner's Monthly* and other national magazines. His most famous work was a 246-line operetta, "Christmas-Night in the Quarters" (*Scribner's*, 1878). A white narrator frames the events while four African Americans—a wagon driver, fiddle player, banjo picker, and preacher—contribute to the festivities at Uncle Johnny Booker's holiday ball.

Russell tried to pursue a literary career in New York and in New Orleans, but depression, alcoholism, and physical exhaustion, made more severe by helping his father nurse yellow fever patients in 1878, ruined his health. He was only twenty-six when he died from pneumonia in New Orleans, on December 23, 1879.

Russell left his mark on American dialect literature, and is part of an influential white nineteenth-century southern local color movement that sought to represent African American experience and expression to a largely white readership. Earlier in the century, William Gilmore Simms, Harriet Beecher Stowe, and Stephen Foster contributed to the southern local color dialect tradition that Russell helped promulgate. In the next century, fellow Mississippian William Faulkner owned an edition of Russell's poems.

Joel Chandler Harris was particularly indebted to Russell, praised his work in an appreciative letter to Russell's sister, and wrote an introduction to the 1888 edition of thirty-one of his poems—including poetry in Irish and Scots brogue—that was also reprinted in the expanded 1917 edition of forty poems. Scholars and critics will continue to debate the cultural validity of Russell's and other white writers' representations of African American experience.

WORKS: *Poems by Irwin Russell* (1888; enl. 1917).

—R. BRUCE BICKLEY, JR.

ARCHIBALD RUTLEDGE (1883–1973). Archibald Hamilton Rutledge, first poet laureate of South Carolina, was born on October 23, 1883, in McClellanville, S.C., the son of Henry Middleton and Margaret Hamilton Rutledge. His ancestors included a chief justice of the Supreme Court, a signer of the Declaration of Independence, and a governor of South Carolina. He was educated at Porter Military Academy in Charleston and Union College in New York. In the period from 1904 until his retirement in 1937, he taught in and became head of the English department at Mercersburg Academy in Pennsylvania. In 1907 he married Florence Louise Hart. They had three sons—Archibald, Jr., Henry Middleton, and Irvine Hart. Florence Louise died in 1934, and in 1936 Rutledge married Alice Lucas, a childhood sweetheart.

Beloved by his admirers, Rutledge received many tributes to his literary efforts: seventeen honorary degrees and more than thirty medals, including the John Burroughs Medal for nature writing, election to the American Society of Arts and Letters, and appointment in 1934 as poet laureate of South Carolina.

In most of his writing, Rutledge applauds the beauties and traditions of Hampton Plantation, the Rutledge ancestral home built in 1730. His poetry is reminiscent of the lyricists of the Old South—

Simms, Wilde, and Pinkney. His short stories and personal essays recount his hunting, appreciation of nature, and experiences with relatives and friends. Most of his more than one thousand poems and articles contributed to popular magazines and literary journals later appeared in book form.

After his retirement, Rutledge returned permanently to South Carolina, continued to write, and restored the old Hampton Plantation, part of which he deeded to the state in 1970. He died on September 15, 1973, a few miles from Hampton at Summer Place, the log house retreat in which he had been born.

WORKS: *The Heart's Quest* (1904). *Under the Pines and Other Poems* (1906). *The Banners of the Coast* (1908). *Spirit of Mercersburg* (1909). *New Poems* (1915). *Tom and I on the Old Plantation* (1918). *Songs from a Valley* (1919). *Old Plantation Days* (1921). *Plantation Game Trails* (1921). *South of Richmond* (1923). *Days Off in Dixie* (1924). *Heart of the South* (1924). *Collected Poems* (1925). *A Monarch of the Sky* (1926). *Children of Swamp and Wood* (1927). *Life's Extras* (1928). *Bolio and Other Dogs* (1930). *The Flower of Hope* (1930). *Peace in the Heart* (1930). *Veiled Eros* (1933). *When Boys Go Off to School* (1935). *Wild Life of the South* (1935). *Brimming Chalice* (1936). *An American Hunter* (1937). *It Will Be Daybreak Soon* (1938). *The Sonnets of Archibald Rutledge* (1938). *Rain on the Marsh* (1940). *Christ Is God* (1941). *Home by the River* (1941). *Love's Meaning* (1943). *Hunter's Choice* (1946). *The Beauty of the Night* (1947). *God's Children* (1947). *The Angel Standing; or, Faith Alone Gives Poise* (1948). *The Everlasting Light and Other Poems* (1949). *A Wildwood Tale: A Drama of the Open* (1950). *Beauty in the Heart* (1953). *The Heart's Citadel and Other Poems* (1953). *Brimming Tide and Other Poems* (1954). *Those Were the Days* (1955). *Bright Angel and Other Poems* (1956). *Santee Paradise* (1956). *From the Hills to the Sea: Fact and Legend of the Carolinas* (1958). *Deep River: The Complete Poems of Archibald Rutledge* (1960; rev. 1966). *The World around Hampton* (1960). *The Ballad of the Howling Hound and Other Poems* (1965). *Willie Was a Lady* (1966). *How Wild Was My Village* (1969). *I Hear America Singing* (1970). *Poems in Honor of South Carolina's Tricentennial* (1970). *The Woods and Wild Things I Remember* (1970). *Voices of the Long Ago: Bible Stories Retold* (1973). *Hunting and Home in the Heartland: The Best of Archibald Rutledge* (1992). *Tales of Whitetails: Rutledge's Great Deer Hunting Stories* (1992). *America's Greatest Game Bird: Archibald Rutledge's Turkey-Hunting Tales* (1994). *Bird Dog Days, Wingshooting Ways* (1998).

—HAROLD WOODELL

ABRAM RYAN (1838–1886). In the words of one of his contemporaries, Abram Joseph Ryan was characterized by "the dreamy mysticism of the poet . . . which marked him off from all other men." In many respects he was indeed an anomaly. Born of Irish Catholic stock and educated largely in the North, he was redoubtably southern in his loyalties. The long-haired poet-priest wrote poems haunted with loss and redeemed by faith.

Part of the mystery of Abram Ryan inheres in his birthplace, because many of his devotees thought of him as "Irish" and thus Irish-born. The weight of the evidence suggests that he was born in Hagerstown, Md., on February 5, 1838. He was ordained in the evangelically oriented Vincentian Order on September 12, 1860. Never commissioned, he served as an unofficial chaplain for the Confederate army—going AWOL from the Vincentians, as it were—and contemporaneous sources corroborate his presence at the defeat at Missionary Ridge, while rumors place him at many other battles.

The war crushed Ryan. After his brother was slain in action he penned "In Memory of My Brother" and "In Memoriam." Father Ryan was born for causes, and he raised "Erin's Flag" alongside "The Sword of Robert Lee." (When Ryan's niece was asked who killed Christ, she reportedly replied, "O yes I know, the Yankees.") Of his widely circulated poems, "March of the Deathless Dead" won widespread acclaim. Ryan's preeminent "The Conquered Banner," which was "read or sung in every Southern household," in an oft-repeated blurb from one of Ryan's eulogists, remains an important fixture in anthologies of Confederate literature. It has resurfaced recently in Confederate flag debates. Ryan has a cameo as a character in Margaret Mitchell's *Gone with the Wind*. In reality, he shared the stage with

Jefferson Davis and General P. G. T. Beauregard on separate occasions, and baptized General James Longstreet after he was shunned by southerners who deemed him a scalawag.

Remarkably peripatetic for his day, Ryan served many churches before settling down at St. Mary's parish in Mobile, Ala. He edited the *Banner of the South* and later a Catholic weekly, the *Morning Star and Catholic Messenger*. He died while visiting the Franciscan monastery in Louisville, Ky., and his remains were returned to his beloved Mobile.

Ryan's poems show their age, but a few commentators have urged that they are considerably subtler—within conventional limits—than they appear. Once anthologized alongside Lanier, Poe, and Timrod, Ryan's efforts to literally sacralize the Lost Cause little endear him to contemporary academic opinion. But as he wrote of "hearts that are great," "Earth knows a little—God, the rest."

WORKS: *Father Ryan's Poems* (1879). *Poems, Patriotic, Religious, and Miscellaneous* (1880). *A Crown for Our Queen* (1882). *A Catholic Convention of One* (1886). *Selected Poems of Father Ryan*, ed. Gordon Weaver (1973).

—BRYAN GIEMZA

KALAMU YA SALAAM (1947–). Born Vallery Ferdinand III in New Orleans on March 24, 1947, to Vallery and Inola Copelin Ferdinand, Kalamu ya Salaam (Kiswahili for "Pen of Peace") has enjoyed an immensely varied career as a poet, essayist, dramatist, performing artist, film maker, disc jockey, music producer, promoter, critic, and self-titled "neo-griot." Salaam's wide-ranging activities have been directed toward promoting minority and women's rights and effecting social change. As early as junior high school, Salaam was active with the NAACP and CORE in registering voters and participating in civil rights protests. After graduating from high school in 1964, he attended Carleton College before serving in the U.S. Army from 1965 to 1968. He briefly returned to Carleton before matriculating to Southern University of New Orleans, but was dismissed for participation in student demonstrations. Salaam then took an associate's degree in business from Delgado Community College in New Orleans.

During his college years in New Orleans, Salaam worked in various capacities with Tom Dent and other emerging writers at the Free Southern Theater. The FST's performing ensemble BLKART-SOUTH published Salaam's first book and produced a number of his one-act plays, including "The Picket," "Mama," "Happy Birthday, Jesus," "Black Liberation Army," "Homecoming," and "Black Love Song." Salaam was a founding member of *The Black Collegian* magazine in 1970 and became its editor-at-large in 1983. In 1973 he helped found Ahidiana, a Pan-African nationalist organization that was active until 1984 in promoting the arts, publishing books on human rights (Salaam's among them), and running a school for preschool children. Salaam served as the executive director of the New Orleans Jazz and Heritage Festival from 1983 to 1987.

Inspired by Langston Hughes and poets of the 1960s Black Arts movement, Salaam uses jazz and blues forms in his plays and poems; he created a spoken-word CD, *My Story, My Song*, in 1997. Perhaps most noted as a music critic, he has penned the program books for several jazz festivals and other agencies, and he has won two awards for excellence in writing about music from the American Society for Composers and Publishers. Salaam's written works have been published in a wide variety of journals and anthologies, though now his primary interest lies in electronic media. Salaam is the founder of the NOMMO Literary Society, a creative-writing workshop, and is also a founder of Runagate Multimedia, Inc. He currently leads WordBand, a poetry performance ensemble, and he teaches radio production and digital video workshops for high school students. In 2004 his short story "Alabama" received a Southeastern Science Fiction Award. With his wife, Tayari kwa Salaam (with whom he collaborated on two books for children), and five children, Salaam made his home in New Orleans.

Displaced by Hurricane Katrina in 2005, he created "Listen to the People," a project aiming to collect firsthand accounts of people who experienced that devastating storm and its aftermath.

WORKS: *The Blues Merchant: Songs for Blkfolk*, as Vallery Ferdinand III (1969). *Hofu Ni Kwenu: My Fear Is for You* (1973). *Pamoja Tutashinda: Together We Will Win* (1974). *Ibura* (1976). *Tearing the Roof off the Sucker: The Fall of South Africa* (1977). *South African Showdown: Divestment Now* (1978). *Nuclear Power and the Black Liberation Struggle* (1978). *Revolutionary Love* (1978). *Who Will Speak for Us? New African Folk Tales*, with Tayari kwa Salaam (1978). *Herufi: An Alphabet Reader*, with Tayari kwa Salaam (1978). *Iron Flowers: A Poetic Report on a Visit to Haiti* (1979). *Our Women Keep Our Skies from Falling* (1980). *Our Music Is No Accident* (1987). *A Nation of Poets* (1989). Ed., *WORD UP: Black Poetry of the Eighties from the Deep South* (1990). *What Is Life? A Reclamation of the Black Blues* (1994). Ed., *Fertile Ground: Memoirs and Visions*, with Kysha N. Brown (1996). *Tarzan Can-Not Return to Africa But I Can* (1996). *He's the Prettiest: A Tribute to Big Chief Allison "Tootie" Montana's Fifty Years of Mardi Gras Indian Suiting* (1997). Ed., *From a Bend in the River: One Hundred New Orleans Poets* (1998). Ed., *360: A Revolution of Black Poets* (1998). *The Magic of Juju: An Appreciation of the Black Arts Movement* (1998).

—PETER J. FLORA

EMMA SPEED SAMPSON (1868–1947). The great-granddaughter of George Keats, brother of poet John Keats, Emma Speed Sampson was born on December 1, 1868, at Chatsworth, a farm just outside Louisville, Ky., and spent part of her youth in nearby Shelbyville. She later studied art at the Art Students League in New York and with Charles Lazar in Paris. She taught for a time in Louisville before marrying Henry Aylett Sampson in 1896. After living in various parts of America, the Sampsons moved to Richmond, Va., which became their permanent home.

Shortly after settling in Richmond, the Sampsons were joined by Emma's sister, Nell Speed, who was completing her fourth novel, featuring a college undergraduate named Molly Brown. Nell Speed knew that she was dying, so she convinced her sister to continue the series of books. Thus, at age forty-five, Emma Speed Sampson wrote her first book. This juvenile novel, *Molly Brown's Post-Graduate Days* (1914), was ultimately followed by three more titles in the same series. During the early years of her career, Sampson, using the name of her sister, which had been willed to her, wrote several volumes in the "Tucker Twins" and "Carter Girls" series.

When a fellow author found that these books were required to run 50,000 words but commanded only $200, she admonished Sampson to change publishers. She wrote to Reilly & Lee, the Chicago firm that had published Frances Boyd Calhoun's *Miss Minerva and William Green Hill* (1909). They suggested that she write a sequel to this best-seller, and two months later she complied with *Billy and the Major*. The manuscript was accepted by return mail and was published under Sampson's own name. It was the first of eleven volumes she wrote as continuations of the prototype.

After her husband's death in 1920, Sampson's career became varied. She continued to write—additional "Miss Minerva" titles, an undetermined number of "Campfire Girl" books, several non-series novels, and two "Priscilla" novels for girls (written in collaboration with her daughter, Emma Keats). She continued the "Mary Louise" series that had been begun by L. Frank Baum under the name of Mrs. Edith Van Dyne. She also served for several years on the Virginia board of motion picture censors and was a staff writer for the *Richmond Times-Dispatch*. Sampson died on May 7, 1947.

WORKS: *Billy and the Major* (1918). *Mammy's White Folks* (1919). *Miss Minerva's Baby* (1920). *The Shorn Lamb* (1922). *Miss Minerva on the Old Plantation* (1923). *The Comings of Cousin Ann* (1923). *Masquerading Mary* (1924). *Miss Minerva Broadcasts Billy* (1925). *Miss Minerva's Scallywags* (1927). *Miss Minerva's Neighbors* (1929). *The Spite Fence* (1929). *Miss Minerva's Cook Book* (1931). *Miss Minerva's Goin' Places* (1931). *Miss Minerva's Mystery* (1933). *Miss Minerva's Problem* (1936). *Miss Minerva's Vacation* (1939).

—WELFORD DUNAWAY TAYLOR

FERROL SAMS (1922–). Although well past retirement age, Ferrol Aubrey Sams, Jr., continues to practice medicine and is medical director of the Fayette Medical Clinic in Fayetteville, Ga. He was born on September 26, 1922, at the family homestead in Fayette County, Ga., where his father, F. A. Sams, Sr., was school superintendent. Sambo, as his father nicknamed him and as he is still widely known, attended public schools. He was among thirty-eight graduates of the class of 1938 at Fayetteville High School and was class president and valedictorian. Sams entered Mercer University in Macon, Ga., as a pre-med major. A member of Kappa Alpha fraternity, he also earned membership in Sigma Mu, Mercer's equivalent of Phi Beta Kappa, but chose not to join because the ten-dollar fee was prohibitive during the Depression. Ferrol entered Atlanta's Emory University School of Medicine immediately upon graduation in 1942, but he left to join the U.S. Army Medical Corps, serving as a surgical technician at field hospitals in France. In 1946 he returned to his medical studies at Emory, where he met and married, in 1948, fellow medical student Helen Fletcher. After graduation in 1951 they started a clinic in Fayetteville. They have four children and numerous grandchildren.

At age fifty-eight, the busy doctor began to write, using the materials of his life in rural Georgia for the novel *Run with the Horsemen*. Published in 1982, it was a best-seller in Atlanta for an unprecedented twenty-two weeks. The story of Porter Osborne, Jr., unfolded in a second novel, *The Whisper of the River*, as Sams looked back on his college days at Mercer. His fans had to wait until 1991 for the final novel in the lively, often hilarious, autobiographical trilogy. *When All the World Was Young* recounts Porter's medical school training and his medical service during World War II.

Since 1991 Sams has taught creative writing at Emory. The recipient of numerous awards, including the D.Litt. from Mercer, Emory, Medical University of South Carolina, and Rhodes College, in 1991 he received the Townsend Prize for fiction. He is in great demand as a speaker and donates all honoraria to the Early Years Program for challenged children.

WORKS: *Run with the Horsemen* (1982). *The Whisper of the River* (1984). *Christmas Gift!* (1989). *The Widow's Mite and Other Stories* (1989). *The Passing: Stories* (1990). *When All the World Was Young* (1991). *Epiphany* (1994).

—LINDA WELDEN

DORI SANDERS (1934–). When Louis D. Rubin, Jr., and Shannon Ravenel conspired to establish Algonquin Books of Chapel Hill, one of their goals was to publish books by unknown southern writers whose work would likely be overlooked by publishers in the Northeast. Dori Sanders was one of the beneficiaries of that vision. She was fifty-six years old when Algonquin published *Clover*, her first novel. (Algonquin rejected her first manuscript, but saw the promise and encouraged her to write about what she knew.) *Clover* charmed a host of readers, and Sanders's career as writer was launched, giving encouragement to older women that their stories matter and could find an audience. Sanders's fame grew further after *Clover* was adapted for television.

Sanders's work has encouraged readers to find hope for racial healing and to glimpse the rural world of African Americans. Clover is a ten-year-old black farm girl whose widowed father has married a white woman. He dies in a car accident on his wedding day, and wife and daughter build a life together in the black community. *Her Own Place*, Sanders's second novel, depicts a determined black mother who successfully raises her five children after being abandoned by her husband. After the children are grown, she leaves the farm (bought with money she had earned) and becomes the first black volunteer at the local hospital, successfully making her way among the white workers there. *Dori Sanders' Country Cooking: Recipes and Stories from the Family Farm Stand* shares accounts of her family and affirms the rural life as experienced by Sanders and other African Americans.

A lifelong peach farmer, Dorinda Sanders was born in 1934 on a farm near Filbert, S.C., eighth of the ten children of Marion Sylvester and Cazetta Sylvia Patton Sanders. Her father, a high school principal, had used his earnings to buy the farm that is still home and central to Dori Sanders's life. After their parents' deaths, Dori and her brother Orestus inherited the farm, which has prospered and grown under their care, and Dori continues to sell produce at their roadside stand, gathering stories all the while.

After graduation from Roosevelt High in Clover, S.C., Sanders tried community college for a year, but seems never to have wanted to leave the farming life. Early on, she was taking jobs elsewhere during winter season. She also wrote stories on scraps of paper. An early marriage failed.

Sanders's papers are part of the South Caroliniana Society Manuscripts at the University of South Carolina in Columbia.

WORKS: *Clover* (1990). *Her Own Place* (1993). *Dori Sanders' Country Cooking: Recipes and Stories from the Family Farm Stand* (1995).

—JOSEPH M. FLORA

GEORGE SANDYS (1578–1644). Sandys was an English traveler, poet, colonist, and early foreign service career officer. The seventh and youngest son of Edwin Sandys, archbishop of York, he was born near York, on March 2, 1578. He studied at St. Mary's Hall, Oxford, and Corpus Christi College and in 1596 was admitted to the Middle Temple. Probably about two years later he married Elizabeth Norton, his father's ward. By 1606 the marriage had ended in permanent separation.

In May 1610, Sandys set out on the travels described in *A Relation of a Journey begun An: Dom: 1610,* which went through nine editions during the seventeenth century and was used as source material by Francis Bacon, Thomas Browne, Milton, and other writers. Sandys returned home in March 1612, and was active in the companies established for colonization in America. His brother, Sir Edwin Sandys, had been instrumental in drawing Virginia Company's charter (1609), and George had been a member of the company since 1607. In July 1621 he accompanied his nephew-in-law, the governor, Sir Francis Wyatt, to Virginia as its first resident treasurer and director of industry and agriculture, continuing in these duties when the crown took over government of the colony in 1624. On his return to England (1625), Sandys was made a gentleman of the king's privy chamber. For about fifteen years he was a member of various committees administering the colonies and, finally (1640), agent for the Virginia colony.

On his voyage to, and while in, the New World, Sandys completed a translation of Ovid's *Metamorphoses,* published in 1626. In 1632 he brought out a revised edition that was expanded to include commentaries from numerous other classical authors and many allusions to the Virginia the author had known. On this work, composed in remarkably compressed heroic couplets, Sandys's poetic fame largely rests. His later and less well-known works reflect his interest in theology. Sandys's last years were spent in London, in Oxfordshire with the Falkland circle at Great Tew, and in Kent with Sir Francis Wyatt at Boxley Abbey, where he died in March 1644, being buried at Boxley Church on March 7.

WORKS: *A Relation of a Journey begun An: Dom: 1610. Four Books containing a description of the Turkish Empire, of Egypt, the Holy Land, of the Remote Parts of Italy, and Islands adjoyning* (1615). Trans., Ovid, *Metamorphoses* (1626, 1632). *A Paraphrase upon the Psalmes of David* (1636). *A paraphrase upon the Divine Poems* (1638). Trans., Grotius, *Christus Patiens,* as *Christ's Passion* (1640). *A Paraphrase upon the Song of Solomon* (1641). *The Poetical Works of George Sandys,* 2 vols., ed. Richard Hopper (1872).

—RICHARD BEALE DAVIS

ELISE SANGUINETTI (1926–). Novelist, reporter, reviewer, and columnist Elise Sanguinetti confronted a South conflicted over its racial codes. Her novels contain a wide diversity of characters who struggle to reestablish their sense of identity in the wake of shifting social mores, selective ideals and memories, and defensive stances against popular prejudices about southerners.

Sanguinetti was born Edel Elise Ayers on January 26, 1926, in Anniston, Ala., to Harry Mell and Edel Ytterboe Ayers, publishers of the *Anniston Star* and other newspapers (Sanguinetti's brother, H. Brandt Ayers, serves as publisher and editor of the *Anniston Star;* her husband, Phillip A. Sanguinetti, is the newspaper's president). Sanguinetti spent her freshman college year at St. Olaf College and then took her degree at the University of Alabama, where she studied writing under Hudson Strode; she later briefly attended the University of Oslo in Norway. Being born to a family of newspaper publishers, traveling widely, and living "in the North" with her husband during the early civil rights skirmishes provided Sanguinetti the various perspectives that inform her best-known novel, *The Last of the Whitfields,* developed from her 1960 short story "To You, Frère Twig," originally published in *Mademoiselle* magazine. Often compared favorably to Harper Lee's *To Kill a Mockingbird,* the novel features a coming-of-age story whose protagonist worries about what social advancement she and her brother might be able enjoy in spite of the perceived stigma of being southern. Though Sanguinetti denies that the novel is autobiographic, it illustrates the pervasive confusion she witnessed at the time, as she notes in a 1986 introduction: "Somewhere along the way it occurred to me that we did not know each other. Neither black nor white, nor South and North."

After completing three other novels, *The New Girl* (a sequel to *Whitfields*), *The Dowager* (the title of which refers to Charleston, S.C.), and *McBee's Station,* Sanguinetti focused her energies on her family's publishing enterprises and became an active proponent of Alabama's literary scene.

WORKS: *The Last of the Whitfields* (1962). *The New Girl* (1964). *The Dowager* (1968). *McBee's Station* (1971).

—THOMAS ALAN HOLMES

HERBERT RAVENEL SASS (1884–1958). Novelist, journalist, historian, and naturalist, Herbert Ravenel Sass was born in Charleston, S.C., on November 2, 1884. From his family Sass inherited a lifelong interest in literature, nature, and history, especially the history of South Carolina. His father, George Herbert Sass, was the famous Confederate poet known under the pen name of Barton Grey. His mother, Anna Eliza Ravenel Sass, was the daughter of Harriott Horry Rutledge Ravenel, a distinguished South Carolina writer and wife of Dr. St. Julien Ravenel, the noted scientist and inventor.

Sass was educated at the College of Charleston, where he received a B.A. in 1905, M.A. in 1906, and an honorary Litt.D. in 1922. After graduating from college Sass worked as assistant director of the Charleston Museum. Upon his father's death in 1908 he joined the staff of the *Charleston News and Courier,* where he worked as city editor and later assistant editor until 1924, when he resigned from journalism to pursue a full-time career in freelance writing. As a freelance writer Sass contributed numerous articles, essays, and short stories to the *Saturday Evening Post, Country Gentleman, National Geographic, Collier's, Harper's, Cornhill,* the *Atlantic Monthly,* the *Saturday Review,* and *Good Housekeeping,* among many others. He also wrote several novels and book-length essays.

In later life Sass's concern for the future of South Carolina led him to write more exclusively about its history and politics. He died at his home in Charleston on February 18, 1958, after a lengthy illness.

WORKS: *The Way of the Wild* (1925). *Adventures in Green Places* (1926; enl. 1935). *Gray Eagle* (1927). *War Drums* (1928). *On the Wings of a Bird* (1929). *Look Back to Glory* (1933). Intro., William Smith, *Old Charleston* (1933).

A Carolina Rice Plantation of the Fifties, with Alice R. Huger Smith (1936). *Fort Sumter,* with DuBose Heyward (1938). *Hear Me, My Chiefs!* (1940). *Emperor Brims* (1941). *Charleston Grows* (1949). *Outspoken: 150 Years of the News and Courier* (1953). *The Story of the South Carolina Lowcountry* (1956).

—JAMES A. LEVERNIER

LYLE SAXON (1891–1946). Born in Baton Rouge, La., on September 4, 1891, to Hugh and Katherine Chambers Saxon, Lyle Saxon became one of the more notable men of letters in Louisiana. For his literary and architectural preservation efforts in the French Quarter, he became known as "Mr. New Orleans." After receiving his B.A. from Louisiana State University in 1912, he worked as a reporter in Chicago. In 1918 he came to the *New Orleans Item* and later to the *Times-Picayune,* where he was a feature writer until 1926. Associated with the *Double Dealer,* he contributed stories and articles to magazines and won the O. Henry Memorial Award in 1926; his work was included in *O'Brien's Best Short Stories* in 1927. Not married, he lived in the Vieux Carré of New Orleans, where William Faulkner, Sherwood Anderson, and Roark Bradford were visitors to his home. He later resided at Melrose Plantation in Natchitoches Parish and then at the now-demolished St. Charles Hotel in New Orleans.

His only novel, *Children of Strangers,* reflecting his experience at Melrose Plantation, explores the lives of African Americans in and about the Cane River country. Saxon focuses on Famie, a beautiful mulatto girl who has just turned sixteen. The novel begins at Easter in 1905 and concludes on an ironic note as he punctures some of the illusions that many whites had held about Americans of African descent.

Most of Saxon's writing is nonfiction. In 1927 *Father Mississippi* examined in part a child's (his own) growing up on a river plantation. A year later *Fabulous New Orleans* presented a series of descriptive impressions and stories. In 1929 Saxon finished *Old Louisiana,* a realistic account of plantation life. His biography of the pirate Jean Lafitte was published in 1930. As director of the Federal Writers' Project in Louisiana, he edited the *New Orleans City Guide,* published in 1938, and *A Collection of Folk Tales: Gumbo Ya-Ya,* published by the Folklore Society in 1945. He also coordinated the compilation of the Louisiana section of the "American Guide" series. His colleagues included Edward Dreyer and Robert Tallant. As part of the Federal Writers' Project, he worked with African American Marcus Christian on the Dillard Project, the writing of a history of African Americans in Louisiana. Saxon died on April 9, 1946, with the manuscript of *The Friends of Joe Gilmore* unfinished.

WORKS: *Father Mississippi* (1927). *Fabulous New Orleans* (1928). *Old Louisiana* (1929). *Lafitte the Pirate* (1930). *Children of Strangers* (1937). *New Orleans City Guide* (1938). *A Collection of Louisiana Folk Tales: Gumbo Ya-Ya* (1945). *The Friends of Joe Gilmore* (1948).

—THOMAS BONNER, JR.

GEORGE SCARBROUGH (1915–). Sharecropper's son, farmer, teacher, essayist, novelist, always poet, George Addison Scarbrough has created a niche for himself in Appalachian literature. Born on October 15, 1915, in a clapboard cabin in Patty, Tenn., George was the third of seven children. His father, William Oscar, was an itinerant farmer; his mother, Louise Anabel McDowell, taught her son to read at an early age, using newspapers that insulated the walls of hand-me-down houses sharecroppers called home. His position is not as child of hills and hollows, but of the croplands of native Polk County, always in the mountain's shadow. From this place Scarbrough has—through one novel and five volumes of verse—drawn imagery and found fascination with multiple generations populating Tennessee's southeastern corner.

Scarbrough attended the University of Tennessee at Knoxville, later received the first-ever literary scholarship to the University of the South, and completed his undergraduate degree at Lincoln Memorial University. He earned the M.A., with a creative thesis, at Knoxville. Scarbrough has enjoyed a remarkable career, garnering attention at age twenty-five with fourteen poems in the *Sewanee Review,* and in ensuing decades by publishing in more than seventy journals. Most recent endeavors have involved an ancient Chinese poet, Han Shan, as alter ego. The deeply personal poems are marked by local landscape: Scarbrough's Han Shan could as easily live on Chilhowee as Cold Mountain. The poems have been well received. *Poetry* published nine Han Shan poems, three of which earned the 2000 Hoken Prize. Among his many accolades, the Fellowship of Southern Writers honored Scarbrough with the 2001 James Still Award for Writing of the Appalachian South. In his unpublished journals Scarbrough wrote, "To make an art for a county on the rim of a rock has been all my intent." His contribution to Appalachian literature is an expansion of the region beyond regionalism by making it larger than itself and more universal, and by creating, from its natural beauty and people, true art.

WORKS: *Tellico Blue* (1949). *The Course Is Upward* (1951). *Summer So-Called* (1956). *New and Selected Poems* (1977). *A Summer Ago* (1986). *Invitation to Kim,* ed. Phyllis Tickle (1989).

—RANDY MACKIN

JANET SCHAW (ca. 1739–post-1778). Adventurous, observant, and witty, Janet Schaw, a Scottish gentlewoman, has gained renown for her epistolary journal recording her travels from Scotland to the British West Indies, North Carolina, and Portugal between 1774 and 1776. Her journal was unknown until the twentieth century, when a researcher in the British Museum accidentally discovered her manuscript, cataloged by the not entirely accurate title *Journal of a Lady of a Voyage from Scotland to the West Indies and South Carolina, with an account of personal experiences during the War of Independence and a visit to Lisbon on her return 25 October 1774–December 1775.* The British Museum manuscript is one of three handwritten copies in existence, the other two being copies owned by Mr. Vere Langford Oliver, a historian of Antiqua, and Colonel R. H. Vetch, a relative of the Schaws and Rutherfords. The original manuscript has not yet been found.

Because the lives of most women in the eighteenth century were not a matter of public record, little is known about Janet Schaw. She was born in Lauriston, a suburb of Edinburgh, Scotland, around 1739. She was one of six children of Gideon and Anne Rutherford Schaw. Their family was distinguished; indeed, Janet was the third cousin once removed of Sir Walter Scott. She was obviously well read, for in her journal she refers to the works of Shakespeare, Jonathan Swift, and William Cowper, as well as to the Bible. Janet was somewhere between thirty-five and forty when she traveled from Leith, Scotland, to the West Indies to accompany her brother Alexander to his new home there and then to visit her brother Robert in North Carolina. There is no record that she ever married.

Janet Schaw's journal is most valuable for its lively style and its vivid capturing of the joys and vicissitudes of sea voyages, plantation life in Antiqua and St. Christopher, and pre-Revolutionary activities in the Cape Fear region.

WORKS: *Journal of a Lady of Quality: Being the Narrative of a Journey from Scotland to the West Indies, North Carolina, and Portugal, in the Years 1774 to 1776,* ed. Evangeline Walker Andrews and Charles M. Andrew (1921).

—LYNNE P. SHACKELFORD

ROBERT SCHENKKAN (1953–). Robert Schenkkan, Jr., was born on March 19, 1953, in Chapel Hill, N.C., to Robert Frederic Schenkkan, a writer and television executive, and Jean Schenkkan. He attended the University of Texas at Austin and received his B.A. in 1975. He made his professional stage debut in Chicago that year. Already decided on a stage career, he enrolled in the creative writing program at Cornell, leaving with an M.F.A. in 1977.

Schenkkan established himself as a playwright in the 1980s with a series of plays, primarily one-acts, produced at regional theaters and Off-Broadway. He married the actress Mary Anne Dorward in 1984. Financial struggles had forced him to move west to Los Angeles, and his work as an actor in film and television, though never his primary focus, garnered him his greatest public exposure through his role on *Star Trek: The Next Generation*.

His rise to artistic prominence, however, had quite different sources: the deaths of his mother and his stillborn child, and an encounter with the extremes of wealth and poverty during a visit to the Appalachian hills of eastern Kentucky. Wrestling with the human and environmental degradation he had seen there led Schenkkan to ask larger questions about memory and history in his six-hour masterwork, *The Kentucky Cycle*, which won the 1992 Pulitzer Prize. This cycle follows three Kentucky families over two hundred years and portrays the ways in which violence, brutality, ruthlessness, and greed are subsumed into myths, legends, and histories over time. In *Handler* (2002), Schenkkan turned from the sweep of history and generations to the lives of one couple seeking resurrection and redemption in a snake-handling Holiness church.

Schenkkan has worked widely in Los Angeles as a writer in television and film. His credits include *Tall Tale* (1994), *Crazy Horse* (1996), and an adaptation of Graham Greene's *The Quiet American* (2002). He lives in Seattle with his son and daughter.

WORKS: *Final Passages* (1983). *The Kentucky Cycle* (1992). *Heaven on Earth* (1992). *Four One-Act Plays* (1995). *Dream Thief* (1999).

—DOUGLAS L. MITCHELL

EVELYN SCOTT (1893–1963). Elsie Dunn was born in Clarksville, Tenn., in 1893 to a genteel southern mother and a northern father; the family moved to New Orleans in 1901. In 1913 she eloped with the already married Frederick Creighton Wellman. The couple, who assumed the names Evelyn and Cyril Kay Scott, moved to Brazil. While they struggled with poverty—as she recorded in her memoir *Escapade*—Scott gave birth to her only child.

In 1919 the couple moved to New York; shortly thereafter, Scott published her first volume of poetry, *Precipitations*. A year later, her drama *Love: A Play in Three Acts* was staged by the Provincetown Players. Although Scott published other volumes of poetry, essays, children's fiction, and a second memoir (*Background in Tennessee*), she is best known for her fiction. *The Narrow House*, along with *Narcissus* and *The Golden Door*, comprise a trilogy that in modernist, experimental prose explores psychological, sexual, and ethical turmoil in a southern family. Scott's second trilogy is historical: *Migrations: An Arabesque in Histories* takes place in the antebellum South; *The Wave*, Scott's most popular novel, deals with the Civil War; and *A Calendar of Sin* stretches from Reconstruction to the early twentieth century.

Scott's personal life paralleled the tempestuousness and experimentation of her prose. Her poor physical health was exacerbated by her psychological breakdowns; frequent moves (including stays in Bermuda, England, and Canada) also eroded her stability. Before her divorce from Cyril in 1928, she was sexually involved with William Carlos Williams and others. In 1925 she entered into a relationship with British novelist John Metcalfe, whom she married in 1930. Scott and Metcalfe moved to England in 1944 and remained there until 1953, when they returned to the United States. Rejected by her son and living in a New York hotel with Metcalfe, Scott died of lung cancer in 1963.

WORKS: *Precipitations* (1920). *Love: A Drama in Three Acts* (1921). *The Narrow House* (1921). *Narcissus* (1922). *Escapade* (1923). *In the Endless Sands: A Christmas Book for Boys and Girls,* with Cyril Kay Scott (1925). *The Golden Door* (1925). *Ideals: A Book of Farce and Comedy* (1927). *Migrations: An Arabesque in Histories* (1927). *The Wave* (1929). *Witch Perkins: A Story of the Kentucky Hills* (1929). *On William Faulkner's "The Sound and the Fury"* (1929). *Blue Rum* (1930). *The Winter Alone* (1930). *A Calendar of Sin: American Melodramas* (1931). *Eva Gay: A Romantic Novel* (1933). *Breathe upon These Slain* (1934). *Billy the Maverick* (1934). *Bread and a Sword* (1937). *Background in Tennessee* (1937). *The Shadow of the Hawk* (1941). *The Collected Poems of Evelyn Scott,* ed. Carolina Maun (2004).

—THERESA LLOYD

MOLLY ELLIOT SEAWELL (1860–1916). Born on a plantation in Gloucester County, Va., on October 23, 1860, Molly Seawell was the daughter of John Tyler and Frances Jackson Seawell. Both her father, a lawyer and classics scholar, and her uncle, Joseph Seawell, a seaman, contributed much to her future literary endeavors. She was educated chiefly in the informal fashion at home, but also received some formal instruction at Virginia schools. It was her girlhood in the Tidewater region that perhaps provided the greatest influence on her writing career.

While in Norfolk in 1886, Seawell modestly began her literary duties. A sojourn in Europe added to her storehouse of subject matter, and, upon her return to Virginia, she initiated publication of several magazine pieces under various pen names. Moving to Washington, D.C., she submitted numerous political articles to New York papers and, throughout her years, continued her political involvement, which culminated in the 1903 publication of *Despotism and Democracy,* a critique of society and politics in Washington, and the 1911 publication of *The Ladies' Battle,* an anti-suffragist tract.

By far the most important aspect of her writing was fiction. From her first novel, *Hale-Weston,* in 1889, her fiction was characterized by a lilting, pleasant style with humor and a major emphasis on setting. In variety, the novels range from antebellum Virginia, to English history, to Parisian society, to the American navy, and to Washington fact and fancy.

Several of her works, such as *The Sprightly Romance of Marsac, The History of Lady Betty Stair,* and *The Fortunes of Fifi,* received a certain degree of popular acclaim, although she is little remembered today. Molly Seawell died in Washington, D.C., on November 15, 1916, and was buried in Baltimore.

WORKS: *The Berkeleys and Their Neighbors* (1888). *Hale-Weston* (1889). *Little Jarvis* (1890). *Throckmorton* (1890). *Midshipman Paulding* (1891). *Maid Marian and Other Stories* (1891). *Children of Destiny* (1893). *The Sprightly Romance of Marsac* (1896). *A Strange, Sad Comedy* (1896). *A Virginia Cavalier* (1896). *The History of Lady Betty Stair* (1897). *Twelve Naval Captains* (1897). *The Loves of the Lady Arabella* (1898). *The Lively Adventures of Gavin Hamilton* (1899). *The House of Egremont* (1900). *Papa Bouchard* (1901). *Franceska* (1902). *The Fortunes of Fifi* (1903). *Despotism and Democracy* (1903). *The Chateau of Montplaisir* (1906). *The Victory* (1906). *The Secret of Toni* (1907). *The Last Duchess of Belgarde* (1908). *John Mainwaring, Financier* (1908). *The Imprisoned Midshipman* (1908). *The Whirl: A Romance of Washington Society* (1909). *The Ladies' Battle* (1911). *Betty's Virginia Christmas* (1914). *The Diary of a Beauty* (1915).

—ROBERT M. WILLINGHAM, JR.

JAMES SEAY (1939–). Poet James Seay was born and raised in Panola County, Miss. His father, a heavy-equipment operator, supervised land development projects in Mississippi and the Florida Everglades; his mother was a homemaker. Seay received his B.A. in English at the University of Mississippi, and his M.A. in English from the University of Virginia. Over an eight-year period he held positions teaching English at Virginia Military Institute, the University of Virginia, the University of

Alabama, and Vanderbilt University; since 1974 he has taught at the University of North Carolina at Chapel Hill. His first marriage (to novelist Lee Smith) produced two sons.

Seay has long admired James Dickey and Richard Wilbur, and it is easy to detect their respective influences on his first book, *Let Not Your Hart*; like Dickey's poems, Seay's embrace southern landscape and culture, and like Wilbur's, several adopt a traditional approach to poetic form. His second collection, *Water Tables,* includes some poems that verge on surrealism; it also includes what is probably Seay's best-known poem, "It All Comes Together Outside the Restroom in Hogansville." A limited-edition long poem, *Said There Was Somebody Talking to Him through the Air Conditioner* (reprinted complete in his selected poems, *Open Field, Understory*), considers the complex relationship between fiction and reality, as do several poems in his third collection, *The Light as They Found It.* Seay's recent poems have tended to be more cosmopolitan than his early work, drawing their inspiration from his travel abroad and the work of other, nonsouthern artists.

His awards include the North Carolina Literary and Historical Association's Roanoke-Chowan Award and an award in literature from the American Academy and Institute of Arts and Letters.

WORKS: *Let Not Your Hart* (1970). *Water Tables* (1974). *Said There Was Somebody Talking to Him through the Air Conditioner* (1985). *The Light as They Found It* (1990). *In the Blood*, a documentary film co-written with director George Butler (1990). *Open Field, Understory: New and Selected Poems* (1997).

—ROBERT M. WEST

DAVID SEDARIS (1956–). David Raymond Sedaris was born on December 26, 1956, in Binghamton, N.Y., but spent most of his childhood and early adulthood in Raleigh, N.C. In grade school, Sedaris developed behavioral tics that alarmed his teachers and later became material for his stage and radio performances. Sedaris began college at Kent State University, dropped out, and enrolled at Western Carolina University before finishing a degree at the Art Institute of Chicago in 1987. In 1991 Sedaris moved to New York, where he held a series of menial jobs. One of them, his "performance" as a holiday elf at Macy's, was described in "The SantaLand Diaries" on National Public Radio in 1992.

This merciless and unhealthily absorbing portrait of his employer, his customers, and himself gave Sedaris the adoring national audience he has had ever since. Sedaris belongs to a tradition of writers who are also true performance artists, sometimes scorned by (and scorning) academic culture: he is akin to Twain and Wilde, but also to Sandra Bernhard and David Letterman. In fact, Sedaris has been influenced as much by Steve Martin, soap operas, and his sister, playwright-comedienne Amy Sedaris, as by any authorial tradition. As he has told the *Miami Herald,* "I write, but I'm reluctant to call myself a writer." His absolute contemporaneity also means that Sedaris may be the first author from any region to write of being gay in an absolutely matter-of-fact way. In a testimony to nationwide cultural transformation, his audience has responded accordingly.

In 2001 David Sedaris was named Humorist of the Year by *Time* magazine; in the same year, he received the third Thurber Prize for American Humor. Under the pseudonym The Talent Family, David and Amy Sedaris have written and produced a series of plays, including *Stump the Host, Stitches* (1994), *Incident at Cobbler's Knob* (1994), the Obie Award–winning *One Woman Shoe* (1995), *The Little Frieda Mysteries* (1997), and *The Book of Liz* (published by the Dramatist's Play Service, 2002), which had its debut and a ten-week run at the Greenwich House Theater in New York. It has also been staged by Theatre in the Park in Raleigh.

After making their home in France for several years, Sedaris and his partner, Hugh Hamrick, now live in London.

WORKS: *Barrel Fever: Stories and Essays* (1994). *Holidays on Ice* (1997). *Naked* (1997). *Me Talk Pretty One Day* (2000). *Book of Liz*, with Amy Sedaris (2002). *Dress Your Family in Corduroy and Denim* (2004). Ed., *Children Playing before a Statue of Hercules: An Anthology of Outstanding Short Stories* (2005).

—JOHN JACKSON AND DAVID CASE

MARY LEE SETTLE (1918–2005). Mary Lee Settle was born in Charleston, W.Va., in 1918. She was educated for two years at Sweet Briar College, and she recounts her experiences there in the novel *The Clam Shell*. Leaving Sweet Briar for a career in acting and modeling, Settle moved to Canada and then England. While living in England during World War II, she served in the Women's Auxiliary Air Force and the Office of War Information. These experiences are recorded in *All the Brave Promises*. After the war she moved to New York and began working as an assistant editor at *Harper's Bazaar.*

After a short stint with *Harper's,* Settle realized how much she wanted to be a writer. She returned to England in 1949 and began writing novels and plays, and her first novel, *The Love Eaters,* was published in 1954. An earlier work, *The Kiss of Kin,* was published the following year. She moved back to West Virginia a few years later and began work on the series of books she is best known for, the Beulah Land Quintet. The writing of the quintet, which explores the settlement of West Virginia from 1754 to the present, was supported by two Guggenheim Fellowships (1957–58 and 1959–60).

Settle also writes of her experiences outside of the South. *Celebration* captures the experience of expatriates in London, and *Blood Tie* of expatriates in Turkey. In 1978 *Blood Tie* won the National Book Award. Settle's recent work is also greatly varied: a biography of her grandmother, *Addie: A Memoir*; a novel about an American colonial radical, *I, Roger Williams*; and *Spanish Recognitions: The Road from the Past,* based on her explorations of Spain.

Settle died on September 27, 2005, at her home in Ivy, Va. She may be best remembered for her ability to capture the real story of people and places in fiction, nonfiction prose, and memoir.

WORKS: *The Love Eaters* (1954). *The Kiss of Kin* (1955). *O Beulah Land* (1956). *Know Nothing* (1960); repr. as *Pride's Promise* (1976). *Fight Night on a Sweet Saturday* (1964); rev. and repr. as *The Killing Ground* (1982). *All the Brave Promises: Memories of Aircraft Woman 2nd Class 2146391* (1966). *The Clam Shell* (1971). *Prisons* (1973); published in England as *The Long Road to Paradise* (1974). *Blood Tie* (1977). *The Scapegoat* (1980). *Celebration* (1986). *Charley Bland* (1989). *Turkish Reflections: A Biography of a Place* (1991). *Choices* (1995). *Addie: A Memoir* (1998). *I, Roger Williams* (2001). *Spanish Recognitions: The Road from the Past* (2004).

—CAROLYN PERRY

JEFF SHAARA (1952–). Jeff Shaara was born in New Brunswick, N.J., on February 21, 1952. He is the son of novelist Michael Shaara and Helen Krumwiede Shaara. Jeff Shaara vividly remembers thoroughly exploring—and at times crawling over—the Gettysburg battle terrain with his father in 1964 and in 1970. Already demonstrating strong writing instincts, Jeff Shaara graduated from Florida State University with a B.S. in criminology in 1973. After his father died, Shaara sold his Tampa, Fla., rare coin business and began to write historical novels. He was encouraged by director Ron Maxwell, who had successfully transformed Michael Shaara's Pulitzer Prize–winning novel *The Killer Angels* (1974) into the film *Gettysburg* (1993). The result has been a series of ambitious, highly regarded books that, collectively, more than equal his father's achievement.

For both his Revolutionary War and nineteenth-century war novels, Shaara thoroughly researched letters, diaries, and memoirs; designed narrative units told from multiple points of view, a technique Jeff learned from his father but which now becomes more comprehensive; filled in the family backgrounds and personal and political values for the major characters; and carefully reconstructed battlefield scenes, augmented with detailed campaign maps.

Rise to Rebellion and *The Glorious Cause* treat the tensions leading up to the Revolutionary War and then the long, complex, and uncertain struggle itself. In these two novels, the reader sees how John and Abigail Adams, Ben Franklin, George Washington, British generals Thomas Gage and Charles Cornwallis, American commander Nathaniel Greene, the Marquis de Lafayette, and other important characters play out their memorable roles and invest themselves emotionally in the war—meanwhile negotiating political realities on both sides of the Atlantic.

Shaara's *Gone for Soldiers* portrays Ulysses S. Grant and Robert E. Lee, under their commander General Winfield Scott, as junior officers experiencing battle for the first time in the 1846–48 Mexican American War against the forces of Santa Anna, who is also believably portrayed. *Gods and Generals* is Shaara's "prequel" to *The Killer Angels*, his father's 1974 novel about Gettysburg. Lee, Winfield Scott Hancock, Stonewall Jackson, and Joshua Lawrence Chamberlain play the major roles in *Gods and Generals*, which opens in November 1858 and closes on the eve of Gettysburg in June 1863. *The Last Full Measure* tracks Lee, Grant, and Chamberlain across the bloody final twenty-two months of the Civil War. Ron Maxwell released his television movie *Gods and Generals* in February 2003. Praised for its authenticity, the three-hour-and-forty-five-minute epic lacked the dramatic force to win popular acclaim.

Jeff Shaara lives with his wife, Lynne, in Montana and New York and is writing a book on William Tecumseh Sherman.

WORKS: *Gods and Generals* (1996). *The Last Full Measure* (1998). *Gone for Soldiers: A Novel of the Mexican War* (2000). *Rise to Rebellion* (2001). *The Glorious Cause* (2002). *To the Last Man: A Novel of the First World War* (2004).

—R. BRUCE BICKLEY, JR.

MICHAEL SHAARA (1928–1988). Born on June 23, 1928, in Jersey City, N.J., the son of Michael Joseph, Sr., and Alleene Maxwell Shaara, Michael Shaara boxed eighteen bouts as a prize-fighter, winning seventeen, before sailing as a merchant seaman and serving in the army. He married Helen Krumweide in 1950 and earned his B.A. from Rutgers University in 1951. After graduate study at Columbia and the University of Vermont, in 1952–54, he worked as a policeman in St. Petersburg, Fla., in 1954–55. The Shaaras had two children, Jeffrey and Lila Elise, as Michael was beginning to build a reputation as a fiction writer. Shaara proved to be a popular teacher when he was hired as associate professor of English at Florida State University in 1961. His experiences as a boxer and policeman, a heart attack in his thirties, and Ernest Hemingway's fiction, including a famous line from *A Farewell to Arms*, were the immediate inspirations for his first novel, *The Broken Place*. Earlier, in 1966, the American Medical Association had given Shaara an award for "In the Midst of Life," his article recounting his experiences before and after his heart had stopped for a record-setting fifty-five minutes.

Shaara's son, Jeff, remembers exploring with his father every ridge and hollow of the Gettysburg terrain while his father was obsessively invested in the research for his next novel, his masterpiece, *The Killer Angels*. Its title an ironic spin on Hamlet's speech about man's essential nobility, Shaara's gripping, carefully detailed narrative re-creates the epic Battle of Gettysburg from the viewpoints of the Union's Colonel Joshua Chamberlain and General John Buford, and the Confederacy's General Robert E. Lee and General James Longstreet. Shaara's novel about the battle that cost nearly fifty thousand lives won the 1975 Pulitzer Prize for fiction. Although it was not a commercial success at the time (fifteen publishers had declined it before McKay said yes), some experts judge it the best war novel ever written. When producer-director Ron Maxwell turned the novel into the acclaimed television movie *Gettysburg* (1993), Shaara's 1974 novel vaulted to the top of the *New York Times* best-seller list.

Shaara's next novel, *The Herald,* was a post-apocalyptic, philosophical work of science fiction that explores the aftermath of an experiment in human mass-destruction. The questions the novel raises still resonate for readers living in the shadow of the attack on the World Trade Center on September 11, 2001, and in a world fraught with nuclear and biological warfare dangers. *Soldier Boy* gathers several of Shaara's earlier short stories.

Michael Shaara, in the middle of fighting a long battle with depression, retired from teaching in 1973 after a motor-scooter accident, and he divorced Helen in 1985. He died of another heart attack on May 5, 1988, in Tallahassee, Fla. His last novel, *For Love of the Game,* about a baseball player who is over the hill, was published posthumously in 1991. In 1999 Shaara's novel was made into a movie starring Kevin Costner and Kelly Preston.

WORKS: *The Broken Place* (1968). *The Killer Angels* (1974). *The Herald* (1981); repr. as *The Noah Conspiracy* (1994). *Soldier Boy* (1982). *For Love of the Game* (1991).

—R. BRUCE BICKLEY, JR.

BOB SHACOCHIS (1951–). Born in Pennsylvania and best known as a writer about the Caribbean, Bob Shacochis grew up in Virginia and has made Florida his most permanent adult home.

The grandson of Lithuanian immigrants and the third and last son of the four children of John P. and Helen Levonski Shacochis, Robert G. Shacochis was born in West Pittston, Pa., on September 9, 1951. Graduating from high school in McLean, Va., he earned a bachelor's degree in journalism from the University of Missouri in 1973 and, after having lived in the Caribbean before and during Peace Corps service, returned to Missouri to receive an M.A. in creative writing in 1979. Three years earlier he met Barbara Petersen, who would become his wife. His first published short story appeared in 1980. In 1982 he completed requirements for an M.F.A. at the University of Iowa, where he began to sell stories to national magazines and where the stories for his thesis became the Caribbean core of his first book, *Easy in the Islands.*

A second collection of stories with more varied settings, *The Next New World,* followed. A novel, *Swimming in the Volcano,* which returned readers to the Caribbean, was Shacochis's third book. His fictional themes of love and politics appear separately manifested in two volumes of nonfiction. *Domesticity: A Gastronomic Interpretation of Love* is a collection of columns from *Gentlemen's Quarterly,* and *The Immaculate Invasion* reports on United States military operations in Haiti in the mid-1990s, when Shacochis lived with Special Forces troops there for over a year.

A frequent traveler and sojourner, often in dangerous overseas situations, Shacochis has been a longtime contributing editor of *Harper's* and a correspondent from around the world for a number of other periodicals. He is widely active in professional creative writing circles and has had teaching appointments at such institutions as, most recently, Florida State University and Bennington College. He has been the recipient of many awards and recognitions, including the American Book Award for First Fiction, the Prix de Rome, and a Best American Travel Writing Award.

WORKS: *Easy in the Islands* (1985). *The Next New World* (1989). *Swimming in the Volcano: A Novel* (1993). *Domesticity: A Gastronomic Interpretation of Love* (1994). *The Immaculate Invasion* (1999).

—BERT HITCHCOCK

EVE SHELNUTT (1941–). Eve Shelnutt, poet and short-story writer, was born in Spartanburg, S.C., on August 29, 1941, the second of three daughters, to James Waldrop, a broadcast journalist, and Evelyn Brock Waldrop, a violinist and music teacher. During her childhood, the family moved often, to California and Long Island and throughout the South and Midwest. Shelnutt received a B.A. in English from the University of Cincinnati in 1972, and an M.F.A. in creative writing from the University of North Carolina at Greensboro in 1973. Her marriages, to William Shelnutt and Mark Logan Shelton, ended in divorce. Her son, Greg Shelnutt, is a sculptor and teacher at the University of Mississippi. Eve Shelnutt has taught at Western Michigan University, Goddard College, the University of Pittsburgh, and Ohio University. Since 1994 she has been writer-in-residence at the College of the Holy Cross in Worcester, Mass.

Reflective of her childhood, Shelnutt's stories often center on a mother and two or three daughters, isolated in rented houses, where their sense of rootlessness is intensified by the father's absence. Citing Wallace Stevens and Elizabeth Bishop as formative influences, Shelnutt has eschewed traditional elements of southern fiction, such as gothicism and oral tradition, and rejected conventions of narrative realism, such as chronological sequence and conventional syntax. Her stories are dense and poetic, sometimes dreamlike, often marked by traumatic events of mysterious origin. Similar elements inform her poetry: the dynamics of family relationships, unresolved conflicts, and portents, sometimes violent, of an undisclosed nature.

In addition to scores of poems and stories in some sixty journals, Shelnutt has published many essays on contemporary literature and creative-writing pedagogy and has edited several collections of essays on writing. She has traveled extensively, giving workshops, lectures, and readings at many institutions.

WORKS: *Two Stories* (1977). *The Love Child* (1979). *Descant* (1982). *The Formal Voice* (1982). *Air and Salt* (1983). *The Musician* (1987). *The Magic Pencil: Teaching Children Creative Writing* (1988). *Recital in a Private Home* (1989). *The Writing Room: Keys to the Craft of Fiction and Poetry* (1989). Ed., *Writing—the Translation of Memory* (1990). Ed., *The Confidence Woman: Twenty-six Women Writers at Work* (1991). *First a Long Hesitation* (1992). *My Poor Elephant: Twenty-seven Male Writers at Work* (1992). *The Girl, Painted* (1996).

—ELSA NETTELS

TED SHINE (1931–). Ted Shine was born in Baton Rouge, La., on April 26, 1931, the son of Theodis Wesley and Bessie (Hudson) Shine. He grew up in Dallas, Tex. He studied with Owen Dodson and Sterling Brown at Howard University (B.A., 1953), and his three early 1950s plays *Cold Day in August, Sho Is Hot in the Cotton Patch,* and *Dry August* were first produced there. After a U.S. Army tour in Germany (1955–57), he earned an M.A. in playwriting at the University of Iowa (1958) and later a Ph.D. from the University of California–Santa Barbara (1973). Dedicated to an audience of midcentury African American youth even before the rise of African American consciousness in the 1960s, his plays were comic and satirical, subversive, and revolutionary, his dominant characters mostly women. He was a teacher and friend of playwrights and actors to such a degree that the body of his work is limited—about ninety scripts (including nearly sixty for the *Our Street* television series from 1969 to 1973), about ten of which are published.

Shine taught at Dillard University in New Orleans (1960–61), then at Howard (1961–67), and finally at Prairie View A&M in Texas (1967–98), as chair of the music and drama department for many years. (At least three of his pieces were musicals or ballet.) His honors include a Rockefeller scholarship (1953–55), the Brook-Hines Award for Playwriting, Howard University (1970), and blue-ribbon committees for the advancement of African Americans in the arts. His most important work is *Contribution* (1969), which has been staged by nearly every African American production company. *Contribution* was collected with *Shoes* (1967) and *Plantation* (1970) in *Contributions: Three One-Act Plays*. His scholarly contribution to drama is as co-editor, with James V. Hatch, of several anthologies of plays by African Americans.

WORKS: *Sho Is Hot in the Cotton Patch* (1950). *Morning, Noon, and Night* (1964). *Contributions: Three One-Act Plays* (1970). Ed., *Black Theatre, U.S.A.: Forty-Five Plays by Black Americans, 1847–1974*, with James V. Hatch (1974; rev. and enl. 1996). *The Woman Who Was Tampered with in Youth* (1980). *Good Old Soul* (1983). *Going Berserk* (1984). Ed., *Black Theatre U.S.A.: Plays by African Americans, the Recent Period, 1935–Today*, with Hatch (1996).

—JOHN R. PFEIFFER

SUSAN RICHARDS SHREVE (1939–). Susan Lynn Richards was born on May 2, 1939, in Toledo, Ohio, to Robert and Helen Richards. In early childhood, she suffered several serious illnesses, including polio. In 1943 she moved with her family to Washington, D.C., where she attended Sidwell Friends School. She received a B.A. from the University of Pennsylvania in 1961 and an M.A. from the University of Virginia in 1969. In 1962 she married Porter Shreve, an educator and family therapist; they have four children. In 1987 she and Porter were divorced, and she married her literary agent, Timothy Seldes, with whom she lives in Washington, D.C.

Since 1976 Shreve has been on the faculty of George Mason University, where she founded the M.F.A. creative writing program. As a visiting faculty member, she has taught at several institutions, including Columbia University, Princeton University, and Goucher College. She has also conducted writing workshops and served as president of the PEN/Faulkner Foundation.

From an early age, Shreve has been a prolific writer. By twenty, she had written several novels, none of which were published. After marriage, she devoted herself to teaching and motherhood, but returned to writing in graduate school, where she studied under Peter Taylor. She published her first novel, *A Fortunate Madness*, in 1974. Since then, Shreve has published numerous adult novels, children's books, short stories, and essays. She has also edited several anthologies, some in collaboration with her son Porter. She has received awards from the Guggenheim Foundation and National Endowment for the Arts, an Edgar Allan Poe Award for mystery writing, and American Library Association citations for juvenile and young adult fiction.

Shreve's works draw heavily upon her childhood experiences and those of her own children. Her novels are intensely psychological and develop several recurring themes, including the search for meaning and identity and reconciliation with family and the past.

WORKS. *A Fortunate Madness* (1974). *A Woman Like That* (1977). *The Nightmares of Geranium Street* (1977). *Loveletters* (1978). *Children of Power* (1979). *Family Secrets: Five Very Important Stories* (1979). *The Masquerade* (1980). *Miracle Play* (1981). *The Bad Dreams of a Good Girl* (1982). *The Revolution of Mary Leary* (1982). *Dreaming of Heroes* (1984). *The Flunking of Joshua T. Bates* (1984). *How I Saved the World on Purpose* (1985). *Queen of Hearts* (1986). *Lily and the Runaway Baby* (1987). *Lucy Forever and Miss Rosetree, Shrinks* (1987). *A Country of Strangers* (1989). *The Gift of the Girl Who Couldn't Hear* (1991). *Daughters of the New World* (1992). *Wait for Me* (1992). *The Train Home* (1993). *Amy Dunn Quits School* (1993). *Joshua T. Bates Takes Charge* (1993). *Lucy Forever, Miss Rosetree, and the Stolen Baby* (1994). *The Formerly Great Alexander Family* (1995). *Zoe and Columbo* (1995). Ed., *Skin Deep: Black Women and White Women Write about Race*, with Marita Golden (1995). *The Visiting Physician* (1996). *The Goalie* (1996). *Warts* (1996). *Joshua T. Bates in Trouble Again* (1997). Ed., *Outside the Law: Narratives on Justice in America*, with Porter Shreve (1997). *Glimmer*, as Annie Waters (1997). *Jonah, the Whale* (1998). Ed., *How We Want to Live: Narratives on Progress* (1998). *Ghost Cats* (1999). *Plum and Jaggers* (2000). *Goodbye, Amanda the Good* (2000). Ed.,

Tales out of School: Contemporary Writers on Their Student Years, with Porter Shreve (2000). *Blister* (2001). *Trout and Me* (2002). Ed., *Dream Me Home Safely* (2003).

—Katherine C. Hodgin

ANNE RIVERS SIDDONS (1936–). Siddons was born Sybil Anne Rivers on January 9, 1936, in Atlanta, Ga., the only child of L. Marvin and Katherine Rivers of Fairburn, a small town south of Atlanta where the Rivers family had lived for six generations. As a young woman Siddons enjoyed academic success and the social triumphs of a popular southern belle.

While at Auburn University, Siddons wrote a column for the student newspaper commending Auburn students for not participating in the protests over the matriculation of the first African American student at the University of Alabama. The column, and a follow-up to the piece, resulted in Siddons's being asked to leave the staff of the paper.

Following her graduation in 1958 (B.F.A., illustration), Siddons returned to Georgia to work in advertising. In 1964 she joined the staff of *Atlanta* magazine, where her work often brought her in contact with the civil rights movement. In 1966 she married Heyward Siddons, an advertising executive. Siddons began writing full-time in 1973 when she was contacted by Doubleday and offered a contract.

Siddons's novels replay her experiences of growing up in elite society, subscribing to the codes of propriety, then breaking with tradition and creating a life independent of the "old South" expectations. The heroine is usually a beautiful, intelligent, young southerner who either alienates herself from family and friends by supporting the ideals of the civil rights movement or by pursuing her own interests outside the prescribed roles of her class, or who is removed from her native South either by marriage or divorce and must rely on her inner resources to establish her identity beyond social expectations. These women confront loneliness, abuse, and mental illness to recover themselves.

Since the publication of *Peachtree Road*, Siddons's novels have appeared regularly on best-seller lists. The combined appeal of local color fiction and romantic depictions of the lives of the South's aristocracy accounts in part for Siddons's popularity. She has been praised for her perceptive treatment of women's issues and of the mentally ill, but she is also faulted for her predictable, often melodramatic plots.

works: *John Chancellor Makes Me Cry* (1975). *Heartbreak Hotel* (1976); adapted as the film *Heart of Dixie* (1989). *The House Next Door* (1978). *Go Straight on Peachtree* (1978). *Fox's Earth* (1980). *Homeplace* (1987). *Peachtree Road* (1988). *King's Oak* (1990). *Outer Banks* (1991). *Colony* (1992). *Hill Towns* (1993). *Downtown* (1994). *Fault Lines* (1995). *Up Island* (1997). *Low Country* (1998). *Nora, Nora* (2000). *Islands* (2004).

—Regina Ammon

WILLIAM GILMORE SIMMS (1806–1870). The principal author of the antebellum South and a major figure in American letters until the Civil War obscured his renown, William Gilmore Simms exemplifies the literary vocation in the early nineteenth century. During the many years of his active professional life, he produced poetry, drama, short fiction, novels, a history, a geography, essays, literary criticism, and orations, meanwhile addressing social, political, and literary concerns in his extensive correspondence. A man of many talents and enormous dedication to the cultural life of his region, he edited important newspapers and journals, participated vigorously in southern politics, and energetically promoted various kinds of southern writing.

Simms was born in Charleston on April 17, 1806, to a mother descended from genteel Virginia forebears and a father who had immigrated to South Carolina from Ireland. When the boy was two, his mother died; his grief-stricken father went first to Tennessee and then to Mississippi, leaving Simms to be reared in Charleston by his maternal grandmother. Simms visited his father in the middle 1820s, riding on horseback through Mississippi, Alabama, and Louisiana where he witnessed pioneer and Native American life. Returning to Charleston, he married in 1826; his wife died in 1832. His father, meanwhile, had also died, and in 1831 Simms returned to the Gulf South to settle the estate and to view the strides civilization was making in the area.

Simms's knowledge of southern tidewater and frontier regions, together with his travels in the Appalachian Mountains, formed the basis for poetry, essays, and orations. It also laid the foundation for the major categories of his fiction—tales and novels from *The Yemassee* and such Revolutionary War romances as *The Partisan* to *The Golden Christmas* and *The Cassique of Kiawah*, set in the low country and describing its development from the seventeenth century through the Revolution and the antebellum era, and border and mountain romances from *Guy Rivers* to *Voltmeier* (serialized 1869), portraying the settlement phases of the Gulf and mountain South.

Guy Rivers and *The Yemassee* brought Simms popular success and the financial security that enabled him to marry, in 1836, Chevillette Eliza Roach, the daughter of a plantation owner, a move that cemented his ties to the planting class. He and his wife lived in one of the Roach plantations, Woodlands, where he wrote many of his books, including Revolutionary War romances such as *Mellichampe* and *Pelayo* and other novels of Spanish history. Woodlands also gave Simms a political base: he served in the South Carolina legislature from 1844 to 1846, vigorously supporting sectional interests. The panic of 1837, an economic depression that persisted until the early 1850s, had meanwhile made the publication of long fiction unprofitable. Hence, during the 1840s Simms abandoned novels for other types of writing—biographies of Francis Marion, Captain John Smith, and Nathaniel (which he spelled "Nathanael") Greene; American cultural history in *Views and Reviews*; short fiction in *The Wigwam and the Cabin*; and poetry such as *The Cassique of Accabee*.

By the 1850s, the market for long fiction had recovered, and Simms returned to the Revolutionary War series with four solid books, including the popular *Woodcraft* (originally titled *The Sword and the Distaff*). He also published a novel about Spanish America, *Vasconselos*, and wrote two of his finest works—*The Golden Christmas*, a short novel lightly satirizing antebellum Charleston and plantation life, and *The Cassique of Kiawah*, his last piece of long fiction, in which he explored the foundations of the Carolina colony.

Since the 1830s Simms had defended southern social institutions, including slavery; one of his essays was included in the influential volume *The Pro-Slavery Argument*. Enduring the Civil War in South Carolina, he described it in the searing *Sack and Destruction of the City of Columbia, S.C.* By the conclusion of the war—his plantation destroyed, his wife dead, and his health and finances ruined—he was forced to support his family by his writing, grinding out three novels for publication in obscure periodicals. The effort secured him some measure of financial security but further undermined his health. Surrounded by his children, he died in Charleston on June 6, 1870.

An informed appraisal of Simms's life and career requires a knowledge of several factors: he was a professional man of letters living far from northern publishing centers, a fact that, as he frequently complained, hindered his attention to his literary interests; the economic depression of 1837 forced him away from long fiction shortly after he had captured a national literary audience, preventing him from solidifying his renown; and the Civil War, which kept him from making trips to the North, severely harmed his productivity as well as his literary reputation. By the twenty-first century, with national acrimony over slavery and secession diminished, his life and work had begun to receive the kind of enlightened scholarly attention appropriate for an author who epitomized the literary and cultural concerns of his region.

WORKS: *Monody, On the Death of Gen. Charles Cotesworth Pinckney* (1825). *Early Lays* (1827). *Lyrical and Other Poems* (1827). *The Vision of Cortes, Cain, and Other Poems* (1829). *The Tri-Color; or, the Three Days of Blood, in Paris. With Some Other Pieces* (1830). *Atlantis: A Story of the Sea. In Three Parts* (1832). *The Remains of Maynard Davis Richardson, With a Memoir of His Life* (1833). *Martin Faber: The Story of a Criminal* (1833). *The Book of My Lady: A Melange* (1833). *Guy Rivers: A Tale of Georgia* (1834). *The Yemassee: A Romance of Carolina* (1835). *The Partisan: A Tale of the Revolution* (1835). *Mellichampe: A Legend of the Santee* (1836). *Martin Faber: The Story of a Criminal; and Other Tales* (1837). *Carl Werner: An Imaginative Story; With Other Tales of Imagination* (1838). *Richard Hurdis; or, The Avenger of Blood. A Tale of Alabama* (1838). *Pelayo: A Story of the Goth* (1838). *Southern Passages and Pictures* (1839). *The Damsel of Darien* (1839). *Border Beagles: A Tale of Mississippi* (1840). *The History of South Carolina* (1840). *The Kinsmen; or, The Black Riders of Congaree. A Tale* (1841); repr. as *The Scout; or, The Black Riders of Congaree* (1854). *Confession; or, The Blind Heart. A Domestic Story* (1841). *Beauchampe; or, The Kentucky Tragedy. A Tale of Passion* (1842); repr. 1856: vol. 1 was retitled *Charlemont; or, The Pride of the Village. A Tale of Kentucky*; vol. 2 was retitled *Beauchampe; or, The Kentucky Tragedy. A Sequel to Charlemont*). *Donna Florida: A Tale* (1843). *The Geography of South Carolina* (1843). *The Social Principle: The True Source of National Permanence. An Oration* (1843). *The Life of Francis Marion* (1844). *Castle Dismal; or, The Bachelor's Christmas. A Domestic Legend* (1844). *The Prima Donna: A Passage from City Life* (1844). *The Sources of American Independence: An Oration* (1844). *The Life of Francis Marion* (1844). *Helen Halsey; or, The Swamp State of Conelachita. A Tale of the Borders* (1845). *The Wigwam and the Cabin* (1845). *Count Julian; or, The Last Days of the Goth* (1845). *Views and Reviews in American Literature History and Fiction* (1845). *Grouped Thoughts and Scattered Fancies: A Collection of Sonnets* (1845). *Areytos; or, Songs of the South* (1846). *The Life of Captain John Smith, the Founder of Virginia* (1846). *The Life of the Chevalier Bayard: "The Good Knight"* (1847). *Charleston, and Her Satirists: A Scribblement* (1848). *Lays of the Palmetto: A Tribute to the South Carolina Regiment, in the War with Mexico* (1848). *The Cassique of Accabee: A Tale, With Other Poems* (1848). Ed., *A Supplement to the Plays of William Shakespeare Comprising the Seven Dramas, Which Have Been Ascribed to His Pen but Which are not Included in His Writings in Modern Editions* (1848). *Father Abbot; or, The Home Tourist. A Medley* (1849). *Sabbath Lyrics; or, Songs from Scripture* (1849). *The Life of Nathanael Greene, Major General in the Army of the Revolution* (1849). *The Lily and The Totem: A Series of Sketches, Picturesque and Historical, of the Colonies of Coligni, in North America, 1562–1570* (1850). *The City of the Silent: A Poem . . . Delivered at the Consecration of Magnolia Cemetery* (1850). *Katharine Walton; or, The Rebel of Dorchester. An Historical Romance of the Revolution in South Carolina* (1851). *Norman Maurice; or, The Man of the People: An American Drama. In Five Acts* (1851). *Michael Bonham; or, The Fall of Bexar: A Tale of Texas in Five Parts* (1852). *The Sword and The Distaff; or, "Fair, Fat, and Forty": A Story of the South, at the Close of the Revolution* (1852); later repr. as *Woodcraft; or, Hawks About The Dovecote: A Story of the South at the Close of the Revolution* (1854). *The Golden Christmas: A Chronicle of St. John's, Berkeley* (1852). *As Good as a Comedy; or, The Tennesseean's Story* (1852). *Vasconselos: A Romance of the New World* (1853). *Egeria; or, Voices of Thought and Counsel, For the Woods and Wayside* (1853). *Marie de Berniere: A Tale of the Crescent City*, also entitled *The Maroon: A Legend of the Caribees* (1853). *Poems Descriptive, Dramatic, Legendary and Contemplative* (1853). *South Carolina in the Revolutionary War* (1853). *Southward Ho! A Spell of Sunshine* (1854). *The Forayers; or, The Raid of the Dog-Days* (1855). *Eutaw: A Sequel to The Forayers; or, The Raid of the Dog-Days: A Tale of the Revolution* (1856). *The Cassique of Kiawah: A Colonial Romance* (1859). *Areytos; or, Songs and Ballads of the South: With Other Poems* (1860). *Sack and Destruction of the City of Columbia, S.C.* (1865). Ed., *War Poets of the South* (1866). *The Army Correspondence of Colonel John Laurens in the Years 1777–8, With a Memoir* (1867). *The Sense of the Beautiful: An Address* (1870). *The Letters of William Gilmore Simms*, 6 vols., ed. Mary C. Simms Oliphant and T. C. Duncan Eaves (1952–82). *Voltmeier; or, The Mountain Men* (1969). *Paddy McGann; or, The Demon of the Stump* (1972). *Joscelyn: A Tale of the Revolution* (1975). *The Cub of the Panther: A Hunter Legend of the "Old North State"* (1997).

—MARY ANN WIMSATT

LEWIS P. SIMPSON (1916–2005). Lewis Pearson Simpson was an intellectual historian of the South. He proposed that the literary consciousness in America is special, North *and* South, by virtue of our founding as an Enlightenment project. "Mind," Simpson's term for the primacy of thinking and intention over primordial myths of origin, shapes our national understanding of beginning, purpose, and fate. "History," his term for the irreversible actuality of events, is mind's antagonist. Hence, southern and American literary productions register the ongoing struggle to reconcile what does happen with what mind thinks ought to have happened.

Unlike most critics who specialize in the South, Simpson was an authority on the New England "mind" as well, translated as the myth of Divine Providence, the intentional design and supervision exercised by the Protestant God over Anglo-European explorers and settlers. God had prepared a Garden for his chosen people in the New World, and they were expected to renew the covenant that had lapsed in the Old World. As early as Bradford's *Of Plymouth Plantation,* however, it was clear that success was wanting. Anxiety about the gap between divine promise and human failure dogged the New England mind up to Emerson. In *The Brazen Face of History,* Simpson brings this branch of his work up to Henry James.

In the South, the edenic promise was historically embodied in chattel slavery and the plantation. Almost from the beginning, in the writings of Jefferson (Simpson's touchstone for the antebellum mind of the South), the fatal contradiction wrought its destructive anxiety. Twentieth-century southern writers such as Robert Penn Warren and Walker Percy continued to explore latter-day evolutionary phases of the split southern consciousness. *The Fable of the Southern Writer* is Simpson's summary statement on the tangled progress of mind in the South, as registered in the works of modern southern writers.

Simpson was born on July 18, 1916, in Jacksboro, Tex. He received a B.A. (1938), M.A. (1939), and Ph.D. (1948) from the University of Texas, where he began a teaching career. He married Mary Elizabeth Ellis on July 14, 1941; they had one son, David. In 1948 Simpson arrived at Louisiana State University as an assistant professor, finding there the professional environment he needed.

If there is one southern writer whose intellectual tenacity, sweep, and subtlety of argument closely match Simpson's own, it is Allen Tate. Tate's sense of southern identity—a condition of estrangement for the rooted provincial in the modern moment—is one of Simpson's key concepts. The essays collected in *The Brazen Face of History* trace this estrangement in the lives and works of American writers from Henry James to Walker Percy. For Simpson, as for Tate, the southerner is the only alienated modern mind aware of, and not prone to live with, alienation. Simpson's argument for this condition shows his mastery of Tate's analysis of the southern circumstances of existence: the southerner knows alienation in the ache for the loss of community and order—a state of dispossession more psychic than historical, and thus incurable.

In recent essays in *The Fable of the Southern Writer* Simpson provided glimpses of his own southern boyhood in Jacksboro, Tex., modeling his own expulsion from community and past into the disordered present. He has found Warren's narrator in *All the King's Men,* Jack Burden, an apt literary analogy for his own life. In other essays on Warren as writer and intellectual, Simpson has shown extraordinary insight into Warren, who, if Tate took the South as an idea, took the South as a visceral reality.

Simpson's influence on southern letters is not limited to his publications. As editor of the Library of Southern Civilization series of Louisiana State University Press from 1969 until his retirement in 1987, he played a large part in recovering and keeping in print the pivotal texts that have functioned as the scripture of southern cultural identity. And as co-editor of the *Southern Review* from the inauguration of the new series in 1965 until 1987, he wielded untold influence over the direction of southern literary criticism. Much honored, Lewis Simpson died on April 17, 2005, in Baton Rouge.

WORKS: *The Federalist Literary Mind* (1962). Ed., *Profile of Robert Frost* (1971). Ed., *The Poetry of Community: Essays on the Southern Sensibility of History and Literature* (1972). *The Man of Letters in New England and the South: Essays on the History of the Literary Vocation in America* (1973). *The Dispossessed Garden: Pastoral and History in Southern Literature* (1975). Ed., *The Possibilities of Order: Cleanth Brooks and His Work* (1975). *The Brazen Face of History: Studies in the Literary Consciousness in America* (1980). Ed., *The History of Southern Literature*, with Louis D. Rubin, Jr., Blyden Jackson, Rayburn S. Moore, and Thomas D. Young (1985). Ed., *Selected Stories from the Southern Review, 1965–1985* (1987). Ed., *The Southern Review and Modern Literature, 1935–85* (1988). *Mind and the American Civil War: A Meditation on Lost Causes* (1989). *The Fable of the Southern Writer* (1994).

—MICHAEL KREYLING

CHARLES ALPHONSO SMITH (1864–1924). C. Alphonso Smith, a professor and popularizer of literature, was born in Greensboro, N.C., on May 28, 1864, to Jacob Henry and Mary Kelly Watson Smith. He received his early education in Greensboro and earned an A.B. (1884) and an A.M. (1887) at Davidson College. For four years Smith taught school in small North Carolina towns. In 1889 he matriculated at Johns Hopkins University, where he received his Ph.D. in 1893. In his subsequent academic career, Smith served as a professor of literature at Louisiana State University (1893–1902), the University of North Carolina (1902–9), the University of Virginia (1909–17), and the United States Naval Academy (1917–24). In 1910–11 he was Roosevelt Professor of American History and Institutions at the University of Berlin, the first southerner since the war to occupy that chair. Smith died in Annapolis on June 13, 1924.

After initial work on grammar and syntax, Smith devoted his scholarly attention to the essay, the short story, and oratory, especially of his native region. He edited one volume of *The Library of Southern Literature* and assisted with others. Smith wrote a biography of his boyhood friend William Sydney Porter (who wrote as O. Henry) and a book on Edgar Allan Poe. He also developed an interest in the collecting of ballads, lectured widely on the topic, and helped found the Virginia Folk-Lore Society in 1913. After his death his widow published some of his short pieces on individual southerners and trends in southern literature as *Southern Literary Studies*. Although a university professor, Smith always sought to interest a wider audience in literature. To do so, he frequently employed his considerable talent as a public lecturer and in 1913 published *What Can Literature Do for Me?* which appeared in several editions.

WORKS: *Repetition and Parallelism in English Verse: A Study in the Technique of Poetry* (1894). *An Old English Grammar and Exercise Book with Inflections, Syntax, Selections for Readings, and Glossary* (1896). *An English-German Conversation Book*, with Gustav Kruger (1902). *Our Language* (1903). *Studies in English Syntax* (1906). *Die Amerikanische Literatur: Vorlesungen, Gehalten an der Königlichen, Friedrich-Wilhelms-Universität zu Berlin, von Dr. C. Alphonso Smith* (1912). *What Can Literature Do for Me?* (1913); repr. as *What Reading Can Do for You* (1925). *O. Henry Biography* (1916). *New Words Self-Defined* (1919). *Keynote Studies in Keynote Books of the Bible* (1919). *Edgar Allan Poe: How to Know Him* (1921). *Southern Literary Studies: A Collection of Literary, Biographical, and Other Sketches* (1927).

—GAINES M. FOSTER

CHARLES FORSTER SMITH (1852–1931). Charles Forster Smith was born on June 30, 1852, in what is now Greenwood County, S.C., the fifth of eleven children. His parents were the Reverend James Francis and Juliana Forster Smith. He received his earliest education at neighboring schools before he went in 1868 to Wofford College, S.C., where he received an A.B. in 1872. He also attended Harvard University (one semester, 1874), the University of Berlin (1874–75), and the University of Leipzig (1874–75, 1879–81). At the latter he was awarded a Ph.D. in 1881; his dissertation, *A Study of Plutarch's Life of Artaxerxes, Especial Reference to the Sources,* was published the same year. The University of Arkansas and Wofford College awarded him the honorary LL.D. in 1910.

Smith married Anna L. Du Pre on August 21, 1879, and they were the parents of five children. She died on April 26, 1893.

Smith held teaching positions in Greenwood, S.C., until 1874; at Wofford College (classics and German, 1875–79); at Williams College (assistant professor of Latin and Greek, 1881–82); at Vanderbilt University (professor of modern language, 1882–83, and chair of Greek, 1883–94); at the University of Wisconsin (professor and chairman of the Department of Greek and Classical Philology, 1894–1917, and emeritus, 1917); and at the American School of Classical Studies in Athens (annual professor, 1920–21). At Wofford and Vanderbilt, Smith's close colleague was William Malone Baskervill.

Smith was associate editor of *Classical Philology* from its founding in 1906 to 1931 and president of the American Philological Association in 1902–3. He was the editor of several college texts in the classics and wrote "The South's Contribution to Classical Studies" for volume 7 of *The South in the Building of the Nation* (1909). During his last years he was working on an unfinished book on the Old South. He died on August 3, 1931, in Racine, Wisc.

WORKS: *A Study of Plutarch's Life of Artaxerxes, with Especial Reference to the Sources* (1881). Ed., *Thucydides, Bk. 7* (1886), *Bk. 3* (1894). Trans., Hertzberg, *Geschichte* (1900). Ed., Xenophon, *Anabasis* (1905). Ed., *Herodotus, Bk. 7* (1907). *Reminiscences and Sketches* (1908). Ed., *Thucydides, Bk. 6* (1913). Trans., *Thucydides,* Loeb Classical Library, 4 vols. (1919–23). *Charles Kendall Adams* (1924).

—RANDALL G. PATTERSON

CHARLES HENRY SMITH (1826–1903). Charles Henry Smith, creator of "Bill Arp," was born in Lawrenceville, Ga., on June 15, 1826. One of ten children born to Asahel Reid and Caroline Ann Maguire Smith, he attended Gwinnett County Manual Labor Institute. In 1844 he entered Franklin College (later the University of Georgia) but because of family illness he left in 1847 before completing his degree. Smith married the sixteen-year-old Mary Octavia Hutchins in 1849 and eventually had thirteen children, ten of whom lived to adulthood. After a brief study of the law, Smith became a lawyer traveling for the Georgia circuit court. In 1851 he and his growing family moved to Rome, Ga., where he was elected alderman six times and mayor once.

As an active supporter of the southern cause during the Civil War, Smith procured supplies, tried cases of treason, and served as an officer in the Army of Northern Virginia and in the Forrest Artillery Company. After the war he continued to be active in law, politics, and business until 1877, when he moved to a farm some five miles from Cartersville. His main source of income from then until his death came from his Bill Arp letters and public lectures. His death at Cartersville on August 24, 1903, was mourned by thousands of admiring readers throughout the South.

Smith's contribution to southern literature, the Bill Arp letters, is a series of more than two thousand informal essays written between 1861 and 1903. The persona Bill Arp is a simple, strong, conservative Georgia cracker whose essays, in the form of letters to the editor, chronicle the successes and failures, hopes and frustrations, of an average southerner during the war and Reconstruction. Over the years the voice of Arp changes from that of a semiliterate given to comic misspellings to that of a gentleman, educated and literary. Most of the letters appeared in Atlanta newspapers (the *Southern*

Confederacy and the *Constitution*), and according to one estimate were also printed in over seven hundred newspapers during the peak of their popularity.

WORKS: *Bill Arp, So Called* (1866). *Bill Arp's Peace Papers* (1873). *Bill Arp's Scrap Book: Humor and Philosophy* (1884). *The Farm and the Fireside: Sketches of Domestic Life in War and in Peace* (1891). *A School History of Georgia* (1893). *Bill Arp: From the Uncivil War to Date* (1903).

—HAROLD WOODELL

DAVE SMITH (1942–). Among the strongest southern poets to emerge in the last decades of the twentieth century, Dave Smith has established himself as an enduring American writer.

Smith's life has been a turbulent search for a sense of place and identity. Born on December 19, 1942, in Portsmouth, Va., to Ralph Smith, a naval engineer, and Catherine Mary Cornwell Smith, a civil-service secretary, David Jeddie Smith grew up in a family that shared the common working-class desire for permanence in post-Depression America. In search of stability, Smith's family shuffled around in various suburbs before building their own house. Despite his suburban upbringing, Smith cultivated a respect for the pastoral world during hunting sessions in the Virginian woods with his grandfather and visits with his grandmother in the Chesapeake Bay area. Taking after his father, he became fascinated with fast cars and their representation of escape and freedom. Tragically, his father would die in a car accident before Smith graduated from high school.

The first in his family to enroll in college, Smith attended the University of Virginia, earning a B.A. in 1965. Afterward, he taught high school French and English in Poquoson, Va. He also coached the triad of American sports: baseball, basketball, and football. The physical life of the fishermen in Poquoson, called Bull Island by its inhabitants, would provide an unforgettable contrast with the intellectual and refined environment of Charlottesville. Having absorbed the rhythms and hardships of the watermen's lives as part of his own identity, Smith honored the townsfolk by entitling his first small collection of poems *Bull Island*. In addition to literary inspiration and a sense of community, Poquoson provided him with his wife, Dee.

In 1969 Smith earned an M.A. at Southern Illinois University; his thesis was on the poetry of James Dickey. He then served in the U.S. Air Force for four years, moonlighting as an English instructor at local colleges. Smith continued to write poetry and was even a founding editor of a literary journal, *Back Door*. After the air force, he attended Ohio University, graduating with a Ph.D. in 1976. During his doctoral studies, Smith's literary reputation flourished. Publication of two major collections, *The Fisherman's Whore* and *Cumberland Station*, led to his recognition as one of the leading young American poets.

After graduation, Smith accepted a position as director of the creative-writing program at the University of Utah. During this time he published *Goshawk, Antelope*, a surprising and surreal departure from the regional colorings of his earlier work. Runner-up for the Pulitzer Prize, the collection established Smith as a complex and versatile poet armed with a literary vision unrestrained by a provincial scope.

The itinerancy of Smith's youth followed him into adulthood. Accepting a position at SUNY-Binghamton in 1980, he taught there for a year, followed by a year at the University of Florida. With the publication of *Dream Flights*, another finalist for the Pulitzer Prize, Smith would seal his legacy as an important poet. The same year, he earned a Guggenheim Fellowship. After teaching at Virginia Commonwealth University for several years, Smith moved to Louisiana State University in 1990 to act as co-editor of the *Southern Review*, the journal co-founded by one of his greatest literary influences,

Robert Penn Warren. After twelve years with the *Southern Review*, Smith accepted a position at Johns Hopkins University, where he has taught creative writing since 2002.

WORKS: *Bull Island* (1970). *Mean Rufus Throw Down* (1973). *The Fisherman's Whore* (1974). *Drunks* (1975). *Cumberland Station: Poems* (1976). *In Dark, Sudden with Light* (1976). *Goshawk, Antelope: Poems* (1979). *Apparitions* (1981). *Blue Spruce* (1981). *Dream Flights: Poems* (1981). *Homage to Edgar Allan Poe: Poems* (1981). *Onliness: A Novel* (1981). Ed., *The Pure Clear Word: Essays on the Poetry of James Wright* (1982). *In the House of the Judge* (1983). *Gray Soldiers: Poems* (1984). *Southern Delights: Poems and Stories* (1984). *Local Assays: On Contemporary American Poetry* (1985). Ed., *The Morrow Anthology of Younger American Poets*, with David Bottoms (1985). *The Roundhouse Voices: Selected and New Poems* (1985). *Cuba Night: Poems* (1990). Ed., *The Essential Poe* (1991). *Night Pleasures: New and Selected Poems* (1992). *Fate's Kite: Poems, 1991–1995* (1995). *Floating on Solitude: Three Volumes of Poetry* (1996). *The Wick of Memory: New and Selected Poems, 1970–2000* (2000). *Little Boats, Unsalvaged: Poems, 1992–2004* (2005).

—JASON NEPHI HALL

F. HOPKINSON SMITH (1838–1915). Francis Hopkinson Smith, a descendant of Francis Hopkinson (poet, composer, signer of the Declaration of Independence), was born in Baltimore, Md., on January 9, 1838. Smith's education was earned in Baltimore's iron factories, and while thus employed he learned mechanical engineering and pursued his love of painting and writing. His knowledge of engineering placed him in the construction industry for thirty-plus years. His experience even extended to the construction of the Statue of Liberty's foundation. He died in New York on April 7, 1915.

Smith's writing career began in the 1880s with the publication of a number of his travel books about Europe and Mexico. He began writing fiction, and in those years after the Civil War the southern romantic novel had become popular. Smith, along with his contemporaries John Fox, James Lane Allen, Thomas Dixon, and Thomas Nelson Page, offered a palatable view of the "New South" to book-buying northern audiences. His short stories and novels were best-sellers, and he became a sought-after lecturer in New York. He was so popular, in fact, that Charles Scribner's and Sons collected his works in twenty-three volumes, the last of which was published during the year of Smith's death. His novels covered subjects and settings as far-ranging as the hardscrabble New York waterfront (*Tom Grogan*) and the genteel world of Virginia's landed gentry (*Colonel Carter of Cartersville*). Recent scholarship, though, has portrayed Smith's work as reductionist local color writing that misrepresented the South to a curious northern audience.

Smith's work as an artist is still ardently studied, and his correspondence, writings, and miscellany have been recently collected by the special collections research center at the Syracuse University Library.

WORKS: *Old Lines in New Black and White* (1885). *Well-Worn Roads in Spain, Holland and Italy* (1886). *A White Umbrella in Mexico* (1889). *A Book of the Tile Club* (1890). *Colonel Carter of Cartersville* (1891). *A Day at Laguerre's and Other Days* (1892). *American Illustrators* (1892). *A Gentleman Vagabond and Some Others* (1895). *Tom Grogan* (1896). *Gondola Days* (1897). *Venice of To-Day* (1897). *Caleb West, Master Diver* (1898). *The Other Fellow* (1899). *The Fortunes of Oliver Horn* (1902). *The Under Dog* (1903). *The Wood Fire in No. 3* (1905). *The Tides of Barnegat* (1906). *The Veiled Lady* (1907). *The Romance of an Old-Fashioned Gentleman* (1907). *Peter* (1908). *Forty Minutes Late* (1909). *Kennedy Square* (1911). *The Arm Chair at the Inn* (1912). *Charcoals of New and Old New York* (1912). *In Thackeray's London* (1913). *In Dickens' London* (1914). *Enoch Crane* (1916).

—MATTHEW SCIALDONE

CAPTAIN JOHN SMITH (1580–1631). The first son born to George Smith, yeoman, and Alice Richard Smith, John Smith was baptized in Willoughby, Lincolnshire, on January 9, 1580. The boy

was given some schooling and apprenticed to a merchant, Thomas Sendall. After his father's death in 1596, Smith left Sendall for France to take up soldiering. He returned home briefly in late 1599 or early 1600, before setting out for central Europe to fight with the Austrian empire against the Turks. In Hungary, Smith acquired a reputation for bravery that he exploited in his 1630 autobiography. Taken captive by Turks, Smith escaped and traveled through Russia and Poland before making it back to England in late 1604 or early 1605.

Still restless after eight years of fighting on the Continent, Smith joined the expedition being planned by the Virginia Company and sailed in the first ships for that North American colony in December 1606. Smith, probably the most experienced soldier and adventurer among the initial settlers, was at first suspected of treachery, but from the time of his arrival on the mainland in April 1607, until his departure two and a half years later, he proved his worthiness to the group. In December he was captured by the Algonkians under Powhatan, the supreme ruler of the tribes in eastern Virginia; his version of that episode bequeathed to history the origins of the Pocahontas story. In September 1608 Smith was elected president of the colony. He enacted strict measures both to ensure the Englishmen's survival and to keep the native people in fear of him. Following his injury in a gunpowder explosion, Smith departed for England in October 1609, never to return to Virginia.

Back in England, Smith used his pen to serve as proponent of the colony and critic of Virginia Company policies that he thought inhibited Virginia's success, notably in *The Proceedings*. In 1614 he set out for the New World again, this time on a voyage for New England. After a failed attempt, Smith again sailed for New England in 1615, only to be captured by a French vessel. After his release, he published his *Description of New England* in 1616 but found further doors to adventuring closed to him. Smith spent the next several years in London writing about Virginia and the English colonies throughout North America. His magnum opus, *The Generall Historie*, came about in part as a response to the 1622 Algonkian attacks on Virginia settlements that left hundreds of English dead and many of the rest in a state of starvation. He insisted that sponsors of colonies take a broad view toward colonization, but he found his writings on colonial affairs not greatly accepted. In his last years, he turned more to practical books and his autobiography, one of the first such works in English. He died in London on June 21, 1631.

Smith's many accounts of his experiences have proven to be much more than the reliable sources of information they generally are. His characterization of Powhatan in *The Generall Historie*, for example, whatever its factual basis, shows a clearly literary touch in the portrait of a large, powerful, wily, but eloquent emperor against whom the heroic Captain Smith strives. Even though Smith the soldier did all he could to keep the Algonkians in submission, the writer demonstrates a thorough interest in native practices and language, and records invaluable understandings of a culture that quickly disappeared after the establishment of English hegemony in the region. He also bequeathed to posterity the image of the self-made, self-authored man, one who sought to control the conditions of his own textual reputation. An originator of the captivity story and the personal narrative, a writer unashamed of promoting his own skills and prowess, a stylist of a rough and ready but sometimes poetic prose, and an occasionally deft satirist, Smith provided for southern and American writers in general a rich source of models and material on which to craft later and distinctive literary traditions.

WORKS: *A True Relation of Such Occurrences and Accidents of Noate as Hath Hapned in Virginia* (1608). *A Map of Virginia. With a Description of the Countrey, the Commodities, People, Government and Religion* (1612). *The Proceedings of the English Colonies in Virginia* (1612). *A Description of New England* (1616). *New Englands Trials* (1620; rev. 1622). *The Generall Historie of Virginia, New-England, and the Summer Isles* (1624). *An Accidence or the Path-way to Experience* (1626). *A Sea Grammar* (1627). *The True Travels, Adventures, and Observations of Captaine John Smith* (1630).

Advertisements for the Unexperienced Planters of New England, or Any Where (1631). *The Complete Works*, 3 vols., ed. Philip L. Barbour (1986).

—Jeffrey H. Richards

LEE SMITH (1944–). Lee Smith, only child of Ernest and Virginia Smith, was born on November 1, 1944, in Grundy, Va., a coal-mining town in the southwestern corner of the state. Growing up in a secure family with deep roots in the area, she spent hours watching local people from a perch in her father's dime store and decided, by the age of nine, to be a writer. During her years at Hollins College (1963–67) she discovered, primarily through reading James Still's *River of Earth*, that the southern mountains of her childhood could provide a powerful sense of place. At Hollins she worked with leading southern scholar-writer Louis Rubin, who not only encouraged her efforts but introduced her to the techniques and themes of southern authors, particularly Eudora Welty, Flannery O'Connor, and William Faulkner. They became early models for her developing awareness of the pull of the past and family, the art of storytelling, and the function of voice and speech in delineating character.

In 1966 Smith submitted a creative writing thesis to the Book-of-the-Month Club Writing Fellowship Contest. *The Last Day the Dog Bushes Bloomed*, which won the award, became her first published novel in 1968. Before its appearance, Smith married, in June 1967, poet James Seay. For the next several years his university assignments and the birth of two sons dictated most of Smith's activities. A second novel, *Something in the Wind*, appeared to good reviews in 1971, and while living in Tuscaloosa with her growing family, Smith wrote a story of an Alabama town's sesquicentennial. *Fancy Strut*, published in 1973, was hailed as a comic masterpiece, but her next and much darker work, *Black Mountain Breakdown*, took five years to find a publisher. Like her first two works, *Black Mountain Breakdown* treats a young girl's agonized and socially conditioned search for self, but it also marks the beginning of Smith's understanding of the ways in which her Appalachian heritage could energize not only her settings but the underpinnings of her characters, their voices, and their will to live.

The early 1980s marked a change in direction for Smith on many fronts. Stories that had helped her to win O. Henry awards in 1978 and 1980 were gathered for her first collection, *Cakewalk*, in 1981, but her marriage to Seay ended a year later. In 1981 she joined the creative writing faculty at North Carolina State University in Raleigh, where until her retirement in 1999 she was a major contributor to the program's growing reputation and a mentor to dozens of emerging writers. During this hectic time she also produced her fifth book, *Oral History*, which became a Book-of-the-Month Club selection in 1983. The use of multiple first-person points of view, the historical and geographical scope, the engagement with language through dialect and style, and the several layers of narrative complexity that distinguish *Oral History* made it a breakthrough work. In 1985 she reached another level of success with *Family Linen*, the beautifully crafted story of a family's confrontation with their violent past and their responsibilities for healing one another. This novel was dedicated to Hal Crowther, whom she married in June of that year. The couple live in Hillsborough, N.C.

Smith's willingness to tackle new narrative forms continued throughout the 1980s with the incomparable epistolary novel *Fair and Tender Ladies*. During the 1990s, she was even more productive as a writer while she continued to teach and provide direction for the creative writing program. Her books of this decade included a second collection of short stories, *Me and My Baby View the Eclipse*; *The Devil's Dream*, a generational saga about a family of country musicians; *Saving Grace*, in which Smith's interest in religion is highlighted through the saga of a snake-handling preacher's daughter; the epistolary novella *The Christmas Letters*; and *News of the Spirit*, a third story collection. The opening story here, "The Bubba Stories," is one of Smith's most autobiographical narratives, dealing

with a college girl and would-be writer who makes up the engaging exploits of a wild brother named "Bubba" to impress her friends. Smith's experiences at Hollins in the 1960s also became the source for *The Last Girls,* a widely acclaimed work that had its beginnings in a raft trip that Smith and fourteen of her classmates took down the Mississippi River in the summer of 1966. Some of the brightest moments of her fiction, along with selections from her friend and former student Jill McCorkle, were shaped in 2001 into a popular musical, *Good Old Girls,* which continues to make the rounds of regional theater.

What increasingly distinguishes Smith's fiction over a remarkable thirty-five-year career is her ability to use regional details to enrich complex narratives not bound within regional commonplaces of culture or geography. What make her one of America's leading writers are her generous humor, her empathy for the struggles and endurance of women whose lives within families and communities represent compelling dramas of quiet heroism, her keen ear for the ways that speech reveals spirit, and her insights into the ways that the past inevitably works its web over the present.

WORKS: *The Last Day the Dogbushes Bloomed* (1968). *Something in the Wind* (1971). *Fancy Strut* (1973). *Black Mountain Breakdown* (1980). *Cakewalk* (1981). *Oral History* (1983). *Family Linen* (1985). *Fair and Tender Ladies* (1988). *Me and My Baby View the Eclipse* (1990). *Devil's Dream* (1992). *Saving Grace* (1994). *Christmas Letters* (1996). *News of the Spirit* (1997). Ed., *Sitting on the Courthouse Bench: An Oral History of Grundy, Virginia* (2000). *Conversations with Lee Smith,* ed. Linda Tate (2001). *The Last Girls* (2002). *Angels Passing* (2003).

—LUCINDA H. MACKETHAN

LILLIAN SMITH (1897–1966). From the 1930s through the 1960s, Lillian Smith was perhaps the most courageous and outspoken white southern critic of the South's racial status quo. Lillian Eugenia Smith was born in Jasper, Fla., on December 12, 1897, the daughter of a prosperous businessman and a cultivated mother ("a wistful creature," Smith called her). She received her early education in Florida and Georgia, studied piano at the Peabody Conservatory in Baltimore between 1917 and 1922, and taught music in a Methodist mission school in China from 1922 to 1925. Awakened by her China experience to the evils of racism and classism, Smith returned to her native South with a more critical vision.

During much of the next two decades she directed the summer camp her father had begun in north Georgia; Smith turned that camp, whose clients were the daughters of prominent white southern families, into a laboratory for racial change. She wrote two early novels (one of which was based on her stay in China and both of which were destroyed by fire) and from 1936 to 1946 co-edited *South Today* (also entitled, at various times, *Pseudopodia* and the *North Georgia Review*), a bold journal calling for radical racial change. For many years, Smith lived with her *South Today* co-editor, frequent collaborator, and longtime partner, Paula Snelling.

In 1944, with the publication of *Strange Fruit,* Smith burst on the national scene. A controversial best-seller, the novel dealt with interracial romance, a lesbian relationship, and racial violence. It was followed by several works of fiction and nonfiction, including two very influential works of personal reminiscences and social commentary, *Killers of the Dream* and *The Journey.* In both works Smith attacked southern racial and gender inequities head-on; *Killers of the Dream* has come to be seen as a classic of southern autobiography. In those works and in essays she wrote for the *New Republic,* the *Saturday Review,* and other magazines, she wrote of the South's "dark tangled forest full of sins and boredom and fears" and of the white southern conscience "stretched so tightly on its frame of sin and punishment and God's anger." Her writings brought Smith criticism from fellow white southerners, even liberals such as Atlanta editor Ralph McGill who thought she was proceeding too fast, but the works also brought recognition and admiration from civil rights workers, black and white, in the early 1960s. Suffering from cancer throughout the late 1950s and 1960s, Smith continued to speak boldly. She died on September 28, 1966, in Atlanta.

WORKS: *Strange Fruit* (1944). *Killers of the Dream* (1949; rev. ed. 1961). *The Journey* (1954). *Now Is the Time* (1955). *One Hour* (1959). *Memory of a Large Christmas* (1962). *Our Faces, Our Words* (1964).

—FRED HOBSON

R. T. SMITH (1947–). Rodney Theodore Smith was born on April 13, 1947, in Washington, D.C. His parents, Roland McCall Smith and Mary Helen Thaxton Smith, were native to Griffin, Ga., and Rod's summer visits with grandparents nurtured his southern roots. In 1953 the family moved to Charlotte, N.C. Following graduation from Charlotte's Harding High School, where he played football, wrestled, ran track, and belonged to the chess club, he entered Georgia Tech but soon transferred to the University of North Carolina, first at Charlotte and then at Chapel Hill. After duty with the U.S. Marine Corps in Vietnam, Smith returned to the University of North Carolina at Charlotte, graduating with a B.A. in philosophy in 1969. In 1973, after teaching in public schools, he entered the graduate program in English at Appalachian State University in Boone, N.C., determined to be a writer. He and fellow graduate students founded the Appalachian literary magazine *Cold Mountain Review,* with Smith as first editor. Upon graduation in 1975 with an M.A. in English, Smith accepted a teaching position in the English Department at Auburn University, where he was appointed alumni writer-in-residence in 1983. In 1991 he received a Fellowship in Literature from the National Endowment for the Arts and in 1994 was a resident fellow at the Tyrone Guthrie Centre at Annaghmakerrig, Ireland. Two books of his poetry have been nominated for the Pulitzer Prize. Smith has held many editorial positions, including as contributing editor of *International Poetry Review,* associate editor of *Southern Humanities Review,* and poetry editor of *National Forum.* In 1995 he accepted the editorship of *Shenandoah* at Washington and Lee University and moved to Rockbridge County, Va. His wife is the poet Sarah Kennedy.

WORKS: *Waking under Snow* (1975). *Good Water* (1979). *Rural Route* (1981). *Beasts Did Leap* (1982). *Finding the Path: Poems* (1983). *From the High Dive* (1983). *Roosevelt Unbound* (1984). *Birch-Light* (1986). *Banish Misfortune* (1988). *The Cardinal Heart* (1991). *The Names of Trees* (1991). *Faith: Stories* (1995). *Gristle* (1995). *Hunter-Gatherer* (1996). *Trespasser: Poems* (1996). *Split the Lark: Selected Poems* (1999). *Lilting* (2000). *But with Blood* (2000). *Messenger: Poems* (2001). *R. T. Smith: Greatest Hits: 1975–2001* (2002). Ed., *Common Wealth: Contemporary Poets of Virginia,* with Sarah Kennedy (2003). *The Hollow Log Lounge: Poems* (2003). *Brightwood: Poems* (2004).

—LINDA WELDEN

WILLIAM JAY SMITH (1918–). William Jay Smith was born in Winnfield, La., on April 22, 1918. He began his prodigious writing career at the age of fourteen, with the national publication of one of his poems. Educated domestically and abroad, he received his B.A. (1939) and M.A. (1941) in French from Washington University in Missouri. Following naval service in World War II, Smith continued postgraduate studies a year at Columbia University, and then spent two years as a Rhodes Scholar at Oxford University, after which he continued his studies at the University of Florence in Italy (1948–50). In 1947 Smith married his first wife, Barbara Howes, a poet, with whom he had two sons. He married his second wife, Sonja Haussmann, of Paris, in 1966; they collaborated on the book *Wild Bouquet,* a presentation of nature poems by Harry Martinson.

Smith's eclectic career has bridged the worlds of art, academia, and politics, and includes a two-year term in the Vermont House of Representatives (1960–62). He is the author of more than fifty books of poetry, children's verse, literary criticism, and translations. Smith worked in Washington,

D.C., as the writer-in-residence at Arena Stage (1964–65), followed by a post as poet-in-residence at Williams College in Massachusetts (1959–64, 1966–77), and consultant in poetry at the Library of Congress (1968–70), the position now known as the poet laureate. He returned to Columbia University in 1973 as chairman of the Writing Division of the School of Arts, a position he held until 1975, before teaching at Hollins College in Virginia until 1980, at which point he became a professor emeritus.

A member of the American Academy of Arts and Letters since 1975, Smith has had a long and highly decorated career, including nominations for the National Book Award for two volumes of poetry (1957, 1966). He received the Henry Bellamann Major Award in 1970 and the Russell Loines Award from the National Institute of Arts and Letters for poetry and a grant from the National Endowment for the Arts in 1972, and was a National Endowment for the Arts fellow (1972, 1995) and a National Endowment for the Humanities fellow (1975, 1989). Smith's translations have been similarly lauded, receiving the médaille de Vermeil from the French Academy (1991), the Pro Cultura Hungarica medal from Hungary (1993), and the René Vásquez Díaz Prize from the Swedish Academy (1997).

WORKS: *Poems* (1947). *Celebration at Dark* (1950). *Laughing Time* (1955). *Valéry Larbaud: Poems of a Multimillionaire* (1955). *Selected Writings of Jules Laforgue* (1956). *Bead Curtain: Calligrams* (1957). *Poems 1947–1957* (1957). *American Primitive* (1957). *The Spectra Hoax* (1961). *The Tin Can and Other Poems* (1966). *Poems from France* (1967). *Poetry of William Jay Smith* (1970). *New and Selected Poems* (1970). *The Streaks of the Tulip: Selected Criticism* (1972). *Poems from Italy* (1972). *At Delphi: For Allen Tate on His Seventy-Fifth Birthday, 19 November 1974* (1974). *Queens of Coins* (1975). *Venice in the Fog* (1976). *Verses on the Times* (1978). *Agadir* (1979). *Army Brat: A Memoir* (1980). *The Traveler's Tree* (1980). *Laughing Time: Nonsense Poems* (1980). *Brazilian Poetry, 1950–1980* (1983). *Dutch Interior: Postwar Poetry of the Netherlands and Flanders* (1984). *Poems from Italy* (1985). Trans., Harry Martinson, *Wild Bouquet: Nature Poems,* with Leif Sjöberg (1985). *Arrow in the Wall: Selected Poetry and Prose* (1987). *Life Sentence: Selected Poems* (1990). *Collected Poems: 1939–1989* (1990). *Berlin: The City and the Court* (1996). *Forest of Childhood: Poems from Sweden* (1996). *The World below the Window: Poems 1937–1997* (1998). *What You Have Almost Forgotten: Selected Poems* (1999). *Girl in Glass: Love Poems* (1999). *The Cherokee Lottery* (2000).

—PATRICK SAMWAY, S.J.

E.D.E.N. SOUTHWORTH (1819–1899). From the early 1850s through the 1880s, Emma Dorothy Eliza Nevitte Southworth was one of the most widely read authors of sentimental and melodramatic novels. Her stories, usually set in the South, often featured unconventional, independent heroines who were rewarded for flouting the constraints of traditional female behavior.

Emma D. E. Nevitte was born on December 26, 1819, in Alexandria, Va. Her father died when she was three. She was educated at her stepfather's school in Washington, D.C., then taught there for five years. She spent summers with her father's family in Maryland, observing the rural life often depicted in her novels.

In 1840 she married Frederick Southworth, who abandoned Emma and their two children in 1844. She resumed teaching, supplementing her salary by writing short stories and novellas. The first appeared in the *Baltimore Saturday Visiter* in 1846, and others the next year in the *National Era.* Her first novel, *Retribution,* ran for fourteen installments in the *Era* in 1849 and was so successful that *Harper's* republished it the same year. This book, which launched Southworth's career as a prolific writer of popular fiction, explores the themes of betrayal and infidelity that recur in her work. Her novels were all serialized in newspapers before appearing, often under new titles, in book form.

She moved into Prospect Cottage, overlooking the Potomac, in 1850. Her Georgetown home attracted colleagues and admirers; guests included her friends John Greenleaf Whittier and Harriet Beecher Stowe. Southworth wrote for both the *Era* and the *Saturday Evening Post,* until the *New York*

Ledger signed her to an exclusive contract in 1856. Her melodramatic *The Hidden Hand*, first serialized in 1859, was her most popular tale.

Southworth produced roughly fifty novels between 1849 and 1886. These were notable for extravagant plot contrivances, wry humor, and wronged women forced to make their own way in a world inequitably and ineptly controlled by men. She died at Prospect Cottage on June 30, 1899.

WORKS: *Retribution; or, The Vale of Shadows: A Tale of Passion* (1849). *The Deserted Wife* (1850). *The Mother-in-Law; or, The Isle of Rays* (1851). *Shannondale* (1851). *Virginia and Magdalene; or, The Foster Sisters: A Novel* (1852). *The Discarded Daughter; or, The Children of the Isle: A Tale of the Chesapeake* (1852). *The Curse of Clifton: A Tale of Expiation and Redemption* (1852). *Old Neighbourhoods and New Settlements; or, Christmas Evening Legends* (1853). *The Wife's Victory and Other Nouvellettes* (1853). *The Lost Heiress* (1854). *The Missing Bride; or, Miriam the Avenger* (1855). *India; or, The Pearl of Pearl River* (1856). *Vivia; or, The Secret of Power* (1857). *The Lady of the Isle: A Romance from Real Life* (1859). *The Haunted Homestead and Other Nouvellettes, with an Autobiography of the Author* (1860). *Hickory Hall; or, The Outcast: A Romance of the Blue Ridge* (1861). *The Gipsy's Prophecy: A Tale of Real Life* (1861). *The Broken Engagement; or, Speaking the Truth for a Day* (1862). *Love's Labor Won* (1862). *The Fatal Marriage* (1863). *The Bridal Eve; or, Rose Elmer* (1864). *Allworth Abbey* (1865). *The Bride of Llewellyn* (1866). *The Fortune Seeker* (1866). *The Coral Lady; or, The Bronzed Beauty of Paris* (1867). *Fair Play; or, The Test of the Lone Isle* (1868). *How He Won Her: A Sequel to "Fair Play"* (1869). *The Changed Brides* (1869). *The Bride's Fate* (1869). *The Family Doom; or, The Sin of a Countess* (1869). *The Maiden Widow: A Sequel to "The Family Doom"* (1870). *The Christmas Guest: A Collection of Stories* (1870). *Cruel as the Grave* (1871). *Tried for Her Life, a Sequel to "Cruel as the Grave"* (1871). *The Lost Heir of Linlithgow* (1872). *A Noble Lord: The Sequel to "The Lost Heir of Linlithgow"* (1872). *A Beautiful Fiend: A Novel* (1873). *Victor's Triumph: The Sequel to "A Beautiful Fiend"* (1874). *The Mystery of Dark Hollow* (1875). *The Spectre Lover* (1875). *Ishmael; or, In the Depths* (1876). *Self-Raised; or, From the Depths: A Sequel to "Ishmael; or, In the Depths"* (1876). *The Red Hill Tragedy: A Novel* (1877). *The Fatal Secret* (1877). *The Bride's Ordeal: A Novel* (1878). *Phantom Wedding; or, The Fall of the House of Flint* (1878). *Sybil Brotherton: A Novel* (1879). *When Love Commands* (1880). *Why Did He Wed Her?: A Novel* (1884). *A Deed without a Name: A Novel* (1886). *Dorothy Harcourt's Secret* (1886). *To His Fate* (1886). *The Hidden Hand; or, Capitola the Madcap* (1888). *Unknown: A Novel* (1889). *Love's Bitterest Cup* (1889). *Nearest and Dearest: A Novel* (1889). *Little Nea's Engagement: A Sequel to "Nearest and Dearest"* (1889). *A Leap in the Dark: A Novel* (1889). *The Unloved Wife: A Novel* (1890). *Lilith: A Novel: A Sequel to "The Unloved Wife"* (1890). *For Woman's Love: A Novel* (1890). *An Unrequited Love: A Sequel to "For Woman's Love"* (1890). *The Lost Lady of Lone* (1890). *The Struggle of a Soul: A Sequel to "The Lost Lady of Lone"* (1890). *Gloria: a Novel* (1891). *David Lindsay: A Sequel to "Gloria"* (1891). *"Em": A Novel* (1892). *Em's Husband: A Novel* (1892). *A Skeleton in the Closet* (1893). *Brandon Coyle's Wife: A Sequel to "A Skeleton in the Closet"* (1893). *Only a Girl's Heart: A Novel* (1893). *The Rejected Bride: Only a Girl's Heart / 2d series* (1894). *Gertrude Haddon: Only a Girl's Heart / 3d series* (1894). *The Widows of Widowville* (1894). *Capitola's Peril: A Sequel to "The Hidden Hand"* (1907). *The Trail of the Serpent; or, The Homicide at Hawke Hall* (1907). *A Tortured Heart: Being Part Second of "The Trail of the Serpent"* (1907). *The Test of Love: Being the Third and Last Part of "The Trail of the Serpent"* (1907).

—NANCY GRAY SCHOONMAKER

ALFRED BENNETT SPELLMAN (1935–). Son of schoolteachers, Alfred Bennett Spellman, Jr., was born on August 7, 1935, in Nixonton, N.C. With his younger brother, Roland, he grew up in nearby Elizabeth City, attending public schools. In 1952 he entered Howard University, where he was immediately drawn to the artistic fervor. A member of the Howard Players theater group, he also wrote poems and shared them with fellow students, including Amiri Baraka (then known as LeRoi Jones) and Lucille Clifton. He was greatly influenced by Sterling Brown, the poet who was his teacher in several courses.

After receiving his B.A. in history and political science in 1956, Spellman entered Howard's law school, but following Baraka's lead, he departed in 1958 for New York City. There he turned his attention to the arts—writing poems and hosting a morning radio show while he worked at various jobs. He was caught up in the black aesthetic movement as well as the turbulent anti–Vietnam War movement.

In 1965 he published *The Beautiful Days and Others*, his only collection of poems, following it the next year with *Four Lives in the Bebop Business*, which profiles the lives of four jazz musicians: Cecil Taylor, Ornette Coleman, Herbie Nicols, and Jackie McLean. In the early 1970s he wrote and produced two shows for television, *Ebony Beat* and *Ebony Beat Junior*. His shows *Say Brother* and *Essays in Black Music* were syndicated throughout New England.

In 1967 Spellman returned to the South. Living in Atlanta, he promoted African American music and culture, teaching at Emory University and Atlanta University Center. In 1973 he accepted a teaching position at Harvard. With his wife and two children, he left Boston in 1978 for Washington, D.C., where he joined the staff of the National Endowment for the Arts, directing the funding of art programs for minority and rural populations.

Although Spellman does not have an extensive body of poetry, his work has been anthologized frequently. Those who have praised it include Langston Hughes and Gwendolyn Brooks.

WORKS: *The Beautiful Days and Others* (1965). *Four Lives in the Bebop Business* (1966). *Black Music* (1970).

—JOSEPH M. FLORA

ANNE SPENCER (1882–1975). Born on February 6, 1882, in Henry County, Va., Annie Bethel Scales spent most of her childhood with her mother in Bramwell, W.Va., after her parents separated about 1887. Barely literate when in 1893 her mother enrolled her in Virginia Seminary in Lynchburg., Va., at age fourteen she wrote her first poem, "The Skeptic," motivated by her disagreement with religious doctrine taught at the seminary. Annie progressed rapidly in her studies and graduated from the secondary division of the seminary in 1889. After two years of teaching primary school in rural West Virginia, she married her classmate Edward A. Spencer in 1901 and moved to Lynchburg, where she lived for the remaining seventy-four years of her life.

Spencer spent most of her adulthood reading and writing, cultivating her flower garden, and working actively in community affairs. Her efforts to help organize the Lynchburg chapter of the NAACP in 1917–18 brought her into contact with James Weldon Johnson, then field secretary for the organization. While a guest at the Spencers' home, Johnson accidentally found some of her poetry and arranged for its publication in *Crisis*, an organ of the NAACP. Always modest about her writings, Spencer did not write with the intent of seeing her works in print. In every case her literary friends arranged for the publication of her poems. During the decade original pieces by Anne Spencer were published in *Crisis*, *Opportunity*, and other magazines and were included in several anthologies.

From 1924 to 1946 she was librarian at Dunbar High School, having charge of the first library in Lynchburg to serve black patrons. Beginning in the 1920s, for four decades her home at 1313 Pierce Street was frequented by such prominent persons as Johnson, Countee Cullen, W. E. B. Du Bois, and Langston Hughes. After the early 1950s Spencer lived an increasingly secluded life. When she died in July 1975, she was working on a free verse poem of seven cantos about the illustrious abolitionist John Brown. Spencer's poems have appeared in French and Spanish translations and have been widely anthologized since the 1920s; they are collected in J. Lee Greene's *Time's Fading Garden*.

WORKS: J. Lee Greene, *Time's Fading Garden: Anne Spencer's Life and Poetry* (1977).

—J. LEE GREENE

ELIZABETH SPENCER (1921–). Elizabeth Spencer was born on July 19, 1921, in Carrollton, a small Mississippi hill town that is depicted in many of her books, especially the fictional *Voice at the Back*

Door and her widely praised memoir *Landscapes of the Heart.* Her parents, James Luther and Mary James McCain Spencer, were affluent and somewhat conservative members of Carrollton society, a tightly knit social fabric she would eventually struggle to escape, both in her fiction as well as in her life.

Spencer earned her B.A. (1942) at Belhaven College in Jackson, Miss., where she met Eudora Welty when the older woman came to speak to the Belhaven Literary Society, over which Spencer presided. They became lifelong friends, supporting each other both personally and artistically as their reputations and circles of influence grew.

From Belhaven, Spencer went on to study at Vanderbilt University, where she earned an M.A. (1943) while studying under Donald Davidson, among others. At Vanderbilt, Spencer was both witness to and a part of the later stages of the Southern Renascence. Through Davidson, she met Robert Penn Warren and other influential southern writers, who would support her early efforts at writing fiction.

After graduating from Vanderbilt, Spencer taught English at Northwest Junior College in Senatobia, Miss. (1943–44), and at Ward-Belmont in Nashville (1944–45) before becoming a reporter for the *Nashville Tennessean* (1945–46). She began writing serious fiction during this period, and her first novel, *Fire in the Morning,* appeared in 1948. Spencer had just begun teaching English at the University of Mississippi, where she remained until 1951. After the success of her first two novels, she received a Guggenheim Fellowship (1953) and went to live in Italy, where she met her future husband, Englishman John Rusher. Italy became a second home to Spencer in the years that followed and served as the setting for *The Light in the Piazza,* perhaps her best-known book.

Spencer married Rusher on September 29, 1956. That year the appearance of *The Voice at the Back Door,* a novel about race relations in the South, although widely celebrated, alienated Spencer from her family. In 1958 she and Rusher settled in Montreal, where they would maintain primary residence for almost thirty years. During the 1960s and 1970s, Spencer published a series of increasingly sophisticated novels set in Italy as well as Canada and the United States. Her reputation was greatly enhanced by the 1981 publication of her collected *Stories,* which included a sparkling foreword by her longtime friend Welty and garnered rave reviews from scholars and writers alike.

In 1986, at the urging of their friend Louis Rubin, Spencer and her husband moved to Chapel Hill, N.C., abandoning the cold and snow of Montreal. Spencer taught creative writing at the University of North Carolina, while continuing to write, publishing a number of prize-winning stories and the 1991 novel *The Night Travellers,* about the social paroxysms of the Vietnam era, as well as her 1998 memoir, *Landscapes of the Heart.*

Since Rusher's death in 1998, Spencer has continued to live and work in Chapel Hill, having returned to the South both physically and spiritually, and adding to the distinguished body of her work. Spencer's reputation has also continued to rise, first with publication of *The Southern Woman: New and Selected Fiction* in a Modern Library edition in 2001 and then by the success on Broadway in 2005 of the musical *The Light in the Piazza.*

WORKS: *Fire in the Morning* (1948). *This Crooked Way* (1952). *The Voice at the Back Door* (1957). *The Light in the Piazza* (1961). *Knights and Dragons* (1966). *No Place for an Angel* (1968). *Ship Island and Other Stories* (1969). *The Snare* (1972). *The Stories of Elizabeth Spencer* (1981). *Marilee: Three Tales* (1981). *The Salt Line* (1985). *Jack of Diamonds and Other Stories* (1988). *For Lease or Sale* (1989). *The Night Travellers* (1991). *On the Gulf* (1991). *The Light in the Piazza and Other Italian Tales* (1996). *Landscapes of the Heart: A Memoir* (1998). *The Southern Woman: New and Selected Fiction* (2001).

—TERRY ROBERTS

LAURENCE STALLINGS (1894–1968). Laurence Tucker Stallings, whose life and writing were dominated by World War I, was born in Macon, Ga., on November 25, 1894. Physically active as a boy, he was captivated by stories from the southern past, especially those of chivalric heroism from the Civil War. Entering Wake Forest College in 1912, he played football and was an excellent student. In 1917, a year after graduation, he joined the Marines and was wounded at Belleau Wood in June 1918, a wound that necessitated the amputation of his right leg in 1922. Later that year he joined the *New York World*.

Stallings's literary career began sensationally. His autobiographical novel *Plumes*, which contrasted his chivalric idealism through college with his bitter despair following the war, was widely hailed as an example of postwar disillusionment. His first play, *What Price Glory*, written with Maxwell Anderson, succeeded tremendously in using the war to symbolize a world without meaning. With Anderson he quickly wrote two more plays that failed commercially, though one, *First Flight* (1925), is an interesting tall tale about Andrew Jackson in North Carolina. Before leaving the *World* in 1926, he also wrote the highly acclaimed motion picture *The Big Parade*.

Stallings published short stories (uncollected) into the early 1930s, dramatized Hemingway's *A Farewell to Arms*, compiled *The First World War: A Photographic History*, and produced a play, *The Streets Are Guarded* (1944; unpublished). But after leaving the *World* his literary career was virtually over. Retiring to North Carolina in 1927, he returned to New York for newspaper work in the early 1930s, then went to Hollywood in 1934. Following duty in World War II, he settled in Whittier, Calif., where he died on February 29, 1968. The major work of his last years was a narrative history of American soldiers in World War I, *The Doughboys*.

WORKS: *Plumes* (1924). *Three American Plays*, with Maxwell Anderson (1926). *The First World War: A Photographic History* (1933). *The Doughboys: The Story of the AEF, 1917–1918* (1963).

—LAURENCE G. AVERY

MAX STEELE (1922–2005). Born Henry Maxwell Steele in Greenville, S.C., on March 30, 1922, he received his early education there. Service in the U.S. Army Air Force, Weather Wing (1942–46), interrupted his undergraduate studies at Furman University (1939–41) and the University of North Carolina (1942). As a meteorology cadet he studied at Vanderbilt University (1943–44) and the University of California–Los Angeles (1944). He received the B.A. from the University of North Carolina in 1946. He did graduate work in painting at the Académie Julien (1951) and in French literature and language at the Sorbonne, University of Paris (1952–54), while acting as advisory editor to the *Paris Review*. His first published story appeared in *Harper's* in August 1944. He married Diana Whittinghill on December 31, 1960. They had two sons: Oliver Whittinghill and Kevin Russell. The marriage ended in divorce, but the parents' living arrangements gave the sons easy access to both.

Steele is probably best known for his humor and wry wit and as a short-story writer. His only novel, *Debby*, received both the Harper Prize and the Mayflower Award in 1950. He also received the Eugene F. Saxton Memorial Trust Award in 1950, and the O. Henry Prize in 1955 and 1969 for short stories included in those collections. Other awards include National Endowment for the Arts and Humanities grants (1967, 1970); D.Litt., Belmont Abbey (1970); Standard Oil Award for Excellence in Undergraduate Teaching (1971); and Distinguished Alumnus Award, Furman University (1971). He presented a series of lectures on the short story at the University of North Carolina under the Rankin Faculty Support Fund (2002–3).

Steele's teaching career was largely connected with the University of North Carolina at Chapel Hill, where he began as a lecturer in 1956 and from which he retired as professor and director of the creative writing program in 1988. He also taught at the University of San Francisco (1962–64).

The skillful construction of Steele's fiction reveals vivid images with little drama; the substance of the stories involves innocence meeting experience. Readers must reexamine and reevaluate their lives from the child's perspective, observing and learning from expression and manner with an overlay of humor. Steele's focused and imaginative eye catches and freezes that moment when all becomes clear. Memory and its retrospective vision, he seems to say in his fiction, expose the meaning of life in recalled images frozen at the crux of change. His use of humor—wry, ribald, or ironic—makes the revelation bearable. He died August 1, 2005, in Chapel Hill.

WORKS: *Debby* (1950); repr. as *The Goblins Must Go Barefoot* (1966). *Where She Brushed Her Hair and Other Stories* (1968). *The Cat and Coffee Drinkers* (1969). *The Hat of My Mother* (1988).

—JEANNE R. NOSTRANDT

WILBUR DANIEL STEELE (1886–1970). A celebrated short-story writer, Wilbur Daniel Steele was born on March 17, 1886, in Greensboro, N.C., to the Reverend Wilbur Fletcher Steele and Rose Wood Steele. He was the youngest of three children. In 1889 his father moved his family to Germany, where he studied for a graduate degree in theology. Three years later, the Steele family, now with four children, moved to Colorado, where the Reverend Steele was a professor of theology at the University of Denver.

Wilbur Daniel Steele received a bachelor's degree from the University of Denver in history and economics in 1907. That year he enrolled in the Boston Museum School of Fine Arts to study painting, and a year later he traveled to France and Italy, where he wrote his first story. When he returned to the United States, he settled in Provincetown, Conn., and decided to become a writer. Steele published his first short story, "On the Ebb Tide," a maritime farce, in *Success* magazine in 1910 and his first novel, *Storm*, in 1914. A year later he co-founded the Provincetown Players.

In 1913 he married Margaret Thurston, whom he had met at art school six years before. They had two sons, Thurston and Peter, born in 1916 and 1918. The wanderlust that marked Steele's youth continued throughout his life. In 1917 he traveled to the Caribbean for *Harper's*, and in 1920–22 he traveled throughout Africa and Europe. In 1929 he moved to Chapel Hill, N.C., where, two years later, his wife died suddenly of pneumonia. In 1932 Steele married actress Norma Mitchell in London and moved to Hamburg, Conn. Together they wrote *Post Road*, a comic mystery play, which ran for 212 performances on Broadway in 1934–35.

In 1943 Steele went on a flying trip across South America for *Cosmopolitan*. This penchant for travel informed his writing, and many of his early works are set in faraway places, such as the South Seas, Arabia, and Africa. "Lands End" (1918), "The Shame Dance" (1923), and his novels *Taboo* and *Isles of the Blest* contain rich descriptions of sea and jungle landscape reminiscent of Joseph Conrad's fiction. Steele's stories also rely heavily on melodramatic plots and the effects of narrative point of view. The events of "The Man Who Saw through Heaven" (1927) are narrated not as they happen, but after the fact as the narrator heard them recounted to him. "Footfalls" (1929) and "How Beautiful with Shoes" (1932), which was adapted for the stage and ran unsuccessfully for eight performances on Broadway in 1935, utilize multiple narrative points of view to achieve surprise endings. Several of Steele's later works feature the southern and the western United States. Most notable is the humorous ghost story "Can't Cross Jordan by Myself" (1931) set in Charleston, S.C. His last four novels—*That Girl from Memphis, Diamond Wedding, Their Town,* and *The Way to the Gold* are set in the American West. When Twentieth Century Fox bought the film rights for *The Way to the Gold*, Steele and his wife retired to Connecticut, where he died on May 26, 1970.

Steele was prolific, producing seven collections of short stories, ten novels, and three plays. Although his work has declined in popularity since the 1930s, he was considered during his lifetime to be one of America's premier short story writers. Between the end of World War I and the Great Depression, he won eleven O. Henry awards, more than any other writer, and in jest some called the award the "Wilbur Daniel Steele Memorial Prize."

WORKS: *Storm* (1914). *Land's End and Other Stories* (1918). *The Shame Dance and Other Stories* (1923). *The Giants Stair* (1924). *Isles of the Blest* (1924). *Taboo* (1925). *The Terrible Woman and Other One Act Plays* (1925). *Urkey Island* (1926). *The Man Who Saw through Heaven and Other Stories* (1927). *Meat* (1928). *Tower of Sand and Other Stories* (1929). *Undertow* (1930). *Post Road* (1935). *Sound of Rowlocks* (1938). *That Girl from Memphis* (1945). *The Best Stories of Wilbur Daniel Steele* (1946). *Diamond Wedding* (1950). *Full Cargo: More Stories* (1951). *Their Town* (1952). *The Way to the Gold* (1955).

—Matthew Spangler

JAMES STERLING (1701–1763). Born in obscurity in Downrass, King's County, Ireland, James Sterling earned his B.A. at Trinity College, Dublin, in 1720. Perhaps the earliest Irish tragic playwright, he saw two of his plays performed on the Irish stage before taking Holy Orders in 1733 and entering the king's service as an army chaplain. Leaving behind his *Poetical Works,* Sterling emigrated to North America in 1737 for a clerical career.

Eventually settling in Kent County on Maryland's Eastern Shore, Sterling married and prospered in his rural parish from 1740 until his death. Securing passage back to England in 1751, he lobbied successfully for a lucrative appointment as collector of customs at Chester on the Chesapeake Bay. Opposition to Sterling's secular self-promotion frustrated his more grandiose economic schemes, but he returned to Maryland in 1752 a man of unshakable means. In publicly disseminated sermons and magazine poetry, he celebrated America as a land of economic opportunity, natural beauty, and colonial loyalty during the last ten years of his life. He died on November 10, 1763.

Sterling's literary reputation rests largely on his competent, if rarely distinguished, neoclassic verse, his early application of sentimentalism to American subjects, and his literary nationalism. These qualities are evident in his major poems, *An Epistle to the Hon. Arthur Dobbs, Esq.* and "A Pastoral." The *Epistle* mixes neoclassic genres to praise Dobbs, an American explorer-hero, to describe the American wilderness, and to speculate on the advantages to trade of the discovery of the Northwest Passage. "A Pastoral" yokes a pastoral elegy mourning the death of Alexander Pope with a progress piece portraying the westward movement of the arts to the New World.

WORKS: *The Rival Generals: A Tragedy* (1722). *The Love of Hero and Leander* (1728). *The Poetical Works of the Rev. James Sterling* (1734). *The Parricide: A Tragedy* (1736). *An Epistle to the Hon. Arthur Dobbs, Esq.* (1752). "A Pastoral" (1758).

—William L. Andrews

JAMES STILL (1906–2001). Born on July 16, 1906, and raised in Chambers County, Ala., James Still spent his adult life in eastern Kentucky. Most of Still's writings—including his acclaimed novel *River of Earth,* award-winning short stories, poetry, children's literature, and folklore collections—are set in the Kentucky hills, where he lived from 1931 until his death on April 28, 2001.

Still studied literature at Lincoln Memorial University and Vanderbilt University, then earned a library science degree from the University of Illinois. Accepting a position as librarian at the Hindman Settlement School (located in Knott County, Ky.) in 1931, Still began to write prolifically. His poems and short stories, which explored the natural world and aspects of Appalachian folklife, were soon appearing in nationally distributed periodicals; his short stories were regularly included in the annual anthology *O. Henry Memorial Prize Stories* (in 1937, 1938, 1939, and 1941). In 1937 the Viking Press published a volume of Still's poetry, *Hounds on the Mountain*. In 1939, to devote more time to writing, he moved into a remote hundred-year-old log house eleven miles from Hindman. In 1940 Viking issued his novel *River of Earth*, for which Still was named co-recipient of the prestigious Southern Author's Award. Viking compiled a collection of his short stories, *On Troublesome Creek*, in 1941.

Drafted in 1942, Still served in Africa and the Middle East during World War II. In 1945 he returned to his log house to recover from physical and psychic wartime wounds. While his fiction was subsequently selected for the *Best American Short Stories* anthology (in 1946, 1950, and 1952), Still's literary productivity decreased. In 1952 he resumed his affiliation with Hindman Settlement School. After a ten-year stint as that school's librarian, he accepted a teaching position in Morehead State University's English department. In the 1970s, retired from academia, he spent several winters traveling in Mexico and Central America. By the late 1970s, Still's work was being rediscovered and republished. During the 1980s and 1990s, residing in Knott County, Still frequently spoke and read at schools across Appalachia. Still's admirers gave him the sobriquet "the dean of Appalachian literature." Authors as diverse as Wendell Berry, Fred Chappell, Wilma Dykeman, Jim Wayne Miller, Gurney Norman, and Lee Smith have publicly declared their appreciation for Still and his work.

WORKS: *Hounds on the Mountain* (1937). *River of Earth* (1940). *On Troublesome Creek* (1941). *Pattern of a Man* (1976). *Sporty Creek* (1977). *The Run for the Elbertas* (1980). *The Wolfpen Poems* (1986). *Jack and the Wonder Beans* (1991). *The Wolfpen Notebooks: A Record of Appalachian Life* (1991). *From the Mountain, from the Valley: New and Collected Poems* (2001).

—TED OLSON

WILLIAM STITH (1707–1755). Minister and historian of Virginia, William Stith was born in 1707, the son of Captain John Stith of Charles County, Va., and Mary Randolph Stith, daughter of William Randolph. After attending the Grammar School of the College of William and Mary, Stith entered Queen's College, Oxford University, on May 21, 1724, and received his B.A. on February 27, 1728. He was ordained a minister in the Anglican Church on April 12, 1731, and returned to Williamsburg.

Stith was elected master of the Grammar School of William and Mary College on October 25, 1731, and he also acted as chaplain to the Virginia House of Burgesses. In July 1736 he became minister of Henrico Parish, Henrico County, where he remained for sixteen years. On July 13, 1738, he married his cousin, Judith Randolph, daughter of Thomas Randolph. Late in 1751 Stith was chosen as minister of St. Ann's Parish, but before he took this post, he was appointed the third president of the College of William and Mary on August 14, 1752. During this time, Stith also served as minister of York-Hampton Parish in York County. He was president of William and Mary until his death on September 19, 1755.

Stith published three sermons in the 1740s and 1750s but he is best known for *The History of the First Discovery and Settlement of Virginia*, published at Williamsburg in 1747. Using the accounts of Captain John Smith and of Robert Beverley and the unpublished records in the possession of William Byrd II and his uncle, Sir John Randolph, Stith carried his account of the founding of Virginia through 1624. Although Thomas Jefferson believed Stith's "details often too minute to be tolerable," and though Stith's account is partisan and critical of the policies of James I, his *History* is still a valuable source for information about early Virginia. Discouraged by the Virginians' reception of his *History*, Stith did not continue the work.

WORKS: *A Sermon Preached Before the General Assembly at Williamsburg, March 2, 1745–46* (1746). *The History of the First Discovery and Settlement of Virginia: Being an Essay Towards a General History of the Colony* (1747). *The Sinful-*

ness and Pernicious Nature of Gaming: A Sermon Preached Before the General Assembly of Virginia (1752). *The Nature and Extent of Christ's Redemption: A Sermon Preached Before the General Assembly* (1753).

—ROBERT BAIN

JAMES HOWELL STREET (1903–1954). James Howell Street achieved national popularity with his historical novels and his tales about dogs. Born in Lumberton, Miss., on October 15, 1903, Street worked as a journalist, traveled throughout the western United States, served as a Baptist minister, and married Lucy Nash O'Briant by the time he was twenty. Resigning his ministry in 1925, Street returned to journalism and worked for such publications as the *Pensacola Journal*, the Arkansas *Gazette*, and the *New York World-Telegram*. During this period he published *Look Away!: A Diary of Dixie Life*, a collection of sketches about Mississippi. In 1937, he sold his first story, "Nothing Sacred," to Hollywood—the proceeds of which allowed him to begin writing fiction full time.

In subsequent years, Street placed stories with such popular publications as *Colliers, Saturday Evening Post,* and *Cosmopolitan.* In 1940 he published *Oh, Promised Land,* his first novel in a series of five southern historical novels, including *Tap Roots, By Valour and Arms, Mingo Dabney,* and *Tomorrow We Reap.* These works follow generations of the Dabney family of Lebanon, Miss., through the nineteenth century. Street also had popular success with his dog tales *The Biscuit Eater* and *Good-bye, My Lady,* both of which were made into movies. Street drew on his experience as a Baptist minister to write *The Gauntlet* and its sequel, *The High Calling.*

The Street family—James, Lucy, and their three children—moved around the South until they settled in Chapel Hill, N.C., in 1945. James Street lived and wrote there until his death in 1954. A collection of his articles on the South appeared posthumously as *James Street's South.*

WORKS: *Look Away! A Dixie Notebook* (1936). *Oh, Promised Land* (1940). *The Biscuit Eater* (1941). *In My Father's House* (1941). *Tap Roots* (1942). *By Valour and Arms* (1944). *Short Stories* (1945). *The Gauntlet* (1945). *Tomorrow We Reap* (1949). *Mingo Dabney* (1950). *The High Calling* (1951). *The Velvet Doublet* (1953). *The Civil War: An Unvarnished Account of the Late but Still Lively Hostilities* (1953). *Good-Bye, My Lady* (1954). *The Revolutionary War: Being a De-Mythed Account of How the Thirteen Colonies Turned a World Upside Down* (1954). *James Street's South* (1955). *Captain Little Ax* (1956). *Pride of Possession* (1960).

—ANDREW B. LEITER

MARY DALLAS STREET (1885–1951). The daughter of a Philadelphia beauty and a Richmond railroad businessman, Mary Dallas Street enjoyed the privileges made possible by Mary Gormley's cultural sophistication and George Levick Street's money. She was born in Richmond on May 31, 1885. She had a masculine frame and a high-strung flamboyance, which was hardly endearing to the literary community and social circle that were seemingly her birthright.

Street attended St. Catherine's School, founded by Miss Jenny Ellett, in Richmond before continuing her studies in Chestnut Hill, Pa. Travel, horseback riding, and club membership consumed most of her youth. At age thirty-six, she was invited—rather her invitation was compelled by Miss Ellett—to join Emily Clark (Balch), Margaret Freeman (Cabell), and Hunter Stagg in founding the *Reviewer.* Street's generous financial support of the magazine during the early 1920s was coupled with her literary contributions: twelve book reviews, six poems, five short stories, three sketches, and one editorial. Except for the *Reviewer* contributions, Street published nothing until 1936 when her first novel appeared. Another decade of silence—punctuated only in 1944 by an award-winning, but unpublished, short story entitled "Of Time Itself"—preceded her second novel.

Street experienced much heartache in her life, not the least of which was the disjunction between her deep desire to be a writer and her pale talent. Her parents' deaths ignited a long-standing feud with her younger brother, George, Jr., who found his sister distasteful and presumptuous; she never received her full share of their father's estate, though for years lawyers tried to secure it. However, she kept her parents' house on West Franklin, sharing it with Gertrude Maxton Lewis. Together, the writer and schoolteacher hosted teas, entertaining the best of Richmond's literary circle. Gertrude's death in 1932 devastated Street, and she moved to New York City in 1935. She returned to Virginia only a short time before her death in 1951, willing her estate to Miss Isabel Machay Kearney, lately of New York, but a native of Virginia. Street was buried, without her brother's attendance, in Richmond's Hollywood Cemetery.

WORKS: *At Summer's End* (1936). *Christopher Holt* (1946).

—MELISSA GRAHAM MEEKS

T. S. STRIBLING (1881–1965). A pioneer realist in the southern literary renascence, Thomas Sigismund Stribling was born in Clifton, Tenn., on March 4, 1881. His father had been a Union soldier, his mother's family had fought for and supported the Confederacy, and he would subsequently draw from this rich legacy for his most significant literary work.

Educated at Florence (Ala.) Normal and the law school of the University of Alabama, Stribling served a lengthy apprenticeship, writing Sunday school and adventure stories and a light, melodramatic novel, *The Cruise of the Dry Dock*. He married Luella Kloss in 1930.

Though Stribling would continue to write other novels and stories of the light and didactic variety in the 1920s and 1930s, his primary métier became the serious iconoclastic novel of social realism. Beginning with *Birthright* and continuing through *These Bars of Flesh*, he produced eight novels exposing social issues of various kinds and magnitude. His principal work in the iconoclastic vein was a popular trilogy—*The Forge, The Store,* and *Unfinished Cathedral*—set in and around Florence, Ala., and covering a historical time frame from the outbreak of the Civil War through the boom period of the 1920s. *The Store* was awarded the Pulitzer Prize in 1933. In 1973 Cleanth Brooks, R. W. B. Lewis, and Robert Penn Warren cited Stribling as the only other southern novelist to aim at "Faulkner's scope and his panoramic vision of the history of the South."

In the 1940s and 1950s, however, Stribling wrote mainly detective and mystery stories, which were published in *Ellery Queen, Famous Detective,* and other magazines. Also during this period, Stribling worked on his autobiography, *Laughing Stock,* which was published posthumously, and several novels and philosophical works, none of which were published. By the 1960s, Stribling and his earlier literary contributions had been virtually forgotten. He died on July 8, 1965, in Florence, Ala.

WORKS: *The Cruise of the Dry Dock* (1917). *Birthright* (1922). *Fombombo* (1923). *Red Sand* (1924). *Teeftallow* (1926). *Bright Metal* (1928). *East Is East* (1928.) *Clues of the Caribbees: Being Certain Criminal Investigations of Henry Poggioli, Ph.D.* (1929). *Strange Moon* (1929). *Backwater* (1930). *The Forge* (1931). *The Store* (1932). *Unfinished Cathedral* (1934). *The Sound Wagon* (1935). *These Bars of Flesh* (1938). *Best Dr. Poggioli Detective Stories* (1975). *Laughing Stock: The Posthumous Autobiography of T. S. Stribling* (1982).

—ED PIACENTINO

DAVID HUNTER STROTHER (1816–1888). David Hunter Strother, whose nom de plume was "Porte Crayon," was born to John and Elizabeth Pendleton Hunter Strother on September 26, 1816, in Martinsburg, Va., now West Virginia. After a year at Jefferson College in Canonsburg, Pa., Strother studied art with Samuel F. B. Morse in New York in 1836–38. In 1840 he traveled to Europe to further his art training, living in Paris, Florence, and Rome, and some of his letters home were published in the local newspaper. He returned to Martinsburg in 1843. During the next several years, he worked for the family inn in Berkeley Springs, Va., pursuing a part-time career as painter and illustrator. He married Ann Doyne Wolff on May 15, 1849, and by her would have a daughter, Emily.

In 1851, on a sporting trip to the Blackwater River, he made drawings that would be used in cousin Philip Pendleton Kennedy's 1853 book about that experience. This led to his illustrating John Pendleton Kennedy's re-issue of *Swallow Barn* and his own contract with Harper Brothers to provide prose and ink sketches of a second trip to the Blackwater. Strother remained busy as a writer and illustrator of travel narratives and was the first journalist on the scene for the aftermath of John Brown's raid, a month before his wife died. He married Mary Eliot Hunter in 1861. During the Civil War, he served with the Union army as a topographer and kept an extensive diary of his experiences. After the war, he continued his previous work in journalism, but interest in his writing dwindled. He served six years as a consul to Mexico (1879–85) before returning to West Virginia, where he died on March 8, 1888.

Strother's sketches mix whimsy, reportage, and backwoods humor. He took more particular interest in African Americans, both in his drawings and writing, than many of his white contemporaries. His diary, only a small portion of which is published, provides a realistic, often sardonic look at a war that put him at odds with many of his Virginia friends and family.

WORKS: *Virginia Illustrated: Containing a Visit to the Virginia Canaan, and the Adventures of Porte Crayon and His Cousins* (1857). *The Capital of West Virginia and the Great Kanawha Valley* (1872). *Historical Address* (1876). *The Old South Illustrated,* ed. Cecil D. Eby, Jr. (1959). *A Virginia Yankee in the Civil War: The Diaries of David Hunter Strother,* ed. Eby (1961).

—JEFFREY H. RICHARDS

DABNEY STUART (1937–). Dabney Stuart was born on November 4, 1937, in Richmond, Va. His father ran a hardware company. The future poet would often visit his father's warehouse on Saturday mornings and exuberantly slide down a metal chute leading from the top level to the shipping dock. His mother would recite Poe's "The Raven" to him when he had trouble falling asleep at night. Other vivid childhood memories include awkward family gatherings with his paternal grandparents and happy summer vacations at his maternal grandparents' home in Hampton, Va.

After attending public school in Richmond, Stuart graduated from Davidson College in 1960. Since 1965 he has taught at Washington and Lee University, where he is a professor of English. Stuart married Sandra Westcott in 1983. He has a daughter and two sons by previous marriages. Many of Stuart's poems and stories focus upon his complex, ambivalent feelings about kinship, marriage, and separation.

Stuart is the author of more than a dozen collections of poems. His earliest work is in the formalist tradition that dominated American verse in the 1950s and early 1960s. His later books, predominantly in free verse, contain multiple voices, surrealistic juxtapositions, and oblique social satire. Throughout his career, however, certain themes remain constant: a distaste for greed and crass commercialism; a fear of social and sexual repression; a suspicion of patriotism; and an affection for family loyalty, verbal ingenuity, and laughter. A recent collection, *Settlers,* shows both a haunting awareness of the poet's mortality and a strong devotional spirit—especially in "George Herbert" and the long "God" sequence.

Since 1991 Dabney Stuart has published three collections of short stories. *The Way to Cobbs Creek*, through the character of Mark Random, explores the intricate son/father/grandfather relationships found throughout Stuart's verse.

WORKS: *The Diving Bell* (1966). *A Particular Place* (1969). *Friends of Yours, Friends of Mine* (1974). *The Other Hand* (1974). *Round and Round* (1977). *Nabokov: The Dimensions of Parody* (1978). *Rockbridge Poems* (1981). *Common Ground* (1982). *Don't Look Back* (1987). *Narcissus Dreaming* (1990). *Sweet Lucy Wine* (1991). *Light Years: New and Selected Poems* (1994). *Second Sight: Poems for Paintings by Carroll Cloar* (1996). *Long Gone* (1996). *The Way to Cobbs Creek* (1997). *Settlers* (1999). *Strains of the Old Man* (1999). *No Visible Means of Support* (2001). *The Man Who Loves Cézanne* (2003). *Family Preserve* (2005).

—GILBERT ALLEN

JESSE STUART (1906–1984). Jesse Stuart was born on August 8, 1906, in W-Hollow, Greenup County, Ky. He was one of the seven children born to Mitchell and Martha Hilton Stuart. After working in Harlan County steel mills, Stuart attended Lincoln Memorial University in Harrogate, Tenn. Graduating in 1924, he returned to his home as principal of Warnock High School (1929), then Greenup High School, and at age twenty-four became the youngest school superintendent in Kentucky. After graduate study at Vanderbilt (1931–32) he returned to the Greenup schools. He spent 1937–38 in Scotland on a Guggenheim grant. On October 14, 1939, Stuart married fellow teacher Naomi Deane Norris; their only child, Jessica Jane, was born in 1942. During World War II he served in the U.S. Naval Writing Division.

His book of poems *Harvest of Youth*, published in 1930, was the first of over sixty volumes Stuart would produce in a prolific publishing career. His most important book of poems, *Man with a Bull-Tongue Plow*, included over seven hundred poems.

Passionately committed to his mountain region of northeast Kentucky, Stuart made it central to all that he wrote. In addition to poetry, he wrote fiction, essays, and an autobiography. His novel *Taps for Private Tussie* won the Thomas Jefferson Southern Award and was a Book of the Month Club selection. Stuart's best-known works are *The Thread That Runs So True*, a book on teaching now established as a classic, and *The Best-Loved Stories of Jesse Stuart*. If his fame is now mainly local, it is because he often overplayed local color and the pathos of poverty and suffering.

In 1954 Stuart was named poet laureate of Kentucky and in 1955 awarded the Academy of American Poets Award for distinguished service to American poetry. His influence continues through the establishment of the Jesse Stuart Foundation (1979), which promotes and preserves the legacy of Jesse Stuart and the Appalachian way of life. He died on February 17, 1984, and was buried in Plum Grove Cemetery in Greenup County.

WORKS: *Harvest of Youth* (1930). *Man with a Bull-Tongue Plow* (1934). *Head O'W-Hollow* (1936). *Beyond Dark Hills* (1938). *Trees of Heaven* (1940). *Men of the Mountains* (1941). *Taps for Private Tussie* (1943). *Mongrel Mettle* (1944). *Album of Destiny* (1944). *Foretaste of Glory* (1946). *Tales from the Plum Grove Hills* (1946). *The Thread That Runs So True* (1949). *Hie to the Hunters* (1950). *Clearing in the Sky and Other Stories* (1950). *Kentucky Is My Land* (1952). *The Good Spirit of Laurel Ridge* (1953). *The Year of My Rebirth* (1956). *Plowshare in Heaven* (1958). *Huey, The Engineer* (1960). *God's Oddling* (1960). *Hold April* (1962). *A Jesse Stuart Reader* (1963). *Save Every Lamb* (1964). *Daughter of the Legend* (1965). *My Land Has a Voice* (1966). *Mr. Gallion's School* (1967). *Stories by Jesse Stuart* (1968). *Come Gentle Spring* (1969). *Old Ben* (1970). *Seven by Jesse* (1970). *To Teach, to Love* (1970). *Autumn Love Song* (1971). *Come Back to the Farm* (1971). *Come to My Tomorrowland* (1971). *Dawn of Remembered Song* (1972). *Tennessee Hill Folk* (1972). *The Land beyond the River* (1973). *Thirty-two Votes before Breakfast* (1974). *My World* (1975). *Up the Hollow from Lynchburg* (1975). *The World of Jesse Stuart: Poems* (1975). *The Only Place We Live* (1976). *The Seasons of Jesse Stuart* (1976). *Honest Confessions of a Literary Son* (1977). *Dandelion on the Acropolis* (1978). *The Kingdom Within* (1979). *Last Sandstones and the Lonely Skies and Other Essays* (1979). *If I were Seventeen Again and Other Essays* (1980). *Land of the Honey-Colored Word* (1981). *The Best Loved Stories of Jesse Stuart* (1982). *Songs of a Mountain Plowman* (1986). *Cradle of the Copperheads* (1988). *Split Cherry Tree* (1990). *Jesse Stuart on Education* (1992). *Come Back to the Farm* (2001).

—GAIL GALLOWAY ADAMS

RUTH McENERY STUART (1852?–1917). Ruth McEnery Stuart was a writer of fiction, and some verse, set in Louisiana and Arkansas. Although there is uncertainty over the year of her birth, most likely she was born on February 19, 1852, in Marksville, Avoyelles Parish, La. She grew up in New Orleans. Her mother was of Scotch ancestry, her father an Irish-American cotton merchant. Married in 1879 to an Arkansas cotton planter, Alfred Oden Stuart, she was a widow four years later. She returned to New Orleans, where she began to write fiction.

Stuart's first story was published in 1888, and, benefiting from the ready national market for picturesque southern literature, she published prolifically for two decades thereafter. Shortly after her first stories were accepted she moved to New York, where she was befriended by Charles Dudley Warner and other literary figures. She never again lived in the South (although she did visit Louisiana twice later in her life) but lived in New York with her sister Sarah and, until his untimely death in 1904, her only son. During the 1890s and early 1900s Stuart's short novels and collections of magazine stories sold well and were positively reviewed. She herself was a fashionable hostess for literary gatherings. She gave many readings on the lecture circuit, often with such writer-friends as Mary Eleanor Wilkins Freeman, and she was consistently a strong advocate for female suffrage.

Outside of some lyric poems based on southern songs and several magazine articles about the South, Stuart's writing consists of seven short novels and many short stories, almost all in the category usually described as "local color." Some of her early fiction is set among the Italians and Sicilians of New Orleans, people she portrays as unpleasant and often violent. Some of her best work is about people, mostly whites but some blacks, in the fictional town of Simpkinsville, Ark. In these tales, in her final novel set in a Virginia sanitarium, and in several other stories Stuart touches upon gender-related issues, but always tentatively. Most of her tales and novels revolve around African Americans or black-white relationships in Louisiana, always from a sentimental, patronizing, reactionary perspective. Stuart's popular fiction was one of those cultural influences persuading northern white readers that sectional reconciliation, with the fate of southern blacks being left to whites who "understood" them best, was a good thing. With no intended irony, Hyder Rollins in 1916 testified to her success by saying that her black characters were more realistic than those of Thomas Nelson Page, Joel Chandler Harris, or even Paul Laurence Dunbar and that she presented "the illiterate, happy-go-lucky, good-natured Negro who is typical of the new South."

WORKS: *Carlotta's Intended* (1891). *A Golden Wedding and Other Tales* (1893). *Carlotta's Intended and Other Tales* (1894). *The Story of Babette, a Little Creole Girl* (1894). *Gobolinks; or, Shadow-Pictures for Young and Old*, with Albert Bigelow Paine (1896). *Sonny* (1896; later editions published as *Sonny, a Christmas Guest*). *Solomon Crow's Christmas Pockets and Other Tales* (1896). *The Snow-Cap Sisters: A Farce* (1897). *In Simpkinsville: Character Tales* (1897). *Moriah's Mourning, and Other Half-Hour Sketches* (1898). *Holly and Pizen and Other Stories* (1899). *The Woman's Exchange of Simpkinsville* (1899; separate edition of story included in *A Golden Wedding*). *Napoleon Jackson: The Gentleman of the Plush Rocker* (1902). *George Washington Jones: A Christmas Gift That Went A-Begging* (1903). *The River's Children: An Idyl of the Mississippi* (1904). *The Second Wooing of Salina Sue and Other Stories* (1905). *Aunt Amity's Silver Wedding and Other Stories* (1909). *The Unlived Life of Little Mary Ellen* (1910; separate edition of story included in *In*

Simpkinsville). *Sonny's Father* (1910). *The Haunted Photograph* [and other stories] (1911). *Daddy Do-Funny's Wisdom Jingles* (1913). *The Cocoon: A Rest-Cure Comedy* (1915). *Plantation Songs and Other Verse* (1916).

—JOHN E. BASSETT

WILLIAM STYRON (1925–). The only child of William Clark Styron, a shipyard engineer who suffered from depression, and Pauline Margaret Abraham Styron, William Styron was born in Newport News, Va., on June 11, 1925. Styron spent one year at Davidson College in North Carolina before transferring to Duke University in 1943 and entering the Marine Corps V-12 program. After Marine Training Camp and officers' candidate school, Styron was sent to Okinawa in 1945, arriving just as the war ended. Subsequently, Styron returned to Duke, graduating in May 1947. After graduation, he moved to New York City, where he worked as an editor for McGraw-Hill. Dissatisfied with what turned out to be a mundane job and with his strict employers, Styron rebelled by coming to work late, dosing off during meetings, and blowing plastic bubbles out an office window. He was fired after a few months.

During this time, Styron also began taking classes with Hiram Haydn at the New School for Social Research. With guidance and encouragement from Haydn, Styron began work on his first novel, *Lie Down in Darkness*, which details the tragic descent of a young woman into suicide and her disintegrating Virginia family. Also in 1951, Styron was briefly recalled to active duty in the Marines, but he was discharged because of cataracts. *Lie Down in Darkness* was an immediate critical and commercial success; Styron was rewarded with the Prix de Rome Fellowship from the American Academy of Arts and Letters. That same year, he traveled around Europe, settling in Paris with his soon-to-be wife, Rose Burgunder. While in Paris, Styron wrote *A Long March*, based on his experiences in the Marines.

In 1954 Styron and his wife returned to Roxbury, Conn., where they have lived ever since. Set in Rome, his next novel, *Set This House on Fire*, concerns three American expatriates. With his next work, Styron returned to a subject that had interested him since childhood: the Southampton, Va., slave uprising of 1831. In *Confessions of Nat Turner* he crafted an introspective and psychological account of the enigmatic leader of the uprising. The book received the Pulitzer Prize in 1968, but Styron's portrayal of Turner brought him immediate and sharp criticism, especially from some African American authors who believed that Styron had little understanding of the slave experience and that Styron's Turner, who had homoerotic tendencies and lusted for a white woman, was demeaning to the African American community and even racist.

After writing a play, *In the Clap Shack*, Styron returned to fiction with *Sophie's Choice*. Set in 1947, *Sophie's Choice* focuses upon the relationships between a young southern writer, based on Styron himself, a ravaged Polish Holocaust survivor who gradually reveals her scarred past, and her brilliant but unstable lover. Styron's greatest commercial success to date, *Sophie's Choice* remained on the *New York Times* best-seller list for forty weeks, won the American Book Award for Fiction, and was made into an Academy Award-winning film by Alan Pakula.

In the 1980s, Styron began work on a new novel set during World War II, but he had trouble completing it and began suffering from severe depression, which became the basis for his critically acclaimed memoir, *Darkness Visible*. Styron returned to fiction with autobiographical stories of his youth in *A Tidewater Morning*. He has received both the National Medal of Arts and the Common Wealth Award. Unquestionably he ranks among the most important southern writers of the twentieth century.

WORKS: *Lie Down in Darkness* (1951). *The Long March* (1956). *Set This House on Fire* (1960). *Confessions of Nat Turner* (1967). *In the Clap Shack* (1973). *Sophie's Choice* (1979). *This Quiet Dust and Other Writings* (1982). *Darkness Visible: A Memoir of Madness* (1990). *A Tidewater Morning: Three Tales from Youth* (1993).

—DANIEL GRASSIAN

VIRGIL SUÁREZ (1962–). The only son of a seamstress working the sweatshops, Virgil Suárez was born in Havana, Cuba, in 1962 and raised in the United States starting in 1974. He is married to Delia Peoy and has two daughters, Alexandra and Gabriela. Suárez earned his M.F.A. in creative writing from Louisiana State University in 1987 and is now professor of English at Florida State University, where he teaches creative writing. Suárez's writings have centered on the themes of immigration, exile, and acclimatization, tragic and comic, to life and culture in the United States.

Suárez is the author of several novels and numerous stories, translations, essays, and poems. His publications have appeared in innumerable journals. He frequently reviews books for the *Los Angeles Times*, the *Miami Herald*, and the *Philadelphia Inquirer*. He has edited several anthologies of Latino/a literature.

Suárez's first novel, *Latin Jazz*, chronicles the experiences of a Cuban American family in Los Angeles by adopting the narrative perspectives of each of the family members. His second novel, *The Cutter*, deals with the desperate attempts of a young sugarcane cutter to leave Cuba and join his family in the United States. *Havana Thursdays* and *Going Under* cast a critical eye at middle-class Cuban American life in Miami. *Havana Thursdays* brings together a family of exceptional women who are attending a funeral and learning to make painful assessments of their lives. *Going Under* is the chronicle of a Cuban American yuppie who is sold on the American Dream, yet is nervous and blind to the consequences of his feverish chase up the ladder of success. He loses sight of the important elements in his life: family, friends, and identity. Suárez's collection of short fiction, *Welcome to the Oasis*, portrays a new generation of young Hispanics who struggle to integrate themselves into American culture while attempting to preserve valuable pieces of their heritage.

An energetic performer, Suárez has won several literary prizes and has conducted readings, workshops, and lectures at universities, colleges, schools, book fairs, libraries, prisons, and community groups nationally and internationally.

WORKS: *Latin Jazz* (1989). *The Cutter: A Novel* (1991). Ed., *Iguana Dreams: New Latino Fiction*, with Delia Poey (1992). *Welcome to the Oasis and Other Stories* (1992). *Havana Thursdays: A Novel* (1995). Ed., *Paper Dance: Fifty-five Latino Poets*, with Hernández Cruz and Leroy V. Quintana (1995). *Going Under: A Novel* (1996). Ed., *Little Havana Blues: A Cuban-American Literature Anthology*, with Poey (1996). *Spared Angola: Memories from a Cuban-American Childhood* (1997). *In the Republic of Longing: Poems* (1999). Ed., *American Diaspora: Poetry of Displacement*, with Ryan G. Van Cleave (2001). *Banyan: Poems* (2001). *Palm Crows* (2001). *Guide to the Blue Tongue: Poems* (2002). *Infinite Refuge* (2002). Ed., *Like Thunder: Poets Respond to Violence in America*, with Van Cleave (2002). *Landscapes and Dreams* (2003). Ed., *Vespers: Contemporary American Poems of Religion and Spirituality*, with Van Cleave (2003). Ed., *Red, White, and Blues: Poets on the Promise of America*, with Van Cleave (2004).

—R. BRUCE BICKLEY, JR.

WALTER SULLIVAN (1924–). Novelist and critic Walter L. Sullivan is significant to southern literature for his role in preserving and interpreting the literary tradition of the Fugitives and Agrarians, many of whom he knew well thanks to his long career at Vanderbilt University. His ideas—like those of other critics of his generation, such as Hugh Holman, Louis D. Rubin, Jr., and Lewis P. Simpson—helped shape the discipline and practice of southern literature.

Sullivan was born on January 4, 1924, in Nashville, Tenn., to Walter Laurence and Aline (Armstrong) Sullivan. During World War II, from 1943 to 1946, he served as a first lieutenant in the U.S. Marine Corps. In 1947 he married Jane Harrison, with whom he had three children. He earned his B.A. in 1947 from Vanderbilt and an M.F.A. in 1949 from the University of Iowa's Writers' Workshop, where he had studied beside and befriended Flannery O'Connor. From 1949 until his retirement in 2001, he served on the faculty of Vanderbilt's English department and was a colleague of several Fugitives and Agrarians. In 1980 he helped host a fiftieth-anniversary celebration of the Agrarians' *I'll Take My Stand,* attended by the movement's remaining members Lyle Lanier, Andrew Lytle, and Robert Penn Warren. He was a founding member of the Fellowship of Southern Writers and led the Society for the Study of Southern Literature from 1975 to 1978. He lectured nationwide and produced lectures on southern literature for Voice of America in 1972 and 1977.

Sullivan authored three novels, several critical books, a historical collection, a memoir of Allen Tate, and dozens of essays, many of which appeared in the *Sewanee Review.* A short story, "Elizabeth," won an O. Henry Award, third prize, in 1980. His novels, set in Tennessee, tell love stories complicated by social and personal history. His criticism traces the decline of southern literature after the Southern Renascence in the post-Freudian erosion of metaphysical structures that endow art with cultural meaning. In his explorations of the relationship of the writer to society, Sullivan calls for a rejuvenation of literature through a renewed search for community and myth.

WORKS: *Sojourn of a Stranger* (1957). *The Long, Long Love* (1959). *Death by Melancholy: Essays on Modern Southern Fiction* (1972). *A Requiem for the Renascence: The State of Fiction in the Modern South* (1976). Ed., *A Band of Prophets: The Vanderbilt Agrarians after Fifty Years,* with William C. Havard (1982). *Writing from the Inside,* with George Core (1983). *Allen Tate: A Recollection* (1988). *In Praise of Blood Sports and Other Essays* (1990). *A Time to Dance* (1995). Ed., *The War the Women Lived: Female Voices from the Confederate South* (1995).

—SCOTT HICKS

HOLLIS SUMMERS (1916–1987). Hollis Spurgeon Summers was born in Eminence, Ky., on June 21, 1916. He graduated from Georgetown College in 1937, receiving his M.A. from Middlebury College in 1943 and his Ph.D. from the University of Iowa in 1949. His long, distinguished, and varied teaching career began at Holmes High School in Covington, Ky., and continued with positions as a professor of literature and creative writing at Georgetown College (1944–49), the University of Kentucky (1949–59), and Ohio University in Athens (1959–86). His awards and honors include the *Saturday Review* poetry award (1957), a Danforth Lectureship (1963–64), a grant from the National Endowment for the Arts (1975), a Fulbright Lectureship (1978), and lectureships at writers' conferences, including Bread Loaf. He married Laura Vimont Clarke in 1943 and had two children. He died in Athens, Ohio, on November 14, 1987, and was buried in Millersburg Cemetery in Kentucky.

Summers's career is marked by an extensive publication record in three genres: poetry, fiction, and editing. In the first stage of his career, roughly 1948–58, he published four novels rooted in the places and family situations that marked his small-town Kentucky childhood as the son of a Baptist minister. He also began to publish poems in various literary journals in the early 1950s. Poetry remained his focus for the next decade, during which he produced four books of verse. During the 1970s and 1980s, he published a mixture of poetry and fiction and the last of the three literature anthologies he edited. Summers's work tends to be lapidary, socially acute, and deliberately unsentimental, with a sly humor and a sophistication of tone and technique.

WORKS: *City Limit* (1948). *Brighten the Corner* (1952). Ed., *Kentucky Story: A Collection of Short Stories* (1954). *Teach You a Lesson*, as Jim Hollis, with James Rourke (1956). *The Weather of February* (1956). *The Walks Near Athens* (1959). Ed., *Literature: An Introduction*, with Edgar Whan (1960). *Someone Else: Sixteen Poems about Other Children* (1962). Ed., *Discussions of the Short Story* (1963). *Seven Occasions* (1965). *The Peddler and Other Domestic Matters* (1967). *The Day after Sunday* (1968). *Sit Opposite Each Other* (1970). *Start from Home* (1972). *The Garden* (1972). *How They Chose the Dead* (1973). *Occupant Please Forward* (1976). *Standing Room* (1984). *Other Concerns and Brother Clark* (1988).

—AMY E. WELDON

JOHN BANISTER TABB (1845–1907). John Banister Tabb was born on March 22, 1845, the son of John Yelverton, a planter, and Marianna Bertrand Archer Tabb. The infant Tabb was nursed by Jenny Thompson, whom he later commemorated fondly in a poem titled "Mammy." Tabb grew up surrounded by the considerable natural beauty of Amelia County, Va. Just before the Civil War erupted, Mary Ruffin—daughter of hot-headed agrarian Edward—rejected his courtship. Tabb's poor eyesight precluded most military service but did not prevent him from serving on a blockade runner stationed in Wilmington, N.C. (a place Tabb remembered principally for the large number of "buzzards" living there). His naval journeys took him to San Salvador, Havana, and London, among other places. He ran the blockade successfully, and upon his capture near Beaufort, N.C., he cheekily described his place of residence as "England, France, Scotland, Canada, and Bermuda."

Unceremoniously delivered to prison at Bull Pen, Point Lookout, Md., Tabb struck up a friendship with fellow prisoner and poet Sidney Lanier. The two remained friends for life. The reverses of war made for bleak prospects when Tabb returned home. He flirted with becoming a pianist and an Episcopalian priest before converting to Catholicism in 1872. He eventually entered St. Mary's seminary in Baltimore, and on December 20, 1884, was ordained a Roman Catholic priest after a prolonged period of coming-to-faith that strained his staunchly Anglican family.

Tabb resumed teaching at St. Charles's College in Ellicott City, Md., from which he had graduated in 1875. There he was remembered as a magister supreme and a notably strict grammarian (his students used his own hornbook, *Bone Rules; or, Skeleton of English Grammar*). It was there that he wrote most of his poems, until incipient blindness forced his retirement in 1907. Two years later, on November 19, 1909, Tabb died in Ellicott City.

Like Poe, Tabb believed that the short lyric was the ideal form. Readers of Tabb's poems will note their consonance with fellow Catholic-Confederate Father Ryan, particularly in his powerful treatment of religious material. But Tabb shied away from Lost Cause formulas and instead wrote wonderfully spare poems, metaphysical in their treatment of nature and spirit ("The Ring"). Other poems treat his literary forebears ("Keats" and "Milton," for example). In its precocious imagism, some of Tabb's work foreshadows the moderns that followed him.

WORKS: *Poems* (1882). *An Octave to Mary* (1893). *Poems* (1894). *Bone Rules; or, Skeleton of English Grammar* (1897). *Lyrics* (1897). *Child Verse* (1899). *Two Lyrics* (1900). *Later Lyrics* (1902). *The Rosary in Rhyme* (1904). *Quips and Quiddits: Ques for the Qurious* (1907). *A Selection of the Verses of John B. Tabb*, ed. Alice B. Meynell (1907). *Later Poems* (1910). *The Poetry of Father Tabb*, ed. F. A. Litz (1928).

—BRYAN GIEMZA

PATRICK TAILFER (fl. 1733–1741). Although virtually no extant documents support claims about his early life, Patrick Tailfer appears to have been born and schooled in Scotland, taken medical training from the University of Edinburgh, received a grant in the new colony of Georgia, and emigrated to Savannah in 1734, arriving on August 1. Before long, Tailfer became identified with a malcontent party resisting Governor James Oglethorpe's authoritarian, if utopian, vision for the colony. The physician's land proved to be far from Savannah. Rather than remain a planter, he decided to practice medicine in town, complaining meanwhile to the government about land policies. After threatening to do so, Tailfer, with two other men connected to him, Hugh Anderson and David Douglas, moved to South Carolina. The three published a book, *A True and Historical Narrative of the Colony of Georgia,* in 1741, but thereafter Tailfer, along with the others, disappears from the public record.

Historians assign primary authorship of the narrative to Tailfer. His book employs a variety of satirical strategies to criticize the Georgia government, and Oglethorpe in particular. According to Tailfer, Georgia was a land of disappointments settled by people lured by false claims. Despite a surface tone of respect, Tailfer styles the governor a *"Perpetual Dictator"* who allows public buildings and works to fall into ruins. Two of his chief complaints have to do with Georgia's original ban on slavery and the colony's restrictive laws that make sale and improvement of one's land difficult. With an eye toward South Carolina, a place Tailfer calls a *"Land of Liberty,"* the author ironically desires the liberty that slavery makes possible. Having finally moved to Carolina, he looks back on his former home with small pity and much scorn, making it the subject of a withering and often humorous attack that adds its portion to an eighteenth-century tradition of southern satire.

WORKS: *A True and Historical Narrative of the Colony of Georgia, in America,* with Hugh Anderson and David Douglas (1741; ed. Clarence L. Ver Steeg, 1960).

—JEFFREY H. RICHARDS

HARDIN E. TALIAFERRO (1811–1875). Hardin Edwards Taliaferro, the author of *Fisher's River (North Carolina) Scenes and Characters,* was born March 4, 1811, on a farm on the Little Fisher River in Surry County, N.C. During his boyhood, Taliaferro heard local yarn spinners relate humorous and sometimes tall-tale anecdotes, some of which he would subsequently modify for inclusion in *Fisher's River,* a collection of backwoods sketches and tales in the tradition of old southwestern humor.

In 1829, when Taliaferro was eighteen, he moved to Roane County, Tenn., to join his three older brothers in the farming and tanning business. Developing an interest in the ministry, but in need of further education, he attended nearby Madisonville Academy. A year later he married Elizabeth Henderson, the daughter of a Madisonville, Tenn., printer. In 1835 Taliaferro and his family migrated to Talladega, Ala., where he combined preaching in small Baptist churches, farming, and running a tanyard. During the next thirty-eight years Taliaferro became widely respected in the Alabama Baptist Church, faithfully pastoring churches in several areas of the state, serving on important church committees, and editing and writing for the Tuskegee-based *Southwestern Baptist.* In 1857, as the result of a personal crisis regarding his religious faith, Taliaferro published *The Grace of God Magnified,* a graphic and allusive book describing his spiritual despondency and recovery.

Returning to Surry County for a visit in the summer of 1857 provided Taliaferro the inspiration for *Fisher's River,* his most significant book. He continued to write humorous backwoods sketches, nine of which were published in the *Southern Literary Messenger* in the early 1860s.

After the Civil War, Taliaferro continued to live in Tuskegee, Ala., where he opened his own tanyard and edited the *Tuskegee News,* a weekly newspaper. In 1869 he was selected by the American Baptist Home Mission Society to help train former African American slaves for entry to the Baptist ministry. He died in Loudon, Tenn., on November 2, 1875.

WORKS: *The Grace of God Magnified: An Experimental Tract* (1857). *Fisher's River (North Carolina) Scenes and Characters, by "Skitt" "Who Was Raised Thar"* (1859). *Carolina Humor: Sketches by Harden E. Taliaferro* (1938). *The Humor of H. E. Taliaferro*, ed. Raymond C. Craig (1987).

—ED PIACENTINO

DONNA TARTT (1963–). Donna Tartt was born in Greenwood, Miss., in 1963. On the advice of Willie Morris, Tartt left the University of Mississippi and attended the liberal arts college Bennington. It was during her second year at Bennington that she began writing *The Secret History*, which was published to widespread acclaim in 1992. Reviewers and critics were swift to make connections with *Crime and Punishment*, *The Great Gatsby*, the *Bacchae*, *Brideshead Revisited*, and Hitchcock's *Rope* and with contemporary campus novels, notably Bret Easton Ellis's *Less Than Zero* and *The Rules of Attraction*. The comparison defined *The Secret History* as inheriting and developing a broad and eclectic cultural territory.

Tartt's novel explores the murder of Bunny Corcoran, an apparently perfect crime that goes hideously wrong when his body is covered by a chance snowfall, leading to a major manhunt. The novel is notable for the way in which it anatomizes the subsequent guilt of Bunny's murderers, also his friends and fellow students, and traces their ghastly trajectory from innocence to corruption. Richard Papen, the novel's narrator, goes on to study Jacobean drama, a genre that allows him to explore the themes of his own narrative, of "sin unpunished, of innocence destroyed."

The same theme pervades Tartt's second novel, *The Little Friend*, published in 2002. As with *The Secret History*, the novel opens with an enticing and shocking prologue: the death of a small boy, Robin Cleve Dufresnes, found hanging from a tupelo tree on Mother's Day. Twelve years later, his sister Harriet, a baby at the time of his death, sets out to avenge him by tracking down Danny Ratliff, one of Robin's classmates. The plot and counterplot are deftly twined and twisted around adventure narratives, southern Baptist preachers, snake handlers, and racial tensions in a vividly realized portrait of two different southern families, the dirt-poor Ratliffs and the respectable, once-moneyed Dufresneses.

Smarting from the loss of privacy engendered by the overnight success of *The Secret History*—often named as the perfect example of the perfectly hyped novel—the shy writer removed herself from the limelight. Tartt spent ten years writing *The Little Friend*, keeping her schedule, and her life, largely to herself.

WORKS: *The Secret History* (1992). *The Little Friend* (2002).

—TRACY HARGREAVES

ALLEN TATE (1899–1979). John Orley Allen Tate was born in Winchester, Clarke County, Ky., on November 19, 1899. His parents, John Orley and Eleanor Varnell Tate, came of Scots-Irish and English stock by way of Virginia and Maryland, of both Protestant and Catholic traditions. The family moved so often that Tate's early education was somewhat checkered. His love of music led him to study for a time in the Cincinnati Conservatory, where his talent was deemed unexceptional.

So he enrolled at Vanderbilt College in 1918 and enjoyed the tutelage of mentors who ignited his love of literature. He studied under John Crowe Ransom, who was astonished by the wide reading and intellectual prowess of his pupil. Donald Davidson took a similar interest in Tate and invited him to join the Fugitives, a collective of extraordinarily talented southern poets and writers who launched *The Fugitive* literary magazine in 1922. The same year, Tate graduated magna cum laude and initiated a lifelong friendship with Robert Penn Warren. Thus young Tate served as a founding editor of the publication often credited with launching the Southern Literary Renascence. Stylistically, Tate was heavily influenced by modernist poets and kindred spirit T. S. Eliot. Within the Fugitives, Tate's classicism counterbalanced Ransom's romanticism.

Tate married novelist Caroline Gordon in 1925 and decamped for New York's literary hub, where the couple shared quarters with Hart Crane. By the time he turned twenty-six, Tate had written the poem that would forever cling to his name—and establish his critical reputation. "Ode to the Confederate Dead" captured many of the tensions that troubled Tate's worldview: community and place, solipsistic self-awareness, and lost identity. After publishing *Mr. Pope and Other Poems,* he accepted a Guggenheim Fellowship for two years in France, where he joined Gertrude Stein's clubby circle of American expatriates in Paris. He also published two biographies during the period: *Stonewall Jackson* and *Jefferson Davis.*

When Tate returned to Tennessee in 1930, the Agrarian movement was rising from the ashes of the expired Fugitive project. Galvanized by the Scopes trial and reunited with old friends, Tate had been rethinking his earlier views of southern stagnation and American "universality." He invested his considerable energies in the Agrarian movement. Tate's "Remarks on the Southern Religion," his contribution to the manifesto *I'll Take My Stand,* was perhaps the most subtle of the lot. Recognizing the international dimensions of the Agrarian agenda, he joined forces with English Distributists in *Who Owns America? A New Declaration of Independence.* By the mid-1930s financial pressure compelled the writer to phase in a collegiate teaching career. In 1938 he published *The Fathers.* The novel, his sole venture into extended fiction, critically considered the effects of materialistic Snopesism on older southern orders.

Tate taught at many institutions before settling into a tenured position at the University of Minnesota in 1951; he taught there until his retirement in 1968. His academic career enlarged his reputation as a critic, particularly within the formalist New Critic school, but he took on varied challenges with characteristic energy. He was chair of poetry for the Library of Congress (1943–44) and edited the *Sewanee Review* (1944–47). Practicing his professed need for a religion that rejected the imperatives of scientific "progress," Tate converted to Roman Catholicism in 1952. He divorced Gordon in 1959 and remarried twice, first to Gordon then to Helen Heinz. In 1968 he retired to Sewanee, where he lived and periodically lectured until his death on February 9, 1979.

Tate counted some of the finest writers and poets of his day among his friends, and he mentored many, including the poets Randall Jarrell and Robert Lowell. His talents indelibly impressed southern criticism, poetry, and letters; the vitality of his mind permanently changed the perception of the southern intellectual.

WORKS: *The Golden Mean and Other Poems,* with Ridley Willis (1923). *Mr. Pope and Other Poems* (1928). *Stonewall Jackson, the Good Soldier: A Narrative* (1928). *Jefferson Davis, His Rise and Fall: A Biographical Narrative* (1929). "Remarks on the Southern Religion," in *I'll Take My Stand: The South and the Agrarian Tradition,* by Twelve Southerners (1930). *Poems: 1928–1931* (1932). *The Mediterranean and Other Selected Poems* (1936). *Reactionary Essays on Poetry and Ideas* (1936). *Who Owns America? A New Declaration of Independence,* with Herbert Agar (1936). *Selected Poems* (1937). *The Fathers* (1938). *Reason in Madness: Critical Essays* (1941). *Sonnets at Christmas* (1941). *The Winter Sea* (1944). *Poems: 1920–1945* (1947). *Poems: 1922–1947* (1948). *On the Limits of Poetry: Selected Essays, 1928–1948* (1948). *The Hovering Fly and Other Essays* (1949). *The Forlorn Demon: Didactic and Critical Essays* (1953). *The Man of Letters in the Modern World: Selected Essays, 1928–1955* (1955). *Collected Essays* (1959). *Collected Poems* (1960). *Essays of Four Decades* (1968). *The Swimmers and Other Selected Poems* (1971). *The Literary Correspondence of Donald Davidson and Allen Tate,* ed. Donald Davidson (1974). *Memoirs and Opinions, 1926–1974* (1975). *Collected Poems: 1919–1976* (1977). *The Poetry Reviews of Allen Tate, 1924–1944* (1983). *The Lytle-Tate Letters: The Correspondence of*

Andrew Lytle and Allen Tate , ed. Thomas Daniel Young and Elizabeth Sarcone (1987). *Cleanth Brooks and Allen Tate: Collected Letters, 1933–1976*, ed. Alphonse Vinh (1998).

—BRYAN GIEMZA

ELEANOR ROSS TAYLOR (1920–). A native of Stanly County, N.C., Eleanor Ross Taylor, one of the writing Rosses, first published poems as a child on the "Sunshine Page" of the *Charlotte Observer*, receiving a cash award of two dollars for each poem. Her brother Fred pursued a career as a journalist, while her sister Jean Ross Justice, wife of poet Donald Justice, and her brother James wrote fiction. Her niece, Heather Ross Miller, is accomplished in both genres.

Taylor chose to attend the Woman's College of the University of North Carolina in Greensboro because she respected the English department and writing faculty there. As a student she was taught and encouraged in her craft by visiting writers Allen Tate and Caroline Gordon. A scholarship to Vanderbilt enabled her to study with Donald Davidson, and led to her meeting author Peter Taylor, her future husband. Marriage to Taylor led to a sojourn at Kenyon College and friendship with the John Crowe Ransoms. Returning to Woman's College as a faculty wife, Taylor began publishing her poems, benefiting from the critical attention of Randall Jarrell. In 1967 the Taylors moved to Charlottesville, Va., where Peter accepted a position with the University of Virginia.

Continuing to live in Charlottesville and to write poems noted for their wry humor and tightly crafted lines, Taylor published her fifth book of poems, *Late Leisure*, in 1999. Taylor is the subject of *The Lighthouse Keeper: Essays on the Poetry of Eleanor Ross Taylor* (2001), edited by Jean Valentine. The poet has been awarded the Shelley Memorial Prize from the Poetry Society of America (1998), the Virginia Prize for Poetry from the Library of Virginia (2000), and the Aiken Taylor Award for Modern Poetry (2001).

WORKS: *Wilderness of Ladies* (1960). *Welcome Eumenides* (1972). *New and Selected Poems* (1983). *Days Going, Days Coming Back* (1992). *Late Leisure* (1999).

—BES STARK SPANGLER

HENRY TAYLOR (1942–). Poet Henry Splawn Taylor was born and raised in Loudoun County, in rural northern Virginia. His mother taught elementary school, after a brief stint as an economist with the federal government; his father was a dairy farmer for two decades, then a high school English teacher. The father's interest in poetry helped shape the son's, as the poem "To Hear My Head Roar" explains. Taylor's rural upbringing was also influential, as it gave his poetry much of its *mise en scène;* particularly notable is the recurrence of poems about horses, which he learned to ride competitively.

Taylor's oeuvre is marked by great range of tone. His books include many humorous poems, among them parodies ("Mr. James Dickey in Orbit"), amusing anecdotes ("Tradition and the Individual Talent"), and incisive epigrams ("To an Older Poet"). One collection, *Brief Candles*, consists entirely of light verse. Generally, however, he juxtaposes his comic work with more sober narratives and meditations, and many of his poems (such as "Things Not Solved Though Tomorrow Came" and "Landscape with Tractor") are startlingly dark.

That tonal variety is matched by technical versatility. Taylor writes both free verse and metrical poetry, and he has often adopted fixed forms, such as the sonnet, the sestina, and the ballade. He is also technically inventive: for example, "To Hear My Head Roar" adapts terza rima by substituting the repetition of whole words for rhyme.

Taylor earned a B.A. in English from the University of Virginia and an M.A. in creative writing from Hollins College. He taught at several colleges and universities before retiring from American University in 2003. He lives in Bethesda, Md., with his wife Mooshe; he has two sons from a previous marriage. His awards include two NEA Fellowships, the American Academy of Arts and Letters' Witter Bynner Prize, and the Pulitzer Prize (for *The Flying Change*).

WORKS: *The Horse Show at Midnight* (1966). *Poetry: Points of Departure* (1974). *An Afternoon of Pocket Billiards* (1975). Ed., *The Water of Light: A Miscellany in Honor of Brewster Ghiselin* (1976). Trans., Euripides, *Children of Herakles*, with Robert A. Brooks (1981). *The Flying Change* (1985). *Compulsory Figures: Essays on Recent American Poets* (1992). *Understanding Fiction: Poems, 1986–1996* (1996). Trans., Vladimir Levchev, *Leaves from the Dry Tree* (1996). Trans., Levchev, *Black Book of the Endangered Species*, with Levchev (1999). *Brief Candles: 101 Clerihews* (2000). *Crooked Run: Poems* (2006).

—ROBERT M. WEST

PETER TAYLOR (1917–1994). Matthew Hillsman Taylor, Jr., was born in Trenton, Tenn., on January 8, 1917. He adopted the name "Peter" only as an adult. His parents, both of whom were Taylors (though unrelated and from opposite ends of the state) were products of lines going back to the earliest days of the region and distinguished by personages well known in Tennessee history. Most notable was Peter Taylor's maternal grandfather, a U.S. senator who in 1884 ran against his brother and their father for the governorship, a political race attracting national attention and dubbed "the War of the Roses." All of this history Peter Taylor drew upon in his fiction and plays. He drew as well on his father's career—first as a country attorney, then as a corporation lawyer, and at his pinnacle as president of an insurance company—and the family moves from Trenton to Nashville to St. Louis and finally to Memphis, this last a result of his father's betrayal by his best friend during the Great Depression.

In school at St. Louis's fashionable Country Day in 1932 when the family removed to Memphis to start over again, he was then placed in a large public school, Central High. His first clash with his formidable and overbearing father came upon graduation, when Hillsman Taylor prohibited his son's accepting a scholarship to Columbia University, and Peter Taylor refused to enter college and instead took a newspaper job. The Darwinian and Freudian power struggle between father and son was to become a central theme for Taylor as a writer.

The following spring, he enrolled at a local liberal arts college, Southwestern, to study under Allen Tate and wrote his first short stories (which were published in a short-lived little magazine in Mississippi, *River*). Tate advised Taylor to transfer to Vanderbilt the next fall to study under his own mentor, John Crowe Ransom. There Taylor became centrally involved personally, though not philosophically, in the Fugitive-Agrarian axis, and after a year at Vanderbilt and a year working as a realtor, he followed Ransom to Kenyon College, where he graduated in 1940. At Kenyon he found a sympathetic group of fellow writers with whom he kept in close touch, lifelong, most notably the poet and critic Randall Jarrell and Taylor's roommate, the poet Robert Lowell.

After graduation, he followed Lowell and Lowell's wife Jean Stafford to Louisiana State University to study under Cleanth Brooks and Robert Penn Warren. Leaving school before the end of the term (but after two stories had been accepted by the *Southern Review*), he returned to Memphis and was drafted. Before being sent overseas, he married the North Carolina poet Eleanor Ross, then under the tutelage of Donald Davidson at Vanderbilt. Returning to America at the end of World War II without ever having seen combat, Taylor took his first academic position, at Woman's College of North Carolina in Greensboro. Teaching stints would follow at Indiana, Chicago, Kenyon, Ohio State, and Harvard, punctuated by returns to Greensboro, a measure of the restlessness that was manifested also in Taylor's buying and selling over thirty residences. In 1967 he moved to the University of Virginia, where he taught until retirement in 1983.

The Best American Short Stories 1942 had included Taylor's story "The Fancy Woman," and for decades his stories would be selected for this series and the annual *O. Henry* volumes. Taylor's first collection, *A Long Fourth,* was published in 1948 with an introduction by Robert Penn Warren. It was favorably reviewed and brought him to the attention of the literary world if not the general public. In 1948 Taylor also began a long association with the *New Yorker.*

In 1959 his "Venus, Cupid, Folly and Time" won the O. Henry first prize. A decade later, just as his *Collected Stories* was being published, he was inducted into the National Institute of Arts and Letters. In 1978 Taylor won the Gold Medal for the Short Story given by the American Academy and Institute, and he was inducted into the academy in 1983. A wide readership continued to elude him, however, until the publication of his novel *A Summons to Memphis,* for which he was awarded the Pulitzer Prize and the Ritz-Hemingway Award. He is considered by many fellow writers and critics a master of the short-story form, some of his later stories being among his best work.

As age and ill health began to mark him, Taylor proved his devotion to his art, publishing a volume of stories and a novel in the last two years of his life. He died on November 2, 1994, in Charlottesville and was buried in Sewanee, Tenn. Misread occasionally as a regional writer of manners exhibiting Agrarian influence (which his work lacks almost totally), Taylor is now recognized as a devoted craftsman dealing in profound psychological soundings, the tension between the individual and the social order, and the complex issue of freedom.

WORKS: *A Long Fourth and Other Stories* (1948). *A Woman of Means* (1950). *The Widows of Thornton* (1954). *Tennessee Day in St. Louis* (1957). *Happy Families Are All Alike: A Collection of Stories* (1959). *Miss Lenora When Last Seen and Fifteen Other Stories* (1964). *The Collected Stories of Peter Taylor* (1969). *Presences: Seven Dramatic Pieces* (1973). *In the Miro District and Other Stories* (1977). *The Early Guest (a sort of story, a sort of play, a sort of dream)* (1982). *The Old Forest and Other Stories* (1985). *A Stand in the Mountains* (1986). *A Summons to Memphis* (1986). *The Oracle at Stoneleigh Court: Stories* (1993). *In the Tennessee Country* (1994).

—HUBERT H. MCALEXANDER

JOHN TAYLOR OF CAROLINE (1753–1824). John Taylor of Caroline is known for his celebration of scientific agriculture and defense of states' rights, including slavery. Born on December 19, 1753, to James and Ann Pollard Taylor of Caroline County, Va., he was raised by his uncle, Edmund Pendleton, after his father's death (ca. 1756).

He was classically educated by private tutors and attended the College of William and Mary. He studied law with Pendleton, joining the bar in 1774. He served in the Revolutionary army in 1775–79 and 1781, earning the rank of lieutenant colonel. He served in the Virginia legislature in 1779–81, 1783–85, and 1796–1800, and in the U.S. Senate in 1792–94, 1803–4, and 1822–24. In 1783 he married Lucy Penn, the daughter of a prominent lawyer and planter. He sided with Thomas Jefferson on most issues until 1809, when he broke ranks with both Jefferson and the Federalist Alexander Hamilton. Taylor fathered eight children and amassed three large plantations before his death on August 21, 1824.

Taylor is best known for *Arator: Being a Series of Agricultural Essays, Practical and Political* and *An Inquiry into the Principles and Policies of the Government of the United States,* works that explore the issues that later would spark the Civil War. *Arator* promotes agricultural reform and inveighs against northern capitalism, coupling a Jeffersonian celebration of the landed farmer with scientific agricultural advice. *An Inquiry*—deemed by Charles Beard "among the two or three really historic contributions to

[American] political science"—argues for the protection of agrarian democracy against an engulfing federal government. Taylor's corpus, Richard Gray posits, offers one of the first examples of "Southern rhetoric"—a peculiar conflation of "past" and "rural" that finds its way into the works of writers from Jefferson to John Pendleton Kennedy to Donald Davidson and the Agrarians.

WORKS: "Remonstrance of Virginia" (March 1781), *Tyler's Quarterly Historical and Genealogical Magazine* 12 (July 1930): 40–41. *An Examination of the Late Proceedings in Congress, Respecting the Official Conduct of the Secretary of the Treasury* (1793). *Definition of Parties* (1794). *An Enquiry into the Principles and Tendencies of Certain Public Measures* (1794). *An Argument Respecting the Constitutionality of the Carriage Tax* (1795). *A Defense of the Measures of the Administration of Thomas Jefferson*, as Curtis (1804). *A Pamphlet, Containing a Series of Letters* (1809). *Arator: Being a Series of Agricultural Essays, Practical and Political* (1813, 1814, 1817, 1818). *An Inquiry into the Principles and Policy of the Government of the United States* (1814). *Construction Construed, and Constitutions Vindicated* (1820). *Tyranny Unmasked* (1822). *New Views of the Constitution of the United States* (1823).

—SCOTT HICKS

JOHN REUBEN THOMPSON (1823–1873). John Reuben Thompson was born on October 23, 1823, in Richmond, Va., and grew up there. He attended the University of Virginia, receiving his Bachelor of Laws in 1845, but soon abandoned practicing law for literature.

A poet of some merit, he is better known as owner and editor of the *Southern Literary Messenger*, where he drew around him the best literary talent of the South, notably William Gilmore Simms, Henry Timrod, Paul Hamilton Hayne, and Philip Pendleton Cooke. A popular lecturer, Thompson contributed to northern magazines, working particularly with Whittier and Bryant. Whittier wrote to Hayne, "To thee, and John R. Thompson . . . the South must look, for its literary leaders."

He worked closely with Poe and wrote "The Genius and Character of Edgar Allan Poe," which he gave many times as a lecture. He spent six months of 1854 in England and Europe, sending travel articles back to the *Messenger* and visiting with Tennyson, Thackeray, Dickens, Carlyle, Macaulay, and the Brownings.

In 1860 Thompson left the editorship of the *Southern Literary Messenger* to become editor of the *Southern Field and Fireside* for one year and then devoted himself to helping the Confederacy during the war. Many of his best-known poems are war lyrics: "Lee to the Rear," "The Battle Rainbow," "Music in Camp," and "General J. E. B. Stuart." From 1864 to 1866 he was back in England, to serve on the staff of the *Index* (official organ of the Confederate States in London), and visited again with his literary friends, spending much time in the homes of Tennyson and Carlyle. Probably few American writers have worked as closely with as many literary figures in England and America as did Thompson. These friendships fitted in well with his work as literary editor, and some of these writers advised him about his own poetry.

Upon his return home he wrote for many journals, and Bryant soon offered him the literary editorship of the *New York Evening Post*, a position that he held until his death on April 30, 1873, in New York City.

WORKS: *Poems of John R. Thompson*, ed. John S. Patton (1920). Ed., *The Genius and Character of Edgar Allan Poe*, with James H. Rindfleische (1929).

—JOHN O. EIDSON

MAURICE THOMPSON (1844–1901). James Madison Thompson was born on September 9, 1844, in Fairfield, Ind. He legally changed his name to James Maurice Thompson, dropping his first name, James, from his signature in 1875. There is evidence he used the pseudonym Bowman, and he carried the nickname Matt. The son of a Primitive Baptist preacher, Thompson spent brief periods in Indiana, Missouri, and Kentucky before settling with his family in Gordon County, Ga., in 1855.

The Civil War brought swift closure to Thompson's sylvan childhood and he enlisted in the 63rd Georgia Regiment in December 1862. He surrendered at Kingston, Ga., on May 12, 1865. In 1868 he left Georgia for Crawfordsville, Ind., and secured employment as a civil engineer for John Lee, a railroad section contractor, and married Lee's daughter, Alice. Thompson purchased a law library, gave up engineering, and entered the legal profession, but his love of letters eventually doomed what might have been a successful career at the bar. With improved finances, he closed the law practice to devote full time to his writing in 1884.

Thompson's southern roots did not run deep. Lucinda MacKethan counts him a "literary opportunist of the clearest stripe" who wrote formulaic potboilers with vague southern settings. He ranged into poetry, fiction, nature sketches, and literary criticism that espoused the values of nonsectarian Christianity, Manifest Destiny, and small-town Victorian gentility. He was, at bottom, more Hoosier than southerner.

Civic minded, Thompson participated in local politics, was elected to the Indiana State Legislature, was later appointed Indiana state geologist, and in 1888 was a delegate to the Democratic National Convention. In 1878 he published *The Witchery of Archery*, igniting a national interest in archery. The following year, he became a founding member of the National Archery Association and was installed as its first president. On the sixtieth anniversary of the National Archery Association in 1939, it created its highest award, the J. Maurice Thompson Medal of Honor, in his memory.

WORKS: *Hoosier Mosaics* (1875). *The Witchery of Archery* (1878). *How to Train in Archery* (1879). *A Tallahassee Girl* (1882). *His Second Campaign* (1883). *Songs of Fair Weather* (1883). *Claude's Big Trout* (1884). *At Love's Extremes* (1885). *A Red-headed Family* (1885). *By-Ways and Bird Notes* (1885). *The Boys' Book of Sports and Outdoor Life* (1886). *A Banker of Bankersville* (1886). *Sunshine and Song* (1887). *Sylvan Secrets* (1887). *A Fortnight of Folly* (1888). *The Story of Louisiana* (1888). *Poems* (1892). *A Shadow of Love* (1892). *Lorel Hasardour* (1892). *The Ethics of Literary Art* (1893). *The King of Honey Island* (1893). *Lincoln's Grave* (1894). *The Ocala Boy* (1895). *Stories of Indiana* (1898). *Stories of the Cherokee Hills* (1898). *My Winter Garden* (1900). *Alice of Old Vincennes* (1900). *Sweetheart Manette* (1901). *Rosalynde's Lovers* (1901).

—CLIFFORD HUNTINGTON, JR.

WILLIAM TAPPAN THOMPSON (1812–1882). William Tappan Thompson was born on August 31, 1812, in Ravenna, Ohio, the son of David and Catherine Kerney Thompson. His formal education ended when, being orphaned at the age of fourteen, he went to Philadelphia to work in the office of the *Daily Chronicle*. By 1830 he had moved to Tallahassee in the employ of James D. Westcott, then secretary of the territory of Florida. In 1835 he was employed by A. B. Longstreet on the *States' Rights Sentinel* in Augusta, Ga., where he married in 1837, and in March 1838 founded the *Mirror*. He also served briefly in 1836 in the Seminole campaign in Florida. Early in 1842 he merged the *Mirror* with the Macon *Family Companion* to form the *Family Companion and Ladies' Mirror*.

The popularity during the 1830s of Seba Smith's Major Jack Downing, Longstreet's *Georgia Scenes*, and the Crockett stories provided Thompson with models for humorous sketches of rustic life. The first Pineville story appeared in the *Family Companion and Ladies' Mirror* in March 1842; the first Major Jones letter, in the same journal in June 1842. Shortly thereafter the journal failed, and Thompson became editor of the *Southern Miscellany* in Madison, Ga., where some thirty letters appeared between August 20, 1842, and February 9, 1844. In 1843 the first sixteen letters were collected in a pamphlet as a subscription premium for the *Miscellany*, constituting the first edition of *Major Jones's*

Courtship. An enlarged second edition of twenty-six letters appeared in 1844; an eighth edition in 1847 added two more letters. By 1900 the work had been reprinted nearly thirty times.

In the character of Major Joseph Jones, Thompson expressed in native dialect, and from a realistic and humorous perspective, the tastes and morals of a middle-class southern farmer-townsman. Kindly, domestically committed, yet shrewdly enjoying human frailty, Major Jones gave a large reading public hearty amusement without the distressing overtones of cruelty and animalism that emerge from the stories of Sut Lovingood or Simon Suggs.

Despite the popularity of his creation, Thompson profited little from the Major Jones books, but he enjoyed increasing success as an editor and publisher. In 1850 he founded the *Savannah Morning News,* which he actively edited until his death on March 24, 1882.

WORKS: *Major Jones's Courtship* (1843, 1844, 1847). *Major Jones's Chronicles of Pineville* (1845). *John's Alive; or, The Bride of a Ghost* (1846). *Major Jones's Sketches of Travel* (1848). *Polly Peablossom's Wedding* (1851). *Rancy Cottem's Courtship* (1879).

—OTIS WHEELER

THOMAS BANGS THORPE (1815–1878). Descended from seventeenth-century New England settlers, Thorpe was born on March 1, 1815, in Westfield, Mass., to Thomas and Rebecca Farnham Thorpe. His father, a Methodist minister, died when Thomas was four, and his mother took the family to live first with her parents in Albany, and later to New York City. In 1830 Thorpe studied art with John Quidor. From 1834 until 1836 he attended Wesleyan University, where he was friendly with the sons of southern planters being educated there.

In 1836, for his health, he moved to Louisiana, where he lived in St. Francisville, Baton Rouge, and New Orleans, painting portraits for the planters. Dissatisfied with the economic and social position of the artist in the South, he began, in 1843, to publish a series of Louisiana newspapers, hold minor political offices, and support Whig candidates and causes. In 1852 he ran for state superintendent of education, lost with his party, and shortly moved back to New York City. During the Civil War he served as colonel with the Union forces in New Orleans. After the war he returned to New York to continue painting and writing until his death, on September 20, 1878.

As early as 1839 Thorpe had begun contributing sketches of Louisiana and Arkansas frontier life to national journals, such as the New York *Spirit of the Times,* the *Knickerbocker Magazine, Graham's, Harper's,* and others. His one antislavery novel and his essays on art and artists retain a minor significance. "The Big Bear of Arkansas" (*Spirit,* 1841), admired by William Faulkner, can be called, because of Thorpe's skillful use of myth, symbol, and comic meaning, the best single story in the tradition of southwestern humor.

WORKS: *The Mysteries of the Backwoods* (1846). *Our Army on the Rio Grande* (1846). *Our Army at Monterey* (1847). *The Taylor Anecdote Book* (1848). *The Hive of "The Bee-Hunter"* (1854). *The Master's House* (1854). *A New Collection of Thomas Bangs Thorpe's Sketches of the Old Southwest,* ed. David C. Estes (1989).

—MILTON AND PATRICIA RICKELS

RICHARD TILLINGHAST (1940–). Although he has lived mostly outside the South since his college graduation, Richard Tillinghast took a southern orientation and a southern accent with him. His several books of poetry are set in many areas of the nation and many parts of the world, but they often mirror southern reality.

He was born on November 25, 1940, in Memphis, Tenn., son of native New Englander Raymond Charles Tillinghast and Martha Williford, whose Tennessee roots were deep. His upbringing in Memphis was solidly middle class: his father worked for Proctor and Gamble and was an inventor; his mother taught French and Latin. Attracted to drawing and the visual arts, young Richard was also adept in music, playing drums and guitar; in his high school years he and his brother David (banjo) played gigs in clubs and nightspots, some of them very rough venues. The group's repertoire included jazz and rock 'n' roll as well as country and western.

Following graduation from Central High in 1958, Tillinghast entered the University of the South. There he claimed poetry as his passion. At Sewanee he encountered giants of the Southern Renascence and read widely in its literature, and during his senior year worked as an editorial assistant to Andrew Lytle. In the charged cultural struggles of those years, even in protected Sewanee, he allied himself with the forces of change and political activism. During his senior year, he went regularly to the Highlander Folk School, where folk music and the protest movement were joined.

The tendency to activism increased at Harvard, where his primary mentor was Robert Lowell— poet with social consciousness second to none. Tillinghast received his M.A. in 1963. For his Ph.D. (1969), he wrote a dissertation on Lowell. It would become the basis of his critical memoir on that poet, *Damaged Grandeur*.

Tillinghast was living in Berkeley when he finished the dissertation. He had in the meantime married Nancy Pringle in 1965; the next year they traveled widely in Europe, then separated in 1966, divorcing in 1970. In the climate of the times, personal freedom was a priority for Tillinghast. Like many, he was attracted to the "spiritual" subculture. His appointment in the Berkeley English department (1968–73) ended with denial of tenure, to no one's surprise.

Exiting Berkeley, he married Mary Graves, with whom he would have four children and eventually a more settled pattern of life. He returned to teaching in 1976—in the prison program at San Quentin. The University of the South offered him a visiting appointment for 1979–80, an appointment important to the growth of his career, and there he revisited his southern roots for "Sewanee in Ruins"—a long poem reflecting on Sewanee's long history and his own. His graduate alma mater provided a further step to "respectability" by appointing him Briggs-Copeland Lecturer (1980–83). In 1983 fellow southerner George Garrett, then establishing the M.F.A. program at the University of Michigan, invited Tillinghast to a tenured appointment, and Tillinghast has been a part of the Michigan program ever since.

Grants and awards continued to feed Tillinghast's love of travel and other cultures. Especially important among them was an Amy Lowell Trust travel grant that took him to Ireland in 1990–91. He has been a part of the Poets' House in Ireland and returns there regularly. Frequently he gives readings, promoting performance poetry. The compact disc "My Only Friends Were the Wolves" (2003) features his poetry performed with a jazz fusion band.

WORKS: *The Keeper* (1967). *Sleep Watch* (1969). *The Knife and Other Poems* (1980). *Sewanee in Ruins* (1983). *Our Flag Was Still There* (1984). *Twos* (1987). *A Quiet Print in Kinvara* (1991). *The Stonecutter's Hand* (1994). *Damaged Grandeur* (1995). *Today in the Café Trieste* (1997). Ed., *A Visit to the Gallery* (1997). *Six Mile Mountain* (2000).

—JOSEPH M. FLORA

HENRY TIMROD (1828–1867). The only son among the four children of Thyrza Prince and William Henry Timrod, a bookbinder and amateur poet whose shop was a gathering place for local literati, Henry Timrod was born in Charleston, S.C., on December 8, 1828. He was educated at the

Classical School of Christopher Cotes, where Paul Hamilton Hayne, the poet, and Basil L. Gilder-sleeve, the classical scholar, were his classmates and where he received a sound grounding in Greek, Latin, French, history, and mathematics. Later, with the help of a city merchant, he attended the University of Georgia for three terms in 1845–46, continuing his earlier studies but dropping out when financial difficulties occurred. Returning home, he read law with James Louis Petigru, a distinguished barrister and former attorney general of the state, and in the 1850s he taught school, tutored on Carolina plantations, and contributed verse and essays to Charleston newspapers and to the *Southern Literary Messenger* and *Russell's Magazine.*

In *Russell's* (1857–60), a monthly edited by Hayne, Timrod published thirty-seven poems and four essays, including several of his best lyrics of the period—"The Arctic Voyager," "Dreams," and "Preceptor Amat"—and two of his most important essays—"What Is Poetry?" and "Literature in the South." In his poems and in his criticism, Timrod offers a romantic interpretation mindful of Wordsworth and Tennyson that concentrates on unusual sensibility, powerful emotion, and beautiful language. In a later lecture, "A Theory of Poetry" (1863; published in 1901), he adds truth and great moral and philosophical lessons. As for southern writing, he characterizes the author of his region as "the Pariah of modern literature," an artist without honor in his own country and ridiculed in the North as a representative (and often defender) of an outmoded and immoral way of life.

Timrod's poems in *Russell's* and elsewhere in the 1850s led to the publication of the only collection that appeared during his lifetime, *Poems,* in December 1859 (a later gathering is said to have been lost in the blockade during the war). Despite his initial reluctance to support secession, the establishment of the Confederate government and subsequently the beginning of hostilities changed his artistic focus and charged his imagination with fresh vitality, and the meeting of the Confederate Congress in February 1861 led him to publish the original version of "Ethnogenesis," his first ode on a "new nation among nations." In the following September he published a second laureate poem, "The Cotton Boll," celebrating a land blessed with "all the common gifts of God" and prophesying that the Confederacy would share its wealth with the world and "revive the half-dead dream of universal peace." But there were also war poems—"A Cry to Arms," "Carolina," and "Charleston," to name a few—that exhorted southerners to meet and defeat the foe, the "Huns" who "tread thy sacred sands." At the same time, the speaker in "Christmas" yearns for "peace in all our homes / And peace in all our hearts." With these lyrics and with "Spring," "The Two Armies," "Carmen Triumphale" and "The Unknown Dead," Timrod became widely known in the South as the poet laureate of the Confederacy, a reputation confirmed by his ultimate poetic contribution to the war and its result, "Ode Sung on the Occasion of Decorating the Graves of the Confederate Dead, at Magnolia Cemetery, Charleston, S.C., 1866." This is Timrod's most perfect poem and assuredly one of the finest Horatian odes in English.

Although Timrod's most important poetry is related to the war, he composed other verse worthy of note during this period, including "Our Willie," "Katie," and "La Belle Juive." His best concurrent prose, "A Theory of Poetry," a lecture in which he disagrees with Poe's ideas that a long poem (the epic in particular) is a contradiction in terms and that poetry should deal primarily with beauty, and maintains that *Paradise Lost,* for example, has a cumulative effect and a general harmony and unity and that poetry, while including beauty as a source, must also have power and embody great moral truths.

After the war was over in 1865, Timrod worked as an editor and journalist and had little time for poetry. He married Katie Goodwin, his sister Emily's sister-in-law, on February 16, 1864, and their only child, William Henry, was born the following Christmas eve. Also in 1864 a benefactor helped him buy part interest in and become an editor of the *Columbia South Carolinian,* but after Sherman's troops sacked and burned the city in February 1865, Timrod and his family lived hand to mouth, selling furniture and other valuables and reluctantly accepting money from friends, including William Gilmore Simms and Hayne. Concurrently, Timrod's recurrent hemorrhages grew worse, and he died of tuberculosis on October 7, 1867, eighteen years to the day after the death of Poe.

After Poe, Timrod is the most important southern poet of the nineteenth century in the quality of his best verse. Sidney Lanier and Hayne have larger bodies of work, and Hayne, in particular, offers a larger range of subject matter and techniques, but Timrod is a better poet than either of his two contemporaries and, though not a major poet, he is surely a significant minor one.

WORKS: *Poems* (1859). *The Poems of Henry Timrod*, ed. Paul Hamilton Hayne (1873). *Katie* (1884). *Poems of Henry Timrod; With Memoir and Portrait* (1899). *The Uncollected Poems of Henry Timrod*, ed. Guy A. Cardwell (1942). *The Essays of Henry Timrod*, ed. Edd Winfield Parks (1942). *The Collected Poems: A Variorum Edition*, ed. Parks and Aileen Wells Parks (1965).

—RAYBURN S. MOORE

MELVIN BEAUNOROUS TOLSON (1898–1966). The eldest of four children of Alonzo Tolson, a Methodist minister, and Lera Tolson, Melvin Beaunorous Tolson was born on February 6, 1898, in Moberly, Mo. After moving between Iowa and Missouri, the family settled in Kansas City, where Tolson graduated from high school. He distinguished himself as valedictorian, orator, and football captain.

Prior to transferring to Lincoln University near Philadelphia, where he took a B.A. in 1923, Tolson passed his freshman year at Fisk University in Nashville. During his Lincoln matriculation he met and married Ruth Southall. They moved to Marshall, Tex., when Tolson accepted a position teaching drama and debate at Wiley College. The couple reared three sons and one daughter.

Study for an M.A. at Columbia University drew Tolson to Harlem in 1930 as the nation's economic depression waxed and the Harlem Renaissance waned. His thesis, "The Harlem Group of Negro Writers," interpreted the literary movement of which he desired to be a part. Bearing traces of Edgar Lee Masters, the French Symbolists, the American Imagists, and the New Negro, his own poetry was gaining aesthetic momentum.

Rendezvous with America, Tolson's first book of verse, includes his most popular poem, "Dark Symphony," winner of *Poetry*'s Bess Hopkins Award. In 1947, the same year that he accepted a position at Langston University in Oklahoma, Liberia appointed Tolson its poet laureate. Serving as the African nation's laureate, he produced *Libretto for the Republic of Liberia,* an extended ode commemorating Liberia's centennial. Tolson's death eclipsed his most ambitious work, *Harlem Gallery.* Only one of the work's projected five books was completed. It nevertheless stands as a complete work on its own. Tolson died of cancer in Dallas, Tex., on August 29, 1966, one year after Tuskegee made him the first Avalon Professor of the Humanities.

WORKS: *Rendezvous with America* (1944). *Libretto for the Republic of Liberia* (1953). *Harlem Gallery: Book I, The Curator* (1965). *A Gallery of Harlem Portraits,* ed. Robert M. Farnsworth (1979). *Caviar and Cabbage* (1982).

—LA VINIA DELOIS JENNINGS

JOHN KENNEDY TOOLE (1937–1969). Born on December 17, 1937, in New Orleans, La., John Kennedy Toole was the only child of John and Thelma Ducoing Toole. Attractive and precocious, Toole excelled in school and graduated at sixteen. The summer before entering Tulane University, he wrote his first novel. Following graduation from Tulane's English honors program, Toole was awarded a Woodrow Wilson Fellowship at Columbia University. He completed the master's program in a single year and returned to Louisiana in the summer of 1959. Toole took a position as an assistant English professor at Southwestern Louisiana Institute (now University of Louisiana at Lafayette).

Eager to return to New York, Toole accepted an offer from Hunter College, where he taught for a year before being drafted into the army. His fluency in Spanish got him posted at Fort Buchanan, Puerto Rico, in 1961–63. During his service tour in the Caribbean, Toole began writing *A Confederacy of Dunces*. After separating from the service, he returned to New Orleans and taught at St. Mary's Dominican College.

Toole finished *Confederacy* and sent it to Simon and Schuster, where the manuscript caught the attention of Robert Gottlieb. The editor worked with Toole on the novel for several years before returning it, having concluded that the novel had no future. In the last two years of his life, Toole began to suffer from severe headaches and paranoia fueled by alcohol and depression before taking his own life on March 26, 1969, in Biloxi, Miss.

His mother maintained unflagging confidence in her son's genius, finally bringing his novel to the reluctant attention of Walker Percy, who soon recognized its great verve and recommended its publication to Louisiana State University Press. In 1980 *A Confederacy of Dunces* was published, and in the following year it won the Pulitzer Prize for fiction, the first such awarded to an author posthumously. The novel quickly became a best-seller for the press; its protagonist, Ignatius Reilly, took his place with the memorable comic figures of southern literature. Toole's earlier novel *The Neon Bible* was published in 1989.

WORKS: *A Confederacy of Dunces* (1980). *The Neon Bible* (1989).

—RENÉ POL NEVILS AND DEBORAH GEORGE HARDY

JEAN TOOMER (1894–1967). Christened Nathan Pinchback Toomer in 1894, Jean Toomer took the name "Jean" from his admiration of Romain Rolland's epic novel *Jean Christophe* (1913), a portrait of the heroic artist based on Beethoven's life. Like Jean Christophe, Toomer wanted to be a musician before he became a writer, an aspiration given to him in part by the cultured world of the mulatto elite in Washington, D.C., where he was born and where he spent his formative years. His father, Nathan, was (or pretended to be) an affluent planter from Sparta, Ga., and at one time was married to the wealthiest woman of color in the United States, Amanda America Dickson. His mother, Nina, was the daughter of P. B. S. Pinchback, a former slave who became the lieutenant governor of Louisiana during Reconstruction. Toomer himself went to M Street High School (1910–14), a prestigious institution that prepared the African American aristocracy for universities like Howard and Harvard. Toomer had other plans. He briefly studied agriculture at the University of Wisconsin and the Massachusetts College of Agriculture, dropping out of both schools to attend the American College of Physical Training in Chicago (1916).

This nomadic existence created a pattern that would last for most of his life, as he came to live at various times in New York, France, California, New Mexico, and eventually Bucks County, Pa., where he became a Quaker and lived the rest of his life. Along the way, he would marry two white women: the novelist Margery Latimer in 1931 (she died a year later giving birth to their daughter, Margery), and then Marjorie Content, the former wife of Harold Loeb, in 1934. An extraordinarily handsome and charismatic man, Toomer had numerous love affairs with famous women, notably Georgia O'Keeffe, Edna St. Vincent Millay, and Mabel Dodge Luhan. In 1923 he embraced the philosophy of the Russian mystic Georges Gurdjieff, and in 1926 he had a mystical experience that completely changed his life—and his writing. Although he continued to write about social themes, they were now shaped by an obsession with spiritual perfection. He died in 1967, a man forgotten except by those who loved, and kept alive, the one book, *Cane*, for which he is now remembered. As a literary kind, *Cane* is hard to define, but perhaps its form is best described as a hybrid short-story cycle modeled in part on W. E. B. Du Bois's *The Souls of Black Folk*, James Joyce's *Dubliners*, Sherwood Anderson's *Winesburg, Ohio*, and Waldo Frank's *City Block*.

There were two key events in the writing of *Cane*. The first was Toomer's meeting Waldo Frank in the fall of 1920, and the second, his trip in the fall of 1921 to Georgia to become assistant principal at the Sparta Agricultural and Industrial School. The first event was important because Frank introduced Toomer to writers who would inspire him and to literature that would help create a vortex of ideas for *Cane*. The writers—Hart Crane, Sherwood Anderson, Lewis Mumford, Gorham Munson, Paul Rosenfeld, Kenneth Burke, Van Wyck Brooks, and Randolph Bourne—were all associated with the quest of rediscovering America's true literary past, one that would escape the stifling hold placed upon it by the puritan-commercial culture. Toomer was especially excited by the theme of cultural renewal in Frank's *Our America*.

It was the second event, the actual trip south to Sparta, that made Toomer a southern writer. Although he lived in Sparta for less than three months, from September to November 25, 1921, he distilled that experience into a great work of art. At times he was excited by the beauty of the South and by the epiphanic recognition of his racial past. This theme is expressed in the poem "Song of the Son," in which he describes his relationship to an African American folk heritage. Another heritage also surfaced in *Cane*, a horrific past he thought was not his because of his privileged place within Washington's "colored" aristocracy. Terror and beauty would be the twin themes of *Cane*, the legacy that would also haunt the literature of the Harlem Renaissance.

As a work of art, *Cane* is unique, mixing poetry and prose within its tripartite structure and presenting a view of the South in terms that anticipate Faulkner. Toomer depicted the South as a diverse region of racial conflicts and mixed bloodlines. He was especially perceptive in his treatment of African American women, avoiding the previous literary stereotypes that had defined them. Ironically, as *Cane* was being published, Toomer was already refusing to be categorized as a "Negro" writer. In one sense, this position is quite understandable in that *Cane* itself deconstructs the whole notion of race; but, in another sense, Toomer's new attitude was misleading since his African American background was the main source and inspiration for the book.

Rejecting the label of "Negro" writer did nothing to improve his own work. Although he never stopped writing, he published only one book after *Cane*, a collection of aphorisms entitled *Essentials*. Much of his previously unpublished and out-of-print fiction, poems, and essays have now been collected in several volumes.

Two years after Toomer died, *Cane* was republished to the delight of a new generation of readers. And as it had inspired much of the literature of the Harlem Renaissance, it continued to inspire African American writers, especially those who wrote about the South: Richard Wright, James Baldwin, Leon Forrest, David Bradley, Gayl Jones, Alice Walker, and Toni Morrison.

WORKS: *Cane* (1923). *Essentials: Definitions and Aphorisms* (1931). *The Wayward and the Seeking: A Collection of Writings by Jean Toomer*, ed. Darwin T. Turner (1980). *The Collected Poems of Jean Toomer*, ed. Robert B. Jones and Margery Toomer Latimer (1988). *A Jean Toomer Reader: Selected Unpublished Writings*, ed. Frederik L. Rusch (1993). *Jean Toomer: Selected Essays and Literary Criticism*, ed. John Chandler Griffin (1996). *The Uncollected Works of American Author Jean Toomer, 1894–1967*, ed. John Chandler Griffin (2003).

—CHARLES SCRUGGS

WILLIAM PETERFIELD TRENT (1862–1939). William Peterfield Trent was born on November 10, 1862, in Richmond, Va., to Peterfield and Lucy Carter Burwell Trent. Both of his parents had distinguished Virginia ancestors; after serving the Confederacy and sacrificing much of his means to the southern cause, his father, a physician, died in 1875. After attending private schools in Richmond, Trent enrolled at the University of Virginia, where he edited the literary magazine and received a B.Litt. in 1883 and the A.M. in 1884. From 1884 to 1887 he read law and taught in private schools in Richmond. In 1887 he went to Johns Hopkins University for a year of postgraduate study in history and political science.

In 1888 he joined the faculty of the University of the South at Sewanee, Tenn., as professor of English and acting professor of political economy and history. While Trent was at Sewanee, his main interests shifted from history to literature. In 1892 he was a leader in founding the *Sewanee Review* and was its editor for seven years. Always a prolific worker, Trent edited eleven texts, wrote sixty-five articles for periodicals, and published eight books while at Sewanee. A biography of William Gilmore Simms for the American Men of Letters series was controversial in the South, for it contended that slavery had been a great evil in part because it had diverted the talents of a man like Simms from a potentially great achievement in belles lettres to a defense of the peculiar institution.

On December 8, 1896, Trent married Alice Lyman, and they were the parents of a daughter and a son. In 1900 he accepted a professorship of English literature at Barnard College of Columbia University. There Trent continued to be a pioneer in teaching the appreciation of literature for its own sake.

One of the major projects of Trent's career was *The Cambridge History of American Literature,* in four volumes, which he edited with Carl Van Doren, John Erskine, and Stuart P. Sherman (1917–21). Another was the Columbia edition of *The Works of John Milton,* in eighteen volumes (1931–38), which Trent first suggested in 1908; he served as editor-in-chief until ill health forced him to resign in 1925. A paralytic stroke in Paris in the summer of 1927 ended his teaching duties. He died of a heart attack at Hopewell Junction, N.Y., on December 6, 1939.

WORKS: *English Culture in Virginia: A Study of the Gilmer Letters and an Account of the English Professors Obtained by Jefferson for the University of Virginia* (1889). *William Gilmore Simms* (1892). *The Makers of the Union: Benjamin Franklin* (1897). *Southern Statesmen of the Old Regime: Washington, Jefferson, Randolph, Calhoun, Stephens, Toombs, and Jefferson Davis* (1897). Ed., Edgar Allan Poe, *The Raven, The Fall of the House of Usher, and Other Poems and Tales* (1897). Ed., Poe, *The Gold Bug, The Purloined Letter, and Other Tales* (1898). *The Authority of Criticism and Other Essays* (1899). *John Milton: A Short History of His Life and Works* (1899). *Robert E. Lee* (1899). *Verses* (1899). Ed., Robert Louis Stevenson, *The Poems of Robert Louis Stevenson* (1900). Ed., Honoré de Balzac, *The Works of Honoré de Balzac,* 32 vols. (1900). Intro., *Historic Towns of the Southern States* (1900). *War and Civilization* (1901). Ed., Herman Melville, *Typee: Life in the South Seas* (1902). *A History of American Literature, 1607–1865* (1903). *Progress of the United States of America in the Century* (1903). *A History of the United States,* with Charles Kendall Adams (1903). Ed., *Colonial Prose and Poetry,* with Benjamin W. Wells, 3 vols. (1903). *A Brief History of American Literature* (1904). *Greatness in Literature and Other Papers* (1905). Ed., *Southern Writers: Selections in Prose and Verse* (1905). Ed., *The Best American Tales,* with John Bell Henneman (1907). *Longfellow and Other Essays* (1910). *Littérature Américaine* (1911). *An Introduction to the English Classics,* with Charles L. Hanson and William T. Brewster (1911). *Great American Writers,* with John Erskine (1912). *Daniel Defoe: How to Know Him* (1916). Ed., *The Cambridge History of American Literature,* with John Erskine, Stuart P. Sherman, and Carl Van Doren, 4 vols. (1917–21). Ed., Washington Irving, *The Journals of Washington Irving,* with George S. Hellman (1919). *Verse Jottings* (1924). Ed., John Milton, *The Works of John Milton,* with Frank A. Patterson et al., 18 vols. (1931–38).

—RANDALL G. PATTERSON

GEORGE TUCKER (1775–1861). Born in August 1775 to a moderately prosperous merchant family in Bermuda, George Tucker studied Latin and eighteenth-century literature and was tutored by Josiah

Meigs, later the founder and first president of the University of Georgia. Tucker moved to Virginia in 1795 and entered the College of William and Mary. The cousin of jurist and writer St. George Tucker, another Bermudan who moved to Virginia, George Tucker practiced law ineptly while searching for a viable career. His marriage in 1797 to Williamsburg heiress Mary Byrd Farley, the great-great-granddaughter of William Byrd II, was cut short by her death from consumption eighteen months later. Tucker would spend the next two decades in and out of court trying to control at least part of his inheritance from her convoluted will.

Tucker moved to Richmond in 1800, still practicing law desultorily and meanwhile publishing essays and a pamphlet on slave conspiracy. He soon became part of the heady Richmond social and political mix. In 1802 he married Maria Ball Carter, the great-niece of George Washington. In 1806 Tucker had to abandon Richmond society and relocate to property owned by his in-laws in Frederick County, in the Shenandoah Valley; in 1808 he moved to Pittsylvania County, where he tried to restructure his affairs, buying a house and several slaves. Over the next fifteen years, Tucker published a series of essays on national policy and on the moral and economic dilemma of slavery; he was elected to the state legislature in 1816, and then to Congress for three successive terms (1819–25). Meanwhile, his fortunes had taken another turn for the worse and he had to sell his Pittsylvania estate and his slaves at public auction. Tucker's emotional life was made even more stressful by the deaths of two of his six children, Harriet in 1816 and Rosalie in 1818; a son was confined to a mental institution; and his second wife, Maria, died of pregnancy complications in 1823.

In the 1820s James Fenimore Cooper was purportedly earning a $5,000 royalty for each of his novels. Hoping to do as well, Tucker wrote In the Valley of Shenandoah; or, Memoirs of the Graysons, America's first plantation novel—one that anticipates John Pendleton Kennedy's Swallow Barn. Tucker wrote his 650-page novel in only two months, and he typically settled for superficial characters whose dialogue was mannered. Although the book was not a commercial success, Tucker's interest in economic history and his own personal losses helped him create an important and realistic account of the decline and displacement of old-line families by an efficiency-minded, hard-driving middle class of merchants who had little sympathy for Old South noblesse oblige and show. The Graysons lose both their paternal estate near Richmond and their idyllic Shenandoah Valley holdings to bankruptcy, see their plantation values made largely irrelevant, witness the betrayal and death of friends and loved ones, and experience the emotionally wrenching effects of auctioning off loyal and much-loved family slaves. Three decades ahead of Uncle Tom's Cabin, Tucker provides a compelling psychological study of the double bind of owning, respecting, and trying to support slaves as fellow human beings while hating what he flatly calls the moral "disease" of institutionalized, economically embedded slavery and its essential inhumanity.

Tucker's political service, a series of essays on Virginia, and another essay collection on taste, morals, and national policy caught the attention of James Madison and Thomas Jefferson. In 1825, at a starting salary of $1,500, Tucker was appointed professor of moral philosophy at Jefferson's newly opened University of Virginia, a position he would hold for twenty years. Among other subjects, Tucker taught rhetoric, metaphysics, and political economy.

Tucker's second novel, A Voyage to the Moon: With Some Account of the Manners and Customs, Science and Philosophy, of the People of Morosofia, and Other Lunarians, is America's first work of interplanetary science fiction. A Brahmin, who provides the Virgilian voice of reason and wisdom, accompanies the first-person narrator, "Atterley," to the moon and back in a copper spaceship supplied with compressed air metered from a spherical container. The vessel itself is powered by an intriguing magnetic force field emanating from the moon that attracts a mysterious metal bolted to their ship. Tucker uses the travelers' interactions with the inhabitants of the moon to satirize human vanity, politics, economics, belief systems, and the pseudoscience of various "projectors."

In 1828 Tucker married Louisa Thompson, who would be his life-mate during the maturation of his teaching and writing career; Louisa died in 1858. During his middle decades, in addition to studies of American demography and economics and a two-volume life of Jefferson, Tucker wrote his third novel, unpublished until 1977. *A Century Hence; or, a Romance of 1941*, which he apparently drafted in 1841, predates by almost half a century Edward Bellamy's 1888 utopian narrative *Looking Backward: 2000–1887*. Tucker is prescient in envisioning expanded professional roles for women; breaking down water into hydrogen and oxygen fuels and the consequences for the coal-mining states; warfare with Mexico; the rising world-powers of China and Russia; evolving views on marriage and birth control; and the increasing pressures on the world's food supply.

In April 1861, after completing an ambitious and authoritative history of the United States and one more volume on American economics, Tucker died accidentally, hit by falling cargo on a steamboat in Mobile. He left a legacy richer and more complex than many have realized.

WORKS: *Letter to a Member of the General Assembly of Virginia, on the subject of the late Conspiracy of the Slaves with a Proposal for Their Colonization* (1801). *Judge Tucker's Blackstone Proposals for Publishing an American Edition of Blackstone's Commentaries* (1802). *Speech of Mr. Tucker, of Virginia, on the Restriction of Slavery in Missouri Delivered in the House of Representatives of the United States, February 25, 1820* (1820). *Letters from Virginia, Translated from the French* (1816). *Essays on Various Subjects of Taste, Morals, and National Policy* (1822). *The Valley of Shenandoah; or, Memoirs of the Graysons* (1824). *A Voyage to the Moon: With Some Account of the Manners and Customs, Science and Philosophy, of the People of Morosofia and Other Lunarians* (1827). *The Laws of Wages, Profits, and Rent, Investigated* (1837). *The Life of Thomas Jefferson, Third President of the United States. With Parts of His Correspondence Never Before Published, and Notices of His Opinions on Questions of Civil Government, National Policy, and Constitutional Law* (1837). *Defence of the Character of Thomas Jefferson, Against a Writer in the New-York Review and Quarterly Church Journal* (1838). *The Theory of Money and Banks Investigated* (1839). *The Geography of America and the West Indies*, with Wilhelm Wittich, George R. Porter, and George Long (1841). *Progress of the United States in Population and Wealth in Fifty Years, as Exhibited by the Decennial Census* (1843). *Memoir of the Life and Character of John P. Emmet, M.D., Professor of Chemistry and Materia Medica in the University of Virginia* (1845). *Progress of the United States in Population and Wealth in Fifty Years, as Exhibited by the Decennial Census, with an Appendix, Containing an Abstract of the Census of 1850* (1855). *A History of the United States from Their Colonization to the End of the Twenty-Sixth Congress, in 1841* (1856–58). *Political Economy for the People* (1859; 1970). *Essays, Moral and Metaphysical* (1860). *A Century Hence; or, A Romance of 1941* (1977).

—R. BRUCE BICKLEY, JR.

NATHANIEL BEVERLEY TUCKER (1784–1851). The son of St. George and Frances Randolph Tucker and the half-brother of John Randolph of Roanoke, Beverley Tucker was born in Chesterfield County, Va., on September 6, 1784. He graduated from William and Mary in 1801 and practiced law for a time with small success. He served in the War of 1812, and in 1815 moved to Missouri, where he rose to a judgeship. After the deaths of his first two wives, he married again in 1830. He returned to Virginia in 1833 and a year later was appointed professor of law at his alma mater, a post that afforded him a platform for his intransigent defense of state sovereignty. Tucker early espoused a peaceful secession from what he saw as a despotic Union, and he championed a slave-based economy until his death on August 26, 1851.

Tucker's many letters and writings on politics and economics remain valuable to the student of southern nationalism, but his literary reputation must stand upon three novels: *George Balcombe, The*

Partisan Leader, and *Gertrude,* serialized in 1844–45 in the *Southern Literary Messenger. Gertrude* is a sentimental trifle, but *George Balcombe,* set in Virginia and Missouri, won the admiration of William Gilmore Simms and Edgar Allan Poe. The title page of *The Partisan Leader* carried the fictitious date of 1856, suggesting that this forecast of war between the North and South was no mere fancy. Tucker might have been gratified that his prophecy was reprinted in the North in 1861 as *A Key to the Disunion Conspiracy* and in Richmond in 1862 as "A Novel, and an Apocalypse of the Origin and Struggles of the Southern Confederacy." Tucker's literary production was not substantial, but its intense sectionalism and its idealized portraits of plantation society contributed importantly to the later fictional treatment of the Lost Cause.

WORKS: *George Balcombe* (1836). *The Partisan Leader* (1836). *A Discourse on the Importance of the Study of Political Science* (1840). *Gertrude* (1844–45). *A Series of Lectures on the Science of Government* (1845). *The Principles of Pleading* (1846).

—J. V. RIDGELY

ST. GEORGE TUCKER (1752–1827). St. George Tucker was a Renaissance man whose occupations reflected his varied talents. He counted himself a poet, a militiaman, a lawyer, a judge, a professor, a trader, an inventor, and an amateur astronomer. The youngest son of Colonel Harry Tucker, he was born on a Bermuda plantation on July 10, 1752. In 1771 he left for America to continue his law studies at William and Mary. (Williamsburg visitors may find his house on Nicholson Street.) He graduated in 1772 and joined the bar in 1774. In 1775 he glimpsed his future wife, Frances Bland Randolph, a First Family belle. But he scarcely had time to practice law or write love poetry before he was caught up in the turbulence of the Revolutionary War. Despite his Bermuda roots, Tucker was no loyalist, and he served as a lieutenant colonel during the Yorktown campaign.

In 1778 he married Frances and removed to Randolph Plantation near Petersburg. In the years that followed, his wife bore him five children (among them, the jurist Henry St. George Tucker and the novelist Nathaniel Beverley Tucker). Tucker began practicing law, taught law at William and Mary, and eventually served on the Virginia Supreme Court and the U.S. District Court. He wrote all the while, and produced a considerable number of poems in the popular forms of the day, including society poetry and satiric verses. An example is this doggerel: "There was a sorry judge who lived at the Swan by himself / He got but little honor, and he got but little pelf / He drudged and judged from morn to night, no ass drudged more than he / And the more he drudged, and the more he judged, the sorrier judge was he."

But American law students remember Tucker as the "American Blackstone," for his states-friendly redaction of the famed English commentaries. The massive, multivolume work brought English common law jurisprudence to American soil. Yet Tucker's signature is legible in the New World overtures—for example, the glosses on liberty, freedom of the press, and conscience.

Tucker died on November 10, 1827, in Nelson County, Va.

WORKS: *The Knight and the Friars: An Historical Tale* (1786). *Liberty, a Poem; On the Independence of America* (1788). *Dissertation on Slavery: With a Proposal for the Gradual Abolition of It in the State of Virginia* (1796). *Probationary Odes of Jonathan Pindar, Esq.* (1796). *Letters on the Alien and Sedition Laws* (1799). *Blackstone's Commentaries: With Notes of Reference to the Constitution and Laws of the Federal Government of the United States and of the Commonwealth of Virginia* (1803). *The Old Bachelor* (1814). *Hansford: A Tale of Bacon's Rebellion* (1857). *The Poems of St. George Tucker of Williamsburg, Virginia, 1752–1827,* ed. William S. Prince (1977).

—BRYAN GIEMZA

JOSEPH ADDISON TURNER (1826–1868). Joseph Addison Turner, probably best known as Joel Chandler Harris's literary mentor, was in his own right a remarkable Renaissance man in the Thomas Jefferson mold. Turner was born in Putnam County, Ga., on September 23, 1826. From his youth, he loved literature and languages and displayed fierce independence and considerable entrepreneurial energy. He studied mathematics, botany, Latin, Greek, Spanish, and French at nearby Phoenix Academy. After a term at Emory College in Oxford, Ga., Turner read and then practiced law, subscribed to a dozen major British and American periodicals, corresponded with several prominent writers, and launched four short-lived literary journals and a newspaper.

Turner married wealthy Eatontonian Louisa Dennis in 1850 and two years later moved to a thousand-acre plantation he had bought next to his father's plantation, nine miles northeast of Eatonton. In 1853 Joseph's brother William Wilberforce Turner inherited his father's estate, and the Turner sons named their combined plantations Turnwold. In addition to serving for two years as an independent in the Georgia legislature, Joseph operated a tannery, blacksmith, and carpentry shop; manufactured Confederate hats during the Civil War; raised cotton, corn, and cattle; kept detailed ornithological records; and published a quarterly, three books, and several essays and poems in national magazines. He also ran a print shop at Turnwold, from which he published America's only plantation newspaper, *The Countryman.* Turner's weekly, "Independent in Everything, Neutral in Nothing," soon enjoyed an impressive subscription list of two thousand. Turner hired seventeen-year-old Joel Harris to set type for his Washington no. 2 hand-press during the four-year run of the paper, in 1862–66; served as his surrogate father and mentor; taught Harris how to write polished, grammatically correct, and compact paragraphs, essays, and reviews; and then published over thirty of his pieces in *The Countryman.* Turner also recommended selected readings in his extensive plantation library of 1,400 volumes, which included Greek and Latin classics, major British and American authors, and 300 books on the law. Harris's Uncle Remus is a composite of several Turner slaves, from whom he heard in rapt fascination scores of Brer Rabbit trickster tales and other African American folk stories.

Although formerly a slave owner, after the Civil War Turner encouraged the education of freed African Americans and promoted sectional reconciliation—soon to become a major theme in Harris's writings, too. Turner was only forty-one when he died on February 29, 1868, from a bronchial infection. The plantation house on the Old Phoenix Road has been partially restored but is rarely open to visitors. A historic marker commemorates Turnwold and Harris's years there.

WORKS: *Turner's Monthly* (1848). *Red Lion* (1849). *Hasty Plate of Soup* (1852). *Tomahawk* (1853). *Independent Press* (1854–55). *The Cotton Planter's Manual* (1857). *The Discovery of Sir John Franklin and Other Poems* (1858). *Plantation: A Southern Quarterly Journal* (1860). *The Countryman* (1862–66).

—R. BRUCE BICKLEY, JR.

MARK TWAIN (1835–1910). Christened Samuel Langhorne Clemens, the boy who made the pen name Mark Twain famous was born in Florida, Mo., barely a village on the edge of a farming slave-economy. Both his parents had grown up in the border South (Virginia and Kentucky) and would continue to honor its values and customs. In 1839 Samuel's family moved to Hannibal, a raw but growing town north of St. Louis on the Mississippi River. Only hindsight can make his boyhood exceptional for its time and place, and only hagiographers can find signs of future greatness. His family, coping with near poverty, got by respectably. After the death in 1847 of his father, Samuel, who remembered him as upright but distant (in contrast to a lively, imaginative mother), continued to attend school part-time for two years while trying several jobs. In 1851 he started setting type for his older brother

Orion's newspaper and worked up to contributing a few columns. If any nonfamilial aspect of his Hannibal years proved crucial, it was his grounding in the partisan yet intellectually lively world of mid-nineteenth-century journalism.

In 1853, while his family was failing to prosper locally, Sam migrated—eastward after a stop in St. Louis. After stints as a typesetter in Manhattan, Philadelphia, and—later—Cincinnati, he fulfilled the dream of Hannibal boys through his apprenticeship as a steamboat pilot. Licensed in 1859, he performed so well as to get steady work between St. Louis and New Orleans until the Civil War cut off river trade. Though he wrote only a few casual pieces, he would consider his piloting years as heady, engrossing, and revelatory of human nature and would use the leadsman's call of "Mark Twain" (two fathoms or twelve feet deep) for his final pen name.

After stumbling around for two weeks with a pro-Confederate band of militia, he did go west—to the future state of Nevada. Failing to strike his bonanza as a miner, he settled for reporting and yarning on the *Virginia City Territorial Enterprise,* where he bylined Mark Twain in February 1863. Next, in San Francisco, he heightened his visibility with humor that overrode routine journalism and began to demonstrate the range of his genius. Having favored compromise rather than secession, he sounded acceptingly pro-Union by war's end.

By 1866 he had earned enough professional respect for an assignment to cover the Sandwich (Hawaiian) Islands. Then, after back-trailing to the East Coast, he persuaded another California newspaper to subsidize his joining a four-month excursion to western Europe and the Holy Land. His revised and supplemented travel letters made *The Innocents Abroad* into a personal and financial coup. Married to Olivia Langdon, a sheltered twenty-four year old from a wealthy, principled family in Elmira, N.Y., he tried a householder's routine as an editor of the *Buffalo Express.* But he soon committed to a career as writer, lecturer, and topical humorist.

For some readers *Roughing It* identified Twain primarily with the Golden West. Yet his wife and he having agreed on preferring sedate Hartford, Conn., they arranged to build a lavish, fashionable house there by 1874. He added fiction to his repertoire by collaborating with Charles Dudley Warner on *The Gilded Age. The Adventures of Tom Sawyer,* more midwestern than southern in ambience, fixed him in some minds as a nostalgic fabulist of childhood. Increasingly, his activities burst through any rubric. Though active as a citizen of New England, he regularly called on his previous personae. Though a productive author, especially during summers with his family (three daughters by 1880) at Quarry Farm overlooking Elmira, he responded to the demands of Hartford society. Though quick with white-hot resentments, he developed intimate friendships, most notably with William Dean Howells and Joseph H. Twichell, pastor of the Congregational church he grudgingly attended. Though praised as unmistakably western and then as uniquely American, he cultivated British friends, and *A Tramp Abroad* ranged cheerfully over western Europe.

After *The Prince and the Pauper,* a humanitarian romance about Tudor England, *Life on the Mississippi* returned to the river commonly associated today with Twain. Readers favor the chapters about his fumblings as a cub pilot, but two-thirds of the text presents the postbellum South from an implicitly northern attitude. *Adventures of Huckleberry Finn* did present an Old South objectively enough that literary historians debate its sociopolitical thrust then and now. Barely softened by affection, many touches satirized it as of "forty to fifty years ago." For some critics *A Connecticut Yankee in King Arthur's Court* no longer stands as a manifesto for democracy and material progress, but others now reclaim it as a pioneer in time-travel fantasy.

Increasingly distracted by financial setbacks, family tensions, and advancing age, Twain cobbled together *The Tragedy of Pudd'nhead Wilson and The Comedy of Those Extraordinary Twins,* his novel that critics most disagree about both as to its coordinated artistry and its underlying pull, exempli-fied through race, between nature and nurture. However registered by author or reader, the slave-holding South does hold center stage. After the labored *Tom Sawyer Abroad* and the surprisingly ideal-ized *Personal Recollections of Joan of Arc*, Twain—depressed by the death of his oldest daughter—ground out a mixture of drolling and of topical commentary in *Following the Equator*, based on his lecturing tour "around the world" to pay the debts from the collapse of his investments.

Biographers quarrel over Twain's final years: over whether he stayed reasonably constructive or drifted into near-alcoholism; whether his late fables, especially "The Mysterious Stranger" manu-scripts, achieved coherence or doodled inconclusively; whether his outbursts of anti-imperialist satire made up for hobnobbing with financiers; whether he worked out a détente with Christianity or sank into nihilism at Stormfield, his last residence. Though choosing to die in Connecticut, he often rhap-sodized after 1900 about southern landscapes, sounds, and foods.

WORKS: *The Celebrated Jumping Frog of Calaveras County and Other Sketches* (1867). *The Innocents Abroad; or, The New Pilgrims' Progress* (1869). *Mark Twain's (Burlesque) Autobiography and First Romance* (1871). *Roughing It* (1872). *The Gilded Age: A Tale of To-Day* (1873). *Sketches, New and Old* (1875). *The Adventures of Tom Sawyer* (1876). *A Tramp Abroad* (1880). *The Prince and the Pauper: A Tale for Young People of All Ages* (1882). *The Stolen White Elephant Etc.* (1882). *Life on the Mississippi* (1883). *Adventures of Huckleberry Finn* (1885). *A Connecticut Yankee in King Arthur's Court* (1889). *Merry Tales* (1892). *The American Claimant* (1892). *The £1,000,000 Bank-Note and Other Stories* (1893). *Tom Sawyer Abroad* (1894). *The Tragedy of Pudd'nhead Wilson* (1894). *Personal Recollections of Joan of Arc* (1896). *Tom Sawyer Abroad; Tom Sawyer, Detective; and Other Stories* (1896). *Following the Equator* (1897). *How to Tell a Story and Other Essays* (1897). *A Double-Barrelled Detective Story* (1902). *Extracts from Adam's Diary* (1904). *A Dog's Tale* (1904). *King Leopold's Soliloquy* (1905). *What Is Man?* (1906). *Eve's Diary* (1906). *The $30,000 Bequest and Other Stories* (1906). *Christian Science* (1907). *A Horse's Tale* (1907). *Is Shakespeare Dead?* (1909). *Extract from Captain Stormfield's Visit to Heaven* (1909). *Mark Twain's Speeches* (1910, 1923). *The Mysterious Stranger: A Romance* (1916). *Mark Twain's Autobiography* (1924). *Letters from the Earth* (1938, 1962).

—LOUIS J. BUDD

ANNE TYLER (1941–). Over the course of her career, Anne Tyler has demonstrated an unerring eye for the surfaces of the American environment and an unerring ear for the rhythms of American speech. Her novels and stories have won the devotion of readers as well as public recognition and critical acclaim. With the 1989 accolade of the Pulitzer Prize, Tyler's status as an important American writer was assured.

Tyler's life and art have been shaped by a Quaker heritage and a North Carolina childhood. Born in Minneapolis on October 25, 1941, Tyler is the only daughter among the four children of Phyllis Mahon and Lloyd Parry Tyler. The Tylers moved from one "commune-like arrangement" to another seeking to live by some "Emersonian ideal," until, when Anne was six, they settled in a Quaker com-munity in Celo, N.C. Five years later the family moved to Raleigh, where Tyler attended Broughton High School and came under the influence of a gifted teacher. She entered Duke University in 1958, already determined to become a writer. Tyler distinguished herself at Duke, publishing stories in the literary magazine and an anthology of student writing, winning awards for creative writing, and being inducted into Phi Beta Kappa. After her 1961 graduation from Duke, she attended Columbia Univer-sity, where she completed the course work for an M.A. in Russian.

Tyler returned to North Carolina in 1962 and worked at the Duke University library. The following May, she married Taghi Mohammad Modarressi, a young doctor from Iran, and in July the Modar-ressis left for Canada. Tyler continued to write even after accepting a job at the McGill University law library, and soon published three stories and *If Morning Ever Comes. The Tin Can Tree* came out in 1965, the same year that the Modarressis' daughter Tezh was born. Shortly after they moved to Baltimore in 1967, their second daughter, Mitra, was born. Writing mainly at night, Tyler continued to publish short stories and, in 1970, *A Slipping-Down Life.*

Tyler's short fiction has appeared in numerous periodicals and several anthologies, including the *O. Henry Awards Prize Stories* (1969, 1972), the 1976 *Pushcart Prize* collection, and *The Best American Short Stories, 1977.* With Shannon Ravenel, Tyler edited *The Best American Short Stories, 1983* and *Best of the South: From Ten Years of New Stories from the South* (1996). Additionally, from the 1970s to the early 1990s, Tyler regularly reviewed books, at first for the *National Observer* and later for a variety of publications, notably the *New York Times Book Review* and the *New Republic.*

The action of Tyler's fourth novel, *The Clock Winder,* moves from North Carolina to Baltimore, illustrating a thematic concern with the journey of life and marking a transition to the Maryland settings of her subsequent fiction. *Celestial Navigation* and *Searching for Caleb* demonstrated Tyler's increasing power as a novelist, and she soon won the respect of critics. In 1977, the year *Earthly Possessions* was issued, the American Academy and Institute of Arts and Letters honored her with an Award for Literature. *Morgan's Passing* won a Janet Heidinger Kafka Prize and nomination for an American Book Award. *Dinner at the Homesick Restaurant* won a PEN/Faulkner Award for Fiction and more nominations, including one for a Pulitzer. *The Accidental Tourist* garnered the National Book Critics Circle Award as the year's most distinguished work of American fiction and was the basis for a well-received film. *Breathing Lessons,* nominated for a National Book Award, earned Tyler a Pulitzer Prize.

In 1997 Anne Tyler's husband of thirty-four years died; *A Patchwork Planet* is dedicated to his memory. This book's protagonist is a relatively young man, but he is one well acquainted with loss. Although Tyler's sanely comedic worldview still underlies the works of the 1990s, *Saint Maybe* conveys a deepening spiritual concern, and the threat of mortality overshadows *Ladder of Years. Back When We Were Grownups* recounts a widow's explorations of the road not taken. January 2004 marked the widely anticipated release of Tyler's sixteenth published novel, *The Amateur Marriage,* a work, like its predecessors, expressive of the compassion inherent in the truth that she tells about American life.

WORKS: *If Morning Ever Comes* (1964). *The Tin Can Tree* (1965). *A Slipping-Down Life* (1970). *The Clock Winder* (1972). *Celestial Navigation* (1974). *Searching for Caleb* (1975). *Earthly Possessions* (1977). *Morgan's Passing* (1980). *Dinner at the Homesick Restaurant* (1982); Ed., *The Best American Short Stories, 1983,* with Shannon Ravenel (1983). *The Accidental Tourist* (1985). *Breathing Lessons* (1988). *Saint Maybe* (1991). *Tumble Tower* (1993). *Ladder of Years* (1996). Ed., *Best of the South: From Ten Years of New Stories from the South,* with Ravenel (1996). *A Patchwork Planet* (1998). *Back When We Were Grownups* (2001). *The Amateur Marriage* (2004).

—ANNE R. ZAHLAN

ALFRED UHRY (1936–). It is often said that a writer should write about that with which he is most familiar; playwright Alfred Uhry exemplifies this maxim. Born into a middle-class, German-Jewish family in Atlanta, Uhry is best known for plays that address race and cultural relations in the twentieth-century South.

Uhry attended Brown University, where he studied English and worked on student musical-theater productions. After graduation in 1958, he went to New York. While working in advertising, he met and was tutored informally by Frank Loesser, a well-known composer and lyricist for many Broadway musicals. In his Broadway debut, Uhry wrote lyrics for *Here's Where I Belong* (1968), a musicalization of John Steinbeck's *East of Eden* (1952), which closed after one performance. Uhry then taught

Shakespeare at the Calhoun School in New York and worked at the Goodspeed Opera House in East Haddam, Conn., where he adapted books into musicals. His breakthrough Broadway production *The Robber Bridegroom* (1975) played at the Harkness Theatre in October 1975 and for a longer run at the Biltmore Theatre starting in October 1976. Based on Eudora Welty's novel of the same title (1942), *The Robber Bridegroom* was nominated for a Tony Award for best musical in 1976. Uhry later wrote the film scripts for *Mystic Pizza* (1988), *Rich in Love* (1993), and *Paradise Road* (1997).

Uhry's first play, *Driving Miss Daisy*, won a Pulitzer Prize for drama in 1988 and ran for an amazing 1,300 performances at the John Houseman Theatre in New York. The film, for which Uhry wrote the script, won Oscars for best picture, best screenplay based on material from another medium, best Actress (Jessica Tandy), and makeup in 1989. Set in Atlanta, *Driving Miss Daisy* spans several decades and focuses on the relationship between an aging Jewish woman and her African American chauffeur. The second play in what would be known as Uhry's "Atlanta Trilogy," *The Last Night at Ballyhoo*, opened during the 1996 Olympic games in Atlanta; in 1997 it moved to New York, where it received a Tony Award for best play. This comedy addresses societal pretension and cultural difference in Atlanta's Jewish community in 1939. *Parade*, the most somber of these three works, dramatizes the true story of Leo Frank, a Jewish supervisor at an Atlanta pencil factory who was wrongly convicted of raping and murdering a thirteen-year-old girl. When the governor of Georgia commuted Frank's death sentence, which was based on questionable testimony and anti-Semitic sentiment, an angry mob pulled Frank from his jail cell and hanged him from a tree. *Parade* opened at Lincoln Center in December 1998 and received nine Tony nominations the next year, winning for best book of a musical and best score. Uhry's most recent play, *Edgardo Mine*, is set in Bologna in 1858 and dramatizes the story of a Jewish boy taken from his family by the papal guard and put in the care of the Catholic Church.

Uhry holds the distinction of being the only person to receive an Oscar, Tony, and Pulitzer.

WORKS: *Here's Where I Belong* (1968). *The Robber Bridegroom* (1975). *Little Johnny Jones* (1982), *Driving Miss Daisy* (1987). *The Last Night at Ballyhoo* (1996). *Parade* (1998). *The Other Line* (2002). *Edgardo Mine* (2002).

—MATTHEW SPANGLER

ABRAHAM VERGHESE (1955–). Abraham Verghese, M.D., was born on May 30, 1955, in Addis Ababa, Ethiopia. His father, George Verghese, and mother, Miriam (Abraham), were Syrian Christians from the southern Indian state of Kerala. In the 1950s both joined an emigration of several hundred Indian teachers to Ethiopia, part of Emperor Haile Selassie's modernization program. Verghese's birth into the Indian African Diaspora, his minority religion, dark skin, and later home in the rural American South would combine to shape his perspective of the perennial outsider.

Verghese first thought of becoming a journalist. Yielding to a parental push and to the romantic pull of Somerset Maugham's *Of Human Bondage*, he entered medical school. When civil unrest led to the medical school's closing, Verghese left Ethiopia, landing in Newark, N.J., where he briefly worked in a nursing home before continuing his medical education in India. He graduated from the University of Madras in 1979. Verghese soon learned that, for many foreign medical graduates, entry into American medicine is possible only via hospitals in inner-city or rural areas. Verghese did his internal medicine residency at East Tennessee State University in Johnson City, followed by a fellowship in infectious disease at Boston University.

His return to Johnson City as faculty member in 1985 coincided with the surge of AIDS in the United States, including the rural South. By 1989 Verghese was caring for more than eighty HIV-positive patients, mostly gay men who had returned home, ill, from the cities. Serving as primary-care doctor for many of them, he learned of their families, friendships, and secrets. A habitual notebook jotter since childhood, Verghese kept a daily journal in which he chronicled his patients' illnesses and tragic deaths and his own responses. In 1990–91 he attended the Iowa Writers' Workshop; there, under the tutelage of John Irving, he began shaping his journal entries into a memoir.

He completed his second memoir during his years in El Paso, where he headed the division of infectious disease at the Texas Tech medical campus. Using tennis as a motif, the book examines male friendship, drug addiction, and suicide among physicians, and Verghese's own failing marriage. Verghese and Rajani Chacko were divorced in 1996; they have two children, Steven and Jacob. He and his second wife, Sylvia Parra, have a child, Tristan, who was born in 1998. In 2002 Verghese moved to the University of Texas Health Sciences Center, San Antonio, where he is director of the Center for Medical Humanities and Ethics.

Verghese says that he is reluctant to plow his own life for yet another memoir. A novel now in progress will deal with a vocation (doctoring) and three places (India, Africa, and the southern part of North America) that he knows well.

WORKS: *My Own Country: A Doctor's Story of a Town and Its People in the Age of AIDS* (1994). *The Tennis Partner: A Doctor's Story of Friendship and Loss* (1998).

—DONALD L. MADISON

PAULA VOGEL (1951–). Born in Washington, D.C., on November 16, 1951, Paula Vogel grew up in the nation's capital and suburban Maryland, where she was exposed to plays at an early age. Her parents divorced when Vogel was quite young, and it was only in later years, when her beloved brother Carl was dying of AIDS, that she grew to know her father. As a sophomore in high school, her interest in theater was sparked by a drama class and by encouragement from her instructor. She worked as stage manager for school productions, and while she herself didn't perform, she did coach other students in acting.

After failing to win a scholarship to Bryn Mawr College, Vogel enrolled in Catholic University in Washington, D.C., from which she graduated in 1974 with a B.A. in theater. Her application to Yale Drama School was denied, and her early plays were rejected by the prestigious Eugene O'Neill National Playwrights Conference. Undaunted, Vogel attended Cornell University and subsequently taught there from 1977 until 1982. Two years later, she took a position at Brown University, where she also served as head of the M.F.A. playwriting program until 1998. She focused on her own writing and, with other writers, experimented with such devices as composing a work in forty-eight hours. Vogel employed these exercises in her teaching and also used them in composing her Pulitzer Prize–winning play *How I Learned to Drive*.

The Baltimore Waltz, a personal catharsis as well as an homage to her brother, brought Vogel national attention, winning the 1992 Obie Award for Best Play. But it was her 1998 play *How I Learned to Drive* that vaulted her to international acclaim; in addition to the Pulitzer, it earned an Obie and the Drama Desk, Outer Critics Circle, Lortel, and New York Drama Critics awards for best play. Inspired by Vladimir Nabokov's novel *Lolita*, *How I Learned to Drive* tackles the sensitive if not taboo subject of pedophilia from the female's point of view. Such pluck is hardly unusual in Vogel's work, which delves into topics ranging from domestic violence and pornography to prostitution and gender issues. Her plays are known for their astute mixture of comedy and tragedy, often incorporating scatological language and humor. Particular themes include gay and lesbian relationships as well as the contradictory representations of women in American culture.

Vogel has cited as her key influences three playwrights: American John Guare, Cuban American Maria Irene Fornes, and Briton Caryl Churchill. Her current projects include a stage adaptation of John Barth's novel *The Sot-Weed Factor,* a screenplay version of *The Oldest Profession,* and some musical theater. Vogel's honors include a Guggenheim Fellowship, a three-year playwriting residency at Arena Stage (which also commissioned two new plays), induction into the American Academy of Arts and Letters in 2004, the Rhode Island Pell Award in the Arts, the Hull-Warriner Award, The Laura Pels Award, the Pew Charitable Trust Senior Award, AT&T New Plays Award, the Fund for New American Plays, the Rockefeller Foundation's Bellagio Center Fellowship, several National Endowment for the Arts Fellowships, the McKnight Fellowship, the Bunting Fellowship, and the Governor's Award for the Arts.

WORKS: *Lady of the Maggots* (1970). *The Beautiful Quasimodo* (1971). *In Her Own Image* (1972). *The Swan Song of Sir Henry* (1974). *Meg* (1977). *The Last Pat Epstein Show before the Reruns* (1979). *Apple-Brown Betty* (1979). *Desdemona: A Play about a Handkerchief* (1979). *The Lady in Black* (1980). *Bertha in Blue* (1981). *The Oldest Profession* (1981). *And Baby Makes Seven* (1984). *The Baltimore Waltz* (1992). *Hot 'n' Throbbing* (1994). *The Baltimore Waltz and Other Plays* (1996). *How I Learned to Drive* (1997; sound recording, 1998; screenplay, 2000). *The Mammary Plays* (1998). *The Mineola Twins: A Comedy in Six Scenes, Four Dreams and (at Least) Six Wigs* (1999). *Common Ground* (screenplay, 2000). *Splits* (teleplay, 2001). *Long Christmas Ride Home* (2004).

—KAREN C. BLANSFIELD

ELLEN BRYANT VOIGT (1943–). Ellen Bryant was born in Danville, Va., to a Southern Baptist family. She grew up on a farm in the southern-central region of the state with a large extended family nearby. As a child, she studied piano and played at church, school, and other venues. At Converse College in South Carolina, where she met and married Francis George Wilhelm Voigt, she initially studied music and then developed an interest in literature, began to write poetry, and studied in the tradition of New Criticism. She received a B.A. in 1964. She continued her studies in music at the University of Iowa and, as a member of the Writers' Workshop, she studied poetry under the tutelage of Donald Justice. She received an M.F.A. in 1966.

Voigt has taught at Iowa Wesleyan College (1966–69), Goddard College (1970–78), Massachusetts Institute of Technology (1979–82), and Warren Wilson College in North Carolina (1981–present). In 1976, at Goddard, she developed, and then directed, the nation's first low-residency writing program, which became the model for low-residency programs at other institutions. In 1981 she assisted in moving Goddard's program to Warren Wilson College, where she has directed the M.F.A. program. She has also taught at the Aspen, Bread Loaf, Catskills, and Indiana Writers' conferences, among others.

Among the grants and awards she has received are a National Endowment for the Arts grant (1976–77), a Guggenheim Foundation grant (1978–79), the Pushcart Prize (1983 and 1991), the Hanes Prize for Poetry from the Fellowship of Southern Writers (1993, for *Two Trees*), nominations for a National Book Critics Circle Award (1995, for *Kyrie*) and a National Book Award (2002, for *Shadow of Heaven*), and an Academy of American Poets Fellowship (2001). She was inducted into the Fellowship of Southern Writers in 2002. She lives in Marshfield, Vt., and has served as the Vermont state poet (1999–2003).

WORKS: *Claiming Kin* (1976). *The Forces of Plenty* (1983). *The Lotus Flowers* (1987). *Two Trees* (1992). *Kyrie* (1995). Ed., *Poets Teaching Poets: Self and the World,* with Gregory Orr (1996). *The Flexible Lyric* (2001). Ed., *Hammer and Blaze: A Gathering of Contemporary American Poets,* with Heather McHugh (2002). *Shadows of Heaven* (2002).

—JEFF MOCK

JOHN DONALD WADE (1892–1963). Born in Marshallville, Ga., John Donald Wade graduated from the University of Georgia in 1914. One year later, he received an M.A. in English literature from Harvard University. Receiving his doctorate from Columbia University, he began his literary career with the publication of his dissertation, *Augustus Baldwin Longstreet: A Study of the Development of Culture in the South.* The biography met some critical acclaim and established Wade as one of the principal authorities on southern thought.

Wade taught English literature at the University of Georgia from 1919 to 1926. In 1926 he received one of the early Guggenheim Fellowships to research a biography on John Wesley, the father of the Methodist Church. Before returning to Athens, however, a disagreement with the administration over the role of intercollegiate athletics in university policy led to Wade's premature resignation. In 1927–28 he lived in Washington, D.C., editing the *Dictionary of American Biography.* After this brief absence from the academy, Wade became the head of the graduate program at Vanderbilt University in Nashville, Tenn. He quickly became associated with the southern Agrarians, an intellectual group devoted to the preservation of southern culture; his essay "The Life and Death of Cousin Lucius" appeared in the group's publication *I'll Take My Stand* (1930).

Dedicated to the ideas of community espoused in *I'll Take My Stand,* Wade returned to Athens, Ga., to teach literature until he retired in 1944. In 1947 he founded the *Georgia Review,* which he edited until 1950. After years in the academy, Wade returned to Marshallville, Ga., where he worked in his garden and arboretum with his wife Julia Floyd Stovall. Three years after her death in 1959, he married Florence Lester. Just four years later, Wade died in Marshallville, in 1963.

WORKS: *Augustus Baldwin Longstreet: A Study of the Development of Culture in the South* (1924). *John Wesley* (1930). "The Life and Death of Cousin Lucius," in *I'll Take My Stand: The South and the Agrarian Tradition,* by Twelve Southerners (1930). *Selected Essays and Other Writings* (1966). *Agrarian Letters: The Correspondence of John Donald Wade and Donald Davidson, 1930–1939,* ed. Gerald J. Smith (2003).

—HARRIS W. HENDERSON

ALICE WALKER (1944–). Alice Malsenior Walker was born on February 9, 1944, in Eatonton, Ga., the eighth and last child of sharecroppers Willie Lee and Minnie Tallulah Grant Walker. Walker attended a segregated school in rural Georgia that had once been the state prison. She was valedictorian of her class and awarded a rehabilitation scholarship based on a childhood injury. In 1961 Walker entered Spelman College in Atlanta. She transferred to Sarah Lawrence College in New York two years later, and she spent a summer in Africa. When she became pregnant and contemplated suicide, her struggle led to many poems that later appeared in *Once.* Walker would thereafter be identified with concerns of women as well as with the problems of black people. She received her degree from Sarah Lawrence in 1965.

After graduation Walker worked for the welfare department in New York. She left that job for voter registration projects in Georgia, then in 1967 for Mississippi and civil rights programs. In Mississippi she met and married Melvyn Rosenman Leventhal, a Jewish civil rights attorney. Their daughter, Rebecca, was born in 1969. The first legal interracial couple in Mississippi, Walker and her husband later divorced but maintained a cordial relationship.

Walker's first novel, *The Third Life of Grange Copeland,* studied the impact of sharecropping on black men and women. *In Love and Trouble: Stories of Black Women* followed in 1974. She moved to a rural area outside of San Francisco to write *The Color Purple,* which won the American Book Award and the Pulitzer Prize in 1983. Walker was the first African American woman to receive the Pulitzer. The

novel stayed on the *New York Times* best-seller list for over twenty-five weeks, and the subsequent film, directed by Stephen Spielberg, made her a celebrity. The novel and the story collection are the works that account for her commanding presence in college literature courses.

Active in Head Start programs, Walker has been a forceful presence in the academy. She was hugely influential in recovering Zora Neale Hurston from obscurity and into prominence, and she has promoted interest in other African American writers, notably Jean Toomer, Langston Hughes, and Ida B. Wells. She has been writer-in-residence or visiting professor at Jackson State College, Tougaloo College, Wellesley College, the University of Massachusetts at Boston, Yale University, Brandeis University, and the University of California at Berkeley. Walker is a winning force on the platform and especially inspires the rising generation of black women.

Walker is particularly noted for promoting African American women's experiences and perspectives, most notably in her womanist essay collection *In Search of Our Mothers' Gardens*. She also writes about the need for creative outlets, discovering personal potential, sources for spiritual growth, the need and desire for family and community, and survival through affirmation and change. For Walker, art has a moral purpose in our complex world. Her fervor is captured in the title of her 2004 book *Now Is the Time to Open Your Heart*.

WORKS: *Once: Poems* (1968). *The Third Life of Grange Copeland* (1970). *Five Poems* (1972). *In Love and Trouble: Stories of Black Women* (1973). *Langston Hughes, American Poet*, illustrations by Don Miller (1973). *Revolutionary Petunias and Other Poems* (1973). *Meridian* (1976). *Good Night Willie Lee, I'll See You in the Morning* (1979). *I Love Myself When I Am Laughing . . . and Then Again When I Am Looking Mean and Impressive: A Zora Neale Hurston Reader* (1979). *You Can't Keep a Good Woman Down* (1981). *The Color Purple* (1983). *In Search of Our Mothers' Gardens: Womanist Prose* (1983). *Horses Make a Landscape Look More Beautiful: Poems* (1984). *Living by the Word: Selected Writings, 1973–1987* (1988). *To Hell with Dying* (1988). *The Temple of My Familiar* (1989). *Finding the Green Stone* (1991). *Her Blue Body Everything We Know: Earthling Poems, 1965–1990 Complete* (1991). *Possessing the Secret of Joy* (1992). *Warrior Marks: Female Genital Mutilation and the Sexual Blinding of Women* (1993). *Everyday Use* (1994). *Alice Walker: Banned* (1996). *The Same River Twice: Honoring the Difficult: A Meditation on Life, Spirit, Art, and the Making of the Film "The Color Purple" Ten Years Later* (1996). *Anything We Love Can Be Saved: A Writer's Activism* (1997). *By the Light of My Father's Smile: A Novel* (1998). *The Way Forward Is with a Broken Heart* (2000). *Sent by Earth: A Message from the Grandmother Spirit after the Bombing of the World Trade Center and the Pentagon* (2002). *Absolute Trust in the Goodness of the Earth: New Poems* (2003). *A Poem Traveled Down My Arm: Poems and Drawings* (2003). *Now Is the Time to Open Your Heart* (2004).

—LAURA J. BLOXHAM

MARGARET WALKER (1915–1998). Margaret Abigail Walker—poet, scholar, novelist, essayist, educator—was born on July 7, 1915, in Birmingham, Ala., to Sigismond Walker, a Methodist minister, and Marion Dozier Walker, a music teacher—a solid-education, middle-class background that Margaret would utilize. The family moved to New Orleans, La., in 1925. Educated at Gilbert Academy, she took her first two years of college at Dillard before transferring to Northwestern University. She received her B.A. in English from Northwestern University in 1935, and worked with the Federal Writers' Project in Chicago during 1936–39. In Chicago she met many writers; the most significant of them was Richard Wright—her "demonic genius." Walker would eventually write about him and their relationship.

In 1942 Walker published her inaugural volume of poetry, *For My People*, which won the Yale Younger Poets Award. She earned an M.A. in creative writing from the University of Iowa in 1940 and a Ph.D. in 1965. Walker published a revised version of her doctoral dissertation, *Jubilee*, in 1966. The novel captured the as-told-to memories of her maternal grandmother, Elvira Ware Dozier.

In 1943 Walker married Firnist Alexander, an interior designer. The couple moved to Jackson, Miss., and Walker began an eventful teaching career at Jackson State College. The Alexanders raised four children. In 1968 Walker founded the Institute for the Study of History, Life, and Culture of Black People (now the Margaret Walker Alexander National Research Center) at Jackson State. She directed the center until her retirement in 1979. Remaining active as professor emerita, she lectured and toured until her death in the fall of 1998. Counted as a pivotal artist in the transitional generation of African American writers that emerged in the 1930s and 1940s, she was deeply mourned.

WORKS: *For My People* (1942). *Jubilee* (1966). *Prophets for a New Day* (1970). *October Journey* (1973). *A Poetic Occasion*, with Nikki Giovanni (1974). *For Farish Street Green* (1986). *The Daemonic Genius of Richard Wright: A Portrait of the Man, a Critical Look at His Works* (1988). *This Is My Century: New and Collected Poems* (1989). *How I Wrote "Jubilee" and Other Essays on Life and Literature*, ed. Maryemma Graham (1990). *On Being Female, Black, and Free: Essays by Margaret Walker, 1932–1992* (1997).

—TOMEIKO R. ASHFORD

EUGENE WALTER (1921–1998). Eugene Ferdinand Walter was born in Mobile, Ala., and except for a brief stint in the Civilian Conservation Corps in Mississippi, spent the first nineteen years of his life there. During World War II he served for three years as a cryptographer in the Aleutian Islands. After the war he moved to New York, where he worked in the foreign exchange department of the New York Public Library, and became involved with Equity Library Theater and Off-Broadway productions. In 1951 he moved to Paris, where he became an unofficial assistant for the Princess Marguerite Caetani's multilingual literary journal *Botteghe Oscure* and a founding contributor to the *Paris Review* when his short story "Troubadour" was selected for the magazine's first issue. Later Walter moved to Rome to become Princess Caetani's official assistant at her magazine's headquarters. In Rome he met the Italian film director Federico Fellini, and was cast in Fellini's masterpiece *8 1/2*. Walter subsequently became an actor and translator for other famous Italian directors. In 1979 he left Rome to return to Mobile, where he remained until his death in 1998.

As a writer, Eugene Walter is best known for his Lippincott Prize–winning novel *The Untidy Pilgrim* and for the best-selling *American Cooking: Southern Style,* compiled for the Time-Life Foods of the World series. Both works draw heavily on Walter's Mobile upbringing, which was the source of inspiration for most of his best writing. A prize-winning collection of verse, *Monkey Poems,* is less well known because it was not widely published, but deserves to be listed among Walter's most important works.

Walter was involved in many other artistic endeavors and was also renowned as a bon vivant who hosted memorable parties for celebrities and other luminaries. Arguably, his greatest work of art was the life he lived.

WORKS: *Jennie, the Watercress Girl: A Fable for Mobilians and a Few Choice Others* (1946). *Monkey Poems* (1953). *The Untidy Pilgrim* (1954). *Shapes of the River* (1955). *Singerie-Songerie: A Version of Hamlet for Monkeys* (1958). *Love You Good; See You Later* (1964). *Fellini's Satyricon* (1970). *American Cooking: Southern Style* (1971). *The Pokeweed Alphabet; or, A Child's Garden of Vices* (1981). *Delectable Dishes from Termite Hall* (1982). *The Likes of Which* (1985). *The Pack Rat* (1987). *Hints and Pinches* (1991). *Lizard Fever* (1994). *Milking the Moon: A Southerner's Story of Life on This Planet* (2001).

—KATHERINE CLARK

THEODORE WARD (1902–1983). One of the first important African American playwrights of the twentieth century, Theodore Ward was born on September 15, 1902, in Thibodaux, La., one of eleven

children. His mother was a schoolteacher and his father an itinerant peddler whose strong religious views drove him to burn an early play by his son, condemning it as a "work of the devil." In his early teens, soon after his mother's death, Ward left home, working various jobs while continuing his self-education. In 1931 he won a Zona Gale Scholarship in creative writing to the University of Wisconsin at Madison. In 1935 he moved to Chicago, where he became involved with the WPA's Chicago Writers Workshop and the John Reed Club. In 1937 he won second prize in a playwriting contest with *Sick and Tiahd.*

By 1940 Ward had moved to New York, where he helped found the Negro Playwrights Company, designed to provide a venue for African American artists. Its first and only production was Ward's *Big White Fog,* a highly charged play dealing with racism, capitalism, socialist communism, and the Garvey movement. The play had already been staged by the Federal Theatre Project in Chicago despite strong political opposition and potential riots. In 1947, with the assistance of a Theatre Guild Award, Ward completed *Our Lan,*' which some consider his finest work. Exploring the plight of dispossessed slaves in the Reconstruction South, *Our Lan*' had a brief Broadway run, with subsequent revivals in 1967 and 1978.

Ward wrote over thirty plays—most of them dealing with social and political issues—including *Shout Hallelujah!* about construction workers dying of silicosis; *The Daubers,* addressing teenage drug addiction; and *Candle in the Wind,* set in Reconstruction-era Mississippi. He also wrote essays, poetry, and folk operas, but envisioned as his major accomplishment a play about John Brown; though it received only one public production (1950), Ward continued to develop and refine the play for two decades.

Winner of a National Theater Conference Award and a Rockefeller Foundation grant, Ward was also the first African American dramatist to receive a Guggenheim Fellowship. He returned to Chicago in 1964, where he helped found the Louis Theatre and School of Drama, serving as its general manager and artistic director. He died on May 8, 1983.

WORKS: *Big White Fog* (excerpt) in *The Negro Caravan,* ed. Sterling A. Brown et al. (1941). *John Brown* (excerpt) in *Masses and Mainstream* (Oct. 1949). "Analysis of a Play: *Our Lan,*'" in *A Theatre in Your Head,* ed. Kenneth Rowe (1960). *Anthology of the Afro-American in the Theatre: A Critical Approach,* ed. Lindsay Patterson (1968). *The Daubers* (excerpt) in *Black Scenes,* ed. Alice Childress (1971). *Big White Fog* (excerpt) in *Black Theater U.S.A.,* ed. James V. Hatch (1974).

—KAREN C. BLANSFIELD

KITTRELL J. WARREN (1829–1889). One of the last of the humorists of the Old Southwest, Kittrell Warren, the son of a frontier Baptist minister, was born on October 6, 1829, in Clarke Country, Ala. He spent his youth in Houston County, Ga., leaving there in 1837 or 1838 to study and practice law with his older brother in Lee County.

In July 1861 he joined Company B of the Eleventh Georgia Volunteers, with whom he served for the next two years. His Civil War experiences were the basis for two pamphlets. The first, *Ups and Downs of Wife Hunting,* comically treats the subject of courtship. In 1863 he published *History of the Eleventh Georgia Vols,* a eulogistic and commemorative account of his experience with Company B. Warren's final book and his most significant contribution to southern frontier humor, *Life and Public Services of an Army Straggler,* a picaresque narrative, chronicles the misadventures of a Confederate deserter and con artist.

After his military service, Warren was elected to the Georgia Legislature in 1863 as a representative from Lee County, a position he held until 1865. He continued to practice law and served in vari-

ous other posts in Georgia, including solicitor general in 1866, and judge of the county court of Lee County from 1877 to 1884. In the 1880s Warren renewed his interests in writing, holding editorial positions on various newspapers and magazines, including the *Leesburg Telephone,* the *Sumter Republican,* and the *Chattanooga Evening Dispatch.* In 1884 Warren moved to Atlanta and served a short stint as associate editor of the *Sunny South,* a weekly newspaper magazine to which he contributed a column titled "Kit Warren's Musings." In 1886 he became editor of the *Macon Evening News,* but he left after one year to become the managing editor of the *Atlanta Evening Capitol.* His health failing for some time, Warren died on December 28, 1889.

WORKS: *Ups and Downs of Wife Hunting; or, Merry Jokes for Camp Perusal* (1861). *History of the Eleventh Georgia Vols., Embracing the Muster Rolls, Together with a Special and Succinct account of the Marches, Engagements, Casualties, Etc.* (1863). *Life and Public Services of an Army Straggler* (1865).

—ED PIACENTINO

ROBERT PENN WARREN (1905–1989). The oldest of three children, Robert Penn Warren was born on April 24, 1905, in Guthrie, Ky., to Ruth Penn and Robert Franklin Warren, a small-town banker and store owner. Somewhat of a child prodigy, Warren finished high school at fifteen and won an appointment to the United States Naval Academy. While waiting to turn sixteen, the earliest age when he could actually enroll at Annapolis, he suffered a severe eye injury that disqualified him from the Naval Academy, so in the fall of 1921 he entered Vanderbilt University intending to become a chemical engineer. A freshman English class with the poet John Crowe Ransom changed his mind and his major, and soon he was hobnobbing with members of the literary group—notably including Ransom and Allen Tate—who called themselves the Fugitives, in flight from the industrial-commercial culture of the modern South. After graduating summa cum laude in 1925, he went to graduate school at the University of California at Berkeley (M.A., 1927), where he met Emma Brescia, whom he married in 1929. In 1927 he transferred to Yale, but a Rhodes Scholarship in 1928 led him to complete graduate work at Oxford (B.Litt., 1930).

After brief stints of teaching in Tennessee, including at Vanderbilt (1931–34), Warren in 1934 accepted a faculty appointment at Louisiana State University, where he and Cleanth Brooks founded one of the nation's most distinguished literary magazines, the *Southern Review.* Here he also launched his career as a novelist with *Night Rider* and *At Heaven's Gate,* while also publishing volumes of poetry in 1935 and 1942. With Cleanth Brooks he co-edited two textbooks that brought the New Criticism (featuring close textual analysis) into thousands of college classrooms—*An Approach to Literature* and *Understanding Poetry.*

In 1942, when Louisiana State University failed to give Warren a promotion, he accepted a professorship at the University of Minnesota, where he completed his Pulitzer Prize–winning novel *All the King's Men,* a collection of short stories, *The Circus in the Attic,* and a historical novel, *World Enough and Time.* In 1950 he accepted a professorship at Yale, where he taught literature until his retirement in 1975. Meanwhile, his personal life took a dramatic new turn with divorce from Emma Brescia Warren in 1951, marriage to the writer Eleanor Clark in 1952, and first-time fatherhood (of Rosanna in 1953 and Gabriel Penn Warren in 1955). This enhanced domestic life apparently initiated a new surge of creativity in the 1950s, with the hitherto famous novelist now earning most of his plaudits in poetry. An epic poem, *Brother to Dragons,* became the forerunner of a dozen volumes of lyric poetry, including two Pulitzer Prize winners, *Promises* (1957) and *Now and Then* (1978), and the widely admired *Audubon: A Vision.* Other honors for poetry included the Bollingen Prize in 1967 and, in 1986, appointment as the first official poet laureate of the United States.

During these later decades of his life, from the 1950s up to his death on September 15, 1989, Warren's creativity flowed unceasingly through volumes of prose as well as poetry. Two books about race relations, *Segregation* and *Who Speaks for the Negro?* are an important record of his response to the civil rights movement, while *Selected Essays, Democracy and Poetry,* and the landmark two-volume anthology *American Literature: The Makers and the Making*—co-edited with Cleanth Brooks and R. W. B. Lewis—mark the culmination of Warren's literary criticism. Meanwhile, he continued to publish novels: *Band of Angels, The Cave, Wilderness, Flood, Meet Me in the Green Glen,* and *A Place to Come To.*

Across his vast range of books, Warren's primary focus was the struggle for a satisfactory identity—"the American theme," according to Ralph Ellison. Upon the ramifications of this theme—the difficulty of self-knowledge, the problem of evil, the entanglements of history—Warren brought every mode of knowledge to bear, including philosophy, psychology, history, science, religion, and aesthetics. Warren also acknowledged the influence of other writers upon his oeuvre, ranging from Dante and Shakespeare to William James and T. S. Eliot.

His masterpiece, *All the King's Men,* has kept its place in the literary canon. Acclaimed by critics and widely taught in literature courses, it has seen production as a stage drama, a movie, and an opera and continues to elicit a steady stream of critical essays. In 2001, more than fifty years after the novel's publication, Noel Polk provided a new edition, restoring material from Warren's manuscript that was deleted or altered in the original publication. A new film version shot in 2005 has received national interest.

Given his wide range and the high excellence of his literary accomplishment, Warren was arguably the leading man of letters of his generation. In 1988 John Burt's edition of *The Collected Poems of Robert Penn Warren* provided a fitting monument to Warren's poetic genius and position in American letters. All signs are that Warren's work will continue to find popular and critical audiences.

WORKS: *John Brown: The Making of a Martyr* (1929). "The Briar Patch," in *I'll Take My Stand: The South and the Agrarian Tradition,* by Twelve Southerners (1930). *Thirty-Six Poems* (1935). *An Approach to Literature,* with Cleanth Brooks and John Thibaut Purser (1936). Ed., *Southern Harvest: Short Stories by Southern Writers* (1937). *Understanding Poetry: An Anthology for College Students,* with Brooks (1938). *Night Rider* (1939). *Eleven Poems on the Same Theme* (1942). *At Heaven's Gate* (1943). *Understanding Fiction,* with Brooks (1943). *Selected Poems: 1923–1943* (1944). *All the King's Men* (1946). *Blackberry Winter* (1946). *The Circus in the Attic and Other Stories* (1947). *Modern Rhetoric,* with Brooks (1949). *Fundamentals of Good Writing: A Handbook of Modern Rhetoric,* with Brooks (1950). *World Enough and Time: A Romantic Novel* (1950). Ed., *An Anthology of Stories from "The Southern Review,"* with Brooks (1953). Ed., *Short Story Masterpieces,* with Albert Erskine (1954). *Band of Angels* (1955). Ed., *Six Centuries of Great Poetry,* with Erskine (1955). *Segregation: The Inner Conflict in the South* (1956). *Brother to Dragons: A Tale in Verse and Voices* (1953; rev., 1979). *Promises: Poems 1954–1956* (1959). Ed., *A New Southern Harvest: An Anthology,* with Erskine (1957). *Remember the Alamo!* (1958). *Selected Essays* (1958). *The Gods of Mount Olympus* (1959). *How Texas Won Her Freedom: The Story of Sam Houston and the Battle of San Jacinto* (1959). *The Cave* (1959). *The Scope of Fiction,* with Brooks (1960). *All the King's Men: A Play* (1960). *You, Emperors, and Others: Poems 1957–1960* (1960). *Wilderness: A Tale of the Civil War* (1961). *The Legacy of the Civil War: Meditations on the Centennial* (1961). *Flood: A Romance of Our Time* (1964). *Who Speaks for the Negro?* (1965). *Selected Poems: New and Old, 1923–1966* (1966). *A Plea in Mitigation: Modern Poetry and the End of an Era* (1966). Ed., *Faulkner: A Collection of Critical Essays* (1966). Ed., *Randall Jarrell, 1914–1965,* with Robert Lowell and Peter Taylor (1967). *Incarnations: Poems 1966–1968* (1968). *Audubon: A Vision* (1969). *Meet Me in the Green Glen* (1971). *Homage to Theodore Dreiser, August 27, 1871–December 28, 1945, on the Centennial of His Birth* (1971). Ed., *Selected Poems of Herman Melville* (1971). Ed., *John Greenleaf Whittier's Poetry: An Appraisal and a Selection* (1971). *Or Else—Poem/Poems 1968–1974* (1974). *American Literature: The Makers and the Making,* with Brooks and R. W. B. Lewis (1974). *Democracy and Poetry* (1975). *Selected Poems: 1923–1976* (1977). *A Place to Come To* (1977). *Now and Then: Poems 1976–1978* (1978). *Being Here: Poetry 1977–1980* (1980). *Jefferson Davis Gets His Citizenship Back* (1980). *Rumor Verified: Poems 1979–1980* (1981). *Chief Joseph of the Nez Perce* (1983). *New and Selected Poems, 1923–1985* (1985). *A Robert Penn Warren Reader*, ed. Erskine (1987). *Portrait of a Father* (1988). *New and Selected Essays* (1989). *Cleanth Brooks and Robert Penn Warren: A Literary Correspondence*, ed. James A. Grimshaw, Jr. (1998). *Collected Poems of Robert Penn Warren*, ed. John Burt (1998). *Selected Letters of Robert Penn Warren*, vol. 1, *The Apprentice Years, 1924–1934* (2000), ed. William Bedford Clark. *All the King's Men*, restored ed., ed. Noel Polk (2001). *Selected Letters of Robert Penn Warren*, vol. 2, *The "Southern Review" Years, 1935–1942*, ed. Clark (2001). *Selected Poems of Robert Penn Warren*, ed. Burt (2001). *The Cass Mastern Material: The Core of Robert Penn Warren's "All the King's Men,"* ed. James A. Perkins (2005). *Selected Letters of Robert Penn Warren*, vol. 3, *Triumph and Transition, 1943–1952*, ed. Randy Hendricks and Perkins (2005).

—VICTOR H. STRANDBERG

BOOKER T. WASHINGTON (1856–1915). One of the most controversial and enigmatic African American leaders of the late nineteenth and early twentieth century, Booker Taliaferro Washington was thrust into the national spotlight in 1895. Delivering what came to be known as the Atlanta Compromise speech at the Cotton States and International Exposition, Washington defended his philosophy of economic gain over political and social rights with regard to African American progress. Key events in Washington's life prior to this September 18, 1895, address anticipated this moment.

Born near Roanoke, Va., in 1856, Washington spent nine years in slavery, after which time he and his family struggled to survive during the harsh Reconstruction era. After slavery, his family traveled to Malden, W.Va., where his stepfather found work in the salt mines. Soon a still-young Washington would find himself engaged in the same grueling work. Yearning for an education, Washington took every opportunity to steal a glance at a book or to seek assistance from the few learned people available to him. When a school was established nearby, Washington asked permission to attend, though work often prevented a steady education. A major turning point came when he secured employment with Mrs. Viola Ruffner, the northern-born wife of the local salt mines owner. A stern and exacting woman, she taught him the value of efficiency and thoroughness in all labor-intensive duties; she encouraged his attempts to gain an education. Washington's experience with Mrs. Ruffner taught him that he could work amicably with any white person, no matter his or her station in life.

At sixteen, Washington entered Hampton Institute, where he excelled. General Samuel Armstrong, the school's president, hired Washington to teach at Hampton, and recommended him to political leaders in Alabama interested in establishing a school for blacks in Tuskegee. Washington was confirmed in his earlier belief that the black man could, in fact, make his way in the white man's world.

In 1881 Washington traveled to Tuskegee, Ala., to create there an institution similar to Hampton. Understanding that he would need the support of both local blacks and whites, he worked tirelessly to foster positive relations with the white business community. Washington adjusted the curriculum to include home economics for the women and industrial science and agriculture for the men.

Washington worked tirelessly to ensure the success of Tuskegee Institute. He traveled extensively to the North, soliciting funds from the white elite. He was assisted by his wives: first Fannie Norton Smith Washington (with whom he had one daughter, Portia), then Olivia A. Davidson Washington (with whom he had two sons, Booker, Jr., and Ernest Davidson), and finally Margaret James Murray Washington.

Cast into national prominence, Washington spent the latter 1890s flexing his political muscle, while still advocating publicly for patience in the black community regarding political and social equality. When William McKinley was preparing his official cabinet, Washington consulted with the president-elect to urge appointing a black to a high-level federal position. And in the fall of 1901, Washington, in what became a highly controversial event, dined at the White House with President

Theodore Roosevelt and his family. Second to the 1895 speech, the 1901 dinner solidified Washington's influence intraracially and interracially.

The 1901 publication of *Up from Slavery* confirmed Washington as an important national figure. The hugely successful autobiography validated his life and work and served as an influential self-help guide for African Americans. From 1901 until his death in 1915, Washington worked not only in the interest of his beloved Tuskegee, but also in the interest of other black educational institutions and black business leagues. Though he was often criticized for accommodating white supremacist attitudes and structures, Washington shrewdly manipulated the social and political systems designed to impede his progress. His accomplishments clearly attest to both his wisdom and undeniable ability.

WORKS: *The Future of the American Negro* (1899). *The Story of My Life and Work* (1900). *Up from Slavery* (1901).

—CHARLES E. WILSON, JR.

HENRY WATTERSON (1840–1921). Henry Watterson was born with considerable cultural advantage, and he did not waste any of it in his long career in the public eye. Born on February 16, 1840, in Washington, D.C., Watterson was the son of Tabitha (Black) and Harvey Watterson, then serving as a Democrat from Tennessee in the U.S. House of Representatives. Watterson's family moved back and forth between Tennessee and Washington in the 1840s and 1850s, a pattern that made his early life remarkably eventful. As Watterson recalled in *"Marse Henry": An Autobiography,* he met virtually all the major political figures of his lifetime.

Watterson edited the school newspaper at a private academy in Philadelphia (1852–56), and from then on he was a journalist to the core. Before the Civil War, he had brief stints with the *Tribune* and the *Times* in New York City, then the *Daily States* in Washington, D.C., which got him an assignment to meet Abraham Lincoln and cover his inauguration. Once the war began, Watterson went back to Tennessee and served briefly in military campaigns, at one point under General Nathan Bedford Forrest, but brief editorship of the *Rebel* in Chattanooga pointed him again toward his life's work. In 1865, not long after he started a three-year editorship at the *Nashville Republican Banner*, Watterson married Rebecca Ewing of Chattanooga.

In 1868 Watterson headed to Louisville, soon settling into editorship of the *Courier-Journal* for the rest of his career. He promoted generally progressive views in his editorials, nudging the South to industrialize and supporting legal and civil rights for African Americans. Watterson exerted significant influence on the national political scene, especially in presidential elections, and the *Courier-Journal* won two Pulitzer Prizes for editorial writing. Watterson lectured widely and was known as a genial, knowledgeable spokesperson for southern life.

Watterson finished his editorship in 1919, aggressive and vigorous to the end in challenging President Wilson's League of Nations plan. Watterson's editorial style was bold but balanced. In *"Marse Henry,"* he offered kind words for both Abraham Lincoln and Jefferson Davis. Throughout their marriage, the Wattersons enjoyed travel, in America and abroad. Henry Watterson died on December 22, 1921, in Jacksonville, Fla., while traveling.

WORKS: *Oddities in Southern Life and Character* (1883). *The Compromises of Life* (1906). *History of the Manhattan Club* (1915). *"Marse Henry": An Autobiography,* 2 vols. (1919). *The Editorials of Henry Watterson,* ed. Arthur Krock (1923).

—OWEN W. GILMAN, JR.

RICHARD WEAVER (1910–1963). Richard Malcolm Weaver, a "gentleman of the old school," was a brilliant southern scholar and classical rhetorician who stood in the first rank of a conservative renaissance. He was also a latter-day Agrarian greatly influenced by his mentors John Crowe Ransom and Donald Davidson and one of the leading rhetorical theorists of the twentieth century.

Weaver was born in Asheville, N.C., on March 3, 1910, the son of Carrye Lee ("Carrie") Embrye and Richard Malcolm ("Dick") Weaver. He was reared mostly in Lexington, Ky. Apart from his father's death when he was five years old, Weaver's unremarkable middle-class upbringing was distinguished by his academic accomplishments. From the start he proved himself an exceptionally bright student. He breezed through the undergraduate requirements of the University of Kentucky and went on to graduate school at Vanderbilt, where Ransom directed his thesis, "The Revolt against Humanism."

Weaver had been involved in various leftist and liberal movements as a student, but in 1939 he experienced an epiphany that substantially shifted his worldview. He described in correspondence "a kind of religious conversion" to the "Church of Agrarianism." He accepted short-term teaching positions at a number of universities while completing his Louisiana State University dissertation, "The Confederate South, 1865–1910: A Study in the Survival of a Mind and a Culture," under Cleanth Brooks. That work, revised, became the basis for the posthumous *The Southern Tradition at Bay*, which identifies the South as "the last non-materialist civilization in the Western world," an argument that continues to provoke debate in academic circles.

In 1944 Weaver accepted a position teaching English at the University of Chicago, where he worked for the rest of his life. While he was famously Spartan and punctual in his daily habits, his intellectual life was anything but sterile. His first book, *Ideas Have Consequences* (a publisher's title that Weaver deemed "hopelessly banal" next to his chosen "The Adverse Descent"), set down a conservative manifesto that probed nothing less than "the dissolution of the West" through a penetrating exhumation of the history of ideas. Weaver next underscored the ethical dimensions of discourse, and its importance in the southern worldview, in *The Ethics of Rhetoric*. He published widely in the magazines of his day and contributed enthusiastically to *National Review* and *Modern Age*. His substantial enrichment of conservative scholarship has been posthumously recognized through the collection of his many essays and commentaries and in the growing readership of his work. Some of his observations—for example, on the importance of local culture—have flourished in the years following his sudden death by heart attack on April 3, 1963.

WORKS: *Ideas Have Consequences* (1948). *The Ethics of Rhetoric* (1953). *Composition: A Course in Reading and Writing* (1957). *Relativism and the Crisis of Our Time* (1961). *Visions of Order* (1964). *Academic Freedom: The Principle and the Problems* (1965). *Life without Prejudice and Other Essays* (1965). *The Southern Tradition at Bay: A History of Post-bellum Thought*, ed. George Core and M. E. Bradford (1968). *Language Is Sermonic: Richard M. Weaver on the Nature of Rhetoric*, ed. Richard L. Johannesen, Rennard Strickland, and Ralph T. Eubanks (1970). *The Southern Essays of Richard M. Weaver*, ed. George M. Curtis III and James J. Thompson, Jr. (1987). *In Defense of Tradition: Collected Shorter Writings of Richard M. Weaver, 1929–1963*, ed. Ted J. Smith III (2000).

—BRYAN GIEMZA

IDA B. WELLS (1862–1931). Ida Wells was a journalist, pamphleteer, and autobiographer whose work focused on social justice for African Americans, especially in opposition to lynching, disfranchisement, and segregation.

Born Ida Belle Wells in 1862 to slave parents in Holly Springs, Miss., she was the second of eight children. She was baptized in the Methodist Episcopal church and attended Rust College. After her parents and one sibling died in the yellow fever epidemic of 1878, Wells sought a living as a teacher. She moved to Memphis around 1882 and taught in the segregated public schools there for almost ten years. In Memphis, she contested racial segregation in the courts and in the press and developed a spirited defense of African American women like herself who suffered from negative stereotypes and abuse. In the 1880s, Wells briefly considered novel writing, but journalism better met her needs for income, timely social criticism, and political organizing.

In 1892, the year of a triple lynching in Memphis and the height of lynching in the U.S., white reaction to Wells's critique of racial murder turned violent. Escaping to the North, she continued to detail the realities of lynching in a series of lectures, newspaper articles, and pamphlets. The first of her pamphlets was an exposé entitled *Southern Horrors: Lynch Law in All Its Phases,* and it remains a signal intellectual intervention against sexualized racism in U.S. culture. Between 1892 and 1920, she documented lynchings and race riots in a series of eight pamphlets, most of which were self-published.

In 1895, Wells married Ferdinand L. Barnett, a Chicago attorney, and raised a family of four children in that city. Her autobiography, dictated a few years before her death, was edited by her daughter Alfreda M. Duster and published by John Hope Franklin at the University of Chicago Press in 1970.

WORKS: *Southern Horrors: Lynch Law in All Its Phases* (1892). *Why the Colored American Is Not at the World's Columbia Exposition: The Afro-American's Contribution to Columbian Literature* (1893). *United States Atrocities: Lynch Law* (1894). *A Red Record: Tabulated Statistics and Alleged Causes of Lynchings in the United States, 1893, 1894, 1895* (1895). *Lynch Law in Georgia* (1899). *Mob Rule in New Orleans: Robert Charles and His Fight to the Death* (1900). *The East St. Louis Massacre: The Greatest Outrage of the Century* (1917). *The Arkansas Race Riot* (1920). *Crusade for Justice: The Life of Ida B. Wells* (1970).

—PATRICIA A. SCHECHTER

REBECCA WELLS (ca. 1952–). Rebecca Wells has become one of Louisiana's best-known writers. Her novels *Little Altars Everywhere* and *Divine Secrets of the Ya-Ya Sisterhood* gained both popular notice and widespread critical acclaim. The movie version of *Divine Secrets of the Ya-Ya Sisterhood* made its debut in 2002. Wells's work depicts the lives of the Walker family, and the author places particular importance upon the mother-daughter relationship of Vivi and Siddalee set in Thornton. Thornton, in the novels, is a re-creation of the city of Alexandria, where Wells was reared. She depicts the complexity, irony, foibles, and successes of the Walker family with great detail, though she insists that the Walkers are not depictions of her family.

Wells will not divulge the date of her birth, but she was likely reared during the late 1950s and early 1960s. In 1970 she received a B.A. in English from Louisiana State University. (The Library of Congress lists her birth date as 1952, which would make her something of a prodigy.) After graduation, she traveled throughout the United States and attended the Naropa Institute in Boulder, Colo., where she studied with Allen Ginsberg. In New York she studied acting with Maurine Holbert-Hogaboom. Wells performed in many off-Broadway productions, and acting continues to be one of her passions. In 1982 she returned to the West, settling in Seattle, where she founded a chapter of Performance Artists for Nuclear Disarmament (PAND). She continues to live in Seattle with her photographer husband, Tom Schworer. She has maintained a dedication to both drama and fiction writing.

Although Wells's body of work is not large, her novels continue to be popular. Her themes will likely sustain her influence as a contemporary southern writer.

WORKS: *Splittin' Hairs* (1982). *Gloria Duplex* (1987). *Little Altars Everywhere* (1992). *Divine Secrets of the Ya-Ya Sisterhood* (1996). *Ya-Yas in Bloom* (2005).

—LISA ABNEY

EUDORA WELTY (1909–2001). Born in Jackson, Miss., to Mary Chestina Andrews Welty and Christian Webb Welty, Eudora Welty attended the local public schools and Mississippi State College for Women in Columbus. Encouraged by her parents to seek a broad education, she completed her B.A. at the University of Wisconsin and afterwards lived briefly in New York, taking several classes in business at Columbia. Although she lived most of her life in Jackson and frequently set her fiction in Mississippi, her family roots were elsewhere. Her father, an insurance executive, was a native of Ohio, and her mother was from West Virginia. After her father's death in 1931, Welty returned from New York to Mississippi, where she worked for a time as a "junior" publicity agent for the WPA, a job that deepened her knowledge of Mississippi's rural and small-town life. She drew upon this experience for the novels and short stories that marked her long and distinguished career.

Early on, Welty focused her creative ambitions on photography, and the visual imagination and sense of telling detail evident in this work became a hallmark of her fiction. She set her first published story, "Death of a Traveling Salesman" (1936), in backwoods Mississippi, portraying a salesman who confronts the emptiness of his life when he encounters a youthful couple clearly impoverished but fulfilled and vital. One of Welty's most widely read stories, "A Worn Path," from her first collection, *A Curtain of Green,* is located on the Natchez Trace, a setting she would further explore in a short novel, *The Robber Bridegroom,* and especially in the stories of her second collection, *The Wide Net.* Several of these stories take place in an early-nineteenth-century Mississippi, with such historical characters as Aaron Burr, John J. Audubon, the circuit-riding evangelist Lorenzo Dow, and the Natchez Trace outlaw James Murrell.

In *Delta Wedding,* her first full-length novel, Welty portrays a 1927 plantation family caught up in wedding plans. To frame the narrative, she employs the mediating point of view of an eleven-year-old, the visiting cousin Laura, who returns to her mother's home place and family for the eventful wedding. The novel illustrates Welty's merger of a modernist sensibility and style with a vivid regionality—an approach that would characterize much of her fiction. Critics have noted in this novel, as well as in other works, elements suggestive of Virginia Woolf. In what many readers regard as her most experimental and evocative work, *The Golden Apples,* Welty links seven stories of inhabitants of two small Mississippi towns. For these, she draws upon Greek and Irish mythology and Mississippi social history, and she gives a nod as well to a host of other literary precursors from Yeats and Joyce to Faulkner. Although in interviews Welty displayed little interest in feminist theory or activism, in her fiction she repeatedly explores gender relations and cultural forms marked by gender—acts of heroism and sacrifice, "vaunting" and "loving," wandering and hearth tending—and depicting these human predilections as they have been formed and deformed by socializing forces.

Welty's acute ear for language is notable. In *The Ponder Heart,* which has been adapted for stage and film, she composed a dramatic monologue that flows from narrator Edna Earle Ponder's mouth in one seemingly breathless stream. It is a form she practiced in the story "Why I Live at the P.O." and would master in the late novel *Losing Battles,* a composition of nearly four hundred pages of dialogue interrupted only by one brief meditative self-revelation by the boy Virgil. Earlier, in the collection *The Bride of the Innisfallen,* she had turned to foreign settings for several of the stories, reflecting her travel in Great Britain and Europe in the 1940s and 1950s. The volume also included the story "Circe," demonstrating Welty's continuing interest in casting mythological figures in new forms that link classical narrative and modernist introspection. For what would be her final novel, and also winner of the Pulitzer Prize in 1973, *The Optimist's Daughter,* she drew heavily upon details of her mother's life, especially of her youth in West Virginia. She wrote this initially as a novella for the *New Yorker,* a venue for many of her stories, including the prescient fiction based upon the murder of the civil rights leader Medgar Evers, "Where Is the Voice Coming From?" She wrote the story in 1963 immediately after hearing of Evers's death, imagining the murderer and his motivations with striking accuracy, even before details of the crime became known. One of her last stories, "The Demonstrators," also deals with the violence, confusion, and guilt associated with the civil rights movement in the South of the 1960s. Welty's widely admired memoir, *One Writer's Beginnings,* is a revised version of the Massey lectures she delivered at Harvard.

Welty was honored at home and abroad with many awards and recognitions, including O. Henry Prizes for the short story, membership in the National Institute of Arts and Letters, the National Medal of Arts, the National Medal of Literature and Medal of Freedom, the National Endowment for the Humanities' Frankel Prize, even induction into the French Legion of Honor. In 1998 the Library of America published a two-volume collection of her works, marking her as the first living author to be selected for inclusion in the series. Following her death on July 23, 2001, she was honored in formal state ceremonies at the Mississippi old capitol, where hundreds of friends and readers came to pay final respects. She rates among the best southern—and, indeed, among the best American—writers of the twentieth century.

WORKS: *A Curtain of Green* (1941). *The Robber Bridegroom* (1942). *The Wide Net and Other Stories* (1943). *Delta Wedding* (1946). *The Golden Apples* (1949). *The Ponder Heart* (1954). *The Bride of the Innisfallen* (1955). *The Shoe Bird* (1964). *Losing Battles* (1970). *One Time, One Place: Mississippi in the Depression, A Snapshot Album* (1971). *The Optimist's Daughter* (1972). *The Eye of the Story: Selected Essays and Reviews* (1978). *The Collected Stories of Eudora Welty* (1980). *One Writer's Beginnings* (1984). *Photographs* (1989). *A Writer's Eye: Collected Book Reviews* (1994). *Welty: Complete Novels* and *Welty: Stories, Essays and Memoir* (1998).

—PEGGY WHITMAN PRENSHAW

DON WEST (1906–1992). Don West, one of America's leading proletarian poets between the world wars, was born on a farm near Burnt Mountain in Gilmer County, Ga. He lived on his father's hundred-acre farm until he was fifteen, when his father moved to the Georgia lowlands, becoming a sharecropper. West attended the Berry School for indigent mountain children, a school he later attacked in a 1933 letter in the *New Republic.* In Tennessee, West enrolled at Lincoln Memorial University, where he became friends with fellow student Jessie Stuart. Professor Harry Harrison Kroll would become his mentor, as well as Stuart's. West also met Mabel "Connie" Adams at Lincoln, and they soon eloped. Two children would be born of their union.

Graduating in 1925, along with classmates Stuart and James Still, he entered graduate school at Vanderbilt University—but in religion rather than literature. West became an ordained Congregation minister with commitment to the Social Gospel. Observing labor problems in Kentucky mines and North Carolina textile mills, he made his entrance into political activism. In the Depression years he became ever more militant, as his sermons and poems make clear. His work appeared in leftist publications as well as in mainstream religious and regional publications. Throughout his long life he was a fervent advocate for the poor, for workers, and for African Americans. On a scholarship, he studied the Folk School Movement in Scandinavia, which led him to co-found, with Myles Horton, the Highlander Folk School in Monteagle, Tenn. Education and political causes (which resulted in some weeks in prison) continued to characterize his work. Following a grant from the Library of Congress to study Appalachia, he established the Appalachian Folk Life Center in Pipestem, W.Va., dedicated "to a mountain heritage of freedom, self-respect and independence, with human dignity."

From the 1930s into the 1980s, West authored eight poetry collections. By far the most successful was *Clods of Southern Earth,* chosen as the inaugural publication of the New York firm Boni and Graer.

In "Speaking of the Poet," the introduction to *The Road Is Rocky*, West proclaims, "Poetry will come from the South. . . . Our land is more than materialism and greed!" Cleanth Brooks singled out his poem "Southern Lullaby" as "propaganda art" in *Modern Poetry and Tradition;* Langston Hughes noted, "Don West marshals words into poetry to sing for democracy and decency, to puncture and plead, to startle and shock, to point out what America is and what America can be."

West died from heart disease on September 29, 1992, in hospital in Charleston, W.Va., not far from his Cabin Creek home, a setting that reminded West of the battles for a decent life for miners.

WORKS: *Crab-Grass* (1931). *Deep, Deep, Down in Living* (1932). *Between the Plow Handles* (1932). *Toil and Hunger* (1940). *Clods of Southern Earth* (1946). *The Road Is Rocky* (1951). *People's Cultural Heritage in Appalachia* (1971). *Southern Mountain Folk Tradition and the Folksong "Stars" Syndrome* (1972). *Romantic Appalachia; or, Poverty Pays If You Ain't Poor* (1972). *Songs for Southern Workers: 1937 Songbook of the Kentucky Workers Alliance* (1973). *Robert Tharin: Biography of a Mountain Abolitionist* (1973). *Freedom on the Mountains: Excerpts from a Book Manuscript on Southern Mountain History* (1973). *A Time for Anger: Poems Selected from "The Road Is Rocky" and "Clods of Southern Earth"* (1980). *In a Land of Plenty* (1982). *No Lonesome Road: Selected Prose and Poems,* ed. Jeff Biggers and George Brosi (2004).

—GEORGE BROSI

ALEXANDER WHITAKER (1585–1617). An Anglican clergyman, Alexander Whitaker was born at Cambridge, England, in 1585, the son of William and Susan Culverwell Whitaker. His father was a noted Puritan divine who remained inside the Established Church, who was appointed Regius Professor of Philosophy at Cambridge in 1580, and who became master of St. John's College in 1587. By 1595 Whitaker's parents were dead, and a kinsman, Alexander Nowell, apparently helped with his education.

Whitaker spent four years at Eton (1598–1602), and in the fall of 1602 he entered Trinity College, Cambridge, taking a B.A. (1605) and M.A. (1608). Following his ordination in the Church of England in 1609, Whitaker spent two years as a minister in the north of England (probably Yorkshire) before volunteering to go to Virginia as minister and missionary. Late in March 1611, he sailed from London with Sir Thomas Dale and three hundred colonists, reaching Virginia on May 19, 1611.

Soon after, Whitaker joined a group founding a new settlement named Henrico (sometimes called Henricopolis) on the north bank of the James River fifty miles up-river from Jamestown. Whitaker built a parsonage, Rock Hall, on the south bank opposite Henrico. In addition to his duties at Henrico, he ministered to another settlement, Bermuda Hundred, about five miles from Rock Hall.

As early as August 9, 1611, Whitaker wrote to friends in England of his pleasure with the Virginia adventure. His *Good News from Virginia*, completed by July 28, 1612, was not intended for publication, but as a report to the Virginia Company. The company's council, pleased with Whitaker's report, decided to print it so that "the naked and plaine truth may give a just affront to the cunning and coloured falsehoods devised by the enemies of this Plantation." Published in the form of a sermon, Whitaker's *Good News from Virginia* appeared in London in 1613. The forty-five-page pamphlet describes the plenty of the country, urges conversion of the Indians, and argues for continued support of the Virginia colony.

Whitaker's pastoral duties evidently included instructing Pocahontas in Christianity and baptizing her before her marriage to John Rolfe. He drowned crossing the James River in the spring of 1617. He never married.

WORKS: *Good News from Virginia* (1613).

—ROBERT BAIN

DANIEL KIMBALL WHITAKER (1801–1881). Daniel Kimball Whitaker was born on April 13, 1801, in Sharon, Mass., to Mary Kimball and Jonathan Whitaker, a Congregationalist minister. After receiving the A.B. (1820) and the A.M. (1823) at Harvard, he studied theology and was licensed to preach. In 1822–23 he edited the abolitionist and anti-Catholic *Christian Philanthropist* in New Bedford.

In poor health, Whitaker moved south in 1823. He lectured and preached widely and organized a congregation in Augusta, Ga., before abandoning the ministry and settling in South Carolina. In 1828 he married Mary H. Firth, a widow with two large tracts and sixty-two slaves in St. Paul's Parish. As a rice and cotton planter, Whitaker was active in agricultural and literary affairs and actively supported nullification in the early 1830s.

Prepared for the bar under James L. Pettigru, he opened a law office in Charleston. There in 1835 he began the *Southern Literary Journal and Monthly Magazine,* which he edited until 1837. He edited the *Southern Quarterly Review* from its beginning in 1842 through 1847. In 1849 he married a widow, Mary Scrimzeour Furman Miller, a writer of poetry and fiction. With her he edited *Whitaker's Magazine: The Rights of the South* in Charleston and Columbia in 1850–53. After it was absorbed by the *Southern Eclectic,* Whitaker edited the latter in Augusta in 1853–54, with J. H. Fitten and later alone.

Having held a minor position in Washington under Buchanan's administration, he served in Richmond in the C.S.A. Post Office Department and Quartermaster General's Department. After moving to New Orleans in January 1866, he edited the *New Orleans Monthly Review* in 1874–76, attempting to revive it as the *New Orleans Quarterly Review* in 1878 and as the *Southern Quarterly Review* in 1879–80. In 1878 he joined the Roman Catholic Church. He died while visiting in Houston on March 23, 1881.

WORKS: *Sidney's Letters to William E. Channing, D.D., Occasioned by His Letter to Hon. Henry Clay, on the Annexation of Texas to the United States* (1837).

—WILLIAM MOSS

ANDREW WHITE, S.J. (1579–1656). Although biographical details of Father Andrew White's early life are sketchy, he was apparently born in London in 1579. Like other English Catholics, he was educated on the Continent, matriculating at Douai College in April 1593, then entering St. Alban's College, Valladolid. In 1605 he took his vows as a priest at Douai. Following this, a mission to England ended in banishment, White having the misfortune to be there at the time of the Gunpowder Plot. In 1607 he was admitted as a Jesuit novitiate at St. John's College, Louvain. As a Jesuit, White, ignoring a death sentence, held several missionary posts in England, where sometime between 1619 and 1622 he evidently met George Calvert, through whom he became interested in Lord Baltimore's plans to colonize what was to become Maryland.

Before sailing to America with Lord Baltimore on November 22, 1633, Father White, often called the Apostle of Maryland, wrote the first Maryland colonization tract: *A Declaration of the Lord Baltimore's Plantation in Mary-land,* an eight-page pamphlet, revised by Calvert, describing in glowing terms the new colony and the advantages of settling there. After arriving in the New World, he wrote a second promotional tract, *A Relation of the Successful Beginnings of the Lord Baltimore's Plantation in Mary-land,* which enthusiastically described the beauty and bounty of the colony through specific details and incidents set in a narrative frame. White's account of the Indians in particular looks forward to his work in converting them to Christianity and, in the process, to his making of a grammar and dictionary of their language. This tract was followed in 1635 by a third colonization tract, composed largely by Father White, *A Relation of Maryland*.

Father White's work in Maryland, although often interrupted by illness, continued until 1644 or 1645, when he was captured by Virginia Puritans and sent to England for trial on the spurious charge of "being a Priest in England." After several years in Newgate Prison, he was released. He was never able to return to Maryland, living instead on the Continent and then in England, where he is recorded as having died on December 27, 1656.

WORKS: *A Declaration of the Lord Baltimore's Plantation in Mary-land* (1633). *A Relation of the Successful Beginnings of the Lord Baltimore's Plantation in Mary-land* (1634). *A Relation of Maryland* (1635).

—PETER L. ABERNETHY

BAILEY WHITE (1950–). Bailey White was born on May 1, 1950, in Thomasville, Ga. Her father, Robb White, was an author as well as a scriptwriter for television and film. Her mother, Rosalie Mason, was a farmer who also served as director of the local chapter of the Red Cross. Much of White's writing—particularly in her first collection, *Mama Makes Up Her Mind and Other Dangers of Southern Living*—testifies to the strong presence of her mother, whom the author portrays with a balance of satire and affection that has become characteristic of her vignettes of small-town life in southern Georgia.

After graduating from Florida State University in 1973, White spent the next two decades working as a first-grade teacher in Thomasville. During these years she wrote short sketches in her spare time, and she eventually became a popular commentator on National Public Radio. The stories in *Mama Makes Up Her Mind* offer an assortment of eccentric personalities: an aunt with a trained alligator, a cousin with a fear of cows, and a mother whose quail dinner comes from a serendipitous highway accident. Her following book, *Sleeping at the Starlite Motel and Other Adventures on the Way Back Home*, continued in a similar vein, although White now provided further sketches based on her experiences outside her native Georgia. White has also written a novel, *Quite a Year for Plums*, in which she adopts a loose, episodic form to trace a web of relationships in a small Georgia community.

Her distinctive humor and her ability to summon broader human insights from the minutiae of the local have earned her a devoted audience across the nation. Since 1993 White's Thanksgiving stories have been an annual NPR tradition, and she still lives in the house where she was born.

WORKS: *Mama Makes Up Her Mind and Other Dangers of Southern Living* (1993). *Sleeping at the Starlite Motel and Other Adventures on the Way Back Home* (1995). *Quite a Year for Plums* (1998).

—CHAD TREVITTE

JOHN BLAKE WHITE (1781–1859). Born near Eutaw Springs, S.C., on September 2, 1781, John Blake White studied painting in London (where he associated with Benjamin West and Washington Allston), attempted to establish himself as painter in Boston in 1804, practiced law in Charleston for almost two decades, was elected to the South Carolina state legislature in 1818, ran a paper mill in Tusculum, S.C. (1826–32), and was South Carolina's most prolific early-nineteenth-century playwright. White began his dramatic career with *Foscari*, a blank verse tragedy produced at the Charleston Theatre in 1806. A derivative piece set in Venice, *The Foscari* reflects White's interest in the gothic, an interest he indulged further with his next piece, *The Mysteries of the Castle* (produced in Charleston in 1806), a play that features a revenge plot, secret chambers, a mysterious specter, and a climactic explosion. White then turned to contemporary issues, and his last three plays feature two reform pieces, *Modern Honor,* which condemns dueling, and *The Forgers* (published in the *Southern Literary Journal* in 1837), which promotes temperance, and a battle play, *The Triumph of Liberty,* which was not produced.

Outside the theater, White eventually earned a national reputation as a painter, seeing four of his historical pieces hung in the U.S. Capitol and executing portraits of many prominent South Carolinians of his era. He died in Charleston, having been employed in that city's customs house for the last twenty-seven years of his life.

WORKS: *Foscari; or, The Venetian Exile: A Tragedy in Five Acts* (1806). *The Mysteries of the Castle; or, The Victim of Revenge* (1807). *Modern Honor: A Tragedy in Five Acts* (1812). *An Oration . . . in Commemoration of the Adoption of the Federal Constitution* (1815). *The Triumph of Liberty; or, Louisiana Preserved* (1819). *The Forgers: A Dramatic Poem* (1899).

—DANIEL J. ENNIS

WALTER FRANCIS WHITE (1893–1955). Walter White, born in Atlanta, on July 1, 1893, was 1/64th Negro. He had blond hair, blue eyes, and a very light skin; he could have "passed." But the terrible Atlanta race riots, which he witnessed with his father on September 23, 1906, seemed to fix in his mind forever that he was black.

After graduating from Atlanta University in 1916, White worked for an Atlanta insurance company, but in 1918 James Weldon Johnson convinced him to go to New York City to become assistant secretary of the NAACP. In 1922 he married Leah Gladys Powell, and in that same year he met H. L. Mencken, who urged him to write a novel about African American life "from the inside." *The Fire in the Flint* focuses upon an African American doctor, Harvard-trained, who returns to his hometown in Georgia to practice medicine. White's objectives were to show "what an intelligent, educated Negro feels" and to illustrate Mencken's thesis in "The Sahara of the Bozart" that the South had become an intellectual and moral wasteland after the Civil War. White's second novel, *Flight,* was influenced by Sinclair Lewis, who became a close friend. In it, he satirized the stuffy, provincial bourgeoisie of both races. During the 1920s, he recommended young black writers to Carl Van Vechten and Alfred Knopf, who were both interested in promoting the Negro Renaissance.

A major turning point in White's life occurred in 1927 when he went to southern France on a Guggenheim Fellowship, ostensibly to write a novel about three generations of a black family. What he wrote instead was *Rope and Faggot: A Biography of Judge Lynch.* It was not fiction but rather a sociopsychological study of the illegal execution of African Americans. White subsequently gave up his literary career to become more active in politics. In 1931 he replaced Johnson as executive secretary of the NAACP; in 1937 he was awarded the Spingarn Medal for activity against lynching; and in 1942 and 1943 he helped settle the race riots in Detroit and Harlem. He also investigated the alleged mistreatment of black troops in Europe during World War II, and his findings took form in a book, *A Rising Wind.* He and his first wife divorced in 1948. He married Poppy Cannon in 1949, and this marriage to a white woman did some damage to his reputation within the NAACP. Her biography of his last years is titled *A Gentle Knight* (1956). He died on March 21, 1955.

WORKS: *The Fire in the Flint* (1924). *Flight* (1926). *Rope and Faggot: A Biography of Judge Lynch* (1929). *A Rising Wind* (1945). *A Man Called White* (1948).

—CHARLES SCRUGGS

JAMES WHITEHEAD (1936–2003). James Tillotson Whitehead was born on March 16, 1936, in St. Louis, grew up in Jackson, Miss., and graduated from Jackson High School in 1954. He had a football scholarship to Vanderbilt University, where he majored in philosophy. An injury caused him to give up football, but he stayed at Vanderbilt and received a B.A. in philosophy in 1959 and an M.A. in English in 1960. In 1963 he enrolled in the University of Iowa's creative writing program, and received the M.F.A. from Iowa in 1965. In 1965 Whitehead and William Harrison founded the creative writing program at the University of Arkansas, Fayetteville, and he attained the rank of professor in 1973. When Whitehead retired in 1998, the program was recognized as one of the best of its kind in the country.

On the strength of his first volume of poems, *Domains*, Whitehead received the Robert Frost Fellowship in poetry of the Bread Loaf Writers' Conference in 1967. Whitehead's other poetry volumes are *Local Men, Near at Hand*, and the chapbook *Actual Size*. His poems have appeared in many American literary journals, among them *Hollins Critic, Mill Mountain Review, Southern Poetry Review, Southern Review, Poetry Now, Cimarron Review, New Orleans Review*, and *Westview*. His work has also appeared in anthologies, including *An Anthology of Mississippi Writers* (1979), *Articles of War: A Collection of Poetry about World War II* (1990), and *A New Geography of Poets* (1992).

Whitehead's novel, *Joiner*, received considerable critical approval for its depiction of Sonny Joiner, a Mississippi football player who makes it into the pros. Joiner calls his account of his life a "tirade on passion, loyalty, race, religion, ambitions, and death." The novel was among the *New York Times*'s "Notable Books" that year. Whitehead received a Guggenheim Fellowship in fiction in 1972.

At the University of Arkansas, Whitehead was a renowned teacher. Twice he received university teaching awards, and he was a founding member of the University Teaching Academy in 1988. His generosity and kindness to students and colleagues are legendary.

Whitehead died on August 17, 2003, in Fayetteville. He was married to the former Guendaline Graeber, a hospital nurse, and they had seven children.

WORKS: *Domains: Poems* (1966). *Joiner* (1971). *Local Men: Poems* (1979). *Near at Hand: Poems* (1993).

—ETHEL SIMPSON

ALBERY ALLSON WHITMAN (1851–1901). Albery Allson Whitman was born a slave near Munfordville, Ky., on May 30, 1851. Whitman had little recollection of his parents, who both died before the Emancipation Proclamation. Seeking work after the Civil War, Whitman made his way to Ohio. He briefly attended school in Troy, Ohio, and subsequently returned to Kentucky to teach. In 1870 he enrolled in Wilberforce University, where he came under the mentorship of the university's president, Bishop Daniel Alexander Payne. A member of the African Methodist Episcopal Church, Whitman traveled the southern United States as a pastor, serving churches in Texas and Georgia, as well as in Ohio and Kansas. Religious calling notwithstanding, Whitman was an alcoholic.

Whitman was married to a beautiful octoroon, Caddie. Her four daughters, two of whom may only have been Whitman's stepdaughters, had successful careers in vaudeville as the Whitman Sisters. After contracting pneumonia in Alabama, Whitman died within a week in his Atlanta home on June 29, 1901.

Perhaps the greatest African American poet of his time, Whitman influenced both Charles Chesnutt and Paul Laurence Dunbar. He served as a transitional figure between nineteenth- and twentieth-century African American poetic aesthetics. His most famous works include *The Rape of Florida* and *Twasinta's Seminoles*—poems written in the epic, romantic mode, which lauded the "primitive" culture of the Seminoles and the bravery and endurance of southern black people.

WORKS: *Essays on the Ten Plagues and Miscellaneous Poems* (1871?). *Leelah Mislead* (1873). *Not a Man, and Yet Man* (1877). *Twasinta's Seminoles; or, The Rape of Florida* (1884/1885). *World's Fair Poem* (1893). *An Idyll of the South: An Epic Poem in Two Parts* (1901).

—KEITH MITCHELL

TOM WICKER (1926–). Thomas Grey Wicker was born on June 18, 1926, in Hamlet, N.C., a small town near the South Carolina border. Wicker embarked on his career path at the University of North Carolina, where he completed his A.B. in journalism in 1948. In a pattern perhaps more typical of his day, he received an immediate appointment as executive director of the Southern Pines Chamber of Commerce, and married Neva Jewett McLean in 1949; they divorced in 1973. His salad days as an inkslinger began with the editorship of the small-town *Sandhill Citizen* (1949), followed by a stint with *The Robesonian* (1949–50), before he settled in at the *Winston-Salem Journal,* where he started as a copy editor (1951–52) and became sports editor (1954–55) and Washington correspondent and editorial writer (1957–59). Wicker began publishing fiction while working for the *Journal,* initially under the pseudonym Paul Connolly. His first novel, *Get Out of Town,* appeared in 1951.

But Wicker hit his stride with his political journalism. After attending Harvard as a Nieman fellow in 1957–58, he worked briefly for the *Nashville Tennessean* and landed a job as the Washington correspondent for the *New York Times* (1960–64). He was promoted to bureau chief (1964–68), then associate editor (1968–85), and in 1966 began his "In the Nation" column, which ran for an impressive twenty-five years. Wicker covered the Kennedy assassination (which he marked as the definitive moment when television supplanted printed media) and Watergate, leading to his empathic study *One of Us: Richard Nixon and the American Dream.* His coverage of the Attica prison uprising produced the best-selling *A Time to Die,* which received an Edgar Allan Poe Award. Wicker has been a particularly interested observer of American race relations through the years; *Tragic Failure: Racial Integration in America* reveals his ruminations.

Wicker's nonfiction efforts have been more favorably reviewed than his forays in fiction. Nevertheless, in 1998 he published a detective potboiler, *Easter Lilly.* The ensuing years have seen the release of a journalistic memoir and two biographies of American presidents. His papers are archived at the University of North Carolina.

WORKS: *Get Out of Town* (1951). *Tears Are for Angels* (1952). *The Kingpin* (1953). *So Fair, So Evil* (1955). *The Devil Must* (1957). *The Judgment: A Novel* (1961). *Kennedy without Tears: The Man Beneath the Myth* (1964). *Social Justice and the Problems of the Twentieth Century,* with Sidney Hook and C. Vann Woodward (1968). *JFK and LBJ: The Influence of Personality upon Politics* (1968). *Facing the Lions* (1973). *A Time to Die* (1975). *On Press* (1978). *Unto This Hour: A Novel* (1984). *One of Us: Richard Nixon and the American Dream* (1991). *Donovan's Wife* (1992). *Tragic Failure: Racial Integration in America* (1996). *Indictment: The News Media and the Criminal Justice System,* with Wallace Westfeldt (1998). *Easter Lilly: A Novel of the South Today* (1998). *The Nixon Years, 1969–1974: White House to Watergate* (1999). *On the Record: An Insider's Guide to Journalism* (2002). *Dwight D. Eisenhower* (2002). *George Herbert Walker Bush* (2004).

—BRYAN GIEMZA

ALLEN WIER (1946–). Allen Wier was born in San Antonio, Tex., on September 9, 1946, and grew up in Texas, Louisiana, and Mexico, where his father explored the jungles of Veracruz seeking ferns and flowers to import for the wholesale flower business. Wier's fiction—including *Things About to Disappear, Blanco,* and *Departing as Air*—often presents these settings as decidedly stark, dusty landscapes.

In 1997 Weir received the Robert Penn Warren Award, a biennial citation conferred by the Fellowship of Southern Writers to "recognize an outstanding young Southern fiction writer." In 2001 he was voted into the Fellowship of Southern Writers. Wier is also the recipient of a Guggenheim Fellowship, a grant from the National Endowment for the Arts, and a Dobie-Paisano Fellowship from the University of Texas and the Texas Institute of Letters. His fiction, essays, and reviews have appeared in *Southern Review, Georgia Review, Ploughshares, Texas Review,* and the *New York Times.* Wier has completed a long novel, *Tehano,* about the Comanche wars in Texas, and a "literary thriller," *Skin for Skin.*

Weir has taught at Longwood College, Carnegie-Mellon University, Hollins College, the University of Texas, Florida International University, and the University of Alabama; currently he teaches at the University of Tennessee in Knoxville, where he has held the John C. Hodges Chair of Teaching Excellence. He lives in Knoxville with his wife Donnie, a painter, and son Wesley, a musician. Wier's first marriage, to poet Dara Wier, ended in divorce.

WORKS: *Things About to Disappear* (1978). *Blanco* (1978). *Departing as Air* (1983). Ed., *Voicelust: Eight Contemporary Fiction Writers on Style,* with Don Hendrie, Jr. (1985). *A Place for Outlaws* (1989). Ed., *Walking on Water and Other Stories* (1996). *Tehano* (2006).

—Rob Trucks

JAMES WILCOX (1949–). Born in Hammond, La., James Wilcox grew up in a home filled with music. His father was a professor of music at Southeastern Louisiana University. Everyone in his immediate family played a musical instrument, and he played cello in the Baton Rouge Symphony Orchestra during high school. After graduation, he attended Yale University, where he studied under Robert Penn Warren. Through Warren he met Albert Erskine, an editor at Random House, who helped him get into publishing. He worked in publishing for a dozen years, first at Random House and then at Doubleday, before committing to a career as a writer. He now directs the creative writing program at Louisiana State University.

Wilcox's novels depict the lives of the residents of Tula Springs—both those who stay home in this mostly Protestant enclave of southeastern Louisiana and those who leave for the city. Collectively, the books develop an intricate local history of overlapping families and recurring characters and a comic chronicle of a community in transition. Wilcox's first four novels take place entirely in Tula Springs, a town too small to have a Wal-Mart. His fourth book, *Sort of Rich,* represents a gradual geographic and demographic shift as he describes the experiences of an aging Manhattan socialite who moves to Tula Springs with her husband. Recent novels, however, reverse the equation, portraying the lives of Tula Springs expatriates living in New York, where they confront urban situations with rural values. *Plain and Normal,* for example, concerns a former resident of Tula Springs who divorces his wife in order to live an openly gay lifestyle, but he never consummates a homosexual relationship. Although Wilcox's novels tend to be humorous, his characters retain a poignant sense of dignity and, occasionally, a prospect of redemption. Harold Bloom included Wilcox's first novel, *Modern Baptists,* in *American Canon.*

WORKS: *Modern Baptists* (1983). *North Gladiola* (1985). *Miss Undine's Living Room* (1987). *Sort of Rich* (1989). *Polite Sex* (1991). *Guest of a Sinner* (1993). *Plain and Normal* (1998).

—David A. Davis

RICHARD HENRY WILDE (1789–1847). Remembered today chiefly for one poem, "The Lament of the Captive," beginning "My life is like the summer rose," Richard Henry Wilde was born in Dublin, Ireland, on September 24, 1789. The family, consisting of parents Richard and Mary Wilde and six children, settled in Baltimore, Md., in 1796; two additional children were born in Baltimore. In 1802, upon the death of the father, a clothing merchant, the family moved to Augusta, Ga., where Mary Wilde opened a dry goods store and Richard Henry grew to manhood. Educated by his mother and private tutors, Richard Henry worked in a store for a while; then he prepared himself for the law and passed the Georgia bar in 1809. Throughout most of his life, he wrote poetry.

As a lawyer and politician, Wilde received some recognition. He was chosen in 1811 to be attorney-general of Georgia; he served in the national House of Representatives during the years 1815–17 and 1825–35.

After a political defeat in 1835 and the death of his wife, he left for Italy, where he lived from 1835 to 1841. He was joined by his sister and his two sons. He immersed himself in the literature of Italy, translating some Italian poems and writing biographies of Italian literary figures. In 1841 he returned to America, moved from Augusta to New Orleans, and resumed the practice of law. He took an active part in community projects and aided in the establishment of the law school at Tulane. He died during a yellow fever epidemic in New Orleans on September 10, 1847.

WORKS: *Conjectures and Researches Concerning the Love, Madness and Imprisonment of Torquato Tasso* (1842). *Hesperia* (1867). *The Italian Lyric Poets* (1966). *Poems, Fugitive and Occasional* (1966).

—EDWARD L. TUCKER

ELIZA WILKINSON (1757–1813?). Born on February 7, 1757, on the family plantation in Yonge's Island, S.C., Eliza Yonge married Joseph Wilkinson in her teens and was widowed a year later. She married Peter Porcher on January 9, 1786; they had four children, including a son, Francis Yonge Porcher. The date of Eliza Wilkinson's death is unknown.

In 1781 Wilkinson began recounting her Revolutionary War experiences in letters to a friend, copying them into a letterbook that her descendants preserved. In 1832 author Caroline Gilman, whose daughter had married Francis James Porcher, Wilkinson's grandson, began publishing selected letters in her magazine the *Southern Rose Bud*. Gilman's *Letters of Eliza Wilkinson* collects the twelve letters previously published.

Letters presents South Carolina planters as peace-loving, genteel survivors of boorish incursions on their natural right to liberty. Wilkinson describes several instances of the British army's raiding plantations where she happened to be, stealing clothing and jewelry, and showing no deference to "the ladies."

Wilkinson's diction reflects a slaveholder's vantage point. She calls people belonging to her family "servants," but she uses the term *slave* for an enslaved African American in the British army. "Servants" figure as property to be protected (her father was counseled to "move off his furniture and Negroes" at the approach of the British) or as tools: Wilkinson describes how she, her sister, and her mother suffered during one removal when they had to walk "three long miles," noting in passing that their servants were carrying their belongings. Readers in 1839 who shared Wilkinson's view of slavery could thus have interpreted *Letters* as a rebuke to the Abolitionist movement that sought to deprive slave owners of their human property and impede their freedom to maintain a plantation economy.

A copy of Wilkinson's complete letterbook, transcribed in 1905, is at the University of South Carolina.

WORKS: *Letters of Eliza Wilkinson*, ed. Caroline Gilman (1839).

—JULIA EICHELBERGER

SYLVIA WILKINSON (1940–). Sylvia Wilkinson was born on April 3, 1940, in Durham, N.C., the daughter of Thomas Noell and Peggy George Wilkinson. Her career was not one anticipated for a young woman of the 1950s as she entered the Woman's College of the University of North Carolina (now the University of North Carolina at Greensboro), where she received a B.A. in painting and writing in 1962. At Greensboro her teacher Randall Jarrell pronounced that she had "a gift." From Greensboro, in order to develop that gift, Wilkinson proceeded to another institution of women, Hollins College. There she came under the influence of Louis Rubin and earned an M.A. in 1963. She then departed for California and Stanford University on a Wallace Stegner Creative Writing Fellowship.

The novels that she began publishing (starting with *Mosses on the North Side* in 1966) soon validated Jarrell's judgment. Her first three novels were set in eastern North Carolina; she turned to the mountains for her fourth novel. Literary honors began to accrue; these include an award from the Eugene F. Saxon Memorial Trust Fund (1964) and a fellowship from the National Endowment for the Arts (1973–74). Twice she has won the Sir Walter Raleigh Award for North Carolina Fiction. She has taught or served as writer-in-residence at the University of North Carolina at Asheville, the College of William and Mary, Sweet Briar College, Washington University, the University of Wisconsin at Milwaukee, and the University of North Carolina at Chapel Hill. Teachers and teaching have been topics that she found important.

But in the 1970s, Wilkinson's passion increasingly shifted to auto racing—a sport that has become quintessentially southern. The turning was no great shock, for she has always been drawn to the active life. A competitive tennis player in the 1950s, she also enjoyed horseback riding. Auto racing became her passionate interest and avocation. She has published nonfiction about it for both adults and children.

Now living in El Segundo, Calif., Wilkinson is active on the racing circuit, sometimes as a member of a racing team or on a sprint crew, sometimes as a timer.

WORKS: *Moss on the North Side* (1966). *A Killing Frost* (1967). *Cale* (1970). Ed., *Change: A Handbook for the Teaching of Social Studies and English,* with Ed Campbell (1971). *The Stainless Steel Carrot: An Auto Racing Odyssey* (1973). *Shadow of the Mountain* (1977). *Can-Am* (1981). *Endurance Racing* (1981). *Super Vee* (1981). *Champ Cars* (1982). *Bone of My Bones* (1982). *Automobiles* (1982). *Dirt Tracks to Glory: The Early Days of Stock Car Racing as Told by the Participants* (1983). *On the 7th Day God Created the Chevrolet* (1993).

—WAYNE J. POND

BEN AMES WILLIAMS (1889–1953). A popular American writer of the first half of the twentieth century, Ben Ames Williams was born on March 7, 1889, in Macon, Miss., and was the grand-nephew of the Confederate general James Longstreet. His family moved to Jackson, Ohio, when Williams was still an infant. He spent his youth in Ohio, received his education at Dartmouth in Massachusetts, and lived in the Northeast for his adult life.

Williams began his professional life as a journalist, but soon turned to writing short stories. His story "They Grind Exceeding Small" was included in the 1919 *O. Henry Memorial Award Prize Stories,* and Williams found a popular outlet for his fiction in the *Saturday Evening Post.* He was best known for stories about the fictional town of Fraternity, Maine, some of which were collected in *Fraternity Village.* Williams eventually turned to longer fiction, publishing dozens of novels, including sea tales, mysteries, contemporary realism, and historical romance. Several of his novels were best-sellers, and his best-remembered works are *The Strange Woman, Leave Her to Heaven, The House Divided*, and *Owen Glen*.

Despite spending most of his life outside the South, Williams maintained an interest in southern history that led to his most ambitious novel, *The House Divided*. The result of more than a decade of work, this epic encompasses the Civil War and its impact on a southern aristocratic family. Williams's interest in the South also resulted in his historical novel *Great Oaks* about a Georgia island, as well as his edition of *A Diary from Dixie by Mary Boykin Chesnut*. Shortly before his death in 1953, Williams completed *The Unconquered*, a novel of the Reconstruction period and sequel to *The House Divided*.

WORKS: *All the Brothers Were Valiant* (1919). *The Sea Bride* (1919). *The Great Accident* (1920). *Evered* (1921). *Black Pawl* (1922). *Thrifty Stock and Other Stories* (1923). *Sangsue* (1923). *Audacity* (1924). *The Whaler* (1924). *The Rational Hind* (1925). *The Silver Forest* (1926). *Immortal Longings* (1927). *Splendor* (1927). *The Dreadful Night* (1928). *Death on Scurvy Street* (1929). *The Bellmer Mystery* (1930). *Touchstone* (1930). *Great Oaks* (1930). Ed., *Letters from Fraternity* (1931). *An End to Mirth* (1931). *Pirate's Purchase* (1931). *Honeyflow* (1932). *Money Musk* (1932). *Pascal's Mill* (1933). *Mischief* (1933). *Hostile Valley* (1934). *Small Town Girl* (1935). *Charles Bismarck Ames: In Memoriam* (1936). *Crucible* (1937). *The Strumpet Sea* (1938). *Once aboard the Whaler* (1939). *Thread of Scarlet* (1939). *The Happy End* (1939). *Come Spring* (1940). *The Strange Woman* (1941). *Deep Waters* (1942). *Time of Peace: September 26, 1930–December 7, 1941* (1942). Ed., *Amateurs at War: The American Soldier in Action* (1943). *Leave Her to Heaven* (1944). *It's a Free Country* (1945). *House Divided* (1947). *Valley Vixen* (1948). *Lady in Peril* (1948). Ed., *A Diary from Dixie by Mary Boykin Chesnut* (1949). *Fraternity Village* (1949). *Owen Glen* (1950). *The Unconquered* (1953).

—ANDREW B. LEITER

JOAN WILLIAMS (1928–2004). Joan Williams was born on September 26, 1928, in Memphis, Tenn., the only child of Maude Moore and Priestly H. Williams. She attended Miss Hutchinson's School for Girls, where she discovered she wanted to be a writer. After a year at Southwestern College at Memphis, and after a short marriage that was annulled, Williams moved to the Washington, D.C., area, where she continued her education at a community college. She completed a B.A. in English at Bard College in 1950.

During the summer of 1949, Williams read William Faulkner's *The Sound and the Fury* and made a pilgrimage to Oxford to meet the author. Faulkner became both a mentor and a love interest, and he asked her to collaborate with him on a portion of what would become *Requiem for a Nun*. That same summer, Williams won first prize in the Mademoiselle College Fiction Contest for her story "Rain Later," which was published in the August 1949 issue of the magazine.

After Williams's marriage in 1954 to Ezra Brown, a writer for *Sports Illustrated*, her writing was slowed for a time as she focused her attention on her two sons, who were born in 1954 and 1956. By the 1960s, Williams was able to spend more time on her writing. Her first novel, *The Morning and the Evening*, won the John P. Marquand First Novel Award in 1962. The opening chapter of the novel is based on a short story published in the *Atlantic Monthly* as an Atlantic First.

Williams published four more novels and a collection of short stories, including *The Wintering*, a fictionalized account of her relationship with Faulkner. In 1962 Williams received a grant from the National Institute of Arts and Letters. She was also the recipient of a Guggenheim Fellowship.

In the 1990s Williams relocated to Charlottesville, Va., where she lived for several years. Declining health caused her to move to apartment quarters in Atlanta, Ga., where she died on April 11, 2004, shortly after relocating.

WORKS: *The Morning and the Evening* (1961). *Old Powder Man* (1966). *The Wintering* (1971). *County Woman* (1982). *Pariah and Other Stories* (1983). *Pay the Piper* (1988).

—MARY LOUISE WEAKS

JONATHAN WILLIAMS (1929–). Jonathan Williams is celebrated as much for his contributions to the publishing world through the Jargon Society as for his own poetry. Despite a steady stream of his own books, now numbering over fifty, Williams's reputation as a somewhat obscure and iconoclastic poet remains steady. Born in Asheville, N.C., on March 8, 1929, he has continued to publish both his own work and the work of others into the twenty-first century, establishing himself as an eccentric, witty, nonacademic man of letters. Williams's poetry, essays, and editions reflect his multiple interests, which include hiking the Appalachian trail, photography, music, art, book designing, gardening, and world travel.

Williams's academic education includes valuable time spent studying art and serving as a conscientious objector and an influential period at Black Mountain College, followed by time spent in San Francisco absorbing some of the spirit of the Beats. The varied nature of his education came together in the early 1950s when he established the Jargon Society, an alternative publishing company to which he has devoted much of his energy and skill, publishing the work both of his Black Mountain friends and of emerging poets such as Lorine Niedecker and Louis Zukofsky.

His various interests also come together in his books of poetry, which combine lyrical poems made out of clever wordplay, Appalachian and other regional dialects, games, puzzles with photography, drawing, and his book-making and editing talents. When he turns his hand to essays, Williams ranges freely over such topics as jazz, neglected writers and photographers, the natural world, sexuality, and cooking. The results are original celebrations of all the arts, created by one of the South's most original artists.

WORKS: *Garbage Litters the Iron Face of the Sun's Child* (1951). *Red/Gray* (1952). *Four Stoppages* (1953). *The Empire Finals at Verona* (1959). *Amen/Huzza/Selah* (1960). *Elegies and Celebrations* (1962). *Emblems for the Little Dells, and Nooks, and Corners of Paradise* (1962). *In England's Green & (A Garland and A Clyster)* (1962). *Lullabies Twisters Gibbers Drags.* (1963). *Lines about Hills above Lakes* (1964). *Slow Owls* (1964). *NC 64* (1964). *Affilati Attrezze Per I Giardini de Catullo* (1966). *Jonathan Williams' Fifty Epiphytes* (1967). *The Lucidities* (1967). *Polycotyledonous Poems* (1967). *Descant on Rawthey's Madrigal* (1968). *Sharp Tools for Catullan Gardens* (1968). *Mahler* (1969). *An Ear in Bartram's Tree: Selected Poems 1957–67* (1969). *Strung out with Elgar on a Hill* (1970). Ed., *Edward Dahlberg: A Tribute* (1970). *Blues & Roots/Rue & Bluets* (1971). *The Loco Logodaedalist in Situ* (1972). Ed., *Epitaphs for Lorina* (1973). *The Sleep of Reason* (1974). *The Personal Eye* (1974). *Hot What?* (1975). *Madeira & Toasts for Basil Buntings 75th Birthday* (1977). *An Omen for Stevie Smith* (1977). *SuperDuper Zuppa Inglese* (1977). *Untinears & Antennae for Maurice Ravel* (1977) *"I Shall Save One Land Unvisited": Eleven Southern Photographers* (1978). *Elite/Elate Poems: Selected Poems, 1971–75* (1979). *Portrait Photographs* (1979). *Shankum Naggum* (1979). *The Delian Seasons* (1982). *Get Hot or Get Out: A Selection of Poems, 1957–1981* (1982). *The Magpie's Bagpipe: Selected Essays* (1982). *In the Azure over the Squalor* (1983). *Letter in a Klein Bottle* (1984). *St. Eom in the Land of Pasaquan* (1987). *Aposiopeses* (1988). *Dementations on Shank's Mare* (1988). *Le Garage Ravi de Rocky Mount: An Essay on Vernon Burwell* (1988). *Quote, Unquote.* (1989). *Uncle Gus Flaubert Rates the Jargon Society* (1989). *Eight Days in Eire* (1990). *Metafours for Mysophobes* (1990). *Quantulumcumque* (1991). *The History of Radnorshire* (1999). *French Kiss with Death* (1999). *Blackbird Dust* (2000). *A Palpable Elysium* (2002). *Jubilant Thicket* (2005).

—TIMOTHY DOW ADAMS

MILLER WILLIAMS (1930–). Poet Miller Williams was born in Hoxie, Ark. His father was a Methodist (and thus itinerant) minister; the family lived in several Arkansas towns as Williams was growing up. After earning a B.S. in biology from Arkansas State College, he earned an M.S. in zoology at the University of Arkansas. He also completed a year's study toward a Ph.D. in physiology at the University of Mississippi Medical School. His early jobs included teaching science at various schools; traveling as a college sales representative for Harcourt, Brace; and working in a Sears store. His career as an English professor began at Louisiana State University; later positions included appointments at the University of Chile and at Loyola University in New Orleans. Since 1971 he has taught at the University of Arkansas at Fayetteville, where he became the first director of the University of Arkansas Press. His first marriage produced three children, one of whom is the singer Lucinda Williams. He lives in Fayetteville with his second wife, Jordan.

Williams's oeuvre is impressively varied, both in form and substance. He has written many memorable poems in free verse, but he is also an accomplished writer of blank verse, sonnets, villanelles, and poems in other traditional forms. Often his poems are monologues by invented personae; these range from a washed-up stripper ("The Stripper") to an extraterrestrial spy ("Notes from the Agent on Earth: How to Be Human"). His wit shines in his many epigrams, and his speculative intelligence informs his many poems about science and religion.

His awards include the Prix de Rome for Literature, an Academy Award for Literature (both given by the American Academy of Arts and Letters), and the Poets' Prize. He has served as a Fulbright Professor at the National University of Mexico and as a fellow of the American Academy in Rome. In 1997 he read his poem "Of History and Hope" at the second inauguration of President Clinton.

WORKS: *A Circle of Stone* (1964). Ed., *Southern Writing in the Sixties: Fiction,* with J. W. Corrington (1966). Ed., *Southern Writing in the Sixties: Poetry,* with J. W. Corrington (1967). Trans., Nicanor Parra, *Poems and Antipoems* (1967). *So Long at the Fair* (1968). Trans. and ed., *Chile: An Anthology of New Writing* (1968). Ed., *The Achievement of John Ciardi: A Comprehensive Selection of His Poems* (1968). *The Only World There Is* (1971). *The Poetry of John Crowe Ransom* (1971). Trans., Nicanor Parra, *Emergency Poems* (1972). Ed., *Contemporary Poetry in America* (1973). *Halfway from Hoxie: New and Selected Poems* (1973). Ed., *How Does a Poem Mean?* with John Ciardi (rev. ed., 1975). Ed., *Railroad: Trains and Train People in American Culture,* with James Alan McPherson (1976). *Why God Permits Evil* (1977). Ed., *A Roman Collection: Stories, Poems, and Other Good Pieces by the Writing Residents of the American Academy in Rome* (1980). Trans., *Sonnets of Giuseppe Belli* (1981). *Distractions* (1981). Ed., *Ozark, Ozark: A Hillside Reader* (1981). *The Boys on Their Bony Mules* (1983). *Patterns of Poetry: An Encyclopedia of Forms* (1986). *Imperfect Love* (1986). *Living on the Surface: New and Selected Poems* (1989). *Adjusting to the Light* (1992). Ed., John Ciardi, *Stations of the Air* (1993). *Points of Departure* (1995). *The Ways We Touch* (1997). *Some Jazz a While: Collected Poems* (1999). *The Lives of Kelvin Fletcher: Stories Mostly Short* (2002).

—ROBERT M. WEST

SAMM-ART WILLIAMS (1946–). A prolific African American playwright, Samuel Arthur Williams was born in Burgaw, N.C. He knew from an early age that he wanted to be a writer, and the primary encouragement for this ambition came from his mother, Valdosia, who taught English and headed the drama department at C. F. Pope High School, which Williams attended. Under her guidance, he read widely in literature of all genres, including work by many African American writers. Bowing to his family's expectations and anticipating a career in law, he majored in political science at Morgan State College in Baltimore. But subsequent moves to Philadelphia and then New York nurtured and strengthened his writing aspirations, providing venues and connections such as Philadelphia's Freedom Theatre and New York's Playwrights Workshop, fostered by the Negro Ensemble Company, which would produce several of his plays

Williams's first play, *Welcome to Black River*, focuses on two families in 1950s North Carolina—one white, the other black—who are secretly related by blood, and are forced to examine and reconfigure their relationships. Other plays followed, many of them based in his own home territory. But it was his 1979 play *Home* that brought him national acclaim. It centers on a North Carolina farmer incarcerated for refusing to serve in Vietnam and the subsequent repercussions. *Home* earned numerous awards, including a John Gassner Playwriting Medallion, the Outer Critics Circle Award for Best Play, the North Carolina Governor's Award, the NAACP Image Award, and a Recognition Award from the Audience Development Committee (AUDELCO). The play was also nominated for a Tony Award and a Drama Desk Award.

Additional works by Williams include *Do Unto Others*, a story of deceit and revenge; *The Coming*, in which God appears as a character; *Brass Birds Don't Sing*, concerning the inability to escape one's past; *The Sixteenth Round* (originally titled *Pathetique* and incorporating Tchaikovsky's music); *Bojangles*, tracing the career of legendary dancer Bill "Bojangles" Robinson; *Cork*, a tribute to early-nineteenth-century black minstrels who opened doors for later African American actors; and *Eve of the Trial*, a dramatization of Anton Chekhov's short story "Orchards." Many of Williams's works are as yet either unpublished and/or unproduced, including *Kamilla*, *The Last Caravan* (a musical), *Something from Now*, *Break of Day Arising*, *Wee Three and Me*, *Panty Raid*, *Flowers of Winter*, and *Woman of the Town*.

In addition to his stage career, Williams has been active in film and television as a writer, actor, and producer, earning fellowships from the Guggenheim Foundation and the NEA, as well as two Emmy nominations. His television scripts include *John Henry*, *Badges*, *Lenny's Neighborhood*, *Solomon Northup's Odyssey*, and *With Ossie and Ruby*. Television shows for which he has written and/or produced include *Miami Vice*, *Cagney and Lacey*, *Martin*, and *The Fresh Prince of Bel-Air*. Besides his stage appearances, Williams's film and television acting credits include *Dressed to Kill*, *Blood Simple*, *Huckleberry Finn*, *The Women of Brewster Place*, and such soap operas as *Search for Tomorrow*.

WORKS: *Welcome to Black River* (1975). *The Coming* (1976). *Do Unto Others* (1976). *Eve of the Trial* (1976). *A Love Play* (1976). *Brass Birds Don't Sing* (1978). *The Frost of Renaissance* (1978). *Home* (1980). *The Sixteenth Round* (1980). *Friends* (1983). *Bojangles* (1985). *Eyes of the American* (1985). *Cork* (1986). *Eve of the Trial* (1986). *Woman from the Town* (1990). *The Dance on Widow's Row* (2000). *Conversations on a Dirt Road* (2002).

—KAREN C. BLANSFIELD

TENNESSEE WILLIAMS (1911–1983). Thomas Lanier Williams was born on March 26, 1911, to Cornelius Coffin Williams (1879–1957) and Edwina Dakin Williams (1884–1980) in Columbus, Miss., where the genteel Edwina resided with her parents while her husband pursued an itinerant salesman's career early in his ill-fated marriage. The Reverend Walter Dakin (1857–1955) and Rosina Otte Dakin (1863–1944) had come south from Ohio for his education at the University of the South and were living in Columbus in 1907 when their only child married the aggressive, masculine shoe salesman whose connections within the socially prominent Williams, Lanier, Coffin, and Sevier families of eastern Tennessee distantly included the poet Sidney Lanier. The couple's first child, Rose Isabel, was born in 1909, sixteen months before Tom.

Williams's southern childhood within the rectory households of his adored grandparents ended in 1918 when his father, promoted to the International Shoe Company's headquarters, moved the family to St. Louis, where a final child, Walter Dakin, was born the following year. As suggested by *The Glass Menagerie*, familial tensions proliferated, and Williams welcomed visits to the Dakins, a 1928

European tour with his grandfather, and escapes into the writing of fiction, drama, and poetry. After graduating from University City High School in 1929, Williams attended the University of Missouri and Washington University before earning a B.A. from the University of Iowa in 1938. The stresses of these years were numerous: emerging homoerotic desire; his parents' crumbling marriage; mutual acrimony between him and his father heightened by imposed employment at the shoe company in the early 1930s; and, perhaps most significantly, his sister's 1937 diagnosis of schizophrenia, her institutionalization, and her prefrontal lobotomy six years later. And yet Williams, influenced by Lawrence, Chekhov, Ibsen, Rilke, and Hart Crane, wrote steadily, published a number of stories and poems, and saw his full-length plays *Candles to the Sun* and *Fugitive Kind* through St. Louis productions.

When Williams left the city in 1938, he adopted the name Tennessee, shaved three years from his age, and acted with increasing fervency upon his homosexuality in a migratory existence that took him most frequently to New Orleans, Provincetown, Key West, New York, and Europe. With the assistance of noted agent Audrey Wood, who had been impressed by Williams's collection of one-act plays, *American Blues,* submitted to the Group Theatre, he was awarded a Rockefeller Foundation grant and worked briefly as a scriptwriter at Metro-Goldwyn-Mayer. Although both *Battle of Angels,* produced in Boston in 1940, and *You Touched Me!* a collaboration with Donald Windham, were unsuccessful, the "memory play" *The Glass Menagerie* triumphed both in Chicago in 1944 and in New York the following year, won the New York Drama Critics' Circle Award, and marked Williams as a major American playwright.

Over the next two decades, Williams was at the height of his career, producing plays that were critical, popular, and financial successes and often soon adapted into film. *A Streetcar Named Desire,* designated by many as Williams's masterpiece, garnered the Critics' Award and the Pulitzer Prize for drama, as did *Cat on a Hot Tin Roof; The Rose Tattoo* and *The Night of the Iguana* won a Tony and the Critics' Award respectively. Other major plays of this era included *Summer and Smoke* (revised as *The Eccentricities of a Nightingale*), *Camino Real, Orpheus Descending* (a revision of *Battle of Angels*), *Suddenly Last Summer,* and *Sweet Bird of Youth.* Most often set in the South and usually growing out of short fiction or one-act plays, these works typically explore the intricacies of desire and its restraints and, especially in the later plays, tend toward the violent and the grotesque. Critics have praised Williams's lyrical language in particular as well as his complex, sensitively drawn female characters, such as Laura Wingfield, Blanche DuBois, Alma Winemiller, Serefina delle Rose, Margaret Pollitt, and Catherine Holly.

Despite his focus on drama, Williams remained a steady writer of fiction throughout the 1950s, publishing short-story collections and the autobiographical novel *The Roman Spring of Mrs. Stone* as well as the collection of poems *In the Winter of Cities* and the script to the controversial film *Baby Doll.* His circle of literary friends was extensive and included Margo Jones, Carson McCullers, Donald Windham, Gore Vidal, and Christopher Isherwood. Williams also formed longtime companionships—even as he consistently embraced gay promiscuity—with first Pancho Rodriguez y Gonzalez and then Frank Merlo, whose death in 1963 devastated Williams on a level comparable to the deaths of his grandparents.

Throughout the rest of the 1960s and the 1970s Williams grew increasingly dependent on drugs—amphetamines and barbiturates—and alcohol, struggled with depression and hypochondria, and moved frenetically with the assistance of paid companions. His artistic production suffered, and he faced accusations of self-plagiarism, especially as he continued compulsively to write, rewrite, and retitle at all stages of production. Negotiating his institutionalization for drug addiction in 1969 and his break with longtime agent Audrey Wood in 1971, he turned in his writing to the intimacies of his own life, laying them bare in the largely unsuccessful late plays *The Two-Character Play, Out Cry, Small Craft Warnings, The Red Devil Battery Sign, Vieux Carré, A House Not Meant to Stand,* and *Something Cloudy, Something Clear.* The same impulse seems to have propelled his autobiography *Memoirs,* his second novel *Moise and the World of Reason,* and his last collection of poems *Androgyne, Mon Amour.* Other late works include *A Lovely Sunday for Creve Coeur, Clothes for a Summer Hotel,* and *The Notebook of Trigorin,* an adaptation of Chekhov's *The Sea Gull* first produced in 1981. Williams was found dead on February 25, 1983, in a New York hotel, the Elysée, apparently having asphyxiated after swallowing the plastic cap of a medicine bottle. He was buried next to his mother in Calvary Cemetery in St. Louis.

WORKS: *Five Young American Poets* (third series) (1944). *Battle of Angels* (1945). *The Glass Menagerie* (1945). *Twenty-seven Wagons Full of Cotton and Other One-Act Plays* (1946). *You Touched Me!* with Donald Windham (1947). *A Streetcar Named Desire* (1947). *One Arm and Other Stories* (1948). *American Blues: Five Short Plays* (1948). *Summer and Smoke* (1948). *The Roman Spring of Mrs. Stone* (1950). *The Rose Tattoo* (1951). *I Rise in Flame, Cried the Phoenix* (1951). *Camino Real* (1953). *Hard Candy: A Book of Stories* (1954). *Cat on a Hot Tin Roof* (1955). *In the Winter of Cities: Poems* (1956). *Baby Doll* (1956). *Orpheus Descending* [with *Battle of Angels*] (1958). *Suddenly Last Summer* (1958). *Garden District* (1959). *Sweet Bird of Youth* (1959). *Period of Adjustment* (1960). *Three Players of a Summer Game and Other Stories* (1960). *The Night of the Iguana* (1962). *The Milk Train Doesn't Stop Here Anymore* (1964). *Grand* (1964). *The Eccentricities of a Nightingale* (with *Summer and Smoke,* 1964). *The Knightly Quest: A Novella and Four Short Stories* (1966; rev. 1968). *The Gnädiges Fräulein* (1967). *The Mutilated* (1967). *Kingdom of Earth (The Seven Descents of Myrtle)* (1968; rev. 1969). *The Two-Character Play* (1969; rev. 1979). *In the Bar of a Tokyo Hotel* (1969). *Dragon Country: A Book of Plays* (1970). *The Theatre of Tennessee Williams,* 8 vols. (1971–92). *Small Craft Warnings* (1972). *Out Cry* (1973). *Eight Mortal Ladies Possessed: A Book of Stories* (1974). *Moise and the World of Reason* (1975). *Memoirs* (1975). *Tennessee Williams' Letters to Donald Windham, 1940–1965,* ed. Donald Windham (1977). *Androgyne, Mon Amour: Poems* (1977). *Where I Live: Selected Essays,* ed. Christine R. Day and Bob Woods (1978). *Vieux Carré* (1979). *A Lovely Sunday for Creve Coeur* (1980). *Collected Later Poems* (1982). *Clothes for a Summer Hotel: A Ghost Play* (1983). *Stopped Rocking and Other Screenplays* (1984). *Collected Stories* (1985). *Conversations with Tennessee Williams,* ed. Albert J. Devlin (1986). *The Red Devil Battery Sign* (1988). *Five O'Clock Angel: Letters of Tennessee Williams to Maria St. Just, 1948–1982* (1990). *Baby Doll and Tiger Tail: A Screenplay and a Play* (1991). *Something Cloudy, Something Clear* (1995). *The Notebook of Trigorin* (1997). *Not about Nightingales* (1998). *Spring Storm* (1999). *Stairs to the Roof: A Prayer for the Wild of Heart That Are Kept in Cages* (2000). *Tennessee Williams (Volume I: Plays 1937–1955)* and *Tennessee Williams (Volume II: 1957–1980),* ed. Mel Gussow and Kenneth Holditch (2000). *The Selected Letters of Tennessee Williams (Volume 1: 1920–1945),* ed. Albert J. Devlin and Nancy M. Tischler (2000). *Fugitive Kind* (2001). *The Collected Poems of Tennessee Williams,* ed. David E. Roessel (2002).

—GARY RICHARDS

CALDER WILLINGHAM (1922–1995). Calder Baynard Willingham, Jr., was born on December 23, 1922, in Atlanta, Ga., to Calder Baynard Willingham (a hotel manager) and Eleanor Churchill Willcox. Willingham was educated at the Darlington Preparatory School (1936–40), the Citadel (1940–41), and the University of Virginia (1941–43). He married Helene Rothenberg in 1945, and they had one son, Paul Thomas, before the marriage ended. Willingham married Jane Marie Bennett on September 15, 1953, and they had three sons (Fredrick Calder, Mark Osgood, and Christopher) and two daughters (Sara Jane and Pamela). Calder Willingham, Jr., died as a result of lung cancer on February 19, 1995, in Laconia, N.H.

Willingham's first novel, *End as a Man,* written when he was twenty-three years old, is a satire of life in a southern military school. It created controversy, a lawsuit, and a publicized trial against the publisher. *End as a Man* served as the basis for a Broadway play of the same title in 1953 and the film *The Strange One* in 1957. Between 1947 and 1977 Willingham published a total of eleven literary works, the last of which was *The Building of Venus Four.* Willingham is also known for his screenplays, including *Paths of Glory* (1957), which was nominated for a Writers Guild Award; *One-Eyed Jacks* (1961); *The Graduate* (1967), which was nominated for an Academy Award and received a Writers Guild Award and a British Film Academy Award; and *Little Big Man* (1970). Willingham's novels are typically set in the South or deal with southern issues. With the exception of his film *The Graduate,* it is these novels for which Willingham is most remembered.

WORKS: *End as a Man* (1947). *Geraldine Bradshaw* (1950). *Reach to the Stars* (1951). *The Gates of Hell* (1951). *Natural Child* (1952). *To Eat a Peach* (1955). *Eternal Fire* (1963). *Providence Island* (1969). *Rambling Rose* (1972). *The Big Nickel* (1975). *The Building of Venus Four* (1977).

—M. KEVIN QUINN

AUGUSTA JANE EVANS WILSON (1835–1909). Augusta Jane Evans Wilson was one of the most talented domestic sentimental novelists of the nineteenth century, combining idealized characterizations and religious didacticism with philosophical and aesthetic speculation. Born on May 8, 1835, in Columbus, Ga., Augusta endured a childhood marred by her father's financial difficulties. In 1845, after Matthew Evans declared bankruptcy, the family traveled by covered wagon to Texas. Concerned about tense relations with the Mexicans and about Comanche raids, the family returned east in 1849, settling in Mobile, Ala. There Augusta began writing fiction in hopes of alleviating her family's financial woes. On Christmas Day, 1854, she presented her father with a manuscript entitled *Inez: A Tale of the Alamo,* which Harper published the following year.

During her early twenties Evans struggled to reconcile scientific reason with her Christian faith, a struggle reflected in the highly autobiographical *Beulah.* Her second novel brought Evans to the attention of the Yankee editor James Reed Spaulding, whose marriage proposal she accepted in 1860. Once she recognized their irreconcilable differences concerning the southern cause, however, she broke the engagement. During the Civil War, Evans advised southern politicians and military leaders, published articles supporting the Confederacy, served as a volunteer nurse, and published *Macaria; or, Altars of Sacrifice,* which celebrated the southern victories at Bull Run and Manassas.

The pinnacle of Evans's career was the 1866 publication of the phenomenally successful *St. Elmo,* a story of an orphan who becomes a writer and redeemer of a Byronic hero. In 1868 Evans married Colonel Lorenzo Madison Wilson. Together they turned the colonel's estate of Ashland into a showplace renowned for its gardens. After her husband's death in 1891, Wilson resided with her brother Howard in Mobile until his death in 1908. Never fully recovering from her grief, she died of a heart attack on May 9, 1909.

WORKS: *Inez: A Tale of the Alamo* (1855). *Beulah* (1859). *Macaria; or, Altars of Sacrifice* (Confederate edition, 1863; northern edition, 1864). *St. Elmo* (1866). *Vashti; or, Until Death Us Do Part* (1869). *Infelice* (1875). *At the Mercy of Tiberius* (1887). *A Speckled Bird* (1902). *Devota* (1907).

—LYNNE P. SHACKELFORD

E. O. WILSON (1929–). Edward Osborne Wilson, Jr., was born in Birmingham, Ala., on June 10, 1929. After his parents' early divorce, his time was unevenly divided among the homes of several people, including his mother, Inez, and more often his father, an accountant whose alcoholic decline ended in suicide. This itinerant life in diverse southern settings from Florida to Washington, D.C., served to establish the younger Wilson's interest in the natural world, which was a steady companion for an only child. Partial deafness and an injury to his right eye (the result of an encounter with a needlefish) made close observation a preferred mode of inquiry and ants a favorite subject for study.

Wilson attended a number of schools and graduated from Decatur (Ala.) High School. He received a B.S. (1949) and an M.S. (1950) in biology from the University of Alabama. After a stint in the University of Tennessee's graduate school, he earned a Ph.D. (1955) from Harvard University, where he joined the faculty as an assistant professor and rose in the academic ranks, though often at odds with colleagues who championed work at the molecular level rather than research on whole organisms. Wilson explores these events in his autobiography, *Naturalist*.

Unusual among modern scientists, who largely confine themselves to workmanlike descriptions of research findings for their peers, Wilson is known for the breadth and grace of his writing, which crosses disciplines and addresses nonscientific as well as scientific audiences. Two of Wilson's books have won Pulitzer Prizes for general nonfiction: *On Human Nature* and *The Ants*. Several other books—*The Insect Societies*, *Sociobiology: The New Synthesis*, and *The Diversity of Life*—have been finalists for the National Book Award. *The Ants*, an overview of ant biology written in collaboration with Bert Hölldobler, was quickly dubbed "the myrmecologist's Bible." In contrast, harsh criticism and even physical attack followed publication of *Sociobiology*, a book that—like *The Insect Societies* and *On Human Nature*—raised questions about nature's role in preconditioning social behaviors, including among humans. There were charges of prejudice, and in 1978 one protester went so far as to empty a water pitcher over Wilson's head during the Washington, D.C., meeting of the American Association for the Advancement of Science. Despite this rancor, Wilson effectively established sociobiology as a reputable field of study, and he was not dissuaded from continuing to play a public role. He now lends himself to environmental causes, seeking to conserve natural resources while meeting human needs.

Among Wilson's many honors are the National Medal for Science, presented by President Carter (1976), and the Royal Swedish Academy of Science's Crafoord Prize, which recognizes fields not included in the Nobel Prizes (1990). Wilson lives with his wife, Renee, in Lexington, Mass. They have a daughter, Catherine.

WORKS: *The Theory of Island Biogeography*, with Robert H. MacArthur (1967). *Ants of Polynesia (Hymenoptera, Formicidae)*, with Robert W. Taylor (1967). *A Primer of Population Biology*, with William H. Bossert (1971). *The Insect Societies* (1971). *Life on Earth*, with Thomas Eisner, Winslow R. Briggs, and others (1973). Ed., *Scientific American Readings: Ecology, Evolution, and Population Biology* (1974). *Sociobiology: The New Synthesis* (1975). Ed., *Animal Behavior: Readings from Scientific American*, with Eisner (1975). Ed., *The Insects*, with Eisner (1977). *Life: Cells, Organisms, Populations*, with Briggs and Eisner (1977). Ed., *Insects : Readings from Scientific American*, with Eisner (1977). *On Human Nature* (1978). *Caste and Ecology in the Social Insects*, with George F. Oster (1978). *Genes, Mind, and Culture*, with Charles J. Lumsden (1981). *Promethean Fire: Reflections on the Origin of Mind*, with Lumsden (1983). *Biophilia* (1984). Ed., *Biodiversity* (1988). *The Ants*, with Bert Hölldobler (1990). *Success and Dominance in Ecosystems: The Case of the Social Insects* (1990). *The Diversity of Life* (1992). Ed., *The Biophilia Hypothesis*, with Stephen R. Kellert (1993). *Journey to the Ants: A Story of Scientific Exploration*, with Hölldobler (1994). Ed., *Biodiversity II: Understanding and Protecting Our Natural Resources*, with Marjorie L. Reaka-Kudla and Don E. Wilson (1996). *In Search of Nature* (1996). *Consilience: The Unity of Knowledge* (1998). *Biological Diversity: The Oldest Human Heritage* (1999). *The Future of Life* (2002). *Pheidole in the New World : A Dominant, Hyperdiverse Ant Genus* (2003). *Genes, Mind, and Culture: The Coevolutionary Process*, with Lumsden (2005). Ed., *From So Simple a Beginning: Darwin's Four Great Books* (2005). *Nature Revealed: Selected Writings, 1949–2006* (2006).

—AMBER VOGEL

WILLIAM WIRT (1772–1834). Author, attorney, and orator William Wirt embodies the timbre of the early Republic: sentimental and Romantic, yet rational and didactic.

Born on November 8, 1772, in Bladensburg, Md., Wirt was the youngest child of a Swiss immigrant. Orphaned at eight and reared by family, he later studied law, joining the bar in Culpepper, Va., in 1792.

He was married twice: first to Mildred Gilmer, from 1795 until her death in 1799, and then to Elizabeth Gamble, the daughter of a wealthy Richmond merchant, in 1802. He died on February 18, 1834.

Wirt was widely known as a lawyer and a politician. He practiced law in Williamsburg, Norfolk, and Richmond. He was celebrated for his 1800 defense of James Callender against libel charges stemming from the Alien and Sedition Acts and through his 1807 role in the prosecution of Aaron Burr. As a politician, he served as a legislative clerk from 1799 to 1802 and as a lawmaker in the Virginia legislature from 1808 to 1809. Though he declined Thomas Jefferson's call to run for Congress, he accepted President James Madison's 1817 offer to serve as attorney general, a post he held until 1829. In 1832, as the nominee of the Anti-Mason Party, he unsuccessfully opposed incumbent President Andrew Jackson.

Wirt's significance to literary studies lies in his eminence as a familiar essayist in the tradition of Montesquieu and Addison. His *The Letters of the British Spy* and *The Old Bachelor*—collections of essays (some of which were written by Dabney Carr and St. George Tucker, among others) that address society, politics, and oratory—encapsulate his hope that future generations will match their forebears' greatness. But he is perhaps best remembered for his 1817 biography of Patrick Henry, in which he reconstructed for posterity the patriot's "Give me liberty, or give me death!" speech.

WORKS: *An Oration Delivered in Richmond on the Fourth Day of July 1800; the Anniversary of American Independence* (1800). *The Letters of the British Spy,* with others (1803). *The Rainbow, First Series,* with others (1804). *The Two Principal Arguments of William Wirt, esquire, on the Trial of Aaron Burr, for High Treason, and on the Motion to Commit Aaron Burr and Others, for Trial in Kentucky* (1808). *The Sylph* (1810). *The Old Bachelor,* with others (1814). *Sketches of the Life and Character of Patrick Henry* (1817). *A Discourse on the Lives and Characters of Thomas Jefferson and John Adams, Who Both Died on the Fourth of July, 1826. Delivered, at the Request of the Citizens of Washington, in the Hall of Representatives of the United States, on the Nineteenth October, 1826* (1826). *An Address Delivered Before the Peithessophian and Philoclean Societies of Rutgers College . . .* (1830). *Argument Delivered at Annapolis . . .* (1830). *Opinion on the Right of the State of Georgia to Extend Her Laws Over the Cherokee Nation* (1830).

—SCOTT HICKS

THOMAS WOLFE (1900–1938). Thomas Clayton Wolfe was born on October 3, 1900. He had too powerful a father to claim outright or fully the southern Appalachia heritage of his mother's family, the Westalls, who came from mountainous and back-woodsy Yancey County to establish households and businesses in Asheville. William Oliver Wolfe (the W. O. Gant of Wolfe's fiction) was a stonecutter from near Gettysburg, Pa. His marriage to Julia Elizabeth Westall brought together two strong-willed people, for Julia Westall (the Eliza of Wolfe's writings on the Gant family) wanted to make her mark in Asheville. Her Presbyterian allegiances often clashed with the generosity and alcoholic excesses of her husband, but they were both keenly aware of bettering their economic status through shrewd land deals, although Thomas Wolfe casts Eliza as the one with an obsessive desire to buy and sell real estate.

A former teacher herself, Julia appreciated the value of a good education and joined with her husband to send Wolfe to a newly formed preparatory school, the North State Fitting School, a project of John and Margaret Roberts. Wolfe flourished under their instruction, winning honors, developing a deep love of poetry, and forming a special bond with Mrs. Roberts, whom he would later call "the mother of his spirit." When Wolfe was to go off to college, his father declared that Wolfe would not have his expenses paid unless he attended the University of North Carolina. Reluctant to go there, Wolfe eventually prospered in both his studies and extracurricular activities. He began to write poems, plays, and articles for the *Daily Tar Heel,* the student newspaper, and took first place for an essay entitled "The Crisis in Industry" (1919). In Chapel Hill also he was drawn to the philosophical ideas of Horace Williams, who advocated a hybrid line of Hegelian thought.

His taste of dramatic writing under the tutelage of Frederick Koch whetted Wolfe's appetite for further training and led to his enrollment in George Pierce Baker's celebrated workshop in drama at Harvard University. The most promising of the several plays written there was *Welcome to Our City*. Wolfe's unwillingness to trim it led to its rejection by New York City producers and his acceptance of a teaching position at the Washington Square campus of New York University, where from 1924 until 1930 he taught intermittently. With income from his salary and the financial backing of his mother, in 1930 Wolfe made the first of seven trips to Europe.

On the return leg of his first trip, he met Aline Bernstein, a successful stage and costume designer some nineteen years his senior. They became lovers, and it was she (the Esther Jack of Wolfe's posthumous novels) who helped Wolfe understand that his talents were more novelistic than dramatic. The harvest was the manuscript of *Oh Lost*, which Maxwell Perkins trimmed to become *Look Homeward, Angel*, published by Scribner's on October 18, 1929. (The publication of Wolfe's first novel as submitted to Scribner's and published by the University of South Carolina Press in 2000 adds a challenge to critics assessing Wolfe's achievement.) Largely well received elsewhere, *Look Homeward, Angel* raised outcries against it and threats to Wolfe from outraged Ashevillians.

Wanting to prove himself capable of writing works not so overtly autobiographical as *Look Homeward, Angel*, Wolfe turned to different material, but eventually came back to the Gant family and followed the journey of Eugene Gant from North Carolina to Harvard, Europe, and New York, the result of which was *Of Time and the River*, published in 1935 after Perkins wrested the lengthy manuscript from its reluctant author. Wolfe had leaned heavily on Perkins as he melded the materials on the Gants written following the publication of his first novel. His account of that collaborative effort, published in 1936 as *The Story of a Novel*, opened Wolfe and Scribner's to a searing attack by Bernard DeVoto and became a factor in Wolfe's decision to leave Scribner's and sign with Harper. The break with Perkins was emotionally traumatic but creatively necessary, Wolfe finally concluded.

Determined to be more honestly autobiographical, socially conscious, and bitingly satiric henceforward, Wolfe turned to reexamine his experience, creating a new surrogate, eventually named George "Monk" Webber. The work he left behind with his new editor, Edward Aswell, when Wolfe began his fateful journey to the American Northwest was in progress and had to be assembled and "creatively edited," to use the late Richard Kennedy's accurate description, before being published as *The Web and the Rock, You Can't Go Home Again*, and *The Hills Beyond*.

Wolfe's final journey carried him through a swift-paced visit to western national parks, to Seattle, to Vancouver, British Columbia, and finally to Baltimore, where he died on September 15, 1938, at Johns Hopkins Hospital, the victim of tubercular meningitis. His body was interred in the family plot in Asheville's Riverside Cemetery.

WORKS: *The Return of Buck Gavin: The Tragedy of a Mountain Outlaw* (1924). *Look Homeward, Angel* (1929). *Of Time and the River* (1935). *From Death to Morning* (1935). *The Story of a Novel* (1936). *A Note on Experts: Dexter Vespasian Joyner* (1939). *The Face of a Nation: Poetic Passages from the Writing of Thomas Wolfe* (1939). *The Web and the Rock* (1939). *You Can't Go Home Again* (1940). *The Hills Beyond* (1941). *Gentlemen of the Press* (1942). *Thomas Wolfe's Letters to His Mother, Julia Elizabeth Wolfe* (1943). *Mannerhouse* (1948, 1985). *The Years of Wandering in Many Lands and Cities* (1949). *A Western Journal: A Daily Log of the Great Parks Trip, June 20–July 2, 1938* (1951). *The Correspondence of Thomas Wolfe and Homer Andrew Watt* (1954). *The Letters of Thomas Wolfe* (1956). *The Short Novels of Thomas Wolfe* (1961). *The Thomas Wolfe Reader* (1962). *Thomas Wolfe's Purdue Speech: "Writing and Living"* (1964). *The Mountains: A Play in One Act. The Mountains: A Drama in Three Acts and a Prologue* (1970). *The Notebooks of Thomas Wolfe* (1970). *A Prologue to America* (1978). *Welcome to Our City* (1983). *K-19: Salvaged Pieces* (1983). *Beyond Love and Loyalty: The Letters of Thomas Wolfe And Elizabeth Nowell* (1983). *My Other Loneliness: Letters of Thomas Wolfe and Aline Bernstein* (1983). *The Train and the City* (1984): *Holding on for Heaven: The Cables and Postcards of Thomas Wolfe and Aline Bernstein* (1985). *The Hound of Heaven* (1986). *The Complete Stories of Thomas Wolfe* (1987). *The Starwick Episodes* (1989). *Thomas Wolfe's Composition Books: The North State Fitting School, 1912–1915* (1990). *The Autobiographical Outline for "Look Homeward, Angel" by Thomas Wolfe* (1991). *The Good Child's River* (1991). *The Lost Boy: A Novella* (1992). *Thomas Wolfe's Notes on Macbeth* (1992). *[George Webber, Writer]: An Introduction by a Friend* (1994). *The Party at Jack's* (1995). *Antaeus; or, A Memory of Earth* (1996). *Passage to England: A Selection* (1998). *O Lost: A Story of the Buried Life* (2000). *To Loot My Life Clean: The Thomas Wolfe–Maxwell Perkins Correspondence* (2000). *The Medical Students* (2000).

—JOHN L. IDOL, JR.

TOM WOLFE (1931–). Tom Wolfe initially earned his reputation as a leading figure in "New Journalism"—a creative form of nonfiction that uses fictional techniques such as stream-of-consciousness narration, extended dialogue, and shifting points of view. Wolfe regales his audience with humorous and incisive analysis of popular culture, treating subjects ranging from drug and hippie culture to art and architecture. His novels treat issues of greed and materialism that he derides in his nonfiction.

Thomas Kennerly Wolfe, Jr., was born in Richmond, Va., on March 2, 1931. He went to a prestigious high school in Richmond and attended Washington and Lee University in Lexington, Va., where he co-founded the literary journal *Shenandoah* and in 1951 received a B.A. in English. Wolfe, a pitcher, played semiprofessional baseball and tried out for the New York Giants, who cut him during spring training in 1952. Once the desired baseball career became out of the question, Wolfe pursued a doctorate in American Studies at Yale University, completing it in 1957. For approximately ten years Wolfe worked at newspapers, including the *Springfield (Mass.) Union* and the *Washington Post.* As the *Post's* Latin American correspondent, he received the Newspaper Guild's award for foreign reporting in 1961. In the 1960s he became a frequent contributor to periodicals, including the *New York Herald Tribune's* Sunday magazine and *Esquire,* where his style of New Journalism emerged. Wolfe himself assumed the persona of the iconoclastic dandy, his white suit emblazing the role.

Wolfe's first published collection of essays, *The Kandy-Kolored Tangerine-Flake Streamlined Baby,* was followed by other nonfiction on a range of topics, including radical chic and the early days of the American space program. In essays, Wolfe has antagonized leading fiction writers by claiming that they have neglected their responsibility to write socially realistic works. As a result, his own novels, beginning with *The Bonfire of the Vanities,* came under considerable scrutiny by critics and reviewers, and by the fiction writers he disparages. *A Man in Full* also had to live up to the pre-publication publicity of a National Book Award nomination. Although it did not win the award, it debuted at the top of the *New York Times* best-seller list. *I Am Charlotte Summers* satirizes the mores of the twenty-first century college experience.

Most of *A Man in Full* takes place in Atlanta, but the majority of Wolfe's writing has not been about the South or set there, and some may consider his status as southern writer suspect. Although the fictional Ivy League university of *I Am Charlotte Summers* is in Pennsylvania, Charlotte Summers was shaped by a small mountain town in North Carolina. Wolfe and his works will continue to be worthy of study because of their ability to reflect issues and concerns of postmodern society rather than any one region's concerns.

WORKS: *The Kandy-Kolored Tangerine-Flake Streamline Baby* (1965). *The Electric Kool-Aid Acid Test* (1968). *The Pump House Gang* (1968). *Radical Chic & Mau-Mauing the Flak Catchers* (1970). Ed., *The New Journalism* (1973). *The Painted Word* (1975). *Mauve Gloves & Madmen, Clutter & Vine, and Other Short Stores* (1976). *The Right Stuff*

(1979). *In Our Time* (1980). *From Bauhaus to Our House* (1981). *The Purple Decades: A Reader* (1982). *The Bonfire of the Vanities* (1987). *A Man in Full* (1998). *Hooking Up* (2000). *I Am Charlotte Summers* (2004).

—Susie Scifres Kuilan

CHARLES WOODMASON (ca. 1720–ca. 1776). As a genteel landowner in pre-Revolutionary South Carolina, Charles Woodmason wrote verse letters in heroic couplets to *The Gentleman's Magazine* back in England. A little more than a decade later he was a missionary Anglican minister in the primitive South Carolina backcountry, recording in a personal journal and in written sermons his sometimes-sardonic observations on the conditions of frontier life. In the midst of this backcountry experience, Woodmason also wrote a "Remonstrance" to the South Carolina Assembly on behalf of the Regulators, vigilantes trying to awaken genteel Charlestonians to the frontier's need for a concerned, responsive government. Overall, Woodmason left a record that in its sophistication, candor, and moral conviction (or bias) reveals a good deal about the eighteenth-century English upper-class sensibility and the conditions of colonial America.

Woodmason was born in England around 1720. An Anglican and a gentleman, familiar with the culture of London, he first sailed to South Carolina in 1752, leaving behind a wife and son. He became a plantation owner and merchant in Prince Frederick Parish, around the Peedee River, and was elected or appointed to a number of local offices, from Anglican vestryman to justice of the peace, over the next decade. His verse letters reveal a classical education, an awareness of contemporary English literary conventions, and some knowledge of the people, topography, flora, and fauna of his new home. After a brief trip to England in 1762, Woodmason returned to South Carolina as a denizen of Charleston, no longer a planter. He held a number of important civic offices, until in 1765 he sought the job of stamp distributor under the new Stamp Act and thereby walked unawares into a beehive of local hostility.

This negative experience may have influenced Woodmason's decision to become an itinerant Anglican minister to St. Mark's Parish, out in the South Carolina backcountry north and west of Camden. He traveled around three thousand miles a year on horseback and recorded in his journal and sermons his sense of the prevalence of sexual promiscuity, lawlessness, illiteracy, and general brutishness among the population. The New Light Baptists and Scotch-Irish Presbyterians, among other increasingly numerous dissenting sects, seemed to him actually to encourage frontier immorality as well as an irrational, irreverent "enthusiasm." Yet Woodmason at times found himself at least equally at odds with the South Carolina upper classes. His politically effective "Remonstrance" of 1767 expresses articulate, irony-laced outrage at the condescending indifference of the Charleston legislators and clergy, who seemed to conspire to hold the frontiersmen in their barbaric state.

Woodmason's deteriorating health and loyalist sympathies both played a role in his leaving the colonies in 1774. The last record of his life is of a sermon he preached near Bristol, England, in 1776.

WORKS: "Horace, Ode iv, Book I, Imitated," *The Gentleman's Magazine* 23 (May 1953): 240–41. "C. W. in Carolina to E. J. at Gosport," *The Gentleman's Magazine* 23 (July 1753): 337–38. "To Benjamin Franklin, Esq.; of Philadelphia, on His Experiments and Discoveries," *The Gentleman's Magazine* 24 (Feb. 1754): 88. "Horace, Ode iii, Book I, Imitated," *The Gentleman's Magazine* 24 (Aug. 1754): 381. *A Letter from a Gentleman of South-Carolina on the Cultivation of Indico* (1754). "The Art of Manufacturing Indigo in Carolina," *The Gentleman's Magazine* 25 (May and June 1755): 201–3, 256–59. "A Political Problem," *South Carolina Gazette and Country-Journal*, Mar. 28, 1769. The journal, sermons, some letters, and the "Remonstrance" and other political writings are in *The Carolina Backcountry on the Eve of Revolution: The Journal and Other Writings of Charles Woodmason, Anglican Itinerant*, ed. Richard J. Hooker (1953).

—Whit Jones

C. VANN WOODWARD (1908–1999). Sheldon Hackney, another esteemed southern-born historian, once described C. Vann Woodward as "the most admired historian of my time." Comer Vann Woodward was born on November 13, 1908, in Vanndale, Ark. His mother, the former Bessie Vann, was a descendant of the slave owners who founded the town. His father worked in the public school system and became the president of a small college in Georgia. "The Faulknerian repertoire was all represented," Woodward recalled of his hometown. When he was aged ten the family moved to Morrilton, Ark. There he witnessed a Ku Klux Klan rally at a Methodist church that concluded with the Klansmen offering a gratuity to a cooperative minister—an experience that he would long remember.

In good southern fashion, Woodward played high school football to win popularity, a stratagem that apparently worked, though he confessed not to care for it. He set off for two years at Henderson Brown College. Happily for the study of history, he failed chemistry and changed course. He transferred to Emory, where he took one history class and found it dreadfully boring, and received his B.A. in philosophy in 1930. During this time he started teaching freshman composition at Georgia Tech and began rubbing elbows with John Hope Franklin, Jay Saunders Redding, and other black intellectuals at crosstown Atlanta University. A very brief enrollment at Columbia did not take, but his time in New York introduced him to Langston Hughes and other eminent figures of the Harlem Renaissance. Like many of his generation, he went on a *wanderjahr* in Europe. Upon his return he became involved in raising funds for the defense of Angelo Herndon, a black communist in a highly publicized case. He was soon asked to leave Tech because of "budget cuts." Stinging with hard-earned wisdom, Woodward sought fresh knowledge and decamped for Chapel Hill, where he completed his Ph.D. in 1937.

Woodward wrote about the real-life Willie Stark in *Tom Watson, Agrarian Rebel,* which deflated a number of misconceptions about the South, setting the tone for his life's work. He taught briefly at the University of Virginia and the University of Florida before writing *The Battle for Leyte Gulf,* an excursion based on his wartime experiences as a lieutenant in the navy. He then settled in to teach at Johns Hopkins from 1947 until 1961. *Origins of the New South, 1877–1913* proved so seminal that southern historiography arguably has expanded—not amended—his basic outline. But it was his next book, *The Strange Career of Jim Crow,* for which he is most often remembered. The book was required reading for any self-respecting civil rights activist. It was groundbreaking in its approach, as it dispelled the popular notion that segregation in the South had been both de facto and de jure since its inception. Woodward might have heard Martin Luther King, Jr., quote his book from the steps of the Alabama Capitol during the 1965 Selma march. King called *The Strange Career* "the historical Bible of the civil rights movement." And a young lawyer named Thurgood Marshall referred to Woodward's book liberally in honing the arguments of *Brown v. Board of Education.* In similar fashion, Woodward gave South-watchers an enduring touchstone in his widely quoted *The Burden of Southern History.*

In 1961 Woodward became Sterling Professor of History at Yale, where he remained until his retirement in 1977. He continued writing, and thus brought to light the complicated loyalties of a southern lady who endured the Civil War in *Mary Chesnut's Civil War,* for which he won the Pulitzer Prize in 1982.

Woodward's life spans a breathtaking expanse of the twentieth century; he is one of those who seems to have been on the ground floor at every major moment. He canvassed for the Works Progress Administration. He witnessed the intellectual foment of the Harlem Renaissance and modernism. He catalyzed the late phase of the Southern Renascence, when he sometimes served as foil to the Fugitives, and became the philosopher king for a generation of scholars. Many of his students became leading historians. He served in World War II. He weathered McCarthyism and participated in the civil rights movement. He was empanelled to help prepare a study to be used during Nixon's impeachment, and he lived to comment on the move to impeach Clinton. He received every accolade that a principal historian could wish for: Guggenheim Fellowships twice (1946–47, 1960–61), the Bancroft Prize (1952), the Pulitzer and the American Book Award (1982), and enough honorary degrees to wallpaper an office.

Woodward died at his home in Hamden, Conn., on December 17, 1999. Though he lived his life as a self-described southern "exile," Woodward was a maverick who knew how to differentiate between the sinner and the sin. He never trucked with segregation or segregationists, but he loved the region whose conformist "savage ideal" (in the words of Wilbur Cash) he had violated. He adored southern literature and viewed it as peopled with the lessons of history—fitting for a lifelong friend of "Red" (Robert Penn) Warren. He understood that history was indeed stories, and because he could not stand dull ones, he did not write them.

WORKS: *Tom Watson, Agrarian Rebel* (1938). *The Battle for Leyte Gulf* (1947). *Origins of the New South, 1877–1913* (1951). *Reunion and Reaction: The Compromise of 1877 and the End of Reconstruction* (1951). *The Strange Career of Jim Crow* (1955). *The Burden of Southern History* (1960). *The Age of Interpretation* (1961). Ed., *The Comparative Approach to American History* (1968). *American Counterpoint: Slavery and Racism in the North-South Dialogue* (1971). Ed., *Mary Chesnut's Civil War* (1981). Ed., *The Oxford History of the United States* (1982–99). Ed., *The Private Mary Chesnut: The Unpublished Civil War Diaries,* with Elisabeth Muhlenfeld (1984). *Thinking Back: The Perils of Writing History* (1986). *The Future of the Past* (1989). *The Old World's New World* (1991).

—BRYAN GIEMZA

C. D. WRIGHT (1949–). C. D. Wright was born Carolyn Wright in Mountain Home, Ark., on January 6, 1949, and grew up in the Ozark Mountains, living there until she was seventeen. She took the name C. D. to distinguish herself from the poet Carolyne Wright. She moved across the South and into New England while attending colleges and working, settling in to study French at Memphis State University (B.A., 1971), then returning in 1972 to Arkansas to study creative writing at the University of Arkansas (M.F.A., 1976), where she and poet Frank Stanford developed an intimate relationship.

After her graduate studies, she worked for the office of Arkansas Arts and Humanities. After Stanford's suicide in 1978, Wright moved to San Francisco and worked at Intersection Center for the Arts and the Poetry Center at San Francisco State University. A National Endowment for the Arts grant in 1981 allowed her to move to Dolores Hidalgo, Mexico.

Since 1983 Wright has taught at Brown University in Rhode Island, where she has directed the graduate creative writing program (1989–92 and 1998–2001) and where, in 2001, she was named the Israel J. Kapstein Professor of English. She has also taught as a visiting faculty member at Burren School of Art in County Clare, Ireland (1996) and the Iowa Writers' Workshop at the University of Iowa (1996–97). With her husband, the poet Forest Gander, she edits Lost Roads Publishers. They have one son, Brecht.

Wright has received grants from the National Endowment for the Arts (1981–82 and 1988) and the Guggenheim Foundation (1987), the Witter Bynner Prize for Poetry from the American Academy and Institute of Arts and Letters (1986), a General Electric Foundation Award for Younger Writers for the literary essay (1988), a Whiting Foundation Award (1989), a Lila Wallace–Reader's Digest Writers' Award (1992), the Poetry Center Book Award from San Francisco State University (1992, for *String Light*), a Lannan Foundation Literary Award (1999), and the Dorothea Lange–Paul Taylor Prize, with photographer Deborah Luster, from the Center for Documentary Studies at Duke University (2001, for *One Big Self: Prisoners of Louisiana*).

Wright has served as the state poet of Rhode Island (1994–99). Nevertheless, her roots in the Ozarks find their way into her poetry—a poetry that often combines the autobiographical and the political activism of her generation.

WORKS: *Alla Breve Loving* (1976). *Room Rented by a Single Woman* (1977). *Terrorism* (1979). *Translations of the Gospel Back into Tongues* (1982). *Further Adventures with You* (1986). *String Light* (1991). *Just Whistle* (1993). *The Reader's Map of Arkansas* (1994). *The Lost Roads Project: A Walk-in Book of Arkansas* (1994). *Tremble* (1996). *Deepstep Come Shining* (1998). *A Reader's Map of Rhode Island* (1999). *One Big Self: Prisoners of Louisiana*, with photographer Deborah Luster (2002). *Steal Away: New and Selected Poems* (2002).

—JEFF MOCK

CHARLES WRIGHT (1935–). Charles Penzel Wright, Jr., was born on August 25, 1935, to Charles Penzel (1904–1972) and Mary Castelman (Winter) Wright (1910–1964), at Pickwick Dam, Tenn. The family soon moved to Oak Ridge, then after World War II to Kingsport. In 1957 Wright graduated from Davidson College and began four years of military service. Assigned to an army counterintelligence unit in Verona, Italy, he began to read poetry seriously through the work of Ezra Pound. This formative experience may still be felt in Wright's distinctive uses of line and image. Other influences include Eugenio Montale, whose work Wright has translated, as well as Dante and the poets of the T'ang dynasty, in their conjunctions of visionary and sensual worlds.

Wright spent two periods at the Writers' Workshop at the University of Iowa, where he studied under Donald Justice, among others. After receiving an M.F.A. in 1963, he spent a year as a Fulbright scholar at the University of Rome, and then returned to Iowa in 1965–66. In 1968 he lectured in Padua. Since then, he has taught at the University of California at Irvine (until 1983) and at the University of Virginia. He is married with one son.

Wright has been awarded a glittering constellation of awards, including the PEN Translation Prize, the Academy of American Poets' Lenore Marshall Poetry Prize, the Ruth Lilly Poetry Prize, and the Award of Merit Medal from the American Academy of Arts and Letters. *Country Music* garnered Wright a National Book Award. *Black Zodiac* earned him both a Pulitzer Prize and a National Book Critics Circle Award. His poetry joins Zenlike apprehension of Appalachian, Italian, and suburban Virginian landscapes with stern echoes of mortality and high lonesome music from southern white Protestantism. His unhurried poems reach in long lines and precise language for that which is beyond both.

WORKS: *The Grave of the Right Hand* (1970). *Hard Freight* (1973). *Bloodlines* (1975). *China Trace* (1977). Trans., Eugenio Montale, *The Storm and Other Poems* (1978). *The Southern Cross* (1981). *Country Music: Selected Early Poems* (1982). *The Other Side of the River* (1984). Trans., Dino Campana, *Orphic Songs* (1984). *Zone Journals* (1988). *Halflife: Improvisations and Interviews, 1977–87* (1988). *Xionia* (1990). *The World of the Ten Thousand Things: Poems 1980–1990* (1990). *Chickamauga* (1995). *Quarter Notes: Improvisations and Interviews* (1995). *Black Zodiac* (1997). *Appalachia* (1998). *North American Bear* (1999). *Negative Blue: Selected Later Poems* (2000). *A Short History of the Shadow* (2002). *Buffalo Yoga* (2004). *Snake Eyes* (2004). *The Wrong End of the Rainbow* (2005).

—MARGARET MILLS HARPER

RICHARD WRIGHT (1908–1960). Richard Wright, whose novel *Native Son* probably did more than any other single literary event to pave the way for the emergence of black literature after World War II, was born on September 4, 1908, on a cotton plantation twenty-five miles from Natchez, Miss. His father, Nathan, was a mill worker; his mother, Ellen, was a country schoolteacher. His childhood was a series of struggles against impossible obstacles, but it provided as well the subject matter and tone for his greatest writing. Nathan Wright deserted the family when Richard was five. Not long after, Ellen Wright suffered a series of paralytic strokes. As a result, Richard was shuttled back and forth between other members of the family. Finally, at age fifteen, he left home to work as a porter-messenger in Memphis. It was in Memphis that he first decided he wanted to write; and he began reading all the books mentioned in Mencken's *Book of Prefaces.*

After a year in Memphis, Wright migrated farther north to Chicago, a city that remained his home for ten years. He held jobs there as a dishwasher, postal clerk, porter, and life insurance salesman, and at other times subsisted on relief. During this time he continued his reading and began to write; and he became involved in politics, serving as an assistant precinct captain for the Republican Party. In 1933 Wright joined the Communist Party, attracted more by the fact that it included many intellectuals and supported oppressed people of all colors than by its specific political views. With the encouragement of fellow members, he began writing poetry and short stories and reading the avant-garde writers of the period. His work, heavily imbued with the radical passions of the Party, began to appear in *New Masses, Left Front, Partisan Review,* and *International Literature,* and he began work for the Federal Writers' Project. Feeling that his writing career was suffering because of the demands made on his time by the Party in Chicago, in 1937 he moved on to New York, where again he would remain for ten years. This decade was to be the most productive of his life, and at its conclusion he would have an international literary reputation.

In December 1937, after months of frustration during which he had his novels continually turned down by New York publishers, Wright won the $500 first prize in a contest sponsored by *Story* magazine for members of the Federal Writers' Project. This in turn led to Harper's acceptance for book publication *Uncle Tom's Children,* a collection of four long short stories dealing with racism in the South and the terror that it instilled in blacks. On March 1, 1940, Harper's published *Native Son,* and Wright's celebrity was assured. The novel was chosen as a selection by the Book-of-the-Month Club; a stage version by Wright and Paul Green was produced by Orson Welles; and the book sold 200,000 copies in less than three weeks. A novella, "The Man Who Lived Underground" (1942), showed the influence of his reading in Dostoevski. Wright's fictionalized autobiography, *Black Boy,* dealt only with the years before the move to Chicago but did so in such moving and vivid detail that it achieved almost as much popular success as had *Native Son.*

In March 1941, after a brief first marriage to Dhimah Rose Meadman, Wright married Ellen Poplar. In 1946 the Wrights and their daughter, Julia, visited Paris, returning the next year to live there until the end of his life. Wright's later work never achieved either the popularity or the quality of *Native Son* and *Black Boy.* His novel *The Outsider* is interesting chiefly for the influence upon it of Sartrean existentialism. *The Long Dream* is a novel about a young African American in Mississippi. While in France, Wright openly renounced his affiliation with the Communist Party. During the last period of his life, he wrote a series of travel books: *Black Power,* on Africa's Gold Coast; *The Color Curtain,* on the Bandung Conference of Asian and African nations; and *Pagan Spain,* a bitter view of Franco's Spain. He died in Paris of a heart attack on November 28, 1960, hailed at his death as "a great American writer." Two of his works appeared posthumously: *Eight Men,* a collection of short stories, and *Lawd Today,* one of the novels he had unsuccessfully tried to publish during his early days in New York.

WORKS: *Uncle Tom's Children* (1938). *Native Son* (1940). *Twelve Million Black Voices* (1941). *Black Boy* (1945). *The Outsider* (1953). *Savage Holidays* (1954). *Black Power* (1954). *The Color Curtain* (1956). *Pagan Spain* (1957). *White Man, Listen!* (1957). *The Long Dream* (1958). *Eight Men* (1961). *Lawd Today* (1963).

—JACKSON R. BRYER

JONATHAN YARDLEY (1939–). Biographer, editor, critic, social commentator, and prize-winning author of over 3,500 reviews, Jonathan Yardley was born in 1939 in Pittsburgh. His parents were William and Helen Yardley. After attending Groton School, he entered the University of North Carolina, where he edited the student newspaper (1960–61) and was active in social organizations. Following his graduation in 1961 and his marriage in that June, to Rosemary Roberts, a 1960 graduate of the university, he interned with James Reston, the Washington bureau chief for the *New York Times*. He next wrote "News of the Week in Review" for the *Times*. In 1964 he and his wife returned to North Carolina, where for a decade he worked as an editorial writer and book editor for the *Greensboro Daily News*. From 1974 to 1978 he served as the book editor of the *Miami Herald*. In Miami he published his first book, *Ring: A Biography of Ring Lardner*. From the *Herald*, he joined the *Washington Star* as its book editor until the paper ceased publication in 1981. His book reviews brought him a Pulitzer Prize in 1981 and steered him toward the position he has since held as book critic and columnist for the *Washington Post*.

During his tenure at the *Post*, Yardley has published an additional five books, including a biography of novelist Frederick Exley and a history of his own family and their social class, provocatively titled *Our Kind of People*. The latter he views as "a WASP *Roots*," an ironic parallel to Alex Haley's African American saga. In the book's title, Yardley intended to mingle pride and criticism, but it created controversy because to some reviewers it seemed chiefly to suggest an Anglo-Saxon, Protestant snobbery. *Out of Step* collects book reviews, *States of Mind* is a travel account, and *Monday Morning Quarterback* provides cultural and social commentary. In addition to the six books he has written, Yardley has edited a posthumous memoir by H. L. Mencken, *My Life as Author and Editor*, and a selection of Ring Lardner's short stories.

With Rosemary Roberts Yardley, he has two sons, both journalists—James Barrett Yardley with the *New York Times* and William W. Yardley II with the *Miami Herald*, two papers for which their father worked. Through the sons he has five grandchildren. Yardley's marriage to Rosemary Roberts ended in early 1975, and in March of that year he wed Susan L. Hartt, from whom he was divorced in 1998. In March 1999 he married Marie Arana, editor of the *Washington Post Book World* and author of *American Chica: Two Worlds, One Childhood*, a finalist for the 2001 National Book Award in nonfiction. He and Arana live on Capitol Hill in Washington. He has received an honorary doctorate from George Washington University (1987) and a Distinguished Alumnus Award from the University of North Carolina (1989).

WORKS: *Ring: A Biography of Ring Lardner* (1977). *Our Kind of People: The Story of an American Family* (1989). *Out of Step: Notes from a Purple Decade* (1991). *States of Mind: A Personal Journey through the Mid-Atlantic* (1993). Ed., H. L. Mencken, *My Life as Author and Editor* (1993). *Misfit: The Strange Life of Frederick Exley* (1997). Ed., Ring Lardner, *Selected Stories* (1997). *Monday Morning Quarterback* (1998).

—JULIUS ROWAN RAPER

FRANK YERBY (1916–1991). Frank Garvin Yerby, the most prolific African American novelist to date, was born in Augusta, Ga., on September 5, 1916, to Rufus Garvin and Wilhelmina Yerby. He began writing stories and poems at age eight, and he was publishing by the time he reached high school. He earned a B.A. at Paine College in Augusta (1937) and an M.A. at Fisk University in Nashville (1938). He studied further at the University of Chicago before taking positions in the English departments at Florida A&M College (now University) in Tallahassee and Southern University in Baton Rouge. He also participated in the Federal Works Progress Administration's Writers' Project. After his teaching career, he worked as a lab technician for Ford Motor Company (1941–44) and continued to write. In 1944 "Health Card" won the O. Henry Memorial Award prize for a first published short story.

In spite of his early critical success with racial protest stories, the African American protest novels he produced shortly thereafter failed to interest publishers. At this point, he turned to writing what he called "costume novels." These mass-market novels usually involve formulaic adventure-romance along with painstaking historical research. Many of Yerby's thirty-three novels were best-sellers, including his first, *The Foxes of Harrow*. They were popular in the United States and around the world; they have been translated into over a dozen languages, and several were adapted for film. Although most critics were disappointed by what they considered Yerby's lack of political and "literary" commitment, he methodically challenged historical myths throughout his writing career in a form that would actually reach the masses.

Yerby expatriated to Spain in 1955 after spending several years in France. He died in Madrid in 1991. He was survived by his wife, Blanca, and his four children from his first marriage.

WORKS: *The Foxes of Harrow* (1946). *The Vixens* (1947). *The Golden Hawk* (1948). *Pride's Castle* (1949). *Floodtide* (1950). *A Woman Called Fancy* (1951). *The Saracen Blade* (1952). *The Devil's Laughter* (1953). *Benton's Row* (1954). *Bride of Liberty* (1954). *The Treasure of Pleasant Valley* (1955). *Captain Rebel* (1956). *Fairoaks* (1957). *The Serpent and the Staff* (1958). *Jarrett's Jade* (1959). *Gillian* (1960). *The Garfield Honor* (1961). *Griffin's Way* (1962). *The Old Gods Laugh: A Modern Romance* (1964). *An Odor of Sanctity: A Novel of Moorish Spain* (1965). *Goat Song: A Novel of Ancient Greece* (1967). *Judas My Brother: The Story of the Thirteenth Disciple* (1968). *Speak Now: A Modern Novel* (1969). *The Dahomean: A Historical Novel* (1971). *The Girl from Storyville: A Victorian Novel* (1972). *The Voyage Unplanned* (1974). *Tobias and the Angel* (1975). *A Rose for Ana Maria* (1976). *Hail the Conquering Hero* (1977). *A Darkness at Ingraham's Crest: A Tale of the Slaveholding South* (1979). *Western: A Saga of the Great Plains* (1982). *Devilseed* (1984). *McKenzie's Hundred* (1985).

—VALERIE MATTHEWS CRAWFORD

MARLY YOUMANS (1953–). Susan Marlene Youmans was born on November 22, 1953, in Aiken, S.C. The daughter of a chemistry professor, Youmans spent her childhood in Louisiana, Kansas, and Delaware before her family settled in Cullowhee, N.C. Her father, who wrote fiction and poetry in addition to publishing a book and many articles in his field, was an important early influence, as was Youmans's mother, a librarian who kept her daughter well supplied with books. She began writing at an early age and published poems and short stories in various journals while earning degrees at Hollins College, Brown University, and the University of North Carolina at Chapel Hill.

After gaining tenure at the State University of New York, Youmans quit academia and returned to North Carolina to devote herself full-time to writing and raising a family. She published her first book, *Little Jordan*, a lyrical coming-of-age novel set in the Carolinas, soon thereafter. Youmans's second book, *Catherwood*, a historical novel set in the wilds of New York in 1678, was inspired by an anecdote about a folk singer's grandmother, lost in the woods of Vermont and Canada for six months. Her son Ben's obsession with the Civil War led to her third novel, *The Wolf Pit*, which follows the lives of a young Confederate soldier and a mulatto slave girl during the war's darkest days. *The Curse of the Raven Mocker*, a fantasy novel set in the Carolina and Tennessee mountains, and *Claire*, a collection of poems, were both published in 2003. Today she lives in "accidental exile" from the South in Cooperstown, N.Y., with her M.D. husband, Mike Miller, and three children, and continues to write fiction.

WORKS: *Little Jordan: A Novel* (1995). *Catherwood* (1996). *The Wolf Pit* (2001). *The Curse of the Raven Mocker* (2003). *Claire: Poems* (2004). *Ingledove* (2006).

—BRIAN CARPENTER

STARK YOUNG (1881–1963). Stark Young was born on October 11, 1881, in Como, a small town in northern Mississippi. He was the son of Alfred Alexander Young, a doctor and Civil War veteran, and Mary Clark Starks of the aristocratic McGehee family. Young's mother died in 1890 and his father's remarriage when Young was fourteen was accompanied by a move to Oxford, where he entered the university, graduating in 1901. Always having felt stifled by the provinciality and hostility to the arts in a plantation household, Young had long been preparing for the move north that he made shortly after graduation, beginning graduate work at Columbia University and receiving his M.A. in 1902. He went on to teach English at the University of Mississippi, the University of Texas, and Amherst College before severing his academic ties in 1921 and returning to New York as a freelance writer.

Young quickly established himself in New York as a playwright, director, and critic. His romantic plays on historical subjects proved to be of only mild interest. More important was his relationship with Herbert Croly and the *New Republic;* he would eventually serve as theater critic and contributing editor, and his association with the magazine would last (with brief interruptions) until 1947. Through hundreds of articles and reviews and his seminal text, *Theatre Practice,* Young helped bring the craft of drama criticism in America to maturity.

In spite of his success in New York, Young was still haunted by memories of the South he had left behind. During eight years (1926–34), he would wrestle with his homeland through four historical novels and through his involvement with the southern Agrarians. In his novels, Young repeatedly presents a sensitive artistic figure estranged from the beautiful, but ultimately stifling, world of the plantation South. His most important novel, *So Red the Rose,* was his great effort to define the difference between the traditional, communal world of the Old South and the grasping individualism that would overwhelm it.

Though he continued to write important criticism after the 1940s, the next two decades found Young pursuing other interests, most notably painting and his wonderful translations of Chekhov. He suffered a stroke in May 1959, and died in New York on January 6, 1963.

WORKS: *Guenevere: A Play in Five Acts* (1906). *The Blind Man at the Window and Other Poems* (1906). *Addio, Madretta and Other Plays* (1912). *Three One-Act Plays* (1921). *The Queen of Sheba* (1922). *The Flower in Drama* (1923). *The Colonnade* (1924). *The Three Fountains* (1924). *Glamour: Essays on the Art of the Theatre* (1925). *The Saint* (1925). *Sweet Times and The Blue Policeman* (1925). *The Twilight Saint* (1925). *Encaustics* (1926). *Heaven Trees* (1926). *Theatre Practice* (1926). *The Theatre* (1927). Trans., Machiavelli, *Mandragola* (1927). *The Torches Flare* (1928). *River House* (1929). *The Street of the Islands* (1930). "Not in Memoriam, but in Defense," in *I'll Take My Stand: The South and the Agrarian Tradition,* by Twelve Southerners (1930). *So Red the Rose* (1934). *Feliciana* (1935). Trans., Chekhov, *The Sea Gull* (1939). *Artemise* (1942). *Immortal Shadows: A Book of Dramatic Criticism* (1948). *The Pavilion* (1951). *The Flower in Drama and Glamour* (1955). Trans., *Best Plays of Chekhov* (1957). *The Theatre* (1958).

—Douglas L. Mitchell

JOHN YOUNT (1935–). John Alonzo Yount, the only child of a father who was a migratory construction worker and a mother from devout Lutheran stock, was born on July 3, 1935, in Boone, N.C. After attending various high schools as his family moved from town to town, he spent two years in the U.S. Army, intending to become a veterinarian. He then attended Wake Forest and Vanderbilt universities, where he first began to take writing seriously, and attained the B.A. from the latter in 1960. From there he went on to study in the creative writing program at the University of Iowa, receiving the M.F.A. in 1962.

Yount has taught writing and literature at Clemson University and the University of Arkansas, but spent most of his career at the University of New Hampshire, where he is now an emeritus member of the faculty. He has been a recipient of grants and fellowships from the Rockefeller Foundation (1967–68), Guggenheim Foundation (1974), and National Endowment for the Arts (1976). Yount married Susan Childe in 1957, and they had two daughters, Jennifer and Sarah; the Younts divorced in 1986.

Although not prolific (he has called himself an "inveterate reviser"), Yount has received excellent reviews since the mixed reception of his first novel, *Wolf at the Door,* and is acclaimed for both the deep attentiveness of his sentences and his cultural perspicacity. He has achieved a strong reputation from other writers, including Raymond Carver, John Irving, and Andre Dubus. Critics especially extolled his third novel, *Hardcastle,* a story of labor, tumult, and violence in a Kentucky mining town in the 1930s. As a novel of the Great Depression, *Hardcastle* has been compared to *The Grapes of Wrath* in its significance. Yount's most recent novel, *Thief of Dreams,* deals with the struggle to navigate and mend breaches that have opened up between son, mother, and father. It, too, has been applauded for its understatement and integrity. Indeed, a common theme among reviewers has been the complexity underlying the apparent simplicity of Yount's writing.

WORKS: *Wolf at the Door* (1967). *The Trapper's Last Shot* (1973). *Hardcastle* (1980). *Toots in Solitude* (1984). *Thief of Dreams* (1991).

—MATTHEW D. MUTTER

JOHN JOACHIM ZUBLY (1724–1781). Minister, pamphleteer, and delegate to the 1774 Continental Congress in Philadelphia, John Joahcim Zubly lived a remarkable and tumultuous public life in pre-Revolutionary America. A native of St. Gallen, Switzerland, Zubly was born in 1724. After being ordained in the German Church in London, he immigrated to America and eventually settled in Georgia, where he and his wife Ann had three children. In 1760 Zubly accepted a call to the Independent Presbyterian Church in Savannah, and he soon became one of that cosmopolitan city's most important and wealthy citizens, as well as one of the colony's most influential clergymen.

On the great political questions of his day—representation, taxation, and the sovereignty of the British Parliament—Zubly thought and wrote with a keen mind but an ambivalent heart. He published a number of pamphlets during the 1760s and 1770s, contributing significantly to the body of political theory that would ultimately make rebellion justifiable in the minds of many colonists, especially in the southern colonies. Among these, *Calm and Respectful Thoughts on the Negative of the Crown* . . . and *The Law of Liberty* . . . are the most nuanced, demonstrating Zubly's belief in the necessity of genuine representation for the colonies even as he consistently eschews any notions of rebellion. In *The Law of Liberty* Zubly insists that even as he and his fellow colonists petition for true representation, "our interests lie in a perpetual connection with our mother country."

Ultimately, the fervor of revolution made such middle ground untenable. Although he was elected as a delegate to the first Continental Congress, Zubly refused to support rebellion, was accused of disloyalty, and was subsequently marginalized. Upon his return to Georgia, he saw his lands seized, and was forced to flee the colony. After living miserably in the Black Swamp of South Carolina for two years, he was allowed to return to Savannah in 1779. In ill health, he resumed his work there as a pastor, serving his parishioners until he died, practically landless, in 1781.

WORKS: *Leichenpredigt* (1746). *Eine Leicht-Predigt* (1747). *Eine Predigt* (1749). *Evangelisches Zeugnuss. Vom Elend und Erlösung der Menschen in zwei Predigten abgelegt Und auf Hoffnung Mehrer Erbauung dem Druck Überlassen* (1751). *The Real Christians Hope in Death* (1756). *The Stamp-Act Repealed: A Sermon Preached in the Meeting at Savannah in Georgia, June 25th, 1766* (1766). *An Humble Enquiry into the Nature of the Dependency of the American Colonies upon the Parliament of Great-Britain, and the Right of Parliament to Lay Taxes on the Said Colonies* (1769).

A Letter to the Reverend Samuel Frink, A.M., Rector of Christ's Church Parish in Georgia, Relating to Some Fees Demanded of Some of His Dissenting Parishioners (1770). *The Wise Shining on the Brightness of the Firmament and they that turn many unto Righteousness as Stars for ever. A Funeral Sermon Preached at Savannah, in Georgia, Nov. 11, 1770, on the Much Lamented Death of the Rev. George Whitefield, A.M.* (1770). *An Account of the Remarkable Conversion of Jachiel Hirshel, from the Jewish to the Christian Religion* (1770). *The Christian's Gain in Death, Represented in a Funeral Sermon, Preached at Purysbourg, in South-Carolina, Jan. 28, 1770, at the Interment of Mr. Jacob Waldburger* (1770). *The Nature of that Faith without which It Is Impossible to Please God, Considered in a Sermon on Hebrews XI 6* (1772). *Calm and Respectful Thoughts on the Negative of the Crown on a Speaker Chosen and Presented by the Representatives of the People* (1772). *The Faithful Minister's Course Finished: A Funeral Sermon, Preached Aug. 4, 1773, in the Meeting at Midway, Georgia, at the Interment of the Rev. John Osgood* (1773). *The Law of Liberty. A Sermon on American Affairs, Preached at the Opening of the Provincial Congress of Georgia* (1775). *Eine Kurzgefasste historische Nachricht von den Kämpfen der Schweitzer für die Freyheit* [appendix to *The Law of Liberty*] (1775). *Pious Advice. Sermon on the Faith* (1775). *Letter to Mr. Frink* (1775). *To the Grand Jury of the County of Chatham, State of Georgia* (1777).

—H. COLLIN MESSER

CONTRIBUTORS

Peter L. Abernethy
Andrew White, S.J.

Robert D. Abner
Ebenezer Cooke [Cook]

Lisa Abney
Rebecca Wells

Gail Galloway Adams
Danske Dandridge
Jesse Stuart

Timothy Dow Adams
Jonathan Williams

Gilbert Allen
Dabney Stuart

Richard E. Amacher
William Dawson

Regina Ammon
Truman Capote
Mark Childress
Anne Rivers Siddons

Daniel Anderson
Wyatt Prunty

William L. Andrews
William Wells Brown
Frederick Douglass
Hugh Jones
Solomon Northup
James Sterling

Robert G. Anthony, Jr.
James Boyd
Alexander Garden
John Lawson
Robert Ruark

Tomeiko R. Ashford
Lonne Elder III
Margaret Walker

Laurence G. Avery
Laurence Stallings

James L. Baggett
Vicki Covington

Robert Bain
James Reid
William Stith
Alexander Whitaker

Bruce E. Baker
Grace Lumpkin
Katharine du Pre Lumpkin

K. Huntress Baldwin
George Alsop
William Hand Browne
John Esten Cooke
George Washington Parke
Custis
Frances E. W. Harper
Francis Scott Key
James Innes Randolph, Jr.

John E. Bassett
Ruth McEnery Stuart

John Batteiger
Don Marquis

Margaret D. Bauer
Ellen Gilchrist

Philip D. Beidler
Winston Groom
William March

Alan T. Belsches
Leroy Leatherman

Alfred Bendixen
Charles Gayarré
Adrien-Emmanuel Rouquette

Barbara Bennett
Marianne Gingher
Molly Ivins

Brian J. Benson
Robert Deane Pharr

Leonidas S. Betts
George Frederick Holmes

John T. Bickley
George Cary Eggleston
Thomas Harriott [Harriot]

R. Bruce Bickley, Jr.
Roberto G. Fernández
Joel Chandler Harris
Georgia Douglas Johnson
David Kirby
James Mathewes Legaré
Virginia Moore
Irwin Russell
Jeff Shaara
Michael Shaara
Virgil Suárez
George Tucker
Joseph Addison Turner

David Bjelajac
Washington Allston

Karen C. Blansfield
Pearl Cleage
Horton Foote

Lillian Hellman
O. Henry
Romulus Linney
Marsha Norman
Paula Vogel
Theodore Ward
Samm-Art Williams

Lynn Z. Bloom
Helen Keller
Jill McCorkle

Joseph Blotner
William Clark Falkner
William Faulkner

Laura J. Bloxham
Alice Walker

Kristina D. Bobo
Alice Dunbar-Nelson
Clarence Major
Mary Mebane

Thomas Bonner, Jr.
John Howard Griffin
Berry Morgan
Thomas Hal Phillips
Lyle Saxon

Anne M. Boyle
Caroline Gordon

Robert H. Brinkmeyer, Jr.
Frederick Barthelme
Rick Bass
Barbara Kingsolver

George Brosi
Janice Giles
Don West

Norman D. Brown
William Garrott Brown

Jackson R. Bryer
Richard Wright

Harriette Cuttino Buchanan
Daphne Athas

Louis J. Budd
Mark Twain

Rebecca Roxburgh Butler
Patricia Cornwell
Caroline Miller
Josephine Pinckney

Mark Canada
Hodding Carter
Thomas Holley Chivers
Anne Moody
Edgar Allan Poe

Thomas M. Carlson
Padgett Powell

Brian Carpenter
Marly Youmans

Virginia Spencer Carr
Carson McCullers

David A. Case
Armistead Maupin
David Sedaris (*with John Jackson*)

Katherine Clark
Eugene Walter

Donna Coates
Leon Rooke

Martha E. Cook
Jesse Hill Ford
Brainard Cheney

Raymond A. Cook
Byron Herbert Reece

Stephen Cooper
William Humphrey
Eric Lincoln
James Alan McPherson

Alice R. Cotten
Frances Courtenay Baylor
Paxton Davis
Sophia Bledsoe Herrick

Norlisha F. Crawford
Maya Angelou

Valerie Matthews Crawford
Frank Yerby

David A. Davis
Gustavo Pérez Firmat
Will N. Harben
Etheridge Knight
James Wilcox

Richard Beale Davis
George Sandys

Cynthia B. Denham
Rick Bragg

R. H. W. Dillard
George Garrett

Cy Dillon
David Bottoms

Suzanne Disheroon-Green
Kate Chopin
Grace King
Jayne Anne Phillips

Susan V. Donaldson
Elizabeth Hardwick

Thomas E. Douglass
Breece D'J Pancake

Joyce Dyer
Jim Wayne Miller

Julia Eichelberger
Julia Peterkin
Eliza Lucas Pinckney
Eliza Wilkinson

John O. Eidson
John Reuben Thompson

Daniel J. Ennis
Samuel Henry Dickson
William Ioor
John Blake White

Allison R. Ensor
Sarah Barnwell Elliott
Mary Noailles Murfree

Barbara C. Ewell
Frances Parkinson Keyes

John J. Fenstermaker
Edwin Phillips Granberry

Mary Anne Ferguson
 Lisa Alther

Joseph M. Flora
 Doris Betts
 James Branch Cabell
 Jimmy Carter
 Anna J. Cooper
 John Cotton of Queen's
  Creek, Va.
 Andre Dubus
 Dubose Heyward
 Harper Lee
 Bobbie Ann Mason
 Helen Norris
 Albert Pike
 Ben Robertson
 Dori Sanders
 Alfred Bennett Spellman
 Richard Tillinghast

Peter J. Flora
 John Ed Bradley
 Robert Olen Butler
 Tim Gautreaux
 Tony Kushner
 Anne Rice
 Kalamu ya Salaam

Gaines M. Foster
 Montrose J. Moses
 Charles Alphonso Smith

Warren French
 Joseph Holt Ingraham

Jane S. Gabin
 Sidney Lanier

George Garrett
 Joseph Blotner

Daniel Garrien
 William Mills

Richard Giannone
 Flannery O'Connor

Bryan Giemza
 Conrad Aiken
 Lerone Bennett

J. Gordon Coogler
Ossie Davis
Thomas Cooper De Leon
John Wesley Thompson
 Faulkner III
Shelby Foote
Ernest J. Gaines
F. R. Goulding
Lewis Grizzard
George Wylie Henderson
Charles Kuralt
Margaret Mitchell
Howell Raines
Ishmael Reed
John Shelton Reed
Abram Ryan
John Banister Tabb
Allen Tate
St. George Tucker
Richard Weaver
Tom Wicker
C. Vann Woodward

Owen W. Gilman, Jr.
 John Fox, Jr.
 Barry Hannah
 David Huddle
 Henry Watterson

MaryAnne M. Gobble
 Lewis Nordan
 E. P. O'Donnell

Nicholas Graham
 John Henry Boner
 Thomas Burke
 Angelina Grimké and Sarah
  Grimké
 Elizabeth Keckley
 Doug Marlette
 Joseph Mitchell

Daniel Grassian
 William Styron

Sharon L. Gravett
 Walter Hines Page

Juliana Gray
 Andrew Hudgins

Michael D. Green
 Alexander Posey

J. Lee Greene
 Anne Spencer

James A. Grimshaw, Jr.
 Donald Justice

Jason Nephi Hall
 Dave Smith

Deborah George Hardy
 John Kennedy Toole (*with René
  Pol Nevils*)

Tracy Hargreaves
 Donna Tartt

William Harmon
 A. R. Ammons
 Robert Morgan

Margaret Mills Harper
 Charles Wright

Suzan Harrison
 Olive Ann Burns

Maria P. Hebert
 Alcée Fortier
 Lafcadio Hearn
 Minnie Bruce Pratt

Harris W. Henderson
 John Gould Fletcher
 Augustus Baldwin Longstreet
 John Donald Wade

R. Sterling Hennis
 Clyde Edgerton

Barbara A. Herman
 Alice Adams

Scott Hicks
 Robert Beverley
 Walter Sullivan
 John Taylor of Caroline
 William Wirt

John T. Hiers
 John Bell Hennemann

Samuel S. Hill
Wendell Berry
Will D. Campbell

Bert Hitchcock
James Lane Allen
Joseph Glover Baldwin
Bob Shacochis

Fred Hobson
W. J. Cash
Hinton Helper
Gerald White Johnson
H. L. Mencken
Howard W. Odum
Lillian Smith

Katherine C. Hodgin
Susan Richards Shreve

Inez Hollander
Hamilton Basso

C. Carroll Hollis
Albert Taylor Bledsoe

C. Hugh Holman
William Crafts

Thomas Alan Holmes
Sharyn McCrumb
Elise Sanguinetti

George Hovis
Fred Chappell
Hal Crowther
Allan Gurganus
Randall Kenan

Karen Jean Hunt
John Hope Franklin

Clifford Huntington, Jr.
Maurice Thompson

John L. Idol, Jr.
Mary Boykin Chesnut
James McBride Dabbs
Ben Greer
Theodore O'Hara
Charles Portis
Thomas Wolfe

M. Thomas Inge
Donald Davidson
Mildred Eunice Haun

John C. Inscoe
Richard Malcolm Johnston
Ralph McGill

John Jackson
David Sedaris *(with David A. Case)*

Lawrence Jackson
Ralph Ellison

Robert D. Jacobs
Benjamin Blake Minor
Edward Coote Pinkney

David K. Jeffrey
John Dufresne
Madison Jones

La Vinia Delois Jennings
Alice Childress
Melvin Beaunorous Tolson

Sara Andrews Johnston
Julia Fields

Robert E. Jones
Merrill Moore

Whit Jones
John Beecher
Charles Woodmason

Tessa Joseph
John Henrik Clarke
Langston Hughes
John Oliver Killens

Nancy Carol Joyner
Harriette Arnow

Julie Kane
Vassar Miller

Joseph Kelly
Henry Laurens

William W. Kelly
Mary Johnston

J. Gerald Kennedy
James Dunwoody Brownson
De Bow

Vincent S. Kenny
Paul Green

Gary Kerley
Harry Stillwell Edwards
George Fitzhugh
Charles Colcock Jones, Jr.
Mirabeau Buonaparte Lamar

Kimball King
George Washington Cable
Preston Jones
Thomas Nelson Page

Lovalerie King
George Moses Horton
Harriet A. Jacobs

Michael Kreyling
Taylor Branch
Louis D. Rubin, Jr.
Lewis P. Simpson

Susie Scifres Kuilan
Pat Conroy
Tom Wolfe

John Kwist, Jr.
Babs H. Deal

Barbara Ladd
Rita Mae Brown

Aubrey C. Land
Daniel Dulany, the Elder
Daniel Dulany, the Younger

John Lang
John Ehle

Andrew B. Leiter
Raymond Andrews
John Trotwood Moore
James Howell Street
Ben Ames Williams

George S. Lensing
James Applewhite
James Dickey

James A. Levernier
    Edwin De Leon
    Rowland Rugeley
    Herbert Ravenel Sass

Theresa Lloyd
    Hubert Creekmore
    Evelyn Scott

Michael A. Lofaro
    Davy Crockett
    William Fitzhugh
    Francis Walker Gilmer

Thomas L. Long
    William Byrd II of Westover

John Lowe
    Zora Neale Hurston
    Pinkie Gordon Lane
    Brenda Marie Osbey

Lucinda H. MacKethan
    John Pendleton Kennedy
    Lee Smith

Randy Mackin
    George Scarbrough

Donald L. Madison
    Abraham Verghese

E. T. Malone, Jr.
    Edwin Wiley Fuller

Carol S. Manning
    Ellen Douglas

Julian Mason
    Benjamin Banneker
    Charles W. Chesnutt
    Kaye Gibbons

Hubert H. McAlexander
    Peter Taylor

Robert L. McDonald
    Erskine Caldwell

Michael McFee
    Betty Adcock
    Jack Butler
    Rodney Jones

Kathryn B. McKee
    Sherwood Bonner

Shannon McKenna
    Jan Karon

Melissa Graham Meeks
    Kate Langley Bosher
    Mary Dallas Street

H. Collin Messer
    Murrell Edmunds
    John Grisham
    T. R. Hummer
    Opie Read
    John Joachim Zubly

Mildred R. Mickle
    Tina McElroy Ansa
    Gerald W. Barrax
    Gayl Jones

Jon C. Miller
    Richard Bland
    Charles Hansford
    Robert Munford

Randall M. Miller
    Henry Louis Gates, Jr.

Joseph R. Millichap
    John Bell Clayton
    Harris Downey
    Josephine Humphreys
    Cale Young Rice

Jerry Leath Mills
    Cormac McCarthy
    Tim McLaurin

Douglas L. Mitchell
    Margaret Gibson
    Thomas Jefferson
    Lawrence Naumoff
    Robert Schenkkan
    Stark Young

Keith Mitchell
    Alex Haley
    Albert Murray
    Albery Allson Whitman

Wayne Mixon
    John Spencer Bassett
    Henry Woodfin Grady

Jeff Mock
    Thomas Rabbitt
    Ellen Bryant Voigt
    C. D. Wright

Rayburn S. Moore
    William J. Grayson
    Paul Hamilton Hayne
    Jay Broadus Hubbell
    Alexander Beaufort Meek
    Henry Timrod

Ruth Moose
    Frances Hodgson Burnett
    Alice Caldwell Hegan Rice

Merritt W. Moseley, Jr.
    Roy Blount, Jr.

William Moss
    Daniel Robinson Hundley
    Marion Montgomery
    Daniel Kimball Whitaker

Matthew D. Mutter
    John Yount

John K. Nelson
    James Madison

Elsa Nettels
    James Blair
    Eve Shelnutt

René Pol Nevils
    John Kennedy Toole (with
        Deborah George Hardy)

Elaine Mitchell Newsome
    Randolph Edmonds

Jeanne R. Nostrandt
    William Hoffman
    Max Steele

Farrell O'Gorman
    William Bartram
    John Peale Bishop
    Valerie Martin
    Katherine Anne Porter

Ted Olson
Marilou Awiakta
Forrest Carter
James Still

Amanda Page
Henry Dumas
Rebecca Gilman

Scott J. Parker
Kermit Hunter

Randall G. Patterson
Edwin Mims
Leonidas Warren Payne, Jr.
Charles Forster Smith
William Peterfield Trent

Tony Peacock
Charles Frazier

Carolyn Perry
Dorothy Allison
Susan Ludvigson
Mary Lee Settle

Patsy B. Perry
Benjamin Griffith Brawley
Nikki Giovanni
Leslie Pinckney Hill
Chester Himes
Jay Saunders Redding

John R. Pfeiffer
Percival L. Everett
Ted Shine

Robert L. Phillips, Jr.
Katherine Bellamann
Frances Gaither

Ed Piacentino
Thomas Dixon
Larry L. King
Harry Harrison Kroll
T. S. Stribling
Hardin E. Taliaferro
Kittrell J. Warren

Wayne J. Pond
J. Frank Dobie
Guy Owen
Frances Gray Patton

Sylvia Wilkinson

Tara Powell
Fannie Flagg
Inglis Fletcher
Cathryn Hankla
Reynolds Price

William S. Powell
John Pory

Peggy Whitman Prenshaw
Eudora Welty

Verbie Lovorn Prevost
Madison Smartt Bell
Alexander Hamilton
Arthur Lee
Richard Henry Lee

Allen Pridgen
James Lee Burke
Donald McCaig
Walker Percy
William Alexander Percy

Paul D. Quigley
James Henry Hammond

M. Kevin Quinn
Calder Willingham

Julius Rowan Raper
John Barth
Ellen Glasgow
Willie Morris
Jonathan Yardley

Gary Richards
Peter Steinam Feibleman
William Goyen
Jim Grimsley
Tennessee Williams

Jeffrey H. Richards
Arthur Blackamore
Moncure Daniel Conway
Thomas Cradock
Christopher Gadsden
David Madden
Captain John Smith
David Hunter Strother
Patrick Tailfer

Milton and Patricia Rickels
Henry Clay Lewis [Madison
Tensas]
Charles Fenton Mercer Noland
Thomas Bangs Thorpe

J. V. Ridgely
Nathaniel Beverley Tucker

Diane Roberts
Nanci Kincaid

Mark Allen Roberts
Randall Jarrell

Terry Roberts
John William Corrington
Wilma Dykeman
Elizabeth Spencer

Anne E. Rowe
Carl Hiaasen
Marjorie Kinnan Rawlings
Elizabeth Madox Roberts

Louis D. Rubin, Jr.
Beatrice Ravenel

Richard D. Rust
Alfred Leland Crabb
William Eddis
Jonathan Boucher

Patrick Samway, S.J.
Richard Bausch
John Finlay
William Jay Smith

Mark A. Sanders
Sterling A. Brown

Damon Sauve
Harry Crews

Patricia A. Schechter
Ida B. Wells

Nancy Gray Schoonmaker
Bernice Kelly Harris
Corra Harris
E.D.E.N. Southworth

Richard R. Schramm
James Agee

Matthew Scialdone
  Robert Bolling
  William Alexander Caruthers
  Henry Sydnor Harrison
  F. Hopkinson Smith

Charles Scruggs
  Jessie Redmond Fauset
  Jean Toomer
  Walter F. White

Dorothy McInnis Scura
  Emily Tapscott Clark
  Constance Cary Harrison
    [Mrs. Burton Harrison]
  Charles William Kent
  F. V. Newton Painter

Lynne P. Shackelford
  John Henry Hammond
  Jeff Daniel Marion
  Janet Schaw
  Augusta Jane Evans Wilson

Frank W. Shelton
  Richard Ford

Bland Simpson
  Olive Tilford Dargan
  Ovid Williams Pierce

Ethel C. Simpson
  Donald Harington
  James Whitehead

Bryan C. Sinche
  Hannah Crafts
  Joseph Dumbleton

David Curtis Skaggs
  Thomas Bacon

Merrill Maguire Skaggs
  Beverly Lowry

B. N. Skardon
  William Elliott

John N. Somerville, Jr.
  Richard Dabney
  Samuel Davies
  Charles Edward Eaton
  Hugh Swinton Legaré

T. R. Pearson
  James Ryder Randall

Bes Stark Spangler
  Martha McFerren
  Heather Ross Miller
  Eleanor Ross Taylor

Matthew Spangler
  James Duff
  Lizette Woodworth Reese
  Wilbur Daniel Steele
  Alfred Uhry

Derrick Spradlin
  Richard Lewis

Peter L. Staffel
  Denise Giardina
  Homer H. Hickam, Jr.

Victor Strandberg
  Cleanth Brooks
  Robert Penn Warren

Welford Dunaway Taylor
  Frances Boyd Calhoun
  Amelie Rives [Princess
    Troubetzkoy]
  Emma Speed Sampson

Betty Taylor-Thompson
  Arna Wendell Bontemps

Victor L. Thacker
  Philip Pendleton Cooke

Janice J. Thompson
  Caroline Howard Gilman

Lawrence S. Thompson
  Madison Julius Cawein

Bailey Thomson
  Clarence Cason

Chad Trevitte
  Bailey White

Rob Trucks
  Tony Earley
  Diane McWhorter
  Chris Offutt
  Allen Wier

Edward L. Tucker
  Richard Henry Wilde

Daniel C. Turner
  Yusef Komunyakaa

Jane Gentry Vance
  Irvin Shrewsbury Cobb
  Guy Davenport, Jr.
  R. H. W. Dillard
  Ed McClanahan

Kathryn VanSpanckeren
  Florence King

Amber Vogel
  Thomas Dale
  Rita Dove
  Zelda Fitzgerald
  Earl Hamner
  Mac Hyman
  Martin Luther King, Jr.
  E. O. Wilson

Barbara A. Wade
  Frances Newman

Richard Walser
  John Charles McNeill

Harry L. Watson
  John S. Mosby

Ritchie D. Watson, Jr.
  George William Bagby
  Clifford Dowdey
  Caroline Lee Hentz
  Margaret Junkin Preston

Mary Louise Weaks
  Kelly Cherry
  Shirley Ann Grau
  Mary Hood
  Joan Williams

Amy E. Weldon
  Larry Brown
  Samuel Minturn Peck
  Hollis Summers

Linda Welden
  Ferrol Sams
  R. T. Smith

Sean H. Wells
  Borden Deal

James L. W. West III
  George Washington Harris

Robert M. West
  Kathryn Stripling Byer
  R. S. Gwynn
  William Harmon
  Michael McFee
  Gibbons Ruark
  James Seay
  Henry Taylor
  Miller Williams

Otis Wheeler
  William Tappan Thompson

Tom Williams
  Roark Bradford
  Martha Hall
  Nancy Lemann

Robert M. Willingham, Jr.
  Molly Elliot Seawell

Charles E. Wilson, Jr.
  James Weldon Johnson
  Booker T. Washington

Mary Ann Wimsatt
  Gail Godwin
  William Gilmore Simms

Mark Royden Winchell
  Andrew Lytle
  John Crowe Ransom

Harold Woodell
  Rebecca Harding Davis
  William Price Fox
  Archibald Rutledge
  Charles Henry Smith

Emily Wright
  Beth Henley

Norris Yates
  Johnson Jones Hooper

Anne R. Zahlan
  Anne Tyler

Gary Phillip Zola
  Isaac Harby
  Penina Moïse